third edition

how children
DEVELOP

third edition

how children DEVELOP

Robert Siegler
Carnegie Mellon University

Judy DeLoache
University of Virginia

Nancy Eisenberg
Arizona State University

And Campbell Leaper, University of California–Santa Cruz, reviser of Chapter 15: Gender Development

WORTH PUBLISHERS

This is dedicated to the ones we love

Senior Publisher: Catherine Woods
Senior Acquisitions Editor: Charles Linsmeier
Development Editor: Peter Deane
Executive Marketing Manager: Katherine Nurre
Senior Media Editor: Andrea Musick
Production Editor: Vivien Weiss, Leo Kelly (MPS Limited, A Macmillan Company)
Associate Managing Editor: Tracey Kuehn
Production Manager: Sarah Segal
Art Director: Barbara Reingold
Interior Designer, Cover Designer: Kevin Kall
Photo Editor: Bianca Moscatelli
Photo Researcher: Julie Tesser
Senior Illustration Coordinator: Bill Page
Illustrations: Todd Buck Illustration; Precision Graphics; TSI Graphics, Inc.; MPS Limited, A Macmillan Company
Composition: MPS Limited, A Macmillan Company
Printing and Binding: Worldcolor Versailles

Library of Congress Control Number: 2009941919
ISBN-10: 1-4292-1790-1
ISBN-13: 978-1-4292-1790-3

Printed in the United States of America

Third printing 2011

Worth Publishers
41 Madison Avenue
New York, NY 10010
www.worthpublishers.com

About the Authors

Robert Siegler is the Teresa Heinz Professor of Cognitive Psychology at Carnegie Mellon University. He is author of the cognitive development textbook *Children's Thinking* and has written or edited several additional books on child development. His books have been translated into Japanese, Korean, Spanish, French, and Portuguese. In the past few years, he has presented keynote addresses at the conventions of the Cognitive Development Society, the International Society for the Study of Behavioral Development, the Japanese Psychological Association, the Eastern Psychological Association, and the Conference on Human Development. He also has served as Associate Editor of the journal *Developmental Psychology,* co-edited the cognitive development volume of the 2006 *Handbook of Child Psychology,* and served on the National Mathematics Advisory Panel from 2006–2008. In 2005, Dr. Siegler received the American Psychological Association's Distinguished Scientific Contribution Award.

Judy DeLoache is the William R. Kenan Jr. Professor of Psychology at the University of Virginia. She has published extensively on aspects of cognitive development in infants and young children. Dr. DeLoache has served as president of the Developmental Division of the American Psychological Association and as a member of the executive board of the International Society for the Study of Infancy. She is currently the president-elect of the Cognitive Development Society. She has presented major invited addresses at professional meetings, including the Association for Psychological Science and the Society for Research on Child Development. Dr. DeLoache is the holder of a Scientific MERIT Award from the National Institutes of Health, and her research is also funded by the National Science Foundation. She has been a fellow at the Center for Advanced Study in the Behavioral Sciences and at the Rockefeller Foundation Study Center in Bellagio, Italy. She was recently inducted into the National Academy of Arts and Sciences.

Nancy Eisenberg is Regent's Professor of Psychology at Arizona State University. She is editor or author of numerous books on prosocial, social, and emotional development. For example, she edited *The Handbook on Child Psychology,* Volume III: *Social, Emotional, and Personality Development.* She is also the author of *The Caring Child* and of *The Roots of Prosocial Behavior in Children* (with Paul Mussen). She has been on the board of directors of the Association of Psychological Science, governing council of the Society for Research in Child Development, and the governing council of the American Psychological Association. Dr. Eisenberg was the associate editor of the *Merrill-Palmer Quarterly* and of the *Personality and Social Psychology Bulletin,* was editor of the *Psychological Bulletin,* is the founding editor of *Child Development Perspectives,* is the president-elect of Division 7 (Developmental Psychology) at the American Psychological Association, and served as president of the Western Psychological Association. She has been the recipient of several National Institutes of Health Career Development and Career Scientist awards. She is the 2007 recipient of the Ernest R. Hilgard Award for a Career Contribution to General Psychology, Division 1, American Psychological Association; the 2008 recipient of the International Society for the Study of Behavioral Development Distinguished Scientific Contribution Award; and the 2009 recipient of the G. Stanley Hall Award for Distinguished Contribution to Developmental Psychology, Division 7, American Psychological Association.

Brief Contents

Contents

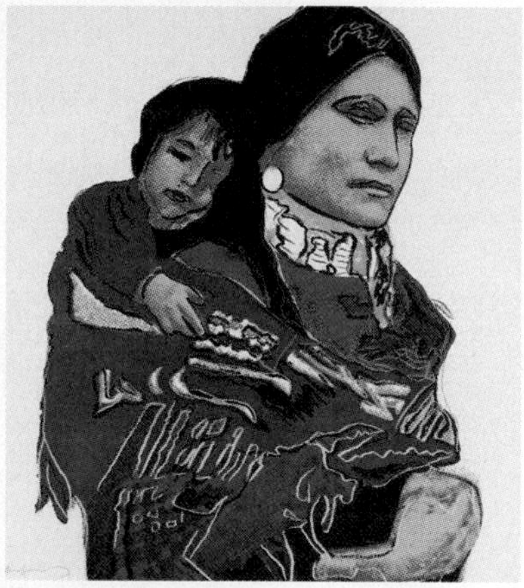

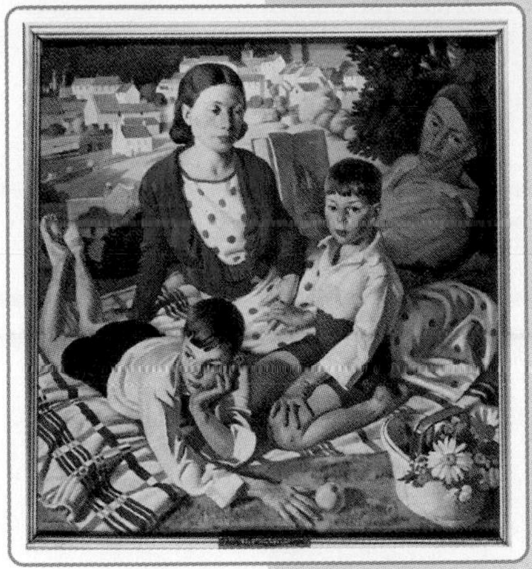

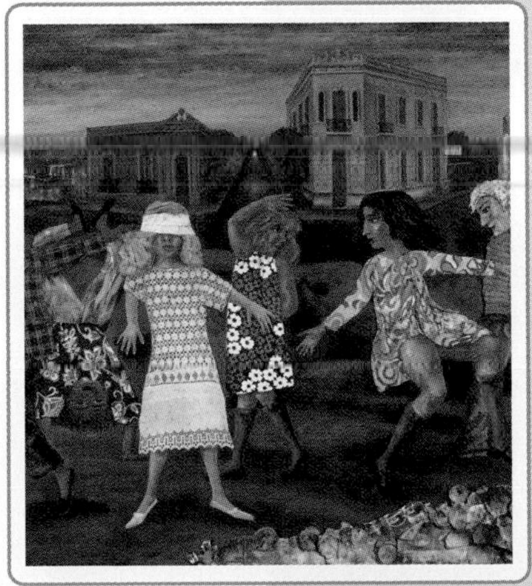

Preface

This is an exciting time in the field of child development. The past decade has brought new theories, new ways of thinking, new areas of research, and innumerable new findings to the field. We originally wrote *How Children Develop* to describe this ever-improving body of knowledge of children and their development and to convey our excitement about the progress that is being made in understanding the developmental process. We are pleased to continue this endeavor with the publication of the third edition of *How Children Develop.*

As teachers of child development courses, we appreciate the challenge that instructors face in trying to present these advances and discoveries—as well as the major older ideas and findings—in a one-semester course. Therefore, rather than aim at encyclopedic coverage, we have focused on identifying the most important developmental phenomena and describing them in sufficient depth to make them meaningful and memorable to students. In short, our goal has been to write a textbook that makes the child development course coherent and enjoyable for students and teachers alike.

Classic Themes

The basic premise of the book is that all areas of child development are unified by a small set of enduring themes. These themes can be stated in the form of questions that child development research tries to answer:

1. How do nature and nurture together shape development?
2. How do children shape their own development?
3. In what ways is development continuous and in what ways is it discontinuous?
4. How does change occur?
5. How does the sociocultural context influence development?
6. How do children become so different from each other?
7. How can research promote children's well-being?

These seven themes provide the core structure of the book. They are introduced and illustrated in Chapter 1, highlighted repeatedly, where relevant, in the subsequent fourteen content chapters, and utilized in the final chapter as a framework for integrating findings relevant to each theme from all areas of development. The continuing coverage of these themes allows us to tell a story that has a beginning (the introduction of the themes), a middle (discussion of specific findings relevant to them), and an ending (the overview of what students have learned about the themes).

We believe that this thematic emphasis and structure will not only help students to understand enduring questions about child development but will also leave them with a greater sense of satisfaction and completion at the end of the course.

Contemporary Perspective

The goal of providing a thoroughly contemporary perspective on how children develop has influenced the organization of our book as well as its contents. Whole new areas and perspectives have emerged that barely existed when most of today's child development textbooks were originally written. The organization of *How Children Develop* is designed to present these new topics and approaches in the context of the field as it currently stands, rather than trying to shoehorn them into organizations that once fit the field but no longer do.

Consider the case of Piaget's theory and current research relevant to it. Piaget's theory usually is presented in its own chapter, three-quarters of which describes the theory in full detail and the rest of which offers contemporary research that demonstrates problems with the theory. This approach often leaves students wondering why so much time was spent on Piaget's theory if modern research shows it to be wrong in so many ways.

The fact is that the line of research that began over 30 years ago as an effort to challenge Piaget's theory has emerged since then as a vital area in its own right—the area of conceptual development. Research in conceptual development provides extensive information on such fascinating topics as children's understanding of human beings, plants and animals, and the physical universe. As with other research areas, most studies in this field are aimed primarily at uncovering evidence relevant to current claims, not those of Piaget.

We adapted to this changing intellectual landscape in two ways. First, our chapter "Theories of Cognitive Development" (Chapter 4) describes the fundamental aspects of Piaget's theory in depth and honors his legacy by focusing on the aspects of his work that have proven to be the most enduring. Second, a first-of-its-kind chapter, "Conceptual Development" (Chapter 7), addresses the types of issues that inspired Piaget's theory but concentrates on modern perspectives and findings regarding those issues. This approach allows us to tell students about the numerous intriguing proposals and observations that are being made in this field, without the artificiality of classifying the findings as "pro-Piagetian" or "anti-Piagetian."

The opportunity to create a textbook based on current understanding also led us to assign prominent positions to such rapidly emerging areas as brain development, behavioral genetics, prenatal learning, infant cognition, acquisition of academic skills, emotional development, prosocial behavior, and friendship patterns. All these areas have seen major breakthroughs in recent years, and their growing prominence has led to even greater emphasis on them in this edition.

Getting Right to the Point

Our desire to offer a contemporary, streamlined approach led to other departures from the traditional organization. It is our experience that today's students take child development courses for a variety of practical reasons and are eager to learn about *children.* Traditionally, however, they have had to wait two or three or even four chapters—on the history of the field, on major theories, on research methods, on genetics—before actually getting to the study of children. We wanted to build on their initial motivation from the start.

Rather than open the book, then, with an extensive examination of the history of the field, we include in Chapter 1 a brief overview of the social and intellectual context in which the scientific study of children arose; then we provide historical background wherever it is pertinent in subsequent chapters. Rather than have an early "blockbuster" theories chapter that covers all the major cognitive and social theories at once (at a point far removed from the content chapters to which the theories apply), we present a chapter on cognitive developmental theories just before the chapters that focus on specific aspects of cognitive development, and we similarly present a chapter on social developmental theories just before the chapters that focus on specific aspects of social development. Rather than have a separate chapter on genetics, we include basic aspects of genetics as part of Chapter 3, "Biology and Behavior," and then discuss the contributions of genetics to some of the differences among individuals throughout the book. When we originally chose this organization, we hoped that it would allow us, from the first weeks of the course, to kindle students' enthusiasm for finding out how children develop. Judging by the overwhelmingly positive response we have received from students and instructors alike, it has.

Features

The most important feature of this book is the exposition, which we have tried to make as clear, compelling, and interesting as possible. As in previous editions, we have given extra attention to making it accessible to a broad range of students.

To further enhance the appeal and accessibility of the text, we have retained three types of discussion boxes that explore topics of special interest. "Applications" boxes focus on how child development research can be used to promote children's well-being. Among the applications that are summed up in these boxes are board-game procedures for improving preschoolers' understanding of numbers; the Carolina Abecedarian Project; interventions to reduce child abuse; programs, such as PATHS, for helping rejected children gain acceptance from their peers; and Fast Track interventions, which help aggressive children learn how to manage their anger and antisocial behavior. "Individual Differences" boxes focus on populations that differ from the norm with regard to the specific topic under consideration, or on variations among children in the general population. Some of these boxes highlight developmental problems such as autism, ADHD, dyslexia, and conduct disorder, while others focus on differences in the development of children that center on attachment status, gender, and cultural differences. "A Closer Look" boxes examine important and interesting research in greater depth than would otherwise be possible: the areas examined range from brain imaging techniques to gender socialization in the family to the developmental impact of homelessness.

We have also retained a number of other features intended to improve students' learning. These features include boldfacing key terms and supplying definitions both within the immediate text and in marginal glossaries; providing summaries at the end of each major section, as well as summaries for the overall chapter; and, at the end of each chapter, posing critical thinking questions intended to promote deeper consideration of essential topics.

New to the Third Edition

We have expanded our coverage of a number of research areas that have become increasingly important in recent years for both the students of child development and the instructors who teach it. In the following paragraphs, we outline some of the highlights of the third edition. Thank you for taking the time to look through the new edition, and we hope you find the changes in the third edition of *How Children Develop* to be useful and practical.

Chapter 15: Gender Development

This engaging chapter has been revised by Campbell Leaper, University of California–Santa Cruz. The chapter explores the development of gender knowledge, gender stereotypes, and gender-typed behavior, and it examines the biological, social, cognitive, and cultural influences that may contribute to patterns of gender development. It also provides a close analysis of gender differences and similarities in key aspects of cognitive and social development.

New and Expanded Coverage

In selecting what to cover from among the many new discoveries about child development, we have emphasized the studies that strike us as the most interesting and important. While retaining and thoroughly updating its essential coverage, the third edition of *How Children Develop* continues to explore a number of fascinating areas in which there has been great progress in the past few years. Among the areas of new and expanded coverage are:

- Gene–environment relations
- Brain development and functioning
- Applications of research to education
- Expanded coverage of dynamic-systems theories and its relevance to various domains
- The impact of socioeconomic status on children's development
- Neural bases of memory development and information processing
- Infants' understanding of other people
- Extensive new research on conceptual development
- Psychological measures of emotion
- Emotional regulation
- Interventions to foster children's social adjustment

Supplements

A variety of excellent teaching and learning tools are available to enrich and reinforce the text.

New! Video Tool Kit for Human Development

The Video Tool Kit for Human Development spans the full range of topics for the child development course, with 100 brief clips of research and news footage on topics ranging from prenatal development to the experience of child soldiers to empathy in adolescence. All these video clips can be assigned to students outside the classroom. A selection of these clips is integrated into approximately 40 interactive student activities that are easily assignable and assessable. The student activities are available exclusively online for this edition. Most instructor clips are available for downloading online, and a subset of more than 100 are available on CD-ROM and closed-captioned DVD.

Instructor's Resource Manual

Written by Lynne Baker-Ward, North Carolina State University, this innovative *Instructor's Resource Manual* includes handouts for student projects, reading lists of journal articles, course-planning suggestions, supplementary readings, and suggestions from the Instructor's Video Tool Kit, in addition to lecture guides, chapter overviews, and learning objectives.

Study Guide

The *Student Study Guide,* written by Jill Saxon, includes, in each chapter, a review of key concepts and multiple-choice and essay questions to help students evaluate their mastery of the material. Learning objectives from the *Instructor's Resource Manual* have been incorporated into each chapter of the *Study Guide* for this new edition.

Test Bank

To ensure seamless coordination between the content that students review and the content on which they are tested, Jill Saxon, who wrote the *Study Guide,* has also written the *Test Bank.* It includes 80 multiple-choice and 20 essay questions for each chapter. Each question is keyed to the textbook by topic, type (factual, definitional or conceptual, or applied), and level of difficulty.

Test Bank on CD-ROM

The *Diploma Test Bank CD-ROM,* on a dual platform for Windows and Macintosh, guides instructors through the process of creating a test and allows them to add, edit, and scramble questions; to change formats; and to include pictures, equations, and media links. The CD-ROM is also the access point for *Diploma Online Testing,* which allows creating and administering examinations on paper, over a network, or over the Internet.

PowerPoint Slides

PowerPoint slides are available in three formats that can be used as they are or can be customized. One set includes all the textbook's illustrations and tables. The second set consists of lecture slides, authored by Dana Narter, University of Arizona, that focus on key themes and terms in the book and include text illustrations and tables. A third set of PowerPoint slides provides an easy way to integrate the Instructor's Video Tool Kit clips into classroom lectures. All these prebuilt PowerPoint presentations are available on CD-ROM or on the companion Web site.

Observation Videos

Journey Through Childhood offers students an opportunity to observe children living in various cultures, from birth through adolescence, in a variety of settings.

Noted experts in child development discuss their work in areas ranging from the biology of early brain development to prosocial behavior in middle childhood. These are available on VHS and DVD.

The *Scientific American* Frontiers Videos

This series for developmental psychology features 17 video clips (lasting 15 minutes each) on a wide range of topics, including gene therapy, infant motor skills development, dyslexia, and memory. A guide to using this video series with specific chapters is included in the *Instructor's Resource Manual.*

Companion Web Site

Created by Rona McCall, Regis College, and Gwynn Dillard, North Carolina State University, the Siegler Companion Web Site (at worthpublishers.com/siegler) provides students with virtual study aids and instructors with a variety of teaching resources. Students will find, at no cost and with no password needed, chapter outlines, annotated Web links to expand on each chapter's coverage, online quizzes to test their knowledge, and interactive flashcards. The password-protected instructors' site offers three prebuilt PowerPoint slide sets (one containing outlines and two containing art) for each chapter and an online quiz gradebook.

Scientific American Reader to Accompany *How Children Develop*

The authors have compiled fifteen *Scientific American* articles relevant to key topics in the text. The selections range from classics such as Harry Harlow's "Love in Infant Monkeys" and Eleanor Gibson and Richard Walk's "The 'Visual Cliff'" to contemporary articles on such topics as the interaction of games and environment in the development of intelligence (Robert Plomin and John DeFries), the effects of child abuse on the developing brain (Martin Teicher), balancing work and family (Robert Pleck), and moral development (William Damon). These articles should enrich students' learning and help them to appreciate the process by which developmental scientists gain new understanding. This premium item can be packaged with the text at no additional cost.

Online Course Materials

As a service to adopters using WebCT or Blackboard course management systems, Worth provides electronic instructor and student resources in the appropriate format. Adopters of *How Children Develop* can request a Blackboard- or WebCT-formatted version of the book's test bank.

Acknowledgments

So many people have contributed (directly and indirectly) to this textbook that it is impossible to know where to start or where to stop in thanking them. All of us have been given exceptional support by our spouses and significant others—Jerry Clore, Jerry Harris, and Xiaodong Lin—and by our children—Benjamin Clore; Michael Harris; and Todd, Beth, and Aaron Siegler—as well as by our parents, relatives, friends, and other loved ones. Our advisors in college and graduate school, Ann Brown, Les Cohen, Harry Hake, Robert Liebert, Paul Mussen, and Jim Pate, helped to launch our careers and taught us how to recognize and appreciate good research. We also have all benefited from collaborators who shared our quest for understanding child development and from a great many exceptionally helpful and generous colleagues, including Karen Adolph, Martha Alibali, Renee Baillargeon, Sharon Carver, Zhe Chen, Richard Fabes, Cindy Fisher, David Klahr, Angel Lillard, Patrick Lemaire, John Opfer, Tracy Spinrad, David Uttal, and Carlos Valiente. We owe special thanks to our assistants, Sheri Towe and Theresa Treasure, who helped in innumerable ways in preparing the book.

We would also like to thank the many reviewers who contributed to this and previous editions: **Lynne Baker Ward,** North Carolina State University; **Hilary Barth,** Wesleyan University; **Christopher Beevers,** Texas University; **Martha Bell,** Virginia Tech; **Cynthia Berg,** University of Utah; **Rebecca Bigler,** Texas University; **Margaret Borkowski,** Saginaw Valley State University; **G. Leonard Burns,** Washington State University; **Myra Cox,** Harold Washington College; **Emily Davidson,** Texas A&M University–Main Campus; **Ed de St. Aubin,** Marquette University; **Marissa Diener,** University of Utah; **Dorothy Fragaszy,** University of Georgia; **Jennifer Ganger,** University of Pittsburgh; **Melissa Ghera,** St. John Fisher College; **Susan Graham,** University of Calgary; **Andrea Greenhoot,** University of Kansas; **Frederick Grote,** Western Washington University; **Alma Guyse,** Midland College; **Lauren Harris,** Michigan State University; **Karen Hartlep,** California State University–Bakersfield; **Patricia Hawley,** University of Kansas–Main; **Susan Hespos,** Northwestern University; **Doris Hiatt,** Monmouth University; **Kathryn Kipp,** University of Georgia; **Rosemary Krawczyk,** Minnesota State University; **Raymond Krukovsky,** Union County College; **Tara Kuther,** Western Connecticut State University; **Kathryn Lemery,** Arizona State University; **Barbara Licht,** Florida State University; **Angeline Lillard,** University of Virginia; **Wayne McMillin,** Northwestern State University; **Scott Miller,** University of Florida; **Keith Nelson,** Pennsylvania State University–Main Campus; **Paul Nicodemus,** Austin Peay State University; **John Opfer,** The Ohio State University; **Ann Repp,** Texas University; **Leigh Shaw,** Weber State University; **Rebekah Smith,** University of Texas–San Antonio; **Mark Strauss,** University of Pittsburgh–Main; **Spencer Thompson,** University of Texas–Permian Basin; **Lisa Travis,** University of Illinois Urbana–Champaign; **Roger Webb,** University of Arkansas–Little Rock; **Keri Weed,** University of South Carolina–Aiken; **Sherri Widen,** Boston College.

We would especially like to thank Campbell Leaper, University of California–Santa Cruz, for his major contributions to the revision of our chapter on gender development (Chapter 15). We are indebted to Campbell for bringing to the third edition his expertise and keen insight in this important area.

Thanks are particularly due to our friends and collaborators at Worth Publishers. As acquisitions editor and publisher, respectively, Charles Linsmeier and Catherine Woods provided exceptional support and any number of excellent suggestions. We would also like to thank Marge Byers, who nurtured our first edition from its inception and helped us to realize our vision. Peter Deane, our development editor, is in a class by himself in both skill and dedication. Peter's creative thinking and firm understanding of the field enhanced the content of the book in innumerable ways. We are deeply grateful to him. Our thanks go also to our project editors Jaclyn Castaldo, Vivien Weiss, and Tracey Kuehn, art director Barbara Reingold, cover and text designer Kevin Kall, photo editor Bianca Moscatelli, photo researcher Julie Tesser, production manager Sarah Segal, and layout designer MPS Limited for their excellent work. They have helped to create a book that we hope you will find a pleasure to look at as well as to read. Marketing manager Katherine Nurre provided outstanding promotional materials to inform professors about the book. Supplements coordinators Andrea Musick and Stacey Alexander coordinated the superb package of ancillary material.

Finally, we want to thank our "book team" of sales representatives and managers. Tom Kling, Julie Hirshman, Kari Ewalt, Greg David, Tom Scotty, Cindy Rabinowitz, Glenn Russell, and Matt Dunning provided a sales perspective, valuable suggestions, and unflagging enthusiasm throughout this project.

third edition

how children

DEVELOP

HENRI MATISSE, *Face in the Flowers*

1

An Introduction to Child Development

THEMES

Nature and Nurture

❖

The Active Child

❖

Continuity/Discontinuity

❖

Mechanisms of Change

❖

The Sociocultural Context

❖

Individual Differences

❖

Research and Children's Welfare

❖

In 1955, a group of child-development researchers began a unique study. Their goal, like that of many developmental researchers, was to find out how biological and environmental factors influence children's intellectual, social, and emotional growth. What made their study unique was that they examined these diverse aspects of development for all 698 children born that year on the Hawaiian island of Kauai and continued studying the children's development for more than 30 years.

With the parents' consent, the research team, headed by Emmy Werner, collected many types of data about the children. To learn about possible complications during the prenatal period and birth, they examined physicians' records. To learn about family interactions and the children's behavior at home, they arranged for nurses and social workers to observe the families and to interview the children's mothers when the children were 1 year old and again when they were 10 years old. The researchers also interviewed teachers about the children's academic performance and classroom behavior during the elementary school years. In addition, they examined police, family court, and social service records that involved the children, either as victims or perpetrators. Finally, the researchers administered standardized intelligence and personality tests to the children when they were 10 and 18 years old and interviewed them at age 18 and again in their early 30s to find out how they saw their own development.

Results from this study illustrated some of the many ways in which biological and environmental factors combine to influence child development. For example, children who experienced prenatal or birth complications were more likely than others to develop physical handicaps, mental illness, and learning difficulties. But whether they did develop such problems—and if so, to what degree—depended a great deal on their home environment. Such factors as parents' income, educational level, and mental health, together with the quality of the relationship between the parents, exerted particularly important influences on the children's subsequent development. By age 2, toddlers who had experienced severe prenatal or birth problems but who lived in harmonious middle-income families were nearly as advanced in language and motor skills as were children who had not experienced such problems. By the time the children were 10-year-olds, prenatal and birth problems were consistently related to psychological difficulties *only* if the children also grew up in poor rearing conditions.

What of children who faced both biological and environmental challenges—prenatal or birth complications *and* adverse family circumstances? The majority of these children developed serious learning or behavior problems by age 10. By age 18, most had acquired a police record, experienced mental health problems, or become an unmarried parent. However, one-third of such at-risk children showed impressive resilience, growing up into young adults who, in the words of Werner (1989, p. 109), "loved well, worked well, and played well." These children often had been befriended by an adult outside the immediate family—an uncle, aunt, neighbor, teacher, or clergyperson—who helped them navigate through the difficulties and dangers in their environment.

Michael was one such resilient child. Born prematurely, with low birth weight, to teenage parents, he spent the first three weeks of his life in a hospital, separated from his mother. By his 8th birthday, Michael's parents were divorced, his mother had deserted the family, and he and his three brothers and sisters were being raised by their father, with the help of their elderly grandparents. Yet by age 18, Michael was successful in school, had high self-esteem, was popular with his peers, and was a caring young man with a positive attitude toward life. The fact that there are many children like Michael—children who show great resilience in the face of adversity—is among the most heartening findings of research on child development.

Werner's remarkable study, like most studies of child development, raises as many questions as it answers. How, exactly, did the children's biological nature, their family environment, and the environments they encountered outside the family combine to shape their development? Would the same results have emerged if the study had been conducted in, say, a primarily African-American or Latino urban community rather than in the primarily Asian, Native Hawaiian, and northern European rural community studied in Kauai? Was it chance that some children from adverse backgrounds were befriended by adults from outside the immediate family, or did the children's individual characteristics, such as winning personalities, attract the friendship and help they received? Can programs be designed that would allow more children to overcome difficult backgrounds?

Reading this chapter will introduce you to these and other basic questions about child development. Once you have read the chapter, you should have a clear sense of why it is worthwhile to study child development. You should also have an understanding of what researchers are trying to learn about the development of children and what methods they use in this endeavor.

Will these children be resilient enough to overcome their disadvantaged environment? The answer will depend in large part on how many risk factors they face and on their personal characteristics.

© JEFF GREENBERG / THE IMAGE WORKS

Why Study Child Development?

For us, both as researchers and as parents, and for many others, the sheer enjoyment of watching children and trying to understand them is its own justification: What could be more fascinating than the development of a child? But there are also practical and intellectual reasons for studying child development. Understanding how children develop can help parents raise their children more effectively, lead society as a whole to adopt wiser policies regarding children's welfare, and answer intriguing questions about human nature.

Raising Children

Being a good parent is not easy. Among its many challenges are the endless questions it raises over the years. When will my baby start to know who I am? Should I stay at home with her, or should I enroll her in day care so that she can get to know other children? If she starts talking earlier than her friends, does that mean that she is gifted? Will she have the same difficulties learning math that I did? How can I help her deal with her anger?

Child-development research can help answer such questions. For example, one problem that confronts almost all parents is how to promote their children's management of anger and other negative emotions. Research indicates several effective approaches (Denham, 1998, 2006). One is expressing sympathy: when parents respond to their children's distress with sympathy, the children are better able to cope with the situation causing the distress. Another effective approach is helping angry children find positive alternatives to expressing anger. For example, distracting them from the source of their anger and encouraging them to do something they enjoy helps them cope with the hostile feelings.

Posters like this are used in the turtle technique to remind children of ways to control anger.

These strategies are also effective when used by other people who contribute to raising children, such as day-care personnel and teachers. One demonstration of this was provided by a special curriculum that was devised for helping preschoolers (3- and 4-year-olds) who were angry and out of control (Denham & Burton, 1996). With this curriculum, which lasted 32 weeks, preschool teachers helped children recognize their own and other children's emotions, taught them techniques for controlling their anger, and guided them in resolving conflicts with other children. One approach that children were taught for coping with anger was the "turtle technique." When children felt themselves becoming angry, they were to move away from other children and retreat into their "turtle shell," where they could think through the situation until they were ready to emerge from the shell. Posters were placed around the classroom to remind children of what to do when they became angry.

The curriculum was quite successful. Children who participated in it became more skillful in recognizing and regulating anger when they experienced it and were generally less negative. For example, one boy, who had regularly gotten into fights when angry, told the teacher after an argument with another child over a toy, "See, I used my words, not my hands" (Denham, 1998, p. 219). The benefits of this program can be long-term. In one test conducted with children in special education classrooms, positive effects were still in evidence two years after children completed the curriculum (Greenberg & Kusche, 2006). Similar programs have proved valuable for improving emotional understanding and social-interaction skills in elementary school children (Domitrovich, Cortes, & Greenberg, 2007). As this example illustrates, knowledge of child-development research can help teachers as well as parents.

Choosing Social Policies

Another reason to learn about child development is to be able to make informed decisions not just about one's own children but also about a wide variety of social-policy questions that affect children in general. For example, are public resources better spent trying to detect and prevent potential developmental problems in young children who seem at risk for them, or is it more cost-effective to reserve the resources for treating children who have actually developed problems? How much trust should judges and juries place in preschoolers' testimony in child-abuse cases? Should preschool programs that teach academic and social skills be made available to all children from low-income families, and should such programs be followed up beyond the preschool period? How effective are health-education courses aimed at reducing teenage smoking, drinking, and pregnancy, and how can such courses be improved? Child-development research can inform discussion of all of these policy decisions and many others.

Consider the issue of how much trust to put in preschoolers' courtroom testimony. At present, more than 100,000 children testify in legal cases each year (Bruck, Ceci, & Principe, 2006; Ceci & Bruck, 1998). Many of these children are very young: more than 40% of children who testify in sexual-abuse trials, for example, are below age 5, and almost 40% of substantiated sexual abuse cases involve children younger than age 7 (Bruck, Ceci, & Principe, 2006; Gray, 1993). The stakes are obviously extremely high in such cases. If juries believe children who falsely testify that they were abused, innocent people may spend years in jail, and their reputations may be ruined forever. If juries do not believe children who accurately report abuse, the perpetrators will go free and probably abuse other children. So how can we know when to believe young children's testimony? What kind of questioning helps children testify accurately about events that are emotionally difficult for them to discuss? And what kind of questioning biases them to report experiences that never actually occurred?

Psychological research has helped answer such questions. In one experiment, researchers designed a test to see whether biased questioning affects the accuracy of young children's memory for events involving touching one's own and other people's bodies. The researchers began by having 3- to 6-year-olds play a game, similar to "Simon Says," in which the children were told to touch various parts of their body and those of other children. A month later, the researchers had a social worker interview the children about their experiences during the game (Ceci & Bruck, 1998). Before the social worker conducted the interviews, she was given a description of each child's experiences. Unknown to her, the description included inaccurate as well as accurate information. For example, she might have been told that a particular child had touched her own stomach and another child's nose, when in fact the child had touched her own stomach and the other child's foot. After receiving the description, the social worker was given instructions much like those in a court case: "Find out what the child remembers."

As it turned out, the version of events that the social worker had heard often influenced her questions. If, for example, a child's account of an event was contrary to what the social worker believed to be the case, she tended to question the child repeatedly about the event ("Are you sure you touched his foot? Is it possible you touched some other part of his body?"). Faced with such repeated questioning, children fairly often changed their responses, with 34% of 3- and 4-year-olds, and 18% of 5- and 6-year-olds, eventually corroborating at least one of the social worker's incorrect beliefs. Especially alarming, the children became increasingly confident about their inaccurate memories with repeated questioning. Children were led to "remember" not only plausible events that never happened but also unlikely ones that the social worker had been told about. For example, some children "recalled" their knee being licked and a marble being inserted in their ear. Clearly, an interrogator's beliefs about what happened in a given event can influence how young children answer the interrogator's questions about the event.

Studies such as this have yielded a number of conclusions regarding children's testimony in legal proceedings. The most important finding is that when shielded from leading questions, even 3- to 5-year-olds can be reliable witnesses. They often forget details of events, but what they do say is usually accurate (Bruck et al., 2006; Howe & Courage, 1997). At the same time, young children are highly susceptible to leading questions, especially ones asked repeatedly. The younger the children, the more susceptible they are and the more their recall reflects the biases of the interviewer's questions. In addition, realistic props, such as anatomically correct dolls, that are often used in judicial cases in the hopes of improving recall of sexual abuse, actually have the effect of increasing inaccurate claims, perhaps by blurring the line between fantasy play and reality (Pipe et al., 1999; Salmon, 2001). The conclusion from the research is that to obtain accurate testimony, especially from very young children, questions should be stated in a neutral

In courtrooms such as this one, asking questions that will help children to testify accurately is of the utmost importance.

STACY PICK / STOCK BOSTON

fashion that does not presuppose the answer, questions that the child has already answered should not be repeated, and props associated with fantasy play should not be used (Bruck et al., 2006). In addition to helping courts obtain more accurate testimony from young children, such research-based conclusions illustrate how, at a broader level, knowledge of child development can inform social policies.

Understanding Human Nature

A third reason to study child development is to better understand human nature. Many of the most intriguing questions regarding human nature concern children. For example, does learning start only after children are born, or can it occur in the womb? Can later upbringing in a loving home overcome the detrimental effects of early rearing in a loveless institutional setting? Do children vary in personality and intellect from the day they are born, or are they similar at birth, with differences arising only because they have different experiences? Until recently, people could only speculate about the answers to such questions. Now, however, developmental scientists have methods that enable them to observe, describe, and explain the process of development. As a result, our understanding of children, and of human nature, is growing rapidly.

A particularly poignant illustration of the way in which scientific research can increase understanding of human nature comes from studies of how children's ability to overcome the effects of early maltreatment is affected by its timing, that is, the age at which the maltreatment occurs and ends. One such research program has examined children whose early life was spent in horribly inadequate orphanages in Romania in the late 1980s and early 1990s (Kreppner et al., 2007; Nelson et al., 2007; Rutter et al., 2004). Children in these orphanages had almost no contact with any caregiver. For reasons that remain unknown, the communist dictatorship of that era instructed staff workers not to interact with the children even when giving them their bottles. In fact, the staff provided the infants with so little physical contact that the crown of many infants' heads became flattened from the babies' lying on their back for 18 to 20 hours per day.

Shortly after the collapse of communist rule in Romania, a number of these children were adopted by families in Great Britain. When these children arrived in Britain, most were severely malnourished, with more than half being in the lowest 3% of children their age in terms of height, weight, and head circumference. Most also showed varying degrees of mental retardation and were socially immature. The parents who adopted them knew of their deprived backgrounds and were highly motivated to provide loving homes that would help the children overcome the damaging effects of their early mistreatment.

This infant is one of the children adopted from a Romanian orphanage in the 1990s. How successfully he develops will depend not only on the quality of caregiving he receives in his adoptive home but also on the amount of time he spent in the orphanage and the age at which he was adopted.

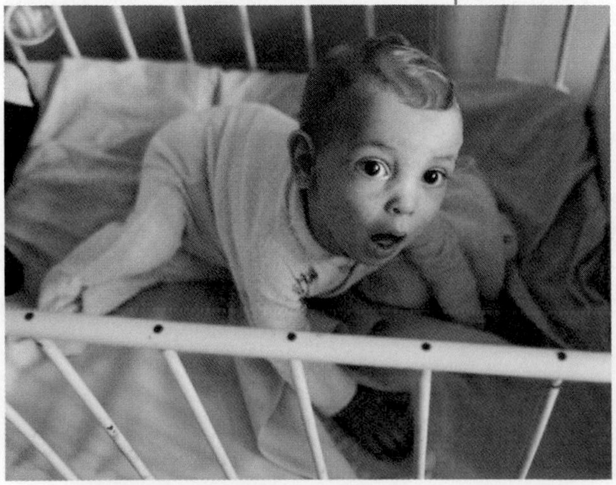
PETER TURNLEY / CORBIS

To evaluate the long-term effects of their early deprivation, the physical, intellectual, and social development of about 150 of the Romanian-born children was examined at age 6 years and again at age 11 years. To provide a basis of comparison, the researchers also followed the development of a group of British-born children who had been adopted into British families before they were 6 months of age. Simply put, the question was whether human nature is sufficiently flexible that the Romanian-born children could overcome the extreme deprivation of their early experience, and if so, would that flexibility decrease with the children's age and the length of the deprivation.

By age 6, the physical development of the Romanian-born children had improved considerably, both in absolute terms and in relation to the British-born comparison group. However, the Romanian children's early experience of deprivation continued to influence their development, with the extent of negative effects depending on how long the children had been institutionalized. Romanian-born children who were adopted by British families before age 6 months, and who had therefore spent the smallest portion of their early lives in the orphanages, weighed about the same as British-born children when both were 6-year-olds. Romanian-born children adopted between the ages of 6 and 24 months, and who therefore had spent more of their early lives in the orphanages, weighed less; and those adopted between the ages of 24 and 42 months weighed even less (Rutter et al., 2004).

Intellectual development showed a similar pattern. The Romanian-born children who had been adopted before age 6 months demonstrated levels of intellectual competence at 6 years comparable to those of the British-born comparison group. Romanian-born children adopted between the ages of 6 and 24 months did somewhat less well, and those adopted between the ages of 24 and 42 months did even more poorly. A sense of the magnitude of the long-term effects of institutionalization is conveyed by the percentage of the Romanian-born children with intellectual retardation. Among children adopted before 6 months of age, 2% scored in the retarded range at age 6 years, the same percentage as in the British population as a whole. In contrast, among children who spent between 24 and 42 months in the institutions, 33% scored in the retarded range at age 6 years (Rutter et al., 2004).

The early experience in the orphanages had similar damaging effects on the children's social development (Kreppner et al., 2007; O'Connor & Rutter, 2000; Rutter et al., 2004). Almost 20% of the Romanian-born children who were adopted after age 6 months showed extremely abnormal social behavior at age 6 years (versus 3% of the British-born comparison group). Particularly striking was that they often seemed not to differentiate between their parents and unfamiliar adults—they tended to be unusually friendly to strangers, and more often than other children their age were willing to go off with them. In addition, the Romanian-born children often did not look to their parents for reassurance in anxiety-provoking situations. They also tended not to form friendships with peers.

When the children's intellectual and social development was examined again at age 11, the length of time spent in the Romanian orphanages continued to influence their development. Despite five more years with their adoptive families, the 11-year-olds who earlier had spent more than 6 months in the orphanages showed deficits as great as those they had demonstrated as 6-year-olds (Beckett et al., 2006; Kreppner et al., 2007). For example, on tests of intelligence on which the average score is 100, children who spent their first 6 to 24 months in the Romanian orphanages had average scores of 86 at both 6 years and 11 years, and those who spent their first 24 to 42 months in the orphanages had average scores of 77 at 6 years and 83 at 11 years. In contrast, their peers who had moved to Britain before age 6 months had typical average scores at both 6 and 11 years (102 and 101).

These findings reflect a basic principle of child development that is relevant to many aspects of human nature: *The timing of experiences influences their effects.* In the present case, children were sufficiently flexible to overcome the effects of living in the loveless, unstimulating institutions if the deprivation lasted no longer than the first 6 months of their lives, but living in the institutions beyond that time had effects that were rarely overcome, even when children spent subsequent years in loving and stimulating environments. The adoptive families clearly made a huge positive difference in their children's lives, but for most children adopted after age 6 months, effects of their early deprivation remained years later.

review: There are at least three good reasons to learn about child development. The first is to gain information and understanding that can help parents raise their own children successfully. The second is to gain insight into social-policy issues related to children and to help society adopt policies that promote children's well-being. The third is to better understand human nature in general.

Historical Foundations of the Study of Child Development

From ancient Greece to the early years of the twentieth century, a number of profound thinkers observed and wrote about children. Their goals were like those of contemporary researchers: to help people become better parents, to improve children's well-being, and to understand human nature. Unlike contemporary researchers, they usually based their conclusions on unsystematic observations of small numbers of children whom they happened to encounter. Still, the issues they raised are sufficiently important, and their insights sufficiently deep, that their views continue to be of interest.

Early Philosophers' Views of Children's Development

Some of the earliest recorded ideas about children's development were those of Plato and Aristotle. These classic Greek philosophers, who lived in the fourth century B.C., were particularly interested in how children's development is influenced by their nature and by the nurture they receive.

Both Plato and Aristotle believed that the long-term welfare of society depended on the proper raising of children. Careful upbringing was essential because children's basic nature would otherwise lead to their becoming rebellious and unruly. Plato viewed the rearing of boys as a particularly demanding challenge for parents and teachers:

> Now of all wild things, a boy is the most difficult to handle. Just because he more than any other has a fount of intelligence in him which has not yet "run clear," he is the craftiest, most mischievous, and unruliest of brutes.
>
> (*Laws,* bk. 7, p. 808)

Consistent with this view, Plato emphasized self-control and discipline as the most important goals of education (Borstelmann, 1983).

Aristotle agreed with Plato that discipline was necessary, but he was more concerned with fitting child-rearing to the needs of the individual child. In his words:

> It would seem . . . that a study of individual character is the best way of making education perfect, for then each [child] has a better chance of receiving the treatment that suits him.
>
> (*Nicomachean Ethics,* bk. 10, chap. 9, p. 1180)

Plato and Aristotle differed more profoundly in their views of how children acquire knowledge. Plato believed that children are born with innate knowledge.

For example, he believed that children are born with a concept of "animal" that, from birth onward, automatically allows them to recognize that the dogs, cats, and other creatures they encounter are animals. In contrast, Aristotle believed that all knowledge comes from experience and that the mind of an infant is like a blackboard on which nothing has yet been written.

Roughly 2000 years later, the English philosopher John Locke (1632–1704) and the French philosopher Jean-Jacques Rousseau (1712–1778) refocused attention on the question of how parents and society in general can best promote children's development. Locke, like Aristotle, viewed the child as a tabula rasa, or blank slate, whose development largely reflects the nurture provided by the child's parents and the broader society. He believed that the most important goal of child-rearing is the growth of character. To build children's character, parents need to set good examples of honesty, stability, and gentleness. They also need to avoid indulging the child, especially early in life. However, once discipline and reason have been instilled,

> authority should be relaxed as fast as their age, discretion, and good behavior could allow it. . . . The sooner you treat him as a man, the sooner he will begin to be one.
>
> (Cited in Borstelmann, 1983, p. 20)

In contrast to Locke's advocating discipline before freedom, Rousseau believed that parents and society should give children maximum freedom from the beginning. Rousseau claimed that children learn primarily from their own spontaneous interactions with objects and other people, rather than through instruction by parents or teachers. He even argued that children should not receive any formal education until about age 12, when they reach "the age of reason" and can judge for themselves the worth of what they read and are told. Before then, they should be allowed the freedom to explore whatever interests them.

Although formulated long ago, these and other philosophical positions continue to underlie many contemporary debates, including whether children should receive direct instruction in desired skills and knowledge or be given maximum freedom to discover the skills and knowledge for themselves. As we will see in later chapters, these philosophical positions are likewise relevant to such debates as whether intelligence and personality are basically fixed at birth or change profoundly with children's experiences, and whether language is acquired through mechanisms that are unique to people and to language or is acquired through mechanisms that other species also possess and that are used to learn other skills as well.

Social Reform Movements

Another precursor of the contemporary field of child psychology was early social reform movements devoted to improving children's lives by changing the conditions in which they lived. During the Industrial Revolution of the eighteenth and nineteenth centuries, a great many children in Europe and the United States worked as poorly paid laborers with no legal protections. Some were as young as 5 and 6 years old; many worked up to 12 hours a day in factories or mines, often in extremely hazardous circumstances. These harsh conditions concerned a number of social reformers, who began to study how such circumstances might be affecting the children's development. For example, in a speech before the British House of

© BETTMANN / CORBIS

During the eighteenth, nineteenth, and early twentieth centuries, many young children worked in coal mines and factories. Their hours were long, and the work was often unhealthy and dangerous. Concern over the well-being of such children led to some of the earliest research on child development.

Commons in 1843, the Earl of Shaftesbury noted that the narrow tunnels where children dug out coal

> [have] very insufficient drainage [and] are so low that only little boys can work in them, which they do naked, and often in mud and water, dragging sledge-tubs by the girdle and chain. . . . Children of amiable temper and conduct, at 7 years of age, often return next season from the collieries greatly corrupted . . . with most hellish dispositions.
>
> (Quoted in Kessen, 1965, pp. 46–50)

The Earl of Shaftesbury's effort at social reform brought partial success—a law forbidding employment of girls and of boys under age 10. In addition to bringing about the first child labor laws, this and other early social reform movements established a legacy of research conducted for the benefit of children and provided some of the earliest recorded descriptions of the adverse effects that harsh environments can have on their development.

Darwin's Theory of Evolution

Later in the nineteenth century, Charles Darwin's work on evolution inspired a number of scientists to propose that intensive study of children's development might lead to important insights into the nature of the human species. Darwin himself was interested in child development and in 1877 published an article entitled "A Biographical Sketch of an Infant," which presented his careful observations of the motor, sensory, and emotional growth of his infant son, William. Darwin's "baby biography"—a systematic description of William's day-to-day development—represented one of the first methods for studying children. Such intensive studies of individual children's growth continue to be a distinctive feature of the modern field of child development. Darwin's evolutionary theory also continues to influence the thinking of modern developmentalists on a wide range of topics: infants' attachment to their mothers (Bowlby, 1969), innate fear of natural dangers such as spiders and snakes (Rakison & Derringer, 2008), sex differences (Geary, 2009), aggression and altruism (Tooby & Cosmides, 2005), and the mechanisms underlying learning (Siegler, 1996).

The Emergence of Child Development as a Discipline

At the end of the nineteenth century and the beginning of the twentieth, child development emerged as a formal field of inquiry. A number of European and North American universities established departments of child development, and the first professional journals devoted to the study of child development were founded. The French researcher Alfred Binet and his colleagues pioneered the systematic testing of children's intelligence and were among the first to investigate differences among children of the same age. The American researchers G. Stanley Hall and, somewhat later, Arnold Gesell presented questionnaires to large numbers of parents, teachers, and children in order to detail numerous aspects of development—from the feeding schedules of infants and the toilet training of toddlers to the play activities of preschoolers, the social relationships of elementary school students, and the physical and psychological changes experienced by adolescents.

Also emerging during this period were the first theories of child development that incorporated research findings. One prominent theory, that of the Austrian psychiatrist Sigmund Freud, included results from Freud's explorations of hypnosis with his patients and from his analysis of their recollections of their dreams and childhood experiences. According to Freud's *psychoanalytic theory,* biological drives, especially sexual ones, are a crucial influence on development. Another prominent theory of the same era, that of the American psychologist John Watson, was based primarily on the results of experiments that examined learning in animals and children. Watson's *behaviorist theory* proposed that children's development is determined by environmental factors, especially the rewards and punishments that follow particular events and behaviors.

By current standards, the research methods on which these theories were based were crude. Nonetheless, these early scientific theories were better grounded in research evidence than were their predecessors, and, as you will soon see, they inspired more sophisticated thinking about how development occurs and more sophisticated methods for studying it.

review: Philosophers such as Plato, Aristotle, Locke, and Rousseau, and early scientific theorists such as Darwin, Freud, and Watson, raised many of the deepest issues about child development. These issues included how nature and nurture influence development, how best to raise children, and how knowledge of children's development can be used to advance their welfare. Although the work of these thinkers often lacked scientific rigor, it helped set the stage for modern perspectives on these and other fundamental issues.

Enduring Themes in Child Development

The modern study of child development begins with a set of fundamental questions. Everything else—theories, concepts, research methods, data, and so on—is part of the effort to answer these questions. Although experts in the field might choose different particular questions as the most important, there is widespread agreement that the seven questions in Table 1.1 are among the most important. These questions form a set of themes that we will highlight throughout the book as we examine specific aspects of child development. In this section, we introduce and briefly discuss each question and the theme that corresponds to it.

TABLE 1.1

Basic Questions About Child Development

1. How do nature and nurture together shape development? *(Nature and nurture)*
2. How do children shape their own development? *(The active child)*
3. In what ways is development continuous, and in what ways is it discontinuous? *(Continuity/discontinuity)*
4. How does change occur? *(Mechanisms of developmental change)*
5. How does the sociocultural context influence development? *(The sociocultural context)*
6. How do children become so different from each other? *(Individual differences)*
7. How can research promote children's well-being? *(Research and children's welfare)*

1 *Nature* and *Nurture*: How Do Nature and Nurture Together Shape Development?

The most basic question about child development is how nature and nurture interact to shape the developmental process. **Nature** refers to our biological endowment, in particular, the genes we receive from our parents. This genetic inheritance influences every aspect of our make-up, from broad characteristics such as physical appearance, personality, intellectual ability, and mental health to specific preferences, such as our political attitudes and our propensity for thrill-seeking (Plomin, 2004; Rothbart & Bates, 2006). **Nurture** refers to the wide range of environments, both physical and social, that influence our development, including the womb in which we spend the prenatal period, the homes in which we grow up,

nature our biological endowment; the genes we receive from our parents

nurture the environments, both physical and social, that influence our development

THE EVERETT COLLECTION

Could appropriate nurture have allowed the Three Stooges to become upper-class gentlemen?

the schools that we attend, the broader communities in which we live, and the many people with whom we interact.

Popular depictions of the nature–nurture issue often present it as an either/or question: "What determines how a person develops, heredity *or* environment?" However, this either/or phrasing of the question is deeply misleading. Every characteristic that we possess—our intellect, our personality, our physical appearance, our emotions—is created through the *joint* workings of nature and nurture, that is, through the constant interaction of our genes and our environment. Accordingly, rather than asking whether nature or nurture is more important, developmentalists ask how nature *and* nurture work together to shape development.

That this is the right question to ask is illustrated by findings on the development of schizophrenia. Schizophrenia is a serious mental illness characterized by hallucinations, delusions, disordered thinking, and irrational behavior. Although most children of schizophrenic parents do not themselves develop the illness, their probability of developing it is much higher than that of other children, even when they are adopted as infants and therefore are not exposed to their parents' schizophrenic behavior (Kety et al., 1994). Among identical twins, whose genes are identical, if one twin has schizophrenia, the other twin has a nearly 50% chance of also having schizophrenia, which is far greater than the chance of children in general having schizophrenia. Thus, children's genes influence their likelihood of becoming schizophrenic. At the same time, the environment is also clearly influential, since roughly 50% of children who have an identical twin with schizophrenia do not become schizophrenic themselves, and children who grow up in troubled homes are more likely to become schizophrenic than are children raised in a normal household. Most important, however, is the interaction of genes and environment. A study of adopted children, some of whose biological parents were schizophrenic, indicated that the only children who had any substantial likelihood of becoming schizophrenic were those who had a schizophrenic parent *and* who also were adopted into a troubled family (Tienari et al., 1990).

How nature and nurture interact is a major theme in all areas of child development research. Consider two more examples of such nature–nurture interactions, one concerning the development of conscience, the other concerning the development of intelligence. Among children born with a fearful temperament, a strong conscience at age 5 years is associated with gentle maternal discipline; in contrast, among fearless children, a strong conscience at age 5 is associated with an especially close and positive mother–child relationship, regardless of the type of discipline the mother uses (Kochanska, 1997a). Turning to intellectual development, the relation between IQ and the quality of a child's home environment is stronger among children from impoverished families than among children from more affluent families (Turkheimer et al., 2003). As these examples illustrate, to say that either nature or nurture is more important than the other, or even that the two are equally important, is to oversimplify the developmental process. All developmental outcomes result from the constant interaction of nature *and* nurture.

2 *The Active Child:* How Do Children Shape Their Own Development?

With all the attention that is paid to the role of nature and nurture in development, many people overlook the ways in which children's actions contribute to their own development. Even in infancy and early childhood, this contribution can be seen in a multitude of ways, including attentional patterns, language use, and play.

Children first begin to shape their own development through their selection of what to pay attention to. Even newborns prefer to look toward things that move and make sounds. This preference helps them learn about important parts of the world, such as people, other animals, and inanimate moving objects such as cars and trucks. When looking at people, infants' attention is particularly drawn to faces, especially their mother's face: given a choice of looking at a stranger's face or their mother's, even 1-month-olds choose to look at Mom's (Bartrip, Morton, & de Schonen, 2001). At first, infants' attention to their mother's face is not accompanied by any visible emotion, but by the end of the 2nd month, infants smile and coo more when focusing intently on their mother's face than at other times. This smiling and cooing by the infant, in turn, elicits further smiling and talking by the mother, which elicits further cooing and smiling by the infant, and so on (Lavelli & Fogel, 2005). In this way, infants' preference for attending to their mother's face leads to reciprocal interactions that can strengthen the mother–infant bond.

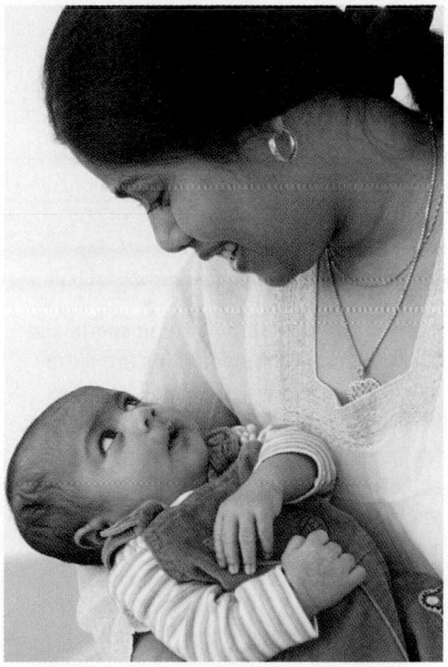

One of the earliest ways children shape their own development is through their choice of where to look. From the first month of life, seeing Mom is a high priority.

Once children begin to speak, usually between 9 and 15 months of age, their contribution to their own development becomes more evident. For example, toddlers (1- and 2-year-olds) often talk when they are alone in a room. Only if children were internally motivated to learn language would they practice talking when no one was present to react to what they are saying. Many parents are startled when they hear this "crib speech" and wonder if something is wrong with a baby who would engage in such odd-seeming behavior. However, the activity is entirely normal, and the practice probably helps toddlers improve their speech.

Young children's play provides many other examples of how their internally motivated activity contributes to their development. Children play by themselves for the sheer joy of doing so, but they also learn a great deal in the process. Anyone who has seen a baby bang a spoon against different parts of a high chair or intentionally drop food on the floor would agree that, for the baby, the activity is its own reward. At the same time, the baby is learning about the noises made by colliding objects, about the speed at which objects fall, and perhaps about the limits of his or her parents' patience.

Young children's fantasy play seems to make an especially large contribution to their knowledge of themselves and other people. Starting at around age 2 years, children sometimes pretend to be different people in make-believe dramas. For example, they may pretend to be superheroes doing battle with monsters or play the role of parents taking care of babies. In addition to being inherently enjoyable, these make-believe scenes appear to teach children valuable lessons, such as how to cope with fears and understand their own and others' reactions (Howes & Matheson, 1992; Smith, 2003).

Play contributes to children's development in many ways, including the spatial understanding and attention to detail required to do puzzles.

In some ways, children's contribution to their own development increases as they grow older (Scarr & McCartney, 1983). When children are young, their parents largely determine their environments, deciding whether or not they will attend day care, where they will play and with whom, what kind of after-school activities they will participate in, and so on. In contrast, older children and adolescents choose many environments, friends, and activities for themselves. Their choices can exert a large impact on their future. To cite just one example, students who participate in one or more extracurricular activities, such as an athletic team or club, for at least a year between 6th and 10th grade are more likely to complete high school, and less likely to be arrested, than are initially similar peers who do not participate in extracurricular activities (Mahoney, 2000). Thus, children contribute to their own development from early in life, and their contributions seem to increase as they grow older.

DAVID YOUNG-WOLFF / PHOTOEDIT

Adolescents who participate in sports and other extracurricular activities are more likely to complete high school, and less likely to get into trouble, than peers who are not engaged in these activities. This is an example of how children contribute to their own development.

3 *Continuity/Discontinuity:* In What Ways Is Development Continuous, and in What Ways Is It Discontinuous?

Some scientists envision children's development as a **continuous** process of small changes, like that of a pine tree growing taller and taller. Others see the process as a series of sudden, **discontinuous** changes, like the transition from caterpillar to cocoon to butterfly (Figure 1.1). The debate over which of these views is more accurate has continued for decades.

Researchers who view development as *discontinuous* start from a common observation: children of different ages seem *qualitatively different.* A 4-year-old and a 6-year-old, for example, seem to differ not just in how much they know but in the whole way they think about the world. To appreciate these differences, consider two conversations between Beth, the daughter of one of the authors, and Beth's mother. The first conversation took place when Beth was 4 years old, the second,

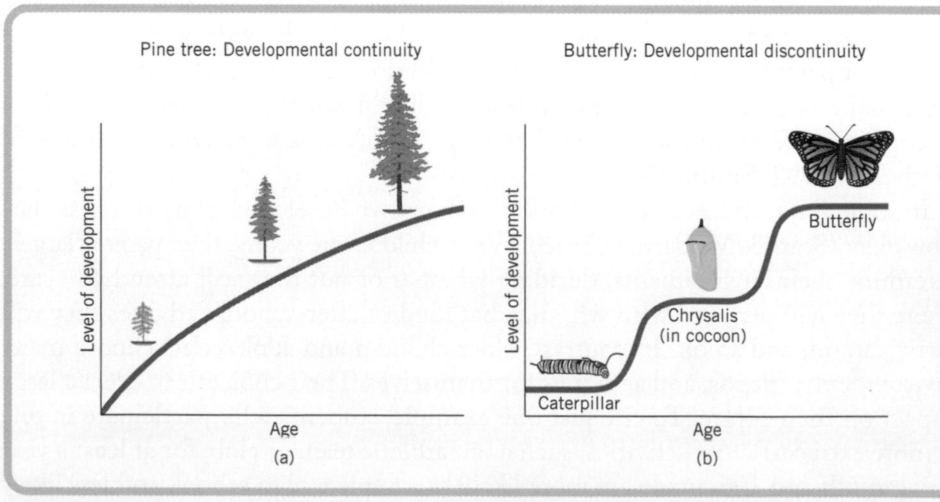

FIGURE 1.1 Continuous and discontinuous development Some researchers see development as a continuous, gradual process, akin to a tree's growing taller with each passing year. Others see it as a discontinuous process, involving sudden dramatic changes, such as the transition from caterpillar to cocoon to butterfly. Both views fit some aspects of child development.

continuous development the idea that changes with age occur gradually, in small increments, like that of a pine tree growing taller and taller

discontinuous development the idea that changes with age include occasional large shifts, like the transition from caterpillar to cocoon to butterfly when she was 6. Both conversations occurred after Beth had watched her mother pour all the water from a typical drinking glass into a taller, narrower glass. Here is the conversation that occurred when Beth was 4:

Mother: Is there still the same amount of water?
Beth: No.
Mother: Was there more water before, or is there more now?
Beth: There's more now.
Mother: What makes you think so?
Beth: The water is higher; you can see it's more.
Mother: Now I'll pour the water back into the regular glass. Is there the same amount of water as when the water was in the same glass before?
Beth: Yes.
Mother: Now I'll pour all the water again into the tall thin glass. Does the amount of water stay the same?
Beth: No, I already told you, there's more water when it's in the tall glass.

TONY FREEMAN / PHOTOEDIT

Children's behavior on Piaget's conservation-of-liquid problem is often used to exemplify the idea that development is discontinuous. The child first sees equal amounts of liquid in similarly shaped glasses and an empty, differently shaped glass. Then, the child sees the liquid from one glass poured into the differently shaped glass. Finally, the child is asked whether the amount of liquid remains the same or whether one glass has more. Young children, like this boy, are unshakable in their belief that the glass with the taller liquid column has more liquid. A year or two later, they are equally unshakable in their belief that the amount of liquid in each glass is the same.

Two years later, Beth responded to the same problem quite differently:

Mother: Is there still the same amount of water?
Beth: Of course!

What accounts for this change in Beth's thinking? Ordinary observations of water being poured cannot explain why the change occurred when it did; Beth had seen water poured many times before she was 4, yet failed to develop the understanding that the volume of water remains constant. Experience with the specific task also does not explain the timing of the change: between the first and second incidents, Beth was never asked whether the amount of water remained the same when water was poured from a typical glass to a taller, narrower one. Then why, as a 4-year-old, would Beth be so confident that pouring the water into the taller, narrower glass increased the amount, and, as a 6-year-old, be so confident that it did not?

The water-pouring procedure is actually a classic technique designed to test children's level of thinking. It has been used with thousands of children around the world, and virtually all the children studied, no matter what their culture, have shown the same types of changes in reasoning as Beth did (though usually at somewhat older ages). Further, such age-related differences in understanding pervade children's thinking. Consider two letters to Mr. Rogers, one sent by a 4-year-old and one by a 5-year-old (Rogers, 1996, pp. 10–11):

Dear Mr. Rogers,
I would like to know how you get in the TV. (Robby, age 4)

Dear Mr. Rogers,
I wish you accidentally stepped out of the TV into my house so I could play with you. (Josiah, age 5)

Clearly, these are not ideas that an older child would entertain. As with Beth's case, we have to ask, "What is it about 4- and 5-year-olds that leads them to form such improbable beliefs, and what changes occur that makes such notions laughable to 6- and 7-year-olds?"

One common approach to answering these questions comes from **stage theories,** which propose that development occurs in a progression of distinct age-related stages, much like the butterfly example in Figure 1.1. According to these theories, a child's entry into a new stage involves relatively sudden, qualitative changes that affect the child's thinking or behavior in broadly unified ways and move the child from one coherent way of experiencing the world to a different coherent way of experiencing it. Among the best-known stage theories is Jean Piaget's theory of **cognitive development,** that is, the development of thinking and reasoning. This theory holds that between birth and adolescence, children go through four stages of cognitive growth, each characterized by distinct intellectual abilities and ways of understanding the world. For example, according to Piaget's theory, 2- to 5-year-olds are in a stage of development in which they can focus on only one aspect of an event, or one type of information, at a time. By age 6 or 7, children enter a different stage, in which they can simultaneously focus on and coordinate two or more aspects of an event and can do so on many different tasks. According to this view, when confronted with a problem like the one that Beth's mother presented to her, most 4- and 5-year-olds focus on the single dimension of height, and therefore perceive the taller, narrower glass as having more water. In contrast, some 6-year-olds and most 7-year-olds consider both relevant dimensions of the problem simultaneously. This allows them to realize that although the column of water in the taller glass is higher, the column also is narrower, and the two differences offset each other.

In the course of reading this book, you will encounter a number of other stage theories, including Sigmund Freud's theory of psychosexual development, Erik Erikson's theory of psychosocial development, and Lawrence Kohlberg's theory of moral development. Each of these stage theories proposes that children of a given age show broad similarities across many situations and that children of different ages tend to behave very differently.

Such stage theories have been very influential. In the past 20 years, however, many researchers have concluded that, in most aspects of development, changes are gradual rather than sudden, and that development occurs skill by skill, task by task, rather than in a broadly unified way (Courage & Howe, 2002; Elman et al., 1996; Fischer & Biddell, 2006; Thelen & Smith, 2006). This view of development is less dramatic than that of stage theories, but a great deal of evidence supports it. One such piece of evidence is the fact that a child often will behave in accord with one proposed stage on one task but in accord with a different proposed stage on another task (Fischer & Biddell, 2006). This variable level of reasoning makes it difficult to view the child as being "in" either stage.

Much of the difficulty in deciding whether development is continuous or discontinuous is that the same facts can look very different, depending on one's perspective. Consider the seemingly simple question of whether children's height increases continuously or discontinuously. Figure 1.2a shows a boy's height, measured yearly from birth to age 18 (Tanner, 1961). When one looks at the boy's height at each age, development seems smooth and continuous, with growth occurring rapidly early in life and then slowing down.

However, when you look at Figure 1.2b, a different picture emerges. This graph illustrates the same boy's growth, but it depicts the amount of growth from one

stage theories approaches that propose that development involves a series of discontinuous, age-related phases

cognitive development the development of thinking and reasoning

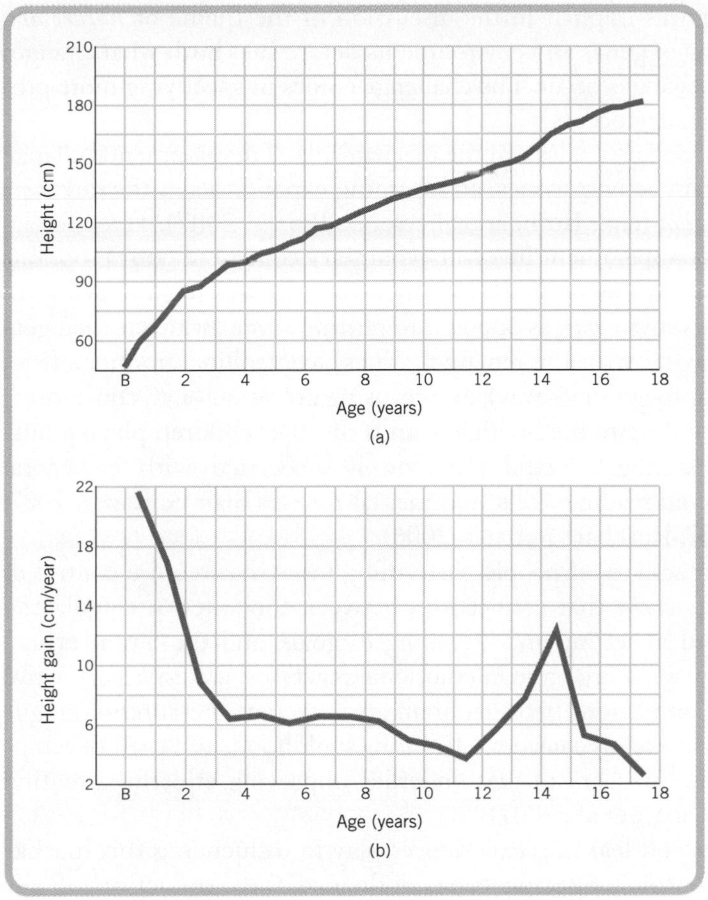

FIGURE 1.2 Continuous and discontinuous growth Depending on how it is viewed, changes in height can be viewed as either continuous or discontinuous. (a) Examining a boy's height at yearly intervals from birth to 18 years makes the growth look gradual and continuous (from Tanner, 1961). (b) Examining the increases in the same boy's height from one year to the next over the same period shows rapid growth during the first three years, then slower growth, then a growth spurt in adolescence, then a rapid decrease in growth; viewed this way, growth seems discontinuous.

year to the next. The boy grew every year, but he grew most during two periods: from birth to age 3, and from ages 12 to 15. These are the kinds of data that lead people to talk about discontinuous growth and about a separate stage of adolescence that includes a physical growth spurt.

So, is development fundamentally continuous or fundamentally discontinuous? The most reasonable answer seems to be, "It depends on how you look at it and how often you look." Imagine the difference between the perspective of an uncle who sees his niece every two or three years and that of the niece's parents, who see her every day. The uncle will almost always be struck with the huge changes in his niece since he last saw her. The niece will be so different that it will seem that she has progressed to a higher stage of development. In contrast, the parents will most often be struck by the continuity of her development; to them, she usually will just seem to grow up a bit each day. Throughout this book, we will be considering the changes, large and small, sudden and gradual, that have led some researchers to emphasize the continuities in development and others to emphasize the discontinuities.

4 *Mechanisms of Developmental Change:* How Does Change Occur?

Perhaps the deepest mystery about children's development is expressed by the question "How does change occur?" In other words, what are the mechanisms that produce the remarkable changes that children undergo with age and experience?

A very general answer was implicit in the discussion of the theme of *nature and nurture*. The interaction of genes and environments determines both what changes occur and when those changes occur. The challenge comes in specifying more precisely how any given change occurs.

One particularly interesting analysis of the mechanisms of developmental change involves the role of brain activity, genes, and learning experiences in the development of *effortful attention* (e.g., Rothbart, Sheese, & Posner, 2007). Effortful attention is an aspect of temperament involving voluntary control of one's emotions and thoughts. It includes processes such as inhibiting impulses (e.g., obeying requests to put all of one's toys away, as opposed to putting some away but then getting distracted and playing with the remaining ones); controlling emotions (e.g., not crying when failing to get one's way); and focusing attention (e.g., concentrating on one's homework despite the inviting sounds of other children playing outside). Difficulty in exerting effortful attention is associated with behavioral problems, weak math and reading skills, and mental illness (Blair & Razza, 2007; McClelland et al., 2007; Rothbart & Bates, 2006).

Studies of the brain activity of people performing tasks that require control of thoughts and emotions show that connections between the anterior cingulate, a brain structure involved in setting and attending to goals, and the limbic area, a part of the brain that plays a large role in emotional reactions, are especially active (Etkin et al., 2006). Connections between brain areas such as the anterior cingulate and the limbic area develop considerably during childhood, and their development appears to be one mechanism that underlies improving effortful attention during childhood (Rothbart et al., 2007).

What role do genes and learning experiences play in influencing this mechanism of effortful attention? Specific genes influence the production of key **neurotransmitters**—chemicals involved in communications among brain cells—and individual variations in these genes are associated with the quality of performance on tasks that require effortful attention (Canli et al., 2005; Diamond et al., 2004; Rueda et al., 2005). These genetic influences do not occur in a vacuum, however. As we have noted, the nature of the environment plays a crucial role in the expression of genes. In the present case, infants with a particular form of one of the genes in question show differences in effortful attention related to the quality of parenting they receive, with lower quality of parenting being associated with lower ability to regulate attention (Sheese, Voelker, Rothbart, & Posner, 2007).

Children's experiences also can change the wiring of the brain system that produces effortful attention. Rueda and colleagues (2005) presented 6-year-olds with a 5-day training program that used computerized exercises to improve capacity for effortful attention. Examination of electrical activity in the anterior cingulate indicated that those 6-year-olds who had been presented the computerized exercises showed improved effortful attention. These children also showed improved performance on intelligence tests, which makes sense given the sustained effortful attention required by such tests. Thus, the experiences that children encounter influence their brain processes and gene expression, just as brain processes and genes influence children's reactions to experiences. More generally, a full understanding of the mechanisms that produce developmental change requires specifying how genes, brain structures and processes, and experiences interact to generate both general developmental trends and differences among children of particular ages.

neurotransmitters chemicals involved in communications among brain cells

5 *The Sociocultural Context:* How Does the Sociocultural Context Influence Development?

sociocultural context the physical, social, cultural, economic, and historical circumstances that make up any child's environment

Children grow up in a particular set of physical and social environments, in a particular culture, under particular economic circumstances, at a particular point in history. Together, these physical, social, cultural, economic, and historical circumstances constitute the **sociocultural context** of a child's life. This sociocultural context influences every aspect of children's development.

The most obviously important parts of children's sociocultural contexts are the people with whom they interact—parents, grandparents, brothers, sisters, day-care workers, teachers, friends, classmates, and so on—and the physical environment in which they live—their house, day-care center, school, neighborhood, and so on. Another important but less tangible part of the sociocultural context is the institutions that influence children's lives: school systems, religious institutions, sports leagues, social organizations (such as boys' and girls' clubs), and so on.

Yet another important set of influences are the general characteristics of the child's society: its wealth and technological advancement; its values, attitudes, beliefs, and traditions; its laws and political structure; and so on. For example, the simple fact that most toddlers and preschoolers growing up in the United States today go to day care or other forms of child care outside their homes reflects a number of these less tangible sociocultural factors, including (1) the historical era (50 years ago, far fewer children in the United States attended day-care centers); (2) the economic structure (most women with young children work outside the home); (3) cultural beliefs (for example, that receiving child care outside the home does not harm children); and (4) cultural values (for example, the value that mothers of young children should be able to work outside the home if they wish). Attendance at day-care centers, in turn, partly determines the people children meet and the activities in which they engage.

One method that developmentalists use to understand the influence of the sociocultural context is to compare the lives of children who grow up in different cultures. Such comparisons often reveal that practices that are rare or nonexistent in one's own culture are common in, and have important advantages for, other cultures. The following comparison of young children's sleeping arrangements in different societies illustrates the value of such cross-cultural research.

In most families in the United States, newborn infants sleep in their parents' bedroom, either in a crib or in the same bed. However, when infants are 2 to 6 months old, parents usually move them to another bedroom where they sleep alone (Greenfield, Suzuki, & Rothstein-Fisch, 2006). This seems only natural to most people raised in the United States. From a worldwide perspective, however, such sleeping arrangements are highly unusual. In most other societies, including industrialized nations such as Italy, Japan, and Korea, babies almost always sleep in the same bed as their mother for the first few years, and somewhat older children also sleep in the same room as their mother, sometimes in the same bed (e.g., Nelson, Schiefenhoevel, & Haimerl, 2000; Whiting & Edwards, 1988). Where does this leave the father? In some cultures, the father sleeps in the same bed with mother and

OWEN FRANKEN / CORBIS

In many countries, including Denmark, the country in which this mother and child live, mothers and children sleep together for the first several years of the child's life. This sociocultural pattern is in sharp contrast to the U.S. practice of having infants sleep separately from their parents soon after birth.

baby; in others, he sleeps in a separate bed or in a different room; and in a few others, he sleeps in a different house altogether.

How do these differences in sleeping arrangements affect children? To find out, researchers interviewed mothers in middle-class U.S. families in Salt Lake City, Utah, and in rural Mayan families in Guatemala (Morelli, Rogoff, Oppenheim, & Goldsmith, 1992). These interviews revealed that by age 6 months, the large majority of the U.S. children had begun sleeping in their own bedroom. As the children grew out of infancy, the nightly separation of child and parents became a complex ritual, surrounded by activities intended to comfort the child, such as telling stories, reading children's books, singing songs, and so on. One mother said, "When my friends hear that it is time for my son to go to bed, they teasingly say, 'See you in an hour'" (Morelli et al., 1992, p. 608). About half of the children were reported as taking a comfort object, such as a blanket or teddy bear, to bed with them.

In contrast, interviews with the Mayan mothers indicated that their children typically slept in the same bed with them until the age of 2 or 3 and continued to sleep in the same room with them for years thereafter. The children usually went to sleep at the same time as their parents. None of the Mayan parents reported bedtime rituals, and almost none reported their children taking comfort objects, such as dolls or stuffed animals, to bed with them. In addition, none of the Mayan children were said to suck their thumbs when they went to bed, unlike many children in the United States.

Why do sleeping arrangements differ across cultures? One possibility that springs to mind is that people in other cultures, particularly impoverished ones like that of the Mayan, lack the space needed for separate bedrooms. However, interviews with the Mayan parents indicated that the crucial consideration for them in determining sleeping arrangements was not space, but rather, cultural values. Mayan culture prizes interdependence among people. The Mayan parents expressed the belief that having a young child sleep with the mother is important for developing a good parent–child relationship, for avoiding the child's becoming distressed at being alone, and for helping parents spot any problems the child is having. They often expressed shock and pity when told that infants in the United States typically sleep separately from their parents (Greenfield et al., 2006). In contrast, U.S. culture prizes independence and self-reliance, and the U.S. mothers expressed the belief that having babies and young children sleep alone promotes these values, as well as allowing intimacy between husbands and wives (Morelli et al., 1992). These differences illustrate both how practices that strike us as natural may differ greatly across cultures and how the simple conventions of everyday life often reflect deeper values.

Contexts of development differ not just between cultures but within them as well. In modern multicultural societies, many contextual differences are related to ethnicity, race, and **socioeconomic status (SES)**—a measure of social class that is based on income and education. Virtually all aspects of children's lives, from the food they eat to the parental discipline they receive to the games they play, are influenced by ethnicity, race, and SES.

The socioeconomic context exerts a particularly large influence on children's lives. In economically advanced societies, including the United States, most children grow up in comfortable circumstances, but millions of other children do not. In 2006, about 14% of U.S. families with children had incomes below the poverty line (in that year, $16,242 for a family of three with one adult and two children). In absolute numbers, that translates into about 13 million children growing up in

socioeconomic status a measure of social class based on income and education poverty (U.S. Census Bureau, 2007). As shown in Table 1.2, poverty rates are especially high in black and Hispanic families and in families of all races that are headed by single mothers. Poverty rates are also very high among the roughly 25% of children in the United States who are either immigrants or the children of immigrants—roughly twice as high as among children of native-born parents (Hernandez, Denton, & Macartney, 2008; Smeeding, 2008).

Children from poor families tend to do less well than other children in many ways (Evans et al., 2005; Morales & Guerra, 2006). In infancy, they are more likely to have serious health problems. In childhood, they are more likely to have social/emotional or behavioral problems. Throughout childhood and adolescence, they tend to have smaller vocabularies, lower IQs, and lower math and reading scores on standardized achievement tests. In adolescence, they are more likely to have a baby or drop out of school (Evans et al., 2005; Luthar, 1999; McLoyd, 1998).

These negative outcomes are not surprising when we consider the huge array of disadvantages that poor children face. Compared with children who grow up in more affluent circumstances, they are more likely to live in dangerous neighborhoods, to attend inferior day-care centers and schools, and to be exposed to high levels of air and water pollution (Dilworth-Bart & Moore, 2006; Evans, 2004). In addition, poor children more often grow up in single-parent homes and are more likely to be living with neither biological parent. Their parents read to them less and talk to them less, provide fewer books in the home, and are less involved in their schooling. The accumulation of these disadvantages, rather than any single one of them, seems to be the greatest obstacle to poor children's chances for successful development (Morales & Guerra, 2006; Sameroff et al., 1993).

And yet as we saw in Werner's study of the children of Kauai, described at the beginning of the chapter, many children do overcome the obstacles that poverty presents. Such resilient children tend to have three characteristics: positive personal qualities, such as high intelligence, an easygoing personality, and adaptability to change; a close relationship with at least one parent; and a close relationship with at least one adult other than their parents, such as a grandparent, teacher, coach, or family friend (Masten, 2007). Thus, although poverty poses serious obstacles to successful development, many children, with the help of adults in their families and communities, do surmount them.

TABLE 1.2

Percentages of U.S. Families with Children Under Age 18 Below Poverty Line in 2006

Group	% in Poverty
Overall U.S. population	14
White, non-Hispanic	8
Black	28
Hispanic	23
Asian or Pacific Islander	10
Married Couples	7
White, non-Hispanic	4
Black	11
Hispanic	16
Asian or Pacific Islander	8
Single parent: Female head of household	38
White, non-Hispanic	30
Black	45
Hispanic	42
Asian or Pacific Islander	27

Source: U.S. Census Bureau, 2007

6 *Individual Differences:* How Do Children Become So Different from One Another?

Anyone who has experience with children is struck by their uniqueness—their differences not only in physical appearance but in everything from activity level and temperament to intelligence, persistence, and emotionality. These differences among children emerge quickly. Some infants in their first year are shy, others outgoing (Kagan, 1998). Some infants play with or look at objects for prolonged periods of time; others rapidly shift from activity to activity. Even children in the same family often differ substantially, as you probably already know if you have siblings.

Scarr (1992) identified four factors that can lead children from a single family (as well as children from different families) to turn out very different from each other:

1. Genetic differences
2. Differences in treatment by parents and others
3. Differences in reactions to similar experiences
4. Different choices of environments

The most obvious reason for differences among children is that, except for identical twins, every individual is genetically unique. All other siblings (including fraternal twins) share 50% of their genes and differ in the other 50%.

© PICTURE CONTACT / ALAMY

Different children, even ones within the same family, often react to the same experience in completely different ways.

A second major source of variation among children is the variation from one child to another in treatment received from parents and other people. This differential treatment is often associated with preexisting differences in the children's characteristics. For example, parents tend to provide more sensitive care to easygoing infants than to difficult ones; by the second year, parents of difficult children are often angry with them even when the children have done nothing wrong in the immediate situation (van den Boom & Hoeksma, 1994). Teachers, likewise, react to children's individual characteristics. For example, they tend to provide positive attention and encouragement to pupils who are learning well and are well behaved, but with pupils who are doing poorly and are disruptive, they tend to be openly critical and to deny the pupils' requests for special help (Good & Brophy, 1996).

In addition to being shaped by objective differences in the treatment they receive, children also are influenced by their subjective interpretations of the treatment. A classic example occurs when each of a pair of siblings feels that their parents favor the other. Siblings also often react differently to events that affect the whole family. In one study, for example, 69% of negative events, such as parents' being laid off or fired, elicited fundamentally different reactions from siblings (Beardsall & Dunn, 1989). Some children were extremely concerned at a parent's loss of a job; others were confident that everything would be okay.

A fourth major source of differences among children relates to the previously discussed theme of the *active child:* As children grow older, they increasingly choose activities and friends for themselves and thus influence their own subsequent development. They may also accept or choose niches for themselves: within a family, one child may become "the smart one," another "the popular one," another "the bad one," and so on (Scarr & McCartney, 1983). A child labeled by family members as "the smart one" may strive to live up to the label; so, unfortunately, may a child labeled "the troublemaker."

As discussed in the section on nature and nurture and in the section on mechanisms of development, differences in biology and experience interact with each other in complex ways to create the infinite diversity of human beings in the world. Thus, a study of 11- to 17-year-olds found that the grades of children who were highly engaged with school changed in more positive directions than would have been predicted by their genetic background or family environments alone (Johnson, McGue, & Iacono, 2006). The same study revealed that children of high intelligence were less negatively affected by adverse family environments than were other children. Thus, children's genes, their treatment by other people, their subjective reactions to their experiences, and their choice of environments interact in ways that contribute to differences among children, even ones in the same family.

7 *Research and Children's Welfare:* How Can Research Promote Children's Well-Being?

Improved understanding of child development often leads to practical benefits. Several examples have already been described, including the program for helping children deal with their anger and the recommendations for fostering valid eyewitness testimony from young children.

Another type of practical benefit that child-development research has yielded is early diagnosis of developmental problems, when they can be corrected most easily and completely. For example, some infants are born with cataracts, areas of cloudiness in the lens of the eye that interefere with sharply focused vision. Such cataracts sometimes are dense, requiring surgery as early in life as possible. With milder cataracts, however, ophthalmologists often cannot determine through examining the cataract alone whether the loss of vision is sufficient to warrant surgery (Lewis & Maurer, 2005).

Standard techniques for evaluating vision require patients to report what they see; infants, of course, cannot provide such verbal reports. However, a child-development research method known as *preferential looking* allows infants' behavior to speak for them. This method builds from research showing that infants who can see the difference between a simple pattern and a solid gray field consistently prefer to look at the pattern. This is true even when the pattern is just a set of vertical stripes. Therefore, to diagnose the effects of an infant's cataracts, an opthalmologist or researcher presents the infant with cards, each of which has a gray area on one half and a white area with black stripes on the other. By varying the spacing of the black stripes and the contrast between them and the white areas, and then observing which half of the card the infant looks at, the examiner can tell when the infant is no longer able to differentiate the black-and-white area from the gray area. The point at which this happens allows assessment of the extent of the visual impairment. This preferential-looking procedure has proved useful in determining whether infants from age 2 months onward need corrective surgery (Maurer, Lewis, Brent, & Levin, 1999).

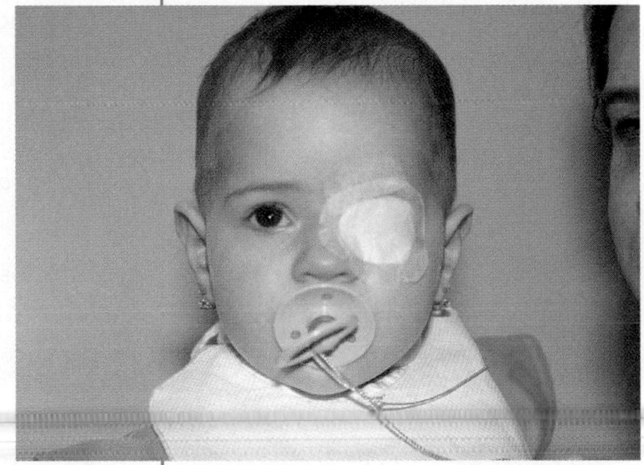

An infant who was born with a cataract that impaired her vision in one eye. The best treatment for such problems is to surgically remove the cataract from the affected eye soon after birth and to keep a patch on the unaffected eye to force use of the previously deprived eye. This infant had surgery soon after birth to remove the cataract; now in her 20s, her vision in the treated eye is quite good.

Child-development research also has been applied to improving education. One important example involves studies of how people's beliefs about intelligence influence their learning. Carol Dweck and her colleagues (Dweck, 1999; Dweck & Leggett, 1988) have found that some children (and adults) believe that intelligence is a fixed entity. They see each person as having a certain amount of intelligence that is set at birth and cannot be changed by experience. Other children (and adults) believe that intelligence is a changeable characteristic that increases with learning and that the time and effort people put into learning is the key determinant of their intelligence.

In general, people who believe that intelligence increases with learning react to failure in more effective ways (Dweck, 1999). When they fail to solve a problem, they tend to persist on the task and try harder. Such persistance in the face of failure is an important quality. As the famous British Prime Minister Winston Churchill once said, "Success is the ability to go from one failure to another with no loss of enthusiasm." In contrast, people who believe that intelligence is a fixed entity tend to give up when they fail, because they think the problem is too hard for them.

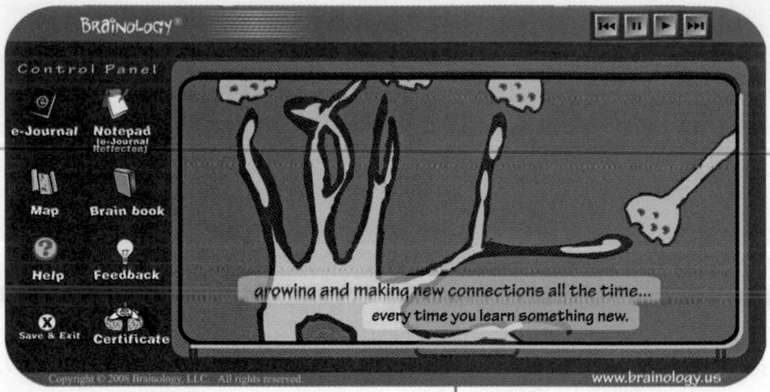

Screenshot from Brainology, a commercially available educational program based on the findings of Blackwell, Trzesniewski, and Dweck (2007). The software, like the research study, emphasizes that learning makes children smarter by building new connections within the brain.

Building on this research regarding the relationship between beliefs about intelligence and persistence in the face of difficulty, Blackwell, Trzeniewski, and Dweck (2007) devised an effective educational program for middle school students from low-income backgrounds. They presented some randomly selected students with research findings about how learning alters the brain in ways that improve subsequent learning and thus "makes you smarter"; other randomly selected students from the same classrooms were presented with information about how memory works. The researchers predicted that the students who were told about the effects learning has on the brain would change their beliefs about intelligence in ways that would help them persevere in the face of failure. In particular, Blackwell and colleagues predicted that the changed beliefs would improve students' learning of mathematics, an area in which children often experience failure before success.

This prediction was borne out. Children who were presented information about how learning changes the brain and enhances intelligence subsequently improved their math grades, whereas the other children did not. Children who initially believed that intelligence was an inborn, unchanging quality, but who came to believe that intelligence reflected learning, showed especially large improvements. Perhaps most striking, when the children's teachers, who did not know which type of information each child had received, were asked if any of their students had shown unusual improvement in motivation or performance, the teachers cited more than three times as many students who had been given information about how learning builds intelligence. One such student's progress was described by his teacher as follows:

> L, who never puts in any extra effort and doesn't turn in homework on time, actually stayed up late working for hours to finish an assignment early so I could review it and give him a chance to revise it. He earned a B+ on the assignment (he had been getting C's and lower).
>
> (Blackwell et al., 2007, p. 256)

In subsequent chapters, we review many additional examples of how child development research is being used to promote children's welfare.

review:

The modern field of child development is in large part an attempt to answer a small set of fundamental questions about children. These include:

1. How do nature and nurture jointly contribute to development?
2. How do children contribute to their own development?
3. Is development best viewed as continuous or discontinuous?
4. What mechanisms produce development?
5. How does the sociocultural context influence development?
6. Why are children so different from one other?
7. How can we use research to improve children's welfare?

Methods for Studying Child Development

As illustrated in the preceding section, modern scientific research has advanced the understanding of fundamental questions about child development well beyond that of the historical figures who first raised the questions. This progress is not due to modern researchers being smarter or working harder than the great thinkers of the past. Rather, it reflects the successful application of the scientific method to the study of child development. In this section, we describe the scientific method and examine how its use has advanced understanding of child development.

The Scientific Method

The basic assumption of the **scientific method** is that all beliefs, no matter how probable they seem and no matter how many people share them, may be wrong. Therefore, until beliefs have been tested, they must be viewed as **hypotheses**, that is, as educated guesses, rather than as truth. If a hypothesis is tested, and the evidence repeatedly does not support it, the hypothesis must be abandoned no matter how reasonable it may have seemed.

Use of the scientific method involves four basic steps:

1. Choosing a question to be answered
2. Formulating a hypothesis regarding the question
3. Developing a method for testing the hypothesis
4. Using the data yielded by the method to draw a conclusion regarding the hypothesis

To illustrate these steps, let's make the *question to be answered* "What abilities predict which preschoolers will become good readers?" A reasonable *hypothesis* might be "Preschoolers who can identify the separate sounds within words will become better readers than those who cannot." A straightforward *method* for testing this hypothesis would be to select a group of preschoolers, test their ability to identify the separate sounds within words, and then, several years later, test the reading skills of the same children. Research has, in fact, shown that preschoolers who are aware of the component sounds within words later read more skillfully than do their peers who lack this ability (Ehri et al., 2001; Rayner et al., 2001). These results support the *conclusion* that preschoolers' ability to identify sounds within words predicts their later reading skill.

The first, second, and fourth of these steps are not unique to the scientific method. As we have seen, great thinkers of the past also asked questions, formulated hypotheses, and drew conclusions that were reasonable given the evidence available to them. What distinguishes scientific research from nonscientific approaches is the third step, the methods used to test the hypotheses. These research methods, and the high-quality evidence that they yield, allow investigators to progress beyond their initial hypotheses so that they can draw firmly grounded conclusions.

The Importance of Appropriate Measurement

In order for the scientific method to work, researchers must use measures that are directly relevant to the hypotheses being tested. A researcher who hypothesized that one curriculum was more effective than another probably would measure children's percentage of correct answers following exposure to each curriculum. The reason is that the hypothesis concerns which curriculum will produce greater knowledge, and correct answers are a good measure of knowledge. In contrast, a researcher who hypothesized that infants prefer bright colors to pale ones might present infants with identical shapes in bright and pale colors and measure the amount of time the infants looked at each one. The reason is that the hypothesis concerns visual preferences, and relative looking time is a good measure of such preferences.

Regardless of the particular measure used, many of the same criteria determine whether a measure is a good one. One key criterion has already been noted—the

scientific method an approach to testing beliefs that involves choosing a question, formulating a hypothesis, testing the hypothesis, and drawing a conclusion

hypotheses educated guesses

reliability the degree to which independent measurements of a given behavior are consistent

interrater reliability the amount of agreement in the observations of different raters who witness the same behavior

test–retest reliability the degree of similarity of a child's performance on two or more occasions

validity the degree to which a test measures what it is intended to measure

internal validity the degree to which effects observed within experiments can be attributed to the variables that the researcher intentionally manipulated

external validity the degree to which results can be generalized beyond the particulars of the research

measure must be directly relevant to the hypothesis. Two other qualities that good measures must possess are *reliability* and *validity.*

Reliability **Reliability** refers to the degree to which independent measurements of a behavior under study are consistent. One important type of consistency, **interrater reliability,** indicates how much agreement there is in the observations of different raters who witness the same behavior. Sometimes the observations are qualitative, as when raters classify a baby's attachment to her mother as "secure" or "insecure." Other times the observations are quantitative, as when raters score on a scale of 1 to 10 how upset babies become when they are presented with an unfamiliar noisy toy or a boisterous stranger. In both cases, interrater reliability is attained when the raters' observations are in close agreement. Without such close agreement, one cannot have confidence in the research findings, because there is no way to tell which (if any) rating was accurate.

A second important type of consistency is **test–retest reliability.** This type of reliability is attained when measures of a child's performance on the same test, administered under the same conditions, are similar on two or more occasions. Suppose, for example, that researchers presented a vocabulary test to a group of children on two occasions one week apart. If the test is reliable, those children who scored highest on the first testing should also score highest on the second, because none of the children's vocabularies would have changed much over such a short period. As in the example of interrater reliability, a lack of test–retest reliability would make it impossible to know which result (if either) accurately reflected each child's knowledge.

Validity The **validity** of a test or experiment refers to the degree to which it measures what it is intended to measure. Researchers strive for two types of validity: internal and external. **Internal validity** refers to whether effects observed within experiments can be attributed with confidence to the conditions that the researcher is testing. For example, suppose that a researcher tests the effectiveness of a type of psychotherapy for depression by administering it to a number of depressed adolescents. If three months later many of the adolescents are no longer depressed, can it be concluded that this type of psychotherapy caused the improvement? No, because the students' recovery may have been due to the mere passage of time. Moods fluctuate, and many adolescents who are depressed at any given time will be happier at a later date even without psychotherapy. In this example, the passage of time is a source of internal invalidity, because the factor believed to cause the improvement (the psychotherapy) may have had no effect.

External validity, in contrast, refers to the ability to generalize research findings beyond the particulars of the research in question. Studies of child development are almost never intended to apply only to the particular children and methodologies involved in a given study. Rather, the goal is to draw conclusions that apply to children and research methods more generally. Thus the findings of a single experiment are only the first step in determining the external validity of the results. Additional studies with participants from different backgrounds and with different particular methods are invariably needed to establish the external validity of the findings. (Table 1.3 summarizes the key properties of behavioral measures.)

TABLE 1.3

Key Properties of Behavioral Measures

Property	Question of Interest
Relevance to hypotheses	Do the hypotheses predict in a straightforward way what should happen on these measures?
Interrater reliability	Do different raters who observe the same behavior classify or score it the same way?
Test–retest reliability	Are the scores or classifications that children receive on the measure stable over time?
Internal validity	Can effects within the experiment be attributed to the variables that the researcher intentionally manipulated?
External validity	How widely can the findings be generalized to different children, measures, and experimental procedures than the ones in the study?

Contexts for Gathering Data About Children

Researchers obtain data about children in three main contexts: *interviews, naturalistic observation,* and *structured observation.* In the following sections, we consider how gathering data in each context can help answer different questions about children.

structured interview a research procedure in which all participants are asked to answer the same questions

clinical interview a procedure in which questions are adjusted in accord with the answers the interviewee provides

Interviews

The most obvious way to collect data about children is to go straight to the source and ask the children themselves about their lives. One type of interview, the **structured interview,** is especially useful when the goal is to collect self-reports on the same topics from everyone being studied. For example, Valeski and Stipek (2001) asked kindergartners and 1st graders questions regarding their feelings about school (How much does your teacher care about you? How do you feel when you're at school?) and also questions about their beliefs about their academic competence (How much do you know about numbers? How good are you at reading?). The children's general attitude toward school and their feelings about their relationship with their teacher proved to be positively related to their beliefs about their competence in math and reading. Asking large numbers of children identical questions about their feelings and beliefs provides a quick and straightforward way for researchers to learn what is typical at different ages and how the beliefs and feelings are related to each other.

A second type of interview, the **clinical interview,** is especially useful for obtaining in-depth information about an individual child. In this approach, the interviewer begins with a set of prepared questions, but if the child says something intriguing, the interviewer can depart from the script to follow up on the child's lead.

The usefulness of clinical interviews can be seen in the case of Bobby, a 10-year-old child who was assessed for symptoms of depression (Schwartz & Johnson, 1985). When the interviewer asked him about school, Bobby said that he did not like it because the other children disliked him and he was bad at sports. As he put it, "I'm not really very good at anything" (p. 214). To explore the source of this sad self-description, the interviewer asked Bobby what he would wish for if three wishes could be granted. Bobby replied, "I would wish that I was the type of boy my mother and father want, I would wish that I could have friends, and I would wish that I wouldn't feel sad so much" (p. 214). Such heartrending comments provide a sense of the painful subjective experience of this depressed child, one that would be impossible to obtain from methods that were not tailored to the individual.

As with all contexts for collecting data, interviews have both strengths and weaknesses. On the positive side, they yield a great deal of data quite quickly and can provide in-depth information about individual children. On the negative side, answers to interview questions often are biased. Children (like adults) often report past events inaccurately. Many avoid disclosing facts that put them in a bad light, distort the way that events happened, and fail to understand their own motivations (Wilson & Dunn, 2004). These

One-on-one clinical interviews like this one can elicit unique in-depth information about a child.

VOISIN / PHOTO RESEARCHERS

limitations have led increasing numbers of researchers to use observational methods in which they witness the behavior of interest for themselves.

Naturalistic Observation

When the primary research goal is to describe how children behave in their usual environments—homes, schools, playgrounds, and so on—**naturalistic observation** is the method of choice. In this approach to gathering data, observers try to remain unobtrusively in the background in the chosen setting, so as not to influence the behaviors they are observing.

A classic example of naturalistic observation is Gerald Patterson's (1982) comparative study of family dynamics in troubled and "typical" families. The troubled families were defined by the presence of at least one child who had been labeled "out of control" and referred for treatment by a school, court, or mental health professional. The typical families were defined by the fact that none of the children in them showed signs of serious behavioral difficulties. Income levels and children's ages were the same for the troubled and typical families.

To observe the frequency with which children and parents engaged in negative behaviors—teasing, yelling, whining, criticizing, and so on—research assistants repeatedly observed dinnertime interactions in both troubled and typical homes. In order to accustom family members to his or her presence, the research assistant for each family made several home visits before beginning to collect data. During the actual observations, the assistant sat quietly in the background and avoided interacting with family members.

© BILLY E. BARNES / PHOTOEDIT

Psychologists sometimes observe family interactions around the dinner table, because mealtime comments can evoke strong emotions.

The researchers found that both parents and children in the troubled families acted differently from their counterparts in the typical families. Parents in the troubled families were more self-absorbed and less responsive to their children than were parents in the typical households. Children in the troubled families responded to parental punishment by becoming more aggressive, whereas children in the typical households responded to punishment by becoming less aggressive. In the troubled families, interactions often fell into a vicious cycle in which:

- The child acted in a hostile or aggressive manner, for example, by defying a parent's request to clean up his or her room.
- The parent reacted angrily, for example, by shouting at the child to obey.
- The child escalated the level of hostility, for example, by yelling back.
- The parent ratcheted up the aggression yet further, perhaps by spanking the child.

As Patterson's study suggests, naturalistic observations are particularly useful for illuminating common everyday social interactions, such as those between children and parents.

Although naturalistic observation yields detailed information about certain aspects of children's everyday lives, it also has important limitations. One is that naturally occurring contexts vary on many dimensions, and it is often hard to know which ones influenced the behavior of interest. For example, while it was clear in the Patterson study that the troubled families' interactions differed from those of the more harmonious families, the interactions and family histories differed in so many ways that it was difficult to identify their specific contributions to the current

naturalistic observation examination of ongoing behavior in an environment not controlled by the researcher situation. A second limitation of naturalistic studies is that many important behaviors occur only occasionally in the everyday environment, which reduces researchers' opportunities to learn about them. A means for overcoming both limitations is the method known as structured observation.

Structured Observation

When using **structured observation,** researchers design a situation that will elicit behavior relevant to a hypothesis and then observe how different children behave in the situation. The researchers then relate the observed behaviors to characteristics of the child, such as age, gender, or personality, and to the child's behavior in other situations that are also observed.

In one such study, Kochanska, Coy, and Murray (2001) investigated how the mother–child relationship influences 2- and 3-year-olds' willingness to comply with their mothers' requests that they forgo appealing activities and participate in unappealing ones. The researchers invited mothers to bring their toddlers to a laboratory room equipped with a number of especially attractive toys sitting on a shelf and a great many less attractive toys scattered around the room. Each mother was asked to tell her child that he or she could play with any of the toys *except* the ones on the shelf. Raters observed children over the next few minutes and classified them as complying with their mother's request wholeheartedly, grudgingly, or not at all. Then the experimenter asked the mother to leave the room and, through a one-way mirror, observed whether the child played with the "forbidden" toys in the mother's absence. The researchers found that children who had earlier complied wholeheartedly with their mother's request not to play with the forbidden toys were less likely to play with them in her absence than were children who had complied only grudgingly or not at all. The compliant children later were more likely to also comply with their mother's request that they engage in an unappealing activity (picking up a large number of toys from the floor and putting them away). When retested near their 4th birthday, most children showed the same type of compliance as they had as toddlers. Overall, the results indicated that the quality of young children's compliance with their mother's requests is a somewhat stable, general property of the mother–child relationship.

This type of structured observation offers an important advantage over naturalistic observation: it ensures that all the children being studied encounter identical situations. This allows direct comparisons of different children's behavior in a given situation and, as in the research just discussed, also makes it possible to establish the generality of each child's behavior across different tasks. On the other hand, structured observation does not provide as extensive information about individual children's subjective experience as do interviews, nor can it provide the opened-ended, everyday kind of data that naturalistic observation can yield.

In short, the ideal data-gathering situation depends on which qualities are most important for the goals of the research. (Table 1.4 summarizes the advantages and disadvantages of interviews, naturalistic observation, and structured observation as contexts for gathering data.)

COURTESY OF SUWANNA AND DAVID SIEGLER

Temptation is everywhere, but children who are generally compliant with their mother's requests when she is present are also more likely to resist temptation when she is absent (like this boy, the nephew of one of the authors, whose reach, despite appearances, stopped just short of the cake).

Correlation and Causation

People differ along an infinite number of **variables,** that is, attributes that vary across individuals and situations, such as age, sex, activity level, socioeconomic status, particular experiences, and so on. A major goal of child-development research

structured observation a method that involves presenting an identical situation to each child and recording the child's behavior

variables attributes that vary across individuals and situations, such as age, gender, and expectations

TABLE 1.4

Advantages and Disadvantages of Three Contexts for Gathering Data

Data-Gathering Situation	Features	Advantages	Disadvantages
Interview	Children answer questions asked either in person or on a questionnaire	Can reveal children's subjective experience. Structured interviews are inexpensive means for collecting in depth data about individuals. Clinical interviews allow flexibility for following up unexpected comments.	Reports are often biased to reflect favorably on interviewee. Memory of interviewee often inaccurate and incomplete. Prediction of future behaviors often is inaccurate.
Naturalistic observation	Activities of children in everyday settings are observed.	Useful for describing behavior in everyday settings. Helps illuminate social interaction processes.	Difficult to know which aspects of situation are most influential. Limited value for studying infrequent behaviors.
Structured observation	Children are brought to laboratory and presented prearranged tasks.	Ensures that all children's behaviors are observed in same context. Allows controlled comparison of children's behavior in different situations.	Context is less natural than in naturalistic observation. Reveals less about subjective experience than interviews.

is to determine how these and other major variables are related to each other, both in terms of associations and in terms of cause–effect relations. In the following sections, we consider the research designs that are used to examine each type of relation.

Correlational Designs

The primary goal of studies that use **correlational designs** is to determine whether children who differ in one variable also differ in predictable ways in other variables. For example, a researcher might examine whether toddlers' aggressiveness is related to the number of hours they spend in day care or whether adolescents' popularity is related to their self-control.

The association between two variables is known as their **correlation.** When variables are strongly correlated, knowing a child's score on either variable allows accurate prediction of the child's score on the other. For example, the fact that the number of hours per week that children spend reading correlates highly with their reading-test scores (Guthrie, Wigfield, Metsala, & Cox, 1999) means that a child's reading-test score can be accurately predicted if one knows how much time the child spends reading. It also means that the number of hours the child spends reading can be predicted if one knows the child's reading-test score.

Correlations can be either positive or negative in direction. The direction is positive when high (or low) values of one variable are associated with high (or low) values of the other; the direction is negative when high values of one are associated with low values of the other. Thus, the correlation between time spent reading and reading-test scores would be positive, because children who spend high amounts of time reading also have high reading-test scores. An example of a negative correlation

correlational designs studies intended to indicate how variables are related to each other

correlation the association between two variables

correlation coefficient a statistic that indicates the direction and strength of a correlation

direction-of-causation problem the concept that a correlation between two variables does not indicate which, if either, variable is the cause of the other

third-variable problem the concept that a correlation between two variables may stem from both being influenced by some third variable would be that between obesity and running speed; the more obese the child, the slower his or her running speed would tend to be.

Both the direction and strength of a correlation are indicated by a statistic called the **correlation coefficient,** which can range from 1.0 to –1.0. When the direction of the correlation is positive, the number is preceded by a positive sign or no sign. When the direction is negative, the number is preceded by a minus sign. In Figures 1.3a and 1.3b, variables 1 and 2 are positively related (that is, the higher the value of variable 1, the higher the value of variable 2). Conversely, in Figures 1.3c and 1.3d, variables 1 and 2 are negatively related (that is, the higher the value of variable 1, the lower the value of variable 2).

The strength of the relation between the two variables is indicated by the number within the correlation coefficient. The higher the absolute value (the closer to 1.0 or –1.0), the stronger the relation between the variables; correspondingly, the lower the absolute value (the closer to 0), the weaker the relation. Thus, the correlations shown in Figures 1.3a and 1.3c, 1.00 and –1.00, are equally strong—the strongest possible—even though the directions of the relations are opposite. In both relations, knowing the value of variable 1 allows us to know the exact value of variable 2. The relations in Figures 1.3b and 1.3d are weaker, but they are still informative, in the sense that knowing the value of variable 1 allows a fairly accurate prediction of the value of variable 2. For example, in Figure 1.3d, if we know that the value of variable 1 is relatively high, we can predict that the value of variable 2 is relatively low, though we cannot know the exact value. Finally, the value of the correlation coefficient in Figure 1.3e is 0. In this situation, knowing the value of variable 1 is useless for predicting the value of variable 2; if the value of variable 1 is high, the value of variable 2 is equally likely to be high, medium, or low.

Correlation Does Not Equal Causation

When two variables are strongly correlated and there is a plausible cause–effect relation between them, it often is tempting to infer that one causes the other. However, this inference is not justified, for two reasons. The first is the **direction-of-causation problem:** a correlation does not indicate which variable is the cause and which the effect. In the above example of the correlation between time spent reading and reading achievement, greater time spent reading *might* cause increased reading achievement. On the other hand, the cause–effect relation could run in the opposite direction: greater reading skill might cause children to spend more time reading, because it makes reading more enjoyable. Alternatively, both could be true.

The second reason that correlation does not imply causation is the **third-variable problem:** the correlation between two variables may actually be the result of some third, unspecified variable. In the reading example, for instance, growing up in an intellectual home environment may be the cause of both the greater time spent reading and the greater reading achievement.

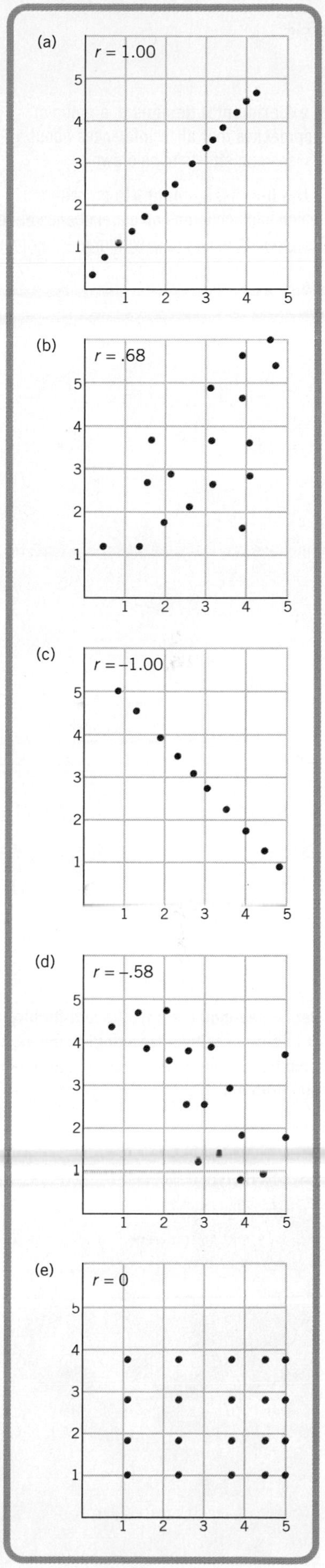

FIGURE 1.3 Five correlations (a) The strongest possible positive correlation; without exception, knowing the value of one variable indicates the exact value of the other, with higher values on one variable indicating higher values on the other. (b) A strong but imperfect positive correlation; a higher value of one variable tends to go with a higher value of the other. (c) The strongest possible negative correlation; without exception, knowing the value of one variable indicates the exact value of the other, with higher values on one variable indicating lower values on the other. (d) A strong but imperfect negative correlation. (e) A total lack of correlation; any value of one variable is equally likely to be accompanied by any value of the other.

experimental designs a group of approaches that allow inferences about causes and effects to be drawn

random assignment a procedure in which each child has an equal chance of being assigned to each group within an experiment

If correlation does not imply causation, why do researchers often use correlational designs? One major reason is that the influence of variables of great interest—age, sex, race, and social class among them—cannot be studied experimentally (see the next section) because researchers cannot manipulate them; that is, they cannot assign participants to one sex or another, to one SES or another, and so on. Consequently, these variables must be studied through correlational methods. Correlational designs are also of great use when the goal is to describe relations among variables rather than to identify cause–effect relations among them. If, for example, the research goal is to discover how moral reasoning, empathy, anxiety, and popularity are related to each other, correlational designs would almost certainly be employed.

Experimental Designs

If correlational designs are insufficient to indicate cause–effect relations, what type of approach is sufficient? The answer is **experimental designs.** The logic of experimental designs can be summarized quite simply: If children in one or more comparable groups are exposed to a particular experience and subsequently behave differently from the children in the group(s) not exposed to the experience, then the subsequent differences in behavior must have resulted from the differences in experience.

Two techniques are crucial to experimental designs: *random assignment* of participants to the groups, and *experimental control.* **Random assignment** involves assigning the participants to one experimental group or another according to chance—by flipping a coin, for example—so that the groups are comparable at the outset. This comparability is crucial for being able to infer that it was the varying experiences to which the groups were exposed in the experiment that caused the later differences between them. Otherwise, those differences might have arisen from some preexisting difference between the people in the groups.

Say, for example, that researchers wanted to compare the effectiveness of two interventions for helping depressed mothers improve their relationship with their infant—providing the mothers with home visits from trained therapists or providing them with supportive phone calls from such therapists. If the researchers provided the home visits to families in one neighborhood and the supportive phone calls to families in another neighborhood, they would be unable to tell whether any differences in mother–infant relationships following the experiment were caused by differences between the effectiveness of the two types of support or by differences between the families in the two areas. Depressed mothers in one neighborhood might suffer from less severe forms of depression than mothers in the other, or they might have greater access to other support, such as mental health centers or parenting programs.

Depressed mothers often have difficulty providing sensitive parenting; home visits from trained therapists can help alleviate this problem.

In contrast, when groups are created through random assignment and include a reasonably large number of participants (typically 20 or more per group), initial differences between the groups tend to be minimal. For example, if, from the same two neighborhoods, 40 families with mothers suffering from depression are divided randomly into two experimental groups, each group is likely to have roughly equal numbers of families from each neighborhood. Similarly, each group is likely to include a few mothers who are extremely depressed, a few with mild forms of depression, and many in between, as well as a few infants who have been severely affected by their mother's depression, a few who have been minimally affected, and many in between. The logic implies that groups created through random assignment should be comparable on all variables except the different treatment that people in the experimenetal groups encounter during the experiment. Such an experiment was in fact conducted, and it showed that home visits helped depressed mothers more than supportive phone calls did (von Doesum et al., 2008).

The second essential characteristic of an experimental design, **experimental control,** refers to the ability of the researcher to determine the specific experiences that children in each group encounter during the study. In the simplest experimental design, one with two conditions, the groups are often referred to as the "experimental group" and the "control group." Children in the **experimental group** are presented with the experience of interest; children in the **control group** are treated identically except that they are not presented with the experience of interest or are presented with a different experience that is expected to have less effect on the variables being tested.

The experience that children in the experimental group receive and that children in the control group do not is referred to as the **independent variable.** The behavior that is hypothesized to be affected by exposure to the independent variable is referred to as the **dependent variable.** Thus, if a researcher hypothesized that showing children an anti-bullying film would reduce their rate of bullying, the researcher might randomly assign some children in a school or day camp to view the film and other children in the same school or camp to view a film about a different topic. In this case, the anti-bullying film would be the independent variable, and the amount of bullying that children subsequently engaged in after watching it would be the dependent variable. If the independent variable had the predicted effect, the children exposed to it would show reduced rates of bullying, whereas the children who watched the other film would not.

One illustration of how experimental designs allow researchers to draw conclusions about causes and effects is a study that tested the hypothesis that television shows running in the background lower the quality of infants' and toddlers' play (Schmidt et al., 2008). The independent variable was whether or not a television program was on in the room where the participants were playing; the dependent variables were a variety of measures of children's attention to the television program and of the quality of their play. The TV program that was playing was *Jeopardy*, which presumably would have been of little interest to the 1- and 2-year-olds in the study; indeed, they looked at it an average of only once per minute and only for a few seconds at a time. Nonetheless, the television show disrupted the children's play, reducing the length of play episodes and the children's focus on their play. These findings indicate that there is a causal, and negative, relation between background exposure to television shows and the quality of young children's play.

Experimental designs are the method of choice for establishing causal relations, a central goal of scientific research. However, as noted earlier, experimental designs cannot be applied to all issues of interest; for example, the reasons why boys tend to be more aggressive than girls are of great interest, but children cannot be randomly assigned to gender. In addition, many experimental studies are conducted in laboratory settings, which improves experimental control but

experimental control the ability of researchers to determine the specific experiences that children have during the course of an experiment

experimental group a group of children in an experimental design who are presented the experience of interest

control group the group of children in an experimental design who are not presented the experience of interest but in other ways are treated similarly

independent variable the experience that children in the experimental group receive and that children in the control group do not receive

dependent variable a behavior that is measured to determine whether it is affected by exposure to the independent variable

TABLE 1.5

Advantages and Disadvantages of Correlational and Experimental Designs

Type of Design	Features	Advantages	Disadvantages
Correlational	Comparison of existing groups of children or examination of relations among each child's scores on different variables.	Only way to compare many groups of interest (boys–girls, rich–poor, etc.). Only way to establish relations among many variables of interest (IQ and achievement, popularity and happiness, etc.).	Third-variable problem. Direction-of-causation problem.
Experimental	Random assignment of children to groups and experimental control of procedures presented to each group.	Allows causal inferences because design rules out direction-of-causation and third-variable problems.	Need for experimental control often leads to artificial experimental situations. Cannot be used to study many differences and variables of interest, such as age, sex, and temperament.

can raise doubts about the external validity of the findings. (The advantages and disadvantages of correlational and experimental designs are summarized in Table 1.5.)

Designs for Examining Development

A great deal of research on child development focuses on the ways in which children change or remain the same as they grow older and gain experience. To study development over time, investigators utilize three research designs: cross-sectional, longitudinal, and microgenetic.

Cross-Sectional Designs

The most common and easiest way to study changes and continuities with age is to use the **cross-sectional** approach. This method compares children of different ages on a given behavior, ability, or characteristic, with all the childen being studied at roughly the same time. For example, in one cross-sectional study of how friendship patterns change with age, researchers asked 6th to 12th graders to name their best friend and up to 10 other friends in their school (Urberg, Degirmencioglu, Tolson, & Halliday-Scher, 1995). The research indicated that some aspects of friendship changed with age; for example, older children named fewer friends than did younger children, but those they named were more likely to name them as friends as well. Other aspects of friendship did not change during the age span examined. For example, at all ages, children who were part of the ethnic majority at their school were more likely to have their choices of friends reciprocated than were children who were part of the minority.

Cross-sectional designs are useful for revealing similarities and differences between older and younger children. However, they do not yield information about the stability of individual differences over time or about the patterns of change shown by individual children. This is where longitudinal approaches are especially valuable.

cross-sectional design a research method in which children of different ages are compared on a given behavior or characteristic over a short period of time

longitudinal design a method of study in which the same children are studied twice or more over a substantial period of time

Longitudinal Designs

The **longitudinal** approach involves following a group of children over a substantial period of time (usually two or more years) and observing changes and continuities

MASTER FILE / RADIUS IMAGES

Being excluded is no fun for anyone. Longitudinal research has been used to determine whether the same children are unpopular year after year or whether popularity changes over time.

in these children's development at regular intervals during that time. In one longitudinal study, Brendgen et al. (2001) examined children's popularity with classmates each year from the time they were 7-year-olds to the time they were 12-year-olds. The popularity of most children proved to be quite stable over this period; a substantial number of children were popular in the large majority of years, and quite a few others were unpopular throughout. At the same time, some individuals showed idiosyncratic patterns of change from year to year; the same child might be popular at age 8, unpopular at age 10, and of average popularity at age 12. Such findings about the stability of individual differences over time and about individual children's patterns of change could only have been obtained in a longitudinal design.

If longitudinal designs are so useful for revealing stability and change over time, why are cross-sectional designs more common? The reasons are mainly practical. Studying the same children over long time periods involves the difficult and time-consuming task of locating the children for each reexamination. Inevitably, some of the children move away or drop out of the study for other reasons. Such loss of participants may call into question the external validity of the findings, because the children who do not continue may differ from those who participate throughout. (For example, children may drop out because they feel that they are performing poorly on the examinations; their dropping-out would therefore likely skew the findings.) Another threat to the external validity of longitudinal designs is the possible effects of the repeated testing. For example, repeatedly taking IQ tests could familiarize children with the type of items on the tests, thus improving the children's scores. For these reasons, longitudinal designs are used primarily when the main issues are stability and change in individual children over time, issues that can be studied only longitudinally. When the central developmental issue involves age-related changes in typical performance, cross-sectional studies are more commonly used.

Microgenetic Designs

An important limitation of both cross-sectional and longitudinal designs is that they provide only a broad outline of the process of change. **Microgenetic designs,** in contrast, are specifically designed to provide an in-depth depiction of the processes that produce changes (Kuhn & Franklin, 2006; Miller & Coyle, 1999; Siegler, 2006). The basic idea of this approach is to recruit children who are thought to be on the verge of an important developmental change, heighten their exposure to the type of experience that is believed to produce the change, and then intensively study the change *as it is occurring.* Microgenetic designs are like longitudinal ones in repeatedly testing the same children over time. They differ in that microgenetic studies typically include a greater number of sessions presented over a shorter time period than in a longitudinal study.

Siegler and Jenkins (1989) used a microgenetic design to study how young children discover the **counting-on strategy** for adding two small numbers. This strategy involves counting up from the larger addend the number of times indicated by

microgenetic design a method of study in which the same children are studied repeatedly over a short period of time

counting-on strategy counting up from the larger addend the number of times indicated by the smaller addend

BOB DAEMMRICH / STOCK BOSTON

Discovering how to solve problems is an inherently rewarding experience. Microgenetic designs can provide insight into both the process of discovery and children's emotional response to it.

the smaller addend; for example, when asked the answer to 3 + 5, a child who was counting-on would say or think "6, 7, 8" before answering "8." Prior to discovering this strategy, children usually solve addition problems by counting from 1. Counting from the larger addend rather than from 1 reduces the amount of counting, producing faster and more accurate solutions.

To observe the discovery process, the researchers selected 4- and 5-year-olds who did not yet use counting-on but who knew how to add by counting from 1. They presented these children with 30 sessions of seven addition problems each—far more addition problems than they would normally encounter before entering school—and videotaped each child's behavior on every problem. This approach allowed the researchers to identify exactly when each child discovered the counting-on strategy.

Although some children discovered the new strategy quickly, others required more than 200 problems before discovering it, and others never discovered it. Examination of the problems immediately preceding the discovery revealed a surprising fact: necessity is not always the mother of invention. Quite a few children discovered the counting-on strategy while working on easy problems that they previously had solved correctly by counting from 1.

The microgenetic method also revealed that children's very first use of the new strategy often was accompanied by insight and excitement, like that shown by Lauren:

> *Experimenter:* How much is 6 + 3?
> *Lauren: (long pause)* 9.
> *E:* OK, how did you know that?
> *L:* I think I said . . . I think I said . . . oops, um . . . 7 was 1, 8 was 2, 9 was 3.
> *E:* How did you know to do that? Why didn't you count 1, 2, 3, 4, 5, 6, 7, 8, 9?
> *L: (with excitement)* 'Cause then you have to count all those numbers.
>
> (Siegler & Jenkins, 1989, p. 66)

Despite her insightful explanation of counting-on and her excitement over discovering it, Lauren, and most other children, only gradually increased their use of the new strategy on the problems that they were given after the discovery. Other microgenetic studies have also shown that generalization of new strategies tends to be gradual (Kuhn & Franklin, 2006).

As this example illustrates, microgenetic methods provide insight into the process of change and into individual differences in change processes over brief periods. However, unlike standard longitudinal methods, microgenetic designs do not yield information about stability and change over long time periods. They therefore are typically used when the basic pattern of age-related change has already been established and the goal becomes to understand how the changes occur. (Table 1.6 outlines the strengths and weaknesses of the three approaches to studying changes with age and experience: cross-sectional, longitudinal, and microgenetic designs.)

Ethical Issues in Child-Development Research

All research with human beings raises ethical issues, and this is especially the case when the research involves children. Researchers have a vital responsibility to anticipate potential risks that the children in their studies may encounter, to minimize

TABLE 1.6

Advantages and Disadvantages of Designs for Studying Development

Design	Features	Advantages	Disadvantages
Cross-sectional	Children of different ages are studied at a single time.	Yields useful data about differences among age groups. Quick and easy to administer.	Uninformative about stability of individual differences over time. Uninformative about similarities and differences in individual children's patterns of change.
Longitudinal	Children are examined repeatedly over a prolonged period of time.	Indicates the degree of stability of individual differences over long periods. Reveals individual children's patterns of change over long periods.	Difficult to keep all participants in study. Repeatedly testing children can threaten external validity of study.
Microgenetic	Children are observed intensively over a relatively short time period while a change is occurring.	Intensive observation of changes while they are occurring can reveal process of change. Reveals individual change patterns over short periods in considerable detail.	Does not provide information about typical patterns of change over long periods. Does not reveal individual change patterns over long periods.

such risks, and to make sure that the benefits of the research outweigh any potential harm.

The Society for Research on Child Development, an organization devoted to research on children, has formulated a code of ethical conduct for investigators to follow (SRCD, 1999, pp. 283–284). Some of the most important ethical principles in the code are:

- Be sure that the research does not harm children physically or psychologically.
- Obtain informed consent for participating in the research, preferably in writing, from parents or other responsible adults and also from children if they are old enough that the research can be explained to them. The experimenter should inform children and relevant adults of all aspects of the research that might influence their willingness to participate and should explain that refusing to participate will not result in any adverse consequences to them.
- Preserve individual participants' anonymity, and do not use information for purposes other than that for which permission was given.
- Discuss with parents or guardians any information yielded by the investigation that is important for the child's welfare.
- Try to counteract any unforeseen negative consequences that arise during the research. If such negative consequences arise, redesign procedures to avoid similar problems.
- Correct any inaccurate impressions that the child may develop in the course of the study. When the research has been completed, explain the general findings to participants at a level they can understand.

Recognizing the importance of such ethical issues, universities and governmental agencies have established institutional review boards made up of independent scientists and sometimes others from the community. These boards evaluate the proposed research to ensure that it does not violate ethics guidelines. However, the individual investigator, who knows the most about the research and is in the best position to anticipate potential problems, bears the ultimate responsibility for seeing that his or her study meets high ethical standards.

review:

The scientific method, in which all hypotheses are treated as potentially incorrect, has allowed contemporary understanding of child development to progress well beyond the understanding of even the greatest thinkers of the past. This progress has been built on a base of four types of innovations:

1. Measures that are reliable and valid
2. Data-gathering situations that yield useful information about children's behavior, such as interviews, naturalistic observations, and structured observations
3. Designs that allow identification of associations and cause–effect relations among variables, notably correlational and experimental designs
4. Designs that allow analysis of the continuities and changes that occur with age and experience, notably cross-sectional, longitudinal, and microgenetic designs

Conducting scientific experiments also requires meeting high ethical standards, including not in any way harming the children who participate; obtaining informed consent for their participation in the research; preserving anonymity of all participants; and, after the study, explaining the findings to parents and, when possible, to children, at a level they can understand.

Chapter Summary

Why Study Child Development?

- Learning about child development is valuable for many reasons: it can help us become better parents, inform our views about social issues that affect children, and improve our understanding of human nature.

Historical Foundations of the Study of Child Development

- Great thinkers such as Plato, Aristotle, Locke, and Rousseau raised basic questions about child development and proposed interesting hypotheses about them, but they lacked the scientific methods to answer them. Early scientific approaches, such as those of Freud and Watson, began the movement toward modern research-based theories of child development.

Enduring Themes in Child Development

- The field of child development is an attempt to answer a set of fundamental questions:
  1. How do nature and nurture together shape development?
  2. How do children contribute to their own development?
  3. In what ways is development continuous, and in what ways is it discontinuous?
  4. How does change occur?
  5. How does the sociocultural context influence development?
  6. How do children become so different from each other?
  7. How can research promote children's well-being?
- Every aspect of development, from the most specific behavior to the most general trait, reflects both people's biological endowment (their nature) and the experiences that they have had (their nurture).
- Even infants and young children actively contribute to their own development through their attentional patterns, use of language, and choices of activities.
- Most developments can appear either continuous or discontinuous, depending on how often and how closely we look at them.
- The mechanisms that produce developmental changes involve a complex interplay among genes, brain structures, neurotransmitters, and experiences.
- The contexts that shape development include the people with whom children interact directly, such as family and friends; the institutions in which they participate, such as schools and religious organizations; and societal beliefs and values, such as those related to race, ethnicity, and social class.
- Individual differences, even among siblings, reflect differences in children's genes, in their treatment by other people, in their interpretations of their own experiences, and in their choices of environments.
- Principles, findings, and methods from child-development research are being applied to improving the quality of children's lives.

Methods for Studying Child Development

- The scientific method has made possible great advances in understanding children. It involves choosing a question, formulating a hypothesis relevant to the question, developing a method to test the hypothesis, and using data to decide whether the hypothesis is correct.
- For a measure to be useful, it must be relevant to the hypothesis, reliable, and valid. Reliability means that independent observations of a given behavior are consistent. Validity means that a measure assesses what it is intended to measure.

- Among the main situations used to gather data about children are interviews, naturalistic observation, and structured observation. Interviews are especially useful for revealing children's subjective experience. Naturalistic observation is particularly useful when the primary goal is to describe how children behave in their everyday environments. Structured observation is most useful when the main goal is to describe how different children react to the identical situation.
- Correlation does not imply causation. The two differ in that correlations indicate the degree to which two variables are associated, whereas causation indicates that changing the value of one variable will change the value of the other.
- Correlational designs are especially useful when the goal is to describe relations among variables or when the variables of interest cannot be manipulated due to technical or practical considerations.
- Experimental designs are especially valuable for revealing the causes of children's behavior.
- Data about development can be obtained through cross-sectional designs (examining different children of different ages), through longitudinal designs (examining the same children at different ages), or through microgenetic designs (presenting intensive experience over a relatively short period and analyzing the change process in detail).
- It is vital for researchers to adhere to high ethical standards. Among the most important ethical principles are striving to ensure that the research does not harm children physically or psychologically; obtaining informed consent from parents and, where possible, from children; preserving participants' anonymity; informing parents of anything needed to preserve the child's welfare; counteracting any negative outcomes that arise in the research; and correcting any inaccurate impressions that children form during the study.

Critical Thinking Questions

1. Do children have different natures, or are differences among children purely due to differences in their experiences? What personal observations, research findings, and reasoning leads to your conclusion?
2. Why do you think that the children who spent less than 6 months in orphanages in Romania were able to catch up physically, intellectually, and socially, whereas those who spent more time there have not been able to catch up? Do you think that they will catch up in the future?
3. In what ways is it fortunate and in what ways unfortunate that children shape their own development to a substantial extent?
4. Did reading about sleeping arrangements in the United States and in other cultures influence what you would like to do if you have children? Explain why or why not.
5. Given what you learned in this chapter about child-development research, can you think of practical applications of the research (other than the ones described) that seem both feasible and important to you?

Key Terms

nature, p. 11
nurture, p. 11
continuous development, p. 14
discontinuous development, p. 14
stage theories, p. 16
cognitive development, p. 16
neurotransmitters, 18
sociocultural context, p. 19
socioeconomic status, p. 20
scientific method, p. 25
hypotheses, p. 25
reliability, p. 26
interrater reliability, p. 26
test-retest reliability, p. 26
validity, p. 26
internal validity, p. 26
external validity, p. 26
structured interview, p. 27
clinical interview, p. 27
naturalistic observation, p. 28
structured observation, p. 29
variables, p. 29
correlational designs, p. 30
correlation, p. 30
correlation coefficient, p. 31
direction-of-causation problem, p. 31
third-variable problem, p. 31
experimental designs, p. 32
random assignment, p. 32
experimental control, p. 33
experimental group, p. 33
control group, p. 33
independent variable, p. 33
dependent variable, p. 33
cross-sectional design, p. 34
longitudinal design, p. 34
microgenetic design, p. 35
counting-on strategy, p. 35

MARC CHAGALL, *Pont Marie,* 1945–1950

2

Prenatal Development and the Newborn Period

THEMES

Nature and Nurture

The Active Child

Continuity/Discontinuity

The Sociocultural Context

Individual Differences

Research and Children's Welfare

Picture the following scenario. A developmental psychologist is investigating a very young research subject's perceptual capacities and ability to learn from experience. First, she plays a loud sound through a speaker near the subject's ear. She notes that the subject moves vigorously in response and concludes that the subject can hear the sound. Now she continues to play the same tone, over and over. As everyone else in the lab gets tired of repeatedly hearing the same sound, so, apparently, does the subject, who responds less and less to the repetitions of the sound and eventually does not react to it at all. Has the subject learned to recognize the sound or just gone to sleep? To find out, the researcher next presents a different sound, to which the subject responds vigorously. The subject seems to have recognized a difference between the new sound and the old one, suggesting that some simple learning has occurred. Wanting to see if the subject is capable of learning something more complex and in a more natural setting, the researcher sends the subject home, asking the subject's mother to read aloud to the subject from a Dr. Seuss book for several minutes a day for six weeks. The idea is to see whether the subject later shows any recognition of the passages that were read. But before the researcher sees the subject again, something quite important happens: the subject is born!

This scenario is not at all fanciful. Indeed, as you will discover later in this chapter, it is an accurate description of a fascinating and informative study that helped to revolutionize the understanding of prenatal development (DeCasper & Spence, 1986). As you will also discover in this chapter, researchers have been asking many questions about the sensory and learning capabilities of fetuses. And they have been finding that while in the womb, fetuses can detect a range of stimuli coming from the outside world and can learn from their experience and remain affected by it after birth.

In this chapter, we will examine the extraordinary course of prenatal development—a time of astonishingly rapid and dramatic change. In addition to discussing the normal processes involved in prenatal development, we will consider some of the ways in which these processes can be disrupted if the fetus is exposed to certain environmental hazards. We will also examine the birth process and what the infant experiences during this dramatic turning point, as well as some of the most salient aspects of neonatal behavior. Finally, we will outline problems associated with premature birth.

In our discussion of the earliest periods of development, most of the themes we described in Chapter 1 will play prominent roles. The most notable will be *nature and nurture,* as we emphasize how every aspect of development before birth results from the continual interplay of biological and environmental factors. The *active child* theme will also be featured, because the activity of the fetus contributes in numerous vital ways to its development. In fact, as you will see, normal prenatal development depends on certain fetal behaviors. Another theme we will highlight is the *sociocultural context* of prenatal development and birth, as we note substantial cultural variation in how people think about the beginning of life and how they handle the birth process. The theme of *individual differences* comes into play at many points, starting with gender differences in survival rates from conception on. The theme of *continuity/discontinuity* is also prominent: despite the dramatic contrast between prenatal and postnatal life, the behavior of newborns shows clear relations to their behavior and experience inside the womb.

Finally, the theme of *research and children's welfare* is central to our discussion of how poverty can affect prenatal development and birth outcomes and to our description of intervention programs designed to foster the development of preterm infants.

Prenatal Development

Hidden from view, the process of prenatal development has always been mysterious and fascinating, and beliefs about the origins of human life and development before birth have been an important part of the lore and traditions of all societies (see DeLoache & Gottlieb, 2000). (Box 2.1 describes one set of cultural beliefs about the beginning of life that are quite unlike those of Western societies.)

When we look back in history, we see great differences in how people have thought about prenatal development. In the fourth century B.C., Aristotle posed the fundamental question about prenatal development that was to underlie Western

a closer look 2.1

Beng Beginnings

Few topics have generated more intense debate and dispute in the United States in recent years than the issue of what point in development marks the beginning of life—the moment of conception or somewhere between conception and birth. The irony is that few who engage in this debate recognize how complex the issue is or the degree to which societies throughout the world have different views on it.

One example of this variety comes from the Beng, a people in the Ivory Coast of West Africa, who believe that every newborn is a reincarnation of an ancestor (Gottlieb, 2004). According to the Beng, in the first weeks after birth, the ancestor's spirit, its *wru*, is not fully committed to an earthly life and therefore maintains a double existence, traveling back and forth between the everyday world and *wrugbe*, or "spirit village." (The term can be roughly translated as "afterlife," but "before-life" might be just as appropriate.) It is only after the umbilical stump has dropped off that the newborn is considered to have emerged from *wrugbe* and to be a person. If the newborn dies before this, there is no funeral, for the infant's passing is simply conceived as a return in bodily form to the space that the infant was still psychically inhabiting.

These beliefs underlie many aspects of Beng infant-care practices. One is the application, many times a day, of an herbal mixture to the newborn's umbilical stump to hasten its drying out and dropping off. In addition, there is the constant danger that the infant or young child will become homesick for its life in *wrugbe* and decide to leave its earthly existence. To prevent this, parents try to make their babies comfortable and happy so they will want to stay in this life. Among the many recommended procedures is elaborately decorating the infant's face and body so that the infant will be attractive and elicit attention from others. Sometimes diviners are consulted, especially if the baby seems to be unhappy; a common diagnosis for prolonged crying is that the baby wants a different name, one from its previous life in *wrugbe*.

So when does life begin for the Beng? In one sense, a Beng individual's life begins well before birth, since he or she is a reincarnation of an ancestor. In another sense, however, life begins sometime after birth, when the individual is considered to have become a person.

COURTESY OF ALMA GOTTLIEB

The mother of this Beng baby has spent considerable time painting the baby's face in an elaborate pattern. She does this every day in an effort to make the baby attractive so other people will help keep the baby happy in this world.

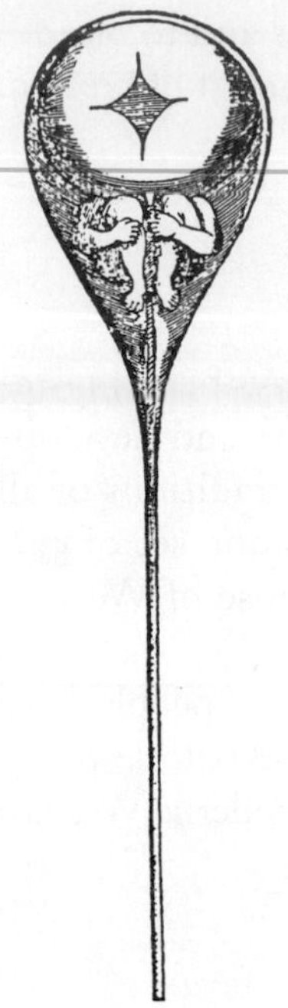

FIGURE 2.1 Preformationism A seventeenth-century drawing of a preformed being inside a sperm. This drawing was based on the claim of committed preformationists that when they looked at samples of semen under the newly invented microscope, they could actually see a tiny figure curled up inside the head of the sperm. They believed that the miniature person would enlarge after entering an egg. As this drawing illustrates, we must always take care not to let our cherished preconceptions so dominate our thinking that we see what we want to see—not what is really there. (From Moore & Persaud, 1993, p. 7)

thought for the next fifteen centuries: Does prenatal life start with the new individual already preformed, composed of a full set of tiny parts, or do the many parts of the human body develop in succession? Aristotle rejected the idea of preformation in favor of what he termed **epigenesis**—the emergence of new structures and functions during development (a view of development that, in more complex form, is highly influential today; Wolpert, 1991). Seeking support for his idea, he took what was then a very unorthodox step: he opened fertile chicken eggs and saw for himself chick organs in various stages of development. Nevertheless, the idea of preformation persisted long after Aristotle, degenerating into a dispute about whether the miniature, preformed human was lodged inside the mother's egg or the father's sperm (see Figure 2.1).

The notion of preformation may strike you as a bit simpleminded. Remember, however, that our ancient forebears had no way of knowing about the existence of cells and genes or about behavioral development in the womb. Many of the mysteries that perplexed our ancestors have now been solved, but as is always true in science, new mysteries have replaced them.

Conception

Each of us originated as a single cell that resulted from the union of two highly specialized cells—a sperm from our father and an egg from our mother. These **gametes,** or germ cells, are unique not only in their function but also in the fact that each one contains only half the genetic material found in other cells. Gametes are produced through a special type of cell division in which the eggs and sperm receive only one member from each of the 46 chromosome pairs contained in all other cells of the body. This reduction to 23 chromosomes in each gamete is necessary for reproduction, because the union of egg and sperm must contain the normal amount of genetic material (23 *pairs* of chromosomes). A major difference in the formation of these two types of gametes is the fact that almost all the eggs a woman will ever have are formed during her own prenatal development, whereas men produce vast numbers of new sperm continuously.

The process of reproduction starts with the launching of an egg (the largest cell in the human body) from one of the woman's ovaries into the fallopian tube (see Figure 2.2). As the egg moves through the tube toward the uterus, it emits a chemical substance that acts as a sort of beacon, a "come hither" signal that attracts sperm toward it. If an act of sexual intercourse takes place near the time the egg is released, **conception,** the union of sperm and egg, will be possible. In every ejaculation, as many as 500 million sperm are pumped into the woman's vagina. Each sperm, a streamlined vehicle for delivering the man's genes to the woman's egg, consists of little more than a pointed head packed full of genetic material (the 23 chromosomes) and a long tail that whips around to propel the sperm through the woman's reproductive system.

To be a candidate for initiating conception, a sperm must travel for about 6 hours, journeying 6 to 7 inches from the vagina up through the uterus to the fallopian tube. The rate of attrition on this journey is enormous: of the millions of sperm

epigenesis the emergence of new structures and functions in the course of development

gametes (germ cells) reproductive cells—egg and sperm—that contain only half the genetic material of all the other cells in the body

conception the union of an egg from the mother and a sperm from the father

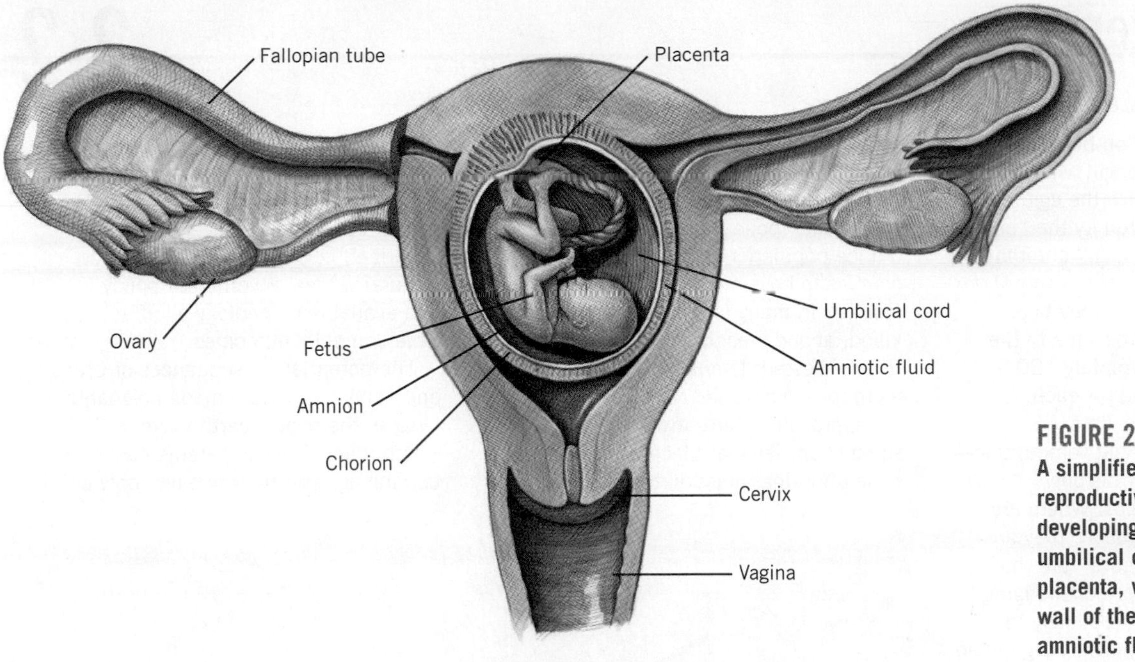

FIGURE 2.2 Female reproductive system A simplified illustration of the female reproductive system, with a fetus developing in the uterus (womb). The umbilical cord runs from the fetus to the placenta, which is burrowed deeply into the wall of the uterus. The fetus is floating in amniotic fluid inside the amniotic sac.

that enter the vagina, only about 200 ever get near the egg (see Figure 2.3). There are many causes for this high failure rate. Some failures are due to chance: many of the sperm get tangled up with other sperm milling about in the vagina, and others simply happen into the fallopian tube that does not currently harbor an egg. Other failures have to do with problems with the sperm themselves: a substantial portion have serious genetic or other defects that prevent them from propelling themselves vigorously enough to reach and fertilize the egg. Thus, any sperm that do get to the egg are relatively likely to be healthy and structurally sound, revealing a Darwinian-type "survival of the fittest" process operating during fertilization. (Box 2.2 describes the consequences of this selection process for the conception of males and females.)

FIGURE 2.3 (a) Sperm nearing the egg Of the millions of sperm that started out together, only a few ever get near the egg. The egg is the largest human cell (the only one visible to the naked eye), but sperm are among the smallest. **(b) Sperm penetrating the egg** This sperm is whipping its tail around furiously to drill itself through the outer covering of the egg.

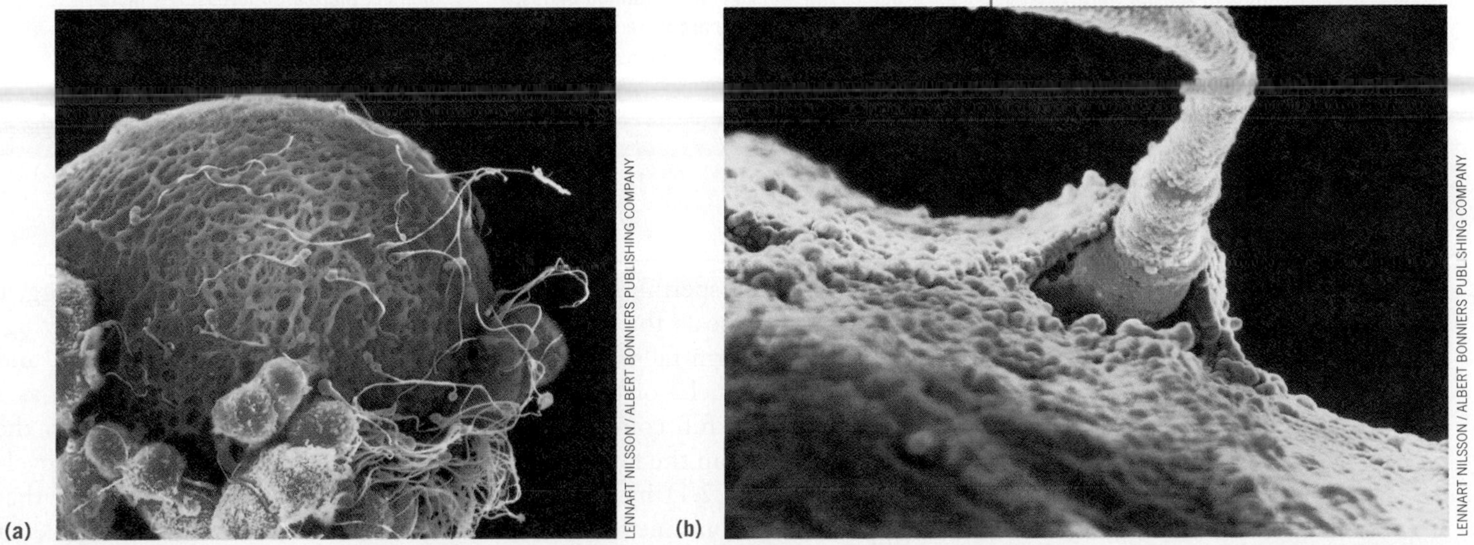

individual differences 2.2

The First—and Last—Sex Differences

The proverbial competition between the sexes might be said to begin with millions of sperm racing to fertilize the egg, a race won much more often by the "boys." Those sperm that possess a Y chromosome (the genetic basis for maleness) are lighter and swim faster, so they beat those bearing an X chromosome to the egg. As a result, approximately 120 to 150 males are conceived for each 100 females.

The girls win the next big competition—survival. The ratio at birth is only 106 males to 100 females. Where are the missing males? Obviously, they are miscarried at a much greater rate than females. Birth is also more challenging for boys, who are 50% more likely to need a cesarean delivery. This heightened vulnerability is not limited to surviving the prenatal period. Boys also suffer disproportionately from most developmental disorders, including language and learning disorders, dyslexia, attention-deficit disorder, mental retardation, and autism. The greater fragility of males continues throughout life, as reflected in the graph. Adolescent boys are more impulsive and take more risks than girls, and they are more likely to commit suicide or die violently.

Differential survival is not always left in the hands of nature. In many societies, both historically and currently, male offspring are more highly valued than females, and parents resort to infanticide to avoid having daughters. For example, Inuit families in Alaska traditionally depended on male children to help in the hunt for food, and in former times, Inuit girls were often killed at birth. Chinese parents, in both the past and present, count on their sons to take care of them in their old age. In modern China, the "one-child" policy, a measure designed to reduce population growth by forbidding couples to have more than one child, has resulted in many female babies being killed, abandoned, or given up for adoption to Western families in order to make room for a male child. A more technological approach is currently practiced in some countries that place a premium on male offspring: prenatal tests are used to determine the gender of the fetus, and female fetuses are selectively aborted. These cases dramatically illustrate the contextual model of development described in Chapter 1, showing how cultural values, government policy, and available technology all affect developmental outcomes.

The potential consequences of China's one-child policy were made poignantly clear in the deadly earthquake of 2008 in which many Chinese parents past childbearing age lost their one and only child.

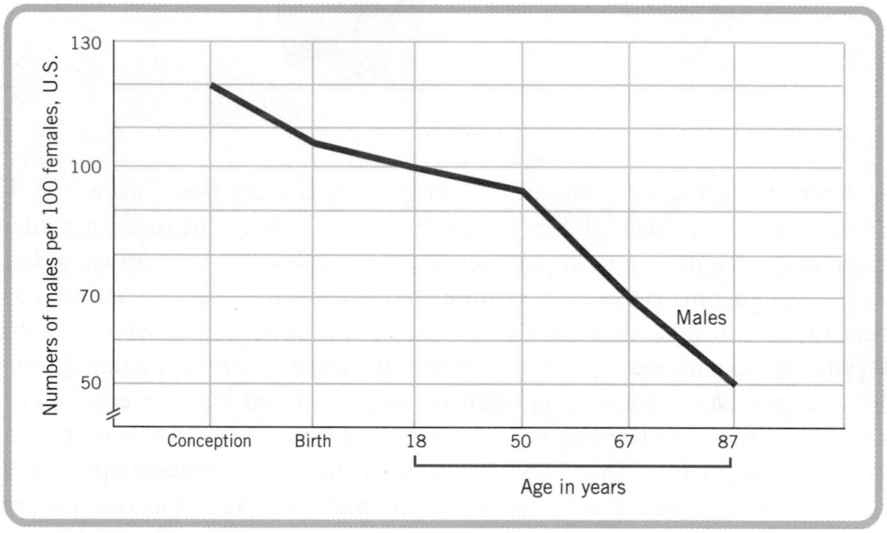

Source: Lerner & Libby (1976)

Males are more vulnerable than females across the life span. In the United States, at conception, there are more males than females, but that advantage quickly disappears. The two sexes become equal in number at around 18 years of age; from then on, there are increasingly more females than males in the population, particularly in old age.

As soon as one sperm's head penetrates the outer membrane of the egg, a chemical reaction seals the membrane, preventing other sperm from entering. The tail of the sperm falls off, the contents of its head gush into the egg, and within hours the nuclei of the two cells merge. The fertilized egg, known as a **zygote,** now has a full complement of human genetic material, half from the mother and half from the father. The first of the three periods of prenatal development (see Table 2.1) has begun and, if everything proceeds normally, that development will continue for approximately 9 months (on average, 38 weeks or 266 days).

zygote a fertilized egg cell

TABLE 2.1

Periods of Prenatal Development

Conception to two weeks	Germinal	Begins with conception and lasts until the zygote becomes implanted in the uterine wall. Rapid cell division takes place.
3rd to 8th week	Embryonic	Following implantation, major development occurs in all the organs and systems of the body. Development takes place through the processes of cell division, cell migration, cell differentiation, and cell death, as well as hormonal influences.
9th week to birth	Fetal	Continued development of physical structures and rapid growth of the body. Increasing levels of behavior, sensory experience, and learning.

Developmental Processes

Before describing the course of prenatal development, we need to briefly outline four major developmental processes that underlie the transformation of a zygote into an **embryo** and then a **fetus**. The first is *cell division.* Within 12 hours or so after fertilization, the zygote divides into two equal parts, each containing a full complement of genetic material. These two cells then divide into four, those four into eight, those eight into sixteen, and so on. Through continued cell division over the course of 38 weeks, the barely visible zygote becomes a newborn consisting of trillions of cells.

A second major process, which occurs during the embryonic period, is *cell migration,* the movement of newly formed cells from their point of origin in the embryo to somewhere else. Among the many cells that migrate are the neurons that originate deep inside the embryonic brain and then, like pioneers settling new territory, travel to the outer reaches of the developing brain.

The third process in prenatal development is *cell differentiation.* Initially, all embryonic cells, also known as **stem cells**, are equivalent and interchangeable: none has any fixed fate or function. After several cell divisions, however, cells start to specialize in terms of both structure and function. In humans, stem cells develop into roughly 350 different types of cells, which perform particular functions on behalf of the organism. (Because of their flexibility, very early embryonic stem cells offer the hope of treating a variety of illnesses, including Parkinson disease and leukemia. Injected into a person suffering from illness or injury, stem cells have the potential to develop into healthy cells to replace diseased or damaged ones.)

The process of differentiation is one of the major mysteries of prenatal development. Since all cells in the body have the identical set of genes, what determines which type of cell a given stem cell will become? One key determinant is which genes in the cell are "switched on" or expressed (see Box 2.3). Another is the cell's location, because its further development is influenced by what is going on in its neighboring cells.

The initial flexibility and subsequent inflexibility of cells, as well as the importance of location, is vividly illustrated by classic research with frog embryos. If the region of a frog embryo that would normally become an eye is grafted onto its belly area very early in development, the transplanted region will develop as a normal part of the belly. Thus, although the cells were initially in the right place to become an eye, they had not yet become specialized. If performed later on, the same

embryo the name given to the developing organism from the 3rd to 8th week of prenatal development

fetus the name given to the developing organism from the 9th week to birth

stem cells embryonic cells, which can develop into any type of body cell

a closer look 2.3

Phylogenetic Continuity

At various times throughout this book, we will describe research done with nonhuman animals to make some point about human development. In doing so, we subscribe to the principle of **phylogenetic continuity**—the idea that because of our common evolutionary history, humans share some characteristics and developmental processes with other living things. Indeed, you share most of your genes with your dog, cat, or hamster. In Chapter 3, we will consider how the part of our genetic heritage that we do not share with other mammals makes us all so different.

The assumption that animal models of behavior and development can be useful and informative for human development underlies a great deal of research. For example, much of our knowledge about the dangers of alcohol consumption by pregnant women comes from research with animals. Because scientists suspected that drinking alcohol while pregnant caused the constellation of defects now known as fetal alcohol spectrum disorder (page 62), they experimentally exposed fetal mice to alcohol. One result of this intervention was that the newborn mice had misformed facial features remarkably similar to the facial anomalies of children born to alcoholic mothers. This fact increased researchers' confidence that the problems commonly associated with fetal alcohol syndrome are, in fact, caused by alcohol rather than by some other factor.

One of the most fascinating discoveries in recent years, discussed later in this chapter, is the existence of fetal learning. Well before this phenomenon was demonstrated for human fetuses, it was documented in research on one of comparative psychologists' favorite creatures—the rat. Some natural preferences exhibited by newborn rat pups, including preferences important for survival, are based on learning that took place in the womb. To survive, newborns must find a milk-producing maternal nipple. How do they know where to go? The answer is that they search for something familiar to them. In the birth process, the nipples on the underside of the mother rat's belly get smeared with amniotic fluid. The scent of the amniotic fluid is familiar to the pups from their time in the womb, and it lures the babies to where they need to be—with their noses, and hence their mouths, near a nipple (Blass, 1990).

How do we know that newborn rats' first nipple attachment is based on their recognition of amniotic fluid? For one thing, when researchers washed the mother's belly clean of amniotic fluid, her pups failed to find her nipples, and if half her nipples were washed, the pups were attracted to the unwashed ones with amniotic fluid still on them (Blass & Teicher, 1980). Even more impressive, when researchers introduced odors or flavors into the amniotic fluid, either by directly injecting them or by adding them to the mother's diet, her pups preferred those odors and tastes after birth (Hepper, 1988; Pedersen & Blass, 1982; Smotherman & Robinson, 1987). These and other experimental demonstrations of fetal learning in rodents inspired developmental psychologists to look for similar processes in human fetuses. As you will see later, they found them.

KAREN HUNTT / NATIONAL GEOGRAPHIC IMAGE COLLECTION

Child and chimp have 99% of their genes in common.

operation results in an eye—alone and unseeing—lodged in the frog's belly (Wolpert, 1991).

The fourth developmental process is something you would not normally think of as developmental at all—*death*. However, the selective death of certain cells is the "almost constant companion" to the other developmental processes we have described (Wolpert, 1991). The role of this genetically programmed "cell suicide," known as **apoptosis**, is readily apparent in hand development (see Figure 2.4): the formation of fingers depends on the death of the cells in between the ridges in the hand plate. In other words, dying is part of the developmental program for those cells that selectively disappear from the hand plates.

phylogenetic continuity the idea that because of our common evolutionary history, humans share many characteristics, behaviors, and developmental processes with other animals, especially mammals

apoptosis genetically programmed cell death

In addition to these four developmental processes, we need to call attention to the influence of hormones on prenatal development. For example, hormones play a crucial role in sexual differentiation. All human fetuses, regardless of the genes they carry, can develop either male or female genitalia. What causes development to proceed one way or the other is the presence or absence of testosterone, a male hormone. If testosterone is present, male sex organs develop; if it is absent, female genitalia develop. The source of this influential hormone is the male fetus itself. Around the 8th week after conception, the testes begin to produce testosterone, and this self generated substance changes the fetus forever. This is just one of the many ways in which the fetus acts as an instigator of its own development.

We now turn our attention to the general course of prenatal development that results from all the preceding influences, as well as other developmental processes.

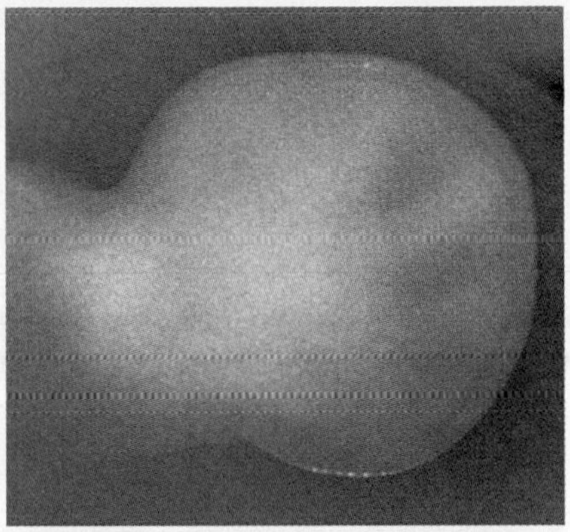

LENNART NILSSON FROM *A CHILD IS BORN* / BONNIER FAKTA

FIGURE 2.4 Embryonic hand plate Fingers will emerge from the hand plate of this 7-week-old embryo. The fingers are formed as a result of the death of the cells between the ridges you can see in the plate. If these cells did not expire, the baby would be born with webbed rather than independent fingers.

Early Development

On its journey through the fallopian tube to the womb, the zygote doubles its number of cells roughly twice a day. By the 4th day after conception, the cells arrange themselves into a hollow sphere with a bulge of cells, called the *inner cell mass,* on one side.

This is the stage at which **identical twins** most often originate. They result from a splitting in half of the inner cell mass, and thus they both have exactly the same genetic makeup. In contrast, **fraternal twins** result when two eggs happen to be released from the ovary into the fallopian tube and both are fertilized. Because they originate from two different eggs and two different sperm, fraternal twins are no more alike genetically than pairs of nontwin siblings.

By the end of the 1st week following fertilization, if all goes well (which it does for less than half the zygotes that are conceived), a momentous event occurs—implantation, the process in which the zygote embeds itself in the uterine lining and becomes dependent on the mother for sustenance. Well before the end of the 2nd week, it will be completely embedded within the uterine wall.

After implantation, the embedded ball of cells starts to differentiate. The inner cell mass will become the embryo, and the rest of the cells will become an elaborate support system—including the *amniotic sac* and *placenta*—that enables the embryo to develop. The inner cell mass is initially a single layer thick, but during the 2nd week, it folds itself into three layers, each with a different developmental destiny. The top layer becomes the nervous system, the nails, teeth, inner ear, lens of the eyes, and the outer surface of the skin. The middle layer eventually becomes muscles, bones, the circulatory system, the inner layers of the skin, and other internal organs. The bottom layer develops into the digestive system, lungs, urinary tract, and glands. A few days after the embryo has differentiated into these three layers, a U-shaped groove forms down the center of the top layer. The folds at the top of the groove move together and fuse, creating the **neural tube** (Figure 2.5). One end of the neural tube will swell and develop into the brain, and the rest will become the spinal cord.

The support system that is developing simultaneously with the embryo is elaborate and essential to its development. As noted above, one key element of this support system is the **amniotic sac,** a membrane filled with a clear, watery fluid in which the fetus floats. The amniotic fluid operates as a protective buffer for the developing fetus in several ways, such as providing it with a relatively even temperature and cushioning it against jolting. As you will soon see, because the amniotic

identical twins twins that result from the splitting in half of the zygote, resulting in each of the two resulting zygotes having exactly the same set of genes

fraternal twins twins that result when two eggs happen to be released into the fallopian tube at the same time and are fertilized by two different sperm; fraternal twins have only half their genes in common.

neural tube a groove formed in the top layer of differentiated cells in the embryo that eventually becomes the brain and spinal cord

amniotic sac a transparent, fluid-filled membrane that surrounds and protects the fetus

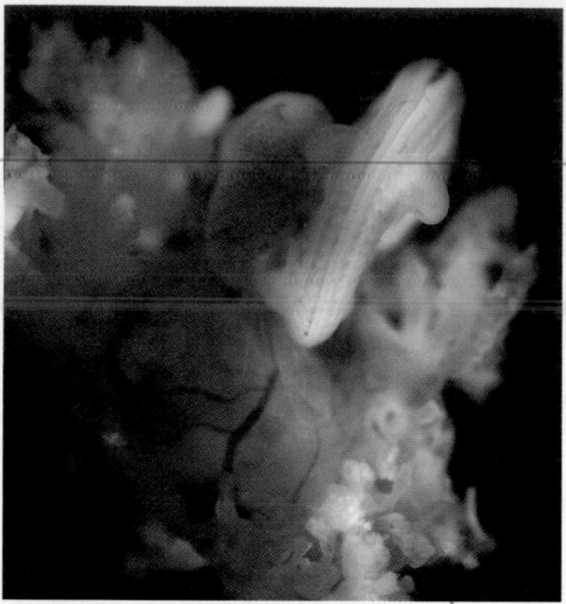

LENNART NILSSON FROM *A CHILD IS BORN* / BONNIER FAKTA

FIGURE 2.5 Neural tube In the 4th week, the neural tube begins to develop into the brain and spinal cord. In this photo, the neural groove, which fuses together first at the center and then outward in both directions as if two zippers were being closed, has been "zipped shut" except for one part still open at the top. Spina bifida, a congenital disorder in which the skin over the spinal cord is not fully closed, can originate at this point. After closing, the top of the neural tube will develop into the brain.

fluid keeps the fetus afloat, it also enables the fetus to exercise its tiny, weak muscles relatively unhampered by the effects of gravity.

The second key element of the support system, the **placenta,** is a unique organ that permits the exchange of materials carried in the bloodstreams of the fetus and its mother. It is an extraordinarily rich network of blood vessels, including minute ones extending into the tissues of the mother's uterus, with a total surface area of about 10 square yards—approximately the amount of driveway covered by the family car (Vaughn, 1996). Blood vessels running from the placenta to the embryo and back again are contained in the **umbilical cord.**

At the placenta, the blood systems of the mother and fetus come extremely close to one another, but the placenta prevents their blood from actually mixing. However, the placental membrane is semipermeable, meaning that some elements can pass through it but others cannot. Oxygen, nutrients, minerals, and some antibodies—all of which are just as vital to the fetus as they are to you—are transported to the placenta by the mother's circulating blood. They then cross the placenta and enter the fetal blood system. Waste products (e.g., carbon dioxide, urea) from the fetus cross the placenta in the opposite direction and are removed from the mother's bloodstream by her normal excretory processes.

The placental membrane also serves as a defensive barrier against a host of dangerous toxins and infectious agents that can inhabit the mother's body and could be harmful or even fatal to the fetus. Unfortunately, being semipermeable, the placenta is not a perfect barrier, and, as you will see later, a variety of harmful elements can cross it and attack the fetus. One other function of the placenta is the production of hormones, including *estrogen,* which increases the flow of maternal blood to the uterus, and *progesterone,* which suppresses uterine contractions that could expel the fetus prematurely (Nathanielsz, 1994).

An Illustrated Summary of Prenatal Development

The course of prenatal development from the 4th week on is illustrated in Figures 2.6 through 2.13, and significant milestones are highlighted in the accompanying text. The fetal behaviors that are mentioned will be discussed in detail in a later section. Notice that earlier development takes place at a more rapid pace than later development and that the areas nearer the head develop earlier than those farther away (e.g., head before body, hands before feet)—a general tendency known as **cephalocaudal development.**

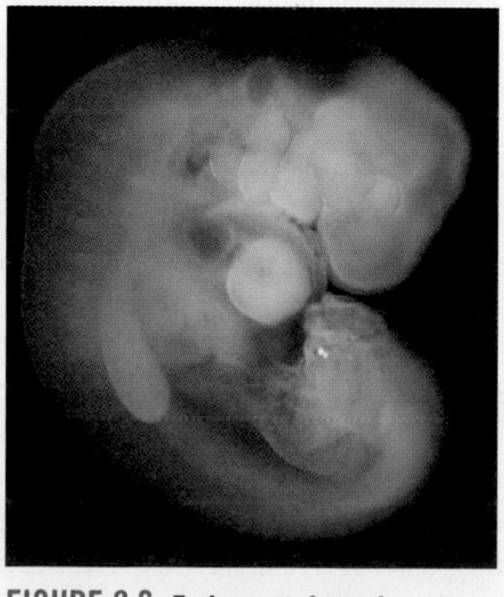

LENNART NILSSON FROM *A CHILD IS BORN* / BONNIER FAKTA

FIGURE 2.6 Embryo at 4 weeks

Figure 2.6: At 4 weeks after conception, the embryo's tiny body is curved so tightly that the head and the tail-like structure at the other end are almost touching. Several facial features have their origin in the set of four folds in the front of the embryo's head; the face gradually emerges as a result of these tissues moving and stretching, as parts of them fuse and others separate. The round area near the top of the head is where the eye will form, and the round gray area near the back of the "neck" is the

placenta a support organ for the fetus; it keeps the circulatory systems of the fetus and mother separate, but as a semipermeable membrane permits the exchange of some materials between them (oxygen and nutrients from mother to fetus and carbon dioxide and waste products from fetus to mother)

umbilical cord a tube containing the blood vessels connecting the fetus and placenta

cephalocaudal development the pattern of growth in which areas near the head develop earlier than areas farther from the head primordial inner ear. A primitive heart is visible; it is already beating and circulating blood. An arm bud can be seen in the side of the embryo; a leg bud is also present but less distinct.

Figure 2.7: (a) In this 5½-week-old fetus, the nose, mouth, and palate are beginning to differentiate into separate structures. (b) Just three weeks later, the nose and mouth are almost fully formed. Cleft palate, one of the most common birth defects worldwide, involves malformations (sometimes minor, sometimes major) of this area. This condition originates sometime between 5½ and 8 weeks prenatally—precisely when these structures are developing.

Figure 2.8: The head constitutes roughly half the length of this 9-week-old fetus, and its bulging forehead reflects the extremely rapid brain growth that has been going on for weeks. Rudimentary eyes and ears are forming. All the internal organs are present, although most must undergo further development. Sexual differentiation has started. Ribs are visible; fingers and toes have emerged, and nails are growing. The umbilical cord connecting the fetus to the placenta is shown (the fetal membranes have been pulled to the side). Spontaneous movements occur, but because the fetus is so small and is floating in amniotic fluid, these movements cannot be felt by the mother.

Figure 2.9: This picture of an 11-week-old fetus was produced by a new noninvasive technique for creating three-dimensional images of the body. The image clearly shows the heart, which has achieved its basic adult structure. You can also see the developing spine and ribs, as well as the major divisions of the brain.

Figure 2.10: During the last 5 months of prenatal development, the growth of the lower part of the body accelerates. The fetus's movements have increased dramatically: the chest makes breathing movements, and some reflexes—grasping, swallowing, sucking—are present. The intense kick dealt by this 16-week-old fetus will be felt by its mother, although only as a mild "flutter." A different camera

(a)

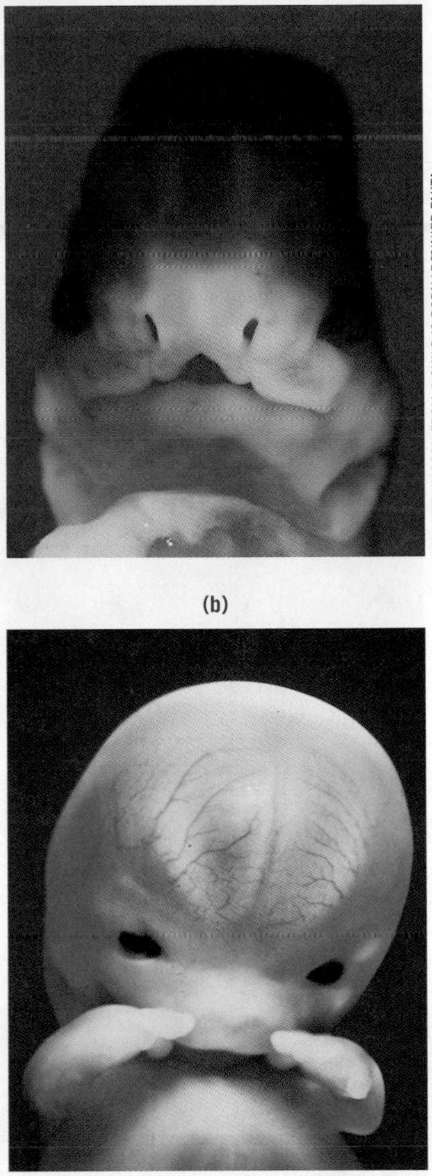

LENNART NILSSON FROM *A CHILD IS BORN* / BONNIER FAKTA

(b)

LENNART NILSSON FROM *A CHILD IS BORN* / BONNIER FAKTA

FIGURE 2.7 **Face development from 5½ to 8½ weeks**

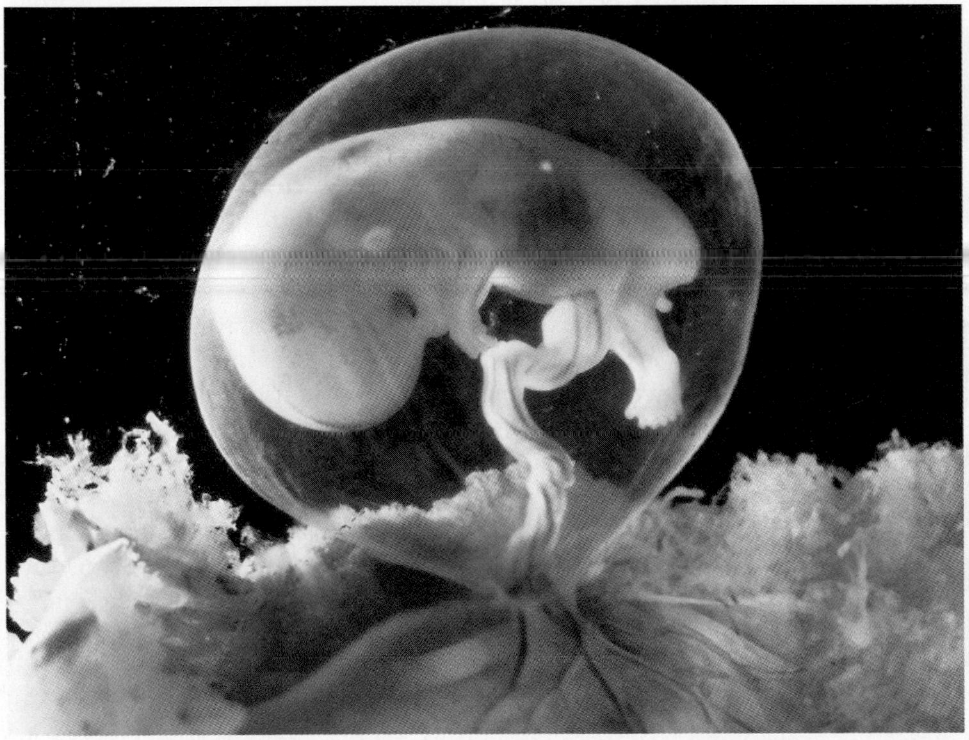

LENNART NILSSON FROM *A CHILD IS BORN* / BONNIER FAKTA

FIGURE 2.8 **Fetus at 9 weeks**

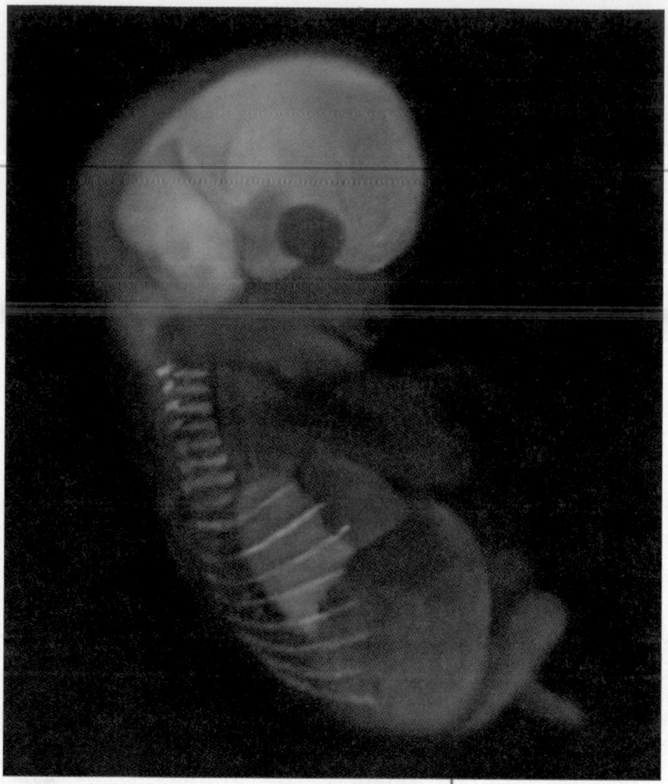

ANATOMICAL TRAVELOGUE / PHOTO RESEARCHERS, INC.

FIGURE 2.9 Fetus at 11 weeks

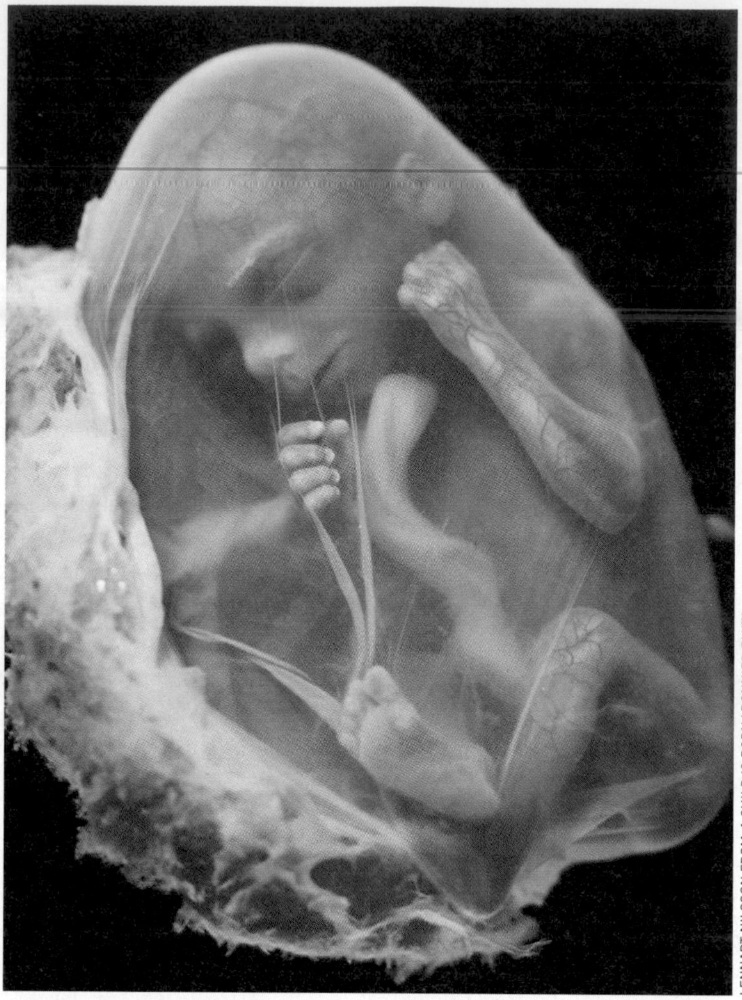

LENNART NILSSON FROM *A CHILD IS BORN* / BONNIER FAKTA

FIGURE 2.10 Fetus at 16 weeks

LENNART NILSSON FROM *A CHILD IS BORN* / BONNIER FAKTA

FIGURE 2.11 Fetus at 18 weeks

angle of this fetus would reveal whether it is boy or girl, as the external genitalia are substantially developed at this point.

Figure 2.11: This 18-week-old fetus is clearly sucking its thumb, in much the same way it will as a newborn. The fetus is covered with very fine hair, and a greasy coating protects its skin from its long immersion in liquid.

Figure 2.12: By the 20th week, the fetus spends increasingly more time in a head-down position. The components of facial expressions are present—the fetus can raise its eyebrows, wrinkle its forehead, and move its mouth. As the fetus rapidly puts on weight, free space in the amniotic sac decreases and, as a consequence, so do fetal movements.

Figure 2.13: The 28th week marks the point at which the brain and lungs are sufficiently developed that a fetus born at this time would have a chance of surviving on its own, without medical intervention. The eyes can open, and they move, especially during periods of REM (rapid eye movement) sleep. The auditory system is now functioning, and the fetus hears and reacts to a variety of

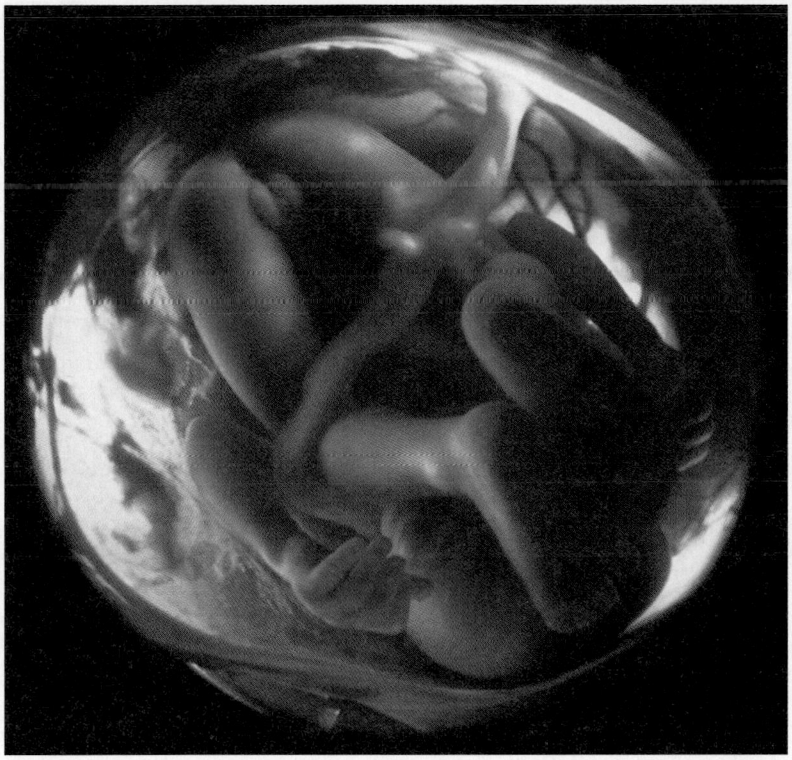

LENNART NILSSON FROM *A CHILD IS BORN* / BONNIER FAKTA

FIGURE 2.12 Fetus at 20 weeks

sounds. At this stage of development, the brain waves of the fetus are very similar to those of a newborn. During the last 3 months of prenatal development, the fetus grows dramatically in size, essentially tripling its weight. The mother becomes increasingly uncomfortable, and so, presumably, does the fetus in the cramped confines of the womb.

The typical result of this 9-month period of rapid and remarkable development is a healthy newborn.

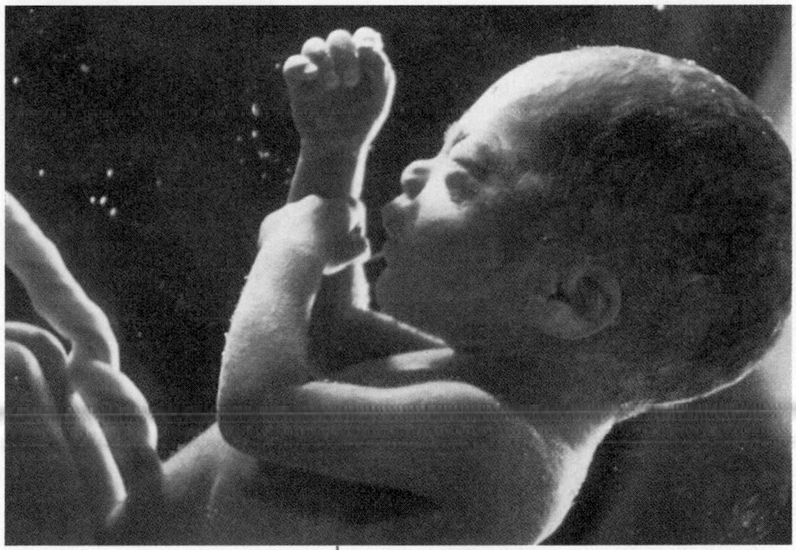

PETIT FORMAT / NESTLE / SCIENCE SOURCE / PHOTO RESEARCHERS, INC.

FIGURE 2.13 Fetus at 28 weeks

Fetal Behavior

As we have noted, the fetus is an active participant in, and contributor to, its own physical and behavioral development. Indeed, the normal formation of organs and muscles depends on fetal activity, and the fetus rehearses the behavioral repertoire it will need at birth.

Movement

Every mother knows that her baby was active in the womb, but few realize how early their child started moving. From 5 or 6 weeks after conception, the fetus moves spontaneously, starting with a simple bending of the head and spine that is soon followed by the onset of numerous kinds of increasingly complex movements over the next weeks (De Vries, Visser, & Prechtl, 1982). One of the earliest distinct

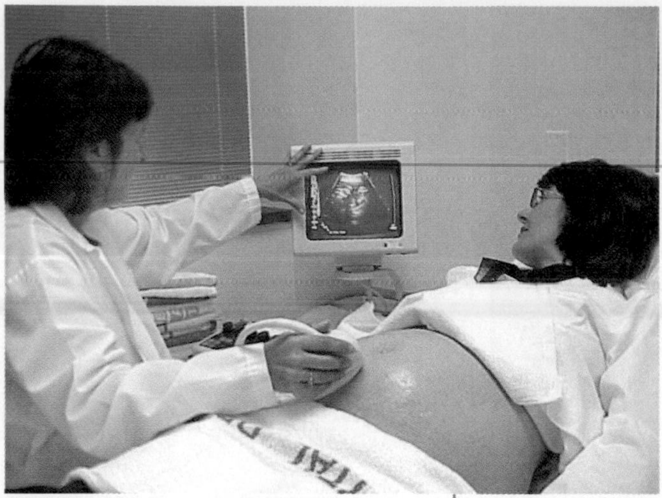

COURTESY JANET DIPIETRO

Developmental psychologist Janet DiPietro is using ultrasound to study the movement patterns of this woman's fetus.

patterns of movement to emerge (at around 7 weeks) is, remarkably enough, hiccups. Why? According to research, hiccups "remain as poorly defined for the fetus as they are for the adult" (Stark & Myers, 1995, p. 61). In other words, no one knows.

The fetus also moves its arms and legs, wiggles its fingers, grasps the umbilical cord, moves its head and eyes, and yawns. Complete changes of position are achieved by a kind of backward somersault. These various movements are initially jerky and uncoordinated but gradually become more integrated. By 12 weeks, most of the movements that will be present at birth have appeared (De Vries et al., 1982), although the mother is still unaware of them.

Presaging the newborn skill of thumb-sucking, more than half of the arm movements of 19- to 35-week-old fetuses result in contact between their hand and mouth (Myowa-Yamakoshi & Takeghita, 2006). Later on, when mothers can readily feel the movement of their fetuses, their reports reveal that how much a fetus moves—its activity level—is quite consistent over time: some fetuses are characteristically very active, whereas others are more sedentary (Eaton & Saudino, 1992). There is prenatal-to-postnatal *continuity* in these individual differences in that more active fetuses turn out to be more active infants (DiPietro, Costigan, Shupe, Pressman, & Johnson, 1998). Further, fetuses that have regular periods of sleep and waking are likely to have similarly regular sleep times as newborns (DiPietro et al., 2002).

A particularly important form of fetal movement is *swallowing*. The fetus drinks amniotic fluid, which passes through its gastrointestinal system. Most of the fluid is then excreted back out into the amniotic sac. One benefit of this activity is that the tongue movements associated with drinking and swallowing promote the normal development of the palate (Walker & Quarles, 1962). In addition, the passage of amniotic fluid through the stomach and intestines helps those organs mature properly, so that the digestive system is functional at birth. Thus, swallowing amniotic fluid prepares the fetus for survival outside the womb.

A second form of fetal movement anticipates the fact that at birth the newborn must start breathing. For that to happen, the lungs and the rest of the respiratory system, including the muscles that move the diaphragm in and out, must be mature and functional. Beginning as early as 10 weeks after conception, the fetus promotes its respiratory readiness by exercising its lungs through "fetal breathing," moving its chest wall in and out (Nathanielsz, 1994). No air is taken in, of course; rather, small amounts of amniotic fluid are pulled into the lungs and then expelled. Unlike real breathing, which must be continuous, fetal breathing goes on only about 50% of the time (James, Pillai, & Smoleniec, 1995).

Behavioral Cycles

Once the fetus begins to move at 5 to 6 weeks, it is in almost constant motion for the next month or so. Then periods of inactivity gradually begin to occur. Rest–activity cycles—bursts of high activity alternating with little or no activity for a few minutes at a time—emerge as early as 10 weeks and become very stable during the second half of pregnancy (Robertson, 1990). In the latter half of the prenatal period, the fetus moves only about 10 to 30% of the time (DiPietro et al., 1998). Fetuses that are anencephalic (a rare condition in which the cerebral cortex is missing) remain highly active throughout pregnancy, suggesting that the cortex is involved in the inhibition of fetal movement (James et al., 1995).

"It's a baby. Federal regulations prohibit our mentioning its race, age, or gender."

Longer-term patterns, including daily (circadian) rhythms, also become apparent, with the fetus being less active in the early morning and more active in the late evening (Arduini, Rizzo, & Romanini, 1995). This confirms the impression of most pregnant women that their fetuses wake up and start doing acrobatics just as they themselves are trying to go to sleep.

Near the end of pregnancy, the fetus spends more than three-fourths of its time in quiet and active sleep states like those of the newborn (James et al., 1995) (see page 70). The active sleep state is characterized by REM, just as it is in infants and adults.

Fetal Experience

There is a popular idea—promoted by everyone from scholars to cartoonists—that we spend our lives longing for the peace and quiet we experienced in our mother's womb. But is the womb a haven of peace and quiet? Although the uterus and the amniotic fluid buffer the fetus from much of the stimulation impinging on the mother, research has made it clear that the fetus experiences an abundance of sensory stimulation.

Sight and Touch

Although it is not totally dark inside the womb, the visual experience of the fetus is presumably negligible. The fetus does, however, experience tactile stimulation as a result of its own activity. In the course of moving around, its hands come into contact with other parts of its body: as noted, fetuses have been observed grasping their umbilical cords, rubbing their faces, and sucking their thumbs (Figure 2.11). As the fetus grows larger, it increasingly often bumps against the walls of the uterus.

Taste

The amniotic fluid that the fetus swallows contains a variety of flavors (Maurer & Maurer, 1988). The fetus can detect these flavors and likes some better than others. Indeed, the fetus has a sweet tooth. The first evidence of fetal taste preferences came from a medical study performed over 60 years ago (described by Gandelman, 1992). A physician named DeSnoo devised an ingenious treatment for women with excessive amounts of amniotic fluid. He injected saccharin into their amniotic fluid, hoping that the fetus would help the mother out by ingesting increased amounts of the sweetened fluid, thereby diminishing the excess. To find out if his procedure worked, DeSnoo experimented with two groups of pregnant women. With one group, he injected the womens' amniotic fluid with both saccharin and a dye that shows up in urine; with the other group, he injected just the dye. He reasoned that the more of the sweetened fluid the fetus drank, the more dye it would take in and pass across the placenta to the mother. Thus, to see if the addition of a sweet flavor increased intake of amniotic fluid, all he had to do was assess how much dye showed up in the mothers' urine. DeSnoo found that the urine of mothers who had the saccharin-dye combination injected into their amniotic fluid was more tinted than that of mothers who had received only the dye. The fact that the fetuses in this study drank more amniotic fluid when it had been sweetened demonstrated that taste sensitivity and flavor preferences exist before birth.

Smell

Amniotic fluid also takes on odors from what the mother has eaten (Mennella, Johnson, & Beauchamp, 1995). Obstetricians have long reported that during birth they can smell scents like curry and coffee in the amniotic fluid of women who had recently consumed them. Indeed, human amniotic fluid has been shown to be rich in odorants (although many do not sound very appealing—including those described as being pungently rancid, goaty, or having a "strong fecal note") (Schaal, Orgeur, & Rognon, 1995). Through fetal breathing, amniotic fluid comes into contact with the fetus's odor receptors. Hence, scientists have concluded that the fetus has olfactory experience.

Hearing

Picture serious scientists hovering over a pregnant woman's bulging abdomen, ringing bells, striking a gong, clapping blocks of wood together, and even sounding an automobile horn—all to see if her fetus reacts to auditory stimulation. (Remind you of the opening to this chapter?) Such research has demonstrated that external sounds that are audible to the fetus include the voices of people talking to the woman. In addition, the prenatal environment includes many maternal sounds—the mother's heartbeat, blood pumping through her vascular system, her breathing, her swallowing, and various rude noises made by her digestive system. A particularly prominent and frequent source of sound stimulation is the mother's voice as she talks, with the clearest aspects being the general rhythm, intonation, and stress pattern of her speech.

The fetus responds to these various sounds from at least the 6th month of pregnancy on. During the last trimester, external noises elicit changes in fetal movements and heart rate (Kisilevsky, Fearon, & Muir, 1998; Lecanuet et al., 1995; Zimmer, Chao, Guy, Marks, & Fifer, 1993). The fetus's heart rate also decelerates briefly when the mother starts speaking (Fifer & Moon, 1995). (Transitory heart-rate deceleration is a sign of interest.) The fetus's extensive auditory experience with human voices has some lasting effects, as we discuss in the next section.

The fetus of this pregnant woman may be eavesdropping on her conversation with her friends.

Fetal Learning

In the preceding sections, we have emphasized the impressive behavioral and sensory capabilities of the fetus in the early stages of development. Even more impressive is the extent to which the fetus learns from many of its experiences in the last 3 months of pregnancy, after the central nervous system is adequately developed to support learning.

Direct evidence for human fetal learning comes from studies of habituation, one of the simplest forms of learning (Thompson & Spencer, 1966). **Habituation** involves a decrease in response to repeated or continued stimulation (see Figure 2.14). If you shake a rattle beside an infant's head, the baby will likely turn toward it. At the same time, the infant's heart rate may slow momentarily, which, as noted above, indicates interest. If you repeatedly shake the rattle, however, the head-turning and heart-rate changes will decrease and eventually stop. This decreased response is evidence of learning and memory: only if the infant remembers the stimulus from one presentation to the next can the stimulus lose its novelty. When a new stimulus occurs, the habituated response recovers (increases). Shaking a bell, for example, may reinstate the head-turning and heart-rate responses. (Developmental psychologists have exploited habituation to study a great variety of topics that you will read about in later chapters.)

habituation a simple form of learning that involves a decrease in response to repeated or continued stimulation

In one habituation study of prenatal learning of speech sounds, a team of French investigators (Lecanuet et al., 1995) repeatedly presented fetuses in their 9th month of gestation with a syllable pair—"babi." (A recording of the syllable pair was played through a speaker placed over the mother's abdomen.) The initial presentations elicited a brief but noticeable deceleration in the fetus's heart rate. As the sound was repeated, the heart rate returned to normal. Then the order of the two syllables was reversed, creating the new stimulus "biba." At this point, the infant's heart rate once again decelerated. Thus, the fetus had habituated to the familiar stimulus (i.e., had learned to recognize it) and could discriminate between one syllable pair and another. Fetuses pay attention to and habituate to a wide variety of sounds in addition to human voices (e.g., Kisilevsky & Muir, 1991; Lecanuet et al., 1995). The earliest time at which fetal habituation has been observed is 32 weeks, indicating that the central nervous system is sufficiently developed at this point for learning and memory to occur (Sandman, Wadhwa, Hetrick, Porto, & Peeke, 1997).

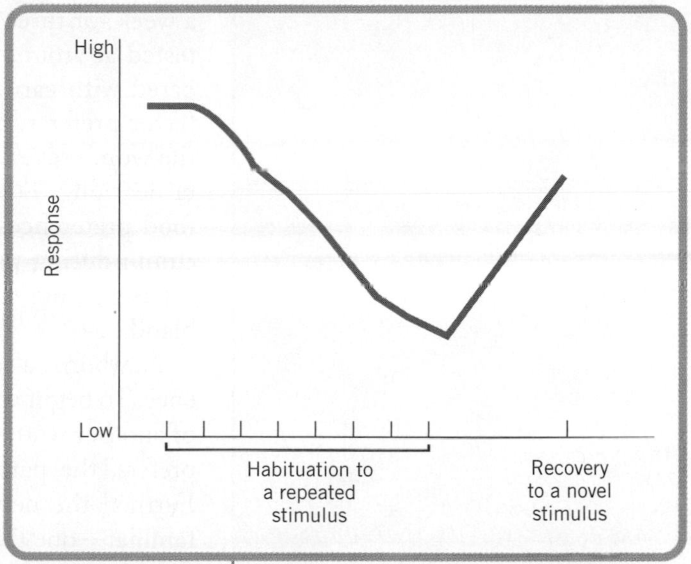

FIGURE 2.14 Habituation Habituation occurs in response to the repeated presentation of a stimulus. As the first stimulus is repeated and becomes familiar, the response to it gradually decreases. When a novel stimulus occurs, the response recovers. The decreased response to the repeated stimulus indicates the formation of memory for it; the increased response to the novel stimulus indicates discrimination of it from the familiar one, as well as a general preference for novelty.

The effects of prenatal learning have also been observed after birth. In a classic study, Anthony DeCasper and Melanie Spence (1986) asked pregnant women to read aloud twice a day from *The Cat in the Hat* (or another Dr. Seuss book) during the last 6 weeks of their pregnancy. Thus, the women's fetuses were repeatedly exposed to the same highly rhythmical pattern of speech sounds. The question was whether they would recognize the familiar story after birth. To see, the researchers tested them as newborns. The infants were fitted with miniature headphones and given a special pacifier to suck on (see Figure 2.15). When the infants sucked in one particular pattern, they heard the familiar story through the headphones, but when they sucked in a different pattern, they heard an unfamiliar story. The babies quickly increased their sucking in the pattern that enabled them to hear the familiar story. Thus, these newborns apparently recognized and preferred the story they had heard in the womb.

Newborns also have a natural preference for a familiar smell—the scent of the amniotic fluid in which they lived for the previous 9 months. In one set of studies that shows this preference, newborns were presented with two pads, one saturated with their own amniotic fluid and the other saturated with the amniotic fluid of a different baby. With the two pads located on either side of their head, the infants revealed a preference for the scent of their own amniotic fluid by keeping their head oriented longer toward that scent (Marlier, Schaal, & Soussignon, 1998; Varendi, Porter, & Winberg, 2002).

Long-lasting preferences based on prenatal experience have been demonstrated for taste (Mennella, Jagnow, & Beauchamp, 2001). Pregnant women were asked to drink carrot juice four days

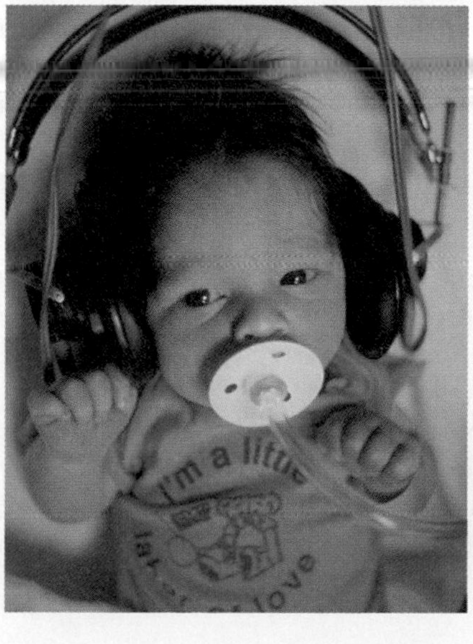

MELANIE SPENCE, UNIVERSITY OF TEXAS

FIGURE 2.15 Prenatal learning This newborn can control what he gets to listen to. His pacifier is hooked up to a computer, which is in turn connected to a tape player. If the baby sucks in one pattern (predetermined by the researchers), he will hear one tape. If he sucks in a different pattern, he will hear a different tape. Researchers have used this technique to investigate many questions about infant abilities, including the influence of fetal experience on newborn preferences.

a week for three weeks near the end of their pregnancy. When their babies were tested at around 5½ months of age, they reacted more positively to cereal prepared with carrot juice than to the same cereal prepared with water. Thus, the flavor preferences of these babies reflected the influence of their experience in the womb several months earlier. This finding reveals a *persistent* effect of prenatal learning. Further, it may shed light on the origins and strength of cultural food preferences. A child whose mother ate a lot of chili peppers, ginger, and cumin during pregnancy, for example, might be more favorably disposed from the beginning to Indian food than would a child whose mother's diet was more bland.

Newborns also show numerous auditory preferences based on prenatal experience. To begin with, they prefer to listen to their own mother's voice over the voice of another woman; in other words, the fetus learns to recognize, and subsequently prefers, the particular voice it has heard the most (DeCasper & Fifer, 1980). Further, the newborn prefers a version of its mother's voice that sounds most familiar—one that has been filtered to sound the way it did in the womb (Moon & Fifer, 1990; Spence & Freeman, 1996). Finally, newborns would rather listen to the language they heard in the womb than to another language (Mehler et al., 1988; Moon, Cooper, & Fifer, 1993). French newborns prefer listening to French over Russian, for example.

There can be little question that the human fetus is listening and learning. Does this mean that parents-to-be should sign up for programs that promise to "educate your unborn child"? Such programs exhort the mother-to-be to talk to her fetus, read books to it, play music for it, and so on. Some also urge the father-to-be to speak through a megaphone aimed at his wife's bulging belly in the hope that the newborn will recognize his voice as well as the mother's. Is there any point in such exercises?

Probably not. Although it seems possible that hearing Dad's voice more clearly and more frequently might lead the newborn to prefer it over unfamiliar voices, such a preference develops very quickly after birth anyway. And it is quite clear that some of the advertised advantages of prenatal training would not occur. Because of the level of development of the fetus's brain, it would be impossible for it to learn the meaning of words or any kind of factual knowledge, no matter how much the mother-to-be might read aloud. The fetus will only learn about her voice and the general patterns of her language—not any specific content. We suspect that the craze for "prenatal education" will go the way of other ill-conceived attempts to shape early development to adult desires.

Hazards to Prenatal Development

Thus far, our focus has been on the normal course of development before birth. Unfortunately, prenatal development is not always free of error or misfortune. The most dire, and by far the most common, misfortune is spontaneous abortion—commonly referred to as miscarriage. In the United States, the best estimate is that around 45% or more of pregnancies end in miscarriage prior to the 3rd week, before the woman has any idea she is pregnant (Moore & Persaud, 1993). The majority of embryos that are miscarried very early have severe defects, such as a missing chromosome or an extra one, that make further development impossible. Of pregnancies that women are aware of, 15% to 20% end in a miscarriage.

Few couples realize how common this experience is, making it all the more painful if it happens to them.

Most infants who survive the danger of miscarriage are born fully normal. This is the case for well over 90% of all newborns in the United States today, and most of the rest have only minor defects. There are, however, numerous factors operating before birth that can cause less fortunate outcomes. Genetic factors, which are the most common, will be discussed in the next chapter. Here, we consider some of the environmental influences that can have harmful effects on prenatal development.

MICHAEL S. YAMASHITA / CORBIS

Victims of "Minamata disease" caused by mercury pollution in Minamata Bay.

Environmental Influences

In the spring of 1956, two sisters were brought to a Japanese hospital, delirious and unable to walk. Their parents and doctors were mystified by the sudden deterioration in the girls, described as having been "the brightest, most vibrant, cutest kids you could imagine." The mystery intensified as more children and adults developed nearly identical symptoms. The discovery that all the disabled patients were from the small coastal town of Minamata suggested a common cause for what was referred to as the "strange disease" (Newland & Rasmussen, 2003; Smith & Smith, 1975).

That cause was eventually traced to the tons of mercury that had been dumped into Minamata Bay by a local petrochemical and plastics factory. For years, the residents of Minamata had been catching and consuming fish that had absorbed mercury from the polluted waters of the bay. By 1993, over 2000 children and adults had been diagnosed with what had come to be known as "Minamata disease"—methyl-mercury poisoning (Harada, 1995). At least 40 children had been poisoned prenatally by mercury in the fish eaten by their pregnant mothers and were born with cerebral palsy, mental retardation, and a host of other neurological disorders.

The tragedy of Minamata Bay provided some of the first clear evidence of the seriously detrimental impact that environmental factors can have on prenatal development. As you will see, a vast array of environmental agents have the potential to cause harm during the prenatal period. These environmental agents, called **teratogens,** can cause prenatal damage ranging from relatively mild and easily corrected problems to fetal death.

A crucial factor in the severity of the effects of potential teratogens is timing (one of the basic developmental principles discussed in Chapter 1). Many teratogens cause damage only if exposure to them occurs during a **sensitive period** in prenatal development (see Figure 2.16). Each of the major organ systems has its own sensitive period, which is the time when its basic structures are being formed. There is no more dramatic or straightforward illustration of the importance of timing than the thalidomide tragedy that occurred in the 1960s. Many pregnant

teratogen an external agent that can cause damage or death during prenatal development

sensitive period the period of time during which a developing organism is most sensitive to the effects of external factors; prenatally, the sensitive period is when the fetus is maximally sensitive to the harmful effects of teratogens

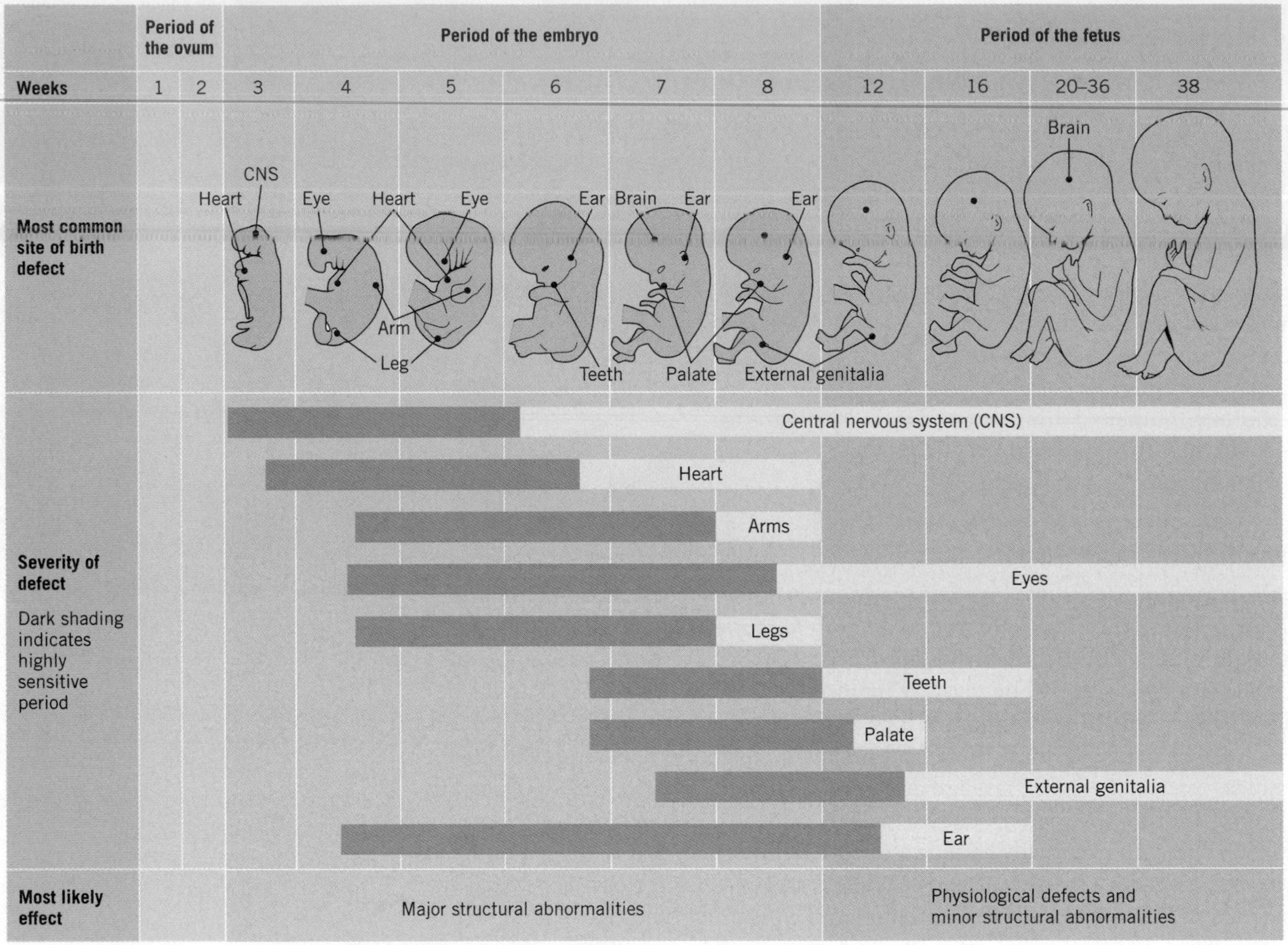

FIGURE 2.16 Sensitive periods of prenatal development **The most sensitive or critical period of prenatal development is the embryonic period. During the first two weeks, before implantation in the uterus, the zygote is generally not susceptible to environmental factors. Every major organ system of the body undergoes all or a major part of its development between the 3rd and the end of the 8th week. The dark green portions of the bars in the figure denote the times of most rapid development when major defects originate. The light green portions indicate periods of continued but less rapid development when minor defects may occur. (Adapted from Moore & Persaud, 1993)**

women who took this new, presumably safe sedative gave birth to babies with major limb deformities; some babies were born with no arms and with flipperlike hands growing out of their shoulders. However, these serious defects occurred only if the pregnant woman took the drug between the 4th and 6th week after conception, the time when her fetus's limbs were emerging and developing (look again at Figures 2.6 to 2.13). Taking thalidomide either before the arms or legs started to develop or after they were basically formed had no harmful effect.

As you can see in Figure 2.16, the sensitive period for many organ systems—and hence the time when the most significant teratogenic damage can result from something the mother does or experiences—occurs before the woman might realize she is pregnant. Because a substantial proportion of all births are unplanned, sexually active people of childbearing age need to be aware of behaviors that could compromise the health of a child they might conceive.

Another crucial factor influencing the severity of teratogenic effects is the amount and length of exposure. Most teratogens show a **dose–response relation:** the greater the fetus's exposure to a potential teratogen, the more likely it is that fetus will suffer damage and the more severe any damage is likely to be.

Avoiding environmental agents that have teratogenic effects is complicated by the fact that they often cannot be readily identified. One reason is that they frequently occur in combination, making it difficult to separate out their effects. For families living in urban poverty, for example, it is hard to tease apart the effects of poor maternal diet, exposure to airborne pollution, inadequate prenatal care, and psychological stress resulting from unemployment, single parenthood, and living in crime-ridden neighborhoods. Furthermore, the presence of multiple factors can have a *cumulative* impact. A given agent may have little discernible effect by itself but might have an impact in combination with other harmful agents. For example, marginal nutrition during fetal development may have little lasting impact on its own, but it can later lead to obesity and higher risk for diabetes and heart disease if the individual is raised in an environment of nutritional abundance. The later emergence of effects of prenatal experience is referred to as *fetal programming,* because experiences during the prenatal period "program the physiological set points that will govern physiology in adulthood" (Coe & Lubach, 2008).

PAUL FIEVEZ / BIPS / GETTY IMAGES

This young artist was damaged while in the womb—his mother took the drug thalidomide. She must have taken the drug in the second month of her pregnancy, the time when the arm buds develop—an unfortunate example providing clear evidence of the importance of timing in how environmental agents can affect the developing fetus.

The effects of teratogens can also vary according to *individual differences* in genetic susceptibility (probably in both the mother and the fetus). Thus, a substance that is harmless to most people may trigger problems in a minority whose genes predispose them to be affected by it.

Finally, identifying teratogens is further complicated by the existence of *sleeper effects,* in which the impact of a given agent may not be apparent for many years. For example, the hormone DES was commonly given between the 1940s and 1960s to prevent miscarriage, with no apparent ill effects on babies born to women who had taken it. However, in adolescence and adulthood, these offspring turned out to have elevated rates of cervical and testicular cancer.

Having discussed some of the basic factors involved in teratogenic influences, we will now briefly examine a few specific teratogens. An enormous number of potential teratogens have been identified, but we will focus only on some of the most common ones, emphasizing in particular those that are related to the *behavior* of the pregnant woman. Table 2.2 includes the agents discussed in the text as well as several additional ones, but you should be aware that there are numerous other agents known to be, or suspected of being, hazardous to prenatal development.

Legal drugs Although many prescription and over-the-counter drugs are perfectly safe for pregnant women to take, some are not. Pregnant women (and women who have reason to think they might be or might soon become pregnant) should take drugs only under the supervision of a physician. The two legal "drugs" that cause by far the most havoc for fetal development are cigarettes (nicotine) and alcohol.

dose–response relation a relation in which the effect of exposure to an element increases with the extent of exposure (prenatally, the more exposure a fetus has to a potential teratogen, the more severe its effect is likely to be)

TABLE 2.2

Some Environmental Hazards to Fetus or Newborn

Drugs	Maternal Disease
Alcohol	AIDS
Birth control pills (sex hormones)	Chicken pox
Cocaine	Chlamydia
Heroin	Cytomegalovirus
Marijuana	Gonorrhea
Methadone	Herpes simplex (genital herpes)
Tobacco	Influenza
Environmental Pollutants	Mumps
Lead	Rubella (German measles)
Mercury	Syphilis
PCBs	Toxoplasmosis

Note: This list of dangerous elements is not comprehensive; there are many other agents in the environment that can have a negative impact on developing fetuses or on newborns during the birth process.

CIGARETTE SMOKING We all know that smoking is unhealthy for the smoker, and there is an abundance of evidence that it is not good for the smoker's fetus either. When a pregnant woman smokes a cigarette, she gets less oxygen, and so does her fetus. One sign of this is that the fetus makes fewer breathing movements after Mom lights up. In addition, the fetuses of smokers metabolize some of the cancer-causing agents contained in tobacco. And because the mother-to-be inhales cigarette gases when someone else, such as the father, is smoking nearby, passive smoking can also have an indirect effect on fetal oxygen.

The main consequence that maternal smoking has for the fetus is retarded growth and low birth weight, both of which compromise the health of the newborn. In addition, evidence suggests that smoking may be linked to increased risk of SIDS (sudden infant death syndrome, discussed in Box 2.4) and a variety of problems, including lower IQ, hearing deficits, and cancer.

In spite of the well-established negative effects of maternal smoking on fetal development, nearly 13% of women in the United States smoke during their pregnancies (Center for Disease Control and Prevention, 2007). The rate is especially high (over 19%) for pregnant 18- and 19-year-olds. Most of these women also continue to smoke after giving birth; thus, their children are exposed to a known teratogen before birth, as well as to a known health hazard after birth. Given that the negative effects of maternal smoking on fetal development are well publicized, you may not find it surprising that mothers who nevertheless smoke during pregnancy are less sensitive and less warm in interactions with their young infants (Schuetze, Eiden, & Dombkowski, 2006).

PHOTRI / JACK NOVAK / CORBIS STOCK MARKET

This woman is endangering the health of her fetus.

ALCOHOL Alcohol is currently considered "the most common human teratogen" (Ramados et al., 2008). Maternal alcohol use is the most common cause of injury to the fetal brain and is generally considered to be the most common preventable cause of mental retardation and birth defects in the United States. This is partly because approximately 50% of women of childbearing age drink alcohol, and 15% to 20% continue to drink after learning they are pregnant (Sokol, Delaney-Black, & Nordstrom, 2003).

When a pregnant woman drinks, the alcohol in her blood crosses the placenta into both the fetus's bloodstream and the amniotic fluid. Thus, the fetus gets alcohol directly and also by drinking an amniotic-fluid cocktail. Concentrations of alcohol in the blood of mother and fetus quickly become equal, but the fetus has less ability to metabolize and remove alcohol from its blood, so it remains in the fetus's system longer. Immediate behavioral effects on the fetus include altered activity levels and abnormal startle reflexes (Little, Hepper, & Dornan, 2002).

fetal alcohol spectrum disorder (FASD) the harmful effects of maternal alcohol consumption on a developing fetus. Fetal alcohol syndrome (FAS) involves a range of effects, including facial deformities, mental retardation, attention problems, hyperactivity, and other defects. Fetal alcohol effects (FAE) is a term used for individuals who show some, but not all, of the standard effects of FAS.

In the long run, maternal drinking can result in various forms of **fetal alcohol spectrum disorder** (FASD) (Sokol et al., 2003), especially when a fetus is exposed to large amounts of alcohol over a long period of time. Babies born to alcoholic women often exhibit a condition known as *fetal alcohol syndrome* (FAS) (Jacobson &

applications 2.4

Face Up to Wake Up

For parents, nothing is more terrifying to contemplate than the death of their child. New parents are especially frightened by the specter of **SIDS—sudden infant death syndrome.** SIDS refers to the sudden, unexpected, and unexplained death of an infant less than 1 year of age. The most common SIDS scenario is that an apparently healthy baby, usually between 2 and 5 months of age, is put to bed for the night and found dead in the morning. Although SIDS is rare, in developing countries, more children under the age of 1 year die of it than of all other causes combined. In the United States, where the SIDS incidence is 2 to 3 deaths per 1,000 births, victims are more likely to be male, from a low-SES family, and African American or Native American (Task Force on Sleep Position and Sudden Infant Death, 2000).

The causes of SIDS are still not fully understood, but Lewis Lipsitt (2003) has proposed that SIDS may involve an inadequate reflexive response to respiratory occlusion—that is, an inability to remove or move away from something covering the nose and mouth. He believes that infants are particularly vulnerable to SIDS between 2 and 5 months of age because that is when they are making a transition from neonatal reflexes under the control of lower parts of the brain (the brainstem) to deliberate, learned behaviors mediated by higher brain areas (cerebral cortex). A waning and "disorganized" respiratory-occlusion reflex during this transition period may make infants less able to effectively pull their head away from a smothering pillow or to push a blanket away from their face.

In spite of the lack of certainty about the causes of SIDS, researchers have identified several steps that parents can take to decrease the risk to their baby. The most important one is putting infants on their back to sleep, reducing the possibility of anything obstructing their breathing. Research has firmly established that sleeping on the stomach increases the risk of SIDS more than any other single factor (e.g., Willinger, 1995). A campaign encouraging parents to put their infants to sleep on their backs—the "back to sleep movement"—has contributed to a dramatic reduction in the number of SIDS victims.

Second, to lower the risk of SIDS, parents should not smoke. If they do smoke, they should not smoke around the baby. Infants whose mothers smoke during pregnancy and/or after the baby's birth are more than 3½ times more likely to succumb to SIDS than are babies not exposed to smokers in their home (Anderson, Johnson, & Batal, 2005).

Third, babies should sleep on a firm mattress with no pillow. Soft bedding can trap air around the infant's face, causing the baby to breathe in its own carbon dioxide instead of oxygen.

Fourth, infants should not be wrapped in lots of blankets or clothes. Being overly warm is associated with SIDS.

One unanticipated consequence of the "back to sleep" movement has been that infants today start crawling slightly later than those in previous generations, presumably because of reduced opportunity to strengthen their muscles by pushing up off their mattress. Parents are now encouraged to give their babies supervised play time on their tummies to exercise their muscles during the day.

BANANASTOCK / FOTOSEARCH

"Face Up to Wake Up." The parents of this infant are following the good advice of the foundation dedicated to lowering the incidence of SIDS worldwide. Since the inauguration of this campaign, SIDS in the United States has declined to half its previous rate (Task Force on Sleep Position and Sudden Infant Death, 2000).

Jacobson, 2002; Jones & Smith, 1973; Streissguth, 2001; Streissguth, Bookstein, Sampson, & Barr, 1993). The most obvious symptoms of FAS are facial deformities like those shown in Figure 2.17. Other FAS effects can include varying degrees of mental retardation, attention problems, and hyperactivity. Many children who were prenatally exposed to alcohol and show similar but fewer symptoms are diagnosed with *fetal alcohol effects* (FAE) (Mattson, Riley, Delis, & Jones, 1998). Even

SIDS (sudden infant death syndrome) the sudden, unexpected death of an infant less than 1 year of age that has no identifiable cause

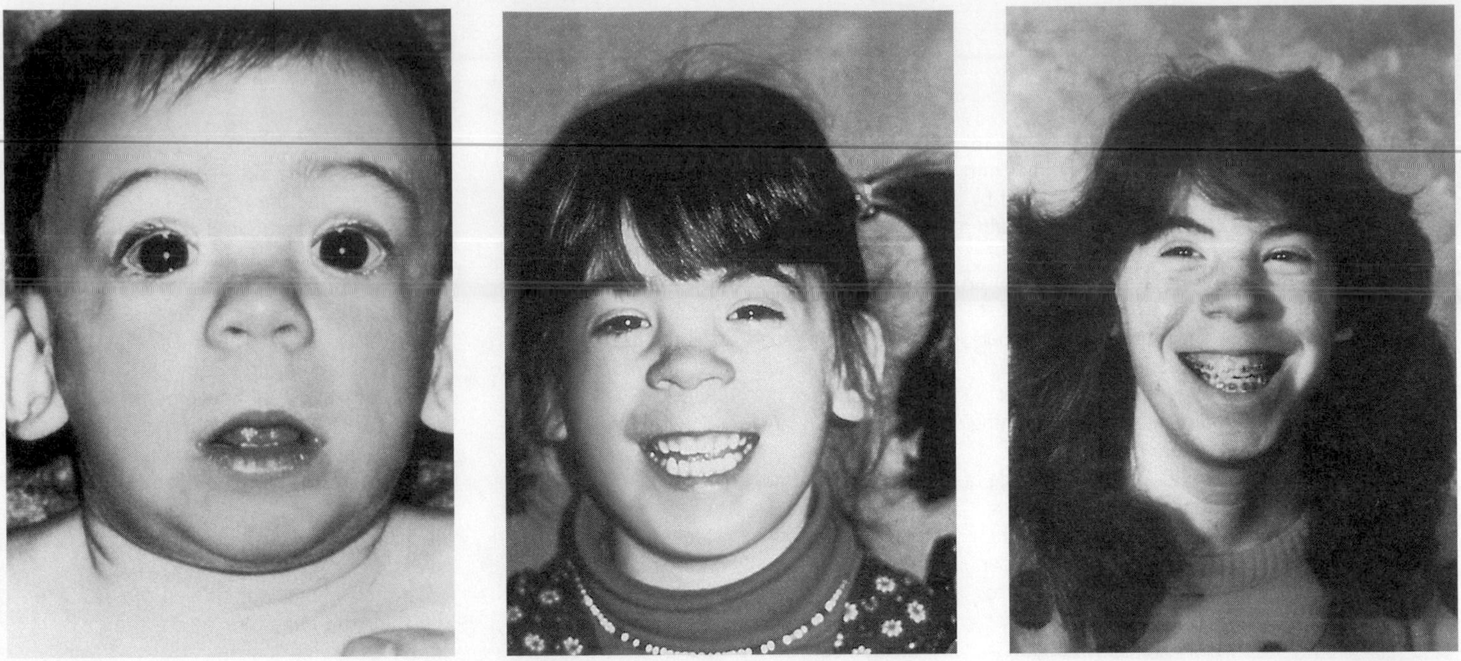

FIGURE 2.17 Effects of FAS This child of an alcoholic mother, shown as an infant, a preschooler, and a school-age child, displays the symptoms of fetal alcohol syndrome (FAS). The characteristic features caused by extensive exposure to alcohol in the womb include facial abnormalities (a smooth upper lip, short nose, and narrow, widely spaced eyes), as well as neuropsychological deficits (including attention, learning, and memory problems). Roughly 1 in every 1000 infants born in the United States has FAS.

moderate drinking during pregnancy (i.e., less than one drink per day) can have both short- and long-term negative effects on development. So can occasional drinking if it involves binge drinking (more than five drinks per episode) (e.g., Hunt, Streissguth, Kerr, & Olson, 1995; Sokol et al., 2003).

Given the potential outcomes and the fact that no one knows if there is a safe level of alcohol consumption for a pregnant woman, the best approach for expectant mothers is to avoid alcohol altogether.

Illegal drugs Approximately 4% of pregnant women in the United States (and worldwide) use common illicit drugs, incuding marijuana, cocaine, ecstasy, and methamphetamine (DHHS, 2006). Almost all commonly abused illegal drugs have been shown to be, or are suspected of being, dangerous for prenatal development. It has proved difficult to pin down exactly how dangerous particular ones are, however, because pregnant women who use one illegal substance often use others and often smoke cigarettes and drink alcohol as well (Frank et al., 2001; Lester, 1998; Smith et al., 2006).

Prenatal exposure to marijuana, the illegal substance most commonly used by women of reproductive age in the United States, is suspected of affecting memory, learning, and visual skills after birth (Fried & Smith, 2001; Mereu et al., 2003). Cocaine in its various forms is the second most common illegal drug abused by young American women (Substance Abuse and Mental Health Services Administration, 2004). Although some early reports of devastating effects from cocaine use during pregnancy turned out to be exaggerated, such use has been associated with fetal growth retardation and premature birth (Hawley & Disney, 1992; Singer et al., 2002). In addition, infants who endured prenatal exposure to cocaine have impaired ability to regulate arousal and attention (e.g., DiPietro, Suess, Wheeler, Smouse, & Newlin, 1995; Lewkowicz, Karmel, & Gardner, 1998). Especially distressing is the case of newborns born to coke-addicted mothers, because they have to go through withdrawal just like a reforming addict (Kuschel, 2007).

Longitudinal studies of the development of cocaine-exposed children have reported persistent, although sometimes subtle, cognitive and social deficits

(Lester, 1998). These deficits can be ameliorated to some degree, as suggested by improved outcomes among affected children who were adopted into supportive middle-class families (Koren et al., 1998).

Environmental pollutants The bodies and bloodstreams of most Americans (including women of childbearing age) contain a noxious mix of toxic metals, synthetic hormones, and various ingredients of plastics, pesticides, and herbicides that can be teratogenic (Moore, 2003). Echoing the story of Minamata disease, evidence has accumulated that mothers whose diet was high in Lake Michigan fish with high levels of PCBs (polychlorinated biphenyls) had newborns with small heads. The children with the highest prenatal exposure to PCBs had slightly lower IQ scores as long as 11 years later (Jacobson & Jacobson, 1996; Jacobson, Jacobson, Padgett, Brumitt, & Billings, 1992).

Occupational hazards Another category of worrisome environmental agents are those in the workplace. Many women have jobs that bring them into contact with a variety of potentially hazardous elements. Tollbooth collectors, for example, are exposed to high levels of automobile exhaust; farmers, to pesticides; and factory workers, to numerous chemicals. As Figure 2.18 shows, even noise pollution can negatively affect fetal development. Employers and employees alike are grappling with how to protect pregnant women from potential teratogens without subjecting them to job discrimination.

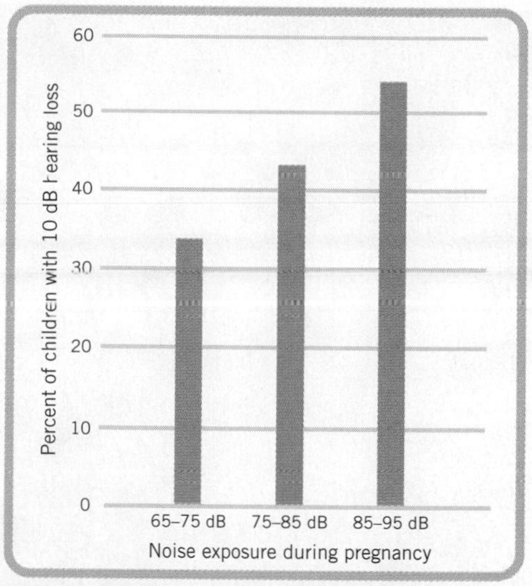

Source: Lalande et al., 1986

FIGURE 2.18 Hearing loss in children whose mothers worked in a noisy factory while pregnant The greater the noise a pregnant woman was exposed to, the greater the hearing impairment of her child.

Maternal Factors

Because the mother-to-be constitutes the most immediate environment for her fetus, certain of her characteristics can affect prenatal development. These characteristics include age, nutritional status, health, and stress level.

Age A pregnant woman's age is related to the outcome of her pregnancy. Infants born to girls 15 years or younger are three to four times more likely to die before their first birthday than are those whose mothers are between 23 and 29 (Phipps, Blume, & DeMonner, 2002). Although the high rate of pregnancies among young teenagers in the United States has declined in recent years, it remains a cause for concern for this and many other reasons. A different cause for concern that has recently arisen has to do with the increasing age of first-time mothers, primarily due to two factors: many women have postponed having children into their 30s or 40s in order to pursue careers, and improved techniques have been developed to help childless couples conceive and bear children. Older mothers are at greater risk for many negative outcomes for themselves and their fetus, including chromosomal abnormalities in the fetus (see Chapter 3) and birth complications.

Nutrition The fetus depends on its mother for all its nutritional requirements. If a pregnant woman has an inadequate diet, her unborn child may also be nutritionally deprived (Pollitt et al., 1996). An inadequate supply of specific nutrients or vitamins can have dramatic consequences. For example, women who get too little folic acid (a form of B vitamin) are at high risk for having an infant with a neural-tube defect such as spina bifida (see Figure 2.5). General malnutrition affects the growth of the fetal brain: newborns who received inadequate nutrients while in the womb tend to have smaller brains containing fewer brain cells than do well-nourished newborns. They also tend to be unresponsive and irritable (Lozoff, 1989).

RICKEY ROGERS / REUTERS / LANDOV

These poor Brazilian parents are worrying about how they are going to feed their children—a situation all too common throughout the world.

Because malnutrition is more common in impoverished families, it often coincides with the host of other risk factors associated with poverty, making it difficult to isolate its effects on prenatal development (Lozoff, 1989; Sigman, 1995). However, one unique study of development in very extreme circumstances made it possible to assess certain effects of malnutrition *independent of socioeconomic status* (Stein et al., 1975). In parts of Holland during World War II, people of all income and education levels suffered severe famine. Later, the health records of those Dutch women who had been pregnant during this time of general malnourishment were examined. Their babies were, on average, underweight at birth, but the severity of effects depended on how early in their pregnancy the women had become malnourished. Those who became malnourished only in the last few months of pregnancy tended to have slightly underweight babies with relatively small heads. However, those whose malnutrition started early in their pregnancy often had very small babies with serious physical defects.

Disease Although most maternal illnesses that occur during a pregnancy have no impact on the fetus, some do. For example, if contracted early in pregnancy, rubella (the three-day measles) can have devastating developmental effects, including major malformations, deafness, blindness, and mental retardation. Any woman of childbearing age who does not have immunities against rubella should be vaccinated before becoming pregnant.

The sexually transmitted diseases (STDs) that have become increasingly common throughout the world are quite hazardous to the fetus. Cytomegalovirus, a type of herpes virus that is present in 50% to 80% of the adult population in the United States, is currently the most common cause of congenital infection. It can damage the fetus's central nervous system and cause a variety of other serious defects. Genital herpes can also be very dangerous: if the infant comes into contact with active lesions in the birth canal, blindness or even death can result. HIV infection is sometimes passed to the fetus in the womb or during birth, but the majority of infants born to women with HIV or AIDS do not have the disease. HIV can also be transmitted through breast milk after birth.

Evidence has been accumulating for effects of maternal illness on the development of *psychopathology* later in life. For example, the incidence of schizophrenia is higher for individuals whose mothers had influenza (flu) during the first trimester of pregnancy (Brown et al., 2004). Maternal flu may interact with genetic or other factors to lead to mental illness.

Maternal emotional state For centuries, people have believed that a woman's emotions can affect her fetus. This view is now supported by research (DiPietro, 2004; Huizink, Mulder, & Buitelaar, 2004). For example, the fetuses of women who reported higher levels of stress during pregnancy were more physically active throughout their gestation than were the fetuses of women who felt less stressed (DiPietro, Hilton, Hawkins, Costigan, & Pressman, 2002). Such effects can continue after birth. In a study that involved more than 7000 pregnant women and their infants, maternal anxiety and depression during pregnancy were assessed. The higher the level of distress the pregnant women reported, the higher the incidence of behavior problems in their children at 4 years of age—including hyperactivity and inattention in boys, conduct problems in girls, and emotional problems in both boys and girls (O'Connor, Heron, Golding, Beveridge, & Glover, 2002). The specific reasons for these relations between maternal anxiety and depression during pregnancy and the outcome for children are not fully clear at this point, but it is a topic of intense interest.

review:

The most rapid period of development starts at conception, with the union of egg and sperm, and continues for roughly 9 months, divided into three developmental periods—germinal, embryonic, and fetal. The processes through which prenatal development occurs include cell division, cell migration, cell differentiation, and cell death. Every major organ system undergoes all or a substantial part of its development between the 3rd and 8th week following conception, making this a sensitive period for potential damage from environmental hazards.

Scientists have recently learned an enormous amount about the behavior and experience of the developing organism, which begins to move at 5 to 6 weeks after conception. Some behaviors of the fetus contribute to its development, including swallowing amniotic fluid and making breathing motions. The fetus has relatively rich sensory experience from stimulation both within and outside the womb, and this experience is the basis for fetal learning. Researchers have recently established some persistent effects of fetal learning after birth.

Many environmental agents can have a negative impact on prenatal development, with cigarette smoking, alcohol consumption, and environmental pollution being the most common problems in the United States. Maternal factors (malnutrition, illness, emotional state, etc.) can also cause problems for the developing fetus and child. Timing is crucial for exposure to many teratogens; the severity of effects is also related to the amount and length of exposure, as well as to the number of different negative factors with which a fetus has to contend.

The Birth Experience

Approximately 38 weeks after conception, contractions of the muscles of the uterus begin, initiating the birth of the baby. Typically, the baby has already contributed to the process by rotating itself into the normal head-down position. In addition, the maturing lungs of the fetus may release a protein that triggers the onset of labor. Uterine contractions, as well as the baby's progress through the birth canal, are painful for the mother, so women in labor are often given pain-relieving drugs. Although these drugs can help the mother get through childbirth more comfortably, they do not help her baby. Many obstetric medications slow labor, and anything that prolongs labor increases the chance of oxygen deprivation, thereby increasing the risk of brain damage. Also, delivery drugs given to the mother can result in a "drugged" baby—a newborn with a decreased supply of oxygen who is less attentive, has poorer muscle tone, exhibits less vigorous reflexes, and so forth (Brackbill, McManus, & Woodward, 1985; Brazelton, Nugent, & Lester, 1987). The extent of these effects depends on which particular drugs are used and how high the dosage is. Fortunately, the effects are generally not long-lasting.

Is birth as painful for the newborn as it is for the mother? Actually, there is good reason to doubt that birth is particularly painful for the baby. Compare how much pain you feel when you pinch and pull on a piece of skin on your forearm versus when you wrap your hand around your forearm and squeeze as tightly as you can. The stretching is painful, but the squeezing is not. The mother's pain comes from her tissues being greatly stretched, but the baby experiences squeezing. Hence, the experiences of the two participants are not really comparable (Maurer & Maurer, 1988). Childbirth programs designed to prevent birth from being painful and traumatic for newborns are probably based on faulty premises.

Further, the squeezing that the fetus experiences during birth serves several important functions. First, it temporarily reduces the overall size of the fetus's disproportionately large head, allowing it to pass safely through the mother's pelvic bones. This is possible because the skull is composed of separate plates that can overlap one another slightly during birth (see Figure 2.19). The squeezing of the fetus's head during birth also serves to stimulate the production of hormones that help the fetus withstand mild oxygen deprivation during birth and to regulate breathing after birth. The squeezing of the fetus's body also forces amniotic fluid out of the lungs, in preparation for the newborn's first, crucial gasp of air (Lagercrantz & Slotkin, 1986; Nathanielsz, 1994). This first breath usually comes by way of the birth cry, which is a very efficient mechanism for jump-starting respiration: a good, lusty cry not only obtains some essential oxygen but also forces open the small air sacs in the lungs, making subsequent breaths easier. An important disadvantage of Caesarean deliveries (in which the fetus is surgically removed from the womb) is the enhanced likelihood of respiratory problems.

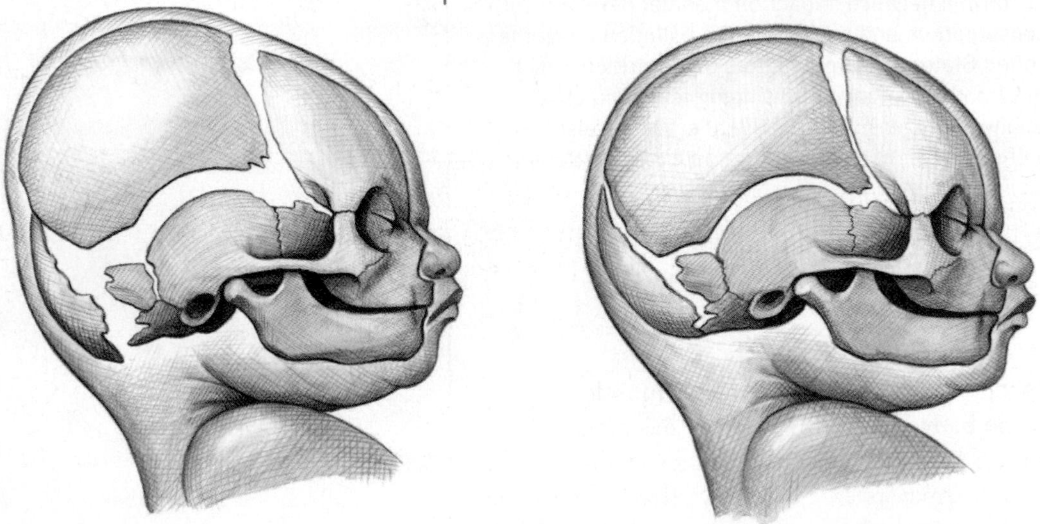

FIGURE 2.19 Head plates Pressure on the head during birth can cause the separate plates of the skull to overlap, resulting in a temporarily misshapen head. Fortunately, the condition rapidly corrects itself after birth. The "soft spot," or fontanel, is simply the temporary space between separate skull plates in the top of the baby's head.

Diversity of Childbirth Practices

Although the biological aspects of birth are pretty much the same everywhere, childbirth practices vary enormously. As with many human behaviors, what is considered a normal and desirable birth custom in one society may seem strange or deviant—or even dangerous—in another.

All cultures pursue the dual goals of safeguarding the *survival and health* of both the mother and the baby and ensuring the *social integration* of the new person. Groups differ, however, regarding the relative importance they give to these goals. An expectant mother on the South Pacific island of Bali assumes that her husband and other kin, along with any children she may already have, will all want to be present at the joyous occasion of the birth of a new child. Her female relatives, as well as a midwife, actively help her throughout the birth, which occurs in her home. Having already been present at many births, the Balinese woman knows what to expect from childbirth, even when it is her first child (Diener, 2000).

A very different scenario has been traditional in the United States, where the woman in labor usually withdraws almost totally from her everyday life. In most cases, she enters a hospital to give birth, typically attended by only one person or the very few people most emotionally close to her. The birth is supervised by a variety of medical personnel, most of whom are strangers. Unlike her Balinese counterpart, the first-time American mother has probably never witnessed a birth, so she may not have very realistic expectations about the birth process. Also, unlike the situation in most other societies, she has a 31% chance of having a cesarean delivery—a rate that has steadily increased in the United States for many years (Hamilton, Martin, & Ventura, 2007).

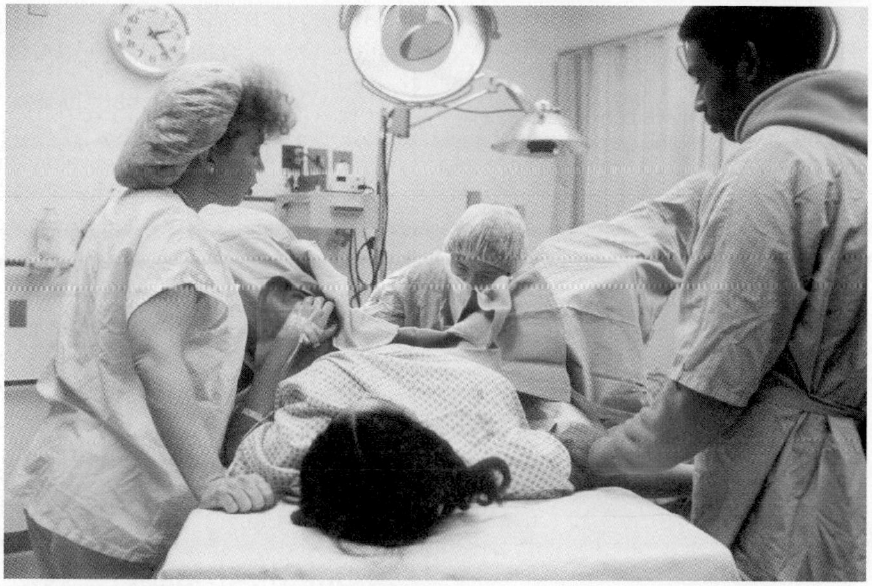

HARRIET GANS/THE IMAGE WORKS

The medical model of childbirth prevails in the United States.

Underlying the Balinese approach to childbirth is great emphasis on the social goal of immediately integrating the newborn into the family and community—hence the presence of many kin and friends to support mother and baby. In contrast, modern Western groups have elevated the physical health of the mother and newborn above all other concerns. The belief that childbirth is safer in a hospital setting outweighs the resulting social isolation of mother and baby.

COURTESY OF ROBBIE DAVIS-FLOYD

This childbirth in Brazil is quite different from the norm in the United States. The baby was born at home, welcomed by his father, older brother, and grandmother. Also present are an obstetrician and midwife who assisted with the birth.

The practices of both societies have changed to some degree. In the United States, the social dimensions of birth are increasingly recognized by doctors and hospitals. As in Bali, various family members—sometimes even including the parents' other children—are encouraged to be present to support the laboring mother and to share a family experience. An increasingly common practice in the United States is the use of *doulas,* individuals trained to assist women in terms of both emotional and physical comfort during labor and delivery. This shift has been accompanied by more moderate use of delivery drugs, thereby enhancing the woman's participation in childbirth and her ability to interact with her newborn. In addition, many expectant parents attend childbirth education classes, where they learn some of what their Balinese counterparts picked up through routine attendance at births. Social support is a key component of these programs; the pregnant woman's husband or some other supportive person is trained to assist her during the birth. Such childbirth programs are generally beneficial (Lindell, 1988), and obstetricians routinely advise expectant couples to enroll in them. At the same time that these changes are occurring in the United

state level of arousal and engagement in the environment, ranging from deep sleep to intense activity

REM (rapid eye movement) sleep an active sleep state characterized by quick, jerky eye movements under closed lids and associated with dreaming in adults

non-REM sleep a quiet or deep sleep state characterized by the absence of motor activity or eye movements and regular, slow brain waves, breathing, and heart rate

autostimulation theory the idea that brain activity during REM sleep in the fetus and newborn facilitates the early development of the visual system

States, in traditional, nonindustrialized societies like Bali, Western medical practices are increasingly adopted in an effort to improve newborn survival rates.

review: Research on the birth process has revealed that many aspects of the experience of being born, including squeezing in the birth canal, have adaptive value and increase the likelihood of survival for the newborn. Great differences exist across cultures in beliefs and practices related to childbirth, with one clear difference having to do with the emphasis on the social aspects of birth.

The Newborn Infant

A healthy newborn is ready and able to continue the developmental saga in a new environment. The baby begins interacting with that environment right away, exploring and learning about both the physical and social entities in it. Newborns' exploration of this uncharted territory is very much influenced by their state of arousal.

State of Arousal

State refers to a continuum of arousal, ranging from deep sleep to intense activity. As you well know, your state dramatically affects your interaction with the environment—with what you notice, do, learn, and think about. It also affects the ability of others to interact with you. State is an even more important mediator of young infants' experience of the world around them.

Figure 2.20 depicts the average amount of time in a 24-hour period that Western newborns typically spend in each of six states, ranging from quiet sleep to crying. Within this general pattern, however, there is a great deal of individual variation. Some infants cry relatively rarely, whereas others cry for hours every day; some babies sleep much more, and others much less, than the 16-hour average shown in the figure. Some infants spend more than the average of 2½ hours in the awake-alert state, in which they are fairly inactive but attentive to the environment. To appreciate how these differences might affect parent–infant interaction, imagine yourself as the parent of a newborn who cries more than the average, sleeps little, and spends less time in the awake-alert state. Now imagine yourself with a baby who cries relatively little, sleeps well, and spends an above-average amount of time quietly attending to you and the rest of his or her environment (see Figure 2.21). Clearly, you would have many more opportunities for pleasurable interactions with the second newborn.

The two newborn states that are of particular concern to parents—sleeping and crying—have both been studied extensively.

FIGURE 2.20 Newborn states This figure shows the average proportion of time, in a 24-hour day, that Western newborns spend in each of six states of arousal. There are substantial individual and cultural differences in how much time babies spend in the different states.

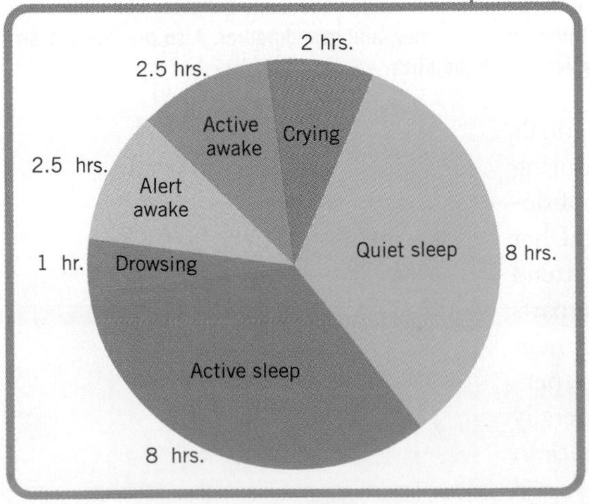

Sleep

Figure 2.22 summarizes several important facts about sleep and its development, two of which are of particular importance. First, "sleeping like a baby" means, in part, sleeping a lot; on average, newborns sleep twice as much as young adults do. Total sleep time declines regularly during childhood and continues to decrease, although more slowly, throughout life.

Second, the pattern of two different sleep states—*REM sleep* and *non-REM sleep*—changes dramatically with age. **REM (rapid eye movement) sleep** is an active sleep state that is associated with dreaming in adults and is characterized by quick, jerky eye movements under closed lids; a distinctive pattern of brain activity; body movements; and irregular heart rate and breathing. **Non-REM sleep,** in contrast, is a quiet or deep sleep state characterized by the absence of motor activity or eye movements and regular, slow brain waves, breathing, and heart rate. As you can see in Figure 2.22, at birth, REM sleep constitutes fully 50% of a newborn's total sleep time. The proportion of REM sleep declines quite rapidly to only 20% by 3 or 4 years of age and remains low for the rest of life.

Why do infants spend so much time in REM sleep? Some researchers believe that it helps develop the infant's visual system. The normal development of the human visual system, including the visual area of the brain, depends on visual stimulation, but relatively little visual stimulation is experienced by either the fetus in the womb or by the newborn in its bed. According to the **autostimulation theory** of REM sleep, the high level of internally generated brain activity that occurs during REM sleep helps to make up for the natural deprivation of visual stimulation and hence facilitates the early development of the visual system in both fetus and newborn (Roffwarg, Muzio, & Dement, 1966). This theory is supported by a study showing that newborns who had been given a high level of extra visual

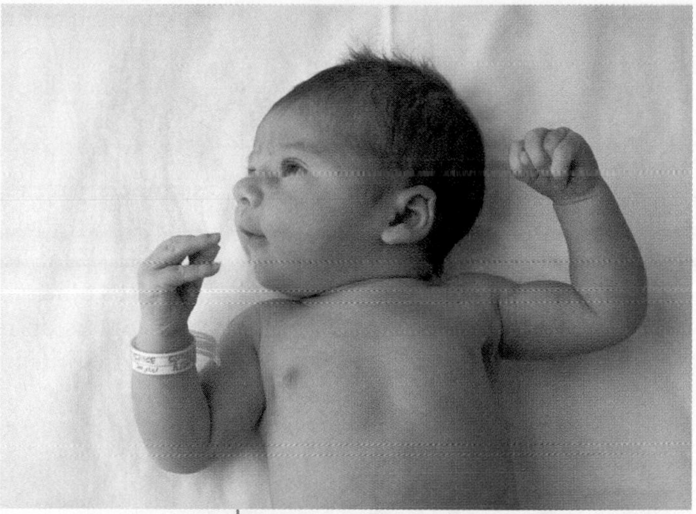

FRANK SITEMAN / STOCK BOSTON / PICTUREQUEST

FIGURE 2.21 Quiet-alert state **The parents of this quiet-alert newborn have a good chance of having a pleasurable interaction with the baby.**

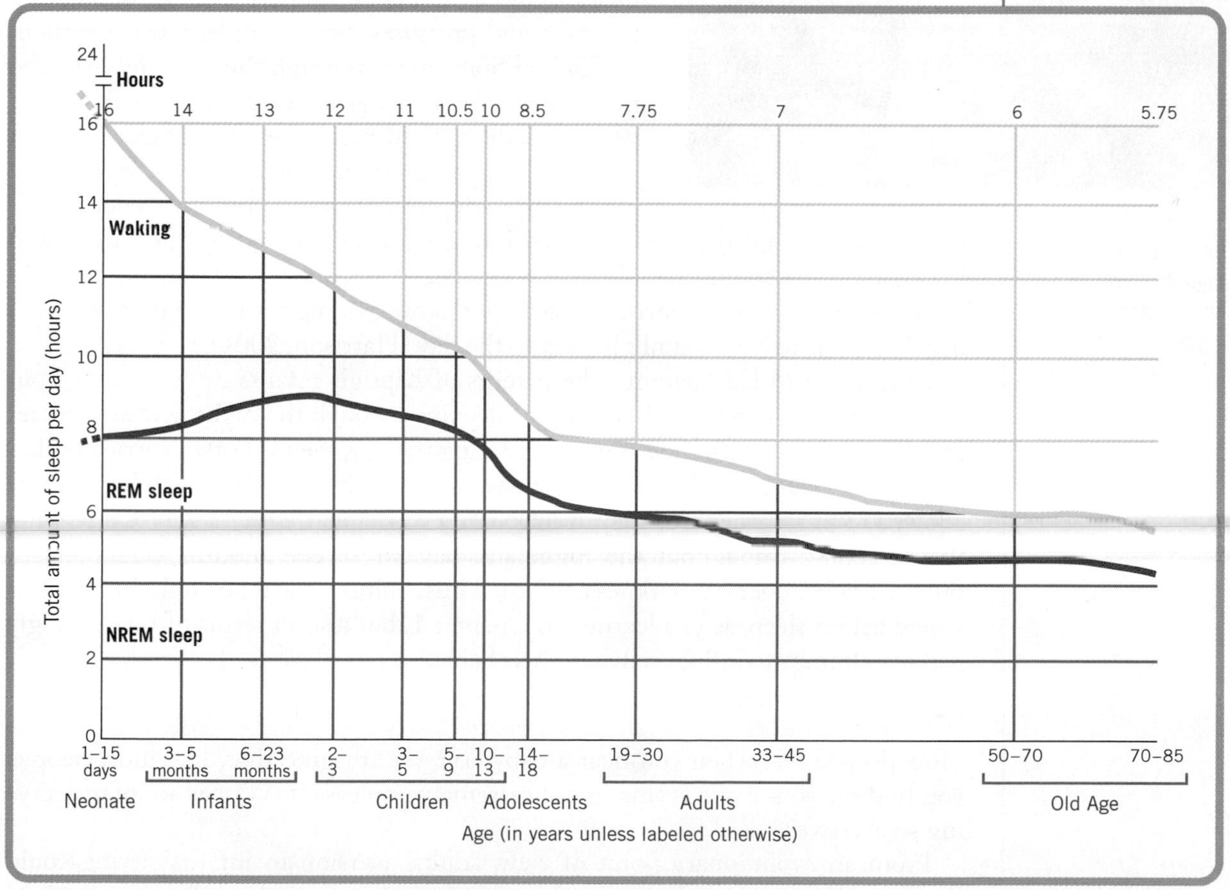

FIGURE 2.22 Total sleep and proportion of REM and non-REM sleep across the life span **Newborns average a total of 16 hours of sleep, roughly half of it in REM sleep. The total amount of sleep declines sharply throughout early childhood and continues to decline much more slowly throughout life. From adolescence on, REM sleep constitutes only about 20% of total sleep time. (Adapted from Roffwarg, Muzio, & Dement, 1966, and from a later revision by these authors)**

stimulation during the day spent less of their subsequent sleep time in REM sleep than did infants exposed to lower levels of visual stimulation (Boismeyer, 1977).

Another distinctive feature of sleep in the newborn period is that napping newborns may actually be learning while asleep. In one study that investigated this possibility, infants were exposed to recordings of Finnish vowel sounds while they slumbered in the newborn nursery. When tested in the morning, their brain activity revealed that they recognized the sounds they had heard while asleep (Cheour et al., 2002). The reason newborns can learn to recognize speech sounds, and presumably other forms of auditory stimulation, in their sleep is that during sleep their brains do not become disconnected from external stimulation to the same extent that the brains of older individuals do.

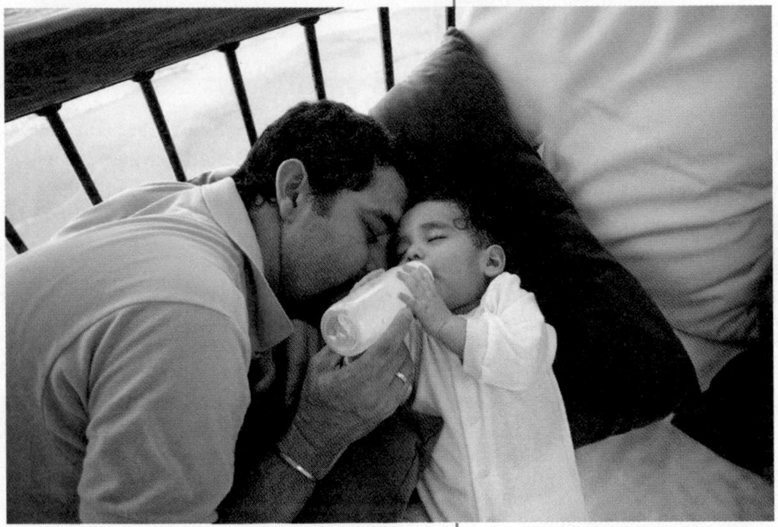

© GETTY IMAGES / PURESTOCK

Most American parents want to avoid the 2 A.M. fate of this young father. They regard their baby's sleeping through the night as a developmental triumph—the sooner, the better.

Another difference between the sleep of young infants and older individuals (not reflected in Figure 2.22) is in sleep–wake cycles. Newborns generally cycle between sleep and waking states several times in a 24-hour period, sleeping slightly more at night than during the day (Whitney & Thoman, 1994). Although newborns are likely to be awake during part of their parents' normal sleep time, they gradually develop the more mature pattern of sleeping through the night.

The age at which infants' sleep patterns come to match those of adults depends very much on cultural practices and pressures. For example, most infants in the United States sleep through the night by around 4 months of age—a change actively encouraged by their parents. Indeed, tired parents employ many different strategies to get their infants to sleep through the night, from adopting elaborate, often extended bedtime rituals intended to lull the baby into dreamland to gritting their teeth and letting the baby cry himself or herself to sleep. (Note: one little-known but particularly useful strategy for encouraging longer periods of nighttime sleeping is exposing the infant to bright sunlight during the day [Harrison, 2004].)

In contrast to U.S. parents, the parents of Kipsigis infants in rural Kenya put little or no importance on their infants' sleeping through the night. Kipsigis babies are almost always with their mothers. During the day, they are often carried on her back as she goes about her daily activities, and at night they sleep with her and are allowed to nurse whenever they awaken. As a consequence, these babies distribute their sleeping throughout the night and day for several months (Harkness & Super, 1995; Super & Harkness, 1986). Thus, cultures vary not only in terms of where babies sleep, as you learned in Chapter 1, but also in terms of how strongly parents attempt to influence when their babies sleep.

Crying

How do you feel when you hear a baby cry? We imagine that, like most people, you find the sound of a crying infant extremely unpleasant. Why is an infant's crying so aversive?

From an evolutionary point of view, adults' aversion to infants' crying could have adaptive value. Infants cry for many reasons—including illness, pain, and hunger—that require the attention of caregivers. Adults' high level of motivation to stop an infant's crying prompts them to take care of the infant's needs and hence promotes the infant's survival. This fact has led some researchers to suggest that in times of hardship, such as famine, cranky babies are more likely to survive than are placid ones, possibly because their distress elicits adult attention and they consequently get more than their share of scarce food resources (DeVries, 1984).

Parents, especially first-timers, are often puzzled and anxious about why their baby is crying. Indeed, one of the most frequent complaints pediatricians hear concerns what parents think is excessive crying (Barr, 1998; Harkness et al., 1996). With experience, parents become better at interpreting their infants' crying, identifying characteristics of the cry itself (a sharp, piercing cry usually signals pain, for example) and considering the context (such as when the infant's last feeding was) (Green, Jones, & Gustafson, 1987).

Crying increases from around 2 weeks of age to a peak at 6 weeks, but then declines to about an hour a day for the rest of the first year (St. James-Roberts & Halil, 1991). On a daily basis, the peak time for crying is late afternoon or evening. The phenomenon of "evening crying," which can be quite disappointing to parents looking forward to interacting with their baby at the end of the workday, may be due to an accumulation of excess stimulation over the course of the day.

The nature of crying and the reasons for it change with development. Early on, crying reflects discomfort from pain, hunger, cold, or overstimulation, although, from the beginning, infants also cry from frustration (Lewis, Alessandri, & Sullivan, 1990; Stenberg, Campos, & Emde, 1983). Crying gradually becomes more of a communicative act; the crying of older babies often seems geared to "tell" caregivers something and to get them to respond (Gustafson & Green, 1988).

Soothing What works best to console a crying baby? Most of the traditional standbys—rocking, singing lullabies, holding the baby up to the shoulder, giving the baby a pacifier—work reasonably well (R. Campos, 1989; Korner & Thoman, 1970). In general, many effective soothing techniques involve moderately intense and continuous or repetitive stimulation. The combination of holding, rocking, and talking or singing relieves an infant's distress better than any one of them alone (Jahromi, Putnam, & Stifter, 2004).

One very common soothing technique is **swaddling,** which involves wrapping a baby tightly in cloths or a blanket, thereby restricting limb movement. The tight wrapping provides a constant high level of tactile stimulation and warmth. This technique is practiced in cultures as diverse and widespread as those of the Navajo and Hopi in the American Southwest (Chisolm, 1963), the Quechua in Peru (Tronick, Thomas, & Daltabuit, 1994), and rural villagers in Turkey (Delaney, 2000). Another traditional approach, distracting an upset infant with interesting objects or events, can also have a soothing effect, but the distress often resumes as soon as the interesting stimulus is removed (Harman, Rothbart, & Posner, 1997).

Touch can also have a soothing effect on infants. In interactions with an adult, infants fuss and cry less, and they smile and vocalize more, if the adult pats, rubs, or strokes them (Field et al., 1996; Peláez-Nogueras, Field, Hossain, & Pickens, 1996; Stack & Arnold, 1998; Stack & Muir, 1992). Carrying young infants, as is routinely done in many societies around the world, reduces the amount of crying that they do (Hunziker & Barr, 1986).

In laboratory studies, placing a small drop of something sweet on a distressed newborn's tongue has been shown to have a dramatic calming effect (Barr et al., 1994; Blass & Camp, 2003; Smith & Blass, 1996). A taste of sucrose has an equally dramatic effect on pain sensitivity; newborn boys who are given a sweetened pacifier to suck during circumcision

swaddling a soothing technique, used in many cultures, that involves wrapping a baby tightly in cloths or a blanket

Carrying infants close to the parent's body results in less crying. Many Western parents are now emulating the traditional carrying methods of other societies around the world.

PHOTODISC

cry much less than babies who do not receive this simple intervention (Blass & Hoffmeyer, 1991).

Response to distress One question that often concerns parents is whether they should respond as quickly and consistently as possible to their infant's signals of distress. Will such a response reward the infant for crying and hence increase how much he or she cries, or will it instill a sense of confidence and actually lead to less fussing and crying? It appears that, as is so often the case, the middle road is probably best. In a longitudinal study, Hubbard and van IJzendoorn (1991) found that infants whose mothers waited for a few minutes before responding to their cries tended to cry less often than did infants whose mothers responded more rapidly. Assessing the severity of the infant's distress before responding may be the key factor. If a parent responds quickly to severe distress but delays responding to minor upset, the infant may learn to cope with less serious problems on his or her own and hence end up crying less overall.

Colic No matter how or how much their parents try to soothe them, some infants are prone to excessive, inconsolable crying for no apparent reason during the first few months of life, a condition referred to as **colic.** Not only do "colicky" babies cry a lot, but they also tend to have high-pitched, particularly unpleasant cries (Stifter, Bono, & Spinrad, 2003). Unfortunately, colic is not a rare condition: more than one in ten young U.S. infants—and their parents—suffer from it. Fortunately, it typically ends by around 3 months of age and leaves no ill effects (Stifter & Braungart, 1992; St. James-Roberts, Conroy, & Wilsher, 1998). One of the best things parents with a colicky infant can do is seek social support, which can provide relief from the stress, frustration, and sense of inadequacy and incompetence they may feel because they are unable to relieve their baby's distress.

Negative Outcomes at Birth

Although most recognized pregnancies in an industrialized society result in the full-term birth of a healthy baby, sometimes the outcome is less positive. The most dire result, obviously, is the death of an infant. A much more common negative outcome is low birth weight, which, if extreme, can have long-term consequences.

Infant Mortality

Infant mortality—death during the first year after birth—has become a relatively rare event in the Western industrialized world, thanks to decades of improvements in public health and general economic levels. In the United States, the 2007 infant mortality rate was 6.3 deaths per 1000 live births, the lowest in American history.

Although the U.S. infant mortality rate is at an all-time low in absolute terms, it is high in comparison with that of other industrialized nations. As Table 2.3 shows, the United Nations estimates that for the period of 2005–2010, the United States will have ranked 20th in the world in terms of the number of infants who fail to survive their first year. The *relative* ranking of the United States has generally gotten worse over the past several decades, because the infant mortality rates in many other countries have had a higher rate of improvement.

The rates of infant mortality are starkly different for subsets of the U.S. population. African-American infants are more than twice as likely to die before their first birthday as Euro-American infants are. Indeed, the infant mortality rate for African Americans is similar to the rates of many underdeveloped countries.

Why do more babies die in the United States—the richest country in the world—than in 19 other countries? Why are African-American infants' chances of survival

colic excessive, inconsolable crying by a young infant for no apparent reason

infant mortality death during the first year after birth so much poorer than those of Euro-American infants? There are many reasons, most having to do with poverty. For example, many low-income mothers-to-be, including a disproportionate number of African Americans, have no health insurance and have limited access to good health and prenatal care (Cohen & Martinez, 2006). In contrast, all the countries that rank above the United States with respect to infant mortality have some form of government-sponsored health care that guarantees pregnant women prenatal care at low or minimal cost.

In less developed countries, especially those suffering from a breakdown in social organization due to war, famine, major epidemics, or persistent extreme poverty, the infant mortality rates can be staggering. A particularly poignant example involved the poorest areas of a small city in northeast Brazil, where extreme poverty, chaotic social services, disrupted families, and an infant mortality rate as high as 90% set up conditions for a vicious cycle (Scheper-Hughes, 1992). Because any baby born in this area had a very high risk of dying and family resources were so slim, mothers looked for some evidence that a new baby "wanted to live" before investing very much in the child, either economically or emotionally. They tended to feed and care for the infant only minimally while engaging in "watchful waiting" for signs of "child sickness" (symptoms of which are the same as those of malnutrition and dehydration). Thus, underfeeding and neglect produced an infant who displayed evidence that he or she had "no knack for life" or "wanted to die," leading to further deprivation and neglect. When the almost inevitable occurred and the baby died, the mother was not supposed to express grief, because a mother's tears would "make the road from heaven to earth slippery," and the baby would "lose his footing and fall."

TABLE 2.3

Infant Mortality Worldwide: Prospects for 2005–2010

Country	Deaths per 1000 births	Country	Deaths per 1000 births
Finland	3.0	Ireland	5.1
Japan	3.0	Luxembourg	5.1
Spain	3.4	Canada	5.2
Norway	3.9	United Kingdom	5.3
Austria	4.1	Greece	5.9
Czech Republic	4.2	New Zealand	6.3
France	4.2	**United States**	**6.8**
Germany	4.3	Hungary	7.2
Denmark	4.4	Poland	7.5
Switzerland	4.5	Slovak Republic	7.6
Italy	4.7	Mexico	20.1
Belgium	4.9	Turkey	38.3
Australia	5.0		

Source: United Nations. (2007). World population prospects: The 2006 revision. New York: United Nations.

Low Birth Weight

The average newborn in the United States weighs 7½ pounds (most are between 5½ and 10 pounds). Infants who weigh less than 5½ pounds (2500 grams) at birth are considered to be of **low birth weight (LBW)**. Some LBW infants are referred to as **premature** or preterm, because they are born at 35 weeks after conception or earlier, instead of the normal term of 38 weeks. Other LBW infants are referred to as **small for gestational age:** they may be either preterm or full-term, but they weigh substantially less than is normal for their gestational age.

Just over 8% of all U.S. newborns are of LBW (National Center for Health Statistics, 2005). The rate for African Americans is nearly twice as high (13.3%) and is strongly associated with poverty. Worldwide, the vast majority (96%) of LBW infants live in developing countries (WHO, 2005). As a group, LBW newborns have a heightened level of medical complications, as well as higher rates of neurosensory deficits, more frequent illness, lower IQ scores, and lower educational achievement. Very LBW babies (those weighing less than 1500 grams, or 3.3 pounds) are particularly vulnerable.

There are numerous causes of LBW and prematurity, including many of the infant-mortality risk factors discussed earlier. Another cause is the increased rate of twin, triplet, and other multiple births that have recently skyrocketed as a result of the development of increasingly successful treatments for infertility. (Box 2.5 discusses some of the challenges faced by parents of LBW infants.)

low birth weight (LBW) a birth weight of less than 5½ pounds (2500 grams)

premature any child born at 35 weeks after conception or earlier (as opposed to the normal term of 38 weeks)

small for gestational age babies that weigh substantially less than is normal for whatever their gestational age

applications 2.5

Parenting a Low-Birth-Weight Baby

Parenthood is challenging under the best of circumstances, but it is especially so for the parents of a preterm or LBW baby. First, they have to accept their disappointment over the fact that they do not have the perfect baby they imagined, and they may also have to cope with feelings of guilt ("What did I do wrong?"), inadequacy ("How can I take care of such a tiny, fragile baby?"), and fear ("Will my baby survive?"). Caring for a healthy baby takes a great deal of time, but caring for an LBW baby can be especially time-consuming and stressful and, if the infant requires extended intensive care treatment, very expensive.

Parents of an LBW baby have a great deal to learn. In the hospital, they need to learn how to interact successfully with a fragile baby confined to an isolette, with its tiny body hooked up to life-support equipment. When their infant comes home, the parents have to cope with a baby that is relatively passive and unresponsive and at the same time be careful not to overstimulate the infant in an effort to get some response (Brazelton et al., 1987; Patteson & Barnard, 1990). LBW infants also tend to be more fussy than the average baby and more difficult to soothe when they become upset (Greene, Fox, & Lewis, 1983). To compound matters, they often have a high-pitched cry that is particularly unpleasant (Lester et al., 1989).

Another problem for parents is the fact that LBW infants have more trouble falling asleep, waking up, and staying alert than do infants of normal birth weight, and their feeding schedules are less regular (DiVitto & Goldberg, 1979; Meisels & Plunkett, 1988). Thus, it takes longer for the baby to get on a predictable schedule, making the parents' life more hectic.

Parents need to understand that their preterm baby's early development will not follow the same timetable as a full-term infant's: developmental milestones will be delayed. For example, their infant will not begin to smile at them at around 6 weeks; instead, they may have to wait several more weeks for their baby to look them in the eye and break into a heart-melting smile. Thus, preterm infants are not only more challenging to care for but in many ways they are also less rewarding to interact with. One consequence is that children who were born preterm are more often victims of parental child abuse (Bugental, 2003; Frodi & Lamb, 1980; Parke & Collmer, 1975).

One step that can be helpful to parents of an LBW or preterm infant is learning more about infant development. An intervention program that trained mothers how to interpret their preterm babies' signals resulted in gains in the children's mental-test performance (Achenbach, Phares, Howell, Rauh, & Nurcombe, 1990). More general knowledge about infants can also be helpful. Preterm infants whose mothers had a relatively high level of knowledge about infancy performed better on a developmental test than did a group of preterm infants whose mothers were less knowledgeable about babies (but were otherwise comparable) (Dichtelmiller, Meisels, Plunkett, Bozynski, & Mangelsdorf, 1992).

In addition, any parent who is trying to deal with an LBW baby or an infant with other problems would do well to seek social support—from a spouse or partner, other family members, friends, or a formal support group. One of the best-documented phenomena in psychology is that we all cope better with virtually any life problem when we have support from other people.

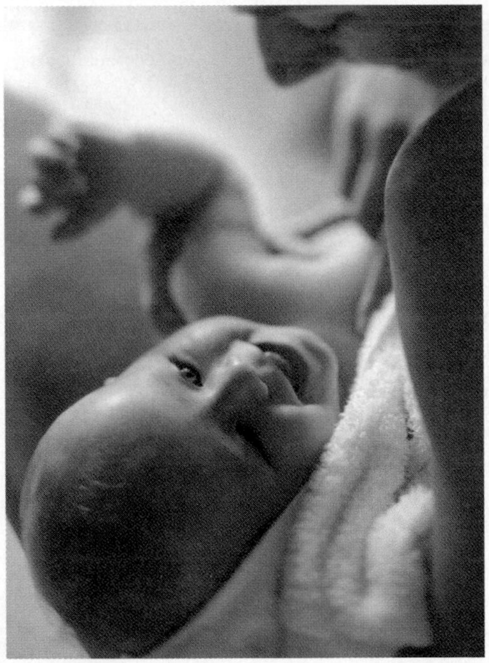

JAING JIN / SUPERSTOCK

Parents of an LBW baby usually have to wait longer to experience the joy of their child's first social smile.

Long-term outcomes What outcome can be expected for LBW newborns who survive? This question becomes increasingly important as newborns of ever lower birth weights—some as low as 800 grams (about 1.76 pounds)—are kept alive by modern medical technology. The answer includes both bad news and good news.

The bad news is that, as a group, children who were LBW infants have a higher incidence of developmental problems; the lower their birth weight, the more likely they are to have persistent difficulties (e.g., Muraskas, Hasson, & Besinger, 2004). They suffer from somewhat higher levels of hearing, language, and cognitive impairments. In preschool and elementary school, they are more likely to be distractible and hyperactive and to have learning disabilities. This group is also more likely to experience a variety of social problems, including poor peer and parent–child relations

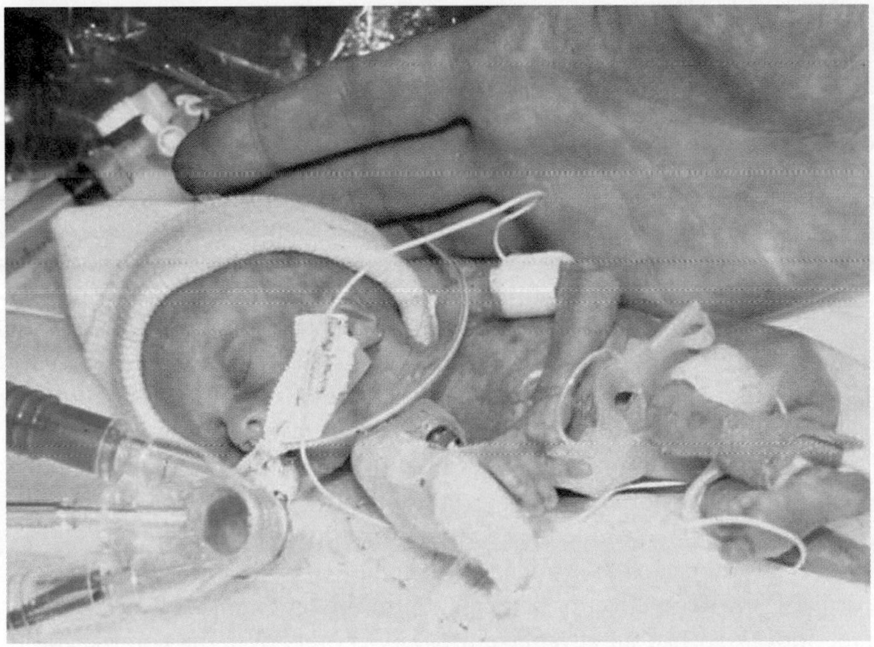

(a)

FIGURE 2.23 Small miracles Shown here is (a) one of the smallest newborns ever to survive and (b) the same child at 14 years of age. Born in 1989 after just 27 weeks of gestation, Madeline weighed a mere 9.9 ounces—approximately the equivalent of three bars of soap. Extremely low-birth-weight infants tend to suffer serious disabilities, but Madeline is remarkably healthy, other than being a bit small for her age and having asthma. She entered high school as an honor student and enjoys playing her violin and rollerblading. (b)

(Landry et al., 1990). Finally, adolescents who were LBW babies are less likely to complete high school than their siblings (Conley & Bennett, 2002).

The good news is that the *majority* of LBW children turn out quite well. The negative effects of their birth status gradually diminish, with children who were slightly to moderately underweight as newborns generally ending up within the normal range on most developmental measures (Kopp & Kaler, 1989; Liaw & Brooks-Gunn, 1993; Meisels & Plunkett, 1988; Vohr & Garcia-Coll, 1988). Figure 2.23 depicts a particularly striking example of this fact (Muraskas et al., 2004).

Intervention programs What can be done to improve the chances that a given LBW infant will overcome his or her poor start in life? A variety of intervention programs for LBW newborns offer a prime example of our theme about the role of research in improving the welfare of children. In many of them, parents are active participants, a marked change from past practice. Hospitals formerly did not allow parents to have any contact with their LBW infants, mainly because of fear of infection. Parents are now encouraged to have as much physical contact and social interaction with their hospitalized infant as the baby's physical condition allows.

One widely implemented intervention for hospitalized newborns is based on the idea that the touching newborns normally experience as they are picked up, cuddled, caressed, and carried around is a vital part of their life. Many LBW infants experience little stimulation of this kind because of the precautions that must be taken with them, including keeping them in special isolettes, hooked up to various life-support machines. To compensate, Tiffany Field and her colleagues (Field, 2001; Field, Hernandez-Reif, & Freedman, 2004) developed a special therapy that involves massaging LBW babies and flexing their arms and legs (Figure 2.24). LBW babies who receive this therapy are more active and alert and gain weight

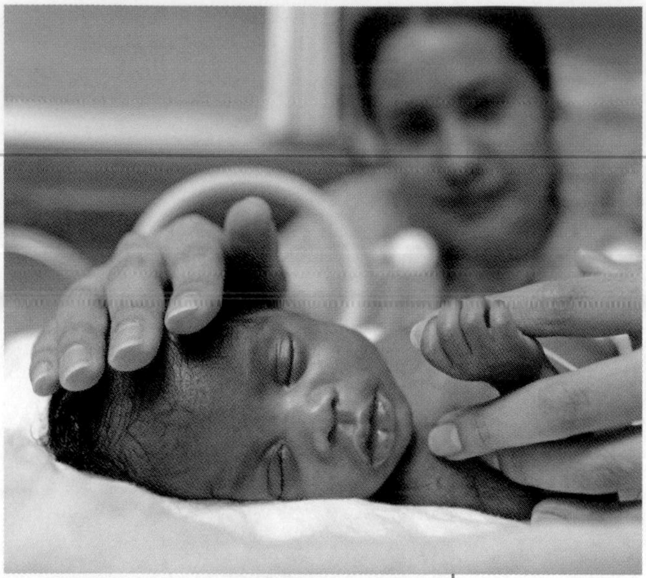

© LOUIE PSIHOYOS / SCIENCE FACTION / CORBIS

FIGURE 2.24 Infant massage Everybody enjoys a good massage, but hospitalized newborns particularly benefit from extra touching.

faster than those who are not massaged. As a consequence, they get to go home earlier.

A large number of intervention programs for LBW newborns extend beyond their hospital stay, some for several years (e.g., Ramey & Campbell, 1992). The most extensive, both in terms of number of children involved (985) and the length and extent of the intervention and follow-up, is the Infant Health and Development Project (IHDP). This program was especially well designed. For one thing, the infants were randomly assigned to either the intervention group or the control group. For another, all the children were provided good health care, which ensured that this crucial factor could not affect the outcome of the research. In addition, the intervention lasted for three years and included an intensive early-childhood education program, as well as home visits that, among other things, encouraged the parents' continued participation in the program.

Repeated assessments of the children have consistently revealed a positive effect of participation in the program. At 3 years of age, the intervention group had an advantage of 14 IQ points over the control group, although the difference was larger for the LBW children who had been relatively heavier at birth—2000 to 2500 grams versus less than 2000 grams. The story was similar at 5 and 8 years of age, although the difference between the intervention and control groups had become smaller. In the most recent follow-up assessment of the participants, at age 18 (McCormick et al., 2006), differences favoring the intervention group were still observed, although only for those teenagers who had been the heavier LBW newborns. The researchers concluded that their results provide support for preschool-based early intervention to promote the development of severely at-risk infants, but they also noted that such interventions are less likely to be successful with children who were extremely small newborns.

The IHDP story illustrates three important general points relevant to intervention efforts designed for high-risk infants. First, many intervention programs produce gains, but often they are relatively modest and diminish over time. Second, the success of any intervention depends on the initial health status of the infant. Like IHDP, many programs for LBW babies have been of more benefit to those infants who are less tiny to begin with. This fact is cause for concern, as modern medical technology makes it possible to save the lives of ever-smaller infants who have a high risk of permanent, serious impairment. The third point is the importance of cumulative risk: the more risks the infant endures, the lower the chances of a good outcome. Because this principle is so important for all aspects of development, we will examine it in greater detail in the following section.

Multiple-Risk Model

Risk factors tend to occur together. For example, a woman who is so addicted to alcohol, cocaine, or heroin that she continues to abuse the substance even though she is pregnant is likely to be under a great deal of stress and unlikely to eat well, take vitamins, earn a good income, seek prenatal care, or take good care of herself in other ways. Further, whatever the cumulative effects of these prenatal risk factors, they will likely be compounded by the mother's continuation of her unhealthy lifestyle and by her resulting inability to provide good care for her child (e.g., Weston, Ivins, Zuckerman, Jones, & Lopez, 1989).

As you will see repeatedly throughout this book, a negative developmental outcome—whether in terms of prenatal or later development—is more likely when there are multiple risk factors. In a classic demonstration of this fact, Michael Rutter (1979) reported a heightened incidence of psychiatric problems among English children growing up in families with four or more risk factors (including marital distress, low SES, paternal criminality, and maternal psychiatric disorder) (Figure 2.25). Thus, the likelihood of developing a disorder is slightly elevated for the child of parents who fight a lot; but if the child's family is also poor, the father engages in criminal behavior, and the mother suffers from emotional problems, the child's risk is multiplied nearly tenfold. Similar risk patterns have been reported for IQ (Sameroff, Seifer, Baldwin, & Baldwin, 1993) and social-emotional competence (Sameroff, Seifer, Zax, & Barocas, 1987).

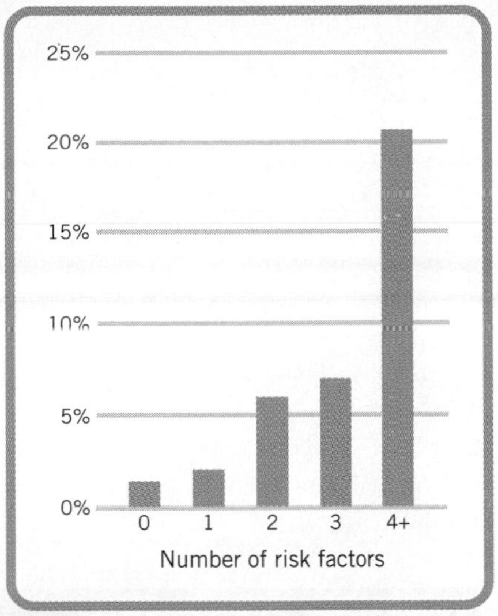

FIGURE 2.25 Multiple risk factors Children who grow up in families with multiple risk factors are more likely to develop psychiatric disorders than are children from families with only one or two problematic characteristics (Rutter, 1979).

Poverty as a Developmental Hazard

Because it is such an important point, we cannot emphasize enough that the existence of multiple risks is strongly related to socioeconomic status. Consider some of the factors we have discussed that are known to be dangerous for fetal development: inadequate prenatal care, poor nutrition, illness, emotional stress, cigarette smoking, drug abuse, and exposure to environmental and occupational hazards. All these factors are more likely to be experienced by a woman living below the poverty line than by a middle-class woman. It is no wonder, then, that, on the whole, the outcome of pregnancy is less positive for infants of lower-SES parents than for babies born to middle-class parents (Kopp, 1990; Minde, 1993; Sameroff, 1986). Nor should it be surprising that among LBW infants, the eventual developmental outcome is poorer for those in lower-SES families (Drillien, 1964; Gross et al., 1997; Kalmar, 1996; Largo et al., 1989; Lee & Barratt, 1993; McCarton et al., 1997; Meisels & Plunkett, 1988).

An equally sad fact is that in many countries, minority families are overrepresented in the lowest SES levels. Although 17% of all children in the United States live in families whose income places them below the poverty line, 33% of African-American and 27% of Latino children live in poverty (Fass & Cauthen, National Center for Children in Poverty, 2007). Thus, their socioeconomic status places many minority fetuses, newborns, and children at increased risk for developmental difficulties.

Risk and Resilience

There are, of course, individuals who, faced with multiple and seemingly overwhelming developmental hazards, nevertheless do well. In studying such children, researchers employ the concept of **developmental resilience** (Garmezy, 1983; Masten, Best, & Garmezy, 1990; Sameroff, 1998). Resilient children—like those in the Kauai study discussed in Chapter 1—often have two factors in their favor: (1) certain personal characteristics, especially intelligence, responsiveness to others, and a sense of being capable of achieving their goals, and (2) responsive care from someone. Recall that in the Kauai study, a crucial factor in the outcome of children who had a problematic start in life was whether some person took an active interest in their welfare.

In summary, development is highly complex, from the moment of conception to the moment of birth. As you will see throughout this book, that complexity continues. Although early events and experiences can profoundly affect later development, developmental outcomes are never a foregone conclusion.

review: The experience of newborn infants is mediated by internal states of arousal, ranging from deep sleep to intense crying, with large individual differences in the amount of time spent in the different states. Newborns spend roughly half their time asleep, but after early infancy, the amount of sleep declines steadily for many years. Researchers believe that the large proportion of sleep time that newborns spend in REM sleep is important for the development of the visual system and brain. Infants' crying is a particularly salient form of behavior for parents, and it generally elicits attention and

developmental resilience successful development in spite of multiple and seemingly overwhelming developmental hazards caretaking. Effective soothing techniques provide moderately intense, continuous, or repetitive stimulation. How parents respond to their young infant's distress is related to later crying.

Negative outcomes of pregnancy are higher for minorities and for families living in poverty. The United States ranks 20th in the world in terms of infant mortality. Just over 8% of all infants born in the United States are of low birth weight. Although most will suffer few lasting effects, the long-term outcome of severely LBW babies is often problematic. Several large-scale intervention programs have successfully improved the outcome of LBW infants.

According to the multiple-risk model, the more risks that a fetus or child faces, the more likely the child is to suffer from a variety of developmental problems. Low SES is associated with many developmental hazards. Despite facing multiple risks, many children nevertheless show remarkable resiliency and thrive.

Chapter Summary

Prenatal Development

- Nature and nurture combine forces in prenatal development. Much of this development is generated by the fetus itself, making the fetus an active player in its own progress. Substantial continuity exists between what goes on before and after birth in that infants demonstrate the effects of what has happened to them in the womb.
- Prenatal development begins at the cellular level with conception, the union of an egg from the mother and a sperm from the father to form a single-celled zygote. The zygote multiplies and divides on its way through a fallopian tube.
- The zygote undergoes the processes of cell division, cell migration, cell differentiation, and cell death. These processes continue throughout prenatal development.
- When the zygote becomes implanted on the uterine wall, it becomes an embryo. From that point, it is dependent on the mother to obtain nourishment and oxygen and to get rid of waste products through the placenta.
- Fetal behavior begins 5 or 6 weeks after conception with simple movements, undetected by the mother, that become increasingly complex and organized into patterns. Later, the fetus practices behaviors vital to independent living, including swallowing and a form of intrauterine "breathing."
- The fetus experiences a wealth of stimulation both from within the womb and from the external environment. The fetus learns from this experience, as demonstrated by studies showing that both fetuses and newborns can discriminate between familiar and novel sounds, especially in language, and exhibit persistent taste preferences developed in the womb.
- There are many hazards to prenatal development. The most common fate of a fertilized egg is spontaneous abortion (miscarriage). A wide range of environmental factors can be hazardous to prenatal development. These include teratogens from the external world and certain maternal characteristics, such as age, nutritional status, physical health, behavior (especially the use of legal or illegal drugs), and emotional state.

The Birth Experience

- Approximately 38 weeks after conception, the baby is ready to be born. Usually, the behavior of the fetus helps to initiate the birth process.
- Being squeezed through the birth canal has several beneficial effects on the newborn, including preparing the infant to take his or her first breath.
- How the process of childbirth is managed varies greatly from one society to another and is in part related to which goals and values are emphasized by the culture.

The Newborn Infant

- Newborns' state of arousal ranges from deep sleep to active crying.
- The amount of time infants spend in the different arousal states varies greatly, both across individuals and across cultures.
- REM sleep seems to compensate for the lack of visual stimulation that results from the newborn's sleeping many hours a day.
- The sound of a baby crying is a very aversive stimulus for others, and adults employ many strategies to soothe distressed infants.
- The infant mortality rate in the United States is higher than that of 19 other nations. It is much higher for babies born to low-SES parents.
- Infants born weighing less than 5½ pounds (2500 grams) are referred to as being of low birth weight. LBW infants are at risk for a variety of developmental problems, and the lower the birth weight, the greater the risk of enduring difficulties.
- A variety of intervention programs have been designed to improve the course of development of LBW babies, but the success of such programs depends very much on the number of risk factors that threaten the baby.

- The multiple-risk model refers to the fact that infants with a number of risk factors have a heightened likelihood of continued developmental problems. Poverty is a particularly insidious risk to development, in part because it is inextricably linked with numerous negative factors.
- Some children display resilience even in the face of substantial risk factors. Resilience seems to result from certain personal characteristics and from attention and emotional support from other people.

Critical Thinking Questions

1. A recent cartoon showed a pregnant woman walking down a street carrying a tape player with a set of very large headphones clamped around her protruding abdomen. What point was it making? What research might provide the basis for her behavior, and what assumptions is she making about what the result might be? If you or your partner were pregnant, do you think you would do something like this?
2. We hear a great deal about the terrible and tragic effects that illegal drugs like cocaine and diseases like AIDS can have on fetal development. But what two maternal behaviors associated with prenatal harm are actually the *most common* in the United States today, and what are some of the effects they can have?
3. Suppose you were in charge of a public health campaign to improve prenatal development in the United States and you could focus on only one factor. What would you target and why?
4. Describe some of the cultural differences that exist in beliefs and practices with respect to conception, pregnancy, and childbirth. Is there any practice of another culture that appeals to you more than practices with which you are familiar?
5. Are you more encouraged or more discouraged by the results of intervention programs such as the IHDP? What would it take to make their gains larger and longer lasting?
6. Speculate on why the infant mortality rate in the United States has steadily gotten worse compared with that of other countries.
7. Explain the basic idea of the multiple-risk model and how it relates to poverty in terms of prenatal development and birth outcomes.

Key Terms

epigenesis, p. 44
gametes (germ cells), p. 44
conception, p. 44
zygote, p. 46
embryo, p. 47
fetus, p. 47
stem cells, p. 47
phylogenetic continuity, p. 48
apoptosis, p. 48
identical twins, p. 49
fraternal twins, p. 49
neural tube, p. 49
amniotic sac, p. 49
placenta, p. 50
umbilical cord, p. 50
cephalocaudal development, p. 50
habituation, p. 56
teratogen, p. 59
sensitive period, p. 59
dose–response relation, p. 61
fetal alcohol spectrum disorder (FASD), p. 62
SIDS (sudden infant death syndrome), p. 63
state, p. 70
REM (rapid eye movement) sleep, p. 70
non-REM sleep, p. 71
autostimulation theory, p. 71
swaddling, p. 73
colic, p. 74
infant mortality, p. 74
low birth weight (LBW), p. 75
premature, p. 75
small for gestational age, p. 75
developmental resilience, p. 79

PABLO PICASSO, *Woman Drawing Surrounded by Her Children*, 1950

3

Biology and Behavior

THEMES

Nature and Nurture

The Active Child

Continuity/Discontinuity

Mechanisms of Change

Individual Differences

Research and Children's Welfare

Several years ago, one of your authors received a call from the police. A city detective wanted to come by for a chat about some street and traffic signs that had been stolen—and also about the fact that one of the culprits was the author's 17-year-old son. In an evening of hilarious fun and poor judgment, the son, along with two friends, had stolen more than a dozen city signs and then concealed them in the family attic. His upset parents wondered how their sweet, sensitive, kind, soon-to-be Eagle Scout son (who can be seen in his innocent days on pages 136 and 584) could have failed to foresee the consequences of his actions.

Many parents have similarly wondered how their once-model children could have morphed into thoughtless, irresponsible, self-absorbed, impolite, bad-tempered individuals simply by virtue of entering adolescence. Parents are not the only ones surprised by the change in the behavior of their offspring: teenagers themselves are often taken aback and mystified as to what has come over them. One 14-year-old girl lamented: "Sometimes, I just get overwhelmed now. . . . There's all this friend stuff and school and how I look and my parents. I just go in my room and shut the door. . . . I don't mean to be mean, but sometimes I just have to go away and calm down by myself." And a 15-year-old boy expressed similar concerns: "I get in trouble a lot more now, but it's for stuff I really didn't mean. . . . I forget to call home. I don't know why. I just hang out with friends, and I get involved with that and I forget. Then my parents get really mad, and then I get really mad, and it's a big mess" (Strauch, 2003).

New insights into these often abrupt developmental changes have come through research into the biological underpinnings of behavioral development. Researchers now suspect that many of the behavioral changes that are distressing both to adolescents and their parents may be related to dramatic changes in brain structure and functioning that occur during adolescence. Evidence is also accumulating for the role of genetic predispositions in these and other changes.

Understanding the biological underpinnings of behavioral development is, of course, essential to understanding development at any point in the life span. The focus of this chapter is on the key biological factors that are in play from the moment of conception through adolescence, including the inheritance and influence of genes, the development and early functioning of the brain, and important aspects of physical development and maturation. Every cell in our bodies carries the genetic material that we inherited at our conception and that continues to influence our behavior throughout life. Every behavior we engage in is directed by our brain. Everything we do at every age is mediated by a constantly changing physical body—one that changes very rapidly and dramatically in the first few years of life and in adolescence, but more slowly and subtly at other times.

Several of the themes that were set out in Chapter 1 figure prominently in this chapter. Issues of *nature and nurture*, as well as *individual differences* among children, are central throughout this whole chapter and especially the first section, which focuses on the interaction of genetic and environmental factors in development. In our extensive discussions of the role of genetic factors in development and of the processes involved in the development of the brain and its relation to behavior, *mechanisms of change* are prominent. *Continuity* in development is also highlighted throughout the chapter. We again emphasize the activity-dependent nature of developmental processes and the role of the *active child* in charting the course of his or her own development.

Nature and Nurture

Everything about you—from your physical structure, intellectual capacity, and personality characteristics to your preferences in hobbies and food—is a joint consequence of the interaction between the genetic material you inherited from your parents and the environments you have experienced from conception to the present moment. These two factors—heredity and environment—work in concert to influence both the ways in which you are like other people and the ways in which you are unique.

The phenomenal athletic ability of tennis greats Venus and Serena Williams is almost certainly due to the *combination* of nature—the genes they inherited from their parents—and nurture—the extensive coaching they received from their father and the tireless emotional support their mother provided.

Long before there was any understanding of the principles of heredity, people were aware that some traits and characteristics "run in families" and that this tendency was somehow related to procreation. For as long as there have been domesticated animals, for example, farmers have practiced selective breeding to improve certain characteristics of their livestock—the size of their horses; the milk yield of their goats, cows, or yaks. People have also long been aware that the environment plays a role in development—that a nutritious diet, for example, is necessary for livestock to produce a good milk supply or fine-quality wool. When scientists first began to investigate the contributions of heredity and environment to development, they generally emphasized one factor or the other as the prime influence—heredity *or* environment, nature *or* nurture. In nineteenth-century England, for example, Francis Galton (1869), a cousin of Charles Darwin, identified men who had achieved "eminence" in a variety of fields and concluded that talent runs in families, because very close relatives of an eminent man (his father, brother, son) were more likely to be high achievers themselves than were less close relatives.

Among Galton's cases of closely related eminent men were John Stuart Mill and his father, both respected English philosophers. However, Mill himself pointed out that most of Galton's eminent men were members of well-to-do families. In his view, the relation between the achievement of these eminent men and their kinship had less to do with biological ties than with the fact that they were similar in economic well-being, social status, education, and other advantages and opportunities. In short, according to Mill, Galton's subjects rose to eminence more because of environmental factors than hereditary ones.

genome the complete set of genes of any organism

Our modern understanding of how characteristics are transmitted from parent to offspring originated with insights achieved by Gregor Mendel, a nineteenth-century Austrian monk who observed patterns of inheritance in the pea plants in his monastery garden. Some aspects of these inheritance patterns were later discovered to occur in all living things. A much deeper understanding of how genetic influences operate came with James Watson and Francis Crick's 1953 identification of the structure of DNA, the basic component of hereditary transmission.

"We think it has something to do with your genome."

Since that landmark discovery, enormous progress has been made in deciphering the genetic code. Researchers have mapped the entire **genome**—the complete set of genes—of several species of plants and animals, including chickens, mice, chimpanzees, and humans. The expectation is that examining the genomes of such a diverse set of species will provide knowledge not only about those species but also about human evolution and the way genes function. Comparisons of the genomes of various species have already revealed much about our human genetic endowment, and they have provided numerous surprises.

One surprise was the number of genes that humans have: the current estimate of around 26,000 genes is far fewer than had been expected (Pennisi, 2003). Another major surprise was that most of those genes are also possessed by all living things. We humans share a large proportion of our genes with bears, barnacles, beans, and bacteria. Most of our genes are devoted, in decreasing order, to making us animals, vertebrates, mammals, primates, and—finally—humans. As a consequence of the small total number of genes we possess and the fact that so few of them are uniquely human, another surprise is that the basis of individual differences among people is quite slim: we differ from one another by only about 1 to 1.5% of our genes.

As researchers have achieved better understanding of the role of hereditary factors in development, they have also come to appreciate the limits of what these factors can account for on their own. Similarly, as knowledge has grown concerning the influence of experience on development, it has become clear that experience alone rarely provides a satisfactory account. Development results from the close and continual interplay of nature *and* nurture—of genes *and* experience—and this interplay is the focus of the following section.

Genetic and Environmental Forces

The interplay of genes and experience is exceedingly complex. To simplify our discussion of interactions among genetic and environmental factors, we will organize it around the model of hereditary and environmental influences shown in Figure 3.1. Three key elements of the model are the **genotype**—the genetic material an individual inherits; the **phenotype**—the observable expression of the genotype, including both body characteristics and behavior; and the **environment**—every aspect of the individual and his or her surroundings other than the genes themselves.

These three elements are involved in four relations that are fundamental in the development of every child: (1) the parents' genetic contribution to the child's genotype; (2) the contribution of the child's genotype to his or her own phenotype; (3) the contribution of the child's environment to his or her phenotype; and

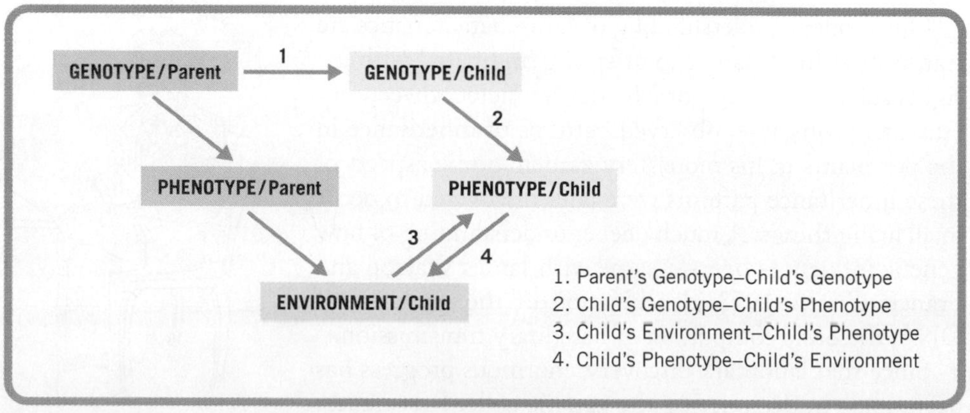

FIGURE 3.1 Development Development is a joint function of genetic and environmental factors. The four numbered relations are discussed in detail in the text.

genotype the genetic material an individual inherits

phenotype the observable expression of the genotype, including both body characteristics and behavior

environment every aspect of an individual and his or her surroundings other than genes

(4) the influence of the child's phenotype on his or her environment. We will now consider each of these four relations.

1. Parent's Genotype–Child's Genotype

Relation 1 involves the transmission of genetic material—chromosomes and genes—from parent to offspring. The nucleus of every cell in the body contains **chromosomes**, long threadlike molecules made up of two twisted strands of **DNA (deoxyribonucleic acid)**. DNA carries all the biochemical instructions involved in the formation and functioning of an organism. These instructions are "packaged" in **genes**, the basic unit of heredity in all living things. Genes are sections of chromosomes. More specifically, each gene is a segment of DNA that is the code for the production of particular *proteins*. Some proteins are the building blocks of the body's cells; others regulate the cells' functioning. Genes affect development and behavior only through the manufacture of proteins—"DNA's information translated into flesh and blood" (Levine & Suzuki, 1993, p. 19).

Human heredity Humans normally have a total of 46 chromosomes in the nucleus of every cell, except egg and sperm cells. (Recall from Chapter 2 that, as a result of the type of cell division that produces germ cells, eggs and sperm each contain only 23 chromosomes.) These 46 chromosomes are actually 23 pairs (Figure 3.2). With one exception—the sex chromosomes—the two members of each chromosome pair are of the same general size and shape (roughly the shape of the letter X). Further, each chromosome pair carries, usually at corresponding locations, genes of the same type—that is, sequences of DNA that are relevant to the same traits. One member of each chromosome pair was inherited from each parent. Thus, every individual has two copies of each gene, one on the chromosome inherited from the father and one on the chromosome from the mother. Your children will each receive half of your genes, and your grandchildren will have one-quarter (just as you have half your genes in common with each of your parents and one-fourth with each grandparent).

Sex determination As noted, the **sex chromosomes**, which determine an individual's sex, are an exception to the general pattern of chromosome pairs being the same size and shape and carrying corresponding genes. Females have two identical, largish sex chromosomes, called X chromosomes, but males have one X chromosome and one much smaller Y chromosome (so called because it has the shape of the letter Y). Because a female has only X chromosomes, the division of her germ cells results in all her eggs having an X. However, because a male is XY, half his sperm contain an X chromosome and half contain a Y. For this reason, it is *always* the father who determines the sex of offspring: if an X-bearing sperm fertilizes an egg, a female (XX) zygote results; if the egg is fertilized by a Y-bearing sperm, the zygote is male (XY). It is the *presence* of a Y chromosome—not the fact of having only one X chromosome—that makes an individual male. A gene on the Y chromosome encodes the protein that triggers the prenatal formation of testes by activating genes on other

chromosomes molecules of DNA that transmit genetic information; chromosomes are made up of DNA

DNA (deoxyribonucleic acid) molecules that carry all the biochemical instructions involved in the formation and functioning of an organism

genes sections of chromosomes that are the basic unit of heredity in all living things

sex chromosomes the chromosomes (X and Y) that determine an individual's gender

FIGURE 3.2 Karyotype This photograph, called a karyotype, shows the 23 pairs of chromosomes in a male human. The pairs of chromosomes have been arranged together in the photo, numbered according to size. The two members of the 23rd pair—the sex chromosomes—differ markedly in size; the Y chromosome that determines maleness is much smaller than the X chromosome. A woman's karyotype would contain two X chromosomes.

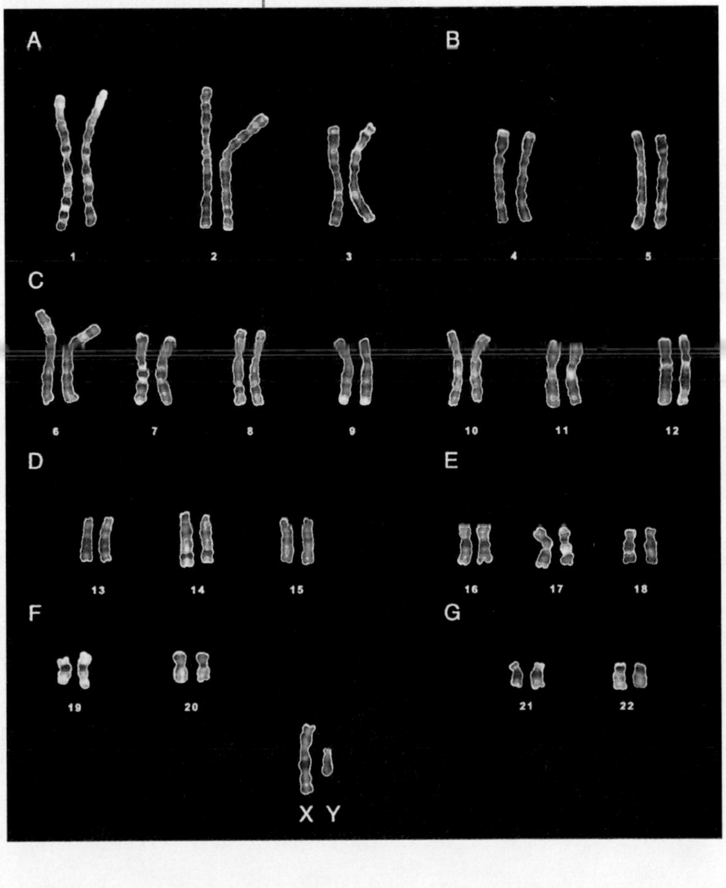

LEONARD LESSIN / PHOTO RESEARCHERS, INC.

R. ELLIS / CORBIS SYGMA

These Elvis impersonators look like Elvis, sneer like Elvis, and even sing like Elvis (sort of). But they are not the King. The probability that any two humans have the same genotype is essentially zero.

chromosomes. Subsequently, the testes produce the hormone testosterone, which takes over the molding of maleness (Jegalian & Lahn, 2001).

Diversity and individuality As we have seen, genes guarantee that we will be similar in certain ways to other people both at the species level (we are all bipedal and have opposable thumbs, for example) and at the individual level (i.e., family resemblances). Genes also guarantee differences at both levels. Several mechanisms contribute to genetic diversity among people.

One such mechanism is **mutation**, a change in a section of DNA. Some mutations are random, spontaneous errors, while others are caused by environmental factors. Most are harmful. Those that occur in germ cells can be passed on to offspring; many inherited diseases and disorders originate from a mutated gene. (Box 3.1, pages 92–93, discusses the genetic transmission of diseases and disorders.)

Occasionally, however, a mutation that occurs in a germ cell or early in prenatal development makes individuals more viable, that is, more likely to survive, perhaps by increasing their resistance to some disease or by increasing their ability to adapt to some crucial aspect of their environment. Such mutations provide the basis for evolution. This is because a person with the favorable mutated gene is more likely to survive long enough to produce offspring, who, in turn, are likely to possess the mutated gene, thus heightening their own chance of surviving and reproducing. Across generations, these favorable genes proliferate in the gene pool of the species.

A second mechanism that promotes variability among individuals is the *random assortment* of chromosomes in the formation of egg and sperm. During germ-cell division, the 23 pairs of chromosomes are shuffled randomly, with chance determining which member of each pair goes into each new egg or sperm. This means that, for each germ cell, there are 2^{23}, or 8.4 million, possible combinations of chromosomes. Thus, when a sperm and an egg unite, the odds are essentially zero that any two individuals—even members of the same family—would have the same genotype (except, of course, identical twins). Further variation is introduced by the fact that when germ cells divide, the two members of a pair of chromosomes sometimes swap sections of DNA. As a result of this process, referred to as **crossing over**, some of the chromosomes that parents pass on to their offspring are constituted differently from their own.

2. Child's Genotype–Child's Phenotype

We now turn to Relation 2 in Figure 3.1, the relation between one's genotype and one's phenotype. Our examination of the genetic contribution to the phenotype begins with a key fact: although every cell in your body contains copies of all the genes you received from your parents, only some of those genes are expressed. At any given time in any cell in the body, some genes are active (turned on), while others are not. Some genes that are hard at work in neurons, for example, are totally at rest in toenail cells. There are several reasons for this.

Gene expression: Developmental changes How is it that people get to be so different from one another when they share the vast majority of their genes in common? An important part of the answer has to do with which particular genes are active at any given point in development.

A given gene influences development and behavior only when it is turned on, and human development proceeds normally, from conception to death, only if genes get switched on and off in the right place, at the right time, and for the right

mutation a change in a section of DNA

crossing over the process by which sections of DNA switch from one chromosome to the other; crossing over promotes variability among individuals length of time. Some genes are turned on in only a few cells and for only a few hours and then are switched off permanently. This pattern is typical during embryological development when, for example, the genes that are turned on in certain cells lead them to specialize for arm, hand, and fingerprint formation. Other genes are involved in the basic functioning of almost all cells almost all the time.

The switching on and off of genes is controlled primarily by **regulator genes.** The activation or inactivation of one gene is always part of a chain of genetic events. When one gene is switched on, it causes another gene to turn on or off, which has an impact on the status of yet other genes. Thus, genes never function in isolation. Instead, they belong to extensive networks in which the expression of one gene is a precondition for the expression of another, and so on. The continuous switching on and off of genes underlies development throughout life, from the initial prenatal differentiation of cells to the gene-induced events of puberty to many of the changes related to aging.

External factors can affect the switching on and off of genes. A dramatic example is the effect of thalidomide on limb development, described in Chapter 2. This sedative interfered with the normal activation pattern of genes in the prenatal process of limb formation. Another example comes from the fact that visual experience is necessary for the normal development of the visual system, because it causes certain genes to switch on, and they in turn switch on others.

The fact that regulator genes can repeatedly switch other genes on and off in different patterns means that a given gene can function multiple times in multiple places during development. All that is required is that the gene's expression be controlled by different regulator genes at different times. This on-again, off-again functioning of individual genes results in enormous diversity in genetic expression. By analogy, consider the fact that this book is written with only 26 letters and probably only a few thousand different words made up of combinations of those letters. The meaning comes from the order in which the letters occur, the order in which they have been "switched on and off" by the authors.

Gene expression: Dominance patterns Many of an individual's genes are never expressed, and many others are only partially expressed. One reason for this is the fact that about a third of human genes have two or more different forms, known as **alleles.** The alleles of a given gene influence the same trait or characteristic (e.g., eye color), but they contribute to different developmental outcomes (e.g., brown, blue, hazel, gray eyes).

Let's consider the simplest pattern of gene expression—the one discovered by Mendel and referred to as the *dominant-recessive pattern.* Some genes have only two alleles, one of which is **dominant** and the other **recessive.** In this pattern, a person can inherit either two of the same allele—two dominant or two recessive—and thus be **homozygous** for the trait in question; or the person can inherit two different alleles—one dominant and the other recessive—and thus be **heterozygous** for the trait. When an individual is homozygous, with either two dominant or two recessive alleles, the corresponding trait will be expressed. When an individual is heterozygous for a trait, the instructions of the dominant allele will be expressed (see Figure 3.3).

regulator genes genes that control the activity of other genes

alleles two or more different forms of a gene

dominant allele the allele that, if present, gets expressed

recessive allele the allele that is not expressed if a dominant allele is present

homozygous having two of the same allele for a trait

heterozygous having two different alleles for a trait

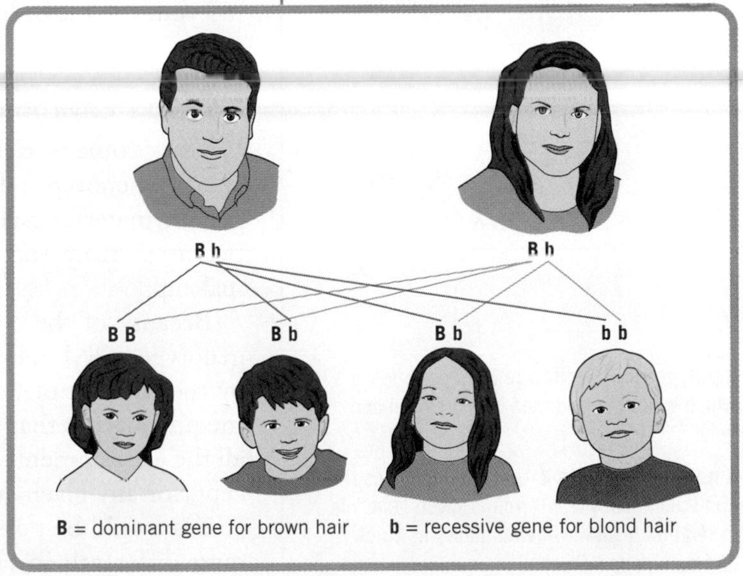

FIGURE 3.3 Mendelian inheritance patterns Pictured here are the Mendelian inheritance patterns for the offspring of two brown-haired parents who are both heterozygous for hair color. The allele for brown hair (B) is dominant, and that for blond hair (b) is recessive. Note that these parents have three chances out of four of producing children with brown hair. They have two chances in four of producing brown-haired children who carry the gene for blond hair.

To illustrate, let us consider two traits of no importance to human survival: the ability to roll one's tongue lengthwise and curliness of hair. If you can roll your tongue lengthwise into the shape of a tube, then at least one, but not necessarily both, of your parents must also possess this remarkable but useless talent. From this statement (and Figure 3.3), you should be able to figure out that tongue rolling is governed by a dominant allele. In contrast, if you have straight hair, then both of your parents must carry an allele for this trait, although it is possible that neither of them actually has straight hair. This is because straight hair is governed by a recessive gene, and curly hair is governed by a dominant gene. Thus, Moe and Larry, with their radically different hairdos shown on page 12, could have had the same parents, both with hair like Larry's. They could not, however, have had parents who had hair like Moe's.

The sex chromosomes present an interesting wrinkle in the story of dominance patterns. The Y chromosome, being smaller than the X chromosome, has only about a third as many genes on it. Suppose, then, that a woman inherits a recessive allele on the X chromosome from her mother. Chances are, she will have a dominant allele on the chromosome from her father to suppress it. Now suppose that a man inherits the same recessive allele on the X chromosome from his mother. Chances are, because of the much smaller size of the Y chromosome he inherits from his father, he will not have a dominant allele to override it, so he will develop the trait. This difference in sex-linked inheritance is one reason for the greater vulnerability of males described in Chapter 2 (Box 2.2, page 46): they are more likely to suffer a variety of inherited disorders caused by recessive alleles on their X chromosome (see Box 3.1, pages 92–93).

Only a few human traits follow the simple Mendelian pattern, in which there are two alleles, one dominant and one recessive, affecting one particular trait. Instead, a single gene can affect multiple traits; both alleles can be fully expressed or blended in heterozygous individuals; and some genes are expressed differently depending on whether they are inherited from the mother or from the father.

Inheritance patterns are even more complicated for most of the traits and behaviors that are of primary interest to behavioral scientists. These traits, such as shyness, aggression, thrill-seeking, and empathy, involve **polygenic inheritance**, in which several different genes contribute to any given phenotypic outcome. There is great variability among people on such characteristics as being able or unable to roll your tongue or having curly or straight hair.

3. Child's Environment–Child's Phenotype

We now come to Relation 3 in our model—the impact of the environment on the child's phenotype. (Remember, the environment includes everything not in the genetic material itself.) As the model indicates, the child's observable characteristics result from the interaction of environmental factors and the child's genetic makeup.

Because of the continuous interaction of genotype and environment, a given genotype will develop differently in different environments. This idea is expressed by the concept of the **norm of reaction** (Dobzhansky, 1955), which refers to all the phenotypes that could theoretically result from a given genotype in relation to all the environments in which it could survive and develop. According to this concept, for any given genotype developing in varying environments, a range of outcomes would be possible. A child with a given genotype would probably develop quite differently in a loving, supportive family than he or she would in an alienated,

polygenic inheritance inheritance in which traits are governed by more than one gene

norm of reaction all the phenotypes that can theoretically result from a given genotype in relation to all the environments in which it can survive and develop

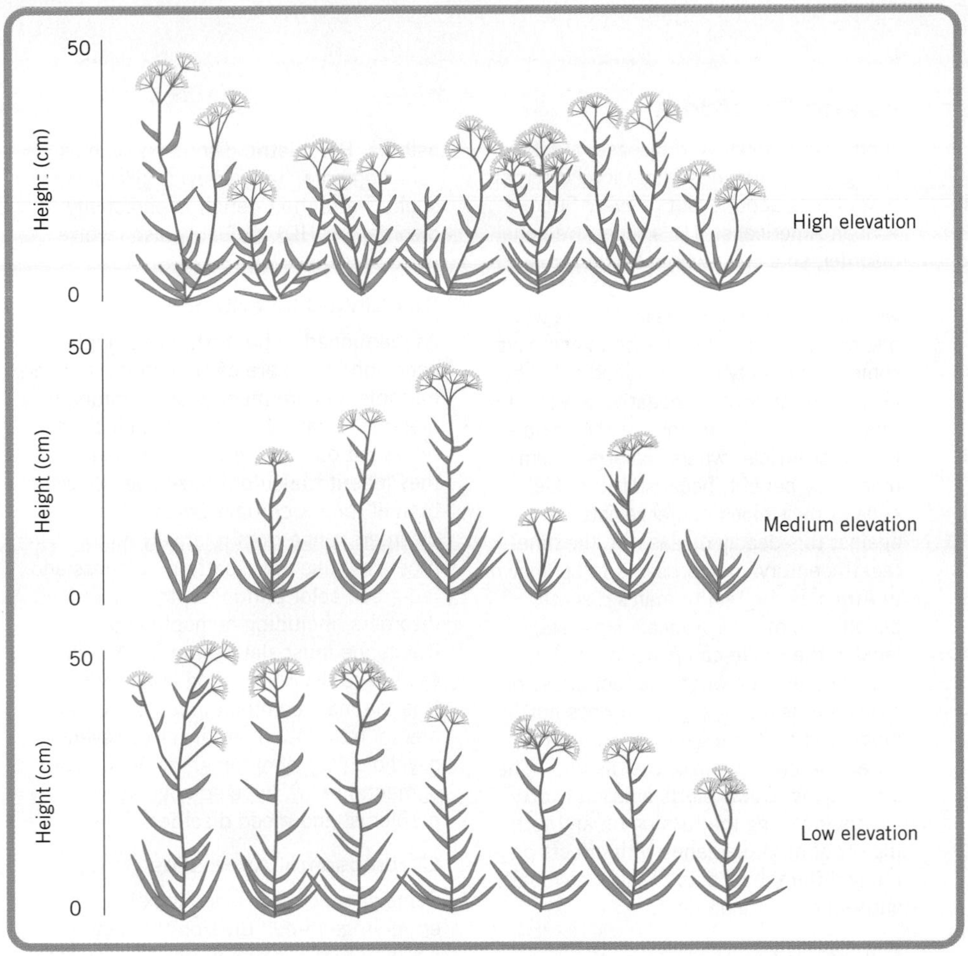

FIGURE 3.4 The norm of reaction concept This classic figure illustrates how a given genotype can develop differently in different environments. Three cuttings were made from each of seven individual plants; thus, the cuttings in each set of three had identical genes. The three cuttings from each plant were then planted at three different elevations, ranging from sea level to high mountains. The question of interest was whether the orderly differences in height that were observed at the low elevation would persist at the two higher elevations. As you can see, the order of the heights of the plants is neither orderly nor consistent across the different environments. For example, the first plant on the left that is the tallest one at sea level and at high elevation is one of the shortest at medium elevation. The fourth plant is tallest at the medium elevation and shortest at the highest. Notice that not a single plant is always either the tallest or the shortest across the three elevations. "The phenotype is the unique consequence of a particular genotype developing in a particular environment" (Lewontin, 1982, pp. 22–23).

abusive family. Figure 3.4 offers a classic illustration of the norm of reaction in a genotype–environment interaction.

Examples of genotype–environment interaction Genotype–environment interactions can be studied directly through research in which scientists randomly assign animals with known genotypes to be raised in a wide variety of environmental conditions. If genetically identical animals develop differently in different environments, researchers can infer that environmental factors must be responsible. Scientists cannot, of course, randomly assign humans to different rearing conditions, but we still have powerful examples of genotype–environment interactions for humans.

One such example is **phenylketonuria (PKU)**, a disorder related to a defective recessive gene on chromosome 12. Individuals who inherit this gene from both parents cannot metabolize phenylalanine, an amino acid present in many foods and in artificial sweeteners. If they eat a normal diet, phenylalanine accumulates in the bloodstream, causing impaired brain development that results in severe mental retardation. However, if infants with the PKU gene are identified shortly after birth and placed on a stringent diet free of phenylalanine, retardation can be avoided. Thus, a given genotype results in quite different phenotypes—severe retardation or relatively normal intelligence—depending on environmental circumstances.

phenylketonuria (PKU) a disorder related to a defective recessive gene on chromosome 12 that prevents metabolism of phenylalanine

applications

Genetic Transmission of Diseases and Disorders

More than 5000 human diseases and disorders—many of them extremely rare—are presently known to have genetic origins. In our discussion of some of these genetically transmitted disorders, we focus on behaviors and psychological symptoms associated with them. However, most of these disorders also involve a variety of physical effects as well, often including unusual physical appearance (e.g., distorted facial features), organ defects (e.g., heart problems), and atypical brain development. These and other genetically based conditions can be inherited in several different ways.

Dominant–Recessive Patterns

Many conditions show straightforward Mendelian (dominant–recessive) patterns of inheritance, occurring only when an individual has two recessive alleles for the condition. Recessive-gene diseases include PKU (discussed on page 91) and sickle-cell anemia (discussed in the next column), as well as Tay-Sachs disease, cystic fibrosis, and many others. Disorders that are caused by a dominant gene include Huntington disease and neurofibromatosis. Severe speech and language difficulties that are common in a particular family in England have been traced to a mutation of a single gene (referred to as FOXP2) that acts in a dominant fashion (see Marcus & Fisher, 2003).

In some cases, a single gene can have both harmful and beneficial effects. One such case is sickle-cell disease, a debilitating and sometimes fatal blood disorder that affects about 1 out of every 500 African Americans. It is a recessive-gene disorder, so a child who inherits two sickle-cell genes (one from both parents) will suffer from the disease. People with one normal and one sickle-cell gene have some abnormality in their blood cells, but usually experience no negative effects. In fact, if they live in regions of the world—like West Africa—where malaria is common, they benefit, because the sickle cells in their blood confer resistance against this deadly disease. In the nineteenth century, malaria came to be known in Africa as the "white man's disease" because so many European explorers, lacking the sickle-cell gene, died of it.

Note that even when the root cause of a disorder is a single gene, it does not mean that that one gene is responsible for all manifestations of the disorder. The single gene simply starts a cascade of events involving the turning on and turning off of multiple genes with effects on many different aspects of the individual's subsequent development.

Polygenic Inheritance

Many common human diseases and disorders are believed to result from multiple inherited genes, often in conjunction with environmental factors. Among the many diseases in this category are some forms of cancer and heart disease, as well as asthma. Psychiatric disorders, such as schizophrenia, and behavior disorders, such as attention-deficit hyperactivity disorder (ADHD), probably also involve multiple genes.

Sex-Linked Inheritance

As mentioned in the text, some single-gene conditions are carried on the X chromosome and are much more common in males. (Females can inherit such conditions, but only in the very rare event that they inherit the culprit recessive alleles on both of their X chromosomes.) Sex-linked disorders range from relatively minor problems, like male-pattern baldness and red-green color blindness, to very serious disorders, including hemophilia and Duchenne muscular dystrophy. Another sex-linked disorder is fragile-X syndrome. It is the most common inherited form of mental retardation and involves several psychological symptoms, including developmental delay, hyperactivity, attention problems, and mood disorders.

Chromosomal Anomalies

Some genetic disorders originate with errors in germ-cell division that result in a zygote that has either more or less than the normal complement of chromosomes. Most such zygotes cannot survive, but some do. Down syndrome most commonly originates when the mother's egg cells do not divide properly, and an egg that is fertilized contains an extra copy of chromosome 21. The probability of such errors in cell division increases with age, with the incidence of giving birth to a child with Down syndrome being markedly higher for women over 35. The child pictured at left shows some of the facial features common to individuals with Down syndrome, which is also marked by mental retardation (ranging from mild to

RICHARD HUTCHINGS / SCIENCE SOURCE / PHOTO RESEARCHERS, INC.

One of the most common identifiable causes of mental retardation is Down syndrome, which occurs in about 1 of every 1000 births in the United States. The risk increases dramatically with the age of the parents, especially the mother; by the age of 45, a woman has 1 chance in 32 of having a baby with Down syndrome. The degree of retardation varies greatly and depends in part on the kind of care and encouragement children receive.

severe), a number of physical problems, and a sweet temperament.

Other genetic disorders arise from extra or missing *sex* chromosomes. For example, males with Kleinfelter syndrome have an extra X chromosome (XXY). Females with Turner syndrome, which affects 1 in 2500 females, have only one X (XO). Turner syndrome is characterized by short stature and stunted sexual development at puberty. The particular type of problems that girls with Turner syndrome experience depends on whether their solitary X came from their mother or their father. Those whose X came from their mother have more social and academic difficulties than do those who inherited their sole X chromosome from their father. This is an example of a gene that functions differently depending on the parent from whom it was inherited.

Gene Anomalies

Just as genetic disorders can originate from extra or missing chromosomes, so too can they result from extra, missing, or abnormal genes. For example, scientists have identified a genetic disorder that seems to be linked to some cases of sudden infant death syndrome (see page 63). Some SIDS victims have two abnormal copies of a gene located on chromosome 6 (Puffenberger et al., 2004). Williams syndrome is a rare disorder involving a variety of impairments, most noticeably in spatial and visual skills, but relatively less impairment in language ability (which has made it of great interest to language researchers) (Bellugi et al, 1999; Mervis et al., 2000). This condition has been traced to the deletion of a small section of approximately 20 genes on chromosome 7.

LEVINE & SUZUKI, 1993

Several cases of XY females have been detected through testing done to prevent males competing as females in the Olympics. Spanish athlete Maria Jose Martinez Patino (an XY female) was barred from Olympic competition for many years after her condition was discovered through genetic testing. She eventually won the right to compete in the 1992 Barcelona games.

Regulator Gene Defects

Many disorders are thought to originate from defects in regulator genes, which, as discussed on page 89, control the expression of other genes. For example, a defect in the regulator gene that initiates the development of a male can interrupt the normal chain of events, occasionally resulting in a newborn that has female genitalia but is genetically male. Such cases often come to light when a young woman fails to begin menstruating or when a fertility clinic discovers that the reason a couple has failed to conceive is that the person trying to get pregnant is genetically male.

Unidentified Genetic Basis

In addition to the known gene-disorder links, there are many syndromes whose genetic origins are clear from their inheritance patterns but whose specific genetic cause has yet to be identified. For example, dyslexia is a highly heritable reading disability that probably stems from a variety of gene-based conditions. Another example is Tourette syndrome. Individuals with this disorder generally display a variety of tics, ranging from involuntary twitching and jerking to a compulsive blurting out of obscenities. Research suggests that Tourette syndrome probably involves dominant, recessive, and intermediate inheritance, making precise determination of the cause very difficult (Olson, 2004).

Autism spectrum disorder (ASD), which includes both autism and Asperger syndrome, involves a wide range of deficits in social skills and communication. Approximately 1 in 150 U.S. children between ages 3 and 10 have been diagnosed as having ASD, with boys being 3 to 4 times more likely to be identified as having the disorder than are girls (Goldberg, 2007). Individuals with Asperger syndrome typically exhibit poor communication skills, intense preoccupation with a narrow topic, lack of empathy, and physical clumsiness. Individuals with autism have more severe versions of the same characteristics. The spectrum includes individuals with not only a range of disabilities but, in some cases, remarkable talents in a narrowly focused area, such as mathematics or drawing. Although the specific genetic basis for autism spectrum disorder has not been identified, the syndrome is known to be highly heritable.

The number of individuals diagnosed with autism has increased rapidly over the past few decades. Part of the increase is believed to be due to greater awareness of the syndrome, leading to a higher level of detection by parents, teachers, and doctors. Researchers have been searching for environmental factors that might be responsible for some of the increase. Many candidates are under investigation, including maternal infections, immune reactions, and stress, but to date no *conclusive* evidence has been found for any of them.

One factor that was highly publicized as a possible cause has been *definitively* ruled out—the MMR vaccine that is routinely given to young children to prevent measles, mumps, and rubella (Centers for Disease Control, 2009; McMahon et al., 2008). Parents who deny their children this important vaccine are needlessly putting them at risk for the illnesses that the vaccine prevents.

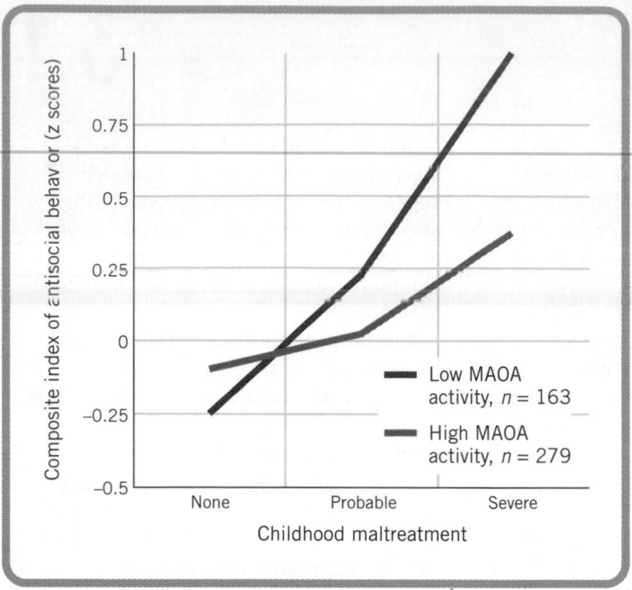

FIGURE 3.5 Genotype and environment This graph shows the level of antisocial behavior observed in young men as a function of the degree to which they had been maltreated in childhood. As this figure shows, those young men who had experienced severe maltreament were in general more likely to engage in antisocial behavior than were those who had experienced none. However, the effect was much stronger for those individuals who had a relatively inactive MAOA gene. (Adapted from Caspi et al., 2002, p. 852)

A second example of a genotype–environment interaction comes from research showing an effect of abusive parenting on children with a particular genotype (Caspi et al., 2002). The researchers wanted to determine why some children who experience severe maltreatment become violent and antisocial as adults, whereas others who are exposed to the same abuse do not. The results, shown in Figure 3.5, revealed the importance of a *combination* of environmental *and* genetic factors leading to antisocial outcomes—suffering abusive treatment as a child *and* possessing a particular variant of MAOA, an X-linked gene known to inhibit brain chemicals associated with aggression. Young men who had a relatively inactive version of the MAOA gene, and who had experienced severe maltreatment, grew up to be more antisocial than other men. More concretely, 85% of the maltreated group with the relatively inactive gene developed some form of antisocial behavior, and they were almost 10 times more likely to be convicted of a violent crime. The important point here is that neither factor by itself (possessing the inactive MAOA gene or being abused) predisposed boys to become highly aggressive; the higher incidence of antisocial behavior was observed only for the group with both factors. As the authors note, knowledge about specific genetic risk factors that make people more susceptible to particular environmental effects could strengthen multiple-risk models, such as those discussed in the previous two chapters.

Parental contributions to the child's environment Obviously, a highly salient and important part of a child's environment is the parents' relationship with the child—the manner in which they interact with him or her, the general home environment they provide, the experiences they arrange for the child, the encouragement they offer for particular behaviors, attitudes, and activities, and so on. Less obvious is the idea that the environment that parents provide for their children is due in part to their own genetic makeup. Parents' behavior toward their children (e.g., how warm or reserved they are, how patient or short-fused) is genetically influenced, as are the kinds of preferences, activities, and resources to which they expose their children (Plomin & Bergman, 1991). Thus, the child of a parent with a high level of musical ability is likely to hear more music while growing up than is a child of less musically talented parents. Parents who are skilled readers and enjoy and value reading are likely to read often for pleasure and information and are likely to have lots of books and magazines around the house. They are also more likely to read frequently to their children and to take them to the library. In contrast, parents for whom reading is challenging and not a source of pleasure are less likely to provide a highly literate environment for their children (Scarr, 1992).

This parent enjoys reading novels for pleasure and reads extensively for her work. She is providing a rich literary environment for her young child. The child may become an avid reader both because her mother's genetic makeup contributed to her enjoyment of reading and because of the physical environment (lots of books) and the social environment (encouragement of an interest in books) that the mother has provided.

4. Child's Phenotype–Child's Environment

Finally, Relation 4 in the model restates the *active child* theme—the child as a source of his or her own development. As noted in Chapter 1, children are not just the passive recipients of a preexisting environment. Rather, in two important ways they are active creators of the environment in which they live. First, by virtue of their nature and behavior, they actively evoke certain kinds of responses from others (Scarr, 1992; Scarr & McCartney, 1983). Babies who enjoy being cuddled are more likely to receive cuddling than are squirmy babies. Impulsive children hear "No," "Don't," "Stop," and "Be careful" more often than inhibited children do. Indeed, the degree to which parent–child relationships are mutually responsive is largely a function of the child's genetically influenced behavioral characteristics (Deater-Deckard & O'Connor, 2000).

The second way in which children create their own environment is by actively selecting surroundings and experiences that match their interests, talents, and personality characteristics (Scarr, 1992). As soon as infants become capable of self-locomotion, for example, they start selecting certain objects in the environment for exploration. Some very young children (especially boys) develop extremely intense interests in particular kinds of objects or activities that do not stem from parental encouragement (DeLoache, Simcock, & Macari, 2008). For example, many little boys become obsessed with vehicles and construction equipment. Other young children develop idiosyncratic and even quite peculiar interests (e.g., blenders, roadkill). For many parents, the origin of these preschool passions is totally obscure, and occasionally worrisome, because they do not realize how common these intense interests actually are.

Beginning in the preschool years, children's friendship opportunities increasingly depend on their own characteristics, as they choose playmates and pals with whom they feel compatible—the "birds of a feather flock together" phenomenon. And, as noted in Chapter 1, with age, children play an ever more active role in selecting their own environment. As they gain more autonomy, they increasingly select aspects of the environment that fit their temperament and abilities. To go back to the reading example, children who enjoy reading will read more books than will children who find reading tedious. The more they read, the more skillful readers they become, leading them to choose increasingly more challenging books, which, in turn, leads them to acquire advanced vocabulary and enhanced general knowledge, resulting in greater success in school.

Our discussion of the four kinds of gene–environment interactions has emphasized the vast complexity of the developmental process, highlighting the fact that great progress has nevertheless been made in understanding how genes function in the development of individuals. Still, the conceptualization we have presented of this process is greatly simplified. Indeed, many geneticists predict that recent discoveries—discoveries that go far beyond the scope of this book—will eventually reveal vastly greater complexities in the precise functioning of genes and their role in development than anyone had previously imagined.

Behavior Genetics

The rapidly expanding area known as **behavior genetics** is concerned with how variation in behavior and development results from the interaction of genetic and environmental factors. Behavior geneticists ask the same sort of question Galton asked about eminence: "Why are people different from one another?" Why, in any

behavior genetics the science concerned with how variation in behavior and development results from the combination of genetic and environmental factors

heritable refers to any characteristics or traits that are influenced by heredity

multifactorial refers to traits that are affected by a host of environmental factors as well as genetic ones

group of human beings, do we vary in terms of how smart, sociable, depressed, aggressive, and religious we are? The answer given by behavior geneticists is that all behavioral traits are **heritable;** that is, they are all influenced to some degree by hereditary factors (Bouchard, 2004; Turkheimer, 2000). As noted, the kind of traits that have been of particular interest to behavior geneticists—intelligence, sociability, mood, aggression, and the like—are polygenic, that is, affected by the combination of many genes. They are also **multifactorial,** that is, affected by a host of environmental factors as well as genetic ones. Thus, the sources of variation are vast.

To fully answer Galton's question, behavior geneticists try to tease apart genetic and environmental contributions to the differences observed among a population of people or other animals. Two premises underlie this endeavor: (1) To the extent that genetic factors are important for a given trait or behavior, individuals who are genotypically similar should be phenotypically similar. In other words, behavior patterns should "run in families": children should be more similar to their parents and siblings than to second- or third-degree relatives or unrelated individuals. (2) To the extent that shared environmental factors are important, individuals who have been reared together should be more similar than people who have not.

Behavior Genetic Research Designs

As it was for Galton, the mainstay of modern behavior-genetics research is the *family study.* In order to examine genetic and environmental contributions to a given trait or characteristic, behavior geneticists first measure that trait in people who vary in terms of genetic relatedness—parents and their children, identical and fraternal twins, nontwin siblings, and so on. Next, they assess how highly correlated the measures of the trait are among individuals who vary in the degree to which they are genetically related. (As you may recall from Chapter 1, a correlation coefficient expresses the extent to which two variables are related; the higher the correlation, the more precisely scores on one variable can be predicted from scores on the other.) Finally, behavior geneticists compare the resulting correlations to see if they are (1) higher for closely related individuals than for less closely related people, and (2) higher for individuals who share the same environment than for people who do not.

There are several specialized family-study designs that are particularly helpful in assessing genetic and environmental influences. One is the *twin-study* design, which compares the correlations for identical (monozygotic, or MZ) twins with those for same-sex fraternal (dizygotic, or DZ) twins. As you will recall, identical twins have 100% of their genes in common, whereas fraternal twins are only 50% genetically similar (just like nontwin siblings). For twins who grow up together, the degree of similarity of the environment is generally assumed to be equal. Both types of twins shared the same womb, were born at the same time, have lived in the same family and community, and are always the same age when tested. Thus, with different levels of genetic similarity and essentially equal environmental similarity, the difference between the correlations for the two types of twins is treated as an index of the importance of genetic factors in development. If the correlation between identical twins on

"The title of my science project is 'My Little Brother: Nature or Nurture.'"

a given trait or behavior is substantially higher than that between fraternal twins, it is assumed that genetic factors are substantially responsible for the difference.

Another family-study design used for assessing genetic and environmental influences is the *adoption* study. In this approach, researchers examine whether adopted children's scores on a given measure are correlated more highly with those of their biological parents and siblings or with those of their adoptive parents and siblings. Genetic influences are inferred to the extent that children resemble their biological relatives more than they do their adoptive ones.

The ideal behavior-genetics design—the *adoptive twin* study—compares identical twins who grew up together versus identical twins who were separated shortly after birth and raised apart. If the correlations for twins reared apart are similar to those for twins reared together, it suggests that environmental factors have little effect. Conversely, to the extent that the correlations between identical twins who grew up in different environments are lower than those for identical twins who grew up together, environmental influence is inferred. Box 3.2 describes some of the remarkable findings that have emerged from studies of twins reared apart, as well as some of the problems with such research.

Family studies of intelligence The most common focus of behavior-genetics family studies has been intelligence. Table 3.1 summarizes the results of over 100 family studies of IQ through adolescence. The pattern of results reveals both genetic and environmental influences. Genetic influence is shown by generally higher correlations for higher degrees of genetic similarity. Most notable is the finding that identical (MZ) twins resemble one another in IQ more than do same-sex fraternal (DZ) twins. At the same time, environmental influences are reflected in the fact that identical twins are not identical in terms of IQ. Further evidence for an environmental role is that MZ twins who are reared together are more similar than those reared apart.

After adolescence, the picture is quite different from that presented in Table 3.1. In adulthood, the correlation for identical twins remains about the same as in the table (above .80), but the correlation for fraternal twins is lower (around .40, compared with .60 in the table) (Pedersen, Plomin, Nesselroade, & McClearn, 1992). The correlation for genetically unrelated individuals who were reared together is essentially zero (McGue, Bouchard, Iacono, & Lykken, 1993).

These patterns are consistent with the idea that people actively construct their environment—the phenotype–environment correlation (Relation 3) discussed earlier (McGue et al., 1993; Scarr & McCartney, 1983). As children get older, they increasingly control their own experiences, and their parents have less influence over their activities. It may be that identical twins' IQs remain similar into adulthood because their common genetic predispositions lead them to select similar intellectual stimulation, whereas the IQs of fraternal twins become increasingly dissimilar because they choose divergent experiences for themselves (Scarr & McCartney, 1983).

TABLE 3.1

Summary of Family Studies of Intelligence

	Average Familial IQ Correlations (R)	
Relationship	**Average R**	**Number of Pairs**
	Reared-together biological relatives	
MZ twins	0.86	4672
DZ twins	0.60	5533
Siblings	0.47	26,473
Parent–offspring	0.42	8433
Half-siblings	0.35	200
Cousins	0.15	1176
	Reared-apart biological relatives	
MZ twins	0.72	65
Siblings	0.24	203
Parent–offspring	0.24	720
	Reared-together nonbiological relatives	
Siblings	0.32	714
Parent–offspring	0.24	720

Note: MZ = monozygotic; DZ = dizygotic. Source: McGue, Bouchard, Iacono, & Lykken (1993)

individual differences 3.2

Identical Twins Reared Apart

Oskar Stohr and Jack Yufa are identical twins who were separated shortly after their birth in Trinidad. Oskar was raised by his grandmother in Germany as a Catholic and a Nazi. Jack was raised by his father, in the Caribbean, as a Jew. Despite their very different backgrounds, when the brothers first met as middle-aged men recruited for a research study in Minneapolis, they discovered a remarkable number of similarities between them:

> They like spicy foods and sweet liqueurs, are absent-minded, have a habit of falling asleep in front of the television, think it's funny to sneeze in a crowd of strangers, flush the toilet before using it, store rubber bands on their wrists, read magazines back to front, dip buttered toast in their coffee. Oskar is domineering toward women and yells at his wife, which Jack did before he was separated.
>
> (Holden, 1980, p. 1324)

Jack and Oskar are participants in the Minnesota Study of Twins Reared Apart, an extensive research project on identical twins separated early in life (Bouchard, Lykken, McGue, Segal, & Tellegen, 1990). Over 100 pairs of such twins have been located, recruited for the study, and brought to Minneapolis to undergo an extensive battery of physiological and psychological tests. Many twin siblings were meeting for the first time since infancy. (The reunited twins in the photo at right showed almost as many striking similarities as did Jack and Oskar, including their choice of occupation as firemen.) The motivation for this large-scale study is to examine genetic and environmental contributions to development and behavior by examining individuals who are genetically identical but who grew up in different environments.

The Minnesota team of investigators has been struck by the extent of similarity they have found in the separated twins they have studied; they have identified genetic contributions to "almost every behavioral trait so far investigated from reaction time to religiosity" (Bouchard et al., 1990). Particularly strong correlations have been found for traits as diverse as IQ, reaction to stress, aggression, and traditionalism.

BOB SACHA

Identical twins Gerald Levey and Mark Newman were separated at birth and reared separately in middle-class Jewish homes in the New York area. When reunited at the age of 31, they discovered they were both firemen with droopy moustaches who wore aviator-style sunglasses.

As striking as the similarities between separated twins may be, there are several problems with automatically assuming that these similarities are attributable to genetic factors. One issue is the practice of selective placement: adoption agencies generally try to place children with families of the same general background and race, so the environments of the separated siblings are often similar in many ways. It is extremely rare for separated twins to be raised like Jack and Oskar, with different languages, religions, and cultures. In fact, the majority of the twins in most behavior-genetics studies are from predominantly white, middle-class families in Western countries. As behavior geneticists Levine and Suzuki (1993) commented:

> Take one of those kids and put him in a really different environment, like in a family of bushmen in Africa, or in a farming village in mainland China, and then come back twenty years later and see if you find two firemen who dress the same!
>
> (p. 241)

Heritability

In their approach to the nature–nurture question, many behavior geneticists attempt to quantify the degree to which genes contribute to various traits. To estimate how much of the variability in measures of a given trait is attributable to genetic and environmental factors, they derive heritability estimates from correlations of the type shown in Table 3.1. **Heritability** is a statistical estimate of how much of the measured variance on a trait among individuals in a given population is attributable to genetic differences among those individuals.

heritability a statistical estimate of the proportion of the measured variance on a trait among individuals in a given population that is attributable to genetic differences among those individuals

A crucial point to understand about heritability estimates is that they tell us nothing about the relative contributions of genetic and environmental factors to the development of an *individual.* Instead, they estimate how much of the variation among *a given population of people* is due to differences in their genes. The heritability estimate for intelligence, for example, is generally considered to be approximately 50% (Bouchard, 2004; Plomin, 1990). This means that, *for the population studied*, roughly 50% of the variation in IQ scores is due to genetic differences among the members of the population. (It does *not* mean that 50% of your IQ score is due to your genetic makeup and 50% is due to your experience.) Note that this heritability estimate indicates that the environmental contribution to the variation in IQ is also approximately 50%.

Behavior-genetic analyses have been applied to many diverse aspects of human behavior, several of which you will encounter in other chapters of this book. To cite just a few examples, substantial heritability has been reported for infant activity level (Saudino & Eaton, 1991), temperament (Goldsmith, Buss, & Lemery, 1997), reading disability (DeFries & Gillis, 1993), and antisocial behavior (Gottesman & Goldsmith, 1994). Substantial heritability has even been reported for divorce (McGue & Lykken, 1992) and TV viewing (Plomin, Corley, DeFries, & Fulker, 1990).

The implausibility of there being "broken home" or "couch potato" genes raises an important point: despite the common use of the phrase, there are no genes "for" particular behavior patterns. As we stressed before, genes do nothing more than code for proteins, so they affect behavior only insofar as those proteins affect the sensory, neural, and other physiological processes involved in behavior. Thus, the heritability estimate for divorce may be related to a genetic predisposition to, say, seek out novelty, and that for TV viewing may be related to a genetically based low activity level or short attention span.

Heritability estimates have been criticized, both from within psychology (e.g., Gottlieb, Wahlsten, & Lickliter, 1997; Lerner, 1995) and from outside it (e.g., Levine & Suzuki, 1993; Lewontin, 1982). Part of the criticism stems from ways that heritability is often misinterpreted. One very common misunderstanding involves the application of the concept of heritability to individuals, despite the fact that, as we have emphasized, *heritability applies only to populations*.

In addition, *a heritability estimate applies only to a particular population living in a particular environment at a particular time*. Consider the case of height. Research conducted almost exclusively with North Americans and Europeans—most of them white and adequately nourished—puts the heritability of height at around 90%. But what if some segment of this population had experienced a severe famine during childhood, while the rest remained well fed? Would the heritability estimate for height still be 90%? No—because the variability due to environmental factors would *increase* dramatically, and hence the variability that could be attributed to genetic factors would *decrease* to the same degree. The principle of variable heritability is seen in the IQ correlations shown in Table 3.1, with the heritability estimates derived from them differing for the same individuals in childhood and adulthood.

Further, it is known that heritability estimates can differ markedly for groups of people who grow up in very different environmental circumstances. In the United States, for example, heritability estimates differ considerably as a function of socioeconomic status, as shown by a large twin study that included families across the SES spectrum (Turkheimer, Haley, Waldron, D'Onofrio, & Gottesman, 2003). In this study, almost 60% of the variance in IQ among the sample of families living in poverty was accounted for by shared environment, with almost none of it attributable to genetic similarity. The pattern for affluent families is the opposite, with genetic factors contributing more than environmental ones. Although it is not fully clear what is responsible for these differing levels of heritability, this study and related research suggests that qualitatively different developmental forces may be operating in poor versus affluent environments.

A related, frequently misunderstood point is that *high heritability does not imply immutability*. The fact that a trait is highly heritable does not mean that there is little point in trying to improve the course of development related to that trait. Thus, for example, the fact that the heritability estimate for IQ is relatively high does not mean that the intellectual performance of young children living in poverty cannot be improved by appropriate intervention efforts (as discussed in the preceding two chapters).

Finally, because they are relevant only within a given population, heritability estimates tell us *nothing* about differences *between groups*. The heritability score for IQ, for example, provides little insight into the meaning of differences in the IQ scores of different groups of Americans. Euro-Americans, on average, score 15 points higher on IQ tests than African Americans do. Some people mistakenly assume that because IQ is estimated to be 50% heritable, the difference between these two groups' IQ scores is genetically based. This assumption is unwarranted, given the large overall disparities between the two groups in family income and education, quality of neighborhood schools, health care, and myriad other factors.

Environmental Effects

Every examination of genetic contributions to behavior and development is also, necessarily, a study of environmental influences: estimating heritability automatically estimates the proportion of variance not attributable to genes. Because heritability estimates rarely exceed 50%, a large contribution from environmental factors is usually indicated.

Behavior geneticists try to assess the extent to which aspects of an environment shared by biologically related people make them more alike and to what extent nonshared experiences make them different. The most obvious source of shared environment is growing up together in the same family, and a standard estimate of shared-environment effects is based on the degree of similarity among adoptive siblings—that is, biologically unrelated individuals who grew up together (Plomin, DeFries, McClearn, & Rutter, 1997). Shared-environment effects are inferred from greater similarity between twins or other relatives than is accounted for by their genetic relatedness. For example, substantial shared-environmental influence has been inferred for positive emotion in toddlers and young children because fraternal and identical twins who were reared together were equally similar in the degree to which they showed pleasure (Goldsmith et al., 1997).

Behavior geneticists have reported surprisingly little effect of shared environment on some other aspects of development. For example, with respect to personality, the correlations for adoptive siblings are often near zero (Rowe, 1994). The same is true for some types of psychopathology, including schizophrenia (Gottesman, 1991). Being adopted into a family with a schizophrenic sibling does not increase the risk that a child will become schizophrenic. In addition, the risk of schizophrenia is the same for the biological child of a schizophrenic

The similarity between these identical twins (in red shirts) may be enhanced by environmental factors. Sharing the same general body build and motor abilities, their enjoyment of athletics exposes them to similar environmental experiences outside their family. Being of similar intelligence, they are likely to have relatively similar experiences in school. Later, they may enjoy similar success in dating and end up marrying women of similar social class.

HUGES MARTIN/CORBIS

parent regardless of whether the child is raised by that parent or is adopted away at birth (Kety et al., 1994).

Nonshared-environment effects have to do with the fact that even children who grow up in the same family do not have all their experiences in common—either inside or outside the family.

Within the family, siblings may have quite different experiences because of their different birth order. In a large family, the oldest child may have been reared by relatively young, energetic, but inexperienced, parents, whereas a much younger sibling will be parented by older, more sedentary, but more knowledgeable, individuals who are likely to have more resources available than they did when younger. In addition, as discussed in Chapter 1, siblings may experience their parents' behavior toward them differently (the "Mom always loved you best" syndrome). They may also be affected quite differently by an event they experience in common, such as the divorce of their parents (Hetherington & Clingempeel, 1992). Finally, siblings may be highly motivated to differentiate themselves from one another (Sulloway, 1996). The younger sibling of a star student may strive to be a star athlete instead, and a child who observes a sibling disappearing into a self-destructive pattern of drug and alcohol abuse may become determined to follow a different path.

Siblings can also have highly divergent experiences outside the family, partly as a result of belonging to different peer groups. Highly active brothers who both like physical challenges and thrills will have very different experiences if one takes up rock climbing while the other hangs out with delinquents. Idiosyncratic life events—suffering a serious accident, having an inspiring teacher, being bullied on the playground—can contribute further to making siblings develop differently. The primary effect of nonshared environmental factors is to increase the differences among family members (Plomin & Daniels, 1987).

review:

The four relations shown in Figure 3.1 depict the complex interplay of genetic and environmental forces in development. (1) The course of children's development is influenced by the genetic heritage they receive from their mother and father, with their sex determined solely by their father's chromosomal contribution. (2) The relation between children's genotype and phenotype depends in part on dominance patterns in the expression of some genes, but most traits of primary interest to behavioral scientists are influenced by multiple genes (polygenic inheritance). (3) As the norm-of-reaction concept specifies, any given genotype will develop differently in different environments. A particularly salient part of children's environment is their parents, including their parents' own genetic makeup, which influences how parents behave toward their children. (4) Children's own genetic makeup influences how they select and shape their own environment and the experiences they have in it.

The field of behavior genetics is concerned with how development results from the interaction of genetic and environmental factors. Using the family-study methodology, behavior geneticists compare the correlations among individuals who vary in the degree of genetic relatedness and in similarity of their rearing environments. Heritability estimates indicate the proportion of the variance among individuals in a given population on a given trait that is attributable to genetic differences among them. Most behavioral traits that have been measured show substantial heritability; at the same time, heritability estimates reveal the close partnership of heredity and environment in development and the fallacy of considering the influences of nature and nurture as independent of one another.

neurons cells that are specialized for sending and receiving messages between the brain and all parts of the body, as well as within the brain itself

cell body a component of the neuron that contains the basic biological material that keeps the neuron functioning

dendrites neural fibers that receive input from other cells and conduct it toward the cell body in the form of electrical impulses

axons neural fibers that conduct electrical signals away from the cell body to connections with other neurons

Brain Development

As you will see, the collaboration between nature and nurture takes center stage in the development of the brain and nervous system. Before discussing developmental processes in the formation of the brain, however, we need to consider the basic components of this "most complex structure in the known universe" (Thompson, 2000, p. 1).

Fundamental to all aspects of behavioral development is the development of the central nervous system (CNS) and especially the brain. The brain is the font of all thought, memory, emotion, imagination, personality—in short, the behavior, capacities, and characteristics that make us who we are. The central role of the brain in human behavior was recognized as early as 3000 B.C. by the Egyptians. According to one ancient text, "If thou examinist a man having a smash in his temple . . . If thou callest to him he is speechless and cannot speak" (quoted in Changeux, 1985, p. 4).

Structures of the Brain

In our examination of the structures of the brain, we focus our discussion on two that are central to behavior—the neuron and the cortex, as well as some of their substructures.

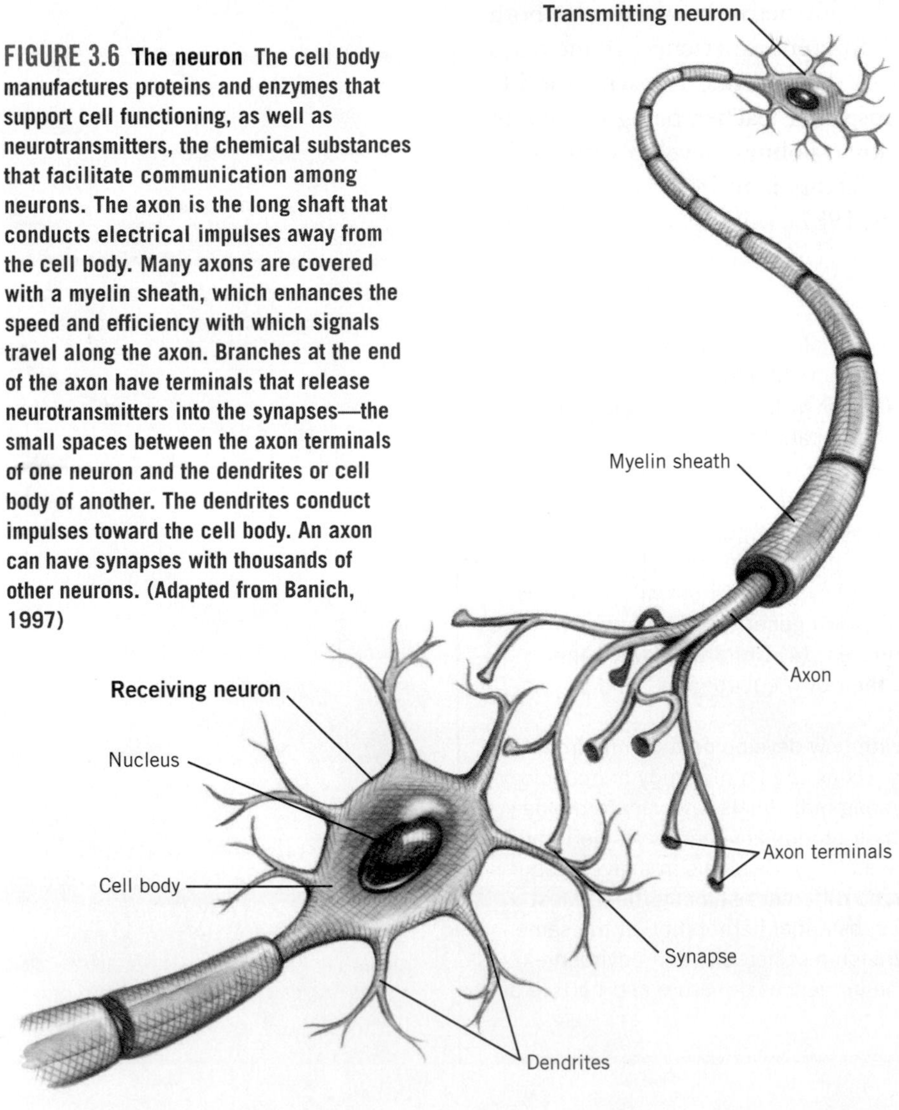

FIGURE 3.6 The neuron The cell body manufactures proteins and enzymes that support cell functioning, as well as neurotransmitters, the chemical substances that facilitate communication among neurons. The axon is the long shaft that conducts electrical impulses away from the cell body. Many axons are covered with a myelin sheath, which enhances the speed and efficiency with which signals travel along the axon. Branches at the end of the axon have terminals that release neurotransmitters into the synapses—the small spaces between the axon terminals of one neuron and the dendrites or cell body of another. The dendrites conduct impulses toward the cell body. An axon can have synapses with thousands of other neurons. (Adapted from Banich, 1997)

Neurons

The business of the brain is information. The basic units of the brain's remarkably powerful informational system are its more than 100 billion **neurons** (Figure 3.6), which constitute the gray matter of the brain. These cells are specialized for sending and receiving electrical messages between the brain and all parts of the body, as well as within the brain itself. *Sensory neurons* transmit information from sensory receptors that detect stimuli in the external environment or within the body itself; *motor neurons* transmit information from the brain to muscles and glands; and *interneurons* act as intermediaries between sensory and motor neurons.

Although they vary substantially in size, shape, and function, all neurons comprise three main components: (1) a **cell body,** which contains the basic biological material that keeps the neuron functioning; (2) **dendrites,** fibers that receive input from other cells and conduct it toward the cell body in the form of electrical impulses; and (3) an **axon,** a fiber (anywhere from a few micrometers to over a meter in length) that conducts electrical signals away from the cell body to connections with other neurons.

Neurons communicate with one another at **synapses,** which are microscopic junctions between the axon terminal of one neuron and the dendritic branches of another. In the process, electrical and chemical messages cross the synapses and cause the receiving neurons either to fire, sending a signal on to other neurons, or to be inhibited from firing. The total number of synapses is staggering—many trillions—with some neurons having as many as 15,000 synaptic connections with other neurons.

Glial Cells

Glial cells, the brain's white matter, make up nearly half the human brain, outnumbering neurons 10 to 1. They perform a variety of critical functions, including the formation of a **myelin sheath** around axons, which insulates them and increases the speed and efficiency of information transmission. Glial cells also play a role in communication within the brain by influencing the formation and strengthening of synapses and by communicating among themselves in a network separate from the neural network (Fields, 2004). Many people with schizophrenia or bipolar disorder have a defect in the gene that regulates production of myelin.

The Cortex

The **cerebral cortex,** the surface of which is shown in Figure 3.7, is considered the "most human part of the human brain" (McEwen & Schmeck, 1994). Over the course of human evolution, the brain expanded greatly in size. Almost all of this increase occurred in the cerebral cortex, which constitutes 80% of the brain, a much greater proportion than in other species (Kolb & Whishaw, 1996). The folds and fissures that are apparent in Figure 3.7 form during development as the brain grows within the confined space of the skull; these convolutions make it possible to pack more cortex into the limited space.

The cortex plays a primary role in a wide variety of mental functions, from seeing and hearing to reading, writing, and doing arithmetic, to feeling compassion

synapses microscopic junctions between the axon terminal of one neuron and the dendritic branches or cell body of another

glial cells cells in the brain that provide a variety of critical supportive functions

myelin sheath a fatty sheath that forms around certain axons in the body and increases the speed and efficiency of information transmission

cerebral cortex the "gray matter" of the brain that plays a primary role in what is thought to be particularly humanlike functioning, from seeing and hearing to writing to feeling emotion

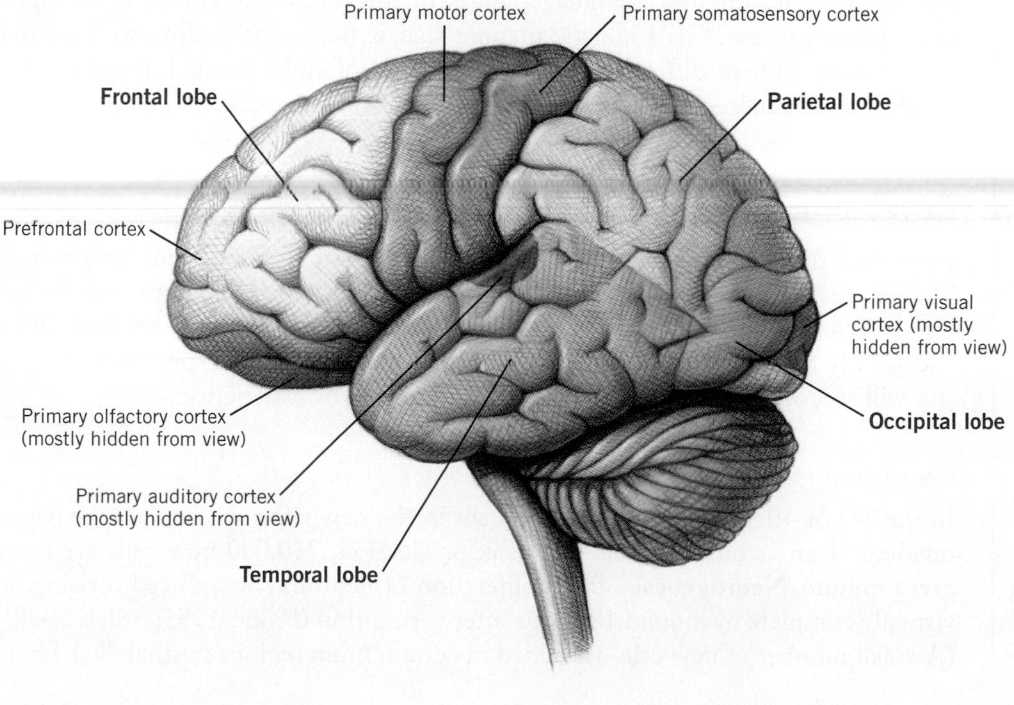

FIGURE 3.7 The human cerebral cortex This view of the left hemisphere of an adult brain shows the four major cortical regions—known as the lobes—which are divided from one another by deep fissures. Each of the primary sensory areas receives information from a particular sensory system, and the primary motor cortex controls the body's muscles. Information from multiple sensory areas is processed in association areas.

and communicating with others. As Figure 3.7 shows, the major areas of the cortex—the **lobes**—can be characterized in terms of the general behavioral categories with which they are associated. The **occipital lobe** is primarily involved in processing visual information. The **temporal lobe** is associated with memory, visual recognition, and the processing of emotion and auditory information. The **parietal lobe** is important for spatial processing. It is also involved in the integration of information from different sensory modalities, and it plays a role in integrating sensory input with information stored in memory and with information about internal states. The **frontal lobe,** the brain's "executive," is involved in many uniquely human abilities. It is particularly important for foresight—planning ahead and organizing behavior to achieve a goal. Information from multiple sensory systems is processed and integrated in the **association areas** that lie in between the major sensory and motor areas.

Although it is convenient to think of different cortical areas as if they were functionally specific, they are not. It has become increasingly clear that complex mental functions are mediated by multiple areas of the brain. A given area may be critical for some ability, but that does not mean that control of that ability is located in that one area. (Box 3.3 examines some of the techniques that researchers use to learn about brain functioning.)

Cerebral lateralization The cortex is divided into two separate halves, or **cerebral hemispheres.** For the most part, sensory input from one side of the body goes to the opposite side of the brain, and the motor areas of the cortex control movements of the opposite side of the body. Thus, if you pick up a hot pot with your right hand, it is the left side of the brain that registers the pain and sends the message to let go immediately.

The left and right hemispheres of the brain communicate with one another primarily by way of the **corpus callosum,** a dense tract of nerve fibers that connect them. The two hemispheres are specialized for different modes of processing, a phenomenon referred to as **cerebral lateralization.** For example, in most people, the left hemisphere processes information in a piecemeal, linear manner as required for logical analysis, language, and sequential tasks; in contrast, the right hemisphere processes in a holistic manner that is better for dealing with spatial information. (These differences are characteristic of right-handed, but not left-handed, individuals—lefties' brains are less clearly lateralized.)

Developmental Processes

How does the incredibly complex structure of the human brain come into being? You will not be surprised to hear that, once again, a partnership of nature and nurture is involved. Some aspects of the construction of the brain are set in motion and tightly controlled by the genes, relatively independent of experience. But, as you will see, other aspects are profoundly influenced by experience.

Neurogenesis and Neuron Development

In the 3rd or 4th week of prenatal life, cells in the newly formed neural tube begin dividing at an astonishing rate—at peak production, 250,000 new cells are born every minute. **Neurogenesis,** the proliferation of neurons through cell division, is virtually complete by around 18 weeks after conception (Rakic, 1995; Stiles, 2008). (A small number of new cells are added in certain brain regions postnatally.) Thus,

lobes major areas of the cortex associated with general categories of behavior

occipital lobe the lobe of the cortex that is primarily involved in processing visual information

temporal lobe the lobe of the cortex that is associated with memory, visual recognition, and the processing of emotion and auditory information

parietal lobe governs spatial processing as well as integrating sensory input with information stored in memory

frontal lobe associated with organizing behavior; the one that is thought responsible for the human ability to plan ahead

association areas parts of the brain that lie between the major sensory and motor areas and that process and integrate input from those areas

cerebral hemispheres the two halves of the cortex; for the most part, sensory input from one side of the body goes to the opposite hemisphere of the brain

corpus callosum a dense tract of nerve fibers that enable the two hemispheres of the brain to communicate

cerebral lateralization the specialization of the hemispheres of the brain for different modes of processing

neurogenesis the proliferation of neurons through cell division

a closer look 3.3

Mapping the Mind

Developmental researchers employ a variety of techniques to determine what areas of the brain are associated with particular behaviors, thoughts, and feelings and how brain functions change with age. The existence of increasingly powerful techniques for investigating brain function has sparked a revolution in the understanding of the brain and its development. Here, we provide examples of the techniques most often used to map the mind and its workings in children.

Neuropsychological Approach

Researchers have long drawn inferences about brain function from the effects of brain damage on behavior. If a particular function is lost or impaired following damage to a given area of the brain, it is evidence that this part of the brain must be involved in that function. In the 1800s, Paul Broca concluded that a particular area of the cortex was involved in language production, because people with damage to that area had difficulty processing speech.

A good example of the neuropsychological approach comes from classic research by Adele Diamond (1991), who has demonstrated that healthy human infants and adult monkeys with lesions in the prefrontal cortex make similar kinds of errors in searching for objects they observed hidden first in one location and then another (see the photos below). Diamond concluded that in both humans and monkeys, the prefrontal cortex is involved in coordinating two skills essential to the search task—*remembering* the current location of an object and *inhibiting* the tendency to respond to its previous location. She inferred that the monkey's poor performance was due to the damage done to this area and that the infants' failure was due to immaturity of the same part of the brain.

Electrophysiological Recording

One of the techniques most often used by developmental researchers to study brain function is based on EEG (electroencephalographic) recordings of electrical activity generated by neurons. EEG is completely noninvasive (the recordings are obtained through electrodes that simply rest on the scalp), so this method can be used successfully with children and even infants (see photo at right). EEG recordings have provided valuable information about a variety of brain-behavior relations.

EEG **This cap holds electrodes snugly against the baby's scalp, enabling researchers to record electrical activity generated from all over the baby's brain.**

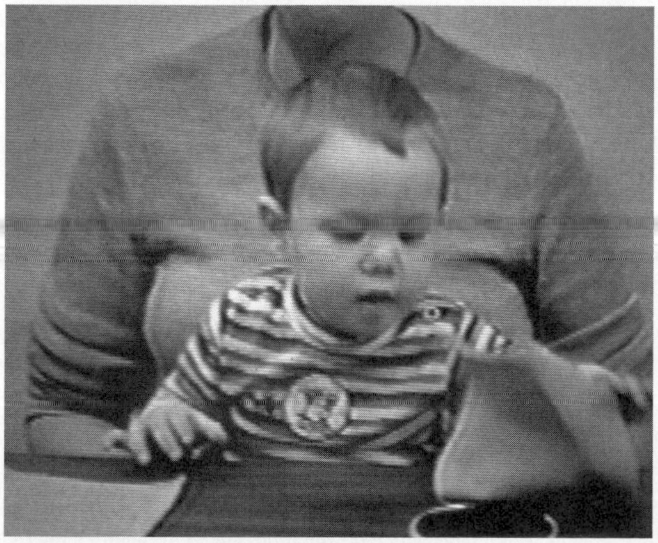

Animal–human parallel **Nine-month-old infants and adult monkeys make similar errors in a search task. After retrieving a desirable object from one location, both baby and monkey repeat their previous action and mistakenly search where they found it before. (From Diamond, 1991)**

(***a closer look*** *is continued on the next page)*

(continued from the previous page)

Researchers have discovered that in infants, just as in adults, greater electrical activity on the left side of the frontal area is associated with positive emotions such as joy, whereas negative emotions, such as anger or fear, involve greater activity on the right side (Sutton & Davidson, 1997). In playful, pleasurable interactions with their mothers, for example, babies generally show greater activation in the left frontal area of the brain. However, infants of depressed mothers do not show these differences, suggesting that interacting with their mothers may not be highly pleasurable (Dawson, Klinger, Panagiotides, Spieker, & Frey, 1992).

An electrophysiological technique that is very useful for studying the relation between brain activity and specific kinds of stimulation is the recording of **ERPs (event-related potentials)**, that is, changes in the brain's electrical activity that occur in response to the presentation of a particular stimulus. One contribution these measures have made is revealing continuity over time. For example, studies of ERPs to auditory stimuli have shown that newborns' ability to discriminate among speech sounds is directly related to their language skills at 3 years of age (Molfese & Molfese, 1994).

ERP measures have also proved useful in studying the development of memory. In one study, 9-month-old infants were shown how to assemble pieces to construct a toy. A week later their ERP responses were recorded when they were presented with the toy pieces that had been in the demonstration and with novel ones (Carver, Bauer, & Nelson, 2000). A month later, they were tested to see if they remembered how to assemble the toy. The pattern of ERP responding (shown in the figure below) from the month before predicted the infants' performance on the memory test: only those infants whose ERP indicated that they had discriminated between the novel and familiar toy pieces the month before knew how to make the novel toy. Thus, an ERP measure of recognition memory was related to later behavioral measures of recall memory.

Functional Magnetic Resonance Imaging (fMRI)

Functional MRI uses a powerful magnet to produce colorful images representing cerebral blood flow in different areas of the brain. These images enable researchers to pinpoint which areas of the brain are active during particular mental states and in response to particular stimuli. Because a person must be able to tolerate the noise and close confinement of an MRI machine and must be able to remain very still, most developmental fMRI studies have been done with children 6 years of age or older.

An ever-increasing amount of research has been done using fMRI to examine developmental changes in brain-behavior relations with respect to a variety of particular topics (e.g., memory development, emotion processing, reading skills, atypical development such as ADHD, and so on). The first figure on page 107 illustrates one of the interesting patterns that have been found with respect to cognitive development: children often show higher overall levels of brain activation than adults do in a given task, suggesting less efficient processing (e.g., Casey et al., 1995).

Positron Emission Tomography (PET)

PET, another brain-imaging technique, has provided some important information about brain development. However, because PET scans require injecting radioactive material into the brain to be imaged, this technique is used primarily for diagnostic purposes. PET scans done with children from birth to adulthood revealed changes in metabolic activity in the brain that closely parallel the changes in synaptic density shown in the pair of PET images on page 107 (Chugani, Phelps, & Mazziotta, 1987).

Other Techniques

Although the above are the main techniques that have been used in developmental research to date, advances are being made at a rapid pace, and several new techniques that are on the horizon will no doubt eventually be adapted for developmental studies. "There is universal agreement that the twenty-first century will be a time of unprecedented discoveries linking the anatomical structures and physiological systems of the brain to the human mind" (Posner, Rothbart, Farah, & Bruer, 2001, p. 293).

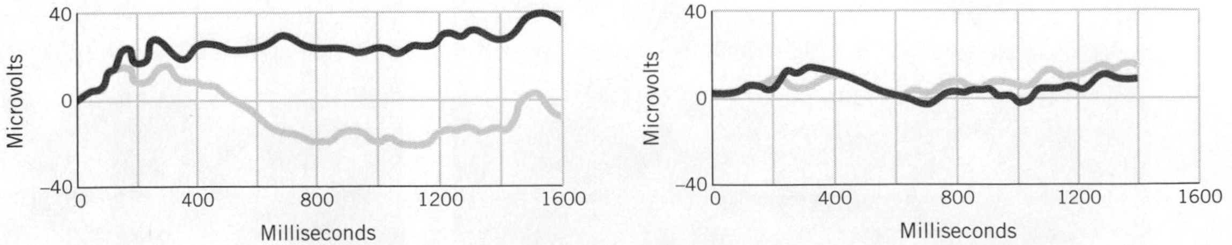

ERP responses This figure shows ERP waveforms in response to novel (red line) and familiar (yellow line) stimuli. The infants who later recalled how to assemble a toy (left panel) had clearly discriminated between the familiar and novel items on an earlier recognition test. The infants who did not recall the assembly sequence (right panel) had not discriminated between the components on the earlier test. (Adapted from Carver et al., 2000)

ERPs (event-related potentials) changes in the brain's electrical activity that occur in response to the presentation of a particular stimulus

3.3

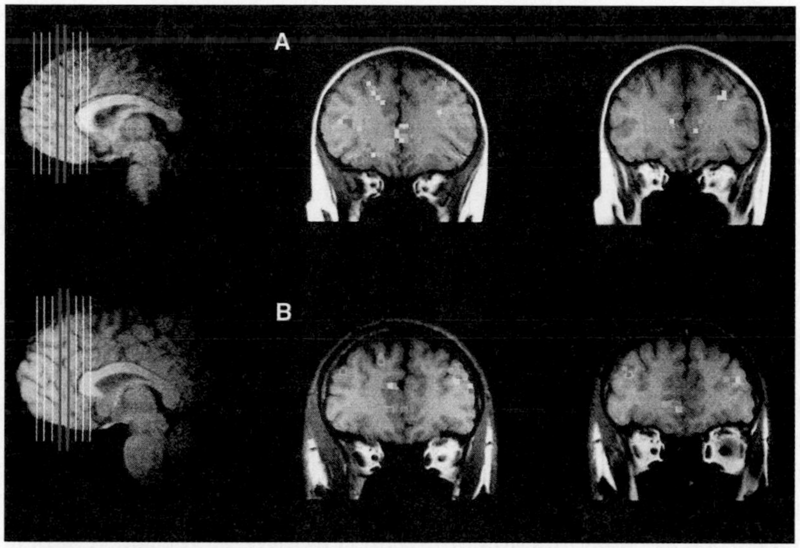

fMRI images The figure shows fMRI images of the brains of a 9-year-old (panel A) and a 24-year-old (panel B) in a standard cognitive task that requires responding to some stimuli but inhibiting responding to others. (The images to the left show the "slices" of the brain averaged together in the images on the right.) The results show that the location of activation in the prefrontal cortex did not differ between children and adults, but the overall extent of activation was greater for the children (Casey, 1999).

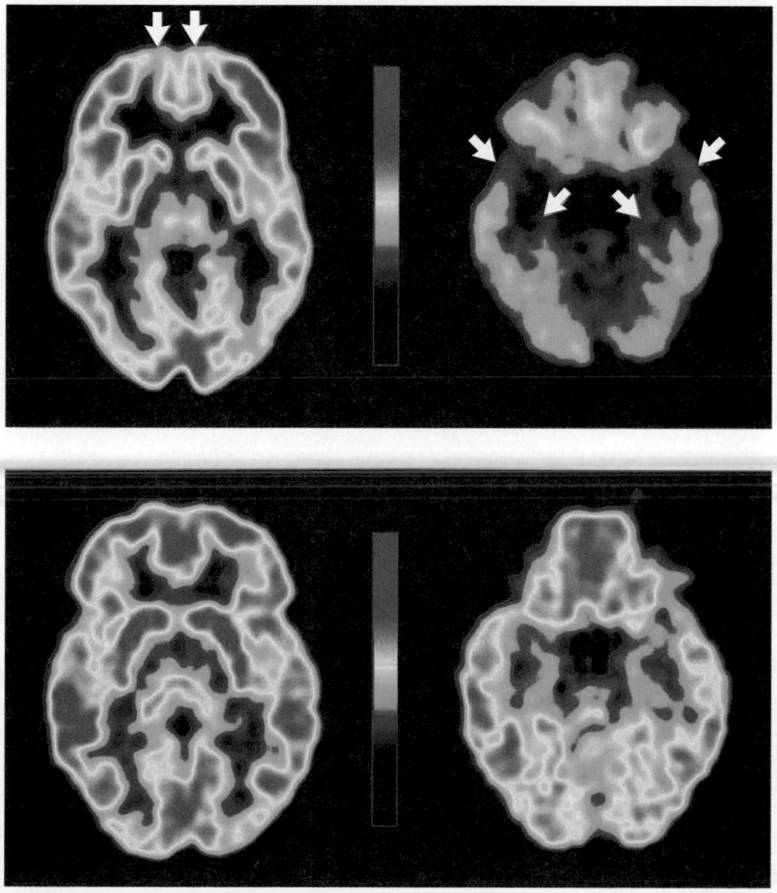

PET images The upper panel shows two sections of the brain of a 9½-year-old girl who spent her first 32 months in a Romanian orphanage before being adopted. The lower panel shows two sections of the brain of a 10½-year-old girl who had a normal home environment. Areas of greater brain activity show up as bolder concentrations of red, whereas deep blue indicates low activity. The arrows in the upper panel point to the areas of unusually low metabolic activity in the brain of the Romanian child.

almost all of the roughly 100 billion neurons you currently possess have been with you since before you were born.

After their "birth," neurons begin the second developmental process, which involves migration to their ultimate destinations. Some neurons are pushed along passively by the newer cells formed after them, whereas others actively propel themselves toward their ultimate location.

Once neurons reach their destination, cell growth and differentiation occur. Neurons first grow an axon and then a "bush" of dendrites (refer back to Figure 3.6). Thereafter they take on specific structural and functional characteristics as they form the different structures of the brain. Axons elongate as they grow toward specific targets, which, depending on the neuron in question, might be anything from another neuron in the brain to a bone in the big toe. The main change in dendrites is "arborization"—an enormous increase in the size and complexity of the dendritic "tree" that results from growth, branching, and the formation of **spines** on the branches. This arborization enormously increases the dendrites' capacity to form connections with other neurons. In the cortex, the period of most intense growth and differentiation comes after birth.

The process of **myelination**, the formation of the insulating myelin sheath around some axons, begins in the brain before birth and continues into early adulthood. As noted earlier, a crucial function of myelin is to increase the speed of neural conduction. The various cortical areas become myelinated at very different rates, possibly contributing to the different rates of development for various behaviors. Particularly dramatic increases in myelination occur in the frontal lobes during adolescence (Durston et al., 2001).

Synaptogenesis

One result of the extraordinary growth of axonal and dendritic fibers is a wildly exuberant generation of neuronal connections. In a process called **synaptogenesis,** each neuron forms synapses with thousands of others, resulting in the formation of the trillions of connections referred to earlier. Figure 3.8 shows the time course of synaptogenesis in the cortex. As you can see, it begins prenatally and proceeds very rapidly both before birth and for some time afterward. Note that both the timing and rate of synapse production vary for different cortical areas; synapse generation is complete much earlier in the visual cortex, for example, than in the frontal area.

Synapse Elimination

We now come to what is one of the most remarkable facts about the development of the human brain. The explosive generation of neurons and synapses during synaptogenesis, which is largely under genetic control, results in a huge surplus—many more neural connections than any one brain can use (Huttenlocher, 1994; Rakic, 1995). This overabundance of synapses includes an excess of connections between different parts of the brain: for example, many neurons in what will become the auditory cortex are linked with those in the visual area, and both of these areas are overly connected to neurons involved in taste and smell. As a consequence of this hyperconnectivity, newborns may experience synesthesia—the blending of different types of sensory input (Maurer & Mondloch, 2004). Because of the extra connections between auditory and visual cortex, they may, for example, have visual experience as a result of auditory stimulation, experiencing a sound as being of a particular color.

spines formations on the dendrites of neurons that increase the dendrites' capacity to form connections with other neurons

myelination the formation of myelin (a fatty sheath) around the axons of neurons that speeds and increases information-processing abilities

synaptogenesis the process by which neurons form synapses with other neurons, resulting in trillions of connections

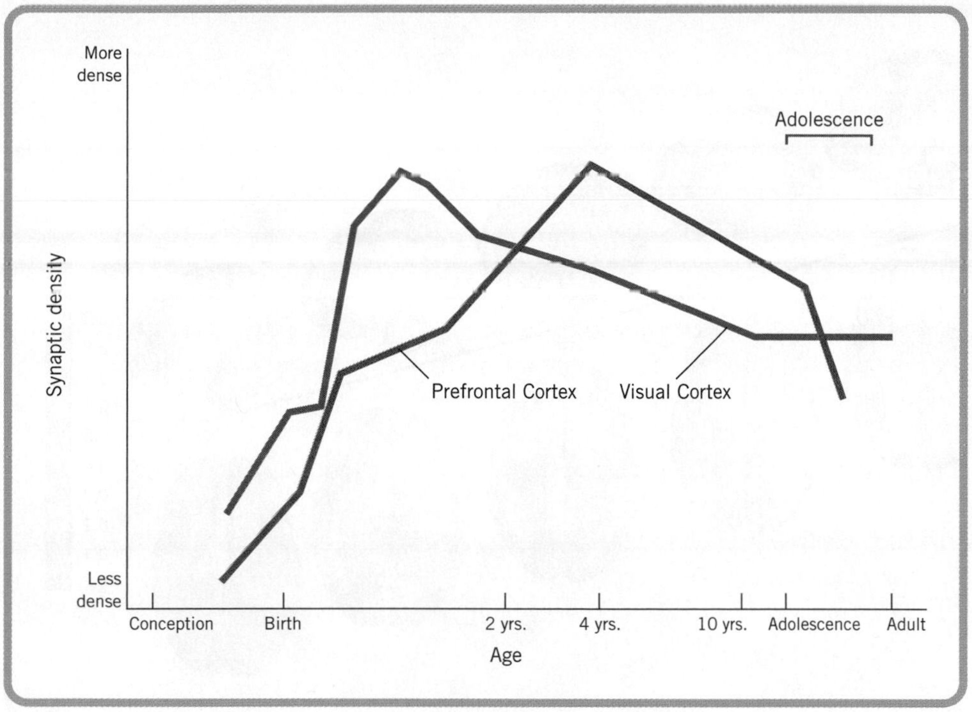

FIGURE 3.8 Synapse production and elimination Mean synaptic density (the number of synapses in a given space) first increases sharply as new synapses are overproduced and later declines gradually as excess synapses are eliminated. Note that the time scale is compressed at later stages. (From Huttenlocher & Dabholkar, 1997)

Approximately 40% of this great synaptic superfluity gets eliminated in a developmental process known as **synaptic pruning.** As you learned in the previous chapter, death is a normal part of development, and nowhere is that more evident than in the systematic pruning of excess synapses that continues for years after birth. This pruning occurs at different times in different areas of the brain (Huttenlocher & Dabholkar, 1997). You can see from Figure 3.8 that the elimination of synapses in the visual cortex begins near the end of the first year of life and continues until roughly 10 years of age, whereas synapse elimination in the prefrontal area shows a slower time course. During peak pruning periods, as many as 100,000 synapses may be eliminated per second (Kolb, 1995)!

In the past decade, researchers have discovered what they think may be a second wave of overproduction and pruning of synapses. The brain undergoes explosive changes in adolescence that are akin to those in the first few years of life (Giedd et al., 1999; Gogtay et al., 2004). Although the amount of white matter in the cortex shows a steady increase from childhood well into adulthood, the amount of gray matter increases dramatically starting around 11 or 12 years of age. The increase in gray matter proceeds rapidly, peaks around puberty, and then begins to decline as some of it is replaced by white matter (see Figure 3.9). The last area of the cortex to mature is the dorso-lateral prefrontal cortex, which is vital for regulating attention, controlling impulses, foreseeing consequences, setting priorities, and other higher-level functions. It does not reach adult dimensions until after the age of 20. It is believed that the rapid increase in gray matter may be related to the impulsive, irrational behavior characteristic of adolescents (including street-sign stealing) and that the subsequent decrease may underlie the development of impulse control, foresight, planfulness, and other aspects of mature adult cognition.

You will notice that Figure 3.8 does not show a second proliferation and reduction of synaptic density in adolescence. One of the reasons for this is that the figure is based on cross-sectional research in which the brains of individuals of different ages were examined only at autopsy. The new data showing substantial

synaptic pruning the normal developmental process through which synapses that are rarely activated are eliminated

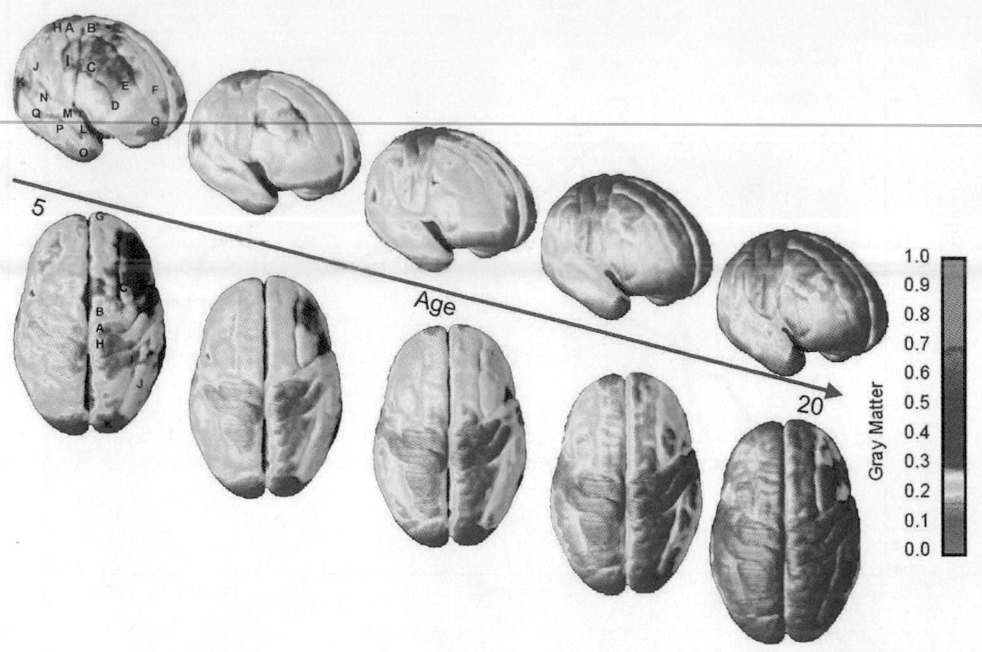

FIGURE 3.9 Brain maturation These views of the right side and top of the brain of 5- to 20-year-olds illustrate maturation over the surface of the cortex. The averaged MRI images come from participants whose brains were scanned repeatedly at 2-year intervals. The bluer the image, the more mature that part of the cortex is (i.e., the more gray matter has been replaced with white matter). Notice that the parts of the cortex associated with more basic functions (i.e., the sensory and motor areas toward the back) mature earlier than the areas involved in higher functions (i.e., attention, executive functioning). Notice particularly that the frontal areas, involved in executive functioning, approach maturity only in late adolescence. (From Gogtay et al., 2004)

development in the adolescent brain come from longitudinal research in which the same individuals' brains were scanned repeatedly over several years. The dramatic changes that appear in individuals were not evident when the brains of separate groups of different ages were studied. (See the discussion of developmental research designs in Chapter 1.)

The Importance of Experience

What determines which of the brain's excess synapses will be pruned and which maintained? Experience plays a central role in what is essentially a case of "use it or lose it." In a competitive process that has been dubbed "neural Darwinism" (Edelman, 1987), those synapses that are frequently activated are selectively preserved (Changeux & Danchin, 1976). The more often a synapse is activated, the stronger the connection becomes between the neurons involved. Conversely, when a synapse is rarely active, it is likely to disappear: the axon of one neuron withdraws and the dendritic spine of the other is "pruned away."

The obvious question now is, Why does the human brain—the product of millions of years of evolution—take such a devious developmental path, producing a huge excess of synapses, only to get rid of a substantial proportion of them? The answer appears to be evolutionary economy. The capacity of the brain to be molded or changed by experience, referred to as **plasticity,** means that less information needs to be encoded in the genes. This economizing may, in fact, be a necessity: although almost half of the entire set of human genes is thought to be involved in the formation and functioning of the nervous system, this number is enough to specify only a very small fraction of the normal complement of neurons and neural connections. To complete the final wiring of the brain, nurture joins forces with nature.

plasticity the capacity of the brain to be affected by experience

The collaboration between nature and nurture in building the brain occurs differently for two kinds of plasticity. One kind involves the general experiences that almost all normal infants have just by virtue of being human. The second kind involves specific, idiosyncratic experiences that children have as a result of their particular life circumstances—such as growing up in the United States or in the Amazon rain forest, experiencing frequent cuddling or abuse, being an only child or one of many siblings, and so on.

Experience-Expectant Processes

William Greenough refers to the role of general human experience in shaping brain development as **experience-expectant plasticity.** According to this view, the normal wiring of the brain is in part a result of the kinds of general experiences that have been present throughout human evolution, experiences that every human who inhabits any reasonably normal environment will have—patterned visual stimulation, voices and other sounds, movement and manipulation, and so forth (Greenough & Black, 1992). Consequently, the brain can "expect" input from these reliable sources to fine-tune its circuitry, as synapses that are frequently activated are strengthened and stabilized and those that are rarely activated are "pruned." Thus, our *experience* of the external world plays a fundamental role in shaping the most basic aspects of the *structure* of our brain.

One fundamental benefit of experience-expectant plasticity is that, because experience helps shape the brain, fewer genes need to be dedicated to normal development. Another is that the brain is better able to recover from brain injury, as other areas can assume the function that would have been performed by the damaged area. The younger the brain when damaged, the more likely recovery is.

The downside of experience-expectant plasticity is that it is accompanied by *vulnerability*. If for some reason the experience that the developing brain is "expecting" to fine-tune its circuits is not present, whether because of inadequate stimulation or impaired sensory receptors, development may be compromised. A good example of this vulnerablility comes from children who are born with cataracts that obscure their vision. The longer a cataract remains in place after birth, the more impaired the child's visual acuity will be once it is removed. Dramatic improvement typically follows early removal, although some aspects of visual processing (especially of faces) remain affected (LeGrand, Mondloch, Maurer, & Brent, 2003; Maurer & Lewis, 2001; Maurer, Lewis, Brent, & Levin, 1999). Presumably, the lasting deficits of late cataract removal occur because synapses that would normally have been activated by visual stimulation after birth were pruned due to the lack of that stimulation.

When an expected form of sensory experience is absent, what happens to areas of the brain that normally would have become specialized as a result of that experience? A wealth of data from animals indicates that such areas can become at least partially reorganized to serve some other function. Evidence of such plasticity and reorganization in humans comes from Helen Neville's (1990) studies of congenitally deaf adults who, as children, had learned American Sign Language (ASL), a full-fledged, visually based, language. Deaf individuals rely heavily on peripheral vision for language processing; they typically look into the eyes of a person who is signing to them, while using their peripheral vision to monitor the hand and arm motions of the signer. ERP recordings of brain activity (see Box 3.3) showed that deaf individuals' responses to peripheral visual stimuli are several times stronger than those of hearing people. In addition, their responses are distributed differently

experience-expectant plasticity the process through which the normal wiring of the brain occurs in part as a result of experiences that every human who inhabits any reasonably normal environment will have across brain regions. Thus, due to the lack of auditory experience, brain systems that would normally be involved in hearing and in spoken-language processing become organized to process visual information instead.

Similar evidence of early brain reorganization comes from research with blind adults. When tested for their ability to discriminate changes in musical pitch, adults who were born blind or became blind quite early performed much better than those who had become blind later in life (Gougoux et al., 2004). Presumably, connections between visual and auditory cortex were preserved in individuals with early-onset blindness, giving them extra "brain power" to apply to the auditory task. Consistent with this idea, brain-imaging research suggests that parts of the visual cortex contribute to superior sound localization ability in adults with early-onset blindness. A related result is that congenitally blind individuals show activation in the "visual" cortex when reading Braille (Sadato, Pascual-Leone, Grafman, & Deiber, 1998).

Sensitive periods As suggested by the foregoing examples, a key element in experience-expectant plasticity is timing. There are a few sensitive periods when the human brain is especially sensitive to particular kinds of external stimuli. It is as though a time window were temporarily opened, inviting environmental input to help organize the brain. Gradually, the window closes. The neural organization that occurs (or does not occur) during sensitive periods is typically irreversible.

As we discussed in Chapter 1, the extreme deprivation that the Romanian orphans suffered early in life, when children normally experience a wealth of social and other environmental stimulation, is considered by some to be an example of a sensitive-period effect. Some investigators speculate that adolescence, when rapid changes are occurring in the brain, may be another sensitive period for various aspects of development.

Experience-Dependent Processes

The brain is also sculpted by idiosyncratic experience through what Greenough calls **experience-dependent plasticity.** Neural connections are created and reorganized throughout life as a function of an individual's experiences. (If you remember anything of what you have been reading in this chapter, it's because you have formed new neural connections.)

The role of experience-dependent plasticity is revealed in comparisons of animals who are reared either in complex environments full of objects to explore or in bare laboratory cages. The brains of rats (and cats and monkeys) that grow up in a complex environment have more dendritic spines on their cortical neurons, more synapses per neuron, and more synapses overall, as well as a generally thicker cortex and more of the supportive tissues (such as blood vessels and glial cells) that maximize neuronal and synaptic function. All this extra hardware seems to have a payoff: rats reared in a complex environment perform better in a variety of learning tasks (e.g., Juraska, Henderson, & Muller, 1984).

Highly specific effects of experience on brain structure also occur. For example, rats that are trained to use just one forelimb to get a food reward have increased dendritic material in the particular area of the motor cortex that controls the movement of the trained limb (Greenough, Larson, & Withers, 1985). In humans, research on musicians has revealed that, compared with a control group, violinists and cellists had increased cortical representation of the fingers of the left

experience-dependent plasticity the process through which neural connections are created and reorganized throughout life as a function of an individual's experiences

BILL GREENOUGH

As a result of growing up in a complex environment full of stimulating objects to explore and challenges to master, the brains of these rats will contain more synapses than if they had been reared in unstimulating laboratory cages.

hand (Elbert, Pantev, Wienbruch, Rockstroh, & Taub, 1995). In other words, after years of practice, more cortical cells were devoted to receiving input from and controlling the fingers that manipulate the strings of the instruments. Similarly, in skilled Braille readers, the cortical representation of the left hand—the hand they use to read Braille text—is enlarged (Pascual-Leone et al., 1993).

Effects of specific experience are also evident in fMRI studies of individuals with *dyslexia,* a severe reading problem in people with normal intelligence and schooling (see page 327). One example involves a remedial reading program in which 2nd and 3rd graders with dyslexia received training in recognizing the correspondence between speech sounds and letters (Blachman et al., 2004). After the training, not only did the children show marked improvement in their reading ability, but fMRI imaging revealed increased activity in their left-brain areas that was similar to the activity in the brains of good readers. The specific effects of one's reading experience also show up in the fact that distinctly different brain networks are involved in reading Chinese characters versus an alphabetic script (such as English). Research using fMRI scans has revealed that the pattern of brain activity associated with dyslexia in 10- to 12-year-old Chinese children is different from that seen in dyslexic English readers (Siok, Perfetti, Jin, & Tan, 2004).

How would the cortical representations of their hands differ for these professional musicians?

DAVE ZAJAC, *THE HERALD* / AP / WIDE WORLD PHOTOS

CALEB RAYNE / *BANGOR DAILY NEWS* / THE IMAGE WORKS

Brain Damage and Recovery

As noted previously, because of its plasticity early in life, the brain can become rewired—at least to some degree—after suffering damage. Thus, in certain respects, children who suffer from brain damage have a better chance of recovering lost function than do adults who suffer similar damage. The strongest evidence for this comes from young children who suffer damage to the language area of the cortex. These children generally recover and rarely have aphasia—or loss of language—later in life. This is because after the damage has occurred, language functions shift to other areas in the young brain. As a result, language is spared. In contrast, adults who sustain the same type of brain damage undergo no such reorganization of language functions and may have a permanent loss in the ability to comprehend or produce speech. Greater recovery from early brain injury has also been observed for functions other than language. For example, producing appropriate facial expressions is more difficult for adults who had damage to the frontal area of the cortex during adulthood than for adults whose frontal lobe injury occurred in childhood (Kolb, 1995).

It is not always true, however, that the chance of recovery from early brain injury is greater than it is for later injury. Likelihood of recovery depends on how extensive the damage is and what aspect of brain development is occurring at the time of the damage. Consider, for example, the offspring of Japanese women who, while pregnant, were exposed to massive levels of radiation from the atomic bombs dropped on Hiroshima and Nagasaki in 1945. The rate of mental retardation was much higher for surviving children whose exposure had occurred very early in prenatal development, during the time of rapid neurogenesis and migration of neurons (Otake & Schull, 1984). Similarly, brain injury during the first year of life generally results in more severe impairment in IQ than does later comparable injury (Kolb, 1995).

Furthermore, even when children appear to have made a full recovery from an early brain injury, deficits may emerge later. This was demonstrated in a study in which cognitive performance was compared for a group of children who had been born with cerebral damage and a control group of children with no brain damage (Banich, Levine, Kim, & Huttenlocher, 1990). As Figure 3.10 shows, the two groups of children did not differ in their performance on two subscales of an IQ test at 6 years of age. However, as the normal children's performance improved

FIGURE 3.10 Emergent effects of early brain damage At 6 years of age, children with congenital brain damage scored the same as normal children on two subscales of an intelligence test. However, the children with brain damage failed to improve and fell progressively farther behind the normal children, so that by adolescence there were large differences between the two groups. (Data from Banich et al., 1990; figure from Kolb, 1995)

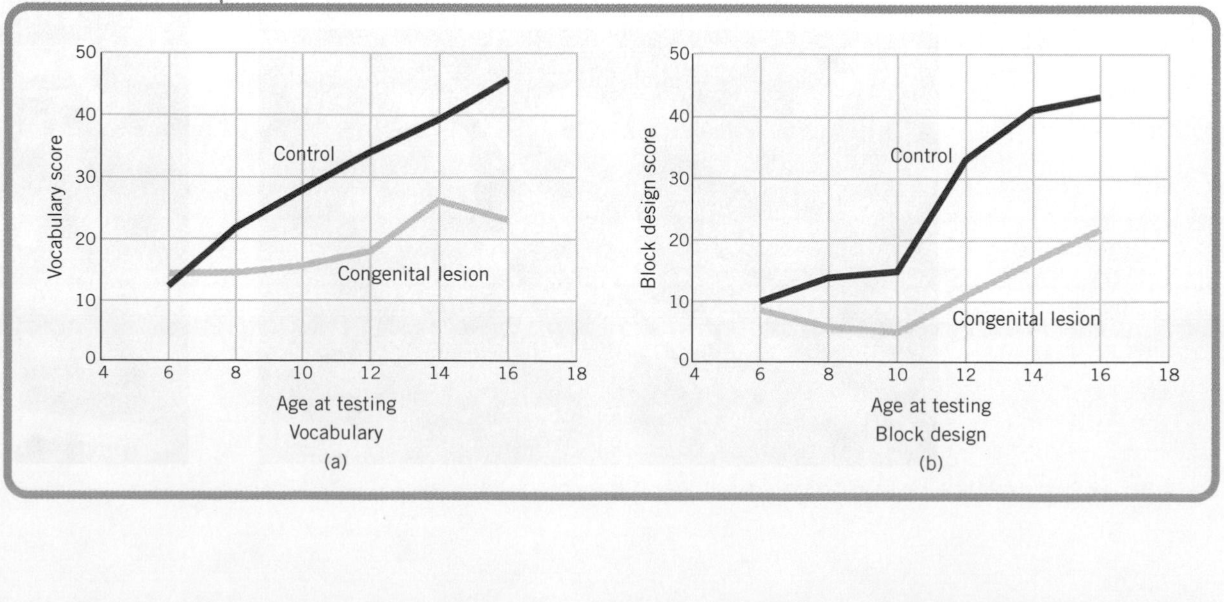

with age, that of the brain-damaged children did not, and they fell progressively behind. This result illustrates the difficulty of predicting the development of children with cerebral injuries; behavior that appears normal early on may deteriorate.

Based on these various aspects of plasticity, we can generalize that the worst time to suffer brain damage is very early, during prenatal development and the first year after birth, when neurogenesis is occurring and basic brain structures are being formed. The "best" time appears to be in early childhood, when synapse generation and pruning are occurring—that is, when plasticity is highest—making rewiring of the brain and hence recovery of function possible.

review:

Nature and nurture cooperate in the construction of the human brain. Some important brain structures include the neurons, which communicate with one another at synapses; the cortex, in which different functions are localized in different areas; and the cerebral hemispheres, which are specialized for different kinds of processing. The processes involved in the development of the brain include neurogenesis and synaptogenesis, followed by the systematic elimination of some synapses and the preservation of others as a function of experience.

Two forms of plasticity contribute to the development of behavior. As a result of experience-expectant plasticity, the brain is shaped by experiences that are available to every normal individual in interaction with every normal environment. Through experience-dependent plasticity, the brain is also structured by an individual's idiosyncratic life experiences. Because of the importance of experience in brain development, sensitive periods exist during which specific experience must be present for normal development. Timing is also a crucial factor in the ultimate impact of brain damage.

The Body: Physical Growth and Development

In Chapter 1, we emphasized the multiple contexts in which development occurs. Here we focus on the most immediate context for development—the body itself. Everything we think, feel, say, and do involves our physical selves; behavior is embodied, and changes in the body lead to changes in behavior. In this section, we present a brief overview of some aspects of physical growth, including some of the factors that can disrupt normal development. Nutritional behavior, a vital aspect of physical development, is featured as we consider the regulation of eating. We concentrate particularly on one of the consequences of poor regulation—obesity. Finally, we focus on the opposite problem—undernutrition.

Growth and Maturation

Compared with most other species, humans undergo a prolonged period of physical growth. The body grows and develops for 20% of the human life span, whereas mice, for example, grow during only 2% of their life span. Figure 3.11 shows the most obvious aspects of physical growth: we get 3 times taller and 15 to 20 times heavier between birth and age 20. The figure shows averages, of course, and there are obviously great individual differences in height and weight, as well as in the timing of physical development.

Growth is uneven over time, as you can tell from the differences in the slopes in Figure 3.11. The slopes are steepest when the most rapid growth is occurring—in the first two years and in early adolescence. Early on, boys and girls grow at

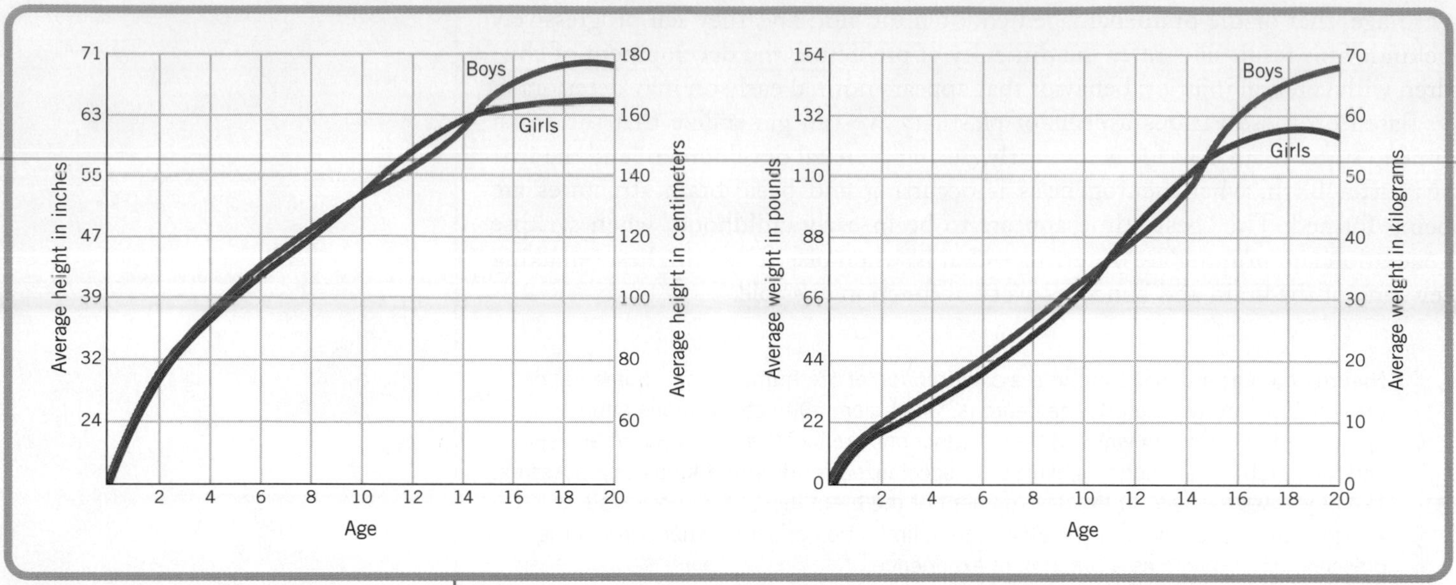

FIGURE 3.11 Growth curves Growth curves for height and weight from birth to 20 years of age. The steeper the slope, the more rapid the change in height or weight. These curves are based on the measurements of 175 well-nourished Americans; very different patterns would be observed for individuals developing in poorer areas of the world. (From R. M. Malina, 1975)

roughly the same rate, and they are essentially equal in height and weight until around 10 to 12 years of age. Then girls experience their adolescent growth spurt, at the end of which they are somewhat taller and heavier than boys. (Remember those awkward middle-school years when the girls towered over the boys, much to the discomfort of both?) Adolescent boys experience their growth spurt about two years after the girls, permanently passing them in both height and weight. Full height is achieved, on average, by around the age of 15½ for girls and 17½ for boys.

Growth is also uneven across the different parts of the body. Following the principle of cephalocaudal development described in Chapter 2, the head region is initially relatively large—fully 50% of body length at 2 months of age—but only about 10% of body length in adulthood. The gawkiness of young adolescents stems in part from the fact that their growth spurt begins with dramatic increases in the size of the hands and feet; it's easy to trip over your own feet when they are disproportionately larger than the rest of you.

Body composition also changes with age. The proportion of body fat is highest in infancy, gradually declining thereafter until around 6 to 8 years of age. In adolescence, it decreases in boys but increases in girls, and that increase helps trigger the onset of menstruation. The proportion of muscle grows slowly until adolescence, when it increases dramatically, especially in boys.

Variability

There is great variability across individuals and groups in all aspects of physical development, as reflected in the following examples. The average child growing up in North America or northern Europe is around 4 inches taller than the average child in Kenya, India, or New Guinea (Eveleth & Tanner, 1990). In the United States, the rate of maturation is generally somewhat faster for African-American children than for their Euro-American peers.

This variability in physical development is due to both genetic and environmental factors. Genes affect growth and sexual maturation in large part by influencing the production of hormones, especially growth hormone (secreted by the pituitary gland) and thyroxine (released by the thyroid gland). The influence of environmental factors is particularly evident in **secular trends,** marked changes in physical development that have occurred over generations. In contemporary industrialized nations, adults are several inches taller than their same-sex great-grandparents were. This change is assumed to have resulted primarily from improvements in nutrition and general health. Another secular trend in the United States today involves girls' beginning to menstruate a few years earlier than their ancestors did, a change attributed to the general improvement in nutritional status of the population.

Environmental factors can also play a role in disturbances of normal growth. For example, severe chronic stress, such as that associated with a home environment involving serious marital discord, alcoholism, or child abuse, can impair growth by lowering the pituitary gland's production of growth hormone (Powell, Brasel, & Blizzard, 1967). A combination of genetic and environmental factors is apparently involved in nonorganic **failure-to-thrive (FTT),** a condition in which infants become malnourished and fail to grow or gain weight for no obvious medical reason. FTT is associated with disturbances in mother–infant interaction that are thought to stem from characteristics of both child and mother (Bithoney & Newberger, 1987; Drotar, 1992). Some mothers experience difficulty and frustration coping with infants who, for example, do not display much interest in food or who may have trouble staying awake to feed. The frustrated mother of a very poor eater may "run out of tricks" to get her baby to eat, eventuating in the child's becoming malnourished (Maldonado-Duran, 2000). If the parents develop improved strategies for coping with their child's feeding problems and the chronically stressful situation is improved, the infant is likely to show quick catch-up growth.

secular trends marked changes in physical development that have occurred over generations

failure-to-thrive (nonorganic) (FTT) a condition in which infants become malnourished and fail to grow or gain weight for no obvious medical reason

Nutritional Behavior

The health of our bodies depends on what we put into them, including the amount and kind of food we eat. Thus, the development of eating or nutritional behavior is a crucial aspect of child development from infancy onward.

Infant Feeding

Like all mammals, human newborns obtain life-sustaining nourishment through suckling, although they require more assistance in this endeavor than do most other mammals. Throughout nearly the entire history of the human species, the only or primary source of nourishment for infants was breast milk. Mother's milk has many virtues (Newman, 1995). It is naturally free of bacteria, strengthens the infant's immune system, and contains the mother's antibodies against infectious agents the baby is likely to encounter after birth. However, in spite of the well-established nutritional superiority of breast milk, as well as the fact that it is free, the majority of infants in the United States are exclusively or predominantly formula-fed.

In developed countries, infant formula can support normal growth and development, although with a somewhat higher rate of infections than with breast milk. In undeveloped countries, however, formula feeding can exact a costly toll. Much of the world does not have safe water, so infant formula is often mixed with polluted water in unsanitary containers. Furthermore, poor, uneducated parents often dilute the formula in an effort to make the expensive powder last longer. In

RICK GOMEZ/CORBIS

By breastfeeding her infant, this mother is providing her baby with the many advantages breast milk has over formula.

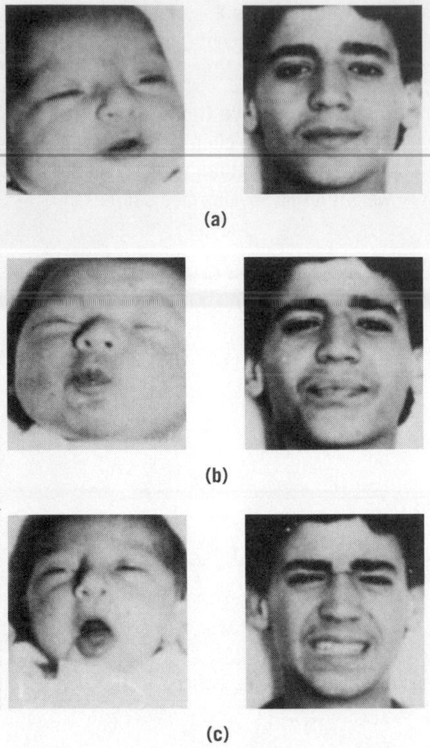

FIGURE 3.12 Taste preferences Taste preferences and reactions to different flavors are very similar in newborns and adults. (a) A sweet solution evokes a hint of a smile, (b) a sour solution causes a pucker, and (c) a bitter solution elicits a grimace.

such circumstances, parents' attempts to promote the health of their babies end up having the opposite effect (Popkin & Doan, 1990).

Development of Food Preferences and the Regulation of Eating

Food preferences are a primary determinant of what we eat throughout life, and some of these preferences are clearly innate. Figure 3.12 depicts some of the unlearned, reflexive facial expressions that newborns as well as adults make in response to three basic tastes—sweet, sour, and bitter (Rosenstein & Oster, 1988; Steiner, 1979). Newborns' strong preference for sweetness is reflected both in their smiling in response to sweet flavors and in the fact that they will drink larger quantities of sweetened water than plain water. These innate preferences may have an evolutionary origin, since poisonous substances are often bitter or sour but almost never sweet.

Infants' taste sensitivity is evident in their reactions to their mother's milk, which can take on the flavor of what she eats. Babies nurse longer and take more breast milk when their mother has ingested either garlic or vanilla flavors, but they drink less breast milk after she has downed a beer (Menella & Beauchamp, 1993a, 1993b, 1996).

From infancy on, experience has a major influence on what foods children like and dislike and on what and how much they eat. For example, preschool children's liking for particular foods increases if they observe other children enjoying them (Birch & Fisher, 1996). Children's eating is also influenced by what foods their parents encourage and discourage. This influence does not always work in the way the parents intend, however. For example, standard parental strategies of cajoling and bribing young children to eat new or healthier foods—"If you eat your spinach, you can have some ice cream"—can be doubly counterproductive. The most probable result is that the child will dislike the healthy food even more and have an even stronger preference for the sweet, fatty food used as a reward (Birch & Fisher, 1996). (See Box 3.4 for recommendations on feeding young children.)

Many parents become needlessly concerned with how much their young children eat. They might, however, put less effort into trying to control their children's eating behavior if they realized that young children are actually quite good at regulating the amount of food they consume. Research has shown that preschool children adjust how much they eat at a given time based on how much they consumed earlier. For example, children were found to eat less for lunch if they had been served a snack earlier than if they had not had the snack (Birch & Fisher, 1996). (In contrast, a group of adults ate pretty much the same amount of a meal whether they had a snack earlier or not.)

In general, children whose parents try to control their eating habits tend to be worse at regulating their food intake themselves than are children whose parents allow them more control over what and how much they eat (Johnson & Birch, 1994). Parents' overregulation of their children's eating behavior can have continuing effects. Adults who reported that their parents used food to control their behavior were more likely to be struggling with their weight and with binge eating (Puhl & Schwartz, 2003).

Obesity

So many people have difficulty regulating their eating appropriately that the most common dietary problems in the United States are related to overeating and its

applications 3.4

Eat Your Peas, Please

Parents can have a powerful impact on what their young children eat, as well as on their children's ability to regulate their own diet in the long run. Research has established that some common parental practices have unintended negative consequences on children's self-regulation and that other approaches are beneficial. The accompanying list of dos and don'ts are adapted from Birch and Fisher (1996).

It is unlikely that changes in parents' behavior alone will be enough to counter the soaring rates of childhood obesity. Fortunately, many schools have begun serving more nutritious foods, including those available in vending machines. Another helpful step, proposed by the Institute of Medicine (2004), would be for the food, beverage, and entertainment industries to discontinue targeting their advertising of high-fat, high-sugar foods and drinks to children and adolescents.

Dos and Don'ts on Feeding Children (Adapted from Birch & Fisher, 1996)

DO

- Take responsibility for what foods are available to your child.
  - Make sure the child has access primarily to healthful foods.
  - Allow some junk foods, but only a limited amount. The probable result of prohibiting all junk food is increased liking for it.
- Expect an initial negative reaction to any new food.
  - Present new foods repeatedly, encouraging your child to take a small bite.
  - Communicate an expectation that the child will try new foods.
- Assume your child can appropriately regulate how much to eat from a variety of nutritious foods.
- Expect variability in the amount and kind of food eaten at a given meal; children vary widely in how much they eat from meal to meal, but they eat consistent amounts over 24-hour periods.
- Encourage your child to learn to regulate his or her own eating behavior.

DON'T

- Don't let your child select what to eat from an unlimited set of foods.
  - Be aware that the probable result of giving children full control over their food choices is a diet heavy in sugar and fat.
- Don't assume from an initial rejection of a new food that it will continue to be rejected.
- Don't force or coerce your child to eat; any short-term success will be negated by the creation of counterproductive likes and dislikes.
- Don't expect consistency in how much your child eats from one meal to the next.
- Don't try to control your child's eating behavior.
  - Don't force your child to eat a specific amount that you think he or she should consume; doing so undermines children's ability to regulate how much they eat.
  - Don't reward your child for eating nonpreferred foods; this will decrease your child's liking for them even further.
  - Don't use a preferred but nonnutritious food as a reward; doing so will probably make your child like it even more.

many consequences. In an epidemic of obesity, over two-thirds of American adults are currently considered to be overweight, and almost half of them are obese. Fully 5% of all American adults are *extremely* obese. Obesity is an expanding problem, not just among Americans but also among indigenous people in many developing countries (Abelson & Kennedy, 2004). This situation exists largely because societies all over the world are increasingly adopting a "Western diet" of foods high in fat and sugar and low in fiber. Fast-food restaurants have proliferated around the globe; indeed, after Santa Claus, Ronald McDonald is the second most recognized figure worldwide (Brownell, 2004).

The proportion of American children and adolescents who are overweight has *tripled* in the past four decades (see Figure 3.13), with the increase being especially marked for Latinos and African Americans. The outlook for these heavy children is troubling, because they are likely to struggle with weight problems throughout their lives. Further, there is a good chance that they will adopt a variety of unhealthy measures to fight their weight problems—skipping meals, fasting, smoking, taking diet pills, and even undergoing liposuction, all of which can lead to further health problems.

FIGURE 3.13 Overweight—a growing problem The proportion of children in the United States who are overweight has tripled in the past four decades.

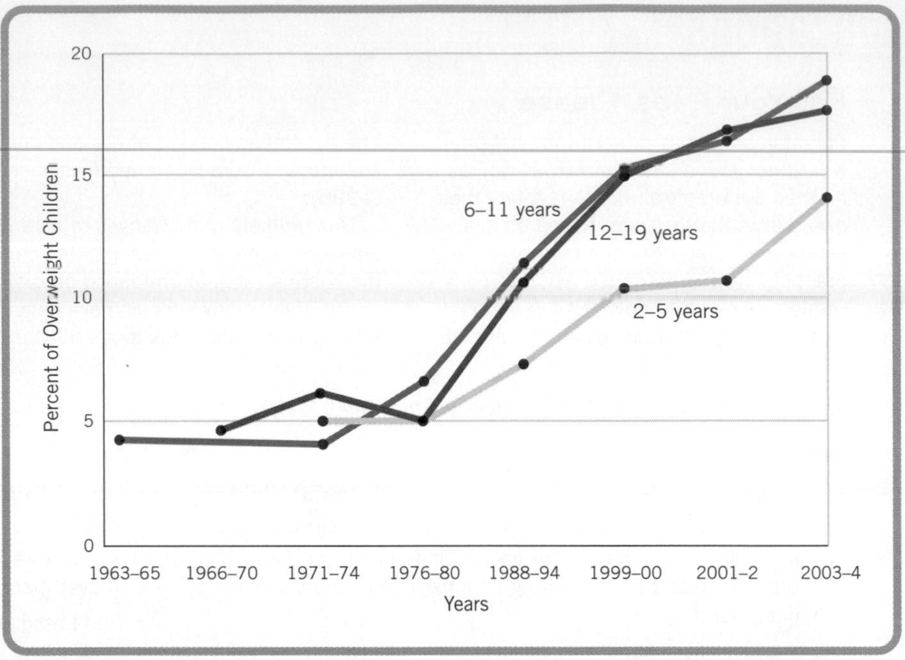

Source: National Health Examination Surveys II (ages 6–11) and III (ages 12–17). National Health and Nutrition Examination Surveys I, II, III, and 1999–2004, NCHS, CDC.

Two important questions need to be addressed: Why do some people but not others become overweight, and why is there an epidemic of obesity? As Figure 3.14 suggests, both genetic and environmental factors play roles. Genetic factors are reflected in the findings (1) that the weight of adopted children is more strongly correlated with that of their biological parents than with that of their adoptive parents, and (2) that identical twins, including those reared apart, are more similar in weight than fraternal twins are (Plomin et al., 1997). Even the *speed* of eating, which is related both to how much is eaten in a given meal and to the weight of the eater, shows substantial heritability (Llewellyn et al., 2008). Thus, genes affect individuals' susceptibility to gaining weight and how much food they eat in the first place, making it relatively difficult or easy for them to avoid becoming part of the obesity epidemic.

NATIONAL GALLERY OF CANADA, OTTAWA: JACOB JORDAENS, AS THE OLD SING, SO THE YOUNG PIPE, 1638

FIGURE 3.14 "Fat runs in families" The overweight diners in this painting are all genetically related, and they are all overeating.

Environmental influences also play a major role in this epidemic, as is obvious from the fact that a much higher proportion of the population of the United States is overweight now than in previous times. Indeed, some have argued that becoming obese in the United States could be considered a normal response to the contemporary American taste for high-fat, high-sugar foods in ever larger portion sizes (Brownell, 2003; see Figure 3.14). A host of other factors fuel the ever-expanding waistlines of today's children. Families more often eat out, frequently at fast-food or "all you can eat" buffet-style restaurants where they consume large portions of relatively high-calorie foods (Krishnamoorthy, Hart, & Jelalian, 2006). Children get less exercise as a result of rarely walking to school. At school, they frequently have no physical education programs or recess activities and are often able to purchase cafeteria lunches consisting of high-fat foods (e.g., pizza, hamburgers) and high-calorie soft drinks. Young couch potatoes, many of whom spend more than 5 hours a day in front of the TV consuming junk food as they are subjected to a barrage of advertisements for more high-fat, nonnutritious fast food, are much more likely to be obese than are children who watch for 2 hours or less (Robinson, 2001).

TRAE PATTON / NBCU PHOTO BANK

By exercising together, this overweight mother and daughter may be taking one of the most effective steps they can toward weight control.

Obesity puts people at risk for a wide variety of serious health problems, including heart disease and diabetes. In addition, many obese people suffer the consequences of negative stereotypes and discrimination in areas ranging from housing to college admissions (Friedman & Brownell, 1995). A particularly striking example is the case of a Tennessee woman who was refused a seat in a movie theater on the grounds that she constituted a fire hazard (Allison & Pi-Sunyer, 1994).

Overweight children and teenagers suffer a variety of other social problems as well. For example, overweight adolescents tend to be either socially isolated or on the fringe of their social networks (Strauss & Pollack, 2003). Also, teens who reported being teased about their weight had considered suicide more often than had their slimmer peers (M. Eisenberg, Neumark-Sztainer, & Story, 2003).

There is, unfortunately, no easy cure for obesity in children. Some long-term success has been reported for a family-based weight-loss program in which both parents and children modified their eating and exercise patterns and reinforced each others' progress (Epstein et al., 1994). Support from family and friends is important in children's successful maintenance of changes in their eating behavior and activity level. Some hope for the general obesity problem comes from the fact that public awareness is now focused on the severity of the problem and the many factors that contribute to it.

Undernutrition

At the same time that many people in relatively rich countries are overeating their way to poor health, the health of people in developing nations is compromised by their not getting enough to eat. Fully one-fourth of all children (and 40% of those under the age of 5) living in these countries are undernourished (UNICEF, 2007). The nutritional deficits they experience can involve an inadequate supply of total calories, of protein, of vitamins and minerals, or any combination of these deficiencies. Severe malnutrition of infants and young children is most common in developing and/or war-torn countries.

Undernutrition and malnutrition are virtually always associated with poverty and myriad related factors, ranging from limited access to health care (the primary cause in the United States) to warfare, famine, and natural disasters. The interaction of malnutrition with poverty and other forms of deprivation adversely affects

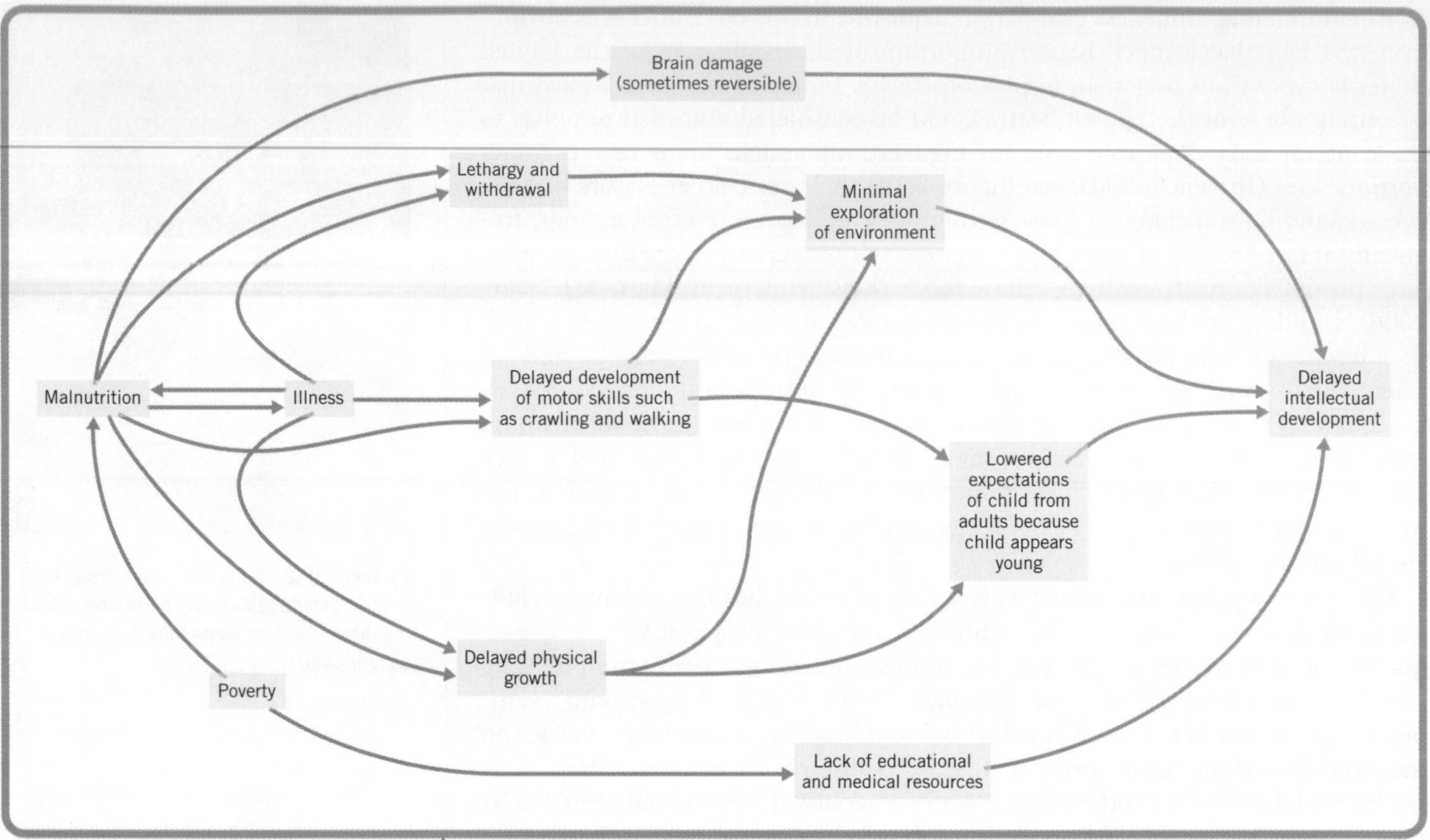

FIGURE 3.15 Malnutrition and cognitive development Malnutrition, combined with poverty, affects many aspects of development and can lead to impaired cognitive abilities. (From Brown & Pollitt, 1996)

all aspects of development. Figure 3.15 presents a model of how the complex interaction of these multiple factors impairs cognitive development (Brown & Pollitt, 1996). As you can see, malnutrition can have direct effects on the structural development of the brain, general energy level, susceptibility to infection, and physical growth. With inadequate energy, malnourished children tend to reduce their energy expenditure and withdraw from stimulation, making them quiet and passive in general, less responsive in social interactions, less attentive in school, and so on. Apathy, slowed growth, and delayed development of motor skills also retard the children's exploration of the environment, further limiting their opportunities to learn.

Additionally, because of their small size and delayed development, malnourished children may be perceived as being younger and less competent than they actually are, leading adults to expect and demand less of them. When relatively little is expected from them by their parents and teachers, they are unlikely to derive the same benefits from attending school that a healthy child gets, thereby losing out further on one of the most important sources of intellectual growth. All these factors, exacerbated by a generally impoverished environment and inadequate resources, converge to lead to delayed intellectual development.

Can anything be done to help malnourished and undernourished youngsters? Because so many interacting factors are involved in the problem, it is not easy to do so, but neither is it impossible, as shown by several large-scale intervention efforts throughout the world. For example, in one long-term project led by Ernesto Pollitt in Guatemala, a high-protein dietary supplement administered starting in infancy correlated with an increase in performance on tests of cognitive functioning in adolescence (Pollitt, Gorman, Engle, Martorell, & Rivera, 1993). Although it is possible to improve the developmental status of malnourished children, it would be better, both for the children themselves and for society in general, to prevent the occurrence of malnutrition in the first place. As Brown and Pollitt (1996) note: "On balance, it seems clear that prevention of malnutrition among young children remains the best policy—not only on moral grounds but on economic ones as well" (p. 702).

review:

Sound nutritional behavior is vital to general health. Preferences for certain foods are evident from birth on, and, as children develop, what they choose to eat is influenced by many factors, including the preferences of their friends and their parents' attempts to influence their eating behavior. Obesity among both adults and children has increased dramatically in the United States and much of the rest of the world in recent decades, as exposure to rich foods in large portions has increased and physical activity has decreased. However, throughout the world, the most common nutritional problem is undernutrition, which is very closely associated with poverty. The combination of malnutrition and poverty is particularly devastating to development.

Chapter Summary

Nature and Nurture

- The complex interplay of nature and nurture was the constant theme of this chapter. In the drama of development, genotype, phenotype, and environment all play starring roles, and the plot moves forward as they interact in many obvious and many not-so-obvious ways.
- The starting point for development is the genotype—the genes inherited at conception from one's parents. Only some of those genes are expressed in the phenotype, one's observable characteristics. Whether or not some genes are expressed at all is a function of dominance patterns. Gene expression, the switching on and off of genes over time, underlies many aspects of development.
- The eventual outcome of a given genotype is always contingent on the environment in which it develops. Parents and their behavior toward their children are a salient part of the children's environment. Parents' behavior toward their children is influenced by their own genotypes. Similarly, the child's development is influenced by the aspects of the environment he or she seeks out and the different responses the child's characteristics and behavior evoke from other people.
- The field of behavior genetics is concerned with the joint influence of genetic and environmental factors on behavior. Through the use of a variety of family-study designs, behavior geneticists have discovered a wide range of behavior patterns that "run in families." Many behavior geneticists use heritability estimates to statistically evaluate the relative contributions of heredity and environment to behavior.

Brain Development

- A burgeoning area of developmental research focuses on the development of the brain—the most complex structure in the known universe. Neurons are the basic units of the brain's informational system. These cells transmit information via electrical signals. Impulses are transmitted from one neuron to another at synapses.
- The most human part of the human brain is the cortex, because it is involved in a wide variety of higher mental functions. Different areas of the cortex are specialized for general behavioral categories. The cortex is divided into two cerebral hemispheres, each of which is specialized for certain modes of processing, a phenomenon known as cerebral lateralization.
- Brain development involves several processes, beginning with neurogenesis and differentiation of neurons. In synaptogenesis, an enormous profusion of connections among neurons is generated, starting prenatally and continuing for the first few years after birth. Through synaptic pruning, excess connections among neurons are eliminated.
- Experience plays a crucial role in the strengthening or elimination of synapses and hence in the normal wiring of the brain. The fine-tuning of the brain involves experience-expectant processes, in which existing synapses are preserved as a function of stimulation that virtually every human encounters, and experience-dependent processes, in which new connections are formed as a function of learning.
- Plasticity refers to the fact that nurture is the partner of nature in the normal development of the brain. This fact makes it possible in certain circumstances for the brain to rewire itself

in response to damage. It also makes the developing brain vulnerable to the absence of stimulation at sensitive periods in development.

- The ability of the brain to recover from injury depends on the age of the child. Very early damage, when neurogenesis and synaptogenesis are occurring, can have especially devastating effects. Damage during the preschool years, when synapse elimination is occurring, is less likely to have permanent harmful effects.

The Body: Physical Growth and Development

- Humans undergo a particularly prolonged period of physical growth, during which growth is uneven, proceeding more rapidly early in life and in adolescence. Secular trends have been observed in increases in average height and weight.
- Food preferences begin with innate responses by newborns to basic tastes, but additional preferences develop as a result of experience. Parents have a large impact on their children's ability to successfully regulate their own eating. Problems with the regulation of eating are evident in the United States, where an epidemic of obesity is clearly related to both environmental and genetic factors.
- In most of the rest of the world, the dominant problem is getting enough food, and nearly half of all the children in the world suffer from undernutrition. Inadequate nutrition is closely associated with poverty, and it leads to a variety of behavioral and physical problems in virtually every aspect of the child's life. Prevention of undernutrition is needed to allow millions of children to develop normal brains and bodies.

Critical Thinking Questions

1. A major focus of this chapter was the interaction of nature and nurture. Consider yourself and your family (regardless of whether you were raised by your biological parents). Identify some aspect of who you are that illustrates each of the four relations described in the text, and answer these questions. (a) How and when was your sex determined? (b) What are some alleles you are certain or relatively confident you share with other members of your family? (c) What might be an example of a gene–environment interaction in your parents' behavior toward you? (d) Give an example of your active selection of your own environment that might have influenced your subsequent development.
2. "50% of a person's IQ is due to heredity and 50% to environment." Discuss what is wrong with this statement, describing both what heritability estimates mean and what they do not mean.
3. Relate the developmental processes of synaptogenesis and synapse elimination to the concepts of experience-expectant and experience-dependent plasticity.
4. What aspects of brain development do researchers think may be related to the traits and behaviors of adolescents?
5. Think back over the last day or so. What aspects of your environment may relate to the epidemic of obesity described in this chapter?
6. Consider Figure 3.15, which addresses malnutrition and cognitive development. Imagine an undernourished 6-year-old child living in the United States. Go through the figure and generate a specific example of something that might happen to this child at each point in the diagram. Now do the same for a 6-year-old living in a poor, war-torn country.

Key Terms

genome, p. 85
genotype, p. 86
phenotype, p. 86
environment, p. 86
chromosomes, p. 87
DNA (deoxyribonucleic acid), p. 87
genes, p. 87
sex chromosomes, p. 87
mutation, p. 88
crossing over, p. 88
regulator genes, p. 89
alleles, p. 89
dominant allele, p. 89
recessive allele, p. 89
homozygous, p. 89
heterozygous, p. 89
polygenic inheritance, p. 90
norm of reaction, p. 90
phenylketonuria (PKU), p. 91
behavior genetics, p. 95
heritable, p. 96
multifactorial. p. 96
heritability, p. 98
neurons, p. 102

cell body, p. 102
dendrites, p. 102
axons, p. 102
synapses, p. 103
glial cells, p. 103
myelin sheath, p. 103
cerebral cortex, p. 103
lobes, p. 104
occipital lobe, p. 104
temporal lobe, p. 104
parietal lobe, p. 104
frontal lobe, p. 104
association areas, p. 104
cerebral hemispheres, p. 104
corpus callosum, p. 104
cerebral lateralization, p. 104
neurogenesis, p. 104
ERPs (event-related potentials), p. 106
spines, p. 108
myelination, p. 108
synaptogenesis, p. 108
synaptic pruning, p. 109
plasticity, p. 110
experience-expectant placticity, p. 111
experience-dependent plasticity, p. 112
secular trends, p. 117
failure-to-thrive (nonorganic) (FTT), p. 117

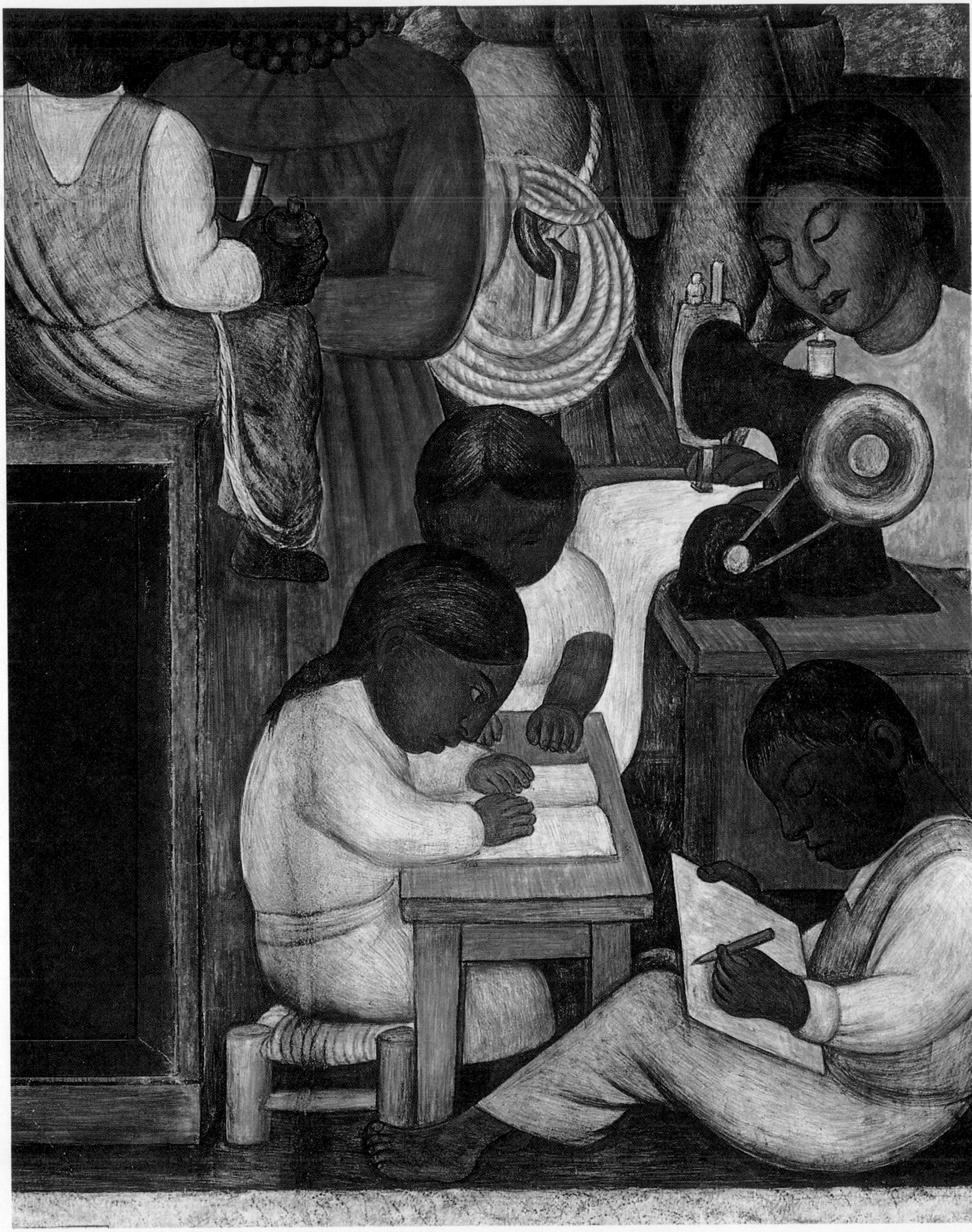

DIEGO RIVERA, *Fin del Corrido*, c. 1922–1928

4

Theories of Cognitive Development

THEMES

Nature and Nurture

The Active Child

Continuity/Discontinuity

Mechanisms of Change

The Sociocultural Context

Research and Children's Welfare

A 7-month-old boy, sitting on his father's lap, becomes intrigued with the father's glasses, grabs one side of the frame, and yanks it. The father says, "Ow!" and his son lets go, but then reaches up and yanks the frame again. The father readjusts the glasses, but his son again grasps them and yanks. How, the father wonders, can he prevent his son from continuing this annoying routine without causing him to start screaming? Fortunately, the father, a developmental psychologist, soon realizes that Jean Piaget's theory of cognitive development suggests a simple solution: put the glasses behind his back. According to Piaget's theory, removing an object from a young infant's sight should lead the infant to act as if the object never existed. The strategy works perfectly; after the father puts the glasses behind his back, his son shows no further interest in them and turns his attention elsewhere. The father silently thanks Piaget.

This experience, which one of us actually had, illustrates in a small way how understanding theories of child development can yield practical benefits. It also illustrates three broader advantages of knowing about such theories:

1. Developmental theories provide a framework for understanding important phenomena. Theories help to reveal the significance of what we observe about children, both in research studies and in everyday life. Someone who witnessed the glasses incident but who did not know about Piaget's theory might have found the experience amusing but insignificant. Seen in terms of Piaget's theory, however, this passing event exemplifies a very general and profoundly important developmental phenomenon: infants below 8 months of age react to the disappearance of an object as though they do not understand that the object still exists. In this manner, theories of child development place particular experiences and observations in a larger context and deepen our understanding of their meaning.

2. Developmental theories raise crucial questions about human nature. Piaget's theory about young infants' reactions to disappearing objects was based on his informal experiments with infants younger than 8 months of age. Piaget would cover one of their favorite objects with a cloth or otherwise put it out of sight and then wait to see if they tried to retrieve the object. They rarely did, leading Piaget to conclude that before the age of 8 months, infants do not realize that hidden objects still exist. Other researchers have challenged this explanation. They argue that infants younger than 8 months do in fact understand that hidden objects continue to exist but lack the memory or problem-solving skills necessary for using that understanding to retrieve hidden objects (Baillargeon, 1993). Despite these disagreements about how best to interpret young infants' failure to retrieve hidden objects, researchers agree that Piaget's theory raises a crucial question about human nature: Do infants realize from the first days of life that objects continue to exist when out of sight, or is this something that they learn later? More significant, do young infants understand that people continue to exist when they cannot be seen? Do they fear that Mom has disappeared when she is no longer in sight?

3. Developmental theories lead to a better understanding of children. Theories also stimulate new research that may support the theories' claims, fail to support them, or require refinements of them, thereby improving our understanding of children. For example, Piaget's ideas led Munakata and her colleagues (1997) to test whether 7-month-olds' failure to reach for hidden objects was due to their lacking the motivation or the reaching skill to retrieve them. To find out, the researchers created a situation similar to Piaget's object-permanence experiment, except that they placed the object, an attractive toy, under a transparent cover rather than under an opaque one. In this situation, infants quickly removed the cover and regained the toy, thus demonstrating that they were both motivated to obtain it and sufficiently skilled to do so. This finding seemed to support Piaget's original interpretation. In contrast, an experiment conducted by Diamond (1985) indicated a need to revise Piaget's theory. Using an opaque covering, as Piaget did, Diamond varied the amount of time between when the toy was hidden and when the infant was allowed to reach for it. She found that even 6-month-olds could locate the toy if allowed to reach immediately, that 7-month-olds could wait as long as 2 seconds and still succeed, that 8-month-olds could wait as long as 4 seconds and still succeed, and so on. Diamond's finding indicated that memory for the location of hidden objects, as well as the understanding that they continue to exist, is crucial to success on the task. In sum, theories of child development are useful because they provide frameworks for understanding important phenomena, raise fundamental questions about human nature, and motivate new research that increases understanding of children.

ELIZABETH CREWS

The author whose son loved to grab his glasses is not the only one who has encountered this problem. If the parent in this picture had the good fortune to have read this textbook, she may have solved the problem in the same way.

Because child development is such a complex and varied subject, no single theory accounts for all of it. The most informative current theories focus primarily either on cognitive development or on social development. Providing a good theoretical account of development in either of these areas is an immense challenge, because each of them spans a huge range of topics. Cognitive development includes the growth of such diverse capabilities as perception, attention, language, problem solving, reasoning, memory, conceptual understanding, and intelligence. Social development includes the growth of equally diverse areas: emotions, personality, relationships with peers and family members, self-understanding, aggression, and moral behavior. Given this immense range of developmental domains, it is easy to understand why no one theory has captured the entirety of child development.

Therefore, we present cognitive and social theories in separate chapters. We consider theories of cognitive development in this chapter, just before the chapters on specific areas of cognitive development, and consider theories of social development in Chapter 9, just before the chapters on specific areas of social development.

This chapter examines five theoretical perspectives on cognitive development that are particularly influential: the Piagetian perspective, the information-processing perspective, the core-knowledge perspective, the sociocultural perspective, and the dynamic-systems perspective. We consider each perspective's fundamental assumptions about children's nature, the central developmental issues on which the perspective focuses, and practical examples of the perspective's usefulness for helping children learn.

These five theoretical perspectives are influential in large part because they provide important insights into the basic developmental themes described in Chapter 1. Each perspective addresses all the themes to some extent, but each emphasizes different ones. For example, Piaget's theory focuses on *continuity/discontinuity* and the *active child,* whereas information-processing theories focus on *mechanisms of change* (Table 4.1). Together, the five perspectives allow a broader appreciation of cognitive development than any one of them does alone.

TABLE 4.1

Main Questions Addressed by Theories of Cognitive Development

Theory	Main Question Addressed
Piagetian	Nature–nurture, continuity/discontinuity, the active child
Information-processing	Nature–nurture, how change occurs
Core-knowledge	Nature–nurture, continuity/discontinuity
Sociocultural	Nature–nurture, influence of the sociocultural context, how change occurs
Dynamic-systems	Nature–nurture, the active child, how change occurs

Piaget's Theory

Jean Piaget's studies of cognitive development are a testimony to how much one person can contribute to a scientific field. Before his work began to appear in the early 1920s, there was no recognizable field of cognitive development. Nearly a century later, Piaget's theory remains the best-known cognitive developmental theory in a field replete with theories. What accounts for its longevity?

One reason is that Piaget's observations and descriptions of children vividly convey the flavor of their thinking at different ages. Another reason is the exceptional breadth of the theory. It extends from the first days of infancy through adolescence and examines topics as diverse as conceptualization of time, space, distance, and number; language use; memory; understanding of other people's perspectives; problem solving; and scientific reasoning. Even today, it remains the most encompassing theory of cognitive development. Yet a third source of its longevity is that it offers an intuitively plausible depiction of the interaction of nature and nurture in cognitive development, as well as of the continuities and discontinuities that characterize intellectual growth.

YVES DEBRAINE / BLACK STAR

Jean Piaget, whose work has had a profound influence on developmental psychology, observing children at play.

View of Children's Nature

Piaget's fundamental assumption about children was that from birth onward they are active mentally as well as physically, and that their activity greatly contributes to their own development. His approach is often labeled *constructivist,* because it depicts children as constructing knowledge for themselves in response to their experiences. Three of the most important of children's constructive processes, according to Piaget, are generating hypotheses, performing experiments, and drawing conclusions from observations. If this description reminds you of scientific problem solving, you are not alone: the "child as scientist" is the dominant metaphor in Piaget's theory. Consider this description of his infant son:

> Laurent is lying on his back. . . . He grasps in succession a celluloid swan, a box, etc., stretches out his arm and lets them fall. He distinctly varies the position of the fall. When the object falls in a new position (for example, on his pillow), he lets it fall two or three more times on the same place, as though to study the spatial relation.
>
> (Piaget, 1952b, pp. 268–269)

In simple activities such as Laurent's game of "drop the toy from different places and see what happens," Piaget perceived the beginning of scientific experimentation.

This example also illustrates a second basic Piagetian assumption: Children learn many important lessons on their own, rather than depending on instruction from adults or older children. To further illuminate this point, Piaget cited a friend's recollection from childhood:

> He was seated on the ground in his garden and he was counting pebbles. Now to count these pebbles he put them in a row and he counted them one, two, three up to 10. Then he finished counting them and started to count them in the other direction. He began by the end and once again he found that he had 10. He found this marvelous. . . . So he put them in a circle and counted them that way and found 10 once again.
>
> (Piaget, 1964, p. 12)

This incident also highlights a third basic assumption of Piaget's: Children are intrinsically motivated to learn and do not need rewards from adults to do so. When they acquire a new capability, they apply it as often as possible. They also reflect on the lessons of their experience, because they want to understand themselves and everything around them.

Central Developmental Issues

In addition to his view that children actively shape their own development, Piaget offered important insights regarding the roles of nature and nurture and of continuities and discontinuities in development.

Nature and Nurture

Piaget believed that nature and nurture interact to produce cognitive development. In his view, nurture includes not just the nurturing provided by parents and other caregivers but every experience the child encounters. Nature includes the child's maturing brain and body; the child's ability to perceive, act, and learn from experience; and the child's motivation to meet two basic functions that are central to cognitive growth: adaptation and organization. **Adaptation** is the tendency to respond to the demands of the environment in ways that meet one's goals. **Organization** is the tendency to integrate particular observations into coherent knowledge. Because both adaptation and organization involve children's response to experience, it can be said that part of children's nature is to respond to their nurture.

Sources of Continuity

Piaget depicted development as involving both continuities and discontinuities. The main sources of continuity are three processes—*assimilation, accommodation*, and *equilibration*—that work together from birth to propel development forward.

Assimilation is the process by which people incorporate incoming information into concepts they already understand. To illustrate, when one of our children was 2 years old, he saw a man who was bald on top of his head and had long frizzy hair on the sides. To his father's great embarrassment, the toddler gleefully shouted, "Clown, clown." (Actually, it sounded more like "Kown, kown.") The man apparently looked enough like a "kown" that the boy could assimilate him to his clown concept.

Accommodation is the process by which people adapt their current understandings in response to new experiences. In the "kown" incident, the boy's father explained to his son that the man was not a clown and that even though his hair looked like a clown's, he was not wearing a funny costume and was not doing silly things to make people laugh. With this new information, the boy was able to accommodate his clown concept to the standard one, allowing other men with bald pates and long side hair to pass by in peace.

Equilibration is the process by which people balance assimilation and accommodation to create stable understanding. Equilibration includes three phases. First, children are satisfied with their understanding of a phenomenon; Piaget labeled this a state of *equilibrium*, because children do not see any discrepancies between their observations and their understanding of the phenomenon. Then, new information leads children to perceive that their understanding is inadequate. Piaget said that children at this point are in a state of *disequilibrium*, because they recognize shortcomings in their understanding of the phenomenon but cannot generate a superior alternative. Finally, children develop a more sophisticated understanding that eliminates the shortcomings of the old one. This new understanding provides

adaptation the tendency to respond to the demands of the environment in ways that meet one's goals

organization the tendency to integrate particular observations into coherent knowledge

assimilation the process by which people translate incoming information into a form that fits concepts they already understand

accommodation the process by which people adapt current knowledge structures in response to new experiences

equilibration the process by which children (or other people) balance assimilation and accommodation to create stable understanding

EVERETT COLLECTION

Perhaps toddlers yelling "Kown, kown" set Larry on his career path.

a more stable equilibrium, in the sense that a broader range of observations can be understood within it.

To illustrate how equilibration works, suppose that a 5-year-old girl believes that only animals are living things, because only they can move in ways that help them survive. (This is, in fact, what most 4- to 7-year-olds in a wide range of cultures believe [Inagaki & Hatano, 2008]; they know that plants grow and need food, but they do not conclude from this knowledge that plants are living things.) Sooner or later, the girl will realize that plants also move in ways that promote their survival (e.g., toward sunlight). This new information would be difficult for her to assimilate into her previous thinking. The resulting disparity between the girl's previous understanding of living things and her new knowledge about plants would create a state of disequilibrium, in which she was unsure what it means to be alive. Later, her thinking would accommodate to the new information about plants. That is, she would realize that animals and plants both move in adaptive ways and that because adaptive movement is a key characteristic of living things, plants as well as animals must be alive (Opfer & Gelman, 2001; Opfer & Siegler, 2004). This constitutes a more advanced equilibrium, because subsequent information about plants and animals will not contradict it. Through innumerable such equilibrations, children extend their understanding of the world around them.

Sources of Discontinuity

Although Piaget placed some emphasis on continuous aspects of cognitive development, the most famous part of his theory concerns discontinuous aspects, which he depicted as distinct *stages* of cognitive development. Piaget viewed these stages as products of the basic human tendency to organize knowledge into coherent structures. Each stage represents a coherent way of understanding one's experience, and each transition between stages represents a discontinuous intellectual leap from one coherent way of understanding to the next, higher one. The following are the central properties of Piaget's stage theory:

1. *Qualitative change.* Piaget believed that children of different ages think in qualitatively different ways. For example, he proposed that children in the early stages of cognitive development conceive of morality in terms of the consequences of a person's behavior, whereas children in later stages conceive of it in terms of the person's intent. A 5-year-old would judge someone who accidentally broke a whole jar of cookies as having been more naughty than someone who deliberately stole a single cookie; an 8-year-old would have the opposite assessment. This difference represents a *qualitative change,* because the two children are basing their moral judgments on entirely different criteria.

2. *Broad applicability.* The type of thinking characteristic of each stage influences children's thinking across diverse topics and contexts.

3. *Brief transitions.* Before entering a new stage, children pass through a brief transitional period in which they fluctuate between the type of thinking characteristic of the new, more advanced stage and the type of thinking characteristic of the old, less advanced one.

4. *Invariant sequence.* Everyone progresses through the stages in the same order and never skips a stage.

Piaget hypothesized that people progress through four stages of cognitive development: the *sensorimotor* stage, the *preoperational* stage, the *concrete operational* stage, and the *formal operational* stage. In each stage, children exhibit new abilities that allow them to understand the world in qualitatively different ways than they had previously.

1. In the **sensorimotor stage** (birth to age 2 years), infants' intelligence develops, and is expressed, through their sensory and motor abilities. They use these abilities to perceive and explore the world around them, gaining information about the objects and people in it and constructing rudimentary forms of fundamental concepts such as time, space, and causality. Throughout the sensorimotor period, infants live largely in the here and now: their intelligence is bound to their immediate perceptions and actions.
2. In the **preoperational stage** (ages 2 to 7 years), toddlers and preschoolers become able to represent their experiences in language and mental imagery. This allows them to remember the experiences for longer periods of time and to form more sophisticated concepts. However, as suggested by the term *preoperational,* Piaget's theory emphasizes young children's inability to perform *mental operations*, that is, forms of reasoning that are part of an organized system of mental activities. Lacking such well-organized systems, children are unable to form certain ideas, such as the idea that pouring water from one glass into a differently shaped glass does not change the amount of water.
3. In the **concrete operational stage** (ages 7 to 12 years), children can reason logically about concrete objects and events; for example, they understand that pouring water from one glass to a differently shaped one leaves the amount of water unchanged. However, they have difficulty thinking in purely abstract terms and in generating scientific experiments to test their beliefs.
4. In the final stage of cognitive development, the **formal operational stage** (age 12 years and beyond), children can think deeply not only about concrete events but also about abstractions and purely hypothetical situations. They also can perform systematic scientific experiments and draw appropriate conclusions from them, even when the conclusions differ from their prior beliefs.

With this overview of Piaget's theory, we can consider in greater depth some of the major changes that take place in each stage.

The Sensorimotor Stage (Birth to Age 2 Years)

One of Piaget's most profound insights was his realization that the roots of adult intelligence are present in infants' earliest behaviors, such as their seemingly aimless sucking, flailing, and grasping. He recognized that these behaviors are not random but instead reflect an early type of intelligence involving sensory and motor activity. Indeed, many of the clearest examples of the *active child* theme come from Piaget's descriptions of the development of what he called "sensorimotor intelligence."

Over the course of the first two years, according to Piaget, infants' sensorimotor intelligence develops tremendously. The sheer amount of change may at first seem astonishing. However, when we consider the immense variety of new experiences that infants encounter during this period, and the tripling of brain weight between birth and age 3 (with weight being an index of brain development during this period), the huge increase in infants' cognitive abilities seems more comprehensible. The profound developments that Piaget described as occurring during infancy call

sensorimotor stage the period (birth to 2 years) within Piaget's theory in which intelligence is expressed through sensory and motor abilities

preoperational stage the period (2 to 7 years) within Piaget's theory in which children become able to represent their experiences in language, mental imagery, and symbolic thought

concrete operational stage the period (7 to 12 years) within Piaget's theory in which children become able to reason logically about concrete objects and events

formal operational stage the period (12 years and beyond) within Piaget's theory in which people become able to think about abstractions and hypothetical situations

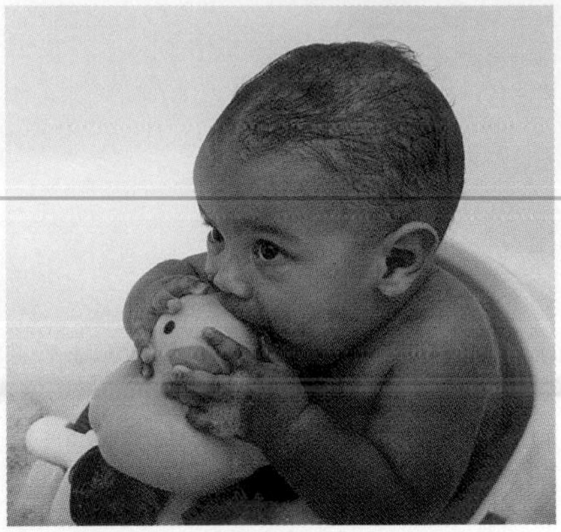

DAVID YOUNG-WOLFF / PHOTOEDIT

Piaget proposed that when infants suck on objects, they not only gain pleasure but also knowledge about the world beyond their bodies.

attention to a general principle: Children's thinking grows especially rapidly in the first few years.

Infants are born with many reflexes. When objects move in front of their eyes, they visually track them; when objects are placed in their mouths, they suck them; when objects come into contact with their hands, they grasp them; when they hear noises, they turn their heads toward them; and so on. Piaget believed that these simple reflexes and perceptual abilities are essential tools for building intelligence.

Even during their first month, infants begin to modify their reflexes to make them more adaptive. At birth, for example, they suck in a similar way regardless of what they are sucking. Within a few weeks, however, they adjust their sucking according to the object in their mouth. Thus, they suck on a milk-yielding nipple in a way that enhances the efficiency of their feeding and that is notably different from the way they suck on a finger or even a pacifier. As this example illustrates, from the first days out of the womb, infants accommodate their actions to the parts of the environment with which they interact.

Over the course of the first few months, infants begin to organize separate reflexes into larger behaviors, most of which are centered on their own bodies. Instead of having two separate reflexes, one of grasping objects that touch their palms and another of sucking on objects that come into their mouths, infants become able to integrate these actions. When an object touches their palm, they can grasp it and bring it to their mouth. Thus, their reflexes serve as building blocks for more complex behaviors.

In the middle of their first year, infants become increasingly interested in the world around them—people, animals, toys, and other objects and events beyond their own bodies. A hallmark of this shift is the repetition of actions on the environment that produce pleasurable or interesting results. Repeatedly banging rattles, for example, is a favorite activity for many infants at this time.

Piaget (1954) made a striking and controversial claim about a deficiency in infants' thinking during this period—the one referred to in the chapter-opening anecdote about the father hiding his glasses. The claim was that through the age of 8 months, infants lack **object permanence,** the knowledge that objects continue to exist even when they are out of view. This claim was based largely on Piaget's observations of his own children, Laurent, Lucienne, and Jacqueline. The following account of an experiment with Laurent reflects the type of observation that inspired Piaget's belief about object permanence:

> At age 7 months, 28 days, I offer him a little bell behind a cushion. So long as he sees the little bell, however small it may be, he tries to grasp it. But if the little bell disappears completely he stops all searching. I then resume the experiment using my hand as a screen. Laurent's arm is outstretched and about to grasp the little bell at the moment I make it disappear behind my hand which is open and at a distance of about 15 cm. from him. He immediately withdraws his arm, as though the little bell no longer existed.
>
> (Piaget, 1954, p. 39)

Thus, in Piaget's view, for infants younger than 8 months, the adage "out of sight, out of mind" is literally true. They are able to mentally represent only objects that they can perceive at the moment.

By the end of the first year, infants search for hidden objects rather than act as if they had vanished, thus indicating that they mentally represent the objects' continuing existence even when they no longer see them. These initial representations of objects are fragile, however, as reflected in the **A-not-B error.** In this error, once

object permanence the knowledge that objects continue to exist even when they are out of view

A-not-B error the tendency to reach for a hidden object where it was last found rather than in the new location where it was last hidden

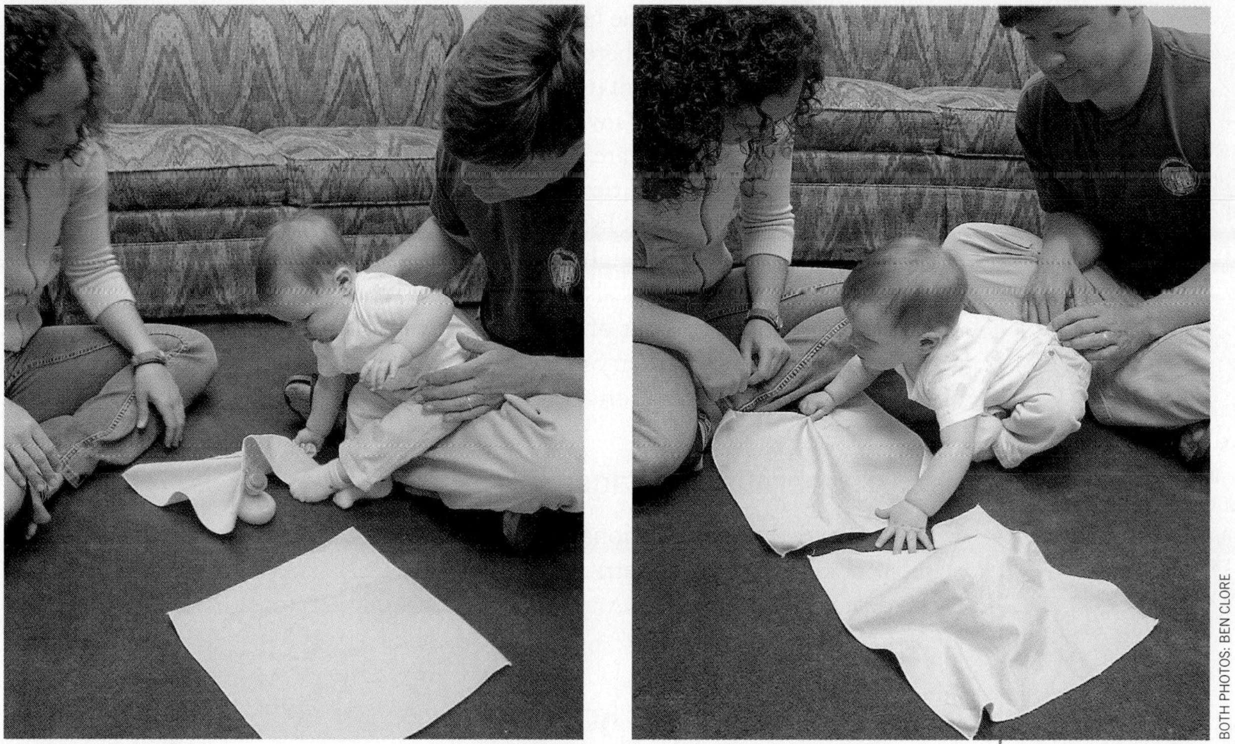

FIGURE 4.1 Piaget's A-not-B task A child looks for and finds a toy under the cloth where it was hidden (left frame). After several such experiences, the toy is hidden in a different location (right frame). The child continues to look where he found the toy previously rather than where it is hidden now. The child's ignoring the visible protrusion of the toy under the cloth in the right frame illustrates the strength of the inclination to look in the previous "hiding place."

8- to 12-month-olds have reached for and found a hidden object several times in one place (location A), when they see the object hidden at a different place (location B) and are prevented from immediately searching for it, they tend to reach where they initially found the object (see Figure 4.1). Not until around their first birthday do infants consistently search first at the object's current location.

At around 1 year of age, infants begin to actively and avidly explore the potential ways in which objects can be used. The "child as scientist" example presented earlier, in which Piaget's son Laurent varied the positions from which he dropped different objects to see what would happen, provides one instance of this emerging competency. Similar examples occur in every family with infants. Few parents forget their 12- to 18-month-olds' sitting in their high chairs, banging various objects against the chair's tray—first a spoon, then a plate, then a cup—seemingly fascinated by the distinctive sounds made by the different objects. Nor do they forget their infants' dropping various bathroom articles into the toilet, or showering a bag of flour over the kitchen floor, just to see what happens. Piaget regarded such actions not as bad behavior but rather as the beginnings of scientific experimentation.

In the last half year of the sensorimotor stage (ages 18 to 24 months), according to Piaget, infants become able to form enduring mental representations. The first sign of this new capability is **deferred imitation,** that is, the repetition of other people's behavior minutes, hours, or even days after it occurred. Consider Piaget's observation of 1-year-old Jacqueline:

> Jacqueline had a visit from a little boy . . . who, in the course of the afternoon, got into a terrible temper. He screamed as he tried to get out of a playpen and pushed it backward, stamping his feet. . . . The next day, she herself screamed in her playpen and tried to move it, stamping her foot lightly several times in succession.
> (Piaget, 1951, p. 63)

deferred imitation the repetition of other people's behavior a substantial time after it originally occurred

This toddler's techniques for applying eye makeup may not exactly mirror those he has seen his mother use, but they are close enough to provide a compelling illustration of deferred imitation, a skill that children gain during their second year.

Piaget indicated that Jacqueline had never before thrown such a tantrum. Presumably, she had watched and remembered her playmate's behavior, maintained a representation of it overnight, and imitated it the next day.

When we consider Piaget's whole account of cognitive development during infancy, several notable trends are evident. At first, infants' activities center on their own bodies; later, their activities include the world around them. Early goals are concrete (shaking a rattle and listening to the sound it makes); later goals often are more abstract (varying the heights from which objects are dropped and observing how the effects vary). Infants also become increasingly able to form mental representations, moving from "out of sight, out of mind" to remembering a playmate's actions from a full day earlier. Such enduring mental representations make possible the next stage, preoperational thinking.

The Preoperational Stage (Ages 2 to 7)

Piaget viewed the preoperational period as including a mix of striking cognitive acquisitions and even more striking limitations. Perhaps the foremost acquisition is the development of *symbolic representations;* among the most notable weaknesses are *egocentrism* and *centration.*

Development of Symbolic Representations

Have you ever seen preschoolers use two popsicle sticks to represent a gun or a banana to represent a telephone? Forming such personal symbols is common among 3- to 5-year-olds. It is one of the ways in which they exercise their emerging capacity for **symbolic representation**—the use of one object to stand for another. Typically, these personal symbols physically resemble the objects they represent. The popsicle sticks' and banana's shape somewhat resemble those of a gun and a telephone receiver.

FIGURE 4.2 **A 4-year-old's drawing of a summer day** Note the use of simple artistic conventions, such as the V-shaped leaves on the flowers (Dennis, 1992, p. 234).

As children develop, they rely less on self-generated symbols and more on conventional ones. For example, when 5-year-olds play games involving pirates, they might wear a patch over one eye and a bandana over their head because that is the way pirates are commonly depicted. Heightened symbolic capabilities during the preoperational period are also evident in the growth of drawing. Children's drawings between ages 3 and 5 make increasing use of symbolic conventions, such as representing the leaves of flowers as V's (Figure 4.2).

Egocentrism

FIGURE 4.3 **Piaget's three-mountains task** When asked to choose the picture that shows what the doll sitting in the seat across the table would see, most children below age 6 choose the picture showing how the scene looks to them, illustrating their difficulty in separating their own perspective from that of others.

Although Piaget noted important growth in children's thinking during the preoperational stage, he found the limitations of this period to be more intriguing, and more revealing of children's preoperational understanding. As noted, one important limitation is **egocentrism,** that is, perceiving the world solely from one's own point of view. An example of this limitation involves preschoolers' difficulty in taking other people's spatial perspectives. Piaget and Inhelder (1956) demonstrated this difficulty by having 4-year-olds sit at a table in front of a model of three mountains of different sizes (Figure 4.3). The children were asked to identify which of several photographs depicted what a doll would see if it were sitting on chairs at various locations around the table. Solving this problem required children to recognize that their own perspective was not the only one possible and to imagine what the view would be from another location. Most 4-year-olds, according to Piaget, cannot do this.

symbolic representation the use of one object to stand for another

egocentrism the tendency to perceive the world solely from one's own point of view

centration the tendency to focus on a single, perceptually striking feature of an object or event

conservation concept the idea that merely changing the appearance of objects does not change their key properties

The same difficulty in taking other people's perspectives is seen in quite different contexts, for example, in communication. As illustrated in Figure 4.4, preschoolers often talk right past each other; they seem blithely unaware that their listener is paying no attention whatsoever to what they are saying. Preschoolers' egocentric communication also is evident when they make statements that assume knowledge that they themselves possess but that their listeners lack. For example, 2- and 3-year-olds frequently tell preschool teachers or parents things like, "He took it from me," in situations where the adult has no idea what person or object the child is referring to. Egocentric thinking is also evident in preschoolers' explanations of events and behavior. Consider the following interviews with preschoolers that occurred in the original version of the TV show *Kids Say the Darndest Things:*

Interviewer: Any brothers or sisters?
Child: I have a brother a week old.
I: What can he do?
C: He can say "Mamma" and "Daddy."
I: Can he walk?
C: No, he's too lazy.

Interviewer: Any brothers or sisters?
Child: A 2-months-old brother.
I: How does he behave?
C: He cries all night.
I: Why is that, do you think?
C: He probably thinks he's missing something on television.

(Linkletter, 1957, p. 6)

FIGURE 4.4 Egocentrism An example of young children's egocentric conversations.

Over the course of the preoperational period, egocentric speech becomes less common. An early sign of progress is children's verbal quarrels, which become increasingly frequent during this period. The fact that a child's statements elicit a playmate's disagreement indicates that the playmate is at least paying attention to the differing perspective that the other child's comment implies. Children also become better able to envision spatial perspectives other than their own during the preoperational period. Of course, we all remain somewhat egocentric throughout our lives, but most of us do improve.

Centration

A related limitation of preschoolers' thinking is **centration,** that is, focusing on a single, perceptually striking feature of an object or event to the exclusion of other relevant but less striking features. Children's approaches to balance-scale problems provide a good example of centration. If presented with a balance scale like that in Figure 4.5 and asked "Which side will go down?," 5- and 6-year-olds center on the amount of weight on each side, ignore the distance of the weights from the fulcrum, and say that whichever side has more weight will go down (Inhelder & Piaget, 1958).

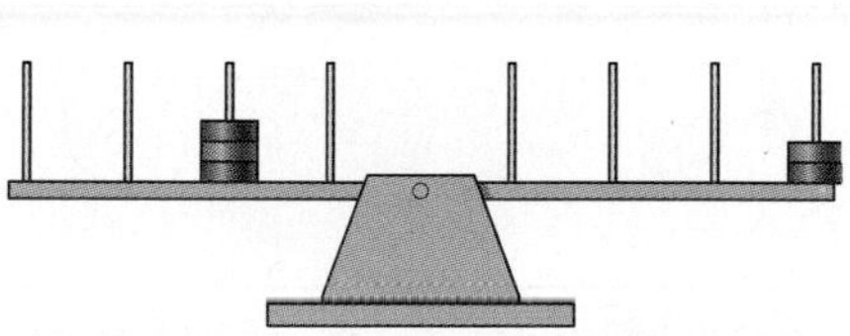

FIGURE 4.5 The balance scale When asked to predict which side of a balance scale, like the one shown above, would go down if the arm were allowed to move, 5- and 6-year-olds almost always center their attention on the amount of weight and ignore the distances of the weights from the fulcrum. Thus, they would predict that the left side would go down, although the right side actually would.

Another good example of centration comes from Piaget's research on children's understanding of conservation. The idea of the **conservation concept** is that merely changing the appearance or arrangement of objects does not necessarily change their key properties, such as quantity of material. Three variants of the concept that are commonly studied in 5- to 8-year-olds are conservation of liquid quantity, conservation of solid quantity, and conservation of number (Piaget, 1952a). In all three cases, the tasks used to measure children's understanding

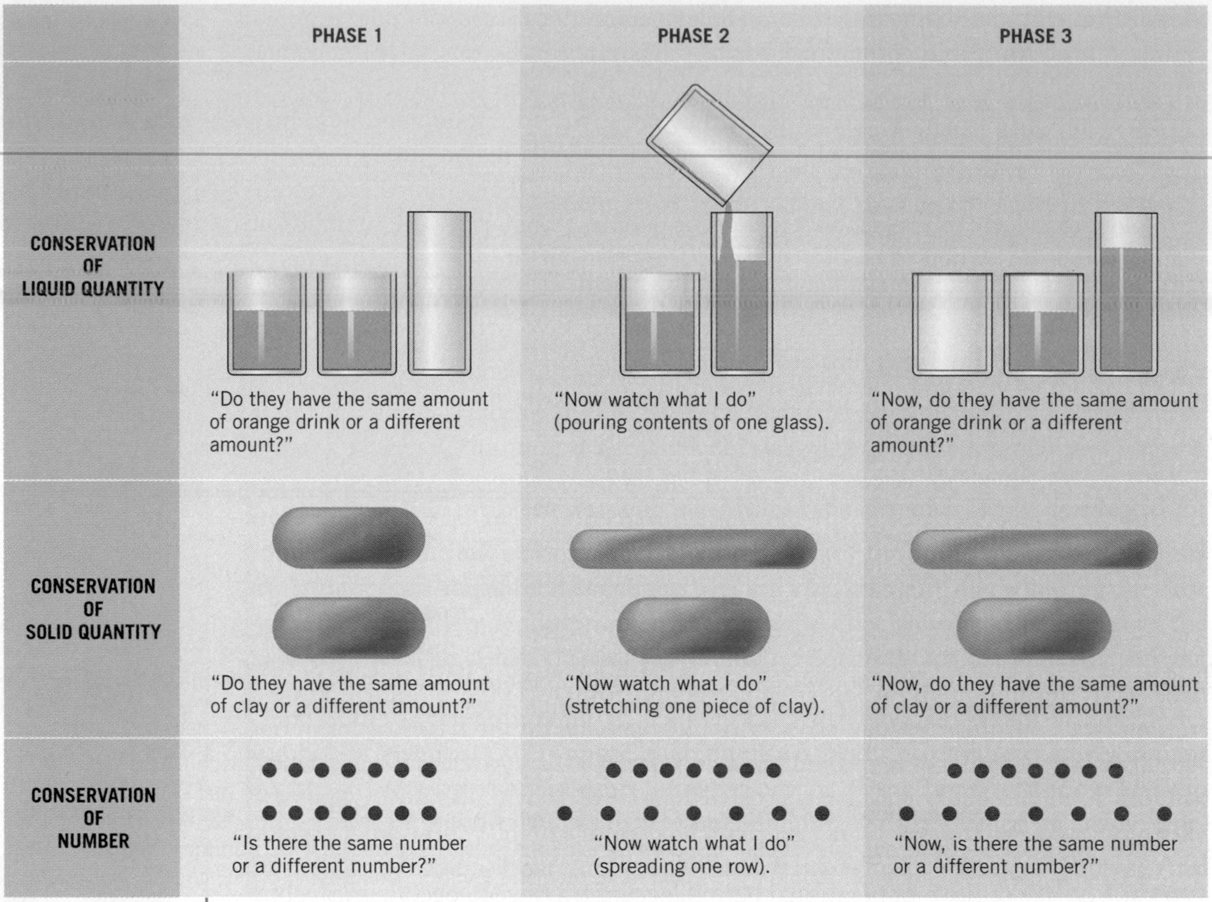
PHASE 1
PHASE 2
PHASE 3
CONSERVATION OF LIQUID QUANTITY
"Do they have the same amount of orange drink or a different amount?"
"Now watch what I do" (pouring contents of one glass).
"Now, do they have the same amount of orange drink or a different amount?"
CONSERVATION OF SOLID QUANTITY
"Do they have the same amount of clay or a different amount?"
"Now watch what I do" (stretching one piece of clay).
"Now, do they have the same amount of clay or a different amount?"
CONSERVATION OF NUMBER
"Is there the same number or a different number?"
"Now watch what I do" (spreading one row).
"Now, is there the same number or a different number?"

FIGURE 4.6 Procedures used to test conservation of liquid quantity, solid quantity, and number Most 4- and 5-year-olds say that the taller liquid column has more liquid, the longer sausage has more clay, and the longer row has more objects.

employ a three-phase procedure (Figure 4.6). First, as in the figure, children see two objects or sets of objects—two glasses of orangeade, two clay sausages, or two rows of pennies—that are identical in number or quantity. Once children agree that the dimension of interest (e.g., the amount of orangeade) is equal in both items, the second phase follows. Here, children observe a transformation of one object or set of objects that makes it look different but does not change the dimension in question. A glass of orangeade might be poured into a taller, narrower, glass; a short, thick clay sausage might be molded into a long, thin sausage; or a row of pennies might be lengthened. Finally, in the third phase, children are asked whether the dimension of interest, which they earlier had said was equal for the two objects or sets of objects, is still equal.

The large majority of 4- and 5-year-olds answer "no." On conservation-of-liquid-quantity problems, they claim that the taller, narrower glass has more orangeade; on conservation-of-solid-quantity problems, they claim that the long, thin sausage has more clay than the short, thick one; and so on. Children of this age make similar errors in everyday contexts; for example, they often think that if a child has one fewer cookie than another child, a fair solution is to break one of the short-changed child's cookies into two pieces (Miller, 1984).

A variety of weaknesses that Piaget perceived in preoperational thinking contribute to these difficulties with conservation problems. Preoperational thinkers center their attention on the single, perceptually salient dimension of height or length, ignoring other relevant dimensions. In addition, their egocentrism leads to their failing to understand that their own perspective can be misleading—that just because a tall narrow glass of orangeade or a long thin clay sausage looks as though it has more orangeade or clay than a shorter, wider one does not mean that it really does. Children's tendency to focus on static states of objects (the appearance of the objects before and after the transformation) and to ignore the transformation that was performed (pouring the orangeade or reshaping the clay) also contributes to their difficulty in solving conservation problems.

In the next period of cognitive development, the concrete operations stage, children largely overcome these and other related limitations.

The Concrete Operations Stage (Ages 7 to 12)

At around age 7, according to Piaget, children begin to reason logically about concrete features of the world. Development of the conservation concept exemplifies this progress. Although few 5-year-olds solve any of the three conservation tasks described in the previous section, most 7-year-olds solve all of them. The same progress in thinking also allows children in the concrete operations stage to solve many other problems that require attention to multiple dimensions. For example, on the balance-scale problem, they consider distance from the fulcrum as well as weight.

However, this relatively advanced reasoning is, according to Piaget, limited to concrete situations. Thinking systematically remains very difficult, as does reasoning about hypothetical situations. These limitations are evident in the types of experiments that concrete operational children perform to solve the pendulum problem (Inhelder & Piaget, 1958) (Figure 4.7). In this problem, children are presented a pendulum frame, a set of strings of varying length with a loop at each end, and a set of metal weights of varying weight, any of which can be attached to any string. When the loop at one end of the string is attached to a weight, and the loop at the other end is attached to the frame of the pendulum, the string can be swung. The task is to perform experiments that indicate which factor or factors influence the amount of time it takes the pendulum to swing through a complete arc. Is it the length of the string, the heaviness of the weight, the height from which the weight is dropped, or some combination of these factors? Think for a minute: How would you go about solving this problem?

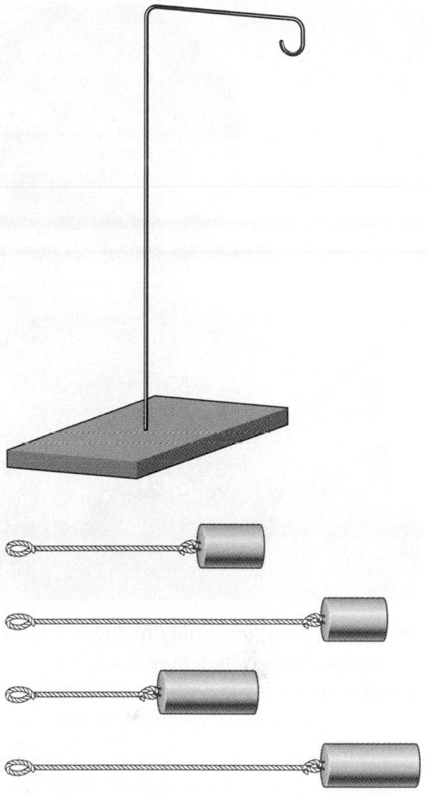

FIGURE 4.7 Inhelder and Piaget's pendulum problem The task is to compare the motions of longer and shorter strings, with lighter and heavier weights attached, in order to determine the influence of weight, string length, and dropping point on the time it takes for the pendulum to swing back and forth. Children below age 12 usually perform unsystematic experiments and draw incorrect conclusions.

Most concrete operational children begin their experiments believing that the heaviness of the weight is the most important factor, quite likely the only important one. This belief is not unreasonable; indeed, most adolescents and adults share it. What distinguishes the children's reasoning from that of older individuals lies in how they test their beliefs. Typically, children design unsystematic experiments from which no clear conclusion can be drawn. For example, they might compare the travel time of a heavy weight on a short string dropped from a high position to the travel time of a light weight on a long string dropped from a lower position. When the first string goes faster, they conclude that, just as they had thought, heavy weights go faster. This premature conclusion, however, reflects their limited ability to think systematically or to imagine all possible combinations of variables; they do not seem to imagine that the faster motion might reflect the length of the string or the height from which the string was dropped, rather than the weight of the object.

The Formal Operations Stage (Age 12 and Beyond)

Formal operational thinking, which includes the ability to think abstractly and to reason hypothetically, is the pinnacle of the Piagetian stage progression. The

MARK RICHARDS / PHOTOEDIT

Teenagers' emerging ability to understand that the reality in which they live is only one of many possible realities contributes to many of them developing a taste for science fiction.

difference between reasoning in this stage and in the previous one is clearly illustrated by formal operational reasoners' approach to the pendulum problem. Framing the problem more abstractly than do children in the concrete operations stage, they see that any of the variables—weight, string length, and dropping point—might influence the time it takes for the pendulum to swing through an arc, and that it therefore is necessary to test the effect of each variable systematically. To test the effect of weight, they compare times to complete an arc for a heavier weight and a lighter weight, attached to strings of equal length and dropped from the same height. To test the effect of string length, they compare the travel times of a long and a short string, with equal weight dropped from the same position. To test the influence of dropping point, they vary the dropping point of a given weight attached to a given string. Such a systematic set of experiments allows the formal operational reasoner to determine that the only factor that influences the pendulum's travel time is the length of the string; neither weight nor dropping point matters.

Piaget believed that unlike the previous three stages, the formal operations stage is not universal: not all adolescents (or adults) reach it. For those adolescents who do reach it, however, formal operational thinking greatly expands and enriches their intellectual universe. Such thinking makes it possible for them to see the particular reality in which they live as only one of an infinite number of possible realities. This insight leads them to think about alternative ways that the world could be and to ponder deep questions concerning truth, justice, and morality. It no doubt also helps account for the fact that many people first acquire a taste for science fiction during adolescence. The alternative worlds depicted in science-fiction stories appeal to adolescents' emerging capacity to think about the world they know as just one of many possibilities and to wonder whether a better world is possible. Inhelder and Piaget (1958) aptly expressed the intellectual power that formal operational thinking provides adolescents: "Each one has his own ideas (and usually he believes they are his own) which liberate him from childhood and allow him to place himself as the equal of adults" (pp. 340–341).

The attainment of such systematic formal operational reasoning does not mean that adolescents will always reason in advanced ways, but it does, according to Piaget, mark the point at which adolescents attain the reasoning powers of intelligent adults. (Some ways in which Piaget's theory can be applied to improving education are discussed in Box 4.1.)

Piaget's Legacy

Although much of Piaget's theory was formulated many years ago, it remains a very influential approach to cognitive development. Some of its strengths were mentioned earlier. It provides a good overview, with countless fascinating observations, of what children's thinking is like at different points in development (see Table 4.2). It offers a plausible and appealing perspective on children's nature. It surveys a remarkably broad spectrum of developments and covers the entire age span from infancy through adolescence.

However, subsequent analyses (Flavell, 1971, 1982; Miller, 2002) have also identified some crucial weaknesses in Piaget's theory. The following four weaknesses are particularly important:

1. The stage model depicts children's thinking as being more consistent than it is. According to Piaget, once children enter a given stage, their thinking consistently shows the

applications 4.1

Educational Applications of Piaget's Theory

Piaget's view of children's cognitive development holds a number of general implications for how children should be educated (Ginsburg & Opper, 1988; Piaget, 1970). Most generally, it suggests that children's distinctive ways of thinking at different ages need to be considered in deciding how to teach them. For example, children in the concrete operational stage would not be expected to be ready to learn purely abstract concepts such as inertia and equilibrium state, whereas adolescents in the formal operational stage would be. Taking into account such general age-related differences in cognitive level before deciding when to teach particular concepts is often labeled a "child-centered approach."

A second implication of Piaget's approach is that children learn by interacting with the environment, both mentally and physically. One research demonstration of this principle involved promoting children's understanding of the concept of speed (Levin et al., 1990). The investigation focused on problems of a type beloved by physics teachers: "When a race horse travels around a circular track, do its right and left sides move at the same speed?" It appears obvious that they do, but in fact they do not. The part of the horse toward the outside of the track is covering a slightly greater distance in the same amount of time as the part toward the inside and therefore is moving slightly faster.

Levin and her colleagues devised a procedure that allowed children to actively experience how different parts of a single object can move at different speeds. They attached one end of a 7-foot-long metal bar to a pivot that was mounted on the floor. Then, one by one, 6th graders and an experimenter took four walks around the pivot while holding onto the bar. On two of the walks, the child held the bar near the pivot and the experimenter held it at the far end; on the other two walks, they switched positions (see figure). After each walk, children were asked whether they or the experimenter had walked faster.

The differences in the speeds required for walking while holding the inner and the outer parts of the metal bar were so dramatic that the children generalized their new understanding to other problems involving circular motion, such as cars moving around circular tracks on a computer screen. In other words, physically experiencing the concept accomplished what years of formal science instruction usually fail to do. As one boy said, "Before, I hadn't experienced it. I didn't think about it. Now that I have had that experience, I know that when I was on the outer circle, I had to walk faster to be at the same place as you" (Levin et al., 1990). Clearly, relevant physical activities, accompanied by questions that call attention to the lessons of the activities, can foster children's learning.

A child and an adult holding onto a bar as they walk around a circle four times. On the first two trips around, the child holds the bar near the pivot; on the second two, the child holds it at its end. The much faster pace needed to keep up with the bar when holding onto its end led children to realize that the end was moving faster than the inner portion (Levin, Siegler, & Druyan, 1990).

TABLE 4.2

Piaget's Stages of Cognitive Development

Stage	Approximate Age	New Ways of Knowing
Sensorimotor	Birth to 2 years	Infants know the world through their senses and through their actions. For example, they learn what dogs look like and what petting them feels like.
Preoperational	2–7 years	Toddlers and young children acquire the ability to internally represent the world through language and mental imagery. They also begin to be able to see the world from other people's perspectives, not just from their own.
Concrete operational	7–12 years	Children become able to think logically, not just intuitively. They now can classify objects into coherent categories and understand that events are often influenced by multiple factors, not just one.
Formal operational	12 years onward	Adolescents can think systematically and reason about what might be as well as what is. This allows them to understand politics, ethics, and science fiction, as well as to engage in scientific reasoning

characteristics of that stage across diverse concepts. Subsequent research, however, has shown that children's thinking is far more variable than this depiction suggests. For example, most children succeed on conservation-of-number problems by age 6, whereas most do not succeed on conservation-of-solid-quantity problems until age 8 or 9 (Field, 1987). Piaget recognized that such variability exists but was unable to explain it successfully.

2. Infants and young children are more cognitively competent than Piaget recognized. Piaget presented children with relatively difficult tests of understanding. This led him to miss infants' and young children's earliest knowledge of these concepts. For example, Piaget's test of object permanence required children to reach for the hidden object several seconds after it is hidden; as Piaget claimed, children do not do this until 8 or 9 months of age. However, alternative tests of object permanence, which analyze infants' eye fixations immediately after the object has disappeared from view, indicate that infants have some grasp of the continuing existence of objects by 3 months of age (Baillargeon, 1987; 1993).

3. Piaget's theory understates the contribution of the social world to cognitive development. Piaget's theory focuses on how children come to understand the world through their own efforts. From the day that children emerge from the womb, however, they live in an environment of adults and older children who shape their cognitive development in countless ways. A child's cognitive development reflects the contributions of other people, as well as of the broader culture, to a far greater degree than Piaget's theory acknowledges.

4. Piaget's theory is vague about the cognitive processes that give rise to children's thinking and about the mechanisms that produce cognitive growth. Piaget's theory provides any number of excellent descriptions of children's thinking. It is less revealing, however, about the processes that lead children to think in a particular way and that produce changes in their thinking. Assimilation, accommodation, and equilibration have a general air of plausibility, but how they operate is far from clear.

These weaknesses of Piaget's theory do not negate the magnitude of his achievement: it remains one of the major intellectual accomplishments of the twentieth century. However, appreciating the weaknesses as well as the strengths of his theory is necessary for understanding why alternative theories of cognitive development have become increasingly prominent.

In the remainder of this chapter, we consider the four most prominent alternative theories: *information-processing, dynamic-systems, core-knowledge,* and *sociocultural.* Each type of theory can be seen as an attempt to overcome a major weakness of Piaget's approach. Information-processing theories emphasize precise characterizations of the processes that give rise to children's thinking and the mechanisms that produce cognitive growth. Core-knowledge theories emphasize infants' and young children's early understandings that may have an innate, evolutionary basis. Sociocultural theories emphasize the ways in which children's interactions with the social world, both with other people and with the products of their culture, guide cognitive development. Dynamic-systems theories emphasize the variability of children's behavior and how the child's developing physical and mental capabilities and the particulars of the situation contribute to that variability. In addition, theorists of all four persuasions agree that children's thinking is more variable than Piaget's stage theory suggests.

review:

Piaget's theory of cognitive development emphasizes the interaction of nature and nurture, continuities and discontinuities, and children's active contribution to their own development. Piaget believed that a maturing brain, growing abilities to perceive and act, and increasingly rich and varied experiences interacting with the environment allow children to adapt to an expanding range of circumstances.

According to Piaget, the continuities of development are produced by assimilation, accommodation, and equilibration. Assimilation involves adapting incoming information to fit current understanding. Accommodation involves adapting one's thinking toward being more consistent with new experiences. Equilibration involves balancing assimilation and accommodation in a way that creates stable understandings.

As depicted by Paiget, the discontinuities of cognitive development involve four discrete stages: the sensorimotor stage (birth to age 2), in which infants begin to know the world through the perceptions of their senses and through their motor activities; the preoperational stage (ages 2 to 7), in which children become capable of mental representations but tend to be egocentric and to focus on a single dimension of an event or problem; the concrete operational stage (ages 7 to 12), in which children reason logically about concrete aspects of the environment but have difficulty thinking abstractly; and the formal operational stage (age 12 and beyond), in which preadolescents and adolescents become capable of abstract thought.

Among the most important strengths of Piaget's theory are its broad overview of development, its plausible and attractive perspective on children's nature, its inclusion of varied tasks and age groups, and its endlessly fascinating observations. Among the theory's most important weaknesses are its overstatement of the consistency of children's thinking, its underestimation of infants' and young children's cognitive competence, its lack of attention to the contribution of the social world, and its vagueness regarding cognitive mechanisms.

Information-Processing Theories

SCENE: DAUGHTER AND FATHER IN THEIR YARD. A PLAYMATE RIDES IN ON A BIKE

Child: Daddy, would you unlock the basement door?
Father: Why?
C: 'Cause I want to ride my bike.
F: Your bike is in the garage.
C: But my socks are in the dryer.

(Klahr, 1978, pp. 181–182)

What reasoning could have produced this girl's enigmatic comment, "But my socks are in the dryer"? David Klahr, an eminent information-processing theorist, formulated the following model of the thought process that led to it:

Top goal: I want to ride my bike.
Bias: I need shoes to ride comfortably.
Fact: I'm barefoot.

Subgoal 1: Get my sneakers.
Fact: The sneakers are in the yard.
Fact: They're uncomfortable on bare feet.

task analysis the research technique of identifying goals, relevant information in the environment, and potential processing strategies for a problem

structure the basic organization of the cognitive system, including its main components and their characteristics

processes the specific mental activities, such as rules and strategies, that people use to remember and to solve problems

Subgoal 2: Get my socks.
Fact: The sock drawer was empty this morning.
Inference: The socks probably are in the dryer.
Subgoal 3: Get them from the dryer.
Fact: The dryer is in the basement.
Subgoal 4: Go to the basement.
Fact: It's quicker to go through the yard entrance.
Fact: The yard entrance is always locked.
Subgoal 5: Unlock the door to the basement.
Fact: Daddies have the keys to everything.
Subgoal 6: Ask Daddy to unlock the door.

Klahr's analysis of his daughter's thinking illustrates several notable characteristics of information-processing theories.[1] One is the precise specification of the processes involved in children's thinking. Klahr attempted to identify his daughter's exact goals, the environmental obstacles she anticipated, and the reasoning that led her to the strategy of asking him to unlock the basement door.

Klahr's approach is referred to as **task analysis**—that is, the identification of goals, relevant information in the environment, and potential processing strategies. Such an approach helps information-processing researchers understand and predict children's behavior and allows them to perform rigorous experimental tests of precise hypotheses regarding how development occurs. In some cases, it also allows them to formulate computer simulations, a type of mathematical model that expresses ideas about mental processes in particularly unambiguous ways. For example, Klahr and Wallace (1976) formulated computer simulations of the knowledge and mental processes that led young children to fail on conservation problems and of the somewhat different knowledge and mental processes that allowed older children to succeed on them.

A second distinctive feature that is evident in Klahr's information-processing analysis is an emphasis on thinking as an activity that occurs over time, with numerous distinct mental operations underlying a single behavior. In his analysis, Klahr depicts his daughter as generating a sequence of subgoals, inferences, and relevant facts, one after another, in planning how to reach the overall goal of riding her bike in comfort.

A third distinctive characteristic of information-processing theories is their emphasis on structure and processes. **Structure** refers to the basic organization of the cognitive system, including the main components of the system and their characteristics. Increasingly, information-processing approaches are linking hypothesized cognitive structures to specific brain areas (see Figure 4.8 on page 147). **Processes** refer to the vast number of specific mental activities, such as the use of rules and strategies, that people devise to aid memory and solve problems. Which rules and strategies children use, and how those rules and strategies change with age and experience, are among the major issues addressed by information-processing approaches.

[1] Here and throughout this section, we use the plural term "information-processing *theories*" rather than the singular term "information-processing *theory*" because information theories consist of a variety of related approaches, rather than reflecting the unified ideas of a single theorist such as Piaget. For the same reason, in subsequent sections we refer to "core-knowledge theories," "sociocultural theories," and "dynamic-systems theories."

View of Children's Nature

Information-processing theorists view children as undergoing continuous cognitive change. That is, they see children's cognitive growth as occurring constantly, in small increments, rather than broadly and abruptly. This depiction differs from Piaget's belief that children progress through qualitatively distinct, broadly applicable stages, separated only by relatively brief transition periods.

The Child as a Limited-Capacity Processing System

In trying to understand the differences in children's thinking at various ages, information-processing theorists draw comparisons between the information processing of computers and that of humans. A computer's information processing is limited by its hardware and by its software. The hardware limitations relate to both the computer's memory capacity and its efficiency in executing basic operations. The software limitations relate to the strategies and information that are available for particular tasks. People's thinking is limited by the same factors: memory capacity, efficiency of thought processes, and availability of useful strategies and knowledge. In the information-processing view, cognitive development arises from children's gradually surmounting their processing limitations through (1) expansion of the amount of information they can process at one time, (2) increasingly efficient execution of basic processes, and (3) acquisition of new strategies and knowledge.

The Child as Problem Solver

Also central to the view of human nature held by information-processing theories is the assumption that children are active problem solvers. As suggested by Klahr's analysis of his daughter's behavior, **problem solving** involves a goal, a perceived obstacle, and a strategy or rule for overcoming the obstacle and attaining the goal. A description of a younger child's problem solving reveals the same combination of goal, obstacle, and strategy:

> Georgie (a 2-year-old) wants to throw rocks out the kitchen window. The lawnmower is outside. Dad says that Georgie can't throw rocks out the window, because he'll break the lawnmower with the rocks. Georgie says, "I got an idea." He goes outside, brings in some green peaches that he had been playing with, and says: "They won't break the lawnmower."
>
> (Waters, 1989, p. 7)

In addition to illustrating the goal–obstacle–strategy sequence, this example highlights another basic tenet of information-processing approaches: Children's cognitive flexibility helps them pursue their goals. These goals may not always be ones that their parents would approve, but even young children show great ingenuity in surmounting the obstacles imposed by their parents, the physical environment, and their own processing and knowledge limitations.

Central Developmental Issues

Like all the theories described in this chapter, information-processing theories examine how *nature and nurture* work together to produce development. What makes information-processing theories unique is their emphasis on precise descriptions of *how change occurs.* The way in which information-processing theories address

problem solving the process of attaining a goal by using a strategy to overcome an obstacle the issues of nature and nurture and how change occurs can be seen particularly clearly in their accounts of the development of memory and problem solving.

The Development of Memory

Memory is central to everything we do. The skills we use on any task, the language we employ when writing or speaking, the emotions we feel on a given occasion—all of these depend on our memory of past experiences and the knowledge acquired through them. Indeed, without memory of our experiences, we would lose our very identity.

Components of the memory system In their attempt to understand the development of memory, information-processing theorists distinguish among three key memory structures: sensory memory, long-term memory, and working memory. **Sensory memory** refers to the fleeting retention of sights, sounds, and other sensations that have just been experienced. This information is briefly held in raw form until it either is identified and moved to working memory or is lost. Thus, if a child reads a sentence about a bird, the visual appearance of the letters *b-i-r-d* enters into sensory memory while the word is being identified. **Long-term memory** refers to information retained on an enduring basis, for example, the child's general knowledge about birds. **Working memory** (sometimes referred to as *short-term memory*) refers to a kind of workspace in which we gather, attend to, and actively process information from sensory memory and long-term memory. Thus, in the reading example, the meaning of "bird" would emerge as working memory integrates the sensory memory of the letters *b-i-r-d* on the page with knowledge about birds from long-term memory.

Information-processing theorists distinguish among these three memory structures because they differ in important ways, including the length of time they can retain information, how much information they can store, the neural mechanisms through which they operate, and their course of development. Sensory memory can hold a small-to-moderate amount of information for a fraction of a second. The brain areas that are called into play vary according to the sensory modality through which the information was obtained. Thus, the visual cortex would be especially active in sensory memory for sights, the auditory cortex would be especially active in sensory memory for sounds, and so on (Eichenbaum, 2003). The capacity of sensory memory is relatively constant over much of development, though it does increase somewhat (Cowan et al., 1999).

Working memory, like sensory memory, is limited in both capacity and duration. Depending on the task and the individual's abilities, age, and knowledge of the material, it can hold and operate on between 1 and 10 items (words, numbers, etc.) for periods ranging from a fraction of a second to about a minute (Smith & Jonides, 1998). Also like sensory memory, working memory comprises separate subsystems for storing information from different sensory modalities—a visual-spatial system for storing visual information, a verbal system for storing auditory information, and so on.

Correspondingly, the brain areas that are most active in working-memory processing vary with the type of information being processed and the type of processing being done. For retention of visual information, a network involving right-hemisphere areas of the frontal and parietal lobes seems to play a particularly active role; for retention of auditory information, corresponding areas in the left hemisphere tend to be particularly active.

sensory memory the fleeting retention of sights, sounds, and other sensations that have just been experienced

long-term memory information retained on an enduring basis

working (short-term) memory a kind of workspace in which information from sensory memory and long-term memory is brought together, attended to, and processed

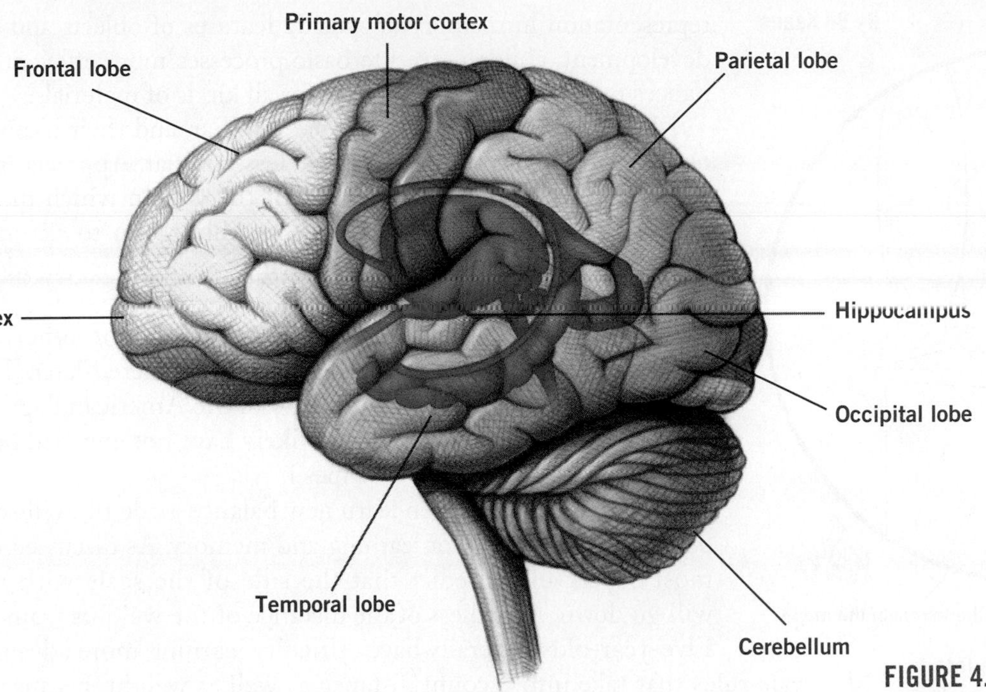

FIGURE 4.8 The memory system is not located in any single brain area; instead, areas throughout the brain make major contributions to memory.

Unlike sensory memory, however, working memory also includes an executive system for regulating attention, planning, and action. The prefrontal cortex plays an especially large role in such executive activities (Anderson, 2005; Nelson, Thomas, & de Haan, 2006). The basic organization of working-memory subsystems seems to be constant from early in childhood, but its capacity and speed of operation increase greatly over the course of childhood and adolescence (Gathercole, Pickering, Ambridge, & Wearing, 2004).

In contrast to the severe limits on the capacity and duration of sensory and working memory, long-term memory can retain an unlimited amount of information for unlimited periods of time. To cite one notable example, research shows that people who studied Spanish or algebra in high school often retain a substantial amount of what they learned in the subject 50 years later, despite both their not having used the information in the interim and their having accumulated vast stores of other skills, concepts, and knowledge in long-term memory over that period (Bahrick, 1987). Neural systems relevant to long-term retention are widely distributed throughout the cortex, with the area of the brain that is most active at any given time depending on the kind of information that is being processed. For example, the hippocampus and the temporal lobe of the cortex tend to be especially active in memory for facts about the world, whereas the motor cortex and cerebellum tend to be especially active in memory for actions (Nelson, Thomas, & de Haan, 2006; see Figure 4.8).

Explanations of memory development Information-processing theorists try to explain both the processes that make memory as good as it is at each age and the limitations that prevent it from being better. These efforts have focused on three types of capabilities: basic processes, strategies, and content knowledge.

BASIC PROCESSES The simplest and most frequently used mental activities are known as **basic processes.** They include *associating* events with each other, *recognizing* objects as familiar, *recalling* facts and procedures, and *generalizing* from one instance to another. Another basic process, which is key to all the others, is **encoding,** the

basic processes the simplest and most frequently used mental activities

encoding the process of representing in memory information that draws attention or is considered important

THE FAMILY CIRCUS By Bil Keane

"Mirror, mirror, on the wall, who's the fairest of the mall?"

Misencoding common sayings can lead to memorable confusions.

representation in memory of specific features of objects and events. With development, children execute basic processes more efficiently, which enhances their memory and learning for all kinds of materials.

Most of these basic processes are familiar, and their importance, obvious. However, encoding is probably less familiar. Appreciating its importance requires some understanding of the way in which memory works. People often think of memory as something akin to an unedited video recording of our experiences. Actually, memory is far more selective. People *encode* information that draws their attention or that they consider relevant, but they fail to encode a great deal of other information. Information that is not encoded is not remembered later. This failure is probably evident in your own memory of the American flag; although you have seen it many times, you most likely have not encoded how many red stripes and how many white stripes it has.

Studies of how children learn new balance-scale rules illustrate the importance of encoding for learning and memory. As discussed on page 137, most 5-year-olds predict that the side of the scale with more weight will go down, regardless of the distance of the weights from the fulcrum. Five-year-olds generally have difficulty learning more advanced balance-scale rules that take into account distance as well as weight, because they do not encode information about distance of the weights from the fulcrum. Teaching them to encode distance enables them to learn more advanced balance-scale rules that peers who were not taught to encode distance have trouble learning (Siegler, 1976; Siegler & Chen, 1998).

Like improved encoding, improved speed of processing plays a key role in the development of memory and learning. As shown in Figure 4.9, processing speed increases most rapidly at young ages but continues to increase through adolescence (Kail, 1991, 1997; Luna et al., 2004).

Two biological processes that contribute to faster processing are myelination and increased connectivity among brain regions (Luna et al., 2004). As discussed in Chapter 3, from the prenatal period through adolescence, increasing numbers of axons of neurons become covered with myelin, the fatty insulating substance that promotes faster and more reliable transmission of electrical impulses in the brain. Myelination seems to contribute to greater speed of processing not only by enhancing the efficiency of neural communication but also by enhancing the ability to resist distractions (Dempster & Corkill, 1999; Wilson & Kipp, 1998). Increasing connectivity among brain regions also increases processing capacity and speed by expanding the resources that can be marshaled for a given task and the efficiency of communication among brain areas. As noted in Chapter 3, such increased connectivity is especially prominent in later childhood and adolescence.

STRATEGIES Information-processing theories point to the acquisition and growth of strategies as another major source of the development of memory and learning. A number of these strategies emerge between ages 5 and 8 years, among them the strategy of **rehearsal,** the repeating of information over and over in order to remember it. The following newspaper item illustrates the usefulness of rehearsal for remembering information verbatim:

> A 9-year-old boy memorized the license plate number of a getaway car following an armed robbery, a court was told Monday. . . . The boy and his friend . . . looked in the drug store window and saw a man grab a 14-year-old cashier's neck. . . . After the robbery, the boys mentally repeated the license number until they gave it to police.
>
> (*Edmonton Journal,* Jan. 13, 1981, cited in Kail, 1984)

rehearsal the process of repeating information over and over to aid memory of it

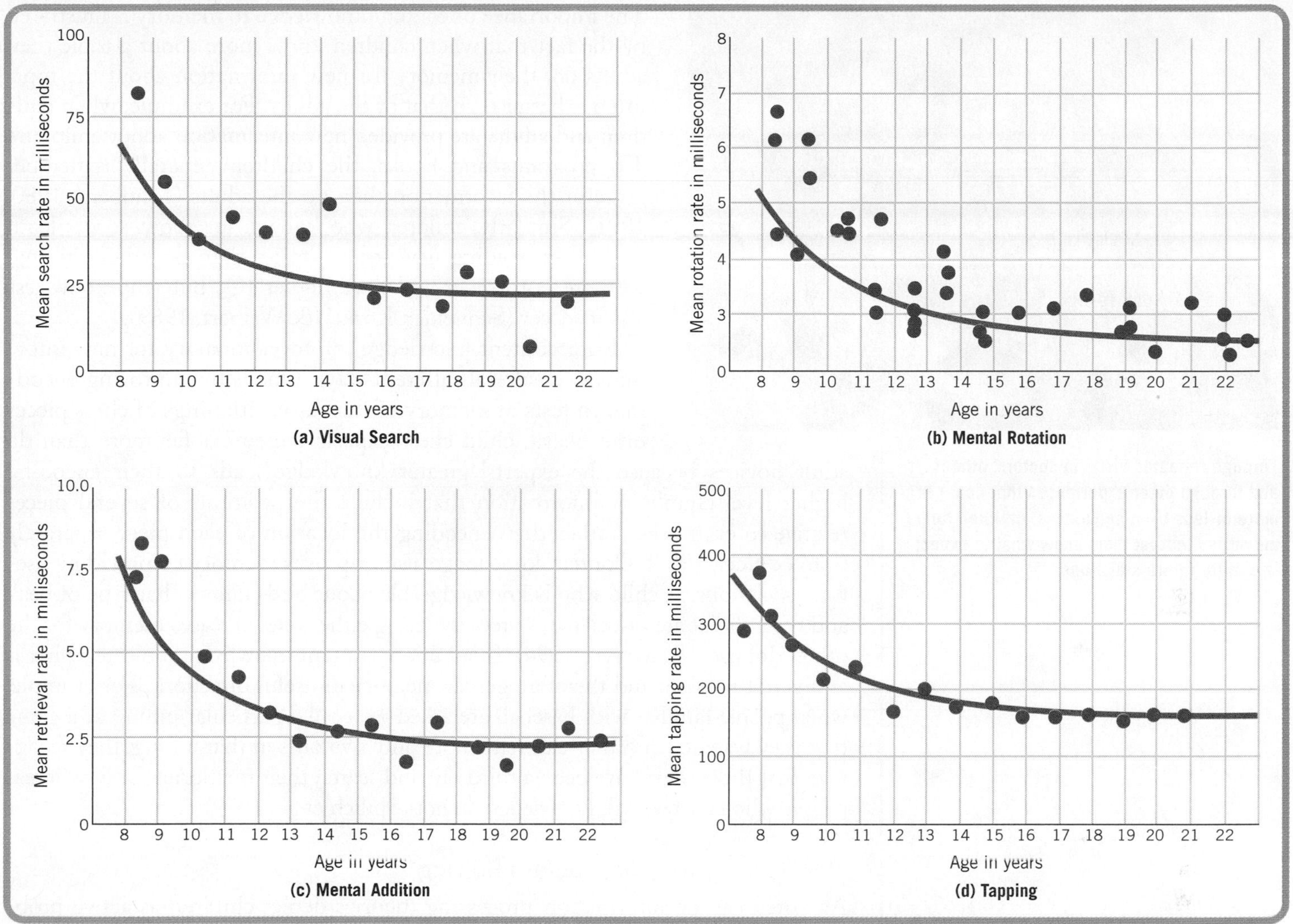

FIGURE 4.9 Increase with age in speed of processing on four tasks Note that on all four tasks, the increase is rapid in the early years and more gradual later. Note: lower numbers indicate faster processing rates. (Data from Kail, 1991)

Had the boys witnessed the same event when they were 5-year-olds, they probably would not have rehearsed the numbers and would have forgotten the license number before the police arrived.

Another widely used memory strategy that becomes increasingly prevalent during the early school years is **selective attention,** the process of intentionally focusing on the information that is most relevant to the current goal. If 7- and 8-year-olds are shown objects from two different categories (e.g., several toy animals and several household items) and are told that they later will need to remember the objects in only one category (e.g., "You'll need to remember the animals"), they focus their attention on the objects in the specified category and remember more of them. In contrast, given the same instructions, 4-year-olds pay roughly equal attention to the objects in both categories, which reduces their memory for the objects they need to remember (DeMarie-Dreblow & Miller, 1988).

CONTENT KNOWLEDGE Information-processing theories also point to a third explanation of development of memory and learning: improved content knowledge. With age and experience, children's knowledge about almost everything increases. Their greater knowledge improves recall of new material by making it easier to integrate the new material with existing understanding (Pressley & Hilden, 2006).

selective attention the process of intentionally focusing on the information that is most relevant to the current goal

Through repeated visits to doctors' offices and through other experiences that occur in more or less fixed sequences, children form memories that let them know what to expect in similar future situations.

The importance of content knowledge to memory is illustrated by the fact that when children know more about a topic than adults do, their memory for new information about the topic often is better than that of the adults. For example, when children and adults are provided new information about children's TV programs and books, the children generally remember more of the information than do the adults (Lindberg, 1980, 1991). Similarly, children who know a lot about soccer learn more from reading new soccer stories than do other children who are both older and have higher IQs but who know less about soccer (Schneider, Korkel, & Weinert, 1989).

Prior content knowledge improves memory for new information in several different ways. One is by improving encoding. In tests of memory of various positionings of chess pieces on a board, child chess experts remember far more than do adult novices because the experts' greater knowledge leads to their encoding higher-level chunks of information that include the positions of several pieces relative to each other rather than encoding the location of each piece separately (Chi & Ceci, 1987). Content knowledge also improves memory by providing useful associations. A child who is knowledgeable about birds knows that type of beak and type of diet are associated, so remembering either one increases memory for the other (Johnson & Mervis, 1994). In addition, content knowledge indicates what is and is not possible and therefore guides memory in useful directions. For example, when people familiar with baseball are asked to recall a particular inning of a game that they watched and they can remember only two outs in that inning, they recognize that there must have been a third out and search their memories for it, whereas people who lack baseball knowledge do not (Spilich et al., 1979).

The Development of Problem Solving

As noted earlier, information-processing theories depict children as active problem solvers whose use of strategies often allows them to overcome limitations of knowledge and processing capacity. In this section, we present an information-processing perspective on the development of problem solving in general—the overlapping-waves approach—and also examine two particularly important problem-solving processes: planning and analogical reasoning.

The overlapping-waves approach Piaget's theory depicted children of a given age as using a particular strategy to solve a particular class of problems. For example, he described 5-year-olds as solving conservation-of-number problems (Figure 4.6) by choosing the longer row of objects, and 7-year-olds as solving the same problems by reasoning that if nothing was added or subtracted, the number of objects must remain the same. According to **overlapping-waves theory,** however, children actually use a variety of approaches to solve this and other problems (Siegler, 1996). For example, examining 5-year-olds' reasoning on repeated trials of the conservation-of-number problem reveals that most children use at least three different strategies (Siegler, 1995). The same child who on one trial incorrectly reasons that the longer row must have more objects will on other trials correctly reason that just spreading a row does not change the number of objects, and on yet other trials will count the number of objects in the two rows to see which has more.

overlapping-waves theories an information-processing approach that emphasizes the variability of children's thinking

Figure 4.10 presents the typical pattern of development envisioned by the overlapping-waves approach, with strategy 1 representing the simplest strategy, and strategy 5, the most advanced. At the youngest age depicted, children usually use strategy 1, but they sometimes use strategy 2 or 4. With age and experience, the strategies that produce more successful performance become more prevalent; new strategies also are generated and, if they are more effective than previous approaches, are used increasingly. Thus, by the middle of the age range in Figure 4.10, children have added strategies 3 and 5 to the original group and have almost stopped using strategy 1.

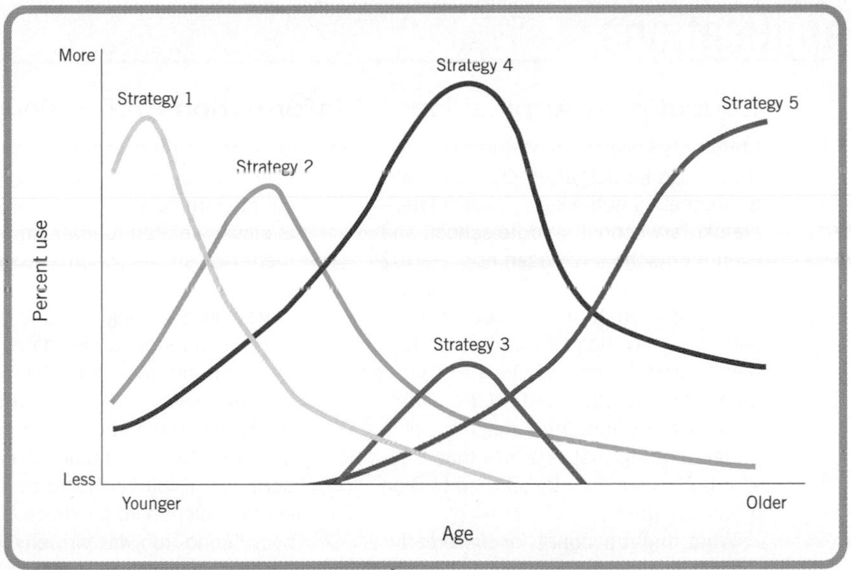

FIGURE 4.10 The overlapping-waves model The overlapping-waves model proposes that, at any one age, children use multiple strategies; that with age and experience, they rely increasingly on more advanced strategies (the ones with the higher numbers); and that development involves changes in use of existing strategies as well as discovery of new approaches.

This model has been shown to accurately characterize children's problem solving in a wide range of contexts. Among the areas in which individual children have demonstrated the use of several strategies for solving a given problem are arithmetic, time-telling, reading, spelling, scientific experimentation, biological understanding, descent of ramps, recall from memory, and understanding of false beliefs (see pages 269–270) (Amsterlaw & Wellman, 2004; Kuhn & Franklin, 2006; Lee & Karmiloff-Smith, 2002; Miller & Coyle, 1999; Siegler, 2006). For example, in descending relatively steep ramps, an individual toddler will sometimes crawl, sometimes slide on her belly, sometimes slide on her behind, sometimes slide head first, sometimes slide feet first, sometimes inch along in a sitting position, and sometimes refuse to go down at all (Adolph, 1997).

Such strategic variability allows children to adjust to the varying challenges that life presents. In the case of ramp descent, for example, 1-year-olds usually crawl or walk down ramps that are not inclined enough to pose the risk of a fall, slide down somewhat steeper ramps on their bellies or behinds, and refuse to descend very steep ramps in any manner. Consistent with the view that variable strategy use is adaptive, the more strategies children know, the better their problem solving and learning tend to be (Goldin-Meadow & Alibali, 2002; Kuhn & Franklin, 2006). (Box 4.2 illustrates how this focus on strategic development can improve education.)

Planning Early in development, children learn an important fact about problem solving: they often are more successful if they plan before acting. Children begin to form simple plans by their 1st birthday. In one demonstration of this capability, Willatts (1990) presented 12-month-olds with a solid barrier, behind which lay a cloth with a string attached and a toy that was too far away for the baby to reach (Figure 4.11). Sometimes the toy was attached to the string; other times it

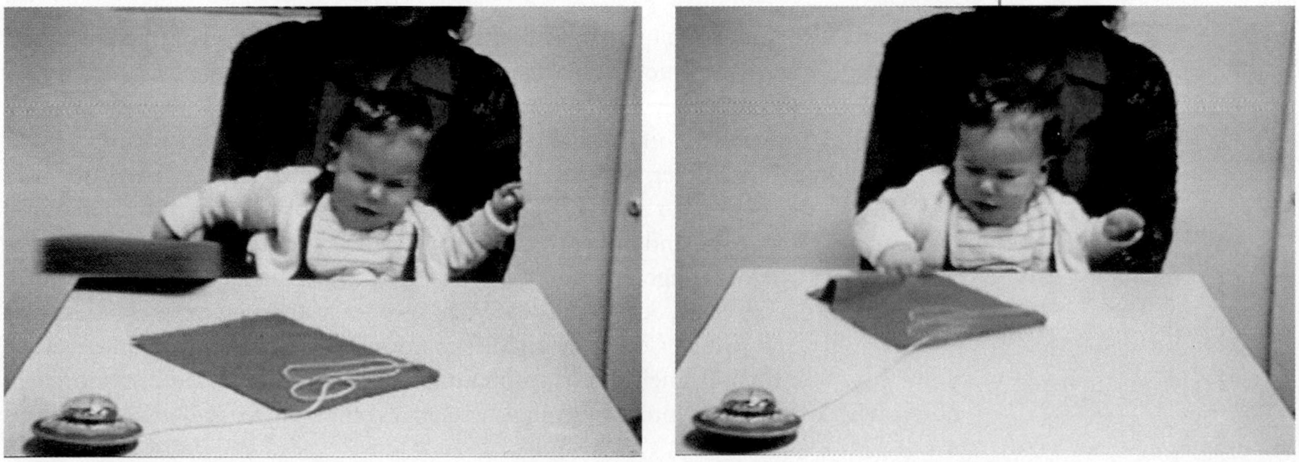

COURTESY OF PETER WILLATTS, UNIVERSITY OF DUNDEE, SCOTLAND

FIGURE 4.11 Planning Procedure used by Willatts (1990) to examine 12-month-olds' planning. To get the attractive toy, the baby needed to knock the barrier out of the way (left frame) and then pull in the towel connected by the string to the toy (right frame).

applications 4.2

Educational Applications of Information-Processing Theories

Children's knowledge of numbers when they begin kindergarten predicts their mathematics achievement years later—in elementary school, middle school, and even high school (Duncan et al., 2007; Stevenson & Newman, 1986). It is especially unfortunate, then, that kindergartners from low-income families lag far behind middle-income peers in counting, number recognition, arithmetic, and knowledge of numerical magnitudes (e.g., understanding that 7 is less than 9 and that both are closer to 10 than to 0 on a number line).

What might account for these early differences in numerical knowledge of children from different economic backgrounds? An information-processing analysis suggested that numerical experience, in particular experience playing numerical board games like Chutes and Ladders, might be important. In Chutes and Ladders, players must move a token across 100 consecutively numbered squares, advancing on each turn by the number of spaces determined by a spinner. The higher the number of the square on which a child's token rests at any given point in the game, the greater the number of number names the child is likely to have spoken and heard, the greater the distance the child has moved the token, the greater the time the child has been playing the game, and the greater the number of discrete moves the child has made with the token. These verbal, spatial, temporal, and kinesthetic cues provide a broadly based, multisensory foundation for knowledge of numerical magnitudes, a type of knowledge that is closely related to mathematics achievement test scores (Booth & Siegler, 2006; 2008).

Ramani and Siegler (2008) applied this information-processing analysis to improving the numerical understanding of low-income preschoolers. The researchers randomly assigned 4- and 5-year-olds from low-income families to either an experimental number-board condition or a control color-board condition. The number-board condition was virtually identical to the first row of the Chutes and Ladders board; it included 10 squares numbered consecutively from left to right. On each turn, the child spun a spinner that yielded a "1" or a "2" and moved his or her token the corresponding number of squares on the board, stating the number on each square in the process. For example, if a player's token was on the square with the "4," and the player spun a "2," the player would say, "5, 6" while moving the token from the "4" to the "6." Children in the color-board condition played the same game, except that their board had no numbers and the players would say the name of the color of each square as they advanced their token. Children in both conditions were given a pretest that examined their knowledge of numbers before playing the game, and then played the game for four 15-minute sessions over a two-week period. At the end of the fourth session, the children were given a posttest on their knowledge of numbers; nine weeks later, they were given a follow-up test identical to the pretest and posttest.

On the posttest, children who played the number-board game showed improved knowledge of the numbers 1 through 10 on all four number tasks that were presented—counting, reading of numbers, magnitude comparisons, and estimates of the locations of numbers on a number line. Significantly, all the gains were maintained on the follow-up test nine weeks later. In contrast, children who played the color-board game showed no improvement in any aspect of number knowledge. Moreover, children's reports of how often they played Chutes and Ladders and other board games at home was positively correlated with their initial knowledge on all four numerical tasks, and middle-income children reported playing numerical board games (though not video games) much more often than children from low-income backgrounds.

A subsequent study (Siegler & Ramani, 2009) demonstrated that playing the 1–10 board game also improves preschoolers' ability to learn the answers to arithmetic problems. Taken together, this evidence suggests that numerical board games represent a quick, effective, and inexpensive means of improving the numerical knowledge of low-income children before they begin formal education.

was not. The babies were quicker to try to get the toy when it was attached to the string than when it was not. Willatts's analysis of the children's information processing indicated that they had formulated a three-step plan for reaching the goal: remove the obstacle, pull in the cloth, and grab the string to get the toy.

As children grow older, they make plans for a wide variety of situations and problems, such as how to get to friends' houses, what books to read for reports, when to study for tests, and how to get their way with parents. This planning helps them solve a broader range of problems than they would be able to solve without planning (Hudson, Sosa, & Schapiro, 1997).

Despite the advantages of planning, many young children fail to plan in situations in which it would help their problem solving (Berg et al., 1997). The question is why. Information-processing analyses suggest that one reason why planning is difficult for young children is that it requires inhibiting the desire to solve the problem immediately in favor of first trying to construct the best strategy. As suggested by the challenge that games such as "Simon Says" and "Mother May I" represent for preschoolers, children below age 5 or 6 years tend to have special difficulty inhibiting the desire to act (Dempster, 1995; Diamond, Kirkham, & Amso, 2002), a tendency that is even greater in young children with learning problems (Winsler et al., 1999). This difficulty in inhibiting action is largely due to the fact that the frontal lobe, which plays an important part in inhibition, is one of the last parts of the brain to mature, with substantial maturation occurring between age 5 and adolescence (Diamond & Amso, 2008).

A second reason why planning is difficult for young children is that they tend to be overly optimistic about their abilities and think that they can solve problems more effectively than they are actually able to (Bjorklund, 1997; Schneider, 1998). This overconfidence can lead them to not plan, because they think they will succeed without doing so. Their overoptimism also can lead young children to act rashly. For example, 6-year-olds who overestimate their physical abilities have more accidents than do children who evaluate their abilities more realistically (Plumert, 1995). Even 12-year-olds leave less distance between themselves and oncoming vehicles when crossing streets than do adults (Plumert, Kearney, & Cremer, 2004). As these examples imply, brain maturation and experiences that reduce overoptimism and demonstrate the value of planning lead to increases in the frequency and quality of planning that continue into adolescence and beyond (Chalmers & Lawrence, 1993).

PHOTOS COURTESY OF JODIE PLUMERT

Young children's overoptimism sometimes leads them to engage in dangerous activities. This particular plan worked out fine, but not all do.

Analogical reasoning People often understand new problems by drawing analogies to familiar ones. For example, Goswami (2001) found that reminding 3- and 4-year-olds of the story "Goldilocks and the Three Bears" helped them solve analogous problems in which they needed to rank objects on dimensions such as temperature (boiling hot, hot, and warm food). Information-processing analyses indicate that, as in this example, successful analogical reasoning requires ignoring superficial dissimilarities (whether the objects are bears or food) and focusing on underlying parallel relations (the ordering from greatest to least).

As with planning, a rudimentary form of analogical reasoning emerges around a child's 1st birthday. This early competence, however, is initially limited to situations in which the new problem closely resembles the old. Thus, when 10-month-olds saw their mothers demonstrate how to solve the barrier and toy problem shown in Figure 4.11, they applied the lesson to new parallel problems only when the new problems duplicated the old in several superficial ways—such as the colors, sizes, shapes, and locations of objects (Chen, Sanchez, & Campbell, 1997).

Superficial similarity between the original and new problems continues to influence analogical reasoning well beyond infancy. Even in middle childhood, younger children often require more surface similarity to draw an analogy than do older ones (Gentner & Markman, 1997). When asked to explain the statement "A camera is like a tape recorder," for example, 6-year-olds tend to cite superficial similarities, such as that both are often black; in contrast, 9-year-olds tend to cite deeper similarities, such as that both devices are used to record information (Gentner et al., 1995). The 9-year-olds' deeper understanding of the nature of tape recorders and cameras enables them to see analogies between the two devices that the less knowledgeable 6-year-olds miss.

review: Information-processing theories envision children as active learners and problem solvers who continuously devise means for overcoming their processing limits and reaching their goals. Sensory memory, working memory, and long-term memory are key structures, whose capacity and processing speed influence all information processing. Planning and analogical reasoning are among the cognitive activities that information-processing theories envision as contributing most to the development of problem solving. Cognitive growth in general, and development of memory and learning in particular, are seen as involving increasingly efficient execution of basic operations, construction of more effective strategies, and acquisition of new content knowledge.

Core-Knowledge Theories

I didn't break the lamp, and I won't do it again.

—3-year-old, speaking to her mother (cited in Vasek, 1986)

Although transparent from an adult's perspective, this 3-year-old girl's attempted cover-up reflects surprisingly sophisticated reasoning. She realizes that her mother does not know all that she herself knows about how the lamp was broken, so she attempts to deny responsibility. At the same time, she knows that her mother may not believe her, so she hedges her bets. The girl's skill at deception is typical for her age. When more than 50 3-year-olds were encouraged by an experimenter to deceive another adult as to the whereabouts of a "treasure" the children had seen a doll hide, the majority destroyed clues to the treasure's location that the doll had "accidentally" left on the scene and lied when asked about where the treasure was hidden (Chandler, Fritz, & Hala, 1989).

Such studies of deception illustrate two characteristic features of research inspired by **core-knowledge theories.** One is that the research focuses on areas—such as understanding of other people's goals and intentions—that have been important throughout human evolutionary history. Other key areas similarly viewed as core knowledge include recognizing the difference between living and nonliving things, identifying human faces, finding one's way around the environment, and learning language.

A second feature of the core-knowledge approach that is reflected in deception studies is the assumption that in certain areas of probable importance in human evolution, young children reason in ways that are considerably more advanced than Piaget suggested were possible. If children under the age of 6 or 7 were completely egocentric, they would assume that other people's knowledge is the same as their own, in which case, there would be no point to making a false statement, because the other person would know it was false. In fact, as we will see, deception studies like the one described above indicate that children as young as 3 years old not only can understand that other people can be fooled but also act on that understanding. The question is how children come to have such sophisticated knowledge so early in life.

THE FAMILY CIRCUS **By Bil Keane**

"Mommy, how much grape juice would be bad for the rug?"

Indirect ways of breaking bad news are a specialty of young children and reflect their understanding that other people's reactions might not be the same as their own.

core-knowledge theories approaches that emphasize the sophistication of infants' and young children's thinking in areas that have been important throughout human evolutionary history

View of Children's Nature

Core-knowledge theories depict children as active learners. As discussed above, for example, research from the core-knowledge perspective shows that 3-year-olds understand deception much better when they are actively involved in perpetrating the deceit than when they merely witness the same deception being perpetrated by others (Carlson, Moses, & Hix, 1998; Sullivan & Winner, 1993). In this respect, the core-knowledge perspective on children's nature resembles that of Piagetian and information-processing theories.

The way in which core-knowledge theories differ most dramatically from Piagetian and information-processing theories is in their view of children's innate capabilities. Piaget and most information-processing theorists believe that children enter the world equipped with only general learning abilities and that they must actively apply these abilities to gradually increase their understanding of all types of content. In contrast, core-knowledge theorists view children as entering the world equipped not only with general learning abilities but also with specialized learning mechanisms, or mental structures, that allow them to quickly and effortlessly acquire information of evolutionary importance. Where the central metaphors within Piagetian and information-processing theories are, respectively, the child as scientist and the child as computational system, the central metaphor in the core-knowledge approach is the child as well-adapted product of evolution. This metaphor is strikingly apparent in the following statement:

> The brain is no less a product of natural selection than the rest of the body's structures and functions. . . . Hearts evolved to support the process of blood circulation, livers evolved to carry out the process of toxin extraction, and mental structures evolved to enable the learning of certain types of information necessary for adaptive behavior.
>
> (Gelman & Williams, 1998, p. 600)

Research on infants' face perception supports the view that people possess specialized learning mechanisms for acquiring information important to survival. From birth onward, brain structures outside the cortex, in particular the superior colliculus, bias infants to prefer looking at faces over other objects (de Haan, Johnson, & Halit, 2003). If infants were not biased to look at faces, they probably would take much longer to learn to recognize their parents and others on whom their survival depends.

Core-knowledge theorists, in particular the noted linguist Noam Chomsky (1988), have proposed that children also have specialized language-learning mechanisms that allow them to rapidly master the complicated systems of grammatical rules that are present in all human languages. One type of evidence for such mechanisms is the universality of language acquisition. Virtually all children in all societies master the basic grammar of their native language quickly and effortlessly, even though adults almost never directly instruct them. In contrast, understanding other complex rule systems—such as those in geometry, logic, and kinship relations (e.g., second cousin, twice removed)—is not universal and requires direct instruction from adults and considerable effort from children.

Another reason for believing that children possess mechanisms that are specialized for learning language is that certain areas in the middle of the left hemisphere of the brain are consistently active in processing grammar. Any damage to those left-hemisphere areas harms grammatical competence to a much greater extent than does similar damage to the corresponding areas of the brain's right hemisphere. The behavioral and physiological data together provide good reason to believe that people possess specialized mechanisms for learning language. Thus, whereas Piaget and information-processing theorists depict intelligence as a unified whole that generates understanding of all domains, core-knowledge theorists depict intelligence as a mixture of general learning abilities and powerful specialized abilities that help children learn to solve evolutionarily important problems, that is, problems that have been important for survival throughout human existence.

Central Developmental Issues

Like Piaget and information-processing theorists, core-knowledge theorists believe that development is produced by the interaction of nature and nurture. Unlike most theorists who take those approaches, however, core-knowledge theorists believe that children's nature includes either an innate understanding of crucial concepts or specialized learning abilities that allow them to form the concepts quickly and effortlessly.

Domain Specificity

The basic understandings proposed by core-knowledge theorists are assumed to be **domain specific,** that is, limited to a particular area, such as living things or inanimate objects. Domain-specific understandings in these areas allow infants to distinguish between living and nonliving things; to anticipate that nonliving physical objects they encounter for the first time will remain stationary unless an external force is applied to them; to anticipate that animals they encounter for the first time might well move on their own; and to learn quickly in these and other areas of probable evolutionary importance. Core-knowledge theorists also have emphasized children's early understanding of other central domains including language, space, number, and people. This research will play an important role in the next three chapters.

Children's Informal Theories

A number of core-knowledge theorists have proposed that young children actively organize their understanding of the most important domains into informal theories (Carey, 1985; Gelman, 2003). In particular, they maintain that children form naive theories of *physics* (knowledge of objects), *psychology* (knowledge of people), and *biology* (knowledge of plants and animals). As rudimentary and informal as these theories may be, they share three important characteristics with formal scientific theories:

1. They identify fundamental units for dividing up all objects and events into a few basic categories.
2. They explain many phenomena in terms of a few fundamental principles.
3. They explain events in terms of unobservable causes.

Each of these characteristics is evident in preschoolers' understanding of biology (Evans, 2008; Gelman, 2003; Inagaki & Hatano, 2008). Consistent with the first characteristic, preschoolers divide all objects into people, other animals, plants, and nonliving things. Consistent with the second characteristic, preschoolers understand broadly applicable principles, such as that a desire for food and water underlies many behaviors of animals. Consistent with the third characteristic, preschoolers know that vital activities of animals, such as reproduction and movement, are caused by something inside the animals themselves, as opposed to the external forces that determine the behavior of objects.

domain specific limited to a particular area, such as living things or people

Why would children form intuitive theories of physics, biology, and psychology? According to core-knowledge theorists Henry Wellman and Susan Gelman (1998), the reason probably lies in our evolutionary past. Children have always needed to know about physical objects in order to perceive the environment accurately and to move around in it safely. They have needed to know about animals and plants to avoid predators and poisons. They have needed to understand other people in order to communicate their wants and needs and to pursue shared goals. Again, the core-knowledge metaphor of the child as a well-equipped product of evolution is clear.

When do children first possess such core theories? Spelke (e.g., 2003) speculates that infants begin life with a primitive theory of physics, that is, of inanimate objects. This theory includes the knowledge that the world contains physical objects that occupy space, move only in response to external forces, move in continuous ways through space rather than jumping from one position to another, and cannot simultaneously occupy the same space as another object. One source of evidence for this view is Baillargeon's (1987, 1994) finding that 3-month-olds show surprise when, thanks to a clever research arrangement of mirrors, a solid object appears to move through the space occupied by another solid object.

Wellman and Gelman (1998) suggested that the first theory of psychology may emerge at around 18 months of age, and the first theory of biology at around 3 years. The first theory of psychology is organized around the understanding that other people's actions, not just one's own, reflect their goals and desires. For example, 2-year-olds realize that another person will want to eat if he or she is hungry, regardless of whether they themselves are. The first theory of biology is organized around the realization that people and other animals are living things, different from nonliving things and plants. For example, 3- and 4-year-olds realize that animals, but not manufactured objects, move on the basis of their own power (Gelman, 2003).

© GEORGE D. LEPP / CORBIS

The joy that animals bring children may provide part of the motivation for the children's informal theories of living things.

Of course, a huge amount of development occurs beyond these initial theories. Some of the development involves building on the original organization and filling in details. For example, even 3-month-olds understand that an object (e.g., a glass) will fall unless at least some of it is supported by another object (e.g., a table), but not until about 7 months of age do infants understand that the object also will fall if only a small portion of it is supported (Baillargeon, 1994). In other cases, children may replace rudimentary theories with more advanced ones. Children's initial biological theory distinguishes animals from inanimate objects and plants; not until the age of 7 years are children convinced that the category of living things includes plants as well as animals (Inagaki & Hatano, 2008).

Due to the many fascinating discoveries that core knowledge has yielded about children's earliest understandings, and due to the light that this research has shed on human nature, core-knowledge theories have become increasingly popular in recent years. This research is examined in greater depth in Chapter 7. We close this section's overview by examining educational implications of the core-knowledge approach (Box 4.3).

applications 4.3

Educational Applications of Core-Knowledge Theories

Operating from the principle that people's existing knowledge greatly influences their learning, Hatano and Inagaki (1996) noted several implications of findings regarding children's naive theories of biology that could be used to help children gain a more advanced understanding of the subject. One such implication is that by the time children enter kindergarten, their theory of unobservable causes—such as those related to animals' vital activities—can be built upon to teach them concepts that are usually thought to be beyond their grasp. For example, they can understand that invisible germs cause diseases and that invisible genes cause resemblances between parents and children (Kalish, 1996; Springer, 1996).

A second instructional implication derives from a more specific finding: children's early theories of biology are influenced by their knowledge about human beings. Young children extrapolate from what they know about people to predict the qualities of other animals, a process known as **personification** (Carey, 1985; Inagaki & Hatano, 2008). Although personification leads to many valid conclusions, it also interferes with understanding of some biological concepts. For example, it makes it difficult for children to understand that plants are alive, because plants clearly do not form intentions and pursue goals in the same sense as people do. Instructional programs that emphasize that plants actually do move in ways that help them function—for example, stems' moving toward sunlight and roots' moving toward water—can help young children overcome such misconceptions (Opfer & Siegler, 2004).

review: Core-knowledge theorists envision children as well-equipped products of evolution. Such theories focus on development of understanding in domains of likely evolutionary importance, such as space, time, language, biology, and so on. Researchers who take this approach have demonstrated that infants and young children possess surprising understanding of these domains. Core-knowledge theorists believe that this early competence is made possible by innate, domain-specific understanding and specialized learning mechanisms. Children are viewed as active thinkers who form theories that divide objects and events into a few basic categories, reflect certain fundamental principles, and explain events in terms of unobservable causes.

Sociocultural Theories

A mother and her 4-year-old daughter, Sadie, assemble a toy, using a diagram to guide them:

> *Mother:* Now you need another one like this on the other side. Mmmmm . . . there you go, just like that.
> *Sadie:* Then I need this one to go like this? Hold on, hold on. Let it go. There. Get that out. Oops.
> *M:* I'll hold it while you turn it. *(Watches Sadie work on toy)* Now you make the end.
> *S:* This one?
> *M:* No, look at the picture. Right here *(points to diagram)*. That piece.
> *S:* Like this?
> *M:* Yeah.
>
> (Gauvain, 2001, p. 32)

This interaction probably strikes you as completely unexceptional—and it is. From the perspective of **sociocultural theories,** however, it and thousands of other everyday interactions like it are of the utmost importance, because they are the mechanisms that move development forward.

One noteworthy characteristic of the event, from the sociocultural perspective, is that Sadie is learning to assemble the toy in an interpersonal context.

personification generalizing knowledge about people to infer properties of other animals

sociocultural theories approaches that emphasize that other people and the surrounding culture contribute to children's development

Through guided participation, parents can help children not only accomplish immediate goals but also learn skills, such as how to use written instructions and diagrams to assemble objects.

Sociocultural theorists emphasize that much of development takes place through direct interactions between children and other people—parents, siblings, teachers, playmates, and so on—who want to help children acquire the skills and knowledge valued by their culture. Thus, whereas Piagetian, information-processing, and core-knowledge theories emphasize children's own efforts to understand the world, sociocultural theories emphasize the developmental importance of children's interactions with other people.

The interaction between Sadie and her mother is also noteworthy because it exemplifies **guided participation,** a process in which more knowledgeable individuals organize activities in ways that allow less knowledgeable people to engage in them at a higher level than they could manage on their own (Rogoff, 2003). Sadie's mother, for example, holds one part of the toy so that Sadie can screw in another part. On her own, Sadie would be unable to screw the two parts together and therefore could not improve her skill at the task. Similarly, Sadie's mother points to the relevant part of the diagram, enabling Sadie to decide what to do next and also to learn how diagrams convey information. As this episode illustrates, guided participation often occurs in situations in which the explicit purpose is to achieve a practical goal, such as assembling a toy, but in which learning occurs as a by-product of the activity.

A third noteworthy characteristic of the interaction between Sadie and her mother is that it occurs in a broader cultural context. This context includes not only other people but also the innumerable products of human ingenuity that sociocultural theorists refer to as **cultural tools:** symbol systems, artifacts, skills, values, and so on. In the example of Sadie and her mother, the relevant symbol systems include the language they use to convey their thoughts and the diagram they use to guide their assembly efforts; the relevant artifacts include the toy and the printed sheet on which the diagram appears; the relevant skills include the proficiency in language that allows them to communicate with each other and the procedures they use to interpret the diagram; and the values include the culture's approval of parents interacting with their children in the way that Sadie's mother does and of young girls' learning mechanical skills. In the background are broader technological, economic, and historical factors. Indeed, the interaction itself would not be occurring were it not for the technology needed to manufacture toys and print diagrams, an economy that allows parents the leisure for such interactions, and a history leading up to the symbol systems, artifacts, skills, and values reflected in the interaction. Thus, sociocultural theories can help us appreciate the many aspects of culture embodied in even the smallest everyday interactions.

View of Children's Nature

The giant of the sociocultural approach to cognitive development, and in many ways its originator, was the Russian psychologist Lev Semyonovich Vygotsky. Although Vygotsky and Piaget were contemporaries, much of Vygotsky's most important work was largely unknown outside the Soviet Union until the 1970s. Its appearance created a stir, in part because Vygotsky's view of children's nature was so different from Piaget's.

guided participation a process in which more knowledgeable individuals organize activities in ways that allow less knowledgeable people to learn

cultural tools the innumerable products of human ingenuity that enhance thinking

DAVIDSON FILMS, INC.

The Russian psychologist Lev Vygotsky, the founder of the sociocultural approach to child development.

Vygotsky's Theory

As noted earlier, Piaget depicted children as little scientists, trying to understand the world on their own. Vygotsky, in contrast, portrayed them as social beings, intertwined with other people who are eager to help them gain skills and understanding. Where Piaget viewed children as intent on mastering physical, mathematical, and logical concepts that are the same in all times and places, Vygotsky viewed them as intent on participating in activities that happen to be prevalent in their local setting. Where Piaget emphasized qualitative changes in thinking, Vygotsky emphasized continuous, quantitative changes. These Vygotskyian views gave rise to the central metaphor of sociocultural theories: children as social beings, shaped by, and shaping, their cultural contexts.

Vygotsky's emphasis on children as social beings is evident in his perspective on the relation between language and thought. Whereas Piaget viewed the two as largely unrelated, Vygotsky (1934–1962) viewed them as integrally related; in particular, he believed that thought is internalized speech and that thought originates in large part in statements that parents and other adults make to children.

To illustrate the process of internalizing speech, Vygotsky described three phases of its role in the development of children's ability to regulate their own behavior and problem solving. At first, children's behavior is controlled by other people's statements (as in the example of Sadie and her mother assembling the toy); then, children's behavior is controlled by their own **private speech,** in which they tell themselves aloud what to do, much as their parents might have earlier; and then their behavior is controlled by internalized private speech (thought), in which they silently tell themselves what to do. The transition between the second and third phases often involves whispers or silent lip movements; in Vygotsky's terms, the speech "goes underground" and becomes thought. Private speech is most prevalent between ages 4 and 6 years, although older children and adults also use it on challenging tasks, such as assembling model airplanes or following complex directions (Winsler et al., 2003). In addition, the progression from external to internalized speech emerges not only with age but also with experience; children generate a considerable amount of overt private speech when they first encounter a challenging task, but the amount lessens as they master it (Berk, 1994).

private speech the second phase of Vygotsky's internalization-of-thought process, in which children develop their self-regulation and problem-solving abilities by telling themselves aloud what to do, much as their parents did in the first stage

A Mayan mother teaches her daughter weaving skills by involving her in the process. The inclination to teach and the ability to learn from teaching are among the most distinctly human characteristics.

BOB DAEMMRICH / STOCK BOSTON

Children as Teachers and Learners

Contemporary sociocultural theorists, such as Michael Tomasello (2001), have extended Vygotsky's insights. Tomasello proposed that the human species has two unique characteristics that are crucial to the ability to create complex, rapidly changing cultures. One of these is the inclination to teach others of the species; the other is the inclination to attend to and learn from such teaching. In every human society, adults communicate facts, skills, values, and traditions to their young. This is what makes culture possible; as Isaac Newton noted, it enables the new generation to stand on the shoulders of the old and thus to see farther. The inclination to teach emerges very early: all normal 2-year-olds spontaneously point to objects to call other people's attention to what they themselves find interesting. Only humans engage in such rudimentary teaching behaviors that are not directly tied to survival. This inclination to teach and to learn from teaching is what enables children to be socialized into their culture and to pass that culture on to others.

Children as Products of Their Culture

Sociocultural theorists believe that many of the *processes* that produce development, such as guided participation, are the same in all societies. However, the *content* that children learn—the particular symbol systems, artifacts, skills, and values—vary greatly from culture to culture and shape thinking accordingly.

One example of the impact of culturally specific content comes from a study of long-term analogical reasoning (Chen, Mo, & Honomichi, 2004). American and Chinese college students were asked to solve two problems. One problem required a solution akin to the strategy of leaving a trail of bright stones in "Hansel and Gretel," a tale well known to the American students but unknown to the Chinese. The American students were far more successful in solving that problem, and many of them alluded to the fairy tale even though they had not heard it in many years. The other problem required a solution analogous to a fairy tale that was well known to the Chinese students but unknown to the Americans. In this case, the Chinese students were vastly superior in solving that problem, and many alluded to the relevant fairy tale.

Children's memories of their own experiences also reflect their culture. When 4- to 8-year-olds from China and the United States were asked to describe their earliest memories, their descriptions differed in ways that reflected their culture's attitudes and values (Wang, 2007). Chinese culture prizes and promotes interdependence among people, especially among close relatives. European-American culture, in contrast, prizes and promotes the independence of individuals. Consistent with these cultural emphases, the Chinese children's reports included more references to other people, whereas those of the American children included more references to the child's own feelings and reactions. Thus, the attitudes and values of a culture, as well as its artifacts and technologies, shape the thoughts and memories of people in that culture.

ARIEL SKELLEY / CORBIS STOCK MARKET

As illustrated by this photo of an East Asian father teaching his children to use an abacus, the tools available in a culture shape the learning of children within that culture.

Central Developmental Issues

Vygotsky and contemporary sociocultural theorists have proposed a number of specific ideas about *how change occurs* through social interaction. One of these ideas—guided participation—has already been discussed. In this section, we examine two related concepts that play prominent roles in sociocultural analyses of change: intersubjectivity and social scaffolding.

Intersubjectivity

Sociocultural theorists believe that the foundation of human cognitive development is our ability to establish **intersubjectivity,** the mutual understanding that people share during communication (Gauvain, 2001; Rommetveit, 1985). The idea behind this imposing term is both simple and profound: effective communication requires participants to focus on the same topic, and also on each other's reaction to whatever is being communicated. Such a "meeting of the minds" is indispensable for effective teaching and learning.

intersubjectivity the mutual understanding that people share during communication

LAURA DWIGHT

Joint attention, the process through which social partners focus on the same external object, underlies the human capacity to teach and to learn from teaching.

The roots of intersubjectivity are evident early in infancy. By age 2 to 3 months, infants show greater animation and interest when their mothers respond to their actions than when their mothers behave in ways that are independent of those actions (Murray & Trevarthen, 1985). By age 6 months, infants can learn novel behaviors by observing other people's behavior (Collie & Hayne, 1999).

These developments set the stage for the emergence of a process that is at the heart of intersubjectivity—**joint attention.** In this process, infants and their social partners intentionally focus on a common referent in the external environment. The emergence of joint attention is evident in numerous ways. Between the ages of 9 and 15 months, infants increasingly look toward the objects that their social partners are looking at, adjust where they are looking if the partner looks at a new object, and actively direct a partner's attention toward objects that interest them (Adamson, Bakeman, & Deckner, 2004; Akhtar & Gernsbacher, 2008; Moore, 2008).

Joint attention greatly increases children's ability to learn from other people. One important example involves language learning. When an adult tells a toddler the name of an object, the adult usually looks or points directly at it; children who are looking at the same object are in a better position to learn what the word means than ones who are not (Baldwin, 1991). Indeed, the degree of success infants have in following other people's gaze predicts their later vocabulary development (Brooks & Meltzoff, 2008). The effectiveness of such joint attention is also reflected in the fact that the younger the age at which infants begin to show joint attention, the faster their subsequent language acquisition (Carpenter, Nagell, & Tomasello, 1998).

Intersubjectivity continues to develop well beyond infancy, as children become increasingly able to take the perspectives of other people. For example, 4-year-olds are more likely than 3-year-olds to reach agreement with peers on the rules of games they are about to play and the roles that each child will assume (Goncu, 1993). The continuing development of such perspective-taking abilities also leads to school-age children's increasing ability to teach and learn from each other (Gauvain, 2001).

Social Scaffolding

When putting up tall buildings, construction workers use metal frameworks called scaffolds, which allow them to work high above the ground. Once a building's main structure is in place, it can support further work on its own, thus allowing the scaffolding to be removed. In an analogous fashion, children's learning is aided by **social scaffolding,** in which more competent people provide a temporary framework that supports children's thinking at a higher level than children could manage on their own (Wood, Bruner, & Ross, 1976). Ideally, this framework includes explaining the goal of the task, demonstrating how the task should be done, and helping the child execute the most difficult parts. This, in fact, is the way parents tend to teach their children (Pratt, Kerig, Cowan, & Cowan, 1988; Saxe, Guberman, & Gearhart, 1987; Wood, 1986). Through the process of social scaffolding, children become capable of working at a higher level than if they had not received such help. At first, this higher-level functioning requires extensive support; then it requires less and less and eventually it becomes possible without any support. The higher the quality of the scaffolding—that is, the more that instructional

joint attention a process in which social partners intentionally focus on a common referent in the external environment

social scaffolding a process in which more competent people provide a temporary framework that supports children's thinking at a higher level than children could manage on their own efforts are directed at the upper end of the child's capabilities—the greater the learning (Conner, Knight, & Cross, 1997; Gauvain, 2001). The goal of social scaffolding—to allow children to learn by doing—is the same as that of guided participation, but scaffolding tends to involve more explicit instruction and explanation, whereas guided participation tends to involve adults' organizing tasks so that children can take increasingly active and responsible roles in them.

© SIMON MARCUS / CORBIS

By providing their children with social scaffolding, parents enable them to play with toys and other objects in more advanced ways than would otherwise be possible, which helps the children learn.

The quality of scaffolding tends to increase with increases in the age and experience of those providing it. Adults' scaffolding tends to be of higher quality than children's, and older children's, of higher quality than younger ones'. In part, this is because adults usually encourage learners to participate actively in the task and help them learn strategies for proceeding independently in the future (Gauvain, 2001). Children, in contrast—even ones who are as knowledgeable about a task as adults are—often just tell less knowledgeable peers what to do or do the task themselves. Not surprisingly, 5- to 9-year-olds who have previously solved problems with their parents do better on similar new problems than peers who have previously solved the same kinds of problems with other children (Radziszewska & Rogoff, 1988).

One particularly important way in which parents use scaffolding is in helping children form autobiographical memories, explicit memories of events that took place at specific times and places in the individual's past (Nelson & Fivush, 2004). Autobiographical memories include information about one's goals, intentions, emotions, and reactions relative to these events. Over time, these memories become strung together into a more or less coherent narrative about one's life.

When discussing past experiences with their young children, some mothers encourage them to provide many details about past events and often expand on the children's statements. Such a mother might reply to her toddler's statement "Bird fly away" by saying, "Yes, the bird flew away because you got very close to it and it was scared of you." Such statements help children remember their experiences by improving their encoding of key information (distance from the bird) and their appreciation of the causal relations among events (Boland, Haden, & Ornstein, 2003; McGuigan & Salmon, 2004). Other mothers ask fewer questions and rarely elaborate on what their children say. Children whose mothers use the more elaborative style remember more about the events than do children whose mothers rarely elaborate (Haden, Hayne, & Fivush, 1997; Harley & Reese, 1999; Leichtman et al., 2000). (As discussed in Box 4.4, concepts from sociocultural theories have also proved useful for improving education in classrooms.)

The importance of the sociocultural persective in understanding cognitive development will be especially clear in the upcoming chapters on language development, conceptual development, and intelligence.

applications 4.4

Educational Applications of Sociocultural Theories

For some time, the educational system of the United States has been criticized for promoting rote memorization of facts rather than deep understanding; for promoting competition rather than cooperation among students; and for generally failing to create enthusiasm for learning (Bruner, 1996; National Research Council, 2001). The emphasis of sociocultural theories on the role of culture in learning implies that one way to improve schooling is to change the culture of schools. The culture should be one in which instruction is aimed at deep understanding, in which learning is a cooperative activity, and in which learning a little makes children want to learn more.

One impressive attempt to meet these goals is Ann Brown's (1997) *community-of-learners* program. Its efforts to build communities of learners have focused on 6- to 12-year-olds, most of them African-American children attending inner-city schools in Boston, Massachusetts, and Oakland, California. The main curriculum consists of projects that require research on some large topic, such as interdependence between animals and their habitats. The class divides into small groups, each of which focuses on a particular aspect of the topic. With the topic of the interdependence between animals and habitats, for example, one group might study predator–prey relations; another, reproductive strategies; another, protection from the elements; and so on.

At the end of roughly 10 weeks, new groups are formed, each including one child from every original group. Children in the new groups are asked to solve a problem that encompasses all the aspects studied by the previous groups, such as designing an "animal of the future" that would be particularly well adapted to its habitat. Because each child's participation in the previous group has resulted in the child's gaining expertise on the aspect of the problem studied by that group, and because no other child in the new group has that expertise, all of the children's contributions are essential for the new group to succeed. This has been labeled the *jigsaw approach,* because, as in a jigsaw puzzle, each piece is necessary for the solution.

A variety of people help foster such communities of learners. Classroom teachers introduce the big ideas of the unit, encourage the class to pool its knowledge to achieve deeper understanding, push children to provide evidence for their opinions, and ask them to summarize what they know and to identify new learning goals. Outside experts are brought to classrooms to lecture and answer questions about the topic. Children and teachers exchange e-mails with groups at other schools who are working on the same problem to see how they are approaching issues that arise.

Communities of learners provide both cognitive and motivational benefits for children. Participation in such groups helps children to become increasingly adept at constructing high-quality solutions to the problems they try to solve. It also helps them learn such general skills as identifying key questions and comparing alternative solutions to a problem. Finally, because the children all depend on each other's contributions, the community-of-learners approach encourages mutual respect and individual responsibility for the success of the entire group. In short, the approach creates a culture of learning.

review: Sociocultural approaches view children as social beings, shaped by, and shaping, their cultural contexts. These approaches emphasize that children develop in a cultural context of other people and human inventions, such as symbol systems, artifacts, skills, and values. Through guided participation, more knowledgeable people help children gain skills in using these cultural tools; using the tools, in turn, further transforms children's thinking. Culture is made possible by the human propensity to think and learn and by our ability to establish intersubjectivity with other people. Through processes such as social scaffolding and the creation of communities of learners, older and more skilled individuals help children acquire the skills, knowledge, and values of their culture.

Dynamic-Systems Theories

Like all biological processes, thinking serves an adaptive purpose: it enables people and other animals to devise plans for attaining goals. However, attaining goals also requires the ability to take action; without this ability, thinking would be pointless. What purpose would it serve for an infant to figure out that she needed to remove an obstacle to obtain a toy if she were incapable of moving the obstacle and accurately reaching for and grasping the toy? As this analysis implies, any variable that influenced the infant's ability to execute the plan—for example, her ability to accurately perceive the toy's position and to maintain a stable posture while reaching—would influence her likelihood of achieving the goal. However, despite this inherent connection between thinking and acting, most theories of cognitive development have focused exclusively on thinking and ignored the development of the actions that allow children to realize the fruits of their mental labor.

dynamic-systems theories a class of theories that focus on how change occurs over time in complex systems

One increasingly influential exception to this generalization is **dynamic-systems theories,** which are a class of theories that focus on how change occurs over time in complex systems. Research that reflects this perspective indicates that detailed analyses of the development of even basic actions, such as crawling, walking, reaching, and grasping, yield surprising and impressive insights into how development occurs. For example, dynamic-systems research has shown that improved reaching influences the development of infants' free (i.e., spontaneous) play with objects. In particular, it allows infants to play with objects in more advanced ways, such as organizing them into categories or interesting configurations (Spencer et al., 2006; Thelen & Corbetta, 1994). Dynamic-systems research also has shown that the onset of crawling changes infants' relationships with family members, who may be thrilled to see their baby attain an important motor milestone but also may find themselves having to be much more watchful and controlling as the child tries to explore anything he or she can get to (Campos, Kermoian, & Zumbahlen, 1992).

Another contribution of dynamic-systems research has been to demonstrate that the development of seemingly simple actions is far more complex and interesting than previously realized. For example, such research has overturned the traditional belief that physical maturation leads infants to attain motor milestones in stages, at roughly the same age, in the same way, and in a steady progression. It has shown instead that individual children acquire skills at different ages and in different ways, and that their development entails regressions as well as progress. One example of this type of research is a longitudinal study of the development of infants' reaching conducted by Esther Thelen, who, along with her colleague Linda Smith, was the cofounder of the dynamic-systems approach to cognitive development. In this particular study, Thelen and colleagues (1993) repeatedly observed the reaching efforts of four infants during their first year. Using high-speed motion-capture systems and computer analysis of the infants' muscle movements, they found that due to individual differences in such factors as the infants' physiology, activity level, arousal, motivation, and experience, each child faced different challenges in his or her attempts to master reaching. The following observations illustrate some of the complexities these researchers discovered, including fluctuations in infants' developmental progress, variability in the ages at which they reach developmental milestones, and the differing challenges they must overcome:

> Infants differed dramatically in the ages of the transition (from no reaching to reaching). Whereas Nathan reached first at 12 weeks, Hannah and Justin did not attain this milestone until 20 weeks of age. [In addition,] the infants showed periods of rapid change, plateaus, and even regressions in performance . . . three of the four infants showed an epoch where straightness and smoothness appeared to get worse after some improvement . . . Finally, there was in Nathan, Justin, and Hannah a rather discontinuous shift to better, less variable performance . . . Gabriel's transition to stability was more gradual.
>
> (Thelen & Smith, 1998, pp. 605, 607)

The electrodes attached to the arms of this baby in Esther Thelen's lab are connected to a computer, so the infant's reaching movements can be analyzed in great detail.

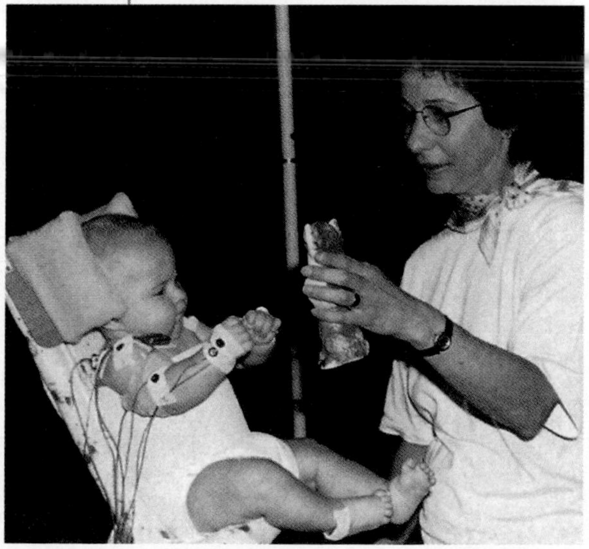

COURTESY OF ESTHER THELEN

> Infants must individually discover the appropriate speeds from the background of their characteristic styles. Gabriel, for example, had to damp down his very vigorous movements in order to successfully reach, and he did. In contrast, Hannah, who moved slowly and spent considerable time with her hands flexed near her face, had to activate her arms more to extend them out in front of her. . . . Reaching is thus sculpted from ongoing movements of the arms, through a process of modulating what is in place . . . As infants become older, their attention becomes more focused, and their perceptual discrimination improves, and their memories get better, and their movements become more skilled. A rich, complex, and realistic account of change must include this dynamic interplay.
>
> (Thelen, 2001, pp. 172, 182)

These quotations help to convey what is meant by the label "dynamic systems." As suggested by the term *dynamic*, these theories depict development as a process in which change is the only constant. Whereas most approaches to cognitive development hypothesize that development entails long periods of relatively stable stages, rules, or core theories separated by relatively brief transition periods, dynamic-systems theories propose that at all points in development, thought and action change from moment to moment in response to the current situation, the child's immediate past history, and the child's longer-term history of actions in related situations. Thus, Thelen and Smith (1998) noted that the development of reaching included regressions as well as improvements, and Thelen (2001) described how differences in Hannah's and Gabriel's early reaches influenced their later path to skilled reaching.

As suggested by the second term in the label, this theory depicts each child as a well-integrated system, in which many subsystems—perception, action, attention, memory, language, social interaction, and so on—work together to determine behavior. For instance, dynamic-systems analyses have revealed that performance on tests of object permanence, Piaget's classic measure of infants' cognitive development, is affected not only by conceptual understanding but also by a host of other factors, including changes in attention, perception, memory, and motor skills (see discussion of the A-not-B error on pages 168–169.) The assumptions that development is dynamic and that it functions as an organized system are central to the theory's perspective on children's nature.

View of Children's Nature

Dynamic-systems theories are the newest of the five types of theories discussed in this chapter, and their view of children's nature incorporates influences from each of the others. Like Piaget's theory, dynamic-systems theories emphasize children's innate motivation to explore the environment; like information-processing theories, they emphasize precise analyses of problem-solving activity; like core-knowledge theories, they emphasize early emerging competencies; and like sociocultural theories, they emphasize the formative influence of other people. These similarities to other theories, as well as differences from them, are evident in dynamic-systems theories' emphasis on motivation and the role of action.

Motivators of Development

To a greater extent than any of the other theories except Piaget's, dynamic-systems theories emphasize that from infancy onward, children are strongly motivated to learn about the world around them and to explore and expand their own capabilities (von Hofsten, 2007). This motivation to explore and learn is clearly apparent in the fact that children persist in practicing new skills even when they possess well-practiced skills that are more efficient. Thus, toddlers persist in their first unsteady efforts to walk, despite the fact that crawling would get them where they want to go more quickly and without the risk of falling (Gibson & Pick, 2000).

Unlike Piaget's theory, but like sociocultural and some core-knowledge theories, dynamic-systems theories also emphasize infants' interest in the social world as a crucial motivator of development. As noted in our discussion of the *active child* in Chapter 1, even newborns prefer attending to the sounds, movements, and features of the human face over almost any alternative stimuli. By 10 to 12 months of age, infants' interest in the social world is readily apparent in the emergence of intersubjectivity (page 161), as infants quite consistently look where the people interacting with them are looking and direct the attention of others to things they themselves find interesting (Deák, Flom, & Pick, 2000; von Hofsten, Dahlström, & Fredricksson, 2005). Dynamic-systems theorists have emphasized that observing other people, imitating their actions, and attracting their attention are all potent motivators of development (Fischer & Bidell, 2006; von Hofsten, 2007).

The Centrality of Action

Dynamic-systems theories are unique in their pervasive emphasis on how children's specific actions shape their development. Piaget's theory asserts the role of actions during the sensorimotor stage, but dynamic-systems theories place greater emphasis than any other theory on how actions contribute to development throughout life. This focus on the developmental role of action has led to a number of interesting discoveries. For example, reaching for objects helps infants infer the goals of other people's reaches (von Hofsten, 2007). These inferences appear to reflect the operation of *mirror neurons*, neurons that are activated when one observes another person perform a given goal-directed action, in effect, neurally "mirroring" the observed behavior as though one were performing it oneself (Umiltá et al., 2001). Such neurons are thought to enable infants to understand other people's reaches by mapping the sight of them onto the infants' motor and goal representations of their own reaches. Another example of infants' learning from actions comes from research in which infants were outfitted with Velcro mittens that enabled them to "grab" and explore Velcro-covered objects that they otherwise could not have picked up. After two weeks of experience grabbing the Velcro-covered objects with the Velcro-covered mittens, infants showed greater ability to grab and explore ordinary objects without gloves than did other infants of the same ages (Needham, Barrett, & Peterman, 2002).

The ways in which children's actions shape their development extend well beyond reaching and grasping in infancy. Actions influence categorization: in one study, encouraging children to move an object up and down led to their categorizing it as one of a group of objects that were easiest to move in that way, whereas encouraging children to move the same object side to side led them to categorize it as one of a group of objects that were easiest to move in that way (Smith, 2005). Actions also affect vocabulary acquisition and generalization (Gershkoff-Stowe, Connell, & Smith, 2006; Samuelson & Horst, 2008): for example, experimental manipulations that lead children to state an incorrect name for an object impair the child's future attempts to learn the object's correct name. In addition, actions shape memory, as demonstrated by research in which children's past attempts to locate and dig up objects they had earlier seen being hidden in a sandbox alter their recall of where they saw the objects being subsequently rehidden. That is, their new searches are in-between the past and present locations, as if they were a compromise between their memory of the new hiding place and of the location where they had originally looked (Schutte, Spencer, & Schöner, 2003; Zelazo, Reznick, & Spinazzola, 1998). Even in adulthood, categorization, vocabulary acquisition, conceptual understanding, and memory are influenced by actions (Barsalou, 2005). Thus, just as thinking shapes actions, actions shape thinking.

Central Development Issues

Two developmental issues that are especially prominent in dynamic-systems theories are how the cognitive system organizes itself and how it changes.

Self-Organization

Dynamic-systems theories view development as a process of self-organization in which "pattern and order emerge from interactions of the components of a complex system without explicit instruction either in the organism itself or from the environment" (Thelen & Smith, 1998, p. 564). In other words, development is neither innately specified in the genome nor wholly dependent upon instruction from other people. Instead, the child's interactions with the physical and social environments produce an organized, flexible, and adaptive behavioral system. Although these ideas regarding self-organization resemble Piaget's concepts of assimilation, accommodation, and equilibration, as well as core-knowledge concepts regarding children's theories, dynamic-systems research has demonstrated more precisely how the organizational process operates.

Self-organization involves bringing together and integrating components as needed to adapt to a continuously changing environment (Spencer et al., 2006). The organizational process is sometimes called *soft assembly*, because the components and their organization change from moment to moment and situation to situation, rather than being governed by rigid rules that are consistently applied across time and situations. The types of research to which this perspective leads are illustrated particularly well by certain studies of the A-not-B error that 8- to 12-month-olds typically make in Piaget's classic object-permanence task. As noted earlier, this error involves infants' searching for a toy where they had previously found it (location A), rather than where they last saw it being hidden (location B). Piaget (1954) explained the A-not-B error by hypothesizing that before their 1st birthday, infants lack a clear concept of the permanent existence of objects.

In contrast, viewing the A-not-B error from a dynamic-systems perspective suggested that many factors other than conceptual understanding influence performance on the object permanence task. In particular, Smith, Thelen, Titzer, and McLin (1999) argued that babies' previous reaching toward location A produces a habit of reaching there, which influences their behavior when the object is subsequently hidden at location B. On the basis of this premise, the researchers made several predictions that were later borne out. One was that the more often babies had found an object by reaching to one location, the more likely they would be to reach there again when the object was hidden at a different location. Also supported was the prediction that increasing the memory demands of the task by not allowing infants to search for the object for 3 seconds after it was hidden at the B location would increase the likelihood of infants' reaching to location A (Clearfield et al., 2009). The reasoning here was that the strength of the new memory would fade rapidly relative to the fading of the habit of reaching to the A location. Dynamic-systems theory also suggested that infants' attention would influence their object-permanence performance. Consistent with this view, manipulating infants' attention by tapping one of the locations just as the infants were about to reach usually resulted in their reaching to the tapped location, regardless of where the object was hidden.

In perhaps the most striking test of such predictions, researchers demonstrated that putting small weights on infants' wrists after the infants had reached to location A but before the object was hidden at location B improved object-permanence performance (Diedrich, Thelen, Smith, & Corbetta, 2000). The researchers had predicted this effect by reasoning that the addition of the wrist weights would require the use of different muscle tensions and forces to reach for the object and consequently would disrupt the infants' habit of reaching to the A location. Thus, rather than providing a pure measure of conceptual understanding, performance on the object-permanence task appears to also reflect the combined influence of the strength of the habit of reaching to location A, the memory demands of the current task, the infants' current focus of attention, and the match between the muscular forces required to reach in the old and new situations.

How Change Occurs

Dynamic-systems theories posit that changes occur through mechanisms of variation and selection that are analogous to those that produce biological evolution (Fischer & Biddell, 2006; Steenbeek & Van Geert, 2008). In this context, *variation* refers to different behaviors being generated to pursue the same goal. As noted in Chapter 1, for example, to add two small numbers, a 1st grader might sometimes count from 1, other times count from the larger number, and yet other times retrieve the answer from memory. *Selection* involves an increasing choice of behaviors that are effective in meeting goals and a decreasing choice of less effective behaviors. For example, over the course of 1st grade, children increasingly retrieve answers to the simpler problems (e.g., 3 + 3), increasingly count from the larger addend when that is easy to do (e.g., 3 + 9), and decreasingly count from 1 on both types of problems (Geary, 2006).

The variability of behavior often waxes and wanes in a cyclical fashion over the course of learning (Siegler, 2006). On number-conservation problems, for example, children first use a variety of incorrect approaches, then converge on a single incorrect approach (the longer row has more objects), then oscillate between that approach and the correct approach of considering on whether any objects were added or subtracted, and finally consistently use the correct approach (Siegler, 1981; 1995).

Such variation is important, because children whose initial goal-directed behavior varies to a greater extent tend to learn more from relevant experience. For example, children who initially use a greater number of strategies to solve number-conservation problems learn more from feedback on the correctness of their answers (Church & Goldin-Meadow, 1986; Siegler, 1995). This positive relation between variability and learning has emerged in numerous contexts, including mathematical reasoning (Alibali & Goldin-Meadow, 1993), scientific reasoning (Perry & Lewis, 1999; Schauble, 1996), and logical deduction (van der Maas & Molenaar, 1992). A possible explanation for the positive relation between variability and learning may be that using multiple approaches to achieving a goal may indicate openness to new experiences and approaches (Goldin-Meadow, 2001).

Children's selection among alternative approaches reflects several influences (Siegler, 2006). Most important is the *relative success* of each approach in meeting a particular goal: as children gain experience, they increasingly rely on approaches that produce desired outcomes. Another important consideration is *efficiency*: children increasingly choose approaches that meet goals more quickly or with less effort than do other approaches. A third consideration is *novelty*, the lure and challenge of trying something new. Children sometimes choose new approaches that are no more efficient, or even less efficient, than an established alternative but that have the potential to become more efficient. They may try to walk down steep ramps when it would be quicker and less dangerous to slide down them (Adolph, 1997), and they use newly generated memory and arithmetic strategies when older approaches temporarily would be equally or more effective (Miller & Seier, 1994; Siegler & Jenkins, 1989). Such a novelty preference tends to be adaptive, because with practice, a strategy that is initially less efficient than existing approaches often becomes more efficient (Wittman, Daw, Seymour, & Dolan, 2008). As discussed in Box 4.5, the insights that dynamic-systems theories have brought to the question of how change occurs has led to useful applications as well as theoretical progress.

applications **4.5**

Educational Applications of Dynamic-Systems Theories

As noted in Chapter 2 (page 76), children born prematurely with low birth weight are more likely than other children to encounter developmental difficulties; one of these is the slower emergence and refinement of reaching (Fallang, Saugstad, Grogaard, et al., 2003). These delays in reaching slow the development of brain areas involved in reaching (Martin, Choy, Pullman, & Meng, 2004) and limit infants' ability to explore and learn about objects (Lobo, Galloway, & Savelsbergh, 2004). A variety of seemingly reasonable efforts to improve preterm infants' reaching, such as guiding their arms through reaching movements, have yielded discouraging results (Blauw-Hospers & Hadders-Algra, 2005).

In contrast, a recent intervention based on dynamic-systems research was quite successful (Heathcock, Lobo, & Galloway, 2008). This intervention was inspired by Thelen and colleagues' (1993) finding that a slowness to self-initiate arm activity impedes the development of reaching and by Needham and colleagues' (2002) finding that providing young infants with experience in reaching for and grabbing Velcro-patched objects while wearing Velcro-covered mittens improves the infants' later ability to reach for and grab ordinary objects barehanded.

The researchers began their intervention by requesting that caregivers of preterm infants in an experimental group provide the infants with special movement experiences. Specifically, the caregivers were asked to encourage infants' arm movements by (1) tying a bell to the infants' wrists so that arm movements would make it ring, presumably motivating further movements, and (2) placing Velcro mittens on the infants' hands to allow them to reach for and grab Velcro-patched toys held in front of them. The caregivers were asked to do this at home five times per week for eight weeks.

Caregivers of preterm infants in a control group were asked to provide their infants with special social experiences that included singing to and talking with the infants on the same intervention schedule as the experimental group's. Periodically, the infants in both groups were brought to the lab to allow project personnel to observe their reaching and exploration under controlled circumstances and during free play.

As might be expected, the reaching of preterm infants in both groups improved over the eight weeks of the study. However, the infants in the experimental group improved to a greater degree. They more often touched toys that were held in front of them, and more often did so with the inside rather than the outside part of their hand, as is needed for grasping objects. The difference between infants in the experimental and control groups grew steadily over the course of the laboratory observations. Especially impressive, infants who were given the movement experience actually reached more often at the end of the experiment than did full-term same-age peers who were not given the movement experience. Such experiences may also help preterm infants avoid other types of cognitive and motor impairments that are partially caused by delayed development of reaching.

review:

Dynamic-systems theories view children as ever-changing, well-integrated organisms that combine perception, action, attention, memory, language, and social influences to produce actions that satisfy goals. From this perspective, children's actions are shaped by both their remote and recent past history, their current physical capabilities, and their immediate physical and social environment. The actions, in turn, are viewed as shaping the development of categorization, conceptual understanding, memory, language, and other capabilities. Dynamic-systems theories are unique in their emphasis on how children's actions shape their development and in the range of developmental influences they consider with regard to particular capabilities.

Chapter Summary

Theories of development are important because they provide a framework for understanding important phenomena, raise major issues regarding human nature, and motivate new research. Five major theories of cognitive development are Piagetian, information-processing, core-knowledge, sociocultural, and dynamic-systems.

Piaget's Theory

- Among the reasons for the longevity of Piaget's theory are that it vividly conveys the flavor of children's thinking at different ages, extends across a broad range of ages and content areas, and provides many fascinating and surprising observations of children's thinking.
- Piaget's theory is often labeled "constructivist," because it depicts children as actively constructing knowledge for themselves in response to their experience. The theory posits that children learn through two processes that are present from birth—assimilation and accommodation—and that they balance their contributions through a third process, equilibration. These processes produce continuities across development.
- Piaget's theory divides cognitive development into four broad stages: the sensorimotor stage (birth to age 2), the preoperational stage (ages 2 to 7), the concrete operations stage (ages 7 to 12), and the formal operations stage (age 12 and beyond). These stages reflect discontinuities in development.
- In the sensorimotor stage, infants' intelligence is expressed primarily through motor interactions with the environment. Infants gain understanding of concepts such as object permanence and become capable of deferred imitation during this period.
- In the preoperational stage, children become able to represent their experiences in language, mental imagery, and thought, but because of cognitive limitations such as egocentrism and centration, they have difficulty solving many problems, including Piaget's various tests of conservation and tasks related to taking the perspective of others.
- In the concrete operations stage, children become able to reason logically about concrete objects and events but have difficulty reasoning in purely abstract terms and in succeeding on tasks requiring hypothetical thinking, such as the pendulum problem.
- In the formal operations stage, children gain the cognitive capabilities of hypothetical thinking.
- The primary weaknesses of Piaget's theory are that it depicts children's thinking as being more consistent than it is, underestimates infants' and young children's cognitive competence, understates the contribution of the social world to cognitive development, and only vaguely describes the mechanisms that give rise to thinking and cognitive growth.

Information-Processing Theories

- Information-processing theories focus on the specific mental processes that underlie children's thinking. Even in infancy, children are seen as actively pursuing goals, encountering processing limits, and devising strategies that allow them to surmount the processing limits and attain the goals.
- The development of memory and learning in large part reflects improvements in basic processes, strategies, and content knowledge.
- Basic cognitive processes allow infants to learn and remember from birth onward. Among the most important basic processes are association, recognition, generalization, and encoding.
- The use of strategies enhances learning and memory beyond the level that basic processes alone could provide. Rehearsal and selective attention are two important strategies.
- Increasing content knowledge enhances memory and learning of all types of information.
- Among the leading contributors to the growth of problem solving are the development of planning and analogical reasoning.

Core-Knowledge Theories

- Core-knowledge theories are based on the view that children begin life with a wide range of specific cognitive competencies.
- Core-knowledge approaches also hypothesize that children are especially adept at acquiring evolutionarily important information, such as language, spatial layouts, and face recognition.
- These approaches also posit that, from early ages, children organize information about the most important domains into informal theories, such as theories of physics, biology, and psychology.

Sociocultural Theories

- Starting with Vygotsky's theory, sociocultural theories have focused on the way that the social world molds development. These theories emphasize that development is shaped not only by interactions with other people and the skills learned from them but also by the artifacts with which children interact and the values and traditions of the larger society.
- Sociocultural theories view humans as differing from other animals in their propensity to teach and their ability to learn from teaching.
- Establishing intersubjectivity between people through joint attention is essential to learning.
- Sociocultural theories describe people as learning through guided participation and social scaffolding, in which others who are more knowledgeable support the learner's efforts.

Dynamic-Systems Theories

- Dynamic-systems theories view change as the one constant in development. Rather than depicting development as being organized into long periods of stability and brief periods of dramatic change, these theories propose that there is no period in which substantial change is not occurring.
- These theories also view each person as a unified system that, in order to meet goals, integrates perception, action, categorization, motivation, memory, language, conceptual understanding, and knowledge of the physical and social worlds.
- Dynamic-systems theories view development as a self-organizing process that brings together components as needed to adapt to a continuously changing environment.
- Attaining goals requires action as well as thought. Thought shapes action, but it also is shaped by action.
- Just as variation and selection produce biological evolution, they also produce cognitive development.

Critical Thinking Questions

1. Piaget's theory has been prominent for more than 80 years. Do you think it will continue to be prominent for the next 20 years as well? Why or why not?
2. Do you think that the term *egocentric* is a good description of preschoolers' overall way of seeing the world? On the basis of what you learned in this chapter and your own experience, explain your answer and indicate in what ways preschoolers are egocentric and in what ways they are not.
3. Information-processing analyses tend to be more specific about cognitive processes than do analyses generated by other theories. Do you see this specificity as an advantage or a disadvantage? Why?
4. Does the evolutionary perspective of core-knowledge theories seem sound to you? Explain and give examples of how learning in core-knowledge domains may or may not have contributed to human evolution.
5. Imagine that you are trying to help a 6-year-old learn a skill that you possess. Using the ideas of guided participation and social scaffolding, describe how you might go about this task.
6. Dynamic-systems theories reflect influences of each of the other theories reviewed in this chapter. Which theoretical influence do you think is strongest: Piagetian, information-processing, core-knowledge, or sociocultural? Explain your reasoning.

Key Terms

adaptation, p. 131
organization, p. 131
assimilation, p. 131
accommodation, p. 131
equilibration, p. 131
sensorimotor stage, p. 133
preoperational stage, p. 133
concrete operational stage, p. 133
formal operational stage, p. 133
object permanence, p. 134
A-not-B error, p. 134
deferred imitation, p. 135
symbolic representation, p. 136
egocentrism, p. 136
centration, p. 137
conservation concept, p. 137
task analysis, p. 144
structure, p. 144
processes, p. 144
problem solving, p. 145
sensory memory, p. 146
long-term memory, p. 146
working (short-term) memory, p. 146
basic processes, p. 147
encoding, p. 147
rehearsal, p. 148
selective attention, p. 149
overlapping-waves theories, p. 150
core-knowledge theories, p. 154
domain specific, p. 156
personification, p. 158
sociocultural theories, p. 158
guided participation, p. 159
cultural tools, p. 159
private speech, p. 160
intersubjectivity, p. 161
joint attention, p. 162
social scaffolding, p. 162
dynamic-systems theories, p. 165

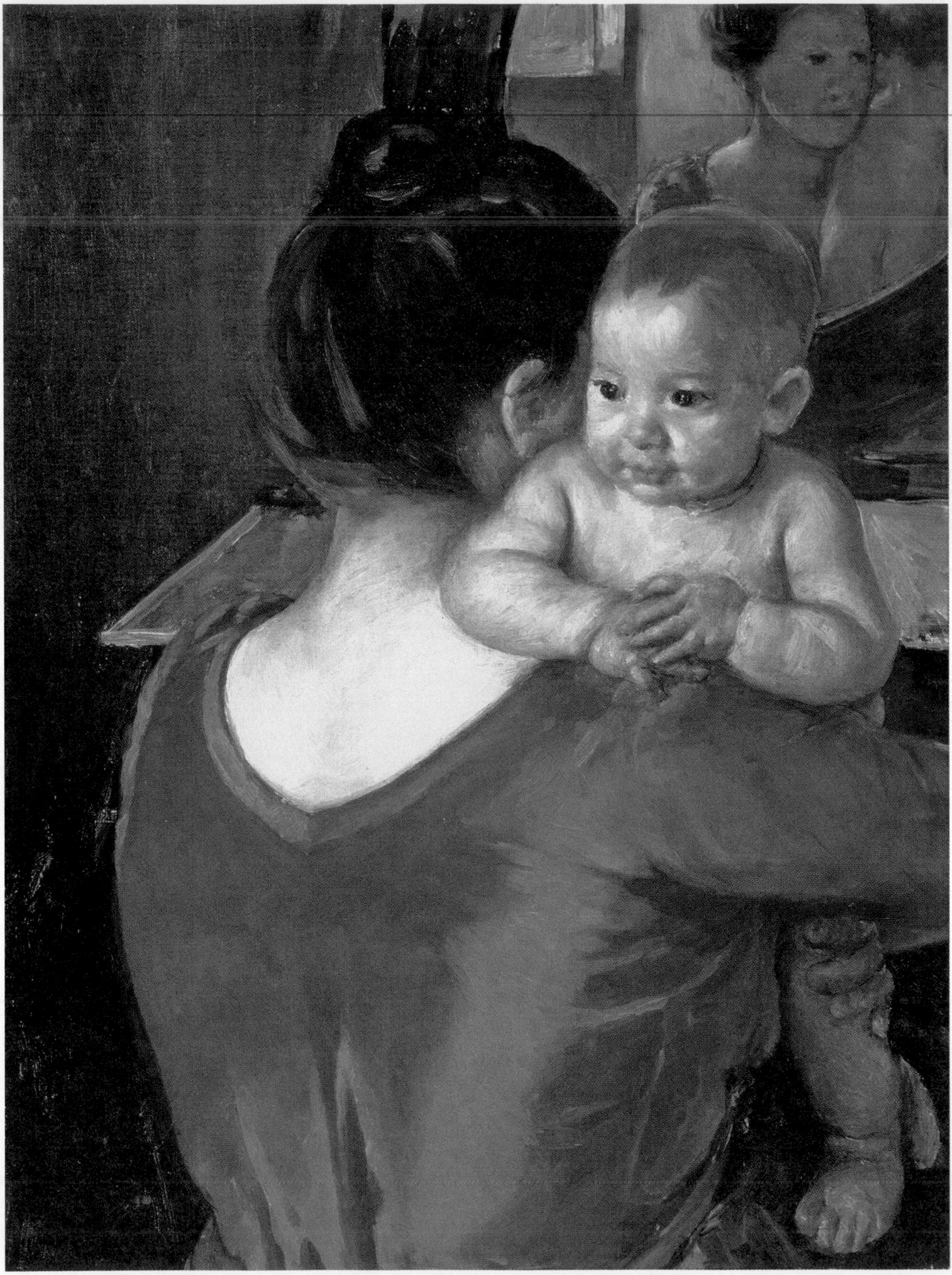

MARY STEVENSON CASSATT, *Mother and Child,* 1900

5

Seeing, Thinking, and Doing in Infancy

THEMES

Nature and Nurture

❖

The Active Child

❖

Continuity/Discontinuity

❖

Mechanisms of Change

❖

The Sociocultural Context

❖

Individual Differences

❖

Four-month-old Benjamin, perched on the kitchen counter in his infant seat, is watching his parents wash the dinner dishes. What he observes includes two people who move on their own, as well as a variety of glass, ceramic, and metal objects of differing sizes and shapes that move only when picked up and manipulated by the people. Other elements of the scene never move. As the people go about their task, distinctive sounds emanate from their moving lips, while different sounds occur as they deposit silverware, skillets, glasses, and sponges on the kitchen counter. At one point, Benjamin sees a cup completely disappear from view when his father places it on the counter behind a cooking pot; it reappears a moment later when the pot is moved. He also sees objects disappear as they pass through the suds and into the water, but he never sees one object pass through another. The objects that are placed on the counter stay put, until Benjamin's father puts a crystal goblet on the counter with more than half of its base hanging over the counter's edge. The crashing sound that follows startles all three people in the room, and Benjamin is further startled when the two adults begin emitting sharp, loud sounds toward one another, quite unlike the soft, pleasant sounds they had been producing before. When Benjamin begins crying in response, the adults rush to him, patting him and making soft, especially pleasant sounds to him.

This example, to which we will return throughout the chapter, illustrates the enormous amount of information that is available for an infant to observe and learn from in even the most everyday situations. In learning about the world through such situations, Benjamin, like most infants, avidly explores everything and everyone around him, using every tool he has: he gathers information by looking and listening, as well as by tasting, smelling, and feeling. His area of exploration will gradually expand as he becomes capable first of reaching for objects and then of manipulating them, making it possible for him to discover more about them. When he starts to move around under his own power, even more of the world will become available to him, including things his parents would prefer that he not investigate, such as electrical outlets and kitty litter. Never will Benjamin explore so voraciously or learn so rapidly as in the first few years of his young life.

In this chapter, we discuss development in four closely related areas: perception, action, learning, and cognition. Our discussion focuses primarily on infancy. One reason for concentrating on this period is that extremely rapid developmental change occurs in all four areas during the first two years of a child's life. A second reason is the fact that development in these four domains is particularly intertwined in this period: the minirevolutions that transform infants' behavior and experience in one domain lead to minirevolutions in others. For example, the dramatic improvements in visual abilities that occur in their first few months enable infants to see more of the people and objects around them, thereby greatly increasing the opportunities they have to learn new information.

A third reason for concentrating on infancy in this chapter is the fact that the majority of recent research on perceptual and motor development has been done with infants and young children. There is also a large body of fascinating research on learning and cognition in the first few years. We will review some of this research here and cover subsequent development in these areas in later chapters. A final reason for focusing on infants in this chapter is that the methods used to investigate infants' development in these four domains are, of necessity, quite different from those that researchers are able to use to study older children.

Our examination of key developments in infancy will feature several enduring themes. The *active child* theme is vividly embodied by infants' eager exploration of their environment. *Continuity/discontinuity* comes up repeatedly in research that addresses the relation between behavior and development in infancy and development later in life. In some sections, the *mechanisms of change* theme is also prominent, as we explore the role that variability and selection play in infants' development. In our discussion of early motor development, we will examine contributions made by the *sociocultural context.*

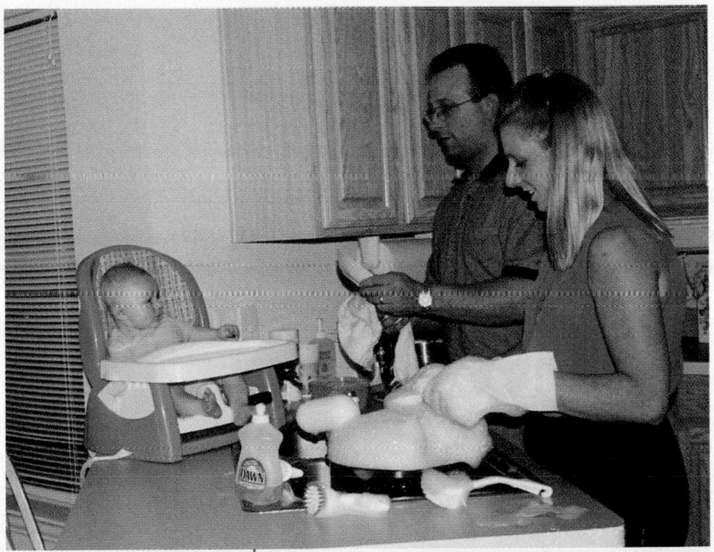

OWCZAR / VISUALS UNLIMITED

Baby Benjamin looking and listening as his parents do the dishes.

The theme that most pervades this chapter, however, is the interaction of *nature and nurture* in development. For at least 2,000 years, a not always amicable debate has existed between those philosophers and scientists who have emphasized innate knowledge in accounting for human development and those who have emphasized learning (Spelke & Newport, 1998). These different emphases are quite evident in the core-knowledge accounts reviewed in Chapter 4. The desire to shed light on this age-old debate is one reason that an enormous amount of research has been conducted in the past few decades on perception, action, learning, and cognition in infancy. As you will see, what developmental scientists have recently learned about babies has revealed that their development is even more complicated and remarkable than previously suspected.

Perception

Parents of new babies cannot help wondering what their children experience—how much they can see, how well they can hear, whether they connect sight and sound (as in our opening vignette), and so on. William James, one of the earliest psychologists, believed that the world of the newborn is a "big blooming, buzzing confusion." Due to remarkable advances in the study of early sensation and perception, modern researchers do not share his view. They have demonstrated that infants come into the world with all their sensory systems functioning to some degree and that subsequent development occurs at a very rapid pace. **Sensation** refers to the processing of basic information from the external world by the sensory receptors in the sense organs (eyes, ears, skin, etc.) and brain. **Perception** is the process of organizing and interpreting sensory information about the objects, events, and spatial layout of the world around us. In our opening example, sensation involved light and sound waves activating receptors in Benjamin's eyes, ears, and brain; perception involved, for example, his experiencing the visual and auditory stimulation provided by the crashing goblet as a single coherent event.

In this section, we devote the most attention to vision, both because of its fundamental importance to humans and because so much more research has been conducted on vision than on the other senses. We will also discuss hearing and, to a lesser degree, taste, smell, and touch, as well as the coordination between these multiple sensory modalities.

sensation the processing of basic information from the external world by the sensory receptors in the sense organs (eyes, ears, skin, etc.) and brain

perception the process of organizing and interpreting sensory information

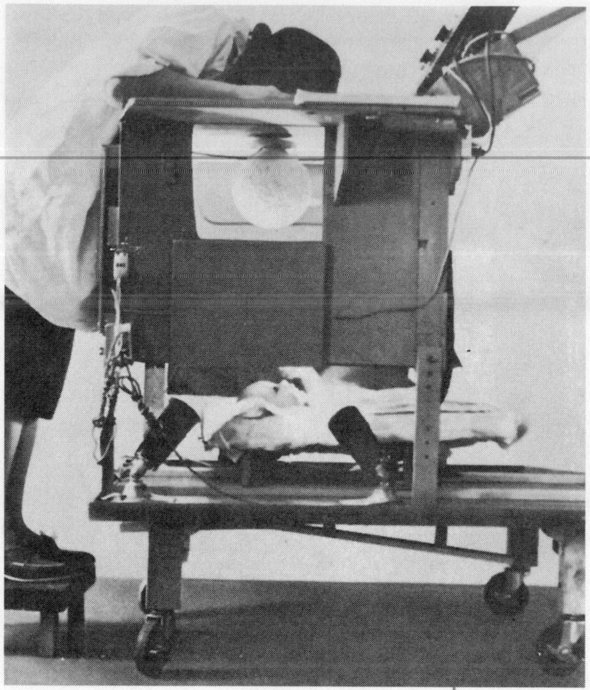

DAVID LINTON / *SCIENTIFIC AMERICAN* (204), PP. 66–72

This simple apparatus, the so-called Fantz box, was designed by Robert Fantz to present visual stimuli to infants. Looking through a peephole in the top of the box, the researcher could clearly see the direction of the baby's gaze. Using handheld buttons, she recorded how long the infant looked at the stimuli presented on the box's ceiling. This relatively primitive apparatus was eventually replaced by much more elaborate and precise equipment, but the basic logic of the more technologically sophisticated equipment used today is exactly the same as that of the Fantz box.

Vision

Humans rely more heavily on vision than most species do: roughly 40 to 50% of our mature cerebral cortex is involved in visual processing (Kellman & Arterberry, 2006). As recently as a few decades ago, it was generally assumed that newborns' vision was so poor as to be barely functional. However, once researchers started carefully studying the looking behavior of newborns and young infants, they discovered that this assumption was incorrect. In fact, newborns begin visually exploring the world minutes after leaving the womb. They scan the environment, and when their gaze encounters a person or object, they pause to look at it (Haith, 1980). Although newborns do not see as clearly as adults do, their vision improves extremely rapidly in their first months.

The evidence that enables us to say this so confidently was made possible by the invention of a variety of ingenious research methods. The first breakthrough was achieved with the **preferential-looking technique,** a method for studying visual attention in infants. In this technique, pioneered by Robert Fantz (1961), different visual stimuli are typically displayed on two side-by-side screens. If an infant looks longer at one of the two stimuli, the researcher can infer that the baby is able to discriminate between them and has a preference for one over the other. Fantz established that newborns, just like everyone else, would rather look at something than at nothing. When a pattern of any sort—black and white stripes, newsprint, a bull's-eye, a schematic face—was paired with a plain surface, the infants preferred (i.e., looked longer at) the pattern.

Another method that is used to study sensory and perceptual development in infants is *habituation,* which you encountered in Chapter 2 as a research tool used in studying fetal development. This procedure involves repeatedly presenting an infant with a given stimulus until the infant's response to it habituates, that is, declines. Then a novel stimulus is presented. If the infant's response increases, the researcher infers that the baby can discriminate between the old and new stimulus. Although extremely simple, habituation and preferential-looking procedures have turned out to be enormously powerful for studying infants' perception and understanding of the world.

Visual Acuity

As discussed in Chapter 1, the preferential-looking method enabled early researchers to assess infants' **visual acuity,** that is, to determine how clearly they can see. This procedure has enabled researchers to discover a great deal about infants' basic sensory abilities and looking preferences. For example, infants generally prefer to look at patterns of high visual contrast—such as a black-and-white checkerboard (Banks & Dannemiller, 1987). This is because young infants have poor **contrast sensitivity:** they can detect a pattern only when it is composed of highly contrasting elements. One reason for this poor contrast sensitivity is the immaturity of infants' **cones,** the light-sensitive neurons that are highly concentrated in the *fovea* (the central region of the retina) and are involved in seeing fine detail and color. In infancy, the cones have a different size and shape and are spaced farther apart than in adulthood (Kellman & Arterberry, 2006). As a consequence, newborns' cones catch only 2% of the light striking the fovea, compared with 65% for adults (Banks & Shannon, 1993). This is partly why in their first month, babies have only about 20/120 vision (a level of acuity that would enable an adult to read the large E at the top of a standard

preferential-looking technique a method for studying visual attention in infants that involves showing infants two patterns or two objects at a time to see if the infants have a preference for one over the other

visual acuity the sharpness of visual discrimination

contrast sensitivity the ability to detect differences in light and dark areas in a visual pattern

cones the light-sensitive neurons that are highly concentrated in the fovea (the central region of the retina) eye chart). Subsequently, visual acuity develops so rapidly that by 8 months of age, infants' vision approaches that of adults, with full adult acuity present by around 6 years of age (Kellman & Arterberry, 2006).

Another restriction on young infants' visual experience is that, for the first month or so, they do not share adults' experience of a richly colorful world. At best, they can distinguish some shades from white (Adams, 1995). By 2 or 3 months of age, infants' color vision is similar to that of adults (Kellman & Arterberry, 2006). Indeed, it is similar to the extent that 4- and 5-month-olds prefer (look longest at) the same basic colors that adults rate as most pleasant—red and blue (Bornstein, 1975). They also perceive the boundaries between colors in more or less the same way as adults do: they respond equivalently to two shades that adults label as the same color (e.g., "blue"), but they discriminate between two shades that adults refer to with different color names (e.g., "blue" and "green") (Bornstein, Kessen, & Weiskopf, 1976).

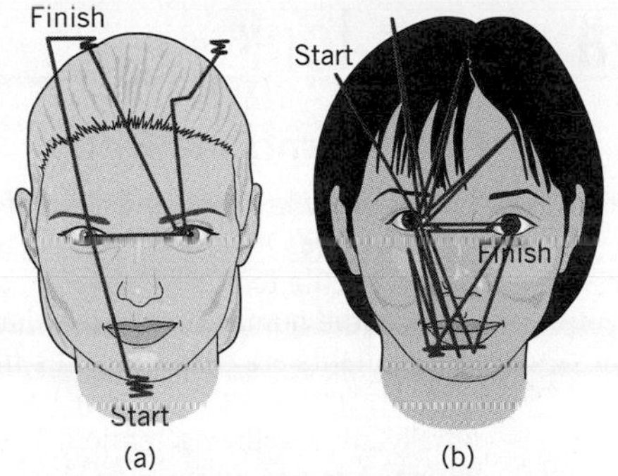

FIGURE 5.1 Visual scanning The lines superimposed on these face pictures show age differences in where two babies fixated on the images. (a) A 1-month-old looked primarily at the outer contour of the face and head, with a few fixations of the eyes. (b) A 2-month-old fixated primarily on the internal features of the face, especially the eyes and mouth. (From Maurer & Salapatek, 1976)

Visual Scanning

As noted, newborns start visually scanning the environment right away. From the beginning, they are attracted to moving stimuli. However, they have trouble tracking these stimuli because their eye movements are jerky and often do not stay with whatever they are trying to visually follow. Not until 2 or 3 months of age are infants able to track moving objects smoothly, and then they are able to do so only if an object is moving slowly (Aslin, 1981).

Another limitation on young infants' visual experience of the world (and therefore on what they can learn) is that their visual scanning is restricted. With a simple figure like a triangle, infants younger than 2 months old look almost exclusively at one corner. With more complex shapes, they tend to scan only the outer edges (Haith, Bergman, & Moore, 1977; Milewski, 1976). Thus, as Figure 5.1 shows, when 1-month-olds look at a line drawing of a face, they tend to fixate on the perimeter—on the hairline or chin, where there is relatively high contrast with the background. By 2 months of age, infants scan much more broadly, enabling them to pay attention to both overall shape and inner details (see Box 5.1 on the next page).

Pattern Perception

Accurate visual perception of the world requires more than acuity and systematic scanning; it also requires analyzing and integrating the separate elements of a visual display into a coherent pattern. To perceive the face in Figure 5.1, as 2-month-olds apparently do, they must integrate the separate elements.

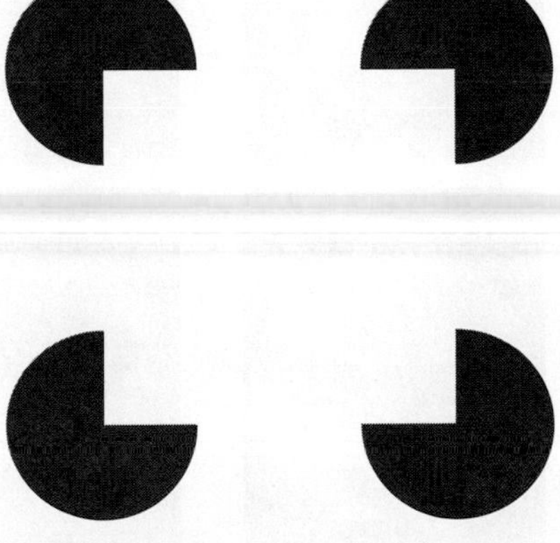

FIGURE 5.2 Subjective contour When you look at this figure, you no doubt see a square—what is called a subjective contour, because it does not actually exist on the page. Seven-month-olds also detect the illusory square. (From Bertenthal, Campos, & Haith, 1980)

A striking demonstration of integrative pattern perception in infancy comes from research using the stimulus shown in Figure 5.2. When you look at it, you no doubt perceive a square, even though no square actually exists. This perception of subjective contour results from your active integration of the separate elements in the stimulus into a single pattern. If you simply looked at the individual shapes in turn, no square would pop out. Like you, 7-month-olds perceive the subjective square in Figure 5.2 (Bertenthal, Campos, & Haith, 1980), indicating that they integrate the separate elements to perceive the whole.

Infants are also able to perceive coherence among moving elements. In research by Bennett Bertenthal and his colleagues (Bertenthal, 1993; Bertenthal, Proffitt, & Kramer, 1987), infants watched a film of moving points of light. Adults who watch this film immediately and confidently identify what they see as a person walking; the moving lights appear to be (and are) attached to the major joints and head of an adult. Five-month-olds apparently see the same thing; they

a closer look

Beauty and the Baby

A particularly fascinating aspect of infant perception has to do with the reaction of human infants to that most social of all stimuli—the human face. As we have noted, infants are drawn to faces from birth, leading researchers to ask what initially attracts their attention. The answer, it seems, is a very general bias toward configurations with more elements in the upper half than in the lower half—something that characterizes all human faces (Simion, Valenza, Macchi Cassia, Turati, & Umilta, 2002; Macchi Cassia, Turati, & Simion, 2004) (see the images in the first column).

From paying lots of attention to real faces, infants very quickly come to recognize and prefer their own mother's face. After about 12 hours' cumulative exposure to Mom over the first few days after birth, infants look longer at her face than at the face of another woman (Bushnell, 1998; Bushnell, Sai, & Mullin, 1989; Pascalis et al., 1995).

With exposure to many different faces over their first months, infants gradually develop a well-organized perceptual prototype for human faces. The formation of this detailed face prototype then facilitates discrimination between different faces. Evidence for the formation of a general face prototype in the first year comes from an intriguing study of infants' and adults' ability to discriminate between individual human faces and individual monkey faces. Adults, 9-month-olds, and 6-month-olds can all readily discriminate between two human faces. However, adults and 9-month-olds have a great deal of difficulty telling the difference between one monkey face and another (Pascalis, de Haan, & Nelson, 2002). Surprisingly, 6-month-olds are just as good at discriminating between monkey faces as they are at discriminating between human faces.

The researchers concluded that the 9-month-olds and adults rely on a detailed prototype of the human face to discriminate between people, but this prototype does not help them tell the difference between monkeys. The fact that the 6-month-olds discriminated equally well between human and monkey faces suggests that their prototype for the human face is not so detailed and tightly organized as it soon will be.

Consistent with this account is research showing effects of experience on face recognition. In one study, 6-month-olds had daily experience at home for three months with pictures of monkeys. When they were then tested at 9 months of age, they retained their ability to distinguish between monkey faces (Pascalis et al., 2005). A related study showed that 3-month-old infants prefer female over male faces—unless their primary caretaker is their father (Quinn, Yahr, Kuhn, Slater, & Pascalis, 2002). Thus, infants appear to develop a preference for the type of face they see most often.

With age, the emotional content of faces plays an increasing role in infants' response to them. Although infants come to discriminate among some facial expressions as early as 4 months of age, they do not reliably prefer one over the other (Nelson, 1987; Walker-Andrews, 1997). Between 5 and 7 months of age, infants notice the connection between emotional expressions in faces and voices (Soken & Pick, 1992; Walker-Andrews, 1997). When they hear a happy voice, they look preferentially at a smiling face, and they look longer at an angry face when they hear an angry voice. By the end of their first year, they generally prefer smiling faces to fearful or angry ones. Thus, infants only gradually come to understand the significance of different facial expressions. The development of expertise in face processing requires visual input to the right hemisphere during infancy. Adults whose early visual experience was restricted to only the left

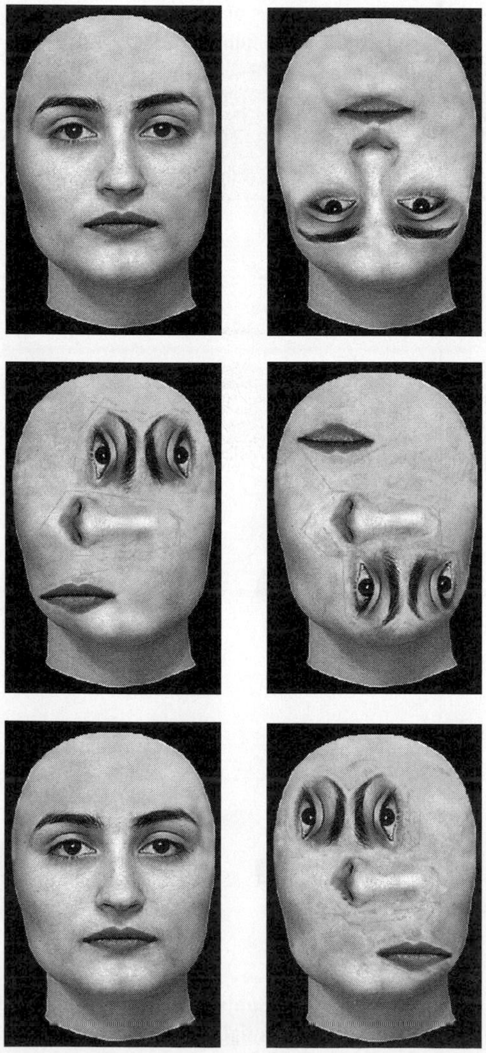

Newborns look longer at the left-hand column of these three pairs of stimuli, revealing a general preference for top-heavy stimuli that contributes to their preference for human faces (Simion et al., 2002; Macchi Cassia et al., 2004). Notice that this simple preference is all that is needed to result in newborns' spending more time looking at their mother's face than at anything else.

5.1

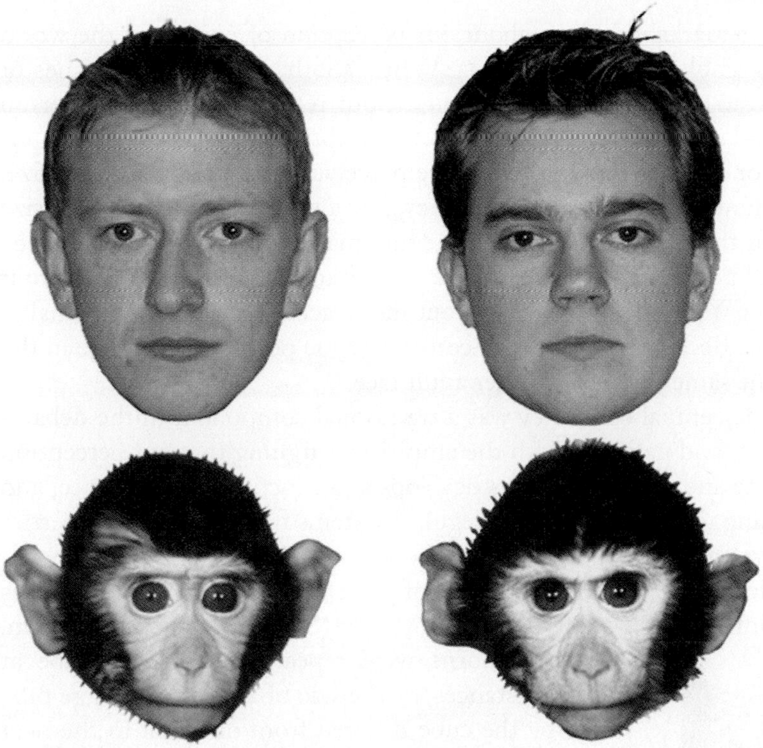

COURTESY OF OLIVIER PASCALIS

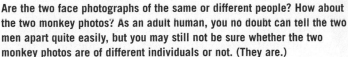

Are the two face photographs of the same or different people? How about the two monkey photos? As an adult human, you no doubt can tell the two men apart quite easily, but you may still not be sure whether the two monkey photos are of different individuals or not. (They are.)

COURTESY OF BEN GLORE

This toddler is reacting more positively to this very attractive young woman than he likely would to an unattractive individual.

hemisphere (which can be caused by a cataract on one eye) have seriously impaired face perception (LeGrand, Mondloch, Maurer, & Brent, 2003).

One of the most intriguing aspects of infants' facial preferences is the fact that, along with all the rest of us, babies like a pretty face. From birth, infants look longer at faces that are judged by adults to be highly attractive than at faces judged to be less appealing (Langlois, Ritter, Roggman, & Vaughn, 1991; Langlois et al., 1987; Rubenstein, Kalakanis, & Langlois, 1999; Slater et al., 1998, 2000).

Older infants' preference for prettiness, like adults', also affects their behavior toward real people. This was demonstrated in an extraordinarily clever and well-designed study in which 12-month-olds interacted with a woman whose face was either very attractive or very unattractive (Langlois, Roggman, & Rieser-Danner, 1990). The first key feature of this study was that the attractive woman and the unattractive woman were one and the same!

This duality of appearance was achieved through the use of extremely natural-looking professional masks that were applied before the woman interacted with the infants. On a given day, the young woman who would test the babies emerged from her makeup session looking either fabulous or not so fabulous, depending on which mask she was wearing. The masks conformed to what adults judge to be a very attractive face and a relatively unattractive one. When interacting with the woman, the infants behaved differently as a function of which mask she was wearing. They were more positive, became more involved in play, and were less likely to withdraw when she was wearing the attractive mask than when she had on the unattractive one.

A second key feature of this study—the control that makes the results so strong is that the young woman never knew on any given day which mask she had on. Thus, the children's behavior could not have been cued by her behavior; it could only have been due to her pretty or homely appearance.

look longer at the point-light displays that suggest human movement than at ones that do not.

Object Perception

One of the most remarkable things about our perception of objects in the world around us is how stable that perception is. When another person approaches or moves away from us, or slowly turns in a circle, our retinal image of the person changes in size and shape, but we do not have the impression that the person gets larger or smaller or changes shape. Instead, we perceive a constant shape and size, a phenomenon known as **perceptual constancy.** For a good demonstration of size constancy, look in the mirror and notice that the image of your face seems to be the normal size of a face. Then steam up the mirror and trace the outline of your face on the mirror. You will find that the outline is actually a great deal smaller than your real face. Because of perceptual constancy, you perceive the image in the mirror as being the same size as any other adult face.

The origin of perceptual constancy was a traditional component in the debates between empiricists and nativists, with the empiricists arguing that our perception of the constant size and shape of objects develops as a function of experience, and the nativists arguing that this perceptual regularity stems from inherent properties of the nervous system.

The nativist view is supported by evidence of perceptual constancy in newborns and very young infants. In a study of size constancy (Slater, Mattock, & Brown, 1990), newborns were repeatedly shown a cube at varying distances, so the size of the retinal image projected by the cube differed from one trial to the next (see Figure 5.3). The question was whether the newborns would perceive these events as multiple presentations of a single object or as similar objects of different sizes. To answer this question, the researchers subsequently presented the newborns with the original cube and a second one that was identical except that it was twice as large. The crucial factor was that the second cube was twice as far away as the original one, so it produced the same-size retinal image as the original. The infants looked longer at the new cube, indicating that they saw it as different in size from the original one. This, in turn, revealed that they had perceived the multiple presentations of the original cube as a single object of a constant size, even though its retinal size varied. Thus, visual experience is not necessary for size constancy (Granrud, 1987; Slater & Morison, 1985).

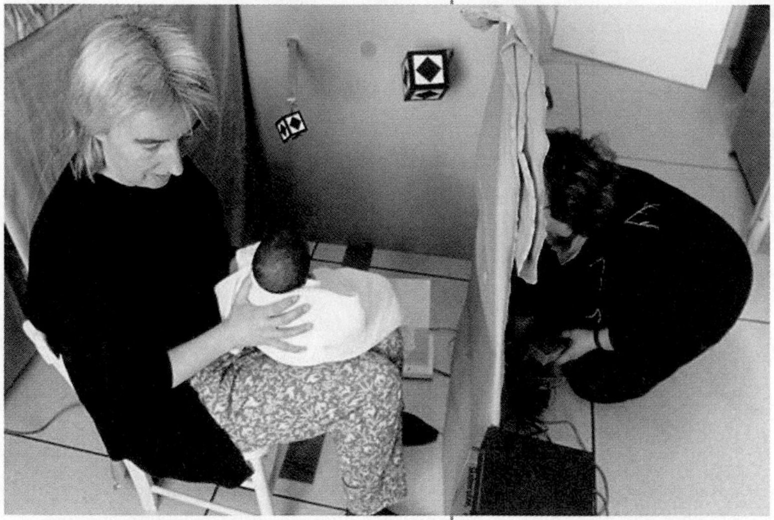
COURTESY OF ALAN SLATER

FIGURE 5.3 If this infant looks longer at the larger but farther-away cube, researchers will conclude the child has size constancy.

Another crucial perceptual ability is **object segregation,** the perception of separate objects in a visual array. To appreciate the importance of this ability, look around and try to imagine that you are seeing the scene and the objects in it for the first time. How can you tell where one object starts and another one ends? A gap between two objects provides clear evidence of two separate entities, and young infants are sensitive to this information (Spelke & Newport, 1998). But what if there are no visible gaps? Suppose, for example, that as baby Benjamin watches his parents washing dishes, he sees a cup sitting on a saucer. Will he perceive this arrangement as one or two objects? Lacking experience with china, Benjamin may

perceptual constancy the perception of objects as being of constant size, shape, color, etc., in spite of physical differences in the retinal image of the object

object segregation the identification of separate objects in a visual array

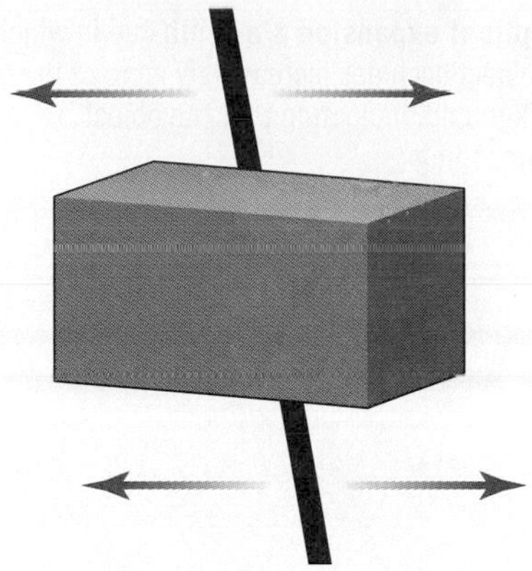
(a)

(b)

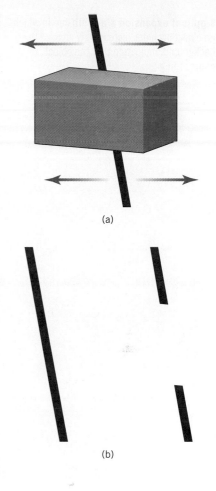

FIGURE 5.4 Object segregation Infants who see the combination of elements in (a) perceive two separate objects, a rod moving behind a block. After habituating to the display, they look longer at two rod segments than at a single rod (b), indicating that they find the single rod familiar but the two segments novel. If they first see a display with no movement, they look equally long at the two test displays. This result reveals the importance of *movement* for object segregation. (From Kellman & Spelke, 1983)

be unsure: the difference in shape suggests two objects, but the common texture suggests only one. Now suppose that Ben's mother picks up the cup to dip it in the suds. Will he still be uncertain? No, because even for an infant, the independent motion of cup and saucer signals that they are separate things.

The importance of motion for object segregation in infants was initially demonstrated in a classic experiment by Kellman and Spelke (1983). First, 4-month-olds were presented with a display, shown in Figure 5.4a, which adults perceive as a single rod moving back and forth behind a block of wood. After habituating to the display, the infants were shown the two test displays in Figure 5.4b. The investigators reasoned that if the infants, like adults, assumed that there was a single rod behind the block during habituation, they would look longer at the two rod segments because that display would be novel. This is exactly what the babies did.

What caused the infants to assume that the two rod segments they could see were a single, unitary object? The answer is *common movement*, the fact that the two segments always moved together in the same direction and at the same speed. Four-month-olds who saw a display that was the same as the one in Figure 5.4a, except that the rod was stationary, looked equally long at the two test displays. In the absence of common movement, the display was ambiguous.

Common movement is such a powerful cue that it makes even perceptually distinct elements seem to be a unitary object. It does not matter if the two parts of the object moving behind the block differ in color, texture, and shape, nor does it make much difference how they move (side to side, up and down, etc.) (Kellman & Spelke, 1983; Kellman, Spelke, & Short, 1986). For infants, it is common movement that conveys oneness.

As they get older, infants use additional sources of information for object segregation, including their general knowledge about the world (Needham, 1997; Needham & Baillargeon, 1997). Consider the rather peculiar-looking displays shown in Figure 5.5. The differences in color, shape, and texture between the box and the tube in Figure 5.5a suggest that there are two separate objects, although you cannot really be sure. However, your knowledge that objects cannot float in

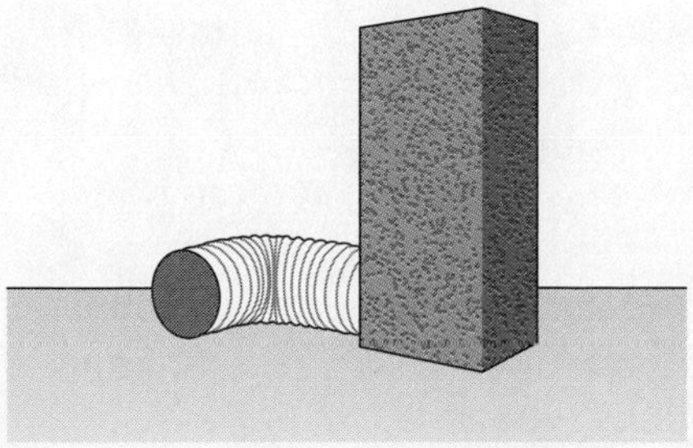
(a)

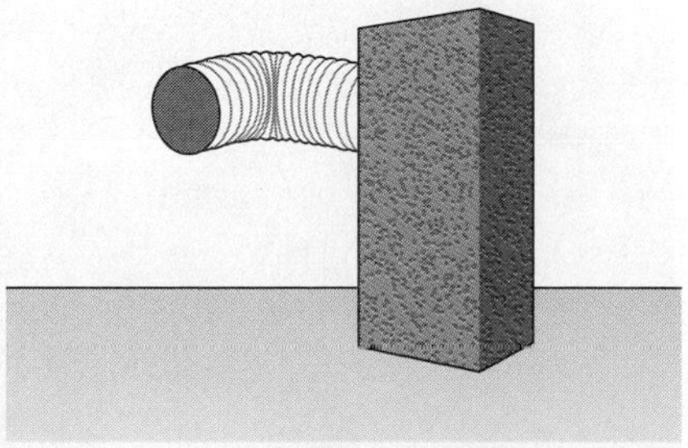
(b)

FIGURE 5.5 Knowledge and object segregation (a) It is impossible to know for sure whether what you see here is one object or two. (b) Because of your knowledge about gravity and support, you can be sure that this figure is a single (albeit very odd) object. (From Needham, 1997)

optical expansion a depth cue in which an object occludes increasingly more of the background, indicating that the object is approaching

midair tells you that Figure 5.5b has to be a single object; that is, the tube must be attached to the box.

Like you, 8-month-olds interpret these two displays differently. When they see a hand reach in and pull on the tube in Figure 5.5a, they look longer (presumably they are more surprised) if the box and tube move together than if the tube comes apart from the box, indicating that they perceive the display as two separate objects. However, the opposite pattern occurs in Figure 5.5b: now the infants look longer if the tube alone moves, indicating that they perceive a single object.

Depth Perception

To navigate through our environment, we need to know where we are with respect to the objects and landmarks around us. We use many sorts of depth and distance cues to tell us whether we can reach the coffee cup on our desk or whether the approaching car is far enough away that we can safely cross in front of it. From the beginning, infants are sensitive to some of these cues, and they rapidly become sensitive to the rest.

One cue that infants are sensitive to very early on is **optical expansion,** in which the visual image of an object increases in size as the object comes toward us, occluding more and more of the background. When an image of an approaching object expands symmetrically, we know that the object is headed right for us, and a sensible response is to duck. Babies cannot duck, but infants as young as 1 month old blink defensively at an expanding image that appears to be an object heading toward them (Ball & Tronick, 1971; Nanez & Yonas, 1994; Yonas, 1981).

EMPEROR AUGUSTUS AND THE SIBYL, 1535 BY PARIS BARDONE (1500–1571) PUSHKIN MUSEUM, MOSCOW, RUSSIA / BRIDGEMAN ART LIBRARY

FIGURE 5.6 Pictorial cues This Renaissance painting contains multiple examples of pictorial cues. One is interposition—nearer objects occlude ones farther away. The convergence of lines in the distance is another. To appreciate the effectiveness of a third cue—relative size—compare the actual size of the man on the steps in the foreground to the actual size of the woman in the blue dress.

Another depth cue that emerges early is due to the simple fact that we have two eyes. Because of the distance between them, the retinal image of an object at any instant is never quite the same in both eyes. Consequently, the eyes never send quite the same signal to the brain—a phenomenon known as **binocular disparity.** The closer the object we are looking at, the greater the disparity between the two images; the farther away the object, the less the disparity. In a process known as **stereopsis,** the visual cortex computes the degree of disparity between the eyes' differing neural signals and produces the perception of depth. This form of depth perception emerges quite suddenly at around 4 months of age and is generally complete within a few weeks (Held, Birch, & Gwiazda, 1980), presumably due to maturation of the visual cortex.

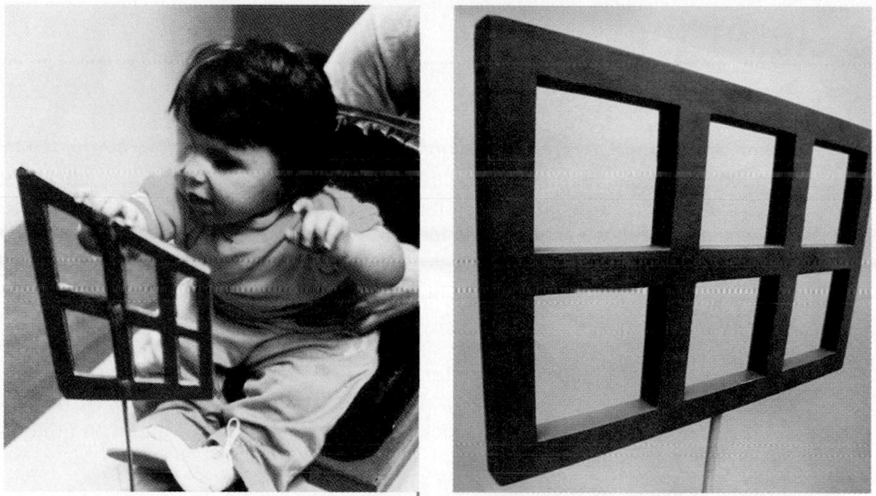

BOTH: COURTESY OF ALBERT YONAS

FIGURE 5.7 Monocular depth cues This 7-month-old infant is using the monocular depth cue of relative size. Wearing an eye patch to take away binocular depth information, he is reaching to the longer side of a trapezoidal window. This behavior indicates that the baby sees it as the nearer, and hence more readily reachable, side of a regular rectangular window. (Yonas et al., 1978)

At around 6 or 7 months of age, infants begin to become sensitive to a variety of **monocular** depth cues (so called because they denote depth even if only one eye is open) (Yonas, Elieff, & Arterberry, 2002). These cues are also known as **pictorial cues**, because they can be used to portray depth in pictures. Three of them, including relative size, are presented in Figure 5.6.

In one of the earliest—and cleverest—studies of infants' sensitivity to monocular depth cues, Yonas, Cleaves, and Pettersen (1978) capitalized on the fact that infants will reach toward whichever of two objects is nearer. The investigators put a patch over one eye of 5- and 7-month-olds (so binocular depth information would not be available) and presented them with a trapezoidal window with one side considerably longer than the other (Figure 5.7). (When viewed by an adult with one eye closed, the window appears to be a standard rectangular window sitting at an angle with one side closer to the viewer.) The 7-month-olds (but not the younger babies) reached toward the longer side, indicating that they, as you would, perceived it as being nearer, providing evidence that they used relative size as a cue to depth. (Box 5.2 reviews research on infants' perception of pictures.)

Auditory Perception

Another rich source of infants' information about the world is sound. The human auditory system is relatively well developed at birth, although newborns can still be characterized as a bit hard of hearing (Trehub & Schellenberg, 1995). The faintest sound a newborn responds to is roughly four times louder than the quietest sound an adult can detect (Maurer & Maurer, 1988). Not until 5 to 8 years of age does hearing approach adult levels.

When they hear a sound, newborns tend to turn toward it, a phenomenon referred to as **auditory localization** (Morrongiello, Fenwick, Hillier, & Chance, 1994). One dedicated scientist tested his 10-minute-old daughter while still in the delivery room and found that she turned her head toward a clicking sound he made (Wertheimer, 1961). Because they turn their heads very slowly, newborns are most likely to localize the source of a sound that continues for several seconds (Clarkson & Clifton, 1991).

binocular disparity the difference between the retinal image of an object in each eye that results in two slightly different signals being sent to the brain

stereopsis the process by which the visual cortex combines the differing neural signals caused by binocular disparity, resulting in the perception of depth

monocular or **pictorial cues** the perceptual cues of depth (such as relative size and interposition) that can be perceived by one eye alone

auditory localization perception of the location in space of a sound source

a closer look 5.2

Picture Perception

A special case of perceptual development concerns pictures. Paintings, drawings, and photographs are ubiquitous in modern societies, and we acquire an enormous amount of information through them. When can infants perceive and understand these important cultural artifacts?

Even young infants perceive pictures in much the same way that you do. In a classic study, Hochberg and Brooks (1962) raised their own infant son with no exposure to pictures at all: no art or family photos; no picture books; no patterns on sheets, clothing, or toys. They even removed the labels from canned foods. Nevertheless, when tested at 18 months, the child readily identified people and objects in photographs and line drawings. Later research established that infants as young as 5 months old can recognize people and objects in photographs and drawings of them (e.g., DeLoache, Strauss, & Maynard, 1979; Dirks & Gibson, 1977), and even newborns can recognize two-dimensional versions of three-dimensional objects (Slater, Rose, & Morison, 1984).

Despite their precocious perception of pictures, infants do not understand their nature. The four babies shown here—two from the United States and two from a rural village in West Africa—are all manually exploring depicted objects. Although these babies can perceive the difference between pictures and objects, they do not yet understand what two-dimensionality means; hence, they attempt to treat pictured objects as if they were real objects—with an inevitable lack of success. By 19 months of age and after substantial experience with pictures, American infants no longer manually investigate pictures, apparently having learned that pictures are to look at and talk about, but not to feel, pick up, or eat (DeLoache, Pierroutsakos, Uttal, Rosengren, & Gottlieb, 1998; Pierroutsakos & DeLoache, 2003). In short, they have come to understand the symbolic nature of pictures and appreciate that a depicted object stands for a real object (Preissler & Carey, 2003).

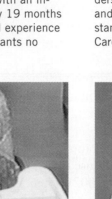

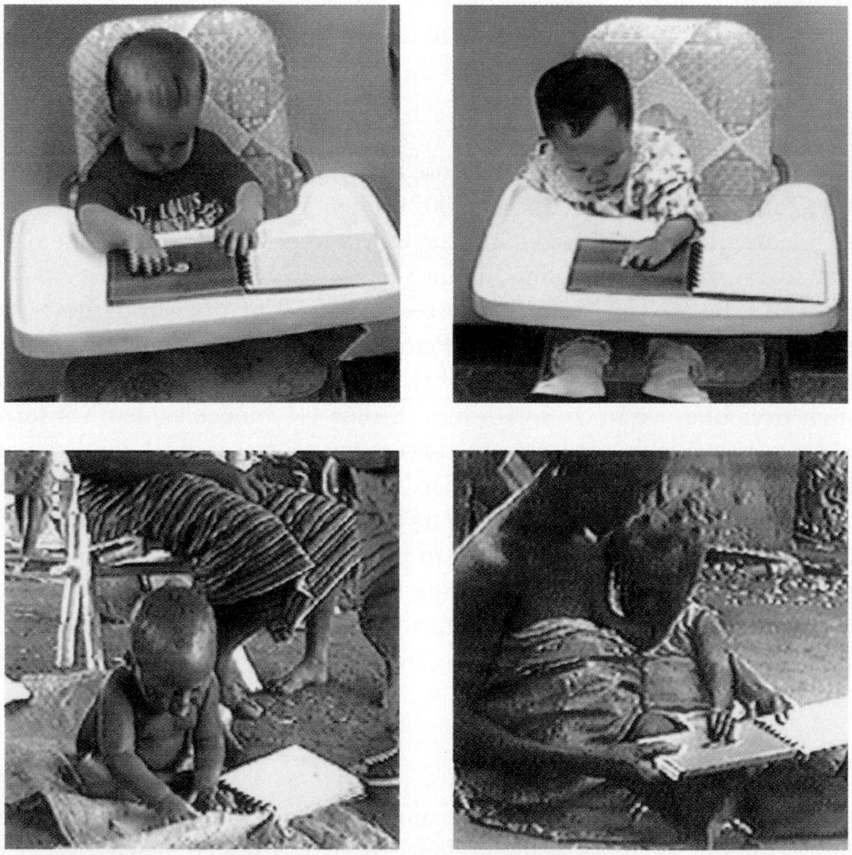

ALL: COURTESY OF DELOACHE, PIERROUTSAKOS, UTTAL, ROSENGREN, AND GOTTLIEB

These 9-month-old infants—two from the United States and two from West Africa—are responding to pictures of objects as if they were real objects. They do not yet know the true nature of pictures. (From DeLoache, Pierroutsakos, Uttal, Rosengren, & Gottlieb, 1998)

Infants are adept at perceiving patterns in the streams of sound they hear. They are remarkably proficient, for example, at detecting subtle differences in the sounds of human speech, an ability we will review in detail in our discussion of language development in Chapter 6. Here we will focus on another realm in which infants display an impressive degree of auditory sensitivity—music.

Music Perception

Infants are sensitive to music, as evidenced by the fact that caregivers the world over sing to their babies (Trehub & Schellenberg, 1995). In the United States, for example, 60% of parents sing or play music to their children every day (Custodero, Britto, & Brooks-Gunn, 2003). Recent research shows that infants' response to music is similar to that of adults.

From Pythagoras to Galileo to the present day, many scholars have argued that consonant tones are inherently pleasing to human ears, whereas dissonance is unpleasant (Schellenberg & Trehub, 1996; Trehub & Schellenberg, 1995). To see if infants agree, researchers employ a simple but reliable procedure. A picture of something that an infant might find attractive is attached to the front of a speaker. Then the music starts, leading the infants to look toward the sound source. The length of time they look at the speaker (or the picture on it) is taken as a measure of their interest in, or preference for, the music emanating from the speaker. Studies have shown that infants pay more attention to a consonant version of a piece of music, whether folk song or minuet, than to a dissonant one (Trainor & Heinmiller, 1998; Zentner & Kagan, 1996, 1998).

Infants also respond to rhythm in music. Although they do not exactly tap their toes in time to the beat, they do move to it, bouncing perceptibly while listening to lively, rhythmic band music (Trehub, 1993). Infants are likewise sensitive to temporal organization in music. In one study, for example, infants as young as $4\frac{1}{2}$ months listened longer to Mozart minuets with 1-second pauses inserted between natural musical phrases than to the same music with the pauses inserted in the middle of the phrases (Krumhansl & Jusczyk, 1990).

Equally impressive is infants' sensitivity to melody. After being habituated to a simple melody, 5-month-olds heard the same melody played at a higher or lower pitch. The infants remained habituated: it was the same song to them. However, when the identical notes were played in a different order (thereby destroying the melodic pattern), the babies showed renewed interest (Chang & Trehub, 1977). Thus, the infants responded like adults, who perceive a melody to be the same regardless of whether it is played on a piccolo or a tuba, but perceive it to be a different tune if the notes are rearranged. Further, infants' detection of melody relies primarily on right-hemisphere processing, just as it does in most adults (Balaban, Anderson, & Wisniewski, 1998).

Taste and Smell

As you learned in Chapter 2, sensitivity to taste and smell develops before birth, and newborns show an innate preference for sweet flavors. Preferences for smells are also present very early in life. Newborns prefer the smell of the natural food source for human infants—breast milk (Marlier & Schaal, 2005). Smell plays a powerful role in how a variety of infant mammals learn to recognize their mothers. It probably does the same for humans, as shown by studies in which infants chose between the scent of their own mother and that of another woman. A pad that an infant's mother had worn next to her breast was placed on one side of the infant's head and a pad worn by a different woman was placed on the other side. Two-week-old infants turned more often and spent more time oriented to the pad infused with their mother's unique scent (MacFarlane, 1975; Porter et al., 1992).

Initially, every object that a baby can pick up goes into his or her mouth for oral exploration—whether or not it will fit. Later, infants begin to visually explore objects, thereby showing an interest in the object itself.

Touch

Another important way that infants learn about the environment is through active touch, whether with their hands and fingers or mouth and tongue. Oral exploration dominates for the first few months, as infants mouth and suck on their own fingers and toes, as well as virtually any object they come into contact with. (This is why it is so important to keep small, swallowable objects away from babies.) Through their ardent oral exploration, babies presumably learn about their own bodies (or at least the parts they can get their mouths on), as well as about the texture, taste, and other properties of the objects they encounter.

From around the age of 4 months, as infants gain greater control over their hand and arm movements, manual exploration increases and gradually takes precedence over oral exploration. Infants actively rub, finger, probe, and bang objects, and their actions become increasingly specific to the properties of the objects. For example, they tend to rub textured objects and bang rigid ones. Increasing manual control facilitates visual exploration in that infants can hold interesting objects in order to examine them more closely, rotating the objects to view them from different angles and transferring them from hand to hand to get a better view (Bushnell & Boudreau, 1991; Lockman & McHale, 1989; Rochat, 1989; Ruff, 1986).

Intermodal Perception

Most events that both adults and infants experience involve simultaneous stimulation through multiple sensory modalities. In the crystal-goblet-falling-on-tile-floor event witnessed by Benjamin, both visual and auditory stimulation were provided by the shattering glass. Through the phenomenon of **intermodal perception,** the combining of information from two or more sensory systems, Ben's parents perceived the auditory and visual stimulation as a unitary, coherent event. It is likely that 4-month-old Ben did, too.

According to Piaget (1954), information from different sensory modalities is initially separate, and only after some months do infants become capable of forming associations between how things look and how they sound, taste, feel, and so on. In contrast, Eleanor Gibson (1988) and her colleagues (e.g., Bahrick, Lickliter, & Flom, 2004; Spelke, 1979) argue that, from very early on, infants integrate information from different senses. A very simple example is newborns' auditory localization: their turning toward a sound they hear indicates that they expect a sound to be associated with an object.

Very young infants also link their oral and visual experience. In studies with newborns (Kaye & Bower, 1994) and 1-month-olds (Meltzoff & Borton, 1979), infants sucked on a pacifier that they were prevented from seeing. They were then shown a picture of the pacifier that had been in their mouth and a picture of a novel pacifier of a different shape or texture. The infants looked longer at the pacifier they had sucked on. Thus, these infants could visually recognize an object they had experienced only through oral exploration.

intermodal perception the combining of information from two or more sensory systems

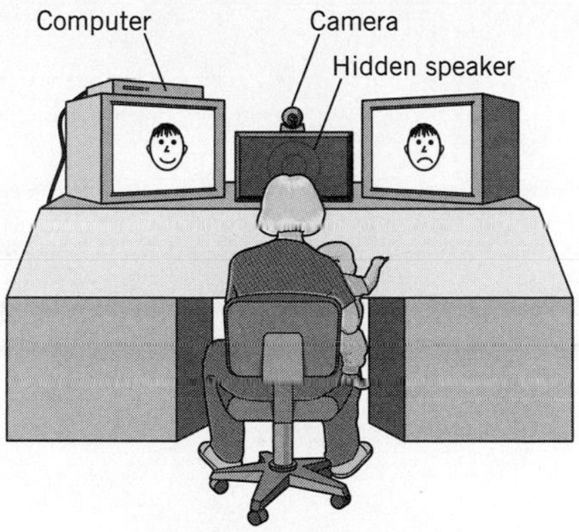

A set-up like this one enables researchers to study auditory–visual intermodal perception. The two computer screens display different films, one of which is coordinated with a soundtrack. The video camera records the infant's looking toward the two screens.

When infants become capable of exploring objects manually, they readily integrate their visual and tactile experience. In one study, for example, 4 month olds were allowed to hold and feel, but not see, a pair of rings that were connected by either a rigid bar or a string. When the babies were shown both types of rings, they recognized the ones they had previously explored with their hands (Streri & Spelke, 1988). Infants can also detect a relation between their own limb movements and a video display of those movements (Rochat & Morgan, 1995; Schmuckler, 1996).

Using a very clever technique, researchers have discovered that infants also possess a variety of forms of auditory–visual intermodal perception. This technique involves simultaneously presenting two dissimilar films, side by side, while playing a soundtrack that is synchronized with one of the films but not the other. If an infant responds more to the film that goes with the soundtrack, it is taken as evidence that the infant detects the common structure in the auditory and visual information.

In a classic study using this procedure, Elizabeth Spelke (1976) showed 4-month-olds two videos, one of a person playing peekaboo and the other of a hand beating a drumstick against a block. The infants responded more to the film that matched the sounds they were hearing. When they heard a voice saying "Peekaboo," they looked more at the person, but when they heard a beating sound, they looked longer at the hand. In subsequent studies, infants showed finer discriminations. For example, 4-month-olds responded more to a film of a "hopping" toy animal in which the sounds of impact coincided with the animal's landing on a surface than they did to a film in which the impact sounds occurred while the animal was in midair (Spelke, 1979).

Similar studies have found that infants seem especially sensitive to the relation between human faces and voices. When 4-month-olds are shown side-by-side films of a person talking while they are listening to a soundtrack that matches one of the films, they look longer at the face whose lip movements are synchronized with the speech they hear (Spelke & Cortelyou, 1980; Walker-Andrews, 1997). Four-month-olds even detect the relation between specific speech sounds, such as "a" and "i," and the specific lip movements associated with them (Kuhl & Meltzoff, 1982, 1984). By 5 months of age, infants associate facial expressions with the emotional tones in voices (Walker-Andrews, 1997). For example, while listening to a sad voice, they look longer at a sad face.

review:

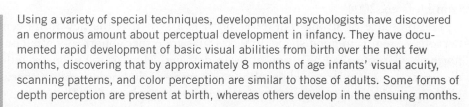

Using a variety of special techniques, developmental psychologists have discovered an enormous amount about perceptual development in infancy. They have documented rapid development of basic visual abilities from birth over the next few months, discovering that by approximately 8 months of age infants' visual acuity, scanning patterns, and color perception are similar to those of adults. Some forms of depth perception are present at birth, whereas others develop in the ensuing months.

By 5 to 7 months of age, infants actively integrate separate elements of visual displays to perceive coherent patterns. They use many sources of information, including movement and their knowledge of their surroundings, for object segregation.

Research on auditory perception has shown that right from birth, babies turn toward sounds they hear. They are quite sensitive to music and display some of the same musical preferences adults do, such as a preference for consonance over dissonance. Smell and touch both play an important role in infants' interaction with the world around them. The crucial ability to link what they perceive in separate modalities to experience unitary, coherent events is present in a simple form at birth, but more complex associations develop gradually. Thus there is much in recent research to encourage anyone of a nativist persuasion. At the same time, most perceptual skills also show development over time, much of which clearly involves learning.

Motor Development

As you learned in Chapter 2, human movement starts well before birth, as the fetus floats weightlessly in amniotic fluid. After birth, the newborn's movements are jerky and relatively uncoordinated, in part because of physical and neurological immaturity and in part because the baby is experiencing the full effects of gravity for the first time. As you will see in this section, the story of how the uncoordinated newborn, a prisoner to gravity, becomes a competent toddler confidently exploring the environment is remarkably complicated.

Reflexes

Newborns start off with some tightly organized patterns of action known as neonatal **reflexes.** Some reflexes, such as withdrawal from a painful stimulus, have clear adaptive value; others have no known adaptive significance. In the *grasping* reflex, newborns close their fingers around anything that presses against the palm of their hand. When stroked on the cheek near their mouth, infants exhibit the *rooting* reflex, turning their head in the direction of the touch and opening their mouth. Thus, when their cheek comes into contact with their mother's breast, they turn toward the breast, opening their mouth as they do. Oral contact with the nipple then sets off a *sucking* reflex, followed by the *swallowing* reflex, both of which increase the baby's chance of getting nourishment and ultimately of surviving. These reflexes are not *fully* automatic; for example, a rooting reflex is more likely to occur when an infant is hungry.

No benefit is known to be associated with other reflexes, such as the *tonic neck* reflex: when an infant's head turns or is turned to one side, the arm on that side of the body extends, while the arm and knee on the other side flex. It is thought that the tonic neck reflex involves an effort by the baby to get and keep its hand in view (von Hofsten, 2004).

The presence of strong reflexes at birth is a sign that the newborn's central nervous system is in good shape. Reflexes that are either abnormally weak or abnormally vigorous may be a sign of brain damage. Most of the neonatal reflexes disappear on a regular schedule, although some—including coughing, sneezing, blinking, and withdrawing from pain—remain throughout life. Persistence of a neonatal reflex beyond the point at which it is expected to disappear can indicate a neurological problem.

reflexes innate, fixed patterns of action that occur in response to particular stimulation

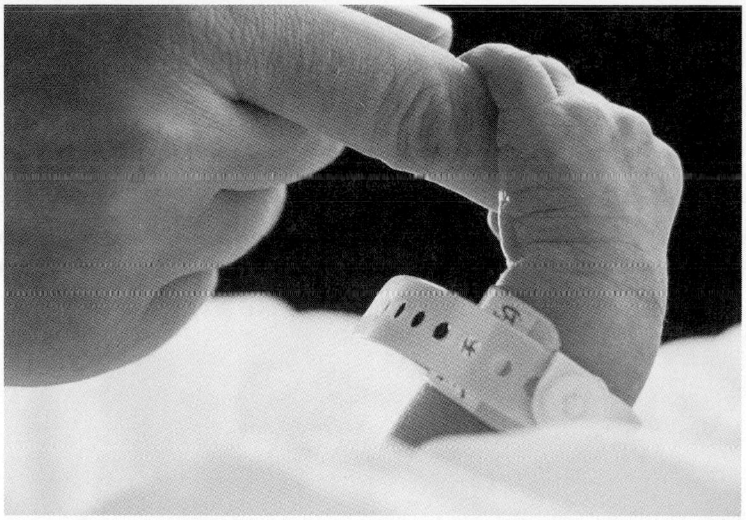

CHRISTOPHER BRISCOE / PHOTO RESEARCHERS, INC.

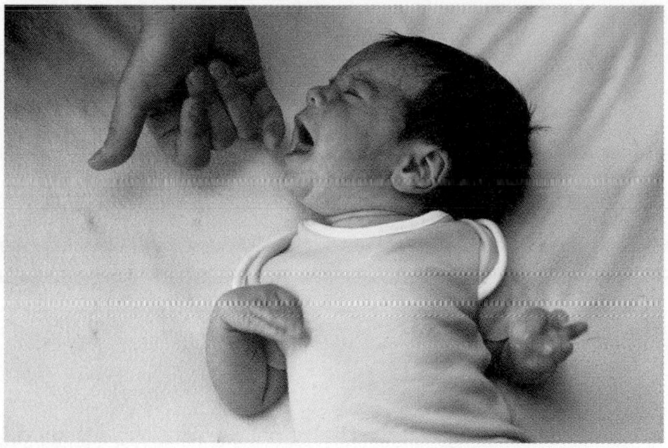

ELIZABETH CREWS / THE IMAGE WORKS

(b) Rooting

Neonatal reflexes: (a) Grasping

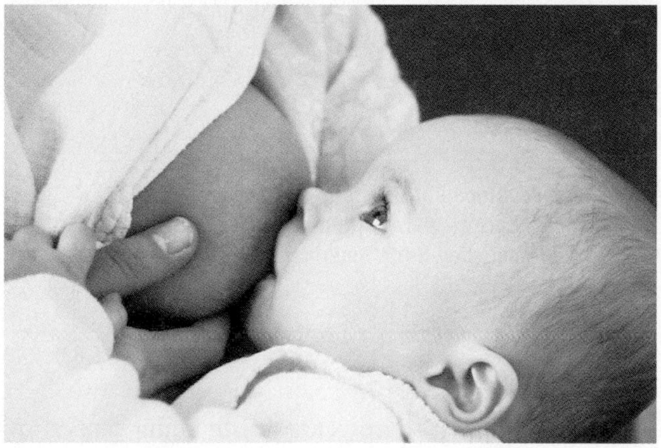

LAURENT / RAVO-VISON / BSIP / SCIENCE SOURCE / PHOTO RESEARCHERS, INC.

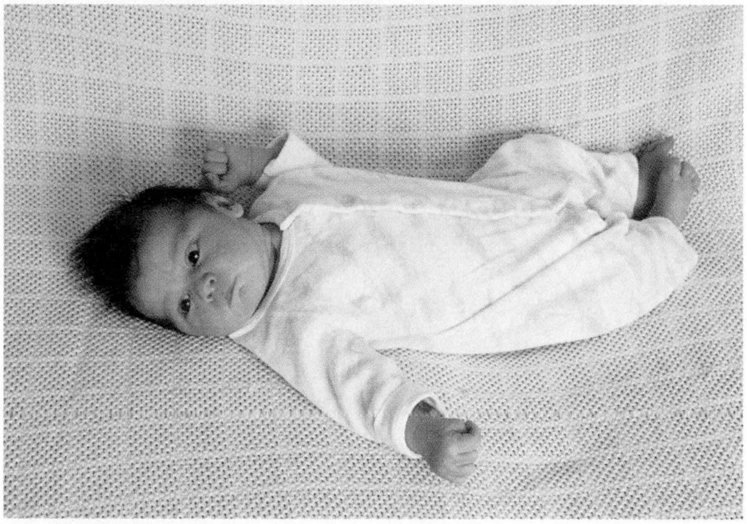

LAURA DWIGHT / PETER ARNOLD, INC.

(c) Sucking

(d) Tonic neck reflex

Motor Milestones

Infants progress quickly in acquiring the basic movement patterns of our species, shown in Figure 5.8. As you will see, the achievement of each of the major "motor milestones" of infancy, especially walking, constitutes a major advance in the infant's experience of the world.

The average ages that Figure 5.8 gives for the development of each of these important motor skills are based on research with Western, primarily North American, infants. Keep in mind that cultural factors can affect the course of motor development and that the degree to which motor skills are encouraged varies from one society to another. In fact, some cultures actively *discourage* early locomotion. In modern urban China, for example, infants are typically placed on beds and surrounded by thick pillows to keep them from crawling on the dirty floor (Campos et al., 2000). These restrictions make it difficult for infants to develop the muscle strength required to support their upper trunk, which is necessary for crawling. Among the Ache, a nomadic people who live in the rain forest of

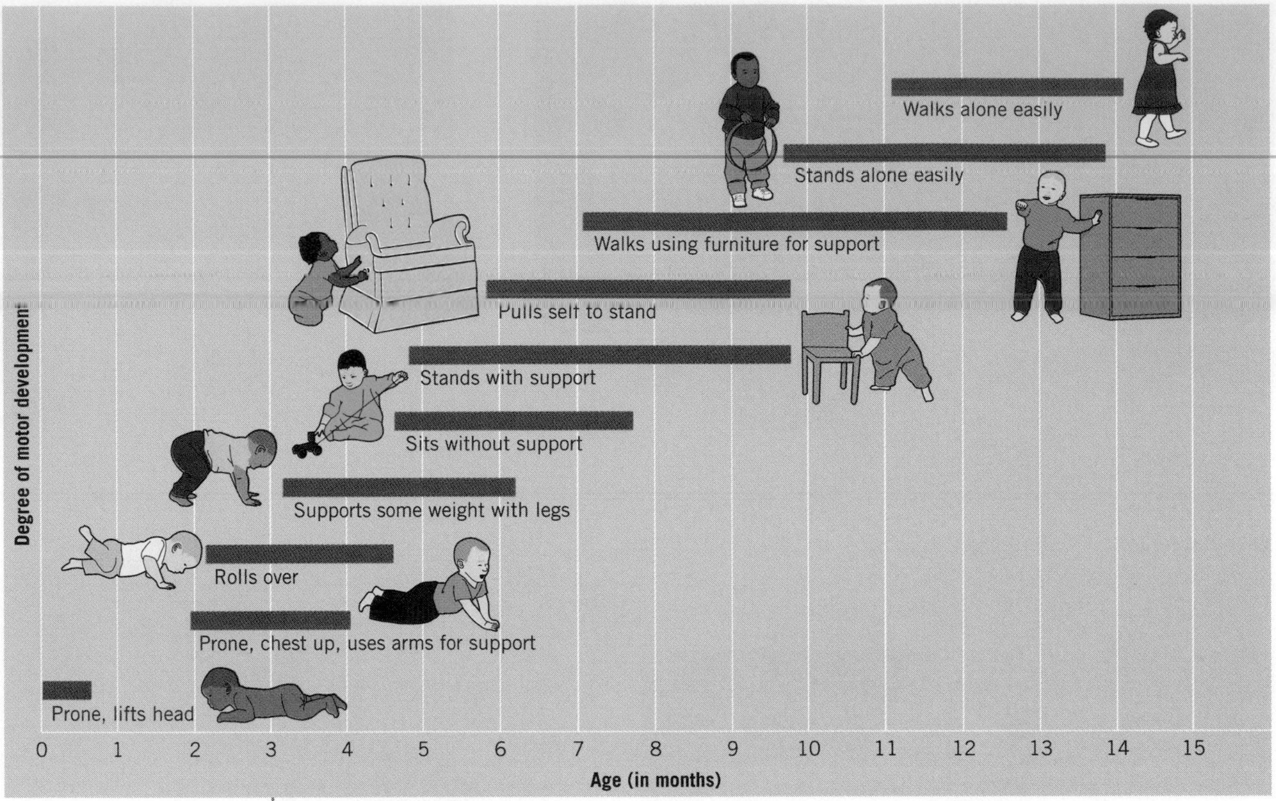

FIGURE 5.8 The major milestones of motor development in infancy The average age and range of ages for achievement of each milestone are shown. Note that these age norms are based on research with healthy, well-nourished North American infants.

To encourage her infant to sit independently, this Kipsigis mother in rural Kenya has dug a small hole in the sand to prop up the baby. This mother believes it is important to help infants develop motor skills (Super, 1976).

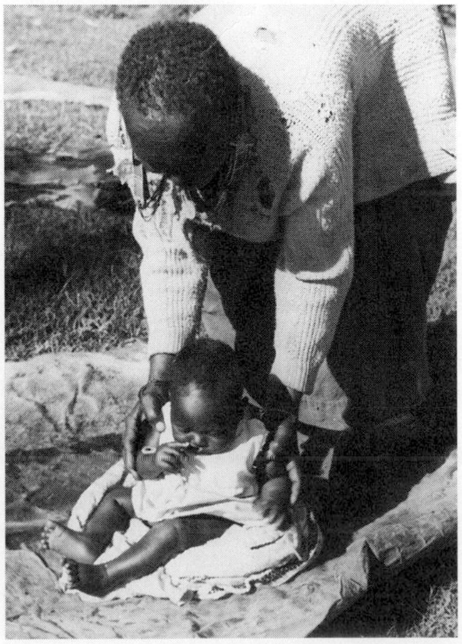

COURTESY OF C. M. SUPER

Paraguay, infants spend almost all of their first three years of life being carried by their mothers or kept very close to her due to safety concerns. These infants thus get relatively little opportunity early on to exercise their locomotor skills (Kaplan & Dove, 1987).

In direct contrast, the Kipsigis in rural Kenya actively encourage the motor development of their infants; for example, they help their babies practice sitting by propping them up in shallow holes dug in the ground to support their backs (Super, 1976). Other groups, in West Africa and the West Indies, institute an aggressive program of massage, manipulation, and stimulation designed to facilitate their infants' motor development (Gottlieb, 2004; Hopkins & Westra, 1988).

These widely varying cultural practices can have an impact on infants' development. Researchers have documented somewhat slower motor development in Ache and Chinese infants compared with the norms shown in Figure 5.8; Kipsigis babies and the infants who undergo exercise regimes, on the other hand, are advanced in their motor-skill development.

Current Views of Motor Development

Impressed by the orderly acquisition of skills reflected in Figure 5.8, two early pioneers in the study of motor development, Arnold Gesell and Myrtle McGraw, concluded that infants' motor development is governed by maturation of the

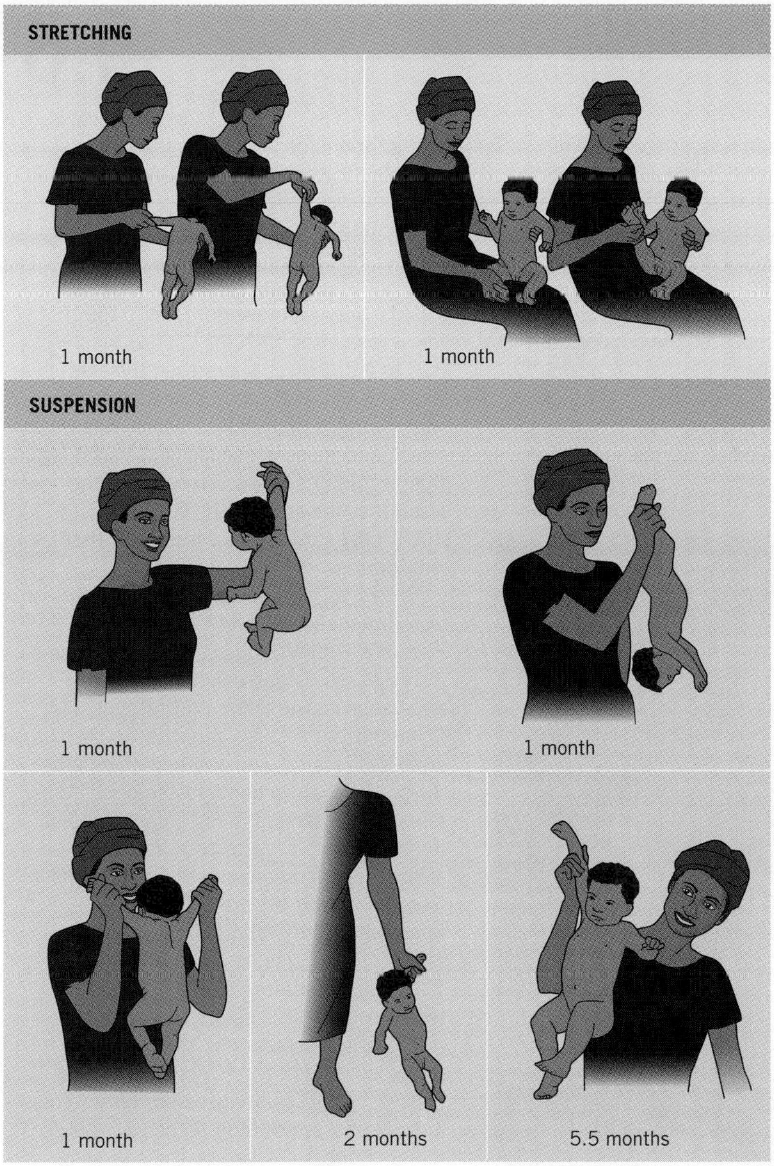

Mothers in Mali believe it is important to exercise their infants to promote their physical and motor development. The maneuvers shown here do not harm the babies and do hasten their early motor skills. (Adapted from Bril & Sabatier, 1986)

cortex (Gesell & Thompson, 1938; McGraw, 1943). In contrast, current theorists, many of whom take a dynamic-systems approach (see Chapter 4), emphasize that early motor development results from a confluence of numerous factors that include developing neural mechanisms, increases in infants' strength, posture control, balance, and perceptual skills, as well as changes in body proportions and motivation (Bertenthal & Clifton, 2006; Lockman & Thelen, 1993; von Hofsten, 2004). (Box 5.3 on the next page offers a detailed account of a program of research exemplifying this approach.)

Think for a moment about how each of these factors plays a part in the gradual transition from newborns unable even to lift their head to toddlers who walk independently, holding their upper body erect while coordinating the movement of their legs that have grown strong enough to support their weight. Every milestone in this transition is fueled by what infants can perceive of the external world and their motivation to experience more of it. The vital role of motivation is especially clear in infants' determined efforts to walk when they can get around much more

a closer look 5.3

"The Case of the Disappearing Reflex"

One of the primary proponents of the dynamic systems point of view we discussed in Chapter 4 was Esther Thelen. Early research by Thelen and her colleagues provides an excellent example of this approach to investigating motor development, as well as a good example of how to formulate hypotheses and test them in general. In one study, they held infants under the arms and submerged them waist-deep in water. As you read the following paragraphs, see how soon you can figure out the rationale for this somewhat strange-sounding, but in fact extremely clever and informative, experiment.

This particular study was one in a series of investigations of what Thelen (1995) referred to as "the case of the disappearing reflex." The reflex in question, the **stepping reflex,** can be elicited by holding a newborn under the arms so that his or her feet touch a surface; the baby will reflexively perform stepping motions, lifting first one leg and then the other in a coordinated pattern as in walking. The reflex typically disappears at around 2 months of age. It was long assumed that the stepping reflex disappears from the infant's motor repertoire as a result of cortical maturation.

However, the results of a classic study by Zelazo, Zelazo, and Kolb (1972) were inconsistent with this view. In this research, 2-month-old infants were given extra practice exercising their stepping reflex; as a result, the infants continued to show the reflex long after it would otherwise have disappeared. Other research also showed persistence of the stepping pattern long beyond 2 months of age. For one thing, the rhythmical kicking that babies engage in when they are lying down on their back involves the same pattern of alternating leg movement as stepping does. However, unlike stepping, kicking continues throughout infancy (Thelen & Fisher, 1982). For another, when 7-month-olds in whom the stepping reflex has disappeared are supported on a moving treadmill, they step smartly (Thelen, 1986). If the stepping reflex can be prolonged or elicited long after it is supposedly scheduled to disappear, cortical maturation cannot account for its vanishing. Why then does it normally disappear?

COURTESY OF ESTHER THELEN

This infant, who no longer shows a stepping reflex on dry land, does show it when suspended in water.

A clue was provided by the observation that chubbier babies generally begin walking (and crawling) somewhat later than slimmer ones. Thelen reasoned that infants' very rapid weight gain in the first few weeks after birth may cause their legs to get heavier faster than they get stronger. More strength is needed to step while upright than to kick while lying down, and more is needed to lift a fat leg than a thin one. Thus, Thelen hypothesized that the solution to the mystery might have more to do with brawn than with brains.

To test this hypothesis, two elegant experiments were conducted (Thelen, Fisher, & Ridley-Johnson, 1984). In one, the researchers put weights, roughly equivalent to the amount of fat typically gained in the first few months, on the ankles of infants who still had a stepping reflex. The babies suddenly stopped stepping. In the second study, infants who no longer showed a stepping reflex were suspended waist-deep in a tank of water (see the photo). As predicted, with the buoyancy of the water supporting their weight, the babies resumed stepping. Thus, the scientific detective work of these investigators established that the normal disappearance of the stepping reflex is not, as was previously assumed, caused by cortical maturation; rather, the movement pattern (and its neural basis) remains but is masked by the changing ratio of leg weight to strength. Only by considering multiple variables simultaneously was it possible to solve the mystery of the disappearing reflex.

efficiently by crawling. All parents—and many researchers—have the impression that infants derive pleasure from pushing the envelope of their motor skills.

The Expanding World of the Infant

Infants' mastery of each of the milestones shown in Figure 5.8 greatly expands their world: there is more to see when they can sit up, more to explore when they can reach for things themselves, and even more to discover when they can move about on their own. In this section, we consider some of the ways that motor development affects infants' experience of the world.

stepping reflex a neonatal reflex in which an infant lifts first one leg and then the other in a coordinated pattern like walking

Reaching

The development of reaching sets off a minirevolution in the infant's life: "once infants can reach for and grasp objects, they no longer have to wait for the world to come to them" (Bertenthal & Clifton, 2006). However, reaching takes time to develop. That is because, as discussed in Chapter 4, this seemingly simple behavior actually involves a complex interaction of multiple, independent components, including muscle development, postural control, development of various perceptual and motor skills, and so on (Spencer, Vereijken, Diedrich, & Thelen, 2000; Thelen et al., 1993).

Initially, infants are limited to **prereaching movements**—clumsy swiping toward the general vicinity of objects they see (von Hofsten, 1982). At around 3 to 4 months of age, they begin successfully reaching for objects, although their movements are initially somewhat jerky and poorly controlled.

prereaching movements clumsy swiping movements by young infants toward the general vicinity of objects they see

At around 7 months, as infants gain the ability to sit independently, their reaching becomes quite stable, and the trajectory of their reaches is consistently smooth and straight to the target (Spencer et al., 2000; Thelen et al., 1993; von Hofsten, 1979, 1991). Infants' sphere of action is enlarged by the achievement of stable sitting and reaching, because they can now lean forward to capture objects previously out of reach (Bertenthal & Clifton, 2006; Rochat & Goubet, 1995).

Infants seem to rely on the "feel" of their hand and arm movement, as shown by the fact that vision is not necessary for accurate reaching: 4- to 8-month-old infants in a completely dark room can successfully nab an invisible object that is making a sound (Clifton, Rochat, Litovsky, & Perris, 1991). In addition, when reaching for objects they can see, infants rarely reach for ones that are too distant, suggesting that they have some sense of how long their arms are (Bertenthal & Clifton, 2006).

With age and practice, infants' reaching shows increasingly clear signs of anticipation; for example, when reaching toward a large object, infants open their fingers widely and adjust their hand to the orientation of the desired object (Lockman, Ashmead, & Bushnell, 1984; Newell, Scully, McDonald, & Baillargeon, 1989). Furthermore, like an outfielder catching a fly ball, infants can make contact with a moving object by anticipating its trajectory and aiming their reach slightly ahead of it (Robin, Berthier, & Clifton, 1996; von Hofsten, Vishton, Spelke, Feng, & Rosander, 1998). Most impressive, 10-month-olds' approach to an object is affected by what they intend to do after they get their hands on it. Like adults, they reach faster for an object that they plan to throw than for one they plan to use in a more precise fashion (Claxton, Keen, & McCarty, 2003). As Figure 5.9 illustrates, infants' anticipation skills are still limited.

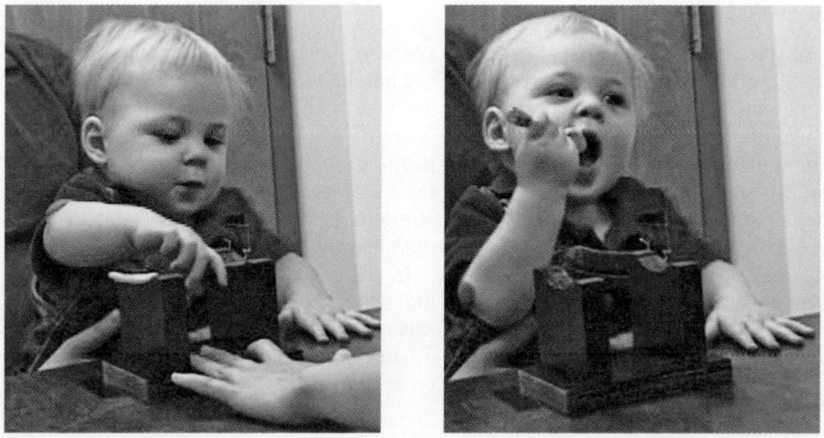

COURTESY OF RACHEL KEEN

FIGURE 5.9 This right-handed 14-month-old—a participant in research by Rachel Keen and colleagues—is having a hard time getting the applesauce he has been offered into his mouth. As the photo on the left shows, he has been presented the spoon with its handle to his left, but he has grabbed it with his dominant right hand, which makes it extremely difficult to keep the spoon upright on its way to his mouth. A spill ensued.

"FIRST STEPS, AFTER MILLET," BY VINCENT VAN GOGH. THE METROPOLITAN MUSEUM OF ART

Van Gogh's painting, "First Steps," may have been inspired by the joy that most parents feel at seeing their baby walk alone for the first time and the joy the baby feels taking those first steps.

Self-Locomotion

At around 8 months of age, infants become capable for the first time in their lives of **self-locomotion,** that is, of moving around in the environment on their own. No longer limited to being only where someone else carries or puts them, their world must seem vastly larger.

Infants' first success at moving forward under their own power typically takes the form of crawling. (Box 5.4 describes a recent increase in variability in the onset of crawling.) Many (perhaps most) infants begin by belly crawling or using other idiosyncratic patterns of self-propulsion, one of which researchers refer to as the "inchworm belly-flop" style (Adolph, Vereijken, & Denny, 1998). Most belly crawlers then shift to hands-and-knees crawling, which is less effortful and faster.

When infants first begin walking independently, at around 11 to 12 months, they keep their feet relatively wide apart, which increases their base of support; they flex slightly at the hip and knee, thereby lowering their center of gravity; they keep their hands in the air to facilitate balance; and they have both feet on the ground 60% of the time (as opposed to only 20% for adults) (Bertenthal & Clifton, 2006). As they grow larger and gain experience, their steps become longer, straighter, and more consistent. Practice is vital to infants' gradual mastery over their initially weak muscles and precarious balance (Adolph, Vereikjen, & Shrout, 2003).

The everyday life of the newly mobile crawler or walker is replete with challenges to locomotion—slippery floors, spongy carpets, paths cluttered with objects and obstacles, stairs, sloping lawns, and so on. Infants must constantly evaluate whether their developing skills are adequate to enable them to travel from one point to another. Eleanor Gibson and her colleagues found that infants adjust their mode of locomotion according to their perception of the properties of the surface they want to traverse (Gibson et al., 1987; Gibson & Schmuckler, 1989). For example, an infant who had promptly walked across a rigid plywood walkway would prudently revert to crawling in order to get across a water bed. Box 5.5 summarizes a program of research on the early development of locomotion and

self-locomotion the ability to move oneself around in the environment

applications **5.4**

A Recent Secular Change in Motor Development

In the late 1990s, pediatricians noticed a surprising increase in the number of visits they received from parents worried because their infants either began crawling quite late or never crawled at all. Many babies had simply gone from sitting to walking.

The cause for this genuine secular change in motor development seems to be traceable to the campaign, described in Box 2.4 (page 63), to get parents to put their babies to sleep on their backs (Davis, Moon, Sachs, & Ottolini, 1998). As we discussed in Chapter 2, this public health effort has been very successful in changing parents' behavior and has resulted in a remarkable reduction in the incidence of SIDS. However, it appears that regularly lying on their backs makes infants less likely to turn over on schedule. One source of this effect may be motivational: the better view of the environment that they have on their backs may lessen infants' motivation to roll over onto their stomachs, where the view is quite restricted. But, spending less time on their tummies, the babies have less opportunity to discover that they can propel themselves forward by squirming. With less practice pushing themselves up from lying on their stomachs, the infants' arm strength may develop somewhat more slowly.

In any event, the research is reassuring: when observed at 18 months, there was no difference in the development of infants who had or who had not crawled on schedule.

a closer look 5.5

"Gangway—I'm Coming Down"

The interdependence of different developmental domains is beautifully illustrated by a rich and fascinating series of experiments conducted over five decades. This work started with a landmark study by Eleanor Gibson and Richard Walk (1960) that addressed the question of whether infants can perceive depth. It has culminated in research linking depth perception, locomotion, cognitive abilities, emotion, and the social context of development.

To answer the depth-perception question, Gibson and Walk used an apparatus known as the "visual cliff." As the photo shows, the visual cliff consists of a thick sheet of plexiglass that can support the weight of an infant or toddler. A platform across the middle divides the apparatus into two sides. A checked pattern right under the glass on one side makes it look like a solid, safe surface. On the other side, the same pattern is far beneath the glass, and the contrast in the apparent size of the checks makes it look as though there is a dangerous drop-off—a "cliff"—between the two sides.

Gibson and Walk reported that 6- to 14-month-old infants would readily cross the shallow side of the visual cliff. They would not, however, cross the deep side, even when a parent was beckoning to them to come across it. The infants were apparently unwilling to venture over what looked like a precipice—strong evidence that they perceived and understood the significance of the depth cue of relative size.

Karen Adolph, who had been a student of Gibson, has conducted extensive research on the relation between perception and action in infancy. Adolph and her colleagues have discovered surprising discontinuities in infants' learning what they can and cannot accomplish with their developing locomotor and postural skills (Adolph, 1997, 2000, Adolph, Eppler, & Gibson, 1993; Adolph et al., 2003; Eppler, Adolph, & Weiner, 1996). This research exemplifies our theme of *mechanisms of change,* in which variation and selection produce developmental change.

As a way of studying the relation between early motor abilities and judgment, the investigators asked parents to try to entice their infants to lean over or crawl across gaps of varying widths in an elevated surface or to crawl or walk down sloping walkways that varied in how steep they were. Some of these tasks were possible for a given infant; the baby would have no trouble, for example, negotiating a slope of a particular steepness. Others, however, were impossible for that infant. Would the babies identify which tasks were which? (An experimenter always hovered nearby to catch any infant who misjudged his or her prowess.)

The photos on page 198 show how infants behaved on slopes when beckoned by an adult (usually their mother). In their first weeks of crawling, infants (averaging around 8½ months in age) unhesitatingly and competently went down shallow slopes. Confronted with slopes that were too steep to crawl down, the babies typically paused for a moment, but then launched themselves headfirst anyway (requiring the experimenter to catch hold of them). With more weeks of crawling practice, the babies got better at judging when a slope was simply too steep and should be avoided. They also improved at devising strategies to get down somewhat steep slopes, such as turning around and cautiously inching backward down the slope.

However, when the infants started walking, they again misjudged which slopes they could get down using their new mode of locomotion and tried to walk down slopes that were too steep for them. In other words, they failed to transfer what they had learned about crawling down slopes to walking down them. Thus, infants apparently have to learn through experience how to integrate perceptual information with each new motor behavior they develop.

Infants' decisions in such situations also depend on social information. Infants who are close to being able to make it down a relatively steep walkway can be rather easily discouraged from trying to do so by their mother telling them, "No! Stop!" Conversely, enthusiastic

COURTESY OF PROFESSOR JOSEPH J. CAMPOS, UNIVERSITY OF CALIFORNIA, BERKELEY

An infant refusing to cross the deep side of the visual cliff, even though his mother is calling and beckoning to him from the other side.

(**a closer look** is continued on the next page)

(continued from the previous page)

encouragement from a parent can lead an inexperienced crawler or walker to attempt a currently too-steep slope. Thus, the child uses both perceptual and social information in deciding what to do. In this case, the information is obtained through *social referencing,* the child's use of another person's emotional response to an uncertain situation to decide how to behave (see Chapter 10, page 414).

A key finding of Adolph's research is that infants have to learn from experience what they can and cannot do with respect to each new motor skill that they master. Just like the new crawlers and walkers who literally plunge ahead when put atop a sloping walkway, an infant who has just developed the ability to sit will lean too far out over a gap in a platform in an attempt to snag an out-of-reach toy and would fall over the edge if not for the ever-present catcher. And, like the experienced crawlers and walkers who pause to make a prudent judgment about whether or not to try a descent, an infant who has been capable of sitting unsupported for some time can judge whether the gap is too wide to lean across and will stay put if it appears to be so. These highly consistent findings across a variety of motor skills have made a very important contribution to our understanding of how infants learn to interact successfully with their environment.

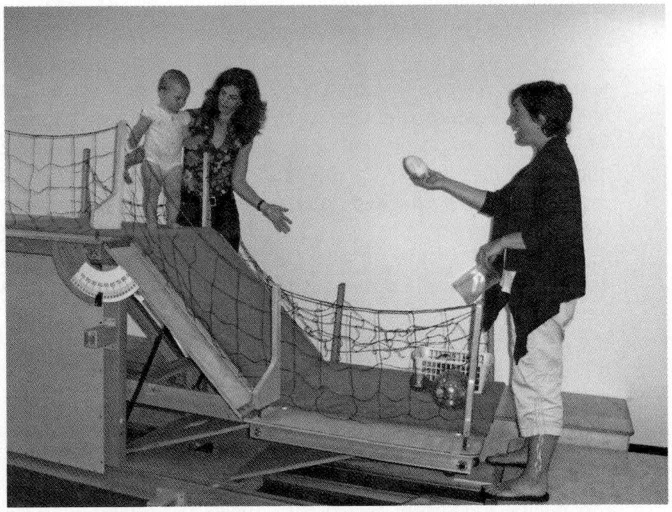

BOTH: COURTESY OF KAREN ADOLPH

Integrating perceptual information with new motor skills. Researcher Karen Adolph will need to rescue the newly crawling young infant on the left, who does not realize that this slope is too steep for her current level of crawling expertise. In contrast, the experienced walker on the right is judiciously deciding that the slope is too steep for him to walk down.

BILL LOSH / FPG / GETTY IMAGES

This toddler is engaged in social referencing; she is using another person's reaction to her behavior to determine whether or not what she's doing is safe.

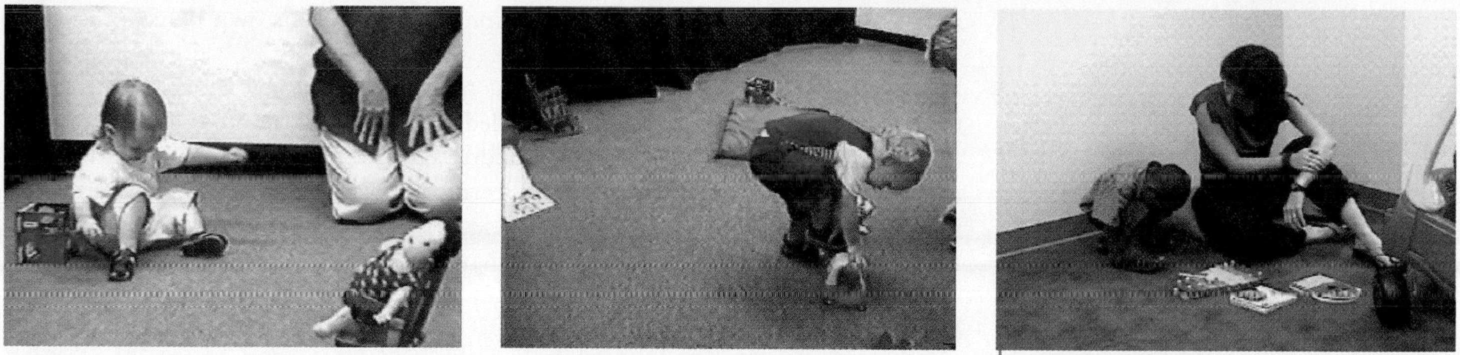

COURTESY OF JUDY DELOACHE

FIGURE 5.10 Scale errors These three children are making scale errors, treating a miniature object as if it were a much larger one. The girl on the left has just fallen off the toy slide she was trying to go down; the boy in the middle is persistently trying to get into a very small car; and the boy on the right is attempting to sit in a miniature chair. (From DeLoache et al., 2004)

other forms of motor behavior in infancy, focusing specifically on the integration of perception and locomotion.

The challenge that young children experience in integrating perceptual information in the planning and execution of actions sometimes results in quite surprising behaviors, especially when children fail to meet the challenge. A particularly dramatic example of failure in the integration of perception and action is provided by **scale errors** (Brownell, Zerwas, & Ramani, 2007; DeLoache, Uttal, & Rosengren, 2004; Ware, Uttal, Wetter, & DeLoache, 2006). In this kind of error, very young children try to do something with a miniature replica object that is far too small for the action to be at all possible. Toddlers will attempt, in all seriousness, to sit in a tiny, dollhouse-sized chair or to get into a small toy car (see Figure 5.10). In committing a scale error, the child momentarily fails to take into account the relation between his or her own body and the size of the target object. These errors are hypothesized to result from a failure to integrate visual information represented in two different areas of the brain in the service of action. With development, the incidence of scale errors diminishes, although even adults make a variety of action errors (e.g., putting a cup of water into the cupboard instead of the microwave or trying to squeeze into a too tight pair of pants).

review:

All normally developing infants display a similar sequence of milestones in the development of motor behavior, starting with a common set of neonatal reflexes. Researchers have increasingly emphasized the pervasive interconnectedness between infants' motor behavior, perception, and motivation, as well as the many ways that infants' experience of the world changes with each advance. In the development of self-locomotion (crawling, walking), infants adopt a variety of different movement patterns to get around and to cope with different environmental challenges. A crucial aspect of development is the ability to make accurate judgments about what actions one is and is not capable of performing, an ability that comes with experience.

Learning

Who do you think learned more today—you or a 10-month-old infant? We'd bet on the baby, just because there is so much that is new to an infant. Think back to baby Benjamin in the kitchen with his parents. A wealth of learning opportunities was embedded in that everyday scene. Benjamin was, for example, gaining experience with some of the differences between animate and inanimate entities; with the particular sights and sounds that go together in events; with the consequences of objects' losing support (including the effect of this event on his parents' emotional

scale error the attempt by a young child to perform an action on a miniature object that is impossible due to the large discrepancy in the relative sizes of the child and the object state); and so on. He also experienced consequences of his own behavior, such as his parents' response to his crying.

In this section, we review six different types of learning by which infants profit from their experience and acquire knowledge of the world. Some of the questions that developmental psychologists have addressed with respect to infants' learning include at what age the different forms of learning appear and in what ways learning in infancy is related to later cognitive abilities. Another important question concerns the extent to which infants find some things easier or more difficult to learn.

Habituation

The simplest and earliest form of learning is recognizing something that has been experienced before. As we discussed in Chapter 2 and again earlier in this chapter, babies—like everybody else—tend to respond relatively less to stimuli they have previously experienced and relatively more to novel ones (see Figure 5.11). The occurrence of habituation in response to repeated stimulation reveals that learning has taken place; the infant has formed a memory representation of the repeated, and now familiar, stimulus. Habituation is highly adaptive: diminished attention to what is old and known enables infants to pay attention to, and learn about, what is new.

The speed with which an infant habituates is believed to reflect the general efficiency of the infant's processing of information. Related measures of attention, including duration of looking and degree of novelty preference, are also taken as measures of speed and efficiency of processing. A substantial and surprising degree of continuity has been found between these measures in infancy and general cognitive ability later in life. Infants who habituate relatively rapidly, who take relatively short looks at visual stimuli, and/or who show a greater preference for novelty tend to have higher IQs when tested as much as 18 years later (Colombo et al., 2004; Rose & Feldman, 1997). Thus, one of the earliest and simplest forms of human learning is fundamental to basic cognitive development.

Perceptual Learning

From the beginning, infants actively search for order and regularity in the world around them, and they learn a great deal from simply paying close attention to the objects and events they perceive. According to Eleanor Gibson (1988), the key process in perceptual learning is **differentiation**—extracting from the events in the environment those elements that are invariant, that remain stable. For example, infants learn the association between tone of voice and facial expression because, in their experience, a pleasant, happy, or eagerly excited tone of voice occurs with a smiling face—not a frowning one—and a harsh, angry tone of voice accompanies a frowning face—not a smiling one. With age and experience, infants

differentiation the extraction from the constantly changing stimulation in the environment of those elements that are invariant, or stable

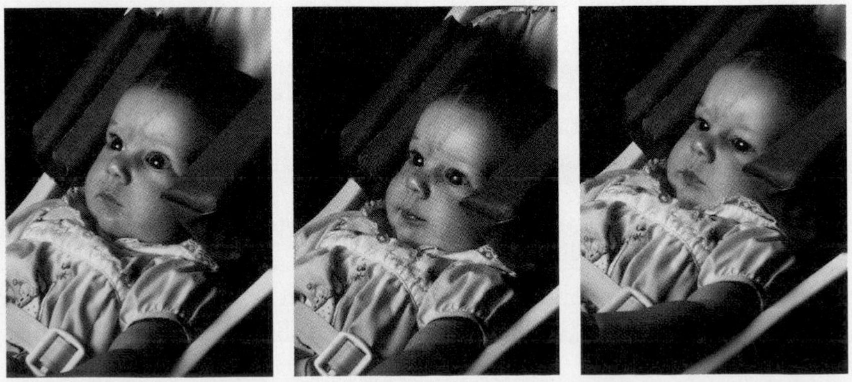

FIGURE 5.11 Habituation This 3-month-old provides a vivid demonstration of habituation. She is seated in front of a screen on which photographs are displayed. At the first appearance of a photo of a face, her eyes widen and she stares intently at it. With three more presentations of the same picture, her interest wanes and a yawn appears. By its fifth appearance, other things are attracting the baby's attention, and by the sixth even her dress is more interesting. When a new face finally appears, her interest in something novel is evident. (From Maurer & Maurer, 1988)

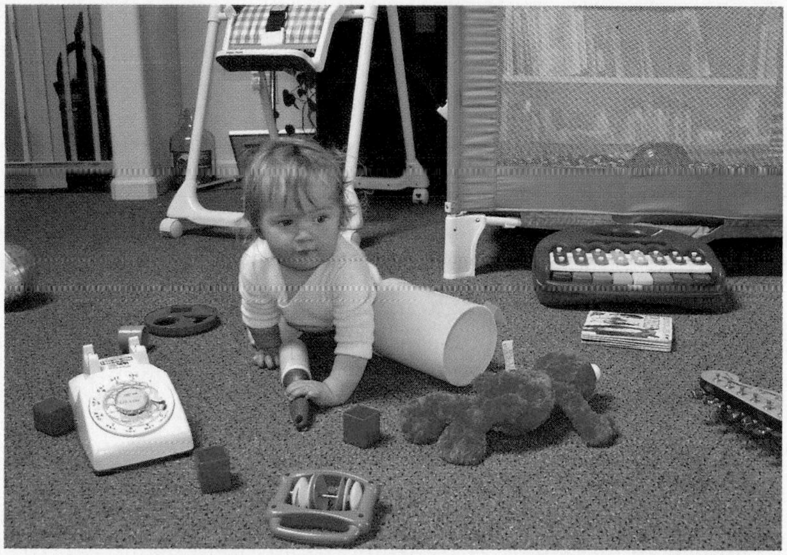

GERI ENGBERT / THE IMAGE WORKS

The objects surrounding this baby offer a variety of affordances. Some can be picked up, but others are too big for the infant's small hands or too heavy for her limited strength. The rattle makes noise when shaken, the piano when banged. Small objects can be inserted into the yellow container, but larger ones won't fit. The stuffed toy can be enjoyably cuddled, but not the telephone. Through interacting with the world around them, infants discover these and many other types of affordances.

become increasingly efficient at extracting relevant information, and they are able to make finer and finer discriminations among stimuli.

A particularly important part of perceptual learning is the infant's discovery of **affordances**—that is, the possibilities for action offered, or afforded, by objects and situations (Gibson, 1988). They discover, for example, that small objects—but not large ones—can be picked up; that liquid can be poured and spilled; that chairs of a certain size can be sat in; and so forth. Infants discover affordances by figuring out the relations between their own bodies and abilities and the things around them. As we discussed earlier, for example, infants come to appreciate that solid, flat surfaces afford stable walking, but squishy, slick, or steeply sloping ones do not (Adolph, 1997; Adolph et al., 2003; Gibson et al., 1987; Gibson & Schmuckler, 1989; Joh & Adolph, 2006; Joh, Adolph, Narayanan, & Dietz, 2007).

affordances the possibilities for action offered by objects and situations

Perceptual learning is involved in many, but not all, examples of intermodal coordination. As we noted previously, learning is not required to detect a unitary event involving sight and sound, so baby Benjamin naturally perceives a single, coherent event the first time he sees and hears a crystal goblet crashing on the floor. However, one does have to learn what particular sights and sounds go together, so only through experience does Ben know that a particular tinkling sound means a glass is being broken. As you have seen, infants are sensitive early on to the synchrony of lip movements and vocal sounds, but they have to learn to relate the unique sight of their mother's face with the unique sound of her voice, which they accomplish by 3½ months of age (Spelke & Owsley, 1979). The necessity for perceptual learning is especially clear for events that involve arbitrary relations, such

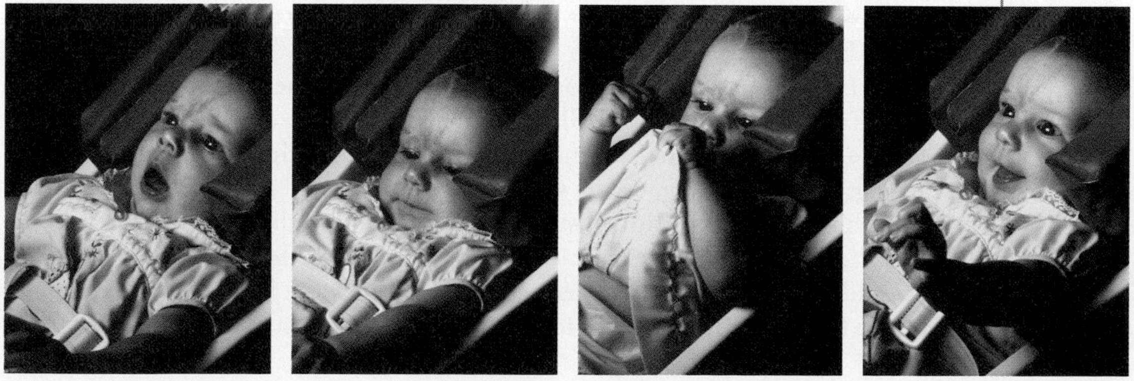

ALL: CHARLES E. MAURER

as an association between the color of a cup and the taste of the food inside. The fact that 7-month-olds can be taught color–taste associations in the lab (Reardon & Bushnell, 1988) would come as no surprise to those parents whose infants clamp their mouths shut at the sight of a spoon conveying anything green.

Statistical Learning

A related type of learning also involves simply picking up information from the environment, specifically, forming associations among stimuli that occur in a statistically predictable pattern (Aslin, Saffran, & Newport, 1998; Kirkham, Slemmer, & Johnson, 2002; Saffran, Aslin, & Newport, 1996). Our natural environment contains a high degree of regularity and redundancy; certain events occur in a predictable order, certain objects appear at the same time and place, and so on. A common example for a baby is the regularity with which the sound of Mom's voice is followed by the appearance of her face.

From quite early on, infants are sensitive to the regularity with which one event follows another. In one study, 2- to 8-month-olds were habituated to six simple visual shapes that were presented one after another with specified levels of probability (Kirkham et al., 2002). For example, three pairs of colored shapes always occurred together in the same order (e.g., a square was always followed by a cross), but the next stimulus could be any of three different shapes (e.g., a cross was followed by a circle, triangle, or square equally often). Thus, the probability that the cross would follow the square was 100%, but the probability that the circle (or triangle or square) would come after the cross was 33%. In a test, the order of appearance of one or more of the shapes was changed. The infants looked longer when the structure inherent in the initial set was violated (e.g., square followed by circle). (Statistical learning has been proposed to be of vital importance in language learning, as we will discuss in Chapter 6.)

Classical Conditioning

Another type of learning, **classical conditioning,** was first discovered by Pavlov in his famous research with dogs (who learned an association between the sound of a bell and the arrival of food and gradually came to salivate at the sound of the bell alone). Classical conditioning plays a role in infants' everyday learning about the relations between environmental events that have relevance for them. Consider young babies' mealtimes, which occur frequently and have a predictable structure. First, the hungry infant is picked up by the mother (with her unique constellation of perceptual features) and held in a particular way. Then a breast or bottle contacts the infant's mouth, eliciting the sucking reflex. The sucking causes milk to flow into the infant's mouth, and the infant experiences the pleasurable sensations of a delicious taste and the satisfaction of hunger. Learning is revealed when an infant's sucking motions begin to occur at the mere sight of the bottle or breast.

In terms of classical conditioning, the nipple in the infant's mouth is an **unconditioned stimulus (UCS)** that reliably elicits a reflexive, unlearned response—in this case, the sucking reflex—the **unconditioned response (UCR).** Learning, or conditioning, occurs when an initially neutral stimulus—the breast or bottle, which is the **conditioned stimulus (CS)**—repeatedly occurs just before the unconditioned stimulus (the baby sees the breast or bottle before receiving the nipple). Gradually, the originally reflexive response—now the learned or **conditioned response (CR)**—comes to occur to the CS (anticipatory sucking movements now

classical conditioning a form of learning that consists of associating an initially neutral stimulus with a stimulus that always evokes a particular reflexive response

unconditioned stimulus (UCS) in classical conditioning, a stimulus that evokes a reflexive response

unconditioned response (UCR) in classical conditioning, a reflexive response that is elicited by the unconditioned stimulus

conditioned stimulus (CS) in classical conditioning, the neutral stimulus that is repeatedly paired with the unconditioned stimulus

conditioned response (CR) in classical conditioning, the originally reflexive response that comes to be elicited by the conditioned stimulus

instrumental or **operant conditioning** learning the relation between one's own behavior and the consequences that result from it

positive reinforcement a reward that reliably follows a behavior and increases the likelihood that the behavior will be repeated begin as soon as the baby sees the breast or bottle). In other words, the sight of the bottle or breast has become a signal of what will follow. Gradually, the infant may also come to associate the mother herself with the whole sequence, including the pleasurable feelings that result from feeding. If so, these feelings could eventually be evoked simply by the presence of the mother. It is thought that many emotional responses are initially learned through classical conditioning.

Instrumental Conditioning

A key form of learning for infants (and everyone else) is learning the consequences of one's own behavior. In everyday life, infants learn that shaking a rattle produces an interesting sound, that cooing at Dad gets him to coo back, and that exploring the dirt in a potted plant leads to a parental reprimand. This kind of learning, referred to as **instrumental conditioning** (or *operant conditioning*), involves learning the relation between one's own behavior and the reward or punishment it results in. Most research on instrumental conditioning in infants involves **positive reinforcement,** that is, a reward that reliably follows a behavior and increases the likelihood that the behavior will be repeated. Such research features a *contingency* relation between the infant's behavior and the reward: if the infant makes the target response, *then* he or she receives the reinforcement. Table 5.1 shows a few examples of the great variety of ingenious situations researchers have engineered in order to examine instrumental learning in infants.

TABLE 5.1

Studying Instrumental Conditioning in Infants

Age Group	Learned Response	Reinforcement
Newborns	Head turn to side	Drink of sucrose water
3 weeks	Sucking pattern	Interesting visual display
5–12 weeks	Sucking pattern	Keep a movie in focus
6 months	Push a lever	Cause a toy train to move along a track

Source: Bruner (1973); Hartshorn & Rovee-Collier (1997); Siqueland & DeLucia (1969); Siqueland & Lipsitt (1966)

One simple but clever instrumental-conditioning procedure for studying learning and memory in young infants was designed by Carolyn Rovee-Collier (1997) and her colleagues. In this procedure, experimenters tie a ribbon around a baby's ankle and connect it to a mobile hanging above the infant's crib (Figure 5.12). In the course of naturally kicking their legs, infants as young as 2 months of age learn within minutes the relation between their leg movements and the enjoyable sight of the jiggling mobile. They then quite deliberately and often joyfully increase their rate of foot kicking. The interesting mobile movement thus serves as reinforcement for the kicking. An additional feature of this procedure is that the intensity of the reward—the amount of movement of the mobile—depends on the intensity of the baby's behavior.

FIGURE 5.12 Contingency This young infant learned within minutes that kicking his leg would cause the mobile to move in an interesting way; he learned the contingency between his own behavior and an external event. Notice the level of concentration he focuses on the mobile that he is controlling.

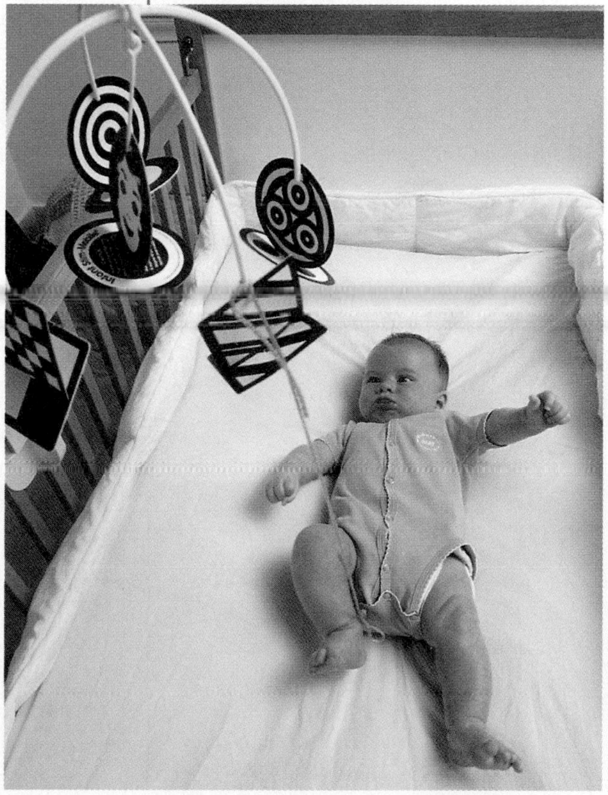

MICHAEL NEWMAN / PHOTOEDIT

Although infants can learn a great variety of contingency relations, there are a number of limitations on the learning process. For example, the younger the infant, the closer together the response and reinforcement have to be both in time and space: young babies learn only if there is a minimal delay between their response and the subsequent reinforcement and only if the reinforcement occurs very near to where the response was made. Thus, they might learn the relation between pressing a button and a light coming on, but only if the light comes on very soon quite near the button (Millar, 1990).

Infants' intense motivation to explore and master their environment, which we have emphasized in our *active child* theme, shows up in instrumental learning situations: infants work hard at learning to predict and control their experience, and they dislike losing control once it has been established. Researchers have described facial expressions of joy and interest seen while infants as young as 2 months old were learning a contingency relation, and expressions of anger when a learned response no longer produced the expected results (Lewis, Alessandri, & Sullivan, 1990; Sullivan, Lewis, & Alessandri, 1992). When newborns failed to receive the sweet liquid they had learned would follow a head-turn response, seven out of eight cried (Blass, 1990).

Infants may also learn that there are situations over which they have no control. For example, infants of depressed mothers tend to smile less and show lower levels of positive affect than do infants whose mothers are not depressed. In part, this may be because infants of depressed mothers learn that their smiling is rarely rewarded by their preoccupied parent (Campbell, Cohn, & Meyers, 1995). More generally, through contingency situations, whether in a lab or an everyday setting, infants learn more than just the particular contingency relations to which they are exposed. They also learn about the relation between themselves and the world and the extent to which they can have an impact on it.

Observational Learning/Imitation

A particularly potent source of infants' learning is their observation of other people's behaviors. Parents, who are often amused and sometimes embarrassed by their toddler's reproduction of their own behavior, are well aware that their offspring learn a great deal through simple observation.

The ability to imitate the behavior of other people appears to be present very early in life, albeit in an extremely limited form. Andrew Meltzoff and Keith Moore (1977, 1983) found that after newborns watch an adult model slowly and repeatedly stick out his or her tongue, they often stick out their own tongue (Meltzoff & Moore, 1977).

By the age of 6 months, infant imitation is quite robust. Six-month-old infants not only imitate tongue protrusion but they also attempt to poke their tongue out to the side when that is what they have seen an adult do (Meltzoff & Moore, 1994). From this age on, the scope of infant imitation expands. Infants begin to imitate novel, and sometimes quite strange, actions they have seen performed on objects. In one procedure that demonstrates this, infants observe an experimenter performing unusual behaviors with objects, such as leaning over from the waist to touch his or her forehead to a box, causing the box to light up. The infants are later presented with the same objects the experimenter had acted on. Infants as young as 6 to 9 months old imitate some of the novel actions they have witnessed, even after a delay of 24 hours (Barr, Dowden, & Hayne, 1996; Bauer, 2002; Hayne, Barr, & Herbert, 2003; Meltzoff, 1988b). Fourteen-month-olds imitate such actions as long as a full week later (Meltzoff, 1988a).

In choosing to imitate a model, infants seem to analyze the reason for the person's behavior. If infants see a model lean over and touch a box with her forehead, they later do the same. If, however, the model remarks that she's cold and tightly clutches a shawl around her body as she leans over and touches a box with her forehead, infants reach out and touch the box with their hand instead of their head (Gergely, Bekkering, & Kiraly, 2002). They apparently reason that the model wanted to touch the box and would have done so in a standard way if her hands had been free. Their imitation is thus based on their analysis of the person's intentions. In general, infants are flexible in learning through imitation: as in the case of touching the box, they can copy either the specific behavior through which a model achieves a goal, or they can employ different behaviors

(a)

(b)

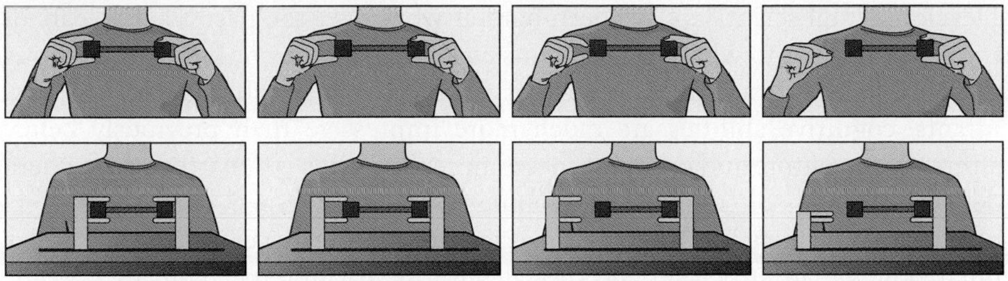

FIGURE 5.13 Imitating intentions
(a) When 18-month-olds see a person apparently try, but fail, to pull the ends off a dumbbell, they imitate pulling the ends off—the action the person intended to do, not what the person actually did. (b) They do not imitate a mechanical device at all. (From Meltzoff, 1995A)

to achieve the same goal the model achieved (Buttelmann, Carpenter, Call, & Tomasello, 2008).

Further evidence of infants' attention to intention comes from research in which 18-month-olds observed an adult attempting, but failing, to pull apart a small dumbbell toy (Meltzoff, 1995). The adult pulled on the two ends, but his hand "slipped off," and the dumbbell remained in one piece (Figure 5.13a). When the infants were subsequently given the toy, they pulled the two ends apart, imitating what the adult had *intended* to do, not what he had actually done. This research also established that infants' imitative actions are limited to human acts. A different group of 18-month-olds watched a mechanical device with pincers grasp the two ends of the dumbbell. The pincers either pulled apart the dumbbell or slipped off the ends (Figure 5.13b). Regardless of what the infants had seen the mechanical device do, they rarely attempted to pull apart the dumbbell themselves. Thus, infants attempt to reproduce the behavior and intentions of other people, but not of inanimate objects.

Babies are by no means restricted to learning from the behavior of live adult models. Infants as young as 15 months of age imitate actions they have seen an adult perform on a video screen (Barr & Hayne, 1999; Meltzoff, 1988a). Peers can also serve as models for young toddlers, as demonstrated by a study in which well-trained 14-month-old "expert peers" performed novel actions (e.g., pushing a button hidden inside a box to sound a buzzer) for their age-mates, either at their preschool or in a laboratory (Hanna & Meltzoff, 1993). When the observer children were tested in their own homes 48 hours later, they imitated what they had seen the child model do earlier.

review:

Infants begin learning about the world immediately. They habituate to repeatedly encountered stimuli, form expectancies for repeated event sequences, and learn associations between particular sights and sounds that regularly occur together. Classical conditioning, which has been demonstrated in newborn and older infants, is believed to be especially important in the learning of emotional reactions. Infants are highly sensitive to a wide range of contingency relations between their own behavior and what follows it. A particularly powerful form of learning for older infants is observational learning: from 6 months of age on, infants learn many new behaviors simply by watching what other people do. Although an enormous amount of learning goes on during the infancy period, some associations or relations are easier for babies to learn than others are. In observational learning, for example, intentionality is a key factor.

Cognition

Clearly, infants are capable of learning in a variety of ways. But do they actually think? This is a question that has intrigued parents and developmental psychologists alike (Kagan, 1972). Baby Benjamin's parents have no doubt looked with wonderment at their child, asking themselves, "What is he thinking? *Is* he thinking?"

Developmental scientists have been hard at work over the past twenty years or so trying to find out to what extent infants engage in cognition (knowledge, thought, reasoning). The resulting explosion of fascinating research has established that infants' cognitive abilities are much more impressive than previously believed, although the nature and origin of these impressive skills is a matter of considerable debate. Theorists of cognitive development vary with respect to the relative roles of nature and nurture, especially in terms of whether development is guided by innate knowledge structures and special-purpose learning mechanisms.

Coming down strongly on the side of nature is the core-knowledge position, which, as discussed in Chapter 4, argues that infants possess innate knowledge in a few domains of particular importance (Carey & Spelke, 1994; Gelman, 2002; Gelman & Williams, 1998; Scholl & Leslie, 1999; Spelke, 2000; Spelke & Kinsler, 2006). Core-knowledge theorists maintain that infants are born with some knowledge about the physical world, such as that two objects cannot occupy the same space and that physical objects move only if something sets them in motion. Other theorists emphasize *specialized* learning mechanisms that enable infants to acquire this kind of knowledge rapidly and efficiently (Baillargeon, 2004; Baillargeon, Kotovsky, & Needham, 1995). According to other theorists, infants' mental representations of the physical world are gradually acquired and strengthened through *general* learning mechanisms (Munakata, McClelland, Johnson, & Siegler, 1997). Finally, at the other end of the spectrum from the core-knowledge theories is the view that infants may not have knowledge representations at all and that much of what has been described as infant cognition may reflect purely perceptual-motor processes (Cohen & Cashon, 2003; Haith & Benson, 1998; Smith, 2003).

Object Knowledge

A large part of what we know about infant cognition has come from research on the development of knowledge about objects, research originally inspired by Jean Piaget's theory of sensorimotor intelligence. As you learned in Chapter 4, Piaget believed that young infants' understanding of the world is severely limited by an inability to mentally represent and think about anything that they cannot currently see, hear, touch, and so on. His tests of *object permanence* led him to infer that when an infant fails to search for an object—even a favorite toy—that has disappeared from sight, it is because the object has also disappeared from the infant's mind.

A substantial body of research has provided strong support for Piaget's original observation that young infants do not manually search for hidden objects. However, as noted in Chapter 4, skepticism gradually arose about his explanation of this fascinating phenomenon, and an overwhelming body of evidence has established that young infants are in fact able to mentally represent and think about the existence of invisible objects and events.

The simplest evidence for young infants' ability to represent an object that has vanished from sight is the fact that they will reach for objects in the dark, that is, they reach for objects they cannot see. When young infants are shown an attractive object and the room is then plunged into darkness, causing the object (and everything else) to disappear from view, most babies reach to where they last saw the object, indicating that they expect it to still be there (Perris & Clifton, 1988; Stack, Muir, Sherriff, & Roman, 1989).

Young infants even seem to be able to think about some characteristics of invisible objects, such as their size (Clifton, Rochat, Litovsky, & Perris, 1991).

When 6-month-olds sitting in the dark heard the sound of a familiar large object, they reached toward it with both hands (just as they had in the light); but they reached with only one hand when the sound they heard was that of a familiar small object.

The majority of the evidence that young infants can represent and think about invisible objects comes from research using the **violation-of-expectancy** procedure. The logic of this procedure is similar to that of the visual-preference method we discussed earlier (page 184). The basic assumption is that if infants observe an event that violates something they know about the world, they will be surprised or at least interested. Thus, an event that is impossible or inconsistent with respect to the infant's knowledge should evoke a greater response (such as longer looking or a change in heart rate) than does a possible or consistent event.

violation-of-expectancy a procedure used to study infant cognition in which infants are shown an event that should evoke surprise or interest if it violates something the infant knows or assumes to be true

The violation-of-expectancy technique was first used in a classic series of studies designed by Renée Baillargeon and her colleagues (Baillargeon, 1987b; Baillargeon, Spelke, & Wasserman, 1985) to see if infants too young to search for an invisible object might nevertheless have a mental representation of its existence. In some of these studies, infants were first habituated to the sight of a solid screen rotating back and forth through a 180° arc (Figure 5.14). Then a box was placed in the screen's path, and the infants saw two test events. In one, the *possible event*, the screen rotated upward, occluding the box as it did so, and stopped when it contacted the box. In the *impossible event*, the screen continued to rotate a full 180°, appearing to pass through the space occupied by the box (which the experimenter had surreptitiously removed).

Infants as young as 3½ months of age looked longer at the impossible event than at the possible one. The researchers reasoned that the full rotation of the screen (to which the infants had previously been habituated) would be more interesting or surprising than the partial rotation *only* if the infants expected the screen to stop when it reached the box. And the only reason for them to have had that expectation was if they thought the box was still present—that is, if they mentally represented an object they could no longer see. The results also indicate that the infants expected the box to remain in place and did not expect the screen to be able to pass through it.

Other studies have shown that young infants' behavior in this situation is influenced by some of the characteristics of the occluded objects, including height (Baillargeon, 1987a, b). They expect the screen to stop sooner for a taller object than for a shorter one. Thus, research using two very different assessments—reaching in the dark and visual attention—provides converging evidence that infants who do not yet search for hidden objects nevertheless can represent their continued existence and some of their properties.

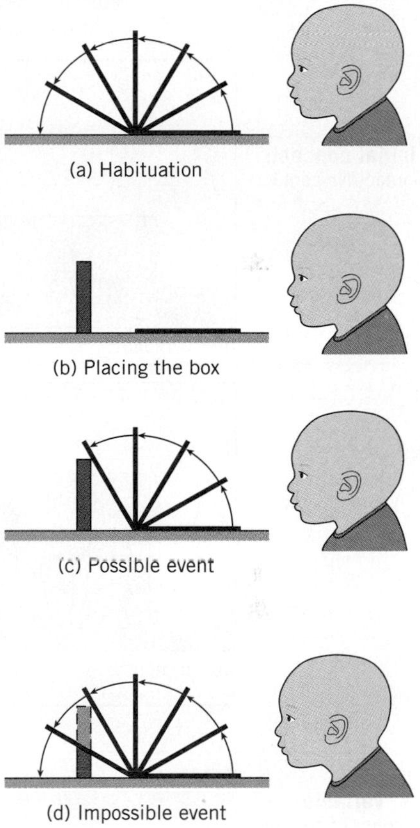

FIGURE 5.14 Possible versus impossible events In a classic series of tests of object permanence, Renée Baillargeon first habituated young infants to the sight of a screen rotating through 180 degrees. Then a box was placed in the path of the screen. In the *possible event,* the screen rotated up, occluding the box, and stopped when it reached the top of the box. In the *impossible event,* the screen rotated up, occluding the box, but then continued on through 180 degrees, appearing to pass through the space where the box was. Infants looked longer at the impossible event, showing that they mentally represented the presence of the invisible box. (From Baillargeon, 1987a)

Physical Knowledge

Infants' knowledge about the physical world is not limited to what they know and are learning about objects. Other research has examined what they know about physical phenomena, such as gravity. Even in the first year of life, infants seem to appreciate that objects do not float in midair, that an object that is inadequately supported will fall, that a nonround object placed on a stable surface will stay put, and so forth. For example, in a series of studies (Kim & Spelke, 1992) in which infants observed a ball being released on a slope, 7-month-olds (but not 5-month-olds) looked longer when the ball moved up the slope than when it moved down, indicating that they had expected the ball to go down. Similarly, they looked longer at an object that traveled more slowly as it rolled down a slope than at one that picked up speed.

Infants also gradually come to understand under what conditions one object can support another. Figure 5.15 summarizes infants' reactions to simple support problems involving boxes and a platform (Baillargeon, Needham, & DeVos, 1992; Needham & Baillargeon, 1993). At 3 months of age, infants are surprised (they look longer) if a box that is released in midair remains suspended (as in Figure 5.15a), rather than falling. However, as long as there is any contact at all between the box and the platform (as in Figure 5.15b and 5.15c), these young infants do not react when the box remains stationary. By approximately 5 months of age, they appreciate the relevance of the type of contact involved in support. They now know that the box will be stable only if it is released on top of the platform, so they would be surprised by the display in Figure 5.15b. Roughly a month later, they recognize the importance of the amount of contact, and hence they look longer when the box in Figure 5.15c stays put with only a small portion of its bottom surface on the platform. Shortly after their 1st birthday, infants also take into account the shape of the object and hence are surprised if an asymmetrical object like that shown in Figure 5.15d remains stable.

Infants presumably develop this progressively refined understanding of support relations between objects as a result of experience. They observe innumerable occasions of adults placing objects on surfaces, and once in a while, as in the crashing crystal observed by baby Benjamin, they see the consequences of inadequate support. And, of course, they collect additional data through their own manipulation of objects, including lots more evidence than their parents would like about what happens when a milk cup is deposited on the very edge of a high chair tray.

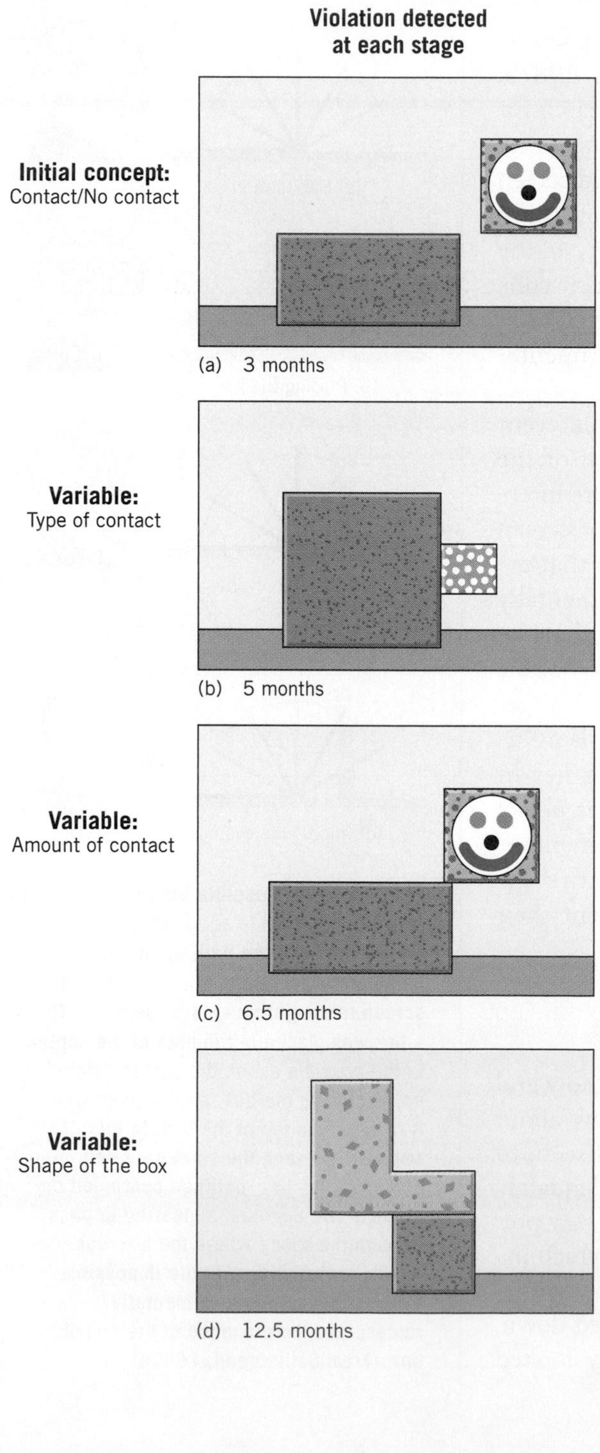

FIGURE 5.15 Infants' developing understanding of support relations Young infants appreciate that an object cannot float in midair, but only gradually do they come to understand under what conditions one object can be supported by another. (Adapted from Baillargeon, 1998)

Social Knowledge

In addition to acquiring knowledge about the physical world, infants need to learn about the social world—about people and their behavior. An important aspect of social knowledge that emerges relatively early is the understanding that the behavior of others is purposive and goal-directed. In research by Amanda Woodward (1998), 6-month-old infants saw a hand repeatedly reach toward one of two objects sitting side by side in a display (see Figure 5.16). Then the position of the two objects was reversed, and the hand reached again. The question was whether the infants interpreted the reaching behavior as directed toward a particular object. They did, as shown by their looking longer when the hand went to the new object (in the old place) than when it reached for the old object it had reached to before. Thus, the infants apparently

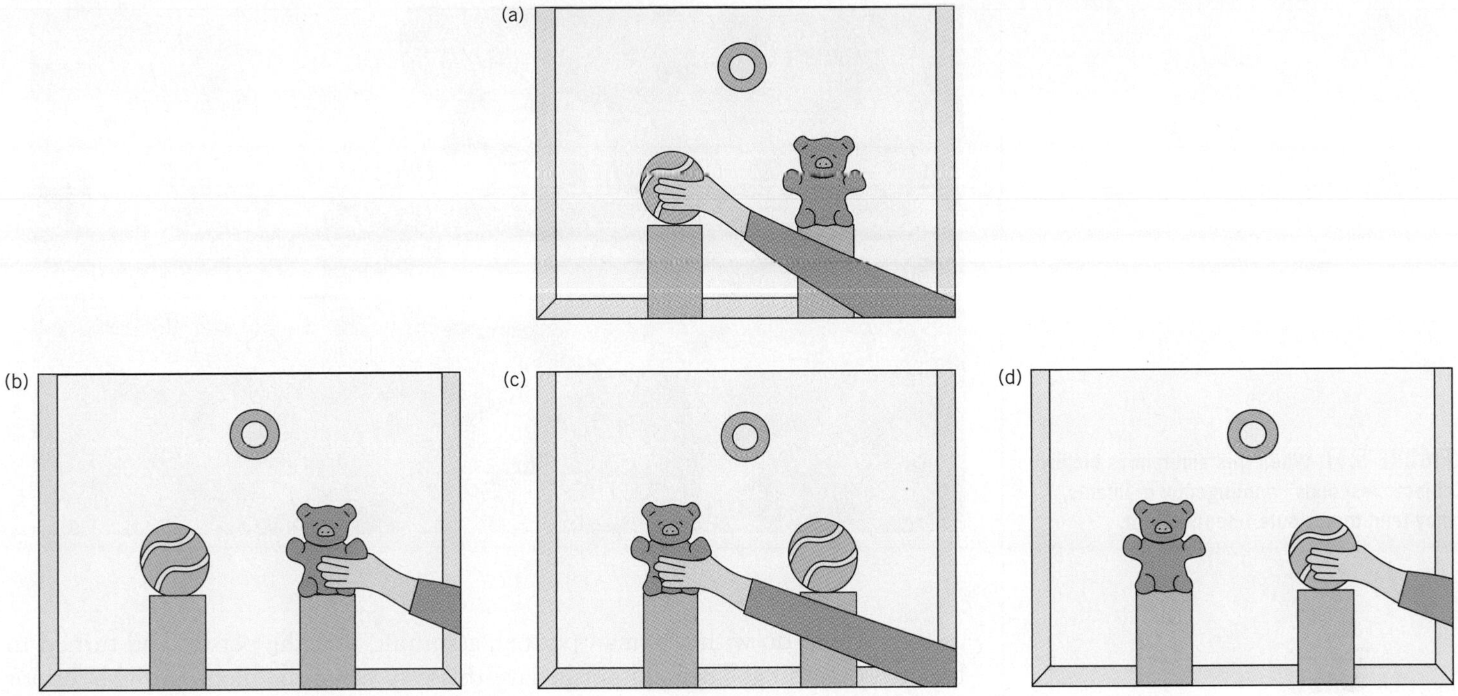

FIGURE 5.16 **Infants were habituated to the event shown in (a), a hand repeatedly reaching for a ball on one side of a display. When tested later with displays (b), (c), and (d), infants who saw the hand reach for the other object looked longer than did those who saw it reach for the ball (regardless of the ball's position). The pattern of results indicates that the babies interpreted the original reaching as object-directed. (Adapted from Woodward, 1998)**

interpreted the reaching behavior as directed toward a particular object. However, this was true only for a human hand; another group of infants did not react the same way when a mechanical arm did the reaching. (This study may remind you of the one by Meltzoff [1995b] in which older infants imitated the actions of a human but not of a mechanical device.)

Subsequent research by Sommerville, Woodward, and Needham (2005) established that infants' understanding of the goal-directed nature of another's actions, as in the above study, is related to their own experience achieving a goal. Three-month-olds, who were not yet able to pick up objects on their own, were fitted with Velcro "sticky mittens" (like those described in Chapter 4) that enabled them to capture Velcro-patched toys. Their brief experience successfully "picking up" objects enabled them to interpret the goal-directed reaching of others in the Woodward procedure described above a few months earlier than they would otherwise have been able to do.

Further understanding of intentionality is revealed by studies showing that older infants even attribute intentions and goals to inanimate entities if the objects seem to "behave" like humans. In research by Susan Johnson, 12- and 15-month-olds were introduced to a faceless, eyeless blob that "vocalized" and moved in response to what the infant or experimenter did, thus simulating a normal human interaction (Johnson, 2003; Johnson, Slaughter, & Carey, 1998) (see Figure 5.17 on the next page). Subsequently, when the blob turned in one direction, the infants looked in that direction. Thus, they seemed to be following the blob's "gaze," just

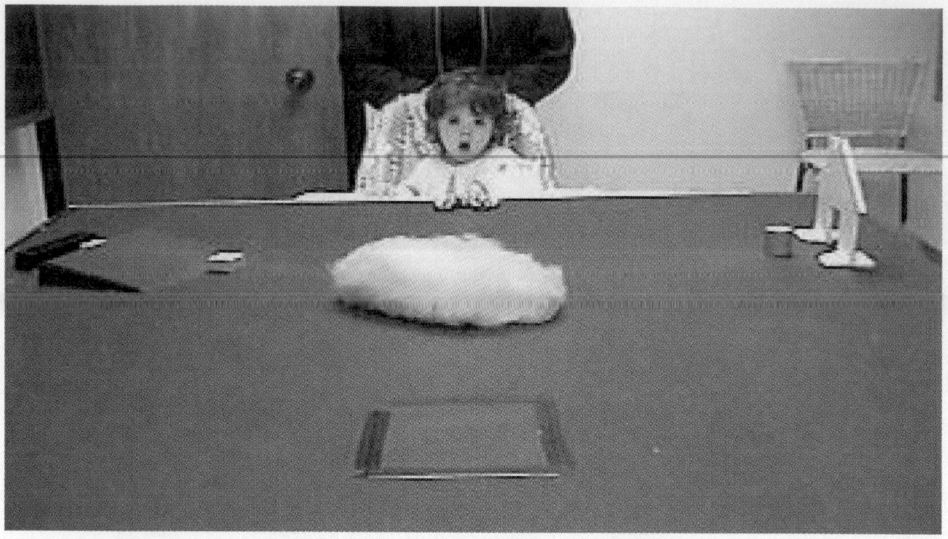

FIGURE 5.17 **When this amorphous blobby object "responds" contingently to infants, they tend to attribute intention to it.**

as they would do with a human partner, assuming that the person had turned to look at something. They did not behave this way when the blob's initial behavior was not contingently related to their own.

Older infants even interpret quite abstract displays in terms of intention and goal-directed action (Csibra et al., 1999, 2003; Gergely et al., 2002). For example, 12-month-olds saw a computer animation of a ball repeatedly "jumping" over a barrier toward a ball on the other side. Adults interpret this display as the jumping ball's "wanting" to get to the other ball. So, apparently, did the infants. When the barrier was removed, the infants looked longer when they saw the ball continue to jump, just as it had done before, than when they saw it move straight to the second ball.

Even younger infants seem to attribute intention with respect to simple displays involving small objects—a ball, cube, and pyramid, each with "googly" eyes attached (Hamlin, Wynn, & Bloom, 2007). Six- and ten-month-olds watched as a red wooden ball—the "climber"—repeatedly "attempted" to climb up a hill, each time falling back to the bottom (see Figure 5.18). Then the climber was either bumped up the hill by the "helper" pyramid or pushed back down by the "hinderer" cube. On the test event, the climber approached either the helper or the hinderer. The infants looked longer when the climber approached the hinderer, indicating that they expected it to go to the helper.

These and related studies indicate that by the middle of their first year, infants have already learned a great deal about how humans behave and how their behavior is related to their intentions and goals. Infants and young children can also draw inferences about other people's knowledge states. For example, 15-month-olds can make inferences about what a person will do based on their knowledge of what the person knows (Onishi & Baillargeon, 2005). In a visual-attention version of the false-belief task (discussed in Chapter 4), infants seem to keep track of what information an adult has about the location of an object. If the object is moved to a new location while an infant—but not the adult—witnesses the move, the infant expects the adult to subsequently search for the object in its *original* location. That is, the infant expects the adult to search where he or she *should believe* the toy to be, rather than in the location where the infant knows it *actually* is. This interpretation

FIGURE 5.18 Viewers of this film—infants and adults alike—readily interpret it in terms of intentional action. They see the circle as "trying" to move up a hill, but then rolling back down, thereby "failing" to achieve its goal of reaching the top. On some trials, after the circle starts to roll back down, the triangle at the top of the screen drops down below the circle and seems to "push" it upward, "helping" it get to the top. On other trials, the square drops down in front of the circle and "hinders" it from going any further toward the top.

is based on the fact that the infants looked longer when the adult searched the object's current location than they did when the adult searched its original location. Thus, this study indicates that 15-month-olds assume that a person's behavior will be based on what the person *believes* to be true, even if the infant knows that the belief is false. This result suggests that there may be very early precursors of a theory of mind.

Looking Ahead

The intense activity focused on cognition in infancy has produced a wealth of fascinating findings. This new information has not, however, resolved the basic issues about how cognition develops in infancy. The evidence we have reviewed reveals a remarkable constellation of abilities and deficits. Infants can be both surprisingly smart and surprisingly clueless (Keen, 2003; Kloos & Keen, 2005). They can infer the existence of an unseen object but cannot retrieve it. They appreciate that objects cannot float in midair but think that any kind and amount of contact at all provides sufficient support. The challenge for theorists is to account for both competence and incompetence in infants' thinking.

review:

Building on the insights and observations of Jean Piaget, and using an array of extremely clever methods, modern researchers have made a host of fascinating discoveries about the cognitive processes of infants. They have demonstrated that infants mentally represent not only the existence of hidden objects but also characteristics such as the object's size, height, and noise-making properties. Infants' understanding of the physical world grows steadily, as shown by their appreciation of support relations and their increasing ability to solve everyday problems. At the same time, their understanding of the social world also increases, as shown, for example, by their interpretation of the intentionality underlying the behavior of actors, both human and animated.

Chapter Summary

Perception

- The human visual system is relatively immature at birth; young infants have poor acuity, low contrast sensitivity, and minimal color vision. Modern research has demonstrated, however, that newborns begin visually scanning the world minutes after birth and that very young infants show preferences for strongly contrasted patterns, for the same colors that adults prefer, and, especially, for human faces.
- Some visual abilities, including perception of constant size and shape, are present at birth; others develop rapidly over the first year. Binocular vision emerges quite suddenly at around 4 months of age, and the ability to identify object boundaries—object segregation—is also present at that age. By 7 months, infants are sensitive to a variety of monocular, or pictorial, depth cues; and pattern perception has developed to the point that infants can perceive illusory (subjective) contours, as adults do.
- The auditory system is comparatively well developed at birth, and newborns will turn their heads to localize a sound. Young infants' remarkable proficiency at perceiving pattern in auditory stimulation underlies their sensitivity to musical structure.
- Infants are sensitive to smell from birth. They learn to identify their mother in part by her unique scent.
- Through active touching, using both mouth and hands, infants explore and learn about themselves and their environment.
- Research on the phenomenon of intermodal perception has revealed that from very early on, infants integrate information from different senses, linking their visual with their auditory, olfactory, and tactile experiences.

Motor Development

- Motor development, or the development of action, proceeds rapidly in infancy through a series of "motor milestones," starting with the reflexes displayed by newborn babies. Recent research has demonstrated that the regular pattern of development results from the confluence of many factors, including the development of strength, posture control, balance, and perceptual skills. Some aspects of motor development vary across cultures as a result of different cultural practices.
- Each new motor achievement, from reaching to self-locomotion, expands the infant's experience of the world but also presents new challenges. Infants adopt a variety of strategies to move around in the world successfully and safely. In the process, they make a variety of surprising mistakes.

Learning

- Various kinds of learning are present in infancy. Infants habituate to repeated stimuli and form expectancies about recurrent regularities in events. Through active exploration, they engage in perceptual learning. They also learn through classical conditioning, which involves forming associations between natural and neutral stimuli, and through instrumental conditioning, which involves learning about the contingency between one's own behavior and some outcome. Babies express enjoyment when learning to control their experience.
- From the second half of the first year on, observational learning—watching and imitating the behavior of other people—is an increasingly important source of information. Infants' assessment of the intention of a model affects what they imitate.

Cognition

- Powerful new research techniques—most notably the violation-of-expectancy procedure—have established that infants display impressive cognitive abilities. Much of this work on mental representation and thinking was originally inspired by Jean Piaget's concept of object permanence. But it has been revealed that, contrary to Piaget's belief, young infants can mentally represent invisible objects and even reason about observed events.
- Other research, focused on infants' developing knowledge of the physical world, has demonstrated their understanding of some of the effects of gravity. It takes babies several months to work out the conditions under which one object can provide stable support for another.
- What infants know about people is a very active area of research. One clear finding is that infants pay particular attention to the intentions of others.
- Although many fascinating phenomena have been discovered in the area of infant cognition, basic issues about cognitive development remain unresolved. Theorists are sharply divided on how to account for the abilities, on the one hand, and the deficiencies, on the other hand, in infants' thinking.

Critical Thinking Questions

1. The major theme throughout this chapter was nature and nurture. Consider the following research findings discussed in the chapter: infants' preference for consonance (versus dissonance) in music, their preference for faces that adults consider attractive, and their ability to represent the existence and even the height of an occluded object. To what extent do you think these preferences and abilities rest on innate factors, and to what extent might they be the result of experience?
2. As you have seen from this chapter, researchers have learned a substantial amount about infants in the recent past. Were you surprised at some of what has been learned? Describe to a friend something from each of the main sections of the chapter that you would never have suspected an infant could do or would know. Similarly, tell your friend a few things that you were surprised to learn infants do not know or that they fail to do.
3. Suppose you were the parent of a young infant, and you were concerned that your baby might not be able to see very well. How could a developmental psychologist test your baby's vision?
4. Explain why researchers did the following things, each of which seems somewhat odd if one does not know the rationale behind it. What hypotheses were they trying to test?
   (a) Suspended infants in water up to their waists
   (b) Put a patch over one eye and showed infants a misshapen window
   (c) "Hid" a toy under a transparent container
   (d) Pretended to be unable to pull the end off a dumbbell

Key Terms

sensation, p. 177
perception, p. 177
preferential-looking technique, p. 178
visual acuity, p. 178
contrast sensitivity, p. 178
cones, p. 178
perceptual constancy, p. 182
object segregation, p. 182
optical expansion, p. 184
binocular disparity, p. 185
stereopsis, p. 185
monocular or pictorial cues, p. 185
auditory localization, p. 185
intermodal perception, p. 188
reflexes, p. 190
stepping reflex, p. 194
prereaching movements, p. 195
self-locomotion, p. 196
scale error, p. 199
differentiation, p. 200
affordances, p. 201
classical conditioning, p. 202
unconditioned stimulus (UCS), p. 202
unconditioned response (UCR), p. 202
conditioned stimulus (CS), p. 202
conditioned response (CR), p. 202
instrumental or operant conditioning, p. 203
positive reinforcement, p. 203
violation-of-expectancy, p. 207

ROMARE BEARDEN, *Early Carolina Morning,* 1978

6

Development of Language and Symbol Use

Nature and Nurture

❖

The Active Child

❖

The Sociocultural Context

❖

Individual Differences

❖

"Woof." (used at the age of 11 months to refer to neighbor's dog)
"Hot." (used at the age of 14 months to refer to stove, matches, candles, light reflecting off shiny surfaces, etc.)
"Read me." (used at the age of 21 months to ask mother to read a story)
"Why I don't have a dog?" (27 months of age)
"If you give me some candy, I'll be your best friend. I'll be your two best friends." (48 months of age)
"Granna, we went to Cagoshin [Chicago]." (65 months of age)
"It was, like, ya' know, totally awesome, dude." (192 months of age)

These utterances, which we will return to throughout the chapter, were all produced by one boy in the process of becoming a native speaker of the English language (Clore, 1981). In beginning to learn his native language, this boy displayed the capacity that most sets humans apart from other species: the creative and flexible use of symbols, including language and many kinds of nonlinguistic symbols (print, numbers, pictures, models, maps, etc.). We use **symbols** to (1) represent our thoughts, feelings, and knowledge, and (2) communicate them to other people. Our ability to use symbols vastly expands our cognitive and communicative power. It frees us from the present, enabling us to learn from the generations of people who preceded us and to contemplate the future. Because symbols are such an important source of learning and knowledge, becoming symbol-minded is a crucial developmental task for all children everywhere in the world (DeLoache, 2005).

In this chapter, we will focus first and primarily on the acquisition of language, the preeminent symbol system—the "jewel in the crown of cognition" (Pinker, 1990). We will then discuss children's mastery and creation of nonlinguistic symbols, such as pictures and models.

The dominant theme in this chapter will once again be *nature and nurture.* Considerable debate has focused on the relative contributions of nature and nurture in children's language development. A related disagreement concerns the extent to which language acquisition is made possible by abilities that are specialized for learning language versus general-purpose cognitive mechanisms that support all sorts of learning.

MYRLEEN FERGUSON CATE / PHOTOEDIT

These children are intent on mastering one of the many important symbol systems in the modern world.

The *sociocultural context* is another theme that is prominent in this chapter. We will frequently discuss research conducted with children from different language communities, citing both similarities and differences in language acquisition across cultures. This comparative work often provides crucial evidence for or against theoretical claims about language development.

A third theme that recurs throughout the chapter is *individual differences.* As you will see, there is great variability in the timing of most aspects of language development. For any given milestone, some children will achieve it much earlier, and some much later, than others. The *active child* theme also puts in repeated appearances here. Infants and young children pay close attention to language and a wide variety of symbolic artifacts, and they work hard at figuring out how to use them to communicate with other people.

Language Development

What is the average 5- to 10-year-old almost as good at doing as you are? Not much, but one very important thing is using language. By 5 years of age, children have mastered the basic structure of their native language, whether spoken or manually signed. The sentences uttered by the average 1st-grade student are just as correct grammatically as those produced by the average college freshman. Although their powers of expression may be less sophisticated than yours and their vocabularies smaller, 1st graders' basic linguistic competence is not.

Using language involves both **language comprehension,** which refers to understanding what others say (or sign or write), and **language production,** which refers to actually speaking (or signing or writing) to others. As you will see repeatedly in this chapter, *language comprehension precedes language production:* children understand words and linguistic structures that other people use before they include them in their own utterances (Goldin-Meadow, Seligman, & Gelman, 1976). This is, of course, not unique to young children; you no doubt understand many words that you never actually use. In our discussion, we will be concerned with developmental processes involved in both comprehension and production, as well as the relation between them.

The Components of Language

Each of the thousands of languages in the world is based on a complex system of rules for combining different kinds of elements at different levels of a hierarchy: sounds are combined to form words, words are combined to form sentences, and sentences are combined to form narratives. Thus, acquiring a language involves learning its sounds and sound patterns, its specific words, and the ways in which the language allows words to be combined. It also involves learning how language is employed for communication with other people. The enormous benefit that emerges from this combinatorial process is **generativity;** using the finite set of words in our vocabulary, we can generate an infinite number of sentences, expressing an infinite number of ideas.

The generative power of language comes at a cost, however, and the cost is complexity. To appreciate the challenge that this complexity presents to children who must master their native language, imagine yourself as a stranger in a strange land. Someone walks up to you and says, "Jusczyk daxly blickets Nthlakapmx." You would have absolutely no idea what this person had just said. Why?

symbols systems for representing our thoughts, feelings, and knowledge and for communicating them to other people

language comprehension understanding what others say (or sign or write)

language production speaking (or writing or signing) to others

generativity refers to the idea that through the use of the finite set of words in our vocabulary, we can put together an infinite number of sentences and express an infinite number of ideas

phonemes the elementary units of meaningful sound used to produce languages

phonological development the acquisition of knowledge about the sound system of a language

morphemes the smallest units of meaning in a language, composed of one or more phonemes

semantic development the learning of the system for expressing meaning in a language, including word learning

syntax rules in a language that specify how words from different categories (nouns, verbs, adjectives, etc.) can be combined

syntactic development the learning of the syntax of a language

pragmatic development the acquisition of knowledge about how language is used

First, you may have difficulty even perceiving some of the sounds that the speaker is uttering. **Phonemes** are the elementary units of sound used to produce languages, and they distinguish meaning. For example, "rake" differs by only one phoneme from "lake" (/r/ versus /l/), but the two words have quite different meanings to English speakers. Languages employ different sets of phonemes; English, for example, uses 45 of the roughly 200 sounds used in the world's languages. The phonemes that distinguish meaning in any one language overlap with, but also differ from, those in other languages. For example, the sounds /r/ and /l/ do not carry different meaning in Japanese. Further, combinations of sounds that are common in one language may never occur in others. When you read the stranger's utterance in the preceding paragraph, you probably had no idea how to pronounce "Nthlakapmx," because the sound combinations that the letters of this word represent do not occur in English. Thus, the first step in children's language learning is **phonological development,** the mastery of the sound system of their language.

Another reason you would not know what the stranger had said to you, even if you could have perceived the sounds being uttered, is that you would have had no idea what the sounds mean. The smallest units of meaning are **morphemes,** which are composed of one or more phonemes. Morphemes, alone or in combination, constitute words. The words *I* and *dog,* for example, are both single morphemes, because each of them refers to a single entity. The word *dogs* contains two morphemes, one designating a familiar furry entity and the second indicating more than one of them. Thus, the second component in language acquisition is **semantic development,** that is, learning the system for expressing meaning in a language, including word learning.

GETTY IMAGES / DIGITAL VISION

In this everyday conversation, these young boys are generating totally novel sentences that are correct in terms of the phonology, semantics, and syntax of their native language. They are also making appropriate pragmatic inferences regarding the content of their partner's utterances.

However, even if you were told the meaning of each individual word the stranger had used, you would still not understand the utterance because, in all languages, meaning depends on how words are put together. To express an idea of any complexity, we combine words into sentences, but only some combinations are permissible. For every language, a large set of rules—the **syntax** of the language—specifies how words from different categories (nouns, verbs, adjectives, etc.) can be combined. In English, many grammatical rules pertain to the *order* in which words can appear in a sentence, because word order affects meaning. "John loves Mary" does not mean the same thing as "Mary loves John." In some other languages, which person is the lover and which the beloved would be conveyed by word endings or subtle differences in sound rather than by word order. The third component in language learning, then, is **syntactic development**, that is, acquiring the rules for combining words in a given language.

Finally, a full understanding of the interaction with the stranger would necessitate some knowledge of the cultural rules for using language. In some societies, it would be quite bizarre to be addressed by a stranger in the first place, whereas in others it's commonplace. **Pragmatic development** refers to acquiring knowledge about how language is used.

Our example of the bewilderment one experiences when listening to someone speak a language one does not know is useful for delineating the components of language use. However, as an analogy to what infants and young children face in learning language, it is limited. An adult who hears someone speaking an unfamiliar language already knows what language is, knows that the sounds the person is uttering constitute words, knows that words are combined to form sentences, knows that only certain combinations are acceptable, and so on. In other words, in contrast to young language learners, adults have considerable **metalinguistic knowledge**—that is, knowledge *about* language, including its properties and how it is used.

Thus, learning to comprehend and produce language involves phonological, semantic, syntactic, and pragmatic development, as well as metalinguistic knowledge about language. The same factors are involved in learning a sign language, in which the basic linguistic elements are gestures rather than sounds. There are over 200 sign languages, including American Sign Language (ASL), which are based on gestures, both manual and facial. They are true languages, and the course of acquisition of a sign language is remarkably similar to that of a spoken language. As you will see, research on the development of sign language has provided a great deal of insight into the nature of language acquisition in general.

What Is Required for Language?

What does it take to be able to learn a language in the first place? Full-fledged language is achieved only by humans, but only if they have experience with other humans using language for communication.

A Human Brain

The key to full-fledged language development is in the human brain. Language is a *species-specific* behavior, in that only humans acquire language in the normal course of development in their normal environment. Furthermore, it is *species-universal* in that virtually all young humans learn language. It takes highly abnormal environmental conditions or relatively severe cognitive impairment to disrupt children's language development.

In contrast, no other animals naturally develop anything approaching the complexity or generativity of human language, even though they can communicate with one another. For example, birds claim territorial rights via birdsong (Marler, 1970), and vervet monkey calls reveal the presence of a predator and indicate whether the predator is a hawk or a snake (Seyfarth & Cheney, 1993).

Researchers have had some success in training nonhuman primates to use complex communicative systems. One of the early efforts was a very ambitious project in which a dedicated couple raised a chimpanzee in their own home, with their own children, to see if the chimp, named Vicki, would learn to speak (Hayes & Hayes, 1951). Although Vicki clearly learned to comprehend some words and phrases, she produced virtually no recognizable words. Concluding that nonhuman primates lack the vocal apparatus for producing speech, later researchers attempted to teach them sign language. Washoe, a chimpanzee, and Koko, a gorilla, became famous for their ability to communicate with their human trainers and caretakers by manual signs (Gardner & Gardner, 1969; Patterson & Linden, 1981). Washoe could label a variety of objects and could make requests ("more fruit," "please tickle") and comments ("Washoe sorry"). The general consensus is that, however impressive Washoe's and Koko's

metalinguistic knowledge an understanding of the properties and function of language—that is, an understanding of language as language

COURTESY OF THE LANGUAGE RESEARCH CENTER, GEORGIA STATE UNIVERSITY, PHOTO BY LIZ PUGH

Panbanisha, a bonobo chimpanzee, communicates with her caretakers by using a specially designed set of symbols that stand for a wide variety of objects, people, and actions.

"utterances" were, they do not qualify as language, because they contained little evidence of syntactic structure (Terrace, Petitto, Sanders, & Bever, 1979; Wallman, 1992).

The most successful sign-learning nonhumans are Kanzi and Panbanisha, two great apes of the bonobo species. Kanzi learned to communicate with humans by using a specially designed keyboard composed of numerous symbols that denote specific objects and actions ("give," "eat," "banana," "hug," etc.) (Savage-Rumbaugh et al., 1993). Kanzi became very adept at using the keyboard to answer questions, to make requests, and even to offer comments. He often combines signs, but whether they can be considered syntactically structured sentences is not clear. Kanzi also understands many words and phrases spoken to him by his human caretakers, and he is even sensitive to word order. For example, when asked to "give the shot [a syringe] to Liz" (a caretaker), he handed the syringe to her; however, when instructed to "give Liz a shot," he touched the syringe to her arm.

Whatever the ultimate decision regarding the extent to which Kanzi, Panbanisha (shown in the photo), or other nonhuman primates should be credited with language, several things are clear. Even the most basic language achievements of nonhuman primates come only after a great deal of concentrated effort by humans to teach the animals, whereas human children master the rudiments of their language by the age of 5 with little explicit teaching. At age 5, human children understand thousands of words, whereas nonhuman primates have relatively small vocabularies. Furthermore, although the most advanced nonhuman communicators combine symbols in utterances, there is little evidence for syntactic structure, which is a defining feature of language (Tomasello, 1994). In short, only the human brain acquires a communicative system with the complexity, structure, and generativity of language.

Brain–language relations A vast amount of research has examined brain–language relations. One thing that is clear is that language processing involves a substantial degree of functional localization. At the broadest level, there are hemispheric differences in language functioning that we discussed to some extent in Chapter 3. For the 90% of people who are right-handed, language is primarily represented and controlled by the left hemisphere of the cerebral cortex. This association was first formally reported in 1861 by Paul Broca, a French physician, whose observations of language deficits in patients with various forms of brain injuries led him to conclude that "we speak with the left hemisphere."

Developmental evidence for language specialization in the left hemisphere also comes from EEG studies showing that, for both adults and children, listening to speech is associated with greater electrical activity in the left hemisphere than in the right. The same is true for young infants, who show greater left-hemisphere activity when listening to speech but greater right-hemisphere response to nonspeech sounds (Molfese & Betz, 1988). Thus, the left hemisphere shows some specialization for language (or language-like stimuli) at a very early age, with the degree of hemispheric specialization for language increasing over time (Mills, Coffey-Corina, & Neville, 1997; Witelson, 1987).

Specialization for language is also evident *within* the left hemisphere (Figure 6.1). Aphasia, the condition in which language functions are severely impaired, can result from damage to some, but not other, parts of the left hemisphere. One form, Broca's aphasia, is typically associated with injury to Broca's area in the front part of the left hemisphere, near the motor cortex. Patients with Broca's aphasia have

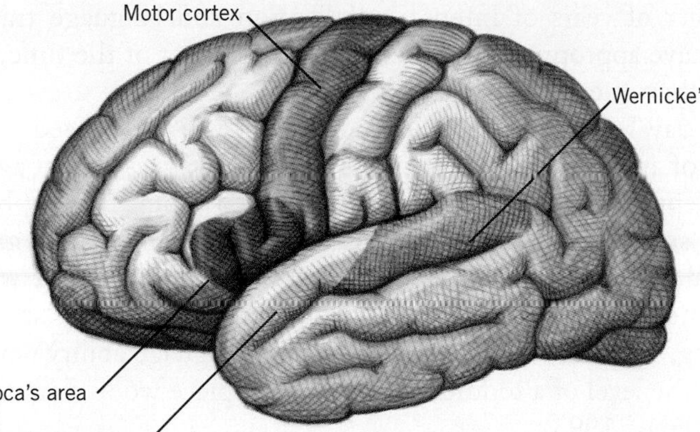

FIGURE 6.1 Lateralization of language In most people, language is primarily represented in the left hemisphere of the cerebral cortex. Damage to Broca's and Wernicke's areas can produce severe impairments in language functions, known as aphasia.

difficulty producing speech; they may say a single word over and over or haltingly produce short strings of words with little or no grammatical structure, as in this example:

> Yes . . . ah . . . Monday . . . and Dad . . . er . . . hospital . . . and ah . . . Wednesday . . . Wednesday, nine o'clock . . . and oh . . . Thursday . . . ten o'clock, ah doctors . . . two . . . an' doctors . . . and er . . . teeth . . . yah.
>
> (Goodglass, 1979, p. 256)

A different aphasia, Wernicke's aphasia (named for the nineteenth-century neurologist who first described it), is typically associated with damage in an area next to the auditory cortex (Wernicke's area). Patients with this type of aphasia have no trouble producing speech, but what they say makes no sense, and their language comprehension is also impaired.

> I feel very well. My hearing, writing has been doing well. Things that I couldn't hear from. In other words, I used to be able to work cigarettes I didn't know how . . . Chesterfeela, for 20 years I can write it.
>
> (Goodglass, 1993, p. 86)

Left-hemisphere damage produces aphasia in deaf signers just as it does for users of spoken language. This suggests that the left hemisphere is actually specialized for the kind of analytic, serial processing required for language, not for the specific modality (spoken words or signs) in which it is expressed (Bellugi, Poizner, & Klima, 1989).

Critical period for language development A considerable body of evidence has given rise to the hypothesis that the early years constitute a **critical period** during which language develops readily. After this period (sometime between age 5 and puberty), language acquisition is much more difficult and ultimately less successful. Relevant to this hypothesis, there are several reports of children who failed to develop language after being deprived of early linguistic input.

The most famous case is that of Victor, the "Wild Child," who had apparently been abandoned by his parents and had lived on his own for many years in the woods near Aveyron, France. When discovered in 1800, the boy, who appeared to be around 12 years of age, was naked, sometimes walked on all fours, and was frightened of people. Although he could make various sounds, he had no language.

critical period for language the time during which language develops readily and after which (sometime between age 5 and puberty) language acquisition is much more difficult and ultimately less successful

After a number of years of intense socialization and language training, Victor learned to behave appropriately in social situations most of the time, but he never learned more than a few words (Lane, 1976).

A modern-day "wild child," Genie, came to light in the United States in 1970. From the age of approximately 18 months until she was rescued at age 13, Genie's parents had kept her tied up and locked alone in a room. During her imprisonment, no one spoke to her; when her father brought her food, he growled at her like an animal. At the time of her rescue, Genie's development was stunted—physically, motorically, and emotionally—and she could barely speak. With intensive training, she made some progress, but her language ability never developed much beyond the level of a toddler's: "Father take piece wood. Hit. Cry" (Curtiss, 1977, 1989; Rymer, 1993).

Do the extraordinary cases of these two children support the critical-period hypothesis? Possibly, but it is difficult to know for sure. It could be that Victor was retarded from infancy and was abandoned for that reason. Genie's failure to develop language might have resulted as much from the bizarre and inhuman treatment she suffered as from the linguistic communication deprivation.

Other areas of research provide much stronger evidence for the critical-period hypothesis. As noted in Chapter 3, adults, who are well beyond the critical period, are more likely to suffer permanent language impairment from brain damage than are children, presumably because other areas of the young brain (but not the older one) are able to take over language functions (see Johnson, 1998). (See Chapter 3, pages 114–115 to review the role of timing in the long-term effects of brain damage.)

Additional strong support for the critical-period hypothesis comes from studies of adults who learned a second language at different ages. Research by Helen Neville and her colleagues (Neville & Bavelier, 1999; Weber-Fox & Neville, 1996) has shown different patterns of cerebral organization in late learners of a second language and in those who learned it early. As Figure 6.2 shows, people who learned English at 4 years of age or later showed less left-hemisphere localization of those aspects of brain organization related to grammatical processing in English than did people who learned the language at a younger age.

In a very important behavioral study, researchers tested the English proficiency of Chinese and Korean immigrants who had come to the United States and had begun learning English either as children or as adults (Johnson & Newport, 1989). The results, shown in Figure 6.3, reveal that knowledge of some fine points of English grammar was related to the age at which these individuals began learning English, but not to the length of their exposure to the language (i.e., how long they had been in America). The most proficient were those who had begun learning English before the age of 7. The same pattern of results has been described for the learning of one's first language. Similarly, the ASL proficiency of deaf adults depends on the age at which they first started learning it—the earlier they began, the more skilled they were as adults (Newport, 1990).

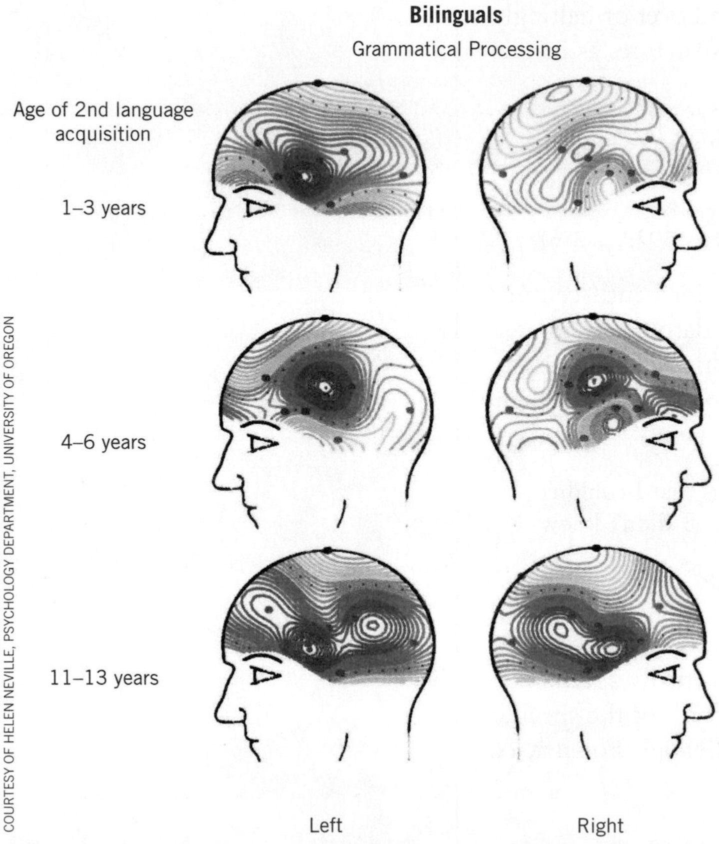

FIGURE 6.2 Hemispheric differences in language processing Adults who learned a second language at 1 to 3 years of age (top pair of images) show the normal pattern of greater activity in the left hemisphere during a test of grammatical knowledge. (Darker colors indicate greater activation.) Those who learned the language later show less localized activity, including more right-hemisphere activity. (Adapted from Neville & Bavelier, 1999)

Elissa Newport (1991) proposed an intriguing hypothesis for these results and for why children are generally better language learners than adults. According to her "less is more" account, perceptual and memory limitations cause young children to extract and store smaller chunks of the language they hear than adults do. Because it is far easier to figure out the underlying structure of shorter samples of speech than longer ones, young learners' limited cognitive abilities may actually make the task of analyzing and learning language easier.

The evidence for a critical period in language acquisition has some very clear practical implications. For one thing, deaf children should be exposed to sign language as early as possible. For another, foreign-language training in the schools, discussed in Box 6.1, should begin in the early grades; by the time students reach high school, their language-learning capability has already declined.

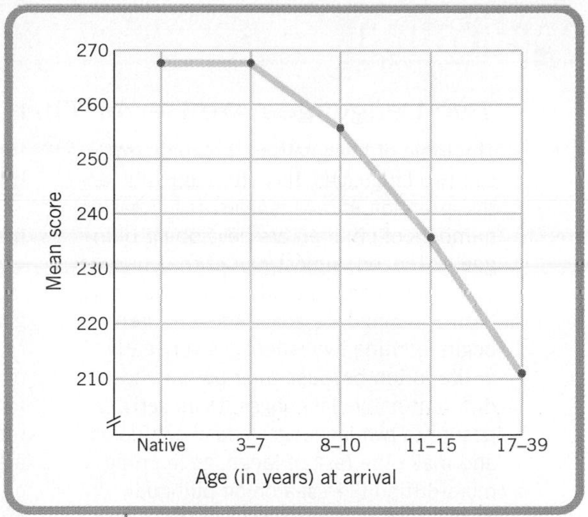

FIGURE 6.3 Test of critical-period hypothesis Performance on a test of English grammar of adults originally from Korea and China is directly related to the age at which they came to the United States and were first exposed to English. The scores of adults who emigrated before the age of 7 are indistinguishable from those of native speakers of English. (Adapted from Johnson & Newport, 1989)

A Human Environment

Possession of a human brain is not enough for language to develop. Children must also be exposed to other people using language—any language, signed or spoken. Adequate experience hearing others talk is readily available in the environment of almost all children anywhere in the world (Jaswal & Fernald, 2002). Like Benjamin watching his parents do the dinner dishes (Chapter 5), infants and young children overhear countless conversations, and in most societies, some speech is specifically directed to them. Much of the speech directed to infants occurs in the context of daily routines—during thousands of mealtimes, diaper changes, baths, and bedtimes, as well as in countless games like peekaboo and "eentsie-weentsie spider." Infants apparently identify speech as something important very early: infants 2 months of age pay attention longer to speech sounds than to nonspeech (Vouloumanos & Werker, 2004).

infant-directed talk (IDT) the distinctive mode of speech that adults adopt when talking to babies and very young children

Infant-directed talk Imagine yourself on a bus; behind you, someone is talking to another person. Could you guess whether that person was addressing an infant or an adult? We have no doubt that you—or anyone else—could, even if you were in another country where you didn't speak the local language. The reason is that in virtually all societies, adults adopt some distinctive mode of speech when talking to babies and very young children. This special way of speaking was originally dubbed "motherese" (Newport, Gleitman, & Gleitman, 1977), but the current term **infant-directed talk (IDT)** recognizes the fact that this special style of speech is not used just by mothers. Indeed, even young children adopt it when talking to babies (Shatz & Gelman, 1973). As we describe the characteristics of IDT, keep in mind that it is not used in all cultures and that the IDT of American mothers tends to be more extreme than that of virtually any other group (Fernald, 1989).

The infant-directed talk used by this father grabs and holds his baby's attention.

MICHAEL NEWMAN / PHOTOEDIT

CHARACTERISTICS OF INFANT-DIRECTED TALK Possibly the most obvious quality of speech directed toward infants is its emotional tone. It is speech suffused with affection—"the sweet music of the species," as Darwin (1877) put it. Another obvious characteristic of IDT is exaggeration (see Boysson-Bardies, 1999). People talking to babies do so in a much higher voice than they

applications 6.1

Two Languages Are Better Than One

The topic of **bilingualism,** the ability to use two languages, has attracted substantial attention in recent years as increasing numbers of children are developing bilingually. Indeed, almost half of the children in the world are regularly exposed to more than one language, and some children begin learning two languages very early in life, often because their parents have different native languages. Does early exposure to two languages cause confusion and make the task of language learning more difficult? Research on bilingual acquisition gives little cause for concern.

For the most part, children who are acquiring two languages do not seem to confuse them; indeed, they appear to build two separate linguistic systems (deHouwer, 1995). They do not mistakenly use the phonological system of one language to pronounce words in the other. Although a word from one language may occasionally get mixed into a sentence in the other, children keep the grammatical rules of the two languages separate.

Learning two languages is, of course, more work than learning just one, and children developing bilingually may initially lag behind slightly on some language measures (Oller & Pearson, 2002). However, both the course and the rate of development are generally very similar for bilingual and monolingual children (deHouwer, 1995). In addition, there are cognitive benefits to bilingualism: children who are competent in two languages perform better on a variety of cognitive tests than do monolingual children (Bialystok, 2009; Bialystok, Shenfield, & Codd, 2000). Thus, the advantages of acquiring two languages outweigh the minor disadvantages.

More difficult issues arise with respect to formal acquisition of a second language later on in school. A major debate in many countries, including the United States and France, has centered around bilingualism in the classroom and what approach to take in educating school-age children who are not fluent in the dominant language of the country. The debate over bilingual education in the United States is extremely complicated and tied up with a host of political, ethnic, and racial issues. One side of this debate advocates total immersion, in which children are communicated with and taught exclusively in English, with the goal of helping them become proficient in English as quickly as possible. The other side recommends an approach that initially provides children with instruction in basic subjects in their native language and gradually increases the amount of instruction provided in English.

In support of the latter view, there is evidence that (1) children often fail to master basic subject matter when it is taught in a language they do not fully understand; and (2) when both languages are integrated in the classroom, children learn the second language more readily, participate more actively, and are less frustrated and bored (Augusta & Hakuta, 1998; Crawford, 1997; Hakuta, 1999). This approach also helps prevent semilingualism—inadequate proficiency in both languages—which can occur if children become less proficient in their original language as a result of being taught a second one in school.

ELIZABETH CREWS / THE IMAGE WORKS

The issue of bilingualism in the classroom has been a topic of intense debate in the United States and other parts of the world. However, research conducted by Ellin Bialystok in areas such as Montreal, where a substantial proportion of the population speak both English and French, reveal a variety of benefits of proficiency in multiple languages.

would ever use with an adult (except possibly a lover), and they make extreme changes in intonation patterns, swooping abruptly from very high-pitched sounds to very low ones. They also talk more slowly and clearly and elongate the pauses between their utterances. All this exaggerated speech is accompanied by exaggerated facial expressions. Many of these characteristics have been noted in adults speaking such languages as Arabic, French, Italian, Japanese, Mandarin Chinese,

bilingualism the ability to use two languages

and Spanish (see Boysson-Bardies, 1999), as well as in deaf mothers signing to their infants (Masataka, 1992).

Although the prevalent emotional tone of IDT is warm and affectionate, parents of older infants vary it to impart important information. For example, a mother's "No" uttered with sharply falling intonation tells the baby that the mother disapproves of something, whereas a cooed "Yeesss" indicates approval. The same intonational qualities are used by mothers to signal approval and disapproval across languages, from English to Italian to Japanese (Fernald et al., 1989). That infants use the intonation of their mothers' messages to interpret meaning was clearly established by Anne Fernald (1989) in a series of clever experiments. In one, 8-month-old infants were presented with an attractive toy, and their mothers either said "Yes, good boy" or "No, don't touch." Half the statements of each type were said in a cooing, encouraging tone of voice and half were said in a sharp, prohibitive tone. The infants played with the toy more when their mother's tone of voice was encouraging, regardless of what she actually said.

Do infants care how they are spoken to? They seem to. In fact, they prefer IDT to speech directed at an adult—even when IDT is spoken to an infant other than themselves (Cooper & Aslin, 1994; Pegg, Werker, & McLeod, 1992) and even when it is in a language other than their own. For example, in one study, both Chinese and American infants listened longer to a Cantonese-speaking Chinese woman talking to a baby than to the same woman talking to an adult friend (Werker, Pegg, & McLeod, 1994). Furthermore, infants (and even adults) learn new words better, whether in their native language or in a foreign one, when the words are presented in IDT than when they are presented in adult-directed speech (Golinkoff & Alioto, 1995; Golinkoff, Alioto, & Hirsch-Pasek, 1996).

BOB AND IRA SPRING / STOCK CONNECTION / PICTUREQUEST

Around the world, parents in some cultures talk directly to their babies, whereas parents in other cultures do not. Almost everywhere, adults and older children use some form of "baby talk" to address infants.

As previously noted, although IDT is very common throughout the world, it is not universal. Among the Kwara'ae of the Solomon Islands in the South Pacific (Watson-Gegeo & Gegeo, 1986), the Kaluli of New Guinea (Schieffelin & Ochs, 1987), and the Ifaluk of Micronesia (Le, 2000), for example, it is believed that infants lack any capacity for understanding speech and that there is therefore no point in speaking to them. When Kaluli infants begin to speak, showing some language understanding, their parents initiate very direct language training, saying words or sentences and instructing their child to repeat what they just said. Crosslinguistic research indicates that whether parents speak directly to their infants or not may affect the speed of their early language learning, but not the level of mastery they eventually achieve (Lieven, 1994).

We thus see that infants begin life equipped with the two basic necessities for acquiring language: a human brain and a human environment. So long as they do not suffer from serious brain injury or developmental disorders or grow up in conditions of extreme social deprivation, they will acquire their native language. We turn now to the many steps through which that remarkable accomplishment proceeds.

The Process of Language Acquisition

Acquiring a language involves both listening and talking (or looking and signing); it requires both comprehending what other people communicate to you and producing intelligible language of your own. Infants start out paying attention to what people say or sign, and they know a great deal about language long before their first linguistic productions.

prosody the characteristic rhythm, tempo, cadence, melody, intonational patterns, and so forth with which a language is spoken

categorical perception the perception of speech sounds as belonging to discrete categories

voice onset time (VOT) the length of time between when air passes through the lips and when the vocal cords start vibrating

Speech Perception

The first step in language learning is the perception of speech. As you saw in Chapter 2, the task usually begins in the womb, as fetuses develop a preference for their mother's voice and the language they hear her speak. The basis for this very early learning is **prosody,** the characteristic rhythm, tempo, cadence, melody, and intonational patterns with which a language is spoken. Differences in prosody are in large part responsible for why languages—from Japanese to French to Swahili—sound so different from one another. Prosody also accounts for why speakers of the same language can sound so different. Contrast the highly expressive speech of British speakers, for example, with the relatively flat speech of Americans.

Beyond prosody, speech perception also involves distinguishing among the speech sounds that make a difference in a given language. To learn English, for example, one must distinguish between *bat* and *pat, dill* and *kill, Ben* and *bed.* Remarkably, infants do not have to learn to hear these differences; young infants perceive many speech sounds in very much the same way that adults do.

Categorical perception of speech sounds Both adults and infants perceive speech sounds as belonging to discrete categories. This phenomenon, referred to as **categorical perception,** has been established by studying people's response to artificial speech sounds. In this research, a speech synthesizer is used to gradually and continuously change one speech sound, such as /b/, into a related one, such as /p/. These two phonemes are on an acoustic continuum; they are produced in exactly the same way, except for one crucial difference—the length of time between when air passes through the lips and when the vocal cords start vibrating. This lag, referred to as **voice onset time (VOT),** is much shorter for /b/ (15 milliseconds) than for /p/ (100 ms). (Try saying "ba" and "pa" alternately several times, and you will likely experience what VOT refers to.) Researchers create tape recordings of artificial speech sounds that vary along this VOT continuum, so that each successive sound is slightly different from the one before, with /b/ gradually changing into /p/. However, adult listeners do not perceive this continuously changing series of sounds (Figure 6.4). Instead, they hear /b/ repeated several times and then hear an abrupt switch to /p/. All the sounds in this continuum that have a VOT of less than 25 ms are perceived as /b/, and all those that have a VOT greater than 25 ms are perceived as /p/. Thus, adults automatically divide the continuous signal into two discontinuous categories—/b/ and /p/.

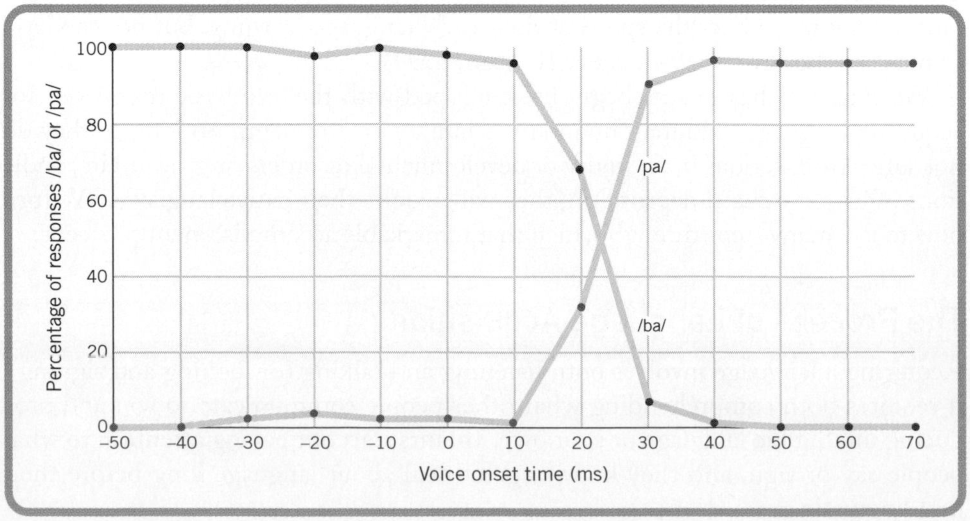

FIGURE 6.4 Categorical perception of speech sounds by adults When adults listen to a tape of artificial speech sounds that gradually change from one sound to another, such as /ba/ to /pa/ or vice versa, they suddenly switch from perceiving one sound to perceiving the other. (Adapted from Wood, 1976)

Young babies make the same kind of sharp distinctions between speech sounds. This remarkable fact was established using the habituation technique familiar to you from previous chapters. In the original, classic study (one of the 100 most frequently cited studies in psychology), 1- and 4-month-olds sucked on a pacifier hooked up to a computer (Eimas et al., 1971). Their sucking caused speech sounds to be played for them to listen to. After hearing the same sound repeatedly, the babies gradually sucked less enthusiastically. Then a new sound was played. If the infants' sucking response to the new sound increased, the researchers inferred that the infants discriminated the new sound from the old one.

The crucial factor in this study was the relation between the new and old sounds—specifically, whether they were from the same or different adult phonemic categories. For one group of the babies, the new sound was from a different adult category; thus, after habituation to a series of sounds that adults perceive as /b/, sucking now produced a sound that adults identify as /p/. For the second group, the new sound was within the same category as the old one (i.e., adults perceive them both as /b/). A critical feature of the study is that for both groups, the new and old sounds differed *equally* in terms of VOT.

As Figure 6.5 shows, after habituating to /b/, the infants increased their rate of sucking when the new sound came from a different phonemic category (/p/ instead of /b/). Habituation continued, however, when the new sound was within the same category as the original one. Since this classic study, researchers have established that infants show categorical perception of numerous speech sounds (Aslin, Jusczyk, & Pisoni, 1998).

One difference between infants' and adults' distinction among speech sounds, however, is that young infants actually make *more* distinctions than adults do. This rather surprising phenomenon occurs because all languages use only a subset of the large variety of phonemic categories that exist. As noted earlier, the sounds /r/ and /l/ make a difference in English, but not in Japanese. Similarly, speakers of Arabic, but not of English, perceive a difference between the /k/ sounds in "keep" and "cool." Adults simply do not perceive most differences in speech sounds that are not important in their native languages, which partly accounts for why it is so difficult for adults to become fluent in a second language.

In contrast, infants can distinguish between phonemic contrasts made in all the languages of the world—about 600 consonants and 200 vowels (Tsao, Liu, & Kuhl, 2004). Research shows that, for example, Kikuyu infants in Africa are just as good as are American babies at discriminating English contrasts not found in Kikuyu (Streeter, 1976). Studies done with infants from English-speaking homes have shown that they can discriminate non-English distinctions made in languages ranging from German and Spanish to Thai, Hindi, and Zulu (Jusczyk, 1997).

This research reveals an ability that is both innate, in the sense that it is present at birth, and independent of experience, because infants can discriminate between speech sounds they have never heard before. Presumably, this capacity for categorical perception of speech sounds is enormously helpful to infants, because it essentially primes them to start learning whichever of the world's languages they hear around them. The crucial role of early speech perception in learning language is reflected in a relation between infants' speech perception skills and their later

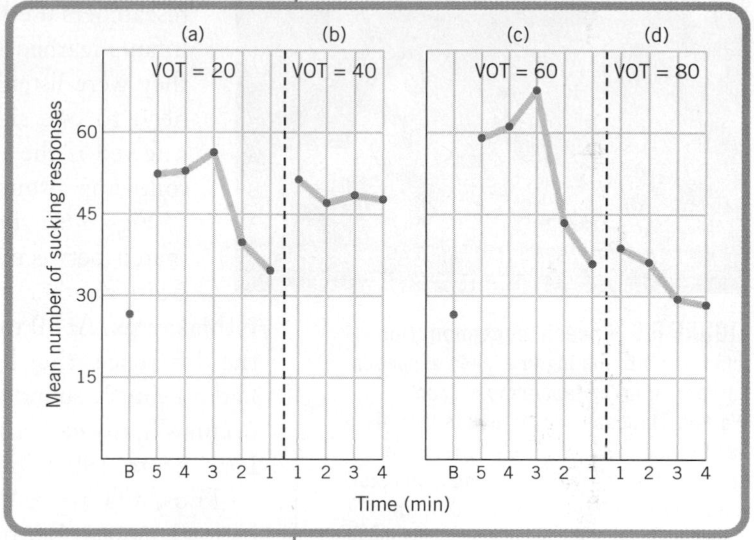

FIGURE 6.5 Categorical perception of speech sounds by infants One- and four-month-old infants were habituated to a tape of artificial speech sounds. (a) One group repeatedly heard a /ba/ sound with a VOT of 20, and they gradually habituated to it. (b) When the sound changed to /pa/, with a VOT of 40, they dishabituated, indicating that they perceived the difference between the two sounds, just as adults do. (c) A different group was habituated to a /pa/ sound with a VOT of 60. (d) When the sound changed to another /pa/ with a VOT of 80, the infants remained habituated, suggesting that, like adults, they did not discriminate between these two sounds. (Adapted from Eimas et al., 1971)

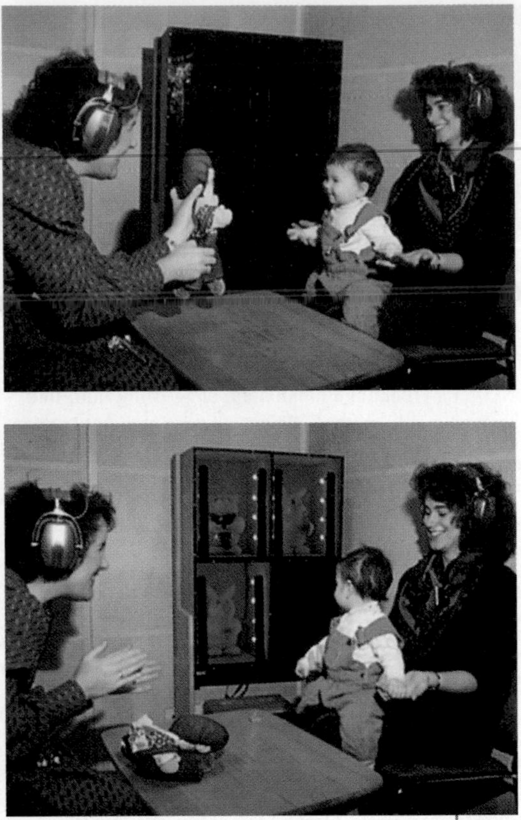

FIGURE 6.6 Speech perception This infant is participating in a study of speech perception in the laboratory of Janet Werker. The baby has learned to turn his head to the sound source whenever he hears a change from one sound to another. A correct head turn is rewarded by an exciting visual display, as well as by the applause and praise of the experimenter. To make sure that neither the mother nor the experimenter can influence the child's behavior, they are both wearing headphones that prevent them from hearing what the baby hears. (From Werker, 1989)

language skills. Babies who were better at detecting differences between speech sounds at 6 months scored higher on vocabulary and grammar tests at 13 to 24 months of age (Tsao, Liu, & Kuhl, 2004).

Developmental changes in speech perception The ability of young infants to discriminate among speech sounds they have never heard before does not last long. By the end of their first year, their speech perception is similar to that of their parents. The initial demonstration of this shift was carried out by Janet Werker and her colleagues, who tested the ability of infants of different ages to discriminate speech sounds (Werker, 1989; Werker & Lalonde, 1988; Werker & Tees, 1984). The infants were all from English-speaking homes, and they were tested with speech contrasts that are not used in English but that are important in two other languages—Hindi and Nthlakapmx (a language spoken by North American Indians in the Pacific Northwest). To test the discriminatory capabilities of 6- to 12-month-old infants, the researchers used a simple conditioning procedure, shown in Figure 6.6. The infants learned that whenever they heard a change in the series of sounds they were listening to, they could see an interesting sight by turning their head to one side. Thus, discrimination between the speech sounds was inferred if the infants quickly turned their heads in the correct direction following a sound change.

Figure 6.7 shows that at 6 to 8 months of age, the infants readily discriminated between the sounds they heard; they could tell one Hindi syllable from another, and they could also distinguish between two sounds in Nthlakapmx. At 10 to 12 months of age, however, the infants no longer perceived the differences they had detected a few months before. Two Hindi syllables that had previously sounded different to them now sounded the same. A similar change occurs slightly earlier for vowels (Kuhl, 1991; Kuhl, Williams, Lacerda, Stevens, & Lindbloom, 1992; Polka & Werker, 1994).

Thus, infants are born with the ability to discriminate between speech sounds in any language, but they gradually begin to specialize, retaining their sensitivity to sounds in the language they hear every day—their native language—but becoming increasingly less sensitive to nonnative speech sounds. This change begins as early as 7 months for some infants. ERP recordings of 7-month-olds' responses to native and nonnative phonemes revealed that some babies were already better at discriminating among sounds in their native language than in another language. Further, those 7-month-olds who had begun to home in on the sounds of their native language later performed better on vocabulary and grammar tests given between 14 and 30 months of age.

Identifying such regularities in speech sounds supports the learning of words. After repeatedly hearing "twang" and "dobu" embedded in a long stream of speech sounds, 17-month-olds readily learned those sounds as labels for objects. Having aleady learned the sound sequences that made up the words apparently made it easier to associate the words with their referents (Estes, Evans, Alibali, & Saffran, 2007).

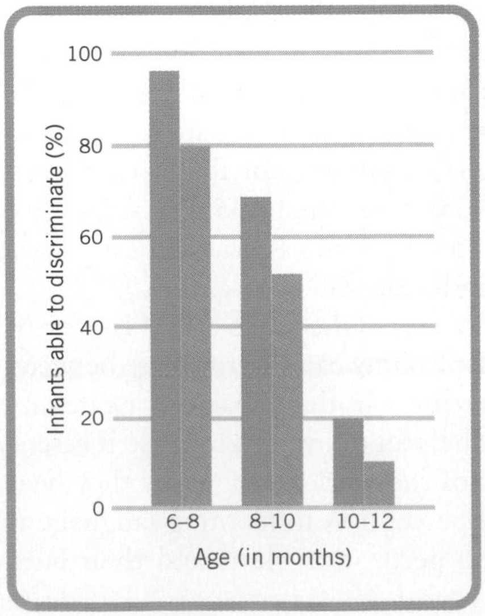

FIGURE 6.7 Percent of infants able to discriminate foreign-language speech sounds Infants' ability to discriminate between speech sounds *not* in their native language declines between 6 and 12 months of age. Most 6-month-olds from English-speaking families readily discriminate between syllables in Hindi (blue bars) and Nthlakapmx (green bars), but most 10- to 12-month-olds do not. (Adapted from Werker, 1989)

Sensitivity to regularities in speech In addition to focusing on the speech sounds that are used in their native language, infants become increasingly sensitive to many of the numerous regularities in that language. One example is stress pattern, an element of prosody. In English, the first syllable in two-syllable words is much more often stressed than the second syllable is (as in "English," "often," and "second"). Nine-month-old American infants attend longer to lists of words that follow this pattern than to words in which the second syllable is stressed (Jusczyk, Cutler, & Redanz, 1993).

The discovery that infants are sensitive to this regular feature of the language they hear was made possible through a very simple procedure designed to assess infants' auditory preferences. Lights mounted near two loudspeakers located in panels on either side of an infant are used to draw the infant's attention to one side or the other. As soon as the infant turns to look at the light, an auditory stimulus is played through the speaker, and it continues as long as the baby is looking in that direction. The length of time the infant spends looking at the light—and hence listening to the sound—is taken as a measure of the degree to which the infant is attracted to that sound. As you will see, this head-turn preference procedure has been used extensively to address a wide variety of questions about language development in infancy.

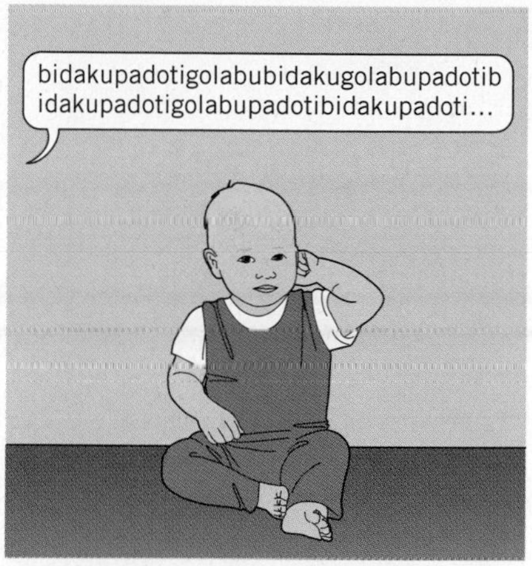

How quickly could you pick out a word from a stream of speech like the one shown here? It takes 8-month-old infants only 2 minutes of listening.

Another regularity to which infants are surprisingly sensitive concerns the **distributional properties** of the speech they hear. In any language, certain sounds are more likely to appear together than are others. Sensitivity to such regularity in the speech stream was demonstrated in an elegant series of statistical-learning experiments in which babies learned new words based purely on regularities in how often a given sound followed another (Aslin, Saffran, & Newport, 1998; Saffran, Aslin, & Newport, 1996). The infants listened to a 2-minute tape of four different three-syllable "words" (e.g., *tupiro, golabu, bidaku, padoti*) repeated in random order with no pauses between the "words." Then, on a series of test trials, the babies were sometimes presented with the "words" they had heard and sometimes with "nonwords"—the same syllables in different combinations. They listened longer to the novel "nonwords." To have formed this preference, the babies must have registered that certain syllables often occurred together in the sample of speech they heard—as when "bi" was always followed by "da" and "da" was always followed by "ku," whereas "ku" was followed by any of three other syllables ("tu," "go," or "pa"). Thus, the infants used recurrent sound patterns to fish words out of the passing stream of speech.

Probably the most salient regularity in what infants and toddlers hear is their own name. As early as 5 months of age, they show the "cocktail party effect," attending selectively to the sound of their own name among a stream of speech sounds they are hearing (Newman, 2005).

As demonstrated in the research on speech perception we have reviewed, infants work very hard right from the beginning to identify patterns in the sounds they hear other people producing. They start out with the ability to make crucial distinctions among speech sounds but then narrow their focus to the sounds that they hear with regularity, the ones that make a difference in their native language. With increasing language exposure, infants come to identify remarkably subtle features in what they hear.

Preparation for Production

In their first months, babies are getting ready to talk. The repertoire of sounds they can produce is extremely limited for the first two months. They cry, sneeze, sigh, burp, and smack their lips, but their vocal tract is not sufficiently developed to allow them to produce anything like real speech sounds. Then, at around 6 to

distributional properties the phenomenon that in any language, certain sounds are more likely to appear together than are others

8 weeks of age, infants suddenly begin producing simple speech sounds—long, drawn-out vowel sounds, such as "ooohh" or "aaahh," or consonant–vowel combinations such as "goo." Lying in their cribs, young infants entertain themselves with vocal gymnastics, switching from low grunts to high-pitched cries, from soft murmurs to loud shouts. They click, smack, blow raspberries, squeal, all with apparent fascination and delight. Through this practice, infants gain motor control over their vocalizations.

At the same time that their sound repertoire is expanding, infants become increasingly aware that their vocalizations elicit responses from others, and they begin to engage in dialogues of reciprocal ooohing and aaahing, cooing and gooing, with their parents. With improvement in their motor control of vocalization, they increasingly imitate the sounds of their "conversational" partners, even producing higher-pitched sounds when interacting with their mothers and lower-pitched sounds when interacting with their fathers (Boysson-Bardies, 1999).

Babbling Sometime between 6 and 10 months of age, but on average at around 7 months, a major milestone occurs: babies begin to babble. Standard babbling involves producing syllables made up of a consonant followed by a vowel ("pa," "ba," "ma") that are repeated in strings ("papapa"). Although it was formerly believed that infants babble a wide range of sounds from their own and other languages (Jakobson, 1941), more recent research has revealed that babies actually babble a fairly limited set of sounds, although some not in their native language are included (Boysson-Bardies, 1999).

A key component in the development of babbling is infants' hearing the sounds they are producing. Although congenitally deaf infants produce vocalizations similar to those of hearing babies until around 5 or 6 months of age, their vocal babbling occurs very late and is quite limited (Oller & Eilers, 1988). (This finding is contrary to earlier claims that deaf infants begin to babble vocally at the same time as hearing babies do—e.g., Lenneberg, 1967.) However, some congenitally deaf babies do "babble" right on schedule—those who are regularly exposed to sign language. According to Petitto and Marentette (1991), at around 8 months of age, deaf infants exposed to ASL begin to babble *manually,* producing repetitive hand movements that are components of full ASL signs, just as vocally babbled sounds are repeated components of words. Thus, like infants learning a spoken language, deaf infants seem to experiment with the elements that are combined to make meaningful words in their native language (Figure 6.8).

As their babbling becomes more varied, it gradually takes on the sounds, rhythm, and intonational patterns of the language infants hear daily. In a simple but clever experiment, French adults listened to the babbling of a French 8-month-old and an 8-month-old from either an Arabic- or Cantonese-speaking family. When asked to identify which baby was the French one in each pair, the adults chose correctly 70% of the time (Boysson-Bardies et al., 1984). Thus, before infants utter their first meaningful words, they are, in a sense, native speakers of a language.

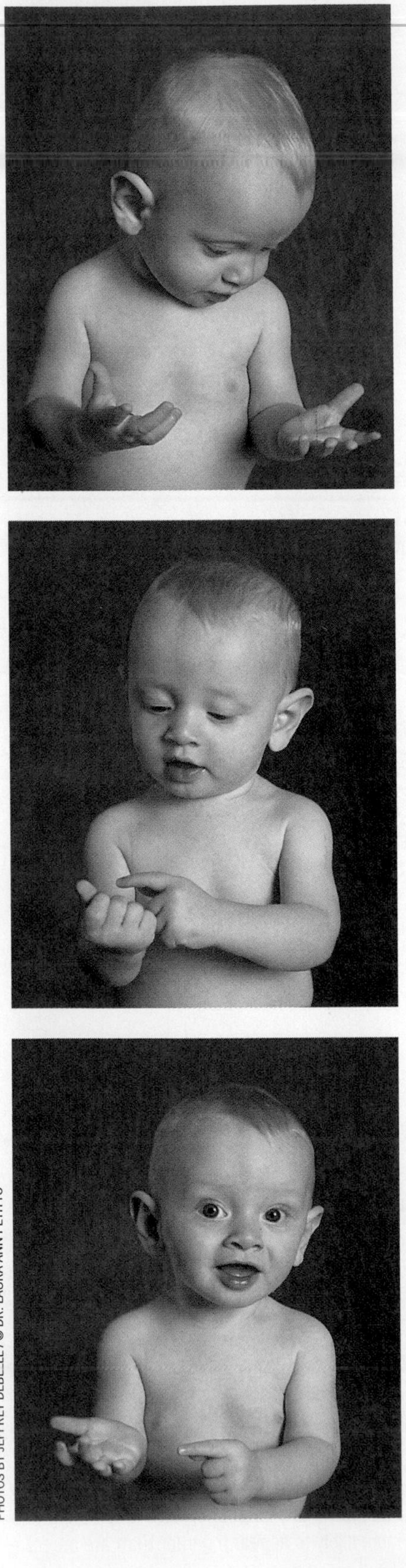

PHOTOS BY JEFFREY DEBELLE / © DR. LAURA ANN PETITTO

FIGURE 6.8 Silent babbling Babies who are exposed to the sign language of their deaf parents engage in "silent babbling." A subset of their hand movements differ from those of infants exposed to spoken language in that their slower rhythm corresponds to the rhythmic patterning of adult sign. (Adapted from Petitto, Holowka, Sergio, & Osstry, 2001)

Early interactions Before we turn to the next big step in language production—uttering recognizable words—it is important to consider the social context that promotes language development in most societies. Even before infants start speaking, they display the beginnings of communicative competence, the ability to communicate intentionally with another person.

The first indication of this communicative competence is turn-taking. In a conversation, mature participants alternate between speaking and listening. Jerome Bruner and his colleagues (Bruner, 1977; Ratner & Bruner, 1978) have proposed that learning to take turns in social interactions is facilitated by parent–infant games, such as peekaboo and "Give-and-Take," in which caregiver and baby take turns giving and receiving objects. (Infants are initially much better at offering an object than they are at relinquishing it.) In these "action dialogues" (Bruner, 1977), the child alternates between active and passive roles, just as one alternates between speaking and listening in conversations. These early interactions provide infants with a scaffold for incorporating words to communicate with others.

As discussed in Chapter 4 (page 161), successful communication also requires *intersubjectivity,* in which two interacting partners share a mutual understanding. The foundation of intersubjectivity is *joint attention,* which, early on, is established by the parent's following the baby's lead, looking at and commenting on whatever the infant is looking at. Around 6 months of age, infants become capable of following the direction of another's gaze, as long as the person is looking at something the infant can see. By 18 months of age, they can use the direction of an adult's gaze to determine the location of an object (Butterworth & Grover, 1988).

A sure method of establishing joint attention with another adult is to point toward whatever you want to talk about. If you try this with a young infant, however, the baby is likely to stare intently at your outstretched finger rather than at the object you are pointing to. But by around 9 months of age, most babies look in the direction in which the finger is pointing. A few months later, they begin to point themselves (Butterworth, 1998), and by 2 years of age, pointing is deliberately employed to direct the attention of another person (Moore & D'Entremont, 2001).

TONY FREEMAN / PHOTO EDIT

This toddler is pointing to get his father to share his attention—to achieve *intersubjectivity.* Once the father identifies the focus of his child's attention, he may even be willing to add it to the shopping cart.

We have thus seen that infants take their time getting ready to talk. Through babbling, they gain some initial level of control over the production of sounds that are necessary to produce recognizable words. As they do so, they already begin to sound like their parents. Through early interactions with their parents, they develop interactive routines similar to those required in the use of language for communication.

First Words

Infants first learn words simply as familiar patterns of sounds without attaching any meaning to them; but then, in a major revolution, words become vehicles of meaning. Thus, infants first *recognize* words, and then they begin to *comprehend* them. Next, they begin producing some of the words they have learned.

Early word recognition The initial task in learning words is picking them out of the speech stream. As noted, the first familiar sound to perceptually pop out of the language a child hears is his or her own name. Infants as young as 4½ months of age will listen longer to a tape repeating their own name than to a tape of a different but similar name (Mandel, Jusczyk, & Pisoni, 1995), and a few weeks later they can pick their own name out of background conversations. This ability helps them learn new words. After hearing "It's Jerry's cup" a number of times, 6-month-old Jerry is more likely to learn the word *cup* than if he had not heard it right after his name (Bortfeld, 2005). At 7 to 8 months of age, infants readily learn to recognize *new* words and remember them for weeks (Jusczyk & Aslin, 1995; Jusczyk & Hohne, 1997). In general, infants are better able to identify word boundaries when they are listening to infant-directed speech rather than to normal speech, so adults' tendency to speak differently to infants pays off (Thiessen, Hill, & Saffran, 2005).

The problem of reference Once infants can recognize recurrent units from the speech they hear, the stage is set for them to make a truly major advance. They are ready to address the problem of **reference,** to start associating words and meaning. Figuring out which of the multitude of possible referents is the right one for a particular word is, as the philosopher Willard Quine (1960) pointed out, a very complex problem. If a child hears someone say "bunny" in the presence of a rabbit, how does the child know whether this new word refers to the rabbit itself, to its fuzzy tail, to the whiskers on the right side of its nose, or to the twitching of its nose? That the problem of reference is a real problem is illustrated by the case of a toddler who thought "Phew!" was a greeting, because it was the first thing her mother said on entering the child's room every morning (Ferrier, 1978).

There is evidence that infants begin associating highly familiar words with their highly familiar referents at around 6 months of age; when 6-month-olds hear either "Mommy" or "Daddy," they look toward the appropriate person (Tincoff & Jusczyk, 1999). Infants gradually come to understand the meaning of less frequently heard words, with the pace of their vocabulary-building varying greatly from one child to another. According to parents' reports on 1,000 children in the United States, 10-month-olds' *comprehension vocabulary*—the words a child understands (but may not be able to say)—ranges from 11 to 154 words (Fenson et al., 1994).

reference in language and speech, the associating of words and meaning

A classic problem posed by philosopher Willard Quine was how someone who does not know the word "rabbit" could figure out exactly what it refers to. The mother in this painting by Titian may be helping her child learn what "rabbit" refers to by drawing the child's attention to the referent of the word.

Early word production Gradually, infants begin to say some of the words they understand, with most producing their first words between 10 and 15 months of age. The term *productive vocabulary* refers to the words a child is able to say.

What qualifies as a "first word"? It can be any specific utterance that the child makes consistently to refer to or to express something. Even with this loose criterion, identification of a child's earliest few words can be problematic. For one thing, doting parents often overinterpret their child's babbling. For another, very early words may differ from the corresponding adult form. For example, *Woof* was one of the first words of the boy whose linguistic progress was illustrated at the beginning of this chapter. It was used to refer to the dog next door—both to excitedly name the animal when it appeared in the neighbors' yard and to wistfully request the dog's presence when it was absent.

Initially, infants' early word production is limited by their ability to pronounce the words they know in a way that an attentive parent can discern their meaning. To make life easier for themselves, infants adopt a variety of simplification strategies (Gerken, 1994). For example, they leave out the difficult bits of words, turning *banana* into "nana," or they substitute easier sounds for hard-to-say ones—"bubba" for *brother,* "wabbit" for *rabbit.* Sometimes they reorder parts of words to put an easier sound at the beginning of the word, as in the common "pasketti" (for *spaghetti*) or the more idiosyncratic "Cagoshin" (the way the child quoted at the beginning of the chapter continued for several years to say *Chicago*). Children's early language is subject to a number of other

individual differences 6.2

Variability in Language Development

Parents often become needlessly concerned if their child seems to lag behind his or her peers in reaching any of the major milestones in language development. When should they worry? It is important that parents understand that there are huge individual differences in many aspects of language acquisition, and *most of them do not predict later problems.*

One form of variation that language researchers have identified is **style,** that is, the strategies young children enlist in beginning to speak. Some children display a **referential** or **analytic style,** whereas others are characterized as having an **expressive** or **holistic style** (Bates, Dale, & Thal, 1995; Bloom, 1975; Nelson, 1973). A third style is referred to as **wait-and-see** (Boysson-Bardies,1999).

Boysson-Bardies (1999) has described these three styles using French infants as examples. Children characterized as *referential* tend to analyze the speech stream into individual phonetic elements and words, and their first utterances tend to be isolated, often monosyllabic words. This style is exemplified by Emilie, whose first 20 words were almost all monosyllables starting with the same three consonants that had dominated her earlier babbling. Thus, from the adult words she heard, she seemed to systematically select those beginning with the sounds she had already mastered. Her simple and efficient strategy enabled Emilie to rapidly increase her vocabulary.

Children characterized as expressive give more attention to the overall sound of language—its rhythmic and intonational patterns—than to the phonetic elements of which it is composed. This style was adopted by Simon, whose strategy might be characterized as "conversation first." Rather than beginning with small units of speech as Emilie did, sociable Simon joined in the conversations of adults with long "sentences" or even "questions," all uttered with perfect French intonational patterns. However, these utterances included hardly any recognizable words.

Children described as "*wait-and-see*" begin to talk late—some of them very late. Henri babbled very little, and even after he understood many words, he rarely said anything beyond "papa," "maman," and "non." Henri had, however, been listening carefully for a long time, because at the age of 20 months he suddenly began saying a large number of clearly articulated words and then rapidly acquired more.

Although these different styles reflect substantial differences in how children go about beginning to talk, they have little if any effect on the ultimate outcome of the process. As noted earlier in the chapter, children also differ dramatically in the age at which they speak their first recognizable word and produce their first sentence, and the size of their early vocabularies varies widely as well. However, most young children who lag behind others or who are below average in productive vocabulary—even those who are far below the norm—catch up within a few years. Therefore, as long as there are no other signs of developmental problems, parents should not worry overly much if their child is a late talker. There is cause for concern, however, about a young child whose *comprehension* of language is lagging, because this kind of delay may signal a hearing problem or cognitive difficulties predictive of later problems (Bates et al., 1995).

Parents who are concerned about their slow-to-talk child can take heart from the fact that Albert Einstein is reported not to have talked before 4 or 5 years of age.

style the strategies that young children enlist in beginning to speak

referential (analytic) style speech strategy that analyzes the speech stream into individual phonetic elements and words; the first utterances of children who adopt this style tend to use isolated, often monosyllabic words

expressive (holistic) style speech strategy that gives more attention to the overall sound of language—its rhythmic and intonational patterns—than to the phonetic elements of which it is composed

wait-and-see style speech strategy that typically involves a late start in speaking, but a large vocabulary once speaking begins

factors that sometimes cause their parents concern. Some of these are discussed in Box 6.2.

Once children start talking, around the end of the first year, what do they talk about? The early productive vocabularies of children in the United States include names for people, objects, and events from the child's everyday life (Clark, 1979; Nelson, 1973). Children name their parents, siblings, pets, and themselves, as well as ecologically important objects such as cookies, juice, and balls. Frequent events and routines are also labeled—"up," "bye-bye," "night-night." Important modifiers are also used—"mine," "hot," "all gone." Table 6.1 reveals substantial crosslinguistic correspondence in the content of the first 10 words of children in the United States, Hong Kong, and Beijing. As the table shows, many of infants' first words in the three societies referred to specific people or were sound effects (Tardif et al., 2008).

TABLE 6.1

Rank Ordered List of Earliest Words in Three Languages*

English (United States)	Putonghua (Hong Kong)	Cantonese (Beijing)
Daddy	**Daddy**	**Mommy**
Mommy	Aah	**Daddy**
BaaBaa	**Mommy**	*Grandma (paternal)*
Bye	*YumYum*	*Grandpa (paternal)*
Hi	*Sister (older)*	**Hello?/Wei?**
UhOh	**UhOh** (Aiyou)	*Hit*
Grr	*Hit*	Uncle (paternal)
Bottle	**Hello/Wei**	Grab/grasp
YumYum	Milk	*Auntie (maternal)*
Dog	Naughty	**Bye**
No	*Brother (older)*	**UhOh** (Aiyou)
WoofWoof	*Grandma (maternal)*	*Ya/Wow*

*Words in boldface were common across all three languages; those in italics were common for two of the languages.

Source: From Tardif, T., Fletcher, P., Liang, W. L., Zhang, Z. X., Marchman, V., & Kaciroti, N. (2008). Babies' First 10 Words. *Developmental Psychology, 44*(4), 929–938.

Nouns predominate in the early productive vocabularies of children learning English, possibly in part because their meanings are easier to pick up from observation than are the meanings of verbs: nouns label entities, whereas verbs represent *relations* among entities (Gentner, 1982). In addition, the proportion of nouns in very young children's vocabularies is related to the proportion of nouns in their mother's speech to them (Pine, 1994); middle-class American mothers (the group most frequently studied) do much more object-labeling for their infants than do mothers in some other cultures, such as Japan (Fernald & Morikawa, 1993).

Initially, infants say the words in their small productive vocabulary only one word at a time. This period of one-word utterances is referred to as the **holophrastic period,** because the child typically expresses a "whole phrase"—a whole idea—with a single word. "Drink" can refer to the child's desire to have his mother pour him a glass of juice. "Juice" could, of course, refer to the very same desire. Children who produce only one-word utterances are not limited to single ideas; they manage to express themselves by stringing together successive one-word utterances. An example is a little girl with an eye infection who pointed to her eye, saying, "Ow," and then after a pause, "Eye" (Hoff, 2001).

The rate of children's vocabulary development is influenced by the sheer *amount* of talk that they hear: the more speech mothers address to their toddlers, the more rapidly the children learn new words (Huttenlocher, Haight, Bryk, Seltzer, & Lyons, 1991). More highly educated mothers talk to their children more than do less-educated mothers, and their children have larger vocabularies than do the children of less-educated parents (Fenson et al., 1994; Hart & Risley, 1994; Huttenlocher et al., 1991).

What young children want to talk about quickly outstrips the number of words in their limited vocabularies, so they make the words they do know perform double duty. One way they do this is through **overextension**—using a given word in a broader context than is appropriate, as when children use *dog* for any four-legged animal, *daddy* for any man, *moon* for a dishwasher dial, or *hot* for any reflective metal (Table 6.2). Most overextensions represent an effort to communicate rather than a lack of knowledge, as demonstrated by research in which children who overextended some words were given comprehension tests (Naigles & Gelman, 1995). In one study, for example, children were shown pairs of pictures of entities for which they generally used the same label—for instance, a dog and a sheep, both of which they normally referred to as "dog." However, when asked to point to the sheep, they chose the correct animal. Thus, these children understood the meaning of the word *sheep,* but because it was not in their productive vocabulary, they used a related word that they could say to talk about the animal.

TABLE 6.2

Examples of Young Children's Overextensions of Word Meaning

Word	Referents
ball	ball, balloon, marble, apple, egg, spherical water tank (Rescorla, 1980)
cat	cat, cat's usual location on top of TV when absent (Rescorla, 1980)
moon	moon, half-moon-shaped lemon slice, circular chrome dial on dishwasher, half a Cheerio, hangnail (Bowerman, 1978)
snow	snow, white flannel bed pad, white puddle of milk on floor (Bowerman, 1978)
baby	own reflection in mirror, framed photograph of self, framed photographs of others (Hoff, 2001)

holophrastic period the period when children begin using the words in their small productive vocabulary one word at a time

overextension the use of a given word in a broader context than is appropriate

Word learning After the appearance of their first words, children typically plod ahead slowly, reaching a productive vocabulary of fifty or so words by around 18 months of age. Suddenly, the plodding is over, as most children begin the "vocabulary explosion," or "word spurt" (Figure 6.9) (Benedict, 1979; Goldfield & Reznick, 1990; McMurray, 2007). Word learning shifts from first gear to overdrive, with new words being said for the first time every day. Children's comprehension vocabulary shows similar rapid growth; from 18 months of age to the time they are in 1st grade, children are estimated to learn an average of 5 to 10 new words every day (Anglin, 1993; Carey, 1978).

What accounts for the speed of young children's word learning? When we look closely, we see that there are multiple sources of support for learning new words, some coming from the people around them, and some generated by the children themselves.

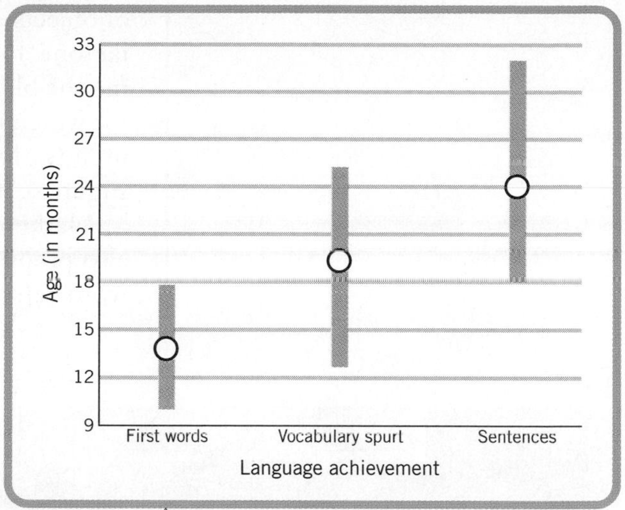

FIGURE 6.9 Language achievement On average, American children say their first word at around 13 months, experience a vocabulary spurt at around 19 months, and begin to produce simple sentences at around 24 months. However, the bars above and below these means show a substantial amount of variability in when different children achieve each of these milestones. (Adapted from Bloom, 1998)

ADULT INFLUENCES ON WORD LEARNING In addition to using IDT, which makes word learning easier for infants, adults make word learning easier for infants by telling them the names of things in ways that highlight their meaning. For example, they put vocal stress on new words and say them in the final position in a sentence—"That's a checchi." Also helpful is adults' tendency to label objects that are already the focus of the child's attention, thereby reducing uncertainty about the referent (Masur, 1982; Tomasello, 1988; Tomasello & Farrar, 1986). Another stimulus to word learning comes from the naming games many families play with young children, asking the child to point to a series of named items—"Where's your nose?" "Where's your ear?" "Where's your tummy?" Repetition also helps; young children are more likely to acquire words their parents use frequently (Huttenlocher et al., 1991).

CHILDREN'S CONTRIBUTIONS TO WORD LEARNING When confronted with novel words whose meaning they do not know, children actively exploit the context in which the new word was used in order to infer its meaning. A classic study by Susan Carey and Elsa Bartlett (1978) demonstrated **fast mapping**—the process of rapidly learning a new word simply from hearing the contrastive use of a familiar word and the unfamiliar word. In the course of everyday activities in a preschool classroom, an experimenter drew a child's attention to two trays—one red, the other an uncommon color the child would not know by name—and asked the child to get "the *chromium* tray, not the red one." The child was thus provided with a contrast between a familiar term (*red*) and an unfamiliar one (*chromium*). From this simple contrast, the children inferred which tray they were supposed to get and that the name of the color of that tray was "chromium." After this single exposure to a novel word, about half the children showed some knowledge of it a week later by correctly picking the *chromium* one from an array of paint chips.

Some theorists have proposed that the many inferences children make in the process of learning words are guided by a number of assumptions (sometimes referred to as principles, constraints, or biases) that limit the possible meanings children entertain for a new word. For example, children expect that a given entity will have only one name, an expectancy referred to as the *mutual exclusivity* assumption by Amanda Woodward and Ellen Markman (1998). Early evidence for this assumption came from a study in which 3-year-olds saw pairs

fast mapping the process of rapidly learning a new word simply from hearing the contrastive use of a familiar and the unfamiliar word of objects—a familiar object for which the children had a name and an unfamiliar one for which they had no name. When the experimenter said, "Show me the blicket," the children mapped the novel label to the novel object, the one for which they had no name (Markman & Wachtel, 1988). Even 13-month-old infants do the same (Woodward, Markman, & Fitzsimmons, 1994). (See Figure 6.10a.)

Markman and Woodward (Markman, 1989; Woodward & Markman, 1998) also propose that a *whole-object* assumption leads children to expect that a novel word refers to a whole object, rather than to a part, property, action, or other

FIGURE 6.10 Pragmatic cues for word learning (a) Because this child already knows the name of the familiar object on the table, she will pick up the novel object when the adult asks her to "show me the blicket."

(b) This child will assume that the novel word she hears the experimenter saying applies to the novel object the experimenter is looking at, even though the child cannot see the object and is looking at a different novel object when she actually hears the word.

COURTESY OF JUDY DELOACHE

(c) This child will learn *gazzer* as the name of the novel object that the adult smiles at triumphantly after she had previously announced that she wanted to find "the gazzer."

aspect of the object. Thus, in the case of Quine's rabbit problem, the whole-object assumption results in children's taking "bunny" to apply to the whole animal, not just to its tail or the twitching of its nose.

In addition to their general tendency to map novel words onto novel objects, children pay attention to the *social context* in which language is used, exploiting a variety of **pragmatic cues** for word learning. For example, children use an adult's focus of attention as a cue to word meaning. In a study by Dare Baldwin (1993), an experimenter showed 18-month-olds two novel objects and then concealed them in separate containers. Next, the experimenter peeked into one of the containers and commented, "There's a modi in here." The adult then removed and gave both objects to the child. When asked for the "modi," the children picked the object that the experimenter had been looking at when saying the label. Thus, the infants used the relation between eye gaze and labeling to learn a novel name for an object before they had ever seen it (see Figure 6.10b).

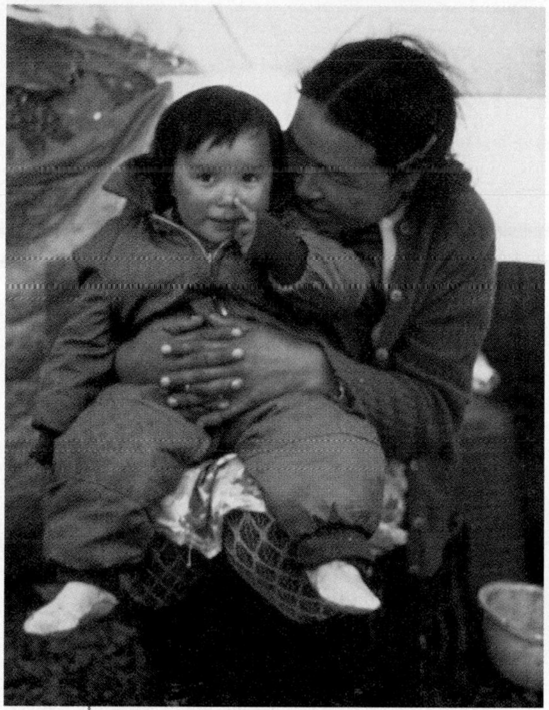
COURTESY OF JEAN BRIGGS

This young Inuit child is playing a naming game; her mother has just asked her to point to her nose.

Another pragmatic cue that children use to draw inferences about a word's meaning is *intentionality* (Tomasello, 2007). For example, in one study, 2-year-olds heard an experimenter announce, "Let's dax Mickey Mouse." The experimenter then performed two actions on a Mickey Mouse doll, one carried out in a coordinated and apparently intentional way, followed by a pleased comment ("There!"), and the other carried out in a clumsy and apparently accidental way, followed by an exclamation of surprise ("Oops!"). The children interpreted the novel verb *dax* as referring to the action the adult seemed to have intended to do (Tomasello & Barton, 1994).

Similarly, 18-month-olds can even use an adult's emotional response to infer the name of a novel object that they cannot see (Tomasello, Strosberg, & Akhtar, 1996). In a study establishing this fact, an adult announced her intention to "find the gazzer." She then picked up one of two objects and showed obvious disappointment with it. When she gleefully seized the second object, the children inferred that it was a "gazzer." (Figure 6.10c depicts another case in which a child infers from an adult's emotional expression the name of an unseen object.)

The degree to which preschool children take a speaker's intention into account is shown by the fact that if an adult labels an object in a way that conflicts with their knowledge of that object, they will nevertheless accept the label if the adult clearly used it intentionally (Jaswal, 2004). When an experimenter simply used the label "dog" in referring to a picture of a catlike animal, preschool children were reluctant to extend the word to other catlike stimuli. They were much more willing to do so when the experimenter made it clear that he really intended his use of the unexpected label by saying, "You're not going to believe this, but this is actually a dog." In general, children's readiness to accept what an adult tells them supports the acquisition of information through reliance on the "testimony" of other people (Harris, 2002; Jaswal, 2004).

In learning new words, young children also use the *linguistic context* in which novel words appear to help infer their meaning. In one of the earliest experiments on language acquisition, Roger Brown (1957) established that the grammatical form of a novel word influences children's interpretation of it. He showed preschool children a picture of a pair of hands kneading a mass of material in a container (Figure 6.11). The picture was described to one group of children as "sibbing," to another as "a sib," and to a third as "some sib." The children subsequently interpreted the new word *sib* as referring to the action, the container, or the material,

pragmatic cues aspects of the social context used for word learning

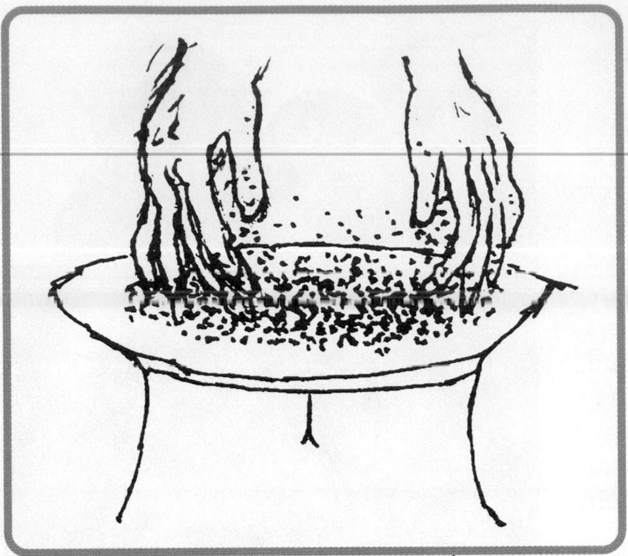

COURTESY OF BRIAN KOVALESKI

FIGURE 6.11 Linguistic context When Roger Brown, a pioneer in the study of language development, described this picture as "sibbing," "a sib," or "some sib," preschool children made different assumptions about the meaning of "sib."

depending on which grammatical form (verb, count noun, or mass noun) of the word they had heard.

Two- and three-year-old children also use the *grammatical category* of novel words to help interpret their meaning (e.g., Hall, Waxman, & Hurwitz, 1993; Markman & Hutchinson, 1984; Waxman, 1990). Hearing "This is a dax" applied to an object, they assume that *dax* refers to that object, as well as to other members of the same category. In contrast, hearing "This is a dax one," they assume that *dax* refers to a property of the object (e.g., its color or texture). These noun-category and adjective-property linkages are even made by infants and toddlers (e.g., Waxman & Hall, 1993; Waxman & Markow, 1995, 1998).

Novel nouns particularly heighten children's attention to shape, possibly because shape is a good cue to category membership. Children readily extend a novel noun to novel objects of the same shape, even when those objects differ dramatically in size, color, and texture (Landau, Smith, & Jones, 1988; Smith, Jones, & Landau, 1992). Thus, a child who hears a U-shaped wooden block called "a dax" will assume that *dax* also refers to a U-shaped object covered in blue fur or to a U-shaped piece of red wire but not to a wooden block of a different shape (Figure 6.12). A shape bias is also evident in young children's spontaneous extension of familiar words to nonsense objects that are vaguely similar to familiar entities (e.g., a cone might be referred to as a "mountain") (Samuelson & Smith, 2005).

Children also use the grammatical structure of whole sentences to figure out meaning—a strategy referred to as **syntactic bootstrapping** (Fisher, 2000; Fisher, Gleitman, & Gleitman, 1991; Yuan & Fisher, 2009). An early demonstration of this phenomenon involved showing 2-year-olds a videotape of a duck using his left hand to push a rabbit down into a squatting position while both animals waved their right arms in circles (Figure 6.13) (Naigles, 1990). (The roles of the rabbit and duck were played by adults in costumes.) As they watched, some children were told "The duck is kradding the rabbit"; the others were told "The rabbit and the duck are kradding." All the children then saw two videos side by side, one showing the duck pushing on the rabbit and the other showing both animals waving their arms in the air. Instructed to "Find kradding," the two groups looked at the event that matched the syntax they had heard while watching the initial video. Those who had heard the first sentence had apparently taken "kradding" to mean what the duck had been doing to the rabbit, whereas those who had heard the second sentence thought it

▌syntactic bootstrapping ▌ the strategy of using the grammatical structure of whole sentences to figure out meaning

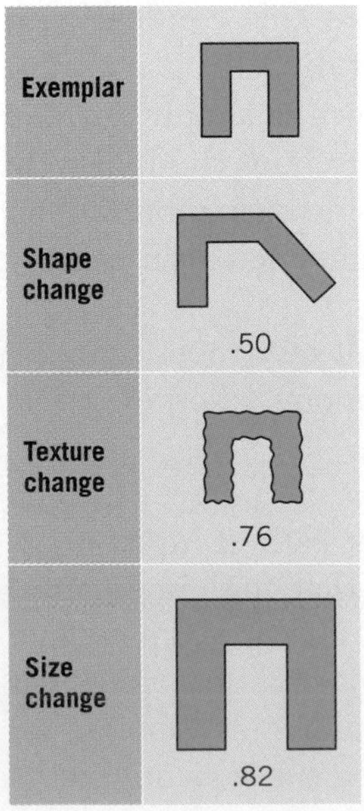

FIGURE 6.12 Shape bias In one of many studies of the shape bias, children were shown the exemplar at the top of this figure and told that it was a "dax" (or some other nonsense word). Then they were asked which of the objects below the exemplar was also a "dax." The numbers under the objects indicate the proportion of children who thought each object was a "dax." As you can see, they most often thought that the word referred to the object that was of the same shape as the exemplar, even if the surface texture or size was different. (Adapted from Landau, Smith, & Jones, 1988)

meant what both animals had been doing. Thus, the children had arrived at different interpretations for a novel verb depending on the *structure* of the sentence in which it was embedded.

As you can see, infants and young children have a remarkable ability to learn new words as object names. Interestingly, they are equally able to learn nonlinguistic "labels" for objects. Infants between 13 and 18 months of age map gestures or nonverbal sounds (e.g., squeaks and whistles) onto novel objects just as readily as they map words (Namy, 2001; Namy & Waxman, 1998; Woodward & Hoyne, 1999). By 20 to 26 months of age, however, they accept only words as names.

In all the above examples of young children's ability to learn new words from various kinds of information, the information was directly provided to them by an adult experimenter. However, in everyday life, children hear lots of language that is not addressed specifically to them. It turns out they can learn new words from overhearing conversations between other people (e.g., hearing an experimenter introduce a novel word to another person) (Akhtar, 2005).

LETITIA R. NAIGLES, UNIVERSITY OF CONNECTICUT

FIGURE 6.13 Syntactic bootstrapping When children in Naigles's (1990) study heard an adult describe this filmed scene as "The duck is kradding the rabbit," they used the syntactic structure of the sentence to infer that *kradding* is what the duck is doing to the rabbit.

Putting Words Together

A major landmark in early language development is achieved when children start combining some words into sentences, an advance that enables them to express increasingly complex ideas. The degree to which children develop syntax, and the speed with which they do it, is what most distinguishes their language abilities from those of nonhuman primates.

First sentences Most children begin to combine words into simple sentences by the end of their second year. However, in another example of comprehension preceding production, young children know something about word combinations well before they produce any. For example, 12- to 14-month-olds listen longer to sentences that have normal word order than to sentences in which word order is scrambled (Fernald & McRoberts, 1995). In another demonstration of infants' sensitivity to word order, Kathy Hirsh-Pasek and Roberta Golinkoff (1991) presented infants with two videotaped scenes—one of a woman kissing some keys while holding up a ball and the other of the woman holding up the keys while kissing the ball. Thus, the same three elements—kissing, keys, and a ball—were present in both scenes. Yet when the infants heard the sentence "She's kissing the keys" or "She's kissing the ball," they looked preferentially at the appropriate scene.

Children's first sentences are two-word combinations; their separate utterances of "More," "Juice," and "Drink" become "More juice" and "Drink juice." These two-word utterances have been described as **telegraphic** speech because, just as in telegrams, nonessential elements are missing (Brown & Fraser, 1963). Consider the following examples of standard two-word utterances: "Read me," "Mommy tea," "Ride Daddy," "Hurt knee," "All wet," "More boy," "Key door," "Andrew sleep" (Braine, 1976). These primitive sentences lack a number of elements that would appear in adult utterances, including function words (such as *a, the, in*), auxiliary verbs (*is, was, will, be*), and word endings (indicating plurals, possessives, or verb tenses). Children's early sentences possess this telegraphic quality in languages as diverse as English, Finnish, Luo (Kenya), and Kaluli (New Guinea) (Boysson-Bardies, 1999).

For young children learning languages like English, in which word order is crucial for meaning, their early, simple sentences follow a consistent word order: a child might say "Eat cookie" but would be unlikely ever to say "Cookie eat." Many

telegraphic speech the term describing children's first sentences that are generally two-word utterances

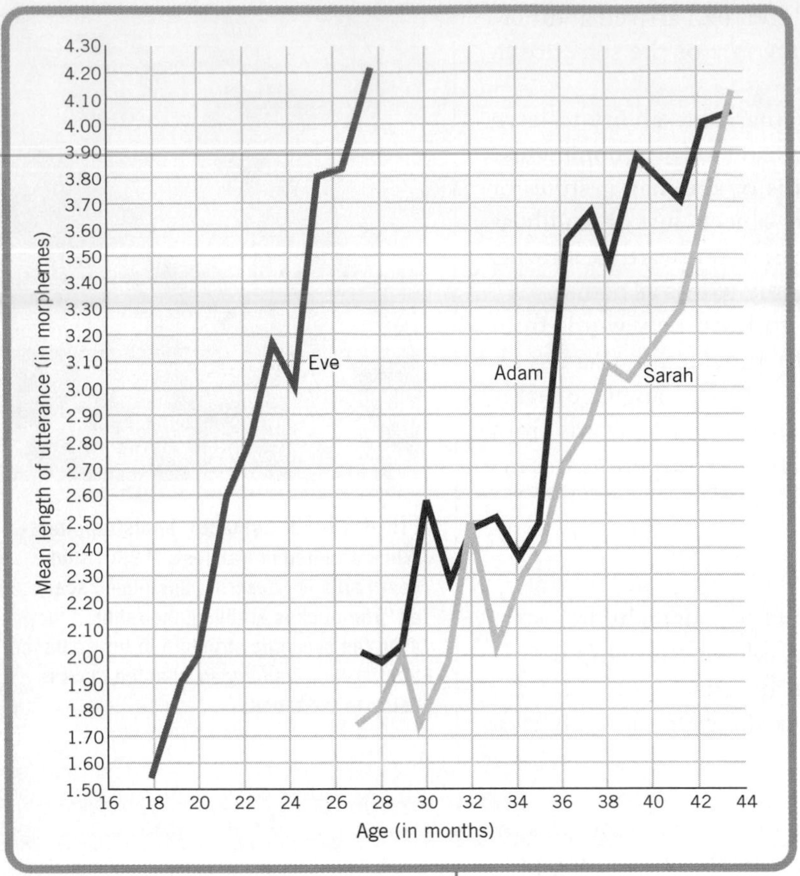

FIGURE 6.14 Length of utterance The relation between age and the mean length of utterance for the three children—Adam, Eve, and Sarah—studied by Roger Brown. (From Brown, 1973)

theorists have cited this preservation of correct word order in young children's early utterances as evidence that they possess grammatical rules similar to those that govern adult speech (e.g., Gleitman, Gleitman, Landau, & Wanner, 1988). Others interpret two-word utterances as governed by grammatical rules, but rules that are unique to the language of children (Bloom, 1970; Braine, 1963). Still others argue that the regularity of early word combinations is primarily a matter of children's imitating the order of words they hear in adult speech (Tomasello, 1992).

Many children continue to produce one- and two-word utterances for some time, whereas others quickly move on to sentences consisting of three or more words. Figure 6.14 shows the rapid increase in the mean length of utterances of three children in Roger Brown's (1973) classic study of language development. As you can see from the figure, Eve started her explosive increase in sentence length much earlier than the other two children did. The length of children's utterances increases in part because they begin to systematically incorporate some of the elements that were missing from their telegraphic speech (deVilliers & deVilliers, 1973). Consider, for example, the sentence "I eating cookies," said by a 2-year-old. A short time before, this child might only have said "Eat cookie" to communicate exactly the same idea. Now, however, three additional elements are present—the first-person pronoun, the *-ing* ending on the verb, and the plural *-s* added to *cookie.* (Sometime soon the child will add the auxiliary verb *am.*)

Once children are capable of producing four-word sentences, typically at around $2^1/_2$ years of age, they begin to produce complex sentences containing more than one clause (Bowerman, 1979): "Can I do it when we get home?" "I want this doll because she's big" (Limber, 1973).

PRACTICE MAKES PERFECT An important source of children's increasing proficiency at using language is their own hard work. Toddlers actively practice their developing language skills, often in solitary practice sessions conducted in their beds before falling asleep. Ruth Weir (1962) put a microphone under her $2^1/_2$-year-old son's crib and recorded his "crib talk"—his exploration and practice of a variety of grammatical forms, as in this example:

Block.
Yellow block.
Look at the yellow block.
There is the light.
Where is the light?
Here is the light.

Grammatical rules As noted above, there is some debate regarding whether the regularity of toddlers' word order reflects an internalization of grammatical rules. The strongest evidence in support of the idea that young children are learning the grammatical rules of their language comes from their production of word endings. In English, the rules for pluralizing nouns and putting verbs into the past tense are, with some exceptions, highly regular: add *-s* to nouns and *-ed* to verbs. These simple rules suffice for the vast majority of English words.

Young children follow these rules, as was established in a classic experiment by Jean Berko (1958) in which young children were shown a picture of a nonsense animal, which the experimenter referred to as "a wug." Then a picture of two of the creatures was produced, and the experimenter said, "Here are two of them; what are they?" Children as young as 4 readily answered correctly: "Wugs." Thus, these children created the correct plural form for a totally novel word.

Other evidence that is consistent with the idea that children learn language rules comes from what they do with word formations that are exceptions to the standard rules. Take the plural of *man* and the past tense of *go,* for example. Children use the correct irregular forms of these words, saying "men" for the plural of *man* and "went" for the past tense of *go.* However, some time after they learn the appropriate regular endings, they start making occasional **overregularization** errors, in which they treat irregular forms as if they were regular. For example, a child who previously said "men" and "went" may begin producing novel forms such as "mans" and "goed," as well as "foots," "feets," "breaked," "broked," and even "branged," and "walkeded" (Berko, 1958; Kuczaj, 1977; Xu & Pinker, 1995). The following dialogue between a 2½-year-old and his father illustrates this kind of error, as well as the difficulty of correcting it:

> *Child:* I used to wear diapers. When I growed up (pause)
> *Father:* When you grew up?
> *Child:* When I grewed up, I wore underpants.
>
> (Clark, 1993)

Before fully mastering irregular forms, children sometimes alternate between overregularization errors and correct irregular word endings (Marcus, 1996; 2004). In this case, according to Marcus, overregulation errors occur when a child fails to retrieve from memory the correct form for a given irregular verb and hence applies the general rule by default. With experience using the language, such retrieval failures occur less frequently, and overregularization errors gradually disappear.

Many syntactic rules have multiple components, and young children master them step by step. One example involves negation. The word *no* is a very useful tool for toddlers, and it accounts for many one-word utterances in children's earliest speech. A little later, *no* is frequently combined with one or two other words to express a variety of meanings, including refusal to do something ("No bath"), the nonexistence of something ("No more cookie"), or denial ("No the sun shining") (Klima & Bellugi, 1967). In young children's early negative sentences, the negative term most often occurs at the beginning of the sentence, and the subject is omitted ("No want juice," "No fit") (Klima & Bellugi, 1966). At around the age of 3, children start to incorporate the negative element into the sentence and add appropriate auxiliary verbs, at which point "No want bath" becomes "I don't want a bath."

Another syntactic rule that children begin to acquire quite early in the preschool period involves the interrogative, which is key to their ability to get desired information from others. Initially, children simply use rising intonation to convert a statement into a query, as in "I ride train?" At around age 2, children who are learning English start asking "wh" questions, that is, questions that focus on who, what, where, when, and why, as well as how. In their earliest "wh" questions, children simply put the "wh" word at the beginning of an affirmative statement

overregularization speech errors in which children treat irregular forms of words as if they were regular

The child in this cartoon has mastered one of the more difficult aspects of English grammar—the passive voice.

(Klima & Bellugi, 1967), as in the plaintive query listed at the beginning of the chapter—"Why I don't have a dog?" Eventually, children work out the correct question form used in English, which requires inverting the subject and verb of the sentence to ask, for example, "Why don't I have a dog?"

Parents play a role in their children's grammatical development, although a more limited one than you might expect. Clearly, they provide a model of grammatically correct speech. In addition, they frequently fill in missing parts of their children's incomplete utterances (Nelson, Denninger, Bonvillian, Kaplan, & Baker, 1984; Newport et al., 1977), as when a parent responds to a child's "No bed" by saying, "You really don't want to go to bed right now, do you?"

One might think that parents also contribute to their children's language development by correcting their frequent speech errors. In fact, parents generally ignore even wildly ungrammatical mistakes, accepting sentences such as "I magicked it," "Me no want go," or "I want dessert in front of dinner" (Becker-Bryant & Polkosky, 2001; Brown & Hanlon, 1970). It would be hard to do otherwise, since so much of children's speech is like this. And, as the parent who tried to correct his son's use of "growed" discovered, such efforts are largely futile anyway. Parents do, however, tend to correct some of their children's utterances—their statements that are factually incorrect. Thus, parents are more concerned with the truth of what their children say than with its grammatical correctness.

Learning how to combine words to create interpretable sentences is the crowning achievement in language acquisition. Possibly no linguistic development is more stunning than the progress children make in a few years from simple two-word utterances to complex sentences that conform to the grammatical rules of the child's language. Even their errors reveal an increasingly sophisticated representation of the grammatical structure of their native language. This accomplishment is made all the more impressive by evidence that parental feedback plays a relatively minor role in it.

Conversational Skills

Young children are eager to participate in conversations with others, but their conversational skills initially lag well behind their burgeoning language skills. For one thing, much of very young children's speech is directed to themselves, rather than to another person. Vygotsky (1962) believed that this *private speech* of young children serves an important regulatory function: children talk to themselves as a strategy to organize their actions (Behrend, Rosengren, & Perlmutter, 1992). Private speech often accompanies solitary play, but as much as half of young children's speech in the company of other children or adults is addressed to themselves (Schoeber-Peterson & Johnson, 1991). Gradually, private speech is internalized as thought, and children become capable of mentally organizing their behavior, so they no longer need to talk out loud to themselves.

▮ **collective monologue** ▮ conversation beween children that involves a series of non sequiturs, the content of each child's turn having little or nothing to do with what the other child has just said

As noted in Chapter 4, when young children converse with other children, their conversations tend to be egocentric. Piaget (1926) labeled young children's talk with their peers as **collective monologues.** Even when they take turns speaking, their conversations tend to be a series of non sequiturs, with the content of each child's turn having little or nothing to do with what the other child has just said. The following conversation between two American preschoolers gives a good idea of what Piaget observed:

Jenny: My bunny slippers . . . are brown and red and sort of yellow and white. And they have eyes and ears and these noses that wiggle sideways when they kiss.
Chris: I have a piece of sugar in a red piece of paper. I'm gonna eat it but maybe it's for a horse.
Jenny: We bought them. My mommy did. We couldn't find the old ones. These are like the old ones. They were not in the trunk.
Chris: Can't eat the piece of sugar, not unless you take the paper off.

(Stone & Church, 1957, pp. 146–147)

Gradually, children's capacity for sustained conversation increases. In a longitudinal study of parent–child conversations of four children from the age of 21 months to 36 months, Bloom, Rocissano, and Hood (1976) found that the proportion of children's utterances that were on the same topic and added new information to what an adult had just said more than doubled (from around 20% to over 40%). In contrast, the proportion of utterances following an adult's statement that were on unrelated topics fell dramatically (from around 20% to almost 0). With peers, children of this age still have considerable difficulty sustaining a dialogue. The conversations of preschool peers are much longer and more complex when they occur in the context of pretend play, in part because pretend play is often based on highly familiar routines, such as cooking or caring for a baby (French, Lucariello, Seidman, & Nelson, 1985; Nelson & Gruendel, 1979).

A particular aspect of young children's conversations that changes dramatically in the preschool period is the extent to which they talk about the past. At most, 3-year-olds' conversations include occasional brief references to past events. In contrast, 5-year-olds produce **narratives**—descriptions of past events that have the form of a story (Miller & Sperry, 1988; Nelson, 1993). One thing that makes longer, more coherent narratives possible is better understanding of the basic structure of stories (Peterson & McCabe, 1988; Shapiro & Hudson, 1991; Stein, 1988).

JEFF GREENBERG / PHOTO EDIT

Parents typically help young children talk about past events. Such conversations contribute to early language development.

Parents actively assist their children to develop the ability to produce coherent accounts of past events by providing what has been referred to as *scaffolding* (discussed in Chapter 4) for their children's narratives (Bruner, 1975). An effective way to structure children's conversations about the past is to ask them elaborative questions, that is, questions that enable them to say something—anything—that advances the story:

Mother: And what else happened at the celebrations?
Child: I don't know.
Mother: We did something special with all the other children.
Child: What was it?
Mother: There were a whole lot of people over at the beach, and everyone was doing something in the sand.
Child: What was it?

narratives descriptions of past events that have the basic structure of a story

Mother: Can't you remember what we did in the sand? We were looking for something.
Child: Umm, I don't know.
Mother: We went digging in the sand.
Child: Umm, and that was when um the yellow spade broke.
Mother: Good girl, I'd forgotten that. Yes, the yellow spade broke, and what happened?
Child: Um, we had to um dig with the other end of the yellow bit one.
Mother: That's right. We used the broken bit, didn't we?
Child: Yeah.

(Farrant & Reese, 2002)

The child in this conversation does not actually say much, but the parent's questions help the child think about the event, and the parent also provides a conversational model. Those toddlers whose parents scaffold their early conversations by asking useful, elaborative questions produce better narratives on their own a few years later (Fivush, 1991; McCabe & Peterson, 1991; Reese & Fivush, 1993).

We thus see that young children put their burgeoning linguistic skills to good use, becoming more effective communicative partners in conversations with other people. Initially, they need substantial support from a more competent partner, but their conversational skills increase quite regularly.

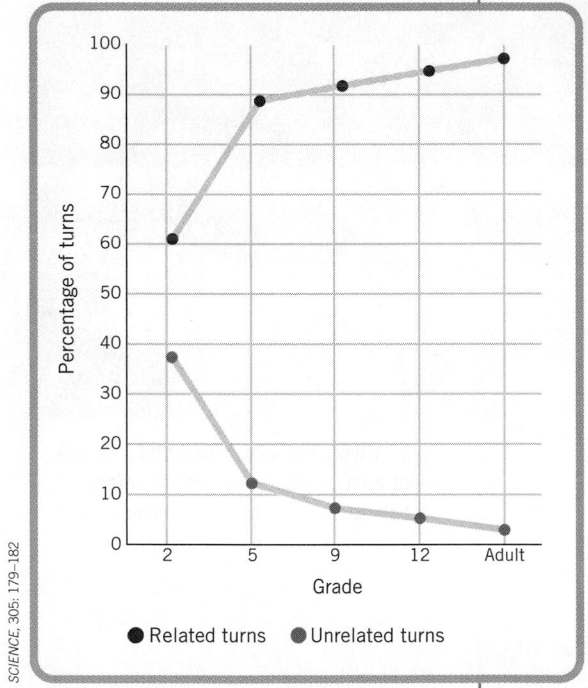

FIGURE 6.15 Conversations become more relevant with age **As children get older, their conversational turns become increasingly more related to what the other person has just said. The proportion of non sequiturs decreases correspondingly.**

Later Development

From 5 or 6 years of age on, children continue to develop language skills, although with less dramatic accomplishments. For example, the ability to sustain a conversation, which grew so dramatically in the preschool years, continues to improve for many years thereafter. Figure 6.15 shows that, as children get older, their conversational contributions are increasingly often related to the topic under discussion. In addition, the length of their dialogues on a single topic increases substantially (Dorval & Eckerman, 1984). School-age children become increasingly capable of reflecting upon and analyzing language, and they master more complex grammatical rules, such as the use of passive constructions.

One consequence of schoolchildren's more reflective and analytic language skills is their increasing appreciation of the multiple meanings of words, which is responsible for the emergence of the endless series of puns, riddles, and "knock-knock" jokes with which primary school children delight themselves and torture their parents (Ely & McCabe, 1994). They also are able to learn the meaning of new words simply from hearing them defined (Pressley, Levin, & McDaniel, 1987), a factor that helps their comprehension vocabulary expand—from the 10,000 words that the average 6-year-old knows to the 40,000 words estimated for 5th graders (Anglin, 1993) to the average college-student vocabulary that has been estimated to be as high as 150,000 words (Miller & Gildea, 1987).

Current Theoretical Issues in Language Development

Clearly, children's early language development represents a prodigious feat, including producing the sounds that make up words in their language (phonological development), learning the meaning of thousands of words (semantic development), and mastering the grammatical structure of the language (syntactic development). By age 5 or 6 years, they have also learned a great deal about the appropriate uses of their language and have become relatively skilled conversationalists (pragmatic

TAXI/GETTY IMAGES

DAVE BARTRUFF / DAHITADELIMONT.COM

COURTESY OF KATE NURRE

RICHARD LORD / THE IMAGE WORKS

According to language theorist Noam Chomsky, all these children rely on the same innate linguistic structures in acquiring their various languages.

development). Theorists of language development have proposed widely varying accounts of this remarkable accomplishment. Although all agree that children acquire language as a result of the interaction between characteristics of the human brain and the language to which they are exposed, they differ sharply with respect to (1) the relative roles of nature and nurture in language development, (2) the degree to which language acquisition is supported by language-specific versus general-purpose cognitive abilities, and (3) the role of social interaction and communication in language development.

Nativist Views

From Plato and Kant to their modern intellectual descendants, nativists have argued that language is too complex to arise from experience alone, so there must be some preexisting, innate structures that enable young humans to acquire it. The most

a closer look

"I Just Can't Talk Without My Hands": What Gestures Tell Us About Language

Most people around the world spontaneously accompany their speech with gestures. The naturalness of gesturing is revealed by the fact that blind people gesture as they speak just as much as sighted individuals do, even when they know their listener is also blind (Iverson & Goldin-Meadow, 1998).

Gesturing starts early: infants often produce recognizable, meaningful gestures before they speak recognizable words. According to Linda Acredolo and Susan Goodwyn (1990), many "baby signs" are invented by children themselves. One participant in their research signed "alligator" by putting her hands together and opening and closing them to imitate snapping jaws; another indicated "dog" by sticking her tongue out as if panting; another signaled "flower" by sniffing. Infants apparently have the cognitive capacity for referring to objects, but they gain earlier motor control of their hands than of their vocal apparatus.

A relation between early gesturing and later vocabulary has recently been reported. In a longitudinal study conducted by Susan Goldin-Meadow and colleagues (Rowe, Ozcaliskan, & Goldin-Meadow, 2008), everyday interactions between 14-month-olds and their mothers were filmed in their own homes. Vocabulary testing of the same children 3 or 4 years later revealed a positive relation: the more the children had used gestures at 14 months, the larger their spoken vocabulary was at 42 months.

Especially dramatic evidence of intimate connections between gesture and language comes from remarkable research on children who have *created* their own gesture-based languages. Goldin-Meadow and colleagues (Feldman, Goldin-Meadow, & Gleitman, 1978; Goldin-Meadow, 2003; Goldin-Meadow & Mylander, 1998) studied congenitally deaf American and Chinese children whose hearing parents had little or no proficiency in any formal sign language. These children and their parents made up "home signs" in order to communicate with one another, but the children's gesture vocabulary quickly outstripped that of their parents.

More important, the children (but not the parents) *spontaneously* imposed a structure—a rudimentary grammar—on their gestures. Both groups of children used a grammatical structure that occurs in some languages but in neither the English nor Mandarin languages of their parents. As a result, the sign systems of the children were more similar to each other than to those of their own parents. The children's signs were also more complex than those of their parents. The tendency of deaf children to *spontaneously* systematize inconsistent input from others has been reported by other researchers as well (Singleton & Newport, 2004).

The most extensive and extraordinary example of language creation by children comes from the invention of Nicaraguan

SUSAN GOODWYN

This young participant in the research of Acredolo and Goodwyn is producing her idiosyncratic "baby sign" for pig.

influential modern version of this point of view was advanced by Noam Chomsky (1957, 1988), a linguist who argues that using a language requires knowledge of a set of highly abstract, unconscious rules. These rules, which Chomsky referred to as **universal grammar,** are common to all languages, and they are what makes it possible for people to learn particular languages. Children are assisted in acquiring their native language by their inborn knowledge of the general form that languages can take. Because of this inborn knowledge, children require only minimal input to trigger language development; simply hearing other people use language is enough to get it going. Chomsky contends that the communicative function of language has little to do with the fundamental nature of language or how it is acquired.

According to the nativist view, the cognitive abilities that support language development are highly specific to language. As Steven Pinker (1994) describes it, language is "a distinct piece of the biological makeup of our brains . . . distinct from more general abilities to process information or behave intelligently" (p. 18).

universal grammar a set of highly abstract, unconscious rules that are common to all languages

6.3

Sign Language (NSL), a completely new language that has been evolving over the past 30 years. In 1979, a large-scale education program for the deaf was begun in the Central American nation of Nicaragua (Senghas & Coppola, 2001). The program brought hundreds of deaf children together in two schools in the city of Managua. For most of the children, it was their first exposure to other deaf youngsters.

The teachers in the school knew no formal sign language, nor did the children, who had only the simple home signs they had used to communicate with their families. The children quickly began to build on one another's existing informal signs, constructing a "pidgin" sign language—a relatively crude, limited communication system. The language was used by the students, both in and outside school, and was learned by each new group of children who entered the community.

SUSAN MEISELAS / MAGNUM PHOTOS, INC.

Nicaraguan deaf children signing together in the language invented in their school.

The impact of having a language was life-altering for these youngsters: Anselmo, a young man who was 7 years old when he first began attending one of the schools, summed up the transformative effect that acquiring a functional language had on his life: "I can remember my childhood, but I can also remember not having any way to communicate. Then my mind was just a blank" (quoted in Osborne, 1999, p. 89).

What happened next was astonishing. As younger students entered the schools, they rapidly mastered the rudimentary system used by the older students and then gradually transformed it into a complex, fully consistent language (NSL) with its own grammar. The most fluent signers in the NSL community were the youngest children, both because NSL had evolved into a real language and because they had acquired it at an earlier age.

These reports of language invention by deaf children are not just fascinating stories: they are also of great theoretical significance. They suggest that "language is so resilient that it can be triggered by exposure to linguistic input that is highly limited and fragmented—an indication of the fundamental innateness of grammar" (Siegal, 2004). The fact that children go beyond the linguistic input they receive, spontaneously refining and systematizing their language, offers support for nativist claims of innate grammatical knowledge that guides language acquisition.

This claim is taken one step further by the **modularity hypothesis,** which proposes that the human brain contains an innate, self-contained language module that is separate from other aspects of cognitive functioning (Fodor, 1983). The idea of specialized mental modules is not limited to language. As you learned in Chapter 4 and will see again in Chapter 7, innate, special-purpose modules have been proposed to underlie a variety of functions, including perception, spatial skills, and social understanding.

Nativist views of language development are supported by the fact that virtually all children exposed to full-fledged language acquire it and by the fact that no other animals do. Demonstrations of critical periods for language development, as well as specific links between brain structures and language abilities, are generally taken as supportive of the nativist position. Probably the strongest support for the idea that children come equipped with some fundamental knowledge of linguistic rules is the research reviewed in Box 6.3 on the *invention* of sign languages by

modularity hypothesis the idea that the human brain contains an innate, self-contained language module that is separate from other aspects of cognitive functioning groups of deaf children with no linguistic input from adults. The fact that these children spontaneously imposed grammatical structure onto their simple sign systems suggests preexisting structural knowledge, especially because aspects of the grammatical system that some of these children invented match that of existing spoken languages.

Nativist views have been criticized for many things, especially for the idea of a universal grammar common to all languages, as well as for the idea that language acquisition is supported by special language-specific mechanisms (Maratsos, 1998; Slobin, 1985). They have also been criticized for focusing almost exclusively on syntactic development while ignoring the importance of the communicative role of language.

Interactionist Views

Interactionist views maintain that virtually everything about language development is influenced by its communicative function. To begin with, children are motivated to interact with others, to communicate their own thoughts and feelings, and to understand what other people are trying to communicate to them (Bloom, 1991; Bloom & Tinker, 2001; Snow, 1999). According to this position, children gradually discover the underlying regularities in language and its use by paying close attention to the multitude of clues available in the language they hear and the social context in which language is used. In a strong version of this general view, Michael Tomasello (2008) argues that language is basically a social skill. The formal structural properties of language that Chomsky believed to be innate are instead mastered in the process of interacting with other people. Language itself is properly thought of as a set of social conventions that enable people to communicate.

Interactionist theories are supported by the basic fact that the main (although not the only) purpose to which infants and young children apply their steadily increasing language skills is communicating with other people. The rapidly accumulating evidence of the remarkable sensitivity of infants and young children to a host of pragmatic cues and their ability to use even quite subtle aspects of the social context to interpret utterances are also consistent with this view. Evidence that undermines the claim for language-specific learning mechanisms supports this position. This includes the fact that the categorical perception of speech sounds discussed earlier has been documented for several different languages, as well as the fact that infants and young children initially accept nonverbal sounds or gestures as labels for objects just as readily as they accept speech sounds.

Critics of the interactionist position contend that even the most diligent attention to language and its accompanying behavior could never reveal the complex, abstract grammatical principles emphasized by Chomsky and other nativists. In this regard, they note that the very impressive demonstrations of infants' and young children's sensitivity to pragmatic cues cited by interactionists have involved semantic (word-learning) development rather than what they see as the more challenging problem of syntactic development.

Connectionist Views

At the opposite end of the theoretical continuum from the nativist view of language development are connectionist theories (e.g., Bates & Elman, 1993). These theories maintain that language development is based not on innate linguistic knowledge or language-specific abilities but on general-purpose learning mechanisms. **Connectionism** is a type of information-processing theory that emphasizes the simultaneous activity of numerous interconnected processing units. Connectionist researchers have developed computer simulations of various aspects of cognitive development, including language acquisition. These programs learn from experience, gradually strengthening certain connections among units in ways that mimic children's developmental progress.

The connectionist view of language development is consistent with the speech-perception research described earlier, documenting young infants' impressive ability to analyze and identify structural features of the language they hear. It is also consistent with statistical-learning accounts of language learning. A good example of the connectionist approach to language development is its account of overregulation errors.

This account is based on computer models of neural networks that have the capacity to modify themselves as a result of input. The model network is provided with a large body of language input similar to what children are exposed to in order to see if the network eventually produces output that simulates the speech of real children.

One of the most successful models focuses on the acquisition of the past tense in English. From input of large numbers of sentences with regular and irregular verbs, neural-network models can learn to form the past tense correctly. Of particular importance is the fact that, in the process, the models make the same kinds of overregularization errors that children make (Rumelhart & McClelland, 1986). Thus, with little built-in (innate) grammatical knowledge and no language-specific learning mechanisms, these models can learn from experience, sometimes displaying patterns of acquisition that are surprisingly similar to those of young children.

Although connectionist accounts have achieved impressive success with respect to modeling a few specific aspects of language development, such as the past tense in English, most aspects of language acquisition have yet to be modeled. In addition, connectionist models are always open to criticism regarding the features that were built into the models in the first place and how well the input provided to them matches the input from which children induce the structure of their language.

review:

The process of comprehending and producing language, whether spoken or signed, involves the development of many different kinds of knowledge and skills. In the space of a few years, children take giant steps in mastering the phonology, semantics, syntax, and pragmatics of their native language. This remarkable achievement is made possible by the joint prerequisites of a human brain and exposure to human communication.

The current theoretical accounts of language development differ with respect to how much emphasis they put on nature and nurture. Nativists like Chomsky and Pinker emphasize innate linguistic knowledge and language-specific learning mechanisms, whereas connectionists argue that language learning can emerge from general-purpose learning mechanisms. Interactionists place particular emphasis on the communicative function of language and children's motivation to understand and interact with other people. The vast literature on language development provides some support for all of these views, but none of them provide the full story of children's acquisition of the "jewel in the crown of cognition."

connectionism a type of information-processing approach that emphasizes the simultaneous activity of numerous interconnected processing units

dual representation the idea that a symbolic artifact must be represented mentally in two ways at the same time—both as a real object and as a symbol for something other than itself

Nonlinguistic Symbols and Development

Although language is our preeminent symbol system, humans have invented a wealth of other kinds of symbols to communicate with one another. Virtually anything can serve as a nonlinguistic symbol so long as someone intends it to stand for something other than itself (DeLoache, 2002, 2004). The list of symbols you regularly encounter is long and varied, ranging from the printed words, numbers, graphs, photographs, and drawings in your textbooks to thousands of everyday items such as TV, movies, computer icons, maps, clocks, and so on. Because symbols are so central to our everyday lives, mastering the various symbol systems important in their culture is a crucial developmental task for all children.

Symbolic proficiency involves both the mastery of the symbolic creations of others and the creation of new symbolic representations. We will first discuss early symbolic functioning, starting with research on very young children's ability to exploit the informational content of symbolic artifacts. Then we will focus on children's creation of symbols through drawing. In Chapter 7, we will consider children's creation of symbolic relations in pretend play, and in Chapter 8, we will examine older children's development of two of the most important of all symbolic activities—reading and mathematics.

Using Symbols as Information

One of the vital functions of many symbols is that they provide useful information. For example, a map—whether a crude pencil sketch on the back of an envelope or a multicolor map in an expensive world atlas—can be crucial for locating a particular place. To use a symbolic artifact such as a map requires **dual representation;** that is, the artifact must be represented mentally in two ways at the same time, as a real object and as a symbol for something other than itself (DeLoache, 2002, 2004).

Very young children can have substantial difficulty with dual representation, limiting their ability to use information from symbolic artifacts (DeLoache, 2004). This has been demonstrated by research in which a young child watches as an experimenter hides a miniature toy in a scale model of the regular-size room next door (Figure 6.16) (DeLoache, 1987). The child is then asked to find a larger version of the toy that the child is told "is hiding in the same place in the big room." Three-year-olds readily use their knowledge of the location of the miniature toy in the model to figure out where the large toy is in the adjacent room. In contrast, most 2½-year-old children fail to find the large toy; they seem to have no idea that the model tells them anything about the room. Because the model is so salient and interesting as a three-dimensional object, very young children have trouble

ALL: COURTESY OF JUDY DELOACHE

FIGURE 6.16 Scale-model task In a test of young children's ability to use a symbol as a source of information, a 3-year-old child watches as the experimenter (Judy DeLoache) hides a miniature troll doll under a pillow in a scale model of an adjacent room. The child searches successfully for a larger troll doll hidden in the corresponding place in the actual room, indicating that she appreciates the relation between the model and room. The child also successfully retrieves the small toy she originally observed being hidden in the model.

managing dual representation and fail to notice the symbolic relation between the model and the room it stands for.

This interpretation received strong support in a study with 2½-year-old children in which reasoning between a model and a larger space was not necessary (DeLoache, Miller, & Rosengren, 1997). An experimenter showed each child a "shrinking machine" (really an oscilloscope with lots of dials and lights) and explained that the machine could "make things get little." The child watched as a troll doll was hidden in a movable tentlike room (approximately 8 feet by 6 feet) and the shrinking machine was "turned on." Then the child and experimenter waited in another room while the shrinking machine did its job. When they returned, a small scale model of the tentlike room stood in place of the original. (Assistants had, of course, removed the original tent and replaced it with the scale model.) When asked to find the troll, the children succeeded.

Why should the idea of a shrinking machine enable these 2½-year-olds to do better? The answer is that if a child believes the experimenter's claims about the shrinking machine, then in the child's mind the model simply *is* the room. Hence, there is no symbolic relation between the two spaces and no need for dual representation.

The difficulty that young children have with dual representation and symbols is evident in other contexts as well. For example, investigators often use anatomically detailed dolls to interview young children in cases of suspected sexual abuse, assuming that the relation between the doll and themselves would be obvious. However, children younger than 5 years of age often fail to make any self–doll connection, so the use of a doll does not improve their memory reports and may even make them less reliable (Bruck, Ceci, Francoeur, & Renick, 1995; DeLoache & Marzolf, 1995; Goodman & Aman, 1990).

Increasing ability to achieve dual representation—to immediately interpret a symbol in terms of what it stands for—enables children to discover the abstract nature of various symbolic artifacts. For example, unlike younger children, school-age children realize that the red line on a road map does not mean that the real road would be red (Liben & Myers, 2007). Older children are also able, when properly instructed, to use objects such as rods and blocks of different sizes that represent different numerical quantities to help them learn to do mathematical operations (Uttal, Liu, & DeLoache, 2006).

Drawing

Drawing pictures is a common symbolic activity that parents in many societies encourage their children to undertake (Goodnow, 1977). When young children first start making marks on paper, their focus is almost exclusively on the activity per se, with no attempt to produce recognizable images. At around 3 or 4 years or age, most children begin trying to draw pictures *of* something; they try to produce representational art.

Initially, children's artistic impulses outstrip their motor and planning capabilities (Yamagata, 1997). Figure 6.17 shows what at first appears simply to be a classic scribble. However, the 2½-year-old

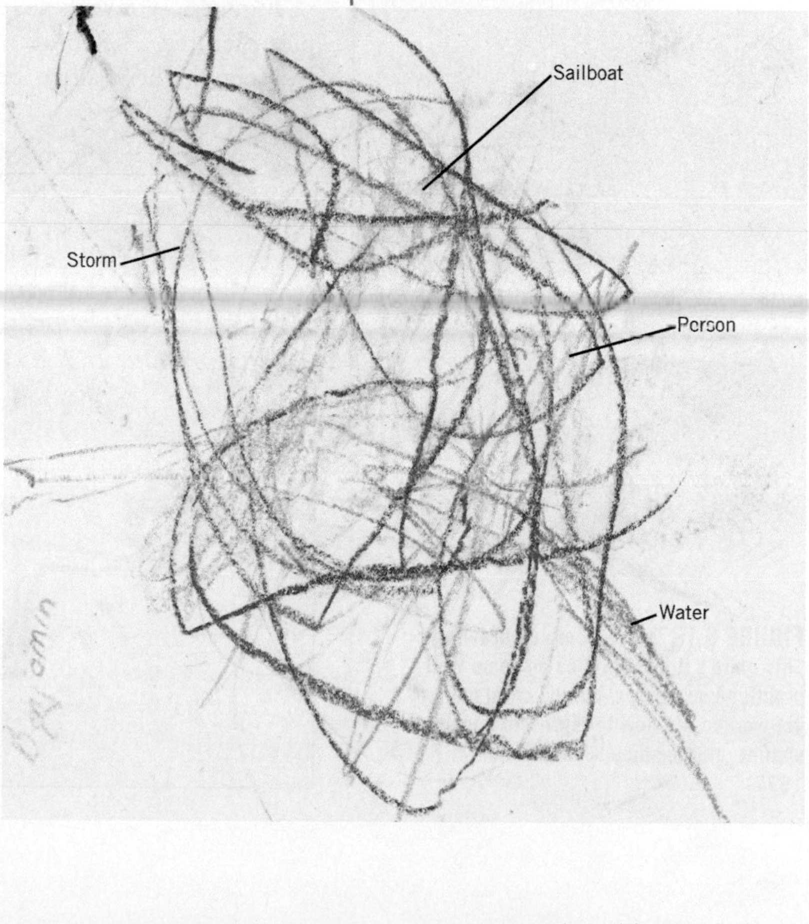

FIGURE 6.17 Early drawing Appearances to the contrary, this is not random scribbling, as shown by what the 2½-year-old who produced it said about his work. As he drew a roughly triangular shape, he said it was a "sailboat." A set of wavy lines was labeled "water." Some scribbled lines under the "sailboat" were denoted as the "person driving the boat." Finally, the wild scribbles all over the rest were "a storm." Thus, each element was representational to some degree, even though the picture as a whole was not.

COURTESY OF JUDY DELOACHE

FIGURE 6.18 Tadpole drawings Young children's early drawings of people typically take a "tadpole" form. (From Goodnow, 1977)

creator of this picture was narrating his efforts as he drew, and a recording of what he said makes it clear that he represented each of the individual elements of his picture reasonably well but was unable to coordinate them spatially on the paper.

The most common subject for young children is the human figure (Goodnow, 1977). Just as infants who are first beginning to speak simplify the words they produce, young children simplify their drawings, as shown in Figure 6.18. Note that to produce these very simple, crude shapes, the child must plan the drawing and must spatially coordinate the individual elements. Even early "tadpole" people have the legs on the bottom and the arms on the side—although often emerging from the head. Gradually, additional elements are incorporated, typically starting with a body drawn beneath the circle that now represents only a head.

Figure 6.19 reveals some of the strategies children use to produce more complex pictures. The child in this case has drawn a picture that includes his home, his school, the road in between them, and four other homes along the road.

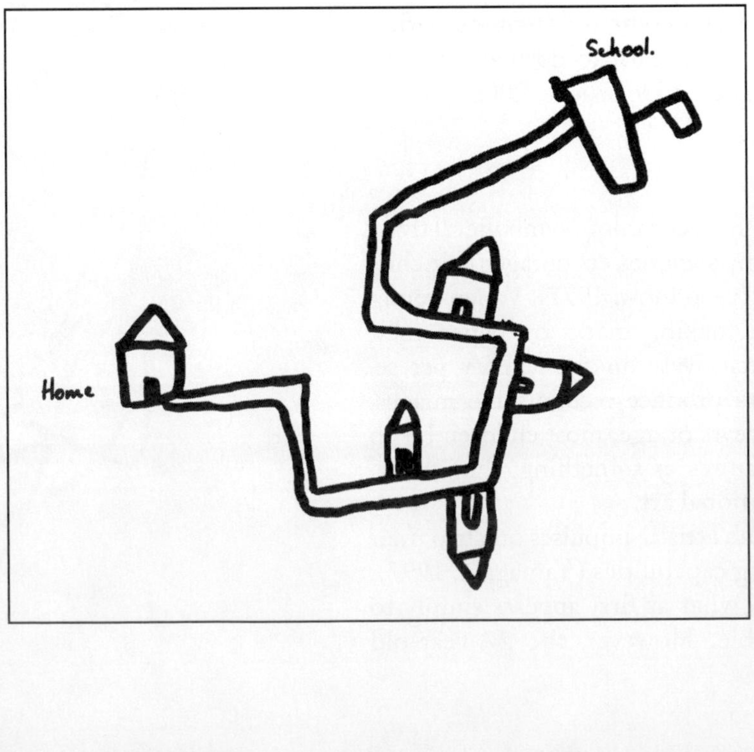

FIGURE 6.19 More complex drawings This child's drawing relies on some well-practiced strategies, but the child has not yet worked out how to represent complex spatial relationships. (From Goodnow, 1977)

One strategy he used was to rely on a well-practiced formula for representing houses: a pentagon with a door and roof line. Another was to coordinate the placement of each house with respect to the road, although at the cost of the overall coordination among the houses. Eventually, some children become highly skilled at representing the relations among the multiple elements in their pictures.

A particularly interesting case of early talent for drawing is Nadia, an autistic child with extraordinary drawing ability who drew the horse and rider in Figure 6.20(a) at the age of 4. Her talent declined dramatically with age (see the second horse in Figure 6.20(b).) Researchers have been particularly interested in autistic individuals who, like Nadia, have exceptional artistic abilities (Selfe, 1995), in part because of the relevance of these rare cases to the modularity hypothesis introduced earlier. Such extraordinary drawing talent amid a range of severe cognitive and (see page 93) is suggestive of an encapsulated ability that is unaffected by general intellectual and other deficits. These cases provide only modest support for the modularity hypothesis, however, because the drawing skill they involve may also arise from the obsessive attention to detail that is common to autism.

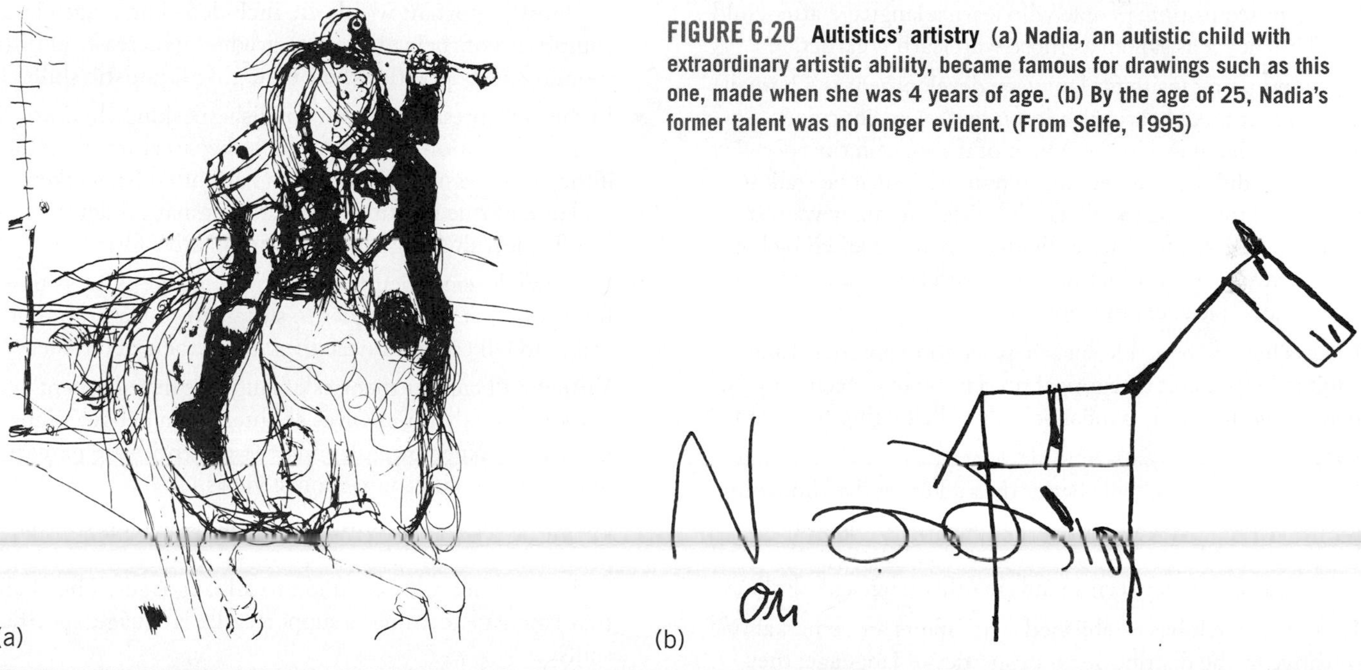

(a) (b)

FIGURE 6.20 Autistics' artistry (a) Nadia, an autistic child with extraordinary artistic ability, became famous for drawings such as this one, made when she was 4 years of age. (b) By the age of 25, Nadia's former talent was no longer evident. (From Selfe, 1995)

review:

Nonlinguistic symbols play an important role in the lives of young children. As they become increasingly sensitive to the informational potential of symbolic objects created by others, children make an important step toward skillful use of the many symbol systems that are key to modern life. A critical factor in understanding and using the symbols created by others is dual representation—the ability to mentally represent both a symbolic object, such as a map or model, and its relation to what it stands for. The ability to *create* symbols is evident in young children's drawings.

Chapter Summary

A critical feature of what it means to be human is the creative and flexible use of a variety of language and other symbols. The enormous power of language comes from generativity—the fact that a finite set of words can be used to generate an infinite number of sentences.

Language Development

- Acquiring a language involves learning the complex system of phonological, semantic, syntactic, and pragmatic rules that govern the sounds, meaning, grammatical structure, and use of the language. The only exception is that sign languages employ gestures rather than sounds as elementary units.
- Language ability is species-specific. The first prerequisite for its full-fledged development is a human brain, areas of which are specialized for the comprehension and production of language. Researchers have succeeded in teaching nonhuman primates remarkable symbolic skills but not full-fledged language.
- The first few years of human life constitute a critical period for language acquisition; people who learn a language after childhood are never as skilled as those who learn it earlier.
- A second prerequisite for language development is a human environment. All hearing children receive an enormous amount of language input. Much of it comes in the special way in which adults and older children in most societies talk to babies. Infant-directed talk (IDT) differs in many ways from speech addressed to older individuals, being marked by higher pitch; extremes in intonation; warm, affectionate tone; and exaggerated facial expressions.
- Infants have remarkable speech-perception abilities. Like adults, they exhibit categorical perception of speech sounds, perceiving physically similar sounds as belonging to discrete categories.
- Young infants are actually better than adults at discriminating between speech sounds not in their native language. As they learn the sounds that are important in that language, their ability to distinguish between sounds in other languages declines.
- Recent research has established that infants are remarkably sensitive to the distributional properties of language; they notice a variety of subtle regularities in the speech they hear and use these regularities to pick out words from the passing stream of speech.
- From their first months, babies are preparing for speech production by making a variety of sounds, steadily gaining motor control over these vocalizations. Infants begin to babble at around 7 months of age. Hearing infants produce sounds like "bababa"; and some deaf infants who are exposed to sign language produce hand movements with the same sort of repetitive pattern. Gradually, vocal babbling begins to sound more like the baby's native language.
- The second half of an infant's first year is also characterized by learning how to interact and communicate with other people, including the ability to establish joint attention with another person by following the direction of that person's gaze or pointing to direct someone else's attention so a topic can be shared.
- Word recognition (associating highly familiar words with their referents) begins to emerge at about 6 months of age.
- The production of recognizable words begins at around 1 year of age. In the holophrastic period, young children say only one word at a time. With their severely limited vocabularies, they often make overextension errors, using a particular word in a broader context than is appropriate.
- At around 18 months of age, a "vocabulary explosion" occurs, as children start learning new words at a very rapid pace. Aided by adults or by their own efforts, they rely on a variety of assumptions and strategies to figure out what new words mean.
- By the end of their second year, most infants produce short sentences, often described as telegraphic speech because only the most important words are included. The length and complexity of their utterances gradually increase, and they spontaneously practice their emerging linguistic skills.
- In the early preschool years, English-speaking children make overregularization errors, in which they treat irregular forms as if they were regular. These errors have often been taken as evidence of rule learning. Further grammatical development involves learning negative and interrogative forms.
- Children develop their burgeoning language skills as they go from collective monologues to sustained conversation—the ability to tell coherent narratives about their experiences.
- Virtually all current theories of language development acknowledge that it involves an interaction between innate factors and experience. Among these theories are nativist, interactionist, and connectionist views.
- Nativists, such as the influential linguist Noam Chomsky, posit innate knowledge of "universal grammar," the set of highly abstract rules common to all languages. They believe that language learning is supported by language-specific skills.
- Interactionist theorists emphasize the communicative context of language development and use. They emphasize the impressive degree to which infants and young children exploit a host of pragmatic cues to figure out what others are saying.
- Connectionists fall at the other end of the theoretical continuum from nativists, arguing that language can develop in the absence of innate knowledge and that language learning requires only powerful general-purpose cognitive mechanisms—that is, that such learning occurs as a result of gradual strengthening of connections in the neural network.

Nonlinguistic Symbols and Development

- Symbolic artifacts like maps or models require dual representation. To use them, children must represent mentally both the object itself as well as its symbolic relation to what it stands for. Toddlers become increasingly skillful at achieving dual representation and using symbolic artifacts as a source of information.
- Drawing is a symbolic activity commonly engaged in by children and encouraged by adults. Young children's early scribbling quickly gives way to the intention to draw pictures *of* something, with a favorite theme being representations of the human figure.
- Developmentalists are interested in the rare cases of autistic children with remarkable artistic skill, in part because of the relevance of these children's isolated skills to the modularity hypothesis. Such skill, however, may also arise from the obsession with detail observed in many autistic individuals.

Critical Thinking Questions

1. Drawing on the many references to parental behaviors relevant to language development that were discussed in this chapter, give some examples of ways parents are known to influence their children's language development.
2. Language development is a particularly complex aspect of child development, and no single theory accounts successfully for all that is known about how children acquire language. Which of the three theoretical views that were presented seem to you to do the best job of explaining what you learned about language development in this chapter?
3. What are overregularization errors, and why do they offer strong evidence for the acquisition of grammatical *rules* by children?
4. Many parallels were drawn between the process of language acquisition in children learning spoken language and in those learning signed language. What do these similarities tell us about the basis for human language?

Key Terms

symbols, p. 216
language comprehension, p. 217
language production, p. 217
generativity, p. 217
phonemes, p. 218
phonological development, p. 218
morphemes, p. 218
semantic development, p. 218
syntax, p. 218
syntactic development, p. 218
pragmatic development, p. 218
metalinguistic knowledge, p. 219
critical period for language, p. 221
infant-directed talk (IDT), p. 223
bilingualism, p. 224
prosody, p. 226
categorical perception, p. 226
voice onset time (VOT), p. 226
distributional properties, p. 229
reference, p. 232
style, p. 234
referential (analytic) style, p. 234
expressive (holistic) style, p. 234
wait-and-see style, p. 234
holophrastic period, p. 236
overextension, p. 236
fast mapping, p. 237
pragmatic cues, p. 239
syntactic bootstrapping, p. 240
telegraphic, p. 241
overregularization, p. 243
collective monologues, p. 244
narratives, p. 245
universal grammar, p. 248
modularity hypothesis, p. 249
connectionism, p. 251
dual representation, p. 252

JOHN GEORGE BROWN (1813–1913), *The Little Joker*

7

Conceptual Development

THEMES

Nature and Nurture

❖

The Active Child

❖

Mechanisms of Change

❖

The Sociocultural Context

❖

Shawna, an 8-month-old, crawls into her 7-year-old brother's bedroom. The room contains many objects: a bed, a dresser, a dog, a baseball, a baseball mitt, books, magazines, shoes, dirty socks, and so on. To her older brother, the room includes furniture, clothing, reading material, and sports equipment. But what does the room look like to Shawna? Infants lack concepts of furniture, reading material, and sports equipment, and also lack more specific, relevant concepts such as baseball mitts and books. Thus, Shawna would not understand the scene in the same way that her older brother would. However, without knowledge of child development research, it would be difficult to anticipate whether a baby as young as Shawna would have formed other concepts relevant to understanding the scene. Would she have formed concepts of living and nonliving things that would help her understand why the dog runs around on its own but the books never do? Would she have formed concepts of heavier and lighter that would allow her to understand why she could pick up a sock but not a dresser? Would she have formed concepts of before and after that would allow her to understand that her brother always puts on his socks before his shoes rather than in the opposite order? Or would it all be a jumble?

As this imaginary scene indicates, concepts are crucial for helping people make sense of the world. But what exactly are concepts, and how do they help us understand?

Concepts are general ideas that organize objects, events, qualities, or relations on the basis of some similarity. There are an infinite number of possible concepts, because there are infinite ways in which objects or events can be similar. For example, objects can have similar shapes (e.g., all football fields are rectangular), materials (e.g., all diamonds are made of compressed carbon), sizes (e.g., all giants are large), tastes (e.g., all candies are sweet), colors (e.g., all colas are brown), functions (e.g., all knives are for cutting), and so on.

Concepts help us understand the world and act effectively in it by allowing us to generalize from prior experience. If we like the taste of one carrot, we probably will like the taste of others. Concepts also tell us how to react emotionally to new experiences, as when we fear all dogs after being bitten by one. Life without concepts would be unthinkable; every situation would be new, and we would have no idea what past experience was relevant in the new situation.

As you will see in this chapter, several themes have been especially prominent in research on conceptual development. One is *nature and nurture:* children's concepts reflect the interaction between their specific experiences and their biological predispositions to process information in particular ways. Another recurring theme is the *active child:* from infancy onward, many of children's concepts reflect their active attempts to make sense of the world. A third major theme is *how change occurs*: researchers who study conceptual development attempt to understand not only what concepts children form but also the processes by which they form them.

Although there is widespread agreement that conceptual development reflects the interaction of nature and nurture, the particulars of this interaction are hotly debated. The controversy parallels the nativist/empiricist controversies described previously in the context of perceptual development (page 182) and language development (pages 246–250). Nativists, such as Liz Spelke (Spelke & Kinzler, in press), Alan Leslie (Scholl & Leslie, 2002), and Karen Wynn (2007) believe that innate understanding of basic concepts plays a central role in development. They argue that infants are born with some sense of fundamental concepts such as time,

concepts general ideas or understandings that can be used to group together objects, events, qualities, or abstractions that are similar in some way space, causality, number, and the human mind, or with specialized learning mechanisms that allow them to acquire rudimentary understanding of these concepts unusually quickly and easily. Within the nativist perspective, nurture is important to children's developing the concepts beyond this initial level, but not for forming the initial understanding.

In contrast, empiricists, such as Scott Johnson (2010), Les Cohen (Cohen & Cashon, 2006), David Rakison (Rakison & Lupyan, 2008), and Marianella Casasola (2010) argue that nature endows infants with only general learning mechanisms, such as the ability to perceive, associate, generalize, and remember. Within the empiricist perspective, the rapid and universal formation of fundamental concepts such as time, space, causality, number, and mind arises from infants' massive exposure to experiences that are relevant to these concepts. Empiricists also maintain that the data on which many nativist arguments are based—data involving infants' looking times in habituation-dishabituation studies—are not sufficient to support the nativists' conclusions that infants understand the concepts in question (Campos et al., 2008; Kagan, 2008). The continuing debate between nativists and empiricists reflects a fundamental, unresolved question about human nature: Do children form all concepts through the same learning mechanisms, or do they also possess special mechanisms for forming a few particularly important concepts?

KENNETH GARRETT / WOODFIN CAMP & ASSOCIATES

What does this infant see when he looks at this room?

The focus of this chapter is on the development of fundamental concepts, the ones that are useful in the greatest number of situations. These concepts fall into two groups. One group of fundamental concepts is used to categorize the kinds of things that exist in the world: people, living things in general, and inanimate objects. The other group of fundamental concepts are dimensions used to represent our experiences: space (where the experience occurred), time (when it occurred), causality (why it occurred), and number (how many times it occurred).

You may have noticed that these fundamental concepts correspond closely to the questions that every news story must answer: Who or what? Where? When? Why? How many? The similarity between the concepts that are most fundamental for children and those that are most important in newspaper stories is no accident. Knowing who or what, where, when, why, and how many is essential for understanding any event.

Because early conceptual development is so crucial, this chapter focuses on development in the first five years. This obviously does not mean that conceptual growth ends at age 5. Beyond this age, children form vast numbers of additional, more-specialized concepts, and understanding of all types of concepts deepens for many years thereafter. Rather, the focus on early conceptual development reflects the fact that this is the period in which children acquire a basic understanding of the most crucial concepts, the ones that are universal across societies, that allow children to understand their own and other people's experiences, and that provide the foundations for subsequent conceptual growth.

Understanding Who or What

To even begin to understand the objects that they encounter, children must answer two key questions: What kinds of things are there in the world? And how are these things related to each other? Dividing the objects they encounter into categories helps children answer both questions.

Dividing Objects into Categories

Beginning early in development, children attempt to understand what kinds of things there are in the world. They start by dividing the objects they perceive into the three most general categories shown at the top of Table 7.1: inanimate objects, people, and other living things (Wellman & Gelman, 1998). Forming these broad divisions is crucial, because different types of concepts apply to different types of objects (Keil, 1979). Some concepts apply to anything—all things, both living and nonliving, have heights, weights, colors, sizes, and so on. Other concepts apply only to living things—only living things eat, drink, grow, and breathe, for example. Yet other concepts—reading, shopping, pondering, and talking—apply to people. These distinctions among the three most general categories are important because they help children make accurate inferences about unfamiliar objects. When told that a platypus is a kind of animal, children know immediately that a platypus can move, eat, grow, reproduce, and so on. The importance of these distinctions also is evidenced by their being the subject of different academic fields: people are the focus of psychology, sociology, and anthropology (among other disciplines); plants and animals are the focus of biology, physiology, and anatomy; and objects are the focus of physics, computer science, and engineering.

The columns within Table 7.1 illustrate a major means by which categorization helps children solve the question of how things in the world are related to each other. Children form **category hierarchies,** that is, categories related by set–subset relations. The furniture/chair/La-Z-Boy example shown in the table is one example. The category "furniture" includes all chairs; the category "chair" includes all La-Z-Boys. Forming such category hierarchies greatly simplifies the world for children by allowing them to draw accurate inferences. If children are told that a La-Z-Boy is a kind of chair, they can use their general knowledge of chairs to infer that people sit on La-Z-Boys and that La-Z-Boys are neither lazy nor boys.

Of course, infants are not born knowing about La-Z-Boys and chairs, nor are they born knowledgeable about the other categories shown in Table 7.1. Thus, one important question is: How do children form categories that apply to all kinds of objects, living and nonliving?

Categorization of Objects in Infancy

Even in the first months of life, infants form categories of objects. Quinn and Eimas (1996), for example, found that as 3- and 4-month-olds were shown a series

TABLE 7.1

Object Hierarchies

Level	Type of Object		
Most General	Inanimate Objects	People	Living Things
General	Furniture, Vehicles . . .	Europeans, Asians . . .	Animals, Plants . . .
Medium	Chairs, Tables . . .	Spaniards, Finns . . .	Cats, Dogs . . .
Specific	La-Z-Boys, Armchairs . . .	Picasso, Cervantes . . .	Lions, Lynxes . . .

category hierarchy categories that are related by set–subset relations, such as animal/dog/poodle of photographs of different cats, they habituated; that is, they looked at new cat photographs for less and less time (Figure 7.1). However, when the infants were subsequently shown a picture of a dog, lion, or other animal, they dishabituated; that is, their looking time increased. Their habituation to the cat photographs suggests that the infants saw all the cats, despite their differences, as members of a single category; their subsequent dishabituation to the photo of the dog or other animal suggests that the infants saw those creatures as members of different categories than the cats. Moreover, 6-month olds displayed similar brain activity when shown sets of pictures of both familiar and unfamiliar cats, whereas their brain activity in response to pictures of unfamiliar dogs differed from that to both sets of cats (Quinn, Westerlund, & Nelson, 2006).

perceptual categorization the grouping together of objects with similar appearances

Infants also can form categories more general than "cats." Behl-Chadha (1996) found that 6-month-olds habituated after repeatedly being shown pictures of different types of mammals (dogs, zebras, elephants, etc.) and then dishabituated when they were shown a picture of a bird or a fish. The infants apparently perceived similarities among the mammals that led to their eventually losing interest in them. The infants also apparently perceived differences between the mammals and the bird or fish that led them to show renewed interest.

As suggested by this example, a key element in infants' categorization abilities is **perceptual categorization,** the grouping together of objects that have similar appearances (Cohen & Cashon, 2006; Madole & Oakes, 1999). Prior to participating in the Behl-Chadha (1996) study, few infants, if any, would have had experience with zebras or elephants. Thus, the distinctions the infants made between these mammals and the birds and fish could only have been based on a perception of the animals' differing appearances.

Infants categorize objects along many perceptual dimensions, including color, size, and movement. Often their categorization is largely based on specific parts of an object rather than on the object as a whole; for example, infants younger than 18 months of age rely heavily on the presence of legs to categorize objects as animals, and they rely heavily on the presence of wheels to categorize objects as vehicles (Rakison & Lupyan, 2008; Rakison & Poulin-Dubois, 2001).

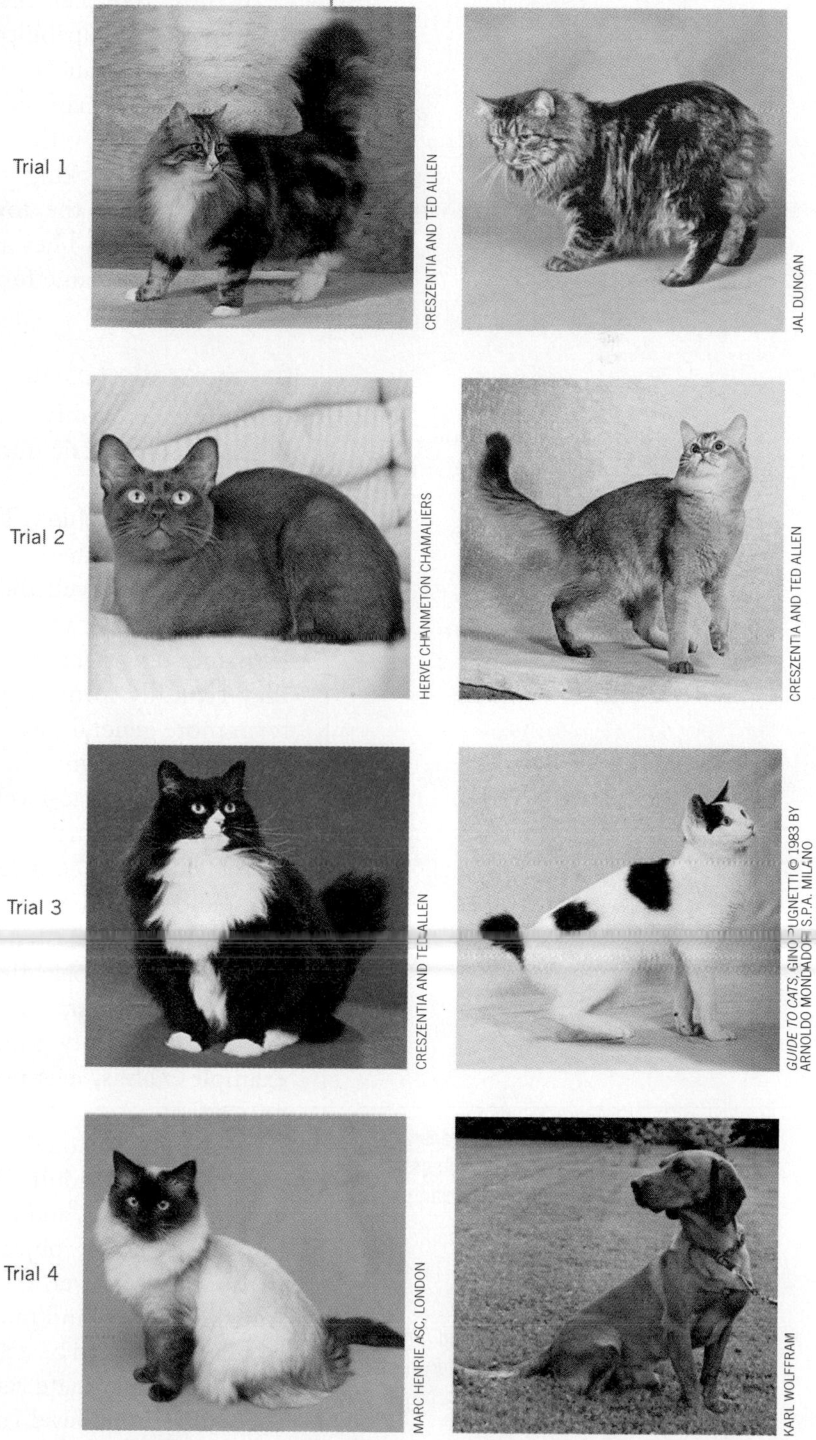

FIGURE 7.1 Infant categorization These photos were used by Quinn and Eimas (1996) to study infant categorization. In their experiment, 3- and 4-month-olds were repeatedly shown photos of pairs of cats that looked quite different from each other (Trials 1–3). After the infants habituated to the cat photos, presentation of a photo of a cat and another animal (Trial 4) led them to look longer at the other animal. Thus, despite lacking knowledge of cats and other animals, infants form categories that allow them to discriminate between members of the category and members of related but different categories.

As children approach their 2nd birthday, they increasingly categorize objects on the basis of overall shape. As discussed in Chapter 6, when toddlers are shown an unfamiliar object and told that it is a "dax," they assume that other objects of the same shape are also "daxes," even when the objects differ from each other in size, texture, and color (Landau, Smith, & Jones, 1998). This is a useful assumption, because for many objects, shape indeed is similar for different members of a category. If we see a silhouette of a cat, hammer, or chair, we can tell from the shape what the object is. However, we rarely can do the same if we know only the object's color or size or texture.

By the end of their first year, infants also form categories on the basis of objects' functions. This capability was evident in a study in which 9- and 10-month-olds were shown castanets that produced clacking sounds when they were squeezed (Baldwin, Markman, & Mellartin, 1993). When the babies were later given a similar-looking toy, they squeezed it in an apparent effort to reproduce the sound. If the similar-looking toy did not make the sound, the infants persisted in squeezing it. (If the toy they were given did not resemble the original, they didn't squeeze it.) They apparently expected that a toy that looked like the original would serve the same function, in this case making the same interesting noise.

Categorization of Objects Beyond Infancy

As children move beyond infancy, they increasingly grasp not only individual categories but also hierarchical and causal relations among categories.

Category hierarchies The category hierarchies that young children form often include three of the main levels in Table 7.1: the general one, which is called the **superordinate level;** the very specific one, called the **subordinate level;** and the medium or in-between one, called the **basic level** (Rosch, Mervis, et al., 1976). As its name suggests, the basic level is the one that children usually learn first. Thus, they typically form categories of medium generality, such as "tree," before they form more general categories such as "plant" or more specific ones such as "oak."

The reasons why children generally form the basic level first are not hard to understand. A basic-level category such as "tree" has a number of consistent characteristics: bark, branches, large size, and so on. In contrast, the more general category "plant" has fewer consistent characteristics: plants come in a wide range of shapes, sizes, and colors (consider an oak, a rose, and grass). Subordinate-level categories have the same consistent characteristics as the basic-level category, and some additional ones—all oaks, but not all trees, have rough bark and pointed leaves, for example. However, it is relatively difficult to discriminate among different subordinate categories within the same basic-level category (oaks versus maples, for example). Thus, it is not surprising that children tend to form basic-level categories first.

It should be noted that very young children's basic categories do not always match those of adults. For example, rather than forming separate categories of cars, motorcycles, and buses, young children seem to group these objects together into a category of "objects with wheels" (Mandler & McDonough, 1998). Even in such cases, however, the initial categories are less general than such categories as "moving things" and more general than ones such as "Toyotas."

Having formed basic-level categories, how do children go on to form superordinate and subordinate categories? Part of the answer is that parents and others use the child's basic-level categories as a foundation for explaining the more specific

superordinate level the most general level within a category hierarchy, such as "animal" in the animal/dog/poodle example

subordinate level the most specific level within a category hierarchy, such as "poodle" in the animal/dog/poodle example

basic level the middle level, and often the first level learned, within a category hierarchy, such as "dog" in the animal/dog/poodle example and more general categories (Gelman, Coley, Rosengren, Hartman, & Pappas, 1998). When parents teach children superordinate categories such as mammals, they typically illustrate the relevant terms with basic-level examples that the child already knows (Callanan, 1990). They might say, "Mammals are animals, like foxes, bears, and cows, that get milk from their mothers when they are babies." Parents also refer to basic-level categories to teach children subordinate-level terms (Callanan & Sabbagh, 2004; Waxman & Senghas, 1992). For example, they might say "A beluga is a kind of whale." Such descriptions allow children to use what they already know about basic-level categories to form superordinate- and subordinate-level categories. The example also illustrates the importance of the social world in explaining how change occurs in conceptual development.

Although parents' explanations clearly enhance children's conceptual understanding, the learning path sometimes involves amusing detours. In one such case, Susan Gelman (2003) gave her 2-year-old son a spoon and a container filled with bite-size pieces of fruit and said "This is a fruit cup." The boy responded to her description by picking up the "cup" and attempting to drink from it. Children's active attempts to understand their experiences lead to many short-lived but interesting concepts such as the "fruit cup."

Causal understanding and categorization Toddlers and preschoolers are notorious for their endless questions about causes and reasons. "Why do dogs bark?" "How does the telephone know where to call?" "Where does rain come from?" Although parents are often exasperated by such questions, their respecting and answering them helps children learn.

Understanding causal relations is crucial in forming many categories. How could children form the category of "light switches," for example, if they did not understand that flipping light switches causes lights to go on and off? To study how an understanding of causes influences category formation, Krascum and Andrews (1998) told 4- and 5-year-olds about two categories of imaginary animals: wugs and gillies. Some of the preschoolers were provided only physical descriptions of the animals: they were told that wugs usually have claws on their feet, spikes on the end of their tails, horns on their heads, and armor on their backs; gillies were described as usually having wings, big ears, long tails, and long toes. Other children were provided the same physical descriptions, plus a simple causal story that explained why wugs and gillies are the way they are. These children were told that wugs have claws, spikes, horns, and armor because they like to fight. Gillies, in contrast, do not like to fight; instead, they hide in trees. Their big ears let them hear approaching wugs, their wings let them fly away to treetops, and so on. After the children in both groups were given the information about these animals, they were shown the pictures in Figure 7.2 and asked which animal was a wug and which was a gilly.

The children who were told why wugs and gillies have the physical features they do were better at classifying the pictures into the appropriate categories. When tested the next day, those children also remembered the categories better than did the children who were given the physical descriptions without explanations. Thus, understanding cause–effect relations helps children learn and remember new categories.

Preschoolers' questions about causes and reasons show that they understand that different categories of objects, such as artifacts and animals, vary in the types of causal relations in which they are typically involved. Artifacts (objects made by

FIGURE 7.2 Cause–effect relations Hearing that wugs are well prepared to fight and gillies to flee helped preschoolers categorize novel pictures like these as wugs or gillies (Krascum & Andrews, 1998). In general, understanding cause–effect relations helps people of all ages learn and remember.

people) usually are designed for specific purposes: forks are for eating food, cups are for drinking liquids, pens are for writing, and so on. In contrast, animals are not *made* for any human purpose (although people often put them to some specific use). The questions that 3- and 4-year-olds typically ask about artifacts and animals show that they understand these categorical differences. Their questions about novel artifacts, for example, focus on the goals that artifacts enable people to pursue (e.g., "What is this for?"). In contrast, preschoolers' questions about animals focus on the animals' own goals ("What do they like to eat?") (Greif, Kemler-Nelson, Keil, & Guitierrez, 2006; Kemler-Nelson, Egan, & Holt, 2004).

Knowledge of Other People and Oneself

Although understanding of oneself and others varies greatly from individual to individual, there is a commonsense level of psychological understanding that just about everybody has. As discussed in Chapter 4 (page 157), this understanding, referred to as **naïve psychology,** is crucial to normal human functioning.

At the center of naïve psychology are two concepts that we all normally use to understand human behavior: desires and beliefs. We apply these concepts almost every time we think about why someone did something. For example, why did Jimmy go to Billy's house? He *wanted* to play with Billy (a desire), and he *expected* that Billy would be at home (a belief). Why did Jenny turn on the TV at 8:00 A.M. on Saturday? She was *interested* in watching "SpongeBob" (a desire), and she *thought* the program was on at that time (a belief).

Three properties of naïve psychological concepts are noteworthy. First, they refer to invisible mental states. No one can see a desire, a belief, a perception, a memory, or the like. We, of course, can see behaviors related to psychological concepts, such as Jimmy's ringing Billy's doorbell, but we can only infer the underlying mental state, such as Jimmy's desire to see Billy. Second, the concepts are all linked to each other in cause–effect relations. Jimmy, for example, might get angry if Billy isn't home because he went to a different friend's house, which could later cause Jimmy to be mean to his younger brother. The third noteworthy property of these naïve psychological concepts is that, as we will presently see, they develop early in life.

Sharp disagreements have arisen between nativists and empiricists regarding the source of this early psychological understanding. Nativists (e.g., Leslie, 2000) argue that the early understanding is possible only because children are born with an innate basic understanding of human psychology. In contrast, empiricists (e.g., Frye, Zelazo, Brooks, & Samuels, 1996; Ruffman, Slade, & Crowe, 2002) argue that experiences with other people and general information-processing capacities are the key sources of the early understanding of other people. There is evidence to support each of these views.

Infants' Naïve Psychology

As we saw in Chapter 5, infants find people interesting, pay careful attention to them, and learn an impressive amount about them in the first year. Even very young infants prefer to look at people's faces rather than at other objects. Infants also imitate people's facial movements, such as sticking out one's tongue, but they do not imitate the motions of inanimate objects. And it is not just the face that interests infants; they also prefer to watch human bodies moving instead of other displays with equal amounts of movement (Bertenthal, 1993).

This early interest in human faces and bodies helps infants learn about people's behavior. Imitating other people and forming emotional bonds with them encourages

naïve psychology a commonsense level of understanding of other people and oneself the other people to interact more with the infants, creating additional opportunities for the infants to acquire psychological understanding.

As noted in earlier discussions, many important aspects of psychological understanding emerge late in the first year and early in the second. One is an understanding of intention, the desire to act in a certain way. Other key psychological concepts that emerge at the same time include joint attention, in which two or more people focus intentionally on the same referent; and intersubjectivity, the mutual understanding that people share during communication (pages 161–162).

One-year-olds' understanding of other people includes an understanding of their emotions. Consider the following incident:

> Michael, 15 months, is struggling with his friend Paul over a toy. Paul starts to cry. Michael appears concerned and lets go of the toy, so Paul has it. Paul continues crying. Michael pauses, then gives his own teddy bear to Paul; Paul continues crying. Michael pauses again, runs to the next room, gets Paul's security blanket, and gives it to him. Paul stops crying.
>
> (Hoffman, 1976, pp. 129–130)

Although interpreting anecdotes is always tricky, it seems likely that Michael understood that giving Paul something desirable might make him feel better (or at least stop his crying). Michael's leaving the room, getting Paul's security blanket, and bringing it back to him suggests that Michael had the further insight that Paul's blanket might be especially useful for soothing his hurt feelings. This interpretation is consistent with a variety of evidence suggesting that 1-year-olds fairly often offer both physical comfort (hugs, kisses, pats) and comforting comments ("You be OK") to unhappy playmates. Presumably, infants' experience of their own emotions and the behaviors that accompany them helps them understand others' emotions when they act similarly (Harris, 2006).

Development Beyond Infancy

In the toddler and preschool periods, children build on their early-emerging psychological understanding to develop an increasingly sophisticated comprehension of themselves and other people and to interact with others in increasingly complex ways. Two areas of especially impressive development are children's understanding of other people's minds and their play with peers.

The growth of a theory of mind Infants' and preschoolers' naïve psychology, together with their strong interest in other people, provides the foundation for the development of a **theory of mind,** an organized, integrated understanding of how psychological processes such as intentions, desires, beliefs, perceptions, and emotions influence behavior. Preschoolers' theory of mind includes, for example, knowledge that beliefs often originate in perceptions, such as seeing an event or hearing someone describe it; that desires can originate either from physiological states, such as hunger or pain, or from psychological states, such as wanting to see a friend; and that desires and beliefs produce actions (Wellman & Gelman, 1998).

One important component of such a theory of mind—understanding the connection between other people's desires and their actions—emerges by the end of the first year. In a study by Phillips, Wellman, and Spelke (2002), 12-month-olds saw an experimenter look at one of two stuffed kittens and say in a joyful voice, "Ooh, look at the kitty!" Then a screen descended, and when it was raised 2 seconds later, the experimenter was holding either the kitty that she had just exclaimed over or the

theory of mind a basic understanding of how the mind works and how it influences behavior other one. The 12-month-olds looked longer when the experimenter was holding the other kitty, suggesting that they expected the experimenter to want to hold the kitty that had just excited her so much and were surprised that she was holding the other one. Eight-month-olds look for similar amounts of time regardless of which kitty the experimenter is holding, suggesting that the understanding that people's desires guide their actions develops toward the end of the first year (Phillips et al., 2002). Consistent with this conclusion, 10-month-olds can use information about a person's earlier desires to predict that person's later desires, but only under virtually identical circumstances (Sommerville & Crane, 2009).

Children's understanding that desires lead to actions is firmly established by age 2 years. Children of this age, for example, predict that characters in stories will act in accord with their own desires, even when those desires differ from the child's wishes (Gopnik & Slaughter, 1991; Lillard & Flavell, 1992). Thus, if 2-year-olds who would rather play with trucks than with dolls are told that a character in a story would rather play with dolls than with trucks, they predict that, given the choice, the character in the story will choose dolls over trucks.

Although most 2-year-olds understand that *desires* can influence behavior, they show little understanding that *beliefs* are likewise influential. Thus, when 2-year-olds were told a story in which a character named Sam believed that the only bananas available were in a cupboard, but they themselves knew that there were bananas in a refrigerator as well, they were no more likely than chance to predict that Sam would act in accord with his own belief and search for bananas only in the cupboard (Wellman & Woolley, 1990).

By age 3 years, children show some understanding of the relation between beliefs and actions. For example, they answer questions such as "Why is Billy looking for his dog?" by referring to beliefs ("He thinks the dog ran away") as well as to desires ("He wants it") (Bartsch & Wellman, 1995). Most 3-year-olds also have some knowledge of how beliefs originate. They know, for example, that seeing an event produces beliefs about it, whereas simply being next to someone who can see the event does not (Pillow, 1988).

At the same time, 3-year-olds' understanding of the relation between people's beliefs and their actions, a key part of their theory of mind, is limited in important ways. These limitations are evident when children are presented with **false-belief problems,** in which another person believes something to be true that the child knows is false. The question is whether the child thinks that the other person will act in accord with his or her own false belief or in accord with the child's correct understanding of the situation. Studying such situations reveals whether children understand that other people's actions are determined by the contents of their own minds, rather than the objective truth of the situation or the child's understanding of it.

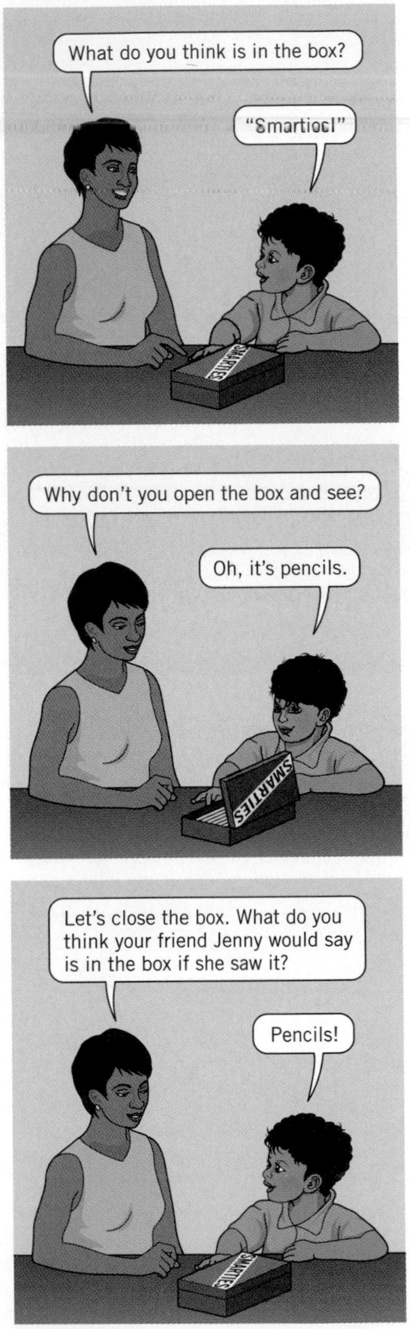

FIGURE 7.3 Testing children's theory of mind The Smarties task is frequently used to study preschoolers' understanding of false beliefs. Most 3-year-olds answer the way the child in this cartoon does, which suggests a lack of understanding that people's actions are based on their own beliefs, even when those beliefs deviate from what the child knows to be true.

In one false-belief problem, preschoolers are shown a box that ordinarily contains a type of candy called Smarties and that has a picture of the candy on it (Figure 7.3). The experimenter then asks what is inside the box. Logically enough, the preschoolers say "Smarties." Next, the experimenter opens the box, revealing that it actually contains pencils. Most 5-year-olds laugh or smile and admit their surprise. When asked what another child would say if shown the closed box and asked to guess its contents, they say the child would answer "Smarties," just as they had. Not 3-year-olds! A large majority claim they always knew what was in the box, and they predict that if some other child were shown the box, that child would also believe that the box contained pencils (Gopnik & Astington, 1988). The 3-year-olds' responses show they have difficulty understanding that other people act on their own beliefs, even when those beliefs are false.

This finding is extremely robust. A review of 178 studies of children's understanding of false beliefs showed that similar results emerged with different forms of the problem, different questions, and different societies (Wellman, Cross, & Watson, 2001). In one noteworthy cross-cultural study, false-belief problems were presented to children attending preschools in Canada, India, Peru, Thailand, and Samoa (Callaghan et al., 2005). Performance improved greatly between ages 3 and 5 years in all five societies, from 14% correct for 3-year-olds to 85% correct for 5-year-olds. Especially striking was the consistency of performance across these very different societies: in no country did 3-year-olds answer more than 25% of problems correctly, and in no country did 5-year-olds answer less than 72% correctly.

Although 3-year-olds generally err on false-belief problems when the problems are presented in the standard way, many children of this age succeed if the task is presented in a manner that facilitates understanding. For example, if an experimenter tells a 3-year-old that the two of them are going to play a trick on another child by hiding pencils in a Smarties box and enlists the child's help in filling the box with pencils, most 3-year-olds correctly predict that the other child will say that the box contains Smarties (Sullivan & Winner, 1993). Presumably, assuming the role of deceiver and hiding the pencils in the candy box helps 3-year-olds see the situation from the other child's perspective. Nonetheless, it is striking just how difficult 3-year-olds find standard false-belief problems. To date, no set of conditions has enabled 3-year-olds to solve standard false-belief questions correctly more often than chance (Harris, 2006).

SUPERSTOCK

Despite leading very different lives, pygmy children in Africa and same-age peers in industrialized North American and European societies respond to the false-belief task in the same way.

Explaining the development of theory of mind People's lives clearly would be very different without a reasonably sophisticated theory of mind. However, the findings on the improvement in normal children's theory of mind between ages 3 and 5 do not tell us what causes the improvement. This question has generated enormous controversy, and currently there is great disagreement about how to answer it.

Investigators who take a nativist position have proposed the existence of a **theory of mind module (TOMM),** a hypothesized brain mechanism devoted to understanding other human beings (Baron-Cohen, 1995; Leslie, 2000). Adherents of this position argue that among typical children exposed to a typical environment, the TOMM matures over the first five years, producing an increasingly sophisticated understanding of people's minds. These investigators cite evidence from brain-imaging studies showing that certain areas of the brain are consistently active in representing beliefs across different tasks, and that the areas are different from those involved in other complex cognitive processes, such as understanding grammar (Saxe & Powell, 2006).

Further evidence that is often cited to support the idea of the TOMM comes from children with autism. As discussed in Box 7.1 on the next page, these children have great difficulty with false-belief problems, a difficulty that appears closely associated with a wide array of limitations in their social interactions. Especially significant to the idea of the TOMM is the discovery that individuals with autism appear to be missing a significant band of tissue in the brain stem (Rodier, 2000). The problem originates in the first month of the prenatal period

false-belief problems tasks that test a child's understanding that other people will act in accord with their own beliefs even when the child knows that those beliefs are incorrect

theory of mind module (TOMM) a hypothesized brain mechanism devoted to understanding other human beings

individual differences 7.1

Children with Autism

Although most children readily handle false-belief problems by the age of 5 years, one group continues to find them very difficult even when they are teenagers: children with autism. As discussed in Chapter 3 (page 93), this syndrome, which strikes roughly 1 in 600 children in the United States, most of them male (Rodier, 2000), involves difficulties in social interaction, communication, and other intellectual and emotional functions.

Autistic children often engage in solitary repetitive behaviors, such as continually rocking back and forth or endlessly skipping around a room. They interact minimally with other children and adults, rarely form close relationships, and tend to be more interested in objects than in people. These problems, among others, have led some researchers to speculate that a failure to understand other people underlies autistic children's limited involvement in the social world.

Recent research supports this hypothesis. Children with autism have trouble establishing joint attention with other people; in fact, there is little evidence that they ever do so (Klin et al., 2004). Compared with both typical children and children with mental retardation, autistic children show less concern when other people appear distressed (Sigman & Ruskin, 1999) or experience circumstances that would lead most people to be distressed (Hobson, Harris, García-Peréz, & Hobson, 2009). Autistic children also tend to have poor language skills (Happé, 1995), which both reflects their lack of attention to other people and limits their opportunities to learn about people's thoughts and feelings through conversation.

In line with these patterns, autistic children are strikingly befuddled by false-belief questions (Baron-Cohen, 1991). For example, fewer than half of 6- to 14-year-olds with autism solve false-belief problems that are easy for typical 4- and 5-year-olds (Peterson, Wellman, & Liu, 2005). Autistic children have some understanding of how desire affects behavior, but the ways in which beliefs influence behavior largely eludes them (Harris, 2006; Tager-Flusberg, 2007). Other groups with limited language skills, such as deaf children who learn to sign relatively late, also show delays in mastering false-belief tasks. However, autistic children differ both from these deaf children and from preschoolers in that they understand false beliefs later than other aspects of psychology that are typically understood after false beliefs (Peterson, Wellman, & Liu, 2005).

Impaired theory-of-mind mechanisms are not the only source of the difficulty that children with autism encounter in understanding other people. More general deficits in planning, adapting to changing situations, and controlling working memory also contribute (Ozonoff et al., 2004). Nonetheless, impaired theory of mind is a source of particular difficulty, especially in understanding situations in which people's beliefs differ from reality (Baron-Cohen, 1993; Tager-Flusberg, 2007). Identifying the difficulty that children with autism have in understanding other people's minds as a major source of the problems encountered in autism may contribute to the development of more effective treatments for this strange and baffling condition.

and may be related to other abnormalities in later developing parts of the brains of autistic children. One area that is typically affected is the amygdala, which plays a crucial role in experiencing and understanding emotions; another is the hippocampus, which plays a crucial role in memory. All these parts of the brain are important for a variety of functions, but abnormalities in them may be especially detrimental to understanding other people.

JAN SONNENMAIR / AURORA

An autistic child, sitting in his mother's lap, shows a distinct lack of interest in her affection. Such lack of interest in other people is common among autistic children and seems related to their very poor performance on tasks that require understanding of other people's minds.

A different explanation of the development of theory of mind is suggested by theorists who take an empiricist stance and maintain that psychological understanding arises from interactions with other people (Jenkins & Astington, 1996; Ruffman, Slade, & Crowe, 2002). They cite evidence that on false-belief tasks, preschoolers who have siblings outperform peers who do not. This finding appears to be especially likely when the siblings are older or of the opposite sex, presumably because interacting with people whose interests, desires, and motives are different from their own broadens children's understanding of the mind (Cassidy et al., 2005; Jenkins & Astington, 1996). From this perspective, the tendency of children with autism not to interact with other people is a major contributor to the children's difficulty in understanding people.

COURTESY OF ALICE AND ROBERT SIEGLER

Sharing experiences with older siblings helps younger siblings understand other people.

A third group of investigators also takes an empiricist stance but emphasizes the growth of general information-processing skills as essential to children's understanding of other people's minds. They cite evidence that understanding false-belief problems is substantially correlated with the ability to reason about complex counterfactual statements (German & Nichols, 2003) and with the ability to inhibit one's own relatively automatic behavioral reactions (Carlson, Mandell, & Williams, 2004; Frye, Zelazo, Brooks, & Samuels, 1996). The ability to reason about counterfactual statements is important because false-belief problems require children to predict what a person would do on the basis of a counterfactual belief. The ability to inhibit relatively automatic reactions is important because false-belief problems also require children to suppress the assumption that the person would act on the truth of the situation. Investigators in this camp argue that typical children under age 4 and children with autism lack the information-processing skills needed to understand others' minds, whereas many typical 4-year-olds and almost all typical 5-year-olds can engage in such processing.

All three explanations seem to have merit. Normal development of brain regions relevant to understanding other people, increasing experience with other people, and improved information-processing capacity all contribute to the growth of psychological understanding during the preschool years. Together, they allow almost all children to achieve a basic, but useful, theory of mind by age 5.

The growth of play Play refers to activities that are pursued for their own sake, without any motivation other than the enjoyment they bring. The earliest play activities, such as banging a spoon on a high-chair tray, tend to be solitary. However, over the next few years, children's increasing understanding of other people contributes to their play becoming more social, as well as more complex.

One early milestone in the development of play is the emergence of **pretend play** at around 18 months of age. When engaged in pretend play, children act as if they were in a different situation than their actual one. They often engage in **object substitution,** ignoring many of a play object's characteristics so that they can pretend that it is something else. A typical example of such object substitution

pretend play make-believe activities in which children create new symbolic relations, for example, using a broom to represent a horse

object substitution a form of pretense in which an object is used as something other than itself

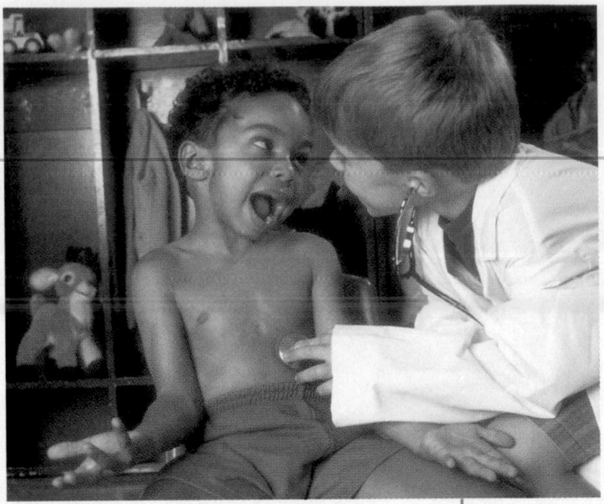

MICHAEL NEWMAN / PHOTOEDIT

Sociodramatic play, in which children create minidramas based on their experiences, both reflects children's understanding of the situation and helps them increase that understanding.

would be a child's cradling a pillow and talking to it as if it were a baby, or talking to a doll as if it were a friend.

About a year later, toddlers begin to engage in **sociodramatic play,** a kind of pretend play in which they enact miniature dramas with other children or adults, such as "mother comforting baby" or "doctor helping sick child" (O'Reilly & Bornstein, 1993). Sociodramatic play is more complex and more social than object substitution. Consider, for example, "tea party" rituals, in which a child and parent "pour tea" for each other from an imaginary teapot, daintily "sip" it, "eat" imaginary cookies, and comment on how delicious they are.

Young children's sociodramatic play is typically more sophisticated when they are playing with a parent or older sibling who can scaffold the play sequence than when they are pretending with a peer (Bornstein, 2006; Lillard, 2006). Such scaffolding during play provides children with opportunities for learning, in particular for improving their storytelling skills (Nicolopoulou, 2006). Consider one mother's comments as her 2-year-old played with two action figures:

> Oh look, Lantern Man is chasing Spider Man. Oh no, he is pushing him down. Spider Man says, 'Help, Lantern Man is grabbing me.' Look, Spider Man is getting away.
>
> (Kavanaugh & Engel, 1998, p. 88)

Such adult elaboration of implicit storylines in children's play provides a useful model for children to follow as they become more verbal.

By the elementary school years, play becomes even more complex and social. It begins to include activities, such as sports and board games, that have conventional rules that participants must follow. The frequent quarrels that arise among young elementary school students regarding who is obeying the rules and playing fair attest to the cognitive and emotional challenges posed by these games (Rubin, Fein, & Vandenberg, 1983).

The quantity of young children's pretend play is related to their understanding of other people's psychological functioning. Children who engage in greater amounts of pretend play tend to show greater understanding of other people's thinking (Lillard, 2006) and emotions (Youngblade & Dunn, 1995). The type of pretend play in which children engage also matters: social pretend play is more strongly related to understanding other people's thinking than is nonsocial pretend play (Harris, 2000). Pretend play may lead toddlers and preschoolers to consider how various situations would make them or their play partner think and feel, and in this way it may increase their understanding of other people. Consistent with this conclusion, children who participate in greater-than-average amounts of pretend play with other children also tend to be popular with their peers and socially mature, perhaps because such play enhances their understanding of other children's feelings (Howes & Matheson, 1992). Thus, although adults often view children's pretend play as unimportant, it is positively related to children's social and intellectual development and may even enhance them.

Children often enjoy having a parent join them in sociodramatic play, which tends to be richer and more informative when the parent provides scaffolding for the play episode. Along with helping to structure the tea-time conversation, the mother in this classic scenario may also be providing her daughter with tips on party etiquette.

LAURA DWIGHT

Knowledge of Living Things

Children find living things fascinating, especially animals. One sign of their fascination is how often their first words refer to animals. In a study of the first 50 words used by children, the two terms that were used by the greatest number of children were "dog" and "cat" (and variants such as "doggie" and "kitty") (Nelson, 1973). "Duck," "horse," "bear," "bird," and "cow" also were among the most common early terms. By the time children are 4 or 5 years old, their fascination with living things translates into an impressive amount of knowledge about them, including knowledge of unobservable biological processes such as inheritance, illness, and healing.

sociodramatic play activities in which children enact minidramas with other children or adults, such as "mother comforting baby"

individual differences 7.2

Imaginary Companions

Many children have an imaginary companion whom they appear to regard as an actual being. Marjorie Taylor (1999) found that 63% of children whom she interviewed at age 3 or 4 years and again at age 7 or 8 years reported having imaginary companions at one or both times. In another study, Taylor and colleagues (2004) found that as many 6- and 7-year-olds as 3- and 4-year-olds said that they had imaginary companions—31% of older children and 28% of younger ones. Hearing a child talk about an invisible friend sometimes leads parents to worry about their child's mental health, but as these statistics show, children's creation of such companions is entirely normal.

Most of the imaginary playmates described by children in Taylor's studies were ordinary boys and girls who happened to be invisible, but others were more colorful. They included Derek, a 91-year-old man who was said to be only 2 feet tall but able to hit bears; "The Girl," a 4-year-old who always wore pink and was "a beautiful person"; Joshua, a possum who lived in San Francisco; and Nobby, a 160-year-old businessman. Other imaginary companions were modeled after specific people: two examples were MacKenzie, an imaginary playmate who resembled the child's cousin MacKenzie, and "Fake Rachel," who resembled the child's friend Rachel.

As with real friends, children have a variety of complaints about their imaginary companions. In a study of 36 preschoolers with imaginary companions, only one child had no complaints; the other 35 children griped that their imaginary companions argued with them, refused to share, failed to come when invited, and failed to leave when no longer welcome (Taylor & Mannering, 2007). In this independence from their creator, the imaginary companions resemble characters invented by novelists, who often report that their characters at times seem to act independently, including making statements the authors did not intend and arguing with and criticizing them (Taylor & Mannering, 2007).

Contrary to popular speculation, Taylor (1999) found that, in terms of broad characteristics such as personality, intelligence, and creativity, children who invent imaginary playmates are no different from children who do not. However, she and other investigators have identified a few, relatively specific differences between these two groups. Children who had created imaginary playmates were more likely (1) to be firstborn or only children; (2) to watch relatively little television; (3) to be verbally skillful; and (4) to have advanced theories of mind (Carlson, Gum, Davis, & Malloy, 2003; Taylor & Carlson, 1997; Taylor et al., 2004). These relations make sense. Being without siblings may motivate some firstborn and only children to invent friends to keep them company; not watching much television frees time for imaginative play; and being verbally skilled and having an advanced theory of mind may enable children to imagine especially interesting companions and especially interesting adventures with them.

Companionship, entertainment, and enjoyment of fantasy are not the only reasons why children invent imaginary companions. Children also use them to deflect blame ("I didn't do it; Blebbi Ussi did"), to vent anger ("I hate you, Blebbi Ussi"), and to convey information that the child is reluctant to state directly ("Blebbi Ussi is scared of falling into the potty"). As Taylor (1999) noted, "Imaginary companions love you when you feel rejected by others, listen when you need to talk to someone, and can be trusted not to repeat what you say" (p. 63). It is no wonder, then, that so many children invent them.

SHERRY WHITMORE

Although the sight of their child feeding someone who isn't there might worry some parents, the majority of children enjoy the company of imaginary friends at some time in early childhood.

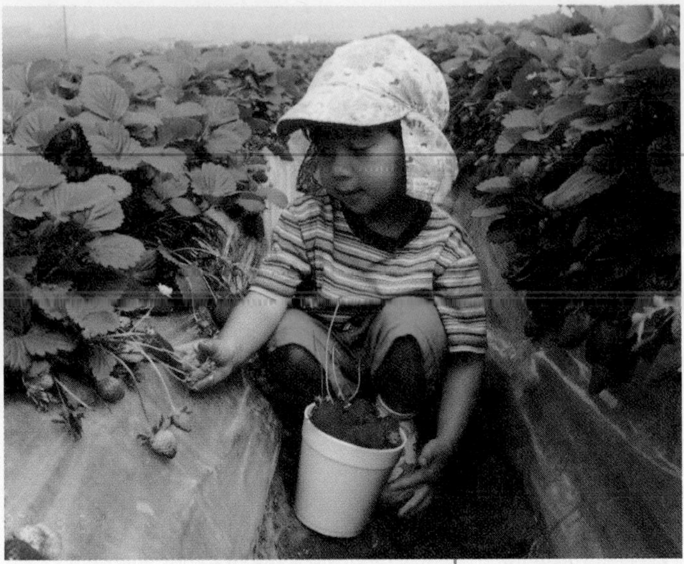
COURTESY OF SUWANNA AND DAVID SIEGLER

Children are interested in living things, plants as well as animals—especially when part of the plant tastes good.

Coexisting with this relatively advanced knowledge, however, are a variety of immature beliefs and types of reasoning. For example, despite the previously mentioned differences in the questions preschoolers ask about animals and artifacts (Greif, Kemler-Nelson, Keil, & Gutierrez, 2006), when preschoolers and older children are asked certain types of "why" questions, the distinction blurs. For example, when Kelemen and DiYanni (2005) asked 6- to 10-year-olds why the first monkey came to exist, they often advanced answers such as "The manager of the zoo-place wanted some" and "So then we had somebody to climb trees." Children advance similar answers to questions about the possible purposes of inanimate natural entities, such as rocks. When 7- and 8-year-olds were asked whether rocks were pointy "because bits of stuff piled up for a long period of time" or "so that animals could scratch on them when they got itchy," most of the 7- and 8-year olds chose the rocks' usefulness for scratching to explain their shape (Kelemen, 1999). Thus, although children's spontaneous questions indicate that they distinguish between animate and inanimate objects, their answers to "why" questions tend to ignore this distinction.

Young children also often err in identifying which things are living and which are not. For example, most 5-year-olds say that plants are not alive, and some say that the moon and mountains are alive (Hatano et al., 1993). Erroneous notions such as these have led some investigators to conclude that children have only a shallow and fragmented understanding of living things until they are 7 to 10 years old (Carey, 1999; Slaughter, Jaakkola, & Carey, 1999). In contrast, other investigators believe that by age 5 years, children understand the essential characteristics of living things and what separates them from nonliving things (Gelman, 2003). A third view is that young children possess both mature and immature theories of living and nonliving things (Inagaki & Hatano, 2008). With this dispute in mind, we will now consider what young children do and do not know about living things and how they acquire knowledge about them.

Distinguishing Living from Nonliving Things

As noted previously, infants in their first year already are interested in people and distinguish them from nonliving things (Figure 7.4). Other animals also attract

BOTH: COURTESY OF DIANE POULIN-DUBOIS

FIGURE 7.4 Distinguishing people from nonliving things These photos show a task used by Poulin-Dubois (1999) to study infants' reactions when they see people and inanimate objects (in this case a robot) engaging in the same action. Both 9- and 12-month-olds show surprise when they see inanimate objects move on their own, suggesting that they understand that self-produced motion is a distinctive characteristic of people and other animals.

infants' interest, though infants act differently toward them than they do toward people. Nine-month-olds, for example, pay more attention to rabbits than they do to inanimate objects, but they smile less at rabbits than they do at people (Poulin-Dubois, 1999; Ricard & Allard, 1993).

These behavioral reactions indicate that infants in their first year distinguish people from other animals and that they distinguish both from inanimate objects. However, the reactions do not indicate when children construct a general category of living things that includes plants as well as animals or when they recognize humans as a type of animal. It is difficult to assess children's knowledge of these and many other properties of living and nonliving things until the age of 3 or 4 years, when they can comprehend and answer questions about these categories. By this age, they clearly know quite a bit about the similarities among all living creatures and about the differences between living creatures and inanimate objects. This knowledge of living things is not limited to visible properties such as having legs, moving, and making distinctive noises. It also extends to biological processes such as digestion and heredity (Gelman, 2003). At least through age 5, however, many children have difficulty understanding that human beings are animals that are similar in many ways to other animals. They frequently deny that people are animals at all (Carey, 1985).

Understanding the life status of plants also presents a challenge to young children. On the one hand, most preschoolers know that plants, like animals but unlike inanimate objects, grow (Hickling & Gelman, 1995; Inagaki & Hatano, 1996), heal themselves (Backscheider, Shatz, & Gelman, 1993), and die (Springer, Nguyen, & Samaniego, 1996). On the other hand, most preschoolers believe that plants are not alive; in fact, it is not until age 7 to 9 years that a clear majority of children realize that plants are living things (Hatano et al., 1993). Part of the reason is that children often equate being alive with being able to move in adaptive ways that promote survival, and the adaptive movements of plants (for example, their bending toward sunlight) are difficult to observe because they occur too slowly (Opfer & Gelman, 2001). Consistent with this interpretation, telling 5-year-olds that plants move toward sunlight and that their roots move toward water so that they can live leads the children to conclude that plants, like animals, are living things (Opfer & Siegler, 2004). More generally, culture and direct experience influence the age at which children understand that plants are, in fact, alive. For example, children growing up in rural areas realize that plants are living things at younger ages than do children growing up in cities or suburbs (Coley, 2000; Ross, Medin, Coley, & Atran, 2003).

Understanding Biological Processes

Preschoolers understand that biological processes, such as growth, digestion, and healing, differ from psychological and physical ones (Wellman & Gelman, 1998). For instance, while 3- and 4-year-olds recognize that desires influence what people do, they also recognize that there are biological processes that are independent of one's desires. This distinction between psychological and biological processes, for example, leads preschoolers to predict that people who wish to lose weight but still eat a lot will not get their wish (Inagaki & Hatano, 1993; Schult & Wellman, 1997). Preschoolers also recognize that properties of living things often serve important functions for the organism, whereas properties of inanimate objects do not. Thus, 5-year-olds recognize that the green color of plants is crucial for them to make food, whereas the green color of emeralds has no function for the emerald (Keil,

1992). The extent of preschoolers' understanding of biological processes can be understood more fully by examining their specific ideas about inheritance, growth, and illness.

Inheritance Although 3- and 4-year-olds obviously know nothing about DNA or the mechanisms of heredity, they do know that physical characteristics tend to be passed on from parent to offspring. If told, for example, that Mr. and Mrs. Bull have hearts of an unusual color, they predict that Baby Bull also will have a heart of that color (Springer & Keil, 1991). Similarly, they predict that a baby mouse will eventually have hair of the same color as its parents, even if it is presently hairless.

Older preschoolers also know that certain aspects of development are determined by heredity rather than by environment. For example, 5-year-olds realize that an animal of one species raised by parents of another species will become an adult of its own species (Johnson & Solomon, 1996).

Coexisting with this understanding are a variety of misguided beliefs about inheritance. Many preschoolers believe that mothers' desires can play a role in their children's inheritance of physical qualities, such as having blue eyes (Weissman & Kalish, 1999). Many preschoolers also believe that adopted children are at least as likely to look like their adoptive parents as like their birth parents (Solomon, Johnson, Zaitchik, & Carey, 1996). In other situations, preschoolers' belief in heredity is too strong, leading them to deny that the environment has any influence. For example, preschoolers tend to believe that differences between boys and girls in play preferences are due totally to heredity (Taylor, 1993).

Related to this general belief in the importance of heredity is one of the most basic aspects of children's biological beliefs—**essentialism,** the view that living things have an essence inside them that makes them what they are (Gelman, 2003). Thus, most preschoolers (as well as most older children and adults) believe that puppies have a certain "dogness" inside them, kittens have a certain "catness," roses have a certain "roseness," and so on. This essence is what makes all members of the category similar to each other and different from members of other categories; for example, their inner "dogness" leads to dogs' barking, chasing cats, liking to be petted, and so on. This essence is viewed as being inherited from one's parents and being maintained throughout the organism's life. Thinking in terms of such essences seems to make it difficult for both children and many adults to understand and accept biological evolution (Evans, 2008). If animals inherit an unchanging essence from their parents, how, they may wonder, would it be possible, say, for mice and whales to have common ancestors?

Growth, illness, and healing Preschoolers realize that growth, like inheritance, is a product of internal processes. They recognize, for example, that plants and animals become bigger and more complex over time due to something going on inside them (again, preschoolers are not sure what) (Rosengren, Gelman, Kalish, & McCormick, 1991). Three- and four-year-olds also recognize that the growth of living things proceeds in only one direction (smaller to larger) at least until old age, whereas inanimate objects such as balloons can become either smaller or larger at any point in time.

Preschoolers also show a basic understanding of illness. Three-year-olds have heard of germs and have a general sense of how they operate. They know that eating food that is contaminated with germs can make a person sick, even if the person is unaware of the germs' presence (Kalish, 1997). Conversely, they realize

essentialism the view that living things have an essence inside them that makes them what they are

"I've been getting in touch with the puppy in me."

A fanciful representation of the inner essence that children believe makes a dog a dog, a cat a cat, and so on.

that psychological processes, such as being aware of germs in one's food, do not cause illness.

Finally, preschoolers know that plants and animals, unlike inanimate objects, have internal processes that often allow them to regain prior states or attributes. For example, 4-year-olds realize that a cat or a tomato plant that is scratched can heal itself but that a scratched car or chair cannot (Backscheider et al., 1993). They also know that when an animal's hair is cut, it will grow back, but that if a doll's hair is cut, it never will. On the other hand, they recognize the limits of such recuperative processes; they understand that both illness and old age can cause death, with death being a state from which no one recuperates (Nguyen & Gelman, 2002).

How Do Children Acquire Biological Knowledge?

As with other aspects of conceptual development, nativists and empiricists have very different ideas regarding the growth of children's biological understanding. Nativists propose that humans are born with a "biology module" much like the theory of mind module described earlier in the chapter. This brain structure or mechanism helps children learn quickly about living things (Atran, 1990, 2002). Nativists support the idea that people have a biology module with three main arguments.

- During earlier periods of our evolution, it was crucial for human survival that children learn quickly about animals and plants.
- Children throughout the world are fascinated by plants and animals and learn about them quickly and easily.
- Children throughout the world organize information about plants and animals in very similar ways (in terms of growth, reproduction, inheritance, sickness, and healing).

Empiricists, in contrast, maintain that children's biological understanding comes from their personal observations and from information they receive from parents, teachers, and the general culture (Callanan, 1990). When mothers in the United States read books about animals to their 1- and 2-year-olds, for example, many of the mothers' comments and questions suggest that animals have intentions

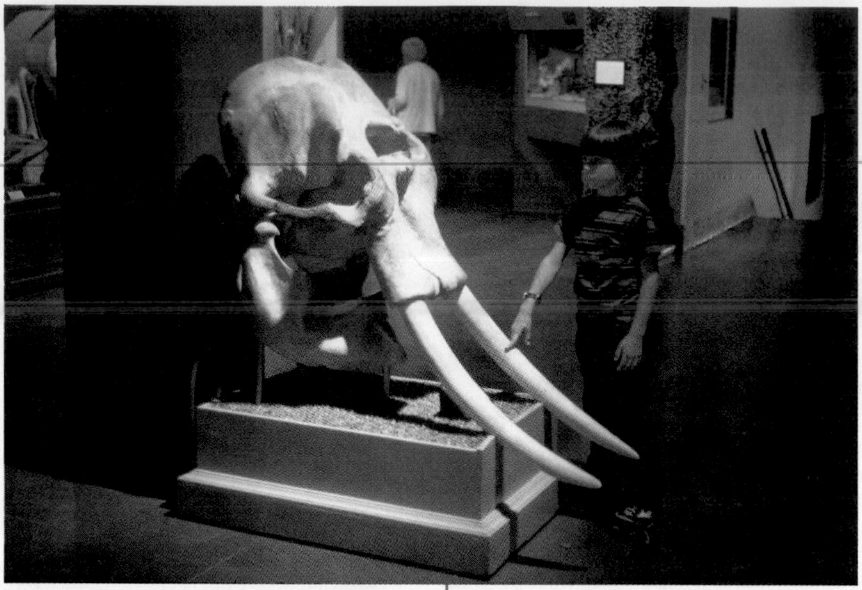

The feelings of awe experienced by many children (and adults) upon seeing remains of great animals of the past and present, such as dinosaurs, elephants, and whales, were a major reason for the founding of natural history museums. Despite all the depictions of monsters and superheroes on television, in movies, and in video games, these fossils and models inspire the same sense of wonder in children growing up today.

and goals; that different members of the same species have a lot in common; and that animals differ greatly from inanimate objects (Gelman et al., 1998). Such parental teaching clearly contributes to children's acquisition of biological knowledge.

Empiricists also note that children's biological understanding reflects the views of their culture. For example, 5-year-olds in Japan are more likely than their peers in the United States and Israel to believe that nonliving things and plants are able to feel physical sensations, such as pain and cold (Hatano et al., 1993). This tendency of Japanese children echoes the Buddhist tradition, still influential in Japanese society, which views all objects as having certain psychological properties.

As with the parallel arguments regarding the sources of psychological understanding, both nature and nurture seem certain to play important roles in the acquisition of biological understanding. Young children are innately fascinated by animals and learn about them much more quickly than about aspects of their environment that they find less interesting. At the same time, the particulars of what children learn obviously are influenced by the information, beliefs, and values conveyed to them by their parents and their society. The challenge remains to specify how children integrate these aspects of nature and nurture to construct sophisticated biological concepts as rapidly as they do.

review:

From early in infancy, children form categories of similar objects. Such categorization helps them infer the properties of unfamiliar objects within a category. For example, if children learn that a new object is an animal, they know that it will grow, move, and eat. Children form new categories, and include new objects within an existing category, on the basis of similarities between the appearance and function of the new object and objects already known to be category members.

One particularly important category is people. From the first days of life, infants are interested in other people and spend a great deal of time looking at them. By age 3 years, they form a simple theory of mind, which includes some understanding of the causal relations among intentions, desires, beliefs, and actions. Not until age 4 or 5 years, however, do most children become able to solve false-belief problems. The development of understanding of other people's minds during the preschool period has been attributed to biological maturation of a theory of mind module, to interactions with other people, and to the growth of information-processing capabilities that allow children to understand increasingly complex social situations.

Another vital category is living things. During the preschool years, children gain a basic understanding of the properties of biological entities: growth, heredity, illness, and death. Not until children go to school, however, do most of them group plants with animals into a single category of living things. Explanations for children's relatively rapid acquisition of biological knowledge include the extensive exposure to biological information provided by families and the broader culture, as well as the existence of brain mechanisms that lead children to be interested in living things and to learn about them quickly and easily.

Understanding Where, When, Why, and How Many

Making sense out of our experiences requires accurately representing not only who or what was involved in an event, but also where, when, why, and how often the event occurred. To grasp the importance of these latter concepts, imagine what life would be like if you lost your understanding of any one of them—for example, your sense of time. Without a sense of time, you would not even know the order in which events occurred. Did you get dressed and then eat breakfast, or did you eat breakfast and then get dressed? Your whole impression of your life as a continuous stream of events would be shattered. Similar problems would arise if you lost your sense of space or causality or number. Reality would resemble a nightmare, in which order and predictability were suspended and chaos ruled.

As described in the previous section, the categories that children need to answer the questions "Who?" and "What?" begin to be formed in infancy, though the understanding deepens for many years thereafter. Development of understanding of space, time, causality, and number follows a similar path. In each case, development begins in the first year of life, but major improvements continue throughout childhood and adolescence.

Space

The nativist/empiricist debate has been vigorous with regard to spatial thinking. Nativists argue that children possess an innate module that is specialized for representing and learning about space and that processes spatial information separately from other types of information (Hermer & Spelke, 1996; Hespos & Spelke, 2004). Empiricists, on the other hand, argue that children acquire spatial representations through the same types of learning mechanisms and experiences that produce cognitive growth in general; that children adaptively combine spatial and nonspatial information to reach their goals through moving around the enviroment; and that language and other cultural tools shape spatial development (Gentner & Broditsky, 2001; Newcombe & Huttenlocher, 2006).

The two sides do agree on some issues. One point of agreement is that from early in infancy, children show impressive understanding of some spatial concepts, such as above, below, left of, and right of (Casasola, 2008; Quinn, 2005). Another common conclusion is that certain parts of the brain are specialized for coding particular types of spatial information. Contrary to the popular notion that spatial thinking occurs solely in the right hemisphere, spatial thinking actually occurs in both brain hemispheres. However, the two sides of the brain differ in the types of spatial information that they most actively process (Newcombe & Huttenlocher, 2000). Certain areas in the right hemisphere are especially active in processing fine-grain, continuous spatial information, such as the information used to recognize faces or to identify objects by means of touch (Wittelson & Swallow, 1988). In contrast, certain areas in the left hemisphere are especially active in processing categorical spatial information, such as the information that a particular object is in the bathroom or next to the television (Chabris & Kosslyn, 1998; Newcombe & Huttenlocher, 2000). The differentiation seems to be present from infancy onward.

Brain activation on a spatial reasoning task As illustrated by the presence of areas of high activation (the areas in color) in both the left and right sides of the brain images, spatial thinking engages both the right and left hemispheres of the brain.

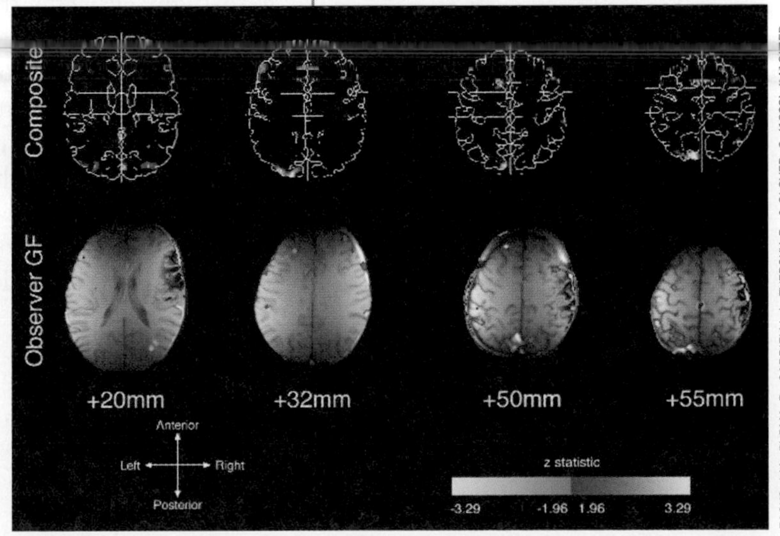

ZACKS, J.M., RYPMA, B., GABRIELLI, J., TVERSKY, B., & GLOVER, G. (1999). IMAGINED TRANSFORMATION OF BODIES: AN FMRI STUDY. *NEUROPSYCHOLOGIA, 37*(9), 1029–1040

An aspect of spatial thinking that is of particular importance is how individuals code space both relative to themselves and relative to the external environment. Below we consider each of these types of spatial coding.

Representing Space Relative to Oneself

From early in infancy, children code the locations of objects in relation to their own bodies. As noted in Chapter 5, when young infants are presented with two objects, they tend to reach for the closer one (von Hofsten & Spelke, 1985). This shows that they recognize which object is closer, as well as the direction of that object relative to themselves.

Over the ensuing months, infants' representations of spatial locations become increasingly durable, enabling them to find objects they observed being hidden some seconds earlier. As discussed in Chapter 4, most 7-month-olds reach to the correct location for objects that were hidden under one of two identical covers 2 seconds earlier but not for objects hidden 4 seconds earlier, whereas most 12-month-olds accurately reach for objects hidden 10 seconds earlier (Diamond, 1985). In part, these increasingly enduring object representations reflect brain maturation, particularly of the dorsolateral prefrontal cortex, an area in the frontal lobe that is involved in the formation and maintenance of plans and in the integration of new and previously learned information (Diamond & Goldman-Rakic, 1989; Nelson, 2006). However, the improved object representations reflect learning as well; infants who are provided a learning experience with a hidden object in one situation show improved location of hidden objects in other situations (Johnson, Amso, & Slemmer, 2003).

Note that all the preceding examples of infants' ability to code space involve the infant remaining in a single location. Piaget (1971) proposed that this is the only kind of spatial coding that infants can do. The reason, according to his theory, is that the only representations infants are capable of forming during the sensorimotor period are **egocentric representations,** in which the locations of objects are coded relative to the infants' immediate position at the time of the coding. As evidence, Piaget reported experiments showing that if infants repeatedly found a toy to their right, they would continue to turn right to find it, even if they were repositioned so that the object was now on their left.

Subsequent studies have obtained similar findings. When 6- and 11-month-olds repeatedly see an interesting sight appear on their right, they initially continue to look to the right, even after they have been turned around 180 degrees so that the interesting sight is now on their left (Acredolo, 1978). Egocentric representation is not absolute, however: if toys are hidden adjacent to a distinctive landmark, such as a large tower, infants usually find the toy despite the change in their own position. Still, the question remains, How do children become able to find objects when their own position has changed and when no landmarks are available to guide their search?

A major factor in helping infants acquire a sense of space independent of their own location appears to be self-locomotion. Thus, infants who crawl, or who have had experience propelling themselves in walkers, more often remember the locations of objects on the object permanence task (page 134) than do infants of the same age without such locomotor experience (Bertenthal, Campos, & Kermoian, 1994; Campos et al., 2000). Similarly, compared with infants who have not yet moved across rooms on their own, those infants who have done so show an earlier understanding of depth and drop-offs on the surfaces they travel; this is evidenced by acceleration in their heart rate as they approach the visual cliff in the procedure described on page 197.

egocentric representations coding of spatial locations relative to one's own body, without regard to the surroundings

The reasons why self-locomotion enhances infants' representation of space should be familiar to anyone who has both driven a car and been a passenger in one. Just as driving requires continuous updating of information about the surroundings, so does crawling or walking. In contrast, just as being a passenger in a car does not require such continuous updating of one's location, neither does being carried.

As would be expected from this analysis, self-locomotion also enhances older children's spatial coding. Striking evidence for this conclusion emerged from a study in which kindergarten classmates were tested in the kitchens of their own homes (Rieser, Garing, & Young, 1994). Some of the kindergartners were asked to stand in place and imagine themselves walking from their seat in the classroom to the teacher's chair and then turning around to face the class. Then they were asked to point from this imagined position to the locations within the classroom of various objects—the fishbowl, the alphabet chart, the coatroom door, and so on. Under these conditions, the 5-year-olds' pointing was very inaccurate. Other kindergartners went through the same procedure, except that they were instructed to actually walk through their kitchen and turn around as they imagined themselves walking to the teacher's chair and then turning to face the class. Under these conditions, the children's pointing to the imagined objects in their imagined classroom was far more accurate. This result, like those described above with infants, highlights the interconnectedness of the system that produces self-generated motion and the system that produces mental representations of space (Adolph & Berger, 2006).

Development of Spatial Concepts in Blind and Visually Impaired People

People often equate spatial thinking with vision, assuming that we can think spatially only about layouts that we have seen. Even in infancy, however, spatial thought can be based on senses other than vision and is possible when vision is not. Thus, when 3-month-olds are brought into a totally dark room in which they cannot see anything, they use sounds emitted by nearby objects to identify the objects' spatial locations and reach for them (Keen & Berthier, 2004).

Although infants can use their auditory sense, among others, to form spatial representations, visual experience during infancy does play an important role in spatial development. Evidence for this conclusion comes from cases in which surgery restored sight to people who were born either blind (Carlson, Hyvarinen, & Raninen, 1986) or with severely impaired vision due to cataracts that prevented patterned stimulation from reaching the retina (Le Grand, Mondloch, Maurer, & Brent, 2001, 2003). The surgery was performed early—on average at 4 months of age—and the people who underwent it had between 9 and 21 years of postsurgical visual experience before being tested. Despite their extensive visual experience after the corrective surgery, most of these people could not use visual information to represent space as well as other people can; problems remained, especially with representations of faces, even 20 years after the surgery (and thus after 20 years of visual experience).

These findings do not mean that children who are born blind cannot represent space. They actually tend to have a surprisingly good spatial sense. On tasks involving the representation of very small spaces, such as being guided in drawing two sides of a triangle on a piece of paper and

Blind adolescents and adults, even those blind from birth, tend to have a quite accurate sense of space, which helps them move around the environment skillfully.

ROBIN SACHS / PHOTOEDIT

then being asked to complete the triangle by drawing the third side themselves, children who are born blind perform as well as sighted children who are blindfolded (Thinus-Blanc & Gaunet, 1997). On tasks involving representation of large spaces, such as those formed by exploring unfamiliar rooms, the spatial representations of people born blind also are surprisingly good, about as good as those formed by sighted people who were blindfolded during the exploration period. Thus, although some spatial skills seem to require early visual experience, many blind people develop impressive senses of space without ever seeing the world.

Representing Space Relative to the External Environment

As we have noted, infants as young as 6 months can use landmarks to code the location of objects they observe being hidden (Lew, Foster, Crowther, & Green, 2004). However, for such young infants to use a landmark successfully, it must be the only obvious landmark in the environment and must be located right next to the hidden object.

With development, infants become increasingly able to choose among alternative potential landmarks. When 12-month-olds are presented a single yellow cushion, a single green cushion, and a large number of blue cushions, they have little trouble finding an object hidden under either the yellow or the green cushion (Bushnell, McKenzie, Lawrence, & Connell, 1995). At 22 months, but not at 16 months, the presence of a landmark improves children's ability to locate an object that is not hidden adjacent to the landmark (Newcombe, Huttenlocher, Drummey, & Wiley, 1998). By age 5 years, children can also represent an object's position in relation to multiple landmarks, such as when it is midway between a tree and a street lamp (Newcombe & Huttenlocher, 2006).

Children, like adults, have more difficulty forming a spatial representation when they are moving around in an environment without distinctive landmarks or when the only landmarks are far from the target location. To understand the challenge of such tasks, imagine that you were walking in an unfamiliar city and did not remember exactly how you had arrived at your current location. How easily could you find your way back to your starting point?

Even toddlers show the required navigational ability to some degree—good enough to lead them in the right general direction (Loomis et al., 1993). In one experiment, 1- and 2-year-olds first saw a small toy hidden in a long, rectangular sandbox and then saw a curtain descend around the sandbox, thus hiding the toy. The toddlers then walked to a different location, after which they were asked to find the toy. Despite no landmarks being present, the toddlers kept track of the hidden toy's location well enough to show better than chance accuracy in their searches (Newcombe et al., 1998).

On the other hand, forming relatively precise coding of locations in the absence of straightforward landmarks continues to be difficult for people well beyond 2 years of age (Bremner, Knowles, & Andreasen, 1994). Six- and seven-year-olds are not very good at it (Overman, Pate, Moore, & Peleuster, 1996), and adults vary tremendously in their abilities to perform this type of navigation. For example, when adults are asked to walk around the perimeter of an unfamiliar college campus and then to walk straight back to the starting point, some are quite accurate but many choose routes that take them nowhere near the original location (Cornell, Heth, Kneubuhler, & Sehgal, 1996).

The degree to which people develop spatial skills is strongly influenced by the importance of such skills in their culture. To demonstrate this point, Kearins

(1981) compared the spatial abilities of seminomadic aboriginal children growing up in the Australian desert with those of Caucasian peers growing up in Australian cities. Spatial ability is essential within aboriginal culture, because much of life within this culture consists of long treks between distant water holes. Needless to say, the aboriginals cannot rely on road signs; they must rely on their sense of space to get to the water. Consistent with the importance of spatial skills within their everyday lives, aboriginal children are superior to their city-dwelling peers in memory for spatial location, even in board games, a context that is more familiar to the urban children (Kearins, 1981). Thus, consistent with the general importance of the sociocultural context, how people make use of spatial thinking in their everyday activities greatly influences their quality of spatial thinking.

PENNY TWEEDIE / PANOS PICTURES

Spatial skills tend to be especially well developed in cultures in which they are crucial for survival.

Time

"What then is time? I know well enough what it is provided nobody asks me; but if I am asked and try to explain, I am baffled."

—*St. Augustine, 398 C.E. (1963)*

As this quotation suggests, even the deepest thinkers, from St. Augustine who wrote in the fourth century to Albert Einstein who wrote in the twentieth, have been mystified by the nature of time. Yet even infants in their first half year have a rudimentary sense of time, including perception of both the order and the duration of events (Friedman, 2008).

Experiencing Time

Probably the most basic sense of time involves knowledge of temporal order, that is, knowing what happened first, what happened next, and so on. Not surprisingly, given how mystifying life would be without such a basic sense of time, infants represent the order in which events occur from as early as the capability can be effectively measured. In one study in which 3-month-olds were presented a series of interesting photos first on their left, then on their left, then on their right, and so on. Within 20 seconds, they began to look to the side where each new photo was to appear even before the photo was presented (Adler, Haith, Arehart, & Lanthier, 2008; Haith, Wentworth, & Canfield, 1993). This looking pattern indicated that 3-month-olds detected the repetitive sequence of events over time and used the information to form expectations of where the next photo would appear. In another experiment, 4-month-olds who were habituated to three objects falling and striking a surface in a constant order dishabituated when there was a change in the order in which the objects fell (Lewkowitz, 2004).

By the end of their first year, infants can remember the order of events for a substantial period. For example, 10-month-olds who saw unusual pairs of actions repeated in the same order a number of times were able to imitate the actions in the correct order three months later (Carver & Bauer, 2001). By age 12 months, infants can see a pair of actions once and then imitate them in the correct order (Bauer, 1995). By 20 months of age, toddlers show similar proficiency with sequences of three events, clearly demonstrating that they can represent which came first, which next, and which last.

Infants also have an approximate sense of the durations of events. In one study, 4-month-olds saw periods of light and darkness alternate every 5 seconds for eight cycles, at which point the pattern was broken by the light's failing to appear. Within half a second of the break, infants' heart rates decelerated, a change, you will recall, that is characteristic of increased attention. In this case, the heart-rate deceleration suggested that the infants had a rough sense of the 5-second interval, expected the light to go on at the end of the interval, and experienced a spike in their attention when it did not appear (Colombo & Richman, 2002).

Infants also can discriminate between longer and shorter durations. The ratio of the durations, rather than differences in their absolute length, is critical for these discriminations (Brannon, Suanda, & Libertus, 2007). For example, 6-month-olds discriminate between durations when their ratio is 2:1 (1 second versus .5 seconds or 3 seconds versus 1.5 seconds) but not when the ratio is 1.5:1 (1.5 seconds versus 1 second or 4.5 seconds versus 3 seconds). Over the course of the first year, the precision of these discriminations increases. Thus, 10-month-olds, unlike 6-month-olds, discriminate when the ratio of the durations is 1.5:1 (though not when it is 1.33:1).

What about longer time periods—periods of weeks, months, or years? It is unknown whether infants have a sense of such long time periods, but preschoolers do possess some knowledge regarding them. For example, when asked which of two past events occurred more recently, most 4-year-olds knew that a specific event that happened a week before the experiment (Valentine's Day) happened more recently than an event that happened seven weeks earlier (Christmas) (Friedman, 1991). However, preschoolers correctly answer such questions only when the more recent event is quite close in time and much closer than the less recent one. Ability to distinguish more precisely among the timing of past events develops slowly during middle childhood (Friedman, 2003). For example, when children who had been presented a distinctive classroom experience were asked three months later to recall the month in which the experience occurred, the percentage of correct recall increased from 20% among 5-year-olds to 46% among 7-year-olds to 64% among 9-year-olds (Friedman & Lyon, 2005).

Understanding of the timing of future events increases during this age range as well (Friedman, 2000, 2003). Preschoolers often confuse the past and the future. For example, 5-year-olds predict a week after Valentine's Day that the next Valentine's Day will come sooner than the next Halloween or Christmas; they also predict that their next lunch is the same amount of time in the future regardless of whether they are tested just before lunch or just after it. Six-year-olds, in contrast, generally predict correctly in both cases. The improvement in children's sense of future time between the ages of 5 and 6 years is probably influenced by 5-year-olds' experience in kindergarten classrooms, where the cycle of seasons, holidays, and daily routines is emphasized.

Children, like adults, are subject to certain illusions about time, in part because of the role of attention in time perception. When 8-year-olds' attention is focused on the passage of time (for example, when they expect a prize at the end of a 2-minute interval), they perceive the duration as longer than the same interval when they are not anticipating a prize. Conversely, when they are very busy, they perceive the duration as shorter than when they have little to do (Zakay, 1992, 1993). Thus, the saying "A watched pot never boils" has psychological merit.

Reasoning about Time

During middle childhood, children become increasingly proficient at reasoning about time. In particular, they become able to infer that if two events started at the same time, but one event ended later than the other, then the event that ended later must have lasted for a greater amount of time.

Children as young as 5 years can sometimes make such logical inferences about time, but they do so only in simple, straightforward situations. For example, when told that two dolls fell asleep at the same time and that one doll awoke before the other, 5-year-olds reason correctly that the doll that slept later also slept longer (Levin, 1982). However, when 5-year-olds see two toy trains travel in the same direction on parallel tracks, and one train stops farther down the track, they usually say that the train that stopped farther down the track traveled for a longer time, regardless of when the trains started and stopped moving (Acredolo & Schmidt, 1981). The problem is that the 5-year-olds' attention is captured by the one train being farther down the track, which leads them to focus on the spatial positions of the trains rather than on their relative starting and stopping times. If this observation reminds you of Piaget's idea of centration (pages 137–138), there is good reason: Piaget's (1969) observations of performance on this task were part of what led him to conclude that children in the preoperational stage often center on a single dimension and ignore other, more relevant ones.

Causality

The famed eighteenth-century British philosopher David Hume described causality as "the cement of the universe." His point was that causal connections unite discrete events into coherent wholes. Consistent with Hume's view, from early in development, children rely heavily on their understanding of causal mechanisms to infer why physical and psychological events occur. When children take apart toys to find out how they work, or ask how flipping a switch makes a light go on, or wonder why Mommy is upset, they are trying to understand causal connections.

Both children and adults appear to have far deeper understanding of psychological causes than of physical ones; for example, kindergartners, 4th graders, and adults all can explain in much greater depth how people's intentions influence their actions than how everyday devices such as toasters and gumball machines work (Keil, 2005; Mills & Keil, 2004). Because we discussed the development of understanding of psychological causes earlier in this chapter, we now focus on the development of understanding of physical causes.

You probably will not be surprised to learn that nativists and empiricists disagree about the origins of understanding of physical causes. The difficulty of making sense of the world without some basic causal understanding, and the fact that children show some such understanding early in infancy, have led nativists to propose that infants possess an innate causal module or core theory that allows them to extract causal relations from the events they observe (e.g., Leslie, 1986; Spelke, 2003). Empiricists, on the other hand, have proposed that infants' causal understanding arises from their observations of innumerable events in the environment (e.g., Cohen & Cashon, 2006; Rogers & McClelland, 2004). As in other contexts, the debate has stimulated many interesting observations and experiments, a few of which we will now review.

Causal Reasoning in Infancy

By 6 months of age, infants perceive causal connections among some physical events (Cohen & Cashon, 2006; Leslie, 1986). In a typical experiment demonstrating infants' ability to perceive such relations, Lisa Oakes and Les Cohen (1995) presented 6- to 10-month-olds a series of video clips in which a moving object collided with a stationary object and the stationary object immediately moved in the way one would expect. Different moving and stationary objects were used in each clip, but the basic "plot" remained the same. After seeing a few of these video clips, infants habituated to the collisions. Then the infants were shown a slightly different clip in which the stationary object started moving before it was struck. Infants looked at this event for a longer time than they had looked during the preceding trials, presumably because the new video clip violated their sense that inanimate objects do not move on their own.

Infants' and toddlers' understanding of physical causality influences not only their expectations about inanimate objects but also their ability to remember and imitate sequences of actions. When 9- to 11-month-olds are shown actions that are causally related (e.g., making a rattle by putting a small object inside two cups that can be pushed together to form a single container), they usually can reproduce the actions (Figure 7.5) (Carver & Bauer, 1999). In contrast, when similar but

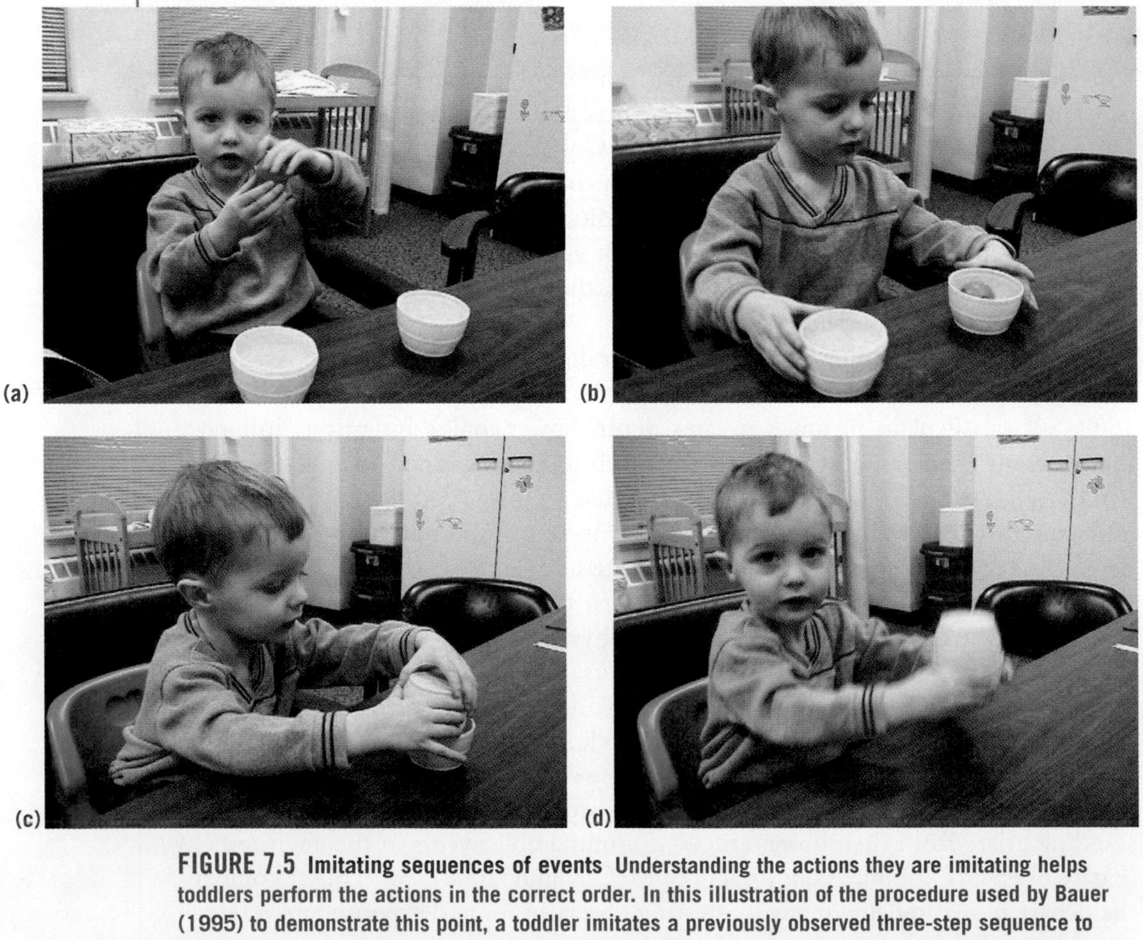

FIGURE 7.5 Imitating sequences of events Understanding the actions they are imitating helps toddlers perform the actions in the correct order. In this illustration of the procedure used by Bauer (1995) to demonstrate this point, a toddler imitates a previously observed three-step sequence to build a rattle. The child (a) picks up a small block; (b) puts it into the bottom half of the container; (c) pushes the top half of the container onto the bottom, thus completing the rattle; and (d) shakes it.

causally unrelated actions are shown, babies do not reliably reproduce them until age 20 to 22 months (Bauer, 2007).

By the end of their second year, and by some measures even earlier, children can infer the causal impact of one variable based on indirectly relevant information about another. Sobel and Kirkham (2006), for example, presented 19- and 24-month-olds a box called a "blicket detector," which, the experimenter explained, played music when a type of object called a blicket was placed on it. Then the experimenter placed two objects, A and B, on the blicket detector, and the music played. When the experimenter next placed object A alone on the blicket detector, the music did not play. Then the children were asked to turn on the blicket detector. The 24-month-olds consistently chose object B, indicating that seeing the ineffectiveness of object A led them to infer that object B activated the blicket detector. In contrast, the 19-month-olds chose object A as often as they did object B, suggesting that they did not draw this inference.

Development of Causal Reasoning Beyond Infancy

Although infants possess some understanding of cause-and-effect by the second half of the first year, they demonstrate such understanding only in situations in which the cause–effect connections are obvious. After infancy, children expand their understanding to include increasing numbers of situations in which the causal connections are less obvious.

One illustration of this growing understanding of causality comes from Chen and Siegler's (2000) study of 1- and 2-year-olds' tool use. The toddlers were presented an attractive toy that was sitting on a table roughly a foot beyond their reach. Between the child and the toy were six potential tools that varied in length and in the type of head at the end of the shaft (Figure 7.6). To succeed on the task, the toddlers needed to understand the causal relations that would make one tool more effective than the others for pulling in the toy. In particular, they needed to understand that a sufficiently long shaft and a head at right angles to the shaft were essential.

The 2-year-olds succeeded considerably more often than the 1-year-olds did in obtaining the toy, both in their initial efforts to get it on their own and after being shown by the experimenter how they could use the optimal tool to obtain it. One reason for the older toddlers' greater success was that they more often used a tool to try to get the toy, as opposed to reaching for it with their hands or seeking their mother's help. Another reason was that the older toddlers chose the optimal tool on a greater percentage of trials on which they used some tool. A third reason was that the older toddlers more often generalized what they had learned on the first problem to new, superficially different problems involving tools and toys with different shapes, colors, and decorations. All these findings indicate that the older toddlers had a deeper understanding of the causal relations between a tool's features and its usefulness for pulling in the toy.

Preschoolers seem to expect that if a variable causes an effect, it should do so consistently (Schulz & Sommerville, 2006). When 4-year-olds see a potential cause produce an effect inconsistently, they infer that some variable that they cannot see must cause the effect; but when the same effect occurs consistently, they do not infer that a hidden variable was important.

FIGURE 7.6 Toddlers' problem solving In the task used by Chen and Siegler (2000) to examine toddlers' causal reasoning and problem solving, choosing the right tool for getting the toy required children to understand the importance of both the length of the shaft and the angle of the head relative to the shaft. Older toddlers' greater understanding of these causal relations led them to more often use tools, rather than just reaching for the toy, and to more often choose the right tool for the task.

SYRACUSE NEWSPAPERS / THE IMAGE WORKS

Most 5-year-olds find magic tricks thrilling, even though a year or two earlier, they would have been left cold by them.

For example, if 4-year-olds saw some dogs respond to petting by eagerly wagging their tails and other dogs respond to petting by growling, they might infer that some variable other than the petting, such as the dogs' friendliness, caused the effect. But if all the dogs they had ever seen looked happy when petted, they would not infer that the dogs' friendliness was relevant.

Preschoolers' emerging understanding that events must have causes also seems to influence children's reactions to magic tricks. Most 3- and 4-year-olds fail to see the point of magic tricks; they grasp that something strange has happened but do not find the tricks humorous or actively try to figure out what caused the strange outcome (Rosengren & Hickling, 2000). By age 5, however, children become fascinated with magic tricks precisely because no obvious causal mechanism could produce the effect (Box 7.3). Many want to search the magician's hat or other apparatus to see how such a stunt was possible. This increasing appreciation that even astonishing events must have causes, along with an increasing understanding of the mechanisms that connect causes and their effects, reflect the growth of causal reasoning.

Number

Like space, time, and causality, number is a central dimension of human experience. It is hard to imagine how the world would appear if we did not have at least a crude sense of number—we would not know how many fingers we have, how many people are in our family, and so on. As with the other concepts we have discussed, the nativist/empiricist debate is in play with regard to the concept of number. Nativists argue that children are born with a core concept of

a closer look

Magical Thinking and Fantasy

Lest you conclude that by age 5, children's causal reasoning is pretty much like that of adults, consider the following conversation between two kindergartners and their teacher:

Lisa: Do plants wish for baby plants?
Deana: I think only people can make wishes. But God could put a wish inside a plant. . . .
Teacher: I always think of people as having ideas.
Deana: It's just the same. God puts a little idea in the plant to tell it what to be.
Lisa: My mother wished for me and I came when it was my birthday.

(Paley, 1981, pp. 79–80)

This is not a conversation that would have occurred with two 10-year-olds. Rather, as noted by Jacqui Woolley, a psychologist who studies preschoolers' fantasies, it reflects one of the most charming aspects of early childhood: preschoolers and young elementary school children "live in a world in which fantasy and reality are more intertwined than they are for adults" (Woolley, 1997).

Young children's belief in fantasy and magic, as well as in normal causes, is evident in many ways. Most 4- to 6-year-olds believe that they can influence other people by wishing them into doing something, such as buying a particular present for their birthday (Vikan & Clausen, 1993). They believe that effective wishing takes a great deal of skill, and perhaps magic, but that it can be done. In related fashion, many believe that getting in good with Santa Claus can make their hopes come true. Children's fantasies can have a dark side as well, such as when they fear that monsters might hurt them (Woolley, 1997). Although this world of the imagination is most striking between ages 3 and 6, aspects of it remain evident for years thereafter. In one study that demonstrated the persistence of magical thinking, many 9-year-olds and some adults reverted to magical explanations when confronted with a trick that was difficult to explain in physical terms (Subbotsky, 2005).

Research has shown that young children not only believe in magic; they sometimes act on their belief in it. In one experiment, preschoolers were told that a certain box was magical and that if they placed a drawing into it and said magical words, the object depicted in the drawing would appear. Then the experimenter left the child alone with the box and a number of drawings. Children put drawings of the most attractive items into the box, said the "magical words," and were visibly disappointed when they opened the box and found only the drawings (Subbotsky, 1993, 1994).

How can we reconcile preschoolers' understanding of physical causes and effects with their belief in magic, wishing, and Santa Claus? The key is to recognize that here, as in many situations, children believe a variety of somewhat contradictory ideas at the same time. They may think number that includes special mechanisms for representing and learning about the relative numbers of objects in sets, counting, and simple addition and subtraction (Brannon, 2006; Wynn, 2000). They also point to specific brain areas that are heavily involved in representing numerical magnitudes (Ansari, 2008) and to the existence of specific neurons that respond most strongly when particular numbers of objects (e.g., 5 objects) are displayed (Nieder, 2005). In contrast, empiricists argue that children learn about numbers through the same types of experiences and learning mechanisms that help them acquire other concepts, and that infants' numerical competence is not as great as nativists claim (Clearfield, 2006; Mix, Huttenlocher, & Levine, 2002). They also note the existence of large differences in numerical understanding among children in different cultures and document the contributions of instruction, language, and cultural values to these differences (Geary, 2006; Miller, Smith, Zhu, & Zhang, 1995). In this section, we review current evidence regarding numerical development, as well as nativist and empiricist perspectives on the evidence.

numerical equality the realization that all sets of N objects have something in common

Numerical Equality

Perhaps the most basic understanding of numbers involves **numerical equality,** the idea that all sets of N objects have something in common. When children recognize, for example, that two dogs, two cups, two balls, and two shoes share the property of "twoness," they have a rudimentary understanding of numerical equality.

Infants as young as 5 months old appear to have some sense of numerical equality, at least as it applies to sets of one, two, or three objects. The evidence for this conclusion comes from studies using the familiar habituation paradigm. In

7.3

that magic or the power of their imagination can cause things to happen, but they may not depend on it when doing so could be embarrassing. In one demonstration of this limited belief in magic and the power of the imagination (Woolley & Phelps, 1994), an experimenter showed preschoolers an empty box, closed it, and then asked them to imagine a pencil inside it. The experimenter next asked the children whether there was now a pencil in the box; many said "yes." Then an adult came into the room and said that she needed a pencil to do her work. Very few of the preschoolers opened the box or handed it to her. Thus, it appeared that many children said the box contained a pencil when no consequences would follow if they were wrong, but they did not believe in magic strongly enough to act in a way that might look foolish to an adult.

How do children move beyond their belief in magic? One means is learning more about real causes; the more children know about the true causes of events, the less likely they are to explain them in magical terms (Woolley, 1997). Another influence is personal experiences that undermine the child's magical beliefs, such as hearing peers pooh-pooh the idea of Santa Claus or seeing two Santa Clauses on the same street. Sometimes, however, children salvage their hopes by distinguishing between flawed manifestations of the magical being and the magical being itself. They may, for example, fervently distinguish between the real Santa Claus and imposters who dress up to look like him.

Belief in magic and fantastic creatures sometimes does not end in childhood. In one study, all 17 college-student participants claimed that they did not believe in magic, yet not one of them was willing to allow someone who was said to be a witch to cast an evil spell on their lives (Subbotsky, 2005). Sampling a broader population, a Gallup poll revealed that more than 20% of American adults believe in ghosts and haunted houses (Gallup & Newport, 1991). Innumerable other adults indulge superstitions such as not walking under ladders, avoiding cracks in sidewalks, and knocking on wood. Apparently, many of us, maybe all, never entirely outgrow magical thinking.

"A real one, or just somebody wearing a funny suit and a painted face?"

these studies, young infants are shown a sequence of pictures, with each picture having the same number of objects but differing in other ways. For example, infants might be shown three stars arranged vertically, then three circles arranged horizontally, then three diamonds arranged diagonally, and so on. After the infants habituate to the pictures of three objects, they are shown a picture with a different number of objects (such as two squares). These studies indicate that 5-month-olds tend to discriminate one object from two, and two objects from three (van Loosbroek & Smitsman, 1990). The tendency is weak—infants' discriminations are often based on the objects' area or perimeter rather than on their number, when both vary (Clearfield & Mix, 1999; Feigenson, Carey, & Spelke, 2002). However, infants also discriminate among small numbers of events, indicating that they do have some sense of number independent of area and perimeter. In one demonstration of this rudimentary numerical understanding, Wynn (1995) showed 6-month-olds a puppet that repeatedly jumped twice. After the infants habituated to this pattern, they were shown the puppet jumping either once or three times. The infants' looking time increased when the number of jumps changed, suggesting that the infants discriminated between two jumps and one or three.

Although infants' recognition of numerical equality is limited to small sets, their recognition of numerical inequality extends to much larger sets. As with discriminations among temporal durations, infants' discriminations among unequal numerical sets depend on the ratio of the number of entities in them. For example, 6-month-olds discriminate between sets of dots or sounds with 2:1 ratios (e.g., 16 versus 8) but not between sets with ratios of 1.5:1 (e.g., 12 versus 8) (Brannon, 2002; Lipton & Spelke, 2003). As with discriminations between temporal durations, numerical-set discriminations become more precise with age: whereas 6-month-olds do not discriminate between ratios of 1.5:1 objects, 9-month-olds do (Wood & Spelke, 2005). However, when discriminating between different numbers of objects, the absolute number of objects also matters: on some tasks, 9- and 11-month-old infants discriminate between one and two objects and between two and three objects, but not between two and four or three and six (Feigenson, Carey, & Hauser, 2002). The reasons for the differing findings are not yet known.

Infants' Arithmetic

Some experts on early understanding of number have concluded that infants also have a basic understanding of arithmetic (R. Gelman & Williams, 1998; Wynn, 1992). The type of evidence on which they base their conclusion is illustrated in Figure 7.7. A 5-month-old sees a doll on a stage. A screen comes up, hiding the doll from the infant's sight. Next, the infant sees a hand place a second doll behind the screen and then sees the hand emerge from behind the screen without the doll, thus seeming to have left the second doll with the first one. Finally, the screen drops down, revealing either one or two dolls. Most 5-month-olds look longer when there is only one doll, suggesting that they expected that $1 + 1$ should equal 2 and that they were surprised when they saw only a single object. Similar results are seen with subtraction: 5-month-olds look longer when the apparent removal of one of two objects results in two objects being present than they do when the removal results in one object being there (Wynn, 1992).

But do these findings show that infants understand arithmetic? The claim that they do has evoked a great deal of argument. One reason for the controversy is that efforts to replicate the original result have had mixed success. Some studies have replicated it (Simon, Hespos, & Rochat, 1995), others have not (Wakeley, Rivera, &

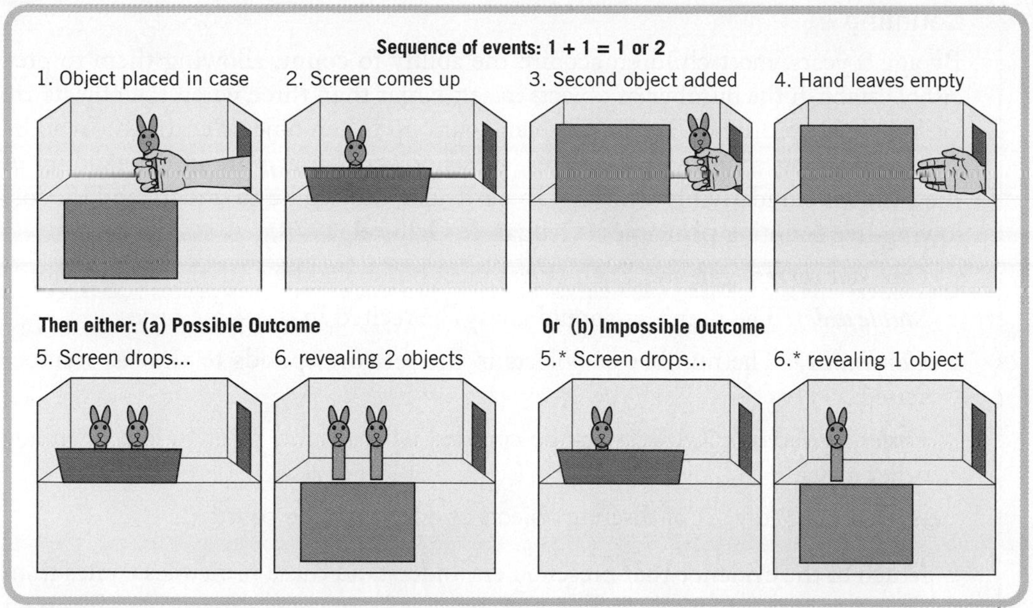
Sequence of events: 1 + 1 = 1 or 2
1. Object placed in case
2. Screen comes up
3. Second object added
4. Hand leaves empty
Then either: (a) Possible Outcome
5. Screen drops...
6. revealing 2 objects
Or (b) Impossible Outcome
5.* Screen drops...
6.* revealing 1 object

COURTESY OF PATRICIA BAUER

FIGURE 7.7 Infants' understanding of addition **On the task used by Wynn (1992) to examine whether infants have a rudimentary grasp of addition, 5-month-olds saw (1) a single doll placed on a stage, (2) a screen raised to hide the doll, (3) a hand with a doll in it move toward and then behind the screen, and (4) the hand return empty after having been behind the screen. Then the screen dropped, revealing either (5 and 6) the possible event of two dolls on the stage or (5* and 6*) the seemingly impossible event of one doll on the stage. Infants younger than 6 months of age looked for a longer time at the seemingly impossible event, suggesting their surprise at seeing one doll rather than two.**

Langer, 2000). A more general reason for the controversy is that, as with the numerical-equality tasks described in the previous section, infants show competence only in situations where the total number of objects is three or fewer. Children do not show similar, precise understanding of the effects of adding two objects to two other objects until they are much older—3 to 5 *years* old (Huttenlocher, Jordan, & Levine, 1994; Starkey, 1992).

The fact that much of infants' numerical competence is limited to sets of three or fewer objects has led a second group of experts (Clearfield & Mix, 1999; Cohen & Marks, 2002; Simon, 1997) to conclude that infants' responses on these tests of arithmetic are based not on understanding of arithmetic but instead on perception. For example, Haith and Benson (1998) proposed that infants rely on **subitizing**, a perceptual process by which adults and children can look at one, two, or three objects and almost immediately form a mental image of how many objects there are. According to this interpretation, infants form an image of the object or objects that are initially presented and of the objects that seem to be added to, or subtracted from, them; if the objects that the infants see at the end of the procedure appear different from the image they originally formed, they look for a longer time. Consistent with this interpretation, when 5-month-olds are tested under conditions that increase the difficulty of forming a mental image (e.g., when they see a hand place one object and then another behind the raised screen but, in contrast to the usual procedure, do not see either object's position until the end), the infants do not show surprise when 1 + 1 = 1 (Uller, Carey, Huntley-Fenner, & Klatt, 1999). Thus, under some circumstances, infants show numerical competence with small sets of objects, but their competence may stem from an ability to form mental images rather than from an understanding of arithmetic.

subitizing a process by which adults and children can look at a few objects and almost immediately know how many objects are present

Counting

By age 3 years, most children acquire the ability to count, allowing them to precisely establish the number of objects in sets larger than three when the objects are visible. The majority of 3-year-olds can count up to ten objects correctly. In addition to learning counting procedures, preschoolers also acquire understanding of the principles underlying counting. In particular, they come to understand the following five counting principles (Gelman & Gallistel, 1978):

One–one correspondence: Each object must be labeled by a single number word.

Stable order: The numbers should always be recited in the same order.

Cardinality: The number of objects in the set corresponds to the last number stated.

Order irrelevance: Objects can be counted left to right, right to left, or in any other order.

Abstraction: Any set of discrete objects or events can be counted.

Much of the evidence that preschoolers understand these principles comes from their judgments when observing two types of counting procedures: incorrect counts and unusual but correct counts. When 4- or 5-year-olds see a puppet counting in a way that violates the one–one correspondence principle—for example, by labeling a single object with two number words (Figure 7.8a)—they consistently say that the counting is incorrect (Frye, Braisby, Lowe, Maroudas, & Nicholls, 1989; Gelman, Meck, & Merkin, 1986). In contrast, when they see the puppet count in ways that are unusual but that do not violate any principle—for example, by starting in the middle of a row but counting all the objects (Figure 7.8b)—they judge the counting to be correct, even though they say that they would not count that way themselves. The preschoolers' realization that procedures that they themselves would not use are nonetheless correct shows that they understand the principles that distinguish correct from incorrect counting.

Although children all over the world learn number words, the rate at which they do so is affected by the specifics of the number system used in their culture. As Kevin Miller and his colleagues note, for example, most 5-year-olds in China can count to 100 or more, whereas most 5-year-olds in the United States cannot count nearly as high (Miller, Smith, Zhu, & Zhang, 1995). Part of the reason for this difference in counting proficiency seems to be the greater regularity of the Chinese number system, particularly with respect to numbers in the teens. In both Chinese and English, the words for numbers greater than 20 follow a regular rule: decade name first, digit name second (e.g., twenty-one, twenty-two, etc.). In Chinese, the words for numbers between 11 and 19 follow the same rule (equivalent to ten-one, ten-two, etc.). In English, however, no simple rule indicates the numbers between 11 and 19; each term has to be learned separately.

FIGURE 7.8 Counting procedures Counting procedures similar to those used by Frye and colleagues (1989) and Gelman, Meck, and Merkin (1986): (a) an incorrect counting procedure; (b) an unusual but correct procedure.

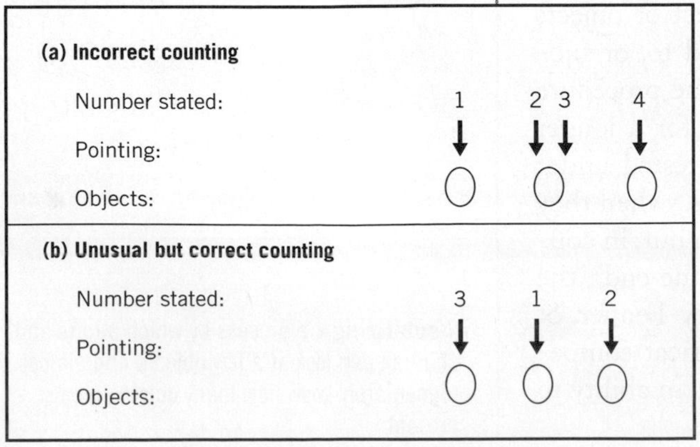

Figure 7.9 illustrates the apparent impact of this cultural difference in number systems. Three-year-olds in the United States and China are comparable in their ability to recite the numbers 1 through 10, which do not follow any obvious rule in either English or Chinese languages. However, Chinese 4-year-olds quickly learn the numbers in the teens and succeeding decades, whereas their U.S. peers experience prolonged difficulty with the teens. The difference in languages is not the only reason why the counting skill of U.S. children lags behind that of children in

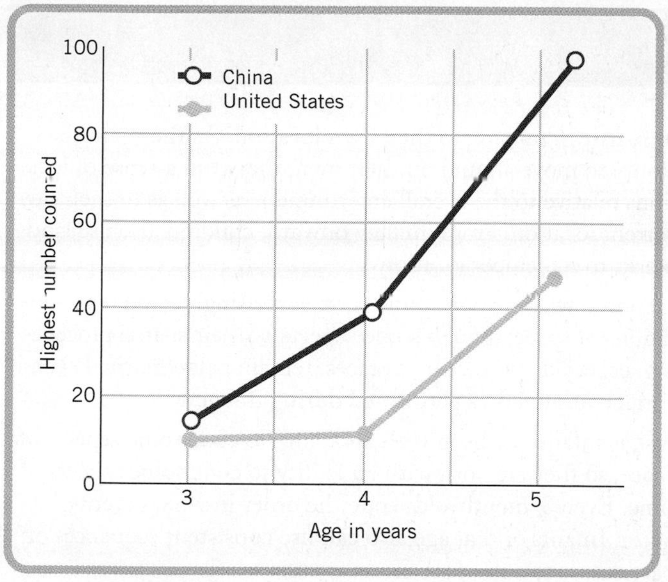

FIGURE 7.9 Counting level Although 3-year-olds in China and the United States can count to about the same point, 4- and 5-year-olds in China can count much higher than their U.S. peers. One reason for the faster development of Chinese children's counting ability appears to be that the Chinese words for numbers in the teens follow a consistent, easily learned pattern, whereas the English words for numbers in the teens must be memorized one by one. (Data from Miller et al., 1995)

China. Chinese culture places a much greater emphasis on mathematical skill than U.S. culture does, and Chinese preschoolers are consequently more advanced than their U.S. peers in numerical skills generally, including arithmetic and number-line estimation (Siegler & Mu, 2008). However, the greater simplicity of the Chinese system for naming numbers in the teens seems to be one contributor to Chinese children's greater counting proficiency.

review:

People, like other animals, are biologically prepared to code specific types of spatial information in specific parts of the brain. From the first year, children represent spatial locations both relative to their own bodies and relative to other features of the environment, such as landmarks. Self-produced movement seems to be crucial in the development of spatial representations.

A rudimentary sense of time also is present extremely early; by age 3 months if not earlier, infants possess a sense of experiential time, the order in which events happened. However, an accurate sense of duration doesn't develop until 3 to 5 years of age, and learning to reason logically about time takes even longer.

A basic understanding of causality emerges extremely early in development. Infants in their first year distinguish between physical causes, in which actions are produced by direct contact, and psychological causes, in which actions are produced by requests, psychological needs, beliefs, and desires. During the preschool and elementary school periods, children become increasingly adept at inferring causal relations, even when the relations are more complex and require deeper understanding of causes, effects, and the mechanisms that link them. However, belief in magic and the supernatural coexist with this growing understanding of causal mechanisms, especially in the preschool years.

A basic recognition of differences between sets of one, two, and three objects or actions is present in the first year. However, not until age 3 or 4 years do children show similar understanding with even slightly larger sets. During the preschool period, children also learn the principles underlying counting, such as that each object must be counted once and only once. By age 5 years, most also learn the counting system of their language. Learning of counting is influenced by the regularity of the number system in the child's language, as well as by the culture's emphasis on mathematics.

Chapter Summary

- To understand their experience, children must learn that the world includes several types of objects: people, other living things, and inanimate objects. Children also need a basic understanding of space, time, causality, and number, so that they will be able to code their experiences in terms of where, when, why, and how often events occurred.

Understanding Who or What

- Infants' early categories of objects are based in large part on perceptual similarity, especially similarity in the shapes of the objects. By the end of the first year, they also form categories of objects that serve the same function.
- By age 2 or 3 years, infants also form category hierarchies: animal/dog/poodle, furniture/chair/La-Z-Boy, and so on.
- From infancy onward, children act differently toward people than toward other animals or inanimate objects. For example, infants smile more at people than at either rabbits or robots.
- By age 4 or 5 years, preschoolers develop a rudimentary but well-organized theory of mind, within which they organize their understanding of people's behavior. A key assumption of this theory of mind is that desires and beliefs motivate specific actions.
- Understanding that other people will act on their beliefs, even when the beliefs are false, is very difficult for 3-year-olds; many children do not gain this understanding until age 5.
- Animals and plants, especially animals, are of great interest to young children. When animals are present, infants and toddlers pay careful attention to them.
- By age 4 years, children develop quite elaborate understanding of living things, including coherent ideas about invisible processes such as growth, inheritance, illness, and healing. Both their natural fascination with living things and the input they receive from the environment contribute to their knowledge about plants and animals.

Understanding Where, When, Why, and How Many

- People, like other animals, are biologically prepared to code space. Early in infancy, they code locations of other objects primarily in relation to their own location. As they gain the ability to move around on their own, they gain a sense of locations relative to the overall environment as well as to their own current location. From infancy onward, children also use landmarks to remember locations.
- Children who are born blind have surprisingly good representations of space, though some aspects of their spatial processing, especially processing of faces, remain below normal even if corrective surgery is performed during infancy.
- Just as infants are born with an ability to code some aspects of space, so they are born with an ability to code some aspects of time. Even 3-month-olds code the order in which events occur. Infants of that age also can use consistent sequences of past events to anticipate future events.
- By age 5 years, children also can reason about time, in the sense of inferring that if two events started at the same time, and one stopped later than the other, that event took longer. However, they can do this only when interfering perceptual cues are absent.
- The development of causal reasoning about physical events also begins in infancy. By 6 to 12 months, infants understand the likely consequences of objects' colliding. Understanding causal relations among actions helps 1-year-olds remember them.
- By 4 or 5 years, children seem to realize that causes are necessary for events to occur. When no cause is obvious, they search for one. During the preschool period, though, many children believe in magic as well as physical cause–effect relations.
- Rudimentary understanding of very small numbers is present from early in infancy. Infants notice numerical differences between small sets of objects and between events that are repeated a different number of times.
- By age 3 years, most children learn to count 10 objects. Their counting seems to reflect understanding of certain principles, such as that each object should be labeled by a single number word. Children's subsequent rate of learning about numbers reflects their culture's number system and the degree to which their culture values numerical knowledge.

Critical Thinking Questions

1. Why is it useful for people to organize categories into hierarchies, such as animal/dog/poodle or vehicle/car/Prius?
2. Did you have an imaginary companion or know someone who did? What functions did the invisible friend serve, and why do you think that you or the other person stopped imagining the companion?
3. Why do you think 5-year-olds are so much better at false-belief problems than 3-year-olds are?
4. Self-produced movement enhances children's representation of space. What evolutionary purpose might this serve?
5. Describe the thoughts that might go through a 5-year-old's mind when the child sees two Santa Clauses walking past each other.
6. Do you think infants possess a basic understanding of arithmetic? Why or why not?

Key Terms

concepts, p. 260
category hierarchy, p. 262
perceptual categorization, p. 263
superordinate level, p. 264
subordinate level, p. 264
basic level, p. 264
naïve psychology, p. 266
theory of mind, p. 267
false-belief problems, p. 268
theory of mind module (TOMM), p. 269
pretend play, p. 271
object substitution, p. 271
sociodramatic play, p. 272
essentialism, p. 276
egocentric representations, p. 280
numerical equality, p. 289
subitizing, p. 291

CHRISTIAN PIERRE, *Miracle of Life*, 1996

8

Intelligence and Academic Achievement

THEMES

Nature and Nurture

The Active Child

Continuity/Discontinuity

Mechanisms of Change

The Sociocultural Context

Individual Differences

Research and Children's Welfare

In 1904, the minister of education of France faced a problem. France, like other western European and North American countries, had recently introduced universal public education, and it was becoming apparent that some children were not learning well. Therefore, the minister wanted a means of identifying children who would have difficulty succeeding in standard classrooms, so that they could be given special education. His problem was how to identify such children.

One obvious way was to ask teachers to indicate which students in their classrooms were encountering difficulty. However, the minister worried that teachers might be biased in their assessments. In particular, he was concerned that some of them would be prejudiced against poor children and would say that they were unable to learn even if they were. He therefore asked Alfred Binet, a French psychologist who had been studying intelligence for 15 years, to develop an easy-to-administer, objective test of intelligence.

The prevailing view at the time was that intelligence is based on simple skills, such as associating objects with the sounds they make (e.g., ducks with quacking, bells with ringing) and detecting whether two objects are the same or different. According to this view, children who are more adept than their peers at such simple skills learn more quickly and thus become more intelligent. The theory was plausible—but wrong. It is now clear that simple skills are only moderately related to broader, everyday indicators of intelligence, such as school performance.

Binet had a different theory. He believed that the key components of intelligence are high-level abilities, such as problem solving, reasoning, and judgment, and he maintained that intelligence tests should assess such abilities directly. Therefore, on the test that he and his colleague Théophile Simon devised—the *Binet-Simon Intelligence Test*—children were asked (among other things) to interpret proverbs, solve puzzles, name objects, and sequence cartoon panels so that the jokes made sense.

Binet's approach was successful in identifying children who would have difficulty learning from classroom instruction. More generally, children's performance on the Binet-Simon test correlated highly not only with their school grades at the time of testing but also with their grades years later. The test was also successful in establishing a goal of intelligence testing that has been pursued ever since—to provide an objective measure of scholastic aptitude that would allow fairer decisions about children's schooling, including which children should be in honors classes, which are in need of special education, which should be admitted to highly selective colleges, and so on.

In addition to the practical impact of his test, Binet's approach to intelligence has continued to influence research on the topic to this day. In most areas of cognitive development—perception, language, conceptual understanding, and so on—the emphasis is on age-related changes: the ways in which younger children differ from older ones. Following Binet's lead, however, research on intelligence has focused on individual differences—on how and why children of the same age differ from each other, and on the continuity of such individual differences over time. The nature of individual differences is one of the enduring themes throughout the field of child development, but the focus on it is especially intense in the study of intelligence.

Questions regarding the development of intelligence excite strong passions, and no wonder. Research in this area raises many of the most basic issues about human nature: the roles of heredity and environment, the influence of ethnic and racial differences, the effects of wealth and poverty, and the possibility of improvement. Almost everyone has opinions, often heartfelt ones, about why some people are more intelligent than others. Intelligence research also has added greatly to the understanding of all of the major themes emphasized in this book; the nature and origins of *individual differences,* the contributions of the *active child* and of the *sociocultural context,* the way in which *nature and nurture* together shape development, the degree of *continuity* in a key human trait, the *mechanisms* that produces changes, and the relation between *research and children's welfare.* Before examining research on the development of intelligence, however, we must examine a question that sounds simple but that actually lies at the heart of many of the controversies: What *is* intelligence?

What Is Intelligence?

Intelligence is notoriously difficult to define, but this has not kept people from trying. Part of the difficulty is that intelligence can legitimately be described at three levels of analysis: as one thing, as a few things, or as many things.

Intelligence as a Single Trait

Some researchers view intelligence as a single entity that influences all aspects of cognitive functioning. Supporting this idea is the fact that performance on almost all intellectual tasks is positively correlated. Children who do well on one intellectual task tend to do well on others, too (Geary, 2005). These positive correlations occur even among dissimilar intellectual tasks—for example, remembering lists of numbers and folding pieces of paper to reproduce printed designs. Such omnipresent positive correlations have led to the hypothesis that each of us possesses a certain amount of ***g*****, or general intelligence,** and that *g* influences our ability to think and learn on all intellectual tasks (Jensen, 1998; Spearman, 1927).

Numerous sources of evidence attest to the usefulness of viewing intelligence as a single entity. Measures of *g,* such as overall scores on intelligence tests, correlate positively with school grades and achievement test performance (Brody, 1992). At the level of cognitive and brain mechanisms, *g* correlates with information-processing speed (Deary, 2000; Geary, 2005), with speed of neural transmission (Vernon et al., 2000), and with brain volume (Wickett, Vernon, & Lee, 2000). Measures of *g* also correlate strongly with people's knowledge of subjects they have not studied in school, such as medicine, law, art history, the Bible, and so on (Lubinski & Humphreys, 1997). Thus, there is good reason to view intelligence as a single entity that involves the ability to think and learn.

Intelligence as a Few Basic Abilities

There also are good arguments for viewing intelligence as more than a single general entity. The simplest such view holds that there are two types of intelligence: *fluid intelligence* and *crystallized intelligence* (Cattell, 1987). **Fluid intelligence** involves the ability to think on the spot, for example, by drawing inferences and understanding relations between concepts that have not been encountered previously. It is closely related to the ability to learn, the speed of information processing, the capacity of working memory, and the ability to control attention (Fry & Hale, 2000; Geary, 2005). Fluid intelligence also is related to brain size, particularly the size of the cortex, and to the amount of activation of specific brain areas, notably the prefrontal cortex and parietal area, on tasks that require attention and problem solving (Deary, 2000; Gray, Chabris, & Braver, 2003).

g (general intelligence) the part of intelligence that is common to all intellectual tasks

fluid intelligence ability to think on the spot to solve novel problems

Crystallized intelligence is factual knowledge about the world: knowledge of word meanings, state capitals, answers to arithmetic problems, and so on. It reflects long-term memory for prior experiences and is closely related to verbal ability. The hippocampus is a particularly crucial brain region for forming the enduring memories on which crystallized intelligence is based (Deary, 2000).

The distinction between fluid and crystallized intelligence is supported by the fact that tests of each type of intelligence correlate more highly with each other than they do with tests of the other type. Thus, children who do well on one test of fluid intelligence tend to do well on other tests of fluid intelligence but not necessarily on tests of crystallized intelligence. In addition, the two types of intelligence have different developmental courses. Crystallized intelligence increases steadily from early in life to old age, whereas fluid intelligence peaks in early adulthood around age 20 and slowly declines thereafter (Salthouse, 2009).

A somewhat more complex view of intelligence proposes that the human intellect is composed of several abilities. One prominent proposal of this type, that of L. L. Thurstone (1938), portrayed intelligence as involving seven **primary mental abilities:** word fluency, verbal meaning, reasoning, spatial visualization, numbering, rote memory, and perceptual speed. The key evidence for the usefulness of dividing intelligence into these seven abilities is similar to that for the distinction between fluid and crystallized intelligence. Scores on various tests of a single ability tend to correlate more strongly with each other than do scores on tests of any of the other abilities. For example, although both spatial visualization and perceptual speed are measures of fluid intelligence, children tend to perform more similarly on two tests of spatial visualization than they do on a test of spatial visualization and a test of perceptual speed. The trade-off between these two views of intelligence is between the simplicity of the crystallized/fluid distinction and the greater precision of the idea of seven primary mental abilities.

Intelligence as Numerous Processes

A third view envisions intelligence as comprising numerous, distinct processes. Information-processing analyses of how people solve intelligence test items (e.g., Carpenter, Just, & Shell, 1990; Siegler & Svetina, 2006) and how they perform everyday intellectual tasks such as reading, writing, and arithmetic (Geary, 2005) reveal that a great many processes are involved. These include remembering, perceiving, attending, comprehending, encoding, associating, generalizing, planning, reasoning, forming concepts, solving problems, generating and applying strategies, and so on. Viewing intelligence as "many things" allows more precise specification of the processes involved in intelligent behavior than do approaches that view it as "one thing" or "a few things."

A Proposed Resolution

How can these competing perspectives on intelligence be reconciled? After studying intelligence for more than half a century, John Carroll (1993, 2005) proposed a grand integration: the **three-stratum theory of intelligence** (Figure 8.1). At the top of the hierarchy is *g;* in the middle are several moderately general abilities (which include both fluid and crystallized intelligence and more specific skills, similar to the seven primary mental abilities); at the bottom are many specific processes. General intelligence influences all of the moderately general abilities, and both general intelligence and the moderately general abilities influence the specific processes. For example, knowing someone's general intelligence allows for a fairly reliable prediction of the person's general memory skills; knowing both of

crystallized intelligence factual knowledge about the world

primary mental abilities seven abilities said by Thurstone to be crucial to intelligence

three-stratum theory of intelligence Carroll's model of intelligence, including *g* at the top of the hierarchy, eight moderately general abilities in the middle, and many specific processes at the bottom

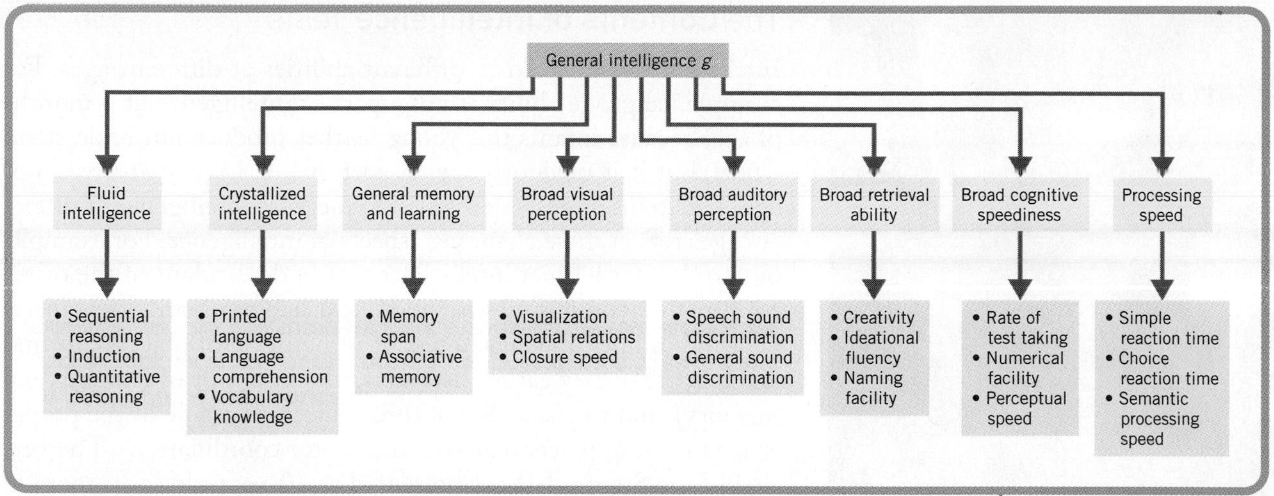

FIGURE 8.1 Carroll's three-stratum theory of intelligence In Carroll's three-stratum theory of intelligence, general intelligence (*g*) influences several intermediate-level abilities, and each intermediate-level ability influences a variety of specific processes. As this model suggests, intelligence can be usefully viewed as a single entity, as a small set of abilities, or as a very large number of particular processes.

them allows quite reliable prediction of the person's memory span; and knowing all three allows very accurate prediction of the person's memory span for a particular type of material, such as words, letters, or numbers.

Carroll's comprehensive analysis of the research literature indicated that all three levels of analysis that we have discussed in this section are necessary to account for the totality of facts about intelligence. Thus, for the question "Is intelligence one thing, a few things, or many things?," the correct answer seems to be "All of the above."

review:

Intelligence can be described at three levels of analysis. It can be viewed as a single general ability to think and learn; as several moderately general abilities, such as spatial, verbal, and mathematical capacities; or as a collection of numerous specific skills, processes, and content knowledge. All three levels are useful for understanding intelligence.

Measuring Intelligence

Although intelligence is usually viewed as an invisible *capacity* to think and learn, any measure of it must be based on *observable behavior*. Thus, when we say that a person is intelligent, we mean that the person acts in intelligent ways. One of Binet's profound insights was that the best way to measure intelligence is by observing people's actions on tasks that require a variety of types of intelligence: problem solving, memory, language comprehension, spatial reasoning, and so on. Modern intelligence tests continue to sample these and other aspects of intelligence.

Intelligence testing is highly controversial. Critics such as Ceci (1996) and Sternberg (2007) argue that measuring a quality as complex and multifaceted as intelligence requires assessing a much broader range of abilities than current intelligence tests include; that current intelligence tests are culturally biased; and that reducing a person's intelligence to a number is simplistic and ethically questionable. In contrast, advocates argue that intelligence tests are better than any alternative method for predicting important outcomes such as school grades, achievement test scores, and occupational success; that they are valuable for making decisions such as which children should be given special education; and that alternative methods for making educational decisions, such as evaluations by teachers or psychologists, may be subject to greater cultural bias. Knowing the facts about intelligence tests and understanding the issues surrounding their use is crucial to generating informed opinions about their potential strengths and liabilities.

SPENCER GRANT / PHOTOEDIT

Many IQ tests measure spatial thinking through tasks like this one. Children are first shown a target pattern, like the one in the notebook on the desk; then they are asked to re-create the target pattern by assembling a set of small blocks, each with different smaller patterns on its six sides. Some children find such tasks stimulating; others find them frustrating.

The Contents of Intelligence Tests

Intelligence is reflected in different abilities at different ages. For example, language ability is not a part of intelligence at 6 months of age, because infants this young neither produce nor understand words, but it is obviously a vital part of intelligence at 6 years of age. The items on tests developed to measure intelligence at different ages reflect these changing aspects of intelligence. For example, on the Stanford-Binet intelligence test (a descendant of the original Binet-Simon test), 2-year-olds are asked to identify the objects depicted in line drawings (a test of recognition of objects), to find an object that they earlier had seen hidden (a test of learning and memory), and to place each of three objects in a hole of the proper shape (a test of perceptual skill and motor coordination). The version of the Stanford-Binet presented to 10-year-olds asks them to define words (a test of verbal ability), to explain why certain social institutions exist (a test of general information and reasoning), and to count the blocks in a picture in which the existence of some blocks must be inferred (a test of problem solving and reasoning).

Intelligence tests have had their greatest success and widest application with children who are at least 5 or 6 years old. The exact abilities examined, and the items used to examine them, vary somewhat from test to test, but there is also considerable similarity among the leading tests.

The most widely used instrument for children 6 years and older is the **Wechsler Intelligence Scale for Children (WISC).** The current edition of this test, the WISC IV, was revised in 2003 to reflect current theoretical conceptions of intelligence and the current population of children in the United States, which is far more culturally and linguistically diverse than it was when the WISC was previously revised in the 1990s. The conception of intelligence underlying the WISC IV is consistent with Carroll's three-stratum framework, proposing that intelligence includes general ability (*g*), several moderately general abilities, and a large number of specific skills. The test yields not only an overall score but also separate scores on four moderately general abilities—verbal comprehension, perceptual reasoning, working memory, and processing speed. These abilities are measured on the test because they reflect skills that are important within information-processing theories, that correlate positively with other aspects of intelligence, and that are related to important outcomes, notably school grades and later occupational success (Flanagan & Kaufman, 2004).

The verbal-comprehension section of the WISC focuses on general knowledge of the world and skill in using language; the perceptual-reasoning section examines spatial and logical abilities; the working-memory section measures ability to hold and manipulate information in short-term memory; and the processing-speed section assesses the ability to focus attention and quickly scan, discriminate, and sequentially order visual information. Each section includes two or three required subtests and one or two that are optional, depending on whether the tester thinks that all the other subtests are valid reflections of the child's capabilities. (If a child's attention wandered during a particular subtest or the child did not understand some of the questions, the tester discards the results of that subtest and substitutes those from the optional subtest.) Figure 8.2 provides examples of the types of items that appear on the WISC (the actual items are protected by copyrights and thus cannot be shown).

Wechsler Intelligence Scale for Children (WISC) a widely used test designed to measure the intelligence of children 6 years and older

Typical Verbal Comprehension Items

Vocabulary **"What is a helicopter?"**
Similarities **"How are a mountain and a river alike?"**

Typical Perceptual Reasoning Items

Block design **"Make these nine blocks look exactly like the picture."**

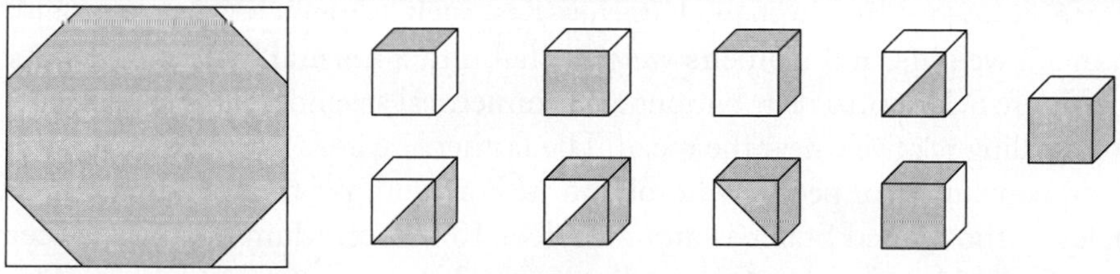

Picture concepts **"Pick an object from each box to make a group of objects that go together."**

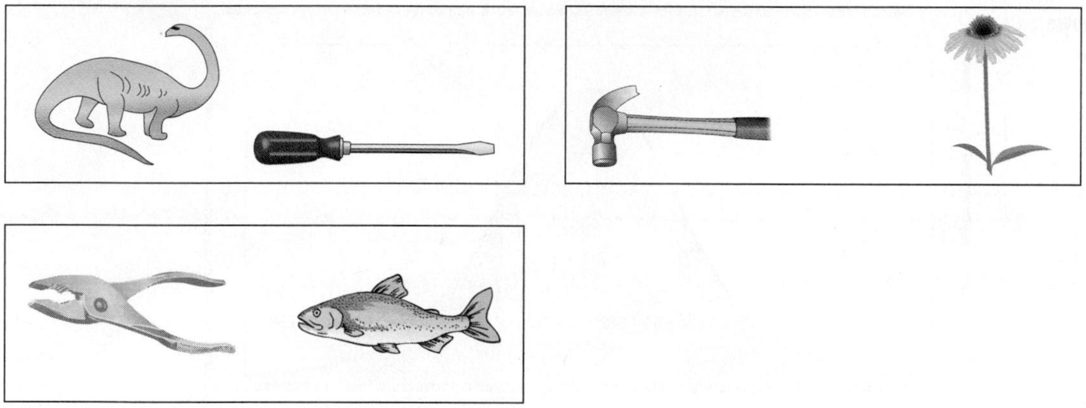

Typical Working Memory Items

Digit span **"Repeat the following numbers in order when I'm finished: 5, 3, 7, 4, 9." "Now say these numbers from last to first: 2, 9, 5, 7, 3."**
Letter-number sequencing **"Repeat the numbers from smallest to biggest, then repeat the letters from earliest to latest in the alphabet: 4, D, 2, G, 7."**

Typical Perceptual Speed Items

Coding **"Under each square, put a plus; under each circle, put a minus; under each triangle, put an X."**

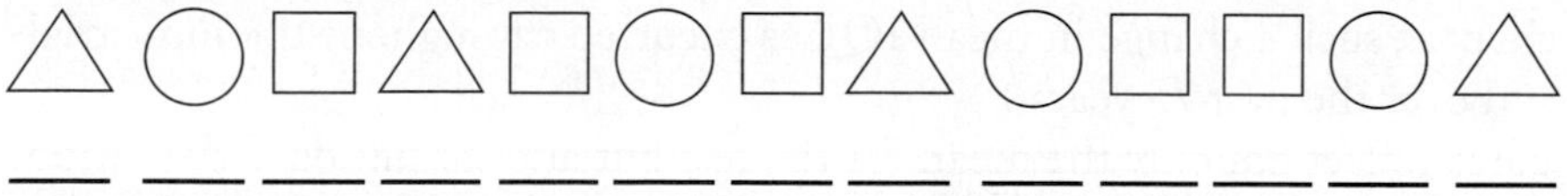

Symbol search **"Does the figure to the left of the line also appear to the right of the line?"**

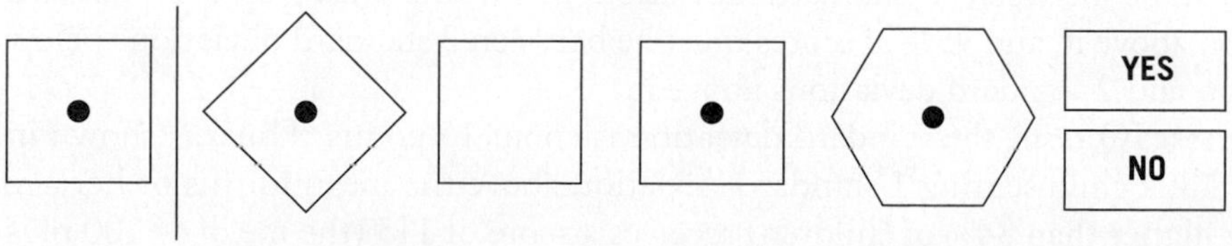

FIGURE 8.2 Types of Items of WISC IV This figure shows examples of the types of items used on the WISC IV to measure children's intelligence. These are not actual items from the test, but rather are items of the same type; copyright laws prevent use of the actual items.

The Intelligence Quotient (IQ)

Intelligence tests such as the WISC and the Stanford-Binet provide an overall quantitative measure of a child's intelligence relative to that of other children of the same age. This summary measure is referred to as the child's **IQ (intelligence quotient).**

Understanding how IQ scores are computed, and why they are computed in this way, requires a little background. Early developers of intelligence tests observed that many easy-to-measure human characteristics, such as men's heights, women's heights, men's weights, and women's weights, fall into a **normal distribution.** As shown in Figure 8.3, normal distributions are symmetrical around a mean value, with most scores falling relatively near the mean. The farther a score is from the mean, the smaller the percentage of people who obtain it. For example, the mean height of adult males in the United States is around 5 feet 10 inches. Many men are 5 feet 9 inches or 5 feet 11 inches, but few men are 5 feet 2 inches or 6 feet 6 inches. The farther a height from the mean, the smaller the number of men of that height.

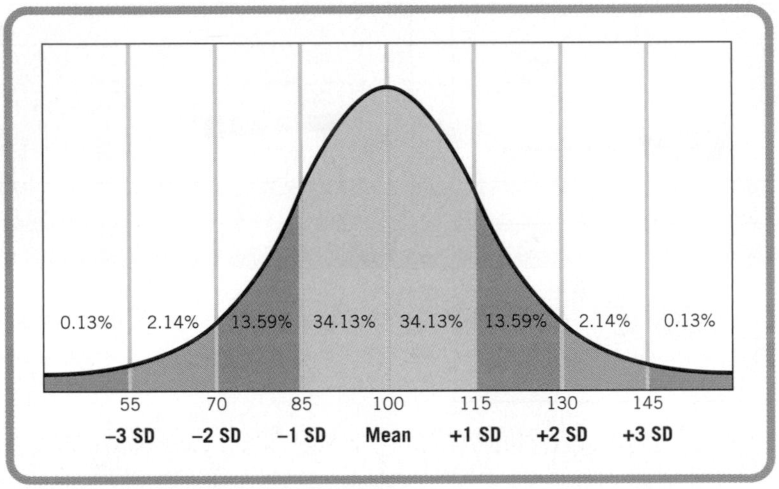

FIGURE 8.3 A normal distribution, shown in both standard deviation units and in the IQ score assigned to that level of performance IQ scores fall into a normal distribution like the one shown here. The numbers along the base of the figure correspond to IQ scores. The number just below each IQ score indicates how many standard deviation units that score is below or above the mean; thus, an IQ of 55 is 3 standard deviations below the mean. The percentages in each interval indicate the percentage of children whose scores fall within that interval; for example, less than 1% of children have IQ scores below 55 and slightly more than 2% score between 55 and 70.

A similar distribution is found in the intelligence test scores of large, representative groups of children of a given age. This normal distribution means that most IQ scores are fairly close to the mean, with few children obtaining very high or very low scores. Early designers of IQ tests made an arbitrary decision that has been maintained ever since: a score of 100 is given to children who score exactly at the mean for their age at the time the test is developed. (The mean score can rise or fall in the years after a particular test is developed and, indeed, as discussed later in this chapter, such a change in mean IQ has occurred throughout the industrialized world over the past 75 years.)

IQ scores reflect not only the mean for the test but also its **standard deviation.** The standard deviation is a measure of the variability of scores within a distribution. By the definition of a normal distribution, 68% of scores in such a distribution must be between 1 standard deviation below the mean and 1 standard deviation above it, and 95% of scores must be between 2 standard deviations below the mean and 2 standard deviations above it.

On most IQ tests, the standard deviation is about 15 points. Thus, as shown in Figure 8.3, a child scoring 1 standard deviation above the mean for his or her age (a score higher than 84% of children) receives a score of 115 (the mean of 100 plus the 15-point standard deviation). Similarly, a child scoring 1 standard deviation

IQ (intelligence quotient) a summary measure used to indicate a child's intelligence relative to that of other children of the same age

normal distribution a pattern of data in which scores fall symmetrically around a mean value, with most scores falling close to the mean and fewer and fewer scores farther from it

standard deviation a measure of the variability of scores in a distribution; in a normal distribution, 68% of scores fall within 1 standard deviation of the mean and 95% of scores fall within 2 standard deviations below the mean (a score higher than only 16% of children) receives a score of 85 (the mean of 100 minus the standard deviation of 15). Figure 8.3 also reflects the fact that about 95% of children obtain IQ scores that fall within 2 standard deviations of the mean (between 70 and 130).

An advantage of this scoring system is that IQs at different ages are easy to compare, despite the great increases in knowledge that accompany development in all children. A score of 130 at age 5 means that a child's performance exceeded that of 98% of age peers; a score of 130 at age 10 or 20 means exactly the same thing. This property has facilitated analysis of the stability of IQ scores over time, a topic we turn to next.

Continuity of IQ Scores

If IQ is a consistent property of a person, then the IQ scores that people obtain at different ages should be highly correlated. Longitudinal studies that have measured the same children's IQ scores at different ages have, in fact, shown impressive continuity from age 5 onward. For example, one study indicated that children's IQs at age 5 correlated .67 with their IQs at age 15 (Humphreys, 1989). This is a quite remarkable degree of continuity over a 10-year period. (Recall from Chapter 1 that a correlation of 1.00 indicates that two variables are perfectly correlated.) Indeed, IQ may be the most stable of all psychological traits (Brody, 1992).

Several variables influence the degree of stability of IQ scores over time. As might be expected, the closer in time that IQ tests are given, the more stability is found. Thus, the same study that found that IQ at ages 5 and 15 correlated .67 also found that IQ at ages 5 and 9 correlated .79 and that IQ at ages 5 and 6 correlated .87. For any given length of time between tests, scores are more stable at older ages. For example, in one study, IQ scores of 4- and 5-year-olds correlated .80, those of 6- and 7-year-olds correlated .87, and those of 8- and 9-year-olds correlated .90 (Brody, 1992).

Although a person's IQ scores at different ages tend to be similar, the scores are rarely identical. Children who take an IQ test at age 4 and again at age 17 show an average change, up or down, of 13 points; those who take the test at ages 8 and 17 show an average change of 9 points; and those who take it at ages 12 and 17 show an average change of 7 points (Brody, 1992). These changes are due at least in part to random variation, for example, in the child's alertness on the test days and in his or her knowledge of the items on the tests. Alterations of the child's environment, for example, through divorce or moving to a better neighborhood, also can have an effect on IQ (Sameroff, Siefer, Baldwin, & Baldwin, 1993).

The IQ scores of children whose parents take an interest in their academic success tend to increase over time.

LAURA DWIGHT

Testing Infants' Intelligence

Measuring infants' intelligence is far more difficult than measuring the intelligence of older children. The main reason is that many abilities that play large roles in later intelligence—language, mathematics, and logical reasoning, for example—are only minimally developed in infancy and therefore cannot be reliably measured at that time. Despite these difficulties, some tests of infants' intelligence have been created. These tests, which measure perception, attention, early vocabulary, and basic motor abilities, have had considerable success in identifying babies with mental deficits and other developmental problems. The tests are less successful, however, in predicting later intelligence of children without such problems (e.g., Colombo, 2001; Colombo & Frick, 1999). In contrast, measures of infants' dishabituation when presented a new stimulus have been shown to be moderately predictive of IQ at ages 11 and 18 *years*, presumably because dishabituation during infancy reflects quality of encoding and recognition memory (Kavšek, 2004; Sigman et al., 1997) (see Box 8.1).

individual differences 8.1

Gifted Children

By the time KyLee was 18 months old, he was fascinated with numbers. His favorite toys were plastic numbers and blocks with numbers on them. As he played with these toys, he said the number names over and over. When he was 2 years old, he saw a license plate with two 8s on it and said "8 + 8 = 16"; neither he nor his parents could explain how he knew this. By age 3 years, KyLee was playing math games on a computer every day. During one such game, he discovered the idea of prime numbers and thereafter was able to identify new prime numbers. Again, neither he nor his parents knew how he did this. Before he entered kindergarten, he could add, subtract, multiply, divide, estimate, and solve complex word problems. When asked if he ever got tired of numbers, he said, "No, never" and said that he was a "number boy" (Winner, 1996, pp. 38–39).

As noted by Ellen Winner, a psychologist who studies intellectually and artistically gifted children, most, like KyLee, show astonishing early facility in a single area: numbers, drawing, reading, music, or some other realm. A smaller number of children are exceptional in a wide range of intellectual areas. These globally gifted children usually display several of the following signs of giftedness from very early in development (Robinson & Robinson, 1992):

- Unusual alertness and long attention span in infancy
- Rapid language development
- Learning with minimal help from adults
- Curiosity—asking deep questions and being dissatisfied with superficial answers
- High energy levels, often bordering on hyperactivity
- Intense reactions to frustration
- Precocious reading and interest in numbers
- Exceptional logical and abstract reasoning
- Unusually good memory
- Enjoyment of solitary play

Exceptional early ability often (though far from always) foreshadows outstanding later achievement. Consider a long-term study of 320 children who took the SAT by age 13 as part of a national talent search and who scored in the top 1 in 10,000 in verbal or math ability. Ten years later, when most of these precocious individuals were 23-year-olds, more than half were enrolled in graduate or professional school (Lubinski, Webb, Morelock, & Benbow, 2001). Among their other accomplishments, various participants had already published 11 articles in scientific and medical journals; adapted Pink Floyd's *The Wall* into a multimedia rock opera; developed one of the most popular video games in the United States; developed a navigation system that was used to land a rocket on Mars; and won major awards in areas ranging from physics to creative writing.

When contacted at age 33, more than half of the original sample had received a PhD, MD, or JD degree (Lubinski, Benbow, Webb, & Bleske-Rechek, 2006). The rate of PhDs was more than 50 times higher than that for the general population, and the rate of patents was 11 times that in the general population. Even within this elite sample, high initial SAT mathematics scores predicted high achievement. For example, the higher the score on the SAT math test at age 13, the greater the number of patents and publications in scholarly journals—especially those in science, engineering, and mathematics—at age 33 (Park, Lubinski, & Benbow, 2008).

Exceptional early ability in an area is no guarantee of outstanding achievement in that area during adulthood. Factors such as amount of interest in the area, willingness to work long hours, creativity, and perseverance in the face of difficulty also are essential for exceptional contributions (Lubinski & Benbow, 2006). Nonetheless, it is impressive how scores on a single test, given at age 13 years, predict exceptional achievement 10 and 20 years later.

ELIZABETH CREWS / THE IMAGE WORKS

Exceptionally early readers, such as this 3½-year-old, often continue to be excellent readers throughout life.

review:

Intelligence tests examine a range of abilities and types of knowledge, including vocabulary, verbal comprehension, arithmetic, memory, and spatial reasoning. The tests are used to obtain a general measure of intelligence, the IQ score. IQ tests are designed to produce average scores of 100, with higher scores indicating above-average intelligence and lower scores below-average intelligence. After age 5 or 6, IQ scores of individual children tend to be quite stable over long periods of time, but they vary somewhat from one testing to the next.

IQ Scores as Predictors of Important Outcomes

Assertions that IQ is a strong predictor of academic, economic, and occupational success are well founded (Sackett, Borneman, & Connelly, 2008; Schmidt & Hunter, 1998). As noted earlier, IQ scores correlate positively and quite strongly with school grades and achievement test performance, both at the time of the test and years later (Geary, 2005); for example, IQ and achievement test performance typically correlate between .50 and .60 (Deary, Strand, Smith, & Fernandes, 2007). IQ scores also correlate positively with long-term educational achievement. In the United States, IQ in 6th grade correlates about .60 with the years of education that a person eventually obtains (Jencks, 1979). Substantial relations between IQ and performance in highly complex occupations are present for at least 10 years after entry into the occupation (Sackett et al., 2008).

In part, the positive relation between IQ and occupational success, including income, is due to the fact that standardized test scores serve as gatekeepers, determining which students are allowed to gain access to the training and credentials required for entry into lucrative professions. Even among people who initially have the same job, however, those with higher IQs tend to perform better, earn more money, and receive better promotions (Schmidt & Hunter, 2004; Wilk, Desmarais, & Sackett, 1995). A child's IQ is more closely related to the child's later occupational success than is the socioeconomic status of the child's family, the school the child attends, or any other variable that has been studied (Ceci, 1993).

As strong a predictor as IQ is of academic, economic, and occupational success, it is far from the only influence. Other characteristics of the child, such as motivation to succeed, conscientiousness, creativity, physical and mental health, and social skills also exert important influences (Roberts et al., 2007; Sternberg, 2004). For example, **self-discipline**—the ability to inhibit actions, follow rules, and avoid impulsive reactions—predicts 8th graders' grades, even after the influence of IQ is taken into account (Duckworth & Seligman, 2005). Similarly, **practical intelligence**—mental abilities not measured on IQ tests but important for success in many situations, such as accurately reading other people's emotions and intentions and motivating others to work effectively as a team—predicts occupational success even after the influence of IQ is taken into account (Cianciolo, Matthew, Sternberg, & Wagner, 2006; Sternberg, 2003). Characteristics of the environment are similarly influential: parents' encouragement and modeling of productive careers predict their children's occupational success (Kalil, Levine, & Ziol-Guest, 2005).

Figure 8.4 illustrates how the same set of data can provide evidence for the importance of both IQ and other factors. Consistent with the importance of IQ, the figure shows that among people with the same level of education, those with higher IQs earn more money. Consistent with the importance of other factors, the figure shows that among people of comparable IQs, those who complete more years of education earn more money. Thus, while IQ is a key contributor to educational, occupational, and economic success, other factors are also influential.

self-discipline the ability to inhibit actions, follow rules, and avoid impulsive reactions

practical intelligence mental abilities not measured on IQ tests but important for success in many situations, such as accurately reading other people's emotions and intentions and motivating others to work effectively as a team

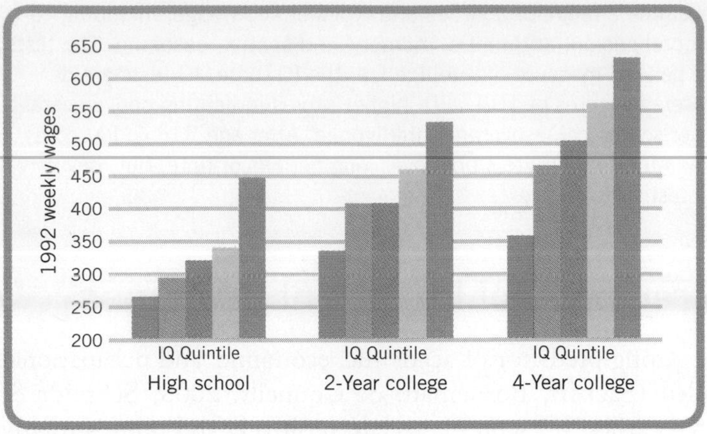

FIGURE 8.4 Effects of IQ and education on income IQ influences income, but so do other factors such as education. The relations are evident in these data, collected in the late 1980s, which indicate the average income of people who received different levels of education and who scored in different quintiles (fifths) of the IQ distribution. Within any given level of education, people of higher IQ earned more. Thus, among people with only a high school education, those who scored in the bottom 20% on an IQ test (the blue bar) averaged only a little more than $250/week, whereas those who scored in the top 20% (the purple bar) averaged almost $450/week. On the other hand, as shown by the purple bars, people in the top 20% in IQ score who had only a high school education earned an average of roughly $450/week, whereas those of comparable IQ but with a four-year college education earned almost $650/week. (Data from Ceci, 1996)

review: IQ scores are positively related to grades in school and achievement test performance, both at the time of the test and in the future. They are also positively related to occupational success in adulthood. However, they are not the only influence on these outcomes. Motivation, creativity, self-discipline, social skills, and a variety of other factors contribute, too.

Genes, Environment, and the Development of Intelligence

No issue in psychology has produced longer or more acrimonious debate than the issue of how heredity and environment influence intelligence. Even people who recognize that intelligence, like all human qualities, is constructed through the continuous interaction of genes and environment often forget this fact and take extreme positions that are based more on emotions and ideology than on evidence. The purpose of the present discussion is to provide a coherent framework for thinking about the complex issues in this area and to summarize what is known.

A useful starting point for thinking about genetic and environmental influences on intelligence is provided by Bronfenbrenner's (1993) ecological model of development (discussed in detail in Chapter 9, pages 362–369). This model envisions children's lives as embedded within a series of increasingly encompassing environments. The child, with a unique set of qualities including his or her genetic endowment and personal experiences, is at the center. Surrounding the child is the immediate environment, especially the people and institutions the child interacts with directly: family, school, classmates, teachers, neighbors, and so on. Surrounding the immediate environment are more distant, and less tangible, environments that also influence development: cultural attitudes, the social and economic system, mass media, the government, and so on. We will now examine how qualities of the child, the immediate environment, and the broader environment contribute to the development of intelligence.

In the movie *My Fair Lady,* Eliza Doolittle found it easier to don the clothing of an upper-class lady than to adopt the haughty reserve viewed as appropriate by that class at that time. This scene from the Ascot opening day, as well as the movie as a whole, makes the argument that differences that might be attributed to nature are actually the product of nurture.

WARNER BROS. / KOBAL COLLECTION

Qualities of the Child

Children contribute greatly to their own intellectual development. The contribution comes about through their genetic endowment, through the reactions they elicit from other people, and through their choice of environments.

Genetic Contributions to Intelligence

As noted in Chapter 3 (pages 97–100), genes have a substantial influence on intelligence. This genetic influence varies greatly with age: it is relatively modest in early childhood and becomes very large by adolescence and adulthood (Bouchard, 2004; Plomin, DeFries, McClearn, & McGuffin, 2001) (Figure 8.5). Correlations between the IQs of identical twins, who have all their genes in common, increase from preschool to adulthood, whereas correlations between the IQs of fraternal twins decrease (McGue, Bouchard, Iacono, & Lykken, 1993). Similarly, the IQs of adopted children and those of their biological parents become increasingly correlated as the children become older, but the IQs of adopted children and their adoptive parents become less correlated as the children become older (Plomin, Fulker, Corley, & DeFries, 1997). One reason for this increasing genetic influence is that some genetic processes do not exert their effects on IQ until later childhood and adolescence. For example, some connections linking areas in the brain that are distant from each other are not formed until adolescence, and the extent of such connections reflects genetic influences (Thatcher, 1992). Another reason is that children's increasing independence with age allows them greater freedom to choose environments that are compatible with their own genetically based preferences, but not necessarily with those of the parents who are raising them (Scarr, 1992).

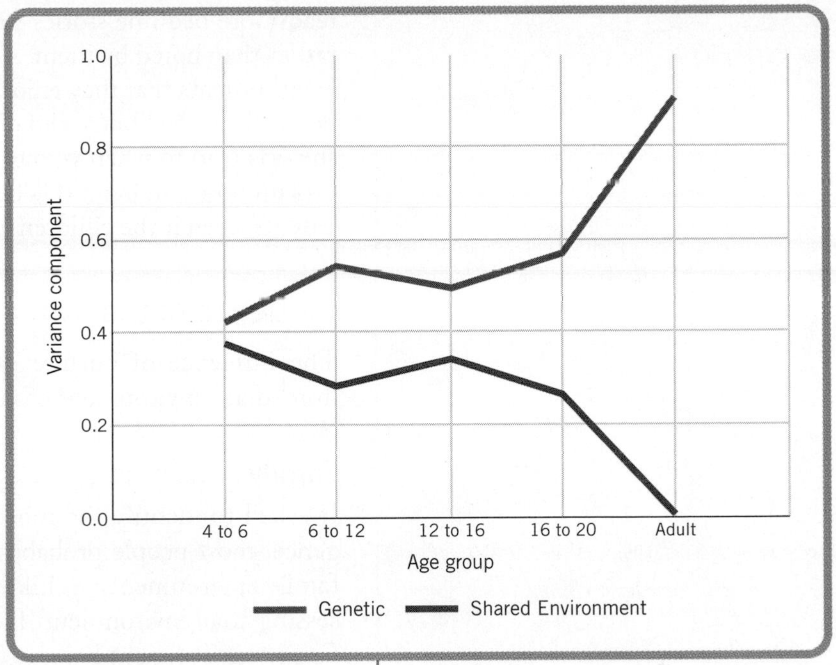

FIGURE 8.5 Increase with age in variance in IQ accounted for by genetics and decrease with age in variance accounted for by shared environment in a predominately middle class sample. (Data from McGue et al., 1993)

Genotype–Environment Interactions

As you will remember from Chapter 3, the environments children encounter are influenced by their genotype. Sandra Scarr (1992) proposed that these gene–environment relations involve three types of effects: passive, evocative, and active. *Passive effects* of the genotype arise when children are raised by their biological parents. These effects occur not because of anything the children do but because of the overlap between their parents' genes and their own. Thus, children whose genotypes predispose them to enjoy reading are likely to be raised in homes with books, magazines, and newspapers, because their parents also like to read. The passive effects of the genotype help explain why IQ correlations between biological parents and their children are higher when the children live with their biological parents than when they live with adoptive parents. *Evocative effects* of the genotype emerge through children's eliciting or influencing other people's behavior. For example, even if a child's parents are not avid readers, they will

Children influence their own development; these children's joyous reactions to their father's reading ensure that he will want to read to them in the future.

PATRICK BENNETT / CORBIS

read more bedtime stories to the child if he or she seems interested in the stories rather than bored by them. *Active effects* of the genotype involve children's choosing environments that they enjoy. A high school student who likes reading will borrow books from the library and obtain books in other ways, regardless of whether he or she was read to when young. The evocative and active effects of the genotype help explain how children's IQs become more closely related to those of their biological parents, even if the children are adopted and never see their biological parents.

Influence of the Immediate Environment

The influence of nurture on the development of intelligence begins with the immediate environment of families and schools.

Family Influences

If asked to identify the most important environmental influence on their intelligence, most people probably would say "my family." Testing the influence of the family environment on children's intelligence, however, requires some means of assessing that environment. How can something as complex and multifaceted as a family environment be measured, especially when it may be different for different children in the same family?

Bettye Caldwell and Robert Bradley (1979) tackled this problem by devising a measure known as the HOME (Home Observation for Measurement of the Environment). This measure samples various aspects of children's home life, including the organization and safety of living space; the intellectual stimulation offered by parents; whether children have books of their own; the amount of parent–child interaction; the parents' emotional support of the child; and so on. Table 8.1 shows the items and subscales used in the original HOME, which was designed to assess

TABLE 8.1

Sample of Items and Subscales on the HOME (Infant Version)

I. Emotional and Verbal Responsivity of Mother
1. Mother spontaneously vocalizes to child at least twice during visit (excluding scolding).
2. Mother responds to child's vocalizations with a verbal response.
3. Mother tells child the name of some object during visit or says name of person or object in a "teaching" style.

II. Avoidance of Restriction and Punishment
4. Mother does not shout at child during visit.
5. Mother does not express overt annoyance with or hostility toward child.
6. Mother does not interfere with child's actions or restrict child's movements more than three times during visit.

III. Organization of Physical and Temporal Environment
7. When mother is away, care is provided by one of three regular substitutes.
8. Child is taken regularly to doctor's office or clinic.
9. Child has a special place in which to keep his or her toys and "treasures."

IV. Provision of Appropriate Play Materials
10. Child has push or pull toy.
11. Child has stroller or walker, kiddie car, scooter, or tricycle.
12. Provides learning equipment appropriate to age—cuddly toy or role-playing toys.

V. Maternal Involvement with Child
13. Mother tends to keep child within visual range and to look at him or her often.
14. Mother "talks" to child while doing her work.
15. Mother structures child's play periods.

VI. Opportunities for Variety of Daily Stimulation
16. Mother reads stories at least three times weekly.
17. Child eats at least one meal per day with mother and father.
18. Child has three or more books of his or her own.

Source: From "174 Children: A Study of the Relationship Between Home Environment and Cognitive Development During the First 5 Years" by R. H. Bradley and B. M. Caldwell, 1984. In A. W. Gottfried, ed. *Home Environment and Early Cognitive Development* (pp. 7–8), New York: Academic Press. Copyright © 1984 by Academic Press. Reprinted by permission.

the family environments of children between birth and age 3. Subsequent versions of the HOME have been developed for application with preschoolers, school-age children, and adolescents (Bradley, 1994).

Throughout childhood, children's IQ scores, as well as their math and reading achievement, are positively correlated with the HOME measure of their family environment (Bradley, Corwyn, Burchinal, McAdoo, & Garcia Coll, 2001). The HOME also predicts future IQ scores. HOME scores of families of 6-month-olds correlate positively with the IQs of the children at age 4 years, and HOME scores of 2-year-olds correlate positively with IQ scores and school achievement of 11-year-olds (Olson, Bates, & Kaskie, 1992). When HOME scores are relatively stable over time, IQ scores also tend to be stable; when HOME scores change, IQ scores also tend to change in the same direction (Bradley, 1989). Thus, assessing varied aspects of a child's family environment allows good prediction of the child's IQ.

TONY FREEMAN / PHOTOEDIT

Stimulating home environments, especially ones in which adults and children undertake challenging tasks together, are associated with high IQs and high achievement in school.

Given this evidence, it is tempting to conclude that better-quality home environments cause children to have higher IQs. Whether that is actually the case, however, is not yet known. The uncertainty reflects two factors. First, the type of intellectual environment that parents establish in the home is almost certainly influenced by their genetic makeup. Second, almost all studies using the HOME have focused on families in which children live with their biological parents. These two circumstances may mean that parents' genes influence both the intellectual quality of the home environment and children's IQs; thus, the home intellectual environment as such may not cause children to have higher or lower IQs. Consistent with this possibility, in the few studies in which the HOME has been used to study adoptive families, the correlations between it and children's IQs are lower than in studies of children living with their biological parents (Plomin, DeFries, McClearn, & Rutter, 1997). Thus, although scores on the HOME clearly correlate with children's IQs, causal relations between the two remain uncertain.

Shared and nonshared family environments When we think of a family's intellectual environment, we usually think of characteristics that are the same for all children within the family: the parents' emphasis on education, the number of books in the house, the frequency of intellectual discussions around the dinner table, and so on. As discussed in Chapter 3, however, each child within a given family also encounters unique, nonshared environments. In any family, only one child can be the firstborn and receive the intense, undivided attention early in life that this status often brings. Similarly, a child who has interests or personality characteristics like those of one or both parents may receive more positive attention than other children in the family. If very deficient homes are excluded from consideration, such within-family variations in children's environment seem to have a greater impact on the development of intelligence than do between-family variations (Petrill et al., 2004). In addition, the influence of nonshared environments increases with

With age, children increasingly shape their own environments in ways that reflect their personality and taste.

age, and the influence of shared environments decreases with age, as children become increasingly able to choose their own environments (Bouchard, 2004; Segal et al., 2007).

The influence of the shared environment varies with the family's socioeconomic status and race. Among 7-year-olds from impoverished backgrounds, the shared environment accounts for far more of the variance in IQ than genetics does. In contrast, among 7-year-olds from affluent families, the relative influence of shared environment and genetics is reversed (Bronfenbrenner & Morris, 2006; Turkheimer et al., 2003). Moreover, parental involvement in schooling, which is one aspect of the shared environment, appears to be more positively related to academic achievement and more negatively relatetd to classroom behavior problems for less-affluent African-American 12- to 16-year-olds than for their more-affluent Euro-American age peers (Hill et al., 2004; Hill & Taylor, 2004). One explanation is that low-income African-American families vary more than do more-affluent Euro-American families in the amount of intellectual stimulation, emotional support, and other relevant qualities parents provide their children. This greater variability may lead to the quality of the family environment being more highly correlated with the intellectual development of children within those families. This is one more illustration of the theme of *nature and nurture* interacting to produce development.

Influences of Schooling

Attending school makes children smarter. One type of evidence for this conclusion came from a study that examined IQ scores of older and younger Israeli children in the 4th, 5th, and 6th grades (Cahan & Cahan, 1989). As indicated by the gradual upward trends in the graphs in Figure 8.6, older children within each grade did somewhat better than younger children within that grade on each part of the test. However, the jumps in the graphs between grades indicate that children who were only slightly older, but who had a year more schooling, did much better than the slightly younger children in the grade below them. For example, on the verbal-oddities subtest (which involves indicating which word in a series does not belong with the others), the results show a small gap between 123- and 124-month-old 4th graders but a large gap between both of them and 125-month-old 5th graders.

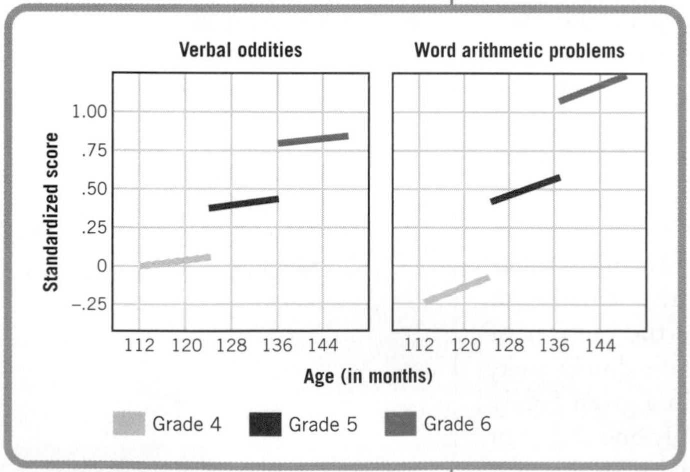

FIGURE 8.6 Relations of age and grade to performance on two parts of an IQ test **The jumps between grade levels indicate that schooling exerts an effect on intelligence test performance beyond that of the child's age. (Data from Cahan & Cahan, 1989)**

Another type of evidence indicating that going to school makes children smarter is that average IQ and achievement test scores rise during the school year and drop during summer vacation (Ceci, 1991; Huttenlocher, Levine, & Vevea, 1998). The way in which these changes vary with children's family backgrounds adds further support to the view that schooling makes children smarter (Alexander & Entwistle, 1996; Entwistle & Alexander, 1992). Children from families of low socioeconomic status and those from families of high socioeconomic status make comparable gains in school achievement during the school year. However, over the summer, the achievement test scores of low-SES children drop, whereas the scores of high-SES children stay constant or rise slightly. The likely explanation is that during the academic year, schools provide children of all backgrounds with relatively stimulating intellectual environments, but when school is not in session, fewer children from low-SES families have the kinds of experiences that would maintain or increase their academic achievement.

Flynn effect the rise in average IQ scores that has occurred over the past 75 years in many countries

Influence of Society

Intellectual development is influenced not only by characteristics of children, their families, and their schools but also by broader characteristics of the economic and social systems within which they develop. One reflection of these influences is that in many countries throughout the world, average IQ scores have risen over the past 75 years, a phenomenon that has been labeled the **Flynn effect** in honor of the researcher who discovered this widespread trend (Flynn, 1987, 2007). In some countries, including the Netherlands and Israel, IQ gains have been as great as 20 points; in the United States, the gains have been roughly 10 points (Dickens & Flynn, 2001; Flynn & Weiss, 2007). Given that the gene pool has not changed appreciably over this period, the increase in IQ scores must be due to changes in the environment.

One clue to the type of environmental change that might be involved is that the increase has been greatest among those in the lower part of the IQ-score distribution. For example, as shown in Figure 8.7, among Danes born from 1942 to 1980, there was no change in the scores of people in the top 10% of the IQ distribution, but there was a large change among those in the bottom 10% (Geary, 2005). Better nutrition, better health care, and universal education seem likely to have had especially positive effects on children from the most deprived backgrounds, who make up a disproportionate number of those with low IQ scores. Consistent with this interpretation, the gains seem to have slowed or stopped in countries—most notably those of Scandinavia—in which even the portions of the population with relatively low incomes have high levels of nutrition, health care, and education (Sundet, Barlaug, & Torjussen, 2004; Teasdale & Owen, 2005).

As suggested by this example, poverty can have a large effect on the development of intelligence. In the following sections, we first consider how poverty affects children's development in different societies and then examine how it contributes to differences in IQ and school achievement among racial and ethnic groups. Next we consider other factors that place intellectual development at risk. Finally, we consider programs aimed at enhancing poor children's intellectual development.

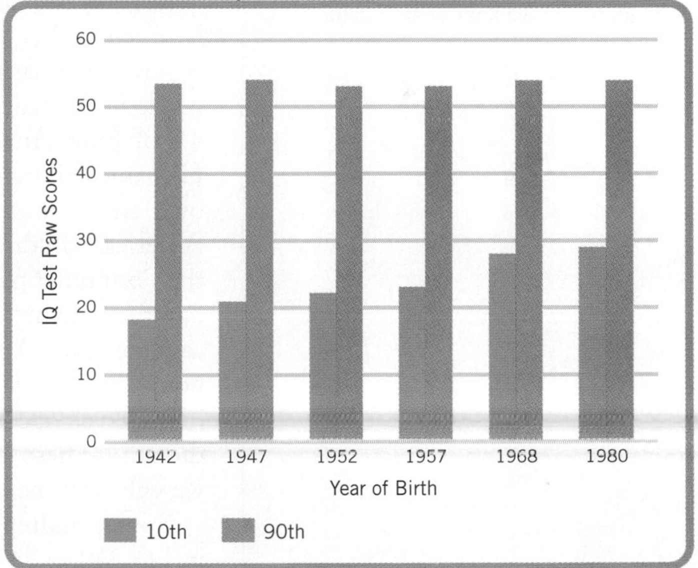

FIGURE 8.7 Changes in IQ over historical time among Danish adults with relatively low IQ scores (10th percentile) and relatively high IQ scores (90th percentile) As these data illustrate, IQ scores have improved considerably over the years among people near the bottom of the distribution but have remained quite constant among people near the top. (Adapted from Geary et al., 2005)

Effects of Poverty

The negative effects of poverty on children's IQ scores are indisputable. Even after taking into account such factors as the mother's education, whether the home is headed by a single mother, and race, the adequacy of family income for meeting family needs is related to children's IQs (Duncan et al., 1998). Further, the more years children spend in poverty, the lower their IQs tend to be.

Poverty can exert negative effects on intellectual development in numerous ways. For example, chronic inadequate diet early in life can disrupt brain development, and missing meals on a given day (e.g., achievement test day) can impair

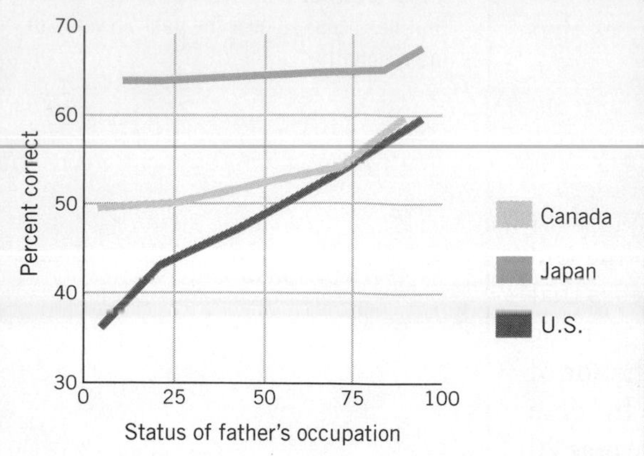

FIGURE 8.8 Relation in three countries between fathers' occupational status and children's math achievement U.S. children whose fathers hold low-status jobs perform far more poorly on math-achievement tests than do children whose fathers hold comparable jobs in Canada or Japan. In contrast, U.S. children whose fathers have high-status jobs perform as well as children whose fathers have comparable jobs in Canada and almost as well as children from similar backgrounds in Japan. (Data from Case et al., 1999)

intellectual functioning on that day. Other factors associated with poverty, such as reduced access to health services, inadequate parenting, and insufficient intellectual stimulation and emotional support in the home, can also hinder intellectual growth.

One source of evidence for the relation between poverty and IQ is the fact that in all countries that have been studied, children from wealthier homes score higher on IQ and achievement tests than do children from poorer homes (Case, Griffin, & Kelley, 1999; Keating & Hertzman, 1999). More telling, in those developed countries where the income gap between rich and poor is widest, such as the United States, the difference between the intellectual achievement of children from rich and poor homes is much larger than in countries in which the gap is smaller—such as the Scandinavian countries and, to a lesser degree, Germany, Canada, and Great Britain. As shown in Figure 8.8, children from affluent families in the United States score about the same on tests of intellectual achievement as do children from affluent families in other countries. In contrast, children from poor families in the United States have achievement test scores far below children from poor families in countries with greater income equality. The key difference is that poor families in the United States are much poorer than their counterparts in many other developed countries. Thus, in 2006, 17% of children in the United States lived in families with incomes below the poverty line (Childstats.gov, 2008), more than double the percentage in Germany and triple the percentage in Switzerland and Sweden a decade earlier (Bound, Duncan, Laren, & Oleinick, 1991).

Within the United States, the percentage of children living in poor families is much higher among African Americans and Latinos than among Euro- and Asian-Americans and is much higher in female-headed families than in families headed by a married couple. In 2006, among families headed by a married couple, 4% of Euro-American children, 12% of African-American children, and 19% of Hispanic children lived in poverty. The corresponding statistics for families headed by a single mother were 33% for Euro-American children, 50% for African-American children, and 47% for Hispanic children (Childstats.gov, 2008). A study that examined families over a six-year period (Duncan et al., 1994) indicated that five times as many African-American families were poor during the entire period as were Euro-American families. Even among children whose families were not poor, nearly 50% of African-American children lived in neighborhoods with a high percentage of poor families, whereas fewer than 10% of Euro-American children did. These economic differences help explain the group differences in IQ that we will examine in the next section.

Some children who live in poverty overcome the odds and do well in school and in life. What distinguishes these *resilient children* (Werner, 1993) from others in similar circumstances? Bradley and his colleagues (1994) identified a group of children who, despite being born into poor families and also being born prematurely, functioned in the normal or superior range on cognitive, social, health, and growth measures at the age of 3 years. The researchers found that the parents of these children protected them in a number of ways from the usual harmful effects of poverty. They were more likely than other impoverished parents to be responsive to their children and to provide them with safe play areas and varied learning materials. Thus, high-quality parenting can help children meet the challenges imposed by poverty.

Race, Ethnicity, and Intelligence

Few claims stir stronger passions than those surrounding assertions that racial and ethnic groups differ in intelligence. It is therefore especially important to know both the facts about this issue and what can and cannot be concluded from them.

One fact is that the *average* IQ scores of children of different racial and ethnic groups *do* differ. For example, the average IQ score of Euro-American children is 10 to 11 points higher than that of African-American children (Dickens & Flynn, 2006). The average scores of Latino and American Indian children fall in the middle of this range, and those of Asian-American children are about 3 points higher than those of Euro-Americans (Ceci, Rosemblum, & Kumpf, 1998; Suzuki & Valencia, 1997). These differences are explained in part by differences in social-class backgrounds. Within each social class, however, differences in mean IQs of African-American and Euro-American children also are present, though they are smaller than the ones that are present when social class is not held constant (Suzuki & Valencia, 1997).

A second fact is that statements about group differences in IQ scores refer to statistical averages rather than to any individual's score. Understanding this second fact is essential for interpreting the first one. Millions of African-American children have IQs higher than the average Euro-American child, and millions of Euro-American children have IQs lower than the average African-American child. There is far more variability *within* each racial group than *between* them. Thus, data on the average IQ of members of an ethnic or racial group tell us nothing about a given individual.

A third fact is that racial/ethnic groups differ in their profile of intellectual abilities as well as in overall scores. A study of 93 American Indian groups indicated that their average score on the performance (e.g., spatial reasoning) part of IQ tests was 100 but that their average score on the verbal part was 83 (Vraniak, 1994). Latino children likewise tend to have higher performance scores than verbal scores (Suzuki & Valencia, 1997), as do Asian-American children (Lynn & Hampson, 1986) and Japanese children who live in Japan (Kodama, Shinagawa, & Motegi, 1978; Suzuki & Valencia, 1997). In contrast, studies of African-American children indicate that their scores on the verbal portion of the IQ tests tend to be higher than their scores on the performance portion (Taylor & Richards, 1991; Vance, Hankins, & McGee, 1979). There are many possible reasons for these differences in profiles of abilities. For example, the superior visual and spatial abilities of Asian-American children have been ascribed to neurological factors, nonverbal communication style, cultural values, and a host of other factors (Sue & Okazaki, 1990).

A fourth crucial fact is that differences in IQ and achievement test scores of children from different racial and ethnic groups describe children's performance only in the environments in which the children live. The findings do not indicate their intellectual potential, nor do they indicate what would happen if the children lived in different environments. In one dramatic illustration of this fact, Scarr and Weinberg (1976, 1983) examined IQ scores of more than 100 African-American children who had been adopted as infants by Euro-American parents. The adoptive parents were above average in income, education, and intelligence (mean IQ = 119), whereas the biological parents were roughly average on these dimensions. When African-American children who were adopted in their first year were tested at around age 7, their mean IQ was 110, higher than that of the average Euro-American child in the United States.

Thus, the current group differences in IQ and achievement test scores in the general population are not inevitable. Indeed, with decreases in discrimination and inequality over the second half of the twentieth century, achievement test differences between Euro-American and African-American children decreased considerably. A rigorous analysis of changes over time in intelligence test scores showed that African-American schoolchildren reduced the gap with Euro-American schoolchildren by 4 to 7 points between 1972 and 2002 (Dickens & Flynn, 2006); achievement test scores have shown the same trend (Brody, 1992).

Risk Factors and Intellectual Development

Articles in popular magazines on how to help all children reach their intellectual potential often focus on a single factor—the need to eliminate poverty, or the need to eliminate racism, or the need to preserve two-parent families, and so on. However, no single factor, or even a small group of factors, is *the* key. Instead, a variety of factors in combination contribute to the problem of substantial numbers of children failing to reach their intellectual potential.

TABLE 8.2

Risk Factors Related to IQ Scores

1. Head of household unemployed or working in low-status occupation
2. Mother did not complete high school
3. At least four children in family
4. No father or stepfather in home
5. African-American family
6. Large number of stressful life events in past few years
7. Rigidity of parents' beliefs about child development
8. Maternal anxiety
9. Maternal mental health
10. Negative mother–child interactions

Source: Sameroff et al., 1993

To capture the impact of these multiple influences, Arnold Sameroff and his colleagues developed an *environmental risk scale* (Sameroff, Seifer, Baldwin, & Baldwin, 1993). The scale was based on a number of features of the environment that put children at risk for low IQs (Table 8.2). Each child's risk score is a simple count of the number of major risks facing the child. Thus, a child growing up with a mother who is unemployed, high in anxiety, a high school dropout, unmarried, and without other risk factors would have a risk score of 4.

Sameroff and his colleagues measured the IQs and environmental risks of more than 100 children when they were 4-year-olds and again when they were 13-year-olds. They found that the more risks in a child's environment, the lower the child's IQ tended to be. As shown in Figure 8.9, the effect was large. The average IQ of children whose environments did not include any of the risk factors was around 115; the average IQ of children whose environments included six or more risks was around 85. The sheer number of risks in the child's environment was a better predictor of the child's IQ than was the presence of any particular risk. Subsequent studies demonstrated similarly strong relations between the number of risk factors and school grades (Gassman-Pines, & Yoshikawa, 2006; Gutman, Sameroff, & Cole, 2003).

This study also provided an interesting perspective on why there is so much stability in children's IQ scores. It is not just that children's genotype remains constant; over time, their environment tends to remain fairly constant as well. The study revealed that there was just as much stability in the number of risk factors in children's environments at ages 4 and 13 years as there was in their IQ scores over that age range.

The number of risk factors in a 4-year-old's environment not only correlates highly with the child's IQ at age 4 but it also predicts the likelihood of changes in the child's IQ between ages 4 and 13. That is, if two children have the same IQ at age 4 but one child lives in an environment with more risk factors, at age 13, the child facing more risks probably will have a lower IQ than that of the other child. Thus, environmental risks seem to have both immediate and long-term effects on children's intellectual development. Genetic contributions cannot be ruled out—anxiety, poor mental health, and other risk factors may be biologically transmitted from parent to child—but the risk factors are definitely associated with low IQ.

Although Sameroff and his colleagues described their measure as a "risk index," it is as much a measure of the goodness of a child's environment as of its potential for harm. High IQs are associated with favorable environments as much as low IQs are associated with adverse ones. Simply put, no one makes it alone: our successes, like our failures, reflect not only our own abilities but also the quality of support provided by our families, other people who influence us, and the broader society.

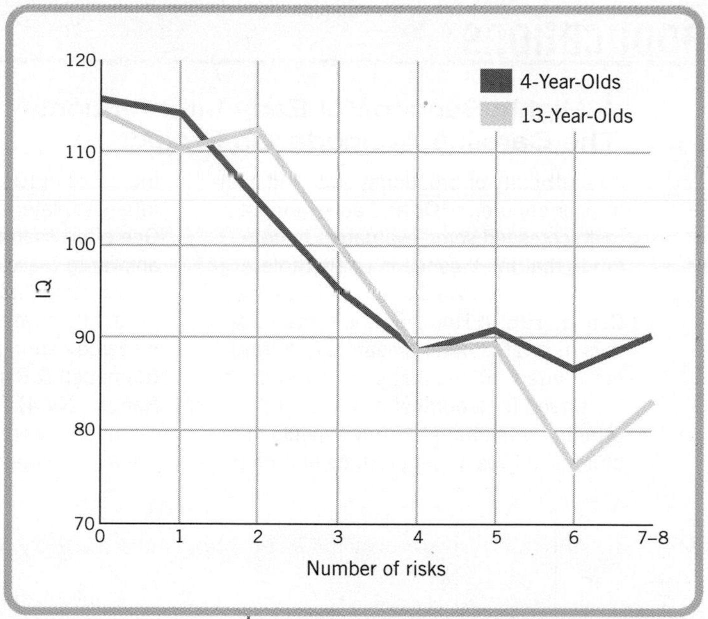

FIGURE 8.9 Risk factors and IQ For both younger and older children, the more risk factors there are in the environment, the lower the average IQ. (Data from Sameroff et al., 1993)

Programs for Helping Poor Children

During the early 1960s, a political consensus developed in the United States proposing that helping children from poor families was an urgent national priority. Psychological research contributed to this consensus by demonstrating that children's environments had significant effects on their cognitive growth (Dennis & Najarian, 1957; Hunt, 1961). As a consequence, over the next few years, many intervention programs were initiated to enhance the intellectual development of preschoolers from impoverished families.

Most of these interventions were small-scale experimental programs, intended to test ideas about the types of intervention that would be most beneficial. Some programs were based on behaviorist theories and emphasized direct instruction, modeling, and reinforcement of the skills needed to learn reading and arithmetic. Other programs were based on Piagetian theory and emphasized providing stimulating environments that would encourage children to construct new skills and concepts without direct instruction or external reinforcement. Yet other programs were an eclectic mix of ideas from behaviorist theory, Piagetian theory, and traditional preschool practices, such as singing songs and telling stories.

In a comprehensive analysis of 11 of the most prominent early-intervention programs—all of which focused on 2- to 5-year-old African-American children from low-income families—Irving Lazar and his colleagues found a consistent pattern (Lazar, Darlington, Murray, Royce, & Snipper, 1982). Participation in the programs, most of which lasted a year or two, initially increased children's IQ scores substantially—by 10 to 15 points. However, over the next two or three years, the gains decreased, and by the fourth year after the end of the programs, no differences were apparent between the IQ scores of participants and those of nonparticipants from the same neighborhoods and backgrounds. Similar patterns emerged in an analysis of programs that emphasized mathematics and reading achievement (McKey et al., 1985).

Fortunately, other effects of these experimental programs were more enduring. Only half as many program participants as nonparticipants were later assigned to special-education classes—14% versus 29%. Similarly, fewer participants were held back in school, more participants subsequently graduated from high school, and fewer had been arrested by age 18 (Reynolds, Temple, Robertson, & Mann, 2001).

This combination of findings may seem puzzling. If the intervention programs did not result in lasting increases in IQ or achievement test scores, why would they applications

A Highly Successful Early Intervention: The Carolina Abecedarian Project

The difficulty of producing enduring gains in poor children's IQs and achievement test scores led some evaluators to conclude that intelligence is unalterable (Jensen, 1973; Westinghouse Learning Center, 1969). However, the same findings motivated other researchers to find out if interventions that started in infancy, continued for a number of years, and attempted to improve many aspects of children's lives might produce enduring increases in IQs, even though briefer, less intensive, later-starting efforts had not. One effort that has yielded a positive answer to these questions is the **Carolina Abecedarian Project,** a program that clearly illustrates the theme of how research can improve children's welfare (Campbell & Ramey, 2007; Ramey & Ramey, 2004).

Children were selected to participate in the Abecedarian (pronounced "a-bee-cee-darian") program on the basis of low family income, the absence of a father in the home, low maternal IQ and education, and other factors that put them at risk for developmental problems. More than 95% of the children who participated were African American. The program was based on seven principles (Ramey & Ramey, 2004):

1. Encourage exploration
2. Mentor basic skills
3. Celebrate developmental advances
4. Rehearse and generalize new skills
5. Protect children from inappropriate disapproval, teasing, and punishment
6. Communicate richly and responsively
7. Guide and limit behavior

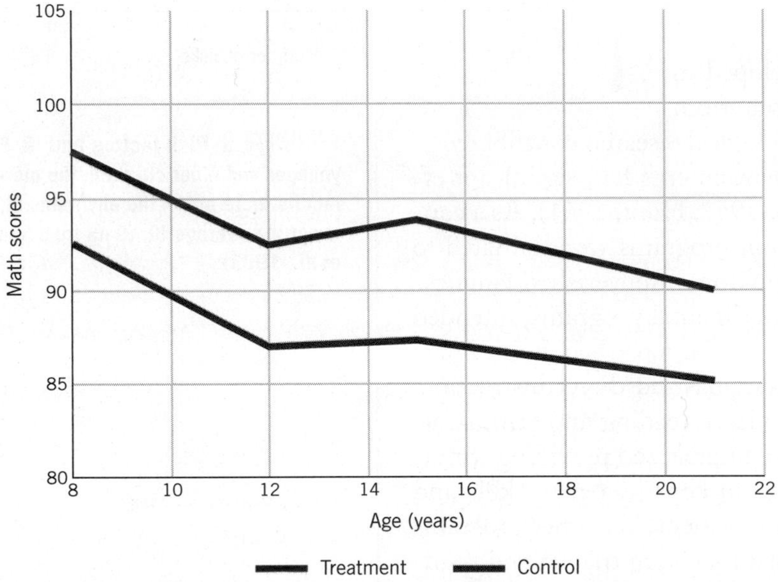

The benefits of participating in the Abecedarian Project remained evident 15 years after the end of the program, as illustrated in this graph of the mathematics achievement of children who participated either in the program or in the control condition. Relative to the average level of mathematics achievement of children in the United States, performance of both groups of children declined somewhat between ages 8 and 21, but at all ages, children who participated in the program performed better than did children from comparably disadvantaged backgrounds who had been in the control condition.

have led to fewer children being assigned to special-education classes or being held back in school? A likely reason is that the interventions had long-term effects on children's motivation and behavior. These effects would help children do well enough in the classroom to be promoted with their classmates.

Participation also led to benefits after children finished school. As adults, former participants in some of the programs used the welfare system less and earned larger salaries than did nonparticipants (Haskins, 1989; McLoyd, 1998). Positive effects such as these suggest that early-intervention programs not only can help participants lead more successful lives but may also more than repay their costs by reducing the need for social services. (As discussed in Box 8.2, at least one specialized, intensive program has shown the possibility of producing enduring gains in IQ and school achievement as well.)

Carolina Abecedarian Project a comprehensive and successful enrichment program for children from low-income families

Project Head Start In response to the same political consensus of the 1960s that led to small-scale early-intervention programs, the U.S. government initiated a

8.2

Children in the program began attending a special day-care center by the time they were 6-month-olds and continued to do so through the age of 5 years. They were at the center for the entire working day (7:45 A.M.–5:30 P.M.) 5 days per week, 50 weeks per year, for 5 years. The teacher–child ratio was optimal: 1:3 for children 3 years old and younger and 1:6 for 4-year-olds. Children 3 years old and younger were provided a program that emphasized general social, cognitive, and motor development; for children over age 3, the program also provided systematic instruction in math, science, reading, and music. At all ages, the program emphasized language development and ensured extensive verbal communication between teachers and children. Program personnel also worked with the children's mothers outside the day-care center to improve their understanding of child development. Families of children in the experimental program were provided nutritional supplements and access to high-quality health care. Families of children in a control group received similar health and nutritional benefits, but the children did not attend the day-care center.

This well-planned, multifaceted program proved to have lasting positive effects on the IQs and achievement levels of children in the experimental group. At the age of 21 years, 15 years after the program had ended, these children had mean IQ scores 5 points higher than the children in the control group: 90 versus 85 (Campbell et al., 2001). Participants' achievement test scores in math and reading also were higher. As with less encompassing intervention programs, fewer participants were ever held back in school or placed in special-education classes. A replication of the program with low-birthweight children demonstrated that the lower the mother's educational level, the greater the difference that the program made (Ramey & Ramey, 2004). The largest effects were on children of high school dropouts, and the next largest was on high school graduates. There were no effects on children whose mother graduated college.

The five years of free, all-day educational child care also had positive effects on the lives of the children's mothers. Sixteen years after the end of the program, mothers of children in the experimental group were more likely to be employed than were mothers of children in the control group and were also more likely to have obtained education beyond high school (Ramey et al., 2000). Teenage mothers showed the largest benefits. In home observations, mothers who participated in the program were rated as having more positive interactions with their children and solving child-rearing problems more effectively (Ramey & Ramey, 2004). These improvements in the mothers' lives and child-rearing skills seem likely to have helped maintain the gains in the children's IQs and academic achievement.

What lessons can be drawn from the Abecedarian Project? One important lesson is the benefit of starting interventions early and continuing them for substantial periods of time. A version of the Abecedarian program that ended at age 3 did not produce long-term effects on intelligence, nor did a program that provided educational support from kindergarten through 2nd grade (Burchinal et al., 1997; Ramey et al., 2000). A second crucial lesson is the need for caregivers to interact with infants in positive, responsive ways. High adult-to-infant ratios in day-care centers make such interactions more likely, as does educating staff members in the need for such interactions. Probably the most important lesson is the most basic: it is possible to design interventions that have substantial, lasting, positive effects on poor children's intellectual development. This knowledge may inspire even more successful efforts to improve the lives of poor children.

large-scale intervention program: Project Head Start. In the past 45 years, this program has provided a wide range of services to more than 25 million children.

At present, Head Start serves more than 900,000 3- to 5-year-olds per year in approximately 2000 centers around the United States (Head Start Bureau, 2007). Most participants are 4-year-olds. The population served is racially and ethnically diverse: according to the most recent data, 31% of Head Start children are African American, 27% are Euro-American,

MICHAEL DOOLITTLE / THE IMAGE WORKS

Children who participate in Head Start programs, like the youngsters pictured here, are in later years less likely to be held back in the same grade and more likely to graduate high school than children from similar backgrounds who did not participate in these programs.

31% Latino, 3% American Indian, and 2% are Asian-American (U.S. Department of HHS, 2005). Almost all the children are from families with incomes below the poverty line, mostly single-parent families. In the program, children receive medical and dental care and nutritious meals, and are provided with a safe and stimulating environment. Many parents of participating children work as caregivers at the Head Start centers, serve on policy councils that help plan each center's directions, and receive help with their own vocational and emotional needs.

Consistent with the findings of the smaller experimental intervention programs that have been aimed at 3- and 4-year-olds, participation in Head Start produces higher IQs and achievement test scores by the end of the program and for a few years thereafter. For example, when children were randomly assigned either to Head Start or to a community-based child-care program of their parents' choice, children in Head Start showed better prereading and prewriting skills (though no better math skills) at the end of a year in the program (Westat, 2005). Beyond the end of Head Start, however, children's performance becomes indistinguishable from that of nonparticipants with similar backgrounds (McKey et al., 1985; McLoyd, 1998). On the other hand, participation in Head Start produces a number of other positive effects that do endure, ones that resemble those produced by the experimental preschool programs: improved social skills and health, lower frequency of being held back in school, greater likelihood of graduating from high school and enrolling in college, and lower rates of drug use and delinquency (Love, Chazan-Cohen, & Raikes, 2007; Zigler & Styfco, 2004). These are important gains and have contributed to the enduring popularity of Head Start.

Among the benefits of Head Start is the provision of nutritious meals for children who otherwise might be at risk for malnutrition.

MARK RICHARDS / PHOTOEDIT

review:

The development of intelligence is influenced by qualities of the child, qualities of the immediate environment, and qualities of the broader society. The child's genetic inheritance is one important influence, an influence that steadily increases over the course of development. The intellectual environment provided by the child's family, and the schooling the child encounters, are also influential, as are the family's economic status and educational level and whether one or two parents are present.

Programs for helping preschoolers who are at risk for low IQs are often beneficial in a variety of ways, though their effect on IQ and achievement test scores usually fades over time. However, at least one early-intervention program, the Abecedarian Project, reports positive effects on IQs and achievement that last into adolescence and adulthood.

Alternative Perspectives on Intelligence

The discussions of intellectual development in this chapter have relied on IQ tests as the main measure of intellectual development. Research using these tests has revealed a great deal about the development of intelligence. However, a number of contemporary theorists have noted that many important aspects of intelligence are not measured by IQ tests. The tests assess verbal, mathematical, and spatial capabilities, but they do not directly examine other abilities that seem to be inherent parts of intelligence: creativity, social understanding, knowledge of one's own strengths and weaknesses, and so on. This perspective has led Howard Gardner and Robert Sternberg to formulate theories of intelligence that encompass a wider range of human abilities than do traditional theories.

Gardner (1993) labeled his approach **multiple intelligence theory.** Its basic claim is that people possess eight kinds of intelligence: the linguistic, logical-mathematical, and spatial abilities emphasized in previous theories and measured on IQ tests, and also musical, naturalistic, bodily-kinesthetic, intrapersonal, and interpersonal abilities (see Table 8.3).

Gardner used several types of evidence to arrive at this set of intelligences. One involved deficits shown by people with brain damage. For example, some brain-damaged patients function well in most respects but have no understanding of other people (Damasio, 1999). This phenomenon suggested to Gardner that interpersonal intelligence was distinct from other types of intelligence. A second type of evidence that Gardner used to identify this set of intelligences was the existence of prodigies, people who from early in life show exceptional

TABLE 8.3

Gardner's Theory of Multiple Intelligences

Type of Intelligence	Description	Examples
Linguistic intelligence	Sensitivity to the meanings and sounds of words; mastery of syntax; appreciation of the ways language can be used	Poet Political speaker Teacher
Logical-mathematical intelligence	Understanding of objects and symbols, of the actions that can be performed on them and of the relations between these actions; ability for abstraction; ability to identify problems and seek explanations	Mathematician Scientist
Spatial intelligence	Capacity to perceive the visual world accurately, to perform transformations upon perceptions and to re-create aspects of visual experience in the absence of physical stimuli; sensitivity to tension, balance, and composition; ability to detect similar patterns	Artist Engineer Chess master
Musical intelligence	Sensitivity to individual tones and phrases of music; an understanding of ways to combine tones and phrases into larger musical rhythms and structures; awareness of emotional aspects of music	Musician Composer
Naturalistic intelligence	Sensitivity and understanding of plants, animals, and other aspects of nature	Biologist
Bodily-kinesthetic intelligence	Use of one's body in highly skilled ways for expressive or goal-directed purposes; capacity to handle objects skillfully	Dancer Athlete Actor
Intrapersonal intelligence	Access to one's own feeling life; ability to draw on one's emotions to guide and understand one's behavior	Novelist Therapist Patient
Interpersonal intelligence	Ability to notice and make distinctions among the moods, temperaments, motivations, and intentions of other people and potentially to act on this knowledge	Political leader Religious leader Parent Teacher Therapist

Source: Gardner (1993)

multiple intelligence theory Gardner's theory of intellect, based on the view that people possess at least eight types of intelligence

Mozart's musical genius was evident from early in childhood, leading some of the greatest musicians of his day to play music with him when he was still a child.

ability in one area but not in others. One such example is Wolfgang Amadeus Mozart, who displayed musical genius while still a child but was unexceptional in many ways. The existence of highly specialized musical talents such as Mozart's provides evidence for viewing musical ability as a separate intelligence.

Gardner proposed that individual children learn best through instruction that allows them to build on their intellectual strengths. Thus, a child who is high in spatial intelligence might learn history best through the extensive use of charts and graphs, whereas a child who is high in social intelligence might learn history best through group discussions and projects. Although Gardner's theory of intelligence is backed by less supporting evidence than traditional theories of intelligence, its emphasis on how instruction can build on individual children's strengths and its optimistic message have caused it to have a large influence on education.

Sternberg (2000) also argued that the emphasis of IQ tests on the type of intelligence needed to succeed in school is too narrow. However, the alternative view of intelligence that he proposed differs from that proposed by Gardner. Sternberg's **theory of successful intelligence** envisions intelligence as "the ability to achieve success in life, given one's personal standards, within one's sociocultural context" (p. 4). In his view, success in life reflects people's ability to build on their strengths, to compensate for their weaknesses, and to select environments in which they can succeed. When people choose a job, for instance, their understanding of the conditions that will motivate them to do their best may be as important to their success as their linguistic, spatial, and mathematical abilities.

Sternberg proposed that the degree to which people succeed in life depends on three types of abilities: analytic, practical, and creative. *Analytic abilities* involve the linguistic, mathematical, and spatial skills that are measured by traditional intelligence tests. *Practical abilities* involve reasoning about everyday problems, such as how to resolve conflicts with other people. *Creative abilities* involve intellectual flexibilty and innovation that allows effective reasoning in novel circumstances.

The recent theories of intelligence proposed by Gardner, Sternberg, and others (e.g., Ceci, 1996) have inspired a rethinking of long-held assumptions about intelligence. Intelligence and success in life clearly involve a broader range of capabilities than those measured by traditional intelligence tests, and it may prove possible to improve the assessment of intelligence by measuring this broader range of capabilities. There is not now, nor will there ever be, a single correct theory of intelligence. What is possible is a variety of theories, and tests based on them, that together reveal the varied ways in which people can be intelligent.

review:

Howard Gardner and Robert Sternberg have formulated new theories of intelligence. Gardner's multiple-intelligence theory proposes that there are eight intelligences: linguistic, logical-mathematical, spatial, musical, naturalistic, bodily-kinesthetic, intrapersonal, and interpersonal. Sternberg's theory of successful intelligence proposes that success in life depends on three types of abilities: analytic, practical, and creative. Both theories conceive of intelligence as a broader set of abilities than have traditional theories.

theory of successful intelligence Sternberg's theory of intellect, based on the view that intelligence is the ability to achieve success in life

Acquisition of Academic Skills: Reading, Writing, and Mathematics

Among the most important uses to which children apply their intelligence is learning the skills and concepts taught at school. Because these skills and concepts are central to succeeding in modern society, and because they are difficult to master, children spend roughly 15,000 hours in school from the 1st through the 12th grade. Much of this time is devoted to learning to read, write, and do math. In this section, we focus on how children acquire these skills and why some children have such difficulty mastering them.

phonemic awareness ability to identify component sounds within words

phonological recoding skills ability to translate letters into sounds and to blend sounds into words

Reading

Many children learn to read effortlessly, either before they go to school or after a small amount of instruction. Others, however, find the learning process difficult and frustrating. You can no doubt remember the painful experience of classmates—and perhaps yourself—seeming to take forever to read aloud simple sentences, even in 2nd and 3rd grade. Why is it that some children learn to read so effortlessly, whereas others experience great difficulty? To answer this question, we must examine the typical path of reading development, as well as how and why children deviate from it.

Chall (1979) described five stages of reading development. These stages provide a good overview of the typical path to mastery:

Stage 0 (birth until the beginning of 1st grade): During this time, many children acquire key prerequisites for reading. These include knowing the letters of the alphabet and gaining **phonemic awareness**, that is, knowledge of the individual sounds within words.

Stage 1 (1st and 2nd grades): Children acquire **phonological recoding skills**, the ability to translate letters into sounds and to blend the sounds into words (informally referred to as "sounding out").

Stage 2 (2nd and 3rd grades): Children gain fluency in reading simple material.

DON SMETZER / PHOTOEDIT

The appeal of nursery rhymes to young children has always been obvious, but only recently have the benefits of such rhymes for phonemic awareness and reading acquisition become known.

Stage 3 (4th through 8th grades): Children become able to acquire reasonably complex, new information from print. To quote Chall, "In the primary grades, children learn to read; in the higher grades, they read to learn" (1979, p. 24).

Stage 4 (8th through 12th grades): Adolescents acquire skill not only in understanding information presented from a single perspective but also in coordinating multiple perspectives. This makes it possible for them to appreciate the subtleties in sophisticated novels and plays, which almost always include multiple viewpoints.

This description of developmental stages provides a general sense of the reading acquisition process and a framework for understanding how particular developments fit into the broader picture.

She fed him, then put him to bed and kissed him goodnight. The little pig kissed her back. This so delighted the woman that she named the pig "Perfect." Perfect could hardly believe it. He had not only found a home, but someone who thought he was perfect.

A WRINKLE IN TIME 27

"I don't know what to do," Meg said.

"You could do your homework, for one thing. Wouldn't your mother help you?"

"If I asked her to."

"Meg, is something troubling you? Are you unhappy at home?" Mr. Jenkins asked.

At last Meg looked at him, pushing at her glasses in a characteristic gesture. "Everything's fine at home."

"I'm glad to hear it. But I know it must be hard on you to have your father away."

Meg eyed the principal warily, and ran her tongue over the barbed line of her braces.

"Have you had any news from him lately?"

Meg was sure it was not only imagination that made her feel that behind Mr. Jenkins' surface concern was a gleam of avid curiosity. Wouldn't he like to know! she thought. And if I knew anything he's the last person I'd tell. Well, one of the last.

The postmistress must know that it was almost a year now since the last letter, and heaven knows how many people she'd told, or what unkind guesses she'd made about the reason for the long silence.

Mr. Jenkins waited for an answer, but Meg only shrugged.

"Just what was your father's line of business?" Mr. Jenkins asked. "Some kind of scientist, wasn't he?"

"He *is* a physicist." Meg bared her teeth to reveal the two ferocious lines of braces.

"Meg, don't you think you'd make a better adjustment to life if you faced facts?"

The books used by 1st graders (left) and 6th graders (right) differ greatly in the number of words per page, the complexity of the ideas, and the background knowledge needed to understand the material. The increased complexity of the older children's readers reflects the remarkable increase in reading skills during this period.

Prereading Skills

Preschoolers acquire certain basic information about reading just from looking at books and having their parents read to them. They learn that (in English and other European languages) text is read from left to right; that after they reach the right end of a line, the text continues at the extreme left of the line below; and that words are separated by small spaces.

Children with well-educated parents also tend to learn the names of most or all of the letters of the alphabet before they enter school. This tends not to be true of children whose parents are poorly educated, however. In one study of beginning kindergartners, 86% of children whose mother graduated from college were proficient in letter recognition, but only 38% of children whose mother did not complete high school were (West, Denton, & Germino-Hausken, 2000).

Kindergartners' mastery of letter names is positively correlated with their later reading achievement through at least 7th grade (Vellutino & Scanlon, 1987). However, there is no causal relation between the two; teaching the names of the letters to randomly chosen preschoolers does not increase their subsequent reading achievement (Adams, 1990). Instead, it appears that other variables, such as children's interest in books and parents' interest in their children's reading, stimulate both early knowledge of the alphabet and later high reading achievement.

Phonemic awareness, on the other hand, is both correlated with later reading achievement and a cause of it. To measure awareness of the component sounds within words, researchers ask children to decide whether two words rhyme, to decide whether they start with the same sound, to identify component sounds within a word, and to indicate what would be left if a given sound were removed from a word. Performance on these phonemic-awareness tasks during kindergarten is the strongest predictor of children's ability to sound out and spell words in the early grades—stronger even than IQ or social-class background (Nation, 2008; Rayner et al., 2001)—and it continues to be related to reading achievement as much as 11 years later, above and beyond the influence of the child's social-class background (MacDonald & Cornwall, 1995). Even more impressive, a review of 52 well-controlled experimental studies indicated that teaching phonemic-awareness skills to 4- and 5-year-olds causes them to become better readers and spellers, with the effects enduring for years after the training (National Reading Advisory Panel, 2000).

Although explicit training can help foster phonemic awareness, most children do not receive such explicit training. Where, then, does phonemic awareness come from in the natural environment? One relevant experience is hearing nursery rhymes. Many nursery rhymes highlight the contribution of individual sounds to differences among words (e.g., "I do not like green eggs and *ham;* I do not like them *Sam* I *am.*") Consistent with this hypothesis, 3-year-olds' knowledge of nursery rhymes correlates positively with their later phonemic awareness, above and beyond their IQs and their mother's educational level (Maclean, Bryant, & Bradley, 1987). Other factors that contribute to the growth of phonemic awareness include growth of working memory, increasingly efficient processing of language, and, especially, reading itself (Anthony & Francis, 2005; McBride-Chang, 2004). Children with greater phonemic awareness read more and read better, which in turn, leads to further increases in their phonemic awareness and in the quantity and quality of their reading.

Word Identification

Rapid, effortless identification of words is crucial not only to reading comprehension but also to the enjoyment of reading. One remarkable finding makes the point: 40% of 4th graders who were poor at identifying words said they would rather clean their rooms than read (Juel, 1988). One child went as far as to say, "I'd rather clean the mold around the bathtub than read." Thus, not only does being poor at word identification make the reading process slow and laborious, it also leads children to read no more than is absolutely necessary, which, in turn, hinders improvement in the reading skills.

Words can be identified in two main ways: *phonological recoding* and *visually based retrieval.* As previously indicated, phonological recoding involves converting the visual form of a word into a verbal, speechlike form and using the speechlike form to determine the word's meaning. **Visually based retrieval** involves processing a word's meaning directly from its visual form.

Most young children use both approaches (Share, 2004), choosing adaptively between them from 1st grade onward. They do so through a **strategy–choice process,** in which they choose the fastest approach that is likely to be correct. In the context of reading, this means that on easy words, children rely heavily on

visually based retrieval proceeding directly from the visual form of a word to its meaning

strategy–choice process procedure for selecting among alternative ways of solving problems

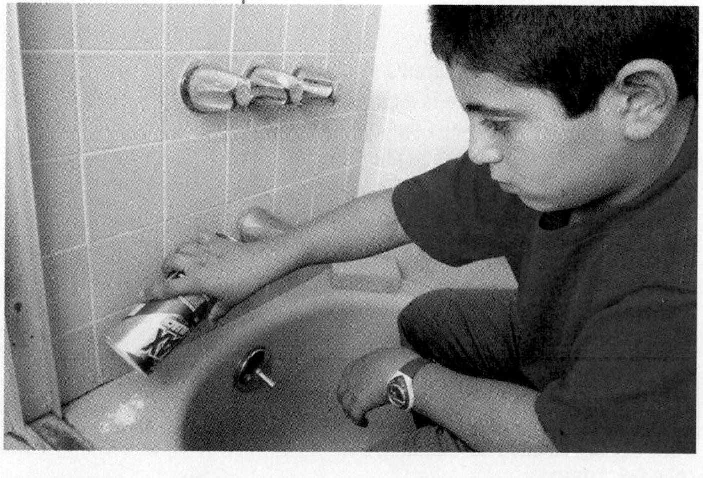

Some children dislike reading so intensely that they would rather scrub the bathtub than read.

MICHAEL NEWMAN / PHOTOEDIT

dyslexia inability to read well despite normal intelligence

phonological processing ability to discriminate and remember sounds within words

the fast but not always accurate approach of retrieval; on hard words, they resort to the slower but surer strategy of phonological recoding. As shown in Figure 8.10, 1st graders are very skillful in adjusting their strategies to the difficulty of the particular word.

The mechanisms underlying this adaptive strategy choice involve a form of associative learning, in which children's past behavior shapes their future behavior (Siegler, 1996). Beginning readers rely heavily on phonological recoding, because the associations between words' visual forms and their sounds are too weak to allow much use of retrieval. Correct use of phonological recoding increases the associations between words' visual forms and their sounds, which in turn allows greater use of visually based retrieval. Consistent with this view, the shift to retrieval occurs most rapidly for words on which children most often execute phonological recoding correctly—words that are short, that have regular letter–sound relations, and that are encountered frequently. Also consistent with this view, children who are better at phonological recoding early in learning stop using that approach earlier, because their past success with it enables them to shift more rapidly to visually based retrieval. A third correct implication is that reading instruction that emphasizes phonics, and the strategy of phonological recoding, should help to produce fast and accurate word identification (Adams, Treiman, & Pressley, 1998; Xue & Meisels, 2004).

With age and experience, vocabulary knowledge becomes an increasingly important influence on word identification, particularly on words with irregular sound–symbol correspondences (Nation, 2008). However, phonological recoding skill also continues to be important, even for adults when they encounter unfamiliar words. (Box 8.3 discusses the relation between poor phonological recoding skills and the reading disability known as dyslexia.)

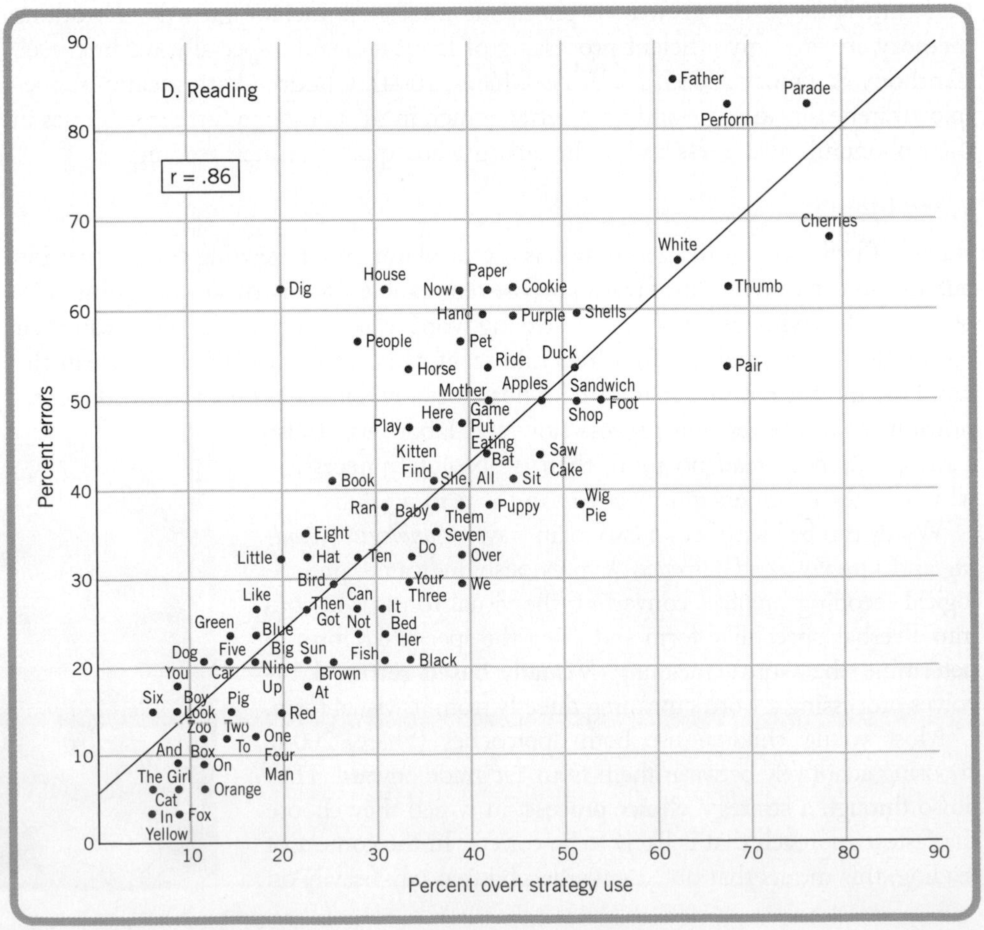

FIGURE 8.10 Young children's strategy choices in reading There is a strong positive correlation between the difficulty of a word, as defined by the percentage of errors children make on it, and the frequency of young children's use of an overt strategy, such as audible phonological recoding, to read it. Thus, on easy words that children almost always read correctly, such as *in*, they rarely used overt strategies to identify the word; but on difficult words that elicit many errors when retrieval is used, such as *parade*, children often fell back on overt strategies such as sounding out. (Siegler, 1986)

individual differences 8.3

Dyslexia

Some children who are of normal intelligence and whose parents encourage them to read nevertheless read very poorly. This inability to read well despite normal intelligence, referred to as **dyslexia,** affects 5% to 10% of children in the United States (Anthony & Francis, 2005). The causes of dyslexia are poorly understood, but genetics are clearly part of the story. If one of a pair of monozygotic twins is diagnosed as dyslexic, the probability of the other twin's being similarly diagnosed is 84%, whereas if the twins are dizygotic, the corresponding probability is 48% (Kovas & Plomin, 2007; Oliver, et al., 2004). The extent of genetic influences varies with parental educational; as with IQ, genetic influences on dyslexia are larger with children of highly educated parents than with children of less educated parents (Friend, DeFries, & Olson, 2008).

At a cognitive level of analysis, dyslexia stems primarily from a general weakness at **phonological processing.** This weakness is evident in poor ability to discriminate between phonemes, poor short-term memory for verbal material (as indicated, for example, by poor ability to recall an arbitrary list of words), and slow recall of the names of objects (Vellutino, Scanlon, & Spearing, 1995; Wimmer, Mayringer, & Raberger, 1999). Determining the sounds that go with vowels is especially difficult for children with dyslexia, at least in English, where a single vowel can be pronounced in many ways (consider the sounds that accompany the letter "a" in "hate," "hat," "hall," and "hard"). Because of this poor phonological processing, dyslexic children have great difficulty mastering the letter–sound correspondences used in phonological recoding, especially in languages with irregular sound–symbol correspondences, such as English (Sprenger-Charolles, 2003).

For example, as shown in the figure, when asked to read pseudowords such as *parding*, dyslexic 13- and 14-year-olds perform at the same level as typical 7- and 8-year-olds (Siegel, 1993). As would be expected from the strategy–choice model described earlier, this difficulty with phonological processing causes most dyslexic children to be poor at visually based retrieval, as well as at sounding out words (Manis, Seidenberg, Doi, McBride-Chang, & Peterson, 1996). The problem can be a lasting one: most individuals who have poor phonological processing skills in early elementary school are poor readers as adults (Wagner et al., 1997). This is especially the case for children from disadvantaged backgrounds: children who come from more advantaged family backgrounds and who attend better schools are more likely to show substantial improvements (Shaywitz, Mody, & Shaywitz, 2006).

Studies of brain functioning support the view that poor phonological processing is at the heart of dyslexia. When dyslexic children read, two areas of their brains are less active than the corresponding areas in typical children reading the same words (Schlaggar & Church, 2009). One such area is directly involved in phonological processing; the other area is involved in integrating visual and auditory data (in this case, integrating the letters on the page with accompanying sounds).

How can dyslexic children be helped? One tempting idea is that because these children have difficulty learning phonics, they would learn better through an approach that deemphasizes letter–sound relations and instead emphasizes either visually based retrieval or reliance on context. These alternative methods work poorly, however (Lyon, 1995). There is simply no substitute for being able to sound out unfamiliar words. Indeed, what seems to work best is to teach children with dyslexia to use strategies that enhance their phonological recoding (Lovett et al., 1994). Effective strategies include drawing analogies to known words with similar spellings; generating alternative pronunciations of vowels when the first attempt at sounding out does not yield a plausible word; and, with long words, "peeling off" prefixes and suffixes and then trying to identify the rest of the word. Using such strategies helps children with dyslexia to improve their reading-achievement scores and spelling (Lovett et al., 1994).

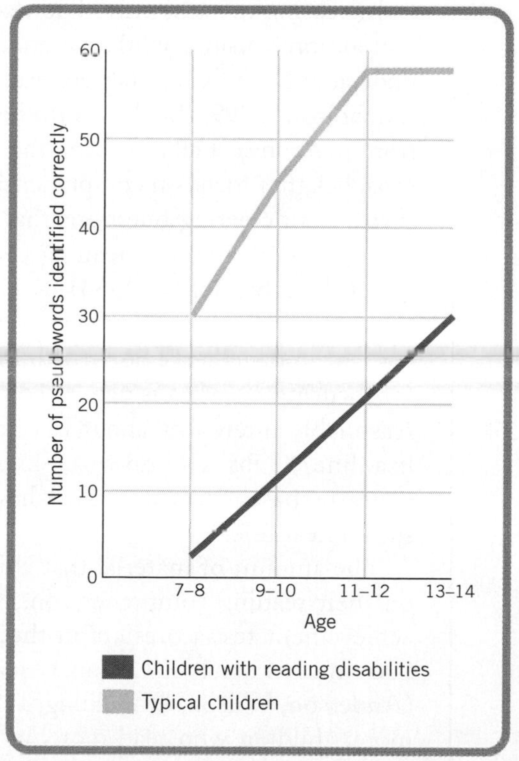

This chart shows the number of pseudowords identified correctly by 7- to 14-year-olds with and without reading disabilities. Note that 13- and 14-year-olds with reading disabilities correctly identified no more items than did typical 7- and 8-year-olds. The poor phonological recoding skills of children with learning disabilities leads them to have special difficulty with pseudowords that, because they are totally unfamiliar, can be pronounced only by using phonological recoding. (Data from Siegel, 1993)

mental model processes used to represent a situation or sequence of events

comprehension monitoring the process of keeping track of one's understanding of a verbal description or text

Comprehension

The point of learning to read individual words is to be able to comprehend the text in which the individual words appear. Reading comprehension involves forming a **mental model** of the situation or idea being depicted in the text and continuously updating it as new information appears (Oakhill & Cain, 2000). All the types of mental operations that influence cognitive development in general—basic processes, strategies, metacognition (knowledge about people's thinking), and content knowledge—also influence the development of reading comprehension.

Basic processes and capacities such as encoding (identification of key features of an object or event) and automatization (executing a process with minimal demands on cognitive resources) are crucial to reading comprehension. The reason is simple: children who are able to identify the key features of stories will be able to understand the story better, and children who are able to automatically identify the key features of words will have more resources left to devote to comprehension. Fast and accurate word identification correlates positively with reading comprehension at all points from the 1st grade through adulthood (Cunningham & Stanovich, 1997).

Development of reading comprehension is also aided by acquisition of reading strategies. For example, good readers proceed slowly when they need to master written material in depth and speed up when they need only a rough sense of it (Pressley & Hilden, 2006). Proficiency in making such adjustments develops surprisingly late, however. Even when 10-year-olds are told that some material is crucial and other material is not, they tend to read all the material at the same speed. In contrast, 14-year-olds skim the nonessential parts and spend more time on the important ones (Kobasigawa, Ransom, & Holland, 1980).

Increasing metacognitive knowledge also contributes to improvements in reading comprehension. With age and experience, readers increasingly monitor their understanding of what they are reading and reread passages they do not understand (Nicholson, 1999). Such **comprehension monitoring** differentiates good readers from poor ones at all ages from the 1st grade through adulthood. Instructional approaches that focus on comprehension monitoring and other metacognitive skills, such as anticipating questions that a teacher might ask about the material, have been found to improve reading comprehension (Palincsar & Magnusson, 2001; Rosenshine & Meister, 1994).

Another powerful influence on the development of reading comprehension is content knowledge. The growth of content knowledge frees cognitive resources for focusing on what is new or complex in the text. It also allows readers to draw reasonable inferences about information left unstated. Thus, when reading the headline "Cubs Thump Sox," knowledgeable readers realize that the headline concerns baseball; it is unclear how less knowledgeable readers would interpret such a headline.

The amount of material that children read varies greatly and has a large effect on their reading comprehension. For example, U.S. 5th graders whose reading-achievement test scores are in the 90th percentile for their grade report roughly 200 times as much discretionary reading as peers who score in the 10th percentile (Anderson, Wilson, & Fielding, 1988). High reading ability leads children to read more; children who read more, in turn, show greater gains over time in reading comprehension than do children of equal ability who read less (Guthrie, Wigfield, Metsala, & Cox, 1999).

Children's reading comprehension is influenced not only by their own activities but also by those of their parents. Being told or read stories by their parents helps preschoolers learn how such stories tend to go, facilitating their understanding of new stories once they start reading themselves. It also enhances their general level of language development (Raikes et al., 2006; Whitehurst & Lonigan, 1998). The amount that parents read to their children during the preschool years also accounts for part of the differences between the reading comprehension skills of children from middle- and low-income families. For example, a study conducted in Israel showed that in an affluent school district with high reading-achievement scores, 96% of parents of preschoolers read to them daily. The same was true of only 15% of parents of preschoolers in a poor district with low scores (Feitelson & Goldstein, 1986).

The straightforward implication of these findings is that if preschoolers from poor families were read to daily, they too would become better readers. The evidence is consistent with this inference. Encouraging low-income parents to actively engage children in the reading process, such as by asking them to relate what is being read to their own experiences or to explain the characters' goals and motivations, helps even more (Zevenburgen & Whitehurst, 2003). Persuading low-income parents to enroll in such programs and read to their children on a continuing basis is not easy, due to time demands and, in many cases, the pressures of being a single parent (Whitehurst et al., 1999); but when parents do so, their children benefit.

Individual Differences

Individual differences in reading tend to be quite stable over time. Children who have relatively advanced reading skills when they enter kindergarten tend to be better readers through elementary, middle, and high school (Duncan et al., 2007; Harlaar, Dale, & Plomin, 2007). Studies of adoptive and nonadoptive siblings and of monozygotic and dizygotic twins indicate that these continuities of individual differences reflect both shared genes and shared environments (Petrill et al., 2006; Wadsworth et al., 2006). As we have noted on several occasions, the genetic and environmental influences are mutually reinforcing: parents who are good and frequent readers are likely to provide both genes and environments that make it likely that their children will be relatively good readers when they are young, which makes it more likely that the children will seek out reading opportunities, which will further improve their reading, and so on (Petrill, Deater-Deckard, Schatschneider, & Davis, 2005).

Writing

Much less is known about the development of children's writing than about the development of their reading, but what is known shows interesting parallels between the two.

Prewriting Skills

The development of writing, like the development of reading, begins before children receive formal schooling. Figure 8.11 displays a typical 3½-year-old's

FIGURE 8.11 A 3½-year-old's effort to write a shopping list for a teddy bear The child's symbols, although unconventional, indicate an understanding that words require separate symbols. (Jones, 1990)

"shopping list." The marks are not conventional letters of the alphabet, but they look vaguely like them and are arranged in a linear horizontal sequence. By age 4, children's "writing" is sufficiently advanced that adults have no trouble distinguishing it from the figures 4-year-olds produce when asked to draw a flower or a house (Tolchnisky, 2003).

Preschoolers' "writing" indicates that they expect meaning to be reflected in print. They use more marks to represent words that signify many objects, such as "forest," than to represent words that signify a single object, such as "tree" (Levin & Korat, 1993). Similarly, when asked to guess which of several words is the name for a particular object, they generally choose longer words for larger objects (Bialystok, 2000). Although written language does not follow this "rule," the children's guess seems reasonable.

Generating Written Text

Learning to write (in the sense of writing an essay or story) is a good deal more difficult than learning to read. This is not surprising, because writing requires focusing simultaneously on numerous goals, both low level and high level. The low-level goals include forming letters, spelling words, and using correct capitalization and punctuation. The high-level goals include making arguments comprehensible without the intonations and gestures that help us express ourselves when we speak, organizing individual points in a coherent framework, and providing the background information that readers need to understand the writing (Berninger & Richards, 2002). The difficulties children have in meeting both the low-level and high-level goals result in their writing the type of story illustrated in Figure 8.12.

FIGURE 8.12 A 4th grader's story The intended title of this story, which was written by a 4th grader, was "The Kid Who Lost Things." See if you can figure out the rest.

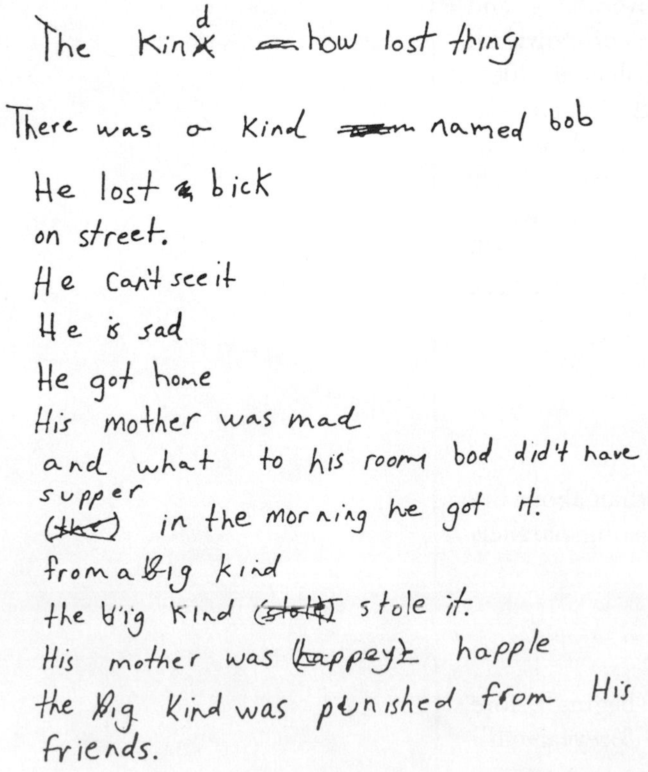
The Kind how lost thing
There was a Kind named bob
He lost bick
on street.
He can't see it
He is sad
He got home
His mother was mad
and what to his room bod did't have
supper
in the morning he got it.
from a big kind
the big Kind stole it.
His mother was happle
the big Kind was punished from His
friends.

As with development of reading comprehension, growth of writing proficiency reflects improvements in basic capacities, strategies, metacognition, and content knowledge. Automatizing low-level skills, such as spelling and punctuation, aids writing not only because correct spelling and punctuation make writing easier to understand but also because automatizing the low-level skills frees cognitive resources for pursuing the higher-level communicative goals of writing. Consistent with this conclusion, children's proficiency at low-level skills such as spelling correlates positively with the quality of the children's essays (Juel, 1994).

Acquisition of strategies also contributes to improvements in writing. One common strategy is to sequence high-level goals in a standard organization that can be used repeatedly.

Harriet Waters, a psychologist whose proud mother saved all of her daughter's "class news" assignments from 2nd grade, was one child who employed such an approach (Waters, 1980). As shown in Table 8.4, in each class news essay, Waters first stated the date, then discussed the weather, and then discussed events of the school day, a strategy that greatly simplified her writing task. For older children, formulating outlines serves a similar purpose of dividing the task of writing into manageable parts: first figure out what you want to say; then figure out how to say it.

Metacognitive understanding plays several crucial roles in writing. Perhaps the most basic type of metacognitive understanding is recognizing that readers may not have the same knowledge as the writer and that one therefore should include all the information that readers will need to allow them to grasp what is being said. Good writers consistently exhibit such understanding by high school; poor writers often do not (Berninger & Richards, 2002). A second crucial type of metacognitive knowledge involves understanding the need to plan one's writing, rather than just jumping in and starting to write. Good writers spend much more time than do poor writers planning what they will say before they begin writing (Kellogg, 1994). Understanding the need for revision is a third key type of metacognitive knowledge. Good writers spend more time revising their already relatively good first drafts than poor writers spend revising their poorer ones (Fitzgerald, 1992).

Fortunately, as with reading, instruction aimed at inculcating metacognitive understanding can enhance writing skills (Graham & Harris, 1996). In particular, the writing of both typical and learning-disabled children improves when they are taught to revise other children's work and to ask themselves several basic questions: Who is the main character in this story? What does the main character do? How do the other characters respond? How does the main character respond to the other characters' responses? What happens in the end? Asking children to reflect on the relative quality of essays written by other children, and on why some essays are better than others, also can improve writing (Braaksma, Rijlaarsdam, van der Bergh, & van Hout-Walters, 2004).

TABLE 8.4

Stories Written at Beginning, Middle, and End of Year for Class News Assignment

SEPTEMBER 24, 1956
Today is Monday, September, 24, 1956. It is a rainy day. We hope the sun will shine.
We got new spelling books. We had our pictures taken. We sang Happy Birthday to Barbara.

JANUARY 22, 1957
Today is Tuesday, January 22, 1957. It is a foggy day. We must be careful crossing the road.
This morning, we had music. We learned a new song.
Linda is absent. We hope she comes back soon.
We had arithmetic. We made believe that we were buying candy. We had fun.
We work in our English books. We learned when to use is and are.

MAY 27, 1957
Today is Monday, May 27, 1957. It is a warm, cloudy day. We hope the sun comes out.
This afternoon, we had music. We enjoyed it. We went out to play.
Carole is absent. We hope she comes back soon.
We had a spelling lesson, we learned about a dozen.
Tomorrow we shall have show and tell.
Some of us have spelling sentences to do for homework.
Danny brought in a cocoon. It will turn into a butterfly.

Source: Waters (1980)

Learning about numbers is harder than it looks.

Finally, as in reading, content knowledge plays a crucial role in writing. Children generally write better when they are familiar with the topic than when they are not (Bereiter & Scardamalia, 1982). Thus, the standard advice "Write what you know" applies to children as well as to aspiring authors.

Mathematics

As discussed in Chapter 7, from early in their first year, infants display a rudimentary sense of number, but one that is limited to sets of three or fewer objects. By the time they are 3 or 4 years old, they supplement this initial competence with skill at counting and with knowledge of the relative sizes of single-digit numbers. These early-emerging numerical competencies provide a base from which children can learn arithmetic and more advanced mathematical skills.

Arithmetic

One striking characteristic of children's arithmetic is the variety of overt strategies that they use to solve problems. When children are 4 or 5 years old, they acquire their first arithmetic strategy, counting from 1 (e.g., solving 2 + 2 by putting up two fingers on each hand and counting "1, 2, 3, 4"). Very quickly, they begin to use the strategy of retrieval (recalling answers from memory) to answer a few simple problems, such as 2 + 2. In 1st grade, when children begin to do arithmetic on a daily basis, they add several new strategies. The most common is *counting from the larger addend* (e.g., solving 3 + 9 by counting, "9, 10, 11, 12"). Another common strategy is *decomposition,* which involves dividing a problem into two easier ones (e.g., solving 3 + 9 by thinking "3 + 10 = 13; 13 − 1 = 12").

Similar use of varied strategies is also present in other arithmetic operations (Geary, 2006). For example, to solve a multiplication problem such as 3 × 4, children

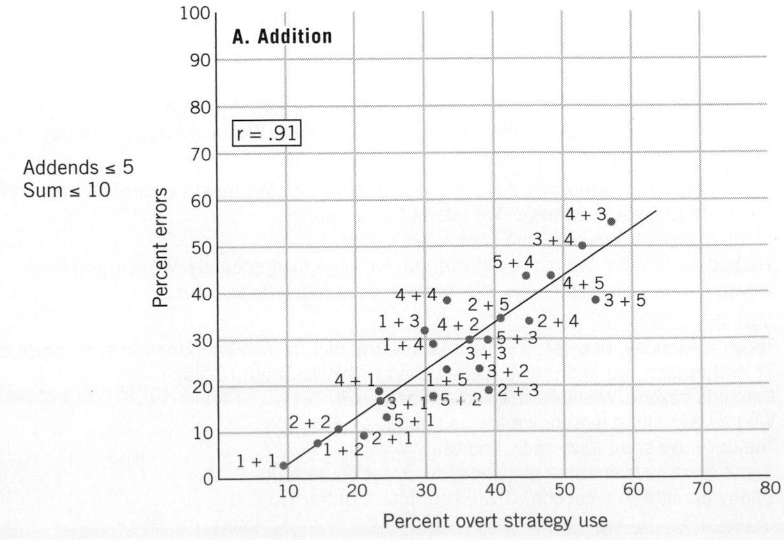

FIGURE 8.13 Young children's strategy choices in addition, subtraction, and multiplication As was illustrated previously with reading (Figure 8.10), there is a strong positive correlation between the difficulty of a problem, as defined by the percentage of errors it elicits, and the frequency of using an overt strategy, such as counting on one's fingers. Thus, on problems that 4- and 5-year-olds found easy, such as 2 + 2, they usually used retrieval. On problems they found difficult, such as 4 + 3, they usually used overt strategies such as counting from 1. (Siegler, 1986)

sometimes write three 4s and add them, sometimes make three bundles of four hatch marks and count them, and sometimes retrieve 12 from memory (Mabbott & Bisanz, 2003). Children also use repeated addition to solve division problems; for example, they might solve 24 ÷ 8 by adding 8 + 8 + 8 and then answering "3" because that was the number of times they added 8 (Robinson et al., 2006). Use of these arithmetic strategies is surprisingly enduring; even college students use strategies other than retrieval on 15% to 30% of single-digit problems (LeFevre et al., 1996).

Just as children's choices among word-identification strategies are highly adaptive, so are their choices among strategies for solving single-digit arithmetic problems (Geary, 2006; Siegler & Shrager, 1984). Even 4-year-olds choose in sensible ways, solving easy problems, such as 2 + 2, quickly and accurately by using retrieval and solving harder problems, such as 5 + 2, less quickly but still accurately by counting (Figure 8.13). As children gain experience with single-digit arithmetic, their strategy choices shift toward increasing use of retrieval. The learning process seems to be the same as with the corresponding shift toward visually based retrieval in reading. The more often children generate the correct answer to a problem, regardless of the strategy they use to generate it, the more often they will be able to retrieve that answer, thereby avoiding the need to use a slower process such as counting (Geary, 2006; Siegler, 1996). (As noted in Box 8.4, although this process usually produces high levels of learning, it goes awry with children who suffer from a general difficulty in thinking about numbers, known as *mathematical disability*).

Conceptual understanding Understanding arithmetic involves more than memorizing answers and problem-solving procedures. It also requires a grasp of underlying concepts and principles. Unfortunately, many children learn procedures that are effective on typical problems without understanding why the procedures are appropriate. Such shallow understanding leads to difficulty when these children encounter novel problems that build on the same underlying concepts but that require different solution procedures.

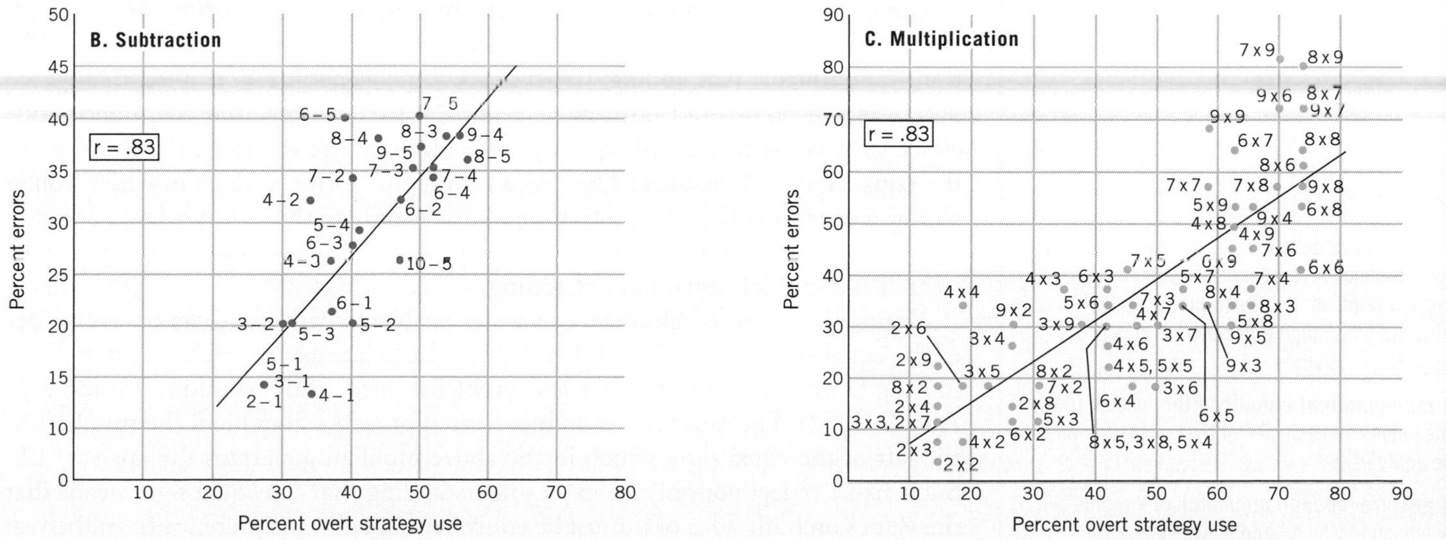

applications 8.4

Mathematical Disabilities

Between 5% and 8% of children perform so poorly in math that they are classified as having mathematical disabilities (Shalev, 2007). These children have IQs in the normal range but are extremely poor at mathematics. They tend to be slow to learn to count, to learn the relative magnitudes of numbers, and to accurately solve single-digit arithmetic problems (Geary, Hoard, Nugnt, & Byrd-Craven, 2007; Jordan, 2007). Their performance improves with experience, but even as adults, most continue to be slow at single-digit arithmetic and to have difficulty with the many mathematical skills that build on it, such as word problems, multidigit arithmetic, and algebra, (Jordan, Levine, & Huttenlocher, 1995; Zawaiza & Gerber, 1993; Zentall & Ferkis, 1993).

Although people often think of mathematics as a type of knowledge that is needed in school but not afterward, testimony from adults with mathematical learning disabilities attests to the debilitating effects of this problem beyond the school years:

> I worked for Nabisco. As a mixer, you had to know the correct scale and formulas. I kept messing up. I lost my job.
>
> (Curry, Schmitt, & Waldron, 1996, p. 63)

> Dairy Queen wouldn't hire me because I couldn't make change in my head.
>
> (Curry et al., 1996, p. 63)

> For as long as I can remember, numbers have not been my friend.
>
> (Blackburn, cited in McCloskey, 2007, p. 415)

Several specific problems contribute to mathematical disabilities (Geary et al., 2007). In severe cases, damage to parts of the brain that are central to numerical processing, such as the intraparietal sulcus, is often the cause (Landerl, Bevan, & Butterworth, 2004; Simon & Rivera, 2007). In less severe cases, a major contributor is minimal exposure to numbers prior to beginning school. Children who started school lacking knowledge of key mathematical concepts and skills that their peers possess and that are crucial for further learning tend to lag far behind throughout school (Duncan et al., 2007). Other variables that are associated with mathematical disabilities, and that may help cause it, are poor working-memory capacity for numbers, slow processing of numerical information, and anxiety about mathematics (Ashcraft, Krause, & Hopko, 2007; McLean & Hitch, 1999).

A variety of programs have been designed to prevent mathematics disabilities by providing preschoolers with the exposure to numerical concepts and skills that many children, particularly those from low-income families, lack. Among the most promising is **Pre-K Mathematics** (Starkey, Klein, & Wakeley, 2004). This program presents preschoolers with a variety of mathematical activities, including ones designed to improve counting, number sense, arithmetic reasoning, spatial sense, geometric reasoning, measurement, and logical relations. Children learn the activities in groups of four to six and are encouraged to discuss the activities with classmates and the teacher. The curriculum also includes a home component, in which parents learn how to help their children learn mathematical concepts and procedures; the parents also are given materials to help their children learn math at home.

Participation in Pre-K Mathematics raises the mathematical skills and conceptual understanding of low-income kindergartners from diverse ethnic and racial groups to levels as high as those of typical middle-income peers. Thus, the program allows these children to start formal schooling with their mathematical knowledge on an equal footing with that of children from more privileged backgrounds.

Conceptual understanding of arithmetic begins developing during the preschool period; for example, many 4-year-olds understand the commutative law of addition, the principle that adding a + b is the same as adding b + a (Canobi et al., 2002). However, it is not until much later that they master other arithmetic concepts, such as **mathematical equality**—the idea that the values on the two sides of the equal sign must balance. The overwhelming majority of cases in which young children encounter the equal sign have numbers only to the left of it (e.g., 3 + 4 = __; 3 + 4 + 5 = __). For purposes of solving such problems, the equal sign can be treated as a kind of signal to start adding.

Eventually, however, children encounter problems with numbers on both sides of the equal sign, such as 3 + 4 + 5 = __ + 5. As late as 4th grade, most children in the United States answer such problems incorrectly (Goldin-Meadow & Alibali, 2002). The most common incorrect approach is to add all the numbers to the left of the equal sign, which in the above problem generates the answer "12." Such errors reflect not only a lack of understanding that the equal sign means that the values on both sides of it must be equivalent but also interference from the vast amount of practice children have had solving typical addition problems, which

Pre-K mathematics a program designed for preschoolers, especially those from low-income families, to prevent mathematics disabilities through exposure to a variety of numerical activities

mathematical equality the concept that the values on each side of the equal sign must be equivalent

gesture–speech mismatches a phenomenon in which hand movements and verbal statements convey different ideas have no number following the equal sign (McNeil & Alibali, 2005). Indeed, explanations that illustrate the concept of the equal sign with typical arithmetic problems that can be solved by adding the numbers to the left of the equal sign—for example, by noting the equality of the left and right sides in 4 + 3 = 7—produce less learning than explanations that simply note, without any example, that the left and right sides must be equal (McNeil, 2008).

In many cases, children's hand gestures reveal that they have somewhat better understanding of mathematical equality than revealed by their answers or explanations. For example, on the problem 3 + 4 + 5 = __ + 5, children often answer "12" and say that they solved the problem by adding 3 + 4 + 5, but when asked to explain how they reached that answer, they point to all four numbers rather than just to the three preceding the equal sign. This pointing suggests an implicit recognition that there is a fourth number to be considered, even though they did not include it in their calculations (Goldin-Meadow & Alibali, 2002). Children who initially show such **gesture–speech mismatches,** in which their gesturing conveys more information than their verbal statements, learn more from instruction than do peers whose gesturing and speech are consistent (that is, those who say "12" and point only to the three numbers preceding the equal sign). The positive relation between gesture–speech mismatches and subsequent learning has emerged on number conservation and physics problems, as well as on mathematical equality problems. These findings illustrate a common conclusion: variability of thought and action (for example, generating diverging gestures and speech or advancing multiple explanations rather than just one) often indicates heightened readiness to learn (Church, 1999; Siegler, 2006; Thelen & Smith, 2006).

MICHAEL NEWMAN / PHOTOEDIT

This child's pointing illustrates a gesture–speech mismatch. He answered "17" to this problem because he added all four of the other numbers. However, his simultaneous pointing to the two 4s suggests that he noticed their equality and found it of interest, despite not utilizing that recognition in generating his answer. Gestures like this one, indicating knowledge not evident in speech, are associated with a high probability of learning from instruction.

Cultural context In some ways, children's approach to arithmetic is relatively constant across cultures; for example, children in a wide variety of cultures use the same strategies and find the same problems easy and difficult (Geary, 2006). However, their approach can also vary with both the cultural context and the verbal context in which the arithmetic problem is presented.

Children who are unskilled at arithmetic in the classroom context sometimes add and subtract much more skillfully in everyday contexts that are familiar and important to them. A particularly vivid illustration of this phenomenon comes from a study of Brazilian children who supplemented their family's meager incomes by selling sweets, soft drinks, and fruit on street corners (Nunes, Schliemann, & Carraher, 1993). The child street vendors ranged in age from 9 to 15 and had attended school—often sporadically—for between one and eight years.

These children showed excellent understanding of arithmetic problems when dealing with them in the course of their street vending but poor understanding when the same problems were presented in the

DAVID FRAZIER / THE IMAGE WORKS

Brazilian children who sell candy, fruit, and other small items at street stands, and who therefore often need to make change for their customers, acquire excellent informal arithmetic skills, despite not attending school. However, the same children do far less well when problems are presented in standard classroom fashion, such as "What is 35 times 4?"

conventional school format. They also used different strategies in the two situations. For example, when the interviewer posed as a customer at one child's stand and asked the cost of four coconuts at 35 cruzeiros per coconut, the child said "Three will be 105, plus 30, that's 135 . . . one coconut is 35 . . . that is . . . 140" (Nunes & Bryant, 1996, p. 106). Thus, the child skillfully divided the problem into simpler parts to solve it.

In contrast, when the same child was asked "What is 35 times 4," he wrote the 35 above the 4 and then said, "4 times 5, 20, carry the 2; 2 plus 3 is 5, times 4 is 20." He then wrote down 20 next to his earlier 0, which resulted in the incorrect answer, 200. Although the two problems were identical mathematically, the differing contexts made them seem quite different to this child. The same was true for the other child vendors. When a problem was presented in the context of vending, it was meaningful to them, and they solved it in a way that reflected its meaning; when the problem was presented as a formal problem, such as 35 times 4, it was meaningless to them, and they tried to solve it by using an algorithm that they did not understand. Making mathematics meaningful to children, and ensuring that they understand underlying concepts as well as procedures, is one of the largest challenges that teachers in all cultures face.

Cross-cultural comparisons of students' mathematical knowledge indicate that some educational systems fare far better than others in helping children understand fundamental concepts and procedures. For example, the Third International Mathematics and Science Study (Gonzales et al., 2004) indicated that throughout East Asia and in some European countries such as Finland and the Netherlands, 4th and 8th graders show more advanced knowledge of mathematical concepts and procedures than do their peers in the United States.

There seem to be two main reasons for the different levels of knowledge in different countries. One is that in the countries with the highest math achievement, teachers and students spend much more time on mathematics than do their counterparts in the United States. The other reason is that math instruction in these countries is more coherent; that is, it makes clear the relations among the relevant concepts and procedures (Hiebert et al., 2005). For example, in Japan, which has been rated in cross-national studies as having particularly coherent math lessons, students often spend an entire class period on a single problem. They first try to solve the problem independently, then they write alternative ways of solving it on the board, and then the whole class discusses why each of several correct approaches is correct and why each of several incorrect approaches is incorrect. The high level of coherence of mathematics instruction seems to contribute to the superior understanding of mathematics shown by Japanese students.

review: Learning to read begins in preschool, when many children come to recognize the letters of the alphabet and gain phonemic awareness. Early in elementary school, children learn to identify words through two main processes—phonological recoding and visually based retrieval—and they choose adaptively between these strategies. Reading comprehension improves through automatization of word identification, development of strategies, and acquisition of metacognition and content knowledge. How much children read and how much their parents read to them also influence reading development.

Learning to write well is difficult. It requires focusing simultaneously on low-level goals (proper spelling, punctuation, and capitalization) and high-level goals (making arguments clear and persuasive). Many Western children enter school knowing that writing proceeds in a horizontal sequence from left to right, that the text on one line continues on the next, and that words are separated by small spaces. Improvements in writing with age and experience reflect automatization of low-level goals, new organizational strategies, growing metacognitive understanding of what readers need to be told, and increasing content knowledge.

Mathematical development follows a similar general pattern. Most children enter school with some useful knowledge, such as knowing how to count from 1 to solve addition problems. Once in school, children learn a wide range of strategies for solving arithmetic and other mathematical problems, and they generally choose among these strategies in sensible ways. Learning mathematics also requires a grasp of underlying concepts and principles, which many students find elusive.

Chapter Summary

- Alfred Binet and his colleague Théophile Simon developed the first widely used intelligence test. Its purpose was to identify children who were unlikely to benefit from standard instruction in the classroom. Modern intelligence tests are descendants of the Binet-Simon test.
- One of Binet's key insights was that intelligence includes diverse high-level capabilities, which need to be assessed in order to measure intelligence accurately.

What Is Intelligence?

- Intelligence can be viewed as a single trait, such as *g;* as a few separate abilities, such as Thurstone's primary mental abilities; or as a very large number of specific processes, such as those described in information-processing analyses.
- Intelligence is often measured through use of IQ tests, such as the Stanford-Binet and the WISC. These tests examine general information, vocabulary, arithmetic, language comprehension, spatial reasoning, and a variety of other intellectual abilities.

Measuring Intelligence

- A person's overall score on an intelligence test, the person's IQ score, is a measure of general intelligence. It reflects the individual's intellectual ability relative to age peers.
- Most children's IQ scores are quite stable over periods of years, though scores do vary somewhat over time.

IQ Scores as Predictors of Important Outcomes

- IQ scores correlate positively with long-term educational and occupational success.
- Other factors, such as social understanding, creativity, and motivation also influence success in life.

Genes, Environment, and the Development of Intelligence

- Development of intelligence is influenced by the child's own qualities, by the immediate environment, and by the broader societal context.
- Genetic inheritance is one important influence on IQ. This influence tends to grow larger with age, in part due to some genes not expressing themselves until late childhood or adolescence, and in part due to genes influencing children's choices of environments.
- A child's family environment, as measured by the HOME, is related to the child's IQ score. The relation reflects within-family influences, such as parents' intellectual and emotional support for the particular child, as well as between-family influences, such as differences in parental wealth and education.
- Schooling positively influences IQ and school achievement.
- Broader societal factors, such as poverty and discrimination against racial and ethnic minorities, also influence children's IQs.
- To alleviate the harmful effects of poverty, the United States has undertaken both small-scale preschool intervention programs and the much larger Project Head Start. Both have initial positive effects on intelligence and school achievement, though the effects fade over time. On the other hand, the programs have enduring positive effects on the likelihood of not being held back in a grade and the likelihood of completing high school.

- Intensive intervention programs, such as the Carolina Abecedarian Project, that begin in the child's first year and provide optimal child-care circumstances and structured academic curricula, have produced increases in intelligence that continue into adolescence and adulthood.

Alternative Perspectives on Intelligence

- New approaches to intelligence, such as Gardner's multiple intelligence theory and Sternberg's theory of successful intelligence, are attempts to broaden traditional conceptions of intelligence.

Acquisition of Academic Skills: Reading, Writing, and Mathematics

- Many children learn letter names and gain phonemic awareness before they start school. Both are correlated with later reading achievement, and phonemic awareness also is causally related to it.
- Word identification is achieved by two main strategies: phonological recoding and visually based retrieval.
- Reading comprehension benefits from automatization of word identification, because the automatization frees cognitive resources for understanding the text. Use of strategies, metacognitive understanding, and content knowledge also influence reading comprehension, as does the amount that parents read to their children and the amount that children read themselves.
- Although many children begin to write during the preschool period, writing well remains difficult for many years for most children. Much of the difficulty comes from the fact that writing requires children to attend simultaneously to low-level processes, such as punctuation and spelling, and to high-level processes, such as anticipating what readers will and will not know.
- As with reading, automatization of basic processes, use of strategies, metacognitive understanding, and content knowledge influence development of writing.
- Most children use several strategies to learn arithmetic, such as counting fingers and retrieving answers from memory. They choose among them in adaptive ways, using the more time-consuming and effortful strategies only on the more difficult problems where such strategies are needed to generate correct answers.
- As children encounter more advanced math, conceptual understanding becomes increasingly important. Many children master procedures but do not understand the meaning of the procedures.

Critical Thinking Questions

1. Intelligence can be viewed as one thing, several things, or many things. List the characteristics that you think are the most important components of intelligence and explain their relevance.
2. Individual differences in intelligence are more stable than individual differences in other areas of psychological functioning such as emotional regulation or aggression. Why do you think this is so?
3. Do you think that in the future, broader theories of intelligence such as Gardner's or Sternberg's will replace the more narrowly focused approaches to intelligence that are currently dominant? Or do you think that the latter approaches will remain dominant? Explain.
4. Participation in Head Start does not lead to higher IQ or achievement test scores by the end of high school, but it does lead to lower rates of dropping out or being placed in special-education classes. Why do you think this is the case?
5. Explain Chall's (1979) statement: "In the primary grades, children learn to read; in the higher grades, they read to learn."

Key Terms

g (general intelligence), p. 299
fluid intelligence, p. 299
crystallized intelligence, p. 300
primary mental abilities, p. 300
three-stratum theory of intelligence, p. 300
Wechsler Intelligence Scale for Children (WISC), p. 302
IQ (intelligence quotient), p. 304
normal distribution, p. 304
standard deviation, p. 304
self-discipline, p. 307
practical intelligence, p. 307
Flynn effect, p. 313
Carolina Abecedarian Project, p. 318
multiple intelligence theory, p. 321
theory of successful intelligence, p. 322
phonemic awareness, p. 323
phonological recoding skills, p. 323
visually based retrieval, p. 325
strategy-choice process, p. 325
dyslexia, p. 327
phonological processing, p. 327
mental model, p. 328
comprehension monitoring, p. 328
Pre-K mathematics, p. 334
mathematical equality, p. 334
gesture–speech mismatches, p. 335

COURTESY OF CHRISTIE'S IMAGES INC., 1989

DOROTHEA SHARP, *Building a Sandcastle*

9

Theories of Social Development

THEMES

Nature and Nurture

The Active Child

Continuity/Discontinuity

Mechanisms of Change

The Sociocultural Context

Individual Differences

Research and Children's Welfare

Imagine yourself interacting with the infant pictured below on the left. What would it be like? You naturally smile and speak in an affectionate tone of voice, and the infant probably smiles and makes happy sounds back at you. If for some reason you speak in a loud, harsh voice, the baby becomes quiet and wary. If you look off to the left, the infant follows your gaze, as though assuming there is something interesting to see in that direction. Of course, the baby does not just respond to what you do; the baby also engages in independent behaviors, examining various objects or events in the room or maybe fussing for no obvious reason. Your interaction with the baby evokes emotions in you—joy, affection, caregiving, and so on. Over time, through repeated interactions, you and the infant learn about each other and smile and vocalize more readily to one another than to someone else.

Now, imagine that you are asked to interact with Kismet, the robot pictured below on the right, just as you would do with a human infant. Although the request might seem strange, Kismet's facelike features make you willing to give it a try. So you smile and speak in an affectionate tone—"Hi Kismet, how are you?" Kismet smiles back at you and gurgles happily. You speak harshly, "Kismet, stop that right now." The robot looks surprised—even a bit frightened—and makes a whimpering sound. You find yourself spontaneously attempting to console Kismet: "I'm sorry; I didn't mean it." After just a few moments, you have lost your feeling of self-consciousness and find the interaction with your new metallic friend remarkably natural. You even start to feel fond of him.

Kismet exists, and "he" behaves pretty much as we have just described him. He was designed by a team of scientists led by Cynthia Breazeal (2002), whose primary goal was to produce a robot that could assist people in a variety of ways. Another of the team's goals was to learn more about the nature of human beings by trying to construct a humanlike robot. Appreciating the fact that humans are a highly social species, the researchers recognized that for Kismet to seem at all humanlike, he would have to behave socially. Because of the extreme complexity of modeling the

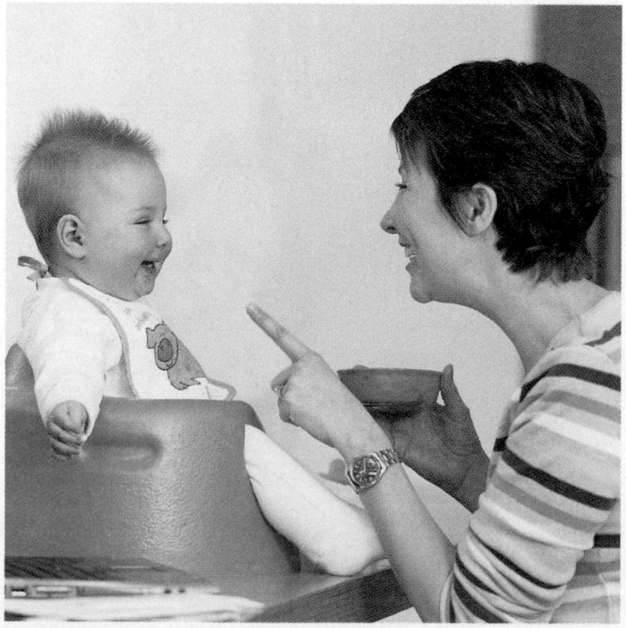

DIGITAL VISION / GETTY IMAGES

A familiar mother–infant interaction involves the mother talking and gesturing and the baby cooing back at her, with both of them expressing lots of positive emotion.

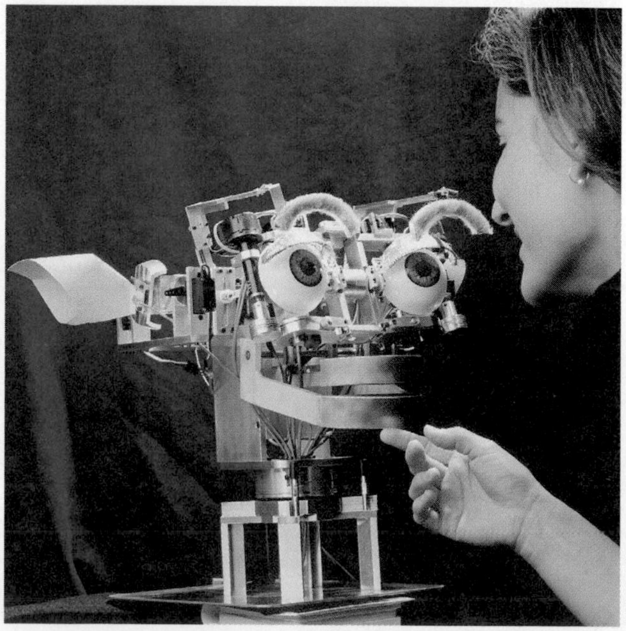

SAM OGDEN

An interaction between Kismet and his designer also involves talking, cooing back and forth, and positive facial expression.

social behavior of adults, they designed Kismet as a sociable, infantlike robot. His behavior is readily interpretable in human terms, and he even seems to have internal mental and emotional states and a personality. Kismet learns from his interactions with people based on their instructions to him and their reactions to his behavior. Through these interactions with others, he figures out how to interpret facial expressions, how to communicate, what behaviors are acceptable and unacceptable, and so on. Thus, Kismet develops over time as a function of the interaction between the "innate" structure built into him and his subsequent socially mediated experience. Just like a baby!

The challenge for Kismet's designers is in many ways like the task of theorists of human development who attempt to account for how children's development is shaped through their interactions with other people. Any successful account of social development must include the many ways we influence one another, starting with the simple fact that no human infant can survive without intensive, long-term care by other people. We learn how to behave based on how others respond to our behavior; we learn how to interpret ourselves based on how others treat us; and we interpret other people by analogy to ourselves—all in the context of social interaction and human society.

In this chapter, we review some of the most important and influential general theories of social development, theories that attempt to account for how children's development is affected by the people and social institutions around them. In our survey of cognitive theories in Chapter 4, we discussed some of the reasons that theories are important (pages 128–129); those reasons apply equally well to theories of social development.

Theories of social development attempt to account for many important aspects of development, including emotion, personality, attachment, self, peer relationships, morality, and gender. In this chapter, we will describe four types of theories that address these topics—psychoanalytic, learning, social cognitive, and ecological. We will discuss the basic tenets of each and examine some of the evidence relevant to them.

Every one of our seven themes appears in this chapter, with three of them being particularly prominent. The theme that pervades this chapter is *individual differences,* as we examine how the social world differentially affects children's development. The theme of *nature and nurture* appears repeatedly, since the theories vary in the degree to which they emphasize biological and environmental factors. The *active child* theme is also a major focus: some of the theories emphasize children's active participation in, and effect on, their own socialization, whereas others view children's development as shaped primarily by external forces.

Psychoanalytic Theories

No psychological theory has had a greater impact on Western culture and on thinking about personality and social development than the psychoanalytic theory of Sigmund Freud. A successor to Freud's theory, the life-span developmental theory of Erik Erikson, has also been quite influential.

View of Children's Nature

In both Freud's and Erikson's theories, development is largely driven by biological maturation. For Freud, behavior is motivated by the need to satisfy basic drives. These drives, and the motives that arise from them, are mostly unconscious, and individuals often have only the dimmest understanding of why they do what they

psychic energy Freud's term for the collection of biologically based instinctual drives that he believed fuel behavior, thoughts, and feelings

erogenous zones in Freud's theory, areas of the body that become erotically sensitive in successive stages of development

do. In Erikson's theory, development is driven by a series of developmental crises related to age and biological maturation. To achieve healthy development, the individual must successfully resolve these crises.

Central Developmental Issues

Three of our seven themes—*continuity/discontinuity, individual differences,* and *nature and nurture*—play prominent roles in psychoanalytic theory. Like Piaget's theory that you encountered in Chapter 4, the developmental accounts of Freud and Erikson are stage theories that stress discontinuity in development. However, within the framework of discontinuous development, psychoanalytic theories stress the continuity of individual differences, emphasizing that children's early experiences have a major impact on their subsequent development. The interaction of nature and nurture arises in terms of Freud and Erikson's emphasis on the biological underpinnings of developmental stages and how they interact with the child's experience.

Freud's Theory of Psychosexual Development

Sigmund Freud (1856–1939), the founder of psychoanalytic theory, was encouraged by his Viennese parents in his academic pursuits: while the rest of the family made do with candles, young Sigmund was provided with an oil lamp to light his studies (Crain, 1985). As a neurologist, Freud became interested in the origins and treatment of mental illness. He was particularly intrigued by the fact that sometimes his patients' neurological symptoms—such as loss of feeling in a hand or blindness—had no apparent physical cause. After listening to his patients talk about their problems, he came to the conclusion that these unexplained symptoms could be attributed to completely unconscious but powerful feelings of guilt, anxiety, or fear—such as the fear of touching or seeing something forbidden. Freud's interest in psychological development grew as he became increasingly convinced that the majority of his patients' emotional problems originated in their early childhood relationships, particularly those with their parents. Freud made fundamental, lasting contributions to developmental psychology, although, as we will discuss later, they had to do with certain broad psychological concepts, not with the specifics of his theory.

In our discussion of Freud's theoretical views, we will focus primarily on their developmental aspects, especially the broad themes that remain influential today.

Basic Features of Freud's Theory

Freud's theory of development is referred to as a theory of *psychosexual* development because he thought that even very young children have a sexual nature that motivates their behavior and influences their relationships with other people. He proposed that children pass through a series of universal developmental stages. According to Freud, in each successive stage, **psychic energy**—the biologically based, instinctual drives that fuel behavior, thoughts, and feelings—becomes focused in different **erogenous zones,** that is, areas of the body that are erotically sensitive (i.e., the mouth, the anus, and the genitals). Freud believed that in each stage, children encounter conflicts related to a particular erogenous zone and that their success or failure in resolving these conflicts affects their development throughout life.

CULVER PICTURES

Sigmund Freud, the father of psychoanalysis, had a lasting impact on developmental psychology through his emphasis on the lifelong impact of early relationships.

The Developmental Process

In Freud's view, development starts with a helpless infant beset by instinctual drives, foremost among them hunger, which creates tension. The young infant has no knowledge of how to reduce it, so the distress associated with hunger is expressed through crying, prompting the mother to breast-feed the baby. (In Freud's day, virtually all babies were breast-fed.) The resulting satisfaction of the infant's hunger, as well as the experience of nursing, is a source of intense pleasure for the infant.

The instinctual drives with which the infant is born constitute the **id**—the earliest and most primitive of three personality structures posited by Freud. The id, which is totally unconscious, is the source of psychic energy. It is the "dark, inaccessible part of our personality . . . a cauldron full of seething excitations" in need of satisfaction (Freud, 1933/1964). The id is ruled by the *pleasure principle*—the goal of achieving maximal gratification maximally quickly. Whether the gratification involves eating, drinking, eliminating, or physical comfort, the id wants it *now.* The id remains the source of psychic energy throughout life, with its operation most apparent in selfish or impulsive behavior in which immediate gratification is sought with little regard for consequences.

During the first year of life, the infant is in Freud's first stage of psychosexual development, the **oral stage,** so called because the primary source of gratification and pleasure is oral activity, such as sucking and eating. "If the infant could express itself, it would undoubtedly acknowledge that the act of sucking at its mother's breast is far and away the most important thing in life" (Freud, 1920/1965). The pleasure associated with breast-feeding is so intense that other oral activities—sucking on a thumb or pacifier, for instance—also provide pleasure.

For Freud, the baby's feelings for his or her mother are "unique, without parallel," and through them the mother is "established unalterably for a whole lifetime as the first and strongest love-object and as the prototype for all later love-relations" (1940/1964).

The infant's mother is also a source of security. However, this security is not free. As always with Freud, there is a dark side: infants "pay for this security by a fear of loss of love" (Freud, 1940/1964). For Freud, common fearful reactions to being alone or in the dark are based on "missing someone who is loved and longed for" (1926/1959).

Later in the first year, the second personality structure, the **ego,** begins to emerge. It arises out of the need to resolve conflicts between the id's unbridled demands for immediate gratification and the restraints imposed by the external world. Whereas "the id stands for the untamed passions," the ego "stands for reason and good sense" (1933/1964). The ego operates under the *reality principle,* trying to find ways to satisfy the id that accord with the demands of the real world. Over time, as it continually seeks resolution between the demands of the id and those of the real world, the ego becomes stronger and more differentiated, eventually developing into the individual's sense of self. Nevertheless, the ego is never fully in control:

> The ego's relation to the id might be compared with that of a rider to his horse. The horse supplies the locomotive energy, while the rider has the privilege of deciding on the goal and of guiding the powerful animal's movement. But only too often . . . the rider [is] obliged to guide the horse along the path by which it itself wants to go.
>
> (Freud, 1933/1964, p. 77)

id in psychoanalytic theory, the earliest and most primitive personality structure. It is unconscious and operates with the goal of seeking pleasure.

oral stage the first stage in Freud's theory, occurring in the first year, in which the primary source of satisfaction and pleasure is oral activity

ego in psychoanalytic theory, the second personality structure to develop. It is the rational, logical, problem-solving component of personality.

anal stage the second stage in Freud's theory, lasting roughly from 1 to 3 years of age, in which the primary source of pleasure comes from defecation

phallic stage the third stage in Freud's theory, lasting from age 3 to age 6, in which sexual pleasure is focused on the genitalia

superego in psychoanalytic theory, the third personality structure, consisting of internalized moral standards

internalization the process of adopting as one's own the attributes, beliefs, and standards of another person

Oedipus complex Freud's term for the conflict experienced by boys in the phallic period because of their sexual desire for their mother and their fear of retaliation by their father. (The complex is named for the king in Greek mythology who unknowingly murdered his father and married his mother.)

During the infant's second year, maturation makes possible the development of control over some bodily processes, including urination and defecation. At this point, the infant enters Freud's second stage, the **anal stage,** which lasts until roughly age 3. In this stage, the child's erotic interests focus on the pleasurable relief of the tension derived from defecation. Conflict ensues when, for the first time, the parents begin to make specific demands on the infant, most notably their insistence on toilet training. In the years to come, parents and others will increase their demands on the child to control his or her impulses and to delay gratification.

Freud's third stage of development, the **phallic stage,** spans the ages of 3 to 6. In this stage, the focus of sexual pleasure again migrates, as children become interested in their own genitalia and curious about those of parents and playmates. Both boys and girls derive pleasure from masturbation, an activity that the parents of Freud's time and place often punished severely.

Freud believed that during the phallic stage, children identify with their same-sex parent, giving rise to gender differences in attitudes and behavior. This identification begins with children's discovery of the vital difference between having and lacking a penis. At this time, a boy takes a strong interest in his penis, "so easily excitable and changeable, and so rich in sensations" (Freud, 1923/1960, p. 246). Freud supposed that girls notice and resent the fact that they do not have one, experiencing what he called *penis envy.*

Freud also believed that young children experience intense sexual desires during the phallic stage, and he proposed that their efforts to cope with them leads to the emergence of the third personality structure, the **superego.** The superego is essentially what we think of as conscience. It enables a child to control his or her own behavior on the basis of beliefs about right and wrong. The superego is based on the child's **internalization,** or adoption, of the parents' rules and standards for acceptable and unacceptable behavior. The superego guides the child to avoid actions that would result in guilt, which the child experiences when violating these internalized rules and standards.

For boys, the path to superego development is through the resolution of the **Oedipus complex,** a psychosexual conflict in which a boy experiences a form of sexual desire for his mother and wants an exclusive relationship with her. Although this idea may seem outlandish, many family stories are consistent with it. For example, when one of our sons was a 5-year-old, he told his mother that he wanted to marry her someday. She said that she was sorry, but she was already married to Daddy, so he would have to marry someone else. The boy replied, "I have a good idea. I'll put Daddy in a big box and mail him away somewhere. Then we can get married!"

Through identifying with his father, this young boy should, according to Freud's theory, develop a strong superego.

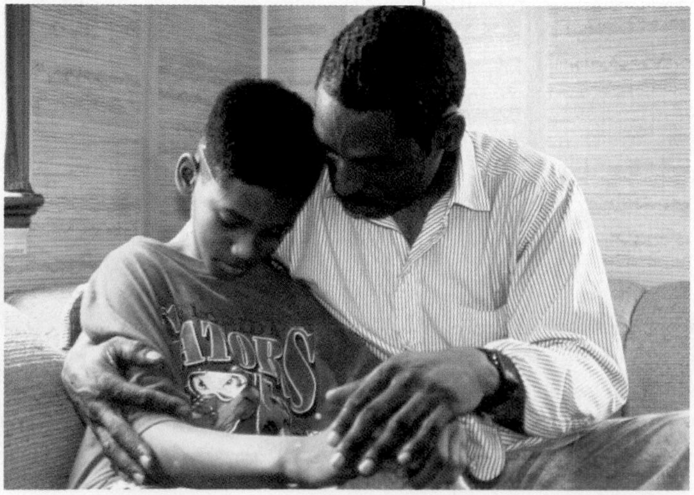

JEFF GREENBERG / PHOTOEDIT

In Freud's account of the Oedipal conflict, the son's desire for his mother and his hostility toward his father are so threatening that the boy's ego protects him through *repression,* banishing his dangerous feelings to the *unconscious,* the mental storehouse where anxiety-producing thoughts and impulses are held hidden from conscious awareness. A consequence of this widespread repression, according to Freud, is *infantile amnesia*—the lack of memories from our first few years that we all suffer. In addition, the boy increases his *identification* with his father: through striving to be like him, the boy *internalizes* his father's values, beliefs, and attitudes, leading to the development of a strong conscience. Freud thought that girls experience a similar but less intense conflict—the **Electra complex,** involving erotic feelings toward the father—which results in their developing a weaker conscience than boys do.

The fourth developmental stage, the **latency period,** lasts from about age 6 to age 12. It is, as its name implies, a time of relative calm. Sexual desires are safely hidden away in the unconscious, and psychic energy gets channeled into constructive, socially acceptable activities, including both intellectual and social pursuits.

The fifth and final stage, the **genital stage,** begins with the advent of sexual maturation. The sexual energy that had been kept in check for several years reasserts itself with full force, although it is now directed toward opposite-sex peers. Ideally, the individual has developed a strong ego that facilitates coping with reality and a superego that is neither too weak nor too strong.

Freud thought that healthy development culminates in the ability to invest oneself in, and derive pleasure from, both love and work. This outcome can be compromised in many ways, however. If fundamental needs are not met during any of the stages of psychosexual development, children may become *fixated* on those needs, continually attempting to satisfy them and to resolve associated conflicts. In Freud's view, these unsatisfied needs, and the person's ongoing attempts to fulfill them, are unconscious and are expressed in indirect or symbolic ways. For example, if an infant's needs for oral gratification are not adequately satisified during the oral stage, later in life the individual may repeatedly engage in substitute oral activities, such as excessive eating, nail-biting, smoking, and so on. Similarly, if toddlers are subjected to very harsh toilet training during the anal stage, they may remain preoccupied with issues related to cleanliness, becoming compulsively tidy and psychologically rigid or extremely sloppy and lax. Thus, in Freud's view, the nature of the child's passage through the stages of psychosexual development shapes the individual's personality for life. (With regard to oral and anal fixations, it is interesting that Freud smoked 20 cigars a day for more than 50 years—in fact, he found it impossible to work without them—and over the same period followed the same ritualized schedule nearly every day.)

Electra complex Freud's term for the conflict experienced by girls in the phallic stage when they develop unacceptable romantic feelings for their father and see their mother as a rival. (The complex is named after a figure in Greek mythology who arranged for the murder of her mother.)

latency period the fourth stage in Freud's theory, lasting from age 6 to age 12, in which sexual energy gets channeled into socially acceptable activities

genital stage the fifth and final stage in Freud's theory, beginning in adolescence, in which sexual maturation is complete and sexual intercourse becomes a major goal

Erikson's Theory of Psychosocial Development

Of the many followers of Freud, none has had greater influence in developmental psychology than Erik Erikson (1902–1994). Erikson accepted the basic elements of Freud's theory but incorporated social factors into it, including cultural influences and contemporary issues, such as juvenile delinquency, changing sexual roles, and the generation gap. Consequently, his theory is regarded as a theory of *psychosocial* development.

The Developmental Process

Erikson proposed eight age-related stages of development that span infancy to old age. Each of Erikson's stages is characterized by a specific *crisis,* or set of developmental issues, that the individual must resolve. If the dominant issue of a given stage is not successfully resolved before maturation and social pressures usher in the next stage, the person will continue to struggle with it. In the following summary of Erikson's stages, we discuss only the first five stages, which focus on development in infancy, childhood, and adolescence.

1. Basic Trust versus Mistrust (the first year). In Erikson's first stage (which corresponds to Freud's oral stage), the crucial issue for the infant is developing a sense of trust—"an essential trustfulness of others as well as a fundamental sense of one's own trustworthiness" (Erikson, 1969, p. 96). If the mother is warm, consistent,

TED STRESHINSKY / CORBIS

Erik Erikson, who was born in Germany, took a long time to settle into a career. Instead of attending college, he wandered around Europe pursuing his interest in art for several years. Eventually he was hired as an art instructor in a school run by Anna Freud, Sigmund Freud's daughter, and became an analyst. He moved to the United States in the early 1930s, when fascism was on the rise in Germany.

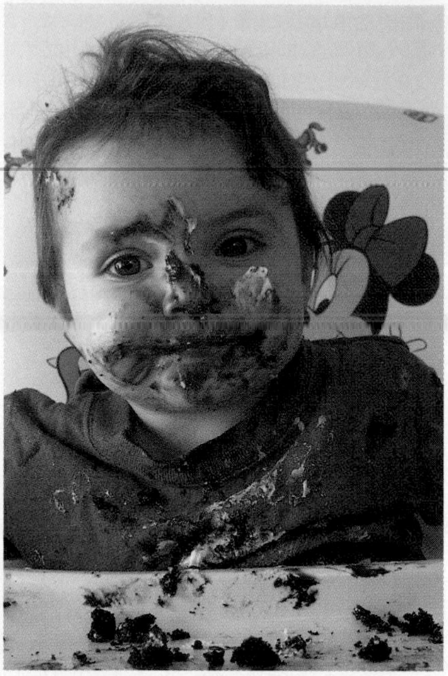

NANCY RICHMOND / THE IMAGE WORKS

This child's parents have not yet succeeded in training her to behave in the socially appropriate way with respect to eating. Once they do, she would feel ashamed to finish a meal looking like this.

and reliable in her caregiving, the infant learns that she can be trusted. More generally, the baby comes to feel good and reassured by being close to other people. If the ability to trust others when it is appropriate to do so does not develop, the person will have difficulty forming intimate relationships later in life.

2. Autonomy versus Shame and Doubt (ages 1 to 3½). The challenge for the child between ages 1 and 3½ (Freud's anal stage) is to achieve a strong sense of autonomy while adjusting to increasing social demands. Going well beyond Freud's focus on toilet training, Erikson pointed out that during this period, the dramatic increases that occur in every realm of children's real-world competence, including motor skills, cognitive abilities, and language, foster children's desires to make choices and decisions for themselves. Infants' new ability to explore the environment on their own changes the family dynamics (as we discussed in Chapter 5), initiating a long-running battle of wills in which parents try to restrict the child's freedom and teach the child what behaviors are acceptable and unacceptable. If parents provide a supportive atmosphere that allows children to achieve self-control without the loss of self-esteem, children gain a sense of autonomy. In contrast, if children are subjected to severe punishment or ridicule, they may come to doubt their abilities or to feel a general sense of shame.

3. Initiative versus Guilt (ages 4 to 6). Like Freud, Erikson saw the time between ages 4 and 6 years as a period during which children come to identify with, and learn from, their parents: "[The child] hitches his wagon to nothing less than a star: he wants to be like his parents, who to him appear very powerful and very beautiful" (Erikson, 1994). The child in this third stage of development is constantly setting goals (building a high tower of blocks, learning the alphabet) and working to achieve them. Like Freud, Erikson believed that a crucial attainment is the development of conscience—the internalization of the parents' rules and standards, and the experiencing of guilt when failing to uphold them. The challenge for the child is to achieve a balance between initiative and guilt. If parents are not highly controlling or punitive, children can develop high standards and the initiative to meet them without being crushed by worry about not being able to measure up.

The vast abundance of cartoons about Freud and psychoanalysis testifies to his enormous impact on society.

4. Industry versus Inferiority (age 6 to puberty). Erikson's fourth stage, which lasts from age 6 to puberty (Freud's latency period), is crucial for ego development.

"To this day, I can hear my mother's voice—harsh, accusing, 'Lost your mittens? You naughty kittens! Then you shall have no pie!' "

"You've got to want to connect the dots, Mr. Michaelson."

During this stage, children master cognitive and social skills that are important in their culture, and they learn to work industriously and to cooperate with peers. Successful experiences give the child a sense of competence, but failure can lead to excessive feelings of inadequacy or inferiority.

5. Identity versus Role Confusion (adolescence to early adulthood). Erikson accorded great importance to adolescence, seeing it as a critical stage for the achievement of a core sense of *identity.* Adolescents change so rapidly in so many ways that they can hardly recognize themselves, either in the mirror or in their minds. The dramatic physical changes of puberty and the emergence of strong sexual urges are accompanied by new social pressures, including a need to make educational and occupational decisions. Caught between their past identity as a child and the many options and uncertainties of their future, adolescents must resolve the question of who they really are or live in confusion about what roles they should play as adults. As you will see in Chapter 11, developmentalists have devoted a good deal of attention to the stage of identity versus role confusion in modern multicultural societies.

Current Perspectives

The most significant of Freud's contributions to developmental psychology were his emphasis on the importance of early experience and emotional relationships and his recognition of the role of subjective experience and unconscious mental activity. Erikson's emphasis on the quest for identity in adolescence has had a lasting impact, providing the foundation for a wealth of research on this aspect of adolescence. The signal weakness of both theories is that their major theoretical claims are stated too vaguely to be testable, and many of their specific elements, particularly in Freud's theory, are generally regarded as highly questionable. Nevertheless, there is no doubt that, historically, Freud's theory has been enormously influential. Further, in recent years, some of Freud's and Erikson's original ideas have reemerged in modified form in psychological research and thinking.

Freud's identification of infantile amnesia, for example, has been supported by a vast literature on the earliest memories that people can recall (Bauer, Wenner, & Kroupina, 2002; Hayne, 2004; Neisser, 2004). Freud was correct in noting that most of us remember almost none of our experiences from our first few years. However, although the precise reasons for the absence of autobiographical memory in the first three years are unknown, virtually no one thinks it is due to repression, as Freud claimed.

Erikson's psychosocial stages of development have also received some support from research on autobiographical memory. In one study, adults between the ages of 62 and 89 were asked to recall up to three memories from each decade of their lives, and the researchers classified their reports with respect to Erikson's stages (Conway & Holmes, 2004). The reported memories of these older adults corresponded quite well with Erikson's stages. For example, memories from the second decade of their lives were predominantly of experiences having to do with identity confusion and establishing a sense of identity.

Another aspect of Freud's theory that has had lasting influence in psychology is his emphasis on the importance of early experience and close relationships, an emphasis that has served as the cornerstone of modern-day attachment research (which you will read about in Chapter 11). This research has established that the nature of infants' relationships with their parents not only affects behavior in infancy but also has important long-term effects on close relationships throughout life (Allen, McElhaney, Kuperminc, & Jodl, 2004; Kobak, Cassidy & Ziv, 2004; Main, 2000).

In addition, Freud's remarkable insight that much of our mental life occurs outside the realm of consciousness is fundamental to modern cognitive psychology and brain science. A recent revolution in many areas of psychology is based on the discovery that a remarkably large proportion of human behavior stems from unconscious processes. According to this research, we are, to a surprising degree, "strangers to ourselves," often acting on the basis of unconscious processes and only later constructing rational accounts of our behavior (Wilson, 2002). In this sense, we experience the "illusion of conscious will," believing that our thoughts are the basis for our behavior, even though those thoughts often come after the brain has already initiated the behavior (Wegner, 2002). Many of us cry out and jump back even before we realize that there is a snake across our path (Ohman & Mineka, 2001).

Our behavior is also influenced by implicit attitudes that we are unaware of, attitudes that are often antithetical to what we consciously believe. For example, many individuals who consider themselves to lack racial prejudice nevertheless unconsciously associate members of some racial groups with a variety of negative characteristics (Greenwald & Banaji, 1995; Nosek & Banaji, 2009). To experience this phenomenon first hand, log onto http://implicit.harvard.edu/implicit and take the Implicit Attitudes Test: the result may surprise you (although it would probably not have surprised Freud).

How might psychoanalytic theories be useful to Kismet's designers? They have already adopted the goal of making Kismet as sociable as possible. Probably the most important further step they can take, based on Freud's and Erikson's theories, is to program Kismet to form a few very close relationships with others. Certain people should become much more important to him than other people with whom he interacts. Ideally, he should derive some sense of security and wellbeing from those relationships. Further, those relationships should have a lasting effect on his internal organization so that they continue to influence him throughout his "life."

review:

The psychoanalytic theories of Sigmund Freud and Erik Erikson propose that social and emotional development proceeds in a series of stages, with each stage characterized by a particular task or crisis that must be resolved for subsequent healthy development. A healthy personality involves an appropriate balance between the three structures of personality—id, ego, and superego. Maturational factors play a key role in both theories. Psychic energy and sexual impulses are emphasized by Freud as major forces in development, whereas Erikson places greater emphasis on social factors. Both theories maintain that early experiences in the context of the family have a lasting effect on the individual's relationships with other people. These theories have had enormous, continuing impact on Western thought and culture.

Learning Theories

I imagine the mind of children as easily turned, this or that way as water itself.

—John Locke

As you may recall from Chapter 1, the empiricist philosopher John Locke believed that experience shapes the nature of the human mind. The intellectual descendants of Locke are psychologists who consider learning from experience to be the primary factor in social and personality development.

View of Children's Nature

In contrast to Freud's emphasis on the role of internal forces and subjective experience, most learning theorists have emphasized the role of external factors in shaping personality and social behavior. They have often made very bold claims about the extent to which development can be guided by how people reward, or reinforce, certain of children's behaviors and punish or ignore others. More contemporary learning theorists have emphasized the importance of cognitive factors and the active role children play in their own development.

Central Developmental Issues

The primary developmental question on which learning theories take a unanimous stand is that of *continuity/discontinuity:* they all emphasize continuity, proposing that the same principles control learning and behavior throughout life and that therefore there are no qualitatively different stages in development. Like information-processing theorists, learning theorists focus on the role of specific *mechanisms of change*—which, in their view, involve learning principles, such as reinforcement and observational learning. They believe that children become different from one another primarily because they have different histories of reinforcement and learning opportunities. The theme of *research and children's welfare* is also relevant here in that therapeutic approaches based on learning principles have been widely used to treat children with a variety of problems.

Watson's Behaviorism

John B. Watson (1878–1958), the founder of behaviorism, believed that children's development is determined by their social environment and that learning through conditioning is the primary mechanism of development (see pages 202–203). He also believed that psychologists should study only objectively verifiable behavior, not the "mind."

The extent of Watson's (1924) faith in the power of conditioning is clear in his famous boast:

> Give me a dozen healthy infants, well-formed, and my own specified world to bring them up in, and I'll guarantee to take any one at random and train him to become any type of specialist I might select—doctor, lawyer, artist, merchant-chief, and yes, even beggar man and thief, regardless of his talents, penchants, tendencies, abilities, vocations, and race of his ancestors.
>
> (p. 104)

On a much less ambitious scale, Watson demonstrated the power of classical conditioning in a famous—and by present standards, unethical—experiment with "Little Albert" (Watson & Rayner, 1920). Watson first exposed 9-month-old Albert to a perfectly nice rat in the laboratory. Initially, Albert reacted positively to the rat. On subsequent exposures, however, the researchers repeatedly paired the presentation of the rat with a loud noise that clearly frightened Albert. After a number of such pairings, Albert became afraid of the rat itself.

Our everyday lives are filled with examples of conditioned responses. Infants and young children, for example, often show fear at the sight of a doctor or nurse in a white coat, based on their previous association between people wearing white coats and painful injections. (To counteract this problem, modern pediatricians often sport lab coats with pictures of cartoon characters, hoping to elicit a positive response in their young patients.)

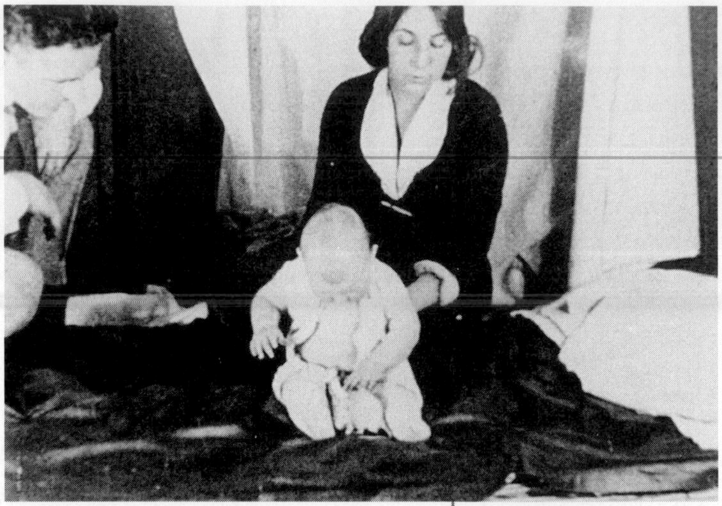

ARCHIVES OF THE HISTORY OF AMERICAN PSYCHOLOGY", THE UNIVERSITY OF AKRON

To demonstrate the power of conditioning, John B. Watson and his assistant Rosemary Raynor conditioned "Little Albert" to fear a white rat. Albert had not been afraid of the rat until its presentation was paired several times with a loud, frightening sound.

Watson's work on classical conditioning laid the foundation for treatment procedures that are based on the opposite process—the deconditioning, or elimination, of fear. A student of Watson's (Jones, 1924) treated 2-year-old Peter, who was deathly afraid of white rabbits (as well as white rats, white fur coats, white feathers, and a variety of other white things). To decondition his fear, the experimenter first gave him a favorite snack. Then, as Peter ate, a white rabbit in a cage was very slowly brought closer and closer to him—but never close enough to make him afraid. After repeatedly being exposed to the feared object in a context in which he experienced no fear but did have the positive experience of his snack, Peter got over his fear. Eventually, he was even able to pet the rabbit. This approach, now known as **systematic desensitization,** has been widely used to rid people of fears and phobias of everything from dogs to dentists.

Believing that he had established the power of learning in development, Watson placed the responsibility for guiding children's development squarely on the shoulders of their parents. In his child-rearing manual, *Psychological Care of Infant and Child* (1928), he offered them stern advice for fulfilling this responsibility. One particular piece of Watson's advice that was widely adopted in the United States was to put infants on a strict feeding schedule. The idea was that the baby would become conditioned to expect a feeding at regular intervals and therefore would not cry for attention in between. To help implement this and other of his strict regimens, Watson advised parents to achieve distance and objectivity in their relations with their children (just as he exhorted psychologists to be objective in their research):

> Treat them as though they were young adults. Dress them, bathe them with care and circumspection. Let your behavior always be objective and kindly firm. Never hug and kiss them, never let them sit on your lap. If you must, kiss them once on the forehead when they say good night. Shake hands with them in the morning. Give them a pat on the head if they have made an extraordinarily good job on a difficult task. Try it out. In a week's time you will find how easy it is to be perfectly objective with your child and at the same time kindly. You will be utterly ashamed of the mawkish, sentimental way you have been handling it.
>
> (pp. 81–82)

Watson's overly strict child-rearing advice gradually fell from favor with the publication and widespread success of Dr. Spock's *The Common Sense Guide to Baby and Child Care* (Spock's thinking about early development and child rearing was very strongly influenced by Freud). However, the behaviorist emphasis on the environment as the key factor in determining behavior persisted in the work of B. F. Skinner.

Skinner's Operant Conditioning

B. F. Skinner (1904–1990) was just as forceful as Watson in proposing that behavior is under environmental control, once claiming that "a person does not act upon the world, the world acts upon him" (Skinner, 1971, p. 211). As described in Chapter 5, a major tenet of Skinner's theory of operant conditioning is that we tend to repeat behaviors that lead to favorable outcomes—that is, reinforcement—and suppress those that result in unfavorable outcomes—that is, punishment. Skinner believed

systematic desensitization a form of therapy based on classical conditioning, in which positive responses are gradually conditioned to stimuli that initially elicited a highly negative response. This approach is especially useful in the treatment of fears and phobias.

intermittent reinforcement inconsistent response to the behavior of another person, for example, sometimes punishing an unacceptable behavior and sometimes ignoring it

behavior modification a form of therapy based on principles of operant conditioning in which reinforcement contingencies are changed to encourage more adaptive behavior that everything we do in life—every act—is an operant response influenced by the outcomes of past behavior.

Skinner's research on the nature and function of reinforcement led to many discoveries, including two that are of particular interest to parents and teachers. One is the fact that *attention* can by itself serve as a powerful reinforcer: children often do things "just to get attention" (Skinner, 1953, p. 78). Thus, the best strategy for discouraging a child who throws temper tantrums from continuing to do so is to ignore that behavior whenever it occurs. The popular behavior-management strategy of *time-out,* or temporary isolation, involves systematically withdrawing attention and thereby removing the reinforcement for inappropriate behavior, with the goal of extinguishing it.

When the toddler son of one of the authors first graduated to a "big-boy bed," he repeatedly got up after having been put to bed, using one pretext after another to join his parents. This undesirable behavior was extinguished in just a few nights by his father, who sat in a chair outside the bedroom door. Every time the child appeared, his father kindly and gently, but firmly and silently, put him back in his bed. The key to this successful intervention was the fact that there was no reinforcement for getting out of bed—no talking, no yelling, no drink of water, no interaction of any sort—in short, none of the potent reinforcers that parental attention provides.

A second important discovery that Skinner made is the great difficulty of extinguishing behavior that has been *intermittently reinforced,* that is, that has sometimes been followed by reward and sometimes not. As Skinner discovered in his research with animals, **intermittent reinforcement** makes behaviors resistant to extinction: if the reward for a behavior is totally withdrawn following intermittent reinforcement, the behavior persists longer than it would if it had always been reinforced. In effect, not having been rewarded every time for a given behavior, an animal does not readily give up the expectation that the next performance of the behavior may produce the reward.

Parents often encourage unwanted behavior in their children by inadvertently applying intermittent reinforcement. They valiantly try not to reward their children's whiny or aggressive demands, but—being human—they sometimes give in. Such intermittent reinforcement is very powerful: if a parent who had occasionally given in to whining never did it again, the child would nevertheless continue to resort to whining for a long time, assuming that because it worked in the past, it might work again. The intermittent-reinforcement effect is one reason most children have at least a few persistent bad habits. Part of the effectiveness of the bedtime example described above was due to the total consistency of the father's behavior.

Skinner's work on reinforcement has led to a form of therapy known as **behavior modification,** which has proven quite useful for changing undesirable behaviors. A simple example of this approach involved a preschool child who spent too much of his time in solitary activities. Observers noticed that the boy's teachers were unintentionally reinforcing his withdrawn behavior: they talked to him and comforted him when he was alone but tended to ignore him when he played with other children. The boy's withdrawal was modified by reversing the reinforcement contingencies: the teachers began paying attention to the boy whenever he joined a group but ignored him whenever he withdrew. Soon the child was spending most of his time playing with his classmates (Harris, Wolf, & Baer, 1967).

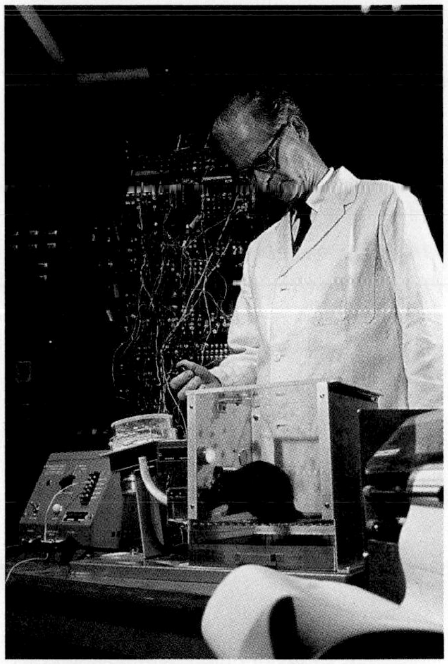

B. F. Skinner, who once appeared in 40th place in a popular magazine's list of the 100 most important people who ever lived (Miller, 2002), believed that children's development is primarily a matter of their reinforcement history.

Although scolding has the goal of causing the child to stop doing something that the parent disapproves of, the fact that it is also a form of paying attention to a child actually reinforces undesirable behaviors and may cause them to persist.

vicarious reinforcement observing someone else receive a reward or punishment

reciprocal determinism Bandura's concept that child–environment influences operate in both directions; children are affected by aspects of their environment, but they also influence the environment

Social Learning Theory

Social learning theory, like other learning theories, attempts to account for personality and other aspects of social development in terms of learning mechanisms. However, in assessing the influence of the environment on children's development, social learning theory emphasizes observation and imitation, rather than reinforcement, as the primary mechanisms of development. Albert Bandura (1977, 1986), for example, has argued that most human learning is inherently *social* in nature and is based on observation of the behavior of other people. Children learn most rapidly and efficiently simply from watching what other people do and then imitating them. Reinforcement can increase the likelihood of imitation, but it is not necessary for learning. Because direct reinforcement is not required for learning, children can learn from symbolic models, that is, from reading books and from watching TV or movies (see Box 9.1).

a closer look

Bandura and Bobo

A series of classic studies by Albert Bandura and his colleagues (Bandura, 1965; Bandura, Ross, & Ross, 1963) will give you a good sense of the kind of questions and methods that typify social learning theory research. The investigators began by having preschool children individually watch a short film in which an adult model performed highly unusual aggressive actions on a Bobo doll (an inflatable toy, with a weight in the bottom so it pops back up as soon as it is knocked down). The model punched the doll, hit it with a mallet while shouting "sockeroo," threw balls at it while shouting "bang bang," and so on.

In one study, three groups of children observed the model receive different consequences for this aggressive behavior. A third of them saw the model be rewarded (an adult gave the model candy and soda and praised the "championship performance"). Another third saw the model punished (scolded) for the aggressive behavior. The remaining children saw the model experience no consequences. The question was whether **vicarious reinforcement**—observing someone else receive a reward or a punishment—would affect the children's subsequent reproduction of the behavior.

After viewing the film, each child was left alone in a playroom with a Bobo doll, and hidden observers recorded whether the child imitated what he or she had seen the model do. Later, whether or not they had imitated the model, the children were offered juice and prizes to reproduce all the model's actions that they could remember.

The results are shown in the figure. The children who had seen the model punished imitated the behavior less than did those in the other two groups. However, the children in all conditions had *learned* from observing the model's behavior and remembered what they had seen; when offered rewards to reproduce the aggressive actions, they did so, even if they had not spontaneously performed them in the initial test.

One particularly interesting feature of this research is the gender differences that emerged: boys were more physically aggressive toward the Bobo doll than girls

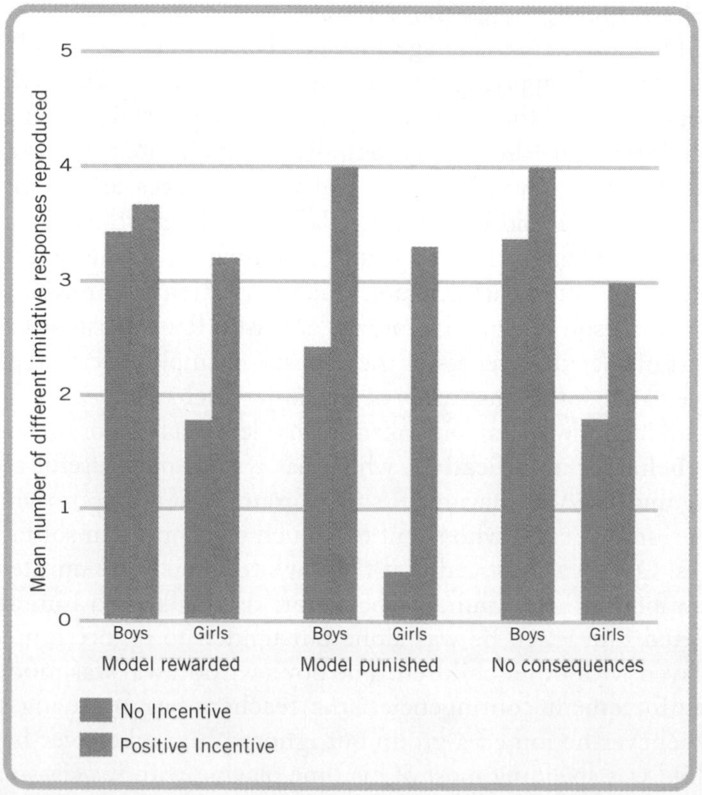

The average number of aggressive behaviors children imitated after seeing a model rewarded, punished, or receiving no consequences for her behavior. In the no-incentive test, the children were simply left alone in the room with the Bobo doll and were given no instructions. In the positive-incentive test, they were offered a reward to do what they had seen the model do. The results clearly show that the children had learned from what they observed and that they had learned more than they initially showed. (Adapted from Bandura, 1965)

Over time, Bandura increasingly emphasized the cognitive aspects of observational learning, eventually renaming his view "social cognitive theory." Observational learning clearly depends on basic cognitive processes of *attention* to others' behavior, *encoding* what is observed, *storing* the information in memory, and *retrieving* it at some later time in order to reproduce the behavior observed earlier. Thanks to observational learning, many young children know quite a bit about adult activities—such as driving a car (you insert and turn the ignition key, press on the accelerator, turn the steering wheel)—long before being allowed to engage in them themselves.

Unlike most learning theorists, Bandura emphasized the active role of children in their own development, describing development as a **reciprocal determinism** between children and their social environment. The basic idea of this concept is that every child has characteristics that lead him or her to seek particular kinds of

9.1

were. However, the girls had learned as much about the modeled behaviors as the boys had, as shown by their increased level of imitation when offered a reward. Presumably, boys and girls generally learn a great deal about the behaviors considered appropriate to both genders but inhibit those they believe to be inappropriate for their own gender.

This classic research thus demonstrates that children can quickly acquire new behaviors simply as a result of observing others, that their tendency to reproduce what they have learned depends on whether the person whose actions they observed was rewarded or punished, and that what children learn from watching others is not necessarily evident in their behavior.

These photographs show an adult performing a series of aggressive actions on a Bobo doll. The boy who had observed the adult's behavior subsequently imitated it when left alone in the room with the Bobo doll. The girl, who did not initially reproduce the model's aggressive actions, did imitate the model's behavior when offered a reward to do so.

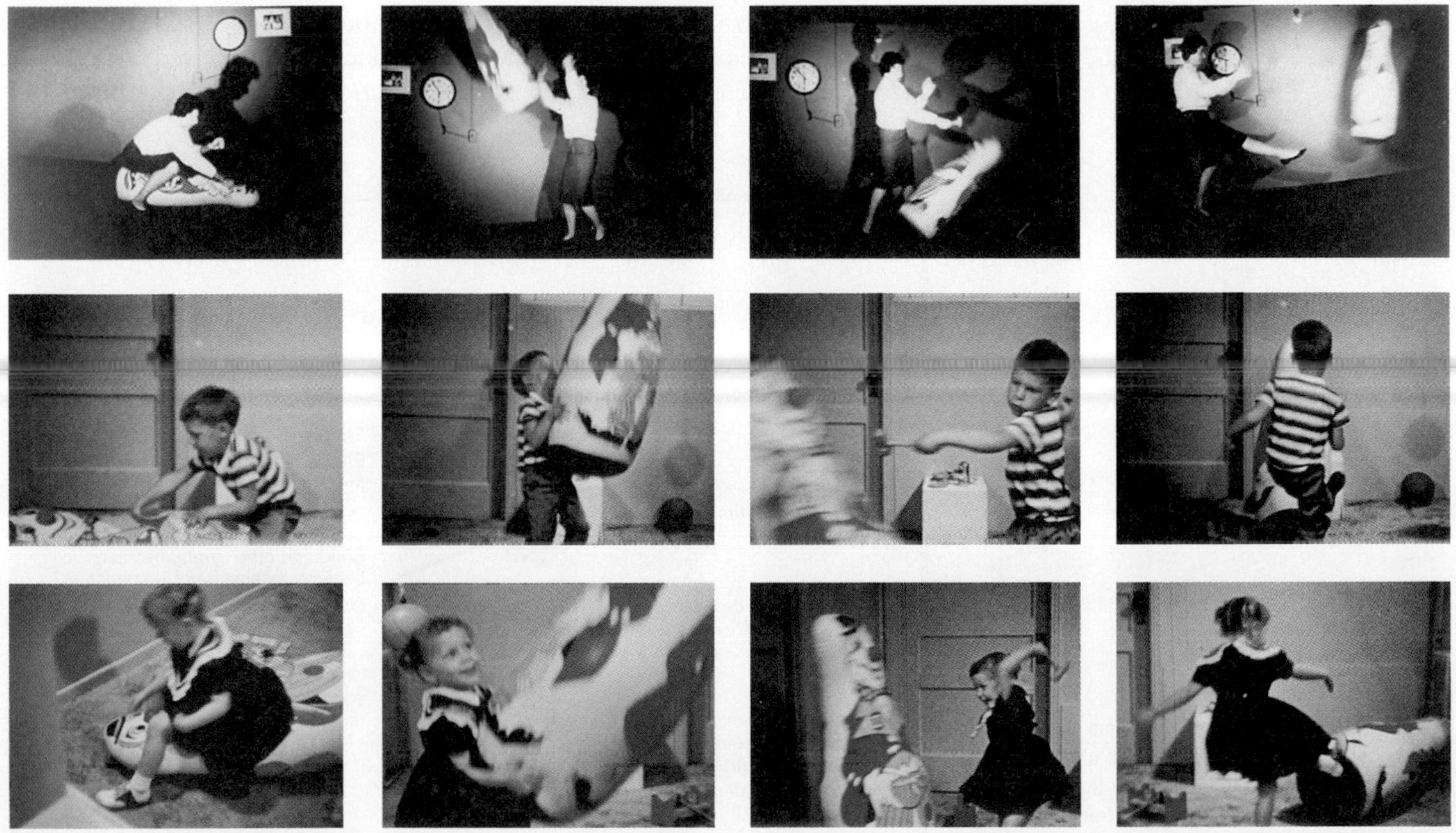

perceived self-efficacy an individual's beliefs about how effectively he or she can control his or her own behavior, thoughts, and emotions in order to achieve a desired goal

A good example of observational learning.

interactions with the external world. The child is affected by these interactions in ways that influence the kinds of interactions he or she seeks in the future. The concept is illustrated in Figure 9.1, depicting a case in which a child's aggressive tendencies have an impact on his playmates and are, in turn, shaped by how those playmates respond.

Bandura has also emphasized the importance of a cognitive factor he calls **perceived self-efficacy**—a person's beliefs about how effectively he or she can control his or her own behavior, thoughts, and emotions in order to achieve a desired goal (Bandura, 1997; Bandura et al., 2003). For example, your *perceived self-efficacy for affect regulation* has to do with your beliefs about how well you can manage your emotional life. In terms of positive affect, your perceived self-efficacy includes your sense of your ability to express affection for another person and to

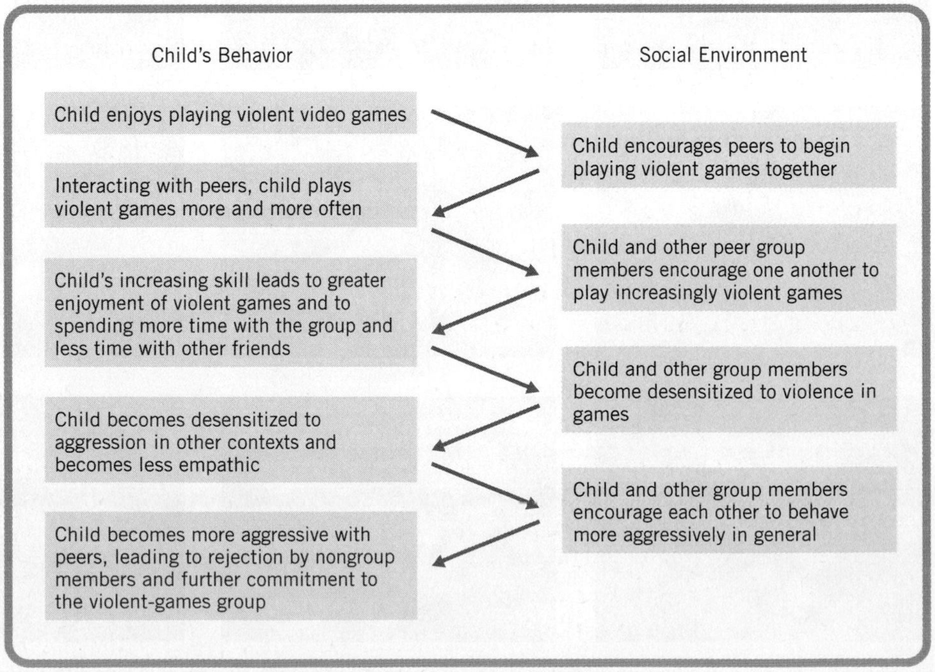

FIGURE 9.1 Reciprocal determinism A hypothetical example showing how a child both influences and is influenced by the social environment. (Based on data from Anderson & Bushman, 2001)

feel satisfaction with your accomplishments. In terms of negative affect, it includes how well you think you can manage fear or anger in the face of threats and provocations and calm yourself after being upset. *Perceived academic self-efficacy* concerns students' beliefs about how well they can regulate their learning activities, master their coursework, and fulfill their own and others' expectations. A person with high academic self-efficacy tends, for example, to arrange the environment to be conducive to effective studying and, when necessary, to seek information and help from teachers and peers.

Perceived self-efficacy in various domains often operate in concert (Bandura et al., 2003). For example, adolescents with low self-efficacy for affect regulation tend to also have low self-efficacy with respect to managing their academic performance. In other words, students who lack confidence in their ability to regulate their emotional life see themselves as incapable of taking charge of their academic work. They are also more likely to engage in delinquent behavior (lying, cheating, theft, aggression, etc.), presumably because feeling incapable of regulating their own behavior undermines their ability to resist negative peer pressures.

Current Perspectives

In contrast to psychoanalytic theories, learning theories are based on principles derived from empirical research. As a result, they allow explicit predictions that can be empirically tested. Partly for this reason, they have inspired an enormous amount of research yielding a great deal of understanding about parental socialization practices and how children learn social behaviors in many domains. They have also led to important practical applications, including clinical procedures of systematic desensitization and behavior modification. The primary weakness of the learning approach is its lack of attention to biological influences and, except for Bandura's theory, to the role of cognition in influencing behavior.

Kismet's designers took learning theories of development to heart from the very beginning by giving him the crucial capacity for learning that is mediated by humans. The emotional and verbal reactions of people to his behaviors instruct him as to the appropriateness of what he has done. He also has the capacity to acquire new behaviors by modeling what he "sees" and "hears" humans do. Kismet's ability to learn from people is a crucial aspect of what makes him seem truly sociable. What would it take for Kismet to acquire a sense of what Bandura refers to as perceived self-efficacy? Could Kismet ever form "beliefs" about what he can and cannot do and base his behavior on those beliefs?

review:

Learning theorists assume that social development is in large part attributable to what children learn through their interactions with other people. Early behaviorists such as Watson and Skinner emphasized the reinforcement history of the individual, believing that children's social behavior is shaped by the pattern of rewards and punishments they receive from others. Social learning theorists, most prominently Albert Bandura, emphasize the role of cognition in social learning, noting that children learn a great deal simply from observing the behavior of other people. Perceived self-efficacy affects the behavior of children in many ways, including the level of effort and persistence they apply to a task. Learning approaches have inspired a variety of treatment methods useful for a wide range of behavioral problems in children.

Theories of Social Cognition

Developmental theories of social cognition have to do with children's ability to think and reason about their own and other people's thoughts, feelings, motives, and behaviors. Like adults, children are active processors of social information. They pay attention to what other people do and say, and they are constantly drawing inferences, forming interpretations, constructing explanations, or making attributions regarding what they observe. They process information about their own behavior and experiences in the same way.

The complexity of children's thinking and reasoning about the social world is related to, and limited by, the complexity of their thought processes in general. After all, the same mind that solves arithmetic and conservation problems also solves problems having to do with making friends and resolving moral dilemmas. With advances in cognitive development in general, the way that children think about themselves and other people deepens and becomes more abstract.

View of Children's Nature

Social cognitive theories provide a sharp contrast to the emphasis that psychoanalytic and learning theories place on external forces as the primary source of development. Instead, social cognitive theories emphasize the process of **self-socialization**—children's active shaping of their own development. According to this view, children's knowledge and beliefs about themselves and other people lead them to adopt particular goals and standards to guide their own behavior.

Central Developmental Issues

The central theme of most relevance to social cognitive theories is the *active child.* Another prominent theme is *individual differences*, particularly in the comparisons that are often drawn between the thinking and behavior of males and females, aggressive and nonaggressive children, and so on. The issue of *continuity/discontinuity* is important in some prominent stage theories that emphasize age-related qualitative changes in how children think about the social world. Information-processing theories, on the other hand, stress continuity in the processes involved in social reasoning. In the following discussions, we will consider these two types of social cognitive theories. The first type is represented by Selman's stage theory of role taking; the second type is represented by Dodge's information-processing theory of social problem solving and by Dweck's attributional account of academic achievement.

Selman's Stage Theory of Role Taking

In formulating his theory of social cognition, Robert Selman (1980; Yeates & Selman, 1989) focused on the development of **role taking**—the ability to adopt the perspective of another person, to think about something from another's point of view. He proposed that such role taking is essential to understanding another person's thoughts, feelings, or motives.

According to Selman, young children's social cognition is quite limited because they lack the ability to role take. Indeed, Selman, like Piaget, suggested that before the age of 6, children are virtually unaware that there is any perspective other than their own; they assume that whatever they think, others will think as well. Perhaps failure to recognize the discrepant view of someone else underlies those endless sibling arguments of the familiar form "'Did,' 'Did not,' 'Did so,' 'Did not.'"

self-socialization the idea that children play a very active role in their own socialization through their activity preferences, friendship choices, and so on

role taking being aware of the perspective of another person, thereby better understanding that person's behavior, thoughts, and feelings

Selman proposed that children go through four increasingly complex and abstract stages in their thinking about other people. In stage 1 (roughly ages 6 to 8), children come to appreciate that someone else can have a perspective different from their own, but they assume that the different perspective is merely due to that person's not possessing the same information they do. In stage 2 (ages 8 to 10), children not only realize that someone else can have a different view, but they also are able to think about the other person's point of view. However, it is not until stage 3 (ages 10 to 12) that children can systematically compare their own and another person's point of view. In this stage, they can also take the perspective of a third party and assess the points of view of two other people. In stage 4 (age 12 and older), adolescents attempt to understand another's perspective by comparing it to that of a "generalized other," assessing whether the person's view is the same as that of most people in their social group.

Notice that in Selman's stages of role taking, as children become less egocentric in their reasoning, they become increasingly capable of considering multiple perspectives simultaneously (e.g., their own, another person's, and "most people's"). This growth in social cognition mirrors the cognitive changes identified by Piaget (and discussed in Chapter 4). Not surprisingly, children's progress through Selman's stages of role taking is strongly related to their progress through Piaget's stages (Keating & Clark, 1980).

DAVID YOUNG-WOLFF / PHOTOEDIT

Many of children's arguments with others stem from their difficulty appreciating that another person can have a different point of view from their own.

Dodge's Information-Processing Theory of Social Problem Solving

The information-processing approach to social cognition emphasizes the crucial role of cognitive processes in social behavior. This approach is exemplified by Kenneth Dodge's analysis of children's use of aggression as a problem-solving strategy (Dodge, 1986; Dodge, Dishion, & Lansford, 2006). In the research on which Dodge's theory was originally based, children were presented stories in which one child suffers because of the actions of another, but the intent of the perpetrator is ambiguous. For example, in one story, as a child is working hard to assemble a puzzle, a peer bumps into the table, scattering the puzzle pieces, and merely says "Oops." Children were asked to imagine themselves as the victim in this scenario and to describe what they would do and why. Some children interpreted the other child's knocking into the table as an accident and said that they would simply ignore the event. Others concluded that the peer bumped the table on purpose, and they reported that they would find a way to get even (many thought that punching the offender would be a good way to achieve that goal).

Dodge and his colleagues have found that some children have a **hostile attributional bias,** that is, a general expectation that others are antagonistic to them (Crick & Dodge, 1994; Graham & Hudley, 1994). This bias leads such children to search for evidence of hostile intent on the part of the peer in the above scenario and to attribute to the peer a desire to harm them. They are likely to conclude that retaliation is the appropriate response to the peer's behavior. Hostile attributional biases become self-fulfilling prophecies: a child's aggressive retaliation to the presumed hostile act of a peer elicits counterattacks and rejection by his or her peers, further fueling the child's belief in the hostility of others.

hostile attributional bias in Dodge's theory, the tendency to assume that other people's ambiguous actions stem from a hostile intent

Dodge has pointed out that school systems have particular problems in dealing with such children. A common strategy is to remove them from regular classrooms

MARY KATE DENNY / PHOTOEDIT

The boy who was spilled on by the other boy seems to have a hostile attributional bias. Because he readily assumes that other people have the intent to harm him, he attributes a hostile intention to the other boy, which leads to a hostile response on that child's part.

because of their disruptive behavior and put them into special classrooms in which they can be more closely supervised (Dodge, Lansford, & Dishion, 2006). However, this approach brings together children with hostile attributional biases, causing other negative consequences. First, it provides these youngsters with evidence supporting their existing expectation of hostility from others, raising the possibility that they will reinforce one another's aggressive tendencies. At the same time, it segregates them from more well-adjusted peers from whom they might learn more moderate attitudes and social strategies.

Dweck's Theory of Self-Attributions and Achievement Motivation

Imagine two grade-school children, Diane and Megan, both hard at work trying to solve math problems, and both initially failing. Coming to the realization that the problems are quite difficult, Diane feels excited about meeting the challenge and works persistently to get the answers. Megan, in contrast, feels anxious and makes only a half-hearted effort to solve the problems. What explains this difference in the children's reaction to failure?

According to Carol Dweck's social cognition perspective (2006), Diane has an *incremental* view of intelligence, the belief that intelligence can be developed through effort. She focuses on mastery—on meeting challenges and overcoming failures, and she generally expects her efforts to be successful. Indeed, her increased effort and persistence following failure will in all likelihood improve her subsequent performance.

Megan, on the other hand, has an *entity* view of intelligence, the belief that her intelligence is fixed. Her goal is to be successful, and as long as she is succeeding, all is well. However, when she fails at something, she feels "helpless." Not succeeding causes her to feel bad and doubt her abilities and self-worth.

Underlying these two patterns of achievement motivation are differences in what attributions children make about themselves, particularly with regard to their sense of their self-worth. Children with an **entity/helpless orientation** tend to base their sense of self-worth on the approval they receive (or do not receive) from other people about their intelligence, talents, and personal qualities. To feel good about themselves, they seek out situations in which they can be assured of success and receive praise, and they avoid situations in which they might be criticized. In contrast, the self-esteem of children with an **incremental/mastery orientation** is based more on their own effort and learning and not on how others evaluate them. Because they do not equate failure on a task with a personal flaw, they can enjoy the challenge of a hard problem and persist in the attempt to solve it.

These different motivation patterns are evident as early as preschool (Smiley & Dweck, 1994). Given a choice of working on a puzzle they have already solved or on one they had previously failed to solve, some 4- and 5-year-old children strongly prefer the one they already know how to do, whereas others want to continue working on the one they had failed to solve.

Older children's cognitions about themselves and their abilities follow a similar pattern but involve more complex concepts and reasoning than those of younger children. Some have what Dweck and her colleagues (Cain & Dweck, 1995; Dweck, 1999; Dweck & Leggett, 1988) refer to as an **entity theory** of intelligence. This theory, like Megan's entity view of intelligence, is rooted in the idea that a person's level of intelligence is fixed and unchangeable. Over time, it comes to include

entity/helpless orientation a general tendency to attribute success and failure to enduring aspects of the self and to give up in the face of failure

incremental/mastery orientation a general tendency to attribute success and failure to the amount of effort expended and to persist in the face of failure

entity theory a theory that a person's level of intelligence is fixed and unchangeable the belief that success or failure in academic situations depends on how smart one is. When evaluating their own performance, children with an entity theory of intelligence focus on outcomes—success or failure—not on effort or learning from mistakes. Thus, when they experience failure (as everyone does some of the time), they think they are not very smart and that there is nothing they can do about it. They feel helpless.

The criticism this teacher is offering this boy on his work could be either beneficial or detrimental, depending on whether she focuses on how smart he is or comments on how his hard work has paid off.

Other children subscribe to an **incremental theory** of intelligence. This theory, like Diane's view of intelligence, is rooted in the idea that intelligence can grow as a function of experience. Children who hold an incremental theory of intelligence believe that academic success is achievable through effort and persistence. When evaluating their performance, they focus on what they have learned, even when they have failed, and they believe that they can do better in the future by trying harder. They feel hopeful.

Given what you have just read, what kind of praise and criticism do you think would reinforce these two patterns? The answer depends on the focus of the feedback. An incremental/mastery pattern is reinforced by focusing on children's effort, praising them for a good effort ("You really worked hard on that," "I like the way you kept at it") and criticizing them for an inadequate one ("Next time you need to put in some more work," "I think you can do better if you try harder"). In contrast, an entity/helpless pattern is reinforced by both praise and criticism focused on children's enduring traits or on the child as a whole ("You're very smart at these problems. I'm proud of you," "You just can't do math. I'm disappointed in you").

Notice that in the long run, doing something that might seem purely positive—praising a child for being good at something—can actually undermine the child's motivation for improvement. Parents and teachers alike should be aware that some kinds of praise are beneficial, whereas others are not.

Current Perspectives

Social cognitive theorists have made several important contributions to the study of social development. One is their strong emphasis on children as active seekers of information about the social world. Another contribution is the insight that the effect of children's social experience depends on their interpretation of those experiences. Thus, children who make different attributions about a given social event (such as someone's causing them harm) or an academic event (such as doing poorly on a test) will respond differently to that event. In addition, a large amount of research has supported the social cognitive position. Although these theories have provided a very healthy antidote to social theories that left children's cognition out of the picture, they too provide an incomplete account. Most notably, they have very little to say about biological factors in social development.

Kismet is designed to shape his own development through his understanding of the behavior of humans toward him—a form of self-socialization emphasized by social cognition theorists. What would it take, however, for Kismet to go further and draw inferences about others' cognitions, feelings, motivations? Will it, for example, ever be possible for him to make different attributions about a given behavior, based on

incremental theory a theory that a person's intelligence can grow as a function of experience subtle aspects of the social context of his history with a person? Even more challenging, will he come to know that people can hold points of view different from one another's and from his own? Finally, can Kismet develop some sense of self-worth that will affect his attributions about himself? These questions about Kismet's potential to mimic social cognition highlight the vast complexity of human social development and the challenge faced by theorists of social development.

review: Theories of social cognition stress the role of cognitive processes—attention, knowledge, interpretation, reasoning, attribution, explanation—in children's social development. A key aspect of these theories is an emphasis on the process of self-socialization, through which children actively shape their own development. Selman's theory of role taking proposes that children go through stages in terms of their ability to appreciate that different people can have different points of view. The information-processing approach taken by Dodge to the study of aggression emphasizes the role of children's interpretation of other people's behavior. Aggressive children often have a hostile attributional bias, a general expectation that other people will be hostile to them. In Carol Dweck's theory of achievement motivation, children's response to their success or failure in an academic situation depends on whether they attribute the outcome to their effort or their intelligence.

Ecological Theories of Development

We now turn to a set of theories united by the fact that they take a very broad view of the context of social development. Virtually all psychological theories, and certainly all that we have reviewed thus far in this chapter, emphasize the role of the environment in the development of individual children. However, the "environment" in many of these theories is narrowly construed as immediate contexts—family, peers, schools. The first two approaches discussed here—ethological and evolutionary psychology views—relate children's development to the grand context of the evolutionary history of our species. The third approach—the bioecological model—considers multiple levels of environmental influence that simultaneously affect development.

View of Children's Nature

Ethological and evolutionary theories view children as inheritors of genetically based abilities and predispositions that underlie most aspects of their behavior. The focus of these theories is largely on aspects of behavior that serve, or once served, an adaptive function.

The bioecological model stresses the effects of context on development, but it also emphasizes the child's active role in selecting and influencing those contexts. Children's personal characteristics—temperament, intellectual ability, athletic skill, and so on—lead them to choose certain environments and also influence the people around them.

Central Developmental Issues

The developmental issue that is front and center in ecological theories is the interaction of *nature and nurture*. The importance of the *sociocultural context* and the *continuity* of development are other implicit emphases in all these theories. The *active role* of children in their own development is another central focus, primarily of the bioecological approach.

Ethological and Evolutionary Theories

Ethological and evolutionary theories are concerned with aspects of human development that are presumed to be based on our evolutionary heritage. These theories primarily focus on species-specific behaviors—behaviors that are common to all humans regardless of the society in which they live.

This famous photograph shows Konrad Lorenz (1952) and a gaggle of Greylag goslings that were imprinted on him and followed him all over his farm. Lorenz discovered that mallard ducklings are more discriminating: they would imprint on him only if he squatted low and dragged himself around, quacking all the while, for hours on end. He was a very dedicated scientist.

Ethology

Ethology, the study of behavior within an evolutionary context, attempts to understand behavior in terms of its adaptive or survival value. According to ethologists, a variety of innate behavior patterns in animals were shaped by evolution just as surely as their physical characteristics were (Crain, 1985).

An ethological approach has frequently been applied to developmental issues. The prototypical, and best-known, example is the study of imprinting made famous by Konrad Lorenz (1903–1989), who is often referred to as the father of modern ethology (Lorenz, 1935, 1952). **Imprinting** is a process in which newborn birds and mammals of some species become attached to their mother at first sight and follow her everywhere, a behavior that ensures that the baby will stay near a source of protection and food. For imprinting to occur, the infant has to encounter its mother during a specific *critical period* very early in life.

The basis for imprinting is not actually the baby's mother per se; rather, the infants of some species are genetically predisposed to follow the first moving object with particular characteristics that they see after emerging into the world. In chickens, for example, imprinting is elicited specifically by the sight of a bird's head and neck regions (Johnson, 1992). Which particular object the individual will dutifully trail after is thus a matter of experience-expectant learning (discussed in Chapter 3). Usually, the first moving object any chick sees *is* its mother, so everything works out just fine.

Although human newborns do not "imprint," they do have strong tendencies that draw them to members of their own species. Examples from Chapter 5 include an innate visual preference for faces that really seems to be an attraction to a face shape with more "stuff" in the top half. Even though it is not a specific human face template, it gets the infant to pay attention to the most significant entities in the environment. Also, like other mammals, human newborns orient to sounds, tastes, and smells familiar from their experience in the womb—a predisposition that inclines them toward their own mother (see Chapter 5). One of the most influential applications of ethology to human development, which we discuss in Chapter 11, is Bowlby's (1969) extension of the concept of imprinting to the process by which infants form emotional attachments to their mother.

Another example of human behavior to which an ethological perspective has been applied is the existence of differences in the play preferences of males and females (which you will read more about in Chapter 15). For example, boys prefer to play with vehicle toys (trucks, cars, etc.), which afford action play, whereas girls prefer dolls, which are conducive to nurturant play. The standard accounts for these differences, which come from social learning and social cognitive theories, maintain that children (especially boys) are encouraged by their parents to play with "gender-appropriate" toys, and they do so because they want to be like others of their own sex.

ethology the study of the evolutionary bases of behavior

imprinting a form of learning in which the young of some species of newborn birds and mammals become attached to and follow adult members of the species (usually their mother)

MYRLEEN FERGUSON CATE / PHOTOEDIT

JULIE HOUCK / STOCK BOSTON

According to evolutionary psychology, gender differences in play probably have their origin in the evolutionary history of the human species, with males being predisposed to dominance, and females, to nurturing.

Recently, some researchers have argued that this is not the whole story and that evolved predispositions fuel these preferences. In one study, for example, newborn girls looked longer at social stimuli—human faces—than at nonsocial stimuli such as mobiles, whereas the reverse was true for boys (Connellan, Baron-Cohen, Wheelwright, Ba'tki, & Ahluwalia, 2001). Similarly, 1-year-old boys watched a video of moving cars longer than one of an active human face, whereas girls did the opposite (Lutchmaya & Baron-Cohen, 2002).

Evolutionary Psychology

A relatively new branch of psychology that is closely related to ethology is evolutionary psychology, which applies the Darwinian concepts of natural selection and adaptation to human behavior (Bjorklund, 2007; Geary, 2009). The basic idea of this approach is that in the evolutionary history of our species, certain genes predisposed individuals to behave in ways that solved the adaptive challenges they faced (obtaining food, avoiding predators, establishing social bonds), thereby increasing the likelihood that they would survive, mate, and reproduce, passing along their genes to their offspring. These adaptive genes became increasingly common and were passed down to modern humans so that many of the ways we behave today are a legacy from our prehistoric ancestors (Geary, 2009).

One of the most important adaptive features of the human species—one that clearly distinguishes us from other species—is the large size of our brains (relative to body size). The trade-off for this is the prolonged period of immaturity and dependence their children go through. We are "a slow-developing, big-brained species" (Bjorklund & Pelligrini, 2001), as illustrated in Figure 9.2. In Chapter 2, we discussed how the size of the human brain at birth is limited by the size of the female pelvis. As modern humans evolved, enlargement of our brains was made possible by birth occurring at a more "premature" stage of development than is characteristic of other mammals. These evolutionary changes were made possible by increased social complexity, which is necessary for successful caregiving of extremely helpless offspring. A related consequence of our large brains and slow development is our species-typical high level of neural plasticity that supports our unequaled capacity for learning from experience. Highlighting the adaptive benefits of our extended immaturity, David Bjorklund (1997) has pointed out that

> a prolonged period of youth is necessary for humans [who,] more than any other species, must survive by their wits; human communities are more complex and diverse than those of any other species, and this requires that they have not only a flexible intelligence to learn the conventions of their societies but also *a long time to learn them.*
>
> (p. 153, emphasis added)

Many evolutionary theorists have suggested that *play,* which is one of the most salient forms of behavior during the period of immaturity of most mammals, is an evolved platform for learning (Bjorklund & Pellegrini, 2001). Children develop motor skills by racing and wrestling with one another, throwing toy spears, or kicking a ball into a goal. They try out and practice a variety of social roles (as mentioned in Chapter 7), enacting what they know about being, say, a parent or a police officer. One of the main virtues of play is that children can experiment in a situation with minimal consequences; no one gets hurt if a baby doll is accidentally dropped on its head or a cap gun is fired at a "bad guy."

To benefit from their protracted immature status, children must, of course, survive it, and their survival and development require that parents spend an enormous amount of time, energy, and resources in raising them (Bjorklund, 2007). Why are parents willing to sacrifice so much for the benefit of their offspring? According to **parental-investment theory** (Trivers, 1972), a primary source of their motivation is the perpetuation of their genes in the human gene pool, which can happen only if their offspring survive long enough to pass those genes on to the next generation.

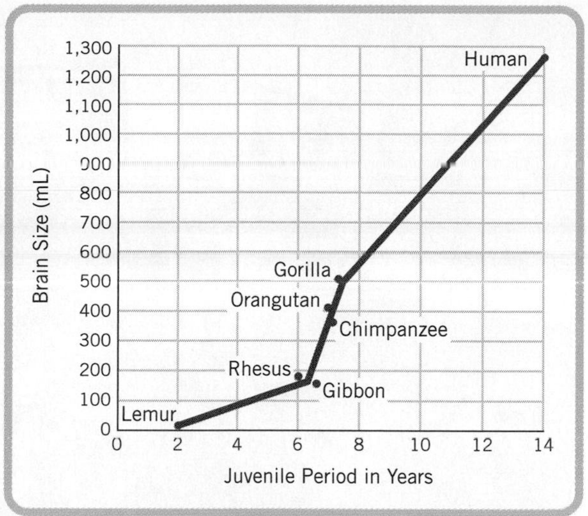

FIGURE 9.2 Brain sizes of various primates and humans Humans are "a slow-developing, big-brained species" compared with other primates. The larger the brain size of various primates, the longer their developmental period. (Adapted from Bonner, 1988)

Parental-investment theory also points to a potential dark side of the evolutionary picture. As Figure 9.3 shows, estimates of the rate of murder committed by stepfathers against children residing with them is hundreds of times higher than the rate for fathers and their biological children. Further, in families in which both natural and stepchildren reside, abusive parents typically target their abuse toward their stepchildren (Daly & Wilson, 1996). Although there are clearly many factors that contribute to these patterns, they are consistent with parent-investment theory; that is, because parenting is so costly, it is not, from an evolutionary point of view, worth investing in children who cannot contribute to the perpetuation of one's own genes.

parental-investment theory a theory that stresses the evolutionary basis of many aspects of parental behavior, including the extensive investment parents make in their offspring

A clear implication of the evolutionary view of development is that radical departures from the species-typical environment could have negative consequences. It is well established that providing young and unborn animals of various species with stimulation that is outside the normal range for their species and age has adverse effects on their development (e.g., Gottlieb, 1992; Kenny & Turkewitz, 1986). For example, while developing inside the egg, bobwhite quails experience no light or visual stimulation. If a piece of the shell is removed, letting in light while the embryo develops, the species-typical behavior of the hatchlings is altered, disrupting normal development (Lickliter, 1995).

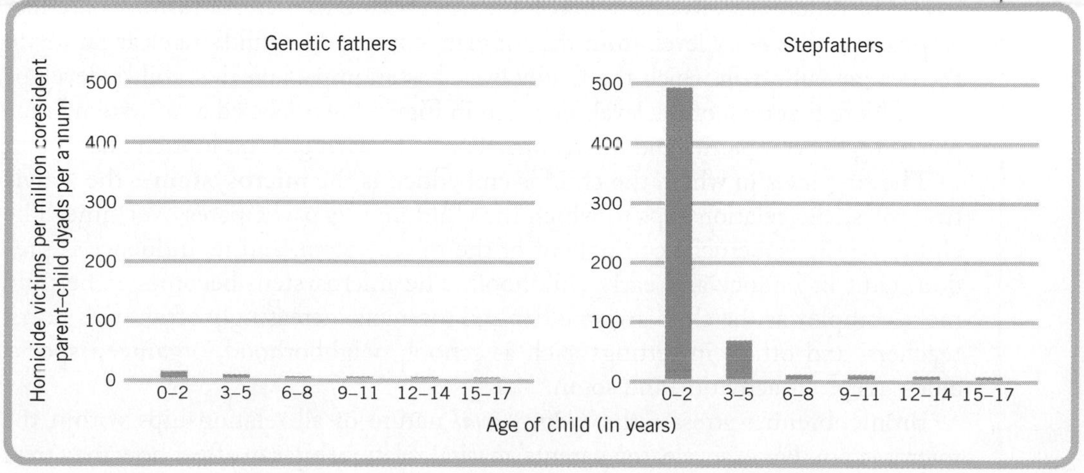

FIGURE 9.3 Estimated rates of child homicide commited by genetic fathers versus stepfathers in Canada from 1974 to 1990 As is shockingly clear, stepchildren, especially very young ones, are much more likely to be murdered by a stepfather than other children are likely to be murdered by their biological fathers. (Adapted from Daly & Wilson, 1996)

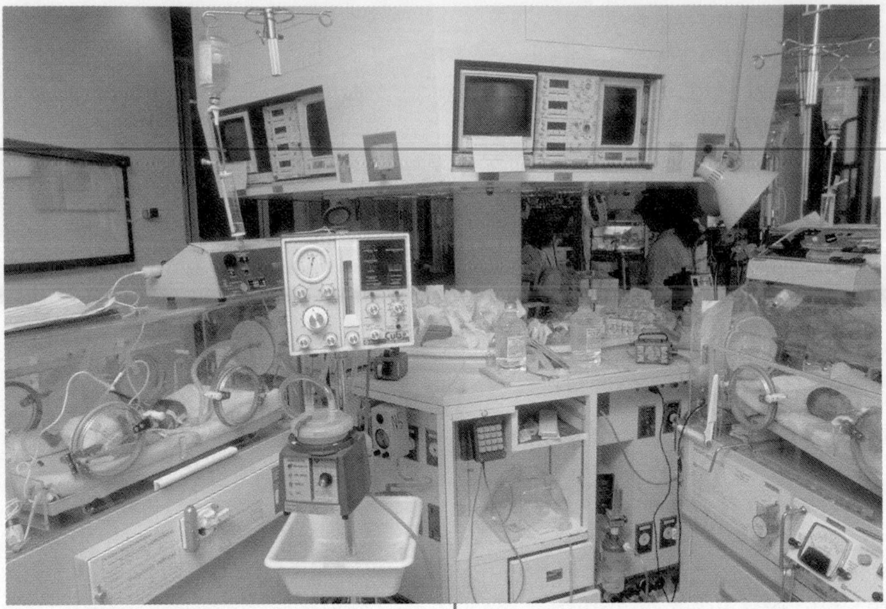
KEN SHERMAN / PHOTOTAKE

The environment that premature infants encounter in a newborn intensive-care unit is radically different from the uterine environment, raising concern that stimulation so different from anything humans encountered in the evolutionary past may be detrimental to development.

Could the same be true for humans? Neonatologist Heideliese Als (2003) believes that we should be concerned about this question with regard to babies born prematurely. As discussed in Chapter 2, modern medicine has enabled increasing numbers of premature infants of ever smaller sizes to survive. However, their first weeks or even months are spent in an environment that is radically different from the species-typical fetal environment. Instead of continued residence in the dark, relatively quiet womb, these babies find themselves in brightly lit, very noisy intensive-care units. Believing that many of the brain and behavioral problems common in premature infants may have to do with this atypical early environment, Als has advocated radical changes in newborn nurseries to simulate the womb environment, including reducing illumination and noise levels.

A related area of concern about potential negative effects of species-atypical stimulation is the current craze for providing extra prenatal stimulation that we discussed in Chapter 2. Our species evolved with a certain amount of stimulation available to the fetus in utero, and a substantial increase in prenatal stimulation might very well have negative consequences.

The Bioecological Model

The most encompassing model of the general context of development is Urie Bronfenbrenner's bioecological model (Bronfenbrenner, 1979; Bronfenbrenner & Morris, 1998). Bronfenbrenner conceptualizes the environment as "a set of nested structures, each inside the next, like a set of Russian dolls" (1979, p. 22). Each structure represents a different level of influence on development (Figure 9.4). Embedded in the center of the multiple levels of influences is the individual child, with his or her particular constellation of characteristics (genes, gender, age, temperament, health, intelligence, physical attractiveness, and so on). Over the course of development, these individual characteristics interact with the environmental forces present at each level. The different levels vary in how immediate their effects are, but Bronfenbrenner emphasizes that *every* level, from the intimate context of a child's nuclear family to the general culture in which the family lives, has an impact on that child's development. Note that each of the levels depicted in Figure 9.4 is labeled as a "system," emphasizing the complexity and interconnectedness of what goes on in each one.

The first level in which the child is embedded is the **microsystem**—the activities, roles, and relationships in which the child *directly* participates over time. The child's family is a crucial component of the microsystem, and its influence is predominant in infancy and early childhood. The microsystem becomes richer and more complex as the child grows older and interacts increasingly often with peers, teachers, and others in settings such as school, neighborhood, organized sports, clubs, religious activities, and so on.

microsystem in the bioecological model, the immediate environment that an individual personally experiences

Bronfenbrenner stresses the *bidirectional* nature of all relationships within the microsystem. For example, the parents' marital relationship can affect how they treat their children, and their children's behavior can, in turn, have an impact on the

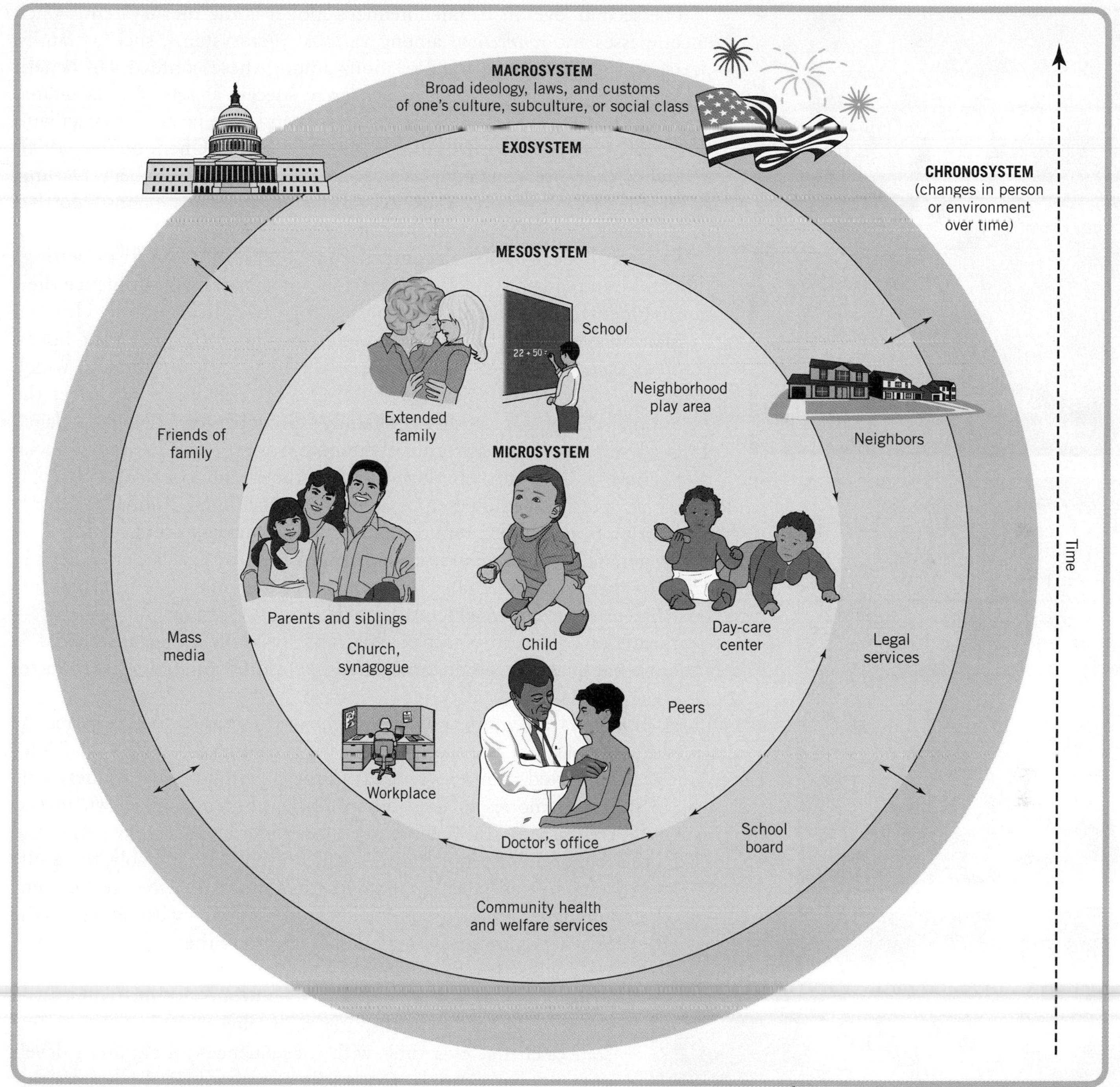

FIGURE 9.4 The bioecological model Urie Bronfenbrenner considers the child's environment as composed of a series of nested structures, including the microsystem (the immediate environment with which the child directly interacts), the mesosystem (the connections that exist among microsystems), the exosystem (social settings the child is not a part of but that still affect him or her), and the macrosystem (the general cultural context in which all the other systems are embedded). This figure illustrates the environment of a child living in the United States. (Adapted from Bronfenbrenner, 1979)

marital relationship. A good, supportive marital relationship helps parents interact more sensitively and effectively with their children (Cowan, Powell, & Cowan, 1998; Cox, Owen, Lewis, & Henderson, 1989), but a chronically fussy baby can create friction and even damage the relationship between parents (Belsky, Rosenberger, & Crnic, 1995).

GETTY IMAGES

BETTMANN / CORBIS

RICHARD HUTCHINGS / PHOTOEDIT

What different experiences were available to these girls born in different historical times? How did their educational and employment opportunities differ?

The second level in Bronfenbrenner's model is the **mesosystem,** which encompasses the *connections* among various microsystems, such as family, peers, and schools. Supportive relations among these contexts can benefit the child. For example, children's academic success at school is facilitated when their parents value scholastic endeavors and have positive contact with their teachers (Luster & McAdoo, 1996; Stevenson, Chen, & Lee, 1993) and when their peers encourage academic achievement (Steinberg, Darling, & Fletcher, 1995). When connections in the mesosystem are nonsupportive, negative outcomes are more likely.

The third level of social context, the **exosystem,** comprises settings that children may not directly be a part of but that can still influence their development. Their parents' workplaces, for example, can affect children in many ways, from the employer's policies about flexible work hours, parental leave, and on-site child care to the general atmosphere in which parents work. Parents' enjoyment or dislike of their work can affect the emotional relationships within the family (Greenberger, O'Neil, & Nagel, 1994). Even something as seemingly remote from the child as the financial success or failure of a parent's employer can be crucial: job loss, for example, is related to abusive or neglectful parenting (Emery & Laumann-Billings, 1998).

The outer level of Bronfenbrenner's model is the **macrosystem,** which consists of the general beliefs, values, customs, and laws of the larger society in which all the other levels are embedded. It includes the general cultural, subcultural, or social-class groups to which the child belongs. Cultural and class differences permeate almost every aspect of children's lives, including differences in beliefs about what qualities should be fostered in children and how best to foster them.

Cultural influences are even apparent in the earliest memories reported by adults in different parts of the world. In a cross-cultural study (Wang, 2006), Euro-Americans reported memories from an earlier age than did Taiwanese participants, and their memories focused on specific events and their own role in those events. In contrast, the Taiwanese more often described everyday events and emphasized the role of other people in the recalled events. Presumably, these differences reflect cultural values that influence what parents encourage their children to talk about, especially with respect to the relative value of focusing on oneself or on others.

Finally, Bronfenbrenner's model also has a temporal dimension, which he has referred to as the **chronosystem.** In any given society, beliefs, values, customs, technologies, and social circumstances change over time, with consequences for children's development. For example, as a result of technological advances that gave rise to the "digital age," children today have access to a vast realm of information and entertainment unimaginable to previous generations. In addition, the impact of environmental events depends on another chronological variable—the age of the child. For example, divorce has different effects on toddlers and teens; it may make both of them unhappy, but only young children are likely to have the extra burden of thinking that the divorce is their fault (Hetherington & Clingempeel, 1992). Another important aspect of the temporal dimension, which we have noted on several occasions, is the fact that as children get older, they take an increasingly active role in their own development, making their own decisions about their friends, activities, and environments. As Box 9.2 on ADHD (pages 370–371) suggests, the chronosystem can even be a factor in developmental disorders.

To illustrate the richness of the bioecological model for thinking about and investigating child development, we will consider three extensive examples in which the interactions among multiple levels of the model are particularly clear and relevant: child maltreatment, children and the media, and SES and development.

Child Maltreatment

One of the most serious threats to children's development in the United States is **child maltreatment,** defined as intentional abuse or neglect that endangers the well-being of anyone under the age of 18. In 2007, an estimated 794,000 children were determined to be victims of child maltreatment, with 62% of them also suffering from neglect (Department of Health and Human Services, 2009). Most of the cases involved maltreatment by parents, most often mothers. The victims included nearly equal numbers of girls and boys, with more than half being 7 years of age or younger and nearly a third being under age 4. More tragic still, over 1500 children—most of them under the age of 6—were killed by a parent or parent figure. Consistent with the bioecological model, a variety of factors, including characteristics of the child, the parents, and the community, have been shown to be involved in the causes and consequences of child abuse.

Causes of maltreatment At the level of the microsystem, certain characteristics of parents increase the risk for maltreatment (Emery & Laumann-Billings, 1998). Among these are low self-esteem, strong negative reactions to stress, and poor impulse control. Parental alcohol and drug dependence also increase the probability of maltreatment. So does an abusive spousal relationship: mothers who are abused by their partner are more likely to pass the abuse on to their children. In addition, certain characteristics of children—including low birth weight, physical or mental handicaps, and difficult temperament—make it more likely that they will suffer abuse at the hands of their parents (e.g., Bugental & Happaney, 2004). Imagine, for example, a child with a mild hearing impairment who, as a consequence, seems unresponsive to her parents, or a child with ADHD who has difficulty complying with his parents' rules. Such children, who are more challenging for parents to cope with, have a heightened risk of being maltreated.

Child maltreatment tends to be associated with additional factors in the mesosystem and exosystem that increase stress on parents. Many of these factors are related to low family income. They include high levels of unemployment, inadequate housing, and community violence (Emery & Laumann-Billings, 1998; Lynch & Cicchetti, 1998).

Often a particularly important exosystem contributor to child maltreatment is a family's social isolation and lack of social support (more common in lower-income families). Such isolation may have multiple reasons—mistrust of other people, a lack of the social skills needed to maintain positive relationships, frequent moves from place to place due to economic factors, or living in a community characterized by violence and transience. The importance of social support is highlighted by the fact that impoverished parents are less likely to maltreat their children if they live in a neighborhood in which there is a prevailing sense of community, with neighbors who care about and help one another (Belsky, 1993; Coulton, Korbin, Su, & Chow, 1995; Garbarino & Kostelny, 1992).

mesosystem in the bioecological model, the interconnections among immediate, or microsystem, settings

exosystem in the bioecological model, environmental settings that a person does not directly experience but that can affect the person indirectly

macrosystem in the bioecological model, the larger cultural and social context within which the other systems are embedded

chronosystem in the bioecological model, historical changes that influence the other systems

child maltreatment intentional abuse or neglect that endangers the well-being of anyone under the age of 18

individual differences

Attention-Deficit Hyperactivity Disorder

Many debilitating syndromes can be profitably examined with the different levels of the bioecological model in mind. Influences and interventions from different levels can make it easier or harder for children to manage their problem. A good case in point is **ADHD—attention-deficit hyperactivity disorder.**

Although the term "ADHD" is relatively new, the syndrome—variously labeled as "hyperactivity," "minimal brain dysfunction," and "attention-deficit disorder" (ADD)—has long been recognized. Children with ADHD tend to be of normal intelligence and do not typically show serious emotional disturbances. However, they have difficulty sticking to plans, following rules and regulations, and persevering on tasks that require sustained attention (especially ones they find uninteresting). Many are hyperactive, constantly fidgeting, drumming on their desks, and moving around. Children with ADHD typically have difficulty acquiring academic skills, such as reading and writing, since these skills require focusing attention for prolonged periods of time. Many also encounter problems with suppressing aggressive reactions when they are frustrated. All these symptoms seem to reflect an underlying difficulty in inhibiting impulses to act (Barkley, 1997). The difficulty is greatest when interesting distractors are present.

According to the National Institute of Mental Health (NIMH), ADHD affects approximately 3% to 5% of U.S. children (2 million). The large majority of children diagnosed with ADHD are boys, but this is partly because boys with ADHD are more likely than girls to engage in disruptive behaviors that lead to their problem being diagnosed (Gaub & Carlson, 1997). Some children with ADHD outgrow their early problems, but most continue to have difficulties into adolescence and adulthood. They are considerably more likely than others to drop out of high school, to have driving accidents, and to commit reckless criminal acts (Green et al., 1997).

The causes of ADHD are quite varied. Genetic factors clearly play a role. If one identical twin has ADHD, the odds are about 50% that the other twin does too, a rate roughly 10 times that among children in general (Silver, 1999). In addition, ADHD in adopted children is associated with ADHD in the biological parent but not in the adoptive parent (Rhee et al., 1999). Further, children with ADHD show reduced electrical activity and blood flow in the frontal lobe, the part of the brain that is most involved in regulation of attention and inhibition of action (Giedd et al., 2001).

Environmental factors in the microsystem also influence the development of ADHD. For example, prenatal exposure to alcohol, which can affect brain development (pages 62–64), is associated with the development of ADHD (Milberger et al., 1997). Parents' behavior toward their children may contribute to the early development of ADHD, as shown by a large study with 5-year-olds, half of whom had been of low birth weight (Tully, Arseneault, Caspi, Moffitt, & Morgan, 2004). Those low-birth-weight children whose mothers expressed a high degree of warmth for them ("He's my ray of sunshine," "She's a delight") were less likely than children of less warm mothers to show symptoms of ADHD.

How children are treated by other people can exacerbate the problem (Hinshaw et al., 1997). For example, parents and teachers often punish children with ADHD for their inattentive and/or disruptive behavior, and peers frequently reject them for the same reason (Campbell, 2000). As a consequence, in addition to their academic problems, children with ADHD have relatively few friends.

Several environmental factors that have often been cited in the media as causes of ADHD actually do *not* contribute to it. Consumption of food additives and sugar, for example, has not been shown to be related to ADHD (Hynd et al., 1991). Similarly, watching action television programs with jump-cut editing does not reduce children's attention span (Huston & Wright, 1998).

Current treament for ADHD involves agents in the microsystem (the family doctor), the exosystem (the drug industry), and the macrosystem (the government). The most common approach taken by physicians is the prescription of stimulant medications, such as Ritalin. Although it seems paradoxical that stimulants could help children who are already overly active, they improve symptoms in 70% to 90% of children for whom they are prescribed. Appropriate medication allows children with ADHD to focus their attention better

Consequences of maltreatment The consequences of child abuse are manifested in the microsystem, the mesosystem, and sometimes even the exosystem (although it can be difficult to be sure to what extent something is a consequence or a contributing factor). In comparison with other children, maltreated children have less secure relationships with their parents, show less empathy for other people, and have lower self-esteem (Cicchetti & Toth, 1998; Main & George, 1985; Smith & Walden, 1999). In elementary school, maltreated children are more aggressive and have more conflict with their peers (Bolger & Patterson, 2001; McCloskey & Stuewig, 2001). Later on, they have difficulty maintaining friendships (Parker & Herrera, 1996; Rogosch, Cicchetti, & Aber, 1995; Salzinger, Feldman, Ng-Mak, Mojica, & Stockhammer, 2001). At school, maltreated children

ADHD (attention-deficit hyperactivity disorder) a syndrome that involves difficulty in sustaining attention

9.2

and to be less distractible. This leads to improved academic achievement, better relationships with classmates, and reduced activity levels (Barbaresi, 2007; Barbaresi et al., 2007). Physicians sometimes prescribe quite large dosages, but small dosages often work as well or even better (Evans et al., 2001).

It is important to realize that the benefits of Ritalin continue only as long as children take the medication. Longer-lasting gains require not only medication but also behavioral treatments, such as teaching children strategies for screening out distractions (Barkley, 1994). The most effective behavioral interventions include working with those who are involved with the children on a daily basis, namely teachers and parents (Pelham & Hoza, 1996). Encouraging teachers to allow children with ADHD to alternate between studying and moving around the classroom, and helping parents muster the patience needed to deal with these challenging children, seem especially effective. Combined, these behavioral interventions and medications benefit a great many children with ADHD.

The availability of medications helpful to those with ADHD is, of course, the result of a perception on the part of drug companies that they can produce, sell, and make a profit from a drug targeted for this problem. It also depends on the medication's receiving a favorable evaluation from the FDA, based on research to determine the drug's efficacy and potential side effects. Thus, the fate of a child in need of medication could be quite different, depending on factors far outside the influence of his or her family.

But would any intervention be necessary in the first place if not every child were expected to spend a substantial amount of time most days sitting quietly at a desk concentrating on tasks that he or she may have little interest in? Pointing to the highest level of the bioecological model—the chronosystem—many have suggested that ADHD may have emerged as a serious problem only in recent times—specifically, only since the advent of compulsory schooling. Before then, an individual who would have suffered attentional problems in a classroom might very well have been able to find a more compatible and less confining niche elsewhere.

DAVID YOUNG-WOLFF / PHOTOEDIT

The short attention span of children with attention-deficit disorder often leads them to distract not only themselves but also other children in their classroom.

are often anxious and inattentive and overly dependent on their teachers for approval and support. They are more than twice as likely as other children to fail a grade (Eckenrode, Laird, & Doris, 1993; Erickson et al., 1989).

In adolescence and adulthood, individuals with a history of maltreatment are at risk for developing serious psychopathologies, including depression, anxiety, substance abuse, eating disorders, sexual dysfunction, hyperactivity, and antisocial behavior (Cicchetti & Toth, 1998; Keiley, Howe, Dodge, Bates, & Pettit, 2001; Kilpatrick et al., 2000). As an indication of how pervasive the effects of maltreatment are, individuals who experience abuse early in life have a higher risk of heart disease in adulthood (Dong et al., 2004). (For a promising approach to preventing child maltreatment, see Box 9.3).

applications 9.3

Preventing Child Maltreatment

Given the multiple factors that contribute to child maltreatment, preventing or ameliorating the problem is extremely difficult. However, one very promising intervention program was developed from research financed by federal funding agencies at the macrosystem level and is carried out at the microsystem level.

BOB KALMAN / THE IMAGE WORKS

The program, reflecting a social cognition perspective, was designed and implemented by Daphne Bugental and her colleagues, who found that many abusive parents have inappropriate models of their relationship with their children. They tend to see themselves and their children as locked in a power struggle—a conflict in which they view *themselves* as the victims (Bugental, Blue, & Cruzcosa, 1989; Bugental & Happaney, 2004). Thus, they might interpret their baby's prolonged crying as evidence that the baby is mad at them, and they might think that a child who continues to beg for a withheld toy or treat is intentionally trying to subvert their authority.

The goal of this program was to help parents at risk for abusing their children achieve more realistic interpretations of their difficulties in caring for their children (Bugental et al., 2002). The intervention involved frequent home visits in which parents were asked to give examples of recent problems they had had with their children and to indicate what they thought had been the cause of the problem. They were then led to identify a cause that did not focus blame on the children (i.e., something other than deliberate misbehavior by their children), as well as to come up with potential strategies for solving the problem.

A particularly important factor in assessing this program is that at-risk families were *randomly assigned* to the intervention condition or to two comparison conditions. Thus, any difference in outcomes could not be due to initial differences among the groups.

The program was remarkably successful: the prevalence of physical abuse in the intervention group was only 4%, compared with around 25% in the two comparison groups. This intervention program, targeted at the microsystem level, suggests that home-visiting programs that focus on altering parents' cognitive interpretations have a high potential for preventing physical maltreatment.

Children and the Media: The Good, the Bad, and the Awful

Another good illustration of the multiple levels in which children's development is embedded is the impact of various media—television programs, movies, video games, and popular music. In terms of the bioecological model, media are situated in the exosystem, but they are subject to influences from the chronosystem, as indicated on page 368; from the macrosystem (including cultural values and government policies); from other elements in the exosystem (such as economic pressures); and from the microsystem (such as parental monitoring). All these factors are at play every time children tune in or boot up.

Early on, when children's in-home screen viewing was mostly limited to TV, some educationally oriented television programming for young children was shown to have beneficial effects (Huston & Wright, 1998). Most notably, watching "Sesame Street" was associated with increases in young children's vocabulary and helped prepare them for school entry, with some positive effects persisting even through high school (Anderson, Huston, Schmitt, Linebarger, & Wright, 2001; Rice, Huston, Truglio, & Wright, 1990).

More recently, concerns have arisen about whether children derive more harm than benefit from their extensive amount of time in front of a variety of screens. American children now spend more time involved in using screen media than in any other activity besides going to school and sleeping. This fact was documented by a national survey conducted by the Kaiser Family Foundation (2005) of media use in households with children between the ages of 2 and 17. Virtually all American homes have one or more television sets, and many children have their own television and computer in their bedrooms. On an average day, the greatest proportion of children's media time is spent in front of a television screen (Kaiser Family Foundation, 2005). Further, students of a wide range of ages use computers for much of their homework. Most of that time, however, they are multitasking—texting friends, exploring the Web, and talking on the phone (Kaiser Family Foundation, 2005; Pew Internet, 2008). In addition, virtually all American teens play electronic games on their computers and cell phones (Pew Internet, 2008). Even very young children are active participants in this media immersion: children 6 years and younger devote more time to entertainment media than to reading, being read to, and playing outside combined (Rideout et al., 2003).

© ALAMY / ALAMY

These children are engaged in a very common activity—playing a video game. It is also increasingly common for children to have television sets in their own rooms.

Concerns about Children's Exposure to Media The nature and amount of children's media exposure has aroused a variety of concerns, ranging from the possible effects of media violence and pornography to those of isolation and inactivity.

MEDIA VIOLENCE Foremost among the concerns that have been raised is fear that a steady diet of watching violent television shows, playing violent video games, and listening to music with violent lyrics will cause children to behave violently. The concern originally arose from the fact that television is awash in violence. The comprehensive National Television Violence Study reported that 61% of programs on television between 1994 and 1997 contained episodes of violence (Wilson et al., 1997). Furthermore, aggression in television programs tends to be glamorized and trivialized—with the violence perpetrated by heroes who are rarely punished or condemned.

Extensive reviews of the vast amount of research on this issue have led researchers to conclude that the scientific debate about whether media violence increases aggression and violence is over: "Research on violent television and films, video games, and music reveals unequivocal evidence that media violence increases the likelihood of aggressive and violent behavior in both immediate and long-term contexts" (Anderson et al., 2003). A recent longitudinal study supported this conclusion, reporting an association between the amount of TV violence that 4th- and 6th-grade children (both boys and girls) watch and their levels of aggressive behavior, including aggressive acts, delinquency, and cruelty (Feshbach & Tangney, 2008).

Exposure to media violence has an impact in four different ways (Anderson et al., 2003). First, seeing actors engage in aggression teaches aggressive behaviors and inspires imitation of them. Second, viewing aggression increases the accessibility of the viewer's own aggressive thoughts, feelings, and tendencies. This heightened aggressive mindset makes it more likely that the individual will interpret new events as involving aggression and will respond aggressively. Further, when aggression-related thoughts are frequently activated, they may become part of the individual's normal internal state. Third, media violence is exciting and arousing for most youth, and their heightened physiological arousal makes them more likely to react violently to provocations right after watching violent films. Finally, frequent long-term exposure to media violence gradually leads to emotional desensitization—a reduction in the level of unpleasant physiological arousal most people experience when observing violence. Because this arousal normally

STONE / GETTY IMAGES

Researchers have concluded that viewing media violence increases the incidence of aggression and violent behavior.

The common practice of spending a great deal of time watching TV while consuming high-fat snacks increases the likelihood of childhood obesity.

helps inhibit violent behavior, emotional desensitization can render violent thoughts and behaviors more likely.

PHYSICAL INACTIVITY Another concern has to do with the fact that a child who is glued to a television or computer screen is not outside playing or otherwise engaging in robust physical activity. In addition, the thousands of TV commercials with which children are bombarded every year (at an advertiser cost of billions of dollars per year) consist largely of advertisements for sugary cereals, candy, and fast food restaurants. The sedentary nature of computer use and television watching, combined with the onslaught of commercials encouraging the consumption of sweet, fatty foods, have been linked to the recent *increase* in childhood obesity discussed in Chapter 3.

SOCIAL ISOLATION Concerns have also been expressed about the solitary nature of children's home use of computer and video games and the possibility that it may rob them of time with friends. However, as noted, much of the time that children spend on the computer is devoted to interpersonal communication via the Internet (Subrahmanyam et al., 2001). In addition, research indicates that moderate video game playing seems to have no significant impact on children's social skills and interactions. In fact, computer games can actually bring together peers and family members who enjoy playing the same games (Colwell, Grady, & Rhiati, 1995).

SOCIAL INEQUITIES Another area of concern centers on the possibility that socioeconomic inequalities will be exacerbated by the "digital divide"—that is, unequal access to and use of computers as a function of SES. Most children have some degree of access to computers at school, but there are great differences between low-SES and high-SES families in terms of the likelihood that computers are available in their homes. Further, higher-SES families are more likely to have newer, more powerful computers and to have more than one of them. Thus, children from higher-SES families are far more likely to be able to use computers to do homework and to use the Internet than are children from poorer families. The disparity in access to computers is less extreme at school, where computers are used extensively in classrooms in low-SES neighborhoods.

PORNOGRAPHY A serious concern for many parents is children's exposure to pornography on television and the Internet, whether inadvertent or intentional. Online pornography is particularly problematic because of its ready availability: in 2009, there were an estimated 4.2 million pornography websites globally—12% of the total of all websites (Ropelato, 2009)! On average, American children first encounter pornography on the Web at the age of 11 (Ropelato, 2009). Research suggests that exposure to pornography can make children and teens more tolerant of aggression toward women, as well as more accepting of premarital and extramarital sex (Greenfield, 2004).

Of special concern is pornography featuring children. Child pornography is a multi-billion-dollar industry and among the fastest-growing criminal segments on the Web (FBI, 2009b). Today, pedophiles commonly use the Web, including chat rooms, to share illegal photographs of children and to lure children into sexual relationships.

The most effective weapons against the various negative effects of media on children operate at the microsystem level, with parents exercising control over their children's access to undesirable media, and at the macrosystem level, with legal controls and government programs designed to minimize the negative features of the media with which children interact. Effective control is complicated, however, by free speech concerns and, in the case of Internet pornography, the global nature of the problem.

SES and Development

As we have frequently noted, the socioeconomic status of their families has profound effects on the development of children. These effects originate at every level of the bioecological model. In the microsystem, children are affected by the nature of their family's housing and their neighborhood, and in the mesosystem, by the condition of their school and the quality of their teachers. Exosystem influences include the nature of the parents' employment or lack of employment. Macrosystem factors include the government policies that affect employment opportunities and establish programs like Head Start geared to low-income families.

Chronosystem factors also come into play with respect to changes over time in the kind and number of jobs that are available. For example, in the United States, the number of well-paying manufacturing jobs has been shrinking for many years, ravaging whole communities with skyrocketing unemployment. The shrinking tax base in those communities results in fewer resources to support schools, playgrounds, and other community resources important for developing children.

The Pervasive Effects of Poverty In many of our discussions throughout this book, we focus on a number of factors that affect the development of children living in poverty. However, the factors we discuss are only the tip of the iceberg. Table 9.1 lists a wide variety of ways that the environment of poor children in the United States differs from that of more affluent children (summarized from Evans, 2004). Many of the items in the table will be familiar to you, but you may never have considered some of the others. As you look over the table, think about how these various aspects of impoverished environments interact and what their cumulative impact might be. Also, consider how the many detrimental factors listed in the table relate to the different levels of the bioecological model, from government priorities and policies to the physical health of the individual child growing up in poverty.

As you look over the table, you should also keep in mind two points from our discussion of the multiple-risk model in Chapter 2. First, it is the *accumulated* exposure to multiple environmental risk factors that is crucial (Evans, 2004). A child whose parents are neglectful might cope reasonably well, but doing so would be more difficult if the child also goes to a poor-quality school in a dangerous neighborhood. Second, individual children differ with respect to how susceptible they are to environmental influences, both positive and negative (Belsky, Bakeman, Kronenberg, & van IJzendorn, 2002).

Because many specific effects of poverty on development are discussed throughout the book, we will not feature them here, but instead will examine a developmental effect of SES that often goes unnoticed: the cost of affluence.

Who do you think attends this school—children from poor or well-to-do families?

J. A. GIORDANO / CORBIS SABA

TABLE 9.1

The Environment of Childhood Poverty

Some ways that the physical and social environments of children growing up in poverty differ from the environments of more well-off children:

PHYSICAL ENVIRONMENT

Home

- Inadequate housing
- Structural deficiencies
- Inadequate heat
- Unsafe drinking water
- Poor air quality in house (including parental smoking)
- Rodent infestation
- Few safety features (e.g., smoke alarms)
- Crowding (number of people in home)
- Small yards (if any)

Neighborhood

- Exposure to toxins
  - Air pollution (e.g., near highways, factories)
  - Water, soil pollution (factories, toxic waste dumps)
  - Exposure to contaminants (lead, pesticides)
- Few parks or open spaces
- Few places for informal gatherings
- Inadequate municipal services (garbage, police, fire)
- Few stores, services, including supermarkets
- Less bus, taxi service
- More bars, taverns
- More physical hazards (traffic volume, street crossings, playground safety)

SOCIAL ENVIRONMENT

Home

- Low parental education
- Low parental income
- Employment instability
- Frequent change of residence
- Social isolation (small social networks)
- Less social support
- Lower marital quality (conflict)
- More domestic violence (spousal, child abuse)
- Higher divorce rate
- More single-parent households
- Harsher, punitive parenting
- Low monitoring of children
- Less emotional support
- More corporal punishment
- Less speech from parents
- Less frequent literacy activities
- Fewer computers/older computers
- Less access to Internet
- More TV watching

School

- Poor quality day care
- Aggressive, violent peers
- Unstable peer relations
- Poorer quality teachers
- High teacher turnover
- High student absenteeism
- Less parent involvement in school
- Less sense of belonging to school
- Inadequate buildings (plumbing, heating, lighting, etc.)
- Overcrowding

Neighborhood

- High crime rates
- High level of violence
- Widespread unemployment
- Fewer positive adult role models
- Few social resources

Source: Evans, G. W. (2004). The environment of childhood poverty. *American Psychologist, 59,* 77–92.

The Costs of Affluence Contrary to popular assumption, growing up in highly affluent families can have negative effects on development. The stereotype of the "poor little rich kid" seems to have some basis in fact. For example, compared with inner-city adolescents, affluent youth report higher levels of anxiety, greater depression, and more use of illicit substances (cigarettes, alcohol, marijuana, and other drugs) (Luthar, 2005). Although adolescents' use of illicit substances is linked with depression and anxiety, it is also associated with popularity, suggesting that peer influences may actively promote this behavior.

In attempting to account for these findings, Luthar and Becker (2002) note that affluent parents tend to pressure their children to excel both academically and in extracurricular activities. At the same time, these parents often provide their children with little support. For example, due to the career demands of the parents and their children's many after-school activities, family time is diminished in many high-income families (Luthar & Latendresse, 2005; Rosenfeld & Wise, 2000). In addition, because of the parents' dual careers, many preteens from upper-income families are home alone after school, unsupervised, for several hours a week (Capizzano, Tout, & Adams, 2002).

A rather remarkable fact is that teens whose family income was fairly low reported higher feelings of closeness with their mothers and fathers than did those whose family income was much higher (U.S. Department of Health and Human

Services, 1999). In addition, the level of happiness reported by youth is not directly related to their family's level of affluence (Csikszentmihalyi & Schneider, 2000).

JENNIE WOODCOCK, REFLECTIONS PHOTOLIBRARY / CORBIS

Teenagers growing up in affluent families are more likely than their peers to smoke, drink alcohol, and use marijuana.

Current Perspectives

The three theoretical positions discussed in this section have all made valuable contributions to developmental science by placing individual development in a much broader context than is typically done in mainstream psychology. All of them challenge researchers to look beyond the lab—far beyond it.

The primary contribution of ethology and evolutionary psychology comes from the emphasis on children's biological nature, including genetic tendencies grounded in evolution. Evolutionary psychology has provided fascinating insights into human development, but it has also come in for serious criticism. One frequent complaint is that, like psychoanalytic theories, many of the claims of evolutionary psychologists are impossible to test. Often, a behavioral pattern that is consistent with an evolutionary account is at least equally consistent with social learning or some other perspective. Finally, evolutionary-psychology theories tend to overlook one of the most remarkable features of human beings, a feature strongly emphasized by Bronfenbrenner—our capacity to transform our environments and ourselves.

Bronfenbrenner's bioecological model has made an important contribution to our thinking about development. His emphasis on the broad context of development and the many different interactions among factors at various levels has highlighted how complex the development of every child is. The main criticism of this model is its lack of emphasis on biological factors.

What is the relevance of ecological theories to Kismet's design? Evolution is basically irrelevant. Evolutionary change does not apply to individual development, and, without the possibility for reproduction, it simply cannot occur.

With respect to the bioecological model, Kismet is developing in an extremely limited microsystem—a lab at MIT—populated with a relatively small number of people. He has no mesosystem at present, although that could change in the future. This fact makes his experience quite different from that of most human children. He could be affected by the macrosystem at any time, if changes in research priorities of the federal government cut off funding for the project. (How sad to think of Kismet falling into poverty.) In terms of the chronosystem, such a remarkable robot was unimaginable until a relatively few years ago, and even more remarkable ones will almost certainly emerge in the relatively near future.

It is interesting that the most difficult parallels to draw between Kismet's development and that of children and theories of social development concern the larger context of human development. Part of what is unique about the human species is the fact that every individual is embedded in multiple layers of human interactions, institutions, traditions, and history.

review:

The theories we have grouped under the label "ecological theories" examine development in a much broader context than those found in other theoretical approaches. Theories of development based on ethology and evolutionary psychology emphasize the influence of the evolutionary history of the human species on the development of individual children. Parental-investment theory proposes that the perpetuation of one's genes underlies the enormous effort that parents invest in raising their children.

Other evolutionary theories emphasize the adaptive function of prolonged immaturity in the development of human children. Urie Bronfenbrenner's highly influential bioecological model conceptualizes the environment in which children develop as a set of nested systems, or contexts. The systems range from aspects of the environment that the individual child directly experiences on a daily basis to the broader society and historical time in which the child lives.

Chapter Summary

Four major types of social development theories present contrasting views of the social world of children.

Psychoanalytic Theories

- The psychoanalytic theory of Sigmund Freud has had an enormous impact on developmental psychology and psychology as a whole, primarily through Freud's emphasis on the importance of early experience for personality and social development, his depiction of unconscious motivation and processes, and his emphasis on the importance of close relationships.
- Freud posited five biologically determined stages of psychosexual development (oral, anal, phallic, latency, genital) in which psychic energy becomes focused in different areas of the body. Children face specific conflicts at each stage, and these conflicts must be resolved for healthy development to proceed. Freud also posited three structures of personality—id (unconscious urges), ego (rational thought), and superego (conscience).
- Freud believed that the Oedipus complex and the Electra complex form the basis for superego (conscience) development, as children identify with and adopt the values of their same-sex parent. He thought that girls develop a weaker conscience than boys do.
- Erik Erikson extended Freud's theory by identifying eight stages of psychosocial development extending across the entire life span. Each stage is characterized by a developmental crisis that, if not successfully resolved, will continue to trouble the individual.

Learning Theories

- John Watson believed strongly in the power of environmental factors, especially reinforcement, to influence children's development.
- B. F. Skinner held that all behavior can be explained in terms of operant conditioning. He discovered the importance of intermittent reinforcement and the powerful reinforcing value of attention.
- Albert Bandura's social learning theory and his empirical research established that children can learn simply by observing other people. Bandura has increasingly stressed the importance of cognition in social learning.

Theories of Social Cognition

- Social cognitive theories assume that children's knowledge and beliefs are vitally important in social development.
- Robert Selman's theory proposes that children go through four stages in the development of the ability to take the role or perspective of another person. They progress from the simple appreciation that someone can have a view different from their own to being able to think about the view of a "generalized other."
- The social information-processing approach to social cognition emphasizes the importance of children's attributions regarding their own and others' behavior. The role of such attribution is clearly reflected in the hostile attributional bias, described by Dodge, which leads children to assume hostile intent on the part of others and to respond aggressively in situations in which the intention of others is ambiguous.
- Dweck's theory of self-attribution focuses on how children's achievement motivation is influenced by their attributions about the reasons for their successes and failures. Children with an incremental/mastery orientation enjoy working on challenging problems and tend to be persistent in trying to solve them, whereas children with an entity/helpless orientation prefer situations in which they expect to succeed and tend to withdraw when they experience failure.

Ecological Theories of Development

- Ethological theories examine behavior within the evolutionary context, trying to understand its adaptive or survival value. The research of Konrad Lorenz on imprinting has been particularly relevant to certain theories of social development in children. Sex differences have been documented in children's toy and play preferences.
- Evolutionary psychologists apply Darwinian concepts of natural selection to human behavior. Characteristic of their approach are parental-investment theory and the idea that the long period of immaturity and dependence in human infancy enables young children to learn and practice many of the skills needed later in life.
- Bronfenbrenner's bioecological model conceptualizes the environment as a set of nested contexts, with the child at the center. These contexts range from the microsystem, which includes the activities, roles, and relationships in which a child directly participates on a regular basis, to the chronosystem, the historical context that affects all the other systems.

Critical Thinking Questions

1. What influences of Freud's theory of development can you identify in modern society?
2. The concept of self-socialization plays a prominent role in social cognitive theories. Explain what is meant by this term. To what extent and in what ways do the other major theories reviewed in the chapter allow for the possibility of self-socialization?
3. Consider your behavior when preparing for and taking tests and when receiving feedback on your academic performance. Do you see yourself as having primarily an incremental/mastery orientation or an entity/helpless orientation to academic achievement?
4. Imagine yourself raising a child. Identify one or two things from each of the four types of theories discussed in this chapter that you think might be helpful to you as a parent.
5. Consider Box 9.2 on attention-deficit hyperactivity disorder (pages 370–371) and analyze what is discussed there in terms of Bronfenbrenner's bioecological model.

Key Terms

psychic energy, p. 344
erogenous zones, p. 344
id, p. 345
oral stage, p. 345
ego, p. 345
anal stage, p. 346
phallic stage, p. 346
superego, p. 346
internalization, p. 346
Oedipus complex, p. 346
Electra complex, p. 347
latency period, p. 347
genital stage, p. 347
systematic desensitization, p. 352
intermittent reinforcement, p. 353
behavior modification, p. 353
vicarious reinforcement, p. 354
reciprocal determinism, p. 355
perceived self-efficacy, p. 356
self-socialization, p. 358
role taking, p. 358
hostile attributional bias, p. 359
entity/helpless orientation, p. 360
incremental/mastery orientation, p. 360
entity theory, p. 360
incremental theory, p. 361
ethology, p. 363
imprinting, p. 363
parental-investment theory, p. 365
microsystem, p. 366
mesosystem, p. 368
exosystem, p. 368
macrosystem, p. 368
chronosystem, p. 368
child maltreatment, p. 369
ADHD (attention-deficit hyperactivity disorder), p. 370

PHILIP EVERGOOD, *Her World*, 1948

10

Emotional Development

THEMES

Nature and Nurture

❖

The Active Child

❖

Continuity/Discontinuity

❖

The Sociocultural Context

❖

Individual Differences

❖

Imagine the following situation. A young girl is taken to a room in her preschool where an experimenter shows her some tasty treats such as M&Ms, marshmallows, or pretzels. Then the experimenter tells the girl that he is going to leave the room "for a while" and that she has two choices. If she waits until he returns to the room, she can have two of the treats. Or if she wishes, she can ring a bell and the experimenter will return immediately—but she will get only one treat. The child is then left alone for a considerable period of time, say 15 to 20 minutes, or until she rings the bell.

Walter Mischel and his colleagues used this procedure in numerous studies with preschoolers and young school-age children to study their ability to delay immediate gratification in order to obtain larger rewards. Videotaping what the children did during the time they were alone with the treats, they found that the children varied in their responses. Some distracted themselves by talking to themselves, singing, trying to sleep, or making up games to play. Others kept looking at the rewards or the bell.

Which children do you think were most successful at curbing their desire for the treat and holding out for the larger reward? Of course, the children who distracted themselves (Mischel, 1981; Rodriguez, Mischel, & Shoda, 1989). More important, the amount of time children were able to delay requesting the treat proved to be a remarkably good predictor of their social and cognitive competence and their coping skills at an older age. For example, ten years after the experiment, the children were rated by their parents with regard to their academic and social competence, as well as their verbal fluency, rational thinking, attentiveness, planfulness, and ability to deal with frustration. Those who had waited the longest in Mischel's experiment were rated higher on these dimensions than were those who had summoned the experimenter back after shorter periods of time (Mischel, Shoda, & Peake, 1988; Peake, Hebl, & Mischel, 2002). In high school, they also obtained higher SAT scores (Shoda, Mischel, & Peake, 1990), and at about age 27, they had achieved a higher educational level, had higher self-esteem, and were reported to be better able to cope with stress. Men in this group also were less likely to have used cocaine or crack in the past year (Ayduk, Mendoza-Denton, Downey, Peake, & Rodriguez, 2000; Mischel & Ayduk, 2004; Peake & Mischel, 2000).

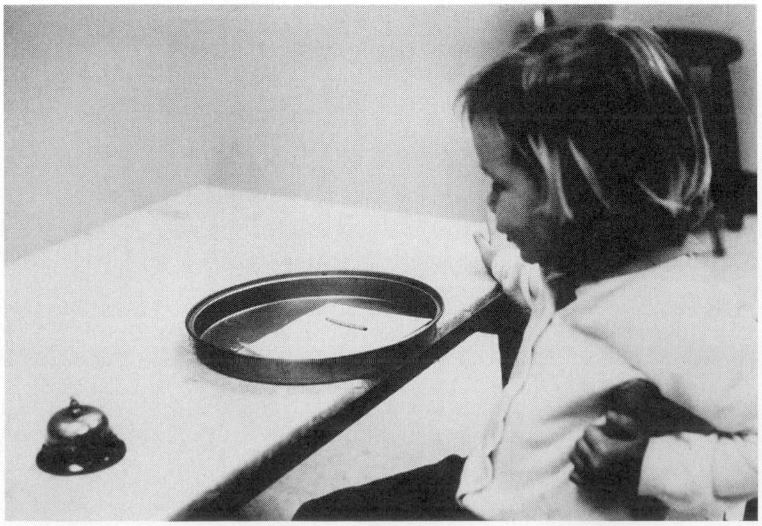

BASED ON MISCHEL, W. EBBESON, E.B., & ZEISS, A.R. (1972). COGNITIVE & ATTENTIONAL MECHANISMS IN DELAY OF GRATIFICATION. *JOURNAL OF PERSONALITY AND SOCIAL PSYCHOLOGY* 21: 204–218

This girl was in one of Mischel's studies of preschoolers' delay of gratification. Children can delay longer if they avert their attention from the desirable object (a pretzel in this study).

That the ability to delay gratification in one situation in preschool predicted social, emotional, and academic competence so many years later illustrates the importance of what has been labeled "emotional intelligence," or "affective social competence." **Emotional intelligence** refers to a set of abilities that are key to competent social functioning. These abilities include being able to motivate oneself and persist in the face of frustration, control impulses and delay gratification, identify and understand one's own and others' feelings, regulate one's moods, regulate the expression of emotion in social interactions, and empathize with others' emotions (Goleman, 1995; Halberstadt, Denham, & Dunsmore, 2001; Matthews, Zeidner, & Roberts, 2002).

The importance of emotional intelligence is reflected in the fact that, more than almost any other measure, it predicts how well people do in life, especially in their social lives. In some cases, it is even more predictive than IQ. For example, in a study in which researchers followed up with 450 boys from impoverished neighborhoods when those boys reached middle age, how well these boys had done at work and in other areas of their lives had relatively little relation to their IQs. Rather, their successfulness corresponded with their ability to manage their frustration, control their emotions, and get along with others (Felsman & Vaillant, 1987). The similarity between the results of this study and the findings of Mischel and his colleagues underscores the point that our emotions, and how we deal with them, play a huge role in the quality of our lives and in our relationships with others.

In this chapter, we examine the development of children's emotions as well as the development of their ability to regulate their emotions and the behavior associated with them. In addition, we discuss the development of children's understanding of emotion, which affects how well they can control their emotions and behavior. In the course of our discussion, we will give particular emphasis to several of our themes. Key among them will be the theme of *individual differences,* as we examine differences among children in various aspects of their emotional functioning. We also discuss the origins of these differences, including heredity, parental socialization practices, cultural beliefs related to emotion, and how the child's behavior in a given context affects his or her physiological reactions. Thus, the themes of *nature and nurture* and the *sociocultural context* will also be prominent. The theme of the *active child* is also touched upon with respect to children's attempts to regulate their own emotions and behavior. Finally, the theme of *continuity versus discontinuity* is discussed briefly in regard to the emergence of self-conscious emotions.

The Development of Emotions in Childhood

Most people take the idea of **emotion** for granted and just equate the term with "feelings." However, developmentalists have a much more complex view of emotions. They see emotions in terms of several components: (1) physiological factors, including heart and breath rate, hormone levels, and the like; (2) subjective feelings; (3) the cognitions that may elicit or accompany subjective feelings; and (4) the desire to take action, including the desire to escape, approach, or change people or things in the environment. A simple example illustrates these components in combination: when people experience fear in response to a growling dog, they typically experience heightened physiological arousal, have the subjective experience of fearfulness, probably are thinking about the ways in which the dog might hurt them, and have the motivation to get away from the dog.

emotional intelligence a set of abilities that contribute to competence in the social and emotional domains

emotion emotion is characterized by physiological responses, subjective feelings, cognitions related to those feelings, and the desire to take action

Although most psychologists share this general view of emotions, they often do not agree on the relative importance of its key components (Saarni et al., 1998; Sroufe, 1995). For example, some theorists believe that cognition plays a much more important role in the experience of emotion than do other theorists. Moreover, there is considerable debate concerning the degree to which emotions are innate versus learned and about when and in what form different emotions emerge during infancy.

Before considering the development of specific emotions in childhood, we first need to examine some of the major views that have been proposed regarding the nature and emergence of emotions.

Theories on the Nature and Emergence of Emotion

The debate about the nature and emergence of emotions in children has deep roots. In *The Expression of the Emotions in Man and Animals,* published in 1872, Charles Darwin argued that the facial expressions for certain basic emotional states are innate to the species—and therefore similar across all peoples—and are found even in very young babies. A corresponding view held by some current investigators such as Silvan Tomkins and Carroll Izard is **discrete emotions theory,** which argues that each emotion is innately packaged with a specific set of physiological, bodily, and facial reactions and that distinct emotions are evident from very early in life (Izard, 2007; Tomkins, 1962).

Other researchers maintain that emotions are not distinct from one another at the beginning of life and that environmental factors play an important role in the emergence and expression of emotions. Some argue, for example, that infants experience only excitement and distress in the first weeks of life, and that other emotions emerge at later ages as a function of experience. According to Alan Sroufe (1979, 1995), there are three basic affect systems—joy/pleasure, anger/frustration, and wariness/fear—and these systems undergo developmental change from primitive to more advanced forms during the early years of life. For example, wariness/fear is first expressed as a startle or pain reaction. At a few months of age, infants start to show wariness of novel situations, and a few months later show clear signs of fear in novel situations. In Sroufe's view, such changes are largely due to infants' expanding social experiences and their increasing ability to understand them.

The role of the environment is also emphasized by theorists who take a **functionalist approach** to understanding emotional development. They propose that the basic function of emotions is to promote action toward achieving a goal in a given context (Campos, Mumme, Kermoian, & Campos, 1994; Saarni et al., 2006). The emotion of fear, for instance, often causes one to flee or otherwise avoid a stimulus that represents a threat. This action helps achieve the goal of self-preservation (see Table 10.1 for other examples). Functionalists such as Joseph Campos have also argued that emotional reactions are affected by social goals and the influence of significant others. For example, young children's experience of emotions such as shame and guilt is related to the values and standards communicated to them by their parents, the manner in which the values and standards are communicated, and the quality of the children's relationships with their parents.

Although these perspectives differ in whether or not they assert that distinct emotions emerge early in life, each with its own set of physiological components, they all agree that cognition and experience shape emotional development. However, few theories within these perspectives offer a detailed description of the emotional processing that accounts for the great variation in emotional experience

discrete emotions theory a theory about emotions, held by Tomkins, Izard, and others, in which emotions are viewed as innate and discrete from one another from very early in life, and each emotion is believed to be packaged with a specific and distinctive set of bodily and facial reactions

functionalist approach a theory of emotion, proposed by Campos and others, that argues that the basic function of emotions is to promote action toward achieving a goal. In this view, emotions are not discrete from one another and vary somewhat based on the social environment.

TABLE 10.1

Characteristics of Some Families of Emotion

Emotion type	Goal connected with the emotion	Meaning regarding the self	Meaning regarding others	Action tendency
Disgust	Avoiding contamination or illness	This stimulus may contaminate me or make me ill	—	Active rejection of the thing causing disgust
Fear	Maintaining one's own physical and psychological integrity	This stimulus is threatening to me	—	Flight or withdrawal
Anger	Attaining the end state that the individual currently is invested in	There is an obstacle to my obtaining my goal	—	Forward movement, especially to eliminate obstacles to one's goal
Sadness	Attaining the end state that the individual currently is invested in	My goal is unattainable	—	Disengagement and withdrawal
Shame	Maintaining others' respect and affection; preserving self-esteem	I am bad (my self-esteem is damaged)	Others notice how bad I am	Withdrawal; avoiding others, hiding oneself
Guilt	Meeting one's own internalized values	I have done something contrary to my values	Someone has been injured by my actions	Movement to make reparation, to inform others, or to punish self

Adapted from Saarni et al. (1998), p. 239

and developmental trajectories across individuals, even among those who share somewhat similar situations or characteristics.

An emerging perspective that explicitly deals with how the child's characteristics and experiences coalesce in emotional processing is *dynamic-systems theory* (see Chapter 4). From a dynamic-systems perspective, novel forms of functioning (emotional or otherwise) arise through the spontaneous coordination of components interacting with each other repeatedly. In these interactions, specific cognitions (including appraisals of events and objects), emotional feelings, and physiological (including neural) events tend to link together more closely with each repeated occasion, forming coherent "emotional interpretations" that become increasingly coordinated each time they are co-activated (Lewis, 2005; also see Camras & Witherington, 2005; Fogel et al., 1992; Izard, Ackerman, Schoff, & Fine, 2000). A dynamic-systems approach to emotional development postulates that emotional reactions develop differently for each person, based on an individual's emotion-related biology and cognitive capacities, his or her experiences, and how these factors tend to coalesce across time in an increasingly coherent and predictable manner.

As you will see in the next section, it is not yet clear to what degree emotions are distinct, emerge early, and can be reliably differentiated. It also is not clear to what degree young children's basic emotions are innate or develop as a consequence of experience.

As is evident from this infant's expression, it often is difficult to identify what negative emotion a young infant is feeling.

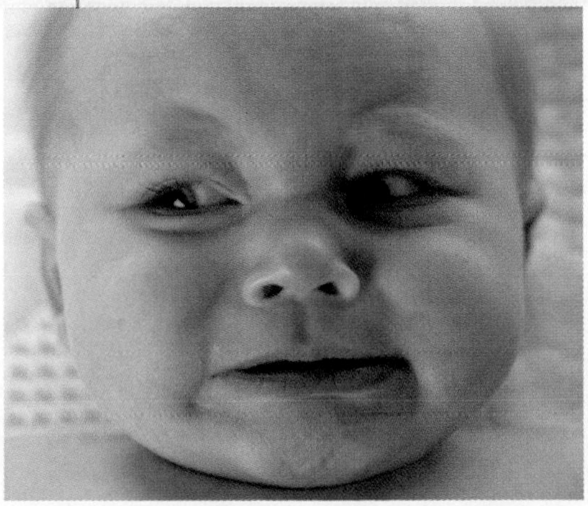

BELYNDA WEBB / SUPERSTOCK

The Emergence of Emotion in the Early Years and Childhood

Parents are likely to think that they see many emotions in their infants, including interest and joy as well as anger, fear, and sadness—even in their 1-month-olds. In fact, however, parents often read into their infant's emotional reaction whatever emotion would seem appropriate in the immediate situation. For example, if an infant reacts negatively when given a

social smiles smiles that are directed at people. They first emerge as early as 6 to 7 weeks of age.

novel toy, the parent may assume that the reaction is fear, when it could just as well be anger or upset at being overstimulated or at having a current activity disrupted.

To make their own interpretations of infants' emotions more objective, researchers have devised highly elaborate systems for identifying the emotional meaning of infants' facial expressions. With these systems, researchers first code dozens of facial cues—whether an infant's eyebrows are raised or knitted together; whether the eyes are wide open, tightly closed, or narrowed; whether the lips are pursed, softly rounded, or retracted straight back; and so on. Then they analyze the combination in which these cues are present. Even with such detailed analysis, however, it is often hard to determine exactly what emotions infants are experiencing, and it is particularly difficult to differentiate among the various negative emotions that young infants express. Correspondingly, getting a clear picture of early emotional development is a more difficult task when it comes to negative emotions than it is with regard to positive emotions.

We begin our examination of the emergence of emotions with the easier task—tracing the early development of positive emotions.

Positive Emotions

The first clear sign of happiness that infants express is smiling. During the first month, they exhibit fleeting smiles, primarily during the REM phase of sleep; after the first month, they sometimes smile when they are stroked gently. These early smiles may be reflexive and seem to be evoked by some biological state rather than by social interaction (Sroufe & Waters, 1976; Wolff, 1987).

Between the third and eighth week of life, infants begin to smile in reaction to external stimuli, including touching, high-pitched voices, or other stimuli that engage their attention (Sroufe, 1995). More important, by the third month of life, and sometimes as early as 6 or 7 weeks of age, babies begin to exhibit **social smiles,** that is, smiles directed toward people (White, 1985). Social smiles frequently occur during interactions with a parent or other familiar people and tend to elicit the adult's delight, interest, and affection (Camras et al., 1991; Huebner & Izard, 1988). In turn, this response usually inspires more social smiling from the infant. Thus, the infant's early social smiles likely promote care from parents and other adults and strengthen the infant's relationships with other people.

In the first weeks of life, infants' smiles tend to be caused by internal factors and are not social.

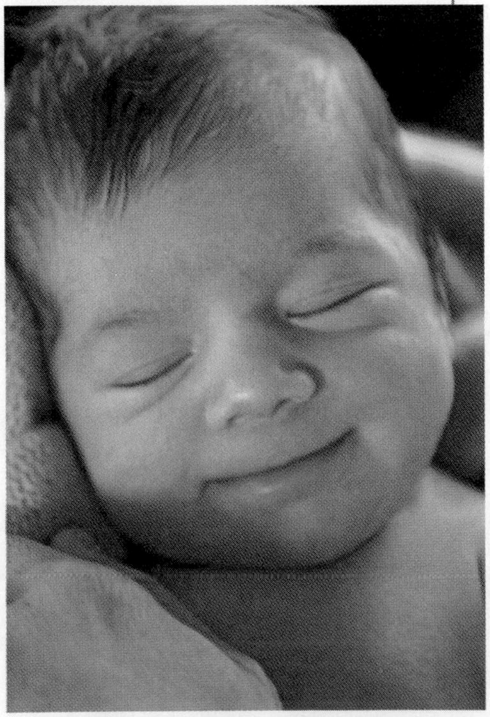

LAURA CIAPPONI / GETTY IMAGES

The social basis of social smiles is highlighted by the fact that although young infants sometimes smile at interesting objects, humans are much more likely to make them smile. This difference was demonstrated in a study in which 3-month-old infants smiled and vocalized much more at people, even strangers, than at puppetlike foam balls that resembled people, were animated, and "talked" to the infant (Ellsworth, Muir, & Hains, 1993).

When infants are at least 2 months of age, they also show happiness in both social and nonsocial contexts in which they can control a particular event. In one study that demonstrated this, researchers divided infants into two groups and attached a string to an arm of each infant. Observing the infants individually, they arranged for infants in one group to hear music whenever they pulled the string and for infants in the other group to hear music at random intervals. The infants who "caused" the music to play by pulling on the string showed more interest and smiling when the music came on than did the infants whose string-pulling had no connection to the music's being played (Lewis, Alessandri, & Sullivan, 1990). This pleasure in controlling events is evident in infants' delight when they can consistently make a noise by shaking their rattle or banging a toy on the floor.

At about 7 months of age, infants start to smile primarily at *familiar* people, rather than at people in general. (In fact, as you will see, unfamiliar people often elicit distress at this age.) These selective smiles tend to delight parents and motivate them to continue interacting with the infant. In turn, infants of this age often respond to parents' playfulness and smiles with excitement and joy, which also prolongs their positive social interactions (Weinberg & Tronick, 1994). Such exchanges of positive affect, especially when they occur with parents and not strangers, make parents feel special to the infant and strengthen the bond between them.

Children's expression of positive emotion increases across the first year of life (Rothbart & Bates, 2006), perhaps because they are able to understand and respond to more interesting and positive events and stimuli. After about 3 or 4 months of age, infants laugh as well as smile during a variety of activities. For example, they are likely to laugh when a parent tickles them or blows on their tummy, bounces them on a knee or swings them around in the air, or shares a favorite activity such as bathing with them. By late in the first year of life, children's cognitive development allows them to take pleasure from unexpected or discrepant events such as Mom's making a funny noise or wearing a goofy hat (Kagan, Kearsley, & Zelazo, 1978).

During the second year of life, children start to clown around themselves and are delighted when they can make other people laugh—as in the case of this 18-month-old who looks at his mother and, fully clothed, sits on his potty:

> *Child:* Poo (grunts heavily). Poo! (grunts). Poo! (gets up, looks at Mother, picks up empty potty, and waves it at Mother, laughing)
>
> (Dunn, 1988, p. 154)

Incidents like this are common in the second year of life and demonstrate infants' desire to share positive emotion and activities with parents.

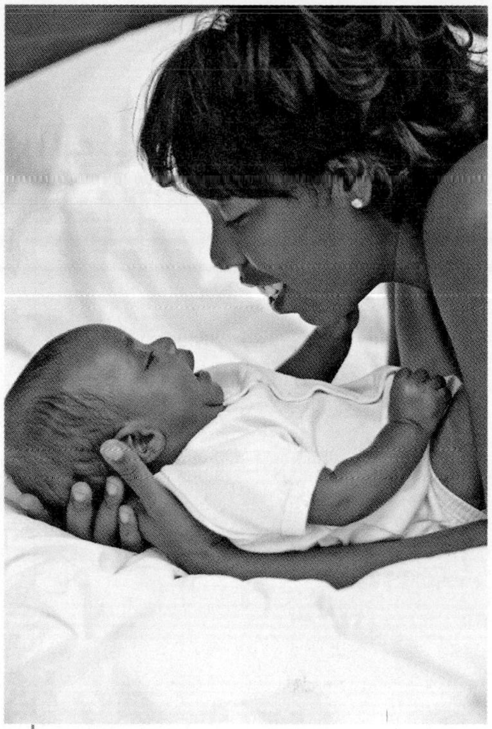

© TOM GRILL / CORBIS

Smiles that arise as a function of social interactions, as contrasted with those associated with strictly biological stimuli, typically first appear during the infant's third month.

Negative Emotions

The first negative emotion that is discernible in newborn infants is generalized distress, which can be evoked by a variety of experiences ranging from hunger and pain to overstimulation. Often expressed with piercing cries and a face screwed up in a tight grimace, this type of distress is unmistakable.

The emergence and development of other negative emotions in infancy are, as noted earlier, more difficult to pin down. A number of studies suggest that negative emotion in young infants continues to be expressed as undifferentiated distress (Oster, Hegley, & Nagel, 1992) and that anger and distress/pain are especially likely to be undifferentiated in most contexts (Camras, 1992). In *some* contexts, however, investigators have been able to differentiate among some negative emotions in fairly young infants. By 2 months of age, for example, facial expressions of what appears to be anger or sadness have been reliably differentiated from one another and from distress/pain in situations such as infants being given an injection during a medical procedure (Izard et al., 1987).

However, the interpretation of negative emotions is complicated by the fact that infants sometimes display negative emotions that seem incongruent with the situation they are experiencing (Camras, 1992; Hiatt, Campos, & Emde, 1979). In the string-pulling study cited earlier, for example, the infants

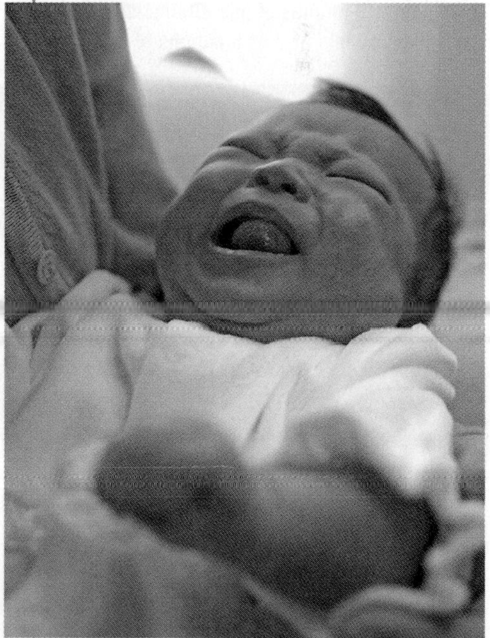

© DOABLE / AMANAIMAGES / CORBIS

Some theorists believe that young infants can experience sadness and anger, whereas others believe that they only experience an undifferentiated state of distress.

who could "control" the music by pulling the string attached to their arms fussed and sometimes expressed anger when pulling the string no longer turned on the music. Other times, however, these infants showed fear when pulling the string no longer produced music (Lewis et al., 1990). In a study in which 11-month-olds in China, Japan, and the United States were put in situations expected to elicit either fear (exposure to a growling gorilla-head toy) or anger (having their arms restrained), they behaved in predictably different ways (e.g., becoming still and breathing more rapidly in the former situation and struggling in the latter); but they did not exhibit distinct facial reactions corresponding to fear and anger in the two contexts (Camras et al., 2007). Incongruities such as these highlight the difficulty of knowing for certain what emotion an infant may be experiencing in certain situations.

Fear and distress Although there is little firm evidence of distinct fear reactions in infants during the first months of life (Witherington, Campos, & Hertenstein, 2001), by 4 months of age, infants do seem wary of unfamiliar objects and events (Sroufe, 1995). Then, at around the age of 6 or 7 months, initial signs of fear begin to appear (Camras et al., 1991), most notably the fear of strangers in many circumstances. This shift likely reflects infants' growing attachment to their parents and their recognition that unfamiliar people do not provide the comfort and pleasure that familiar people do.

Consider the following contrast: At the age of 10 weeks, as Janine was whimpering in her crib, a stranger came over and smiled and talked to her. Janine stopped fussing and smiled at the stranger. At the age of 8 months, Janine is playing on her mother's knee when her mother has to put her down and leave the room to answer the door. A moment later the visitor, a stranger, enters the room without Janine's mother.

> When the visitor enters, Janine cries. The visitor tries to comfort Janine by picking her up and talking softly to her, but she cries still more frantically until her mother returns and holds her. Then Janine calms down and smiles when mother lifts her high in the air in play.
>
> (Bronson, 1972)

STUART COHEN / THE IMAGE WORKS

Young children who were not afraid of strangers at 6 months of age often suddenly show fear of them at 7 or 8 months of age.

In general, the fear of strangers intensifies and lasts until about age 2. However, it should be noted that the fear of strangers is quite variable (Sroufe, 1995), depending on both the infant's temperament (i.e., how fearful the infant is in general) and the specific context, such as whether a parent is present and the manner in which the stranger approaches (e.g., abruptly and excitedly or slowly and calmly).

Other fears also are evident at around the age of 7 months, including fear of novel toys, loud noises, and sudden movements by people or objects, all of which tend to decline after 12 months of age, as shown in Figure 10.1 (Kagan et al., 1978; Scarr & Salapatek, 1970). The emergence of such fears is clearly adaptive. Because babies often do not have the ability to escape from potentially dangerous situations on their own, they must rely on their parents to protect them, and

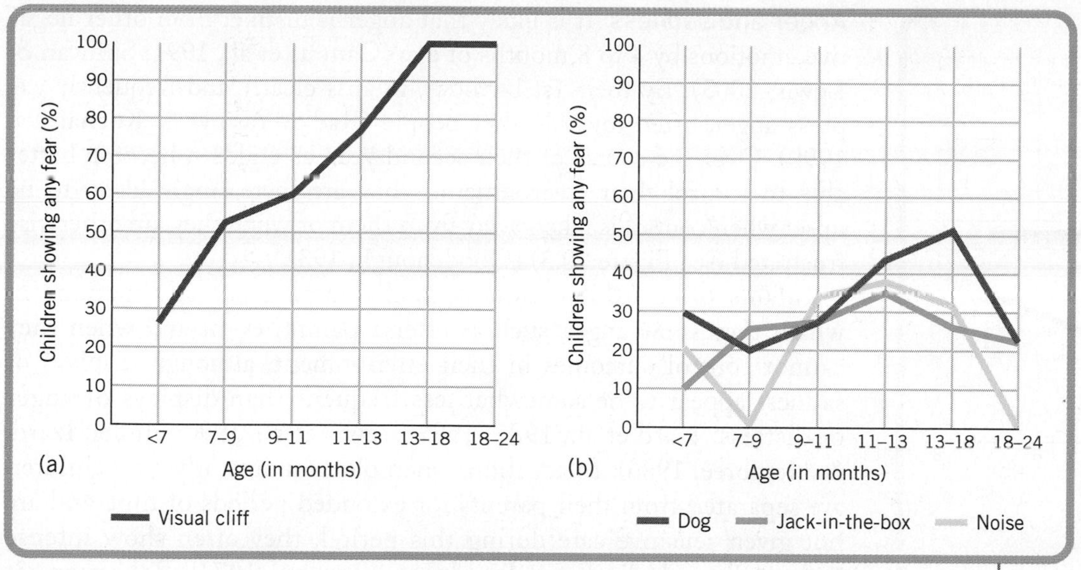

FIGURE 10.1 Percentages of young children showing fear of (a) the visual cliff and (b) dogs, noises, and a jack-in-the-box Children 1½ to 2 years of age show the most fear of the visual cliff. Children show the most fear of the jack-in-the-box and loud noises at about 1 year of age and the most fear of dogs at 1 to 1½ years of age. (Adapted from Scarr & Salapatek, 1970)

expressions of fear and distress are powerful tools for bringing help and support when they are needed.

An especially salient and important type of fear or distress that emerges at about 8 months of age is **separation anxiety**—distress due to separation from the parent that is the child's primary caregiver. When infants experience separation anxiety, they typically whine, cry, or otherwise express fear and upset. However, the degree to which children exhibit such distress varies with the context. For example, infants show much less distress when they crawl or walk away from a parent than when the parent does the departing (Rheingold & Eckerman, 1970). Separation anxiety tends to increase from 8 to 13 or 15 months of age, and then begins to decline (Kagan, 1976).

separation anxiety feelings of distress that children, especially infants and toddlers, experience when they are separated, or expect to be separated, from individuals to whom they are emotionally attached

This pattern of separation anxiety occurs across many cultures, displayed by infants reared in environments as disparate as the United States, Israeli kibbutzim (communal farming communities), and !Kung San hunting-and-gathering groups in the Kalahari Desert in Africa (Kagan, 1976) (see Figure 10.2).

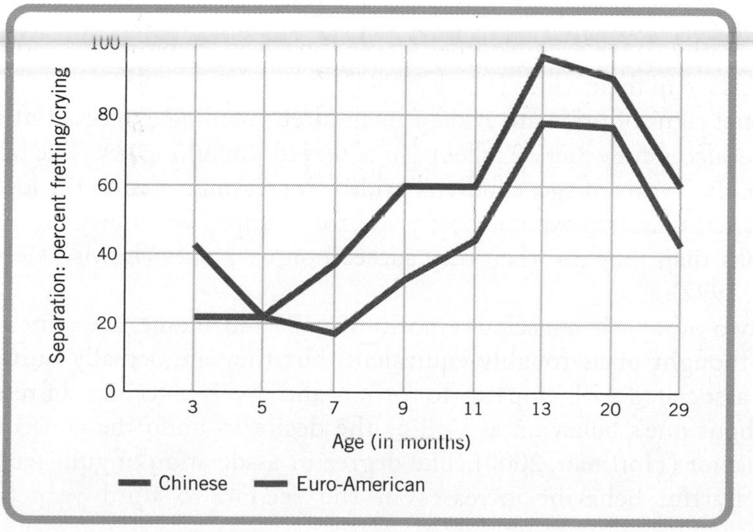

FIGURE 10.2 Percentages of Chinese and Euro-American children at different ages displaying fretting or crying at the departure of mother Children exhibit the most evidence of separation anxiety at about 13 months of age, and Chinese children have been found to display somewhat more anxiety and distress than do Euro-American children. (Adapted from Kagan, Kearsley, & Zelanzo, 1978)

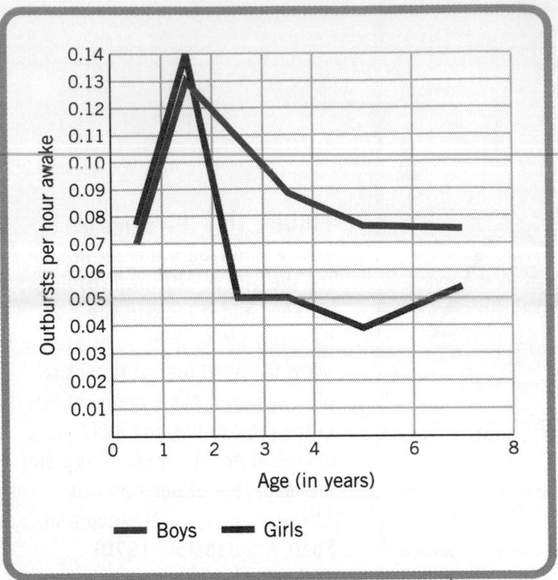

FIGURE 10.3 Frequency of angry outbursts in the home Children display the most anger at home during the second year of life. Displays of anger drop sharply thereafter, especially for girls. (Adapted from Goodenough, 1931)

Anger and sadness It is likely that anger is distinct from other negative emotions by 4 to 8 months of age (Camras et al., 1991; Sullivan & Lewis, 2003). By their 1st birthday, infants clearly and frequently express anger, often toward other people (Radke-Yarrow & Kochanska, 1990). Over the course of their second year, as children become better able to control their environments, they are increasingly likely to be upset when control is taken away from them or when they are otherwise frustrated (see Figure 10.3) (Goodenough, 1931).

Infants often exhibit sadness in the same types of situations in which they show anger, such as after a painful event and when they cannot control outcomes in their environment, although displays of sadness appear to be somewhat less frequent than displays of anger or distress (Izard et al., 1987, 1995; Lewis et al., 1990; Shiller, Izard, & Hembree, 1986). In addition, when older infants or young children are separated from their parents for extended periods of time and are not given sensitive care during this period, they often show intense and prolonged displays of sadness (Bowlby, 1973; Robertson & Robertson, 1971).

The Self-Conscious Emotions: Embarrassment, Pride, Guilt, and Shame

During the second year of life, children begin to show a range of new emotions: embarrassment, pride, guilt, and shame (Stipek, Gralinski, & Kopp, 1990; Thompson, 2006; Zahn-Waxler & Robinson, 1995). These emotions often are called **self-conscious emotions** because they relate to our sense of self and our consciousness of others' reactions to us. Some investigators such as Michael Lewis believe that these emotions emerge in the second year because that is when children gain the understanding that they themselves are entities distinct from other people and begin to develop a sense of self (Lewis, 1998). Such a view implies an abrupt, qualitative change in children's abilities to experience these emotions and suggests discontinuity in emotional development due to the emergence of an underlying cognitive awareness (Lewis, 1998; Mascolo, Fischer, & Li, 2003). The emergence of self-conscious emotions is also fostered by children's growing sense of what adults and society expect of them (Lewis et al., 1992; Mascolo et al., 2003).

At about 15 to 24 months of age, some children start to show embarrassment when they are made the center of attention. Asked to show off an ability or a new piece of clothing, for example, they lower their eyes, hang their head, blush, or hide their face in their hands (Lewis, 1995).

The first signs of pride are evident in children's smiling glances at others when they have successfully met a challenge or achieved something new, like taking their first step. By 3 years of age, children's pride is increasingly tied to the level of their performance. Children express more pride, for example, when they succeed on difficult tasks than they do when they succeed on easy ones (Lewis, Alessandri, & Sullivan, 1992).

The two other self-conscious emotions, guilt and shame, are sometimes mistakenly thought of as roughly equivalent, but they are actually quite distinct. Guilt is associated with empathy for others and involves feelings of remorse and regret about one's behavior, as well as the desire to undo the consequences of that behavior (Hoffman, 2000). The degree of association of guilt feelings with bad or hurtful behavior increases in the second to third year (Aksan &

self-conscious emotions emotions such as guilt, shame, embarrassment, and pride that relate to our sense of self and our consciousness of others' reactions to us

Kochanska, 2005). In contrast, shame does not seem to be related to concern about others. When children feel shame, their focus is on themselves: they feel that they are exposed, and they often feel like hiding (Eisenberg, 2000; Tangney, Stuewig, & Mashek, 2007).

Shame and guilt can be distinguished fairly early, as documented by a study in which researchers arranged for 2-year-olds to play with a doll belonging to an adult (the experimenter). The doll had been rigged so that one leg would fall off during play, while the adult was out of the room. When the "accident" occurred, some toddlers displayed a pattern of behavior that seemed to reflect shame—that is, they avoided the adult when she returned to the room and delayed telling her about the mishap. Other children showed a pattern of behavior that seemed to reflect guilt—that is, they repaired the doll quickly, told the adult about the mishap shortly after she returned to the room, and showed relatively little avoidance of her (Barrett et al., 1993).

Children in the preschool years often exhibit shame or guilt when they do something wrong.

In everyday life, as well, the same situation often elicits shame in some individuals and guilt in others. Which emotion children experience partly depends on parental practices. Studies of North American children have found that they are more likely to experience guilt than shame if, when they have done something wrong, their parents emphasize the "badness" of the behavior ("You did a bad thing") rather than of the child ("You're a bad boy"). In addition, children are more likely to feel guilt rather than shame if their parents help them understand the consequences their actions have for others, teach them the need to repair the harm they have done, avoid publicly humiliating them, and communicate respect and love of their children even when disciplining them (Hoffman, 2000; Tangney & Dearing, 2002).

The situations likely to induce self-conscious emotions in children vary across cultures, as does the frequency with which specific self-conscious emotions are likely to be experienced (Cole, Tamang, & Shrestha, 2006). For example, among traditional Zuni Indians, standing out from others is discouraged. As a result, Zuni children who achieve an individual success, such as doing better than peers on a project, are likely to feel embarrassment or shame (Benedict, 1934). Similarly, the Japanese tend to avoid bestowing praise on the individual because they believe that it encourages a focus on the self rather than on the needs of the larger social group (Lewis, 1992). Correspondingly, Japanese children, in comparison with U.S. children, are less likely to experience pride as a consequence of personal success. Moreover, in many Asian or Southeast Asian cultures that emphasize the welfare of the group rather than the individual, not living up to social or familial obligations is likely to evoke shame or guilt (Mascolo et al., 2003). In such cultures, parents' efforts to elicit shame from their young children are often direct and disparaging (e.g., "You made your mother lose face," "I've never seen any three-year-old who behaves like you") (Fung & Chen, 2001). This kind of explicit belittling appears to have a more positive effect on children in these Asian cultures than it does on children in Western cultures.

Normal Emotional Development in Childhood

The causes of emotions continue to change in childhood. For example, the basis of children's self-esteem or self-evaluation changes with cognitive development and experience (see Chapter 11), and the events that make children feel happiness and pride tend to change accordingly. From early to middle childhood, for instance, acceptance by peers and achieving goals become increasingly important, and successes in these areas become key sources of happiness and pride. What makes children smile and laugh also changes with age. As their language skills develop along with their understanding of people and events, children in the preschool years begin to find verbal jokes funny (Dunn, 1988).

Similar examples can be seen in regard to children's negative emotions. For instance, as children's cognitive ability to represent imaginary phenomena develops in the preschool years, they often start to fear imaginary creatures such as ghosts or monsters. Such fears are uncommon in elementary school children (Silverman, La Greca, & Wasserstein, 1995), probably because children of this age have a better understanding of reality than do younger children. Instead, school-age children's anxieties and fears are generally related to important, real-life issues (albeit sometimes exaggerated), such as challenges at school (tests and grades, being called on in class, and pleasing teachers), health (their parents' and their own), and personal harm (being robbed, mugged, or shot). In one study of U.S. 2nd to 5th graders, 56% of the children reported worries about being physically attacked or otherwise harmed by someone (Silverman et al., 1995).

The causes of anger also change as children develop a better understanding of others' intentions and motives. For example, in the early preschool years, a child is likely to feel anger when harmed by a peer whether or not the harm was intentional. In contrast, children in the early school years are less likely to be angered if they believe that harm done to them was unintentional or that the motive for some harmful action was benign rather than malicious (Coie & Dodge, 1998; Dodge, Murphy, & Buchsbaum, 1984).

The frequency with which specific emotions are experienced also may change in childhood and adolescence. There is some evidence, for example, that over the course of the preschool and early school years, children generally become less emotionally intense and negative (Guerin & Gottfried, 1994; Murphy, Eisenberg, Fabes, Shepard, & Guthrie, 1999). There also is some support for the common assumption that negative emotion increases after middle childhood. Typically, early to middle adolescence is marked by an increase in the frequency or intensity of negative emotions and a decrease in positive emotion. For most youths, the increase is mild (Larson & Lampman-Petraitis, 1989; Larson, Moneta, Richards, & Wilson, 2002; Weinstein, Mermelstein, Hankin, Hedeker, & Flay, 2007), but for a minority, it is quite sharp, often in their relations with their parents (Collins & Steinberg, 2006; Laursen, Coy, & Collins, 1998; see Chapter 12). This negative shift in average emotions generally appears to end by grade 10, and older adolescents also experience less emotional liability (i.e., change from day to day) than do young adolescents (Larson et al., 2002; Weinstein et al., 2007).

Of course, children's emotional states are highly influenced by the world around them, with negative emotion being intensified by stressful conditions. As might be expected, children and adolescents directly exposed to war or terrorism tend to experience unusually high levels of fear, anxiety, and depression (Joshi & O'Donnell, 2003; Shaw, 2003). Exposure to lesser stressors, such as interparental conflict in the home, also appears to increase children's experience of negative emotion (Rhoades, 2008).

It is common for children to experience a modest increase in negative emotions as they move into adolescence. Often this increase is evidenced in family interactions.

© ELLEN SENISI / THE IMAGE WORKS

Depression

Serious bouts of depression are much more common in adolescence than in childhood. Prior to adolescence, a child's chance of experiencing a period of serious depression is less than 1 to 3% (Hammen & Rudolph, 2003; Kessler, 2002). In contrast, the rate of clinical depression that is, depression warranting treatment—is 15% or even higher from about age 15 to 18 years (Hammen & Rudolph, 2003; Hankin et al., 1998), with about 6% of adolescents in this age group experiencing major depression (Kessler, 2002) (see Figure 10.4).

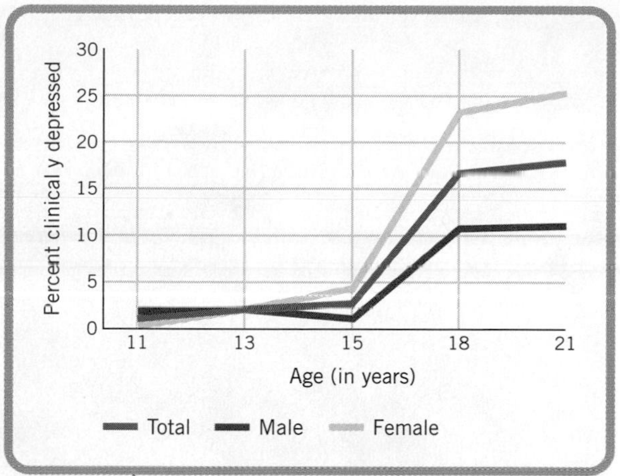

FIGURE 10.4 Development of overall rates of clinical depression by gender and age Rates of depression increase in early adolescence and increase dramatically at age 15 to 18, especially for girls. (Adapted from Hankin et al., 1998)

Major depression is characterized by some combination of the following symptoms, occurring nearly every day: depressed mood most of the time; marked diminished interest or pleasure in almost all activities; significant weight loss; insomnia or excessive sleeping; motor agitation; fatigue or loss of energy; feelings of worthlessness or excessive or inappropriate guilt; diminished ability to think or concentrate; recurrent thoughts of death (Hammen & Rudolph, 2003). Besides these specific diagnostic criteria, social withdrawal and bodily complaints are common in depressed youth, as is anxiety (Turner & Barrett, 2003).

In addition to the adolescents who experience major depression, 11% of U.S. youths experience depressive symptoms that are not severe and persistent enough to be classified as clinical (Hammen & Rudolph, 2003). As discussed in Box 10.1, this rate is even higher for females. For example, in one study, approximately 21% of 11- to 16-year-old females exhibited significant symptoms of nonclinical depression (Cooper & Goodyer, 1993).

individual differences 10.1

Gender Differences in Adolescent Depression

One of the most striking features of adolescent depression is the gender-related differences in its occurrence (Costello et al., 2008; Twenge & Nolen-Hoeksema, 2002). By approximately age 13 to 15 in the United States, girls begin exhibiting higher rates of depression than do boys (Cole et al., 2002; Garber, Keiley, & Martin, 2002; Hankin & Abramson, 1999), and by about age 18, the difference is quite large (see Figure 10.4). Similar gender differences in the patterns of adolescent depression have been found in numerous countries (Galambos, Leadbeater, & Barker, 2004; Hankin et al., 1998; Wichstrom, 1999).

Why are teenage females more likely to experience depression? While there is some evidence for the role of hormones and heredity (Hankin & Abramson, 1999), it seems more likely that the key factor is the greater stress that adolescence represents for females (Petersen, Sarigiani, & Kennedy, 1991), at least in certain cultures. One important stressor can be concerns about one's body and appearance. As discussed in Chapter 15, adolescent females in the United States report greater dissatisfaction with their bodies than males report with theirs. This dissatisfaction, fueled by a cultural obsession with an "ideal" body type attainable only by a few, seems to contribute substantially to low self-esteem and depression in adolescent girls (Compian, Gowen, & Hayward, 2004; Hankin & Abramson, 1999; Harter, 2006; Wichstrom, 1999).

Another stressor for girls can be early puberty, which represents a clear risk for depression. Early maturity may create stress for girls because it often leads to involvement with older adolescent males, who may pressure them to engage in sexual activity, drinking, or delinquency. Many younger girls are not cognitively and socially mature enough to cope with these pressures (Ge, Conger, & Elder, 1996; Ge et al., 2003). Although early puberty is initially related to depression for boys, it does not persist (Ge et al., 2003).

Concerns about peer acceptance can also be a source of stress, and girls appear to be more likely than boys to be upset and depressed by problems in their peer relationships (Hankin, Mermelstein, & Roesch, 2007; Nolen-Hoeksema, 2001). It is also likely that adolescent girls are more prone than their male peers to repeatedly focus on symptoms of their distress ("I'm so fat" or "I'm so tired") and on the meaning of their distress ("What's wrong with my life?") (Nolen-Hoeksema, Larson, & Grayson, 1999). Such thinking appears to increase the chances of females' becoming depressed (Hankin & Abramson, 1999; Nolen-Hoeksema, Stice, Wade, & Bohon, 2007). This may be especially true during puberty because of girls' heightened sensitivity to changes in their bodies and in their relationships with others (Rudolph & Flynn, 2007).

DAVID GROSSMAN / PHOTO RESEARCHERS, INC.

Depression is much more common in adolescent girls than boys and frequently is accompanied by unhappiness with one's appearance and weight.

Some investigators have found that poorer children are especially prone to major depression (Hammen & Rudolph, 2003). In terms of nonclinical symptoms of depression, adolescents' self-reports do not reflect such socioeconomic differences. They do, however, suggest some ethnic differences, with Hispanic children reporting more symptoms of depression than do Euro-American or African-American youth (Twenge & Nolen-Hoeksema, 2002). Moreover, there may be cultural differences in the prevalence of adolescent depression: for example, Chinese adolescents tend to experience depressive symptoms more than do their U.S. counterparts (Greenberger, Chen, Tally, & Dong, 2000).

Children and adolescents who experience depression frequently exhibit behavioral problems such as aggression, stealing, delinquency, and substance abuse (see Chapter 14; Hammen & Rudolph, 2003; Wiesner & Kim, 2006). Not surprisingly, depressed youths often also have difficulties in their relationships with peers (Rudolph, Ladd, & Dinella, 2007).

There are many possible causes of depression. One is heredity, since major depression often runs in families. Children whose mothers are depressed tend to exhibit a pattern of activation in the prefrontal cortex that is associated with greater reactivity to the environment, negative emotionality, and withdrawal; they also may have elevated hormone-based stress reactivity (Cicchetti & Toth, 2006). These biological correlates likely are partly due to a genetic vulnerability, but they also could be exacerbated by problems in parenting that often accompany maternal depression (Cicchetti & Toth, 2006), including insensitivity and disengagement (Campbell, Matestic, von Stauffenberg, Mohan, & Kirchner, 2007; Lau, Rijskijk, Gregory, McGuffin, & Eley, 2007; Lovejoy et al., 2000).

Other family factors likely also contribute to depression in youth. In particular, children's symptoms of depression are frequently associated with low levels of family engagement, support, and acceptance. This pattern is often characterized by parents' punishing or "dampening" responses to their children's expressions of positive emotion and by high levels of negative feedback (Jacquez, Cole, & Searle, 2004; Kim, Ge et al., 2003; McCarty & McMahon, 2003; Yap, Allen, & Ladouceur, 2008). Chronic stress and conflict in the family also predict depression in youth (Brennan, Hammen, Katz, & Le Brocque, 2002; Kim, Capaldi, & Stoolmiller, 2003).

In addition, some investigators emphasize the role that maladaptive belief systems play in the onset and maintenance of depression (Beck, 1983; Hammen & Rudolph, 2003). They argue, for example, that depressed individuals tend to see themselves and others in an excessively negative way and, thus, feel incompetent and worthless and view the world as cruel and unfair (Bohon, Stice, Burton, Fudell, & Nolen-Hoeksema, 2008; Hoffman, Cole, Martin, Tram, & Seroczynski, 2000; Rudolph & Clark, 2001). They may also feel that they cannot change things for the better because they believe that negative events are beyond their control and they do not take credit for their accomplishments (Garber, Keiley, & Martin, 2002; Gregory et al., 2007; Seligman, 1975). Depressed youths also tend to pay excessive attention to the potential causes and negative consequences of their symptoms (Schniering & Rapee, 2004); this rumination can interfere with effective problem solving (Nolen-Hoeksema, 1991; Silk et al., 2003). All these ideas about the causes of depression have received some support from research (Hammen & Rudolph, 2003).

Other investigators argue that youths get depressed because they lack the regulation and skills needed for positive social interactions (e.g., Cole, Luby, & Sullivan, 2008; Kovacs, Joormann, & Gotlib, 2008). This idea is consistent with the finding that negative experiences with peers such as victimization and rejection sometimes appear to contribute to depression (Hawker & Boulton, 2000; Morrow, Hubbard, Rubin, & McAuliffe, 2008), whereas feelings of connection with peers and school are associated with less depression (Costello, Swendsen, Rose, & Dierker, 2008). At the same time, of course, it is also possible that depression contributes to the negative beliefs and self-perceptions, as well as the lack of social skills, that sometimes characterize children who feel depressed (McGrath & Repetti, 2002; Stewart et al., 2004).

In many cases, depression is likely due to a combination of personal vulnerability and external stressful factors (Abela, 2001; Lewinsohn, Joiner, & Rohde, 2001). In one study, for instance, youths who felt that they had little control over their success in school and who demonstrated little investment in school were especially likely to show an increase in depressive symptoms if they also experienced a stressful transition to middle school (Rudolph, Lambert, Clark, & Kurlakowsky, 2001). Other research suggests that the physiological changes of puberty, in combination with increases in stressful peer or familial interactions, may also put youth at risk for depression (see Box 10.1). In addition, the combination of family difficulties (e.g., separation from parents) in early childhood and high levels of interpersonal stress later on may increase youths' vulnerability to depression (Rudolph & Flynn, 2007), perhaps because early stress can affect the child's ability to adapt physiologically years later (Gunnar & Vazquez, 2006).

The most common treatment for depression in youth is drug therapy, but recent concerns have been raised about the possibility that antidepressants may increase the risk of suicidal thinking and behavior for some adolescents. An alternative therapy that has been shown to reduce adolescents' depressive symptoms to some degree involves programs designed to promote optimistic thinking and teach positive problem solving (Gillham, Reivich, Jaycox, & Seligman, 1995; Jaycox, Reivich, Gillham, & Seligman, 1994; Spence, Sheffield, & Donovan, 2003).

review:

Emotions are fundamental to much of human functioning and undergo change in the early months and years of life. Smiles emerge early but do not become social until the second to third month of life, and what makes children smile and laugh changes with age and cognitive development. Distress in newborns involves hunger and various other discomforts, by 6 to 7 months of age, it is often caused by a stranger's approach; and by approximately 8 months of age, it is likely to be triggered by a separation from parents. Separation distress develops in similar ways in various cultures.

It is hard to know exactly when anger emerges because distress/pain and anger are difficult to differentiate early in life. Children may experience anger by the second month of life in response to loss of control. In the first months, it is similarly difficult to differentiate fear from distress, but fear likely has emerged by 6 or 7 months of age, when some children appear to display fear of strangers. Young children also exhibit sadness, especially when they are separated from loved ones for extended periods of time.

The self-conscious emotions—embarrassment, pride, shame, and guilt—emerge somewhat later than do most emotions, probably in the second year of life. Their emergence is tied in part to the development of a rudimentary sense of self and to an appreciation of others' reactions to the self. Situations that evoke these emotions vary across cultures.

Emotions continue to change in their occurrence and causes in childhood and adolescence. Depression increases markedly in adolescence, especially for females. Age-related cognitive, biological, and experiential factors likely account for these changes.

emotional self-regulation the process of initiating, inhibiting, or modulating internal feeling states and related physiological processes, cognitions, and behaviors

Regulation of Emotion

Throughout life, being able to regulate one's emotions is crucial to achieving one's goals. **Emotional self-regulation** is a complex process that involves initiating, inhibiting, or modulating the following aspects of emotional functioning:

1. *Internal feeling states* (the subjective experience of emotion)
2. *Emotion-related cognitions* (e.g., thoughts about one's desires or goals, or one's interpretation of an evocative situation)
3. *Emotion-related physiological processes* (e.g., heart rate and hormonal or other physiological reactions that can change as a function of regulating one's feeling states and thoughts)
4. *Emotion-related behavior* (e.g., actions or facial expressions related to one's feelings)

The emergence of emotional regulation in childhood is a long, slow process. Obviously, young infants are not very good at controlling their emotional reactions. They are easily overwhelmed by loud noises, abrupt movements, hunger, or pain and must rely on their caregivers to settle them down. Older infants also have difficulty dealing with intense emotions such as fear of strangers or of being left alone, and they often run to parents for comfort. Indeed, it takes years for children to develop the abilities to reliably regulate their emotions and control the behaviors associated with them.

The Development of Emotional Regulation

The development of emotional regulation is characterized by three general age-related patterns of change. The first pattern involves infants' transition from their relying almost totally on other people to help them regulate their emotions to their being increasingly able to self-regulate during early childhood. The second pattern involves the use of cognitive strategies to control negative emotions. The third pattern involves the selection of appropriate regulating strategies.

Parents often help young children to regulate themselves by physically calming them or distracting them with an object.

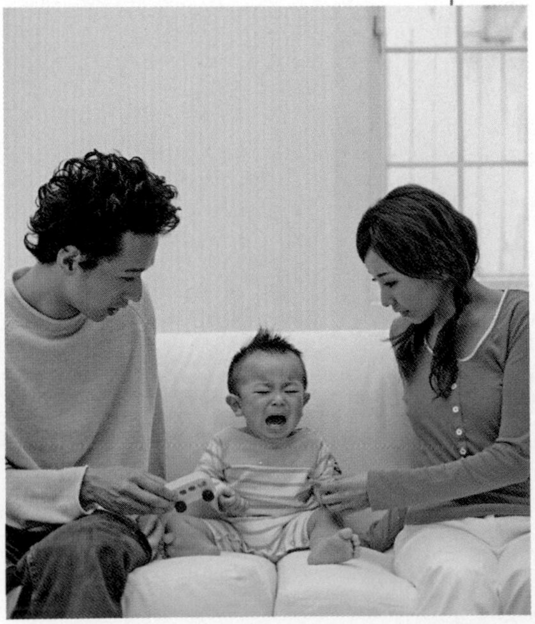

The Shift from Caregiver Regulation to Self-Regulation

When young infants are distressed, frustrated, or frightened, their parents typically try to help them regulate their emotional arousal by attempting to soothe or distract them (Gianino & Tronick, 1988). For example, mothers tend to use caressing and other affectionate behavior to calm a crying 2-month-old and, increasingly over the next few months, include vocalizations (e.g., talking, singing, "shushing") in their calming efforts as well as in their attempts to divert the infant's attention. Holding or rocking upset young infants while talking soothingly to them seems to be the most reliable approach, and feeding them if they are not highly upset is also effective (Jahromi, Putnam, & Stifter, 2004).

By 6 months of age, infants show the first signs of emotional self-regulation. In aversively arousing or uncertain situations, they may reduce their distress by simply averting their gaze unselectively. Occasionally, 6-month-olds can also *self-soothe*—that is, engage in repetitive rubbing or stroking of their body or clothing—or distract themselves by looking specifically at neutral or positive persons or objects rather than at what has upset them. Between ages 1 and 2, infants increasingly distract themselves from distressing stimuli by selectively averting their attention (Grolnick, Bridges, & Connell, 1996; Mangelsdorf, Shapiro, & Marzolf, 1995; Parritz, 1996). Such changes in young children's behavior are probably made possible by their growing ability to control both their own attention and their movements (Ruff & Capozzoli, 2003).

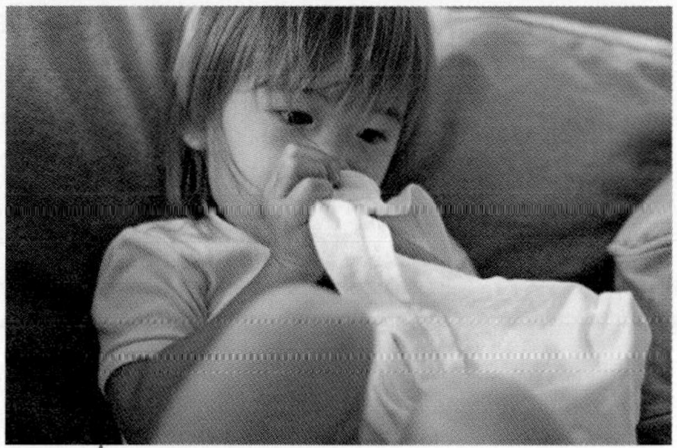

© HELEN LI J / A_AMY

Young children tend to soothe themselves by rubbing their body, sucking a thumb, and clinging to well-loved objects that provide a sense of security.

Over the course of the early years, children develop and improve their ability to distract themselves by playing on their own when distressed. They also become less likely to seek comfort from their parents when they must delay gratification or are upset (Bridges & Grolnick, 1995; Li-Grining, 2007). And because of their growing ability to use language, when they do seek comfort, children are more likely to discuss upsetting emotional situations with parents rather than simply crying (Campos, Frankel, & Camras, 2004; Kopp, 1992). Similarly, instead of pouting or throwing a temper tantrum when they can't have their own way, children can increasingly manage their negative emotional arousal by talking to others and negotiating ways to resolve situations that at least partially meet their own needs (Klimes-Dougan & Kopp, 1999; Kopp, 1992). For example, if a preschooler is unhappy when told by a parent to stop playing and clean up his or her room, the child may verbally protest and lobby for extra play time rather than throwing a fit.

These changes in children's self-regulation are at least partly due to the increasing maturation of the neurological systems—including the portion of the frontal lobes that are central to effortfully managing attention and inhibiting thought and behaviors (Rueda, Posner, & Rothbart, 2004). They are also partly due to changes in what adults expect of children. As children age, adults increasingly expect them to manage their own emotional arousal and behavior. Once children are capable of crawling, for example, they are viewed as more responsible for their behavior and for complying with parental expectations (Campos, Kermoian, & Zumbahlen, 1992). At about 9 to 12 months of age, children start to show awareness of adults' demands and begin to regulate themselves accordingly. For example, they are increasingly likely to comply with simple instructions, such as to not touch dangerous objects.

In the second year of life, children also show increases in the ability to inhibit their motor behavior—such as slowing down their walking when asked to do so (Kochanska, Murray, & Harlan, 2000). Although these abilities are quite limited in the toddler years, they improve considerably by age 3 to 5 (Putnam, Gartstein, & Rothbart, 2006; Reed, Pien, & Rothbart, 1984) and further improve in the school years and beyond (Murphy et al., 1999; Williams, Ponesse, Schacher, Logan, & Tannock, 1999). At the same time, children's ability to regulate their attention is improving (Rothbart & Rueda, 2005). As a result, children are increasingly able to conform to adults' expectations, such as not hurting others when angered and staying seated at school when they would much prefer to get up and talk or play with classmates. In adolescence, the neurological changes that occur in the cortex (see page 109) further contribute to self-regulation and other cognitive functioning. They also likely contribute to the decline in risk-taking and the improvement in judgment that often occur in the transition from adolescence to young adulthood.

NATALIE VALIENTE

This little girl is using signs to communicate that she wants to eat. Children who can indicate their wants and needs with language or signs are less likely to get frustrated and to exhibit unregulated behavior.

social competence the ability to achieve personal goals in social interactions while simultaneously maintaining positive relationships with others

The Use of Cognitive Strategies to Control Negative Emotion

Whereas younger children regulate their negative emotions primarily by using behavioral strategies (e.g., distracting themselves with play), older children are also able to use cognitive strategies to adjust to emotionally difficult situations (Skinner, 2007). Finding themselves caught in unpleasant or threatening circumstances, they may rethink their goals or the meaning of events so that they can adapt gracefully to the situation. This ability helps children avoid acting in ways that might be counterproductive. When children are teased by peers, for example, they may be able to defuse the situation by downplaying the importance of the teasing and not reacting to it in a way that would provoke more teasing.

The Selection of Appropriate Regulatory Strategies

In dealing with emotion, children, over time, improve in their ability to select cognitive or behavioral strategies that are appropriate for the particular situation and stressor (Brenner & Salovey, 1997). One reason is that, with age, children are more aware that the appropriateness of a particular coping behavior depends on their specific needs and goals, as well as on the nature of the problem. For example, children are increasingly likely to realize that it is better to try to find alternative ways to obtain a goal rather than simply give up in frustration when their initial efforts fail (Berg, 1989).

Children's improving ability to use appropriate strategies for dealing with negative situations is also aided by their growing ability to distinguish between stressors that can be controlled (such as homework) and those that cannot be (such as painful medical procedures). Older children, for example, are more aware than younger children that in situations they cannot control, it is easier to manage their emotion by simply adapting to the situation rather than trying to change it (e.g., Altshuler et al., 1995; Hoffner, 1993; Rudolph, Dennig, & Weisz, 1995). Faced with having to undergo major surgery, for instance, older children may adapt by trying to think about the benefits of having the surgery, such as being in better health afterward, or by distracting themselves with enjoyable activities. Younger children, in contrast, are more likely to insist that they do not need the operation.

Children who exhibit positive affect and laughter tend to be well liked by peers.

LAURA DWIGHT

The Relation of Emotional Regulation to Social Competence and Adjustment

As we noted earlier, the development of emotional regulation has important consequences for children, especially with regard to their social competence. **Social competence** is a set of skills that help individuals achieve their personal goals in social interactions while maintaining positive relationships with others (Rubin et al., 1998). A variety of studies indicate that children who have the ability to inhibit inappropriate behaviors, delay gratification, and use cognitive methods of controlling their emotion and behavior tend to be well-adjusted and liked by their peers and adults (Diener & Kim, 2004; Eisenberg, Spinrad, & Eggum, in press; Lengua, Bush, Long, Kovacs, & Trancik, 2008; Wilson, 2003; Zhou et al., 2004).

Moreover, children and adolescents who are able to deal constructively with stressful situations—negotiating with others to settle conflicts, planning strategies to resolve upsetting situations, seeking social support, and so on—generally are better adjusted than are children who lack these skills, including those who avoid dealing with stressful situations altogether (Blair, Denham, Kochanoff, & Whipple, 2004; Compas, Connor-Smith, Saltzman, Thomsen, & Wadsworth, 2001; Jaser et al., 2007). Well-regulated children also do well in school, likely because they are better able to pay attention, are better behaved and liked by teachers and peers, and, consequently, like school better than do their less regulated peers (Eisenberg et al., 2005; Trentacosta & Izard, 2007; Valiente et al., 2007).

review:

Children's efforts to regulate their emotions and emotionally driven behavior change with age. Whereas young infants must rely on adults to manage their emotions, older infants and young children increasingly regulate their own emotions and behavior through such methods as averting their attention, self-soothing, and distracting themselves with activities. Their ability to inhibit their actions also improves with age. Improvements in children's regulatory capacities likely are based on increases in brain maturation that allow them to better control their attention and their own bodies, as well as on changes in adults' expectations of them.

In contrast to young children, who often try to cope with their emotions by taking direct action, older children also are able to use cognitive modes of coping, such as focusing on positive aspects of a negative situation or trying to think about something else altogether. In addition, they are increasingly able to select ways of regulating themselves and coping with stress that are appropriate to the requirements of specific situations.

The abilities to regulate one's emotions and related behavior, and to deal constructively with stressful situations, are associated with high social competence and low levels of problem behavior.

Individual Differences in Emotion and Its Regulation

Although the overall development of emotions and self-regulatory capabilities is roughly similar for all children, there also are very large individual differences in children's emotional functioning. Some infants and children are relatively mellow: they do not become upset easily and they usually do not have difficulty calming down when they are upset. Other children are quite emotional; they get upset quickly and intensely, and their negative emotion persists for a long time. Moreover, children differ in their timidity, in their expression of positive emotion, and in the ways they deal with their emotions. Compare these two 3-year-old children, Maria and Bruce, as they react to Teri, an adult female stranger:

> When Teri walks over to Maria and starts to talk with her, Maria smiles and is eager to show Teri what she is doing. When Teri asks Maria if she would like to go down the hall to the play room (where experiments are conducted), Maria jumps up and takes Teri's hand.
>
> In contrast, when Teri walks over to Bruce, Bruce turns away. He doesn't talk to her and averts his eyes. When Teri asks him if he wants to play a game, Bruce moves away, looks timid, and softly says "no."
>
> (Eisenberg, laboratory observations)

temperament constitutionally based individual differences in emotional, motor, and attentional reactivity and self-regulation that demonstrate consistency across situations, as well as relative stability over time

Children also vary in the speed with which they express their emotions, as illustrated by the differences in these two preschool boys:

> When someone crosses Taylor, his wrath is immediate. There is no question how he is feeling, no time to correct the situation before he erupts. Douglas, though, seems almost to consider the ongoing emotional situation. One can almost see annoyance building until he finally sputters, "Stop that!"
>
> (Denham, 1998, p. 21)

The differences among children in their emotionality and regulation of emotion almost certainly have a basis in heredity (Rothbart & Bates, 2006). However, environmental stressors, including factors as diverse as negative parenting (see below) and instability in an adopted child's placement (Lewis, Dozier, Ackerman, & Sepulveda-Kozakowski, 2007) are related to problems children may have with self-regulation and the expression of emotion. Undoubtedly, a combination of genetic and environmental factors jointly contribute to individual differences in children's emotions and related behaviors.

Temperament

Because infants differ so much in their emotional reactivity, even from birth, it is commonly assumed that children are born with different emotional characteristics. Differences in various aspects of children's emotional reactivity that emerge early in life are labeled as dimensions of **temperament.** Mary Rothbart and John Bates, two leaders in the study of temperament, define temperament as

> constitutionally based individual differences in emotional, motor, and attentional reactivity and self-regulation. Temperamental characteristics are seen to demonstrate consistency across situations, as well as relative stability over time.
>
> (Rothbart & Bates, 1998, p. 109)

Who could resist this toddler? Children who smile easily in new situations—who have an easy temperament—are likely to elicit more positive reactions from adults than children who express a high level of negative emotion.

TRACY SPINRAD

The phrase "constitutionally based" in this definition means biologically based. At the most obvious level, it refers, of course, to genetically inherited characteristics. But it also refers to aspects of biological functioning, such as neural development and hormonal responding, that can be affected by the environment during the prenatal period and after birth. For example, nutritional deficiencies or exposure to cocaine during the prenatal period (Dennis, Bendersky, Ramsay, & Lewis, 2006), as well as a premature birth (Clark, Woodward, Horwood, & Moor, 2008), can affect infants' and young children's ability to regulate their attention and behavior. Similar negative effects can result from sustained elevations of *cortisol* (a hormone that activates energy reserves) due to maternal insensitivity or child abuse during the early years of life (Bugental, Martorell, & Barraza, 2003; Gunnar & Cheatham, 2003). Thus, the construct of temperament is highly relevant to our themes of *individual differences* and the role of *nature and nurture* in development.

The pioneering work in the field of temperament research was the New York Longitudinal Study, conducted by Stella Chess and Alexander Thomas (Thomas & Chess, 1977; Thomas, Chess, & Birch, 1963). These researchers began by interviewing a sample of parents, repeatedly and in depth, about their infants' specific behaviors. To reduce the possibility of bias in the parents' reports, the researchers asked the parents to provide detailed descriptions of their infant's specific behavior rather than interpretive characterizations (e.g. "he's often cranky," "she's interested in everything"). On the basis of those interviews, nine characteristics of children were identified, including such traits as attention span and persistence, quality of mood, adaptability, and activity level. Analyzing the interview results in terms of these characteristics, the researchers classified the infants into three groups: easy, difficult, and slow-to-warm-up.

1. *Easy babies* adjusted readily to new situations, quickly established daily routines such as sleeping and eating, and generally were cheerful in mood and easy to calm.
2. *Difficult babies* were slow to adjust to new experiences, tended to react negatively and intensely to novel stimuli and events, and were irregular in their daily routines and bodily functions.
3. *Slow-to-warm-up babies* were somewhat difficult at first but became easier over time as they had repeated contact with new objects, people, and situations.

Due partly to variations in temperament, children often show very different reactions to the same situation.

ALFRED EISENSTAEDT / TIMEPIX

In the initial study, 40% of the infants were classified as easy, 10% as difficult, and 15% as slow-to-warm-up. The rest did not fit into one of these categories. Of particular importance, some dimensions of children's temperament showed relative stability over time, with temperament in infancy predicting how children were doing years later. For example, "difficult" infants tended to have problems with adjustment at home and at school, whereas few of the "easy" children had such problems. (We will return to the issue of stability of temperament and its social and emotional correlates shortly.)

Since the groundbreaking efforts of Thomas and Chess, researchers have devoted a great deal of effort to refining both the definition of temperament and its measurement (see Box 10.2 on pages 404–406). Unlike Thomas and Chess, many contemporary researchers differentiate among types of negative emotionality and assess different types of regulatory capacities. Recent research suggests that infant temperament is captured by six dimensions (Rothbart & Bates, 1998, 2006):

1. *Fearful distress/inhibition*—distress and withdrawal, and their duration, in new situations.
2. *Irritable distress*—fussiness, anger, and frustration, especially if the child is not allowed to do what he or she wants to do.
3. *Attention span and persistence*—duration of orienting toward objects or events of interest.
4. *Activity level*—how much an infant moves (e.g., waves arms, kicks, crawls).
5. *Positive affect/approach*—smiling and laughter, approach to people, degree of cooperativeness and manageability.
6. *Rhythmicity*—the regularity and predictability of the child's bodily functions such as eating and sleeping.

The terms used by investigators to refer to these dimensions vary somewhat—for example, "irritable distress" may be called "frustration" or "anger"—but these dimensions generally include most of the aspects of temperament that have been studied extensively.

In childhood, the first five of these dimensions (see Table 10.2) are particularly important in classifying children's temperament and predicting their behavior (Rothbart & Bates, 1998). In addition, there is some evidence that a dimension referred to as agreeableness/adaptability may be another important aspect of temperament (Rothbart & Bates, 2006). Agreeableness involves other-oriented emotions and behaviors (e.g., getting along with others and caring about them versus being aggressive and manipulative), as well as the tendency to affiliate with others. Adaptability involves being able to adjust to specific conditions, including the needs and desires of others.

TABLE 10.2

Examples of Items in Mary Rothbart's Temperament Scales

Response scale for items:

1	2	3	4	5	6	7	X
Never	Very rarely	Less than half the time	About half the time	More than half the time	Almost always	Always	Does not apply

Temperament dimension	Sample items in infant scale	Sample items in child scale
Fearful distress	How often during the last week did the baby: —cry or show distress at a loud sound (blender, vacuum cleaner, etc.)? —cry or show distress at a change in parents' appearance (glasses off, shower cap on, etc.)?	—Is not afraid of large dogs and/or other animals (reversed for scoring) —Is afraid of loud noises
Irritability (or distress at limitations in infancy and anger/frustration in childhood)	When having to wait for food or liquids during the last week, how often did the baby: —seem not bothered? —show mild fussing? —cry loudly?	—Has temper tantrums when s/he doesn't get what s/he wants —Gets mad when even mildly criticized
Attention span	How often during the last week did the baby: —look at pictures in books and/or magazines for 5 minutes or longer at a time? —play with one toy or object for 10 minutes or longer?	—When drawing or coloring in a book, shows strong concentration —When building or putting something together, becomes very involved in what s/he's doing, and works for long periods
Activity level	During feeding (during the last week), how often did the baby: —lie or sit quietly? —squirm or kick? —wave arms?	—Tends to run, rather than walk, from room to room —When outside, often sits quietly (reversed for scoring)
Positive affectivity (smiling and laughter)	When tossed around playfully (during the last week), how often did the baby: —smile? —laugh?	—Smiles and laughs during play with parents —Usually has a serious expression, even during play (reversed for scoring)

Adapted from Rothbart Infant Behavior Questionnaire and Child Behavior Questionnaire (Rothbart & Gartstein, 2000)

Stability of Temperament Over Time

As we have seen, temperament, by definition, involves traits that remain relatively stable over time. One example of such stability comes from research indicating that children who exhibited inhibition or fearful distress when presented with novel stimuli as infants also exhibited elevated levels of fear in novel situations at age 2 and elevated levels of social inhibition at age 4½. Similarly, children who are more prone to negative emotion than their peers at age 3 tend to be more emotionally negative than their peers at ages 6 and 8 (Guerin & Gottfried, 1994; Rothbart, Derryberry, & Hershey, 2000); and, across the same age range, those prone to positive affect remain relatively positive (Durbin, Hayden, Klein, & Olino, 2007; Sallquist et al., 2009). Research also indicates that children who are high in the ability to focus attention in the preschool years are high in this ability at age 11 to 12 (Murphy et al., 1999) and that there is stability in attentional and behavioral regulation from childhood into adolescence (Eisenberg, Hofer, et al., 2008) and across adolescence (Ganiban, Saudino, Ulbricht, Neiderhiser, & Reiss, 2008).

JON FEINGERSH / CORBIS STOCK MARKET

A fetus's activity level in the womb appears to be related to some aspects of postnatal temperament. Fetuses who are more active tend to be active, difficult, and nonadaptive in the first half-year of life.

It is important to note, however, that some aspects of temperament tend to be more stable than others. Over the course of infancy, activity level, for example, may be less stable than positive emotionality, fear, and distress/anger (Lemery, Goldsmith, Klinnert, & Mrazek, 1999). During childhood, there can be considerable change in the degree of children's reaction to unfamiliar situations, people, or objects, especially among children who are not at one extreme of reactivity or the other (Kagan, Snidman, & Arcus, 1998; Pfeifer, Goldsmith, Davidson, & Rickman, 2002).

The Role of Temperament in Children's Social Skills and Maladjustment

One of the reasons for researchers' deep interest in temperament is that it plays an important role in determining children's social adjustment. Consider a boy who is prone to anger and has difficulty controlling this emotion. Compared with other boys, he is likely to sulk, to yell at others, and to be defiant with adults and aggressive with peers. Such behaviors often lead to long-term adjustment problems. Consequently, it is not surprising that differences in aspects of temperament such as anger/irritability, positive emotion, and the ability to inhibit behavior—aspects reflected in the difference between difficult and easy temperament—have been associated with differences in children's social competence and maladjustment (Eiden, Colder, Edwards, & Leonard, 2009; Eisenberg et al., 2009; Guerin, Gottfried, & Thomas, 1997; Kochanska, Barry, Aksan, & Boldt, 2008; Rothbart & Bates, 1998, 2006).

Such differences are highlighted by a large longitudinal study in New Zealand conducted by Avshalom Caspi, Terrie Moffitt, Bill Henry, and their colleagues. These researchers found that children who were negative and unregulated as young children tended as adolescents or young adults to have more problems with adjustment, such as not getting along with others, than did peers with different temperaments. They also were more likely to engage in illegal behaviors and to get in trouble with the law (Caspi, Henry, McGee, Moffitt, & Silva, 1995; Caspi & Silva, 1995; Henry, Caspi, Moffitt, & Silva, 1994). In addition, at age 21, they reported getting along less well with whomever they were living with (e.g., roommates) and

a closer look

Measurement of Temperament

Currently a number of different methods are used to assess temperament. In one method, similar to that used by Thomas and Chess, parents or other adults (usually teachers or observers) periodically report on aspects of a child's temperament, such as fearfulness, anger/frustration, and positive affect. These reports, based on observations of the children in various contexts (see Table 10.2), tend to be fairly stable over time and predict general later development in such areas as behavioral problems, anxiety disorders, and social competence (Rothbart, Ahadi, & Evans, 2000; Rothbart & Bates, 1998, 2006).

Laboratory observations have also been used to assess aspects of temperament such as behavioral inhibition, emotionality, and regulatory capacities. In a longitudinal study conducted by Jerome Kagan, for example, investigators observed children's reactions to a variety of novel experiences in early infancy, at age 2, and at age 4½. Across all three ages, about 20% of the children were consistently quite inhibited and reactive when exposed to the unfamiliar stimuli. As infants, they cried and thrashed about when brightly colored toys were moved back and forth in front of their faces or when a cotton swab dipped in dilute alcohol was applied to their nose. At age 2, one-third of these inhibited children were highly fearful in unfamiliar laboratory situations—such as being exposed to a loud noise, the smell of alcohol, and an unfamiliar woman dressed in a clown outfit—and nearly all showed at least some fear in these situations.

Other children were less reactive: as infants, they rarely fussed when they encountered the novel experiences, and at age 2, most showed little or no fear in the unfamiliar situations. At the age of 4½, the children who had been reactive to unfamiliar situations were more subdued, less social, and less positive in their behavior than were the uninhibited children, who were relatively spontaneous, asked questions of the researchers when being evaluated, commented on events happening around them, and smiled and laughed more (Kagan, 1997; Kagan & Fox, 2006; Kagan, Snidman, & Arcus, 1998). Thus, laboratory observations appear to be good measures of behavioral inhibition.

Physiological measures also have proved useful for assessing some aspects of children's temperament. Kagan (1998; Kagan & Fox, 2006), for example, has found that high-reactive and low-reactive children exhibit differences in the variability of their heart rate. Heart-rate variability—how much an individual's heart rate normally fluctuates—is believed to reflect, in part, the way the central nervous system responds to novel situations and the individual's ability to regulate emotion (Porges, Doussard-Roosevelt, & Maiti, 1994; Porges, 2007). Investigators often measure this fluctuation of heart rate in terms of *vagal tone,* an index of how effectively the vagus nerve—which regulates autonomic nervous system functioning—modulates heart rate in accordance with breathing. Children who have heart rates that are constantly high and that vary little as a function of breathing are said to have low vagal tone. These children tend to be negatively reactive and inhibited in response to novel situations.

In contrast, children who have variable and often lower heart rates are said to have high vagal tone. After the first year of life, these children tend to exhibit positive emotions and few negative reactions in novel or even stressful situations, such as when dealing with a new preschool (Calkins, 1997; Porges et al., 1994). Vagal tone after infancy has been linked with interest and attention, as well as with levels of positive expressiveness (Beauchaine, 2001; Rothbart & Bates, 2006).

A vital component of emotion regulation is the ability to modulate vagal tone in challenging situations that require an organized response (Porges, 2007). This ability involves autonomic physiological processes, referred to as *vagal suppression*, that allow the child to shift away from the physiological responses triggered by the situation and to focus on

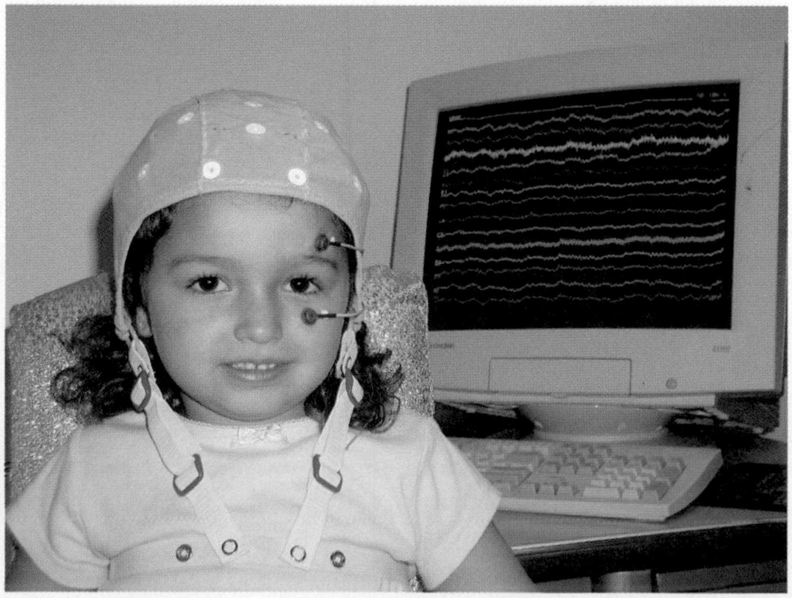

COURTESY OF SEAN FLANAGAN & STACEY BARTON, CHILD DEVELOPMENT LABORATORY, UNIVERSITY OF MARYLAND, COLLEGE PARK

Nathan Fox and his colleagues have found that children who tend to experience positive emotions and approach new situations show a different pattern of EEG activation than children who tend to experience negative emotions and are more inhibited in their behavior. However, it is unclear if EEG patterns change as a function of children's behavior or if brain waves reflect an aspect of physiological functioning that causes these patterns in behavior.

10.2

processing of information relevant to the situation and generating coping strategies. Vagal suppression also allows for higher physiological arousal that can be used to deal with the situation at hand. Vagal suppression during challenging situations has been related to a variety of positive outcomes over the course of childhood, including better regulation of state and more attentional control in infancy (Huffman et al., 1998); fewer behavior problems, higher status with peers, and more appropriate emotion regulation in the preschool years (Calkins & Dedmon, 2000; Calkins & Keane, 2004); and sustained attention in the school years (Suess, Porges, & Plude, 1994; see Thompson, Lewis, & Calkins, 2008).

In addition, children with higher vagal suppression or vagal tone appear less likely to have problem behaviors and anxiety if exposed to stressors such as parental hostility and marital conflict (El-Sheikh, Harger, & Whitson, 2001; El-Sheikh & Whitson, 2006). Findings such as this support the idea that vagal tone and its suppression assess some capacity related to adaptation and emotion regulation.

Another commonly used physiological measure of temperament is electroencephalographic recordings (see Chapter 3, page 105) of frontal-lobe activity. Activation of the left frontal lobe of the cortex as measured with an electroencephalogram (EEG) has been associated with approach behavior, positive affect, exploration, and sociability. In contrast, activation of the right frontal lobe has been linked to withdrawal, a state of uncertainty, fear, and anxiety (Davidson et al., 2003). Thus, when confronted with novel stimuli, situations, or challenges, infants and children who show greater right frontal activation on the EEG are more likely to react with anxiety and avoidance (Calkins, Fox, & Marshall, 1996; Kagan & Fox, 2006), whereas individuals who show left frontal activation are more likely to exhibit a relaxed, often happy mood and an eagerness to engage new experiences or challenges (Davidson et al., 2003; Kagan & Fox, 2006). EEG activation patterns are associated with children's ongoing temperament, not just with their reactions in these specific situations. For example, compared with uninhibited peers, inhibited children showed greater activation in the right frontal area even under resting conditions (Davidson, 1994).

A third physiological measure of temperament is cortisol level. In reaction to stress, the adrenal cortex secretes steroid hormones, including cortisol, which, as noted previously, helps to activate energy reserves (Carter, 1986). Sometimes individual differences in children's cortisol baseline—that is, their typical cortisol level—have been related to high levels of internalizing problems such as inhibition, anxiety, and social withdrawal (Granger, Stansbury et al., 1994; Smider et al., 2002) and to low regulation (Gunnar et al., 2003) and the acting out of behavioral problems (Gunnar & Vazquez, 2006; Shirtcliff et al., 2005; Shoal, Giancola, & Kirillova, 2003). For example, 2-year-olds who, in a relatively nonthreatening situation, exhibit extremely fearful reactions—such as freezing up in their behavior—tend to have higher levels of cortisol in general, not just in such situations (Buss, Davidson, Kalin, & Goldsmith, 2004).

Moreover, cortisol reactivity—the amount of cortisol produced in a given situation—has been linked to temperament differences in emotionality, inhibition, regulation, and maladjustment (Ashman, Dawson, Panagiotides, Yamada & Wilkinson; 2002; Blair et al., 2008; Granger et al., 1998). Cortisol reactivity is related to internalizing problems such as anxiety primarily if a child displays a heightened response to a familiar stressor (Gunnar & Vazquez, 2006). For example, children high in temperamental negative emotionality and low in regulation show larger increases in cortisol levels when they are in less than optimal child-care situations than do other children (Dettling, Parker, Lane, Sebanc, & Gunnar, 2000). As this example suggests, the child's experience with the particular context often needs to be considered when cortisol measures are used to assess temperament.

In one study, for example, children who were active and outgoing tended to show higher cortisol levels when they first entered group care than did anxious and withdrawn children; later in the school year, however, the reverse was true. According to teachers' reports at the time of the second cortisol testing, the former group was higher in popularity and had fewer problems interacting socially. Presumably, the less inhibited children had actively dealt with the new situation, initially creating stress and raising their cortisol levels but subsequently adapting successfully. The inhibited children, in contrast, had avoided the challenges (and stress) of the new situation and were still not well adjusted to it (Gunnar, 1994). The exception is uninhibited children who are also unregulated; they exhibit relatively high cortisol levels at preschool even later in the year, perhaps because their impulsive behavior leads to peer rejection (Gunnar, Sebanc, Tout, Donzella, & van Dulmen, 2003).

Each type of measure of temperament has advantages and disadvantages, and there is considerable debate regarding the merits of the various methods (Kagan, 1998; Kagan & Fox, 2006; Rothbart & Bates, 1998, 2006). The key advantage of parents' reports of temperament is that parents have extensive knowledge of their children's behavior in many different situations. One important disadvantage of this method is that parents may not always be objective in their observations, as suggested by the fact that their reports sometimes do not correspond with what is found with laboratory measures (Seifer, Sameroff, Barrett, & Krafchuk, 1994). Another disadvantage is that many parents do not have wide knowledge of other children's behavior to use as a basis for comparison when reporting on their own children (what is irritability to some parents, for example, may be near-placidness to others).

The key advantage of laboratory observational data is that such data are less likely to be biased than is an adult's personal view of the child. A key disadvantage is that children's behavior usually is observed in only a limited set of

(***a closer look*** *is continued on the next page)*

(continued from the previous page)

circumstances. Consequently, laboratory observational measures may reflect a child's mood or behavior at a given moment, in a particular context, rather than reflecting the child's general temperament.

Physiological measures such as an EEG and vagal tone are also relatively objective and unlikely to be biased, but there is no way to tell whether the processes reflected by physiological measures are a cause or consequence of the child's emotion and behavior in the specific situation. It is unclear, for example, whether left and right frontal lobe activity triggers, or is triggered by, a particular emotional response. Thus, no measure of temperament is foolproof, and it is prudent to measure temperament with a variety of different measures.

experiencing more unemployment. As adults, they tended to have few people from whom they could get social support (Caspi, 2000) and were prone to negative emotions like anxiety, perhaps due to the ill effects of their angry, undercontrolled behavior in childhood and adolescence (Caspi et al., 2003).

Researchers also have found stability with regard to **behavioral inhibition,** the tendency to be high in fearful distress and restrained when dealing with novel or stressful situations. Children who are behaviorally inhibited are more likely than other children to have problems such as anxiety, depression, phobias, and social withdrawal at older ages (Biederman et al., 1990; Hirschfeld-Becker et al., 2007; Moffitt et al., 2007). Thus, different problems with adjustment seem to be associated with different temperaments.

However, how children ultimately adjust depends not only on their temperament but also on how well their temperament fits with the particular environment they are in—what is often called **goodness of fit.** On the basis of their data, Chess and Thomas (1990) argued, for example, that children with difficult temperaments have better adjustment if they receive parenting that is supportive and consistent rather than punitive, rejecting, or inconsistent. In support of their argument, research indicates that children who are impulsive or low in self-regulation seem to have more problems and are less sympathetic to others if exposed to hostile, intrusive, and/or negative parenting rather than to supportive parenting (e.g., Lengua et al., 2000; Hastings & De, 2008; Rubin et al., 1998; Valiente et al., 2004; see Rothbart & Bates, 2006). Similarly, children prone to negative emotions such as anger are more likely to have behavioral problems such as aggression if exposed to hostile parenting or low levels of positive parenting (Calkins, 2002; Morris et al., 2002; Rothbart & Bates, 2006). Thus, children exposed to suboptimal parenting do worse if they have unregulated or reactive temperaments.

Not only are children's maladjustment and social competence predicted by the combination of their temperament and their parents' child-rearing practices, but the child's temperament and parents' socialization efforts also seem to affect one another over time (Belsky et al., 2007; Brody & Ge, 2001; Eisenberg, Fabes et al., 1999; Kim, Conger, Lorenz, & Elder, 2001). For example, parents of negative, unregulated children may eventually become less patient and more punitive with their children; this intensification of disciplining may cause their children to become even more negative and unregulated. Thus, temperament plays a role in the development of children's social and psychological adjustment, but that role is complex and varies as a function of the child's social environment.

behavioral inhibition a temperamentally based style of responding characterized by the tendency to be particularly fearful and restrained when dealing with novel or stressful situations

goodness of fit the degree to which an individual's temperament is compatible with the demands and expectations of his or her social environment

review:

Temperament refers to individual differences in various aspects of children's emotional reactivity, regulation, and other characteristics such as behavioral inhibition and activity level. Temperament is believed to have a constitutional (biological) basis, but it is also affected by experiences in the environment, including social interactions. Temperament tends to be somewhat stable over time, although the degree of its stability varies across the dimensions of temperament and individuals.

Temperament plays an important role in adjustment and maladjustment. A difficult and unmanageable temperament in childhood tends to predict problem behaviors and low social competence in childhood and adulthood, and children who as infants are fearful and negatively reactive to novel objects, places, and people sometimes have later difficulties in interactions with others, including peers. However, children whose temperaments put them at risk for poor adjustment often do well if they receive sensitive and appropriate parenting and if there is a good fit between their temperament and their social environment.

Children's Emotional Development in the Family

It is clear that the dimensions of temperament related to emotional development are linked to heredity. Twin and adoption studies show that, compared with fraternal twins, identical twins are more similar in the intensity of their emotional reactions, shyness, and sociability, as well as in other aspects of temperament and **personality.** Furthermore, biological siblings tend to be more similar to one another in some aspects of temperament than do siblings who are not biologically related. On the basis of such studies, it is estimated that genes account for a substantial portion of the variation in some aspects of temperament (Caspi & Shiner, 2006; Saudino, 2005).

In addition, recent studies of specific genes have showed connections between an individual's genes and aspects of temperament such as self-regulatory capacities (Caspi & Shiner, 2006; Deater-Deckard, Petrill, & Thompson, 2007; Goldsmith, Pollak, & Davidson, 2008). For example, genes related to dopamine and other neurotransmitters that affect voluntary attentional processes (executive attention) appear to be especially relevant for self-regulation (Posner, Rothbart, & Sheese, 2007). The expression of these genes appears to be affected by environmental factors such as quality of parenting or stress, with the most common pattern being that genetic vulnerabilities are most likely expressed when the environment is suboptimal (e.g., Bakermans-Kranenburg, & van Ijzendoorn, 2006; Kochanska, Philibert, & Barry, in press; Sheese, Voelker, Rothbart, & Posner, 2008).

However, some aspects of temperament may be more genetically based than others. For example, studies of toddler twins suggest that heredity plays a moderate role in individual variation in negative emotions, such as anger and social fearfulness, but a much smaller role in positive emotion (Emde et al., 1992; Goldsmith, Buss, & Lemery, 1997; Goldsmith, Lemery, Buss, & Campos, 1999).

Findings in behavioral genetics research also suggest that various environmental factors play an important role in shaping individual differences in temperament, including those related to children's emotionality (Caspi & Shiner, 2006; Deater-Deckard et al., 2007; Goldsmith et al., 1997). Chief among these factors are children's relationships with their parents and their parents' socialization practices.

personality the pattern of behavioral and emotional propensities, beliefs and interests, and intellectual capacities that characterize an individual. Personality has its roots in temperament (and thus has a constitutional basis) but is shaped by interactions with the social and physical world.

Quality of the Child's Relationships with Parents

The quality of children's relationships with their parents can influence their emotional development in several ways. As is discussed fully in Chapter 11, the quality of children's relationships with their parents seems to influence their sense of security and how they feel about themselves and other people (Thompson, 2006). In turn, these feelings affect children's emotionality. For example, children who have secure relationships with their parents tend to show more positive emotion and less social anxiety and anger than do children who are insecurely attached to their parents (e.g., Bohlin, Hagekull, & Rydell, 2000; Denham, Blair, Schmidt, & DeMulder, 2002; Kochanska, 2001). Securely attached children also tend to be more open and honest in their expression of emotion (Becker-Stoll, Delius, & Scheitenberger, 2001; Zimmerman, Maier, Winter, & Grossmann, 2001); they likewise tend to be more advanced in their understanding of emotion, perhaps because their parents are more likely to discuss feelings and other mental states with them (Laible, 2004; Mcquaid, Bigelow, McLaughlin, & MacLean, 2007; Raikes & Thompson, 2006). This enhanced understanding of emotion is likely to help these children recognize when and how to regulate their emotion.

Parental Socialization of Children's Emotional Responding

In addition to being affected by the overall parent–child relationship, children's emotional development is influenced by parents' **socialization** of their children—that is, their direct and indirect influence on their children's standards, values, and ways of thinking and feeling. Parents socialize their children's emotional development through (1) their expression of emotion with their children and other people, (2) their reactions to their children's expression of emotion, and (3) the discussions they have with their children about emotion and emotional regulation. Each of these avenues of socialization can affect not only children's emotional development but also their social competence.

Parents' Expression of Emotion

How parents express their own emotions can have a powerful socializing effect on their children in several ways. To begin with, the emotions expressed in the home may influence children's views about themselves and others in their social world (Dunsmore & Halberstadt, 1997). For example, children exposed to a lot of anger and hostility may come to view themselves as individuals who anger people and may come to believe that most people are hostile. In addition, parents' expression of emotion provides children with a model of when and how to express emotion (Denham, Zoller, & Couchoud, 1994; Dunn & Brown, 1994). This modeling also may affect children's understanding of what types of emotional expressions are appropriate and effective in interpersonal relations (Halberstadt, Cassidy, Stifter, Parke, & Fox, 1995; Morris, Silk, Steinberg, Myers, & Robinson, 2007).

If parents do not talk about emotions but express their feelings nonverbally, for example, their children may come to believe that it is not appropriate to discuss their feelings directly with others. They also may get the message that emotions are basically bad and should be avoided or inhibited. Finally, the parental emotions children are exposed to may affect their level of distress and arousal, and children who are highly aroused tend not to attend to and process important information about ongoing social interactions.

Whatever the underlying process, it is clear that the consistent and open expression of positive or negative emotion in the home is associated with specific

socialization the process through which children acquire the values, standards, skills, knowledge, and behaviors that are regarded as appropriate for their present and future role in their particular culture

BROOKLYN PRODUCTIONS / THE IMAGE BANK / GETTY IMAGES

Children who are exposed to relatively high levels of positive emotion in the family tend to express more positive emotion and are more socially skilled and adjusted than children who are exposed to high levels of negative emotion.

outcomes for children. In a review of a considerable number of studies, Amy Halberstadt and her colleagues found that when positive emotion is prevalent in the home, children tend to express positive emotion themselves. They are socially skilled, able to understand others' emotions (at least in childhood), are low in aggression, are well adjusted, and tend to have high self-esteem (Halberstadt, Crisp, & Eaton, 1999).

In contrast, when negative emotion is prevalent in the home, especially intense and hostile emotion, children tend to exhibit low levels of social competence and to experience and express negative emotion themselves, including depression and anxiety (Crockenberg & Langrock, 2001; Eisenberg et al., 2001; Halberstadt et al., 1999; Stocker, Richmond, Rhoades, 2007). Even when the conflict and anger in the home involve the adults rather than the children directly, there is an increased likelihood that the children will develop behavior problems and deficits in social competence and self-regulation (Cummings & Davies, 2002; Grych & Fincham, 1997; Rhoades, 2008). These outcomes are also more likely when children are exposed to high levels of parental depression (Blandon et al., 2008; Cicchetti & Toth, 2006; Downey & Coyne, 1990).

Of course, parental expression of emotion is not always causally related to positive or negative outcomes in children; children undoubtedly influence the expression of emotion in the home. For example, children who have difficult temperaments or are unmanageable are likely to evoke negative emotion from their parents (Eisenberg, Champion et al., 2008). Moreover, genetic factors may contribute to some of the associations between parental emotion and children's emotions or behavior (Burt, McGue, Krueger, & Iacono, 2005). That is, due to heredity, both parent and child may be prone to anger and impulsive behavior. Thus, both heredity and the kinds of emotions children see and experience in the home undoubtedly play roles in children's emotional and social development.

Parents' Reactions to Children's Emotions

Parents' reactions to their children's negative emotions also seem to affect children's emotional expressivity, as well as their social competence and adjustment.

Consider, for example, the different parental messages conveyed in the following two instances:

> Jeremy . . . watched the movie *Jaws*, against his mother's better judgment. He fearfully, animatedly asked many questions about the movie afterwards, and anxiously discussed it in great detail (e.g., "What was that red stuff?"). His mother and father answered all the questions and supported him as he resolved these things in his mind. Jeremy's emotions were accepted, and he was able to regulate them, as well as to learn about what makes things "scary."
>
> (Denham, 1998, p. 106)

> Scott's parents, who are punitive socializers, show disregard and even contempt when his best friend moves away. These parents tease Scott for his tender feelings, so that in the end he is let down not only by the disappearance of his friend, but by their reactions as well. . . . [H]e is very lonely and still feels very bad.
>
> (Denham, 1998, p. 120)

Parents who, like Scott's, dismiss or criticize their children's expressions of sadness and anxiety communicate to their children that their feelings are not valid. Parents send similar messages when they react to their children's anger with threats, belligerence, or dismissive comments. In turn, their children are likely to be less emotionally and socially competent than are children whose parents are emotionally supportive. They tend, for example, to be lower in sympathy for others, less skilled at coping with stress, and more prone to negative emotions and problem behaviors such as aggression (Eisenberg, Fabes et al., 1996; Fabes et al., 2001; Lunkenheimer, Shields, & Cortina, 2007; Snyder, Stoolmiller, Wilson, & Yamamoto, 2003).

In contrast, parents who are supportive when their children are upset help their children to regulate their emotional arousal and to find ways to express their emotions constructively. In turn, their children tend to be better adjusted and more competent both with peers and academically (Eisenberg, Cumberland, & Spinrad, 1998; Gottman, Katz, & Hooven, 1997; Klimes-Dougan et al., 2007). Parents' supportive reactions to their young children's emotional upsets may be especially helpful in reducing problem behaviors for those children who have difficulty regulating their physiological responses to challenges (see Box 10.2; Hastings & De, 2008).

Parents' Discussion of Emotion

As you will shortly see, children's emotional understanding is a key part of their emotional development and self-regulation. Family conversations about emotion are therefore an important aspect of children's emotional socialization. Parents who discuss emotions with their children teach them about the meanings of emotions, the circumstances in which they should and should not be expressed, and the consequences of expressing or not expressing them (Eisenberg, Cumberland, et al., 1998; LaBounty et al., 2008; Thompson, 2006). An additional help in emotional socialization is *emotion coaching,* in which parents not only discuss emotions with their children but also help them learn ways of coping with their emotions and expressing them appropriately (Gottman et al., 1997; Power, 2004). Children who receive these types of guidance tend to display better emotional understanding than children who do not.

A longitudinal study by Judy Dunn and her colleagues found, for example, that the degree to which children are exposed to, and participate in, discussions of emotions with family members at ages 2 and 3 predicts their understanding of others' emotions until at least age 6 (Brown & Dunn, 1996; Dunn, Brown, & Beardsall, 1991; Dunn, Brown, Slomkowski, Tesla, & Youngblade, 1991). In a similar study, mothers' references to their child's desires at 15 months of age predicted their children's understanding of emotions and use of emotion language at 24 months. Further, mothers' verbal references to others' thoughts and knowledge when describing a series of pictures to their children at 24 months of age predicted children's use of emotion language and understanding of emotion at 33 months of age (Taumoepeau & Ruffman, 2006, 2008). Indeed, in this same study, as well as in another (Ensor & Hughes, 2008), mothers' references to others' mental states predicted children's emotion understanding better than did mothers' references to emotions themselves, perhaps because references to mental states help children understand the thoughts that accompany and motivate emotional states.

Researchers have also found that children whose parents use emotion coaching are more socially competent with peers and less likely to exhibit problem behaviors or depression (Katz & Windecker-Nelson, 2004; Stocker, Richmond, & Rhoades, 2007). Of course, children's own characteristics—such as their ability to sustain attention and their initial understanding of emotions—may affect the degree to which adults talk about emotion with them. For example, in one study, parents engaged in more conversations about emotional past events with their 5- and 6-year-olds if they were relatively well regulated and if their expression of negative emotion was consistent with what their parents expected from a child (Bird, Reese, & Tripp, 2006).

review:

Children's emotional development is influenced by their relationship with their parents: children who have secure relations with their parents tend to show more positive emotion and greater emotional understanding than do children whose relations with their parents are insecure. Another influence on children's emotional development is their parents' socialization of emotional responding, including what emotions parents express with their children and others and how they express them; how parents respond to their children's negative emotions; and whether and how parents discuss emotions with their children.

Culture and Children's Emotional Development

Although people in all cultures appear to experience most of the same basic emotions, there is considerable cultural variation in the degree to which certain emotions are expressed. One reason for this may be genetic, in that people in different racial or ethnic groups may tend, on average, to have somewhat different temperaments. This possibility has been tentatively suggested by cross-cultural studies that were conducted with young infants to minimize the potential for the results to be affected by socialization. One such study found that, in general, 11-month-old Euro-American infants react more strongly to unfamiliar stimuli than do Chinese or Chinese-American babies and cry or smile more in response to evocative events (e.g., scary toys, a vanishing object) (Freedman & Freedman, 1969). Another study found that, compared with Chinese infants, American infants also respond more quickly to negative emotion-inducing events such as having their arm held down so they cannot move it (Camras et al., 1998).

A more obvious contributor to cross-cultural differences in infants' emotional expression is the diversity of parenting practices. In Central Africa, for example, the infants in a Ngandu community fuss and cry more than infants in an Aka community do. This may be attributable to differences in caregiving practices related to the contrasting lifestyles of these two groups. The Aka are hunters and gatherers whose daily foraging activities are carried out by women and children together. Consequently, Aka infants are almost always within arm's reach of someone who can feed or hold them when the need arises. The Ngandu, on the other hand, are farmers, and their infants are left alone more often. Thus, Aka infants may cry and fuss less because they have more physical contact with caregivers and their needs are met more quickly. Of course, genetic factors related to temperament could also contribute to the differences (Hewlett, Lamb, Shannon, Leyendecker, & Scholmerich, 1998).

The influence of cultural factors on emotional expression is strikingly revealed by a comparison of Japanese and American children. In one study, Japanese and American preschoolers were asked to say what they would do in hypothetical situations of conflict and distress, such as being hit, hearing their parents argue, or seeing a peer knock down a tower of blocks they had just built. American preschoolers expressed more anger and aggression in response to these vignettes than did Japanese children. This difference may have to do with the fact that American mothers appear to be more likely than Japanese mothers to encourage their children's emotional expressiveness in situations such as these (Zahn-Waxler, Friedman, Cole, Mizuta, & Hiruma, 1996). This tendency is in keeping with the high value Euro-American culture places on independence, self-assertion, and expressing one's emotions, even negative ones (Zahn-Waxler et al., 1996). In contrast, Japanese culture emphasizes interdependence, the subordination of oneself to one's group, and, correspondingly, the importance of maintaining harmonious interpersonal relationships. Thus, Japanese mothers often may discourage their children from expressing negative emotion (Markus & Kitayama, 1991; Matsumoto, 1996; Mesquita & Frijda, 1992).

Interviews with children in remote villages in Nepal allowed Pamela Cole and her colleagues to examine how Buddhist and Hindu values contribute to children's understanding of emotion.

COURTESY OF PAMELA COLE

Cultures also differ in the degree to which they promote or discourage specific emotions, and these differences are often reflected in parents' socialization of emotion. For example, Chinese culture strongly emphasizes the need to be aware of oneself as embedded in a larger group and to maintain a positive image within that group. Thus, shame would be expected to be a powerful emotion—and a particularly useful one for inducing compliance in children. In fact, Chinese (Taiwanese) parents frequently try to induce shame in their preschool children when they transgress, typically pointing out that the child's behavior is judged negatively by people outside the family and that the child's shame is shared by other family members (Fung & Chen, 2001). Because of this cultural emphasis, it is likely that children in this society experience shame more frequently than children in many Western cultures do.

Another striking example of cultural influences on emotional socialization is provided by the Tamang in rural Nepal. The Tamang are Buddhists who place great value on keeping one's *sem* (mind-heart) calm and clear of emotion, and they believe that people should not express much negative emotion because of its disruptive effects on interpersonal relationships. Consequently, although Tamang parents are responsive to the distress of infants, they often ignore or scold children older than age 2 when those children express anger, and they seldom offer explanations or support to reduce children's anger. Such parental reactions are not typical of all Nepali groups, however; for example, parents of Brahman Nepali children respond to children's anger with reasoning and yielding.

Of particular interest is the fact that although nonsupportive parental behavior comparable to that of the Tamang has been associated with low social competence in U.S. children, it does not seem to have a negative effect on the social competence of Tamang children. Because of the value placed on controlling the expression of emotion in Tamang culture, parental behaviors that would seem dismissive and punitive to American parents likely take on a different meaning for Tamang parents and children and probably have different consequences (Cole & Dennis, 1998; Cole, Tamang, & Shrestha, 2006).

Parents' ideas about the usefulness of various emotions also vary in different cultural and regional groups within the United States. In a study of African-American mothers living in dangerous neighborhoods, mothers valued and promoted their daughters' readiness to express anger and aggressiveness in situations related to self-protection because they wanted their daughters to act quickly and decisively to defend themselves when necessary. One way they did this was to play-act the role of an adversary, teasing, insulting, or challenging their daughters in the midst of everyday interactions. An example of this is provided by Beth's mother, who initiated a teasing event by challenging Beth (27 months old) to fight:

> "Hahahaha, Hahaha. Hahahahah. [Provocative tone:] You wanna fight about it?" Beth laughed. Mother laughed. Mother twice reiterated her challenge and then called Beth an insulting name, "Come on, then, chicken." Beth retorted by calling her mother a chicken. The two proceeded to trade insults through the next 13 turns, in the course of which Beth marked three of her utterances with teasing singsong intonation and aimed a shaming gesture (rubbing one index finger across the other) at her mother. The climax occurred after further mock provocation from the mother, when Beth finally raised her fists (to which both responded with laughter) and rushed toward her mother for an exchange of ritual blows.
>
> (Miller & Sperry, 1987, pp. 20–21)

It is unlikely that mothers in a less difficult and dangerous neighborhood would try to promote the readiness to express aggression in their children, especially in their daughters. Thus, the norms, values, and circumstances of a culture or subcultural group likely contribute substantially to differences among groups in their expression of emotion.

review: Children's tendencies in regard to experiencing and regulating emotions may be affected by differences in temperament among different groups of people. These tendencies may also be influenced by differences in parenting practices, which in turn are often affected by cultural differences in beliefs about what emotions are valued and when and where emotions should be expressed.

Children's Understanding of Emotion

Another key influence on children's emotional reactions and regulation of emotion is their *understanding* of emotion—that is, their understanding of how to identify emotions, as well as their understanding of what emotions mean, their social functions, and what factors affect emotional experience. Because an understanding of emotion affects social behavior, it is critical to the development of social competence. Children's understanding of emotions is primitive in infancy but develops rapidly over the course of childhood.

social referencing the use of a parent's or other adult's facial expression or vocal cues to decide how to deal with novel, ambiguous, or possibly threatening situations

Identifying the Emotions of Others

The first step in the development of emotional knowledge is the recognition of different emotions in others. By 4 to 7 months of age, infants can distinguish certain emotional expressions, such as happiness and surprise (Serrano, Iglesias, & Loeches, 1993; Walker-Andrews & Dickson, 1997). If, for example, they are habituated to pictures of happy faces and then are presented with a picture of a face depicting surprise, they dishabituate, showing renewed interest by looking longer at the new picture. By 7 months of age, infants exhibit different patterns of brain waves when they observe fearful and angry facial expressions, a finding that suggests some ability to discriminate these emotions (Kobiella, Grossmann, Reid, & Striano, 2008). At about this age, infants also start to perceive others' emotional expressions as meaningful. For example, if infants at this age are shown a video in which a person's facial expression and voice are consistent in their emotional expression (e.g., a smiling face and a bubbly voice) and a video in which a person's facial expression and voice are emotionally discrepant (e.g., a sad face and a bubbly voice), they will attend more to the presentation that is emotionally consistent (Walker-Andrews & Dickson, 1997). Infants much younger than 7 months generally do not seem to notice the difference between the two presentations.

As discussed in Chapter 5, at about 8 to 12 months of age, children begin to demonstrate that they can relate facial expressions of emotion and emotional tones of voice to events in the environment. These skills are evident in children's **social referencing**—that is, their use of a parent's or other adult's facial expression or vocal cues to decide how to deal with novel, ambiguous, or possibly threatening situations. In laboratory studies of this phenomenon, infants are typically exposed to novel people or toys while their mother, at the experimenter's direction, shows a happy, fearful, or neutral facial expression. In studies of this type, 12-month-olds tend to stay near their mother when she shows fear; to move toward the novel person or object if she expresses positive emotion; and to move partway toward the person or object if she shows no emotion (Carver & Vaccaro, 2007; Moses, Baldwin, Rosicky, & Tidball, 2001; Saarni, Campos, Camras, & Witherington, 2006).

Similar results have been found in research on 12-month-olds' ability to read their mother's tone of voice. When prevented from seeing their mother's face as they were being presented with novel toys, infants were more cautious and exhibited more fear when the mother's voice was fearful than when it was neutral (Mumme, Fernald, & Herrera, 1996). By 14 months of age, the emotion-related information obtained through social referencing has an effect on children's touching of the object even an hour later (Hertenstein & Campos, 2004).

By the age of 3, children in laboratory studies demonstrate a rudimentary ability to label a fairly narrow range of emotional expressions displayed in pictures or on puppets' faces (Bullock & Russell, 1985; Denham, 1986; Russell & Bullock, 1986). Young children—even 2-year-olds—are skilled at labeling happiness (usually by pointing to pictures that reflect happiness). The ability to label anger and sadness usually emerges in the next year or two, with the ability to label fear, surprise, and disgust gradually appearing in the late preschool and early school years (Eisenberg, Murphy, & Shepard, 1997; Russell & Widen, 2002; Widen & Russell, 2003). (African-American children from disadvantaged backgrounds appear to recognize fear expressions earlier than do Euro-American children, perhaps because they are exposed to more fear-inducing situations in their daily lives [Smith & Walden, 1998].) Most children cannot label more complex emotions such as pride, shame, and guilt until early to mid-elementary school (Saarni et al., 2006).

The ability to discriminate and label different emotions helps children to respond appropriately to their own and others' emotions. If a child understands that he or she is experiencing guilt, for example, the child may understand the need to make amends to diminish the guilt. Similarly, a child who can see that a peer is angry can devise ways to avoid or appease that peer. In fact, children who are more skilled than their peers at labeling and interpreting others' emotions are also higher in social competence (Denham et al., 2003; Feldman, Philippot, & Custrini, 1991; Izard et al., 2008) and lower in behavior problems or social withdrawal (Fine, Izard, Mostow, Trentacosta, & Ackerman, 2003; Schultz, Izard, Ackerman, & Youngstrom, 2001).

Understanding the Causes and Dynamics of Emotion

Knowing the causes of emotions also is important for understanding one's own and others' behavior and motives (Saarni et al., 2006). It likewise is key for regulating one's own behavior and, hence, for social competence (Denham, Blair, et al., 2003; Denham, Caverly, et al., 2002; Schultz et al., 2001). Consider, for example, a child who is being rebuffed or insulted by a friend whom the child has just beaten in a game or on an exam. If the child understands that, in this situation, the friend may be lashing out not because the friend is nasty or a sore loser but because the friend feels threatened and inadequate, the child may be much better able to control his or her own response.

A variety of studies have shown rapid development over the preschool and school years in children's understanding of the kinds of emotions that certain situations tend to evoke in others. In a typical study of this understanding, children are told short stories about characters in situations such as having a birthday party or losing a pet. Children are then asked how the character in the story feels. Even 2-year-olds are fairly accurate at identifying happy situations, indicating their answer by selecting a picture of a happy face from an array of faces depicting a variety of emotions (Michalson & Lewis, 1985). By age 3, children are quite good at identifying happy situations. However, in line with their initial limited ability to identify negative emotions, they are not accurate at identifying sad situations until age 4 (Borke, 1971; Denham & Couchoud, 1990).

Young children have even more difficulty identifying fear- and anger-inducing situations, but their ability to do so increases in the preschool and elementary school years (Eisenberg, Murphy, et al., 1997; Smith & Walden, 1998). Children's ability to understand the circumstances that evoke complex social emotions such as pride, guilt, shame, and jealousy often emerges after age 7, and, according to cross-cultural research that involved children from both Western nations and a remote Himalayan village, this ability is considerable by late elementary school and early adolescence (Harris, Olthof, Terwogt, & Hardman, 1987; Thompson, 1987; Wiggers & van Lieshout, 1985).

Another way to assess children's understanding of the causes of emotions is to record what they say about emotions in their everyday conversations and to ask them to discuss and explain others' emotions. In this kind of research, even

28-month-olds mention emotions such as happiness, sadness, anger, fear, crying, and hurting in appropriate ways in their conversations (e.g., "You sad, Daddy?" or "Don't be mad") and sometimes even mention their causes (e.g., "Santa will be happy if I pee in the potty" or "Grandma mad. I wrote on wall") (Bretherton & Beeghly, 1982).

By age 4 to 6, children can give accurate explanations for why their peers expressed negative emotions in their preschool (e.g., because they were teased or lost the use of a toy) (Fabes et al., 1988). Children get more skilled at explaining the causes of emotion across the preschool and school years (Fabes, Eisenberg, Nyman, & Michealieu, 1991; Saarni et al., 2006; Strayer, 1986). For example, 3rd and 6th graders are more likely than kindergartners to believe that someone caught being dishonest will be scared (Barden, Zelko, Duncan, & Masters, 1980).

With age, children also come to understand that people can feel particular emotions based on reminders of past events. For example, in one study, 3- to 5-year-olds were told stories about children who experienced a negative event and later saw reminders of that event. One story was about a girl named Mary who has a pet rabbit that lives in a typical rabbit cage. One day Mary's rabbit is chased away by a dog and is never seen again. In different versions of the story, Mary later sees one of three reminders of her loss—the culprit dog, her rabbit's cage, or a photograph of her rabbit. At this point, the children were told that Mary started to feel sad and were asked, "Why did Mary start to feel sad right now?" On stories such as these, 39% of 3-year-olds, 83% of 4-year-olds, and 100% of 5-year-olds understood that the story characters were sad because a memory cue had made them think about a previous unhappy event (Lagattuta, Wellman, & Flavell, 1997). Similarly, from ages 3 to 5, children increasingly can explain that when people are in a situation that reminds them of a past negative event, they may worry and change their behavior to avoid future negative events (Lagattuta, 2007). Understanding that memory cues can trigger emotions associated with past events helps children to explain their own and others' emotional reactions in situations that in themselves seem emotionally neutral.

In the elementary school years, children become increasingly sophisticated in their understanding about how, when, and why emotions occur. For example, they become more aware of cognitive processes related to regulating emotion and of the fact that emotional intensity wanes over time. They also come to recognize that people can experience more than one emotion at the same time, including both positive and negative emotions arising from the same source (Harris, 2006; Harter & Buddin, 1987; Pons & Harris, 2005). At around age 10, children begin to understand emotional ambivalence and realize that people can have mixed feelings about events, others, and themselves (Donaldson & Westerman, 1986; Reissland, 1985). Taken together, these developments allow children to better understand the complexities of emotional experience in context.

Children's Understanding of Real and False Emotions

An important component in the development of emotional understanding is the realization that the emotions people express do not necessarily reflect their true feelings (Figure 10.5). The beginnings of this realization are seen in 3-year-olds' occasional (and usually transparent) attempts to mask their negative emotions when they receive a disappointing gift or prize (Cole, 1986). By age 5, children's

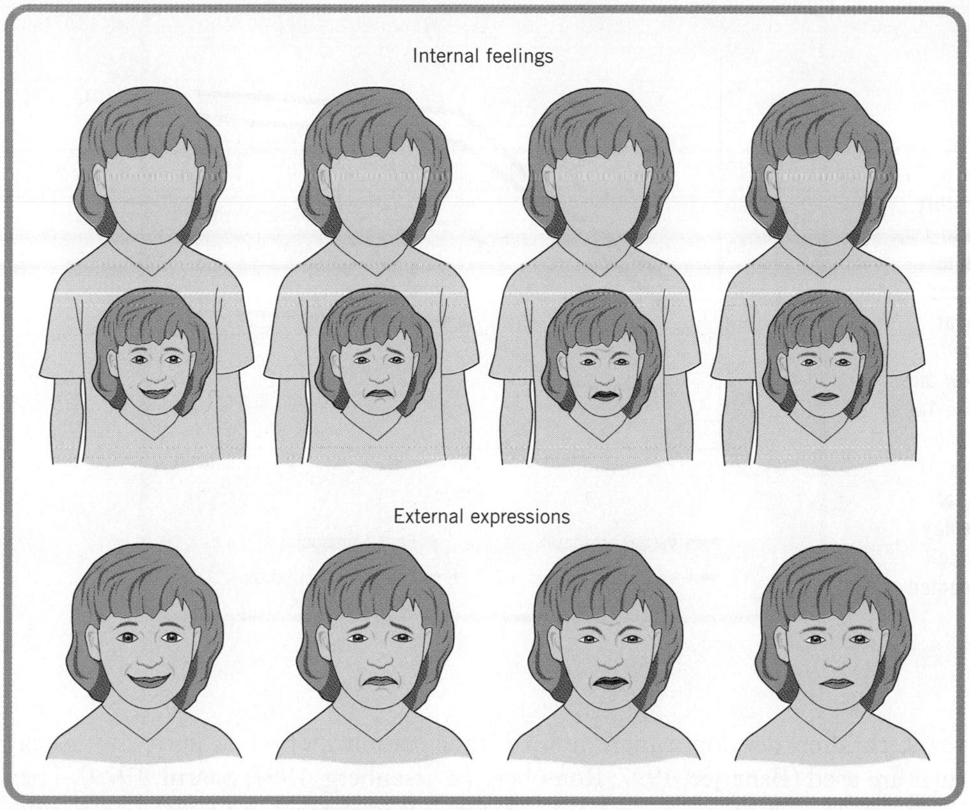

FIGURE 10.5 Facial display figures used in the assessment of expression regulation **The figures on the girl's chest indicate how she feels inside. Children select from the different pictures of facial expressions to indicate what expression the girl would show externally, that is, on her face, as well as internally or on the inside. (Adapted from Jones, Abbey, & Cumberland, 1998)**

understanding of false emotion has improved considerably, as demonstrated in a study that used six stories such as the following:

> Michelle is sleeping over at her cousin Johnny's house today. Michelle forgot her favorite teddy bear at home. Michelle is really sad that she forgot her teddy bear. But, she doesn't want Johnny to see how sad she is because Johnny will call her a baby. So, Michelle tries to hide how she feels.
>
> (Banerjee, 1997)

After children were questioned to ensure that they understood the story, they were presented with illustrations of various emotional expressions and given instructions such as "Show me the picture for how Michelle really feels" and "Show me the picture for how Michelle will try to look on her face." Whereas about half of 3- and 4-year-olds chose the appropriate pictures on four or more of the stories, over 80% of 5-year-olds chose correctly. Studies with both Japanese and Western children also confirm that between 4 and 6 years of age, children increasingly understand that people can be misled by others' facial expressions (Gardner, Harris, Ohmoto, & Hamazaki, 1988; Gross & Harris, 1988).

Part of the improvement in understanding false emotion involves a growing understanding of **display rules**—a social group's informal norms about when, where, and how much one should show emotions and when and where displays of emotion should be suppressed or masked. Over the preschool and elementary school

display rules a social group's informal norms about when, where, and how much one should show emotions and when and where displays of emotion should be suppressed or masked by displays of other emotions

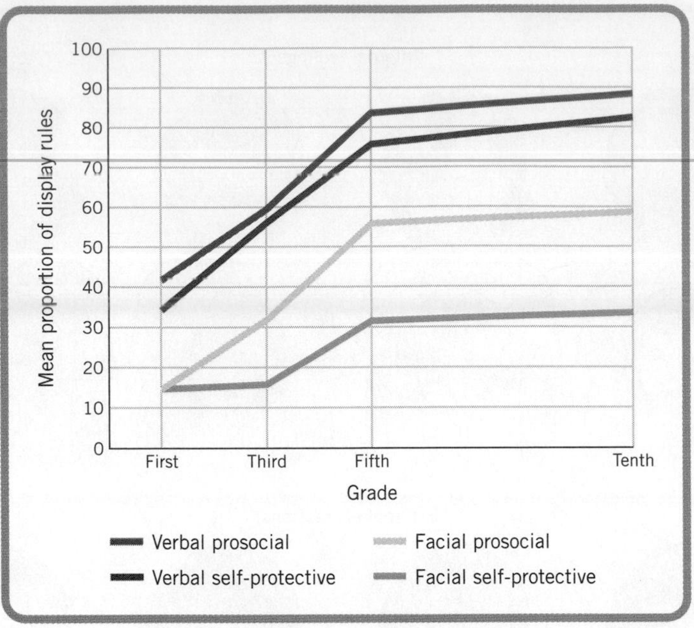

FIGURE 10.6 Mean proportion of display rules as a function of mode of expression (verbal or facial), story type (prosocial or protective), and grade Children in 1st, 3rd, 5th, and 10th grade listened to stories designed to elicit display rules. Then they were asked to predict and explain what the story protagonists would say and what facial expressions the protagonists would show in the emotion-laden situations. Children's knowledge of how and when to control emotional displays increased between 1st and 5th grade and then leveled off. Their understanding was greater for verbal display rules, whereby children monitor, falsify, and inhibit their speech, than for facial display rules. Children also understood prosocial display rules (used to protect another's feelings) better than self-protective display rules (used for personal gain). (Adapted from Gnepp & Hess, 1986)

years, children develop a more refined understanding of when and why display rules are used (Banerjee, 1997; Rotenberg & Eisenberg, 1997; Saarni, 1979). They increasingly understand, for example, that people use verbal and facial display rules to protect others' feelings or their own, as when they pretend to like someone's cooking so as not to hurt the cook's feelings (labeled a *prosocial motive*) or hide their emotions when they themselves are being teased or lose a contest (labeled a *self-protective motive*) (Gnepp & Hess, 1986). (Figure 10.6 shows age-related changes in these types of motives.)

These age-related advances in children's understanding of real versus false emotion and display rules are apparently linked to increases in children's cognitive capacities (Flavell, 1986; Harris, 2000, 2006). For example, children who are higher than their peers in reasoning on Piagetian preoperational and concrete operational conservation tasks (see Chapter 4, pages 137–139) exhibit greater understanding of emotions (Carroll & Steward, 1984).

Social factors also seem to affect children's understanding of display rules. For example, in most cultures, display rules are somewhat different for males and females and reflect societal beliefs about how males and females should feel and behave (Ruble, Martin, & Berenbaum, 2006; van Beek et al., 2006). Elementary school girls in the United States, for instance, are more likely than their male counterparts to feel that openly expressing emotions such as pain is acceptable (Zeman & Garber, 1996). In most cultures, girls are also somewhat more attuned than boys to the need to inhibit emotional displays that might hurt others' feelings (Cole, 1986; Saarni, 1984). This is especially true for girls from cultures such as India, in which females are expected to be deferential and to express only socially appropriate emotions (Joshi & MacLean, 1994). These findings obviously are consistent with the gender stereotypes that girls are more likely both to try to protect others' feelings and to be more emotional than boys.

Parents' beliefs and behaviors—which often reflect cultural beliefs—likely contribute to children's understanding and use of display rules. As we saw earlier, the emphasis placed on controlling emotional displays in Nepal varies by subculture.

Correspondingly, the degree to which Nepalese children report masking negative emotions varies with the degree to which mothers in different Nepalese subcultures report teaching their children how to manage emotions (Cole & Tamang, 1998). A less benign example of parents' influence on children's understanding and use of display rules is the fact that U.S. children are more likely to display knowledge of self-protective display rules (for example, knowing not to display an emotion that would get them in trouble) if they are frequently exposed to hostility in the home (Jones et al., 1998). Thus, children seem to be attuned to display rules that are valued in their culture or that serve an important function in the family.

review:

Children's understanding of emotions plays an important role in their emotional functioning. Although infants can detect differences in different emotional expressions such as happiness and surprise by 4 to 7 months of age, it is not until they are about 7 months of age that they start to treat others' emotional expressions as meaningful. At about 8 to 12 months of age, children begin to connect facial expressions of emotion or an emotional tone of voice with other events in the situation, as evidenced by their use of social referencing. By age 3, children demonstrate a rudimentary ability to label facial expressions and understand simple situations that are likely to cause happiness.

As children move through the preschool and elementary school years, their understanding of emotions and situations that cause emotions grows in range and complexity. In addition, they increasingly appreciate that the emotions people show may not reflect their true feelings.

Chapter Summary

The Development of Emotions in Childhood

- Discrete-emotions theorists believe that each emotion is packaged with a specific set of bodily and facial reactions and that distinct emotions are evident from very early in life. In contrast, functionalists believe that emotions reflect what individuals are trying to do in specific situations—that is, their concerns and goals at the moment—and that there is not a set of innate, discrete emotions but many emotions based on people's many different interactions with the social world.
- From early in life, emotions play an important role in both survival and social communication. Although infants show negative and positive affect from birth, it is not clear whether young infants experience different types of negative emotions such as anger, fear, and sadness.
- Emotions undergo change in the early months and years of life. Smiles become social around the second to third month of life, and what makes children smile and laugh changes with cognitive development.
- Newborns exhibit distress due to discomfort and hunger. By 6 to 7 months of age, they often are distressed when strangers approach them, and by approximately 8 months of age, they tend to get distressed when separated from their parents.
- The social emotions—embarrassment, pride, shame, and guilt—emerge in the second year of life. Their emergence is tied in part to the development of a rudimentary sense of self and to an appreciation of others' reactions to the self.
- In childhood, children's emotional reactions are increasingly influenced by their growing cognitive understandings of events and emotions. For some children, there is an increase in the experience of negative emotion from childhood to adolescence. Rates of clinical and subclinical depression are much higher in adolescence than at younger ages, especially for girls.

Regulation of Emotion

- Emotional self-regulation involves the process of initiating, inhibiting, or modulating internal feeling states and emotion-related physiological processes, cognitions, and behavior in the service of accomplishing one's goals.

- Young infants are not very skilled at regulating themselves and must rely on adults to manage their emotions. However, children's self-regulation improves with age as they increasingly use cognitive strategies and more appropriate and effective means of managing their emotions and behavior. Improvements in children's regulatory capacities are based on increases in both their ability to control their own bodies and their cognitive development, as well as on changes in others' expectations of them.
- Emotional self-regulation generally is associated with high social competence and low problem behavior.

Individual Differences in Emotion and Its Regulation

- Both biological and environmental factors contribute to the differences we see in children's emotions and related behaviors. Temperament, which is believed to have a constitutional basis but also is affected by social experiences, predicts adjustment in childhood and adulthood. However, children with difficult temperaments often do well if they receive sensitive and appropriate parenting.

Children's Emotional Development in the Family

- Children's emotional development is affected by the quality of their early social relationships and their parents' discussion of emotion. High levels of positive emotion in the home are associated with favorable outcomes for children, whereas high levels of negative emotion and punitive reactions to children's displays of negative emotion often are linked to negative developmental outcomes. Parental discussion of emotion or other internal states (e.g., desires, cognitions) may promote children's understanding of emotion and their social competence.

Culture and Children's Emotional Development

- There may be differences in temperament across some cultures, which affect children's tendencies to experience and regulate emotions.
- There are cultural differences in beliefs about what emotions are valued and when emotions should be expressed, and these shape children's expression of emotion.

Children's Understanding of Emotion

- To interact with others effectively, a person must be able to identify others' emotions and have some knowledge of their causes and significance. At about 7 months of age, infants start to treat others' emotional expressions as meaningful. At 8 to 12 months of age, children start to exhibit social referencing.
- By age 2 to 3 years, children demonstrate a rudimentary ability to label facial expressions and simple situations associated with happiness. Children's understanding of facial expressions, the situations that cause emotions, display rules, and the complexities of emotional experience increases in the preschool and elementary school years.

Critical Thinking Questions

1. How might differences in children's intelligence contribute to (a) the emotions they display and (b) their understanding of emotions? What other factors might contribute to children's understanding of their own and others' emotions?
2. List at least five aspects of temperament. What aspects of adults' personality might each predict?
3. Suppose that you wanted to assess changes with age in children's regulation of emotion. Think of five different tasks you could use to assess age-related changes. Which would be best to use in early childhood and which would better reflect changes at older ages?
4. Recall from Chapter 7 the development of children's theory of mind. How might advances in children's understanding of theory of mind relate to their understanding of emotion?

Key Terms

emotional intelligence, p. 383
emotion, p. 383
discrete emotions theory, p. 384
functionalist approach, p. 384
social smiles, p. 386
separation anxiety, p. 389
self-conscious emotions, p. 390
emotional self-regulation, p. 396
social competence, p. 398
temperament, p. 400
behavioral inhibition, p. 406
goodness of fit, p. 406
personality, p. 407
socialization, p. 408
social referencing, p. 414
display rules, p. 417

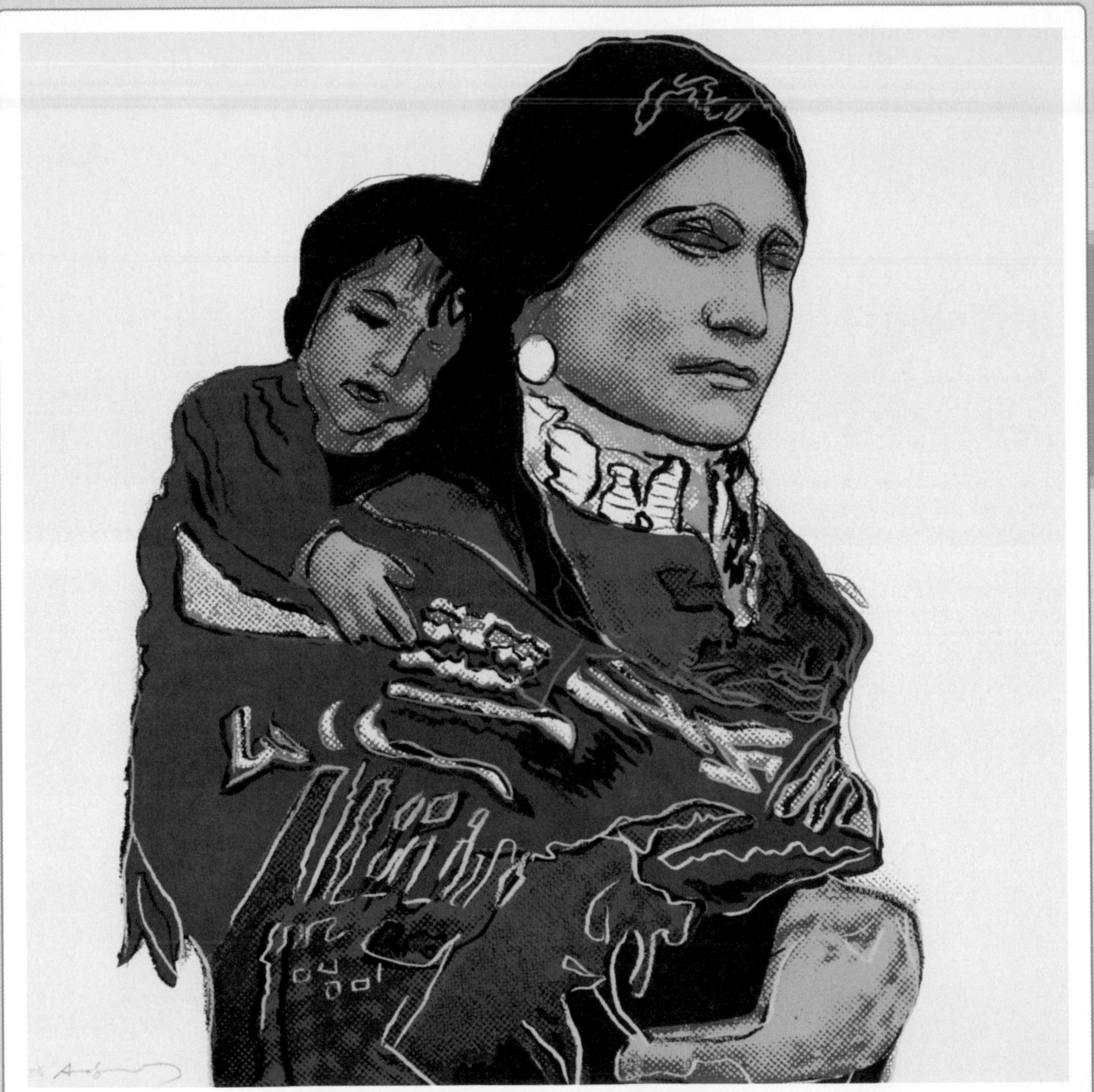

ANDY WARHOL, *Mother and Child, from the Cowboys and Indians Series*, 1986

11

Attachment to Others and Development of Self

THEMES

Nature and Nurture

❖

The Active Child

❖

The Sociocultural Context

❖

Individual Differences

❖

Research and Children's Welfare

❖

Between 1937 and 1943, numerous child-care professionals in both the United States and Europe reported instances of a disturbing phenomenon: children who seemed to have no concern or feeling for anyone but themselves. Some of the children were withdrawn and isolated; others were overactive and abusive toward their peers. By the time they were adolescents, these children often had histories of persistent stealing, violence, and sexual misdemeanors. Many of these children had been reared in institutions in which they received adequate physical care but experienced little social interaction; others had been shifted from foster home to foster home in infancy and early childhood (Bowlby, 1953).

At about the same time, similar disturbances were being observed among children who had been orphaned or separated from their parents during World War II and were in refugee camps or other institutional settings. John Bowlby, an English psychoanalyst who worked with many of these children, reported that they were very listless, depressed or otherwise emotionally disturbed, and mentally stunted. Older refugee children often seemed to have lost all interest in life and were possessed by feelings of emptiness (Bowlby, 1953). These children, like the Romanian orphans discussed in Chapter 1, tended not to develop normal emotional attachments with other people.

On the basis of such observations, René Spitz, a French psychoanalyst who had worked with Freud, conducted a series of classic studies of how the lack of adequate caregiving affects development (Spitz, 1945, 1946, 1949). Spitz filmed infants (a methodological innovation) residing in orphanages, most of whom had been born out of wedlock and had been given up for adoption. The films were extremely poignant and painful to watch. They documented the fact that, despite receiving good institutional care, the infants were generally sickly and physically and developmentally retarded. In many cases, the infants seemed unmotivated to live: their death rate was about 37% over two years, compared with no deaths in an institution where children had daily contact with their mothers. The films' most important contribution, however, was their evidence of intense and prolonged grief and depression in infants who had been separated from their mothers after developing a loving relationship with them. Psychologists of the time did not believe that infants could experience such emotions (Emde, 1994).

Taken together, these early observations also challenged the more central belief, then held by many child-care professionals, that if children in institutions such as orphanages received good physical care, including proper nourishment and health care, they would develop normally. These professionals placed little emphasis on the emotional dimensions of caregiving. As a result of the studies of children who lost their parents in the 1940s, it became generally recognized that, no matter how hygienic and competently managed, institutions like orphanages put babies at high risk because they did not provide the kind of caregiving that enables infants to form close socioemotional bonds. Adoption—the earlier the better—came to be viewed as a far better option.

Another important outcome of the work of Bowlby and others who studied institutionalized children was the beginning of systematic research on how the quality of parent–child interactions affects children's development in families, especially their development of emotional attachments to other people. This research, which continues today, has led to a much deeper understanding of the ways in which the early parent–child emotional bond likely influences children's interactions with others from infancy into adulthood. It has also provided new insight into the development of children's sense of self, as well as of their emotions, including their feelings of self-worth.

In this chapter, we will first explore how children develop **attachments**, that is, close, enduring emotional bonds to parents or other primary caregivers. Then we will examine the ways in which the nature of these attachments to others seems to set the stage for the child's near- and long-term development. As you will see, the attachment process appears to be biologically based yet unfolds in different ways, depending on the familial and cultural context. Thus, the themes of *nature and nurture* and the *sociocultural context* will be important in our discussion of this topic. You will also see that although most children in normal social circumstances do develop attachments to their parents, the quality of these attachments differs in important ways and has implications for each child's social and emotional development. The theme of *individual differences* will therefore figure prominently in our discussion as well. The theme of *research and children's welfare* is also relevant to our examination of experimental interventions designed to enhance the quality of mother–child attachment.

attachment an emotional bond with a specific person that is enduring across space and time. Usually, attachments are discussed in regard to the relation between infants and specific caregivers, although they can also occur in adulthood.

Next we will examine a related issue—the development of children's sense of self—that is, their self-understanding, self-identity, and self-esteem. Although many factors influence these areas of development, the quality of children's early attachments lays the foundation for how children feel about themselves, including their sense of security and well-being. Over time, children's self-understanding, self-esteem, and self-identity are also shaped by how others perceive and treat them, by biologically based characteristics of the child, and by children's developing abilities to think about and interpret their social worlds. Thus, the themes of *nature and nurture, individual differences,* the *sociocultural context,* and the *active child* will be evident in our discussion of the development of self.

The Caregiver–Child Attachment Relationship

Following the very disturbing observations made in the 1930s and 1940s regarding children separated from their parents early in life, researchers began to conduct systematic studies of this phenomenon. Much of the early research, such as that conducted by Spitz, focused on how the development of young children who had been orphaned or otherwise separated from their parents was affected by the quality of the caregiving they subsequently received. The research on children adopted from Romania discussed in Chapter 1 is probably the best known of recent studies on this topic.

Another line of research involved experimental work with monkeys. In some of the most famous research in the whole of psychology, Harry Harlow and his colleagues (Harlow & Harlow, 1965; Harlow & Zimmerman, 1959; Young, Suomi, Harlow, & McKinney, 1973) reared infant rhesus monkeys in isolation from birth, comparing their development with that of monkeys reared normally with their mothers. The isolated babies were well fed and kept healthy, but they had no exposure to their mother or other monkeys. When they finally were placed with other monkeys six months later, they exhibited severe social disturbances. They compulsively bit and rocked themselves and avoided other monkeys completely, apparently incapable of

Harlow's female monkeys who were raised in isolation were poor mothers as adults, turning their backs on their infants, literally and figuratively, and often attacking them. This outcome suggested that "mother love" is essential to normal social and emotional development.

HARLOW PRIMATE LABORATORY, UNIVERSITY OF WISCONSIN

communicating with, or learning from, others. As adults, formerly isolated females had no interest in sex. If they were artificially impregnated, they did not know what to do with their babies. At best, they tended to ignore or reject them; at worst, they attacked them. This research, although examining the effects of the lack of all early social interaction (and not just that with parents), strongly supported the view that children's healthy social and emotional development is rooted in their early social interactions with adults.

Attachment Theory

The findings from observations of children and monkeys separated from their parents were so dramatic that psychiatrists and psychologists were compelled to rethink their ideas about early development. Foremost in this effort was John Bowlby, who proposed **attachment theory,** and his colleague, Mary Ainsworth, who extended and tested Bowlby's ideas.

Bowlby's Attachment Theory

Bowlby's theory of attachment was strongly influenced by several key tenets of Freud's theories, especially the idea that infants' earliest relationships with their mothers shape their later development. However, Bowlby replaced the psychoanalytic notion of a "needy, dependent infant" with the idea of a "competence-motivated infant" who uses his or her primary caregiver as a **secure base** (Waters & Cummings, 2000). The general idea of the secure base is that the presence of a trusted caregiver provides the infant or toddler with a sense of security that allows the child to explore the environment and hence to become generally knowledgeable and competent. In addition, the primary caregiver serves as a haven of safety when the infant feels threatened or insecure, and the child derives comfort and pleasure from being near the caregiver.

Bowlby's idea of the primary caregiver as a secure base was directly influenced by ethological theory, particularly the ideas of Konrad Lorenz (see Chapter 9, page 363). Bowlby proposed that the attachment process between infant and caregiver is rooted in evolution and increases the infant's chance of survival. Just like imprinting, this attachment process develops from the interaction between species-specific learning biases (such as infants' strong tendency to look at faces) and the infant's experience with his or her caregiver. Thus, the attachment process is viewed as having an innate basis, but the development and quality of infants' attachments are highly dependent on the nature of their experiences with caregivers.

According to Bowlby, the initial development of attachment takes place in four phases.

- *Preattachment* (birth to age 6 weeks). In this phase, the infant produces innate signals, most notably crying, that summon caregivers, and the infant is comforted by the ensuing interaction.
- *Attachment-in-the-making* (age 6 weeks to 6 to 8 months). During this phase, infants begin to respond preferentially to familiar people. Typically they smile, laugh, or babble more frequently in the presence of their primary caregiver and are more easily soothed by that person. Like Freud and Erikson, Bowlby saw this phase as a time when infants form expectations about how their caregivers will respond to their needs and, accordingly, do or do not develop a sense of trust in them.

attachment theory theory based on John Bowlby's work that posits that children are biologically predisposed to develop attachments with caregivers as a means of increasing the chances of their own survival

secure base refers to the idea that the presence of a trusted caregiver provides an infant or toddler with a sense of security that makes it possible for the child to explore the environment

- *Clear-cut attachment* (between 6 to 8 months and $1\frac{1}{2}$ years of age). In this phase, infants actively seek contact with their regular caregivers. They happily greet their mother when she appears and, correspondingly, may exhibit *separation anxiety or distress* when she departs (see Chapter 10, pages 389–390). For the majority of children, the mother now serves as a secure base, facilitating the infant's exploration and mastery of the environment.
- *Reciprocal relationships* (from $1\frac{1}{2}$ or 2 years of age on). During this final phase, toddlers' rapidly increasing cognitive and language abilities enable them to understand their parents' feelings, goals, and motives and to use this understanding to organize their efforts to be near their parents. As a result, a more mutually regulated relationship gradually emerges as the child takes an increasingly active role in developing a working partnership with his or her parents (Bowlby, 1969). Correspondingly, separation distress declines.

The usual outcome of these phases is an enduring emotional tie uniting the infant and caregiver. In addition, the child develops an **internal working model of attachment,** a mental representation of the self, of attachment figures, and of relationships in general. This internal working model is based on the young child's discovering the extent to which his or her caregiver could be depended upon to satisfy the child's needs and provide a sense of security. Bowlby believed that this internal working model guides the individual's expectations about relationships throughout life. If caregivers are accessible and responsive, young children come to expect interpersonal relationships to be gratifying and feel that they themselves are worthy of receiving care and love. As adults, they look for, and expect to find, satisfying and security-enhancing relationships similar to the ones they had with their attachment figures in childhood. If children's attachment figures are unavailable or unresponsive, children develop negative perceptions of relationships with other people and of themselves (Bowlby, 1973, 1980; Bretherton & Munholland, 1999). Thus, children's internal working models of attachment are believed to influence their overall adjustment, social behavior, perceptions of others, and the development of their self-esteem and sense of self (Thompson, 2000, 2006).

Ainsworth's Research

Mary Ainsworth, who began working with John Bowlby in 1950, provided empirical support for Bowlby's theory and extended it in important ways. In research conducted in both Uganda (Ainsworth, 1967) and the United States, Ainsworth studied mother–infant interactions during infants' explorations and separations from their mother. On the basis of her observations, she came to the conclusion that two key measures provide insight into the quality of the infant's attachment to the caregiver: (1) the extent to which an infant is able to use his or her primary caregiver as a secure base; and (2) how the infant reacts to brief separations from, and reunions with, the caregiver.

Measurement of Attachment Security in Infancy

With these measures in mind, Ainsworth designed a laboratory test for assessing the security of an infant's attachment to his or her parent. This test is called the **Strange Situation** because it is conducted in a context that is unfamiliar to the child and likely to heighten the child's need for his or her parent. In this test, the infant, accompanied by the parent, is placed in a laboratory playroom equipped with interesting toys. After the experimenter introduces the parent and child to the room,

internal working model of attachment the child's mental representation of the self, of attachment figure(s), and of relationships in general that is constructed as a result of experiences with caregivers. The working model guides children's interactions with caregivers and other people in infancy and at older ages.

Strange Situation a procedure developed by Mary Ainsworth to assess infants' attachment to their primary caregiver

ROBERT MARVIN

Mary Ainsworth developed the laboratory techniques to test and extend Bowlby's pioneering ideas about attachments.

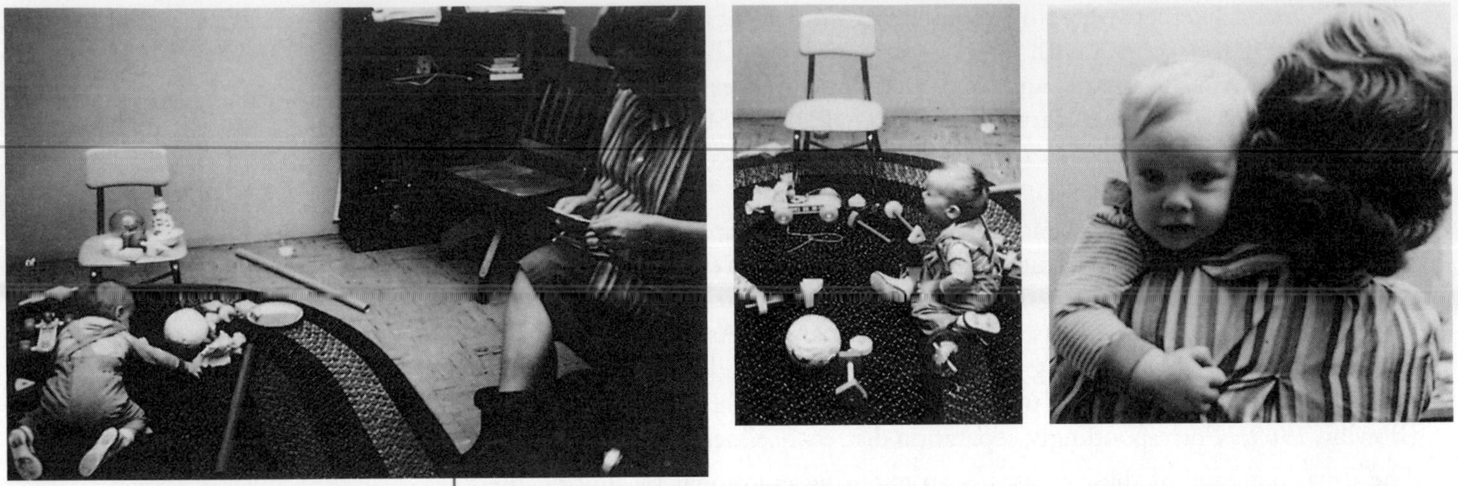

ALL PHOTOS COURTESY OF MARY AINSWORTH

In the Strange Situation, this securely attached child explores the environment when his mother is in the room, cries and stops exploring when she leaves, and is easily calmed by his mother when she returns.

the child is exposed to seven episodes, including two separations from, and reunions with, the parent, as well as two interactions with a stranger—one when the parent is out of the room and one when the parent is present (see Table 11.1). Each episode lasts approximately 3 minutes unless the child becomes overly upset. Throughout these episodes, observers rate infants' behaviors, including their attempts to seek closeness and contact with the parent, their resistance to or avoidance of the parent, their interactions with the stranger, and their interactions with the parent from a distance using language or gestures.

Although this mini-melodrama is a highly artificial situation, it has proven extremely useful in understanding the nature and importance of early parent–child relationships. As Jay Belsky observed of the Strange Situation:

> It may be artificial, but so is a treadmill test for the heart. That's a physical stress test—this is an emotional stress test. They're both artificial, but they're both diagnostic too.
>
> (Quoted in Talbot, 1998, p. 46)

TABLE 11.1

Episodes in Ainsworth's Strange Situation Procedure

Episode	Events	Aspect of Attachment Behavior Assessed
1	Experimenter introduces caregiver and infant to the unfamiliar room; shows toys to baby; then leaves.	None
2	Caregiver and child are alone; caregiver is told not to initiate interaction but to respond to baby as appropriate.	Exploration and use of parent as a secure base
3	Stranger enters and is seated quietly for 1 minute; then talks to caregiver for 1 minute; then tries to interact with the baby for 1 minute.	Reaction to the stranger
4	Mother leaves child alone with the stranger, who lets baby play but offers comfort if needed. Segment is shortened if the baby becomes too distressed.	Separation distress and reaction to stranger's comforting
5	Caregiver calls to baby from outside door, enters the room, and pauses by the door. Stranger leaves. Caregiver lets infant play or may comfort infant if distressed.	Reaction to reunion with parent
6	Parent leaves infant alone in the room. Segment is ended if infant is too distressed.	Separation distress
7	Stranger enters room, greets infant, and pauses. She sits or comforts infant if the infant is upset. Segment is ended if the infant is very upset.	Ability to be soothed by stranger
8	Caregiver calls from outside the door, enters and greets infant and pauses. Caregiver sits if infant is not upset but may provide comfort if infant is distressed. Caregiver allows infant to return to play if interested.	Reaction to reunion

Adapted from Ainsworth et al. (1978)

In her work with the Strange Situation, Ainsworth (1973) discerned three distinct patterns in infants' behavior that seemed to indicate the quality or security of their attachment bond. These patterns—which are reflected in the infant's behavior throughout the Strange Situation, but especially during the *reunions* with the parent—have been replicated many times in research with mothers, and sometimes with fathers. On the basis of these patterns, Ainsworth identified three attachment categories.

The first attachment category—the one into which the majority of infants fall—is **secure attachment**. Babies in this category use their mother as a secure base during the initial part of the session, leaving her side to explore the many toys available in the room. As they play with the toys, these infants occasionally look back to check on their mother or bring a toy over to show her. They are usually, but by no means always, distressed to some degree when their mother leaves the room, especially when they are left totally alone. However, when their mother returns, they make it clear that they are glad to see her, either by simply greeting her with a happy smile or, if they have been upset during her absence, by going to her to be picked up and comforted. If they have been upset, their mother's presence comforts and calms them, often enabling them to explore the room again. About 62% to 68% of typical middle-class children in the United States fall into this category; for infants from lower socioeconomic groups, the rate is significantly lower—slightly less than 50% for childen under 24 months of age (Thompson, 1998; van IJzendoorn, Schuengel, & Bakermans-Kranenberg, 1999).

The other two attachment categories that Ainsworth originally identified involve children who are rated as **insecurely attached,** that is, who have less positive attachment to their caregivers than do securely attached children. One type of insecurely attached infant is classified as **insecure/resistant,** or **ambivalent.** Infants in this category are often clingy from the beginning of the Strange Situation, staying close to the mother instead of exploring the toys. When the mother leaves the room, they tend to get very upset, often crying intensely. In the reunion, the insecure/resistant infant typically reestablishes contact with the mother, only to then rebuff her efforts at offering comfort. For example, the infant may rush to the mother bawling, with outstretched arms, signaling the wish to be picked up and then, as soon as he or she is picked up, arch away from the mother or begin squirming to get free from her embrace. About 9% of typical middle-class children in the United States fall into the insecure/resistant category, but the percentage appears to be somewhat higher in many non-Western cultures (van IJzendoorn et al., 1999).

The other type of insecurely attached infant is classified as **insecure/avoidant.** Children in this category tend to avoid their mother in the Strange Situation. For example, they often fail to greet her during the reunions and ignore her or turn away while she is in the room. Approximately 15% of typical middle-class children fall into the insecure/avoidant category (van IJzendoorn et al., 1999).

Subsequent to Ainsworth's original research, attachment investigators found that the reactions of a small percentage of children in the Strange Situation did not fit well into any of Ainsworth's three categories. These children seem to have no consistent way of coping with the stress of the Strange Situation. Their behavior is often confused or even contradictory. For example, they may exhibit fearful smiles and look away while approaching their mother, or they may seem quite calm and contented and then suddenly display angry distress. They also frequently appear dazed or disoriented and may freeze in their behavior and remain still for a substantial period of time. These infants, labeled **disorganized/disoriented,** seem to have an unsolvable problem: they want to approach their mother, but they also

secure attachment a pattern of attachment in which infants or young children have a high-quality, relatively unambivalent relationship with their attachment figure. In the Strange Situation, a securely attached infant, for example, may be upset when the caregiver leaves but may be happy to see the caregiver return, recovering quickly from any distress. When children are securely attached, they can use caregivers as a secure base for exploration.

insecure attachment a pattern of attachment in which infants or young children have a less positive attachment to their caregiver than do securely attached children. Insecurely attached children can be classified as insecure/resistant (ambivalent), insecure/avoidant, or disorganized/disoriented.

insecure/resistant (or ambivalent) attachment a type of insecure attachment in which infants or young children are clingy and stay close to their caregiver rather than exploring their environment. In the Strange Situation, insecure/resistant infants tend to get very upset when the caregiver leaves them alone in the room, and they are not readily comforted by strangers. When their caregiver returns, they are not easily comforted and both seek comfort and resist efforts by the caregiver to comfort them.

insecure/avoidant attachment a type of insecure attachment in which infants or young children seem somewhat indifferent toward their caregiver and may even avoid the caregiver. In the Strange Situation, they seem indifferent toward their caregiver before the caregiver leaves the room and indifferent or avoidant when the caregiver returns. If they get upset when left alone, they are as easily comforted by a stranger as by a parent.

disorganized/disoriented attachment a type of insecure attachment in which infants or young children have no consistent way of coping with the stress of the Strange Situation. Their behavior is often confused or even contradictory, and they often appear dazed or disoriented

individual differences

Parental Attachment Status

According to attachment theorists, parents have "working models" of attachment relationships that guide their interactions with their children and thereby influence the security of their children's attachment. These **adult attachment models** are based on adults' perceptions of their own childhood relationships with their parents and on the continuing influence of those relationships (Main, Kaplan, & Cassidy, 1985).

Parental models of attachment often are measured with the Adult Attachment Interview (AAI), developed by Mary Main, Carol George, and their colleagues. In this interview, adults are asked to discuss their early childhood attachments and to evaluate them from their current perspectives (Hesse, 1999). For example, they are asked to describe their childhood relationship with each parent, including what their parent did for them when they were hurt or upset; what they remember about separations from the parent; if they ever felt rejected by the parent; and how their adult personalities were shaped by these experiences. These descriptions are used to classify the adults into four major attachment groups—autonomous (or secure), dismissing, preoccupied, and unresolved/disorganized.

Adults who are rated *autonomous,* or *secure,* are those whose descriptions are coherent, consistent, and relevant to the questions. Generally, autonomous adults describe their past in a balanced manner, recalling both positive and negative features of their parents and of their relationships with them. They also report that their early attachments were influential in their development. Autonomous adults discuss their past in a consistent and coherent manner even if they did not have supportive parents.

Adults in the other three categories are considered to be insecure in their attachment status. *Dismissing* adults often insist that they cannot remember attachment-related interactions with their parents, or they minimize the impact that these experiences had on them. They may also contradict themselves when describing their attachment-related experiences and seem unaware of their inconsistencies. For example, they may describe their mother in glowing terms and later talk about how she got angry at them whenever they hurt themselves (Hesse, 1999).

Preoccupied adults are intensely focused on their parents and tend to give confused and angry accounts of attachment-related experiences. A prototypical response is "I got so angry [at my mother] that I picked up the soup bowl and threw it at her" (Hesse, 1999, p. 403). Preoccupied adults often seem to be so caught up in their attachment memories that they cannot provide a coherent description of them. *Unresolved/disorganized* adults appear to be suffering the aftermath of past traumatic experiences of loss or abuse. Their descriptions of their childhood show striking lapses in reasoning and may not make sense. For example, an unresolved/disorganized adult may indicate that he or she believes that a dead parent is still alive or that the parent died because of negative thoughts that the adult had about the parent (Hesse, 1999).

Parents' attachment classification predicts both their sensitivity toward their own children and their children's attachment to them. Autonomous parents tend to be sensitive, warm parents, and their infants usually are securely attached to them (Magai, Hunziker, Mesias, & Culver, 2000; Steele, Steele, & Fonagy, 1996; van IJzendoorn, 1995). Correspondingly, parents in the other three categories tend to have insecurely attached infants, although the relation is not very strong for preoccupied parents (see figure). Unresolved parents are particularly likely to have disorganized infants (Hesse & Main, 2006; Madigan, Moran, Schuengel, et al., 2007), probably partly due to their low sensitivity, negative and controlling parenting, or disengaged, inattentive interactions with their children (Bailey, Moran, Pederson, & Bento, 2007; Busch, Cowan, & Cowan, 2008).

This general pattern of findings has been found in studies in a number of different Western cultures (Hesse, 1999). It is also noteworthy that mothers' attachment scores have been associated not only with those of their infants but also with their own mothers' scores on the AAI (Benoit & Parker, 1994).

The reason for the association between parents' attachment models and the security of their children's attachments is not clear. There is little doubt that autonomous parents are more sensitively attuned to

seem to regard her as a source of fear from which they want to withdraw (Main & Solomon, 1990). About 15% of middle-class American infants fall into this category. However, this percentage may be considerably higher among maltreated infants (van IJzendoorn et al., 1999), among infants whose parents are having serious difficulties with their own working models of attachment (van IJzendoorn, 1995) (see Box 11.1), and among preschoolers from lower socioeconomic backgrounds (Moss et al., 2004; van IJzendoorn et al., 1999).

A key question, of course, is whether there is some similarity between infants' behavior in the Strange Situation and their behavior at home. The answer is yes (Solomon & George, 1999). For example, in comparison with infants who are insecurely attached, 12-month-olds who are securely attached exhibit more enjoyment of physical contact, are less fussy or difficult, and are better able to use their mothers as a secure base for exploration at home (Pederson & Moran, 1996).

adult attachment models working models of attachment in adulthood that are believed to be based upon adults' perceptions of their own childhood experiences—especially their relationships with their parents—and of the influence of these experiences on them as adults

11.1

their children and that this contributes to their children's being securely attached (Pederson, Gleason, Moran, & Bento, 1998). For example, securely attached parents are less angry and intrusive in their interactions with their children than are preoccupied parents (Adam, Gunnar, & Tanaka, 2004). And it may very well be that autonomous adults, who tend to have been securely attached as infants or children (Waters, Merrick, Trebouz, Cromwell, & Albersheim, 2000), are more sensitive and skilled parents because of their own early experiences with sensitive parents (although the evidence for this is somewhat conflicting; Bailey et al., 2007).

However, it is not clear what adults' responses on the AAI actually represent. Although attachment theorists claim that the content and coherence of adults' discussions of their own early childhood experiences reflect the effects of these early experiences, there is little evidence to prove (or disprove) this theory (Fox, 1995; Thompson, 1998). Rather than reflecting their own childhood experiences, adults' discussions of them may instead reflect their personal theories about development and child rearing, their current level of psychological functioning, or their personality, all of which also may affect their parenting. Regardless of the reason, the relation between parents' attachment models and their infants' attachment suggests that parents' beliefs about parenting and about relationships have a powerful influence on the bond between them and their children (Thompson, 1998).

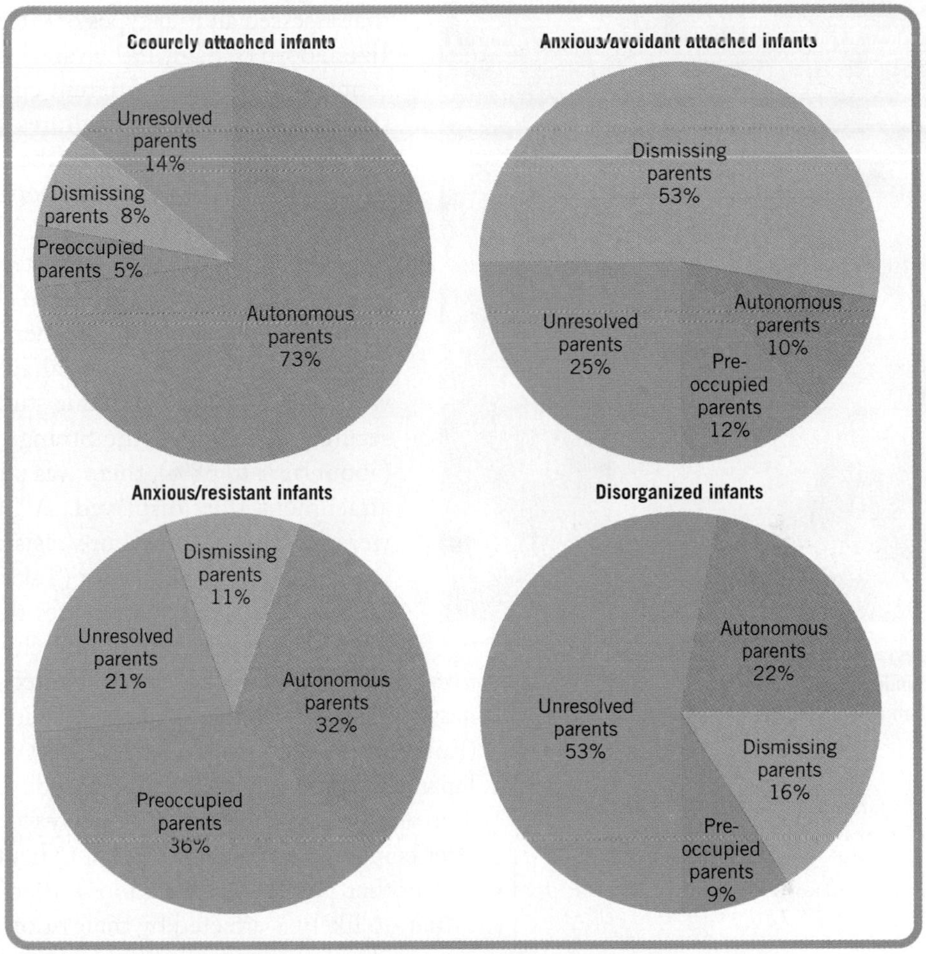

Parents with secure adult attachments tend to have securely attached children. (Adapted from van IJzendoorn, 1995)

Thus, they are more likely to learn about their environments and to enjoy doing so. In addition, children's behavior in the Strange Situation correlates with attachment scores derived from observing children's interactions with their mother over several hours (van IJzendoorn, Vereijken, Bakermans-Kranenburg, & Riksen-Walraven, 2004). As you will shortly see, attachment measurements derived from the Strange Situation also correlate with later behavior patterns.

Cultural Variations in Attachment

Because human infants are believed to be biologically predisposed to form attachments with their caregivers, one might expect attachment behaviors to be similar in different cultures. In fact, in large measure, infants' behaviors in the Strange Situation are similar across numerous cultures, including those of China, western

DON STEVENSON / INDEX STOCK IMAGERY / PICTUREQUEST

The degree to which children are encouraged to be independent varies across cultures and can affect whether or not children are categorized as insecure/resistant.

Europe, and various parts of Africa. In all these cultures, there are securely attached, insecure/resistant, insecure/avoidant, and disorganized infants, with the average percentages for these groupings in non-Western cultures being approximately 8%, 53%, 18%, and 24%, respectively, in those studies that assessed all four types of attachments (rather than only three types; van IJzendoorn & Sagi, 1999; van IJzendoorn et al., 1999). However, these percentages vary across different cultures and studies. Although relatively few studies in non-Western cultures have included the category "disorganized/disoriented," the findings of those that have suggest that the percentage of babies who fall into this category is roughly the same as in Western countries (Behrens, Hesse, & Main, 2007; van IJzendoorn et al., 1999).

Despite these general consistencies in attachment ratings, some interesting and important differences in children's behavior in the Strange Situation have been noted in certain other cultures (van IJzendoorn & Kroonenberg, 1988; Zevalkink, Riksen-Walraven, & Van Lieshout, 1999). For example, while Japanese infants in one study showed roughly the same percentage of secure attachment in the Strange Situation as middle-class U.S. infants do (about 62% to 68%), there was a notable difference in the types of insecure attachment they displayed. All the insecurely attached Japanese infants were classified as insecure/resistant, which is to say that none exhibited insecure/avoidant behavior (Takahashi, 1986).

One possible explanation for this is that Japanese culture exalts the idea of oneness between mother and child; correspondingly, its child-rearing practices, compared with those in the United States, foster greater mother–infant closeness and physical intimacy, as well as infants' greater dependency on their mother (Rothbaum, Pott, Azuma, Miyake, & Weisz, 2000). Thus, in the Strange Situation, Japanese children may desire more bodily contact and reassurance than do U.S. children and therefore may be more likely to exhibit anger and resistance to their mother after being denied contact with her (Mizuta, Zahn-Waxler, Cole, & Hiruma, 1996).

Another possible explanation is that how young children react in the Strange Situation likely is affected by their prior experience with unfamiliar situations and people. Thus, part of the difference in the rates of insecure/resistant attachment shown by Japanese and U.S. infants may be due to the fact that, at the time that many of the studies in question were conducted (the 1980s), very few infants in Japan were enrolled in day care and thus did not experience frequent separations from their mother. Consistent with this argument, a high number of insecure/resistant babies was not found in a more recent study of the reunion behaviors of 6-year-old Japanese children who had all experienced regular separations from their mother due to their having attended preschool (Behrens, Hesse, & Main, 2007). Nor was a high number found in another study of infants in Tokyo who did not attend child care but who had frequent play interactions with other infants, likely sometimes outside the home (Durrett, Otaki, & Richards, 1984). It is therefore possible that differences in children's experiences with separation within or across cultures contribute substantially to the variability in children's behavior in the Strange Situation.

Factors Associated with the Security of Children's Attachment

One obvious question that arises in trying to explain differences in attachment patterns is whether the parents of securely attached and insecurely attached children differ in the way they interact with their children. Evidence suggests that they do.

Parental Sensitivity

ELIZABETH CREWS

The mothers of securely attached infants generally respond warmly to their offspring and are sensitive to their needs.

Attachment theorists have argued that the most crucial parental factor contributing to the development of a secure attachment is **parental sensitivity** (Ainsworth, Blehar, Waters, & Wall, 1978). One key aspect of parental sensitivity is *consistently responsive* caregiving. The mothers of securely attached 1-year-olds tend to read their babies' signals accurately, responding quickly to the needs of a crying baby and smiling back at a beaming one. Positive exchanges between mother and child, such as mutual smiling and laughing, making sounds at one another, or engaging in coordinated play, are a characteristic of sensitive parenting that may be particularly important in promoting secure attachment (De Wolff & van IJzendoorn, 1997; Nievar & Becker, 2007).

In contrast, the mothers of insecure/resistant infants tend to be inconsistent in their early caregiving: they sometimes respond promptly to their infants' distress, but sometimes they do not. These mothers often seem highly anxious and overwhelmed by the demands of caregiving. Mothers of insecure/avoidant infants tend to be indifferent and emotionally unavailable, sometimes rejecting their baby's attempts at physical closeness (Isabella, 1993). Mothers of disorganized/distressed infants sometimes exhibit abusive, frightening, or disoriented behavior and may be dealing with unresolved loss or trauma (Forbes, Evans, Moran, & Pederson, 2007; Madigan, Moran, & Pederson, 2006; van IJzendoorn, Schuengel, & Bakermans-Kranenburg, 1999). In response, their infants often appear to be confused or frightened (Carlson, 1998; Hesse & Main, 2006). By age 3 to 6, perhaps in an attempt to manage their emotion, these children often try to control their parent's activities and conversation either in an excessively helpful and emotionally positive way, basically trying to cheer their mother up, or through hostility and aggression (Moss et al., 2004; Solomon, George, & De Jong, 1995).

The association between maternal sensitivity and the quality of infants' and children's attachment has been demonstrated in numerous studies involving a variety of cultural groups (Posada, Carbonell, Alzate, & Plata, 2004; Valenzuela, 1997; van IJzendoorn et al., 2004). Particularly striking is the finding that infants whose mothers are insensitive show only a 38% rate of secure attachment, which is much lower than the typical rate (van IJzendoorn & Sagi, 1999). An association between fathers' sensitivity and the security of their children's attachment has also been found, though it is somewhat weaker than that for mothers (van IJzendoorn & De Wolff, 1997); and the relation between maternal sensitivity and security of attachment may be somewhat weaker in low-income families than in higher-income families (Nievar & Becker, 2007).

Given that all the research discussed above involves correlations between parental sensitivity and children's attachment status, it is impossible to determine whether parents' sensitivity was actually responsible for their children's security of attachment or was merely associated with it. It could be that some other factor, such as the presence or absence of marital conflict, affected both the parent's sensitivity and the child's security of attachment. However, evidence that parental sensitivity does in fact have a causal effect on infants' attachment has been provided by short-term experimental interventions designed to enhance the sensitivity of mothers' caregiving. These interventions, discussed in Box 11.2, have been found to increase not only mothers' sensitivity with their infants but also the security of

parental sensitivity an important factor contributing to the security of an infant's attachment. Parental sensitivity can be exhibited in a variety of ways, including responsive caregiving when an infant is distressed or upset and engaging in coordinated play with the infant.

applications 11.2

Interventions and Attachment

To determine whether parental sensitivity is *causally* related to differences in security of attachment, researchers have designed special intervention studies. In these studies, parents in an experimental group are first trained to be more sensitive in their caregiving. Later, the attachment statuses of their infants are compared with those of children whose parents, as members of a control group, experienced no intervention (van IJzendoorn, Juffer, & Duyvesteyn, 1995).

An intervention study of this sort was conducted in the Netherlands by Daphna van den Boom (1994, 1995). Infants who were rated as irritable shortly after their birth were selected for the study because some investigators (but not all) have found that irritable infants may be at risk for insecure attachment. When the infants were about 6 months of age, half of their mothers were randomly chosen to be in the experimental group for three months. The mothers in this group were taught to be attuned to their infants' cues regarding their wants and needs and to respond to them in a manner that fostered positive exchanges between mother and child. The remaining mothers formed the control group and received no special training.

At the end of the intervention, mothers in the experimental group were more attentive and responsive to their infants, as well as more stimulating, than those in the control group. In turn, their infants were more sociable, explored the environment more, were better able to soothe themselves, and cried less than did infants whose mothers did not receive the intervention. Especially significant, the rates of secure attachment were notably higher for infants whose mothers were in the experimental group—62% compared with 22%.

In a longitudinal follow-up, the infants and mothers were evaluated again when the children were 18 months, 24 months, and 3½ years of age. At 18 months of age, 72% of the children in the intervention group were securely attached, compared with 26% of the children in the control group. When their infants were 24 months old, mothers in the intervention group were, as earlier, more accepting, accessible, cooperative, and sensitive with their infants than were the control-group mothers, and their children were more cooperative. Similar findings were obtained when the children were 3½ years old.

Experimental interventions also have been used to improve depressed mothers' attachments will their children. As discussed in Chapter 10, depressed mothers tend to have depressed children. The assumption in these intervention studies is that depressed mothers can be provided with skills and knowledge that improve the quality of the mother–infant relationship, which, in turn, reduces depression in children. In one study, for example, investigators taught depressed mothers parenting skills and provided them with information about child development to enhance their coping and social-support skills (Toth, Rogosch, Manly, & Cicchetti, 2006). In another study (van Doesum, Riksen-Qalraven, Hosman, & Hoefnagels, 2008), depressed mothers were videotaped bathing or feeding their infant and then, after viewing the film, were trained to respond to the infant with more sensitive and appropriate communicative behaviors. In addition, training included one or more of the following four techniques: modeling of a positive caregiving by a home visitor; encouraging the mother to change negative patterns of thinking about her infant and about her own parenting skills; providing practical information on child development and behavior; and offering instruction in how to massage the baby.

Both studies were successful in improving the quality of the mother–infant attachment relationship. Based on evidence from experimental studies such as this, it seems clear that parenting sensitivity contributes to infants' and young children's security of attachment.

their infants' attachment (Bakermans-Kranenburg, van IJzendoorn, & Juffer, 2003; van IJzendoorn, Juffer, & Duyvesteyn, 1995). Moreover, in twin studies of infants' attachment, nearly all the variation in attachments was due to environmental factors, including those to which all children in the home were exposed and those that one child but not another experienced (Bokhorst et al., 2003; Roisman & Fraley, 2008).

Does Security of Attachment Have Long-Term Effects?

The reason that developmentalists are so interested in children's attachment status is that securely attached infants appear to grow up to be better adjusted and more socially skilled than do insecurely attached children. One explanation for this may be that children with a secure attachment are more likely to develop positive and constructive internal working models of attachment. (Recall that children's working models of attachment are believed to shape their adjustment and social behavior, self-perceptions and sense of self, and expectations about other people, and there is some direct evidence for this assumption [e.g., Johnson, Dweck, & Chen, 2007].) In addition, children who experience the sensitive, supportive parenting that is associated with secure attachment are likely to learn that it is acceptable to express emotions in an appropriate way and that emotional communication with others is important (Cassidy, 1994; Kerns, Abraham, Schlegelmilch, & Morgan, 2007; Sroufe, 1995). In contrast, insecure/avoidant children, whose parents tend to be nonresponsive to their signals of need and distress, are likely to learn to inhibit emotional expressiveness and to not seek comfort from other people (Bridges & Grolnick, 1995).

Consistent with these patterns, children who were securely attached as infants seem to have closer, more harmonious relationships with peers than do insecurely attached children. For example, they are somewhat more regulated, sociable, and socially competent with peers (Lucas-Thompson & Clarke-Stewart, 2007; Troy & Sroufe, 1987; Vondra, Shaw, Swearingen, Cohen, & Owens, 2001) and, correspondingly, are less anxious (Dallaire & Weinraub, 2007), aggressive, and antisocial (DeMulder, Denham, Schmidt, & Mitchell, 2000; Madigan, Moran, Schuengel, Pederson, & Otten, 2007; NICDH Early Child Care Research Network, 2006). They are also better able to understand others' emotions (Laible & Thompson, 1998; Ontai & Thompson, 2002; Steele, Steele, Croft, & Fonagy, 1999) and display more helping, sharing, and concern for peers (Kestenbaum, Farber, & Sroufe, 1989).

Secure attachment in infancy even predicts positive peer and romantic relationships and emotional health in adolescence (Carlson, Sroufe, & Egeland, 2004; Collins, Hennighausen, Schmit, & Sroufe, 1997). There is also some evidence that although securely and insecurely attached children do not differ in terms of intelligence (Thompson, 1998), securely attached children tend to be more attentive and involved at school than insecurely attached children and to earn higher grades (Jacobsen & Hofmann, 1997).

The general patterns described above hold when children's attachment status has been assessed in infancy or after infancy using a variety of methods besides the Strange Situation (e.g., Allen et al., 2002, 2007; Moss et al., 2004; Schneider, Atkinson, & Tardif, 2001). Clearly, then, children's security of attachment is related to their later psychological, social, and cognitive functioning. However, experts disagree on the meaning of this relationship. As noted, some theorists believe that early security of attachment has important effects on later development because it provides enduring working models of positive relationships (Bowlby, 1973; Fraley, 2002; Sroufe, Egeland, & Kreutzer, 1990). This view implies that the effects of early attachment remain stable over time. Other theorists believe that early security of attachment predicts later development primarily to the degree that the child's environment—including the quality of parent–child interactions does not change (Lamb, Thompson, Gardner, & Charnov, 1985). In other words, early security of attachment predicts children's functioning at an older age because "good" parents tend to remain good parents and "bad" parents tend to remain bad parents. If the parent–child relationship and family circumstances change due to divorce, financial stress, or other factors, including positive ones, the child's attachment and development are likely to change as well.

Empirical findings support both perspectives to some degree. One study reported that even if they functioned poorly during the preschool years, children who had a secure attachment and adapted well during infancy and toddlerhood were more socially and emotionally competent in middle childhood than were their

MARY KATE DENNY / PHOTOEDIT

Toddlers who were securely attached as infants are more likely to engage in prosocial behavior, such as trying to comfort someone who is sad, than are those who were insecurely attached as infants.

peers who had been insecurely attached (Sroufe et al., 1990). This suggests that a child's early attachment has some effects over time. However, although there often is considerable stability in attachment security (Fraley, 2002; Hamilton, 2000), there also is evidence that children's security of attachment can change somewhat as their environment changes—for example, with the onset or termination of stress and conflict in the home (Frosch, Mangelsdorf, & McHale, 2000; Lewis, Feiring, & Rosenthal, 2000; Moss et al., 2004) or a pronounced shift in the mother's typical behavior with the child (Forbes et al., 2007). In such cases, current parent–child interactions or parenting behaviors predict the child's social and emotional competence at that age better than measures of attachment taken at younger ages (Thompson, 1998; Youngblade & Belsky, 1992). Thus, it is likely that children's development can be predicted better from the combination of both their early attachment status and the quality of subsequent parenting than from either factor alone. Finally, it must be emphasized again that most of the research on attachment is correlational, so it is difficult to pin down causal relations.

review:

Evidence of the poor development of infants who are deprived of caring, consistent relationships with an adult led to extensive interest in infants' early attachments. John Bowlby proposed that a secure attachment provides children with a secure base for exploration and contributes to a positive internal working model of relationships in general. According to attachment research, pioneered by Mary Ainsworth, children's attachment relationships with caregivers can be classified as secure, insecure/avoidant, insecure/resistant, and disorganized/disoriented. Children in these categories display similarities across cultures, although the percentage of children in different attachment groups sometimes varies across cultures or subcultures.

Factors that appear to influence the security of attachment include caregivers' sensitivity and responsiveness to children's needs and parents' attachment status. Children's security of attachment to their caregivers predicts the quality of their relationships with family members and peers and their academic skills, all of which are likely to affect how children feel about and evaluate themselves. These relations may hold not only because the sensitivity of parenting in the early years of life has long-term effects but also because sensitive parents usually continue to provide effective parenting, whereas less sensitive parents continue to interact with the children in ways that undermine children's optimal development.

Conceptions of the Self

As we have noted, children's security of attachment to caregivers affects their feelings about themselves, especially in regard to their relationships with other people. Thus, attachment experiences early in life likely color the sense of self that emerges in infancy. However, the development of a sense of self is an ongoing, very complex process that involves much more than early notions of the self.

When we speak of **self,** we are referring to a conceptual system made up of one's thoughts and attitudes about oneself. This conceptual system can include thoughts about one's own physical being (e.g., body, possessions), social characteristics (e.g., relationships, personality, social roles), and "spiritual" or internal characteristics (e.g., thoughts and psychological functioning). It also may include notions about how the self changes or remains the same over time, beliefs about one's own role in shaping these processes, and even reflections on one's own consciousness of selfhood (Damon & Hart, 1988). The development of the self is important because individuals' self-conceptions, including the ways they view and feel about themselves, appear to influence their overall feelings of well-being and competence.

self a conceptual system made up of one's thoughts and attitudes about oneself

The Development of Conceptions of Self

Children's sense of self emerges in the early years of life, especially in their interactions with people who are important to them. It continues to develop into adulthood, becoming more complex as the individual's emotional and cognitive development deepens.

The Self in Infancy

There is compelling evidence that infants have a rudimentary sense of self in the first months of life. As we saw in Chapters 5 and 10, by 2 to 4 months of age, infants have a sense of their ability to control objects outside themselves, as is clear both from their enthusiasm when they can make a mobile move by pulling a string attached to an arm and from their anger when their efforts no longer have an effect. They also seem to have some understanding of their own bodily movements. For example, when viewing live video images of their own leg movements, 3- to 5-month-old infants looked longer and moved their legs more when the video showed their leg movements from a perspective other than their own (e.g., when the right and left legs in the video image appeared to move in opposition to the leg movements the infants were performing) than when the video image showed leg movements as the infants themselves saw them (Rochat & Morgan, 1995). Perhaps their longer looking reflected their surprise at, or interest in, seeing the reversal of their leg movements (Rochat & Striano, 2002).

A sense of self becomes much more distinct at about 8 months of age, when infants react with separation distress if parted from their mother, suggesting that they recognize that they and their mother are separate entities. Further indications that children view others as beings different from themselves are apparent by age 1. As discussed in Chapter 4, around their 1st birthday, infants begin to show joint attention with respect to objects in the environment. For example, they will visually follow a caregiver's pointing finger to find the object that the caregiver is calling attention to, and then turn back to the caregiver to confirm that they are indeed looking at the intended object (Stern, 1985). They sometimes will also give objects to an adult in an apparent effort to engage the adult in their activities (West & Rheingold, 1978).

INFANT LEARNING LABORATORY, INSTITUTE FOR THE STUDY OF CHILD DEVELOPMENT, ROBERT WOOD JOHNSON MEDICAL SCHOOL, MICHAEL LEWIS, PH.D., DIRECTOR

Even young infants seem to experience a sense of mastery and control when they can make a mobile do their bidding by moving their arm.

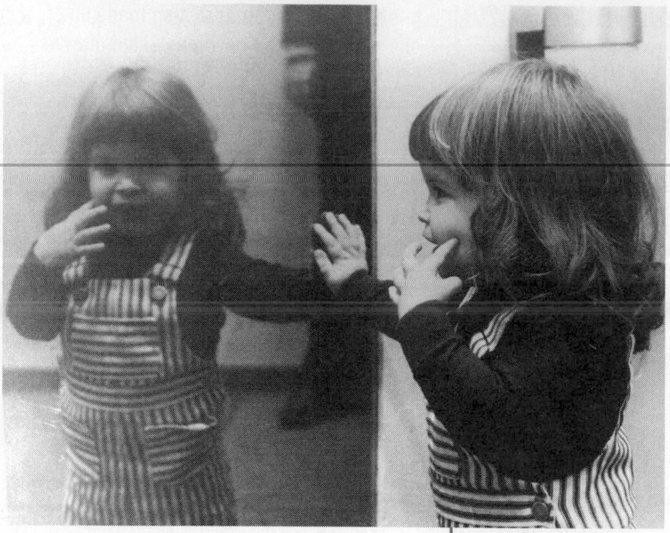

DR. MICHAEL LEWIS, INSTITUTE FOR THE STUDY OF CHILD DEVELOPMENT, ROBERT WOOD JOHNSON MEDICAL SCHOOL, UNIVERSITY OF MEDICINE AND DENTISTRY OF NEW JERSEY, EAST BRUNSWICK, N.J.

In this photo from the original research of Lewis and Brooks-Gunn, the girl recognizes that the child in the mirror with a spot on her cheek is herself.

Infants' emerging recognition of the self becomes more directly apparent by 18 to 20 months of age, when many children can look into a mirror and realize that they are looking at themselves (Asendorpf, Warkentin, & Baudonniere, 1996; Lewis & Brooks-Gunn, 1979; Nielsen, Suddendorf, & Slaughter, 2006). In studies that test this ability, an experimenter surreptitiously puts a dot of rouge on a child's face, places the child in front of a mirror, and then asks the child who the person with the red spot is, or tells the child to clean the spot off the person in the mirror. Children younger than 18 months old often respond by trying to touch the child in the mirror, or they do nothing. By about the age of 18 months, however, many children touch the rouge on their own face, so it is assumed that they realize that the mirror image is a self-reflection.

By age 2, many children can recognize themselves in photographs. In one study, 63% of a group of 20- to 25-month-olds picked themselves out when presented with pictures of themselves and two same-sex, same-age children. By approximately age 30 months, 97% of the children immediately picked their own photograph (Bullock & Lutkenhaus, 1990).

During their third year, children's self-awareness becomes quite clear in other ways as well. As we saw in Chapter 10, 2-year-olds exhibit embarrassment and shame—emotions that obviously require a sense of self (Lewis, 1995, 1998). The strength of 2-year-olds' awareness of self is even more evident in their notorious self-assertion, which has led to the period between ages 2 and 3 to be called the "terrible twos." During this time, children often try to determine their activities and goals independent of, and often in direct opposition to, what their parents (and other adults) want them to do (Bullock & Lutkenhaus, 1990).

Two-year-olds' self-awareness is also evident in, and is enhanced by, their use of language. They can, for example, use pronouns to refer to themselves ("me," "mine") and can label themselves by name (e.g., "Daddy take Julia's book") (Bates, 1990). Young children can also use language to store in memory their own experiences and behavior, giving them access to information about themselves and their past. Thus, language makes it possible for children to construct a narrative of their own "life story" and develop a more enduring picture of the self (Harter, 1998; Thompson, 2006).

Parents contribute to the child's expanding self-image by providing descriptive information about the child ("You're such a big boy"), evaluative descriptions of the child ("You're so smart"), and information about the degree to which the child has met rules and standards ("Good girls don't hit their baby sisters"). As noted in Chapter 4, parents also collaborate in children's construction of autobiographical memory by reminding them of their past experiences (Snow, 1990).

The Self in Childhood

As children progress through childhood, their conception of themselves becomes increasingly complex and encompassing. This developmental pattern in self-understanding has been vividly illustrated by Susan Harter, a leading researcher on children's emerging sense of self. Combining statements made by a wide array of children in a number of empirical studies, Harter has constructed composite examples of children's typical self-descriptive statements at different ages. The following is a composite example of how 3- to 4-year-olds describe themselves:

> I'm three years old and I live in a big house with my mother and father and my brother, Jason, and my sister, Lisa. I have blue eyes and a kitty that is orange and a television in my room. I know all of my ABC's, listen: A, B, C, D, E, F, G, H, J, L, K, O, M, P, Q, X, Z. I can run real fast. I like pizza, and I have a nice teacher at preschool. I can count up to 10, want to hear me? I love my dog Skipper. I can climb to the top of the jungle gym—I'm not scared! I'm never scared! I'm always happy. . . . I'm really strong. I can lift this chair, watch me!
>
> (Harter, 1999, p. 37)

As this composite self-description demonstrates, at age 3 to 4, children understand themselves in terms of concrete, observable characteristics related to physical attributes ("I have blue eyes"), physical activities and abilities ("I can run real fast"), social relationships ("my brother, Jason, and my sister, Lisa"), and psychological traits ("I'm always happy") (Damon & Hart, 1988; Harter, 1999). Their focus on observable features is further reflected by the fact that the prototypical 3-year-old in the example bragged about particular skills such as running fast and did not make generalizations about his/her overall ability as an athlete. Even when the child made a general statement about himself/herself ("I'm really strong"), this statement was closely tied to actual behavior (lifting a chair). Young children also describe themselves in terms of their preferences ("I love my dog Skipper") and possessions ("I have . . . a kitty . . . and a television").

SUPERSTOCK

In describing themselves, young children often make reference to their preferences and possessions such as a family pet.

The composite example reflects another characteristic typical of children's self-concept during the preschool years: their self-evaluations are unrealistically positive. Young children seem to think that they are really like what they want to be (Harter & Pike, 1984; Stipek, Roberts, & Sanborn, 1984). For example, the child in the composite self-description claimed mastery of the ABCs but clearly lacked it. Maintaining positive illusions about themselves is relatively easy for young children because they usually do not consider their own prior successes and failures when assessing their abilities. Even if they have failed badly at a task several times, they are likely to believe that they will succeed on the next try (Ruble, Grosovsky, Frey, & Cohen, 1992).

Children begin to refine their conceptions of self in elementary school, in part because they increasingly engage in **social comparison,** comparing themselves with others in terms of their characteristics, behaviors, and possessions ("He is bigger than me"). At the same time, they increasingly pay attention to discrepancies between their own and others' performance on tasks ("She got an A on the test and I got only a C") (Frey & Ruble, 1985). By middle to late elementary school, children's conceptions of self have begun to become integrated and more broadly encompassing, as is illustrated by the following composite self-description that would be typical of a child between the ages of 8 and 11:

> I'm pretty popular, at least with the girls. That's because I'm nice to people and helpful and can keep secrets. Mostly I am nice to my friends, although if I get in a bad mood I sometimes say something that can be a little mean. . . . At school, I'm feeling pretty smart in certain subjects like Language Arts and Social Studies. . . . But I'm feeling pretty dumb in Math and Science, especially when I see how well a lot of the other kids are doing. Even though I'm not doing well in those subjects, I still like myself as a person, because Math and Science just aren't that important to me. How I look and how popular I am are more important. I also like myself because I know my parents like me and so do other kids. That helps you like yourself.
>
> (Harter, 1999, p. 48)

social comparison the process of comparing aspects of one's own psychological, behavioral, or physical functioning to that of others in order to evaluate oneself

PHOTODISC RED / GETTY IMAGES

In middle childhood, children start to refine their sense of self by comparing their own attributes and behavior with those of peers.

The developmental changes in older children's conceptions of self reflect cognitive advances in their ability to use higher-order concepts that integrate more specific behavioral features of the self. For example, the child in the preceding self-description was able to relate being "popular" to several behaviors, such as being "nice to others" and being able to "keep secrets." In addition, older children can coordinate opposing self-representations ("smart" and "dumb") that, at a younger age, they would have considered mutually exclusive (Harter, 1999; Marsh, Craven, & Debus, 1998). The newfound cognitive capacity to form higher-order conceptions of the self allows older children to construct more global views of themselves and to evaluate themselves as a person overall. These abilities result in a more balanced and realistic assessment of the self, although they also can result in feelings of inferiority and helplessness (see the discussion of achievement motivation in Chapter 9, pages 360–361).

The preceding self-description also reflects the fact that schoolchildren's self-concepts are increasingly based on others' evaluations of them, especially those of their peers. Consequently, their self-descriptions often contain a pronounced social element and focus on characteristics that may influence their place in their social networks, as reflected in the following interview:

> WHAT ARE YOU LIKE? I am friendly.
>
> WHY IS THAT IMPORTANT? Other kids won't like you if you aren't.
>
> (Damon & Hart, 1988, p. 60)

Because older school-age children's conceptions of self are strongly influenced by the opinions of others, children at this age are vulnerable to low self-esteem if others view them negatively or as less competent than their peers (Harter, 2006).

The Self in Adolescence

Children's conceptions of self change in fundamental ways across adolescence, due in part to the emergence of abstract thinking during this stage of life (see Chapter 4, pages 139–140). The ability to use this kind of thinking allows adolescents to conceive of themselves in terms of abstract characteristics that encompass a variety of concrete characteristics and behaviors. Consider the following composite self-description of a young adolescent:

> I'm an extrovert with my friends: I'm talkative, pretty rowdy, and funny. . . . All in all, around people I know pretty well I'm awesome, at least I think my friends think I am. I'm usually cheerful when I'm with my friends, happy and excited to be doing things with them. . . . With my parents . . . I feel sad as well as mad and also hopeless about ever pleasing them. . . . At school, I'm pretty intelligent. I know that because I'm smart when it comes to how I do in classes, I'm curious about learning new things, and I'm also creative when it comes to solving problems. My teacher says so. . . . I can be a real introvert around people I don't know well—I'm shy, uncomfortable, and nervous. Sometimes I'm simply an airhead, I act really dumb and say things that are just plain stupid. . . .
>
> (Harter, 1999, p. 60)

As is evident in this composite example, young people's concern over their social competence and their social acceptance, especially by peers, intensifies in early adolescence (Damon & Hart, 1988). The example also illustrates young adolescents' ability to arrive at higher-level, abstract self-descriptions such as "extrovert" based on personal traits such as "talkative," "rowdy," and "funny."

Particularly notable is the fact that adolescents can conceive of themselves in terms of a variety of selves, depending on the context. The adolescent in the composite, for instance, describes himself/herself as a somewhat different person with friends and with parents, as well as with familiar and unfamiliar people. In part, this may be because young adolescents tend to think about each of their abstract representations of the self separately from other abstractions and cannot integrate them (Higgins, 1991). Consequently, in terms of their overall sense of themselves, it does not overly concern young adolescents that the person they appear to be can vary according to the context (see Figure 11.1).

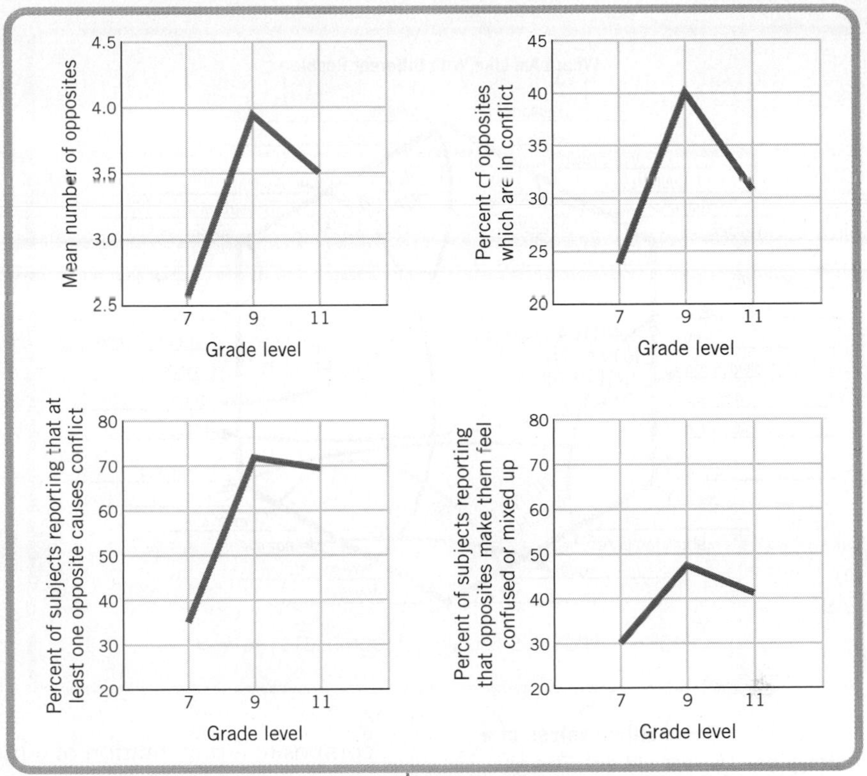

FIGURE 11.1 Developmental differences in adolescents' perceptions of opposing and conflicting self-attributes When asked about their characteristics, 7th graders were much less likely than older adolescents to report contradictions in their characteristics. Older adolescents, especially 9th graders, reported that such contradictions caused them to feel internal conflict such as confusion or negative emotion. (Adapted from Harter & Monsour, 1992)

According to David Elkind (1967), thinking about the self in early adolescence is characterized by a form of egocentrism called the **personal fable,** in which adolescents overly differentiate their feelings from those of others and come to regard themselves, and especially their feelings, as unique and special. They may believe that only they can experience whatever misery or rapture or confusion they are currently feeling. This belief is typified in the adolescent assertion "But you don't know how it feels," or "My parents don't understand me, what do *they* know about what it's like to be a teenager?" (Elkind, 1967; Harter, 1999, p. 76).

The kind of egocentrism that forms the basis for adolescents' personal fables also causes many adolescents to be preoccupied with what others think of them (Elkind, 1967; Harter, 1999; Rosenberg, 1979). This preoccupation is exhibited in what Elkind (1967) has labeled as the adolescent's belief in an **imaginary audience.** According to Elkind, because adolescents are so concerned with their own appearance and behavior, they assume that everyone else is, too. Wherever they are, whatever they are doing, they think that all eyes are upon them, scrutinizing their every blemish or social misstep.

In their middle teens, adolescents often begin to agonize over the contradictions in their behavior and characteristics. They tend to become introspective and concerned with the question of "Who am I?" (Broughton, 1978). Their concern with this question is reflected in the following composite self-description of a 15-year-old:

> What am I like as a person? You're probably not going to understand. I'm complicated! With my really *close* friends, I am very tolerant, I mean I'm understanding and caring. With a *group* of friends I'm rowdier. I'm also usually friendly and cheerful, but I can be pretty obnoxious and intolerant if I don't like how they're acting. . . . I really don't understand how I can switch so fast from being cheerful

personal fable a form of adolescent egocentrism that involves beliefs in the uniqueness of one's own feelings and thoughts

imaginary audience the belief, stemming from adolescent egocentrism, that everyone else is focused on the adolescent's appearance and behavior

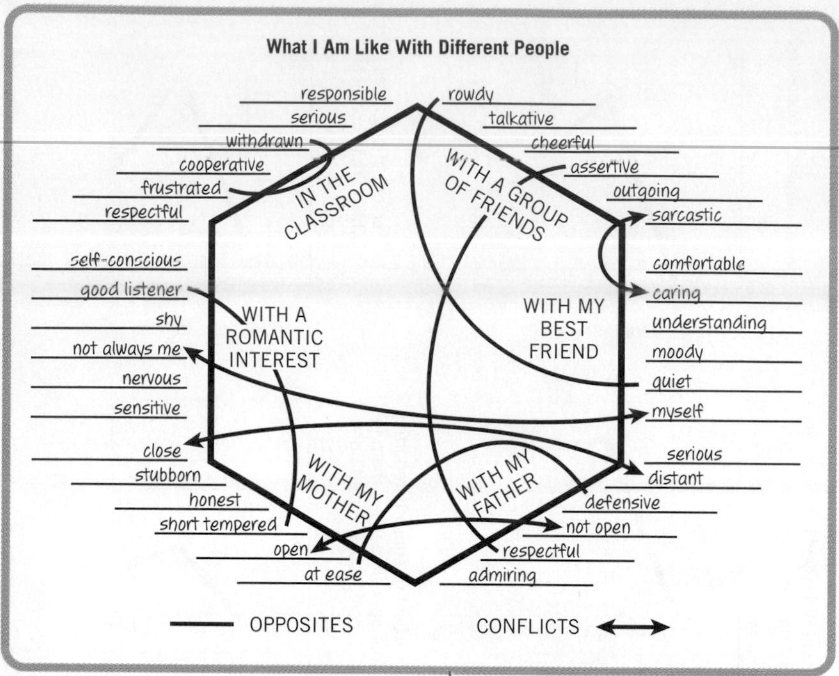

FIGURE 11.2 The multiple selves of a prototypical 15-year-old girl This girl viewed herself as being different in different contexts or with different people. For example, she described herself as open with her mother but not her father, and as quiet with her best friend but rowdy with a group of friends. (Adapted from Harter, 1999)

> with my friends, then coming home and feeling anxious, and then getting frustrated and sarcastic with my parents. Which one is the *real* me?
>
> (Quoted in Harter, 1999, p. 67)

Although adolescents in their middle teens are better than younger adolescents at identifying contradictions in themselves (see Figure 11.2) and often feel conflicted about these inconsistencies, most still do not have the cognitive skills needed to integrate their recognition of these contradictions into a coherent conception of self. As a consequence, adolescents of this age often feel confused and concerned about who they really are. As one teen put it, "It's not right, it should all fit together in one piece!" (Harter, 1999, p. 71; Harter, Bresnick, Bouchey, & Whitsell, 1998).

In late adolescence and early adulthood, the individual's conception of self becomes both more integrated and less determined by what others think. Both of these shifts are captured by Harter's composite representation of a high school senior:

> I'd like to be an ethical person who treats other people fairly. That's the kind of lawyer I'd like to be, too. I don't always live up to that standard; that is, sometimes I do something that doesn't feel that ethical. When that happens I get a little depressed because I don't like myself as a person. But I tell myself that it's natural to make mistakes, so I don't really question the fact that deep down inside, the real me is a moral person. Basically, I like who I am. . . . Being athletic isn't that high on my own list of what is important, even though it is for a lot of the kids in our school. But I don't really care what they think anymore. I *used* to, but now what *I* think is what counts. After all, I have to live with myself as a person and to respect that person, which I do now, more than a few years ago.
>
> (Quoted in Harter, 1999, p. 78)

As in the case of this prototypical senior, older adolescents' conceptions of self frequently reflect internalized personal values, beliefs, and standards. Many of these were instilled by others in the child's life but are now accepted and generated by adolescents as their own. Thus, older adolescents place less emphasis on what other people think than they did at younger ages and are more concerned with meeting their own standards and with their future self—what they are becoming or are going to be (Harter, 1999; Higgins, 1991).

Older adolescents are also more likely to have the cognitive capacity to integrate opposites or contradictions in the self that occur in different contexts or at different times (Higgins, 1991). They may explain contradictory characteristics in terms of the need to be flexible, and may view variations in their behavior with different people as "adaptive" because one cannot act the same with everyone. Similarly, they may integrate changes in emotion under the characteristic "moody." Moreover, they are likely to view their contradictions and inconsistencies as a normal part of being human, which likely reduces feelings of conflict and upset.

Whether older adolescents are able to successfully integrate contradictions in themselves likely depends not only on their own cognitive capacities but also on the help they receive from parents, teachers, and others in understanding the complexity

Feelings of self-worth develop partly from the child's feelings of acceptance in the family.

identity versus identity confusion Erikson's psychosocial stage of development that occurs during adolescence. During this stage, the adolescent or young adult either develops an identity or experiences an incomplete and sometimes incoherent sense of self.

identity achievement an integration of various aspects of the self into a coherent whole that is stable over time and across events

identity confusion an incomplete and sometimes incoherent sense of self that often occurs in Erikson's stage of identity versus identity confusion

of personalities. The support and tutelage of others in this regard allow adolescents to internalize values, beliefs, and standards that they feel committed to and to feel comfortable with who they are (Hart & Fegley, 1995; Harter, 1999).

Identity in Adolescence

Clearly, the question "Who am I?" is a central and often disturbing one for many adolescents. It is also a question that, for many older adolescents, expands well beyond the issue of multiple selves and inconsistent behavior. As they begin to approach adulthood, adolescents must begin to develop a sense of personal identity that incorporates numerous aspects of self, including their values, their belief systems, their goals for the future, and, for some, their sexual identity.

As noted in Chapter 9, Erik Erikson argued that the resolution of these many identity issues is the chief developmental task in adolescence. He referred to the resolution of these issues as the crisis of **identity versus identity confusion**. In his view, the challenge is as follows: "From among all possible and imaginable relations, [the person] must make a series of ever-narrowing selections of personal, occupational, sexual, and ideological commitments" (1968, p. 245). Successful resolution of this crisis results in **identity achievement**—that is, an integration of various aspects of the self into a coherent whole that is stable over time and across events.

During late adolescence, reexamination of one's value system is common; renewed commitment to previously held beliefs on the one hand, or total rejection on the other, are not unusual outcomes.

Erikson's Theory of Identity Formation

According to Erikson, adolescents who fail to attain identity achievement can experience one of several negative outcomes. One such outcome is **identity confusion,** an incomplete and sometimes incoherent sense of self that may cause the adolescent to feel lost, isolated, and depressed. Erikson suggested that some form of identity confusion is very common in adolescence and that it

MICHAEL NEWMAN / PHOTOEDIT

Trying out various "looks" can be an aspect of the self-discovery that occurs among many adolescents in some cultures.

generally lasts for a relatively short time, although it sometimes persists and turns into a more severe psychological disturbance.

Another negative outcome related to the struggle for identity can arise if adolescents commit themselves prematurely to an identity without adequately considering alternative possibilities. This identity choice is called **identity foreclosure.** An example of this category might be a 17-year-old who quits school and goes to work in a dead-end job because he or she does not envision any other options, or a young adolescent who decides to become a doctor simply because his or her parent is one, never considering any other options during high school, college, or medical school.

A different self-defeating outcome of the search for an identity is a **negative identity,** one that is chosen because it represents the opposite of what is valued by people around the adolescent. A typical example would be a minister's child's becoming a drug pusher or a professor's child's dropping out of high school with no occupational goal. For some adolescents, Erikson suggested, taking on a negative identity is a way of getting noticed by significant others when more conventional attempts have failed.

Erikson (1968) argued that because of all the "possible and imaginable" role options that are available in modern society, attaining identity achievement is highly complex and difficult. In light of the negative consequences of failing to achieve a coherent identity, he proposed the importance of a **psychosocial moratorium**—a time-out period during which the adolescent is not expected to take on adult roles and is free to pursue activities that lead to self-discovery. During this period, adolescents can try out new looks, new ways of acting, new ideas about what they want to do for a living, and so forth.

Although Erikson argued that this period of experimentation is important to adolescents' finding the best identity for themselves, a moratorium of this sort is possible or acceptable only in some cultures. Even then, it often is a luxury reserved for the middle and upper classes (i.e., those can who afford the moratorium provided by the college years). If adolescents must work full time to help support their families and themselves, many identity options will be closed to them because of limits on their time and schooling. In addition, in traditional societies where there are few role choices available, a moratorium is unheard of and unnecessary: children know from a very young age what their adult identity will be, and people generally live their lives in the same manner as their parents have.

Research on Identity Formation

Following up on Erikson's depiction of identity formation, a number of researchers looked for ways to measure the identity status of adolescents and to trace the outcome of the various statuses proposed by Erikson. The method most often used for this purpose was devised by James Marcia (1980). In this method, study participants are interviewed to determine the extent of their exploration of, and commitment to, issues related to occupation, ideology (e.g., religion, politics), and sexual behavior. On the basis of their responses, they are classified into one of the following four categories of identity status:

- **Identity-diffusion status.** The individual does not have firm commitments regarding the issues in question and is not making progress toward developing them.
- **Foreclosure status.** The individual has not engaged in any identity experimentation and has established a vocational or ideological identity based on the choices or values of others.

identity foreclosure ▮ premature commitment to an identity without adequate consideration of other options

negative identity ▮ identity that stands in opposition to what is valued by people around the adolescent

psychosocial moratorium ▮ a time-out during which the adolescent is not expected to take on adult roles and can pursue activities that lead to self-discovery

identity-diffusion status ▮ a category of identity status in which the individual does not have firm commitments and is not making progress toward them

foreclosure status ▮ a category of identity status in which the individual is not engaged in any identity experimentation and has established a vocational or ideological identity based on the choices or values of others

- **Moratorium status.** The individual is exploring various occupational and ideological choices and has not yet made a clear commitment to them.
- **Identity-achievement status.** The individual has achieved a coherent and consolidated identity based on personal decisions regarding occupation, ideology, and the like. The individual believes that these decisions were made autonomously and is committed to them.

Researchers using methods similar to Marcia's have found that most young adolescents seem to be in identity diffusion or identity foreclosure, and that the percentage of youth in moratorium status is highest at age 17 to 19 (Nurmi, 2004; Waterman, 1999). In the course of adolescence and early adulthood, people in identity-diffusion and moratorium statuses tend to move into identity-achievement status, whereas those in a foreclosed state often remain there (Berzonsky & Adams, 1999; Meeus, Iedema, Helsen, & Vollebergh, 1999).

Researchers generally have found that, at least in modern Western societies, the identity status of adolescents and young adults is related to their adjustment, social behavior, and personality. Those who have attained identity-achievement status tend to be more socially mature, higher in achievement motivation, and more likely to be involved in their careers. Individuals who have an identity-diffusion status tend to be apathetic, to lack intimate relationships with peers, and to be most at risk for drug abuse (Damon, 1983; Grotevant, 1998; Jones, 1992; Marcia, 1980).

Individuals with a foreclosure status are the most authoritarian in their attitudes (that is, they strongly believe in obeying authority) (Damon, 1983; Marcia & Friedman, 1970; Podd, Marcia, & Rubin, 1970) and are likely to rely on others to make important life decisions for them (Meeus et al., 1999; Orlofsky, 1978; Waterman & Waterman, 1971). Young adults with a diffused or foreclosed status also tend to have difficulty constructing meaning from life events (McLean & Pratt, 2006). Those with a moratorium status tend to be high in anxiety and relatively unhappy, as well as low in authoritarian attitudes. Perhaps because they are in a period of experimentation, they also are relatively likely to have engaged in unprotected sex or to have tried drugs such as marijuana (Damon, 1983; Hernandez & DiClemente, 1992; Jones, 1992; Marcia, 1980; Meeus et al., 1999).

LAURA ZITO

In some traditional cultures, adolescents have few role options and, consequently, know from a young age what their adult identity will be.

Influences on Identity Formation

A number of factors influence adolescents' identity formation. One key factor is the approach parents take with their offspring. Adolescents are more likely to have a foreclosed identity status if their parents are overly protective or employ an *authoritarian* parenting style (that is, a style that is cold and controlling; see page 470) (Berzonsky & Adams, 1999). In contrast, adolescents are more likely to explore identity options if they have at least one parent who encourages in them both a sense of connection with the parent and a striving for autonomy and individuality (Grotevant, 1998; Samuolis, Layburn, & Schiaffino, 2001).

Another factor affecting identity formation is the individual's own behavior. The early use of drugs, for example, appears to undermine adolescents' abilities to develop healthy identities, perhaps because it diverts their attention from school and other activities, such as hobbies and clubs, that provide opportunities for learning and self-exploration (Jones, 1992).

Identity formation is also influenced by both the larger social context and the historical context (Bosma & Kunnen, 2001). As already noted, adolescents from poor communities may have fewer career options due to low-quality schooling, financial limitations, and a lack of career information and role models. Such limitations likely affect some aspects of these adolescents' identity formation.

moratorium status a category of identity status in which the individual is in the phase of experimentation with regard to occupational and ideological choices and has not yet made a clear commitment to them

identity-achievement status a category of identity status in which, after a period of exploration, the individual has achieved a coherent and consolidated identity based on personal decisions regarding occupation, ideology, and the like. The individual believes that these decisions were made autonomously and is committed to them.

The historical context plays a role in identity formation, as well, because of the changes it brings about in identity options over time. Until a few decades ago, for instance, most adolescent girls focused their search for identity on the goal of marriage and family. Even in developed societies, few career opportunities were available to females, and young women who chose a career path instead of, or even in addition to, raising a family were generally regarded as "selfish" by the society at large. Today, women in many cultures are more likely to base their identity on both family and career. Thus, familial, individual, socioeconomic, historical, and cultural factors all contribute to identity development.

review:

Children's self-conceptions change greatly with age, shifting from being very concrete—based on physical characteristics and overt behavior—to being based on internal qualities and the nature of one's relationships with others. Young children tend to view themselves in uniformly positive ways and to overestimate their abilities. Older children are more likely to evaluate themselves on their general level of competence and to assess their own strengths and weaknesses realistically. In late childhood, children increasingly incorporate others' perceptions of themselves into their self-image, and, with age, their conceptions of self also become much more complex and integrated.

Adolescents' self-conceptions are more abstract than younger children's and include the existence of different selves in different contexts. Young adolescents usually are not upset when they perceive discrepancies in their behavior and characteristics across contexts. However, according to Elkind, many young adolescents do develop a form of egocentrism that expresses itself as the "personal fable" and the critical "imaginary audience." In mid-adolescence, teenagers often agonize over the discrepancies they see in themselves and tend to become concerned with the question of "Who am I?" and with what others think of them. In late adolescence and early adulthood, concepts of the self become much more integrated and are more likely to include personal attributes that reflect internalized personal values, beliefs, and standards.

According to Erikson, adolescence is the time of the crisis of identity versus identity confusion, in which the young person must form an identity by making a series of ever-narrowing selections of personal, occupational, sexual, and ideological commitments. A psychosocial moratorium, a time of experimenting with different identities, appears to be healthy in Western cultures but may not be a viable option in some cultures and subcultures. The premature choice of an identity, called identity foreclosure, may prevent the individual from obtaining his or her full potential, as may identity diffusion or the taking on of a negative identity. How and when young people construct their identity are affected by a variety of influences, ranging from personal and familial factors to cultural and historical ones.

Ethnic Identity

The development of identity can present special challenges for minority-group adolescents because it often involves complications related to ethnicity and/or race. In certain contexts, a legitimate distinction can be drawn between the concept of ethnicity (which refers to shared cultural traditions) (Spencer & Markstrom-Adams, 1990) and the concept of race (which refers to a shared biological ancestry). In the context of identity formation, however, the two concepts are, for practical purposes, quite similar. Thus, for the present discussion, we will use the term **ethnic identity** to refer to the degree to which an individual has a sense of belonging to an ethnic or racial group and associates his or her thinking, feelings, and behavior with membership in that ethnic or racial group (Rotheram & Phinney, 1987).

ethnic identity individuals' sense of belonging to an ethnic or racial group, including the degree to which they associate their thinking, perceptions, feelings, and behavior with membership in that group

Ethnic Identity in Childhood

Children's ethnic identity can be viewed as having five components (Bernal, Knight, Ocampo, Garza, & Cota, 1993):

- *Ethnic knowledge.* Children's knowledge that their ethnic group has certain distinguishing characteristics—behaviors, traits, values, customs, styles, and language—that set it apart from other groups.
- *Ethnic self-identification.* Children's categorization of themselves as members of their ethnic group.
- *Ethnic constancy.* Children's understanding that the distinguishing characteristics of their ethnic group do not change across time and place and that they themselves will always be a member of their ethnic group.
- *Ethnic-role behaviors.* Children's engagement in the behaviors that reflect the distinguishing characteristics of their ethnic group.
- *Ethnic feelings and preferences.* Children's feelings about belonging to their ethnic group and their preferences for the characteristics that distinguish the group and for its members.

Ethnic identity develops gradually during childhood, although it does not develop for all ethnic-minority children. Preschool children do not really understand the significance of being a member of an ethnic group, although they may be able to label themselves as "Mexican," "American Indian," "African American," or the like. Even if they engage in behaviors that characterize their ethnic group and have some simple knowledge about the group, they do not understand that ethnicity is a lasting feature of the self (Bernal et al., 1993) (see Table 11.2).

By the early school years, ethnic-minority children know the common characteristics of their ethnic group, start to have feelings about being members of the group, and may have begun to form ethnically based preferences regarding foods, traditional holiday activities, language use, and the like (Ocampo, Bernal, & Knight, 1993). Children tend to identify themselves according to their ethnic group between the ages of 5 and 8 and shortly thereafter begin to understand that their race or ethnicity is an unchanging feature of themselves (Bernal, Knight, Garza, Ocampo, & Cota, 1990; Ocampo, Knight, & Bernal, 1997).

PAUL CHELSEY / STONE / GETTY IMAGES

Much of young children's learning about their ethnic group takes place in the family. Parents teach their children the specific practices associated with their group and can instill in them pride in their ethnic heritage.

TABLE 11.2

Examples of Components of Ethnic Identity in Preschool and the Early School Years

Ethnic-Identity Components	Preschool Level	Early School Level
Ethnic knowledge	Simple, global knowledge	More complex and specific knowledge, including cultural traits
Ethnic self-identification	Empty labels: "I'm Mexican because my mother said so."	Meaningful labels: "I'm Mexican because my parents come from Mexico."
Ethnic constancy	Don't understand	Understand permanence of their ethnicity
Ethnic-role behaviors	Engage in and describe behaviors; may not know why behaviors are ethnic	Engage in more role behaviors; know more about their ethnic relevance
Ethnic feelings and preferences	Undeveloped; do as their families do	Have feelings and preferences

Adapted from Bernal, Knight, Ocampo, Garza, & Cota (1993)

The family and the larger social environment play a major role in the development of children's ethnic identity. Parents and other family members and adults can be instrumental in teaching their children about the strengths and unique features of their ethnic culture and instilling them with ethnic pride (Hughes et al., 2006; Vera & Quintana, 2004). Such instruction can be especially important for the development of a positive ethnic identity when the child's racial or ethnic group is the object of prejudice and discrimination in the larger society (Parke & Buriel, 2006; Spencer & Markstrom-Adams, 1990).

Ethnic Identity in Adolescence

The issue of ethnic identity often becomes much more central in adolescence, as young people try to forge their overall identity (French, Seidman, Allen, & Aber, 2006). Minority-group members in particular may be faced with difficult and painful decisions as they try to decide the degree to which they will adopt the values of their ethnic group or those of the dominant culture (Phinney, 1993; Spencer & Markstrom-Adams, 1990).

One difficulty for ethnic-minority adolescents is that they are more likely than they were at younger ages to be aware of discrimination against their group and consequently may feel ambivalent about the group and their own ethnic status (Greene, Way, & Pahl, 2006; Seaton, Caldwell, Sellers, & Jackson, 2008; Szalacha, Erkut, Coll, Alarcón, Fields, & Ceder, 2003). Ethnic-minority children may also be faced with basic conflicts between the values of their ethnic group and those of the dominant culture (Parke & Buriel, 2006; Qin, 2009). For example, many ethnic groups place a premium on family obligation, including values and behaviors related to children's assistance, support, and respect for members of the nuclear and extended family. Thus, adolescents in traditional Mexican-American families, for instance, may be expected to spend after-school time helping take care of elderly or young family members or earning money for the family. At the same time, the majority culture may be urging them to participate in school-related activities, such as sports, clubs, or study groups, that can lead to expanded opportunities.

For youths of Eastern Asian descent, a focus on family obligation may stand in direct opposition to the emphasis that Western cultures place on autonomy and self-interest, including achieving a career that may take the young adult away from home and family (Fuligni, 2007). Such a clash of values can cause conflict in the family and within adolescents as they attempt to build an identity and develop their values and goals for the future.

Family or peer pressures such as these may help explain why the rate of foreclosed identity is higher among ethnic-minority adolescents than it is among majority adolescents (Spencer & Markstrom-Adams, 1990; Streitmatter, 1988). Indeed, in some minority groups such as certain American Indian tribes, traditional values and activities may be so valued that it is adaptive for youth to simply adhere to them without exploring their identities in any way (Parke & Buriel, 1998; Spencer & Markstrom-Adams, 1990). For these young people, abandoning the accustomed ways of family and community to "make it" in an unfamiliar culture carries a high risk of loneliness and depression.

Extending the work of Erikson, Jean Phinney (Phinney & Kohatsu, 1997) has identified three phases of ethnic-identity development that minority youth often experience:

1. *Ethnic-identity diffusion/foreclosure.* In this phase, many ethnic-minority adolescents have not examined their ethnicity and are not particularly interested

in it. Others, a minority, have internalized the majority society's negative views of their ethnic group.

2. *Ethnic-identity search/moratorium.* Minority youth in this phase develop an interest in learning about their ethnic or racial culture and begin to consider the effects that their ethnicity may have on their life in the present and future. In some cases, this exploration eventually leads to the third phase (Whitehead, Ainsworth, Wittig, & Gadino, 2009).
3. *Ethnic-identity achievement.* This phase is characterized by a more conscious awareness of, and commitment to, one's ethnic group and ethnic identity (Spencer & Markstrom-Adams, 1990).

MICHAEL J. DOOLITTLE / THE IMAGE WORKS

Engaging in activities that promote the welfare of others in their ethnic or racial group may contribute to adolescents' having a positive sense of ethnic identity.

Research suggests that higher levels of ethnic identity are generally associated with high self-esteem, well-being, and low levels of emotional and behavior problems (Berkel et al., 2009; Jones & Galliher, 2007; Kiang et al., 2006; Phinney, Cantu, & Kurtz, 1997).

The exploration of ethnic identity does not always follow this pattern, however. For some ethnic-minority adolescents, an identity search leads to an exploration of majority identities and a lessening of commitment to the ethnic group. However, when ethnic-minority parents actively socialize their children into their ethnic culture, the children tend to have a more positive ethnic identity (McHale et al., 2006; Umaña-Taylor, Bhanot, & Shin, 2008) and appear to be buffered from the negative effects of discrimination (Berkel et al., 2009; Harris-Britt, Valrie, Kurtz-Costes, & Rowley, 2007; Neblett et al., 2008). In some cases, ethnic-minority youth develop a *bicultural identity* that includes a comfortable identification with both the majority culture and their own ethnic culture. Although trying to straddle two cultures can be stressful, for some minority youths, it does not cause distress and may provide some benefits (Fuligni, Yip, & Tseng, 2002; Kiang, Yip, & Fuligni, 2008; LaFromboise, Coleman, & Gerton, 1993).

review:

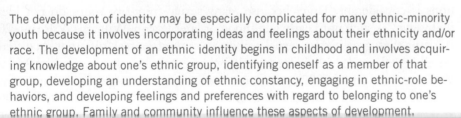

The development of identity may be especially complicated for many ethnic-minority youth because it involves incorporating ideas and feelings about their ethnicity and/or race. The development of an ethnic identity begins in childhood and involves acquiring knowledge about one's ethnic group, identifying oneself as a member of that group, developing an understanding of ethnic constancy, engaging in ethnic-role behaviors, and developing feelings and preferences with regard to belonging to one's ethnic group. Family and community influence these aspects of development.

The achievement of an identity during adolescence can be difficult and painful for minority youth due to their awareness of prejudice against their group. Possible clashes between the values and goals of the group and those of the majority culture can further complicate the process. In adolescence, some minority youth start to actively explore the meaning of their ethnicity and its role in their identity. As a result of this exploration, some adolescents come to embrace their ethnicity; others gravitate toward the majority culture; and still others become bicultural.

Sexual Identity or Orientation

In childhood and especially adolescence, an individual's identity includes his or her **sexual orientation**—that is, a person's preference in regard to erotic feelings toward males or females. The majority of youth are attracted to individuals of the other sex; a sizable minority are not. Dealing with new feelings of sexuality can be

sexual orientation a person's preference in regard to males or females as objects of erotic feelings a difficult experience for any adolescent, but the issue of establishing a sexual identity is much harder for some adolescents than for others.

The Origins of Youths' Sexual Identity

Puberty, when there are large rises in gonadal hormones (Buchanan, Eccles, & Becker, 1992; Halpern, Udry, & Suchindran, 1997), is the most likely time for youth to begin experiencing feelings of sexual attraction to others. Most current theorists believe that whether those feelings are inspired by members of the other sex or one's own is based primarily on biological factors, although the environment may also be a contributing factor (Savin-Williams & Cohen, 2004). Twin and adoption studies, as well as DNA studies, indicate that a person's sexual orientation is at least partly hereditary: identical twins, for example, are more likely to exhibit similar sexual orientations than are fraternal twins (Bailey & Pillard, 1991; Bailey, Pillard, Neale, & Agyes, 1993; Hamer, Hu, Magnuson, Hu, & Pattatucci, 1993). However, biological factors may not directly determine an individual's sexual orientation; rather, they may predispose children to experiences that contribute to their sexual orientation (Bem, 1996).

VINCENT DEWITT / STOCK, BOSTON

Sexual-minority youth deal with many of the same family and identity issues as other adolescents and generally are as adjusted as other teens. However, they face special challenges if their peers and family do not accept their sexual identity.

Sexual Identity in Sexual-Minority Youth

For the majority of youth everywhere, the question of personal sexual orientation never arises, at least at a conscious level. They feel themselves to be unquestioningly heterosexual. For a minority of youth, however, the question of personal sexual identity is a vital one that, initially at least, is often confusing and painful. These are the **sexual-minority youth,** who experience same-sex attractions.

It is difficult to know precisely how many youths are in this category. Although current estimates indicate that only 2 to 4% of high school students in the United States identify themselves as gay, lesbian, or bisexual (Rotheram-Borus & Langabeer, 2001; Savin-Williams & Ream, 2007), the number of youths with same-sex attractions is considerably larger because many sexual-minority youth do not identify themselves as such until early adulthood or later (Savin-Williams & Ream, 2007). It is true that, growing up, sexual-minority youth often feel "different" (a difference possibly reflected in their frequently being labeled sissies or tomboys) (Savin-Williams & Cohen, 2007), and some even display cross-gender behavior from a relatively early age (Drummond, Bradley, Peterson-Badali, & Zucker, 2008). However, it sometimes takes them a long time to recognize that they are lesbian, gay, or bisexual.

Another complicating fact is that, especially for females, there is considerable instability in adolescents' and young adults' reports of same-sex attraction or sexual behavior (Savin-Williams & Ream, 2007). By college age, for example, a number of young women identify themselves as "mostly straight"—that is, mostly heterosexual but somewhat attracted to females (Thompson & Morgan, 2008). One longitudinal study that followed 79 lesbian, bisexual, and unlabeled women aged 18 to 25 found that, over a 10-year period, two-thirds changed the identity labels they had claimed at the beginning of the study and one-third changed labels two or more times (Diamond, 2008).

sexual-minority youth young people who experience same-sex attractions and for whom the question of personal sexual identity is often confusing and painful

In most ways, sexual-minority children and adolescents are developmentally indistinguishable from their heterosexual peers: they deal with many of the same family and identity issues in adolescence and generally function just as well. However, they do face some special challenges. Because being gay, lesbian, or bisexual is viewed negatively by many members of society, it is often difficult for sexual-minority youth to recognize or accept their own sexual preferences. It is usually even more difficult for them to reveal their sexual identity to others—that is, to "come out." However, with the media's increasing attention to, and positive portrayals of, sexual-minority people, more sexual-minority youths in the United States are coming out today, and are doing so at earlier ages, than did any previous cohort (Savin-Williams, 2001b).

The Process of Coming Out

In many cases, the coming-out process for sexual-minority youth involves several developmental milestones. It begins with the *first recognition*—an initial realization that one is somewhat different from others, accompanied by feelings of alienation from oneself and others. At this point, there generally is some awareness that same-sex attractions may be the relevant issue, but the individual does not reveal this to others. Many sexual-minority youth have some awareness of their sexual attractions by middle childhood. In one study, initial same-sex attractions typically were found to occur at age 8 or 9 (see Table 11.3) (Savin-Williams & Diamond, 2000). As one gay male reported:

> Maybe it was the third grade and there was an ad in the paper about an all-male cast for a movie. This confused me but fascinated—intrigued—me, so I asked the librarian and she looked all flustered, even mortified, and mumbled that I ought to ask my parents.
>
> (Quoted in Savin-Williams, 1998a, p. 24)

However, there is great variability in the age at which same-sex attractions are first noticed. Some recall these attractions as part of their earliest memories, whereas others recall not having these feelings until young adulthood (Savin-Williams & Diamond, 2000). Consistent with the findings noted earlier, this variability seems more pronounced among sexual-minority women, a significant number of whom (16% in one study) feel that they were initially heterosexual and

TABLE 11.3

Ages of Identity Milestones for Gay/Bisexual Male Youth in Savin-Williams's Study (all are gay youth who have acknowledged their sexual-minority identity)

Event	Mean Age in Years	Age Range	Percent Who Had Not Experienced the Event
Awareness of same-sex attractions	8	3–17	0%
Knew meaning of *homosexuality*	10	4–19	0%
Applied the term *homosexual* to own attractions	13	5–20	0%
First gay sex	14	5–24	7%
First heterosexual sex	15	5–22	48%
Recognized self as gay/bisexual	17	8–24	0%
First disclosed to another	18	13–25	0%
First same-sex romance	18	11–25	29%
First disclosed to:			
Sibling	19	13–25	38%
Father	19	13–25	44%
Mother	19	13–25	31%
Developed positive sexual identity	19	10–25	23%

These numbers do not apply to samples of young men who have not acknowledged their same-sex attractions.
Adapted from Table 1.2 in R. Savin-Williams, . . . *And Then I Became Gay*. New York: Routledge, 1998, p. 15.

in midlife, after falling in love with a woman, became lesbian (Schneider, 2001). In contrast, the vast majority of sexual-minority men feel that they were always gay and were born that way.

The next milestone is *test and exploration,* a period in which the individual feels ambivalent about his or her same-sex attractions but eventually has limited contact with gays or lesbians and starts to feel alienated from heterosexuality. At the third milestone, *identity acceptance,* there is a preference for social interaction with other sexual-minority individuals. During this period, the person comes to feel more positive about his or her sexual identity and for the first time discloses it to heterosexuals (e.g., family or friends).

The average age at which contemporary sexual-minority youth privately label themselves as gay, lesbian, or bisexual is about 15 years of age (Savin-Williams & Cohen, 2004). Males tend to engage in sexual activity with same-sex partners before identifying themselves as gay, whereas females are more likely to identify themselves as lesbian first (Savin-Williams & Diamond, 2000). Many gay and lesbian youth and young adults, especially females, engage in heterosexual activities prior to, or overlapping with, same-sex activities (Diamond, Savin-Williams, & Dube, 1999).

The final step for some youth is *identity integration,* in which gay, lesbian, and bisexual individuals firmly view themselves as such, feel pride in themselves and their particular sexual community, and publicly come out to many people. Often, arrival at this milestone is accompanied by anger over society's prejudice against members of sexual minorities (Savin-Williams, 1996; Sophie, 1985/1986).

Of course, not all individuals go through all these steps; some never fully accept their own sexuality or discuss it with others. Others—about a third in one study—are "discovered" by their parents and do not disclose their sexual identity by choice (Rotheram-Borus & Langabeer, 2001).

Consequences of Coming Out

Sexual-minority youth typically do not disclose their same-sex preferences to a best friend, a peer to whom they are attracted, or siblings until about 16½ to 19 years of age (D'Augelli & Hershberger, 1993; Herdt & Boxer, 1993; Savin-Williams & Diamond, 2000) and do not tell their parents until a year or two later, if at all (Savin-Williams, 1998b). If they do reveal their sexual identity to their parents, they usually tell their mothers before telling their fathers, often because the mother asked or because they wanted to share that aspect of their life with their mother (Savin-Williams & Ream, 2003a). Another reason may be that fathers often react more negatively than do mothers (Heatherington & Lavner, 2008).

Youths are more likely to come out to a parent, and at a younger age, if they have a close relationship with, and are securely attached to, the parent. If they are from communities or religious or ethnic backgrounds that are relatively low in acceptance of same-sex attractions, they are less likely than other sexual-minority youth to disclose their sexual preference to family members. For example, there is some evidence that non-Caucasian families in the United States, including Latino and Asian-American families, are less accepting of same-sex attractions than are Euro-American families (Dube, Savin-Williams, & Diamond, 2001). The effects of such low cultural acceptance are reflected in this statement from a young Asian-American man:

> I am first generation from Southeast Asia. I am still very culturally bound and my . . . mother can't fathom homosexuality, and many of our friends are the same. So I can't express myself to my culture or to my family. It probably delayed my coming out. I wish I could have done it in high school like other kids.
>
> (Quoted in Savin-Williams, 1998a, pp. 216–217)

Although many parents react in a supportive or only slightly negative manner to their children's coming out, there is good reason for many sexual-minority youth to fear disclosing their sexual identity to their family. It is not unusual for parents to initially respond with anger, disappointment, and especially denial (Savin-Williams & Ream, 2003a). Often parents feel that these attractions violate their religious principles and at the same time imagine that they are somehow responsible for their children's same-sex attractions (Savin-Williams, 2001b). Surveys indicate that about 20 to 40% of sexual-minority youth experience insults or threats from relatives after they reveal their sexual identity, and 5% or so experience physical violence (Berrill, 1990; D'Augelli, 1998). Sexual-minority youth who disclose their sexual identity at a relatively early age, and those who are publicly open about their sexual identity, are most often subjected to abuse in the home or community (Pilkington & D'Augelli, 1995). As might be expected, sexual-minority youth whose parents are accepting of their child's sexual orientation report higher self-esteem and lower levels of depression and anxiety (Floyd, Stein, Harter, Allison, & Ney, 1999; Savin-Williams, 1989a, b).

Fears of being harassed or rejected outside the home cause many sexual-minority youth to hide their sexual identity from peers. In fact, many heterosexual adolescents are not very accepting of same-sex preferences in their peers, and sexual-minority youth report more loss of friendships and worry more about losing friends than do heterosexual youth (Bos et al., 2008; Diamond & Lucas, 2004; Pilkington & D'Augelli, 1995). In most cases, sexual-minority youth disclose their sexual identity first to a sexual-minority friend, and many sexual-minority youth report that having sexual-minority friends is important in providing social support and acceptance (Savin-Williams, 1994, 1998a).

Presumably due to the pressures of coping with their sexuality, sexual-minority youth are prone to experience negative affect, depression, low self-esteem, and low feelings of control in their romantic relationships (Bos et al., 2008; Carver, Egan, & Perry, 2004; Diamond & Lucas, 2004; Safren & Heimberg, 1999). They also report higher levels of school-related problems and substance abuse than do other youth (Bos et al., 2008; Rotheram-Borus & Langabeer, 2001). Finally, sexual-minority youth have higher reported rates of attempted suicide than do their heterosexual peers, with the estimated attempt rates ranging from about 12% to over 50% (D'Augelli, Hershberger, & Pilkington, 2001; Safren & Heimberg, 1999; Savin-Williams & Ream, 2003b). Some of these problems appear to be at least partly due to the relatively poor quality of their relationships with peers and fathers (Bos et al., 2008) and to a heightened tendency for risk-taking among youths who acknowledge their same-sex attraction or act on it (Busseri, Willoughby, Chalmers, & Bogaert, 2008; Savin-Williams, 2006).

It must be noted, however, that these high rates may be misrepresentative because they are often derived from studies of youth who openly identify themselves as gay and who therefore, as mentioned earlier, are at increased risk of abuse or rejection by their family or community. In fact, estimates of suicide and other problems of adjustment are considerably lower for youth who are attracted to same-sex individuals but have not yet identified themselves as gay (Savin-Williams, 2001a). It is likely that dealing with the consequences of being in the sexual minority, rather than same-sex attraction per se, is what contributes to social and psychological problems for youths as they attempt to establish their personal and social identities.

review:

Although in most respects, sexual-minority youth differ little from other youth, they may face special challenges in regard to their identity and disclosing their same-sex preferences to others. Typically, but not always, they move through the milestones of *first recognition, test and exploration, identity acceptance,* and *identity integration.* Many sexual-minority youth have a sense of their sexual attractions by middle childhood, although some individuals report that they first experienced same-sex attractions in middle age. Because many sexual-minority youth initially have difficulty accepting their sexuality and fear revealing their sexual identity to others, they often do not tell others about their sexual preferences until age 16 to 19.

Parents sometimes have difficulty accepting their children's same-sex orientation, and a minority of parents abuse or reject their children for this reason. Although sexual-minority youth usually come out first to a friend, they often fear harassment from peers. Perhaps because of the pressures associated with adjusting to their sexual identity, sexual-minority youth who have openly identified themselves as such to others appear to be more likely than other youth to attempt suicide.

Self-Esteem

A key element of self-concept is **self-esteem,** or one's overall evaluation of the self and the feelings engendered by that evaluation (Crocker, 2001). Self-esteem is important because it is related to how satisfied people are with their lives and their overall outlook. Individuals with high self-esteem tend to feel good about themselves and hopeful in general, whereas individuals with low self-esteem tend to feel worthless and hopeless (Harter, 1999). In particular, low self-esteem in adolescence is associated with problems such as aggression, depression, substance abuse, social withdrawal, and suicidal ideation (Boden, Fergusson, & Horwood, 2008; Donnellan et al., 2005; Rubin, Coplan, & Bowker, 2009). It also predicts certain problems in adulthood, including mental health problems, substance abuse and dependence, criminal behavior, weak economic prospects, and low levels of satisfaction with life and with relationships (Boden et al., 2008; Orth, Robins, & Roberts, 2008; Trzesniewski et al., 2006). However, it is not entirely clear if low self-esteem actually causes such problems or if both are due to a third factor. For example, low self-esteem in children is often associated with their parents' having such characteristics as low education, low income, and teenage maternity, as well as a history of alcohol or illicit drug use and criminal behavior. It may be that these parental characteristics underlie both the children's low self-esteem and their high rates of behavioral and psychological problems (Boden et al., 2008).

Sources of Self-Esteem

A number of factors are related to the development of children's self-esteem. These include their genetic inheritance, the quality of their relationships with others, their appearance and competence, their school and neighborhood, and various cultural factors that impinge on their lives. In addition, how children think about themselves in a wide variety of contexts contributes to their feelings of overall self-worth. Thus, the development of self-esteem offers a highly transparent example of the

self-esteem one's overall evaluation of the worth of the self and the feelings that this evaluation engenders

TABLE 11.4

Sample Items from Susan Harter's Self-Perception Profile for Children, a Commonly Used Measure of Self-Esteem and Self-Perceptions

Really True for Me	Sort of True for Me				Sort of True for Me	Really True for Me
			Scholastic Competence			
☐	☐	Some kids feel that they are very *good* at their school work	BUT	Other kids *worry* about whether they can do the school work assigned to them.	☐	☐
			Social Acceptance			
☐	☐	Some kids find it *hard* to make friends	BUT	Other kids find it's pretty *easy* to make friends.	☐	☐
			Athletic Competence			
☐	☐	Some kids do very *well* at all kinds of sports	BUT	Other kids *don't* feel that they are very good when it comes to sports	☐	☐
			Physical Appearance			
☐	☐	Some kids are *happy* with the way they look	BUT	Others kids are *not* happy with the way they look	☐	☐
			Behavioral Conduct			
☐	☐	Some kids often do *not* like the way they *behave*	BUT	Other kids usually *like* the way they behave	☐	☐
			Global Self-Esteem			
☐	☐	Some kids are often *unhappy* with themselves	BUT	Other kids are pretty *pleased* with themselves	☐	☐

Adapted from Harter (1985)

interaction of *nature and nurture,* including the *sociocultural context.* Moreover, it is a domain of functioning marked by large *individual differences.*

To measure children's self-esteem, researchers ask children, verbally or with questionnaires, about their perceptions of themselves. As reflected in Table 11.4, they assess children's sense of their own physical attractiveness, athletic competence, social acceptance, scholastic ability, and the appropriateness of their behavior. In addition, they ask children about their global self-esteem—how they feel about themselves in general.

FIGURE 11.3 Gender differences in adolescents' concerns about their appearance, social behavior, competence, and conduct Girls report more concerns about their appearance and social behavior, whereas boys report more concerns about their competence and conduct. (Adapted from Harter, 1999)

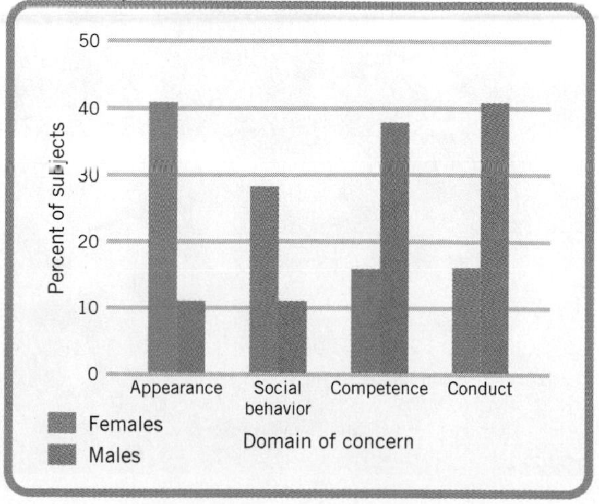

Heredity

Heredity contributes to children's sense of self-worth in several ways. The most obvious of these involve physical appearance and athletic ability, both of which are strongly related to self-esteem. In childhood and adolescence, attractive individuals are much more likely to report high self-esteem than are those who are less attractive (Erkut, Marx, Fields, & Sing, 1998; Harter, 1993; Verkuyten, 1990), possibly because attractive people are viewed more positively by others, and are treated better, than are unattractive people. Perhaps as a consequence, attractive people behave in more socially competent ways and are well-adjusted, which likely enhances their appeal to others (Langlois et al., 2000). The association between self-esteem and attractiveness may be stronger for girls than for boys, particularly in late childhood and adolescence, because girls are much more likely to report concerns about their appearance (see Figure 11.3). This gender difference may partly explain why males report slightly higher self-esteem than do females, especially in late adolescence (Kling, Hyde, Showers, & Buswell, 1999).

In addition, genetically based intellectual abilities and aspects of personality, such as sociability, no doubt play a part in academic and social self-esteem (Harter, 1983; Skinner, Zimmer-Gembeck, & Connell, 1998), although self-esteem may also affect academic competence (Chen, He, & Li, 2004). The hereditary contribution to self-esteem is underscored by the fact that on a variety of dimensions, self-esteem is more similar in identical twins than in fraternal twins and in nontwin siblings than in stepsiblings (McGuire, Neiderhiser, Reiss, Hetherington, & Plomin, 1994).

Interestingly, the genetic contribution to self-esteem appears to be stronger for boys than for girls (Raevuori et al., 2007), perhaps, in part, because of the power and pervasiveness of certain environmental influences on girls' self-esteem. Chief among these are the social norms and media messages regarding the importance of female beauty. A telling example of this is the emphasis that the media and peers put on the desirability of thinness, an emphasis that appears to contribute to some girls' dissatisfaction with their bodies and themselves by the age of 8 (Dohnt & Tiggemann, 2006).

Others' Contributions to Self-Esteem

One of the most important influences on children's self-esteem is the approval and support they receive from others. This idea goes back a full century to Charles Cooley's (1902) proposal of the "looking glass self"—the concept that people's self-esteem is a reflection of what others think of them (see Figure 11.4). More specifically, Cooley maintained that we develop our sense of self-esteem by internalizing the views that important others have of us.

Similar ideas were proposed by Erikson (1950) and Bowlby (1969), who argued that children's sense of self is grounded in the quality of their relationships with others. If children feel loved when young, they come to believe that they are lovable and worthy of others' love; if they feel unloved when young, they come to believe the opposite. This view is supported by links between attachment status and children's self-esteem or positive self-perceptions (Boden et al., 2008; Cassidy, Ziv, Mehta, & Feeney, 2003; Verschueren, Marcoen, & Schoefs, 1996). Moreover, parents who tend to be accepting and involved with their child and who use supportive yet firm child-rearing practices tend to have children with high self-esteem (Awong, Grusec, & Sorenson, 2008; Laible & Carlo, 2004; Lamborn, Mounts, Steinberg, & Dornbusch, 1991). In contrast, parents who regularly react to their children's unacceptable behavior with belittlement or rejection—in effect, condemning the child rather than the behavior—are likely to instill in their children a sense of worthlessness and of being loved only to the extent that they meet parental standards (Harter, 1999, 2006; Heaven & Ciarrochi, 2008).

CINDY CHARLES / PHOTOEDIT

Although far from being the only factors in shaping a child's self-esteem, the quality and nature of interactions with parents and other caregivers are among the more important influences.

Over the course of childhood, children's self-esteem is increasingly affected by peer acceptance (Harter, 1999). Indeed, in late childhood, children's feelings of competence about their appearance, athletic ability, and likability may be affected more by their peers' evaluations than by their parents'. At the same time, it is likely that children's self-esteem affects how peers respond to them. For example, young adolescents with negative self-perceptions tend to disengage from peers, which, in turn, appears to contribute to difficulties in their peer relationships. In contrast, youth who see themselves as competent in their peer relationships tend to be well liked (Caldwell, Rudolph, Troop-Gordon, & Kim, 2004).

Although the approval of others is a major factor in children's self-esteem, adolescents increasingly use internalized standards to evaluate themselves (Connell & Wellborn, 1991; Higgins, 1991). Thus, over time their self-esteem becomes less tied to the approval of others. Adolescent girls' self-esteem, for example, is increasingly linked to their feeling that they can have *relationship authenticity*—that is, that they can be themselves in terms of thoughts and feelings in their social interactions (Impett, Sorsoli, Schooler, Henson, & Tolam, 2008). Experts agree that adolescents who continue to base their self-evaluations on others' standards and approval are at risk for psychological problems, at least in Western industrialized cultures where an autonomous, relatively stable sense of self is valued (Damon & Hart, 1988; Higgins, 1991).

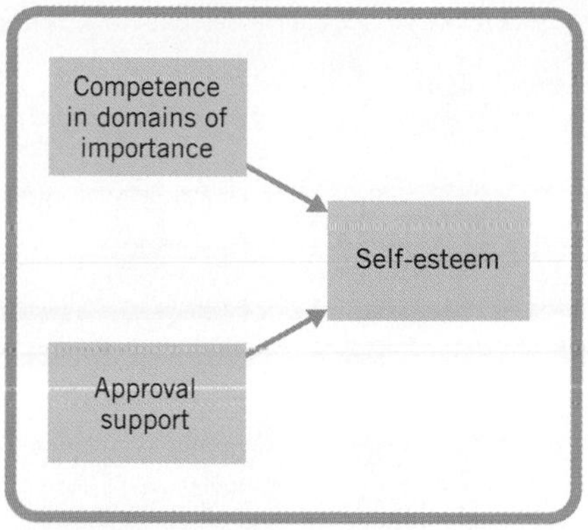

FIGURE 11.4 Factors contributing to children's self-esteem Children's self-esteem is affected by the approval and support they receive from parents, friends, and other people in their communities, as well as by their physical, social, behavioral, and academic competence, which are affected by both environmental and genetic factors. (Adapted from Harter, 1999)

School and Neighborhood

Children's and adolescents' self-esteem can also be affected by their school and neighborhood environments. The effect of the school environment is most apparent in the decline in self-esteem that is associated with the transition from elementary school into junior high (Eccles et al., 1989). The junior high environment often is not a good developmental match for 11- and 12-year-olds because it is difficult for children of that age to make the switch from having one teacher whom they know well and who is well acquainted with their skills and weaknesses to having many teachers who know little about them. In addition, the transition to junior high forces students to enter a new group of peers and to go from the top of one school's pecking order to the bottom of another. Especially in poor, overcrowded, urban schools, young adolescents often do not receive the attention, support, and friendship they need to do well and to feel good about themselves (Seidman, Allen, Aber, Mitchell, & Feinman, 1994; Wigfield et al., 2006).

That children's self-esteem can be affected by their neighborhood is suggested by the evidence that living in poverty in an urban environment, especially in violent neighborhoods, is associated with lower self-esteem among adolescents in the United States (Ewart & Suchday, 2002; Paschall & Hubbard, 1998; Turley, 2003). This may be due to high levels of stress that undermine the quality of parenting, prejudice from more affluent peers and adults, and inadequate material and psychological resources (Walker, Taylor, McElroy, Phillip, & Wilson, 1995).

MARY KATE DENNY / PHOTOEDIT

Children who do poorly at school tend to have lower self-esteem than do their more successful peers. However, children's perceptions of their academic competence tend to be less important to their overall self-esteem than are their perceptions of their appearance.

Self-Esteem in Minority Children

Minority children in the United States generally are more likely than majority (Euro-American) children to live in "undesirable," impoverished neighborhoods and to be subjected to prejudice from both adults and peers, which can undermine children's self-esteem (e.g., Greene et al., 2006; Seaton & Yip, 2009). Because children's self-esteem is strongly influenced by the evaluations of others, it often is assumed that minority children, especially African-American and Latino children, have lower self-esteem than do Euro-American children.

In fact, this is not always true. The self-esteem of young Euro-American children tends to be higher than that of their African-American peers, but after age 10, the trend reverses slightly. This shift most likely occurs because (1) African Americans tend to identify more with their racial group than do Euro-Americans, and (2) African-American culture, more than Euro-American culture, emphasizes desirable aspects of the group's distinctiveness (as reflected in the popular slogan from the 1960s and 1970s, "Black is beautiful"). Because ethnic identity is an important aspect of self-concept for many African Americans, this emphasis on the positive features of being African American may enhance African American adolescents' and adults' self-esteem (Gray-Little & Hafdahl, 2000; Herman, 2004).

Less is known about the self-esteem of Latino and other minority children. Because of the poverty and prejudice that many Latino-Americans experience, one might expect their self-esteem to be consistently much lower than that of Euro-Americans at all ages, and it is, at least through elementary school. Beginning in adolescence, however, this difference becomes much smaller (Twenge & Crocker, 2002). In part, this change may be due to the fact that Latino (e.g., Mexican-American) parents encourage their children's identification with the family and with the larger ethnic group (Parke & Buriel, 2006), which can provide a buffer against some of the negative effects that poverty and prejudice often have on self-esteem. Especially in communities where Latinos are in the majority, Latino youth who identify with their ethnic group, in comparison with those who do not, tend to have higher self-esteem (Umaña-Taylor, Diversi, & Fine, 2002).

Other minority groups in the United States show different patterns of self-esteem. Asian-American children, for example, report higher self-esteem than do Euro-Americans and African Americans in elementary school, but by high school their reported self-esteem is lower than that of Euro-Americans (Herman, 2004; Twenge & Crocker, 2002). As we discuss in the next section, cultural factors may contribute to the lower levels of self-esteem reported in some ethnic-minority groups.

How minority children and adolescents think about themselves is influenced much more strongly by acceptance from their family, neighbors, and friends than by reactions from strangers and the society at large. Thus, minority-group parents can help their children to develop high self-esteem and a sense of well-being by instilling them with pride in their culture and by being supportive (Bámaca et al., 2005; Berkel et al., 2009; Umaña-Taylor, Bhanot, & Shin, 2006). For example, African-American adolescents whose mothers support them and help them to cope with problems hold more positive attitudes toward their race and express greater pride in being African American than do adolescents with less supportive mothers. In turn, this greater pride predicts lower levels of perceived stress and, consequently, better adjustment (Caldwell, Zimmerman, Bernat, Sellers, & Notaro, 2002). Having positive peer and adult role models from their own ethnic group also contributes to children's positive feelings about themselves and their ethnicity (Fischer & Shaw, 1999; Walker et al., 1995).

Culture and Self-Esteem

In various cultures, the sources of self-esteem, as well as its form and function, may be different, and the criteria that children use to evaluate themselves may vary accordingly. It is not surprising, then, that scores on standard measures of self-esteem vary considerably across cultures. Except perhaps in the area of social competence, for example, self-esteem scores tend to be lower in China, Japan, and Korea than in the United States, Canada, Australia, and some parts of Europe (Harter, 1999). These differences seem to be partly due to the greater emphasis that the Asian cultures place on modesty and self-effacement—which results in less positive self-descriptions (Cai, Brown, Deng, & Oakes, 2007; Wang, 2004).

However, this cultural difference probably is not the whole explanation. There appear to be fundamental differences between Asian and Western cultures that affect the very meaning of self-esteem. In Western cultures, it is argued, self-esteem is related to individual accomplishments and self-promotion. In contrast, in Asian societies such as Japan and China, which traditionally have had a collectivist or group orientation, self-esteem is believed to be more related to contributing to the welfare of the larger group and affirming the norms of social interdependence. In this cultural context, self-criticism and efforts at self-improvement may be viewed as evidence of commitment to the group (Heine, Lehman, Markus, & Kitayama, 1999). But in terms of standard measures of self-esteem (i.e., those used by U.S. researchers), this motivation toward self-criticism is reflected as lower self-evaluation.

In addition, in some Asian societies, people tend to be more comfortable acknowledging discrepancies in themselves—for example, the existence of both good and bad personal characteristics—than are people in Western cultures, and this tendency results in reports of lower self-esteem in late adolescence and early adulthood (Hamamura, Heine, & Paulus, 2008; Spencer-Rodgers, Peng, Wang, & Hou, 2004).

RICHARD CUMMINS / CORBIS

Cultures differ in the skills they value. Children learn what abilities are valued in their group through participation in the family and larger community and evaluate their own competence accordingly.

The same types of cultural influences may affect measures of self-esteem in U.S. subcultures that have maintained traditional non-Western ideas about the self and its relation to other people, although in one of the few studies to test the equivalence of measures of self-esteem, Chinese-American, Filipino, and Euro-American adolescents responded to a measure of self-esteem in very comparable ways (Russell, Crockett, Shen, & Lee, 2008). In general, however, cultural values may affect how children and youths evaluate themselves and their strengths and weaknesses.

review:: Many factors affect children's and adolescents' self-esteem. Genetic predispositions, the support and approval of parents and peers, physical attractiveness, academic competence, and social factors such as the neighborhood and school environments all affect how children and youth feel about themselves. Although minority children in the United States often are exposed to prejudice and poverty, supportive families and communities can buffer and even enhance their self-esteem. The sources of self-esteem, as well as its form and function, may differ across cultures, and self-evaluations may differ accordingly.

Chapter Summary

The Caregiver–Child Attachment Relationship

- According to Bowlby's theory, attachment is a biologically based process that is rooted in evolution and increases the helpless infant's chance of survival. A secure attachment also provides children with a secure base for exploration. An outcome of early parent–caregiver interactions is an internal working model of relationships.
- The quality of children's attachment with their primary caregiver has been assessed using Ainsworth's Strange Situation. Children typically are categorized as securely attached, insecurely attached (insecure/resistant, insecure/avoidant), or disorganized/disoriented. Children are more likely to be securely attached if their caregivers are sensitive and responsive to their needs.
- There are similarities in children's attachments across many cultures, although the percentages of children in different attachment categories sometimes vary across cultures or subcultures.
- Parents' attachment status and their working models of relationships are related to the quality of their attachment with their infants. There appears to be some continuity in attachment from childhood to adulthood, unless hardships such as divorce, illness, child maltreatment, or maternal depression occur between childhood and adulthood.
- Intervention programs demonstrate that parents can be trained to be more sensitive, attentive, and stimulating in their parenting and that these changes are associated with increases in infants' sociability, exploration, ability to soothe themselves, and security of attachment.
- Children's security of attachment to their caregivers predicts interpersonal relationships and adjustment.

Conceptions of the Self

- Young children's conceptions of themselves are very concrete—based on physical characteristics and overt behavior—and uniformly positive. With age, conceptions of self increasingly become based on internal qualities and the quality of relationships with others; they also become more realistic, integrated, abstract, and complex.
- According to Elkind, because of their focus on what others think of them, young adolescents think about an "imaginary audience" and develop "personal fables."
- According to Erikson, adolescence is marked by the crisis of identity versus identity confusion. The individual's attempt to construct an identity, as well as whether and when the individual experiences a particular identity status (psychosocial moratorium, identity foreclosure, identity diffusion, or identity achievement), is influenced by personal characteristics and familial and cultural factors.

Ethnic Identity

- In childhood, the development of an ethnic identity involves identifying oneself as a member of an ethnic group, developing an understanding of ethnic constancy, engaging in ethnic-role behaviors, acquiring knowledge about one's ethnic group, and developing a sense of belonging to the ethnic group. Family and community influence these aspects of development.

- In adolescence, minority youth often start to explore the meaning of their ethnicity and its role in their identity. Many ethnic-minority youth initially tend to be diffused or foreclosed in regard to their identities; then they become increasingly interested in exploring their ethnicity (search/moratorium). Some come to embrace their ethnicity (ethnic-identity achievement); others gravitate toward the majority culture; still others become bicultural.

Sexual Identity or Orientation

- Sexual-minority (gay, lesbian, or bisexual) youth are similar to other youth in their development of identity and self, although they face special difficulties. Many have some awareness of their same-sex attractions by middle childhood. The process of self-labeling and disclosure among sexual-minority youth often involves several steps: (1) first recognition, (2) test and exploration, (3) identity acceptance, and (4) identity integration. However, not all individuals go through all these steps, and many have difficulty accepting their sexuality and revealing it to others.

Self-Esteem

- Children's self-esteem is affected by many factors, including genetic predispositions, the quality of parent–child and peer relationships, physical attractiveness, academic competence, and various social factors.
- Although minority children in the United States often are exposed to prejudice and poverty, supportive families and communities can buffer and even enhance their self-esteem.
- Concepts of what a person should be like differ across cultures, with the consequence that self-evaluations and self-esteem scores differ in different cultures.

Critical Thinking Questions

1. Some theorists believe that early attachment relationships have enduring long-term effects. Others think that such effects depend on the quality of the ongoing parent–child relationship, which tends to be correlated with the security of children's early attachment to parents. How do you think researchers might go about examining this issue?
2. Based on what you have read about attachment and the development of the self, what negative effects might children experience as a result of being placed in a series of different foster-care homes? How might these effects vary with the age of the child?
3. What are the similarities and differences in the stages or phases of identity development as discussed by Erikson or Marcia (general identity development), Phinney (ethnic identity), and Savin-Williams (sexual-minority identity)? What factors might contribute to similarities and differences? What variables might be especially relevant for ethnic identity and for identity in regard to sexual orientation?
4. What are some of the practical and conceptual difficulties of determining when children first recognize that they prefer same-sex or other-sex individuals (i.e., are physically attracted to them)?
5. Recall Erikson's psychosocial stages of development (Chapter 9). How might a person's self-esteem be affected by the events and outcomes associated with each of the stages?

Key Terms

attachment, p. 425
attachment theory, p. 426
secure base, p. 426
internal working model of attachment, p. 427
Strange Situation, p. 427
secure attachment, p. 429
insecure attachment, p. 429
insecure/resistant (or ambivalent) attachment, p. 429
insecure/avoidant attachment, p. 429
disorganized/disoriented attachment, p. 429
adult attachment models, p. 430
parental sensitivity, p. 433
self, p. 437
social comparison, p. 439
personal fable, p. 441
imaginary audience, p. 441
identity versus identity confusion, p. 443
identity achievement, p. 443
identity confusion, p. 443
identity foreclosure, p. 444
negative identity, p. 444
psychosocial moratorium, p. 444
identity-diffusion status, p. 444
foreclosure status, p. 444
moratorium status, p. 445
identity-achievement status, p. 445
ethnic identity, p. 446
sexual orientation, p. 449
sexual-minority youth, p. 450
self-esteem, p. 454

BERNARD FLEETWOOD-WALKER, *The Family*, c. 1932

12

The Family

THEMES

Nature and Nurture

❖

The Active Child

❖

The Sociocultural Context

❖

Individual Differences

❖

Research and Children's Welfare

❖

In 1979, the People's Republic of China announced a sweeping new policy that was to affect Chinese families dramatically. Due to the many problems associated with the country's overpopulation, the government ordered a limit of one child per family in urban populations. Backed up by a system of economic rewards for those who complied and financial and social sanctions against those who did not, this policy was quite effective, especially in urban areas. For example, in Shanghai in 1985, 98% of births were first births; across the country, the figure was 68% (Poston & Falbo, 1990).

The one-child policy is controversial at a number of levels and has had a consequence that was unintended and grim: an epidemic of female abortion and infanticide (see page 46). On the benign side, however, the one-child policy provided developmental psychologists an opportunity to study how a particular family structure might affect children's development. Think about the differences in upbringing that might occur when parents have one child as opposed to two or more. To begin with, an only child is likely to receive more individual attention from parents and more of the family's resources. In addition, an only child does not have to cooperate and share with siblings. Because of differences such as these, many people predicted that the new generation of single children raised in the People's Republic of China would be overindulged and have little experience in compromising and cooperating with others. Thus, there was concern that these single children (called "onlies") would become spoiled "little emperors" (Falbo & Poston, 1993). Such a concern was not confined to China. An increase of one-child families in the United States likewise raised worries that single children would become spoiled brats (Falbo & Polit, 1986).

In general, however, there is no consistent support for these concerns. There is some evidence that onlies in China, especially in urban areas, perform better on tests of academic performance and intelligence than do children from families with more than one child (Falbo & Poston, 1993; Falbo, Poston, & Jiao, 1989; Jiao, Ji, & Jing, 1996). And although some initial studies found that only children in China were viewed by peers as more self-interested and less cooperative than children with siblings (e.g., Jiao, Ji, & Jing, 1986), later studies have found little evidence that only children have more behavioral problems (Wang et al., 2000; Zhang, 1997), except perhaps for displays of spoiled behavior from age 3 to 5 (McLoughlin, 2005).

Moreover, large survey studies do not indicate that onlies are more prone to depression and anxiety (Edwards et al., 2005; Hesketh & Ding, 2005), despite the potential for heightened family pressures on them to fulfill parental goals and needs. In fact, there appears to be virtually no difference between onlies and other children in regard to personality or social

ADRIAN BRADWHAW / NEWSMAKERS / GETTY IMAGES

The one-child policy in China provided an opportunity to assess the effects of being an only child. In general, only children in China are as well-adjusted as children from larger families and tend to do better in school. However, the one-child policy has resulted in the birth and survival of far more male children than female children, apparently due to parents' resorting to selective abortion or female infanticide in order to have the opportunity to have a son. During the period of 2000–2004, approximately 124 boys were born for every 100 girls. It is estimated that in 2005 there were 32 million more males than females in China under the age of 20.

behavior, including positive behaviors needed for getting along with others, negative behaviors such as aggression and lying, and respect and support for other family members (Deutsch, 2005; Falbo & Poston, 1993; Fuligni & Zhang, 2004; Poston & Falbo, 1990). The difference between the early and later findings may be due to the possibility that parents' behaviors toward only children have changed as one-child families have become more common and expected, with the consequence that onlies are less likely to be spoiled.

The one-child policy in China is a good example of how the structure of families can change and of how, consistent with Bronfenbrenner's model discussed in Chapter 9, the larger world affects what goes on within families. Culture, as well as social and economic events, can have a tremendous effect on the structure of families and interactions among family members. In industrialized Western societies as well, a variety of social changes in the past 50 years have had marked effects on the structure of the family. For example, families are smaller than in the past, and many more people are choosing to have children outside of wedlock (ChildStats.gov, 2008; Ventura, Martin, Curtin, & Mathews, 1997). In addition, it is not uncommon today for children to be reared by one biological parent or to live in a family in which there have been one or more divorces. Such changes in the family can affect the resources available to the child, as well as the parents' child-rearing practices and behavior.

In this chapter, we examine many developmental aspects of family interaction, including the ways in which parents' approach to parenting can influence their children's development, the ways in which children can influence their parents' parenting, and the ways in which siblings may influence one another. In addition, we consider how family functioning and children's development may have been affected by certain social changes that have occurred in the United States over the past half century—from the increased age of first-time parenthood to increased rates of divorce, remarriage, and maternal employment. We will also consider the impact that factors such as poverty and culture may have on developmental outcomes.

As you will see, the theme of *nature and nurture* is central in the study of the role of the family because a child's heredity and rearing influence each other and jointly affect the child's development. In addition, the theme of the *active child* is evident in our discussion of how children influence the way their parents socialize them. The theme of *sociocultural context* is also key, in that parenting practices are

EYEWIRE / GETTY IMAGES

MONIKA GRAFF / THE IMAGE WORKS

Among the many changes that have occurred in the American family over the past half century is a rise in the age of first marriage.

strongly influenced by cultural beliefs, biases, and goals and are related to different outcomes for children in different cultures. Further, the issue of *individual differences* is a major theme in this chapter because different styles of parenting, child-rearing practices, and family structures are associated with differences in children's social and emotional functioning. Finally, because parenting influences the quality of children's day-to-day experience, as well as children's beliefs and behaviors, understanding patterns of family functioning has relevance for our theme of *research and children's welfare.*

The Nature and Functions of the Family

What is considered a family varies across individuals and cultures. In some cases, for example, a family typically includes several generations and married siblings living together. In other cases—especially in the United States—it often includes just a single parent living alone with his or her children. Despite differences in some characteristics of family structure around the world, how do most families function?

Functions of Families

No matter what their structure or size, families in all societies serve several functions related to child rearing (LeVine, 1988):

1. **Survival of offspring.** Families help to ensure that children survive to maturity by attending to their physical needs, health, and safety.
2. **Economic function.** Families provide the means for children to acquire the skills and other resources that they will need to be economically productive in adulthood.
3. **Cultural training.** Families teach children the basic values of their culture.

The first function is obviously the most fundamental: the goals of the economic and cultural functions are of little importance if children do not survive. Thereafter, however, if children are to fare well, they must learn the skills needed to make a living and the values and norms of the society they live in. Thus, families serve functions that are of fundamental importance for the development of their children.

Family Dynamics

How well a family fulfills its basic child-rearing functions obviously depends on a great many factors. Not the least of these is **family dynamics,** that is, how the family operates as a whole. In subsequent sections, we discuss the ways in which individual family members contribute to a child's development. However, it is important to frame these discussions with a clear appreciation of the overall impact of family dynamics. No member of a family functions in isolation. Families are complex social units whose members are all interdependent and reciprocally influence each other.

Consider the diverse ways in which family members affect one another in the following scenario. A man loses his job due to company cutbacks, and the ensuing stress causes him to become very irritable with both his wife and children.

survival of offspring a function of the family that pertains to ensuring the survival of offspring by providing for their needs

economic function a function of the family that pertains to providing the means for children to acquire the skills and other resources they need to be economically productive as adults

cultural training a function of the family that pertains to teaching children the basic values in their culture

family dynamics the way in which the family operates as a whole

His wife, in turn, has to work extra hours to make ends meet, and her increasing fatigue makes her less patient with the children. The mother's increased workload also means that the couple's 8-year-old daughter is expected to do more of the household chores. This makes the daughter angry because her 6-year-old brother is not required to help her out. Soon the daughter becomes hostile to both her parents and her brother. Not surprisingly, the brother starts to complain about his sister and fight with her, further upsetting the parents. Over time, tension and conflict among all family members increase, adding to the stress created by the family's economic situation.

As researchers have increasingly focused on the complexity of family dynamics, a number of factors have become clear (Parke & Buriel, 1998). First, as illustrated by the foregoing example, family members—mothers, fathers, and children—all influence one another, both directly and indirectly, through their behaviors. Second, family functioning is influenced by the social support that parents receive from kin, friends, neighbors, and social institutions such as schools and churches (Leerkes & Crockenberg, 2003; Parke & Kellam, 1994; Taylor & Roberts, 1995). Thus, the sociocultural context is important for understanding family dynamics and their possible effects on children. Finally, family dynamics must be looked at developmentally. As children grow older, the nature of parent–child interactions changes. For example, as we saw in Chapter 5, when infants begin to walk, parents start to discipline them more because they can more easily defy their parents' wishes and commands, getting themselves into trouble or danger. Thus, as children become increasingly mobile, emotional exchanges between parents and children often include more anger (Campos, Kermoian, & Zumbahlen, 1992). Similarly, when children reach adolescence, there sometimes is increased intensity of conflict between them and their parents over the children's activities or friends (Laursen, Coy, & Collins, 1998). (See Box 12.1 on the next page.)

Family dynamics may also be altered by changes in parents (for example, in their beliefs about child rearing), in the marital relationship (for example, how well the parents are getting along), or in the relationships of other family members (for example, in the level of conflict between siblings). Alterations in the family structure due to births, deaths, divorce, remarriage, or other factors can also influence interactions among family members and may affect family routines and norms. In many cases, the effects of such shifts in family dynamics tend to be gradual and continuous. However, a single event such as a traumatic divorce or the death of a parent may cause a fairly dramatic change in a child's behavior and emotional adjustment.

In thinking about family dynamics, it is also important to keep in mind that biological characteristics (e.g., temperament) of both children and parents, as well as parental behaviors, contribute to the nature of parent–child interactions (Collins, Maccoby, Steinberg, Hetherington, & Bornstein, 2000; Deater-Deckard, 2000; McGuire, 2003). Moreover, the biological characteristics of family members affect family interactions. For example, mothers' negativity toward their children and the degree of control they use appear to be affected partly by children's heredity (including, perhaps, their tendency to experience and express negative emotion), whereas the degree to which mothers are close and affectionate with their children appears to be partly due to mothers' own genetic inheritance (Narusyte et al., 2008; Neiderhiser et al., 2004).

With this larger framework of family dynamics in mind, we now turn to the role that parents play in the socialization of their children.

a closer look 12.1

Parent–Child Relationships in Adolescence

A common stereotype about adolescence is that, inevitably, conflict between parents and their children escalates dramatically and that parents and their adolescent children typically become alienated from each other. However, a good deal of research has shown that this simply is not true in most families (Laursen & Collins, 1994). For example, in a study of approximately 1000 U.S. adolescents from immigrant and native-born families of Mexican, Chinese, Filipino, and European backgrounds, there was little increase in reported conflict between parents and their children from 6th to 10th grades (Fuligni, 1998).

This pattern holds true despite the fact that as children advance through adolescence, they become more willing to disagree openly with their parents and feel that their parents should have less authority over them in personal matters (Fuligni, 1998; Younlss & Smollar, 1985). For the most part, however, disagreements between parents and adolescents, though fairly frequent, are over mundane topics such as attire and hairstyle. Moreover, the increase in mild conflict and bickering between adolescents and their parents in early adolescence is typically followed by the establishment of a relationship that is less contentious and volatile, and more egalitarian (Steinberg, 1990; Steinberg & Morris, 2001).

In a minority of families, however, parent–child conflict in adolescence runs hotter and deeper, often involving issues such as sex, drugs, and choice of friends (Arnett, 1999; Papini & Sebby, 1988). Higher levels of conflict seem especially likely when children attain puberty earlier than their peers do (Collins & Steinberg, 2006; Hill, 1988; Steinberg, 1987, 1988). This may be because early maturation widens the gap between how much autonomy the adolescents themselves think they deserve and how much autonomy their parents are willing to grant them. In addition, children who are unregulated and prone to negative emotions are particularly likely to have heated conflicts with their parents in adolescence about issues such as chores and respecting and getting along with other family members (Eisenberg et al., 2008). Such conflicts between adolescents and their mothers are associated with delinquency and externalizing problems in youths (Eisenberg et al., 2008; van Doorn, Branje, & Meeus, 2008).

Although most parents and their adolescents are not alienated, feelings of closeness and support between them often decline, especially at the beginning of puberty through mid-adolescence (Fuligni, 1998; Shanahan, McHale, Crouter, & Osgood, 2007; Steinberg, 1988; Stemmler & Petersen, 1999). In addition, adolescents spend less time with their parents and more time with peers than do younger children and preadolescents (Dubas & Gerris, 2002; Larson & Richards, 1991). This decline in feelings of closeness is likely due in part to the desire by adolescents to be more autonomous and to an increase in their activities outside the home. Nonetheless, although peers are important confidants for adolescents (see Chapter 13), parents remain a primary source of support.

MONIKA GRAFF / THE IMAGE WORKS

Most adolescents and their parents do not experience high levels of conflict.

review: Families are complex social units that serve diverse functions, including helping offspring to survive, to acquire the skills needed to be economically productive adults, and to learn the values of the culture. Family members' behaviors influence one another and can alter the functioning of the entire family. Moreover, family dynamics are affected by a number of factors, including changes in the parents, changes in the child with development, and changes in family circumstances.

The Influence of Parental Socialization

Socialization is the process through which children acquire the values, standards, skills, knowledge, and behaviors that are regarded as appropriate for their present and future role in their particular culture. Parents typically contribute to their children's socialization in at least three different ways (Parke & Buriel, 1998, 2006):

- *Parents as direct instructors.* Parents may directly teach their children skills, rules, and strategies and explicitly inform or advise them on various issues.
- *Parents as indirect socializers.* Parents provide indirect socialization through their own behaviors with and around their children. For example, through their everyday actions, parents unintentionally demonstrate skills and communicate information and rules. They also model attitudes and behaviors toward others, such as understanding and helpfulness or intolerance and aggression.
- *Parents as social managers.* Parents manage their children's experiences and social lives, including their exposure to various people, activities, and information. This managerial role is especially prominent and influential when children are young. If parents decide to place their child in day care, for example, the child's daily experience with peers and adult caregivers will likely differ dramatically from that of children whose daily care is provided at home by a parent.

Parents use all these ways of socializing their children's behavior and development. However, as you will see, parents differ considerably in how they do so.

Parenting Styles and Practices

parenting styles parenting behaviors and attitudes that set the emotional climate in regard to parent–child interactions, such as parental responsiveness and demandingness

As you undoubtedly recognize from your own experience, parents in different families exhibit quite different **parenting styles,** that is, parenting behaviors and attitudes that set the emotional climate of parent–child interactions. Some parents, for example, are strict rule setters who expect complete and immediate compliance from their children. Others are more likely to allow their children some leeway in following the standards they have set for them. Still others seem oblivious to what their children do. Parents also differ in the overall emotional tone they bring to their parenting, especially with regard to the warmth and support they convey to their children.

In trying to understand the impact that parents can have on children's development, researchers have identified two dimensions of parenting style that are particularly important: (1) the degree of parental warmth, support, and acceptance, and (2) the degree of parenting control and demandingness (Maccoby & Martin, 1983). As you will see, these aspects of parenting—which reflect individual differences in parents—appear to play an important role in shaping individual differences in children.

The pioneering research on parenting style was conducted by Diana Baumrind (1973), who differentiated among four styles of parenting related to the dimensions of support and control. These styles are referred to as *authoritative, authoritarian, permissive,* and *rejecting-neglecting* (Baumrind, 1973, 1991b) (Figure 12.1). The differences in these parenting styles are reflected in the following examples, which depict the way four different mothers respond when they observe their child taking away another child's toy.

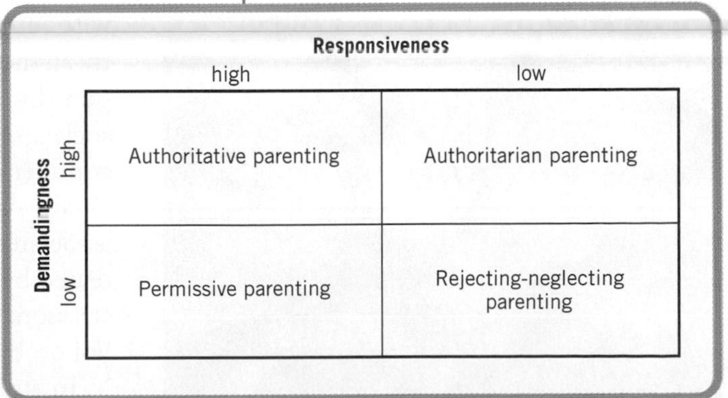

FIGURE 12.1 Parental demandingness and responsiveness The relations of parental demandingness and responsiveness to Baumrind's typology of parenting styles.

Authoritative. When Kareem takes away Troy's toy, Kareem's mother takes him aside, points out that the toy belongs to Troy and that Kareem has made Troy

authoritative parenting a parenting style that is high in demandingness and supportiveness. Authoritative parents set clear standards and limits for their children and are firm about enforcing them; at the same time, they allow their children considerable autonomy within those limits, are attentive and responsive to their children's concerns and needs, and respect and consider their children's perspective.

authoritarian parenting a parenting style that is high in demandingness and low in responsiveness. Authoritarian parents are nonresponsive to their children's needs and tend to enforce their demands through the exercise of parental power and the use of threats and punishment. They are oriented toward obedience and authority and expect their children to comply with their demands without question or explanation.

upset. She also says, "Remember our rule about taking others' things. Now think about how to make things right with Troy." Her tone is firm but not hostile, and she waits to see if Kareem returns the toy.

Authoritarian. When Elene takes Mark's toy, Elene's mother comes over, grabs her arm, and says in an angry voice, "Haven't I warned you about taking others' things? Return that toy now or you will not be able to watch TV tonight. I'm tired of you disobeying me!"

Permissive. When Jeff takes away Angelina's toy, Jeff's mother does not intervene. She doesn't like to discipline her son and usually does not try to control his actions, even though she is affectionate with him in other situations.

Rejecting-Neglecting. When Heather takes away Alonzo's toy, Heather's mother, as she does in most situations, pays no attention. She generally is not very involved with her child and would prefer that her husband deal with disciplining Heather. Even when Heather behaves well, her mother rarely hugs her or expresses approval of Heather or her behavior.

According to Baumrind, **authoritative** parents, like Kareem's mother, tend to be demanding but also warm and responsive. They set clear standards and limits for their children, monitor their children's behavior, and are firm about enforcing important limits. However, they allow their children considerable autonomy within those limits, are not restrictive or intrusive, and are able to engage in calm conversation and reasoning with their children. They are attentive to their children's concerns and needs and communicate openly with their children about them. They also are measured and consistent, rather than harsh or arbitrary, in disciplining them. Authoritative parents usually want their children to be socially responsible, assertive, and self-controlled. Baumrind found that children of authoritative parents tend to be competent, self-assured, and popular with peers. They are also able to behave in accordance with adults' expectations and are low in antisocial behavior. As adolescents, they tend to be relatively high in social and academic competence, self-reliance, and coping skills, and relatively low in drug use and problem behavior (Baumrind, 1991a, 1991b; Driscoll, Russell, & Crockett, 2008; Lamborn, Mounts, Steinberg, & Dornbusch, 1991; Simons & Conger, 2007).

TONY FREEMAN / PHOTOEDIT

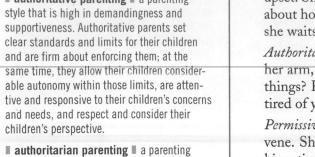

Positive social and academic outcomes seem more likely when levels of parental warmth and control are both high.

Authoritarian parents, much like Elene's mother, tend to be cold and unresponsive to their children's needs. They also are high in control and demandingness and expect their children to comply with their demands without question. Authoritarian parents tend to enforce their demands through the exercise of parental power, especially the use of threats and punishment. Children of authoritarian parents tend to be relatively low in social and academic competence, unhappy and unfriendly, and low in self-confidence, with boys being more negatively affected than girls in early childhood (Baumrind, 1991b). High levels of authoritarian parenting are associated with youths' experiencing negative events at school (e.g., being teased by peers, doing poorly on tests) and ineffective coping with everyday stressors (Zhou et al., 2008), along with depression, delinquency, and alcohol problems (Driscoll et al., 2008).

In studies by Baumrind and many others, parents' control of children's behavior has been measured mostly in terms of the setting and enforcing of limits. Another type of control is psychological control—control that constrains, invalidates, and manipulates children's psychological and emotional experience and expression. Examples include parents' cutting off children when they want to express themselves, threatening to withdraw love and attention if they do not behave as expected, exploiting children's sense of guilt, belittling their worth, and discounting or misinterpreting their feelings. These kinds of psychological control are more likely to be reported by children in relatively poor families. Their use by parents predicts children's depression in late middle childhood and adolescence and delinquent and externalizing problems (e.g., aggression and delinquency) in adolescence (Barber, 1996; Hofer & Eisenberg, in press; Pettit, Laird, Dodge, Bates, & Criss, 2001; Soenens et al., 2008).

Permissive parents are responsive to their children's needs and wishes and are lenient with them. Like Jeff's mother, they are nontraditional and do not require their children to regulate themselves or act in appropriate ways. Their children tend to be impulsive, lacking in self-control, and low in school achievement (Baumrind, 1973, 1991a, 1991b). As adolescents, they engage in more school misconduct and drug or alcohol use than do peers with authoritative parents (Driscoll et al., 2008; Lamborn et al., 1991).

Rejecting-neglecting parents, such as Heather's mother, are disengaged parents, low in both demandingness and responsiveness to their children. They do not set limits for them or monitor their behavior and are not supportive of them. Sometimes they are rejecting or neglectful of their children altogether. These parents are focused on their own needs rather than their children's. Children who experience rejecting-neglecting parenting tend to have disturbed attachment relationships when they are infants or toddlers and problems with peer relationships as children (Parke & Buriel, 1998; Thompson, 1998). In adolescence, they tend to exhibit a wide range of problems, from antisocial behavior and low academic competence to internalizing problems (e.g., depression, social withdrawal), substance abuse, and risky or promiscuous sexual behavior (Baumrind, 1991a, 1991b; Driscoll et al., 2008; Lamborn et al., 1991). The negative effects of this type of parenting continue to accumulate and worsen over the course of adolescence (Steinberg, Lamborn, Darling, Mounts, & Dornbusch, 1994).

In addition to the broad effects that different parenting styles seem to have for children, they also establish an emotional climate that affects the impact of whatever specific parenting practices may be employed (Darling & Steinberg, 1993). For example, children are more likely to view punishment as being justified and indicating serious misbehavior when it comes from an authoritative parent than when it comes from a parent who generally is punitive and hostile. Moreover, parenting style affects children's receptiveness to parents' practices. Children are more likely to listen to, and care about, their parents' preferences and demands if their parents are supportive and generally reasonable than if they are distant, neglectful, or expect obedience in all situations (Grusec, Goodnow, & Kuczynski, 2000; Hoffman, 1983).

Ethnic and Cultural Influences on Parenting

In keeping with our theme of the *sociocultural context,* it is important to note that the effects of different parenting styles and practices may vary somewhat across ethnic or racial groups in the United States. Consider findings regarding restrictive, highly controlling parenting. In contrast to the negative findings for Euro-American children, researchers have found that for African-American children, especially those in low-income families, this kind of parenting (e.g., involving intrusiveness or unilaternal decision making) is associated with positive developmental outcomes such as high academic competence and low levels of deviant behavior (Dearing, 2004; Ipsa et al., 2004; Lamborn, Dornbusch, & Steinberg, 1996; Tamis-LeMonda et al., 2008). Moreover, whereas parental use of physical discipline has been associated with high levels of problem behaviors for Euro-American youths, such punishment is associated with relatively low levels for African-American youths (Deater-Deckard, Dodge, Bates, & Pettit,

permissive parenting a parenting style that is high in responsiveness but low in demandingness. Permissive parents are responsive to their children's needs and do not require their children to regulate themselves or act in appropriate or mature ways.

rejecting-neglecting (disengaged) parenting a parenting style that is low in both responsiveness and demandingness. Rejecting-neglecting parents do not set limits for or monitor their children's behavior, are not supportive of them, and sometimes are rejecting or neglectful. They tend to be focused on their own needs rather than their children's.

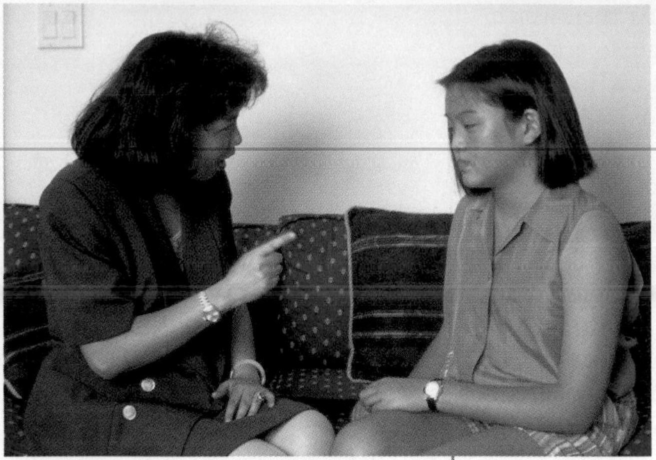

The meaning of parental discipline varies depending on the culture or subculture. For example, authoritarian child-rearing practices seem to be associated with less negative consequences in Chinese and first-generation Chinese-American families than in Euro-American families.

1996; Lansford, Deater-Deckard, Dodge, Bates, & Pettit, 2004), especially when African-American mothers believe measured physical punishment is an appropriate method for correcting misbehavior (McLoyd, Kaplan, Haradway, & Wood, 2007).

One possible explanation for these findings is that many caring African-American parents may feel the need to use authoritarian control to protect their children from special dangers, ranging from the risks found in crime-ridden neighborhoods to the prejudice experienced in predominantly Euro-American, affluent communities (Kelley, Sanchez-Hucies, & Walker, 1993; Parke & Buriel, 2006). In turn, African-American youth may recognize the protective motive in their parents' controlling practices and, consequently, respond relatively positively to their parents' demands. Moreover, because controlling, intrusive parenting is more normative in lower-income African-American than in many middle-class Euro-American communities, it may be interpreted in a more benign manner by African-American children, especially if their parents are warm (Ispa et al., 2004; Tamis-LeMonda et al., 2008).

Indeed, particular parenting styles and practices may also have different meanings, and different effects, in different cultures. For example, in Euro-American families, authoritative parenting, as noted, seems to be associated with a close relationship between parent and child and with children's positive psychological adjustment and academic success. Although a somewhat similar relation between authoritative parenting and adjustment has been found in China, it tends to be much weaker (Chang, Lansford, Schwartz, & Farver, 2004; Nelson, Hart, Yang, Olsen, & Jin, 2006; Zhou et al., 2004, 2008). In fact, some features of parenting that are considered appropriate in traditional Chinese culture are more characteristic of authoritarian parenting than of authoritative parenting. Compared with Euro-American mothers, for example, Chinese-American mothers are more likely to believe that children owe unquestioning obedience to parents and thus use scolding, shame, and guilt to control their children (Chao, 1994). Although such a pattern of parental control generally fits the category of authoritarian parenting, it appears to have few negative effects for Chinese-American and Chinese children, at least prior to adolescence. Rather, for this group, it is primarily physical punishment that is related to negative outcomes (Eisenberg, Chang et al., 2009; Zhou et al., 2004, 2008).

A likely explanation is that in Chinese culture, children (but perhaps not adolescents) may view parental strictness and emphasis on obedience as signs of parental involvement and caring, and as important for family harmony (Chao, 1994; Yau & Smetana, 1996). Consistent with this idea, parents' directiveness with their preschoolers—for example, telling the child what to do—is positively related to parental warmth/acceptance in China but is negatively related to this dimension in the United States (Wu et al., 2002).

Other studies also suggest that authoritarian parenting may have a different meaning in different cultures. For example, in a study of families in Canada, authoritarian control and negative feelings about their children tended to co-occur in mothers from a European background but did not co-occur in mothers from non-Western countries such as Egypt, Iran, India, and Pakistan (Rudy & Grusec, 2006). In another study, parental warmth and the use of harsh control tended to co-occur in Spanish-speaking Mexican-American families but were unrelated to one another in English-speaking Mexican-American families. Although harsh control was associated with more conduct problems for both groups of families, parental acceptance was related to fewer problem behaviors only for Spanish-speaking Mexican-American families (Hill, Bush, & Roosa, 2003). Thus, parental warmth and acceptance, as well as harsh control, seemed to have different meanings in acculturated and less acculturated families.

Because of variations such as these, findings regarding parenting in U.S. families—especially findings that involve primarily Euro-American middle-class families—cannot automatically be generalized to other cultures or subcultures. Rather, the relation of parenting to children's development must be considered in terms of the cultural context in which it occurs. Nonetheless, it should be noted that there are probably more similarities than differences in the parenting values and behaviors of various ethnic groups in the United States, as is strongly suggested by research that controls for socioeconomic status (e.g., Hill et al., 2003; Julian, McKenry, & McKelvey, 1994; Whiteside-Mansell, Bradley, Owen, Randolph, & Cauce, 2003).

The Child as an Influence on Parenting

Among the strongest influences on parents' parenting style and practices are the characteristics of their children, such as their appearance, behavior, and attitudes. Thus, *individual differences* in children contribute to the parenting they receive, which in turn contributes to differences among children in their behavior and personalities.

Attractiveness

Although we might not want to think it is true, children's physical appearance can influence the way their parents respond to them. For example, mothers of very attractive infants are more affectionate and playful with their infants than are mothers of infants with unappealing faces. When in public, mothers of unappealing infants, compared with mothers of appealing ones, are likely to pay attention to other people rather than to their own infants. These mothers are also more likely than other mothers to report that their infants interfere with their lives (Langlois, Ritter, Casey, & Sawin, 1995). Thus, from the first months of life, unattractive infants may experience somewhat different parenting than attractive infants. And this pattern continues, with attractive children, like attractive infants, tending to elicit more positive responses from adults (Langlois et al., 2000).

It is not clear why attractive children receive preferential treatment. However, in line with parental-investment theory discussed in Chapter 9, an evolutionary explanation would propose that parents are motivated to invest more time and energy in

ARIEL SKELLEY / CORBIS

Attractive children tend to elicit positive interactions from adults, which likely helps to foster their social and emotional development.

offspring who are healthy and genetically fit and therefore likely to survive, and it may be that attractiveness is intuited as an indicator of these characteristics (Langlois et al., 2000).

Children's Behaviors and Temperaments

Children's influence on parenting through their appearance is, of course, a passive contribution. Consistent with the theme of the *active child,* children are active contributors to the parenting process as well. Children who are disobedient, angry, or challenging, for example, make it more difficult for parents to use authoritative parenting than do children who are compliant and positive in their behavior (Cook, Kenny, & Goldstein, 1991; Crouter & Booth, 2003).

Differences in children's behavior with their parents—including the degree to which they are emotionally negative, unregulated, and disobedient—can be due to a number of reasons. The most prominent of these are genetic factors related to temperament (Emde et al., 1992; Goldsmith, Buss, & Lemery, 1997). At the same time, studies with twins indicate that environmental factors, likely including social interactions at home, also significantly affect infants' temperament (Roisman & Fraley, 2006).

Children can also learn to be noncompliant through interactions with their parents that reinforce their negative behavior. In resisting their parents' demands, for example, they may become so whiny, aggressive, or hysterical that their parents back down, leading the children to resort to the same behavior to resist future demands (Patterson, 1982). To further complicate matters, children's behavior with their parents can be affected by their perceptions of their parents' attitudes toward them. Even if inaccurate, children's perceptions that their parents are hostile toward them increases the likelihood of their becoming antisocial or depressed (Neiderhiser, Pike, Hetherington, & Reiss, 1998). Thus, children not only elicit positive and negative behaviors from parents but also filter, and react to, parental behaviors based on their own view of those behaviors.

Over time, this mutual influence, or **bidirectionality of parent–child interactions,** reinforces and perpetuates each party's behavior. One study, for example, found that children's low self-regulation at age 6 to 8 (which may have been influenced by maternal behaviors at an earlier age) predicted mothers' punitive reactions (e.g., scolding and rejection) to their children's expressions of negative emotion at age 8 to 10. In turn, mothers' punitive reactions when their children were age 8 to 10 predicted low levels of self-regulation in the children at age 10 to 12 (Eisenberg et al., 1999) (Figure 12.2).

A similar self-reinforcing and escalating negative pattern is common when parents are hostile and inconsistent in enforcing standards of conduct with their adolescent children; their children, in turn, are hostile, insensitive, disruptive, and inflexible with them (Conger & Ge, 1999; Rueter & Conger, 1998) and exhibit increased levels of problem behaviors (Scaramella, Neppl, Ontal, & Conger, 2008). Bidirectional interaction is also a likely key factor in parent–child relationships that exhibit a pattern of cooperation, positive affect, harmonious communication, and coordinated behavior, with the positive behavior of each partner eliciting analogous positive behavior from the other (Aksan, Kochanska, & Ortmann, 2006).

bidirectionality of parent–child interactions the idea that parents and their children are mutually affected by each other's characteristics and behaviors

Socioeconomic Influences on Parenting

Another factor that is associated with parenting styles and practices is socioeconomic status (SES). Parents with low SES are more likely than higher-SES parents to use an

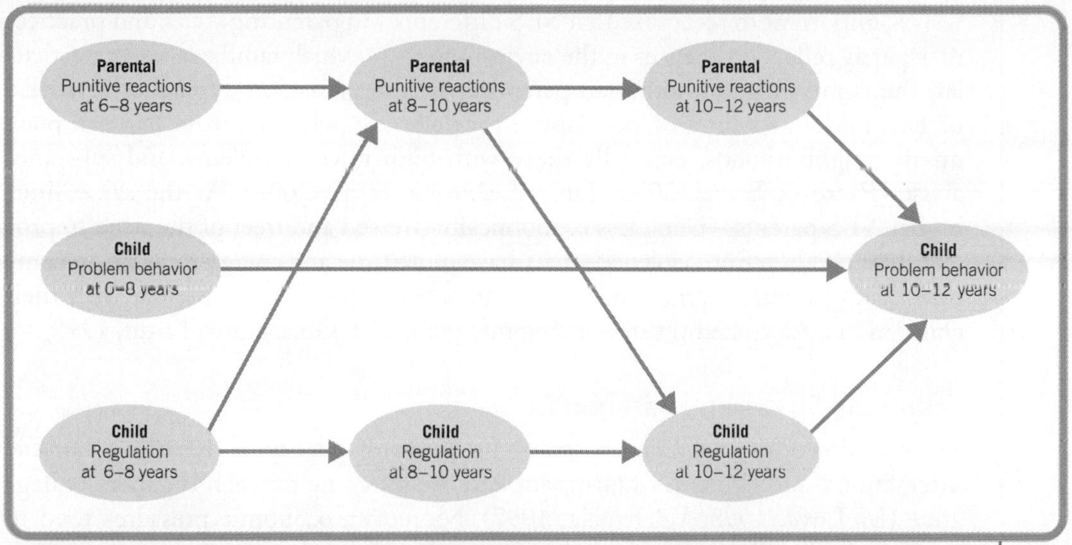

FIGURE 12.2 Bidirectional parent–child interactions **In a study of elementary school children, children's low self-regulation at ages 6 to 8 predicted parents' punitive reactions when the children were 8 to 10 years of age, which in turn predicted relatively low self-regulation at ages 10 to 12. Both parental punitive reactions and relatively low self-regulation at ages 10 to 12, as well as their problem behavior at a younger age, predicted externalizing problem behavior at ages 10 to 12. In addition, parental punitive reactions, children's regulation, and children's problem behavior were all correlated across time. (Adapted from Eisenberg, Guthrie et al., 1999)**

authoritarian and punitive child-rearing style; higher-SES parents tend to use a style that is more authoritative, accepting, and democratic (Pinderhughes, Dodge, Bates, Pettit, & Zelli, 2000; Shaw, Criss, Schonberg, & Beck, 2004). Higher-SES mothers, for example, are less likely than low-SES mothers to be controlling, restrictive, and disapproving in their interactions with their young children, even in African-American families (Tamis-LeMonda et al., 2008) and non-Western cultures (Chen, Dong, & Zhou, 1997; von der Lippe, 1999). In addition, higher-SES mothers talk more to, and elicit more talk from, their children, and they follow up more directly on what their children say. This greater use of language by higher-SES mothers may foster better communication between parent and child, as well as promote the child's verbal skills (Hart & Risley, 1995; Hoff, Laursen, & Tardif, 2002).

Some of the SES differences in parenting style and practices are related to differences in parental beliefs and values (Bornstein & Bradley, 2003; Skinner, 1985). Higher-SES parents are more likely than lower-SES parents to view themselves as teachers rather than as providers or disciplinarians (Hill & Sprague, 1999). Both in the United States and in other Western countries, parents from lower-SES families often promote conformity in children's behavior, whereas higher-SES parents are more likely to want their children to become self-directed and autonomous (Alwin, 1984; Luster, Rhoades, & Haas, 1989).

It is likely that level of education is an important aspect of SES associated with differences in parental values. Highly educated parents tend to hold a more complex view of development than do parents with less education. They are more likely, for example, to view children as active participants in their own learning and development (Johnson & Martin, 1985; Skinner, 1985). Such a view may make high-SES parents more inclined to allow children to have a say in matters that involve them, such as family rules and the consequences for breaking them. Highly educated parents are also more likely to encourage their children to express their thoughts and feelings.

It is important to recognize that SES differences in parenting styles and practices may partly reflect differences in the environments in which families live. In particular, the controlling, authoritarian parenting style that is more typical of low-SES parents may, in some cases, be adaptive for protecting children from harm in poor, unsafe neighborhoods, especially those with high rates of violence and substance abuse (Parke & Buriel, 2006; Tamis-LeMonda et al., 2008). At the same time, higher-SES parents—being less economically stressed and freer of the need to protect their children from violence—may have more time and energy to focus on complex issues in child rearing and may be in a better position to interact with their children in a controlled yet stimulating manner (Hoff-Ginsberg & Tardif, 1995).

Economic Stress and Parenting

Protracted economic stress is a strong predictor of quality of parenting, familial interactions, and children's adjustment and the outcome for each is generally negative (McLoyd, 1998; Valenzuela, 1997). Moreover, economic pressures tend to increase the likelihood of marital conflict and parental depression, which, in turn, makes parents more likely to be uninvolved with, or hostile to, their children (Conger et al., 2002; Keller, Cummings, Davies, & Mitchell, 2008; Parke et al., 2004) and less likely to cooperate and support each other's parenting (Katz & Low, 2004; Margolin, Gordis, & John, 2001; McHale et al., 2004). For both children and adolescents, the nonsupportive, inconsistent parenting associated with economic hardship and living in a poor neighborhood correlates with increased risk for depression, loneliness, unregulated behavior, delinquency, and substance use (Brody et al., 1994; Conger et al., 2002; Kohen, Leventhal, Dahinten, & McIntosh, 2008; Scaramella, Neppl, Ontai, & Conger, 2008).

The quality of parenting and family interactions is especially likely to be compromised for families at the poverty level, which in 2006 included 42% of U.S. single-parent families headed by mothers and 8% of families headed by married adults. All told, about 17% of children under 18 years of age live in poverty in the United States, the highest rate of child poverty among industrialized, Western countries (ChildStats.gov, 2008; see Figure 12.3). At one time or another, a substantial number of families in poverty experience homelessness, which obviously makes effective parenting extremely difficult (see Box 12.2).

One factor that can help moderate the potential impact of economic stress on parenting is having supportive relationships with relatives, friends, neighbors, or others who can provide material assistance, child care, advice, approval, or a sympathetic ear. Such positive connections can help people feel more successful and satisfied as parents and actually be better parents (MacPhee, Fritz, & Miller-Heyl, 1996). Although parental social support generally is associated with better maternal functioning and child outcomes (Feldman & Masalha, 2007; Franz, Lensche, & Schmitz, 2003; Taylor, Seaton, & Dominguez, 2008), it may be less beneficial for those low-income parents in the poorest, most dangerous neighborhoods (Ceballo & McLoyd, 2002).

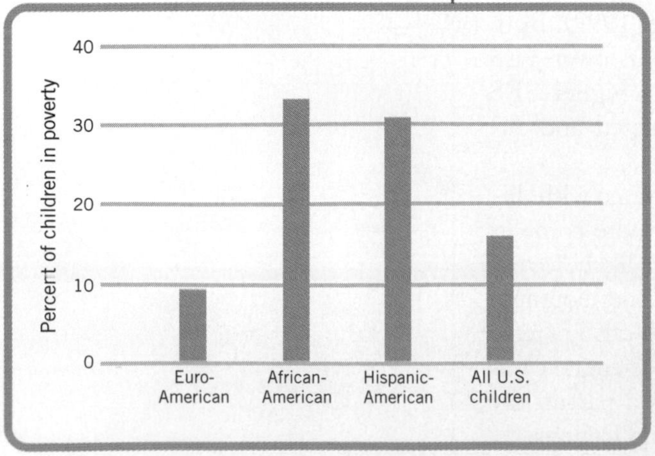

FIGURE 12.3 Child poverty rates in the United States Minority children in the United States—especially African-American and Hispanic-American children—are more than three times as likely to live in poverty than are Euro-American children. (ChildStats.gov, 2005)

a closer look 12.2

Homelessness

It is impossible to know the precise number of homeless children and families in the United States, much less in the world. In some countries, such as India and Brazil, the figure is in the millions (Diversi, Filho, & Morelli, 1999; Verma, 1999). In the United States, it is estimated that 3 million people are homeless at some point over the course of a given year, including 1.3 million children who usually are living with at least one parent (National Law Center on Homelessness and Poverty, 2009).

Homeless children are at risk in a variety of ways. At the most basic level, they are often malnourished and lack adequate medical care. Frequently they are also exposed to the chaotic and unsafe conditions found in many shelters. As might be expected, homeless children's school performance tends to be poor and is commonly accompanied by absenteeism and serious behavioral problems (Masten et al., 1997; Tyler, Whitbeck, Hoyt, & Johnson, 2003). Compared with poor children who are not homeless, homeless children also experience more internalizing problems, such as depression, social withdrawal, and low self-esteem (Buckner, Bassuk, Weinreb, & Brooks, 1999; DiBiase & Waddell, 1995; Rafferty & Shinn, 1991).

When they were young, mothers of homeless families often experienced stressors such as physical and sexual abuse, living on the street, and living in foster care or in an institution (Shinn, Knickman, & Weitzman, 1991). Many homeless men appear to have similar backgrounds (Interagency Council on the Homeless, 1999). In turn, their children are at increased risk both of being sexually abused (Buckner et al., 1999) and of ending up in foster care (Zlotnick, Kronstadt, & Klee, 1998). Thus, the cycle of deprivation, abuse, and disruption of social relationships that contributes to homelessness is likely self-perpetuating.

In adolescence, numerous youths either choose to leave their homes or are kicked out, and many of them live on the streets. Estimates of homeless, runaway, or "thrown away" adolescents in the United States (many of whom may not be included in homeless statistics) range from about 575,000 to over 1.6 million (Urbina, 2009; Wolfe, Toro, & McCaskill, 1999). Predictors of youths' running away include their living in lower-income families and neighborhoods and experiencing peer victimization and school suspension (Tyler & Bersani, 2008). In comparison with other adolescents from the same neighborhoods, these homeless youths generally report having experienced more conflict with, and rejection by, their parents and more parental maltreatment, including physical abuse. These differences in experience seem to be based in part on differences in the parents' behavior or in levels of stress in the home; they do not seem to be due merely to the homeless children's having had more problems of adjustment (Wolfe et al., 1999). Once on the streets, over a third of adolescents are likely to become affiliated with gangs and involved in illegal activities such as dealing drugs, stealing, and prostitution (Unger et al., 1998).

In many third-world countries, homeless children often live with other children on the streets and report doing so because of the loss of their parents or because of sexual, mental, or physical abuse at home (Aptehar & Ciano-Federoff, 1999). In many cases, children living on the streets reside at least part of the time with a parent or other relative (Diversi et al., 1999; Verma, 1999). Some youths report that they stay on the streets in order to enjoy freedom with their friends (Campos et al., 1994; Sampa, 1997).

Life on the streets in most third-world countries is even riskier than it is in the United States. In one study of Brazilian street youth, 75% were engaged in illegal activities such as stealing and prostitution (Campos et al., 1994). The longer these children were on the streets, the more likely they were to be involved in illegal activities. Street children also were at risk for drug abuse and had begun sexual activities at a younger age than their peers who hung out on the street but usually slept in homes. Thus, it is clear that homelessness, wherever it occurs, takes a tremendous toll on the welfare of children and on the larger society.

TONY FREEMAN / PHOTOEDIT

Children in homeless families are at risk for depression, behavioral problems, and academic failure.

DMITRI SHALGANOV / PPI / NEWSMAKERS / GETTY IMAGES

Homeless youth are at high risk for becoming involved in drugs and prostitution.

review:

Styles of parenting are associated with important developmental outcomes. Researchers have delineated four basic parenting styles varying in parental warmth and control: authoritative (relatively high in control but supportive); authoritarian (high in control but low in warmth); permissive (high in warmth and low in control); and rejecting-neglecting (low in both warmth and control). Particular styles of parenting can affect the meaning and impact of specific parenting practices, as well as children's receptiveness to these practices. In addition, the significance and effects of different parenting styles or practices may vary somewhat across cultures.

Education and income are associated with variations in parenting. Economic stressors can undermine the quality of marital and parent–child interactions. Children in poor and homeless families are more at risk for serious adjustment problems, such as depression, academic failure, disruptive behavior at school, and drug use.

Mothers, Fathers, and Siblings

As part of their focus on family dynamics, developmentalists have examined differences in children's interactions with mothers, fathers, and siblings. They have been particularly interested in these two questions: How do mothers and fathers differ in their parenting? How do siblings affect one another?

Differences in Mothers' and Fathers' Interactions with Their Children

It will come as no surprise that there is a great deal of difference, both quantitative and qualitative, between mothers' and fathers' interactions with their children. Although in most Western cultures today spouses share child-care responsibilities to some degree, in the majority of families, mothers—including those who work outside the home—still spend considerably more time with their children than do fathers (Aldous, Mulligan, & Bjarnason, 1998; Dubas & Gerris, 2002; Gaertner, Spinrad, Eisenberg, & Greving, 2007). In the United States, this pattern seems to hold in Latino-, African-, and Euro-American families, continuing from the early years into adolescence (Parke & Buriel, 1998). As might be expected, fathers spend more time with their sons than with their daughters, and mothers spend more time with their daughters than with their sons (Dubas & Gerris, 2002; NICHD Early Child Care Research Network, 2000a). A number of factors can cause fathers to be more likely to spend time with their infants, including their being encouraged to by the mother (Schoppe-Sullivan et al., 2008); their working fewer hours, and the mother's working more, than is typical; and their having an intimate marital relationship (NICHD Early Child Care Research Network, 2000a).

Fathers tend to engage in more physical play with their children than do mothers.

Fathers' participation in child care differs from mothers' not only in amount but in kind. Mothers are more likely to provide physical care and emotional support than are fathers (Moon & Hoffman, 2008; Russell & Russell, 1987). In contrast, fathers in Western industrialized cultures spend a greater proportion of their available time playing with their children than do mothers, both in infancy and childhood, and the type of play they engage in differs from mothers' play as well (Parke & Buriel, 1998). In an Australian study, for example, fathers were more likely to engage their children in physical and outdoor play activities (e.g., rough-and-tumble play and playing ball)

than were mothers (Russell & Russell, 1987). Mothers, on the other hand, tended to play more reserved games (e.g., peekaboo), to teach and read to their children, and to play more with toys indoors (Parke, 1996; Russell & Russell, 1987).

Although these general patterns prevail in many cultures, there are also some cultural variations. Fathers in Sweden, Malaysia, and India, for example, do not report much play at all with their children (Hwang, 1987; Roopnarine, Lu, & Ahmeduzzaman, 1989). Indeed, both mothers and fathers in some cultures simply play less with their children than American parents do (Goncu, Mistry, & Mosier, 2000; Roopnarine & Hossain, 1992). In a study of Gusii infants and parents in Kenya, fathers were seldom seen within 5 feet of their infants, and mothers spent 60% less time playing with infants than American mothers typically do (LeVine et al., 1996). The degree of maternal and paternal involvement in parenting and the nature of parents' interactions with children doubtlessly vary as a function of cultural practices and such factors as the amount of time parents work away from home and children spend at home.

Sibling Relationships

The quality of parents' relationships with their children is related to how well siblings interact.

ARIEL SKELLEY / BLEND IMAGES / CORBIS

Siblings influence each other's development and the functioning of the larger family system in many ways, both positive and negative. They serve not only as playmates for one another but also as sources of support, instruction, security, assistance, and caregiving (Brody, Stoneman, MacKinnon, & MacKinnon, 1985; Gass, Jenkins, & Dunn, 2007; Herrera & Dunn, 1997). Siblings, of course, also can be rivals and sources of mutual conflict and irritation (Vandell, 1987). And in some cases, they can contribute to the development of a sibling's undesirable behaviors, such as disobedience, delinquency, and drinking (Bank, Patterson, & Reid, 1996; McGue, Sharma, & Benson, 1996; Slomkowski, Rende, Conger, Simons, & Conger, 2001), especially if they live in disadvantaged neighborhoods (Brody et al., 2003). Low-quality sibling relationships also are associated with higher levels of siblings' depression (Compton, Snyder, Schrepferman, Bank, & Shortt, 2003; McHale, Whiteman, Kim, & Crouter, 2007; Stocker, Burwell, & Briggs, 2002).

Numerous factors affect whether or not siblings get along with each other. Siblings' relationships tend to be less hostile and more supportive, for example, when their parents are warm and accepting of them (Grych, Raynor, & Fosca, 2004; Ingoldsby, Shaw, & Garcia, 2001; Kim, McHale, Osgood, & Crouter, 2006). Siblings also have closer, more positive relationships if their parents treat them similarly (Brody, Stoneman, McCoy, & Forehand, 1992; McHale, Crouter, McGuire, & Updegraff, 1995). If parents favor one child over another, the sibling relationship may suffer, and the less favored child may experience distress, depression, and other problems with adjustment, especially if the child does not have a positive relationship with his or her parents (Feinberg & Hetherington, 2001; O'Connor, Hetherington, & Reiss, 1998; Shanahan, McHale, Crouter, & Osgood, 2008).

Differential treatment by parents is particularly influential in early and middle childhood, with less favored siblings being likelier to experience worry, anxiety, or

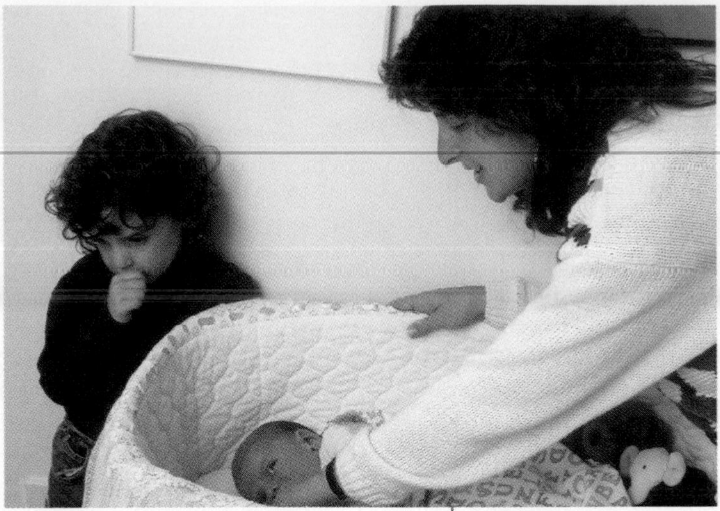

LAURA DWIGHT

Young children are more likely than older children to respond poorly when they perceive an infant sibling receiving more attention than they themselves do.

depression than are their more favored siblings (Coldwell, Pike, & Dunn, 2008; Dunn, 1992). By early adolescence, however, children often view parents' differential treatment of them as justified because of differences they perceive between themselves and their siblings in age, needs, and personal characteristics. When children view differential treatment by parents as justified, they report more positive relationships with their sibling and their parents than when they feel that differential parental treatment is unfair (Kowal & Kramer, 1997; Kowal, Krull, & Kramer, 2004; McHale, Updegraff, Jackson-Newsom, Tucker, & Crouter, 2000).

Cultural values may play a role in children's evaluations of, and reactions to, differential parental treatment. For example, in a study of Mexican-American families, older siblings who embraced the cultural value of *familism,* which emphasizes interdependence, mutual support, and loyalty among family members, were not put at risk of higher levels of depressive symptoms or risky behaviors by their parents' preferential treatment of younger siblings (McHale, Updegraff, Shanahan, Crouter, & Killoren, 2005).

Another factor that can affect the quality of siblings' interactions is the nature of the parents' relationship with each other. Siblings get along better if their parents are getting along with each other (Erel, Margolin, & John, 1998; McGuire, McHale, & Updegraff, 1996). In part, this may be because the parents model positive behavior. In contrast, siblings whose parents fight with each other are likely to have more hostile interactions because their parents not only model negative behavior for their children but also may be less sensitive and appropriate in their efforts to manage their children's interactions with each other (Howe, Aquan-Assee, & Bukowski, 2001).

Rivalry and conflict between siblings tend to be higher in divorced families and in remarried families than in nondivorced families, even between biological siblings. Although some siblings turn to one another for support when their parents divorce or remarry (Jenkins, 1992), they also may compete for parental affection and attention, which often are scarce in these situations. Relationships between half-siblings can be especially emotionally charged, perhaps because the older sibling may resent the younger sibling who is born to both parents in the new marital relationship (Hetherington, 1999). In general, the more a child in a blended family perceives a parent's preferential treatment of a sibling—whether a full sibling or a half-sibling—the worse the child's relationship is with that sibling (Baham, Weimer, Braver, & Fabricius, 2008).

Thus, the quality of sibling relationships differs across families depending on the ways that parents interact with each child and with each other and children's perceptions of their treatment by other family members. Such differences highlight the fact that families are complex, dynamic social systems and that all members contribute to one another's functioning.

review:

Mothers typically interact with their children much more than fathers do. The nature of mother–child and father–child interactions also tends to differ, with fathers engaging in more physical play with their children. Parent–child interactions differ across cultures; for example, in some cultures, parents play little or not at all with their children.

Siblings are important contributors to one another's socialization and development. They can be sources of learning and support for each other, as well as rivalry and conflict. Siblings get along better if they have good relationships with their parents and if they do not feel that their parents treat them differentially. Sibling relationships are, on average, more hostile and conflicted in divorced and remarried families than in nondivorced families. Thus, sibling relationships, like all family relationships, must be viewed in the context of the larger family system.

Changes in Families in the United States

The family in the United States has changed dramatically since the middle of the twentieth century. For example, from the 1950s to 2002, the median age at which people first married rose from age 20 to nearly 25 for women and from age 23 to over 27 for men (Goodwin, McGill, & Chandra, 2009). Over this same period, the economic arrangement of the U.S. family also changed quite strikingly. In 1940, the father was the breadwinner and the mother was a full-time homemaker in 52% of nonfarm families (Hernandez, 1993). In contrast, in 2005, the majority of women with infants and about 73% of mothers with school-aged children worked outside the home (U.S. Bureau of the Census, 2005).

A third change that occurred in the family, partly as a result of the two just mentioned, was that the average age at which women bore children increased, especially within marriages. The mean age of first-time motherhood rose from 21.4 in 1970 to 25.1 in 2002 (Sutton & Mathews, 2004). In the late 1970s, less than 20% of births in the United States were to women over age 30 (Coltrane, 1996); in 2001, the rate was about 37% (Hamilton, Martin, & Ventura, 2007).

Two of the most far-reaching changes in the U.S. family in the past half century have been the upsurge in divorce and the increase in the number of children born to unwed mothers. The divorce rate more than doubled between 1960 and 1980, with nearly one out of two marriages ending in divorce, and this rate has held fairly steady ever since (Coltrane, 1996; Kreider & Fields, 2002). The rise in out-of-wedlock births began in the 1980s, with the number of births among unmarried women increasing from 29 per 1000 women to 48 per 1000 in 2005. In 2006, 38% of all births were to unmarried women, including 92% of births for 15- to 17-year-olds (ChildStats.gov, 2007). (See Figure 12.4.)

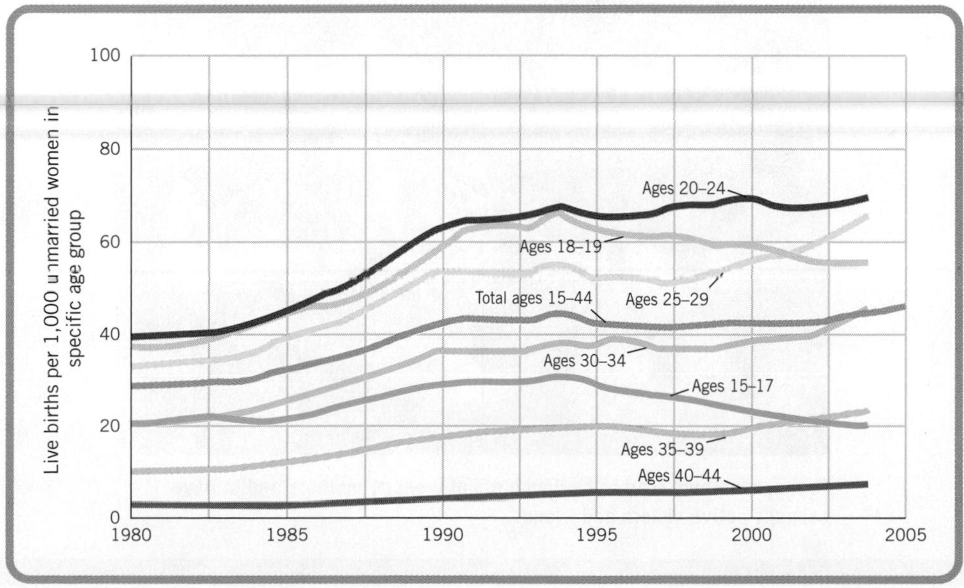

FIGURE 12.4 Birthrates for unmarried women by age of the mother The proportion of births that are to unmarried women in general rose sharply from 1980 to 2005. However, the rate of births to unmarried teens has dropped substantially since 1994, from 32 to 20 per 1000. (Adapted from ChildStats.gov, 2007)

Due both to the increase in divorce and the increase in the birthrate among unmarried women, the percent of children living with two married parents fell from 77% in 1980 to 68% in 2007. In 2007, 23% of children lived with only their mother, 3% lived with only their father, 3% lived with two unmarried parents, and 4% lived with neither parent (ChildStats.gov, 2008). Although people are more likely to divorce than in the past, most divorced people also remarry. Indeed, 54% percent of divorced women remarry after 5 years and 75% remarry within 10 years; these rates are even higher for women in the child-bearing years (Bramlett, & Mosher, 2002). Thus, the number of families including children from one or both parents' prior marriages has increased substantially (Coltrane, 1996).

All these changes in the structure and composition of families have vast implications for an understanding of child development and family life. In the following sections, we will give detailed consideration to the impact of age on parenting, the effects of both divorce and remarriage on children's development, and the issues surrounding maternal employment and child care. We will also consider an

individual differences

Adolescents as Parents

Childbearing in adolescence is a common occurrence in the United States. Among 15- to 17-year-olds in 2006, the rate of births was 22 per 1000 females (Hamilton, Martin, & Ventura, 2007). This rate was substantially below the rate in the 1960s (ChildStats.gov, 2001; Ventura et al., 1997), due in part to the greater availability of birth control and abortions. Nevertheless, the current rate is still much higher than that in other industrialized countries (Coley & Chase-Lansdale, 1998), and in 2006, 92% of all births in this age group were to unmarried mothers (ChildStats.gov, 2008). Thus, births to U.S. teens remains problematic.

A number of factors affect U.S. girls' risk for childbearing during adolescence. Two factors that reduce the risk are living with both biological parents and being involved in school activities and religious organizations (Ellis et al., 2003; Moore, Manlove, Glei, & Morrison, 1998). Factors that substantially increase the risk include being raised in poverty by a single or adolescent mother (Coley & Chase-Lansdale, 1998; Hardy, Astone, Brooks-Gunn, Shapiro, & Miller, 1998), low school achievement and dropping out of school (Freitas, Cais, Stefanello, Botega, 2008), significant family problems (e.g., death of a parent, drug or alcohol abuse in the family; Freitas et al., 2008), and having an older adolescent sibling who is sexually active or is a parent him- or herself (East & Jacobson, 2001; Miller, Benson, & Galbraith, 2001).

For young adolescent girls, having a mother who is cold and uninvolved may increase the risk of their becoming pregnant in later adolescence. In part, this may be because girls whose mothers fit this pattern tend to do poorly in school and hang out with peers who get into trouble, which often leads to risk taking and pregnancy (Scaramella, Conger, Simons, & Whitbeck, 1998). In fact, girls who are at risk for becoming mothers as teenagers tend to have many friends who are sexually active (East, Felice, & Morgan, 1993; Scaramella et al., 1998). It is likely that girls' willingness to engage in sex is influenced by its acceptability in their group of friends.

Having a child in adolescence is associated with many negative consequences for both the adolescent mother and the child (Jaffee, 2002). Motherhood curtails the mother's opportunities for education,

JOHN BERRY / SYRACUSE NEWSPAPERS / THE IMAGE WORKS

Teenage mothers tend to be daughters of teenage mothers and to have sexually active sisters and friends.

additional change in family structure that has recently received a good deal of public attention: the increase in the number of families with lesbian or gay parents.

Older Parents

About 100,000 of the 4,000,000 women who have babies in the United States each year are age 40 or older (U.S. Census Bureau, 2005). The age at which parents have children can affect their parenting in a number of ways. Within limits, having children at a later age has decided parenting advantages. As discussed in Box 12.3, adolescents, whether married or not, are generally less psychologically and financially equipped for parenthood than are older people. Even parents in their early 20s lack the resources of older first-time parents, who tend to have more education, higher-status occupations, and higher incomes. Older parents also are more likely to have planned the birth of their children and to have fewer children overall. Thus, they have more financial resources for raising a family and are less likely to get divorced within 10 years if they are married (Bramlett & Mosher, 2002).

12.3

career development, and normal relationships with peers. Even if teenage mothers marry, they are very likely to get divorced and to spend many years as single mothers (Coley & Chase-Lansdale, 1998; Lamb & Teti, 1991; Moore & Brooks-Gunn, 2002). Indeed, 48% of women who marry before age 18 have disrupted marriages within 10 years compared with only 24% for women who married at age 25 or older (Bramlett & Mosher, 2002). In addition, adolescent mothers often have poor parenting skills and are more likely than older mothers to provide low levels of verbal stimulation to their infants, to expect their children to behave in ways that are beyond their years, and to neglect and abuse them (Culp, Appelbaum, Osofsky, & Levy, 1988; Ekeus, Kyllike, & Anders, 2004; Lamb & Ketterlinus, 1991).

Given these deficits in parenting, it is not surprising that children of teenage mothers are more likely than children of older mothers to exhibit low impulse control, problem behaviors, and delays in cognitive development in the preschool years and thereafter. As adolescents themselves, children born to teenagers have higher rates of academic failure, delinquency, incarceration, and early sexual activity than do adolescents born to older mothers (Coley & Chase-Lansdale, 1998; Moore & Brooks-Gunn, 2002; Wakschlag et al., 2001).

This does not mean that all children born to adolescent mothers are destined to poor developmental outcomes. Adolescent mothers who have more knowledge about child development and parenting and who exhibit more authoritative parenting than most teen mothers do have children who display fewer problem behaviors and better intellectual development (Bates, Luster, & Vandenbelt, 2003; Miller, Miceli, Whitman, & Borkowski, 1996). Moreover, a positive parent–child relationship, including consistent and sensitive parenting, is related to the children of teenage mothers staying in school and obtaining employment in early adulthood (Jaffee, Caspi, Moffitt, Belsky, & Silva, 2001). Overall, then, it appears that the risks faced by children of adolescent mothers are not due so much to the age of their mother as to background factors such as low income, unemployment, and poor education that may affect the quality of parenting and the home environment (Turley, 2003).

A number of factors likewise affect adolescent males' risk for becoming fathers. Chief among these are being poor, being prone to substance abuse and behavioral problems, being involved with deviant peers, and having a police record (Fagot, Pears, Capaldi, Crosby, & Leve, 1998; Miller-Johnson et al., 2004; Moore & Florsheim, 2001).

Many young unmarried or absent fathers see their children regularly, at least during the first few years, but rates of contact decrease over time (Corey & Chase-Lansdale, 1998; Marsiglio, Amato, Day, & Lamb, 2000). In one study, 40% of adolescent fathers had no contact with their 2-year-old children (Fagot et al., 1998). Contact is less likely to be maintained when the unmarried noncohabiting father is an adolescent (Wilson & Brooks-Gunn, 2001). Young unmarried fathers remain more involved with their children if they have a warm, supportive relationship with the mother in the weeks after delivery and if the mother does not experience many stressful life events (particularly financial problems) during and soon after the pregnancy (Cutrona, Hessling, Bacon, & Russell, 1998). They are also more likely to be involved with their infants if they have social support from their parents for the parenting role, and if their level of stress related to fatherhood or other factors is low (Fagan, Bernd, & Whiteman, 2007).

Children of adolescent mothers fare better in their own adolescence if they have a good relationship with their biological father or with a stepfather, especially if he lives with the child. However, exposure to a fathering figure may have little beneficial effect on children of adolescent mothers if the father–child relationship is not positive or the father figure has a criminal history (Furstenberg & Harris, 1993; Jaffee et al., 2001).

An additional benefit for mothers who delay childbearing is that they tend to perform fewer hours of housework, either because they are able to afford household help or because their husbands, also being older and having similar or higher SES characteristics, are more likely than the husbands of young mothers to believe that housework should be shared (Coltrane, 1996). Taken together, these factors help reduce the overall stresses of parenting for mothers.

Older parents also tend to be more positive in their parenting of infants than younger parents are—unless they already have several children. Even in research that involved only people who became parents between the ages of 18 and 25, older mothers and fathers had lower rates of observed harsh parenting with their 2-year-olds. Moreover, the degree of harsh parenting predicted the level of problem behaviors a year later (Scaramella et al., 2008). In another study of mothers aged 16 to 38 who had recently given birth, the older the mother, the more she expressed satisfaction with parenting and commitment to the parenting role. Older mothers also reported greater gratification from their interactions with the baby, displayed more positive emotion toward the baby, and showed greater sensitivity to the baby's cues. Again, however, these positive outcomes did not extend to mothers who already had two or more children. Perhaps because they had less energy to deal with so many children, these mothers tended to exhibit less positive affect and sensitive behavior with their infants than did younger mothers with two or more other children (Ragozin, Basham, Crnic, Greenberg, & Robinson, 1982).

Men who delay parenting until approximately age 30 or later are likewise more positive about the parenting role than are younger fathers (Cooney, Pedersen, Indelicato, & Palkovitz, 1993; NICHD Early Child Care Research Network, 2000a). On average, they tend to be more responsive, affectionate, and cognitively and verbally stimulating with their infants. They are also more likely to provide a moderate amount of child care (Neville & Parke, 1997; NICHD Early Child Care Research Network, 2000a; Volling & Belsky, 1991). These differences may be partly due to older fathers' being better established in their careers, allowing them to focus on their role as father and to be more flexible in their beliefs about acceptable roles and activities for fathers (Coltrane, 1996; Parke & Buriel, 1998).

MICHAEL NEWMAN / PHOTOEDIT

On average, older fathers engage in more verbal interactions with their preschool-age children than do younger fathers.

Divorce

About 20% of first marriages in the United States end in divorce or separation within 5 years and one-third end within 10 years; thus, many children experience divorce (Bramlett & Mosher, 2002). In 2003, 5.7 million U.S. children lived with only their divorced mother, 1.5 million children lived with their divorced father, and several million others lived in reconstituted familes (Child Trends, 2007). Moreover, about 40% of remarriages involving children end in divorce in 10 years (Bramlett & Mosher, 2002). Thus, the effects of divorce and remarriage on children are of great concern.

The Potential Impact of Divorce

Most experts agree that children of divorce are at greater risk for a variety of short- and long-term problems than are most children who are living with both their biological parents. Compared with the majority of their peers in intact families, for example, they are more likely to experience depression and sadness, to have lower self-esteem, and to be less socially responsible and competent (Amato, 2001; Ge, Natsuaki, & Conger, 2006; Hetherington, Bridges, & Insabella, 1998). Boys whose parents divorce are also prone to higher levels of externalizing problem behaviors such as aggression and antisocial behavior, both soon after the divorce and years later (Burt, Barnes, McGue, & Iacono, 2008; Malone et al., 2004). Adolescents whose parents divorce exhibit a greater tendency toward dropping out of school, engaging in delinquent activities and substance abuse, and having children out of wedlock (Amato & Keith, 1991; Hetherington et al., 1998; Simons & Associates, 1996).

As adults, children from divorced and remarried families are at greater risk for divorce themselves (Bumpass, Martin, & Sweet, 1991; Rodgers, Power, & Hope, 1997). Being less likely to have completed high school or college, they often earn lower incomes in early adulthood than do their peers from intact families (Hetherington, 1999). As adults, they are also at slightly greater risk for serious emotional disorders such as depression, anxiety, and phobias (Chase-Lansdale, Cherlin, & Kiernan, 1995).

Despite all these greater risks, most children whose parents divorce do not suffer significant, enduring problems as a consequence (Amato & Keith, 1991). In fact, although divorce usually is a very painful experience for children, the differences between children from divorced families and children from intact families in terms of their psychological and social functioning are small overall (e.g., Burt et al., 2008). In addition, these differences often reflect an extension of differences in the children's and/or their parents' psychological functioning that existed for years prior to the divorce (Clarke-Stewart, Vandell, McCartney, Owen, & Booth, 2000; Emery & Forehand, 1994).

Factors Affecting the Impact of Divorce

A variety of interacting factors seem to predict whether or not the painful experiences of divorce and remarriage will cause children significant or lasting problems. The question here is one of individual differences: Why do some children of divorce do better than others?

Parental conflict One influence on children's adjustment to divorce is the level of parental conflict prior to, during, and subsequent to a divorce (Buchanan, Maccoby, & Dornbusch, 1996). In fact, levels of parental conflict may predict the outcomes for children more than divorce itself. Not only is parental conflict distressing for children to observe, but it also may cause them to feel insecure about their own relationships with their parents, even making them fear that their parents will desert them or stop loving them (Davies & Cummings, 1994; Grych & Fincham, 1997). In addition, when there is parental conflict, fathers tend to have lower-quality relationships with their children, which may contribute to children's adjustment problems (Pruett, Williams, Insabella, & Little, 2003).

Conflict between parents often increases when the divorce is being negotiated and may continue for years after the divorce. This ongoing conflict is especially likely to have negative effects on children if they feel caught in the middle of it, as when they are forced to act as intermediaries between their parents or to inform one parent about the other's activities. Similar pressures may arise if children feel the need to hide from one parent information about, or their loyalty to, the other. Adolescents who feel that they are caught up in their divorced parents' conflict are at increased risk for being depressed or anxious and for engaging in problematic behavior such as drinking, stealing, cheating at school, fighting, or using drugs (Buchanan, Maccoby, & Dornbusch, 1991).

Stress A second factor that affects children's adjustment to divorce is the stress experienced by the custodial parent and children in the new family arrangement. Not only must custodial parents juggle household, child-care, and financial responsibilities that usually are shared by two parents, but they often must do so isolated from those who might otherwise help. This isolation typically occurs when custodial parents have to change their residence and lose access to established social networks, or when friends and relatives—especially in-laws—take sides in the divorce and turn against them. In addition, custodial mothers usually experience a substantial drop in their income, and this financial stress is often associated with problems in their physical health (Wickrama et al., 2006). All this may occur on top of the conflicts related to divorce mentioned above. Not surprisingly, custodial parents, usually mothers, often are not only stressed but also angry, hurt, or depressed.

BRUCE AYRES / STONE / GETTY IMAGES

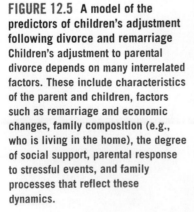

Divorced parents who are single often have to deal with increased levels of stress, which can affect the quality of their parenting.

As a result of all these factors, the parenting of newly divorced mothers, compared with that of mothers in two-parent families, often tends to be characterized by more irritability and coercion, and less warmth, consistency, and supervision of children (Hetherington, 1993; Hetherington et al., 1998; Simons & Johnson, 1996). This is unfortunate because children tend to be most adjusted during and after the divorce if their custodial parent is supportive and uses authoritative parenting (Hetherington, 1993; Simons & Associates, 1996; Steinberg, Mounts, Lamborn, & Dornbush, 1991). Making parenting even more difficult for the mother, noncustodial fathers often are permissive and indulgent with their children (Hetherington, 1989; Parke & Buriel, 1998), increasing the likelihood that children will resent and resist their mother's attempts to control their behavior.

Thus, stressful life experiences during and after divorce often undermine the quality of parenting and of family interactions, which affects children's adjustment (Ge et al., 2006). These stressful life experiences can also have a direct effect on the child's adjustment (Figure 12.5). Having to move because of reduced household

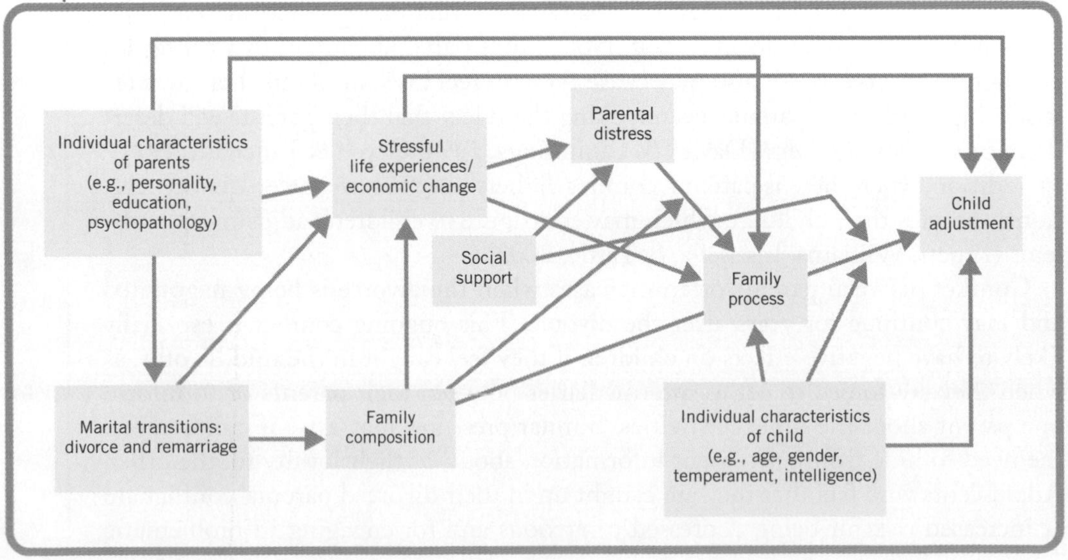

FIGURE 12.5 A model of the predictors of children's adjustment following divorce and remarriage **Children's adjustment to parental divorce depends on many interrelated factors. These include characteristics of the parent and children, factors such as remarriage and economic changes, family composition (e.g., who is living in the home), the degree of social support, parental response to stressful events, and family processes that reflect these dynamics.**

income, for example, may mean that at a time of high emotional vulnerability, a child also has to go through a wrenching transition to a new residence, neighborhood, school, and peer group (Braver, Ellman, & Fabricius, 2003).

Age of the child An additional factor that influences the impact of divorce is the child's age at the time of the divorce. Compared with older children and adolescents, younger children may have more trouble understanding the causes and consequences of divorce. They are especially more likely to be anxious about abandonment by their parents and to blame themselves for the divorce (Hetherington, 1989). As an 8-year-old boy explained, a year after his parents' divorce:

> My parents didn't get along. . . . They used to argue about me all the time when they were married. I guess I caused them a lot of trouble by not wanting to go to school and all. I didn't mean to make them argue. . . .
>
> (Wallerstein & Blakeslee, 1989, p. 73)

This boy firmly believed that he caused the divorce.

The following clinical report presents a picture of how divorce often affects young children:

> When we first saw seven-year-old Ned, he brought his family album to the office. He showed us picture after picture of himself with his father, his mother, and his little sister. Smiling brightly, he said, "It's going to be all right. It's really going to be all right." A year later, Ned was a sad child. His beloved father was hardly visiting and his previously attentive mother was angry and depressed. Ned was doing poorly in school, was fighting on the playground, and would not talk much to his mother.
>
> (Wallerstein & Blakeslee, 1989, p. xvi)

Although older children and adolescents are better able to understand a divorce than are younger children, they are nonetheless particularly at risk for problems with adjustment, including poor academic achievement and negative relationships with their parents. Adolescents who live in neighborhoods characterized by a high crime rate, poor schools, and an abundance of antisocial peers are at especially high risk (Hetherington et al., 1998), most likely because the opportunities to get into trouble are amplified when there is only one parent—who most likely is at work during the day—to monitor the child's activity. College students are less reactive to their parents' divorce, probably because of their maturity and relative independence from the family (Amato & Keith, 1991). With regard to their parents' remarriage, young adolescents appear to be more negatively affected than younger children. One possible explanation for this is that young adolescents' struggles with the issues of autonomy and sexuality are heightened by the presence of a new parent who has authority to control them and is a sexual partner of their biological parent (Hetherington, 1993; Hetherington et al., 1992).

Contact with noncustodial parents Contrary to popular belief, the frequency of children's contact with their noncustodial parent, usually the father, is not, in itself, a significant factor in their adjustment after divorce (Amato & Gilbreth, 1999; Trinder, Kellet, & Swift, 2008). Sadly, this is probably good news, because some data indicate that noncustodial fathers become increasingly uninvolved with their children over time, such that less than 50% of noncustodial fathers see their children more than once a year (Hetherington & Stanley-Hagan, 2002; Parke & Buriel, 1998). What does affect children's adjustment after divorce is the quality of

TONY FREEMAN / PHOTOEDIT

Children of divorce benefit from interaction with noncustodial fathers only if that interaction is of high quality.

the contact with the noncustodial father: children who have contact with competent, supportive, authoritative noncustodial fathers show better adjustment and do better in school than children who have frequent but superficial or disruptive contact with their noncustodial fathers (Amato & Gilbreth, 1999; Hetherington, 1989; Hetherington et al., 1998; Whiteside & Becker, 2000).

Less is known about noncustodial mothers. However, it is clear that they provide more emotional support for their children than noncustodial fathers do and are more likely to maintain contact through letters, phone calls, and overnight visits. The more noncustodial mothers maintain such involvement with their children, the better adjusted their children are (Gunnoe & Hetherington, 2004).

The contribution of long-standing characteristics As noted earlier, it is important to recognize that the greater frequency of problem behaviors in children in divorced and remarried families may not be solely due to the divorce and remarriage. Rather, it sometimes may be related to characteristics of the parents or the children that existed long before the divorce. For example, the parents may have difficulty coping with stress or forming positive social relationships, as suggested by the fact that parents who divorce are more likely than undivorced parents to be depressed, alcoholic, or antisocial, to hold dysfunctional beliefs about relationships, or to lack skills for regulating conflict and negative emotion (Emery, Waldron, Kitzmann, & Aaron, 1999; Jochlin, McGue, & Lykken, 1996; Kurdek, 1993). If it is a factor in the divorce, any one of these characteristics would be likely to undermine the quality of parenting the child receives.

The idea that the greater frequency of problem behaviors in children of divorce may be related to long-standing characteristics of the children themselves is supported by the finding that children of divorce tend to be more poorly adjusted prior to the divorce than are children from nondivorced families (Block, Block, & Gjerde, 1986; Hetherington & Stanley-Hagan, 2002). This difference may be due to stress in the home, poor parenting, or parental conflict prior to divorce. Alternatively or additionally, it may be due to inherited characteristics such as a lack of self-regulation or a predisposition to negative emotion (O'Connor, Caspi, DeFries, & Plomin, 2000). Such characteristics would not only underlie children's adjustment problems but, when expressed in both children and their parents, would also increase the likelihood of divorce (Hetherington et al., 1998; Jochlin et al., 1996). Children with difficult personalities and limited coping capacities may also react more adversely to the negative events associated with divorce than would other children.

Custody of Children After Divorce

In 2003, children living with one divorced parent were more than 4 times as likely to live with their mothers as with their fathers (U.S. Bureau of the Census, 2003b). However, parents sometimes have joint custody of their children. This arrangement is generally associated with better adjustment in children than is sole custody (Bauserman, 2002), but its effects depend in part on the degree of cooperation between ex-spouses. When parents cooperate with each other and keep the children's best interests in mind, children are unlikely to feel caught in the middle than if their parents are in conflict (Maccoby, Buchanan, Mnookin, & Dornbusch, 1993).

Unfortunately, mutually helpful parenting is not the norm (Bretherton & Page, 2004): one study found that once parents had been separated for a year and a half or more, most engaged in conflict or did not deal much with each other (Maccoby et al., 1993).

An Alternative to Divorce: Ongoing Marital Conflict

On the basis of the publicity given to the negative effects that divorce can have on children, some people have argued that it would be better for families if it were more difficult for parents to obtain a divorce. When considering this argument, it is important to realize that sustained marital conflict has negative effects on children at all ages. Infants and children can be harmed by marital conflict because it may cause mothers to be less warm and supportive, undermining parental emotional involvement with the child and the security of the early parent–child attachment (El-Sheikh & Elmore-Staton, 2004; Frosch, Mangelsdorf, & McHale, 2000; Sturge-Apple, Davies, & Cummings, 2006). Preschoolers and older children are especially likely to feel threatened and helpless when there is ongoing parental conflict—even more so if the conflict involves high levels of verbal and physical aggression (Davies, Cummings, & Winter, 2004; Grych, Harold, & Miles, 2003).

Even adolescents often feel threatened by, and responsible for, parental conflict (Buehler, Lange, & Franck, 2007). Children and adolescents exposed to sustained marital conflict tend to be more aggressive and engage in more delinquent behavior than do their peers from less combative family environments (Davies, Sturge-Apple, Cicchetti, & Cummings, 2007; Grych, Raynor, & Fosco, 2004; Lindahl, Malik, Kaczynski, & Simons, 2004). All these outcomes are likely to be exacerbated if the sustained marital conflict leads—as it frequently does—to parental hostility toward the children themselves (Buehler et al., 1997; Harold & Conger, 1997). Further complicating matters is the fact that the relation between marital conflict and children's acting out problem behavior seems to be partly due to genetic factors that affect both parents' and children's behavior (Harden et al., 2007).

NORBERT SCHAFER / CORBIS

The level of parental conflict appears to be an important factor that influences a child's adjustment to divorce.

Stepparenting

In 2007, roughly 6% of U.S. children lived in a household with a stepparent (ChildStats.gov, 2008)—in about 75% of cases, a stepfather (ChildStats.gov, 2007). Because many children who were not living with a stepparent in 2007 had done so in the past, or might do so in the future, it seems likely that the number of children who would experience living with a stepparent by the age of 18 would actually be considerably higher, perhaps three times as high.

The entry of a stepparent into the family is often a very threatening event for children. As described by one long-term study, the child's world is suddenly full of anxious questions:

> What will this new man do for me? Will he threaten my position in the family? Will he interfere with my relationship with Mom and Dad? . . . Is he good for my mom? Will she be in a better mood? Will she treat me better? . . . Will my dad be angry? Will having a stepfather around make Dad want to visit me more or less? . . . Will Mom and Dad ever get remarried now that someone else is in the picture?
>
> (Wallerstein & Blakeslee, 1989, p. 246)

The answers to specific questions like these obviously vary case by case. Nevertheless, investigators have found some general patterns in the adjustments that are required of both children and adults when a remarriage occurs.

Factors Affecting Children's Adjustment in Stepfamilies

The adjustment of children living with a stepparent is influenced by a number of factors, including the child's age at the time of the remarriage. Very young children tend to accept stepparents more easily than do older children and adolescents (Amato & Keith, 1991; Hetherington et al., 1989). In addition, children generally adjust better when all the children are full siblings (Hetherington et al., 1999). One indicator of this is the fact that, in adolescence, children born into blended families have higher rates of delinquency, depression, and detachment from school tasks and relationships than do full siblings living with their biological parents, perhaps due to more conflict in the family (Halpern-Meekin & Tach, 2008).

Another factor affecting children's adjustment is whether the new stepparent is a stepfather or a stepmother. Although most stepfathers want their new families to thrive, they generally feel less close to their stepchildren than do fathers in intact families (Hetherington, 1993). At first, they tend to be polite and ingratiating toward their stepchildren and are not as involved in monitoring or controlling them as are fathers in intact families (Kurdek & Fine, 1993). Nevertheless, on average, conflict between stepfathers and stepchildren tends to be greater than that between fathers and their biological offspring (Bray & Berger, 1993; Hetherington et al., 1992, 1999). It is thus not surprising that children with stepfathers tend to have higher rates of depression, withdrawal, and disruptive problem behaviors than do children in intact families (Hetherington & Stanley-Hagan, 1995).

Preadolescent girls in particular are likely to have problems with their stepfathers. Often the difficulty arises from the fact that prior to the remarriage, divorced mothers have had a close, confiding relationship with their daughters, and the entry of the stepfather into the family disrupts this relationship. These changes can lead to resentment in the daughter and conflict with both her mother and the stepfather (Hetherington et al., 1992; Hetherington & Stanley-Hagen, 2002).

Despite these potential difficulties, the presence of an involved stepfather can bring benefits, including substantially improved family finances and a welcome source of emotional support and assistance for the custodial parent. A new stepfather may be especially helpful both in controlling his stepson and in providing a male role model (Parke & Buriel, 1998). One sign of this is that the increase of delinquency associated with children of divorce is lessened if the adolescent's parent remarries (Burt et al., 2008). Overall, with time, children often become as close to their stepfathers as they are to their nonresidential biological fathers, sometimes even closer (Falci, 2006).

Because there are decidedly fewer stepmothers than stepfathers, much less research has been devoted to their role as stepparents. However, it appears that stepmothers generally have more difficulty with their stepchildren than do stepfathers (Gosselin & David, 2007). Often fathers expect stepmothers to take an active role in parenting, including monitoring and disciplining the child. However, children frequently resent the stepmother's being the disciplinarian. Nonetheless, when it is possible for stepmothers to use authoritative parenting successfully, stepchildren may be better adjusted (Hetherington et al., 1998). Indeed, children of both sexes are most adjusted in stepfamilies when their custodial parent is authoritative in his or her parenting style and the stepparent is warm and involved and supports the custodial parent's decisions rather than trying to exert control over the children independently (Bray & Berger, 1993; Hetherington et al., 1998).

A final factor in children's adjustment in stepfamilies is the attitude of the noncustodial biological parent toward the stepparent and the level of conflict between the two (Wallerstein & Lewis, 2007). If the noncustodial parent has hostile feelings toward the new stepparent and communicates these feelings to the child, the child is likely to feel caught in the middle, increasing his or her adjustment problems (Buchanan et al., 1991). The noncustodial parent's hostile feelings may also encourage the child to behave in a hostile or distant manner with the stepparent. In stepfamilies in which the relations between the noncustodial parent and the stepparent are supportive and the relations between the biological parents are cordial, children tend to have fewer difficulties than those in which hostility between biological parents is evident (Golish, 2003). Thus, the success or failure of stepfamilies is affected by the behavior and attitudes of all involved parties.

Lesbian and Gay Parents

Another way that U.S. families have changed in recent decades is that more lesbian and gay adults are parents. Although the numbers of lesbian and gay parents cannot be estimated with confidence because many conceal their sexual orientation, the most likely figure seems to be between 1 and 5 million (Patterson, 2002).

Most children of lesbian or gay parents are born when their parents are in a heterosexual marriage or relationship. In many cases, the parents divorce when one parent comes out as lesbian or gay. In addition, an increasing number of single and coupled lesbians are choosing to give birth to children, often through the use of artificial insemination. Other lesbians or gay men choose to become foster or adoptive parents, although there sometimes are legal barriers to such adoptions. In some cases, gay men have opportunities to act as stepfathers to the biological children of their partners (Patterson, 2002; Patterson & Chan, 1997).

The question that concerns many people is whether children raised by gay and lesbian parents grow up to be different from other children. According to a limited but growing body of research, they are, in fact, very similar in their development to children of heterosexual parents in terms of adjustment, personality, and relationships with peers (Golombak, Spencer, & Rutter, 1983; Wainright & Patterson, 2006, 2008). They are also similar in their sexual orientation and in the degree to which their behavior is gender-typed (Bailey, Bobrow, Wolfe, & Mikach, 1995; Fulcher, Sutfin, & Patterson, 2008; Golombok et al., 2003), as well as in their romantic involvements and sexual behavior as adolescents (Wainright et al., 2004). Perhaps surprisingly, children of lesbian and gay parents generally report low levels of stigmatization and teasing (Tasker & Golombok, 1995), although they sometimes feel excluded by peers or the target of their gossip (Bos & van Balen, 2008). This relatively low rate of difficulties with peers may be partly due to the fact that children of gay or lesbian parents frequently try to hide their parents' sexual preference from their friends, largely because they fear being labeled by peers as gay or lesbian themselves (Bozett, 1980, 1987; Crosbie-Burnett & Helmbrecht, 1993).

As in families with heterosexual parents, whether or not children of lesbian and gay parents do well seems to depend on family dynamics, including the closeness of the parent–child relationship (Wainright & Patterson, 2008). In addition, children of lesbian parents are better adjusted when their mother and her partner are getting along and are not highly stressed (Chan, Raboy, & Patterson, 1998), when they report sharing child-care duties evenly (Patterson, 1995a), and when they are satisfied with the division of labor in the

BOB DAEMMRICH / STOCK BOSTON

Although it is not extensive, the research to date suggests that the development of children of lesbian and gay parents differs little, if at all, from that of children of heterosexual parents.

home (Chan, Brooks, Raboy, & Patterson, 1998). In families with a gay father and his partner, sons' happiness with their family life is related to the inclusion of the partner in family activities and the son's having a good relationship with the partner as well as with his father (Crosbie-Burnett & Helmbrecht, 1993).

review:

The American family has changed dramatically in recent decades. Adults are marrying later and having children later; more children are born to single mothers; and divorce and remarriage are common occurrences.

Adolescent parents come disproportionately from impoverished backgrounds and are more likely than other teens to have behavioral and academic problems. Adolescent mothers tend to be less effective parents than older mothers, and their children are at risk for behavioral and academic problems and early sexual activity. In contrast, mothers who delay childbearing tend to be more responsive with their children than are mothers who have their first children at a younger age.

Parental divorce and remarriage have been associated with enduring negative outcomes, such as behavioral problems, for only a minority of children. The major factor contributing to negative outcomes for children of divorce is dysfunctional family interactions in which parents deal with each other in hostile ways and children feel caught in the middle. Parental depression and upset, as well as economic pressures and other types of stress associated with single parenting, often compromise the quality of parents' interactions with each other and with their children.

Stepfamilies present special challenges. Conflict is common in stepfamilies, especially when the children are adolescents, and stepparents usually are less involved with their stepchildren than are biological parents. Children do best if all parents are supportive and use an authoritative parenting style.

An increasing number of children live in families in which at least one parent is openly lesbian or gay. There is no evidence that children raised by lesbian or gay parents are more likely to be lesbian or gay themselves or to differ from children of heterosexual parents in their adjustment.

Maternal Employment and Child Care

Paralleling many of the other changes that have occurred in the family over the past half century in the United States, the employment rate for mothers increased more than fourfold. In 1955, only 18% of mothers with children under the age of 6 were employed outside the home; in 2005, 58.5% were employed outside the home (another 4% were in the labor force looking for jobs). In addition, in 2005, 73% of mothers of children age 6 to 18 were employed outside the home, with another 3.5% looking for jobs (Child Health, 2006). In 2002, 55% of mothers of infants worked outside the home (U.S. Census Bureau, Facts for Features, 2005). These changes in the rates of maternal employment reflect a variety of factors, including greater acceptance of mothers' working outside the home, more opportunities in the workplace for women, and increased financial need, often brought about by single motherhood or divorce.

The dramatic rise in the number of mothers working outside the home raised a variety of concerns. Some experts predicted that maternal employment, especially in an infant's first year, would seriously diminish the quality of maternal caregiving and that the mother–child relationship would suffer accordingly. Others worried that "latchkey" children who were left to their own devices after school would get into serious trouble, academically and socially. Over the past two decades, much research has been devoted to addressing such concerns. For the most part, the findings have been reassuring.

The Effects of Maternal Employment

Taken as a whole, research does not support the idea that maternal employment per se has negative effects on children's development. There is little consistent evidence, for example, that the quality of mothers' interactions with their children necessarily diminishes substantially as a result of their employment (Gottfried, Gottfried, & Bathurst, 2002; Hoffman, 1989; Huston & Aronson, 2005; Paulson, 1996). Although working mothers typically spend somewhat less time with their children than do nonworking mothers, the difference in time is not large because relatively less of their caregiving time is spent in household, leisure, organizational, and social activities (Huston & Aronson, 2005). Even in the area of greatest debate—the effects of maternal employment on infants in their first year of life—when negative relations between maternal work and children's cognitive or social behavior have been found, they have not been consistent across studies, ethnic groups, or type of analyses applied to the data (Berger, Grooks-Gunn, Paxson, & Waldfogel, 2008; Burchinal & Clarke-Stewart, 2007).

Overall, what the evidence does suggest is that maternal employment may be associated with negative outcomes for some children under certain circumstances and that it may be associated with positive outcomes in other circumstances. As is discussed shortly, quality of child care provided while mothers work is undoubtedly a critical factor affecting whether maternal employment is associated with cognitive, language, or social problems in young children. Many other factors also are likely to affect whether or not maternal employment is associated with negative outcomes for children. For example, if children are not adequately supervised and monitored after school, their academic performance may suffer (Muller, 1995). However, if employed mothers are involved with their children, and if their children's activities are supervised after school, their children tend to do as well at school as children of mothers who are not employed outside the home (Beyer, 1995). Another factor to consider is that in two-parent families, fathers are often more involved with their young children if mothers work; thus, father involvement may compensate for any decline in maternal involvement (Gottfried et al., 2002).

Studies of older children also reveal contextual variation in the effects that maternal employment can have on children's development. In a large study of elementary school children, sons and daughters of employed mothers had higher scores on math and reading tests than did children of full-time homemakers and were somewhat more assertive and independent (Hoffman & Youngblade, 1999). In addition, girls of employed mothers exhibited higher social adjustment and competence. These positive outcomes seemed to be due, in part, to the fact that employed mothers—especially working-class mothers—were less permissive, coercive, or authoritarian, and more authoritative, in their style of parenting than were the full-time homemakers. One negative outcome was noted in the findings, however: boys who were from middle-class families in which both parents worked exhibited more problem behavior, such as aggression, than did middle-class boys with stay-at-home mothers—perhaps because they had less supervision.

There also appear to be costs and benefits of maternal employment for low-income families, depending on the circumstances. Adolescents in low-income, single-parent, mother-headed families report feeling more positive emotions and higher self-esteem if their mothers are employed full time (Duckett & Richards, 1995). Perhaps this is because maternal employment is an important factor in pulling mother-headed, poor families out of poverty (Harvey, 1999; Lichter & Lansdale, 1995). Moreover, African-American daughters of working mothers are more likely

STEVEN RUBIN / THE IMAGE WORKS

Some research suggests that African-American daughters of working mothers are less likely to quit school than are African-American daughters of mothers who are not employed.

to stay in school than are African-American daughters of unemployed working-class mothers (Wolfer & Moen, 1996). However, there is also some evidence that unmarried mothers with poor-paying jobs may become less supportive of their children and provide a less stimulating home environment after they start working compared with when they were at home full time (Menaghan & Parcel, 1995). This drop in supportiveness is no doubt linked to the fact that single mothers with low-paying jobs are particularly likely to be stressed, unhappy with their jobs, and unable to afford child care or other services to assist them with child rearing.

Maternal employment may have specific benefits for girls. Children of employed mothers are more likely than children of nonemployed mothers to reject the confining aspects of traditional gender roles, and they are more likely to believe that women are as competent as men (Hoffman, 1984, 1989). Children of employed mothers are more likely to be exposed to egalitarian parental roles in the family, and this experience seems to affect girls' feelings of effectiveness (Hoffman & Youngblade, 1999). In addition, daughters of employed mothers tend to have higher aspirations than do peers whose mothers are not employed (Gottfried et al., 2002).

The impact that maternal employment—or the lack thereof—can have on children also depends in part on how the mother is affected by her employment status (Kalil & Ziol-Guest, 2005). Mothers who want to work but do not, for example, sometimes are depressed (Gove & Zeiss, 1987), which can undermine the quality of their parenting. For mothers who want to work and do, employment can have a positive effect on their mood, morale, and sense of effectiveness (Hoffman & Youngblade, 1999), which would be expected to affect the quality of their parenting (Bugental & Johnston, 2000).

As already noted, a factor that is key to how maternal employment affects children's development is the nature and quality of the day care children receive. But there, too, as you will see, the effects vary as a function of the context and the individuals involved.

The Effects of Child Care

Because so many mothers work outside the home, a large number of infants and young children receive care on a regular basis from someone besides their parents. In 2005 in the United States, 61% of children up to age 6 who were not in kindergarten were in nonparental child care on a regular basis (ChildStats.gov, 2008). About 22% were cared for by a relative, 14% were cared for primarily by a nonrelative, and 36% were enrolled in center-based programs, with center-based care occurring much more often for children between 3 and 6 years of age (57%) than for those age 2 or younger (20%) (ChildStats.gov, 2007) (see Figure 12.6). (The percentages noted here total more than 61% because some children were in more than one type of child care.)

In regard to the debate over potential risks and benefits of nonparental child care, some experts have argued that, especially for children from deprived backgrounds, group care, with its wide variety of activities, can provide greater cognitive stimulation than care at home (Consortium for Longitudinal Studies, 1983). Some have also suggested that children in group care learn important social skills through their interactions with peers (Clarke-Stewart, 1981; Volling & Feagans, 1995). Critics counter that enriched cognitive stimulation is provided only by high-quality

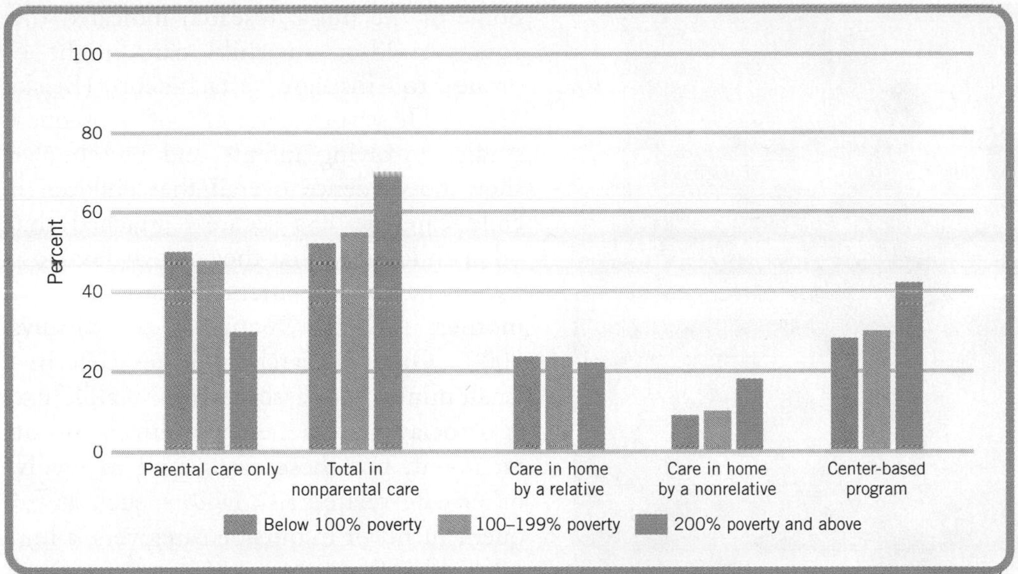

FIGURE 12.6 Percentage of children, from birth through age 6 not yet in kindergarten, in various types of care arrangement, 2005 In 2005, 61% of children (about 12 million) from birth through age 6 received some form of child care from persons other than their parents. Children from families with incomes twice the poverty level are likely to receive nonparental care, especially in centers. (Adapted from ChildStats.gov, 2007)

child care and that much of the child care that is currently available does not provide as much stimulation as care by a parent at home does. Critics also point out that although children in child care may learn social skills from interactions with their peers, they also learn negative behaviors, such as aggression, because of the need to assert oneself in the group setting (Bates et al., 1994; Haskins, 1985).

Probably the greatest concern about child care has been that it might undermine the early mother–child relationship (e.g., Belsky, 1986). For example, on the basis of attachment theory (see Chapter 11), it has been argued that young children who are frequently separated from their mothers are more likely to develop insecure attachments to their mothers than are children whose daily care is provided by their mothers. As you will now see, that concern is largely unwarranted.

Attachment and the Parent–Child Relationship

The issue of whether nonparental child care in the early years interferes with children's attachment relationships to their parents has been examined in many studies.

LAURA DWIGHT

A little more than three-fourths of 4-year-olds in this country are regularly in child care.

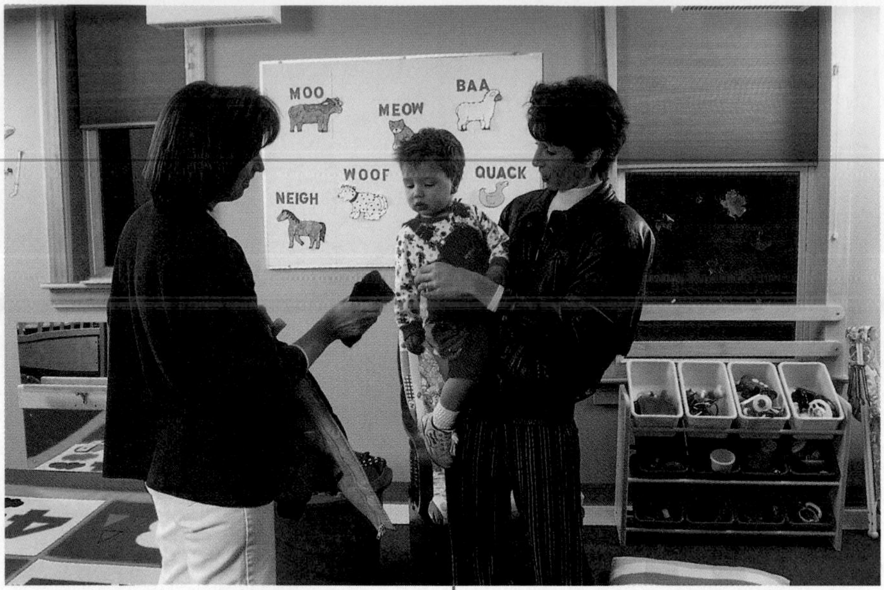

ELLEN B. SENISI

The education and stability of day-care staff are important factors affecting children's development.

Some of the initial research indicated that young children in child care might be prone to insecure attachment (Belsky, 1986). However, a variety of subsequent studies involving infants and preschoolers show no evidence overall that children in child care are less securely attached than other children or that they display less positive behavior in interactions with their mothers (Erel, Oberman, & Yirmiya, 2000). Other research indicates that in a small minority of cases, extensive child care is associated with negative effects on attachment, but these cases tend to involve other care-related risk factors, such as frequent turnover in outside caregivers, a high ratio of infants per caregiver, and poor-quality care at home (Lamb, 1998; Sagi, Koren-Karie, Gini, Ziv, & Joels, 2002).

Similar findings have been shown in a major in-depth study funded by the National Institute of Child Health and Development (NICHD) that has followed the development of approximately 1300 children in various child-care arrangements and in elementary school. This study, begun in 1991, includes families who are from 10 locations around the United States and who vary considerably in their economic status, ethnicity, and race. The study measures (1) characteristics of the families and the child-care setting, and (2) children's attachment to, and interactions with, their mothers, as well as their social behavior, cognitive development, and health status.

An important finding in this study is that how children in nonmaternal care fare is much more strongly related to characteristics of the family—such as level of income, maternal education, maternal sensitivity, and the like—than to the nature of the child care itself. Moreover, any effects that child care might have on development, positive or negative, appear to be very limited in magnitude. Indeed, insecure attachments of a notable degree were predicted only when two conditions existed *simultaneously*—that is, (1) when the children experienced poor-quality child care, had 10 or more hours of child care per week, or had more than one child-care arrangement; *and* (2) when the mothers were not very sensitive or responsive to their children (NICHD Early Child Care Research Network, 1997a).

When children were 24 and 36 months old, the quality of mother–child interaction was, to a slight degree, predicted by the number of hours in child care. Compared with mothers who did not use child care or who put their child in care for fewer hours, mothers of children who were in day care for longer hours tended to be less sensitive with their children, and their children tended to be less positive in interactions with them (NICHD Early Child Care Research Network, 1999). Even in these circumstances, the magnitudes of the effects were small.

Adjustment and Social Behavior

The possible effects of child care on children's self-control, compliance, and social behavior have also been a focus of much concern and research. Here, the findings are mixed. A number of investigators have found that children who are in child care do not differ in problem behavior from those reared at home (Erel et al., 2000; Lamb, 1998). However, findings from the NICHD study indicate that many hours a day in child care or a number of changes in caregivers in the first two years of life predicted lower social competence and more noncompliance with adults at age 2 (NICHD Early Child Care Research Network, 1998a). At 4½ years of age, children in extensive child care were viewed by care providers (but not by mothers) as exhibiting more problem behaviors, such as aggression, noncompliance, and anxiety/depression (NICHD Early Child Care Network, 2006). Of the children in this study who were in day care more than 30 hours a week, 17% showed aggressive behaviors between the ages of 4½ and 6, whereas only 6% of those who spent fewer than 10 hours a week in day care showed such behavior (Douglas, 2001). The relation between more hours in center care and teacher-reported externalizing problems (e.g., aggression, defiance) was also found in the elementary school years but generally was not significant by 6th grade (Belsky et al., 2007). In another large study in Australia, the number of changes in the care-giving situation and the quality of child care were also associated with conduct problems and deficits in social skills (Love et al., 2003).

Significantly, the finding that greater time in child care is related to increased risk for adjustment problems appears not to apply to children from very low-income, high-risk families (Côté, Borge, Geoffroy, Rutter, & Tremblay, 2008). In fact, longer time in child care has been found to be positively related to the better adjustment of such children, unless the quality of care is very poor (Votruba-Drzal, Coley, & Chase-Lansdale, 2004). Similarly, in a large study of children from high-risk families in Canada, physical aggression was less common among children who were in group day care than among those who were looked after by their own families (Borge, Rutter, Côté, & Tremblay, 2004). High-quality child care that involves programs designed to promote children's later success at school may be especially beneficial for disadvantaged children. As in the case of Head Start, discussed in Chapter 8, children who experience these programs show improvements in their social competence and declines in conduct problems (Lamb, 1998; Peisner-Feinberg et al., 2001; Reynolds, Mavrogenes, Bezruczko, & Hagemann, 1996; Webster-Stratton, 1998).

GREENBERG / FOLIO, INC.

For low-income students, some positive academic outcomes that are associated with high-quality preschool child care have been found to persist into elementary grades.

Thus, although most children in child care never develop significant behavior problems, the risk that children from working- and middle-class families will exhibit problem behaviors increases the more hours they spend in child care, especially center care. However, it must be remembered that the background characteristics of children who are in day care for long hours likely differ in a variety of ways (e.g., family income, parental education, parental personality) from the circumstances of those in day care for fewer hours. Therefore, cause-and-effect relations cannot be assumed, even when the effects of some of these factors are taken into account (Bolger & Scarr, 1995; NICHD Early Child Care Research Network, 1997b). Moreover, the number of hours is less relevant than the quality of child care provided: no matter what their SES background, children in high-quality child-care programs tend to be well adjusted and to develop social competencies (Love et al., 2003; NICHD Early Child Care Research Network, 2003c; Votruba-Drzal et al., 2004).

Cognitive and Language Development

The possible effects of child care on children's cognitive and language performance are of particular concern to educators as well as to parents. Research suggests that high-quality child care can have a modest, positive effect on these aspects of children's functioning. The NICHD study found that, overall, the number of hours in child care did not correlate with cognitive or language development when demographic variables such as family income were taken into account. However, higher-quality child care that included specific efforts to stimulate children's language development was linked to better cognitive and language development in the first three years of life (NICHD Early Child Care Research Network, 2000b). By age 4½, children in higher-quality child care (especially center care) scored higher on tests of preacademic cognitive skills, language abilities, and attention than did those in lower-quality care (NICHD Early Child Care Research Network, 2002, 2006; NICHD Early Child Care Research Network & Duncan, 2003b). Higher-quality care also predicted high vocabulary (but not reading and math) scores in elementary school (Belsky et al., 2007).

Other research also suggests that child care may have positive effects on cognition and that these effects are larger for higher-quality centers (Peisner-Feinberg et al., 2001). For example, in Sweden and the United States, a number of researchers have found that children enrolled in out-of-home child care perform better on cognitive tasks, even in elementary school (Erel et al., 2000; Lamb, 1998). In addition, children from low-income families who spend long hours in child care, compared with those who spend fewer hours, tend to show increases in quantitative skills (Votruba-Drzal et al., 2004). It is likely that child care, unless it is low quality, provides greater cognitive stimulation than is available in some low-income homes.

Quality of Child Care

It is not surprising that the quality of child care children receive is related to some aspects of their development. Unfortunately, most child-care centers in the United States do not meet the recommended minimal standards established by such organizations as the American Academy of Pediatrics and the American Public Health Association. These minimum standards include:

- A child-to-caregiver ratio of 3:1 for children aged 6 to 15 months, 4:1 for 2-year-olds, and 7:1 for 3-year-olds
- Maximum group sizes of 6 for 6- to 15-months-olds, 8 for 2-year-olds, and 14 for 3-year-olds
- Formal training for caregivers (including certification or a college degree) in child development, early childhood education, or a related field

In the NICHD study, children in a form of day care that met more of these guidelines tended to score higher on tests of language comprehension and readiness for school, and they had fewer behavior problems at age 36 months. The more standards that were met, the better the children performed at 3 years of age (NICHD Early Child Care Research Network, 1998b). (See Table 12.1 for quality standards set by an early-education association for quality child care.) Quality was generally highest in nonprofit centers that were not religiously affiliated, intermediate in nonprofit religiously affiliated centers and in for-profit independent centers, and lowest in for-profit chains (Sosinsky, Lord, & Zigler, 2007).

However, some research studies in several other countries, as well as in the United States, have found the quality of child care to have little effect on the development

TABLE 12.1

Characteristics of Good Child-Care Programs (WAS 12.2)

Experts in early education recommend that parents assess child-care programs before selecting one for their children. Following are some of the indicators of high-quality child care, set forth by the National Association for the Education of Young Children (1986), that parents should look for. (Note that the standards discussed on page 498 are even more stringent than the standards of this professional association.)

Characteristics of the Staff

1. The adults caring for children enjoy observing and understand how young children learn and grow. They are considerate to children, and their expectations vary according to children's ages and interests. Staff also continue to learn about young children through conferences and other forms of education.
2. The staff continually foster children's emotional and social development. They listen and talk to the children; are consistent and gentle, yet firm, in discipline; help children learn to consider others' feelings and rights; and assist them in learning how to deal with negative emotions constructively.
3. There are enough adults available to work with groups of children and to meet their individual needs. For infants, there should be no more than eight children in the care of at least two adults. Two- and three-year-olds should be in groups of no more than 16, with two adults. Four- and five-year-olds should be in groups of no more than 20 children, with at least two adults.
4. All staff members work together cooperatively. They meet regularly to plan and evaluate the child-care program, and they will adjust daily activities to accommodate children's individual needs and interests.
5. The staff observe and keep records of each child's progress and development. They stress children's accomplishments, use their records to educate parents, and are responsive to parents' concerns about their child's progress.

Program Activities and Equipment

1. The environment fosters children's working and playing together. Staff provide opportunities for both vigorous outdoor play and quiet indoor play, for children to select their own activities, and for children to work alone as well as in small groups. Children also are encouraged to develop self-help skills when they are ready.
2. A quality program provides a wide range of activities and appropriate materials—climbing equipment, blocks, balls, dramatic-play props, art supplies, puzzles, small manipulatable toys, books, and plants or animals and other natural science objects for children to care for or observe. In addition, there are opportunities for activities involving music and movement, such as dance.
3. Children are assisted in increasing their language skills and their understanding of the world. They talk freely among themselves and with adults, and staff talk with children about objects, feelings, experiences, and events. Children are encouraged to solve their own problems and to think independently. Field trips enhance children's learning experiences.
4. The health of the children, staff, and parents is promoted and protected. The staff are alert to health issues—for example, with regard to food, room temperature, and cleanliness—and medical records and emergency information are kept for each child.
5. The facility is safe for children and staff; for example, the facility is free of hazards, toxic materials are locked away, and indoor and outdoor surfaces are cushioned with materials such as carpeting or wood chips.
6. The environment is large enough to allow a variety of activities and equipment. There should be at least 35 square feet of usable playroom floor space indoors per child and 75 square feet of play space outdoors for each child. There is also space for adults to walk between sleeping children's cots and for children's personal items.

Staff Relations with the Community

1. A good program considers and supports the needs of entire families. Parents are welcome to observe the children, discuss policies, and participate in center activities. Staff members share highlights of a child's experiences with parents and are alert to family matters that might affect a child. The staff also respect family members from diverse cultures and backgrounds.
2. Staff are aware of, and contribute to, community resources. For example, they refer family members to appropriate services when needed, share information on community recreational and educational opportunities, and collaborate with other professional groups to provide high-quality child care.
3. Good centers encourage parents who are interested in their programs to observe and ask questions about the facilities, staff, and program philosophy and activities. If staff are not open about these matters, it is likely that the facility does not provide optimal care.

of children from typical families (Scarr, 1998). Studies may differ in their findings because they do not equally assess a wide range of quality in child-care programs, because they differ in the types of families included in the research, or because they differ in the degree to which more concerned parents choose higher-quality centers.

review:

The bulk of recent research on maternal employment indicates that it often benefits children and mothers and that it has few negative effects on children if they are in child care of acceptable quality and are supervised and monitored. Unfortunately, however, in low-income families, especially those headed by a single parent, adequate child care and supervision may not always be possible.

Because so many mothers work, a large proportion of children receive some care from adults other than their parents. Recent research on child care indicates that, on the whole, children's receiving nonmaternal care has small, if any, effect on the quality of the mother–child relationship. Children who spend long hours in centers tend to exhibit more aggressive behavior at schools, but the effects are modest and likely are nonsignificant for high-quality child care. High-quality care does appear to have some modest benfits for cognitive and especially language development. Whether child care has positive or negative effects on children's functioning probably depends on the characteristics of the child, the number of hours in care, parenting at home, and the quality of the care situation.

Chapter Summary

The Nature and Functions of the Family

- Families serve at least three goals with respect to child rearing: helping offspring survive, teaching them the skills they will need to be economically productive as adults, and teaching them the values of the culture.
- How well a family fulfills its functions depends on its family dynamics: all the family members influence one another, and the nature of their interactions shapes children's development.

The Influence of Parental Socialization

- Parents socialize their children's development through direct instruction; through their modeling of skills, attitudes, and behavior; and through their managing of children's experiences and social lives.
- Researchers have identified several types of parenting styles related to the dimensions of warmth and control. Authoritative parents are supportive and relatively high in control; their children tend to be socially and academically competent. Authoritarian parents are low in warmth and high in control; their children tend to be relatively low in social and academic competence, unhappy, and low in self-confidence. Permissive parents are responsive to their children's needs and wishes and low on control; their children tend to be low in self-control and in school achievement. Rejecting-neglecting parents are low in demandingness, support, and control; their children tend to have disturbed attachment relationships during infancy, poor peer relations during childhood, and poor adjustment in adolescence.
- The significance and effects of different parenting styles or practices may vary somewhat across cultures.
- Parenting styles and practices are affected by characteristics of the children, including their attractiveness, behavior, and temperament.
- Parents' beliefs and values tend to differ across social classes, such that lower socioeconomic status tends to be associated with authoritarian parenting.
- Economic stressors can undermine the quality of marital and parent–child interactions, increasing children's risk for depression, academic failure, disruptive behavior, and drug use.
- Homeless children are more likely than other children to show delays in cognitive and language development, to have academic difficulties, and to show problems in adjustment.

Mothers, Fathers, and Siblings

- Mothers typically interact with their children much more than fathers do, and fathers' play tends to be more physical than is mothers'. However, the nature of parent–child interactions differs across cultures.
- Siblings learn from one another, can be sources of support for each other, and sometimes engage in conflict. Siblings get along better if they have good relationships with their parents and if they do not feel that their parents treat them less well than they treat their siblings.

Changes in Families in the United States

- In the United States today, adults are marrying later, more children are being born to single mothers, and divorce and remarriage are common occurrences.
- Mothers who delay childbearing tend to be more responsive with their children and to enjoy motherhood more than mothers who have their first children at a younger age.
- Adolescent parents come disproportionately from impoverished backgrounds and families with cold, uninvolved parents. Adolescent mothers tend to be less effective parents than older parents, and their children are at risk for behavioral and academic problems, delinquency, and early sexual activity. Children of adolescent mothers fare better if their mothers have more knowledge about parenting and if the children themselves have a warm, involved relationship with their fathers.
- Parental divorce and remarriage have been associated with enduring negative outcomes such as behavioral problems for a minority of children. The major factor contributing to negative outcomes for children of divorce is hostile, dysfunctional family interactions, including continuing conflict between ex-spouses.
- Parental depression and upset, as well as other types of stress associated with single parenting, often compromise the quality of divorced parents' interactions with their children.

- Conflict is common in stepfamilies. Children often are hostile toward stepparents, and stepparents usually are less involved with their stepchildren than are biological parents. Children do best if all parents are supportive and use an authoritative parenting style.
- There is no evidence that children raised by lesbian or gay parents differ from children of heterosexual parents in their sexual orientation or adjustment.

Maternal Employment and Child Care

- Children and mothers reap some benefits from maternal employment, and maternal employment has few negative effects on children if they are in child care of acceptable quality and are supervised and monitored by parents.
- Experience with nonmaternal care has small negative effects on the quality of the mother–child relationship for some young children, especially if they are in child care for long hours, the quality of care is low, and their mother is insensitive.
- Child care is associated with a small increase in negative problem behavior for working- and middle-class children but may be associated with improvements in adjustment for low-income children.
- Children in high-quality care do better in their cognitive and language development than children in low-quality care. Whether child care has positive or negative effects on children's functioning probably depends in part on the characteristics of the child, the child's relationship with his or her mother, and the quality of the child-care situation.

Critical Thinking Questions

1. It often is assumed that parental socialization of children's behavior is a bidirectional process, with the parent affecting the child's behavior and the child's behavior also evoking some socialization practices or behaviors. Provide examples of bidirectional causality in regard to (a) the relation between parental punitive practices and children's aggression, and (b) the relation between parental use of punitive control and children's self-regulation.
2. In some cultures, respect of authority, including the authority of parents in general, is valued more than in many Western industrialized countries. How might this cultural variation affect interactions between parents and children and the relation of parenting styles to children's social and emotional development? Similarly, how might living in a culture in which men and women often are separated (e.g., do not eat together) and women are discouraged from going out in public affect parent–child relationships and interactions?
3. Think about the ways your parents interacted with you when you were a child. Based on Baumrind's categories of parenting style, which type of parenting did your mother and/or father display? What specific behaviors did you use to classify their parenting?
4. Make a list of the advantages and disadvantages of joint custody for children of divorce. How would the advantages and disadvantages vary for families in which the parents either (a) argue a lot or get along and (b) live 50 miles apart or 5 miles apart after the divorce?
5. What factors might make it difficult to study children's development in families with gay parents?

Key Terms

survival of offspring, p. 466
economic function, p. 466
cultural training, p. 466
family dynamics, p. 466
parenting styles, p. 469
authoritative parenting, p. 470
authoritarian parenting, p. 470
permissive parenting, p. 471
rejecting-neglecting (disengaged) parenting, p. 471
bidirectionality of parent–child interactions, p. 474

ANTONIO BERNI, *La Gallina Ciega*

13

Peer Relationships

THEMES

Nature and Nurture

❖

The Active Child

❖

Continuity/Discontinuity

❖

The Sociocultural Context

❖

Individual Differences

❖

Research and Children's Welfare

❖

In Chapters 1 and 11, we described the plight of institutionalized orphans who, lacking consistent interaction with a caring adult, developed social, emotional, and cognitive deficits. After World War II, an interesting exception to this pattern was noted by Anna Freud—the daughter of Sigmund Freud—and Sophie Dann (1972/1951). They observed six young German-Jewish children who had been victims of the Hitler regime. Soon after these children were born, their parents were deported to Poland and killed. The children were subsequently moved from one refuge to another until, between the ages of approximately 6 and 12 months, they were placed in a ward for motherless children in a concentration camp. The care they received in this ward was undoubtedly compromised by the fact that their caregivers were themselves prisoners who were undernourished and overworked. Moreover, the rates of deportation and death among the prisoners were high, so it is likely that the children's caregivers changed very frequently.

In 1945, approximately two to three years after the children's arrival at the concentration camp, the camp was liberated; within a month, the six children were sent to Britain. After spending two months in a reception facility, the children, as a group, were sent to various shelters and then, finally, to a country house that had been converted to accommodate orphans.

Given the conditions of their early lives, it is not surprising that these children initially showed a variety of problem behaviors in their new home:

> During the first days after arrival they destroyed all the toys and damaged much of the furniture. Toward the staff they behaved either with cold indifference or with active hostility, making no exception for the young assistant Maureen who had accompanied them from Windermere and was their only link with the immediate past. At times they ignored the adults so completely that they would not look up when one of them entered the room. . . . In anger, they would hit the adults, bite or spit . . . shout, scream, and use bad language.
>
> (Freud & Dann, 1972, p. 452)

These children behaved quite differently with each other, however. They obviously were deeply attached to one another, sensitive to each others' feelings, and

Anna Freud's study of children who lived together in a concentration camp provided evidence of the importance of early peer relationships.

exhibited almost a complete lack of envy, jealousy, and rivalry. They shared possessions and food, helped and protected one another, and admired one another's abilities and accomplishments. The children's closeness is reflected in this brief selection from Freud and Dann's daily observations:

> November 1945—John cries when there is no cake left for a second helping for him. Ruth and Miriam offer him what is left of their portions. While John eats their pieces of cake, they pet him and comment contentedly on what they have given him. . . .
>
> December 1945—Paul loses his gloves during a walk. John gives him his own gloves, and never complains that his hands are cold. . . .
>
> April 1946—On the beach in Brighton, Ruth throws pebbles into the water. Peter is afraid of the waves and does not dare to approach them. In spite of his fear, he suddenly rushes to Ruth, calls out: "Water coming, water coming," and drags her back to safety. . . .

Freud and Dann concluded that the children, although aggressive and difficult for adults to handle, were "neither deficient, delinquent nor psychotic" (p. 473) and that their relationships with one another helped them to master their anxiety and develop the capacity for social relationships.

Freud and Dann's observations provided some of the first evidence that relationships with peers can help very young children develop some of the social and emotional capacities that usually emerge in the context of adult–child attachments. Two decades later, similar findings were obtained in research with monkeys. As discussed in Chapter 10, Stephen Suomi and Harry Harlow raised laboratory monkeys in isolation from other monkeys from birth to 6 months of age. By the end of this period, the isolate monkeys had developed significant abnormalities in behavior such as compulsive rocking and a reluctance to explore. Some of the isolate monkeys were subsequently placed with one or two normal, playful monkeys who were 3 months younger. Over the course of the next several months, the isolate monkeys' abnormal behaviors diminished greatly, and they began to explore their environment and engage in social interactions, demonstrating that peers can provide some of the social and emotional experiences required for normal development in monkeys (Suomi & Harlow, 1972).

Findings such as these do not suggest that peers alone can produce optimal development in young children. However, they do suggest that peers can contribute to children's development in meaningful ways. In fact, in Western societies, children's relationships with other children—their friends and acquaintances at school and in the neighborhood—usually play a very important role in their lives. By middle childhood in the United States, for example, more than 30% of children's social interactions involve peers (Rubin, Bukowski, & Parker, 1998). As they grow older, children spend increasingly more time with peers and interact with a greater number of them. Thus, peer interactions are a context in which children develop social skills and test new behaviors, good and bad.

In this chapter, we consider the special nature of peer interactions and their implications for children's social development. First, we discuss theoretical views on what makes peer interactions special. Then we look at friendships, the most intimate form of peer relationships, and consider questions such as: How do children's interactions with friends differ from those with other peers (nonfriends)? How do friendships change with age? What do children get out of friendships and how do they think about them?

peers people of approximately the same age and status

Next, we consider children's relationships in the larger peer group. These relationships are discussed separately from friendships because they appear to play a somewhat different role in children's development, particularly in regard to the provision of intimacy. We try to answer questions such as: What are the differences among children who are liked, disliked, or not noticed by their peers? Does children's acceptance or rejection by peers have long-term implications for their behavior and psychological adjustment?

In our discussions of friendships as well as more general peer relationships, we will examine *individual differences* among children in their relationships with peers and the ways in which these differences may cause differences in development. In addition, we will focus on the influence that the *sociocultural context* has on peer relationships, the contributions that both *nature and nurture* make to the quality of children's peer relationships, and the role of the *active child* in choosing friends and activities with peers. We will also consider the question of whether changes in children's thinking about friendships exhibit *continuity or discontinuity*. Finally, as an example of *research and children's welfare,* we will examine interventions to improve children's interactions with other children.

What Is Special About Peer Relationships?

Many theorists have argued that peer relationships provide special opportunities for children's development. To begin with, **peers** are, by definition, individuals who are close in age to one another, closer usually than siblings. Thus, in contrast to their status in most of their other relationships, especially those with adults, children are relatively equal in terms of power when they interact with their peers (Furman & Buhrmester, 1985).

Piaget (1932/1965) suggested that because of this relative equality, children tend to be more open and spontaneous with peers when expressing their ideas and beliefs than they are with adults. As Piaget noted, children often accept adults' beliefs and rules on the basis of mere obedience rather than on the basis of understanding or agreement (Youniss, 1980). With peers, on the other hand, children are more likely to openly criticize another's ideas, clarify and elaborate their own ideas, and ask for feedback (Kruger & Tomasello, 1986). In this way, peers jointly construct their own explanations and rules for why or how things work or should work.

Similarly, Vygotsky (1978) suggested that children learn new skills and develop their cognitive capacities in peer interactions. However, unlike Piaget, Vygotsky highlighted the role of cooperation between peers. In particular, he emphasized the ways in which children's working together helps to build new skills and abilities, as well as to convey the knowledge and skills valued by the culture.

Both disagreement and cooperation within the context of peer relationships have been emphasized by theorists as important contributors to children's cognitive development.

SUSIE FITZHUGH

Other researchers have emphasized the social and emotional gains provided by peer interaction. In the preschool and school years, peers are an important source of companionship and assistance with problems and tasks (Youniss, 1980). As children become older, peers may become more important as a source of emotional support. Harry Stack Sullivan (1953) believed that friendships are essential for older children's sense of well-being. He noted that in early adolescence, children begin to develop close, intimate relationships with same-sex peers—what he called "chumships." According to Sullivan, chumships provide children with their first experience of an intimate interpersonal relationship based on reciprocity and exchange between equals. In this relationship, young adolescents become concerned about what they can do to make their chums feel good about themselves and happy. Sullivan suggested that children who are not liked by peers develop feelings of inferiority and loneliness, as well as concerns about their own abilities. As we will discuss later, there is some support for Sullivan's view, although the contribution of friends to children's development is somewhat more complicated than Sullivan's depiction suggests.

In summary, theorists such as Piaget, Vygotsky, and Sullivan have argued that peer relationships provide a unique context for cognitive, social, and emotional development. In their view, the equality, reciprocity, cooperation, and intimacy that can develop in peer relationships enhance children's reasoning ability and their concern for others. The equality and closeness between peers discussed by theorists is most often found in children's friendships. In the next section, we will focus particularly on what friendships are like, how they change with age, and what possible benefits and costs they carry with them.

friendships intimate, reciprocated positive relationships between two people

Friendships

> Kay and Sarah are my *best* friends—we talk and share secret things . . . and we sometimes do things with Jo and Kerry and Sue. Then there's all the rest of the girls—some are nice. But the boys—yuk!
>
> (Annie, aged 8, cited by Dunn, personal communication, 1999)

Annie, the speaker above, a typical 8-year-old, filled in the chart in Figure 13.1 to describe her relationships with the children in her class. She is very good friends with the girls in the inner circle, Kay and Sarah. They play together; share toys, problems, and secrets; and also quarrel. The three girls in the next circle are part of a larger friendship group that includes Annie and her closest friends. Then there are the other children in the class, represented in the outer two circles. As her comments clearly indicate, Annie is closer to the girls than to the boys in this group and undoubtedly plays and talks with the girls more than with the boys. Although Annie does not have close relationships with these girls, she cares about what they think of her, and she and her close friends are interested in, and likely gossip about, what goes on in the larger group.

The children in Annie's inner circle no doubt share characteristics that are common among most close friends. Researchers generally agree that friends are people who like to spend time together and feel affection for one another. In addition, their interactions are characterized by *reciprocities*; that is, friends have mutual regard for one another, exhibit give-and-take in their behavior (such as cooperation and negotiation), and benefit in comparable ways from their social exchanges (Bukowski, Newcomb, & Hartup, 1996). In brief, a **friendship** is an intimate, reciprocated positive relationship between two people.

FIGURE 13.1 A graphic representation of Annie's peer social world Annie's close friends are all girls, as are all of the children with whom she socializes. Most girls in the United States show similar relationship patterns at Annie's age.

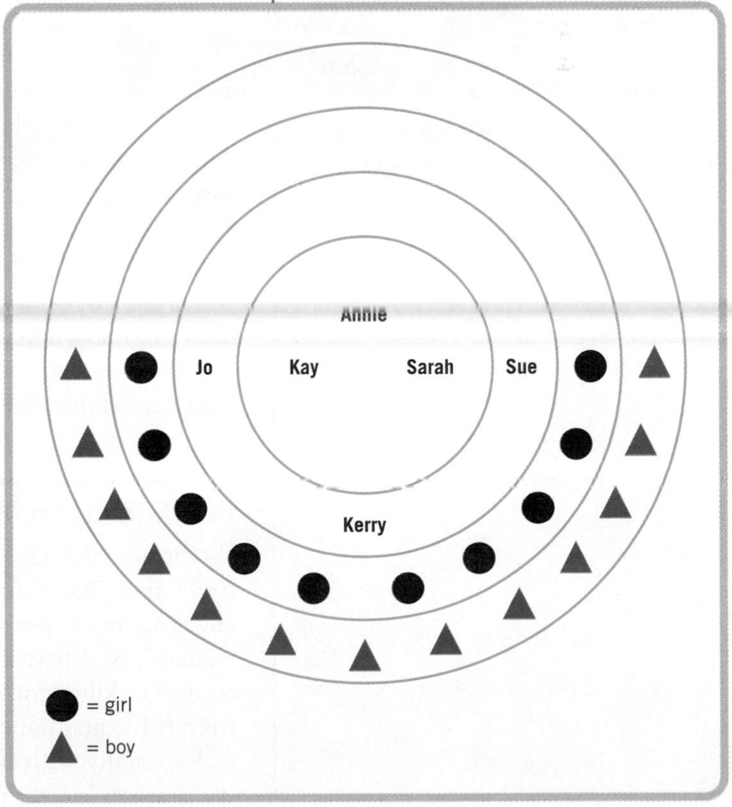

The degree to which the conditions of friendship become evident in peer interactions increases with age during childhood. As you will see, it is not clear whether, by the definition just given, very young children have relationships that qualify as friendships. By the preschool years, however, children often proclaim who their friends are, and the truth of their sentiment is obvious from their interactions with them.

Early Peer Interactions and Friendships

Very young children usually cannot verbally indicate who they like, so researchers must make inferences about children's friendships from observing their behavior with peers. In doing so, researchers have focused particularly on such issues as the age at which friendships first develop, the nature of early friendships, and age-related changes in friendships.

ELIZABETH CREWS

Some researchers believe that friendships may begin as early as 2 years of age or before.

Do Very Young Children Have Friends?

Some investigators have argued that children can have friends by or before the age of 2 (Howes, 1996). Consider the following example:

> Anna and Suzanne are not yet 2 years old. Their mothers became acquainted during their pregnancies and from their earliest weeks of life the little girls have visited each other's houses. When the girls were 5 months old they were enrolled in the same child-care center. They now are frequent play partners, and sometimes insist that their naptime cots be placed side by side. Their greetings and play are often marked by shared smiles. Anna and Suzanne's parents and teachers identify them as friends.
>
> (Howes, 1996, p. 66)

Even 12- to 18-month-olds seem to select and prefer some children over others, touching them, smiling at them, and engaging in positive interactions with them more than they do with other peers (Hay, Caplan, & Nash, 2009; Howes, 1983). In addition, when a preferred peer shows distress, toddlers are three times more likely to respond by offering comfort or by alerting an adult than they are when a nonpreferred peer is upset (Howes & Farver, 1987). Starting at around 20 months of age, children also increasingly initiate more interactions with some children than with others and contribute more when playing games with those children (Ross & Lollis, 1989). By age 3 or 4, children can make and maintain friendships with peers (Dunn, 2004), and by age 3 to 7 years, it is not uncommon for children to have "best friends" that are stable over at least several months' time (Sebanc, Kearns, Hernandez, & Galvin, 2007).

Differences in Young Children's Interactions with Friends and Nonfriends

By the age of 2, children begin to develop several skills that allow greater complexity in their social interactions, including imitating other people's social behavior, engaging in cooperative problem solving, and reversing roles during play (Brownell, Ramani, & Zerwas, 2006; Howes, 1996; Howes & Matheson, 1992). These more complex skills tend to be in greater evidence in the play of friends than of nonfriends (acquaintances) (Werebe & Baudonniere, 1991).

Especially with friends, cooperation and coordination in children's interactions continue to increase substantially from the toddler to the preschool years (Howes

& Phillipsen, 1998). This is especially evident in shared pretend play (Dunn, 2004), which occurs more often among friends than among nonfriends (Howes & Unger, 1989). As discussed in Chapter 7, pretend play involves symbolic actions that must be mutually understood by the play partners, as in the following example:

> Johnny, 30 months, joins his friend Kevin who is pretending to go on a picnic. Johnny, on instruction from 3-year-old Kevin, fills the car with gas, "drives" the car, then gets the food out, pretends to eat it, saying he doesn't like it! Both boys pretend to spit out the food, saying "yuk!," laughing. . . .
>
> (Dunn, personal communication, 1999)

Pretend play may occur more often among friends because friends' experiences with one another allow them to trust that their partner will work to interpret and share the meaning of symbolic actions (Howes, 1996).

While the rate of cooperation and positive interactions among young friends is higher than among nonfriends, so is the rate of conflict. Preschool friends quarrel as much or more with one another as do nonfriends and also more often express hostility by means of assaults, threats, and refusing requests (Fabes, Eisenberg, Smith, & Murphy, 1996; French, Pidada, Denoma, Lawton, & McDonald, 2005; Hartup, Laursen, Stewart, & Eastenson, 1988). The higher rate of conflict for friends is likely due, in part, to the greater amount of time friends spend together.

Although preschool friends are more likely than nonfriends to fight, they also are more likely to resolve conflicts in controlled ways, such as by negotiating, asserting themselves nonaggressively, acquiescing, or simply ceasing the activity that is causing the conflict (Fabes et al., 1996; Hartup et al., 1988) (see Table 13.1). Moreover, friends are more likely than nonfriends to resolve conflicts in ways that result in equal outcomes rather than in one child's winning and another's losing. Thus, after a conflict, friends are more likely than nonfriends to resume their interactions and to have positive feelings for one another.

TABLE 13.1

Strategies Chosen by Schoolchildren When a Peer Says Something Mean to, or About, Them

Percent of Children Selecting Each Strategy When the Peer Is:

	Their Best Friend	Classmate (Neither a Friend nor Enemy)
Talk to friend/classmate	43%	19%
Think about what to do	24%	14%
Hit, kick, yell	9%	10%
Hold anger in	8%	5%
Quit thinking about it	6%	20%
Get away from what happened	4%	17%
Talk to someone else about it	4%	11%
Do nothing	1%	4%

Adapted from Whitesell & Harter, 1996

Developmental Changes in Friendship

In the school years, many of the patterns apparent in the interactions among preschool-age friends and nonfriends persist and become more sharply defined. As earlier, friends, in comparison with nonfriends, communicate more and better with each other and cooperate and work together more effectively (Hartup, 1996). They also fight more often—but again, they also are more likely to negotiate their way out of the conflict (Laursen, Finkelstein, & Betts, 2001). In addition, they now have the maturity to take responsibility for the conflict and to give reasons for their disagreement, increasing the likelihood of their maintaining the friendship (Fonzi, Schneider, Tani, & Tomada, 1997; Hartup, French, Laursen, Johnston, & Ogawa, 1993; Whitesell & Harter, 1996).

While children's friendships remain similar in many aspects as the children grow older, they do change in one important dimension: the level and importance of intimacy. The change is reflected both in the nature of friends' interactions with each other and in the way children conceive of friendship. Between ages 6 and 8,

TABLE 13.2

Dimensions on Which Elementary School Children Often Evaluate Their Friendships

Validation and Caring	
	Makes me feel good about my ideas.
	Tells me I am good at things.
Conflict Resolution	
	Make up easily when we have a fight.
	Talk about how to get over being mad at each other.
Conflict and Betrayal	
	Argue a lot.
	Doesn't listen to me.
Help and Guidance	
	Help each other with schoolwork a lot.
	Loan each other things all the time.
Companionship and Recreation	
	Always sit together at lunch.
	Do fun things together a lot.
Intimate Exchange	
	Always tell each other our problems.
	Tell each other secrets.

Adapted from Parker & Asher, 1993

for example, children define friendship primarily on the basis of actual activities with their peers and tend to define "best" friends as peers with whom they play all the time and share everything (Gummerum & Keller, 2008; Youniss, 1980). At this age, children also tend to view friends in terms of rewards and costs (Bigelow, 1977). In this respect, friends tend to be close by, have interesting toys, and have similar expectations about play activities. Nonfriends tend to be uninteresting or difficult to get along with. Thus, in the early school years, children's views of friendship are instrumental and concrete (Rubin, Bukowski, & Parker, 2006) (see Table 13.2).

In contrast, between the early school years and adolescence, children in both Asian and Western countries increasingly define their friendships in terms of characteristics such as companionship, similarity in attitudes/interests, acceptance, trust, genuineness, mutual admiration, and loyalty (Furman & Buhrmester, 1992; Gummerum & Keller, 2008; McDougall & Hymel, 2007). At about 9 years of age, children seem to become more sensitive to the needs of others and to the inequalities among people. Children define friends in terms of taking care of one another's physical and material needs, providing general assistance and help with schoolwork, reducing loneliness and the sense of being excluded, and sharing feelings. The following descriptions of friends are typical:

> *female, 10:* If you're hurt, they come over and visit.
> *male, 9:* Help someone out. If the person is stuck, show them the answer but tell them why it's the answer.
> *female, 9:* Being nice to each other. If something happened to you, they run over to help you.
> *male, 9:* You're lonely and your friend on a bike joins you. You feel a lot better because he joined you.
>
> (Youniss, 1980, pp. 177–178)

When children are about 10 years old, loyalty, mutual understanding, and self-disclosure become important components of children's conceptions of friendship (Bigelow, 1977). In addition, both preadolescents and adolescents emphasize cooperative reciprocity (doing the same things for one another), equality, and trust between friends (Youniss, 1980). The following descriptions are indicative of how children in this age range view their friends:

> *male, 10:* You exchange kindness for a long time, not just for a day.
> *female, 10:* Somebody you can keep your secrets with together. Two people who are really good to each other.
> *male, 12:* A person you can trust and confide in. Tell them what you feel and you can be yourself with them.
> *female, 13:* They'll understand your problems. They won't always be the boss. Sometimes they'll let you decide; they'll take turns. If you did something wrong, they'll share the responsibility.
> *male, 14:* They have something in common. You hang around with him. . . . We're more or less the same; the same personalities.
>
> (Youniss, 1980, pp. 180–182)

During the elementary-school years, the willingness to lend support and help, including on homework, becomes an important dimension of friendship.

ESBIN-ANDERSON / THE IMAGE WORKS

More than younger children, adolescents use friendship as a context for self-exploration and working out personal problems (Gottman & Mettetal, 1986). Thus, friendships become an increasing source of intimacy and disclosure with age, as well as a source of honest feedback. These changes may explain why adolescents perceive the quality of their friendships as improving from middle to late adolescence and why they value them so highly (Way & Greene, 2006).

What accounts for the various age-related changes that occur in children's friendships, particularly with regard to their conception of friendship? Some researchers have argued that the changes in children's thinking about friendship are qualitative, or *discontinuous*. For example, Selman (1980) suggested that changes in children's reasoning about friendships are a consequence of age-related qualitative changes in their ability to take others' perspectives (see Chapter 9, pages 358–359). In the view of Selman, as well as of Piaget and others, young children have limited awareness that others may feel or think about things differently than they themselves do. Consequently, their thinking about friendships is limited in the degree to which they consider issues beyond their own needs. As children begin to understand others' thoughts and feelings, they realize that friendships involve consideration of both parties' needs so that the relationship is mutually satisfying.

LAURA DWIGHT

Adolescent friends are more likely to share confidences with one another than are younger friends.

Other researchers argue that the age-related changes in children's conceptions of friendships reflect differences in how children think and express their ideas rather than age-related differences in the basic way they view friendships. Hartup and Stevens (1997) maintain that children of all ages consider their friendships "to be marked by reciprocity and mutuality—the giving and taking, and returning in kind or degree" (p. 356). What differs with age is merely the complexity with which children view friendship and describe its dimensions. Nonetheless, these differences likely have important effects on children's behavior with friends and on their reactions to friends' behavior. For example, because 6th graders are more likely than 2nd graders to report that intimacy and support are important features of friendships (Furman & Bierman, 1984), they are more likely to evaluate their own and their friends' behaviors in terms of these dimensions.

The Functions of Friendships

As is clear from their statements about the meaning of friendships, having friends provides numerous potential benefits for children. The most important of these, noted by Piaget, Vygotsky, Sullivan, and others, are emotional support and the validation of one's own thoughts, feelings, and worth, as well as opportunities for the development of important social and cognitive skills.

Support and Validation

Friends can provide a source of emotional support and security, even at an early age. Consider the following fantasy play interaction between Eric and Naomi, two 4-year-olds who have been best friends for some time. In the course of their play, Eric expresses his ongoing fear that other children don't like him and think he's stupid:

Eric: I'm the skeleton! Whoa! [screams] A skeleton, everyone! A skeleton!
Naomi: I'm our friend, the dinosaur.
Eric: Oh, hi Dinosaur. [subdued] You know, no one likes me.

Naomi: [reassuringly] But I like you. I'm your friend.
Eric: But none of my other friends like me. They don't like my new suit. They don't like my skeleton suit. It's really just me. They think I'm a dumb-dumb.
Naomi: I know what. He's a good skeleton.
Eric: [yelling] I am not a dumb-dumb!
Naomi: I'm not calling you a dumb-dumb. I'm calling you a friendly skeleton.

(Parker & Gottman, 1989, p. 95)

In this fantasy play situation, Naomi clearly served as a source of support and validation for Eric. When he expressed concern that others do not like him, she reassured him that she does. And when he confessed that the other children think he, not the skeleton, is dumb, she shifted the focus from him to the fantasy skeleton character, praising the skeleton character to make Eric feel competent ("He's a good skeleton") (Gottman, 1986).

Friends also can provide support when a child feels lonely. School-age children with best friends and with intimate, supportive friendships experience less loneliness than children without a best friend or with friends who are less caring and intimate (Asher & Paquette, 2003; Erdley, Nangle, Newman, & Carpenter, 2001). Moreover, chronic friendlessness predicts internalizing problems such as depression and social withdrawal, which often cause or accompany loneliness (Ladd & Troop-Gordon, 2003; Pedersen, Vitaro, Barker, & Borge, 2007).

The support of friends can be particularly important during difficult periods of transition that involve peers. For example, young children have more positive initial attitudes toward school if they begin school with a large number of established friends as classmates (Ladd & Coleman, 1997; Ladd & Kochenderfer, 1996). In part, this may be because the presence of established friends in the early weeks of school reduces the strangeness of the new environment. Similarly, as 6th graders move into junior high, they are more likely to increase their levels of sociability and leadership if they have stable, high-quality, intimate friendships during this period (Berndt, Hawkins, & Jiao, 1999).

Friendships may also serve as a buffer against unpleasant experiences, such as being yelled at by the teacher, being picked on by peers (Ladd, Kochenderfer, & Coleman, 1996), or being socially isolated (i.e., having low levels of involvement with peers more generally; Laursen, Bukowski, Aunola, & Nurmi, 2007). This buffering effect was made especially clear by a study of elementary school children who were reported to be verbally or physically victimized by their peers. Among this group, the children who showed an increase in adjustment problems a year later (e.g., sadness, loneliness, fearfulness, aggression, and lying or stealing) were those who lacked a **reciprocated best friendship,** that is, a friendship in which two children are best friends to each other (Hodges, Boivin, Vitaro, & Bukowski, 1999).

Victimized children also fare better if they have a number of friendships, if their friends are capable of defending them and are liked by peers (Hodges, Malone, & Perry, 1997), and if their friendships are high-quality—that is, friends are viewed as helpful and providing intimacy and security (Schmidt & Bagwell, 2007). Similarly, children who are rejected or have few friends are less likely to exhibit adjustment problems if they have friendships that provide intimacy and support (Waldrip, Malcolm, & Jensen-Campbell, 2008). Moreover, children who exhibit early problem behaviors—and who are therefore at risk for peer rejection—are less likely to be victimized by peers if they have a reciprocated best friendship than are similar children without one (Schwartz, McFadyen-Ketchum, Dodge, Pettit, & Bates, 1999).

reciprocated best friendship a friendship in which two children view each other as best or close friends

As noted previously, the degree to which friends provide caring and support generally increases from childhood into adolescence. Indeed, around age 16, adolescents, especially girls, report that friends are more important confidants and providers of support than their parents are (Furman & Buhrmester, 1992; Helsen, Vollebergh, & Meeus, 2000; Hunter & Youniss, 1982) (Figure 13.2).

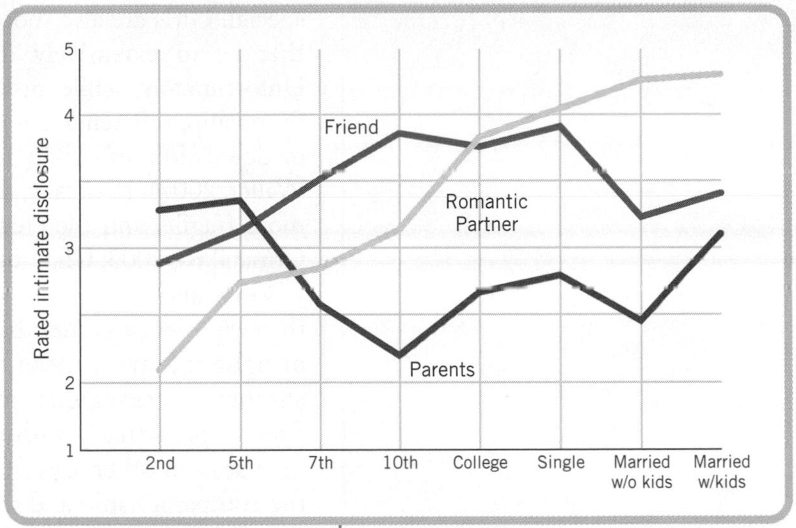

FIGURE 13.2 Age trends in reports of self-disclosure to parents and peers By early adolescence, children disclose more to friends than to their parents. Young adults continue to disclose much more to friends than to their parents, but by college age they disclose most to romantic partners. (Adapted from Burmeister, 1996)

The Development of Social and Cognitive Skills

Friendships provide a context for the development of social skills and knowledge that children need to form positive relationships with other people. As discussed earlier, young children seem to first develop more complex play in interactions with friends; and throughout childhood, cooperation, negotiation, and the like are all more common among friends than among nonfriends. In addition, young children who discuss emotions with their friends and interact in positive ways with them develop a better understanding of others' mental and emotional states than do children whose peer relationships are less close (Hughes & Dunn, 1998; Maguire & Dunn, 1997).

Friendship provides other avenues to social and cognitive development as well. Through gossip with friends about other children, for example, children learn about peer norms, including how, why, and when to display or control the expression of emotions and other behaviors (Gottman, 1986; McDonald, Putallaz, Kupersmidt, & Coie, 2007). As Piaget pointed out, friends are more likely than nonfriends to criticize and elaborate on one another's ideas and to elaborate and clarify their own ideas (Azmitia & Montgomery, 1993; Nelson & Aboud, 1985). This kind of openness promotes cognitive skills and enhances performance on creative tasks (Miell, 2000; Rubin et al., 2006). One demonstration of this was provided by a study in which teams of 10-year-olds, half of them made up of friends and the other half made up of nonfriends, were assigned to write a story about rain forests. The teams consisting of friends engaged in more constructive conversations (e.g., they posed alternative approaches and provided elaborations more frequently) and were more focused on the task than were teams of nonfriends. In addition, the stories written by friends were of higher quality than those written by nonfriends (Hartup, 1996).

TONY FREEMAN / PHOTOEDIT

Interactions with friends provide children with opportunities to get constructive feedback regarding their behavior and ideas.

Gender Differences in the Functions of Friendships

As children grow older, gender differences emerge in what girls and boys feel they get from their friendships. By late elementary school, girls, compared with boys, feel that their friendships are more intimate and provide more validation, caring, help, and guidance (Bauminger, Finzi-Dottan, & Chason, 2008; Rubin et al., 2004; Zarbatany, McDougall, & Hymel, 2000). For instance, girls are more likely than boys to report that they rely on their friends for advice or help with homework, that they and their friends share confidences and stick up for one another, and that their friends tell them that they are good at things and make them feel important and special. Girls are also more likely than boys to *co-ruminate* with their close friends, that is, to extensively discuss problems and negative thoughts and feelings. Unfortunately, while providing support and even increasing the quality of the friendship, this tendency may also reinforce internalizing problems such as anxiety or depression, especially in young adolescent girls (Rose, 2002; Rose, Carlson, & Waller, 2007). Ironically, the very intimacy of girls' best friendships may make them more fragile, and therefore of shorter duration, than those of boys (Benenson & Christakos, 2003; Chan & Poulin, 2007; Hardy, Bukowski, & Sippola, 2002).

Girls and boys are less likely to differ in the amount of conflict and betrayal they experience in their best friendships. For example, they report similar amounts of fighting, saying mean things about the friend to other people, or bugging one another. However, girls report less difficulty than boys in resolving conflict with friends, particularly with regard to being able to talk about how to get over being mad at each other. Boys' and girls' friendships also do not differ much in terms of the companionship and recreational opportunities they provide (e.g., doing things together, going to each other's houses) (Parker & Asher, 1993), although they may differ in the time spent together in various activities (e.g., sports versus shopping).

Effects of Friendships on Psychological Functioning and Behavior over Time

Because friendships fill important needs for children, it might be expected that having friends enhances children's social and emotional health. In fact, having close, reciprocated friendships in elementary school has been linked to a variety of positive psychological and behavioral outcomes for children, not only during the school years but also years later in early adulthood. However, there also may be costs to having friends, if the friends engage in or encourage negative behaviors rather than positive ones (Simpkins, Eccles, & Becnel, 2008).

The Possible Long-Term Benefits of Having Friends

Longitudinal research provides the best data concerning the possible long-term effects of having friends in elementary school. Because this research is generally correlational, however, it is difficult to determine if having friends influences long-term outcomes such as psychological adjustment or if characteristics of the child such as psychological adjustment affect whether the child has friends (Klima & Repetti, 2008).

In one longitudinal study of the correlates of friendships, researchers looked at children when they were 5th graders and when they were young adults. They found that, compared with their peers who did not have reciprocated best friendships, 5th graders who did have them were viewed by classmates as more mature and competent, less aggressive, and more socially prominent (e.g., they were liked by everyone or were picked for such positions as class president or team captain). At approximately age 23, those individuals who had reciprocated best friendships in 5th grade reported higher levels of doing well in college and in their family and social life than did individuals who did not have a reciprocated best friendship. They also reported higher levels of self-esteem, fewer problems with the law, and less psychopathology (e.g., depression; Bagwell, Newcomb, & Bukowski, 1998). Thus, having a reciprocated best friend in preadolescence relates not only to positive social outcomes in middle childhood but also to self-perceived competence and adjustment in adulthood.

The Possible Costs of Friendships

Although friendships are usually associated with positive outcomes, sometimes they are not. Friends who have behavioral problems may exert a detrimental influence, contributing to the likelihood of a child's or adolescent's engaging in violence, drug use, or other negative behaviors. Moreover, friends who are depressed may foster depression in their close friends (Crosnoe & Needham, 2004; Rose, 2002).

Aggression and disruptiveness In the late elementary school years or early adolescence, children who have antisocial and aggressive friends tend to exhibit antisocial, delinquent, and aggressive tendencies themselves, even across time (Brendgen, Vitaro, & Bukowski, 2000; Snyder et al., 2008). However, because the research in this area is correlational, it is unclear to what degree having aggressive friends actually causes children and adolescents to behave aggressively or is merely a correlate of being aggressive (and therefore does not necessarily induce aggressive behavior).

As was discussed in Chapter 3, children's characteristics, such as their activity level or quickness to anger, may influence their choice of environments, including their friends. Thus, aggressive and disruptive children may gravitate toward similar peers for friendship, thereby taking an active role in creating their own peer group (Mrug, Hoza, & Bukowski, 2004). The effect may also be bidirectional (Vitaro, Pedersen, & Brendgen, 2007): through their talk and behavior, boys who are aggressive may socialize and reinforce aggression and deviance in one another by making them seem acceptable (Dishion, Eddy, Haas, Li, & Spracklen, 1997; Piehler, & Dishion, 2007).

Whether having an aggressive friend affects a child's own behavior over time may depend on the child's baseline level of aggression. This possibility was suggested by a longitudinal study that followed three groups of boys who had been assessed as *nondisruptive, highly disruptive,* or *moderately disruptive* (that is, somewhat above average in aggressive and disruptive behavior). The boys who had been assessed as moderately disruptive *and* who also had aggressive, disruptive friends at ages 11 and 12 reported more delinquent acts at age 13 than did boys who were moderately disruptive but did not have disruptive friends. At the same time, boys who had been assessed as either highly aggressive and disruptive or nonaggressive and nondisruptive did not change their behavior, regardless of their friends' behavior (Vitaro, Tremblay, Kerr, Pagani, & Bukowski, 1997). Thus, young adolescents who are somewhat aggressive and disruptive, but who do not yet exhibit a high level of such behavior, seem to be the most vulnerable to the negative influence of aggressive and disruptive friends.

Peers can encourage youths to use alcohol, but it is also the case that youths who are prone to drinking may seek out peers who are similarly inclined.

BOB DAEMMRICH / THE IMAGE WORKS

Alcohol and substance abuse As in the case of aggression, adolescents who abuse alcohol or drugs tend to have friends who do so also (Jaccard, Blanton, & Dodge, 2005; Scholte et al., 2008; Urberg et al., 1997). And again, as in the case of aggression, it is not clear if friends' substance abuse is a cause or merely a correlate of adolescents' substance abuse, or if the relation between the two is bidirectional. On the one hand, there is some evidence that adolescents who are especially susceptible to peer pressure regarding negative or risky behavior select friends who drink and use drugs, which then contributes to their own alcohol and substance use (Schulenberg et al., 1999).

On the other hand, there is some evidence for a more direct causal link: adolescents who start drinking or smoking during the school year tend to have a close friend who was already using alcohol or tobacco (Selfhout, Branje, & Meeus, 2008; Urberg, Degirmencioglu, & Pilgrim, 1997). Youths who are especially susceptible to the influence of their close friends seem particularly vulnerable to any pressure from them to use drugs and alcohol (Allen, Porter, & McFarland, 2006). There is also evidence that adolescents' drinking and their friends' alcohol use appear to mutually affect one another over time so that drinking often escalates among friends (Bray, Adams, Getz, & McQueen, 2003; Popp, Laursen, Kerr, Stattin, & Burk, 2008).

Another factor in the association between adolescents' abuse of drugs and alcohol and that of their peers is likely genetic. Youths with similar genetically based temperamental characteristics such as risk-taking may be drawn both to one another and to alcohol or drugs (Dick et al., 2007; Hill, Emery, Harden, Mendle, & Turkheimer, 2008). Thus, friends' alcohol and drug abuse may be correlated because of their similarity in genetically based characteristics as well as other social processes.

The extent to which friends' use of drugs and alcohol may put adolescents at risk for use themselves seems to depend, in part, on the nature of the child–parent relationship. An adolescent with a drug-using close friend is at risk primarily if the adolescent's parents are cold, detached, and uninclined to monitor and supervise the adolescent's activities (Mounts & Steinberg, 1995; Pilgrim, Luo, Urberg, & Fang, 1999). If the adolescent's parents are authoritative in their parenting, monitoring their child's behavior and setting firm limits but also being warm and receptive to the adolescent's viewpoint (see page 470), the adolescent is more likely to be protected against peer pressure to use drugs (Mounts, 2002).

Children's Choice of Friends

What factors influence children's choices of friends? For young children, proximity is an obvious key factor. Preschoolers tend to become friends with peers who are nearby physically, as neighbors or playgroup members. (As Box 13.1 points out, young children's access to peers can vary widely by culture.) Although proximity becomes less important with age, it continues to play a role in individuals' choices of friends in adolescence and even into adulthood (Clarke-McLean, 1996; Dishion, Andrews, & Crosby, 1995).

In most industrialized countries, similarity in age is also a major factor in friendship, with most children tending to make friends with age-mates (Aboud & Mendelson, 1996; Dishion et al., 1995). In part, this may be due to the fact that in most industrialized societies, children are segregated by age in school: in societies where children do not attend school or otherwise are not segregated by age, they are more likely to develop friendships with children of different ages.

Another powerful factor in friend selection is a child's gender: girls tend to be friends with girls, and boys, with boys. Cross-gender friendships, though not uncommon, tend to be more fragile (Lee, Howes, & Chamberlain, 2007; Maccoby, 2000; see Chapter 15). The preference for same-gender friends emerges in preschool and continues through childhood (Hartup, 1983). The liking of other-gender peers also increases over the course of childhood and into early adolescence (Poulin & Pedersen, 2007), with other-gender close friendships increasing in frequency from 8th to 11th grade (Arndorfer & Stormshak, 2008).

To a lesser degree, children tend to be friends with peers of their own racial/ethnic group, although this tendency varies across groups and contexts. In general, efforts to establish friendships outside one's own racial/ethnic group are less likely to be reciprocated (i.e., mutual) than are efforts within the group (Vaquera & Kao, 2008);

individual differences 13.1

Culture and Children's Peer Experience

Young children's contact with unrelated peers varies considerably around the world. In some communities, such as one in Okinawa, Japan, Beatrice Whiting and Carolyn Edwards (1988) found that children were free to wander in the streets and public areas of town and had extensive contact with peers. In contrast, in some sub-Saharan African societies, children were confined primarily to the family yard and therefore had relatively little contact with peers other than their siblings.

As might be expected, Whiting and Edwards found that children's access to the wider community, including peers, increased with age. However, even when children were aged 6 to 10, there were marked differences in the extent to which their social interactions extended beyond the family. In large measure, these differences were based on parents' attitudes toward childhood peer relationships. For example, in kin-based societies such as Kenya, peer interactions were discouraged:

> Parents feared the inherent potential for competition and conflict; they did not want their children to fight with outsiders and engender spiteful relations or become vulnerable to aggression and sorcery. Moreover, as their children did not attend school, they had no need for them to easily acquire skills of affiliating, negotiating, and competing with nonfamily agemates.
>
> (Edwards, 1992, p. 305)

However, Edwards noted that the situation in Kenya is changing as the economy modernizes and literacy becomes an increasingly valued skill. Parents usually want their children to be educated, and education involves contact with peers. Indeed, in numerous societies, such as the Maisin in Papua New Guinea, levels of interaction with peers who are not from the child's family or clan increased dramatically when Westernized schooling was established (Rogoff, 2003; Tietjen, 2006). Nevertheless, in some groups such as the Maisin, contact between children of different clans still occurred primarily within the school setting, with little such contact outside it.

Cultures differ in terms of the total number of hours that children typically spend with peers. In many cultures, especially in unschooled, nonindustrial populations, boys tend to spend more time with peers than girls do, likely because they are less closely monitored and are allowed greater freedom to be away from home (Larson & Verma, 1999). For example, 6- to 12-year-old Indian boys were found to spend three times as much time with their peers outside their families than girls did (Sarswathi & Dutta, 1986).

Among postindustrial schooled populations, Euro-American, African-American, and European adolescents have been found to spend much more time with peers, especially other-gender peers, than Asian adolescents do (Larson & Verma, 1999). In one study, for example, U.S. adolescents spent 18.4 hours per week with friends outside the classroom, whereas the time their Japanese and Taiwanese counterparts spent in out-of-school peer contact was, respectively, 12.4 and 8.8 hours per week (Fuligni & Stevenson, 1995). Moreover, East Asians tended to spend more of their time with peers studying than did U.S. youth, who were more inclined to engage in leisure activities with peers. Similar differences were evident in time spent dating, with Japanese and Taiwanese 11th graders devoting roughly an hour a week to dating, compared with 4.7 hours per week for U.S. youths.

Adults' expectations in regard to the nature of children's interactions with peers also tend to differ across cultures. For example, there are cultural differences in the degree to which parents expect their children to develop such social skills as negotiating, taking the initiative, and standing up for their rights with peers. Euro-American and Euro-Australian mothers expect their children to develop such skills earlier than do Japanese mothers (Hess, Kashiwagi, Azuma, Price, & Dickson, 1980) and Lebanese-Australian mothers (Goodnow, Cashmore, Cotton, & Knight, 1984). This probably is because the Euro-American and Euro-Australian mothers are influenced by their respective culture's emphasis on personal autonomy and independence and believe that the aforementioned skills are important for success.

Correspondingly, Japanese mothers and Australian mothers of Lebanese heritage are likely to be similarly influenced by their respective cultures' emphasis on the interdependence of family members; therefore, they may be more likely to accept or even encourage dependency in young children (Johnson, 1993; White & LeVine, 1986). Thus, differences in parents' expectations regarding what social skills their children will develop and by what age likely influence what parents teach their children about social interactions with peers.

MORTON BEEBE / CORBIS

In some groups in Kenya, children are discouraged from forming relationships with peers who are not related. Thus, children interact primarily with siblings and adult relatives.

when they are reciprocated, they often are not as long-lasting (Lee et al., 2007). Those youths with cross-racial/ethnic friendships tend to be leaders and relatively inclusive in their social relationships (Kawabata & Crick, 2008).

Beyond these basic factors, a key determinant of liking and friendship is similarity of interests and behavior. By age 7, children tend to like peers who are similar to themselves in the cognitive maturity of their play (Rubin, Lynch, Coplan, Rose-Krasnor, & Booth, 1994) and in the level of their aggressive behavior (Poulin et al., 1997). Between 4th and 8th grade, friends are more similar than nonfriends in their cooperativeness, antisocial behavior, acceptance by peers, and shyness (Chen, Chang, He, & Liu, 2005; Haselager, Hartup, van Lieshout, & Riksen-Walraven, 1998; Rose, Swenson, & Carlson, 2003). Friends are also more similar in their level of academic motivation and self-perceptions of competence (Altermatt & Pomerantz, 2003). Much the same pattern holds for adolescents (Gavin & Furman, 1996; Rubin et al., 2006), with the added dimension that friends also tend to share similar levels of negative emotions such as distress and depression (Haselager et al., 1998; Hogue & Steinberg, 1995).

Thus, birds of a feather do tend to flock together. Similarity probably initially attracts children to one another and then serves to maintain their friendships. In addition, older children tend to dislike peers who differ from them in behavioral style or social acceptance (Nangle, Erdley, Zeff, Stanchfield, & Gold, 2004). The fact that friends tend to be similar on a number of dimensions underscores the difficulty of knowing whether friends actually affect one another's behavior or whether children simply seek out peers who think, act, and feel as they do.

review:

Peers, especially friends, provide intimacy, support, and rich opportunities for the development of play and for the exchange of ideas. Children engage in more complex and cooperative play, and in more conflict, with friends than with nonfriends, and they tend to resolve conflicts with friends in more appropriate ways. With age, the dimensions of children's friendships change somewhat. Whereas young children define friendship primarily on the basis of actual activities with their peers and on the rewards and costs involved, older children increasingly rely on their friends to provide a context for self-disclosure, intimacy, self-exploration, and problem solving. As was suggested by Piaget and Vygotsky, friends also provide opportunities for the development of important social and cognitive skills. However, friends can have negative effects on children if they engage in problematic behaviors such as aggression or substance abuse.

Children tend to become friends with peers who are similar in age, sex, race, and social behavior. This makes it especially difficult to distinguish between characteristics that children bring to friendships and the effects of friends on one another.

Peers in Groups

Let's go back to Annie for a moment. Recall that she not only had a couple of close friends, Kay and Sarah, but she also had a group of friends—Jo, Kerry, and Sue—with whom she "did things" (see Figure 13.1, page 507) and to whom she felt closer than she did to other children in her peer group. This pattern of social relationships is typical. Like Annie, most children usually have one or a few very close friends and some less close additional friends with whom they spend time and share activities. These groups tend to exist within a larger social network of peers that hangs together loosely. Developmentalists have been especially interested in how these peer groups emerge and change with age and how they affect the development of their members.

The Nature of Young Children's Groups

When in a setting with a number of their peers, very young children, including toddlers, sometimes interact in small groups. One striking feature of these first peer groups is the early emergence of status patterns within them, with some children being more dominant and central to group activities than are others (Rubin et al., 2006).

By the time children are preschool age, there is a clear dominance hierarchy among the members of a peer group. Certain children are likely to prevail over other group members when there is conflict, and there is a consistent pattern of winners and losers in physical confrontations. Some ethological theorists believe that dominance hierarchies serve a valuable purpose because they reduce overt aggression among children. In fact, children who lose in conflicts over objects eventually tend to back off to avoid further conflict with the victorious child (Strayer & Strayer, 1976).

As we will discuss shortly, by middle childhood, status in the peer groups involves much more than dominance, and children become very concerned about their peer-group standing. Before examining peer status, however, we need to consider the nature of social groups in middle childhood and early adolescence.

Cliques and Social Networks in Middle Childhood and Early Adolescence

Starting in middle childhood, most children are part of a clique. **Cliques** are friendship groups that children voluntarily form or join themselves. In middle childhood, clique members are usually of the same sex and race and typically number between three and nine (Chen, Chang, & He, 2003; Rubin et al., 2006), with boys' groups tending to be larger than those of girls (Benenson, Morganstein, & Roy, 1998). By age 11, many of children's social interactions—from gatherings in the school lunchroom to outings at the mall—occur within the clique (Crockett, Losoff, & Peterson, 1984). Although friends tend to be members of the same clique, many members of a clique do not view each other as close friends (Cairns, Leung, Buchanan, & Cairns, 1995).

A key feature that underlies cliques and binds their members together is the similarities the members share. Like friends, members of cliques tend to be similar in their degree of academic motivation (Kindermann, 2007; Kiuru, Nurmi, Aunola, & Salmela-Aro, 2009); in their aggressiveness and bullying (Espelage, Holt, & Henkel, 2003; Kiesner, Poulin, & Nicotra, 2003; Salmivalli & Voeten, 2004); and in their shyness, attractiveness, popularity, and adherence to conventional values such as politeness and cooperativeness (Leung, 1996). In one study of 4th and 5th graders, there were five cliques that, based on characteristics of their members, could be described, respectively, as tough, competent, withdrawn, incompetent/aggressive, and average (Kwon & Lease, 2007). Not only do like individuals tend to group together in cliques, but membership in a clique also seems to increase the likelihood that children will exhibit behaviors similar to those of other group members (Espelage et al., 2003).

Despite the social glue of similarity, the membership of cliques tends to be relatively unstable (Cairns et al., 1995). Another study of 4th and 5th graders, for example, found the turnover rate of cliques to be about 50% over eight months (Kindermann, 1993); and in a study of 6th graders, only about 60% of the members of cliques maintained their group ties over the school year (Kindermann, 2007).

cliques friendship groups that children voluntarily form or join themselves

crowds groups of adolescents who have similar stereotyped reputations. Among American high school students, typical crowds may include the "brains," "jocks," "loners," "burnouts," "punks," "populars," "elites," "freaks," or "nonconformists."

The degree to which cliques remain stable appears to depend in large part on whether children are assigned to the same classroom from one year to the next (Neckerman, 1996).

In contrast to the tendency of dominant children to be the central figures in young children's groups, during the school years, girls and boys who are central to the peer group are likely to be popular, athletic, cooperative, seen as leaders, and studious relative to other peers (Farmer & Rodkin, 1996). However, especially in the case of boys, and more especially in the case of aggressive groups of youths, the central figures are sometimes domineering, aggressive, and viewed by peers as "tough" or "cool" (Estell, Cairns, Farmer, & Cairns, 2002; Rodkin, Farmer, Pearl, & Van Acker, 2006).

Cliques in middle childhood serve a variety of functions: they provide a ready-made pool of peers for socializing; they offer validation of the characteristics that the group members have in common; and, perhaps most important, they provide a sense of belonging. By middle childhood, children are quite concerned about being accepted by peers, and issues of peer status become a common topic of children's conversation and gossip (Gottman, 1986; Kanner, Feldman, Weinberger, & Ford, 1987; Rubin et al., 1998). Being accepted by others who are similar to oneself in various ways may provide a sense of personal affirmation, as well as of being a welcomed member of the larger peer group.

Cliques and Social Networks in Adolescence

From age 11 to 18, there is a marked drop in the number of students who belong to a single clique and an increase in the number of adolescents who have ties to many cliques or to students at the margins of cliques (Shrum & Cheek, 1987). In addition, membership in a clique is fairly stable across the school year by 10th grade (Degirmencioglu, Urberg, Tolson, & Richard, 1998).

Children and adolescents in cliques tend to spend a lot of time together and often dress similarly.

DONNA DAY / IMAGE STATE

The dynamics of cliques also vary at different ages in adolescence. During early and middle adolescence, children report placing a high value on being in a popular group and in conforming to the group's norms regarding dress and behavior. Failure to conform—even something as trivial-seeming as wearing the wrong brand or style of jeans or belonging to an afterschool club that is viewed as uncool—can result in being ridiculed or shunned by the group. In comparison with older adolescents, younger adolescents also report more interpersonal conflict with members of their group as well as with members of other groups. In later adolescence, the importance of belonging to a clique and of conforming to its norms appears to decline, as does the friction and antagonism within and between groups of adolescents. With increasing age, adolescents not only are more autonomous but they also tend to look more to individual relationships than to group relationships to fulfill their social needs (Gavin & Furman, 1989; Rubin et al., 1998).

Although older adolescents seem less tied to cliques, they still often belong to crowds. **Crowds** are groups of people who have similar stereotyped reputations. Among high school students, typical crowds may include the "brains," "jocks," "loners," "burnouts," "punks," "populars," "elites," "freaks," "hip-hoppers," "geeks," or "nonconformists/alternatives" (Brown & Klute, 2003; Delsing, Ter Bogt, Engels, & Meeus, 2007; La Greca, Prinstein, & Fetter, 2001). Which crowd adolescents belong to is often not their choice; crowd "membership" is frequently assigned to the individual by the consensus of the peer group, even though the individual may actually spend little time with other members of his or her designated crowd (Brown, 1990).

Being associated with a crowd may enhance or hurt adolescents' reputations and influence how they are treated by peers. Someone labeled a freak, for example, may be ignored or ridiculed by people in groups such as the jocks or populars (Horn, 2003). Thus, it is not surprising that youths in high-status groups tend to have higher self-esteem than that of youths in less desirable crowds (Brown, von Bank, & Steinberg, 2008). Being labeled as part of a particular crowd also may limit adolescents' options with regard to exploring their identities (see Chapter 11). This is because crowd membership may "channel" adolescents into relationships with other members of the same crowd rather than with a diverse group of peers (Brown, 2004; Eckert, 1989). Thus, adolescents in one crowd may be exposed to the acceptance of violence or drugs by peers, whereas members of another crowd may find that their peers value success in academics or sports rather than involvement in illegal or violent activities (La Greca et al., 2001).

Boys and Girls in Cliques and Crowds

In adolescence, girls are more likely than boys to be integrated into cliques and to draw a large percentage of their friends from their own clique (Urberg, Degirmencioglu, Tolson, & Halliday-Scher, 1995). Perhaps because of their tighter connection to a single peer group, girls seem to be more upset than boys are by the arguments and negative interactions that sometimes go on within cliques (Gavin & Furman, 1989). As discussed previously, children tend to affiliate with same-gender peers throughout childhood and into adolescence (see also Chapter 15). However, by 7th grade, about 10% of cliques contain both boys and girls (Cairns et al., 1995). Thereafter, girls and boys tend to associate with one another more, and dyadic dating relationships become increasingly common (Dunphy, 1963; Richards, Crowe, Larson, & Swarr, 1998) (see Box 13.2 on the next page). Consequently, by high school, cliques of friends often include adolescents of both genders (Fischer, Sollie, & Morrow, 1986; La Greca et al., 2001).

Negative Influences of Cliques and Social Networks

Like close friends, members of the clique or the larger peer network can sometimes lead the child or adolescent astray. Preadolescents and adolescents are more likely to smoke, drink, use drugs, goof off in school, or engage in violence, for example, if members of their peer group do so and if they hang out with peers who have been in trouble (Lacourse, Nagin, Tremblay, Vitaro, & Claes, 2003; Loukas, Prelow, Zuizzo, & Allua, 2008; Rose, Chassin, Presson, & Sherman, 1999). Adolescents who have an extreme orientation to peers—that is, who are willing to do anything to be liked by peers—are particularly at risk for such behaviors if engaging in them secures peer acceptance (Fuligni, Eccles, Barber, & Clements, 2001).

Perhaps the greatest potential for negative peer-group influence comes with membership in a **gang,** which is a loosely organized group of adolescents or young adults who identify as a group and often engage in illegal activities. Gang members often say that they join or stay in a gang for protection from other gangs. One male gang member explained that "being cool with a gang" meant that "you don't have to worry about nobody jumping you. You don't got to worry about getting beat up" (quoted in Decker, 1996, p. 253). Gangs also provide members with a sense of belonging and a way to spend their time. Gang members frequently report

gang a loosely organized group of adolescents or young adults who identify as a group and often engage in illegal activities

a closer look 13.2

Romantic Relationships with Peers

In the United States, 25% of 12-year-olds and 70% of 18-year-olds report having had a romantic relationship in the past 18 months (Carver, Joyner, & Udry, 2003). Similar rates have been reported for youth in Europe (Zani, 1991). While only 35% of 14- to 15-year-olds report that their romantic relationships last for at least 11 months, 55% of youth 16 or older do (Collins, 2003).

Participation in mixed-gender peer groups typically precedes involvement in dyadic romantic relationships, with dating emerging out of mixed-gender group affiliations (Collins & Steinberg, 2006; Connolly et al., 2004). From ages 14 to 18, youth tend to balance the time they spend with romantic partners and with same-gender cliques, gradually decreasing the percent of time they spend in mixed-gender groups (Richards et al., 1998). However, by early adulthood, time with romantic partners increases to the point that it is at the expense of involvement with friends and crowds (Reis, Lin, Bennett, & Nezlek, 1993). Less is known about the emergence of romantic relationships among sexual-minority youths: although many report some sexual activity in adolescence (Savin-Williams & Diamond, 2000), whether or not they date depends on the level of acceptance in their social environment (Diamond et al., 1999).

Young adolescents tend to be drawn to, and choose, partners based on characteristics that bring status—such as being stylish in their appearance—and the approval of their peers (Pelligrini & Long, 2007). They also tend to be similar to their romantic partners in levels of popularity, physical attractiveness, and even in their depressive symptoms (Simon, Aikins, & Prinstein, 2008). In contrast, older adolescents are more likely than younger ones to select partners based on compatibility and characteristics that enhance intimacy. With age, romantic relationships are more likely to reflect caring and compromise (Collins, 2003).

For many adolescents, being in a romantic relationship is important for a sense of belonging and status in the peer group (Carlson & Rome, 2007; Connolly, Craig, Goldberg, & Pepler, 1999). Having a high-quality romantic relationship is also associated with feelings of self-worth and, by late adolescence, with a general sense of competence (Collins, Welsh, & Furman, 2009; Connolly & Konarski, 1994). Moreover, such a high-quality relationship can improve functioning in adolescents who are prone to depression, sadness, or aggression (Simon et al., 2008).

However, romantic relationships can also have negative effects on development. Early dating and sexual activity, for example, are associated with increased rates of current and later problem behaviors, such as drinking and using drugs, and with social and emotional difficulties (e.g., Davies & Windle, 2000; Zimmer-Gembeck, Siebenbruner, & Collins et al., 2001). This is especially true if the romantic partner is prone to delinquent behavior (Lonardo, Giordano, Longmore, & Manning, 2009). When a romantic relationship doesn't work out, hurt feelings for one or both partners are par for the course, but girls who are treated badly or are rejected in a relationship seem particularly prone to depression and anxiety (Ellis, Crooks, & Wolfe, 2009).

The quality of adolescents' romantic relationships appears to mirror the quality of their other relationships. Adolescents who have had poor-quality relationships with parents and peers are more likely to experience physical and relational aggression with romantic partners (Stocker & Richmond, 2007; Zimmer-Gembeck, Siebenbruner, & Collins, 2004). In addition, it is believed that adolescents' working models of relationships with parents tend to be reflected in their romantic relationships. This belief is supported by the finding that children who were securely attached at age 12 months were more socially competent in elementary school, which predicted more secure relationships with friends at age 16. The security of these friendships, in turn, predicted more positive daily emotional experiences in romantic relationships at age 20 to 23 and less negative affect in conflict resolution and collaborative tasks with romantic partners (Simpkins et al., 2007). Thus, romantic relationships appear to be affected in multiple ways by youths' history of relationships.

that the most common gang activities are "hanging out" together and engaging in fairly innocuous behaviors (e.g., drinking beer, playing sports, cruising, looking for girls, and having parties) (Decker & van Winkle, 1996). Nonetheless, adolescents tend to engage in more illegal activities such as delinquency and drug abuse when they are in a gang than when they are not (Bjerregaard & Smith, 1993; Craig, Vitaro, Gagnon, & Tremblay, 2002; Esbensen & Huizinga, 1993; see Chapter 14, pages 577–578).

Negative peer-group influences can also exist among college students. For example, students involved in athletics and fraternities or sororities are more likely than other students to engage in binge drinking, in part because the practice tends to be positively sanctioned by those groups as a regular part of their social activities (Carter & Kahnweiler, 2000; Meilman, Leichliter, & Presley, 1999). Further, individuals who started bingeing in adolescence and continued to binge heavily in early adulthood tend to have friends who drank heavily in adolescence (Chassin,

Pitts, & Prost, 2002). Because of the link between bingeing and friends' drinking, and the tendency of friends to drink together as a social activity (Jamison & Myers, 2008), intervention programs designed to reduce binge drinking on campuses sometimes try to address the role of these peer groups in the process (Bishop, 2000; Nelson & Wechsler, 2001).

The potential for peer-group influence to promote problem behavior is affected by family and cultural influences. As noted in our discussion of friendship, having authoritative, involved parents helps protect adolescents from peer pressure to use drugs, whereas having authoritarian, detached parents increases adolescents' susceptibility to such pressure. Those who do not live with their fathers or stepfathers and who have a poor relationship with their mothers may be especially vulnerable to such pressure (Farrell & White, 1998). At the same time, the strength of peer influence on problem behavior can vary by culture and subculture. For example, compared with its strength among Euro-American adolescents, peer influence on the use of drugs, drinking, aggression, or school misconduct appears to be weaker for American Indian youths who live on a reservation and for adolescents in mainland China or Taiwan (Chen, Greenberger, Lester, Dong, & Guo, 1998; Swain, Oetting, Thurman, Beauvais, & Edwards, 1993), perhaps because family sanctions against such behaviors play a more important role in these groups. Although the precise reasons for all these differences in peer-group influence are not yet known, it is clear from findings such as these that family and cultural factors can affect the degree to which peers' behaviors are associated with adolescents' problem behavior.

review:

Very young children often interact with peers in groups, and dominance hierarchies emerge in these groups by preschool age. By middle childhood, most children belong to cliques of same-gender peers who often are similar in their aggressiveness and orientation toward school.

In adolescence, the importance of cliques tends to diminish, and adolescents typically belong to more than one group. The degree of conformity to the norms of the peer group regarding dress, talk, and behavior decreases over the high school years. Nonetheless, adolescents often are members of "crowds" such as the jocks, loners, or brains—that is, groups of people with similar reputations. Even though adolescents often do not choose what crowd they belong to, belonging to a particular crowd may affect their reputations, their treatment by peers, and their exploration of identities.

Peer groups sometimes contribute to the development of antisocial behavior and the use of alcohol and drugs. Membership in a gang is particularly likely to encourage problem behavior. The degree to which the peer group influences adolescents' antisocial behavior or drug abuse appears to vary according to family and cultural factors.

Status in the Peer Group

As noted in the preceding section, older children and adolescents often are extremely concerned with their peer status: being popular is of great importance, and peer rejection can be a devastating experience. Rejection by peers is associated with a range of developmental outcomes for children, such as dropping out of school and problem behaviors, and these relations can hold independent of any effects of having, or not having, close friends (Gest, Graham-Berman, & Hartup, 2001). Because of the central role that peer relations play in children's lives, developmental researchers have devoted a good deal of effort to studying the concurrent and long-term effects associated with peer status.

TABLE 13.3

Common Sociometric Categories

Popular—Children are designated as *popular* if they receive many positive nominations (e.g., for being liked) and few negative nominations (e.g., for being disliked).

Rejected—Children are designated as *rejected* if they receive many negative nominations and few positive nominations.

Neglected—Children are designated as *neglected* if they are low in social impact—that is, if they receive few positive or negative nominations. These children are not especially liked or disliked by peers; they simply go unnoticed.

Average—Children are designated as *average* if they receive an average number of both positive and negative nominations.

Controversial—Children are designated as *controversial* if they receive many positive and many negative nominations. They are noticed by peers and are liked by a quite a few children and disliked by quite a few others.

In this section, we will examine children's status in the peer group, including how it is measured, its stability, the characteristics that determine it, and the long-term implications of being popular with, or being rejected by, peers.

Measurement of Peer Status

The most common method developmentalists use to assess peer status is to ask children to rate how much they like or dislike each of their classmates. Alternatively, they may ask children to nominate some of those whom they like the most and the least or whom they do or don't like to play with. The information from these procedures is used to calculate the children's **sociometric status,** that is, the degree to which the children are liked or disliked by their peers as a group. The most commonly used sociometric system classifies children into five groups: popular, rejected, neglected, average, or controversial (see Table 13.3) (Coie & Dodge, 1988).

Characteristics Associated with Sociometric Status

Why are some children liked better than others? One obvious factor is physical attractiveness. Attractive children are much more likely to be popular than are children who are unattractive (Langlois et al., 2000). This pattern, which emerges in early childhood, is particularly apparent in adolescence. Indeed, physical attractiveness in adolescence may be more important than sociability in contributing to both peer acceptance in a new setting and the development of positive friendships (Hanna, 1998). Peer status is also affected by the status of one's friends: having popular friends appears to boost one's own popularity (Eder, 1985; Sabongui, Bukowski, & Newcomb, 1998). Beyond these simple determiners, sociometric status also seems to be affected by a variety of other factors, including children's social behavior, personality, cognitions about themselves and others, and goals when interacting with peers.

Popular Children

Popular children—those who, in sociometric procedures, are predominantly nominated as liked by peers—tend to have a number of social skills in common. To begin with, they tend to be skilled at initiating interaction with peers and at maintaining positive relationships with others (Rubin et al., 2006). For example, when popular children enter a group of children who are already talking or playing, they first try to see what is going on in the group and then join in by talking about the same topic or engaging in the same activity as the group (Putallaz, 1983). In keeping with this approach, popular children are relatively unlikely to draw unwarranted attention to themselves when entering a group (Dodge, Schlundt, Schocken, & Delugach, 1983).

At a broader level, popular children tend to be cooperative, friendly, sociable, helpful, and sensitive to others, and they are perceived that way by their peers, teachers, and adult observers alike (Dodge, Lochman, Harnish, Bates, & Pettit, 1997; Lansford et al., 2006; Newcomb, Bukowski, & Pattee, 1993; Rubin et al.,

Physically attractive children and teens tend to be more popular than their less attractive peers.

KERI PICKETT / TIMEPIX

2006). They also are not prone to intense negative emotions and regulate themselves well (Eisenberg et al., 1993).

Although popular children often are less aggressive overall than are rejected children (Newcomb et al., 1993), in comparison with children designated as *average* (i.e., those who receive an average number of both positive and negative nominations), they are less aggressive only with respect to aggression related to generalized anger, vengefulness, or satisfaction in hurting others (Dodge, Coie, Pettit, & Price, 1990). With respect to assertive aggressiveness, including pushing and fighting, popular children often do not differ from average children (Newcomb et al., 1993). Highly aggressive children may even have high peer acceptance in some special cases, such as among adolescent males (but not females) who perform poorly in school (Kreager, 2007) or, as noted earlier, in peer groups in which the popular members tend to be relatively aggressive (Dijkstra, Lindenberg, & Veenstra, 2008).

On the question of aggression and popularity, it is important to differentiate between children who are popular in terms of sociometric measures and those who are perceived by peers as being popular with others. Although children who are designated by peers as being someone they like tend not to be particularly aggressive, children who are perceived as having high status in the group—those who are often labeled "popular" by children themselves—tend to be viewed as above average in aggression and use it to obtain their goals (Hawley, 2003; Prinstein & Cillessen, 2003; Sijtsema, Veenstra, Lindenberg, Salmivalli, 2009).

This association between aggression and perceived popularity, although seen to some degree even in preschool (Vaughn et al., 2003), is especially strong in early adolescence; indeed, high-status individuals, particularly girls, are likely to engage in **relational aggression,** such as excluding others from the group, withholding friendship to inflict harm, and spreading rumors to ruin a peer's reputation (Cillessen & Mayeux, 2004; Prinstein & Cillessen, 2003; Rubin et al., 2006). Especially if they are aware that they are perceived as popular, youth who are perceived as having high status tend to increasingly use relational and physical aggression across adolescence, perhaps because they tend to be arrogant and can get away with it (Cillessen & Mayeux, 2004; Mayeux & Cillessen, 2008; Rose, Swenson, & Waller, 2004). By the middle-school years, children with the reputation of being popular sometimes start to shun less popular peers. As a result, they are considered "stuck up" and begin to be viewed with ambivalence by their peers and sometimes even become resented or disliked (Eder, 1985; Merton, 1997).

sociometric status a measurement that reflects the degree to which children are liked or disliked by their peers as a group

popular peer status a category of sociometric status that refers to children or adolescents who are viewed positively (liked) by many peers and are viewed negatively (disliked) by few peers

relational aggression a kind of aggression that involves exclusion from the social group or attempting to do harm to another's relationships with others. It includes spreading rumors about peers, withholding friendship to inflict harm, and ignoring and excluding peers when a child is angry or wants his or her own way.

rejected peer status a category of sociometric status that refers to children or adolescents who are liked by few peers and disliked by many peers

aggressive-rejected children a category of sociometric status that refers to children who are especially prone to physical aggression, disruptive behavior, delinquency, and negative behavior such as hostility and threatening others

Rejected Children

A majority of **rejected** children tend to fall into one of two categories: those who are overly aggressive and those who are withdrawn.

Aggressive-rejected children According to reports from peers, teachers, and adult observers, 40 to 50% of rejected children tend to be aggressive. These **aggressive-rejected children** are especially prone to hostile and threatening behavior, physical aggression, disruptive behavior, and delinquency (Hinshaw, Zupan, Simmel, Nigg, & Melnick, 1997; Newcomb et al., 1993; Pedersen et al., 2007; Rubin et al., 2006). When they are angry or want their own way, many

Children who are accepted by peers tend to find ways to enter into a group without disrupting its activities.

ELLEN B. SENISI

rejected children also engage in relational aggression (Cillessen & Mayeux, 2004; Crick, Casas, & Mosher, 1997; Tomada & Schneider, 1997).

Most of the research on the role of aggression in peer status is correlational, so it is impossible to know for certain whether aggression causes peer rejection or results from it. However, some research supports the view that aggressive behavior often underlies rejection by peers. For example, observation of unfamiliar peers getting to know one another has shown that those who are aggressive become rejected over time (Coie & Kupersmidt, 1983). Other longitudinal research has shown that children who are aggressive, negative, and disruptive tend to become increasingly disliked by peers across the school year (Little & Garber, 1995; Maszk, Eisenberg, & Guthrie, 1999).

As you have seen, however, not all aggressive children are rejected by their peers. Some develop a network of aggressive friends and are accepted in their peer group (Xu, Farver, Schwartz, & Chang, 2004), and some preadolescent boys who start fights and get into trouble are viewed as "cool" and are central in their peer group (Rodkin et al., 2000, 2006). Many of these boys are among those designated as *controversial*—liked by numerous children and disliked by numerous others.

ELIZABETH CREWS

Children who are socially withdrawn miss opportunities to learn social skills and may eventually be rejected by peers, especially if they behave in negative ways.

Withdrawn-rejected children The second group of rejected children are those who are **withdrawn-rejected.** These children, who make up 10 to 25% of the rejected category, are socially withdrawn and wary and, according to some research, are often timid (Cillessen, van IJzendoorn, van Lieshout, & Hartup, 1992; Rubin et al., 2006). They frequently are victimized by peers, and many feel isolated and lonely (Booth-LaForce & Oxford, 2008; Rubin, Coplan, & Bowker, 2009). Friendlessness, friendship instability, and exclusion in 5th grade predict increases in socially withdrawn behavior from 5th to 8th grade, whereas low peer exclusion in 5th grade predicts a decline in social withdrawal across time (Oh et al., 2008). Thus, social withdrawal may be both a cause and consequence of peer exclusion and rejection.

However, research suggests that not all socially withdrawn children are rejected or socially excluded (Gazelle, 2008; Gazelle & Ladd, 2003). In one study of different types of socially withdrawn children, observers kept track of the times kindergarten children played alone, wandered around aimlessly, or merely watched other children (Harrist, Zaia, Bates, Dodge, & Pettit, 1997). In addition, teachers provided information on the children's tendencies to isolate themselves and to exhibit negative emotions and a range of negative behaviors. Assessing the children's sociometric status in kindergarten and over the next few years, the researchers found that *active isolates*—withdrawn children who displayed immature, unregulated, or angry, defiant behavior such as bullying, boasting, and meanness—were particularly likely to be rejected by peers. In kindergarten, 59% of these children were rejected, and only about 14% were popular.

In contrast, children who interacted with peers at a low rate but were viewed by teachers as relatively socially competent were simply neglected—that is, they were not nominated as liked or disliked by peers. Finally, children who were very high in isolated behavior and were viewed by teachers as timid and anxious tended to be average in their sociometric status. Thus, withdrawn behavior in itself was not associated with being rejected by peers; rather, it was withdrawn behavior combined with negative actions or emotions that correlated with rejection.

withdrawn-rejected children a category of sociometric status that refers to rejected children who are socially withdrawn, wary, and often timid

Over the course of childhood, withdrawn behavior seems to become a more reliable predictor of peer rejection. By the middle to late elementary school years, children who are quite withdrawn stand out and tend to be disliked and appear to become increasingly alienated from the group as time goes on (Rubin et al., 1998). In some cases, however, children who are not initially socially withdrawn have social isolation forced upon them as they progress through school (Bowker, Bukowski, Zargarpour, & Hoza, 1998). That is, children who are disliked and rebuffed by peers, often because of their disruptive or aggressive behavior, may increasingly isolate themselves from the group even if they initially were not withdrawn (Coie et al., 1990; Rubin et al., 1998).

Social cognition and social rejection Rejected children, particularly those who are aggressive, tend to differ from more popular children in their social motives and in the way they process information related to social situations. For example, rejected children are more likely than better-liked peers to be motivated by goals such as "getting even" with others or showing them up (Crick & Dodge, 1994; Rubin et al., 2006). As discussed in Chapter 9 (pages 359–360), they also are relatively likely to attribute malicious intent to others in negative social situations, even when the intent of others is uncertain or benign (Crick & Dodge, 1994).

Moreover, rejected children have more trouble than other children do in finding constructive solutions to difficult social situations, such as wanting a turn on a swing when someone else is using it. When asked how they would deal with such situations, rejected children suggest fewer and more hostile, demanding, and threatening strategies than do their more popular peers (Dodge et al., 2003; Harrist et al., 1997; Rubin et al., 1998). (Box 13.3 on the next page discusses programs designed to help rejected children gain peer acceptance.)

Social rejection and self-evaluations Perhaps because of their deficits in social behavior, withdrawn-rejected children, in comparison with other children, have less confidence in their social skills, report being more anxious in peer contexts, and are more likely to blame themselves for their social failures (Hymel, Bowker, & Woody, 1993; Rubin et al., 2006; Wichmann, Coplan, & Daniels, 2004). In contrast, aggressive-rejected children, despite their also lacking important social skills, tend to overestimate their social competence with peers, including the degree to which they are liked and accepted by them (Hymel, Bowker, & Woody, 1993; Patterson, Kupersmidt, & Griesler, 1990). This tendency may create additional problems for these children, leading them to jump into social situations that they cannot handle well and to fail to monitor the outcomes of their actions.

Neglected Children

As noted earlier, some withdrawn children are categorized as **neglected** because they are not nominated by peers as either liked or disliked (Booth-LaForce & Oxford, 2008). These children tend to be less sociable and disruptive than average children (Rubin et al., 1998) and are likely to back away from peer interactions that involve aggression (Coie & Dodge, 1988). Neglected children not only interact less frequently with peers than do children who are average in sociometric status, but they also perceive that they receive less support from peers (Wentzel, 2003); yet they are not particularly anxious about social interactions (Hatzichristou & Hopf, 1996; Rubin et al., 1998). In fact, neglected children display relatively few behaviors that differ greatly from those of many other children (Bukowski, Gauze, Hoza, & Newcomb, 1993). They appear to be neglected primarily because they are not noticed by their peers.

neglected peer status a category of sociometric status that refers to children or adolescents who are infrequently mentioned as liked or disliked; they simply are not noticed much by peers

applications 13.3

Fostering Children's Peer Acceptance

Given the difficult and often painful outcomes commonly associated with a child's being rejected or having few friends, a number of researchers have designed programs to help children in these categories gain acceptance from peers. Their approaches have varied according to what they believe to be the causes of social rejection, but a number of approaches have proved to be useful, at least to some degree.

One common approach involves **social skills training.** The assumption behind this approach is that rejected children lack social skills that promote positive peer relations. These deficits are viewed as occurring at three levels (Mize & Ladd, 1990):

1. *Lack of social knowledge*—Rejected children lack social knowledge regarding the goals, strategies, and normative expectations that apply in specific peer contexts. For example, children engaged in a joint activity usually expect a newcomer to the group to blend in slowly and not to begin immediately pushing his or her own ideas or wishes. Lacking an understanding of this, aggressive-rejected children are likely to barge into a conversation or to try to control the group's choice of activities. In contrast, a withdrawn-rejected child may not know how to start a conversation or contribute to the group's activities when the opportunity arises.
2. *Performance problems*—Some rejected children possess the social knowledge required for being successful in various peer contexts, but they may still act inappropriately because they are unable or unmotivated to use their knowledge to guide their performance.
3. *Lack of appropriate monitoring and self-evaluation*—To behave in a way that is consistent with the interests and actions of their peers, children need to monitor their own and others' social behavior. Such monitoring requires them to accurately interpret social cues regarding what is occurring, what others are feeling and thinking, and how their own behavior is being perceived. Rejected children often cannot engage in such monitoring and thus cannot modify their behavior in appropriate ways.

To help children overcome such deficits, some social-skills training programs teach children to pay attention to what is going on in a group of peers and help them develop skills related to participating with peers. Interventions may include coaching and rehearsing children on how to start a conversation with an unfamiliar peer, how to compliment a peer, how to smile and offer help, and how to take turns and share materials (Oden & Asher, 1977). In other interventions, the emphasis is primarily on teaching children to think about alternative ways to achieve a goal, evaluate the consequences of each alternative, and then select an appropriate strategy. Children may be asked to think about or act out a situation in which they are excluded or teased by peers and to come up with various strategies for handling the situation. The children are then helped to evaluate the strategies and to understand the specific costs and benefits of each (e.g., Coleman, Wheeler, & Webber, 1993).

Recent forms of this sort of program are often multifaceted, including such components as communication skills, anger management, and training in perspective-taking (Reid, Webster-Stratton, & Hammond, 2007; Webster-Stratton, Reid, & Stoolmiller, 2008). Their primary focus is on helping children to better understand and communicate about their own and others' emotions and to regulate their behavior (Domitrovich, Cortes, & Greenberg, 2007; Izard et al., 2008), although training of social-skill strategies also usually occurs to some degree. The general assumption underlying these programs is that children act in more appropriate ways and, consequently, are better liked if their behavior takes into account the feelings of others and is modulated in a manner that is both sensitive and socially appropriate to those feelings.

A notable example of this approach is the PATHS (Promoting Alternative Thinking Strategies) curriculum, in which children learn to identify emotional expressions (e.g., with pictures) and to think about the causes and consequences of different ways of expressing emotions (Domitrovich et al., 2007). In addition, the program provides children with opportunities to develop conscious strategies for self-control through verbal mediation (self-talk) and practicing ways to self-regulate. The approach of PATHS is suggested by the Control Signals Poster (CSP), which is designed to remind children how to deal with troubling social situations:

> The CSP is modeled after a traffic signal, with red, yellow, and green lights. The red light signals children to "Stop—Calm Down." Here, youth are instructed that as challenging social situations occur, they should first "take a long deep breath," calm down, and "say the problem and how they feel." The yellow light signals children to "Slow Down—Think." Here, youth make a plan by considering possible solutions and then selecting the best option. Finally, the green light signals children to "Go—Try My Plan." Below the illustration of the stoplight are the words "Evaluate—How Did My Plan Work?" Students may then formulate and try new plans if necessary.
>
> (Riggs, Greenberg, Kusche, & Pentz, 2006, p. 94)

Programs like this one tend to be successful in fostering knowledge about emotions, self-regulation, and social competence—and sometimes in reducing social withdrawal as well (e.g., Domitrovich et al., 2007; Izard et al., 2008; Riggs et al., 2006). Such improvements have been found especially for children with numerous problem behaviors (Greenberg et al., 1995). The increases in social competence that often result as a consequence of participation in such an intervention would be expected to promote children's social status, although this issue usually has not been specifically tested.

Controversial Children

In some ways, the most intriguing group of children are **controversial** children, who, as indicated, are liked by numerous peers and disliked by numerous others. Controversial children tend to have characteristics of both popular and rejected children (Rubin et al., 1998). For example, they tend to be aggressive, disruptive, and prone to anger, but they also tend to be cooperative, sociable, good at sports, and humorous (Bukowski et al., 1993; Coie & Dodge, 1988). They are very socially active and tend to be group leaders (Coie, Dodge, & Kupersmidt, 1990). Controversial children also tend to be viewed by peers as arrogant and snobbish (Hatzichristou & Hopf, 1996), which could explain why they are disliked by some peers.

social skills training training programs designed to help rejected children gain peer acceptance; they are based on the assumption that rejected children lack important knowledge and skills that promote positive interaction with peers

controversial peer status a category of sociometric status that refers to children or adolescents who are liked by quite a few peers and are disliked by quite a few others

Stability of Sociometric Status

Do popular children always remain at the top of the social heap? Do rejected children sometimes become better liked? In other words, how stable is a child's sociometric status in the peer group? The answer to this question depends in part on the particular time span and sociometric status that are in question.

Over relatively short time periods such as weeks or a few months, children who are popular or rejected tend to remain so, whereas children who are neglected or controversial are highly likely to acquire a different status (Asher & Dodge, 1986; Chen, Rubin, & Li, 1995b; Newcomb & Bukowski, 1984). Over longer periods of time, children's sociometric status is more likely to change. In one study in which children were rated by their peers in 5th grade and again two years later, only children who had initially been rated average maintained their status overall, whereas nearly two-thirds of those who had been rated popular, rejected, or controversial received a different rating later on (Newcomb & Bukowski, 1984). Over time, sociometric stability for rejected children is generally higher than for popular, neglected, or controversial children (Harrist et al., 1997; Parke et al., 1997) and may increase with the age of the child (Coie & Dodge, 1983; Rubin et al., 1998).

Cross-Cultural Similarities and Differences in Factors Related to Peer Status

Most of the research on behaviors associated with sociometric status has been conducted in the United States, but findings similar to those discussed here have been obtained in a wide array of cross-cultural research. In countries ranging from Canada, Italy, and Greece to Indonesia and China, for example, socially rejected children tend to be aggressive and disruptive; and, in most countries, popular (i.e., well-liked) children tend to be described as prosocial and as having leadership skills (Attili, Vermigli, & Schneider, 1997; Chen, Rubin, & Li, 1995a; French, Setiono, & Eddy, 1999; Hatzichristou & Hopf, 1996; Tomada & Schneider, 1997; Xu et al., 2004).

Similar cross-cultural parallels have been found with regard to withdrawal and rejection. Various studies done with schoolchildren in Germany and Italy, for example, have shown that, as in the United States, withdrawal becomes linked with peer rejection in elementary school (Asendorpf, 1990; Attili et al., 1997; Casiglia, Lo Coco, & Zappulla, 1998).

Children who are well liked tend to have similar characteristics in many cultures, as do children who are rejected by their peers.

REIHHARD EISELE / CORBIS

Research has also demonstrated that there are certain cultural and historical differences in the characteristics associated with children's sociometric status. One notable example involving both differences is the status associated with shyness among Chinese children. In studies conducted in the 1990s, Chinese children who were shy, sensitive, and cautious or inhibited in their behavior were—unlike their inhibited or shy Western counterparts—viewed by teachers as socially competent and as leaders, and they were liked by their peers (Chen et al., 1995a, 1995b; Chen, Rubin, Li, & Li, 1999; Chen, Rubin, & Sun, 1992). A probable explanation for this difference is that Chinese culture traditionally values self-effacing, withdrawn behavior, and Chinese children are encouraged to behave accordingly (Ho, 1986).

In contrast, because Western cultures place great value on independence and self-assertion, withdrawn children in these cultures are likely to be viewed as weak, needy, and socially incompetent. However, Chen (Chen, Cen, Li, & He, 2005) has found that since the early 1990s, shy, reserved behavior in Chinese elementary school children has become increasingly associated with lower levels of peer acceptance. Chen argues that the economic and political changes in China in the past decade have been accompanied by an increased valuing of assertive, less inhibited behavior.

Peer Status as a Predictor of Risk

Having an undesirable peer status has been associated with a variety of near- and long-term risks and negative outcomes for children, including inferior academic performance, loneliness, delinquency, and poor adjustment.

Academic Performance

Research in a variety of regions, including North America, China, and Indonesia, indicates that rejected children, especially those who are aggressive, are more likely than their peers to have academic difficulties (Chen, Rubin, & Li, 1997; French et al., 1999; Wentzel, 2009). In particular, they have higher rates of school absenteeism (DeRosier, Kupersmidt, & Patterson, 1994) and lower grade-point averages (Wentzel & Caldwell, 1997). Those who are aggressive are especially likely to be uninterested in school and to be viewed by peers and teachers as poor students (Hymel et al., 1993; Wentzel & Asher, 1995).

Longitudinal research indicates that students' classroom participation is lower during periods in which they are rejected by peers than during periods when they are not, and that the tendency of rejected children to do relatively poorly in school worsens across time (Coie, Lochman, Terry, & Hyman, 1992; Ladd, Herald-Brown, & Reiser, 2008; Ollendick, Weist, Borden, & Greene, 1992). In one study that followed children from 5th grade through the high school years, rejected children were much more likely than other children, especially popular children, to be required to repeat a grade or to be suspended from school, to be truants, or to drop out (Kupersmidt & Coie, 1990) (Figure 13.3). They were also more likely to have difficulties with the law—in many cases, no doubt, deepening their academic difficulties. All told, approximately 25 to 30% of rejected children drop out of school, compared with approximately 8% or less of other children (Parker & Asher, 1987; Rubin et al., 1998). Dropping out may be especially likely for children who feel isolated and lonely at school and who blame rejection by peers for their situation (Hymel, Comfort, Schonert-Reichl, & McDougall, 1996).

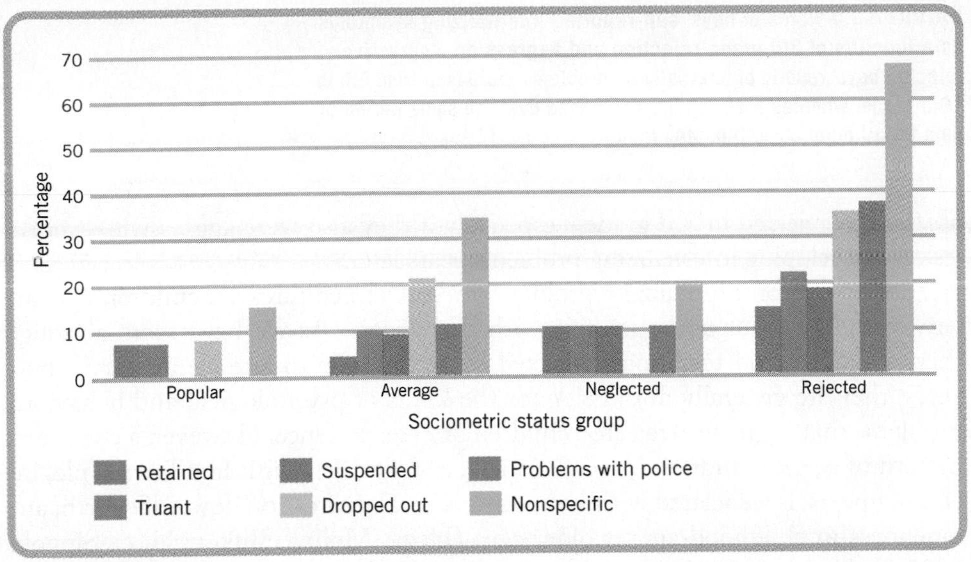

FIGURE 13.3 The relation of children's sociometric status to academic and behavioral problems Children's sociometric status is related to their future problem behaviors. Rejected children are far more likely to be held back in, or suspended from, school, to be truants, to drop out, and to have problems with the police. (Adapted from Kupersmidt & Coie, 1990)

Problems with Adjustment

Children who are rejected in the elementary school years—especially aggressive-rejected boys—are at risk for externalizing symptoms such as aggression, delinquency, hyperactivity and attention-deficit disorders, conduct disorder, and substance abuse (Dodge et al., 2003; Ollendick et al., 1992; Vitaro, Pedersen, & Brendgen, 2007). In one study that followed more than 1000 children from 3rd to 10th grade (Coie, Terry, Lenox, Lochman, & Hyman, 1995), boys and girls who were assessed as rejected in 3rd grade were, according to parent reports, higher than their peers in externalizing symptoms three years and seven years later. In addition, aggressive boys (both rejected and nonrejected) increased in parent-reported externalizing symptoms between grades 6 and 10, whereas other boys did not; and by 10th grade, aggressive-rejected boys were especially high in externalizing symptoms (Figure 13.4). By 10th grade, aggressive-rejected boys themselves reported an average of more than twice the number of symptoms reported by all other boys.

Other research provides evidence that peer rejection may also be associated with internalizing problems such as loneliness, depression, withdrawn behavior, and obsessive-compulsive behavior (Prinstein, Rancourt, Guerry, & Browne, 2009). Girls and boys who were rejected in 3rd grade were, as reported by parents, higher than their peers in internalizing symptoms by 6th grade and 10th grade. Moreover, aggressive-rejected boys themselves reported a marked increase in internalizing symptoms from 6th to 10th grade, whereas all other boys reported a drop in these symptoms (Figure 13.5). Aggressive-rejected girls were viewed by parents as most prone to internalizing problems by grade 10. Thus, both boys and girls who were

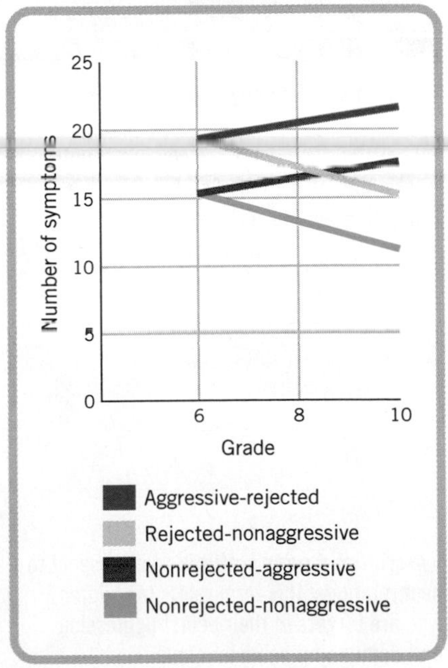

FIGURE 13.4 Rates of parent-reported externalizing symptoms in adolescent males as a function of 3rd-grade rejection and aggression According to parent reports, boys who were assessed as rejected in 3rd grade were, years later, higher than their peers in externalizing symptoms. Aggressive boys (both rejected and nonrejected) increased in parent-reported externalizing symptoms between grades 6 and 10, whereas other boys did not; by 10th grade, aggressive-rejected boys were especially high in externalizing symptoms. (Adapted from Coie et al., 1995)

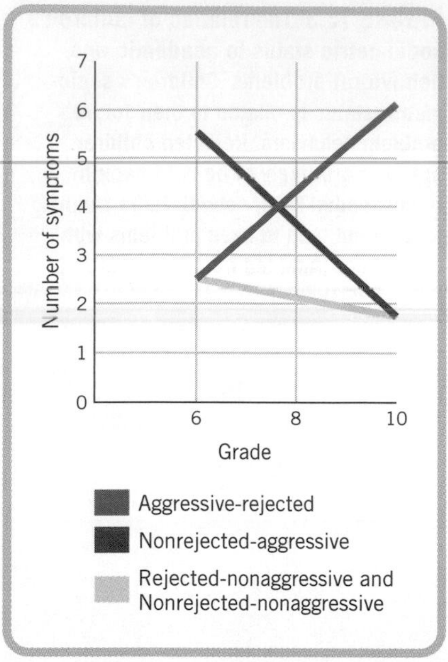

FIGURE 13.5 Rates of boys' self-reported internalizing symptoms as a function of 3rd-grade rejection and aggression Aggressive-rejected boys' reports of internalizing problems increased from 6th to 10th grade, whereas such reports decreased over the same period of time for all other boys. (Adapted from Coie et al., 1995)

assessed as rejected in 3rd grade—especially if they also were aggressive—were at risk for developing internalizing problems years later.

Also at risk for internalizing problems in Western cultures are children who are very withdrawn but nonaggressive with their peers. As we have seen, although these children tend to become rejected by the middle to late elementary school years, they are generally not at risk for the kinds of psychological and behavioral problems that aggressive-rejected children often experience. However, a consistent pattern of social withdrawal, social anxiety, and wariness with familiar people, including peers, is associated with symptoms such as depression, low self-worth, and loneliness in childhood and at older ages (Hoza, Molina, Bukowski, & Sippola, 1995; Rubin et al., 2009). Such a pattern is also associated with less support from peers (La Greca & Lopez, 1998), and shy-anxious children who are excluded by peers are especially likely to develop internalizing problems by mid-elementary school (Gazelle & Ladd, 2003).

SCOTT BARROW, INC. / SUPERSTOCK

Children who are shy with familiar peers are at risk for loneliness and feelings of insecurity. Boys who are shy with familiar peers may also be at risk for negative outcomes as adults.

Children who are socially withdrawn amid familiar peers may differ in important ways from their peers even in adulthood. In a longitudinal study of American children born in the late 1920s, boys who were rated by their teachers as reserved and unsociable were less likely to have been married and to have children than were less reserved boys. They also tended to begin their careers at later ages, had less success in their careers, and were less stable in their jobs. Reserved men who were late in establishing stable careers had twice the rate of divorce and marital separation by midlife as did their less reserved peers.

In contrast, reserved girls were more likely than their less reserved peers to have a conventional lifestyle of marriage, parenthood, and homemaking rather than working outside the home. Thus, a reserved style of interaction at school in childhood was associated with more negative outcomes for men than for women, perhaps because a reserved style was more compatible with the feminine homemaker role of the times than with the demands of achieving outside the home (Caspi, Elder, & Bem, 1988).

A final group of rejected children who may be especially at risk for loneliness and other internalizing problems is **victimized** children, who are targets of their peers' aggression and demeaning behavior. These children tend to be aggressive as well as withdrawn and anxious (Barker, Boivin, Brendgen, Barker et al., 2008; Schwartz, McFadyen-Ketchum, Dodge, Pettit, & Bates, 1998; Snyder et al., 2003), and it may be their aggression that elicits victimization by peers (Barker et al., 2008; Ostrov, 2008). Although the sequence of events is not entirely clear, it appears that children in this group are more likely to be rejected first and then victimized rather than the reverse (Hanish & Guerra, 2000a; Schwartz et al., 1999). Victimization by peers, in turn, likely increases children's aggression, withdrawal, depression, and loneliness (Hanish & Guerra, 2002; Nylund, Bellmore, Nishina, & Graham, 2007; Schwartz et al., 1998), leading to problems at school and absenteeism (Juvonen, Nishina, & Graham, 2000; Kochenderfer & Ladd, 1996).

victimized peer status with respect to peer relations, this term refers to children who are targets of their peers' aggression and demeaning behavior

Unfortunately, peer victimization is not an uncommon event. In one study in the United States, approximately one-fifth of kindergartners were repeatedly victimized by peers (Kochenderfer & Ladd, 1996). Although this rate appears to be lower among older children (Olweus, 1994), peer victimization is a serious problem that warrants concern, especially since the same children tend to be victimized again and again (Hanish & Guerra, 2000b).

Paths to Risk

Clearly, children who are rejected by peers are at risk for academic and adjustment problems. The key question is whether peer rejection actually causes problems at school and in adjustment, or whether children's maladaptive behavior (e.g., aggression) leads to both peer rejection and problems in adjustment (Parker, Rubin, Price, & DeRosier, 1995; Woodward & Fergusson, 1999). Although conclusive evidence is not yet available, findings suggest that peer status and the quality of children's social behavior have partially independent effects on subsequent adjustment (Coie et al., 1992; DeRosier et al., 1994). Thus, it is likely that children's maladaptive behavior and their peer status both play a causal role in their future adjustment—separately and in combination (Fergusson, Woodward, & Horwood, 1999).

Once children are rejected by peers, they may be denied opportunities for positive peer interactions and thus for learning social skills. Moreover, cut off from desirable peers, they may be forced to associate with other rejected children, and rejected children may teach one another, and mutually reinforce, deviant norms and behaviors. The lack of social support from peers also may increase rejected children's vulnerablity to the effects of stressful life experiences (e.g., poverty, parental conflict, divorce), negatively influencing their social behavior even further, which in turn affects both their peer status and adjustment.

review:

Children's sociometric status is assessed by peers' reports of their liking and disliking of one another. On the basis of such reports, children typically have been classified as popular, rejected, average, neglected, or controversial.

Well-liked, popular children tend to be attractive, socially skilled, prosocial, well regulated, and low in aggression that is driven by anger, vengefulness, or satisfaction in hurting others. However, some children who are viewed as popular by their peers are aggressive and not especially well-liked. Some rejected children tend to be relatively aggressive, disruptive, and low in social skills; they also tend to make hostile attributions about others' intentions and have trouble dealing with difficult social situations in a constructive manner. Withdrawn children who are aggressive and hostile as well are also rejected by peers by kindergarten age. In contrast, most children who are withdrawn from their peers but are not hostile and aggressive are at somewhat less risk, although they sometimes become rejected later in elementary school.

Neglected children interact less frequently with peers than do children who are average in sociometric status, and they display relatively few behaviors that differ greatly from those of many other children. Controversial children display characteristics of both popular and rejected children and tend to be very socially active. Children who are neglected or controversial, unlike rejected children, are particularly likely to change their status, even over short periods of time.

Rejection by peers in childhood—especially rejection due to aggression—predicts relatively high levels of subsequent academic problems and externalizing behaviors. Rejected children also tend to become more withdrawn and are prone to loneliness and depression. It is likely that children's maladaptive behavior as well as their low status with peers contribute to these negative developmental outcomes.

The Role of Parents in Children's Peer Relationships

Cliff is having a hard time, . . . he just doesn't have any good friends, says he has no one to do things with . . . he's just not part of the gang. . . . I hate to see him having troubles with the other kids—I keep wondering if I should do something about it, or if he just has to sort it out hisself. . . . And it reminds me of *my* troubles at school.

(quoted in Dunn, personal communication)

The speaker, the mother of 8-year-old Cliff, not only worries about Cliff's problems with his peers but also feels that she may have contributed to them—a common reaction of parents of lonely and rejected children. The idea that parents influence children's ability to relate to peers has a long history, beginning with Freud's emphasis on the importance of the mother–child relationship as a foundation for later personality development and interpersonal relationships. Moreover, attachment theorists (see Chapter 11) as well as social learning theorists (see Chapter 9) have asserted that early parent–child interactions are linked to children's peer interactions at an older age. It also seems likely that children's ongoing relationships with their parents can affect their relationships with their peers.

Relations Between Attachment and Competence with Peers

Attachment theory maintains that whether a child's attachment to the parent is secure or insecure affects the child's future social competence and the quality of the child's relationships with others, including peers. Attachment theorists have suggested that a secure attachment between parent and child promotes competence with peers in at least three ways (Elicker, Englund, & Sroufe, 1992). First, children with a secure attachment develop positive social expectations. They thus are inclined to interact readily with other children and expect these interactions to be positive and rewarding. Second, because of their experience with a sensitive and responsive caregiver, they develop the foundation for understanding reciprocity in relationships. Consequently, they learn to give and take in relationships and to be empathic to others. Finally, children who are securely attached are likely to be confident, enthusiastic, and emotionally positive—characteristics that are attractive to other children and that facilitate social interaction.

BOB DAEMMRICH / STOCK BOSTON

Children who have secure attachment relationships with their parents tend to develop better social skills than do their peers who are not securely attached.

Conversely, attachment theorists argue, an insecure attachment is likely to impair a child's competence with peers. If parents are rejecting and hostile or neglectful, young children are likely to become hostile themselves and to expect negative behavior from other people. They may be predisposed to perceive peers as hostile and, consequently, are likely to be aggressive toward them. These children also may expect rejection from other people and may try to avoid experiencing it by withdrawing from peer interaction (Furman, Simon, Shaffer, & Bouchey, 2002; Renken, Egeland, Marvinney, Sroufe, & Mangelsdorf, 1989).

There is a good deal of evidence to support these theoretical views. Children who do not experience sensitive, responsive parenting and who are not securely attached do, in fact, tend to have difficulties with peer relationships (Fagot, 1997).

Toddlers and preschoolers who were insecurely attached as infants tend to be aggressive, whiny, socially withdrawn, and low in popularity in elementary school (Bohlin, Hagekull, & Rydell, 2000; Burgess, Marshall, Rubin, & Fox, 2003; Erickson, Sroufe, & Egeland, 1985). Throughout childhood, these children, in comparison with securely attached children, express less positive emotion with peers, as well as less sympathy and prosocial behavior, and they demonstrate poorer skills in resolving conflicts (Elicker et al., 1992; Fox & Calkins, 1993; Kestenbaum, Farber, & Sroufe, 1989; Raikes & Thompson, 2008).

Securely attached children, on the other hand, tend to exhibit positive emotions and good social skills and, not surprisingly, tend to be relatively popular with peers—both as preschoolers (La Freniere & Sroufe, 1985) and in elementary school and adolescence (Granot & Mayseless, 2001; Kerns, Klepac, & Cole, 1996; Schneider, Atkinson, & Tardif, 2001). Even in late elementary school, children with more and higher-quality (e.g., more intimate and supportive) friendships tend to be those with a history of a secure attachment (Freitag, Belsky, Grossman, Grossman, & Scheuerer-Englisch, 1996; Schneider, Atkinson, & Tardif, 2001; Simpson, Collins, Tran, & Haydon, 2007).

Thus, security of the parent–child relationship is linked with quality of peer relationships. This link probably arises from both the early and the continuing effect that parent–child attachment has on the quality of the child's overall social behavior. However, it is also possible that characteristics of children, such as sociability, influence both the quality of their attachments and the quality of their relationships with peers.

Quality of Ongoing Parent–Child Interactions and Peer Relationships

Ongoing parent–child interactions are associated with peer relations in much the same way that attachment patterns are. For example, socially competent, popular children tend to have mothers who discuss feelings with them and who use warm control, positive verbalizations, reasoning, and explanations in their approach to parenting (Hart, DeWolf, Wozniak, & Burts, 1992; Lindsey & Mize, 2001; McDowell & Parke, 2009; Raver, Gershoff, & Aber, 2007). This association may occur because such parenting fosters children's self-regulation (Eiden, Colder, Edwards, & Leonard, 2009). Unpopular children, on the other hand, often experience harsh, authoritarian discipline, and their activities tend to go relatively unmonitored (Dishion, 1990; Hart, Ladd, & Burleson, 1990).

In general, fathers' parenting practices appear to be somewhat less related to children's social competence and sociometric status than do mothers' (Eisenberg, Fabes, & Murphy, 1996; Hart et al., 1992). However, the degree to which fathers are affectionate and express positive rather than negative emotions toward their children does predict the positiveness of preschoolers' interactions with close friends (Kahen, Katz, & Gottman, 1994; Youngblade & Belsky, 1992). In addition, boys whose fathers play with them are better liked by peers than are boys whose fathers do not play with them. This may partly be because the rough-and-tumble nature of typical father–son play helps boys learn to interpret others' emotions, and to regulate their own, in physically arousing play (MacDonald & Parke, 1984; Pettit, Brown, Mize, & Lindsey, 1998).

In considering findings such as these, it is generally assumed that quality of parenting influences the degree to which children behave in socially competent ways, which in turn affects whether or not children are accepted by peers. But as in the case of attachment, it is difficult to prove that quality of parenting actually has a causal influence on children's social behavior with peers. It may be that children who are aggressive and disruptive because of constitutional factors (e.g., heredity, prenatal influences) elicit both negative parenting and negative peer responses (Rubin, Nelson, Hastings, & Asendorpf, 1999) (see Chapters 3 and 12); or it may be that both harsh parenting and the children's negative behavior with peers are due to heredity. The most likely possibility is that the causal links are bidirectional—that parents' behavior affects their children's social competence and vice versa—and that both environmental and biological factors play a role in the development of children's social competence with peers.

Parental Beliefs and Behaviors

Parents of socially competent children think about parenting and their children somewhat differently than do parents of children who have low social competence. For one thing, they are more likely to believe that they should play an active role in teaching their children social skills and in providing them with opportunities for peer interaction. They also tend to believe that when their children display inappropriate or maladaptive behavior with a peer (e.g., aggression, hostility, social withdrawal), it is because of the circumstances of the *specific situation,* such as a provocation by the peer or a mutual misunderstanding. In contrast, parents of less socially competent children tend to believe that when their children behave in socially inappropriate ways, it is because of something in their children's nature and that it would thus be very hard to alter such behavior (Rubin et al., 2006). In other words, they tend to believe that their children "were born that way." Of course, it is difficult to know the degree to which parents' beliefs about their children's social competencies are based on realistic perceptions of their offspring or on their own belief systems and personal history (such as the troubles Cliff's mother experienced when she was a schoolchild).

Parents' beliefs about their children's social competence often are reflected in the way they respond to their children. Mothers of children who are socially withdrawn with peers tend to attribute their children's withdrawal to immaturity or character weaknesses, and they react by being protective and trying to solve their children's social problems for them (Mills & Rubin, 1993). Whenever a peer tries to take a toy from their child, for instance, they may scold the peer or remove their child from the play situation. In contrast, mothers of socially competent children would be more likely to give their children a chance to deal with the peer by themselves. Thus, as a result of their beliefs about their children's social competencies, parents often may promote their children's socially adaptive or maladaptive behavior with peers.

Parents may contribute to their children's development of social competence by arranging opportunities for their children to interact with peers.

MICHAEL NEWMAN / PHOTOEDIT

Gatekeeping, Coaching, and Modeling by Parents

Several other dimensions of parent–child interactions may influence children's competencies in peer relationships. These include parents' gatekeeping role in their children's social life, their coaching of social skills, and their modeling of social behavior.

Gatekeeping

As noted in Chapter 12, parents, especially those of young children, act as gatekeepers, controlling where their children go, with whom they interact, and how much time they spend with peers doing various activities. However, some parents are more thoughtful and active in this role than are others (Mounts, 2002). Preschoolers whose parents arrange and oversee opportunities for them to interact with peers tend to be more positive and social with peers, have a larger and more stable set of play partners, and more easily initiate social interactions with peers than do other children—so long as their parents are not overly controlling in this gatekeeping role (Ladd & Golter, 1988; Ladd & Hart, 1992).

Coaching

Preschool children also tend to be more popular if their parents effectively coach them in how to deal with unfamiliar peers. Mothers of accepted children tend to teach their children group-oriented strategies for gaining entry into a group of peers: they may make suggestions about what to say when entering the group, for example, or they may discourage the child from disrupting the group's current activities. In contrast, mothers of children who are low in sociometric status often try to direct the group's activity themselves or urge their child to initiate activities that are inconsistent with what the group is currently doing (Finnie & Russell, 1988; Russell & Finnie, 1990). For reasons that are not yet clear, mothers' coaching may be especially important for enhancing girls' social skills (Pettit et al., 1998).

Modeling

Another way that parents influence their children's competence with peers is by modeling either socially competent or incompetent behaviors (Russell, Pettit, & Mize, 1998). The way they communicate with their children, for example, appears to influence the communication style their children adopt with peers. Parents of rejected children tend to talk at them at length, to talk over them when they are trying to talk, and to respond to them in ways that are unrelated to what their children have just said. Such a parent might ask, "Do you want to go to the park today?" and then say something like "Oh, did your sister have fun last night?" in response to the child's answer. Rejected children, in turn, tend to converse with their peers in a similar manner, talking at the same time as their peers and saying things that do not maintain the thread of the conversation. In contrast, popular children, like their parents, are more likely to engage in turn taking and to stay on the topic in their conversations with peers (Black & Logan, 1995). Thus, children's imitation of their parents' style of conversation may affect the quality of their interactions with, and acceptance by, peers. Children's imitation of parents' behaviors with their friends may account for the fact that the quality of parents' friendships and those of their children tend to be similar (Simpkins & Parke, 2001).

Children who frequently observe their parents express negative emotion—especially hostile, assertive, negative emotion—tend to express more negative emotion themselves and to be less socially skilled than their peers.

TONY FREEMAN / PHOTOEDIT

Family Stress and Children's Social Competence

As discussed in Chapter 12 (page 476), parents who are preoccupied and distressed by problems related to poverty are more likely to be negative and less

FIGURE 13.6 Percentages of children rejected by peers as a function of gender and family income As can be seen in these data from a longitudinal study, elementary school children from families with low incomes are considerably more likely to be rejected than are children from middle-class families. (Adapted from Patterson, Griesler, Vaden, & Kupersmidt, 1992)

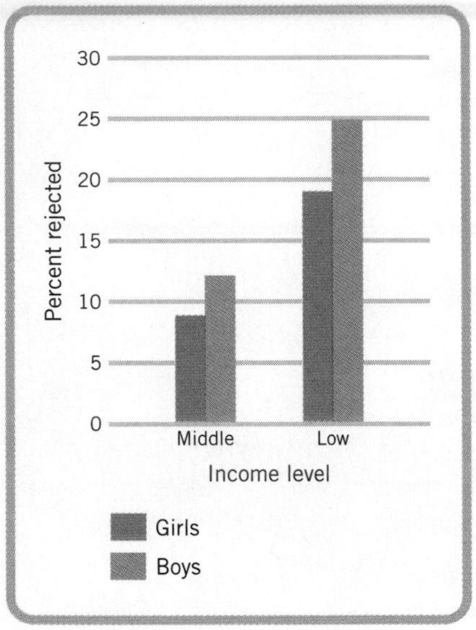

likely to be warm and supportive and to monitor their children's behavior (Lengua, Honorado, & Bush, 2007; McLoyd, 1998; McLoyd, Jayaratne, Ceballo, & Borquez, 1994). Thus, it is not surprising that children from families with fewer economic resources and higher levels of stress (e.g., unemployment, health problems) exhibit less social competence, have fewer friends, and are more likely than other children to be rejected by their peers (Brophy-Herb, Lee, Nievar, & Stollak, 2007; Criss et al., 2002; Dishion, 1990; Patterson, Griesler, Vaden, & Kupersmidt, 1992).

This pattern of findings is illustrated by the data in Figure 13.6, which are from a longitudinal study. In this study, elementary school children from low-income families were considerably more likely to be rejected than were children from middle-class families (boys also were rejected more than girls). Of course, prejudice toward children of lower SES may partly account for this pattern of findings (Eder, 1985). However, it is also likely that the effects of poverty and stress on parenting are reflected in children's compromised social competence.

Marital conflict is another form of family stress that has been associated with the quality of children's peer interactions. In one study, when marital conflict in the home was high, 36-month-olds engaged in more unfriendly and aggressive interactions with peers in day care and displayed less complex types of play and fewer sociable, positive play interactions (Lindsey, Caldera, & Tankersley, 2009). This pattern held especially when the mother–child or father–child attachment was insecure. Moreover, it appeared that marital conflict may have impaired the security of the parent–child attachment and increased the exchange of negative emotions between parent and child; this, in turn, predicted lower-quality behavior with peers. Therefore, the effects of marital conflict on the quality of children's peer interactions was likely due, in part, to compromised interactions between parents and children when the level of marital conflict was high.

review:

Although differences in children's social behavior likely are based in part on constitutional factors that influence temperament and personality, parents appear to influence children's competence with peers. Attachment theorists have suggested that a secure attachment between parent and child promotes peer competence because securely attached children develop positive social expectations, the foundation for understanding reciprocity in relationships, and a sense of self-worth and self-efficacy. In fact, securely attached children tend to be more positive in their behavior and affect, more socially skilled, and better liked than insecurely attached children. Ongoing parent–child interactions show similar associations with peer relations.

Parents can also influence their children's competence with peers through their beliefs, their role as gatekeepers, and the social behaviors they teach and model for their children. It is probable that the causal links between quality of parenting and children's social competence are bidirectional and that both environmental (e.g., parenting, divorce, poverty) and biological factors play a role in the development of children's social competence with peers.

Chapter Summary

What Is Special About Peer Relationships?

- Theorists such as Piaget, Vygotsky, and Sullivan have argued that the equality, reciprocity, cooperation, and intimacy that characterize many peer relationships enhance children's ability to reason and their concern for others.

Friendships

- Consistent with theorists' arguments, peers, especially friends, provide intimacy, support, and rich opportunities for the development of play and for exchange of ideas.
- Even very young children prefer some children over others. Toddlers engage in more complex and cooperative play with friends than with nonfriends, and those who engage in such play exhibit more positive and social behavior with peers when they are older.
- As children grow, friends rely on one another and increasingly provide a context for self-disclosure and intimacy. Adolescent friends, more than younger friends, use friendship as a context for self-exploration, personal problem solving, and as a source of honest feedback.
- Children's conceptions of friends change with age. Young children define friendship primarily on the basis of actual activities with their peers. With age, issues such as loyalty, mutual understanding, trust, cooperative reciprocity, and self-disclosure become important components of friendship.
- As was suggested by Piaget, Vygotsky, and Sullivan, friends provide emotional support; validation or confirmation of the legitimacy of one's own thoughts, feelings, and worth; and opportunities for the development of important social and cognitive skills.
- Having friends is associated with positive developmental outcomes, such as social competence and adjustment. However, friends also may have negative effects on children if they engage in problematic behaviors such as violence or substance abuse.
- Intervention programs can be helpful in teaching children social skills. One common approach, social skills training, involves teaching children skills related to three types of deficits: lack of social knowledge, problems in performing appropriate behaviors, and a lack of appropriate monitoring and self-evaluation. Many recent programs include procedures to foster children's understanding and communication of emotion and their self-regulation.
- Children tend to become friends with peers who are similar in age, sex, and race and who are similar in behaviors such as aggression, sociability, and cooperativeness.
- The degree to which adults encourage children to play with unrelated peers varies greatly in different cultures, as does the degree to which parents expect their children to develop social skills with peers (e.g., negotiating, taking initiative, standing up for their rights). In addition, the hours children spend with unrelated peers varies considerably across cultures.

Peers in Groups

- The size of very young children's playgroups increases with age, and dominance hierarchies emerge by preschool age.
- By middle childhood, most children belong to cliques of same-sex peers, and members of cliques often are similar in their aggressiveness and orientation toward school. Membership in these cliques is not very stable over time.
- In adolescence, the importance of cliques tends to diminish, and adolescents tend to belong to more than one group. With increasing age, adolescents are not only more autonomous but also tend to look more to individual relationships rather than to a social group to fulfill their social needs. Nonetheless, adolescents often are members of crowds. In adolescence, girls and boys associate with one another more with increasing age, both as members of social groups and in dyadic relationships.
- In some circumstances, the peer group may contribute to the development of antisocial behavior, alcohol consumption, and substance use, although youths may also seek out peers who engage in similar levels of these behaviors.

Status in the Peer Group

- On the basis of their sociometric ratings, children typically have been classified as popular, rejected, neglected, average, or controversial.
- Children's status in the larger peer group varies as a function of their social behavior and thinking about their social interactions, as well as their physical attractiveness.
- Popular children—those who rank high on sociometric measures—tend to be socially skilled, prosocial, and well regulated in their expression of emotion and behavior. In contrast, children who are perceived as popular in terms of high status often are aggressive and not always well liked.
- Children who are rejected by their peers often (but not always) are aggressive and/or socially withdrawn. Rejected-aggressive children are low in social skills, tend to make hostile attributions about others' intentions, and have trouble coming up with constructive strategies for dealing with difficult social situations. Withdrawn children who are rejected during preschool tend to be aggressive and hostile.

- Children who are withdrawn from their peers but are not hostile or aggressive are at less risk for rejection during the early school years, although they tend to become rejected later in elementary school. Withdrawn behavior seems to become a more important predictor of peer rejection with increasing age in childhood.
- Neglected children—those who are not nominated by peers as either liked or disliked—tend to be less sociable, aggressive, and disruptive than average children. They display relatively few behaviors that differ greatly from those of many other children.
- Controversial children tend to have characteristics of both popular and rejected children: they tend to be aggressive, disruptive, and prone to anger, as well as helpful, cooperative, sociable, good at sports, and humorous.
- Although children's status with their peers frequently changes over time, those children who are rejected frequently remain rejected. Children who are neglected or controversial are particularly likely to change their status, even over short periods of time.
- In general, in numerous cultures, children who are popular or rejected share similar characteristics. However, reticent behavior may be more valued in some East Asian cultures and has, at least until recently, been related in China to others' perceptions of a child's social competence.
- Rejection by peers in childhood—especially rejection due to aggression—predicts subsequent academic problems, delinquency, substance abuse, social withdrawal, and loneliness and depression. Children who are consistently withdrawn, reticent, and wary with familiar people, including peers, are more likely than less withdrawn children to experience internalizing problems such as depression, low self-worth, and loneliness concurrently and at older ages. It is likely that children's maladaptive behavior and their peer status both play a causal role in their future adjustment—separately and in combination.

The Role of Parents in Children's Peer Relationships

- Consistent with the predictions of attachment theorists, securely attached children tend to be more positive in their behavior and affect, more socially skilled, and better liked than insecurely attached children.
- Parents of socially competent and popular children are more likely than parents of less competent children to use warm control, positive verbalizations, reasoning, and explanations in interactions with their children. They also hold more positive beliefs about their children's abilities. It is likely that the causal links between quality of parenting and children's social competence are bidirectional and that both environmental and biological factors play a role in the development of children's social competence with peers.
- Parents are the gatekeepers of young children's peer interactions in the sense that they organize and control their children's social experiences.
- Parents explicitly teach and model behaviors that children can adopt in their social interactions with peers—such as methods of influencing others and dealing with conflicts.
- Stressors such as poverty and marital conflict appear to have a negative effect on the quality of parenting, which in turn is linked to low peer competence in children.

Critical Thinking Questions

1. What are some of the ways in which same-aged peer relationships and relationships with older or younger siblings might differ? On what dimensions are they typically the same? What might Piaget and Vygotsky say about the different costs and benefits of interactions with same-aged friends and differently-aged siblings?
2. What procedures and methods might someone use to assess which 2-year-old playmates in a group are close friends? How would these methods be the same or different if one were assessing close friendships at ages 6, 11, and 17?
3. List at least five ways in which interactions among friends and among nonfriends in elementary school likely differ (e.g., type of activities, style of interaction). In what ways might such differences, if they exist, influence children's socioemotional development?
4. Consider a child who is growing up in an isolated area with few peers nearby and is being schooled at home. In what ways might his or her daily experience differ from that of children attending school? How might this affect his or her development, positively or negatively? What factors might mitigate or increase these effects?

Key Terms

peers, p. 506
friendships, p. 507
reciprocated best friendship, p. 512
cliques, p. 519
crowds, p. 520
gang, p. 521
sociometric status, p. 524
popular peer status, p. 524
relational aggression, p. 525
rejected peer status, p. 525
aggressive-rejected children, p. 525
withdrawn-rejected children, p. 526
neglected peer status, p. 527
social skills training, p. 528
controversial peer status, p. 529
victimized peer status, p. 532

VICTOR GILBERT, *Make Believe*

14

Moral Development

THEMES

Nature and Nurture

❖

The Active Child

❖

Continuity/Discontinuity

❖

Mechanisms of Change

❖

The Sociocultural Context

❖

Individual Differences

❖

Research and Children's Welfare

❖

In April 1999, Eric Harris and Dylan Klebold, two students at Columbine High School in Littleton, Colorado, killed a dozen students and a teacher and injured 23 other persons. As terrible as this incident was, it could have been much worse. The two adolescents, who had planned the massacre carefully for months, had actually prepared 95 explosive devices, which did not go off due to an electronic failure. One set of explosives was placed a few miles from school and was supposed to explode to distract the police while Harris and Klebold carried out the attack at the school. The second set was supposed to go off in the cafeteria, killing many students and forcing others to flee into the schoolyard, where Harris and Klebold had planned to hide in wait and gun them down. The third set of explosives was planted in the killers' cars in the school parking lot. It was timed to explode after the police and paramedics arrived on the scene, causing more death and chaos. In videotapes made weeks before the attacks, the boys gleefully predicted that they would kill 250 people and bragged about the publicity they would get for their actions. They also made it clear that their attack was payback for having been humiliated and rejected by their peers: on one videotape, Harris, holding a sawed-off shotgun, declared, "Isn't it fun finally to get the respect that we are going to deserve?" (quoted in Aronson, 2000, p. 86).

One might think that Harris and Klebold had suffered terrible childhoods. Yet, from all reports, their parents were probably more supportive than the average parents. And although the pair did endure considerable peer rejection at Columbine, Harris, at least, was a fairly popular student at his school in Plattsburgh, New York, before he moved to Littleton. Explanations for why Harris and Klebold did what they did are not as simple as they might initially seem.

In striking contrast to the lethally self-centered actions of Harris and Klebold, in the midst of the carnage, some students stayed with and tried to assist a teacher and other students who were shot. One boy running for his life helped a badly wounded girl get to an exit. Another boy draped himself over his sister and her friend so that he would be the one to be shot (Gibbs, 1999). These students were concerned with others' lives even when their own were at risk.

The Columbine tragedy, and subsequent incidents like it, are additions to a long list of incidents that raise questions about why some adolescents become involved

GARY CASKEY / REUTERS NEW MEDIA INC. / CORBIS

Although many contributing factors to the Columbine tragedy have been identified, the precise reasons for the actions of Harris and Klebold may never be known. As you will discover in this chapter, moral development—and whether an individual is inclined to prosocial or aggressive, antisocial behavior—depends on the interaction of a great many variables.

in antisocial and illegal behavior, ranging from vandalism and other forms of delinquency to horrific violent crime. The starting point for finding answers to these questions is understanding aspects of children's thinking and behavior that contribute to morality.

To act in moral ways on a regular basis, children must have an understanding of right and wrong and the reasons that actions are moral or immoral. In addition, they must have a conscience, that is, they must be concerned about acting in a moral manner and feel guilty when they do not. When studying moral development, researchers have focused on a number of different questions related to these requirements. How do children think about moral issues and how does this thinking change with age? Does children's reasoning about moral issues relate to their behavior? How early do caring and sharing, or aggression and cruelty, first appear in children? What factors contribute to differences among children in the degree to which they display helpful and caring or antisocial behaviors? Can steps be taken to help children develop caring and helpful behavior and reduce the likelihood of their developing immoral or antisocial behaviors?

We start our discussion of moral development by examining children's moral judgment—that is, how children think about situations involving moral decisions. Then we examine findings on the early emergence of conscience and the development of *prosocial* behaviors—behaviors such as helping and sharing that benefit others. Next, we turn to aggression and other antisocial behaviors such as stealing. As you will see, children's moral development is influenced by advances in their social and cognitive capacities, as well as by genetic factors and environmental factors, including family and cultural influences. Therefore, the themes of *individual differences, nature and nurture,* and the *sociocultural context* will be prominent in our discussions. In addition, theory and research on moral judgment grew out of Piaget's work in this area, which, like his theory on cognitive development (see Chapter 4), involves stages of development and assumes that children actively try to understand the world around them. Consequently, the themes of *continuity/discontinuity, mechanisms of change,* and the *active child* are evident in our consideration of the development of moral judgment. Also in play is the theme of *research and children's welfare,* as we survey intervention programs that are designed to promote prosocial thinking and behavior and prevent antisocial behavior.

Moral Judgment

The morality of a given action cannot be determined at face value. Consider a girl who steals food to feed her starving sister. Stealing is usually regarded as an immoral behavior, but obviously the morality of this girl's behavior is not so clear. Or consider an adolescent male who offers to help fix a peer's bike but does so because he wants to borrow it later, or perhaps wants to find out if the bike is worth stealing. Although this adolescent's behavior may appear altruistic, it is ambiguous at best in the first instance and clearly immoral in the second. These examples illustrate that the morality of a behavior is based partly on the cognitions—including conscious intentions and goals—that underlie the behavior.

Indeed, some psychologists (as well as philosophers and educators) believe that the reasoning behind a given behavior is critical for determining whether that behavior is moral or immoral, and they maintain that changes in moral reasoning form the basis of moral development. As a consequence, much of the research on children's moral development has focused on how children think when they try to

Piaget (1932/1965) argued that in games such as marbles, children learn that rules are a creation of human beings—that they are not absolute but are interpreted, and they can be changed, by the consensus of the peer group.

resolve moral conflicts and how their reasoning about moral issues changes with age. The most important contributors to the current understanding of the development of children's moral reasoning are Piaget and Lawrence Kohlberg, both of whom took a cognitive developmental approach to studying the development of morality.

Piaget's Theory of Moral Judgment

The foundation of cognitive theories about the origin of morality is Piaget's book *The Moral Judgment of the Child* (1932/1965). In it, Piaget describes how children's moral reasoning changes from a rigid acceptance of the dictates and rules of authorities to an appreciation that moral rules are a product of social interaction and hence are modifiable. Piaget believed that interactions with peers, more than adult influence, account for advances in children's moral reasoning.

Piaget initially studied children's moral reasoning by observing children playing games, such as marbles, in which they often deal with issues related to rules and fairness. In addition, Piaget interviewed children to examine their thinking about issues such as transgressions of rules, the role of intentionality in morality, fairness of punishment, and justness when distributing goods among people. In these open-ended interviews, he typically presented children with pairs of short vignettes such as the following:

> A little boy who is called John is in his room. He is called to dinner. He goes into the dining room. But behind the door there was a chair, and on the chair there was a tray with fifteen cups on it. John couldn't have known that there was all this behind the door. He goes in, the door knocks against the tray, bang go the fifteen cups, and they all get broken!
>
> Once there was a little boy whose name was Henry. One day when his mother was out he tried to get some jam out of the cupboard. He climbed up on to a chair and stretched out his arm. But the jam was too high up and he couldn't reach it and have any. But while he was trying to get it he knocked over a cup. The cup fell down and broke.
>
> (Piaget, 1932/1965, p. 122)

After children heard these stories, they were asked which boy was naughtier and why. Children younger than 6 years old typically said that the child who broke 15 cups was naughtier. In contrast, older children said that the child who was trying to sneak jam was naughtier, even though he broke only one cup. Based partly on children's responses to such vignettes, Piaget concluded that there are two stages of development in children's moral reasoning, as well as a transitional period between the stages.

The Stage of the Morality of Constraint

The first stage of moral reasoning, referred to as the *morality of constraint,* is most characteristic of children who have not achieved Piaget's stage of concrete operations—that is, children younger than 7 years old (see Chapter 4). Children in this stage regard rules and duties to others as unchangeable "givens." In their view, justice is whatever authorities (adults, rules, or laws) say is right, and authorities' punishments are always justified. Acts that are not consistent with rules and authorities' dictates are "bad"; acts that are consistent with them are "good." It is in this stage that children believe that what determines whether an action is good or bad is the consequences of the action, not the motives or intentions behind it.

Piaget suggested that young children's belief that rules are unchangeable is due to two factors, one social and one cognitive. First, Piaget argued that parental control of children is coercive and unilateral, leading to children's unquestioning respect for rules set by adults. Second, children's cognitive immaturity causes them to believe that rules are "real" things, like chairs or gravity, that exist outside people and are not the product of the human mind.

The Transitional Period

According to Piaget, the period from about age 7 or 8 to age 10 represents a transition from the morality of constraint to the next stage. During this transitional period, children typically have more interactions with peers than previously, and these interactions are more egalitarian, with more give-and-take, than are their interactions with adults. In games with peers, children learn that rules can be constructed and changed by the group. They also increasingly learn to take one another's perspective and to cooperate. As a consequence, children start to value fairness and equality and begin to become more autonomous in their thinking about moral issues. Piaget viewed children as taking an active role in this transition, using information from their social interactions to figure out how moral decisions are made and how rules are constructed.

The Stage of Autonomous Morality

By about age 11 or 12, Piaget's second stage of moral reasoning emerges. In this stage, referred to as the stage of *autonomous morality* (also called *moral relativism*), children no longer accept blind obedience to authority as the basis of moral decisions. They fully understand that rules are the product of social agreement and can be changed if the majority of a group agrees to do so. In addition, they consider fairness and equality among people as important factors to consider when constructing rules. Children at this stage also believe that punishments should "fit the crime" and that punishment delivered by adults is not necessarily fair. They also consider individuals' motives and intentions when evaluating their behavior; thus, they view breaking one cup while sneaking jam as worse than accidentally breaking 15 cups.

According to Piaget, all normal children progress from the morality of constraint to autonomous moral reasoning. Individual differences in the rate of their progress are due to numerous factors, including differences in children's cognitive maturity, in their opportunities for interactions with peers and for reciprocal role taking, and in how authoritarian and punitive their parents are.

Evaluation of Piaget's Theory

Piaget's general vision of moral development has received some support from empirical research. Studies of children from many countries and various racial or ethnic groups have shown that with age, boys and girls increasingly take motives and intentions into account when judging the morality of actions (Berg & Mussen, 1975; Lickona, 1976). In addition, parental punitiveness, which would be expected to reinforce a morality of constraints, has been associated with less mature moral reasoning and moral behavior (Hoffman, 1983). Finally, consistent with Piaget's belief that cognitive development plays a role in the development of moral judgment, children's performance on tests of perspective-taking skills, Piagetian logical tasks, and IQ tests have all been associated with their level of moral judgment (Berg & Mussen, 1975; Lickona, 1976).

Some aspects of Piaget's theory, however, have been soundly faulted. For example, there is little evidence that peer interaction per se stimulates moral development (Lickona, 1976). Rather, it seems likely that the quality of peer interactions—for example, whether or not they involve cooperative interactions—is more important than mere quantity of interaction with peers. In addition, Piaget underestimated young children's ability to appreciate the role of intentionality in morality. For example, many, though not all, 4- and 5-year-olds do *not* think that a person caused a negative outcome "on purpose" if they have been explicitly told that the person had no foreknowledge of the consequences of his or her action or believed that the outcome of the action would be positive rather than negative (Pellizzoni, Siegal, & Surian, 2009).

In addition, when Piagetian moral vignettes are presented in ways that make the individuals' intentions more obvious—such as by using videotaped dramas—preschoolers and early elementary school children recognize that individuals with bad intentions are naughtier than those with benign intentions (Chandler, Greenspan, & Barenboim, 1973; Grueneich, 1982; Yuill & Perner, 1988). (It is likely that in Piaget's research, young children focused primarily on the consequences of the individuals' actions because consequences were emphasized and very salient in his stories.) Moreover, as you will see later in the chapter, it is clear that young children do not believe that some actions, such as hurting others, are right even when adults say they are.

Whatever its shortcomings, Piaget's theory provided the basis for subsequent research on the development of moral judgment. The most notable example is the more complex and differentiated theory of moral development formulated by Lawrence Kohlberg.

Kohlberg's Theory of Moral Judgment

Heavily influenced by the ideas of Piaget, Kohlberg (1976; Colby & Kohlberg, 1987a) was primarily interested in the sequences through which children's moral reasoning develops. On the basis of a 20-year longitudinal study in which he first assessed children's moral reasoning at ages 10, 13, and 16, Kohlberg proposed that moral development proceeds through a specific series of stages that are discontinuous and hierarchical. That is, each new stage reflects a qualitatively different, more adequate way of thinking than the one before it.

Kohlberg, like Piaget, argued that stages of moral reasoning involve a qualitative change in reasoning and that each stage represents a new way of thinking that replaces the child's thinking at prior, lower levels.

Kohlberg assessed moral judgment by presenting children with hypothetical moral dilemmas and then questioning them about the issues these dilemmas involved. The most famous of these dilemmas concerns a man named Heinz, whose wife was dying from a special kind of cancer:

> There was one drug that the doctors thought might save her. It was a form of radium that a druggist in the same town had recently discovered. The drug was expensive to make, but the druggist was charging 10 times what it cost him to make. The sick woman's husband, Heinz, went to everyone he knew to borrow the money and tried every legal means, but he could only get together about $2,000, which is half of what it cost. He told the druggist his wife was dying, and asked him to sell it cheaper or let him pay later. But the druggist said, "No, I discovered the drug and I'm going to make money from it." So having tried every legal means, Heinz gets desperate and considers breaking into the man's store to steal the drug for his wife.
>
> (Colby & Kohlberg 1987b, p. 1)

LEE LOCKWOOD / TIMEPIX

After relating this dilemma to children, Kohlberg asked them questions such as, Should Heinz steal the drug? Would it be wrong or right if he did? Why? Is it a husband's duty to steal the drug for his wife if he can get it no other way? For Kohlberg, the reasoning behind choices of what to do in the dilemma, rather than the choices themselves, is what reflects the quality of their moral reasoning. For example, the response that "Heinz should steal the drug because he probably won't get caught and put in jail" was considered less advanced than "Heinz should steal the drug because he wants his wife to feel better and to live."

Kohlberg's Stages

On the basis of the reasoning underlying children's responses, Kohlberg proposed three levels of moral judgment—preconventional, conventional, and postconventional, or principled. *Preconventional moral reasoning* is self-centered: it focuses on getting rewards and avoiding punishment. *Conventional moral reasoning* is centered on social relationships: it focuses on compliance with social duties and laws. *Postconventional moral reasoning* is centered on ideals: it focuses on moral principles. Each of these three levels involves two stages of moral judgment (see Table 14.1). However, so few people ever attained Stage 6 (Universal Ethical Principles) of the postconventional level that Kohlberg (1978) eventually stopped scoring it as a separate stage, and many theorists consider it an elaboration of Stage 5 (Lapsley, 2006).

Delinquents tend to use lower-level reasoning than do nondelinquents (Nelson, Smith, & Dodd, 1990). For example, they tend to justify their choice of action in moral conflicts with reasoning based on punishment for "getting caught" or self-gain.

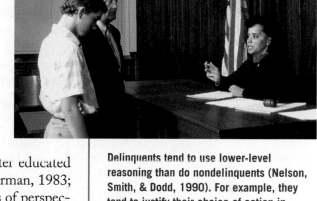

Kohlberg argued that people in all parts of the world move through his stages in the same order, although they differ in how many stages they attain. As in Piaget's theory, age-related advances in cognitive skills, especially perspective taking, are believed to underlie the development of higher-level moral judgment. Consistent with Kohlberg's theory, people who have higher level cognitive skills and who are better educated exhibit higher-level moral judgment (Colby, Kohlberg, Gibbs, & Lieberman, 1983; Mason & Gibbs, 1993; Rest, 1983). Children who exhibit higher levels of perspective taking than their peers also score higher in their moral judgment.

In their initial research, Kohlberg and his colleagues (Colby et al., 1983) studied only boys, whom they followed into adulthood. As shown in Figure 14.1, moral judgment changed systematically with age. When the boys were 10 years old, they

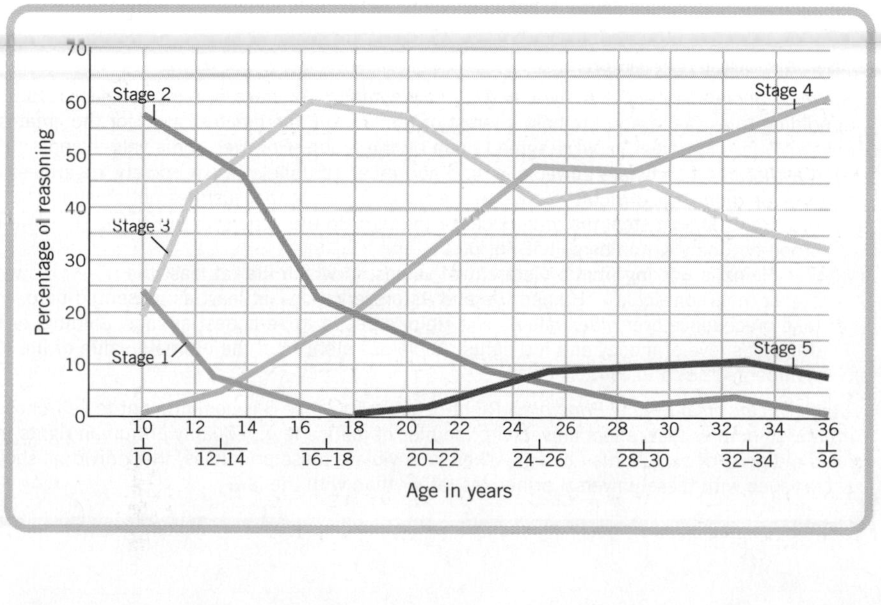

FIGURE 14.1 Mean percentage of moral reasoning at each stage for each age group **This graph shows age trends in moral reasoning in Kohlberg's longitudinal sample. (Adapted from Colby et al., 1983)**

TABLE 14.1

Kohlberg's Levels and Stages of Moral Reasoning

Preconventional Level

Stage 1: Punishment and Obedience Orientation. At Stage 1, what is seen as right is obedience to authorities. Children's "conscience" (what makes them decide what is right or wrong) is fear of punishment, and their moral action is motivated by avoidance of punishment. The child does not consider the interests of others or recognize that they differ from his or her own interests. Examples of reasoning for (pro) and against (con) Heinz's stealing the drug for his wife are as follows:

Pro: If you let your wife die, you will get in trouble. You'll be blamed for not spending the money to save her and there'll be an investigation of you and the druggist for your wife's death.

Con: You shouldn't steal the drug because you'll be caught and sent to jail if you do. If you do get away, your conscience would bother you thinking how the police would catch up with you at any minute (Kohlberg, 1969, p. 381).

Stage 2: Instrumental and Exchange Orientation. At Stage 2, what is right is what is in one's own best interest or involves equal exchange between people (tit-for-tat exchange of benefits).

Pro: If you do happen to get caught, you could give the drug back and you wouldn't get much of a sentence. It wouldn't bother you much to serve a little jail term, if you have your wife when you get out.

Con: He may not get much of a jail term if he steals the drug, but his wife will probably die before he gets out so it won't do him much good. If his wife dies, he shouldn't blame himself, it wasn't his fault she has cancer (Kohlberg, 1969, p. 381).

Conventional Level

Stage 3: Mutual Interpersonal Expectations, Relationships, and Interpersonal Conformity ("Good Girl, Nice Boy") Orientation. In Stage 3, good behavior is doing what is expected by people who are close to the person or what people generally expect of someone in a given role (e.g., "a son"). Being "good" is important in itself and means having good motives, showing concern about others, and maintaining good relationships with others.

Pro: No one will think you're bad if you steal the drug, but your family will think you're an inhuman husband if you don't. If you let your wife die, you'll never be able to look anybody in the face again.

Con: It isn't just the druggist who will think you're a criminal, everyone else will, too. After you steal it, you'll feel bad thinking how you've brought dishonor on your family and yourself; you won't be able to face anyone again (Kohlberg, 1969, p. 381).

Stage 4: Social System and Conscience ("Law and Order") Orientation. Right behavior in Stage 4 involves fulfilling one's duties, upholding laws, and contributing to society or one's group. The individual is motivated to keep the social system going and to avoid a breakdown in its functioning.

Pro: In most marriages, you accept the responsibility to look after one another's health and after their life and you have the responsibility when you live with someone to try and make it a happy life (Colby & Kohlberg, 1987b, p. 43).

In the revised coding manual, Colby and Kohlberg (1987b) provide virtually no examples of Stage 4 reasoning supporting the decision that Heinz should not steal the drug for his wife. However, they provide reasons for not stealing the drug for a pet: Heinz should not steal for a pet because animals cannot contribute to society (p. 37).

Postconventional or Principled Level

Stage 5: Social Contract or Individual Rights Orientation. At Stage 5, right behavior involves upholding rules that are in the best interest of the group ("the greatest good for the greatest number"), are impartial, or were agreed upon by the group. However, some values and rights, such as life and liberty, are universally right and must be upheld in any society, regardless of majority opinion. It is difficult to construct a Stage 5 reason that justifies not stealing the drug.

Pro: Heinz should steal the drug because the right to life supersedes or transcends the right to property (Colby & Kohlberg, 1987b, p. 11).

Pro: Heinz is working from a hierarchy of values, in which life (at least the life of his wife) is higher than honesty. . . . Human life and its preservation—at least as presented here—must take precedence over other values, like Heinz's desire to be honest and law abiding, or the druggist's love of money and his rights. All values stem from the ultimate value of life (Colby & Kohlberg, 1987b, p. 54).

Stage 6: Universal Ethical Principles. Right behavior in Stage 6 is commitment to self-chosen ethical principles that reflect universal principles of justice (e.g., equality of human rights, respect for the dignity of each human being). When laws violate these principles, the individual should act in accordance with these universal principles rather than with the law.

used primarily Stage 1 reasoning (blind obedience to authority) and Stage 2 reasoning (self-interest). Thereafter, reasoning in these stages dropped off markedly. For most adolescents aged 14 and older, Stage 3 reasoning (being "good" to earn approval or maintain relationships) was the primary mode of reasoning, although some adolescents occasionally used Stage 4 reasoning (fulfilling duties and upholding laws to maintain social order). Only a small number of participants, even by age 36, ever achieved Stage 5 (upholding the best interests of the group while recognizing life and liberty as universal values).

There appears to be a modest degree of association between people's level of moral reasoning and the moral level of their behavior. For example, people with higher-level moral reasoning are more likely to behave in a moral manner (Kohlberg & Candee, 1984) and to assist others (Blasi, 1980) and are less likely to engage in delinquent activities (Stams et al., 2006).

Critique of Kohlberg's Theory

Kohlberg's work is important because it demonstrated that children's moral judgment changes in relatively systematic ways with age. In addition, because individuals' levels of moral judgment have been related to their moral behavior, especially for people reasoning at higher levels (e.g., Kutnick, 1985; Underwood & Moore, 1982), Kohlberg's work has been useful in understanding how cognitive processes contribute to moral behavior.

Kohlberg's theory and findings have also produced controversy and criticism. One issue pertains to cultural differences. Although children in many non-Western, nonindustrialized cultures start out reasoning much the way Western children do in Kohlberg's scoring system, their moral judgment within this system generally does not advance as far as that of their Western peers (e.g., Nisan & Kohlberg, 1982; Snarey, 1985). This finding has led to the criticism that Kohlberg's stories and scoring system reflect an intellectualized conception of morality that is biased by Western values (Simpson, 1974). In many non-Western societies, in which the goal of preserving group harmony is of critical importance and most conflicts of interest are worked out through face-to-face contact, issues of individual rights and civil liberties may not be viewed as especially relevant. Moreover, in some societies, obedience to authorities, elders, and religious dictates are valued more than principles of freedom and individual rights.

Another criticism has to do with Kohlberg's argument that change in moral development is discontinuous. Kohlberg asserted that because each stage is more advanced than the previous one, once an individual attains a new stage, he or she seldom reasons at a lower stage. However, research has shown that children and adults alike often reason at different levels on different occasions—or even on the same occasion (Rest, 1979). As a consequence, it is not clear that the development of moral reasoning is qualitatively discontinuous. Rather, children and adolescents may gradually acquire the cognitive skills to use increasingly higher stages of moral reasoning but also may use lower stages when it is consistent with their goals, motives, or beliefs in a particular situation. For example, even an adolescent who is capable of using Stage 4 reasoning may well use Stage 2 reasoning to justify a decision to break the law for personal gain.

A hotly debated issue regarding Kohlberg's theory is whether there are gender differences in moral judgment. As noted previously, Kohlberg developed his conception of moral-reasoning stages on the basis of interviews with a sample of boys. Carol Gilligan (1982) argued that Kohlberg's classification of moral judgment is

prosocial behavior voluntary behavior intended to benefit another, such as helping, sharing, and comforting of others

biased against females because it does not adequately recognize differences in the way males and females reason morally. Gilligan suggested that because of the way they are socialized, males tend to value principles of justice and rights, whereas females value caring, responsibility for others, and avoidance of exploiting or hurting others (Gilligan & Attanucci, 1988). This difference in moral orientation, according to Gilligan, causes males to score higher on Kohlberg's dilemmas than females do.

Contrary to Gilligan's theory, there is little evidence that boys and girls, or men and women, score differently on Kohlberg's stages of moral judgment (Turiel, 1998; Walker, 1984, 1991). However, consistent with Gilligan's arguments, during adolescence and adulthood, females focus somewhat more on issues of caring about other people in their moral judgment (Garmon, Basinger, Gress, & Gibbs, 1996; Jaffee & Hyde, 2000). Differences in males' and females' moral reasoning seem to be most evident when individuals report on moral dilemmas in their own lives (Jaffee & Hyde, 2000). Thus, Gilligan's work has been very important in broadening the focus of research on moral reasoning and in demonstrating that males and females differ somewhat in the issues they focus on when confronting moral issues.

Although Kohlberg's stages probably are not as invariant in sequence nor as universal as he claimed, they do describe changes in children's moral reasoning that are observed in many Western societies. These changes are important because people who reason at higher stages are somewhat more likely to behave in moral ways—such as helping others. Thus, understanding developmental changes in moral judgment provides insight into why, as children grow older, they tend to engage in more prosocial behavior.

Prosocial Moral Judgment

When children respond to Kohlberg's dilemmas, they are choosing between two acts that are wrong—for example, stealing or allowing someone to die. However, there are other types of moral dilemmas in which the choice is between personal advantage versus fairness to, or the welfare of, others (Damon, 1977; Eisenberg, 1986; Skoe, 1998).

To determine how children resolve these dilemmas, researchers present children with stories in which the characters must choose between helping someone or meeting their own needs. These dilemmas are called *prosocial* moral dilemmas and concern **prosocial behavior**—that is, voluntary behavior intended to benefit another, such as helping, sharing, and comforting of others. The following story illustrates the type of dilemma that has been used with children age 4 or older (with slight modifications for the latter group):

> One day a boy named Eric was going to a friend's birthday party. On his way he saw a boy who had fallen down and hurt his leg. The boy asked Eric to go to his house and get his parents so the parents could come and take him to a doctor. But if Eric did run and get the child's parents, he would be late to the birthday party and miss the ice cream, cake, and all the games.
>
> What should Eric do? Why?
>
> (Eisenberg-Berg & Hand, 1979, p. 358)

On these tests, children and adolescents use five stages of prosocial moral reasoning, delineated by Eisenberg (1986), that resemble Kohlberg's stages (see Table 14.2). Preschool children express primarily hedonistic reasoning (Level 1) in which their own needs are central. They typically indicate that Eric should go to the party because he wants to. However, preschoolers also often mention others' physical needs, which suggests that some preschoolers are concerned about other people's welfare

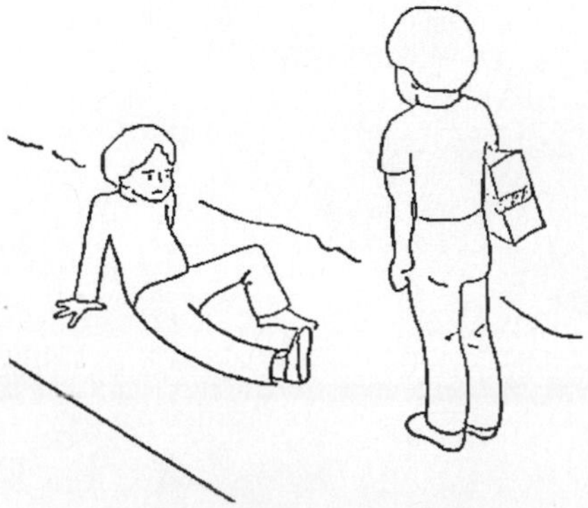

COURTESY OF NANCY EISENBERG

This is one of the pictures that accompany the prosocial moral-reasoning vignette of Eric's birthday-party dilemma.

TABLE 14.2

Levels of Prosocial Behavior

Level 1: Hedonistic, self-focused orientation. The individual is concerned with his or her own interests rather than with moral considerations. Reasons for assisting or not assisting another include direct personal gain, future reciprocation, and concern for the other based on need or affection. (Predominant mode primarily for preschoolers and younger elementary school children.)

Level 2: Needs-based orientation. The individual expresses concern for the physical, material, and psychological needs of others even when those needs conflict with his or her own. This concern is expressed in the simplest terms, without clear evidence of self-reflective role taking, verbal expressions of sympathy, or reference to such emotions as pride or guilt. (Predominant mode for many preschoolers and many elementary school children.)

Level 3: Approval and/or stereotyped orientation. The individual justifies engaging or not engaging in prosocial behavior on the basis of others' approval or acceptance and/or on stereotyped images of good and bad persons and behavior. (Predominant mode for some elementary school and high school students.)

Level 4a: Self-reflective empathic orientation. The individual's judgments include evidence of self-reflective sympathetic responding or role taking, concern with the other's humanness, and/or guilt or positive emotion related to the consequences of one's actions. (Predominant mode for a few older elementary school children and many high school students.)

Level 4b: Transitional level. The individual's justifications for helping or not helping involve internalized values, norms, duties, or responsibilities. They may also reflect concerns for the condition of the larger society or refer to the necessity of protecting the rights and dignities of other persons. These ideals, however, are not clearly or strongly stated. (Predominant mode for a minority of people of high school age or older.)

Level 5: Strongly internalized stage. The individual's justifications for helping or not helping are based on internalized values, norms, or responsibilities; the desire to maintain individual and societal contractual obligations or improve the condition of society; and the belief in the rights, dignity, and equality of all individuals. This level is also characterized by positive or negative emotions related to whether or not one succeeds in living up to one's own values and accepted norms. (Predominant mode for only a small minority of high school students.)

Adapted from Eisenberg (1986)

(Level 2). (For example, they may indicate that Eric should help because the other boy is bleeding or hurt.) Such recognition of others' needs increases in the elementary school years. In addition, in elementary school, children increasingly express concern about social approval and acting in a manner that is considered "good" by other people and society (e.g., they indicate that Eric should help "to be good"; Level 3).

In late childhood and adolescence, children's judgments begin to be based, in varying degrees, on perspective taking (Level 4a—e.g., "Eric should think about how he would feel in that situation") and morally relevant affect such as sympathy, guilt, and positive feelings due to the real or imagined consequences of performing beneficial actions (e.g., "Eric would feel bad if he didn't help and the boy was in pain"). The judgments of a minority of older adolescents reflect internalized values and affect (Levels 4b and 5) related to not living up to those values (e.g., self-censure).

In general, this pattern of changes in prosocial moral reasoning has been found for children in Brazil, Germany, Israel, and Japan (Carlo, Koller, Eisenberg, Da Silva, & Frohlich, 1996; Eisenberg, Boehnke, Schuhler, & Silbereisen, 1985; Fuchs, Eisenberg, Hertz-Lazarowitz, & Sharabany, 1986; Munekata & Ninomiya, 1985). Nevertheless, children from different cultures do vary somewhat in their prosocial moral reasoning. For example, older children (and adults) in some traditional societies in Papua New Guinea exhibit higher-level reasoning less often than do people in Western cultures. However, the types of reasoning they frequently use—reasoning that pertains to others' needs and the relationship between people—are consistent with the values of a culture in which people must cooperate with one another in face-to-face interactions in order to survive (Tietjen, 1986). In nearly all cultures, reasoning that reflects the needs of others and global concepts of good and bad behavior (Kohlberg's Stage 3 and Eisenberg's Level 3) emerges at somewhat younger ages on prosocial dilemmas than on Kohlberg's moral dilemmas.

To measure a child's prosocial moral reasoning, a researcher presents the child with a story that reflects a prosocial moral dilemma. In response to the story about a child on the way to a party who sees an injured boy, a typical response of many 9- or 10-year-olds is, "Help because the boy's leg is hurt and he needs to go to a doctor."

MICHAEL NEWMAN / PHOTOEDIT

With age, children's prosocial moral judgment, like their reasoning on Kohlberg's moral dilemmas, becomes more abstract and based more on internalized principles and values (Eisenberg, 1986; Eisenberg, Carlo, Murphy, & Van Court, 1995). Moreover, paralleling the case with moral reasoning on Kohlberg's measure, those children, adolescents, and young adults who use higher-level prosocial moral reasoning tend to be more sympathetic and prosocial in their behavior than are peers who use lower-level prosocial moral judgment (Eisenberg, 1986; Eisenberg, Miller et al., 1991; Janssens & Dekovic, 1997).

Domains of Social Judgment

In everyday life, children make decisions about many kinds of actions, including whether to follow rules and laws or break them, whether to fight or walk away from conflict, whether to dress formally or informally, whether to study or goof off after school, and so on. Some of these decisions involve *moral judgments;* others involve *social conventional judgments;* and still others involve *personal judgments* (Nucci, 1981; Turiel, 2006).

Moral judgments pertain to issues of right and wrong, fairness, and justice. **Social conventional judgments** pertain to customs or regulations intended to ensure social coordination and social organization, such as choices about modes of dress, table manners, and forms of greeting (e.g., using "Sir" when addressing a male teacher). **Personal judgments** pertain to actions in which individual preferences are the main consideration. For example, within Western culture, the choice of friends or recreational activities usually is considered a personal choice (Nucci & Weber, 1995). These distinctions are important because whether children perceive particular judgments as moral, social conventional, or personal affects the importance they accord them.

Children's Use of Social Judgment

In many cultures, children begin to differentiate between moral and social conventional issues at an early age (Miller & Bersoff, 1992; Nucci, Camino, & Sapiro, 1996; Tisak, 1995). By age 3, they generally believe that moral violations (e.g., stealing another child's possession or hitting another child) are more wrong than social conventional violations (e.g., not saying "please" when asking for something or wearing other-gender clothing). By age 4, they believe that moral transgressions, but not social conventional transgressions, are wrong even if an adult does not know about them and even if adult authorities have not said they are wrong (Smetana & Braeges, 1990). This distinction is reflected in the following excerpt from an interview with a 5-year-old boy:

> *Interviewer:* This is a story about Park School. In Park School the children are allowed to hit and push others if they want. It's okay to hit and push others. Do you think it is all right for Park School to say children can hit and push others if they want to?
> *Boy:* No. It is not okay.
> *Interviewer:* Why not?
> *Boy:* Because that is like making other people unhappy. You can hurt them that way. It hurts other people, hurting is not good.

This boy is firm in his belief that hurting others is wrong, even if adults say it is acceptable. Children tend to justify their condemnation of moral violations by referring to violations of fairness and harm to others' welfare (Turiel, 2008). Compare

moral judgments decisions that pertain to issues of right and wrong, fairness, and justice

social conventional judgments decisions that pertain to customs or regulations intended to secure social coordination and social organization

personal judgments decisions that refer to actions in which individual preferences are the main consideration that reasoning with the boy's response to a question about the acceptability of a school policy that allows children to take off their clothes in hot weather.

> *Interviewer:* I know another school in a different city. . . . Grove School . . . At Grove School the children are allowed to take their clothes off if they want to. Is it okay or not okay for Grove School to say children can take their clothes off if they want to?
> *Boy:* Yes. Because this is the rule.
> *Interviewer:* Why can they have that rule?
> *Boy:* If that's what the boss wants to do, he can do that. . . . He is in charge of the school.
>
> (Turiel, 1987, p. 101)

With regard to both moral and social conventional issues in the family, children and, to a lesser degree, adolescents, believe that parents have authority (Smetana, 1988, Yau, Smetana, & Metzger, 2009). With respect to matters of personal judgment, however, even preschoolers tend to believe that they themselves should have control, and older children and adolescents are quite firm in their belief that they should control choices in the personal domain (e.g., their appearance, how they spend their money, and their choice of friends) at home and school. At the same time, parents usually feel that they should have some authority over their children's personal choices, even into adolescence, so parents and teenagers frequently do battle in this domain—battles that parents often lose (Lins-Dyer & Nucci, 2007; Smetana, 1988; Smetana & Asquith, 1994).

Cultural and Socioeconomic Differences

People in different cultures sometimes vary in whether they view decisions as moral, social conventional, or personal (Shweder, Mahapatra, & Miller, 1987). Take the question of one's obligation to attend to the minor needs of parents and the moderate needs of friends or strangers. Hindu Indians believe that they have a clear moral obligation to attend to these needs (Miller, Bersoff, & Harwood, 1990). In contrast, Americans appear to consider it a matter of personal choice or a combination of moral and personal choice. This difference in perceptions may be due to the strong cultural emphasis on individual rights in the United States and the emphasis on duties to others in India (Killen & Turiel, 1998; Miller & Bersoff, 1995).

Cultural differences with regard to which events are considered moral, social conventional, or personal sometimes arise from religious beliefs (Turiel, 2006; Wainryb & Turiel, 1995). For example, Hindus in India believe that if a widow eats fish, she has committed an immoral act. In Hindu society, fish is viewed as a "hot" food, and eating "hot" food is believed to stimulate the sexual appetite. Consequently, traditional Hindu adults and children assume that a widow who eats fish will behave immorally and offend her husband's spirit. Underlying this belief is the obligation that Hinduism places on a widow to seek salvation and be reunited with the soul of her husband rather than initiating another relationship (Shweder et al., 1987). Of course, for most other people in the world, a widow's eating fish would be considered a matter of personal choice. Thus, beliefs regarding the significance and consequences of various actions in different cultures can influence the designation of behaviors as moral, social conventional, or personal.

Socioeconomic class can also influence the way children make such designations. Research in the United States and Brazil indicates that children

Children in India are much more likely than children in the United States to say that helping other people is a moral obligation, not a matter of personal choice.

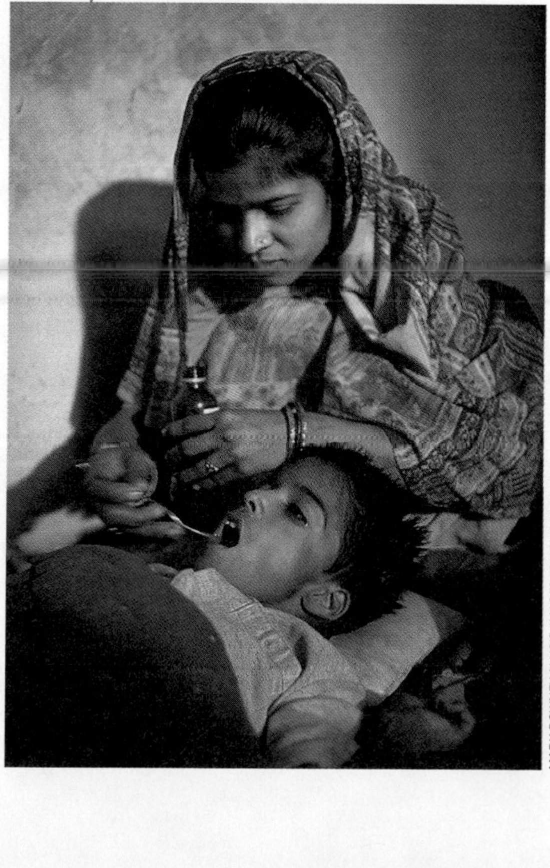

MARK DOWNEY / LUCID IMAGES / PICTUREQUEST

of lower-income families are somewhat less likely than middle-class children to differentiate sharply between moral and social conventional actions and, prior to adolescence, to view personal issues as a matter of choice. These differences may be due to the tendency of individuals of low socioeconomic status both to place a greater emphasis on submission to authority and to allow children less autonomy (Nucci, 1997). This social-class difference in children's views may evaporate as youths approach adolescence, although Brazilian mothers of lower-income youths still claim more control over personal issues than do mothers of middle-income youths (Lins-Dyer & Nucci, 2007).

review:

How children think about moral issues provides one basis for their moral or immoral behavior. Piaget delineated two moral stages—morality of constraint and autonomous morality—separated by a transitional stage. In the first stage, children regard rules as fixed and tend to weigh consequences more than intentions in evaluating actions. According to Piaget, a combination of cognitive growth and egalitarian, cooperative interactions with peers brings children to the autonomous stage, in which they recognize that rules can be changed by group consent and judge the morality of actions on the basis of intentions more than consequences. Aspects of Piaget's theory have not held up well to criticism—for example, children use intentions to evaluate behavior at a younger age than he believed—but his theory provided the foundation for Kohlberg's work on stages of moral reasoning.

Kohlberg outlined three levels of moral judgment—preconventional, conventional, and postconventional—each initially containing two stages (Stage 6 was subsequently dropped). He hypothesized that his sequence of stages reflected age-related discontinuous changes in moral reasoning with age and that children everywhere go through the same stages (although they may stop development at different points). Several aspects of Kohlberg's theory are controversial, including whether children's moral reasoning moves through discontinuous stages of development; whether the theory is valid for all cultures; and whether there are gender differences in moral judgment. Research on other types of moral judgment such as prosocial moral judgment suggests that children's concerns about the needs of others emerge at a younger age than Kohlberg's work indicates. However, with age, prosocial moral reasoning, like Kohlberg's justice-oriented moral reasoning, seems to become more abstract and based on internalized principles.

There are important differences among the moral, social conventional, and personal domains of behavior and judgment—differences that even children know. For example, young children believe that moral transgressions, but not social conventional or personal violations, are wrong regardless of whether adults say they are unacceptable. There are some cultural differences in whether a given behavior is viewed as having moral implications, but it is likely that people in all cultures differentiate among moral, social conventional, and personal domains of functioning.

The Early Development of Conscience

We all are familiar with the notion of a conscience—that voice inside us that pushes us to behave in moral ways and makes us feel guilty if we do not. Stated more formally, **conscience** is an internal regulatory mechanism that increases the individual's ability to conform with standards of conduct accepted in his or her culture. Consistent with Freud's theory (see Chapter 9), it is likely that the conscience of a young child reflects primarily internalized parental standards (although probably the standards of both parents, not just of the same-gender parent). The conscience restrains antisocial behavior or destructive impulses and

conscience an internal regulatory mechanism that increases the individual's ability to conform to standards of conduct accepted in his or her culture promotes a child's compliance with adults' rules and standards, even when no one is monitoring the child's behavior (Kochanska, 2002). The conscience also can promote prosocial behavior by causing the child to feel guilty when engaging in uncaring behavior or failing to live up to internalized values about helping others (Eisenberg, 2000; Hoffman, 1982).

Factors Affecting the Development of Conscience

Although Freud maintained that the conscience emerges as an outcome of identification with the same-gender parent at about age 4 to 6, children actually develop a conscience slowly over time. By age 2, toddlers start to show an appreciation for moral standards and rules and begin to exhibit signs of guilt when they do something wrong (Kopp, 2001; Zahn-Waxler & Robinson, 1995). These two components of conscience—the desire to comply with rules and moral emotion such as guilt—are quite stable in their early development from 22 to 45 months of age (Aksan & Kochanska, 2005; Kochanska, Gross, Lin, & Nichols, 2002). As they mature, children are more likely to take on their parents' moral values, and to exhibit guilt for violating those values, if their parents use disciplinary practices that deemphasize parental power, including rational explanations that help children understand and learn the parents' values (Kochanska & Aksan, 2006; Laible, Eye, & Carlo, 2008; Volling, Mahoney, & Rauer, 2009). Children's adoption of their parents' values is also facilitated by a secure, positive parent–child relationship, which inclines children to be open to, and eager to internalize, their parents' communication of their values (Bretherton, Golby, & Cho, 1997; Kochanska, Barry, Aksan, & Bolt, 2008; Kochanska, Forman, Aksan, & Dunbar, 2005).

Children may develop a conscience in different ways according to their temperament. Toddlers who are prone to fear (e.g., who are fearful of unfamiliar people or situations) tend to exhibit more guilt at a young age than do less fearful children (Kochanska et al., 2002). Moreover, for those infants who are prone to fear, the development of conscience seems to be promoted by the mother's use of gentle discipline that includes reasoning with the child and providing nonmaterial incentives for compliance (Kochanska & Aksan, 2006). When mothers use gentle discipline, fearful children do not become so apprehensive and anxious that they tune out their mother's messages about desired behavior. Gentle discipline arouses fearful children just enough that they attend to and remember what their mother tells them (Kochanska, 1993).

In contrast, gentle discipline seems to be unrelated to the development of conscience in fearless young children, perhaps because it is insufficient to arouse their attention (Kochanska, 1997a). What does seem to foster the development of conscience in fearless children is a parent–child relationship characterized by secure attachment and mutual cooperation (Kochanska & Aksan, 2006). Fearless children appear motivated more by the desire to please their mother than by a fear of her (Kochanska, 1997b). Unfortunately, research on this topic seldom has been conducted with fathers, so it is not known if the findings for the effects of mothers' discipline generalize to fathers' discipline.

SUSIE FITZHUGH

If disciplined in a harsh manner, children who are temperamentally fearful are likely to become too distressed to get their parents' disciplinary message. For such children, parental reasoning is more likely to promote the development of guilt and internalized (i.e., willing and eager) compliance with parental rules and demands.

The early development of conscience doubtlessly contributes to whether children come to accept the moral values of their parents and society; indeed, guilt at 22 and 45 months of age predicts children's morality at 54 months of age (Kochanska et al., 2002), which in turn predicts whether they engage in hurtful or problematic social behavior at 67 months (Kochanska et al., 2008). Therefore, the nature of early parent–child disciplinary interactions sets the stage for children's subsequent moral development.

review: The conscience is believed to reflect internalized moral standards; it restrains the child from engaging in immoral behavior and involves feelings of guilt for misbehavior. Contrary to Freud's beliefs, the conscience emerges slowly over time, beginning before age 2. Children are more likely to internalize parental standards if they have secure attachments with their parents and if their parents use rational explanations in their discipline rather than excessive parental power. Factors that promote the development of conscience differ somewhat for children with different temperaments.

Prosocial Behavior

As we noted earlier, moral behavior is as important for moral development as are moral thinking and moral emotions. The same is true for prosocial behavior; all children are capable of prosocial behaviors, but children differ in how often they engage in these behaviors and in their reasons for doing so. Consider the behavior of the following three preschool children:

> Sara is drawing a picture and has a box of crayons. Erin is sitting across from her, and wants to draw. But Erin has only a single crayon and all the rest are in use by other children. She looks around for crayons of other colors. After a short time, Erin looks somewhat distressed. Sara notices that Erin is looking for crayons and is distressed, so she smiles and hands Erin a few of her own crayons, saying, "Here, do you want to use these?"
>
> Marc is sitting at a table drawing with crayons when Manuel comes over and wants to draw. Manuel can't find any crayons and shows signs of upset. Marc looks at Manuel and then returns to his own drawing. Finally, Manuel asks Marc, "Can I have some crayons?" At first Marc ignores Manuel. After Manuel asks for crayons again, Marc hands Manuel three crayons without any comment or display of emotion.
>
> Sakina is drawing when Darren comes to the table, picks up a piece of paper, and looks around for crayons. When Darren can't find any, he exhibits mild distress and then asks Sakina for some crayons. Sakina just ignores him. When Darren tries to take a crayon that Sakina is not using, Sakina angrily pushes him away.
>
> (Eisenberg, unpublished laboratory observations)

ELIZABETH CREWS

In their second year, most children share objects with their parents and with other children (Hay, Castle, Stimson, & Davies, 1995).

Seeing that someone else is sad or in distress, Sara gladly shares without even being asked. Marc shares only if asked repeatedly. Sakina doesn't share at all and does not seem to care if other children are upset. Do these differences in behavior forecast consistent differences in Sara's, Marc's, and Sakina's positive moral behavior as they are growing up?

The answer is yes: there is some developmental consistency in children's readiness to engage in prosocial behaviors, such as sharing, helping, and comforting (Eisenberg & Fabes, 1998; Knafo et al., 2008). In fact, children who, like Sara, share spontaneously with peers tend to be more concerned with others' needs throughout childhood and adolescence and even in early adulthood. One study found that, in comparison with their peers, for example, they were more likely to assist other people even when doing so involved a cost to themselves. As young adults, they reported that they felt responsible for the welfare of others and that they usually tried to suppress aggression toward others when angered. This view of themselves was supported by friends, who rated them as more sympathetic than study participants who engaged in less spontaneous prosocial behavior in preschool (Eisenberg, Guthrie et al., 1999; Eisenberg, Guthrie et al., 2002). In contrast, children like Sakina are unlikely to be concerned with others' needs and feelings when they are older.

altruistic motives helping others for reasons that initially include empathy or sympathy for others and, at later ages, the desire to act in ways consistent with one's own conscience and moral principles

Of course, not all prosocial behaviors are of equal worth. Compare Qing's sharing of crayons, for instance, with Sara's:

> Qing is drawing and has lots of crayons. Michael sits down, wants to draw, and looks for crayons. He is upset when he can't find any. When he asks Qing for some of her crayons, she says, "I'll give you some crayons if you give me some of your paper."
>
> (Eisenberg, unpublished laboratory observations)

Qing is willing to share, but only for a price. Similarly, some children may help or share to gain social acceptance from peers or to avoid their anger ("I'll share my doll if you'll be my friend"). However, most parents and teachers want children to perform prosocial behaviors not for rewards or social approval but for altruistic motives. **Altruistic motives** initially include empathy or sympathy for others and, at later ages, the desire to act in ways consistent with one's own conscience and moral principles (Eisenberg, 1986).

The Development of Prosocial Behavior

The origins of altruistic prosocial behavior are rooted in the capacity to feel empathy and *sympathy*. As discussed in Chapter 10, *empathy* is an emotional reaction to another's emotional state or condition (e.g., sadness, poverty) that is highly similar to (or consistent with) the other person's state or condition (Eisenberg, 1986; Hoffman, 2000). For example, if a child becomes sad upon observing another person's sadness or pain, the child is experiencing empathy. To experience empathy, children must be able to identify the emotions of others (at least to some degree) and understand that another person is feeling an emotion or is in some kind of need.

RICK RICKMAN / MATRIX

This group of boys shaved their heads to show their sympathy, support, and solidarity with their friend (middle) who was being treated for cancer. Children's ability to sympathize with others appears to increase somewhat with age in early and middle childhood.

ELIZABETH CREWS

ANDY COX / GETTY IMAGES

Young children who view another child's distress sometimes respond with looks of concern or attempts to console or help the distressed peer—about 20% of the time in a study of 16- to 33-month-olds (Howes & Farver, 1987). Even young infants sometimes show interest in a peer's distress.

Sympathy is a feeling of concern for another in reaction to the other's emotional state or condition. Although sympathy often is an outcome of empathizing with another's negative emotion or negative situation, what distinguishes sympathy from empathy is the element of concern: people who experience sympathy for another person are not merely feeling the same emotion as the other person.

An important factor contributing to empathy or sympathy is, obviously, the ability to take the perspective of others. Although early theorists such as Piaget believed that children are unable to do this until age 6 to 7 (Piaget & Inhelder, 1956), it is now clear that children have some ability to understand others' perspectives much earlier (Vaish, Carpenter, & Tomasello, 2009). Some children as young as 6 months old show interest in a peer's distress by leaning or gesturing toward, or touching, the distressed peer (Hay, Nash, & Pedersen, 1981). By 10 to 14 months of age, children sometimes become disturbed and upset when they view other people who are upset (Knafo et al., 2008):

> Jenny [a 14-month-old] observed a crying 6-month-old baby. She watched; tears welled in her eyes; she began to cry.
>
> (Radke-Yarrow & Zahn-Waxler, 1984)

Of course, it may be that infants are not really sympathizing with others' distress; they may become upset merely because they do not differentiate clearly between another person's emotional distress and their own (Hoffman, 1990). Indeed, young children such as Jenny sometimes seek comfort from a parent when they see someone else upset. Or children may be upset both for another person and for themselves (Zahn-Waxler, Radke-Yarrow, & King, 1979).

By 18 to 25 months of age, toddlers in laboratory studies sometimes exhibit concern and share with an adult whose property has been destroyed or taken away, even when the victim does not express an emotional reaction (Vaish et al., 2009). They are also more likely to try to comfort someone who is upset than to become upset themselves, indicating that they know who it is that is suffering. Consider the following example:

> A neighbor's baby cries. Jenny (18 months old) looked startled, her body stiffened. She approached and tried to give the baby cookies. She followed him around and began to whimper herself. She then tried to stroke his hair, but he pulled away. Later, she approached her mother, led her to the baby, and tried to put mother's hand on the baby's head. He calmed down a little, but Jenny still looked worried. She continued to bring him toys and to pat his head and shoulders.
>
> (Radke-Yarrow & Zahn-Waxler, 1984, p. 89)

Martin Hoffman (2000) argued that although young children may be able to take others' perspective in terms of feelings of distress, their efforts to help or comfort are often egocentric. Thus, they are apt to help others in ways that they themselves would like to be helped, not in ways that are most helpful to the other person. For example, a young child who sees a friend in distress may fetch his or her own security blanket rather than that of the distressed friend. However, as children become better able to understand how others think and feel, their helping behavior becomes more sensitive and appropriate for the other person's needs.

In the second and third years of life, the frequency and variety of young children's prosocial behaviors increase. Children not only increasingly comfort others (see Table 14.3) and share objects but also assist adults with various tasks such as sweeping, carrying objects, or setting the table (Rheingold, 1982; Warneken, Chen, & Tomasello, 2006). Moreover, their prosocial behaviors at home often seem to be motivated by concern for others because they frequently show expressions of sympathy when they help or comfort others (Knafo, Zahn-Waxler, van Hulle, Robinson, & Rhee, 2008; Radke-Yarrow & Zahn-Waxler, 1984). As is shown in Table 14.3, 25% of 23 to 25 month olds showed concern when they observed someone in distress that they had not caused themselves.

As should be clear from the table, however, young children do not regularly act in prosocial ways (Lamb & Zakhireh, 1997). Between the ages of 2 and 3, children most often ignore their siblings' distress or need, or they simply watch without intervening. Occasionally, they even make the situation worse with teasing or aggression (Dunn, 1988; see "Aggressive behavior" in Table 14.3). In one study of children in a play-group setting, 16- to 33-month-olds responded to peers' distress only 22% of the time, usually by attempting to intervene on the peer's behalf, comforting the peer, or bringing the peer's distress to the attention of the caregiver (Howes

MARGARET ROSS / STOCK BOSTON

Young children sometimes respond to another's distress with self-focused discomfort or anxiety. Children who experience such personal distress tend to be motivated to make themselves, not the other person, feel better.

TABLE 14.3

Mothers' Reports of the Proportion of Times Children Responded to Others' Distress During the Second Year of Life

	When the child witnesses another's distress			When the child caused another's distress		
	13–15 months	18–20 months	23–25 months	13–15 months	18–20 months	23–25 months
Prosocial behavior	.09	.21	.49	.07	.10	.52
Empathy or sympathy	.09	.10	.25	.03	.03	.14
Aggressive behavior	.01	.01	.03	.01	.04	.19
Self-distress (personal distress)	.15	.12	.07	.34	.41	.33

Adapted from Zahn-Waxler, Radke-Yarrow, Wagner, & Chapman (1992)

& Farver, 1987). Consistent with our discussion in Chapter 13, these children were much more likely to help a friend than to help a child who was not a friend (Eisenberg, Fabes, & Spinrad, 2006; Fujisawa, Kutsukake, & Hasegawa, 2008).

Even at age 3 to 4, children are more inclined to act in selfish than in prosocial ways, although this selfishness decreases with age in the preschool and early school years (Fehr, Bernhard, & Rockenbach, 2008). Children's prosocial behaviors such as helping, sharing, and donating increase in frequency in the toddler years and from the preschool years to adolescence. Older adolescents (e.g., 16-year-olds) are more likely than younger children to share and donate toys or money at a cost to themselves. Thus, in general, children engage in more prosocial behavior with age (Eisenberg & Fabes, 1998; Knafo et al., 2008).

The Origins of Individual Differences in Prosocial Behavior

Although children's prosocial behaviors change with age, consistent with the theme of *individual differences,* there is great variation among children of the same age in their propensity to help, share with, and comfort others. Recall the behaviors of Sara, Marc, and Sakina, the three children described earlier in this chapter. Why do children of the same ages differ so much in their prosocial behavior? To identify the origins of these individual differences, we must consider the themes of *nature and nurture* and *sociocultural context.*

Biological Factors

Many biologists and psychologists have proposed that humans are biologically predisposed to be prosocial (Hastings, Zahn-Waxler, & McShane, 2005). They believe that humans have evolved the capacity for empathy and altruism because these traits increase the likelihood of an individual's genes being passed on to the next generation (Hoffman, 1981). According to this view, people who help others are more likely than less helpful people to be assisted when they themselves are in need and, thus, are more likely to survive and reproduce (Trivers, 1983). In addition, assisting those with whom they share genes increases the likelihood that those genes will be passed on to the next generation (Wilson, 1975). Evolutionary explanations for prosocial behavior, however, pertain to the human species as a whole and do not explain individual differences in empathy, sympathy, and prosocial behavior.

Nonetheless, genetic factors do contribute to individual differences in these characteristics. In twin studies with adults, twins' reports of their own empathy and prosocial behavior are considerably more similar for identical twins than for fraternal twins (Gregory et al., 2009; Knafo & Plomin, 2006b; Knafo et al., 2008). In one of the few twin studies of children's prosocial behavior, researchers observed young twins' reactions to adults' simulations of distress in the home and in the laboratory. They also had the twins' mothers report on their everyday prosocial behavior. On the basis of heritability estimates derived from this study, it appears that the role genetic factors play in the children's prosocial concern for others and in their prosocial behavior increases with age (Knafo et al., 2008).

How do genetic factors affect empathy, sympathy, and prosocial behavior? Most likely, their effects are related to differences in temperament. For example, differences in children's ability to regulate emotion are related to children's empathy and sympathy. Children who tend to experience emotion without getting overwhelmed by it are especially likely to experience sympathy (Eisenberg, Fabes et al., 1996;

Eisenberg, Michalik et al., 2007; Trommsdorff, Friedlmeier, & Mayer, 2007). Another partly genetic factor that affects children's enactment of prosocial behavior is their assertiveness: perspective taking is more likely to lead to prosocial action if children are assertive enough to intervene when they understand that another person needs help. For example, once a child understands that a peer cannot tie the sash of his or her painting apron, the observing child must be confident enough to approach the peer and offer assistance. Nonassertive children may not act prosocially even if they understand the other person's problem and would like to help (Barrett & Yarrow, 1977; Denham & Couchoud, 1991). This is a good example of how children's cognitive functioning and their personality characteristics jointly affect their social behavior.

CHRIS ANDERSON / AURORA

Children are more likely to donate to charity if they see others donate and if adults explain to them how donating helps others.

The Socialization of Prosocial Behavior

A number of environmental factors also contribute to sympathy and prosocial behavior (Knafo & Plomin, 2006a, 2006b; Volbrecht et al., 2007). The primary environmental influence on children's development of prosocial behavior probably is their socialization in the family. Researchers have identified three ways in which parents socialize prosocial behavior in their children: (1) through their modeling and teaching prosocial behavior; (2) through their arranging opportunities for their children to engage in prosocial behavior; and (3) through their methods of disciplining their children and eliciting prosocial behavior from them. Parents also communicate and reinforce cultural beliefs about the value of prosocial behavior (see Box 14.1 on the next page).

Modeling and the communication of values Just as they imitate many other behaviors, children tend to imitate other people's helping and sharing behavior, including even that of unknown peers or adults (Eisenberg & Fabes, 1998). Children are especially likely to imitate the prosocial behavior of adults with whom they have a positive relationship (Hart & Fegley, 1995; Yarrow, Scott, & Zahn-Waxler, 1973). This may help explain the fact that parents and children tend to be similar in their levels of prosocial behavior and sympathy (Clary & Miller, 1986; Eisenberg, Fabes, Schaller, Carlo, & Miller, 1991; Stukas, Switzer, Dew, Goycoolea, & Simmons, 1999), although heredity may also contribute to the similarity between parent and child in sympathy and helpfulness.

In a particularly interesting study, individuals who had risked their lives to rescue Jews from the Nazis in Europe during World War II were interviewed many years later, along with "bystanders" from the same communities who had not been involved in rescue activities (Oliner & Oliner, 1988). When recalling the values that they had learned from their parents and other influential adults, 44% of the rescuers mentioned generosity and caring for others; only 21% of bystanders mentioned the same values. As shown in Table 14.4, bystanders were almost twice as likely as rescuers to cite economic competence as a value learned from their parents.

Bystanders also reported that their parents emphasized ethical obligations to family, community, church, and country, but not to other groups of people. In contrast, rescuers were 7 times more likely than bystanders to report that their parents taught

TABLE 14.4

Values Learned from Parents by Rescuers and Bystanders (Percent of Rescuers and Bystanders Who Reported Learning a Given Type of Value from Parents)

Type of Value	Rescuers (%)	Bystanders (%)
Economic competence	19	34
Independence	6	8
Fairness/equity (including reciprocity)	44	48
Fairness/equity applied universally	14	10
Caring	44	21
Caring applied universally	28	4

Adapted from Oliner & Oliner (1988)

a closer look 14.1

Cultural Contributions to Children's Prosocial and Antisocial Tendencies

The amount of prosocial and antisocial behavior that children display can be influenced by the particular culture they are part of (Graves & Graves, 1983; Turnbull, 1972). For example, children from traditional communities and subcultures (e.g., Mexicans and Mexican-Americans) are more likely to cooperate on laboratory tasks than are children from urban, Westernized groups (Eisenberg & Mussen, 1989; Knight, Cota, & Bernal, 1993). Similar patterns have been found in observations of children interacting at home and in their neighborhoods (Whiting & Edwards, 1988; Whiting & Whiting, 1975): children in traditional societies in Kenya, Mexico, and the Philippines helped, shared, and offered support to others in their families and communities more than did children in the United States, India, and Okinawa. In the more prosocial cultures, children often lived in extended families with many relatives. At a young age, they were assigned chores that were very important for the welfare of other family members, such as caring for younger children and tending herds. As a result of taking on these duties, children may have learned that they were responsible for others and that their helping behavior was expected and valued by adults.

However, there may be cultural differences in the people toward whom children's caring behavior is directed. For example, although Philippine children in one study were more prosocial toward relatives than were U.S. children, U.S. children were more prosocial toward nonrelatives than were Philippine children (de Guzman, Carlo, & Edwards, 2008). Children in traditional cultures may be socialized to help people with whom they have close ties but may be relatively uninclined to help people with whom they don't have a close connection.

The multicultural study cited above also revealed cultural differences in children's aggression (Whiting & Whiting, 1975). Children's tendencies to assault, berate, and scold others were related primarily to family structure and interactions among parents. Children with lower rates of assaulting and reprimanding tended to live in cultures in which fathers were closely involved with their wives and children, helped their wives with the care of infants, and were relatively unlikely to assault their wives. In such family circumstances, children may have learned nonaggressive modes of social interaction from their fathers and were relatively unlikely to have been exposed to aggressive adult models.

Even in various industrial societies today, there are differences in cultural values regarding prosocial and antisocial behavior. For example, the incidence of children's sharing, helping, and comforting is higher in Taiwan and Japan than in the United States (Rao & Stewart, 1999; Stevenson, 1991) and is higher among Asian than among Caucasian schoolchildren living in Hong Kong (Stewart & McBride-Chang, 2000). Chinese and Japanese cultures traditionally place great emphasis on teaching children to share and to be responsible for the needs of others in the group (the family, class, or community). In Japan, there also is an emphasis on creating a "community of learners" in the elementary school classroom—that is, teaching children to respond supportively to one another's thoughts and feelings (M. Lewis, 1995). However, the traditional emphasis on prosocial behavior in many Asian cultures seems to be eroding (Lee & Zhan, 1991), perhaps due to increasing industrialization and exposure to Western culture and values, which are less likely to emphasize the welfare of the larger group.

CATHERINE URSILLO / PHOTO RESEARCHERS, INC.

Cross-cultural research has shown that girls who live in societies where they are expected to take care of younger children are more prosocial than are girls who live in societies that do not have this expectation.

them that values related to caring should be applied to everyone (28% of rescuers; 4% of bystanders):

> "They taught me to respect all human beings."
>
> "He taught me to love my neighbor—to consider him my equal whatever his nationality or religion."
>
> (Oliner & Oliner, 1988, p. 165)

Thus, the values parents convey to their children may influence not only *whether* children are prosocial but also *toward whom* they are prosocial.

One effective way for parents to teach their children prosocial values and behaviors is to have discussions with them that appeal to their ability to sympathize. In laboratory studies, when elementary school children heard adults explicitly point out the positive consequences of prosocial actions for others (e.g., "Poor children . . . would be so happy and excited if they could buy food and toys"), they were relatively likely to donate money anonymously to help other people (Eisenberg-Berg & Geisheker, 1979; Perry, Bussey, & Freiberg, 1981). Children were less likely to donate anonymously if adults simply said that helping is "good" or "nice" and did not provide sympathy-arousing rationales for helping or sharing (Bryan & Walbek, 1970; Eisenberg & Fabes, 1998).

Opportunities for prosocial activities Providing children with opportunities to engage in helpful activities can increase their willingness to take on prosocial tasks at a later time (Eisenberg, Cialdini, McCreath, & Shell, 1987; Staub, 1979). In the home, opportunities to help others include household tasks that are performed on a routine basis and benefit others (Richman, Berry, Bittle, & Himan, 1988; Whiting & Whiting, 1975), although performance of household tasks may foster prosocial actions primarily toward family members (Grusec, Goodnow, & Cohen, 1996). For adolescents, voluntary community service such as working in homeless shelters or other community agencies also can be a way of gaining experience in helping others and deepening feelings of prosocial commitment (Johnson, Beebe, Mortimer, & Snyder, 1998; Lawford et al., 2005; Yates & Youniss, 1996).

Participation in prosocial activities may also provide children and adolescents with opportunities to take others' perspectives, to increase their confidence that they are competent to assist others, and to experience emotional rewards for helping. Even mandatory school-based service activities have been associated with future prosocial values (Hart, Donnelly, Youniss, & Atkins, 2007) and increased voluntary service at a later date for those high school youth who were not initially inclined to engage in such activities (Metz & Youniss, 2003). It should be noted, however, that forcing older adolescents or young adults into service activities can sometimes backfire and undermine their motivation to help (Stukas, Snyder, & Clary, 1999).

Discipline and parenting style High levels of prosocial behavior and sympathy in children tend to be associated with constructive and supportive parenting (Knafo & Plomin, 2006a; Michalik et al., 2007; Moreno, Klute, & Robinson, 2008). In contrast, a parenting style that involves physical punishment, threats, and an authoritarian approach (see Chapter 12) tends to be associated with a lack of sympathy and prosocial behavior in children (Asbury, Dunn, Pike, & Plomin, 2003; Hastings, Zahn-Waxler, Robinson, Usher, & Bridges, 2000; Krevans & Gibbs, 1996).

The way in which parents attempt to directly elicit prosocial behavior from their children is also important. If children are regularly punished for failing to engage in prosocial behavior, they may start to believe that the reason for helping others is primarily to avoid punishment (Dix & Grusec, 1983; Hoffman, 1983). Similarly, if children are given material rewards for prosocial behaviors, they may come to believe that they helped solely for the rewards and, thus, may be less motivated to help when no rewards are offered (Fabes, Fultz, Eisenberg, May-Plumlee, & Christopher, 1989; Warneken & Tomasello, 2008).

What does seem particularly likely to foster children's voluntary prosocial behavior is discipline that involves reasoning. This is especially true when the reasoning points out the consequences of the child's behavior for others (Krevans

SUSIE FITZHUGH

When adults point out the consequences of a child's transgressions for others, children are more likely to respond with sympathy and prosocial behavior in other situations (Eisenberg & Fabes, 1998; Krevans & Gibbs, 1996).

& Gibbs, 1996) and is used by parents who generally are warm and supportive (Hoffman, 1963). Such reasoning also encourages sympathy with others and provides guidelines children can refer to in future situations (Henry, Sager, & Plunkett, 1996; Hoffman, 1983). Maternal use of reasoning (e.g., "Can't you see that Tim is hurt?") seems to increase prosocial behavior even for 1- to 2-year-olds, as long as mothers state their reasoning in an emotional tone of voice (Zahn-Waxler et al., 1979). Emotion in the mother's voice likely catches her toddler's attention and communicates that she is very serious about what she is saying.

The combination of parental warmth and certain parenting practices—not parental warmth by itself—seems to be especially effective for fostering prosocial tendencies in children. Thus, children tend to be more prosocial when their parents are not only warm and supportive but also model prosocial behavior, include reasoning and references to moral values and responsibilities in their discipline, and expose their children to prosocial models and activities (i.e., use authoritative parenting; Hastings, McShane, Parker, & Ladha, 2007; Janssens & Dekovic, 1997; Yarrow et al., 1973).

Because most of the research on the socialization of prosocial responding is correlational in design, it does not allow firm conclusions about cause-and-effect relations. However, some school interventions have been effective at promoting prosocial behavior in children, so environmental factors must contribute to its development (see Box 14.2). The research underlying such interventions indicates that experience in helping and cooperating with others, exposure to prosocial values and behaviors, and adults' use of reasoning in discipline jointly contribute to the development of prosocial behavior.

applications 14.2

School-Based Interventions for Promoting Prosocial Behavior

Knowledge about the socialization of helping and sharing behavior has been used to design school interventions aimed at fostering such behavior. Perhaps the most ambitious of these interventions was the Child Development Project in the East Bay area of San Francisco (Battistich, Solomon, Watson, & Schaps, 1997; Battistich, Watson, Solomon, Schaps, & Solomon, 1991). This longitudinal intervention, which followed children across elementary school, trained teachers in providing opportunities for children to develop a prosocial orientation toward their classmates and the community. The training focused on getting children to do the following:

1. Collaborate with others to achieve common academic and social goals
2. Develop and practice important social competencies such as understanding of others' thoughts and feelings
3. Provide meaningful help to others and receive help when it was needed
4. Discuss and reflect upon the degree to which their own and others' behavior reflects fairness, concern and respect for others, and social responsibility
5. Participate in decision making about classroom norms, rules, and activities and take on responsibility for appropriate aspects of classroom life

The program has led to increases in spontaneous prosocial behavior, conflict-resolution skills, and prosocial moral reasoning (Solomon, Battistich, & Watson, 1993; Solomon, Watson, Delucchi, Schaps, & Battistich, 1988).

The concept of the school as a caring community becomes a central part of similar interventions. The caring school community is one in which teachers and students (1) care about and support one another; (2) share common values, norms, goals, and a sense of belonging; and (3) participate in and influence group decisions. Programs designed to promote caring school communities included many of the components of the original Child Development Project. Findings with diverse samples of children suggest that enhancing a sense of school community not only promotes children's concern for others, fostering prosocial behavior, conflict-resolution skills, and ethical attitudes and values; it also increases academic motivation and liking of school and is associated with fewer problem behaviors and less use of drugs (Battistich, Schaps, Watson, Solomon, & Lewis, 2000; Battistich, Schaps, & Wilson, 2004; Battistich et al., 1997; Solomon et al., 2000).

review:

Prosocial behaviors emerge by the second year of life and increase in frequency during the toddler years. Prosocial behavior continues to increase in frequency and sensitivity in the preschool years and elementary school years. Early individual differences in prosocial behavior predict differences among children in these types of behaviors years later.

Prosocial behavior may increase with age partly due to children's developing abilities to sympathize and take others' perspectives. Differences among children in their empathy, sympathy, personal distress, and perspective taking also contribute to individual differences in children's prosocial behavior. Furthermore, biological factors, which may contribute to differences among children in temperament, likely affect how empathic and prosocial children become.

The development of prosocial behavior also is related to children's upbringing. In general, a positive relationship between parents and children is linked to prosocial moral development, especially when supportive parents use effective parenting practices. Authoritative, positive discipline—including the use of reasoning by parents and teachers and exposure to prosocial models, values, and activities—is associated with the development of sympathy and prosocial behavior. Cultures differ in the degree to which they value and teach prosocial behavior, and these differences are reflected in how much children help, share with, and are concerned about other people.

Intervention programs in schools designed to foster prosocial behavior have been found to increase children's prosocial behavior and prosocial moral reasoning. Such findings convincingly demonstrate that social factors (as well as heredity) contribute to the development of prosocial tendencies.

Antisocial Behavior

Pick up any newspaper and you are inevitably reminded of the violence that is commonplace among youth in urban, industrialized countries, especially in Western societies. In the United States in 2007, juveniles under age 18 were involved in 10% of murder arrests, 13% of aggravated assault arrests, 27% of burglary arrests, 27% of robbery arrests, and 23% of weapons arrests (Pazzanchera, 2009). Statistics like these, along with incidents like the Columbine tragedy described at the beginning of the chapter, raise questions such as: Are youth who commit violent acts already aggressive in childhood? How do levels of aggression change with development? What factors contribute to individual differences in children's antisocial behavior? As we address these issues, the themes of *individual differences, nature and nuture,* the *sociocultural context,* and *research and children's welfare* will be particularly salient.

The Development of Aggression and Other Antisocial Behaviors

Aggression is behavior aimed at harming others (Parke & Slaby, 1983), and it is behavior that emerges quite early. How early? Although conflicts between infants over objects are very common at 12 to 18 months of age, most do not involve aggression (Coie & Dodge, 1998; Hay & Ross, 1982). However, at around 18 months of age, physical aggression such as hitting and pushing begins and increases in frequency until about age 2 or 3 (Alink et al., 2006; Shaw, Gilliom, Ingoldsby, & Nagin, 2003). Then, with the growth of language skills, physical aggression decreases in frequency, and verbal aggression such as insults and taunting increases (Bonica, Arnold, Fisher, Zeljo, & Yershova, 2003; Dionne, Tremblay, Boivin, Laplante, & Pérusse, 2003; Miner & Clarke-Stewart, 2008).

aggression behavior aimed at harming or injuring others

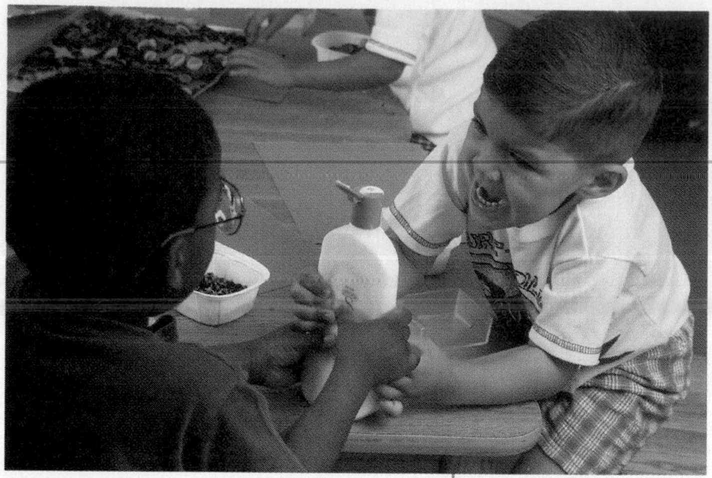

LAURA DWIGHT

Aggressive conflicts over objects are very common among young children.

Among the most frequent causes of aggression in the preschool years are conflicts between peers over possessions (Fabes & Eisenberg, 1992; Shantz, 1987) and conflict between siblings over most anything (Abramovitch, Corter, & Lando, 1979). Conflict over possessions often is an example of **instrumental aggression,** that is, aggression motivated by the desire to obtain a concrete goal, such as gaining possession of a toy or getting a better place in line. Preschool children sometimes also use *relational aggression* (Crick, Casas, & Mosher, 1997), which, as explained in Chapter 13, is intended to harm others by damaging their peer relationships. Among preschoolers, this typically involves excluding peers from a play activity or a social group (Underwood, 2003).

The drop in physical aggression in the preschool years is likely due to a variety of factors, including not only children's increasing ability to use verbal and relational aggression but also their developing ability to use language to resolve conflicts and to control their own emotions and actions (Coie & Dodge, 1998). Thus, overt physical aggression continues to decline in frequency for most children during elementary school, although a relatively small group of children—primarily boys (Moffitt & Caspi, 2001)—develop frequent and serious problems with aggression and antisocial behavior at this age (Cairns, Cairns, Neckerman, Ferguson, & Gariepy, 1989; Shaw et al., 2003).

Whereas aggression in young children is usually instrumental, aggression in elementary school children often is hostile, arising from the desire to hurt another person or the need to protect oneself against a perceived threat to self-esteem (Dodge, 1980; Hartup, 1974). Children who engage in physical aggression tend to also engage in relational aggression (Card, Stucky, Sawalani, & Little, 2008), with the degree to which they use one or the other tending to be consistent across childhood (Ostrov, Ries, Stauffacher, Godleski, & Mullins, 2008; Vaillancourt, Brendgen, Boivin, & Tremblay, 2003). Overall, the frequency of overt aggression decreases for most teenagers (Loeber, 1982), at least after mid-adolescence (Karriker-Jaffe, Foshee, Ennett, & Suchindran, 2008).

In childhood, covert types of antisocial behaviors such as stealing, lying, and cheating also occur with considerable frequency and begin to be characteristic of some children with behavioral problems (Loeber & Schmaling, 1985). In mid-adolescence, serious acts of violence increase markedly, as do property offenses and status offenses such as drinking and truancy (Lahey et al., 2000). As illustrated in Figure 14.2, adolescent violent crime peaks at age 17, when 29% of males and 12% of females report committing at least one serious violent offense. As the figure also shows, male adolescents and adults engage in much more violent behavior and crime than do females (Coie & Dodge, 1998; Elliott, 1994) (see Box 14.3 on page 570)—although in 2007, 29% of the arrests among juveniles were of females (Pazzanchera, 2009), who made up 17% of the juvenile arrests for violent crime and 35% of the juvenile arrests for propery crime.

Consistency of Aggressive and Antisocial Behavior

There is considerable consistency in both girls' and boys' aggression across childhood and adolescence. Although many children decline in their aggression from age 2 to age 8 (Shaw et al., 2003), children—especially boys (Fontaine et al., 2009)—who are the most aggressive and prone to conduct problems such as stealing in middle

instrumental aggression aggression motivated by the desire to obtain a concrete goal

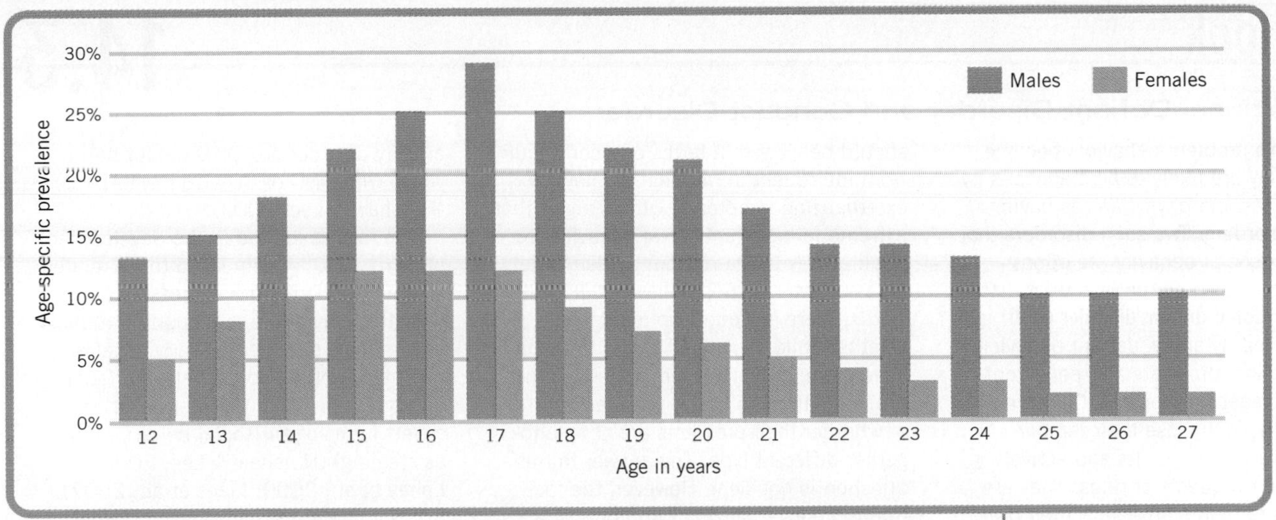

FIGURE 14.2 Prevalence of self-reported violence for males and females at different ages At all ages, males report enacting more violence than do females. (Adapted from Coie & Dodge, 1998)

childhood tend to be aggressive and delinquent in adolescence, more so than children who develop conduct disorders at a later age (Broidy et al., 2003; Lahey, Goodman, et al., 1999; Schaeffer, Petras, Ialongo, Poduska, & Kellam, 2003). In one study, children who had been identified as aggressive by their peers when they were 8 years old had more criminal convictions and engaged in more serious criminal behavior at age 30 than did those who had not been identified as aggressive (see Figure 14.3) (Eron, Huesmann, Dubow, Romanoff, & Yarmel, 1987).

Adolescents most at risk for serious problem behaviors are those who, as elementary school children, engaged in both aggression *and* other antisocial behaviors such as lying and stealing (Loeber, 1982). However, aggression is not a necessary ingredient for later problem behavior. Some children who are not overtly aggressive in childhood simply move from lying, stealing, and property damage in childhood to more serious crimes such as stealing cars, robbery, and selling drugs in adolescence (Loeber et al., 1993).

Many children who are aggressive from early in life have neurological deficits (i.e., brain dysfunctions) that underlie such problems as difficulty in paying attention and hyperactivity (Gatzke-Kopp et al., 2009; Moffitt, 1993a; Speltz, DeKlyen,

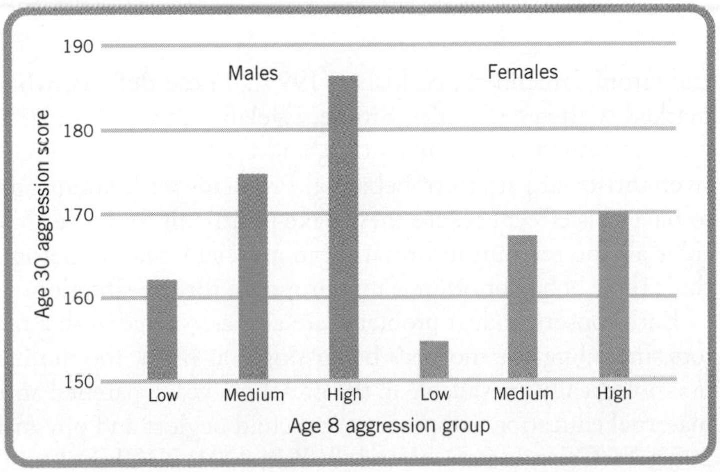

FIGURE 14.3 The relation of peer-nominated aggression at age 8 to self-reported aggression by their peers at age 30 Boys and girls who were nominated as high in aggression at age 8 were higher in self-reported aggression at age 30 than were those of their peers who had been nominated as lower in aggression. (Adapted from Eron, Huesmann, Dubow, Romanoff, & Yarmel, 1987)

a closer look 14.3

Oppositional Defiant Disorder and Conduct Disorder

If children's problem behaviors become serious, they are likely to be diagnosed by psychologists and physicians as having clinical disorders. Two such disorders that involve antisocial behavior are oppositional defiant disorder and conduct disorder. **Oppositional defiant disorder (ODD)** is characterized by angry, defiant behavior that is age-inappropriate and persistent (lasting at least six months). Children with ODD typically lose their temper easily, arguing with adults and actively defying their requests or rules. They are also prone to blame others for their own mistakes or misbehavior and are often spiteful or vindictive. **Conduct disorder (CD)** includes more severe antisocial and aggression behaviors that inflict pain on others (e.g., initiating fights, cruelty to animals) or involve the destruction of property or the violation of the rights of others (e.g., stealing, robberies).

Other diagnostic signs include frequently running away from home, frequently staying out all night before age 13 despite parental prohibitions, or persistent school truancy beginning prior to age 13. To warrant a diagnosis of ODD or CD, children must exhibit multiple, persistent symptoms that are clearly impairing, distinguishing them from those youngsters who display the designated behaviors on an infrequent or inconsistent basis (American Psychiatric Association, 1994; Hinshaw & Lee, 2003).

There is debate in the field regarding how antisocial behavior, including ODD and CD, should be conceptualized. Some experts argue that antisocial behavior should be viewed in terms of a continuum from infrequent to frequent displays of externalizing symptoms. Others argue that extreme forms of antisocial behavior are qualitatively different from garden-variety types of externalizing behaviors. In other words, there is a question regarding whether children with ODD or CD simply have more, or more severe, externalizing problems than do better-adjusted youth, or whether their problems are of an altogether different type. The answer to this question is not clear. However, the fact that more externalizing symptoms at a younger age predict serious diagnosed problems in adolescence or adulthood (Biederman et al., 2008; Cote et al., 2001; Hinshaw & Lee, 2003) is viewed by some as evidence that serious externalizing problems differ in their origins from less severe types of such behavior.

Estimates of the prevalence of ODD and CD range widely (Hinshaw & Lee, 2003). A median prevalence estimate for ODD among U.S. youth is about 3% (Lahey et al., 1999). The American Psychiatric Association (1994) estimates that the rate of CD for children and adolescents is 6 to 16% for males and 2 to 9% for females. In one large study in Canada, the rates were approximately 8% for boys and 3% for girls (Offord, Alder, & Boyle, 1986). The average age of onset for ODD is approximately 6 years of age; for CD it is 9 years of age (Hinshaw & Lee, 2003). A minority of youth with ODD later develop CD. In many instances, youth with ODD or CD also have been diagnosed with other disorders such as anxiety disorder or ADHD (about half of youth with ODD or CD also have ADHD) (Hinshaw & Lee, 2003).

The factors related to the development of CD or ODD are similar to those related to the development of aggression. Genetics play a role, although heritability seems to be stronger for early onset and overt types of antisocial behavior (such as aggression) than for later onset or covert forms of antisocial behavior (such as stealing) (Hinshaw & Lee, 2003; Lahey et al., 2009; Maes et al., 2007). Environmental risks for these disorders include such factors as living in a stressed, lower-SES family; parental abuse; poor parental supervision; and harsh and inconsistent discipline. Peer rejection and associating with deviant peers are also linked with ODD and CD (Hinshaw & Lee, 2003; Loeber & Stouthamer-Loeber, 1986). It is likely that a variety of these factors jointly contribute to children's developing ODD or CD and that the factors which are most important vary, depending on the age of onset, the type of problem behaviors, and individual characteristics of the children, including their temperament and intelligence.

Youth with externalizing problems, and especially with CD, are, by definition, high in aggression and delinquency and therefore are prone to get in trouble with the law. However, programs such as the Fast Track program (described in Box 14.4, page 578) can be used to reduce the risks for these youth (Eyberg et al., 2008).

oppositional defiant disorder (ODD) a disorder characterized by age-inappropriate and persistent displays of angry, defiant, and irritable behaviors

conduct disorder (CD) a disorder that involves severe antisocial and aggression behaviors that inflict pain on others or involve destruction of property or denial of the rights of others

Calderon, Greenberg, & Fisher, 1999). These deficits, which may become more marked with age (Aguilar, Sroufe, Egeland, & Carlson, 2000), can result in troubled relations with parents, peers, and teachers, further fueling the child's aggressive, antisocial pattern of behavior. Problems with attention are particularly likely to have this effect because they make it difficult for these children to carefully consider all the relevant information in a social situation before deciding how to act; thus, their behavior often is inappropriate for the situation.

Early-onset conduct problems are also associated with a range of family risk factors, including the mother's being single at birth, the mother's being stressed and psychologically unavailable in the preschool years, parental antisocial tendencies, low maternal education and poverty, and child neglect and physical abuse (Aguilar et al., 2000; McCabe, Hough, Wood, & Yeh, 2001; NICHD Early Child Care Research

Network, 2004). In contrast, conduct problems that emerge in adolescence are more likely to be associated with being a member of an ethnic minority (especially for African Americans) and interacting with deviant peers (McCabe et al., 2001; McCabe, Rodgers, Yeh, & Hough, 2004; see Chapter 13, pages 514–515, 521–523).

Adolescents with a long childhood history of troubled behavior represent only a minority of adolescents who engage in the much broader problem of "juvenile delinquency" (Hamalainen & Pulkkinen, 1996). Indeed, most adolescents who perform delinquent acts have no history of aggression or antisocial behavior before age 11 (Elliott, 1994). For them, delinquency may occur in response to the normal pressures of adolescence, as when they attempt to assert their independence from adults or win acceptance from their peers. These adolescents typically stop engaging in antisocial behavior later in adolescence or early adulthood (Moffitt, 1993a), although some continue to engage in problem behaviors and to have some problems with their mental health and substance dependence until at least their mid-20s (Moffitt, Caspi, Harrington, & Milne, 2002).

Characteristics of Aggressive-Antisocial Children and Adolescents

Aggressive-antisocial children and adolescents differ, on average, from their nonaggressive peers in a variety of characteristics. These include having a difficult temperament and the tendency to process social information in negative ways.

Temperament and Personality

Children who develop problems with aggression and antisocial behavior tend to exhibit a difficult temperament from a very early age (Rothbart & Bates, 2006). Longitudinal studies have shown, for example, that infants and toddlers who frequently express intense negative emotion and demand much attention tend to have higher levels of problem behaviors such as aggression from the preschool years through high school (Bates, Bayles, Bennett, Ridge, & Brown, 1991; Joussemet et al., 2008; Olson, Bates, Sandy, & Lanthier, 2000). Similarly, preschoolers who exhibit lack of control, impulsivity, high activity level, irritability, and distractibility are prone to fighting, delinquency, and other antisocial behavior at ages 9 through 15; to aggression and criminal behavior in late adolescence; and, in the case of males, to violent crime in adulthood (Caspi, Henry, McGee, Moffitt, & Silva, 1995; Caspi & Silva, 1995; Tremblay, Pihl, Vitaro, & Dobkin, 1994). Some of these children and adolescents tend to feel neither guilt nor empathy or sympathy for others. They are often charming but insincere and callous. The combination of impulsivity, problems with attention, and callousness in childhood is especially likely to predict aggression, antisocial behavior, and run-ins with the police in adolescence (Christian, Frick, Hill, Tyler, & Frazer, 1997; Frick & Morris, 2004; Hastings et al., 2000) and perhaps in adulthood as well (Lynam, 1996).

Social Cognition

In addition to their differences in temperament, aggressive children differ from nonaggressive children in their social cognition. As discussed in Chapter 9, aggressive children tend to interpret the world through an "aggressive" lens. They are more likely than nonaggressive children to attribute hostile motives to others in contexts in which the other person's motives and intentions are unclear (the "hostile attributional bias") (Dodge et al., 2006; MacBrayer, Milich, & Hundley, 2003; Nelson,

Mitchell, & Yang, 2008). Compared with those of nonaggressive peers, their goals in such social encounters are also more likely to be hostile and inappropriate to the situation, typically involving attempts to intimidate or get back at a peer (Crick & Dodge, 1994; Slaby & Guerra, 1988). Moreover, when imagining possible reactions in a negative social situation, aggressive children tend to come up with fewer options than nonaggressive children do, and these options are more likely to involve aggressive or disruptive behavior (Deluty, 1985; Slaby & Guerra, 1988).

In line with these tendencies, aggressive children are also inclined to evaluate aggressive responses more favorably, and competent, prosocial responses less favorably, than do their nonagressive peers (Crick & Dodge, 1994; Dodge, Pettit, McClaskey, & Brown, 1986). In part, this is because they feel more confident of their ability to perform acts of physical and verbal aggression (Quiggle et al., 1992), and they expect their aggressive behavior to result in positive outcomes (e.g., getting their way) and to reduce negative treatment by others (Dodge et al., 1986; Perry, Perry, & Rasmussen, 1986). Given all this, it is not surprising that aggressive children are predisposed toward engaging in aggressive behavior (Dodge et al., 2006). This aggressive behavior, in turn, appears to increase children's subsequent tendency to positively evaluate aggressive interpersonal behaviors, further increasing the level of future antisocial conduct (Fontaine, Yang, Dodge, Bates, & Pettit, 2008).

Proactive aggression (purposeful aggression not evoked by emotion) is used by children to bully others and to get what they want from them.

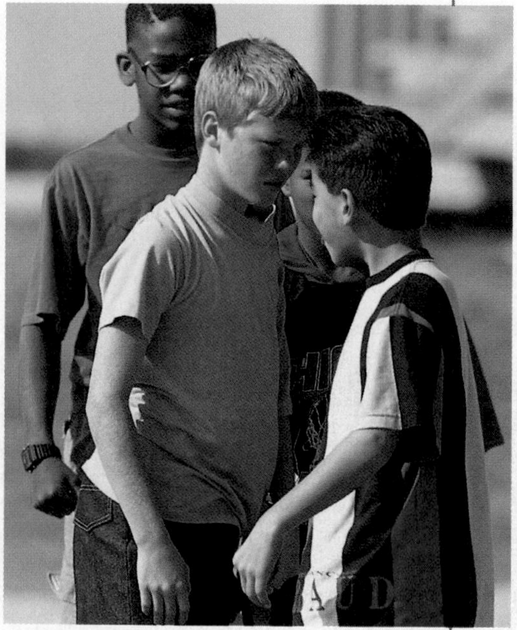

BOB DAEMMRICH / STOCK BOSTON

It is important to note, however, that although all these aspects of functioning contribute to the prediction of children's aggression, not all aggressive children exhibit the same biases in social cognition. Children who are prone to emotionally driven, hostile aggression—labeled **reactive aggression**—are particularly likely to perceive others' motives as hostile (Crick & Dodge, 1996), to initially generate aggressive responses to provocation, and to evaluate their responses as morally acceptable (Dodge, Lochman, Harnish, Bates, & Pettit, 1997). Perhaps this is because many of these children are likely to have suffered abuse (Shields & Cicchetti, 1998). In contrast, children who are prone to **proactive aggression**—unemotional aggression aimed at fulfilling a need or desire—tend to anticipate more positive social consequences for aggression (Crick & Dodge, 1996; Dodge et al., 1997; Sijtsema, Veenstra, Lindenberg, & Salmivalli, 2009).

The Origins of Aggression

What are the causes of aggression in children? Key contributors include genetic makeup, socialization by family members, the influence of peers, and cultural factors.

Biological Factors

Biological factors undoubtedly contribute to individual differences in aggression, but their precise role is not very clear. Twin studies suggest that antisocial behavior runs in families and is partially due to genetic factors (Arsenault et al., 2003; Rhee & Waldman, 2002). In addition, heredity appears to play a stronger role in aggression in early childhood and adulthood than in adolescence, when environmental factors are a major contributor to aggression (Rende & Plomin, 1995; Taylor, Iacono, & McGue, 2001). Heredity also appears to play a stronger role in boys' aggression than it does in girls' (Baker, Raine, Liu, & Jacobson, 2008).

reactive aggression emotionally driven, antagonistic aggression sparked by one's perception that other people's motives are hostile

proactive aggression unemotional aggression aimed at fulfilling a need or desire

We have already noted one genetically influenced contributor to aggression—difficult temperament. Hormonal factors are also assumed to play a role in aggression, although the evidence for this assumption is mixed. For example, testosterone levels seem to be related to activity level and responses to provocation, and high testosterone levels sometimes have been linked to aggressive behavior (Archer, 1991; Hermans et al., 2008). However, the relation of testosterone to aggression, although statistically significant, is quite small (Book, Starzyk, & Quinsey, 2001).

Another biological contributor to aggression discussed earlier is neurological deficits that affect attention and regulatory capabilities (Moffitt, 1993b): children who are not well regulated are likely to have difficulty controlling their tempers and inhibiting aggressive impulses (Eisenberg et al., 2009; Xu, Farver, & Zhang, 2009).

Whatever their specific role, the biological correlates of aggression probably are neither necessary nor sufficient to cause aggressive behavior in most children. Genetic, neurological, or hormonal characteristics may put a child at risk for developing aggressive and antisocial behavior, but whether or not the child becomes aggressive will depend on numerous factors, including experiences in the social world.

Socialization of Aggression and Antisocial Behavior

Many people, including some legislators and judges, feel that the development of aggression can be traced back to socialization in the home. In fact, the quality of parenting experienced by antisocial children is poorer than that experienced by other children (Dodge et al., 2006; Scaramella, Conger, Spoth, & Simmons, 2002). However, the degree to which poor parenting rather than other factors accounts for antisocial behavior is unclear.

Parental punitiveness Many children whose parents often use harsh but nonabusive physical punishment are prone to problem behaviors in the early years, aggression in childhood, and criminality in adolescence and adulthood (Bender et al., 2007; Gershoff, 2002). This is especially true when parents are cold and punitive in general (Deater-Deckard & Dodge, 1997) and when their children have a difficult temperament and are unregulated (Mulvaney & Mebert, 2007; Xu et al., 2009).

It is important to note, however, that the relation between physical punishment and children's antisocial behavior varies across racial, ethnic, and cultural groups. As discussed in Chapter 12, in some cultures and subcultures, physical punishment and controlling parental behaviors are viewed as part of responsible parenting when coupled with parental support and normal demands for compliance. When this is the case, parental punishment tends not to be associated with antisocial behavior because children may tend to see authoritarian parenting as protective and caring (Lansford et al., 2006).

In contrast, abusive punishment is likely to be associated with the development of antisocial tendencies regardless of the group in question (Deater-Deckard, Dodge, Bates, & Pettit, 1995; Luntz & Widom, 1994; Weiss, Dodge, Bates, & Pettit, 1992). Very harsh physical discipline appears to lead to the kinds of social cognition that are associated with aggression, such as assuming that others have hostile intentions, generating aggressive solutions to interpersonal problems, and expecting aggressive behavior to result in positive outcomes (Dodge, Pettit, Bates, & Valente, 1995).

In addition, parents who use abusive punishment provide salient models of aggressive behavior for their children to imitate (Dogan, Conger, Kim, & Masyn,

Parental punitiveness and coercive behavior tend to be associated with adolescents' problematic externalizing behaviors.

TOPHAM / THE IMAGE WORKS

2007). Ironically, children who are subjected to such punishment are likely to be anxious or angry and therefore are unlikely to attend to their parents' instructions or demands or to be motivated to behave as their parents wish them to (Hoffman, 1983).

There probably is a reciprocal relation between children's behavior and their parents' punitive discipline (Cohen & Brook, 1995; Eisenberg, Fabes et al., 1999). That is, children who are high in antisocial behavior or low in self-regulation tend to elicit harsh parenting; in turn, harsh parenting increases the children's problem behavior. Although research findings with adolescents are not all that consistent (Cohen & Brook, 1995; Feldman & Weinberger, 1994; Stice & Barrera, 1995), it is likely that harshly punitive parents and antisocial adolescents also influence one another's behavior in a way that continues this vicious cycle (Sheehan & Watson, 2008).

The relation between punitive parenting and children's aggression may have a genetic component. Parents who are genetically prone to anger and violence will tend to have children with a similar genetic predisposition, and these same parents are more likely than other parents to engage in harsh or punitive parenting. At the same time, however, twin studies indicate that the relation between punitive, negative parenting and children's aggression and antisocial behavior is not due entirely to hereditary factors (Jaffee et al., 2004a, 2004b). For example, punitive parenting is related to differences in identical twins' aggression (Caspi et al., 2004).

Ineffective discipline and family coercion Another factor that can increase children's antisocial behavior is ineffective parenting. Parents who are inconsistent in administering discipline are more likely than other parents to have aggressive and delinquent children (Dumka, Roosa, & Jackson, 1997; Frick, Christian, & Wooten, 1999; Laub & Sampson, 1994). So too are parents who fail to monitor their children's behavior and activities. One reason parental monitoring may be important is that it reduces the likelihood that older children and adolescents will associate with deviant, antisocial peers (Dodge, Greenberg, Malone, 2008; Patterson, Capaldi, & Bank, 1991). It also makes it more likely that parents will know if their children are engaging in antisocial behavior. At the same time, however, parents of difficult, aggressive youth sometimes find that monitoring leads to such conflict with their children that they are forced to back off (Laird et al., 2003).

Ineffective discipline is often evident in the pattern of family interaction described by Patterson (1982, 1995; Snyder, Cramer, Afrank, & Patterson, 2005) and discussed in Chapter 1. In this pattern, the aggression of children who are out of control is often unintentionally reinforced by parents when, their efforts to coerce compliance having failed, they give in to their children's fits of temper and demands (Snyder, Reid, & Patterson, 2003). This may be especially true in the case of out-of-control boys, who are much more likely than other boys to react negatively to their mother's attempts to discipline them (Patterson, Reid, & Dishion, 1992). Whether or not maternal coercion elicits the same pattern of response from girls as from boys is not yet known because most of the relevant research has been done with boys, but there is some reason to believe that it does not (McFadyen-Ketchum, Bates, Dodge, & Pettit, 1996).

Parental conflict Children who are frequently exposed to verbal and physical violence between their parents tend to be more antisocial and aggressive than other children (Cummings & Davies, 2002; Ingoldsby, Shaw, Owens, & Winslow, 1999; Keller, Cummings, Davies, & Mitchell, 2008). This relation holds true even when

BOB DAEMMRICH / THE IMAGE WORKS

Children are more likely to develop aggressive and antisocial behavior if they are exposed to marital conflict, especially violence. Parents who are in unhappy marriages tend to be withdrawn and nonsupportive with their children, which appears to contribute to their children's problems with adjustment.

genetic factors that might have caused it are taken into account (Jaffee et al., 2002). One obvious reason for this is that embattled parents model aggressive behavior for their children. Another is that children whose mothers are physically abused tend to believe that violence is an acceptable, even natural part of family interactions (Graham-Bermann & Brescoll, 2000). Compared with spouses who get along well with each other, embattled parents also tend to be less skilled at parenting and more hostile with their children (Buehler et al., 1997; Emery, 1989; Gonzales, Pitts, Hill, & Roosa, 2000).

As noted in Chapter 12, even when marital conflict results in divorce, the problems may not end: the more children must contend with family transitions such as relocation and remarriage, the more antisocial and delinquent behavior they may exhibit (Capaldi & Patterson, 1991; Malone et al., 2004; Pagani, Tremblay, Vitaro, Kerr, & McDuff, 1998). Furthermore, for a period of time after a divorce, mothers tend to become less supportive toward their children and to be more inconsistent and authoritarian, and thereby less effective, in controlling their children. Such ineffectiveness can lead to a coercive cycle of parenting (Hetherington, Stanley-Hagen, & Anderson, 1989). Thus, parental conflict and its aftermath can increase children's antisocial behavior in a number of different ways.

Socioeconomic status and children's antisocial behavior Children from low-income families tend to be more antisocial and aggressive than children from more prosperous homes (Keiley, Bates, Dodge, & Pettit, 2000; NICHD Early Child Care Research Network, 2004; Stouthamer-Loeber et al., 2002). This pattern is highlighted by the fact that when families escape from poverty, 4- to 7-year-old children tend to become less aggressive and antisocial, whereas remaining in poverty or moving into poverty for the long-term is associated with an increase in children's antisocial behavior (Macmillan, McMorris, & Kruttschnitt, 2004). There are many reasons that might account for such differences in trajectories.

One major reason is the greater amount of stressors experienced by children in poor families, including stress in the family (illness, domestic violence, divorce, legal problems) and neighborhood violence. In addition, as we have seen, low socioeconomic status tends to be associated with living in a single-parent family or being an unplanned child of a teenage parent; stressors of these sorts are linked to increased aggression and antisocial behavior (Dodge, Pettit, & Bates, 1994; Linares et al., 2001; Tolan, Gorman-Smith, & Henry, 2003; Trentacosta et al., 2008).

Because of the many poverty-related stressors faced by their parents, children living in poverty are also frequently exposed to parenting deficits that predict children's antisocial, aggressive behavior. Their parents are more likely than other parents to use erratic, threatening, and harsh discipline and to be lax in supervising their children. They also model more aggression and are more likely to be hostile and reject their children than are parents who do not face the stresses associated with poverty (Conger, Ge, Elder, Lorenz, & Simons, 1994; Dodge et al., 1994; Williams, Conger, & Blozis, 2007).

In addition to all these risk factors, other factors such as the presence of gangs, the lack of jobs for juveniles, and few opportunities to engage in constructive activities such as clubs and sports likely contribute to the antisocial behavior of many youth in poor neighborhoods.

Peer Influence

As we discussed in Chapter 13, aggressive children tend to socialize with other aggressive children, and boys who initially are moderately aggressive become more delinquent over time if they have close friends who are aggressive. Although highly aggressive friends may not directly cause one another's aggressive behavior, they certainly may spur each other on. Moreover, the expression of a genetic tendency toward aggression is stronger for individuals who have aggressive friends (Brendgen et al., 2008).

The larger peer group with whom older children and adolescents socialize may influence aggression even more than their close friends do (Coie & Dodge, 1998). In one study, boys exposed to peers involved in overt antisocial behaviors, such as violence and the use of a weapon, were more than 3 times as likely as other boys to engage in such acts themselves (Keenan, Loeber, Zhang, Southamer-Loeber, & Van Kammen, 1995). Associating with delinquent peers tends to increase delinquency because these peers model and reinforce antisocial behavior in the peer group. At the same time, participating in delinquent activities brings adolescents into contact with more delinquent peers (Lacourse, Nagin, Tremblay, & Vitaro, 2003; Thornberry, Lizotte, Krohn, Farnworth, & Jang, 1994).

Although research findings vary somewhat, it appears that children's susceptibility to peer pressure to become involved in antisocial behavior increases in the elementary school years, peaks at about 8th or 9th grade, and declines thereafter (Berndt, 1979; Brown, Clasen, & Eicher, 1986; Steinberg & Silverberg, 1986). Although not all adolescents are susceptible to negative peer influence (Allen, Porter, & McFarland, 2006), even popular youth in early adolescence tend to increase participation in minor levels of drug use and delinquency if these behaviors are approved by peers (Allen, Porter, McFarland, Marsh, & McElhaney, 2005). However, there are exceptions to this pattern that appear to be related to cultural factors. For example, Mexican-American immigrant youth who are less acculturated, and therefore more tied to traditional values, appear to be less susceptible to peer pressure toward antisocial behavior than are Mexican-American children who are more acculturated. Thus, it may be that peers may play less of a role in promoting antisocial behavior for adolescents embedded in a traditional culture oriented toward adults' expectations (e.g., deference and courtesy toward adults and adherence to adult values) (Wall, Power, & Arbona, 1993).

Gangs An important peer influence on antisocial behavior can be membership in a gang. It has been estimated that in the United States in 2007, there were 27,000 gangs with 788,000 active members (Egley & O'Donnell, 2009). Most gangs are in metropolitan areas, with Los Angeles, for example, reporting that in March 2004, approximately 47,000 youth in that city were gang members (LAPD, 2004). However, since 1993, the presence of gangs in suburban and rural areas has increased (Egley & O'Donnell, 2009; Snyder & Sickmund, 1999; see Table 14.5). In many other countries, youth gangs are likewise becoming, or are likely to become, a serious problem (Vittori, 2007).

TABLE 14.5

Distribution of Estimated Gangs and Gang Members by Area Type, 2007

	Gangs (%)	Gang Members (%)
Rural counties	5.9	2.3
Smaller cities	33.5	16.8
Suburban counties	19.9	25.0
Larger cities	40.7	55.9
Total	**100%**	**100%**

Source: Egley & O'Donnell, 2009

Gangs tend to be composed of young people who are similar in ethnic and racial background. Their membership is about 90% male, though the proportion of female members seems to be increasing (Snyder & Sickmund, 1999). The average age of gang members is between 17 and 18 years, with about half being 18 or older and a small portion being as young as 12 (Egley, 2002).

Adolescents are more likely to join gangs if they come from a neighborhood with a high rate of resident turnover and if they have psychopathic tendencies such as a combination of high hyperactivity, low anxiety, and low prosociality (Dupéré, Lacourse, Willms, Vitaro, & Tremblay, 2007). Adolescents who join gangs also tend to have engaged in antisocial activities and to have had delinquent friends before they joined. However, being in a gang appears to increase adolescents' delinquent and antisocial behavior above their prior levels (Battin, Hill, Abbott, Catalano, & Hawkins, 1998; Lahey, Gordon, Loeber, Stouthamer-Loeber, & Farrington, 1999). Not surprisingly, the longer adolescents remain in a gang, the more likely they are to engage in delinquent and antisocial behavior (Craig, Vitaro, Gagnon, & Tremblay, 2002; Gordon et al., 2004). The specific levels of antisocial behavior typically vary from gang to gang, ranging from graffiti tagging, property destruction, and fighting to robbery and murder. Drug use and drug selling are also common in many gangs (Short, 1996; Taylor et al., 2007).

A. RAMEY / STOCK BOSTON

Gangs often provide youth with a sense of belonging, emblemized by specific gang signs.

Teens who are gang members are responsible for much of the serious violence in the United States. For example, a survey in Denver found that while only 14% of teens were gang members, they were responsible for committing 89% of the city's serious violent crimes (Huizinga, 1997). Much of this violence involves conflict within and between gangs, and gang members are at least 60 times more likely to be killed than are the rest of the population (Howell, 1998). They also are much more likely to be victimized in other ways (e.g., robbed or attacked), apparently in part because of their high involvement in delinquent activities and their ready access to drugs and alcohol (Taylor et al., 2007, 2008).

applications 14.4

The Fast Track Intervention

Psychologists interested in the prevention of antisocial behavior and violence have designed numerous school-based intervention programs. One of the most intensive was Fast Track—a large, federally funded study that was being tested in high-risk schools in four U.S. cities (Conduct Problems Prevention Research Group, 1999a, 1999b). This program was initially implemented for three successive years with almost 400 1st grade classes, half of which received the intervention and half of which served as a control group. The children in both groups tended to come from low-income families, about half of which were minority families (Slough, McMahon, & the Conduct Problems Prevention Research Group, 2008).

There were two major parts of the intervention. In the first part, all children in the intervention classes were trained with a special curriculum designed to promote understanding and communication of emotions, positive social behavior, self-control, and social problem solving (Greenberg, Kusche, Cook, & Quamma, 1995). The children were taught to recognize emotional cues in themselves and to distinguish appropriate and inappropriate behavioral reactions to emotions. They were also taught how to make and keep friends, how to share, how to listen to others, and how to calm themselves down and to inhibit aggressive behavior when they became upset or frustrated.

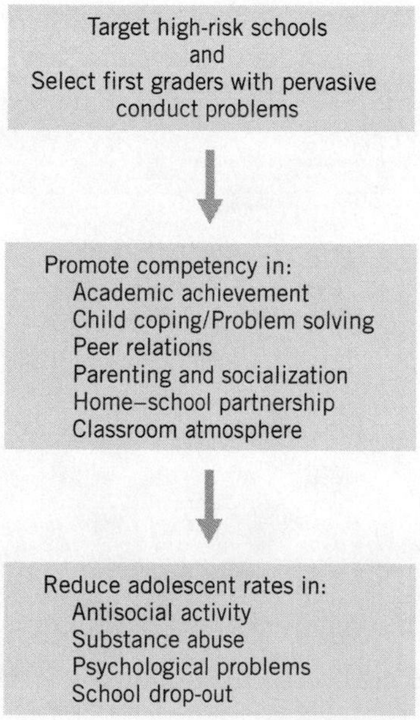

Objectives of the Fast Track project

In the second part of the program, children with the most serious problem behaviors (about 10% of the group) participated in a more intensive intervention. In addition to the school intervention, they attended special meetings throughout the year, receiving social skills training similar to what they experienced in the classroom. They were also tutored in their schoolwork. Their parents received group training that was designed to build their self-control and promote developmentally appropriate expectations for their child's behavior. In addition, the program promoted parenting skills that would improve parent–child interaction, decrease children's disruptive behavior, and establish a positive relationship between parents and the child's school. After 1st grade, the curriculum was continued in the classrooms; other aspects of the intervention outside the classroom were adjusted to the needs of each family and child (Conduct Problems Prevention Research Group, 2004). Meetings with children and parents continued through the 9th grade.

The program was quite successful. In the 1st grade classrooms as a whole, there was less aggression and disruptive behavior and a more positive classroom atmosphere than in the control classes. More important, the children in the intervention group improved in their social and emotional skills (such as recognizing and coping with emotions), as well as in academic skills. They had more positive interactions with peers, were liked more by their classmates, and exhibited fewer conduct problems than the control children. Their parents improved in their parenting skills and were more involved with their children's schooling.

In a follow-up at the end of 3rd grade, 37% of the children in the intervention group were found to be free of serious conduct problems, whereas only 27% of the children who did not receive the intervention were free of problems (Conduct Problems Prevention Research Group, 2002a). Teachers' and parents' reports, as well as information from school records, indicated that there was a modest effect at both home and school; moreover, children in the intervention had lower rates of use of special education services. In 4th and 5th grades, children in the intervention group still exhibited modest improvements in terms of conduct problems, peer acceptance, and lower levels of association with deviant peers. These positive outcomes seemed to be due, in part, to the effects of the intervention on reducing children's hostile attribution biases, fostering their problem-solving skills, and reducing the levels of harsh parental discipline (Conduct Problems Prevention Research Group, 2002b, 2004).

In 9th grade, the intervention appeared to have had a significant positive effect in lowering such externalizing problems as conduct disorder, attention-deficit/hyperactivity disorder, and antisocial behavior—but only among those at highest risk initially (Bierman et al., 2007). In terms of cost, it appears that, given the funds available, the program was not cost-efficient relative to the total sample but was likely cost-effective for children at high risk for externalizing problems (Foster & Jones, 2007). Thus, it is important that children be screened for inclusion in high-cost programs such as Fast Track (Bierman et al., 2007).

Much of the violence in gangs involves members' attempts to gain or preserve status in the group. Violence also often occurs due to competition with, and retaliation against, other gangs. Moreover, gang members sometimes engage in acts of violence together as a means of increasing group solidarity (Decker, 1996; Decker & van Winkle, 1996; Short, 1996).

Because many gang members do not have a high school education or do poorly in school, they are likely to have few opportunities to earn money through legitimate employment. Thus, involvement in illegal gang activities may be the most attractive means they know for obtaining money. As a result, many inner-city gang members continue their membership in gangs rather than entering into conventional adult roles (Decker & van Winkle, 1996; Short, 1996).

Biology and Socialization: Their Joint Influence on Children's Antisocial Behavior

As should be clear by now, it is very difficult to separate the specific biological, cultural, peer, and familial factors that affect the development of children's antisocial behavior (Van den Oord, Boomsma, & Verhulst, 2000). As we have noted, for example, antisocial children sometimes have biologically based characteristics that tend to elicit negative reactions from others, which in turn increases the children's probability of becoming antisocial (Dodge & Pettit, 2003). This is especially the case when children's negative behavior elicits harsh punishment.

The relation between socialization and biology is further complicated by the fact that parents whose children are antisocial and aggressive often are that way themselves and predisposed to punitive parenting (Dogan, Conger, Kim, & Masyn, 2007; Thornberry, Freeman-Gallant, Lizotte, Krohn, & Smith, 2003). Moreover, the effects of parenting on children's aggression sometimes differ depending on the children's temperament—for example, how difficult, active, or unmanageable they are (Bates, Pettit, Dodge, & Ridge, 1998; Colder, Lochman, & Wells, 1997; Rothbart & Bates, 2006).

Nonetheless, parental treatment of children clearly affects children's antisocial behavior. Direct evidence of the role of parental effects can be found in intervention studies. When parents are trained to deal with their children in an effective manner, there are improvements in their children's conduct problems (Connell et al., 2008; Dishion et al., 2008; Hanish & Tolan, 2001). Similar effects have been obtained in intervention studies in schools (see Box 14.4). Moreover, aggressive children exposed to inept, harsh parenting tend to show more antisocial behavior over time (Dodge et al., 2006). Effects such as these indicate that socialization in and of itself plays a role in the development of antisocial behavior.

review:

Aggressive behavior emerges by the second year of life and increases in frequency during the toddler years. Physical aggression starts to decline in frequency in the preschool years; in elementary school, children tend to exhibit more nonphysical aggression (e.g., relational aggression) than at younger ages, and some children increasingly engage in antisocial behaviors such as stealing. Early individual differences in aggression and conduct problems predict antisocial behavior in later childhood, adolescence, and adulthood. Children who first engage in aggressive, antisocial acts in early to mid-adolescence are less likely to continue their antisocial behavior after adolescence than are children who are aggressive and antisocial at a younger age.

Biological factors, including those related to temperament and neurological problems, likely affect how aggressive children become. Social cognition is also associated with aggressiveness in a variety of ways, including the attribution of hostile motives to others, having hostile goals, constructing and enacting aggressive responses in difficult situations, and evaluating aggressive responses favorably.

Children's aggression is affected by a range of environmental factors, as well as by heredity. In general, low parental support, poor monitoring, or the use of disciplinary practices that are abusive or inconsistent are related to high levels of children's antisocial behavior. Parental conflict in the home and many of the stresses associated with family transitions (e.g., divorce) and poverty can increase the likelihood of children's aggression. In addition, involvement with antisocial peers likely contributes to antisocial behavior, although aggressive children also seek out antisocial peers. Cultural values and practices, as communicated in the child's social world, also contribute to differences among children in aggressive behavior. Intervention programs can be used to reduce aggression, which provides evidence of the role of environmental factors in children's aggression.

Chapter Summary

Moral Judgment

- Piaget delineated two age-related moral stages and a transitional period. In the first stage, morality of constraint, young children tend to believe that rules are unchangeable and to weigh consequences more than intentions in evaluating the morality of actions. In the autonomous stage, children realize that rules are social products that can be changed, and they consider motives and intentions when evaluating behavior. Several aspects of Piaget's theory have not held up well to scrutiny, but his theory provided the foundation for subsequent work on moral reasoning.
- Kohlberg outlined three levels of moral judgment—preconventional, conventional, and postconventional—each originally containing two stages (Stage 6 was eventually dropped from Kohlberg's scoring procedure). Kohlberg hypothesized that his sequence of stages reflects age-related, discontinuous (qualitative) changes in moral reasoning that are universal. According to Kohlberg, these changes stem from cognitive advances, particularly in perspective taking. Although there is support for the idea that higher levels of moral reasoning are related to cognitive growth, it is not clear that children's moral reasoning moves through discontinuous stages of development or develops the same way in all cultures and for all kinds of moral issues (e.g., prosocial moral reasoning).
- There are important differences among the moral, social conventional, and personal domains of behavior and judgment. Young children, like older children, differentiate among different domains of social judgment. Which behaviors are considered matters of moral, social conventional, or personal judgment varies somewhat across cultures.

The Early Development of Conscience

- The conscience involves internalized moral standards and feelings of guilt for misbehavior: it restrains the individual from engaging in unacceptable behavior. The conscience develops slowly over time, beginning before age 2. Children are more likely to internalize parental standards if they are securely attached and if their parents do not rely on excessive parental power in their discipline.

Prosocial Behavior

- Prosocial behavior is voluntary behavior intended to benefit another, such as helping, sharing, and comforting others. Young children who are prosocial, especially those who spontaneously engage in sharing that is costly to themselves, tend to be prosocial when older.
- Prosocial behaviors emerge by the second year of life and increase in frequency with age, probably due to age-related increases in children's abilities to sympathize and take others' perspectives. Differences among children in these abilities contribute to individual differences in children's prosocial behavior.
- Heredity, which contributes to differences among children in temperament, likely affects how empathic and prosocial children are.
- A positive parent–child relationship; authoritative parenting; the use of reasoning by parents and teachers; and exposure to prosocial models, values, and activities are associated with the development of sympathy and prosocial behavior. Cultural values and expectations also appear to affect the degree to which children exhibit prosocial behavior and toward whom.
- School-based intervention programs designed to promote cooperation, perspective taking, helping, prosocial values, and the exercise of autonomy are associated with increased prosocial tendencies in children.

Antisocial Behavior

- Aggressive behavior emerges by the second year of life and increases in frequency during the toddler years; physical aggression starts to decline in frequency in the preschool years. In elementary school, children tend to exhibit more nonphysical aggression (e.g., relational aggression) than at younger ages, and some children increasingly engage in antisocial behaviors such as stealing.
- From preschool on, boys are more physically aggressive than girls and more likely to engage in delinquent behavior.

- Early individual differences in aggression and conduct problems predict antisocial behavior in later childhood, adolescence, and adulthood.
- Biological factors that contribute to differences among children in temperament and neurological problems likely affect how aggressive children become. Social cognition also affects aggression: aggressive children tend to attribute hostile motives to others and to have hostile goals themselves.
- Children's aggression is promoted by a range of environmental factors, including low parental support; poor monitoring; abusive, coercive, or inconsistent disciplining; and stress or conflict in the home. In addition, involvement with antisocial peers likely contributes to antisocial behavior, although it is also likely that aggressive children seek out antisocial peers. Aggression also varies somewhat across cultures, suggesting that cultural values, norms, and socialization practices may also contribute to individual differences in aggression and antisocial behavior.
- Children who are diagnosed with antisocial behavior such as conduct disorder (CD) and oppositional defiant disorder (ODD) display relatively severe forms of problematic externalizing behaviors.
- Interventions in high-risk schools designed to promote understanding and communication of emotions, positive social behavior, self-control, and social problem solving can reduce the likelihood that children will develop behavior problems, including aggression.

Critical Thinking Questions

1. Recall a recent moral dilemma in your own life. What sorts of reasoning did you use when thinking about the dilemma? On what dimensions did it differ from Kohlberg's Heinz dilemma? How might these differences have affected your reasoning about this dilemma?
2. How would you design a study to determine why aggressive children and adolescents have aggressive friends? How would you determine whether aggressive youth simply choose aggressive friends or whether aggressive friends tend to make youth become more aggressive?
3. Suppose you wanted to assess children's helping behavior that was altruistic and not due to factors such as the expectation of personal gain or concern about others' approval. How would you design a study to assess altruistic helping in 5-year-olds? Might the procedure differ if you wanted to assess altruistic helping in 16-year-olds?
4. Freud believed that morality does not emerge until the child develops a superego at around 4 to 6 years of age. What evidence contradicts his theory?
5. Using the tenets of social learning theory (see Chapter 9), outline ways that parents might deter the development of aggression in their children.

Key Terms

prosocial behavior, p. 552	conscience, p. 556	oppositional defiant disorder (ODD), p. 570
moral judgments, p. 554	altruistic motives, p. 559	conduct disorder (CD), p. 570
social conventional judgments, p. 554	aggression, p. 567	reactive aggression, p. 572
personal judgments, p. 554	instrumental aggression, p. 568	proactive aggression, p. 572

ROMARE BEARDEN, *Sunday after the Sermon,* 1969

15

Gender Development

THEMES

Nature and Nurture

❖

The Active Child

❖

The Sociocultural Context

❖

Individual Differences

❖

One late summer afternoon, the two children pictured below were playing in the backyard as their mothers, best friends for many years, were having tea on the deck. Colin, who was 5 years old, and Catherine, who was 4½, had played together since infancy. Even though they shared many of the same interests, they also were different in many ways. For example, Catherine hated movies that were the least bit violent or scary: as a toddler she would not even watch *Sesame Street* because she was frightened of Oscar the Grouch. When asked to pause in her play to be photographed, Catherine happily complied and struck an expressive pose. In contrast, Colin loved action films full of car chases, fires, and explosions. His rifle and helmet testify to his fascination with guns and the military. Colin initially resisted the request for a photo. After agreeing, he took an aggressive stance holding his toy gun.

Colin and Catherine exhibit some of the behavioral differences in assertion and affiliation that are often seen between girls and boys. **Assertion** refers to one's attempts to exert influence over the environment, whereas **affiliation** refers to making connections with others. The traditional masculine role in most societies stresses self-assertion over interpersonal affiliation, with corresponding emphases on independence, competition, and task orientation. In contrast, the traditional feminine role stresses affiliation over assertion, with corresponding emphases on interpersonal sensitivity, showing support, and affection (Bassen & Lamb, 2006; Leaper & Smith, 2004). However, the goals of assertion and affiliation are not mutually exclusive: they are often blended together in a style known as **collaboration.** As discussed later in the chapter, collaboration is associated with gender-role flexibility and is more common among girls than boys.

assertion the tendency to take action on behalf of the self through competitive, independent, or aggressive behaviors

affiliation the tendency to affirm connection with others through being emotionally open, empathetic, or cooperative

collaboration a blending of the assertion and affiliation styles of behavior. Associated with gender-role flexibility, it is more common among girls than among boys.

In this chapter, we consider some of the reasons that might account for gender differences or similarities between children like Catherine and Colin. Why do they have different preferences? How representative is their behavior of that of

Although Colin and Catherine are similar in age, some differences in their behavior, attitudes, and interests are apparent. In this chapter, we will compare boys' and girls' development and consider different theoretical perspectives on the development of gender differences.

BOTH: COURTESY OF JUDY DELOACHE

other children of their own gender? Do they consistently demonstrate gender-stereotypical behaviors across different situations?

Developmentalists generally acknowledge the combined influences of biological, psychological, and cultural processes on gender development (Leaper & Friedman, 2007). They differ, however, in how much they stress particular factors. Some researchers argue that differences in boys' and girls' behavior reflect biological differences that have emerged over the course of human evolution (Bjorklund & Pellegrini, 2002; Geary, 1998). In their view, average gender differences in assertive and affiliative preferences and behavior are attributable to genetic sex differences in brain structures and hormone effects. In contrast, other psychologists place more emphasis on socialization and situational demands (Bussey & Bandura, 1999; Martin, Ruble, & Szkrybalo, 2002). These researchers believe that the role of biology in the development of gender-related differences must be considered in the context of the social influences of family, peers, teachers, and the culture at large.

In this chapter, the main question we examine is how similar or different girls and boys are in terms of psychological variables, as well as what might account for any differences. We first consider the biological, cognitive-motivational, and cultural influences that may contribute to gender development. Next, we outline the major milestones in children's development of gender stereotypes and gender-typed behavior. Then we compare what is actually known about the similarities and differences between girls and boys in specific areas of development, including physical development, cognitive abilities and achievement, and personality and social behavior. (Note that throughout our discussion, we use the terms *sex* and *gender* in distinct ways. The term *sex* tends to imply biological origins for any male–female differences. Therefore, we follow the convention of using *gender* as a more neutral term, referring simply to one's social categorization as either female or male, and use the term *sex* only when referring explicitly to biological processes, such as those involving sex hormones or genetic sex.)

Four of our seven themes are particularly prominent in this chapter. The theme of *nature and nurture* appears repeatedly, as perspectives vary in their emphasis on the roles played by biological and environmental factors in gender development. The theme of the *active child* is apparent in cognitive theories of gender development that emphasize children's role in discovering what it means to be male or female and in socializing their peers into gender-appropriate roles. The theme of the *sociocultural context* is reflected in theories that emphasize the central role of teachers, peers, and the media in shaping children's gender development. Finally, the theme of *individual differences* also pervades the chapter, as we attempt to account for the ways in which males and females are similar and different.

Theoretical Perspectives on Gender Development

Researchers variously point to three kinds of influence on gender development. Some investigators argue that behavioral gender differences reflect biological differences between males and females, including the influence of sex hormones and differences in brain structure. Others emphasize the influences of cognition and motivation, holding that children's behavior reflects their learning of the gender-typed roles that they observe in the home and in the larger community. These researchers also note that boys and girls are provided different opportunities and incentives for gender-typed behavior by parents, teachers, and peers. A third approach draws attention to cultural influences and the relative status of women and men in society. As you will see in this section, each perspective has gained some empirical support. Indeed, it is likely that gender development results from the complex interaction of all the factors they highlight.

Biological Influences

Some researchers interested in the biological influences on development try to explain gender differences in behavior according to the presumed adaptive function they played in the story of human evolution. Other biologically oriented researchers focus more directly on identifying hormonal factors and differences in brain functioning as possible influences on gender differences in behavioral development.

Evolutionary Approaches

As discussed in Chapter 9, evolutionary theory proposes that certain characteristics that facilitate survival and the transmission of genes to succeeding generations have been favored over the course of human evolution. Developmental psychologists generally agree that evolution is important for understanding children's development. However, there are different views regarding whether males and females evolved different behavioral dispositions, and if so, to what degree. Two examples of evolutionary approaches in psychology are *evolutionary psychology theory* and *biosocial theory.*

Evolutionary psychology theory According to one version of evolutionary psychology theory, gender differences in certain behavioral dispositions evolved because they offered reproductive advantages (Bjorklund & Pellegrini, 2002; Buss, 1999; Geary, 1998; Kenrick, Trost, & Sundie, 2004). As noted in Chapter 9, studies of children's play behavior show average gender differences that have been interpreted as consistent with the evolutionary perspective. Specifically, boys are more likely to engage in physically active play, including rough-and-tumble play, and, as discussed later in this chapter, they tend to show higher levels of impulsivity and physical aggression.

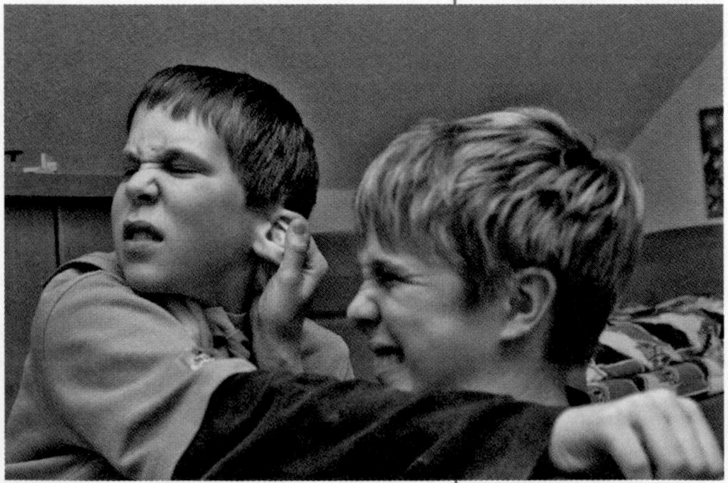

© WOODYSTOCK / ALAMY

Rates of physical aggression with peers tend to be higher for boys than for girls in all cultures that have been studied, although the magnitude of the average gender difference varies across cultures.

Boys also devote considerable effort to jockeying for dominance in groups with their male peers. David Geary (1999) proposed that the play fighting of boys may represent an "evolved tendency to practice the competencies that were associated with male–male competition during human evolution" (p. 31). A propensity to engage in physical aggression is thought to have provided reproductive advantages for males in competition with other males for resources, including access to females. Evolutionary psychologists likewise infer that the greater male propensity toward impulsivity may also have conferred an advantage in seeking mates and in hunting as well (Geary, 2004).

In contrast, girls devote much effort to establishing and maintaining positive social relations, spend time in smaller groups of close female friends, and tend to avoid open conflict in their interactions. Girls also engage in much more play parenting, including play with dolls, than boys do. This makes sense from the evolutionary perspective, given that until quite recently, maternal care in the form of breast-feeding was required for infants' survival. In addition, having an affiliative orientation may have helped women gain assistance with child care, thereby increasing the probability that their offspring would survive long enough to reproduce. Females' greater impulse control is viewed as having been beneficial in the selection of appropriate mates and in inhibiting attention to their own needs in favor of focusing on the needs of their children (Miller, Putcha-Bhagavatula, & Pedersen, 2002).

This version of evolutionary psychology theory is a popular one, but it is also controversial. One major argument against it is that many of its claims cannot be tested (Gould, 1997; Lickliter & Honeycutt, 2003; Wood & Eagly, 2002). In addition, many of the theory's ideas regarding gender differences as evolved dispositions are based not on identified genetic influences but on the assumption that gender differences in behavior reflect different dispositions that were favored during evolution because they were adaptive. Critics complain that this is circular reasoning (i.e., a gender difference occurs because it reflects an evolved disposition; and evidence for this claim is that the gender difference occurs). The theory is also faulted for being deterministic and emphasizing biological constraints on gender development.

An alternative view emphasizes human evolution as maximizing our capacity for behavioral flexibility as an adaptation to environmental variability (Gould, 1997; Lickliter & Honeycutt, 2003). This view also points out that because of their focus on biological constraints in gender development, some versions of evolutionary theory can be construed as a rationalization for the status quo in gender-role inequities (Angier, 1999; Gould, 1997).

Biosocial theory Wendy Wood and Alice Eagly (2002) have offered biosocial theory as an alternative evolutionary approach to understanding gender development. This theory focuses on physical rather than dispositional differences between the sexes and proposes that these differences have behavioral and social consequences. For much of human history, the most important differences have been men's greater average size, strength, and foot speed, and women's childbearing and nursing capacities. Men's physical abilities gave them an advantage for activities such as hunting and combat, both of which, in turn, tended to confer status and social dominance in the society. In contrast, bearing and nursing children limited women's mobility and involvement in many forms of economic subsistence such as hunting.

However, biology is not destiny, according to biosocial theory. In postindustrial societies, men's strength and other physical qualities are not relevant for most means of subsistence. For example, strength is irrelevant to succeeding as a manager, a lawyer, a doctor, or an engineer. Also, reproductive control and day care have enabled women's active involvement in the labor force. Thus, according to biosocial theory, both physical sex differences and the social ecology can shape the different gender roles assigned to men and women, which, in turn, shapes the gender socialization of boys and girls.

Whereas some versions of evolutionary psychology theory have been criticized for emphasizing biological determinants of gender differences, biosocial theory faces the flip side of the argument. Evolutionary psychology theorists assert that the body and the mind evolved together and that biosocial theory addresses only the body's impact on gender development (Archer & Lloyd, 2002; Luxen, 2007). That is, they acknowledge the importance of the physical differences highlighted in biosocial theory but also maintain that the additional impact of evolved behavioral dispositions cannot be overlooked.

Neuroscience Approaches

Researchers who take a neuroscience approach focus on testing whether and how hormones and brain functioning are related to variations in gender development

androgens a class of hormones that normally occur at higher levels in males than in females and that affect physical development and functioning from the prenatal period onward

congenital adrenal hyperplasia (CAH) a condition in which the adrenal glands produce high levels of hormones that have androgen-like effects

organizational hormonal influences the potential result of certain sex-linked hormones affecting brain differentiation and organization during prenatal development or at puberty

activational hormonal influences the potential result of certain fluctuations in sex-linked hormone levels affecting the contemporaneous activation of certain brain and behavioral responses

(Berenbaum, 1998; Hines, 2004). Some of these researchers also frame their work in terms of an evolutionary psychology perspective (Geary, 1998).

Hormones and brain functioning In the study of gender development, much attention has been paid to the possible effects of **androgens,** which are steroid hormones that include testosterone. As discussed in Chapter 2, during normal prenatal development, the presence of androgens, in particular testosterone, leads to the formation of male genitalia in genetic males; in their absence, female genitalia are formed in genetic females.

In rare instances, high levels of androgens are produced during the prenatal development of genetic females. This can lead to **congenital adrenal hyperplasia (CAH),** a condition that involves the formation of ostensibly male (or partly masculinized) genitalia. Researchers have studied girls with CAH to infer the possible organizational influence of androgens on gender development. They have found that, compared with other girls, those with CAH are more likely to choose physically active forms of play, such as rough-and-tumble play, and to avoid sedentary forms of play, such as playing with dolls (Berenbaum & Hines, 1992; Nordenstrom, Servin, Bohlin, Larsson, & Wedell, 2002). This evidence has been used to support the idea that prenatal androgens may contribute to boys' and girls' gender identity (see Box 15.1) and to gender-typed play preferences. In addition, this kind of evidence is sometimes used to support evolutionary accounts of gender development (Alexander, 2003).

Hormones can have *organizational* or *activational* influences on the nervous system. **Organizational influences** occur when certain sex-linked hormones affect brain differentiation and organization during prenatal development or at puberty. For example, sex-related differences in prenatal androgens may partly contribute to average gender differences in certain play preferences (see Berenbaum, 1998). **Activational influences** occur when fluctuations in sex-linked hormone levels influence the contemporaneous activation of certain brain and behavioral responses (Collaer & Hines, 1995). For example, as discussed later, the

a closer look

Gender Identity: More than Socialization?

For most children, their gender identification is consistent with their gender socialization. That is, their view of themselves in terms of their gender is consistent with the gender expectations others hold for them. However, in some rare cases, children believe that their gender is not the one that others take it to be. Studies of such cases suggest that, once established, the child's initial gender identification is often impervious to parental attempts to socialize the child as a member of what the child perceives as the "wrong" gender.

The most dramatic of these cases have involved male infants or toddlers whose genitals were prenatally malformed or seriously damaged postnatally due to accidents and whose parents, following the medical advice then current, had the child's sex "reassigned" to female. Typically, the reassignment process involved reconstructive surgery, estrogen therapy, and female gender socialization. Initially, these cases of sex reassignment were declared to be very successful and were touted as providing strong evidence for the powerful impact of socialization and learning on gender development—a triumph of nurture over nature (Money & Ehrhardt, 1972).

Later it was discovered that, in many cases, the sex reassignments had actually not been successful at all. In one famous case, a male toddler, John, underwent sex reassignment after a failed surgical procedure severely damaged his penis. The child's parents, following the doctors' recommendations, agreed to the required medical interventions and did everything they could to treat their child as a girl, including renaming her Joan, dressing her in girls' clothes, and otherwise encouraging her female identity in every way they could think of. However, from early childhood, Joan preferred to socialize with boys and engaged in typical boy activities. As a result, she was mercilessly teased by her peers.

As she grew up, Joan became increasingly unhappy about her gender, and in body increases the production of androgens in response to perceived threats, with possible implications for gender differences in aggression.

gender self-socialization the process through which children's biases to behave in accord with their gender identity is strengthened by their greater attention to and involvement with entities and activities deemed appropriate to their gender

Brain structure and functioning Male and female brains show some small differences in physical structure (Hines, 2004). One such difference is in the corpus callosum, the connection between the brain's two hemispheres. The corpus callosum tends to be larger and to include more dense nerve bundles in women than in men (Driesen & Raz, 1995). When engaged in cognitive tasks (e.g., deciding if words rhyme or navigating a maze), the male brain tends to show activations in one hemisphere or the other, whereas the female brain tends to show activations in both hemispheres (Shaywitz et al., 1995). However, this particular difference does not appear to result in any advantage to cognitive performance (Halpern, 2000).

One limitation of research documenting sex differences in brain structure is that it is mostly based on brain-imaging studies performed on adults. Since the continual interaction of genes and experience shapes brain development, it is unclear to what extent any differences in the brain's structure or functioning are due to genetic or environmental influences. It is also unclear to what extent these small differences in brain structure determine gender differences in ability and behavior (Halpern, 2000; Halpern et al., 2007).

Cognitive and Motivational Influences

Cognitive theories of gender development emphasize the ways that children learn gender-typed attitudes and behaviors through observation, inference, and practice. According to these explanations, children form expectations about gender that guide their behavior. In this regard, cognitive theories stress children's active **gender self-socialization**. However, cognitive theories also emphasize the role that the environment plays in terms of the different role models, opportunities, and incentives that girls and boys might experience. Four pertinent cognitive theories of gender development are summarized in the following discussion: cognitive developmental theory, gender schema theory, social identity theory, and social cognitive theory.

15.1

her early teens, she began to have suicidal thoughts. At age 14, she confided to the doctor who was overseeing her estrogen therapy that since the 2nd grade she had believed that she was a boy. Shortly thereafter, Joan was told the truth about her gender history, and with great relief, she began the process of reestablishing her true gender as a male (Diamond & Sigmundson, 1997).

Another example of the dominance of gender identification over gender socialization and learning involves children who indicate, almost as soon as they can talk, that their gender is not consistent with their physical sex. For example, a 2-year-old boy may prefer feminine over masculine gender-typed play and may resist adult efforts to treat him as a boy (Zucker & Bradley, 1995). Such discrepant gender identity usually appears very early in development, mostly occurs in boys, and can be difficult to alter even with intensive therapy and parental socialization efforts. These cases, along with examples like the John/Joan case, suggest that gender identification has a biological component. As we have discussed, the biological perspective on gender development points to the impact of sex hormones on the developing fetal brain during prenatal development. Such biological influences seem to contribute to gender identity as well as to behavioral gender differences.

There is currently a debate in psychology about whether children with discrepant gender identities should be classified as having a psychiatric disorder. At present, they are given a diagnosis of *gender identity disorder.* Defenders of maintaining this disorder classification contend that children with discrepant gender identity are distressed and require care (Zucker, 2006). Critics argue that applying a disorder label to children with cross-gender-typed interests merely reflects societal pressures for gender-role conformity (Bartlett, Vasey, & Bukowski, 2000; Zucker, 2006).

JULIA CUMES / THE IMAGE WORKS

As predicted by social learning theory, children learn a great deal about gender roles by observing other people. Television, movies, and videos provide many examples of gender stereotypes for both sexes.

Cognitive Developmental Theory

Lawrence Kohlberg's (1966) cognitive developmental theory of gender-role development reflects a Piagetian framework (reviewed in Chapter 4). Kohlberg proposed that children actively construct gender knowledge in the same way they construct other knowledge about the world. And, just as young children's understanding of the physical world is limited, so is their understanding of the social world, including their knowledge of the meaning and immutability of gender.

Kohlberg maintained that the development of a mature understanding of gender involves a three-stage process. First, young children establish **gender identity:** by about 30 months of age, they learn that they are members of one gender category or the other and begin labeling themselves as either a girl or a boy (Fagot & Leinbach, 1989). However, they do not yet realize that gender is permanent (they think, for example, that a girl could grow up to be a father) (Slaby & Frey, 1975). The next stage, **gender stability,** begins at around 3 or 4 years of age, as children come to realize that gender is stable over time ("I'm a girl, and I'll always be a girl"). However, they are still not clear that gender is independent of superficial appearance and think that a boy who has put on a dress and now looks like a girl has become a girl.

The basic understanding of gender is completed in the third stage, at around 5 to 7 years of age, when children achieve **gender constancy,** the understanding that gender is *consistent* across situations ("I'm a girl, and nothing I do will change that"). Kohlberg noted that this is the same age at which children begin to succeed on Piagetian conservation problems and argued that both achievements reflect the same stage of thinking. Kohlberg maintained that children's understanding that gender remains constant even when superficial changes occur is similar to their understanding that the amount of a substance is conserved even when its appearance is altered (a ball of clay that has been mashed flat is still the same amount of clay; a girl who gets her hair cut short and starts wearing baseball shirts instead of dresses is still a girl). Once gender constancy is attained, according to Kohlberg, children begin to seek out and attend to same-gender models in order to learn how to behave ("Since I'm a girl, I should like to do girl things, so I need to find out what those are").

Research has shown that children's understanding of gender develops in the sequence Kohlberg hypothesized and that the attainment of gender constancy occurs at more or less the same age as success on conservation problems (e.g., Marcus & Overton, 1978; Munroe, Shimmin, & Munroe, 1984). However, as you will shortly see, it is also clear that young children begin showing gender-based preferences for toys, activities, and playmates long before they have a mature understanding of gender. Thus, gender constancy is now viewed as the point at which the child's gender knowledge and behaviors become consolidated.

gender identity awareness of one's own gender

gender stability awareness that gender is stable over time

gender constancy the realization that gender is invariant despite superficial changes in a person's appearance or behavior

Gender Schema Theory

Carol Martin and Charles Halverson (1981) proposed gender schema theory to explain children's gender development (also see Bem, 1981; Liben & Bigler, 2002). In contrast to Kohlberg's view that gender-typed interests emerge after gender constancy is achieved, gender schema theory holds that the motivation to enact gender-typed behavior begins as soon as children can label other people's and their own gender—in other words, when they are toddlers.

According to gender schema theory, children's understanding of gender develops through their construction of **gender schemas.** These are mental representations incorporating everything the child knows about gender, including memory representations of his or her own experience with males and females, gender stereotypes transmitted directly by adults and peers ("boys don't cry," "girls play with dolls"), and messages conveyed indirectly through the media. Children use an *ingroup/outgroup* gender schema to classify other people as being either "the same as me" or not. The motivation for cognitive consistency leads them to prefer, pay attention to, and remember more about others of their own gender. As a consequence, an *own-gender schema* is formed, consisting of detailed knowledge about how to do things that are consistent with one's own gender. Simply learning that an unfamiliar object is "for my gender" makes children like it more.

gender schemas organized mental representations (concepts, beliefs, memories) about gender, including gender stereotypes

To test the impact of gender schemas on children's information processing, an experimenter showed 4- to 5-year-olds unfamiliar, gender-neutral objects and told the children either that the objects were "for boys" or that they were "for girls." (Each of the objects was labeled in one way for some of the children and the opposite way for the others.) Girls reported liking the "girl" objects more than boys did, and vice versa. Girls also believed that other girls would like the "girl" items better than boys would (Martin, Eisenbud, & Rose, 1995). In another study, 4- to 9-year-olds were given boxes of unfamiliar gender-neutral objects described as either "boy" or "girl" things. The children spent more time exploring whichever toys had been labeled as being for their own gender, and a week later, they remembered more about the same-gender items (Bradbard, Martin, Endsley, & Halverson, 1986). In an observational study conducted in a preschool classroom, boys were influenced by the number and the proportion of same-gender children who were playing with a set of toys: they approached toys that were being played with primarily by boys and shunned those that seemed popular mainly with girls (Shell & Eisenberg, 1990).

Gender schemas are also responsible for *biased* processing and remembering of information about gender. As just noted, children tend to remember more about what they observe members of their own gender do than what other-gender individuals do (Signorella, Bigler, & Liben, 1997; Stangor & McMillan, 1992). They are also more likely to accurately encode and remember information about story characters that behave in gender-consistent ways and to forget or distort information that is gender-inconsistent (Liben & Signorella, 1993; Martin & Halverson, 1983). For example, children who heard a story that featured a girl sawing wood often remembered it later as a story about a boy sawing wood, and children who saw pictures that showed a boy playing with a doll and a girl playing with a truck tended to misremember the gender of the children performing the actions (Martin & Halverson, 1983). This tendency to retain information that is schema-consistent and to ignore or distort schema-inconsistent information helps to perpetuate gender stereotypes that have little or no basis in reality.

Although gender schemas are resistant to change, the contents of children's gender schemas can be modified through explicit instruction. Such an approach was demonstrated by Bigler and Liben (1987, 1990), who created a cognitive intervention program in which elementary school children learned that a person's interests and abilities (but not gender) were important for the kind of job that the person could have. (The children were encouraged to see, for example, that if Mary was

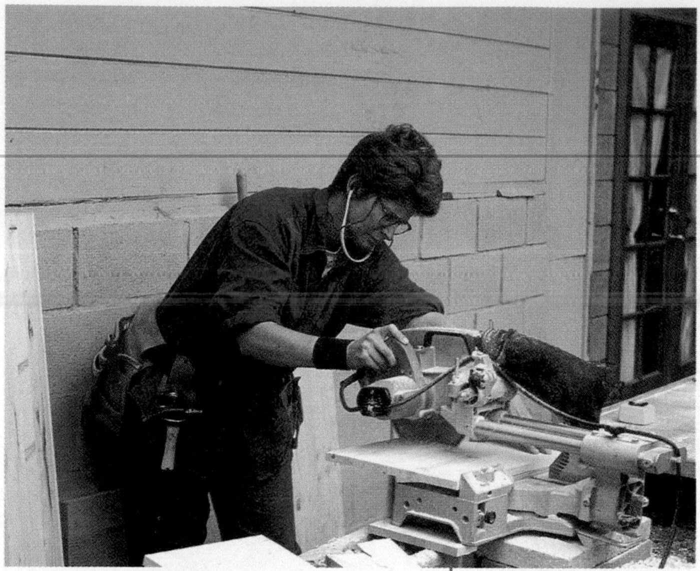

BONNIE KAMIN / PHOTOEDIT

Children's stereotyped beliefs about gender can be changed through cognitive intervention programs. Children who learned that a person's interests and abilities were important for the kind of job that the person could have showed significant reductions in gender stereotypes.

strong and liked to build things, a good job for her would be to work as a carpenter.) Children who participated in this week-long program showed decreased gender stereotyping and also had better memory for gender-inconsistent stimuli, such as a picture of a girl holding a hammer.

Social Identity Theory

Developmental psychologists have highlighted the importance of gender as a social identity in children's development (e.g., Bigler & Liben, 2007; Harris, 1995; Leaper, 2000b; Powlishta, 1995). Indeed, gender may be the *most* central social identity in children's lives (Bem, 1981, 1993). Children's commitment to gender as a social identity is most readily apparent through their primary affiliation with same-gender peers (Leaper, 1994; Maccoby, 1998).

Henri Tajfel and John Turner's (1979) social identity theory addresses the influence of group membership on people's self-concepts and behavior with others. According to this theory, commitment to an ingroup is associated with **ingroup bias,** in which individuals tend to evaluate individuals and characteristics of the ingroup as superior to those of the outgroup. For example, Powlishta (1995) observed that children showed same-gender favoritism when rating peers on likeability and favorable traits. Ingroup bias is related to the process of **ingroup assimilation**, whereby individuals are socialized to conform to the group's norms. That is, peers expect ingroup members to demonstrate the characteristics that define the ingroup. Thus, they anticipate ingroup approval for preferring same-gender peers and same-gender-typed activities, as well as for avoiding other-gender peers and cross-gender-typed activities (Banerjee & Lintern, 2000; Martin, Fabes, Evans, & Wyman, 1999). As a result, children tend to become more gender-typed in their preferences as they assimilate into their same-gender peer groups (Martin & Fabes, 2001).

Social identity theory can help to explain why gender-typing pressures tend to be more rigid for boys than for girls (Leaper, 2000b). According to the theory, group socialization pressures can differ when groups differ in status or power: members of high-status groups, for example, are usually more invested in maintaining group boundaries than are members of low-status groups. In most societies, males are accorded greater status and power than are females. Consistent with social identity theory, boys are more likely than girls to initiate and maintain role and group boundaries (Fagot, 1977; Sroufe, Bennett, Englund, Urban, & Shulman, 1993). Boys are also more likely to endorse gender stereotypes (Rowley, Kurtz-Costes, Mistry, & Feagans, 2007) and to hold sexist attitudes (Brown & Bigler, 2004).

A corollary of social identity theory is that the characteristics associated with a high-status group are typically valued more than those of a low-status group. In male-dominated societies, masculine-stereotyped attributes such as assertiveness and competition tend to be valued more than feminine-stereotyped attributes such as affiliation and nurturance (Hofstede, 2000). Related to this pattern is the tendency of cross-gender-typed behavior to be more common among girls than among boys. Indeed, masculine-stereotyped behavior in a girl can sometimes enhance her status, whereas feminine-stereotyped behavior in a boy typically tarnishes his status (see Leaper, 1994).

ingroup bias tendency to evaluate individuals and characteristics of the ingroup as superior to those of the outgroup

ingroup assimilation process whereby individuals are socialized to conform to the group's norms, demonstrating the characteristics that define the ingroup

Social Cognitive Theory

Kay Bussey and Albert Bandura (1999) proposed a theory of gender development based on Bandura's (1986, 1997) social cognitive theory (see pages 355–356). The theory depicts a *triadic model of reciprocal causation* among personal factors, environmental factors, and behavior patterns. Personal factors include cognitive, motivational, and biological processes. Although the theory acknowledges the potential influence of biological factors, it primarily addresses cognition and motivation. Some key features of the theory include sociocognitive modes of influence, observational learning processes, and self-regulatory processes.

According to social cognitive theory, learning occurs through *tuition*, *enactive experience*, or *modeling*. **Tuition** refers to direct teaching. This occurs during gender socialization, for example, when a father shows his son how to throw a baseball, or a mother teaches her daughter how to change a baby's diaper. **Enactive experience** occurs through experiencing the reactions one's behavior evokes in others. For example, girls and boys commonly get positive reactions for behaviors that are gender-stereotypical and negative reactions for behaviors that are counter-stereotypical (Fagot, 1977). Finally, most learning occurs through modeling. That is, children learn a great deal about gender through observing other people such as their parents, teachers, and peers. (Various forms of gender socialization in the family are described in Box 15.2). Children also learn about gender roles in media such as television, films, and computer games (see Box 15.3).

tuition learning about gender through direct teaching

enactive experience learning about gender through experiencing the reactions one's behavior evokes in others

Observational learning of gender-role information involves four key processes: attention, memory, production, and motivation. To learn new information, it must, of course, be noticed and then stored in memory. As we have noted, children often notice information that is consistent with their existing gender stereotypes. (This is the main premise of gender schema theory.) Next, children need to practice the behavior (production) that they have observed (assuming that the behavior is within their capabilities). Finally, children's motivation to repeat a gender-typed behavior will depend on the external sanctions—that is, the incentives or disincentives—that children experience relative to the behavior. These sanctions can be experienced either directly, as when a parent praises a daughter for helping to prepare dinner, or indirectly, as when a boy observes another boy getting teased for playing with a doll. Over time, external sanctions are usually internalized as personal standards and become self-sanctions that motivate behavior.

According to the social cognitive theory, children monitor their behavior and evaluate how well it matches personal standards. After this evaluation is made, children may feel pride or shame, depending on whether they meet their standards. When individuals experience positive self-reactions for their behavior, they gain the sense of personal agency referred to as *self-efficacy* (see pages 356–357). Self-efficacy can develop gradually through practice (as when a son regularly plays catch with his father), through social modeling (as when a girl observes a female friend do well in math and thinks that maybe she could do well herself), and by social persuasion (as when a coach gives a pep talk to push boys' performance on a baseball team). Researchers consistently find a strong relation between feelings of self-efficacy and motivation. For example, self-efficacy in math predicts girls' as well as boys' likelihood of taking advanced math courses (Stevens, Wang, Olivarez, & Hamman, 2007).

Self-Socialization: A Common Theme in Cognitive Theories

A common underlying premise of all the cognitive theories described here is that gender development is largely a process of self-socialization. They all stress how

a closer look 15.2

Gender Socialization at Home

Parents convey messages about gender in many ways. For example, they frequently assign different household chores to boys and girls. In most U.S. households, boys take out the trash, help wash the car and mow the lawn, and generally are more often responsible for tasks that are performed outside the home and that involve tools and machines. Girls are more often responsible for tasks inside the home, particularly helping to care for younger siblings (Grusec, Goodnow, & Cohen, 1996). This gender-based assignment of chores implies a natural division of labor and may influence boys' and girls' emerging interests and preferences.

Another form of gender socialization has been noted in conversations between parents and children. Parents often convey relatively subtle messages about gender through the use of **gender-essentialist statements** about boys and girls. Gender-essentialist statements are phrased in the timeless present tense, such as "Boys play football" and "Girls take ballet." This linguistic form implies that the activities and implied characteristics in question are and always will be generally true of the group as a whole. In contrast, nonessentialist statements such as "Those girls are taking ballet lessons" carry no such implications. In a study of the comments that mothers made as they read stories to their toddlers or preschool children, nearly all (96%) used gender-essentialist language when referring to the gender of the story characters and activities (Gelman, Taylor, & Nguyen, 2004). They also used gender to distinguish the characters' activities ("Does that look more like a boy job or a girl job?"). Such language use may convey the idea that gender is an important distinction and that gender-related characteristics are universal and stable (Leaper & Bigler, 2004).

Another difference in how parents talk to boys and girls was found in a naturalistic-observation study of parent–child conversations in a science museum. While using interactive exhibits, parents were three times more likely to offer explanations to boys about what they were observing than they were to girls (Crowley, Callanan, Tenenbaum, & Allen, 2001). In a different study, researchers observed that when asked to demonstrate a physics task to their school-age children, fathers used more instructional talk (explanations, use of technical vocabulary) with sons than with daughters (Tenenbaum & Leaper, 2003). Presumably, both sets of findings occurred because adults assumed that boys are more scientifically inclined than girls are.

In their conversations with children, parents and other adults are also much more likely to comment on girls' physical appearance and attire than they are on boys', and to feel that this is natural. Adults' talk about girls' appearance, even if in the form of praise, can lead girls to infer that the way they look is one of the most important things about them. And, unfortunately, in some ways this is true. As we saw in Chapter 11, attractiveness is a much stronger predictor of social acceptance for girls than for boys. A girl's appearance can even influence family relationships, as Glen Elder and his colleagues demonstrated in a study of adults who had grown up in the economic hardship of the Great Depression of the 1930s. Overall, as children, the females in this study had experienced more parental rejection and punishment than had the males, with one exception: highly attractive girls rarely suffered paternal rejection, no matter how severe the economic pressures on the family (Elder, Van Nguyen, & Caspi, 1985).

In most American households, children's chores are assigned in ways that differ by gender: girls are responsible for tasks performed in the home, whereas boys are more often assigned chores that involve machinery and that are performed outside the home.

MICHAEL SILUK/THE IMAGE WORKS

gender-essentialist statements statements about males and females that imply that the descriptions and characterizations contained therein generally apply to all members of the gender in question and always will

applications 15.3

Where Are SpongeSally SquarePants and Curious Jane?

Before reading further, take a moment to list your five favorite television programs. Now count the number of major characters in them who are male and female. Which characters are highly active and/or have positions of power on the show? How would you characterize the general nature of your programs—action-packed adventures, romantic comedies, sports shows, soap operas? What would be different if you made a list of the programs you liked best as a child?

We would be willing to bet that your list of major characters includes more males than females, probably by a substantial degree (except for daytime soap operas). We also suspect that more of our male readers would list action and sports as favorite programs, whereas more of our female readers would have romantic shows or soap operas on their lists. We are also pessimistic that the imbalance of male over female characters would be much different for your current favorite shows versus those you watched in your youth. The reason we feel such confidence in our predictions is that these differences in the gender representation of characters on TV have been very well documented, are very large, and have changed relatively little over the past three decades (Huston & Wright, 1998; Leaper, Breed, Hoffman, & Perlman, 2002; Signorielli, 2001; Thompson & Zerbinos, 1995).

The differential treatment of the sexes in the media is not limited to numerical representations. Portrayals of males and females tend to be highly stereotypical in terms of appearance, personal characteristics, occupations, and the nature of the roles they play. On average, male characters tend to be older and in more powerful roles; females tend to be young, attractive, and provocatively dressed (Calvert & Huston, 1987; Leaper et al., 2002; Signorielli, 2001; Signorielli, McLeod, & Healy, 1994; Thompson & Zerbinos, 1995).

Does it matter that there are large differences in both the number and nature of the portrayals of the sexes on TV? Keep in mind that the average U.S. child between ages 3 and 11 watches 2 to 4 hours of TV a day (Huston & Wright, 1998). In addition, for most young children, television is a major source of information about the world at large (Gerbner, Gross, Morgan, Signorielli, & Shanahan, 2002). From a gender-socialization perspective, the fact that children have so much exposure to highly stereotyped gender models matters a great deal.

There is some evidence for such a supposition. For example, children who watch a lot of TV have more highly stereotypic beliefs about males and females and prefer gender-typed activities to a greater extent than do children who are less avid viewers (McGhee & Frueh, 1980; Oppliger, 2007; Signorielli & Lears, 1992). But since this evidence is correlational, it is difficult to know how to interpret it. However, a different type of evidence suggests that TV watching does, in fact, cause stereotyping. In the early 1980s, television was introduced to an isolated town in Canada. Prior to this, the children of the town, referred to as "Notel," held less stereotyped views of gender than did children from comparison towns that did have access to TV. A few years after TV came to Notel, the children of the town showed a substantial increase in their gender stereotyping (Williams, 1986).

Children are, of course, exposed to media other than television, but similar gender disparities have been documented in them as well. For example, children's books still contain far more male than female characters, and characters of both sexes are often portrayed in gender-stereotypic ways. Males tend to be depicted as active and effective in the world at large, whereas females are frequently passive and prone to problems that require the help of males to solve (Kortenhaus & Demorest, 1993; Tognoli, Pullen, & Lieber, 1994; Turner-Bowker, 1996).

Another medium in which gender differences abound is video games. The most popular games typically feature a high-action format and violent themes, and they are replete with gender stereotypes, as male heroes with bulging biceps rescue scantily clad heroines with bulging bosoms. Partly because of these characteristics, boys are much more avid video game players than girls are, and this difference is cause for some concern. As discussed later, *some* video games that involve fast action and divided attention improve children's attentional and spatial skills (Greenfield, deWinstanley, Kilpatrick, & Kaye, 1994; Okagaki & Frensch, 1996; Subrahmanyam & Greenfield, 1996), and the fact that boys spend more time playing them could widen the gap between male and female spatial abilities.

REUTERS / BEAWIHARTA / LANDOV

Computer games are beginning to displace television as the primary source of children's media entertainment. Unfortunately, like television programming, many computer games portray the sexes in highly stereotyped ways.

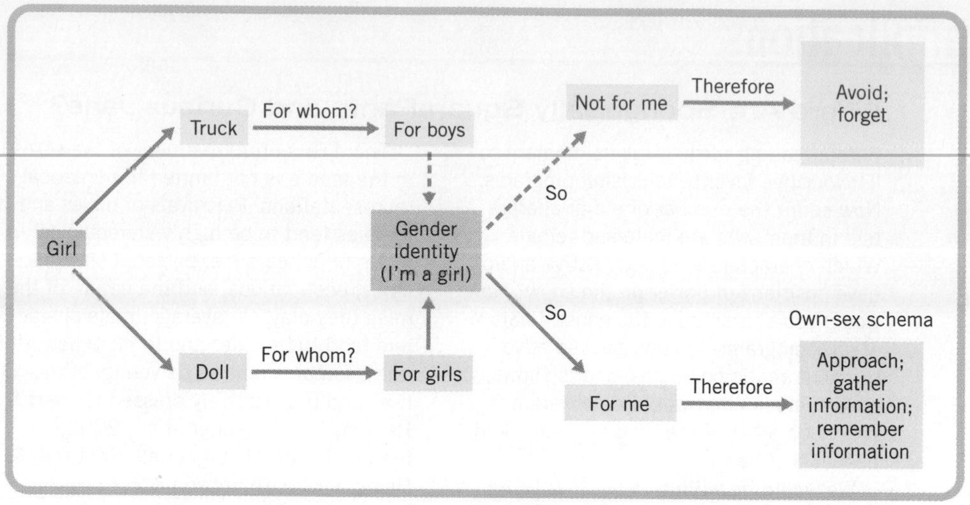

FIGURE 15.1 Gender schema theory According to gender schema theory, children classify new objects and activities as "for boys" or "for girls." They tend to investigate objects and activities that are relevant to their gender and to ignore those that are associated with the other gender.

children's ideas about gender guide their behavior. Figure 15.1 illustrates how this process of gender self-socialization leads children to acquire greater knowledge and expertise with gender-consistent entities. Imagine a young girl presented with the choice between a toy truck and a doll. Her selection will depend on both her gender identity and her knowledge about these specific toys. If she knows that she is a girl (i.e., has gender identity) and knows that trucks are "boy toys" and dolls are "girl toys," she is likely to choose the doll for herself. Through her subsequent exploration of the doll, she will learn more about dolls, how to play with them, what others think about her playing with dolls, and so on. Avoiding the truck, she will learn nothing further about trucks. The power of children's gender self-socialization is familiar to many parents who have tried but failed to get their children to develop in more gender-neutral ways. Despite their parents' efforts, many little boys continue to show no interest in nurturing baby dolls, and many little girls remain devoted to frilly clothing and Barbie dolls.

Cultural Influences

The last set of approaches to understanding gender development stresses the larger cultural and social-structural factors that can shape gender development. These approaches, involving the bioecological systems model and social role theory, emphasize how cultural practices both reflect and perpetuate the gender divisions that are prevalent in a society.

Bioecological Model

As described in Chapter 9, Urie Bronfenbrenner's bioecological model of human development differentiates among interconnected systems, ranging from the microsystem (the immediate environment) to the macrosystem (the culture), that influence children's development (Bronfenbrenner, 1979; Bronfenbrenner & Morris, 1998). A fundamental feature of the macrosystem is its **opportunity structure,** that is, the economic resources it offers and people's understanding of those resources (Ogbu, 1981). Opportunities for members of a cultural community

opportunity structure the economic resources offered by the macrosystem in Bronfenbrenner's bioecological model, and people's understanding of those resources can vary depending on gender, income, and other factors and are reflected by the dominant adult roles within that cultural community.

According to the bioecological approach, child socialization practices in particular microsystems serve to prepare children for these adult roles. Thus, traditional gender-typing practices perpetuate as well as reflect the existing opportunity structures for women and men in a particular community at a particular time in history (Whiting & Edwards, 1988; Wood & Eagly, 2002). To the extent that children's development is largely an adaptation to their existing opportunities, changes in children's macrosystems and microsystems can lead to greater gender equality (see Leaper, 2000b). For example, increased academic and professional opportunities for girls in the United States have led to a dramatic narrowing of the gender gap in math and science within the past 30 years (Halpern et al., 2007).

Social Role Theory A fundamental premise of social role theory is that different expectations for each gender stem from the division of labor between men and women in a given society (Eagly, 1987; Eagly, Wood, & Diekman, 2000). To the extent that family and occupational roles are allocated on the basis of gender, there are different behaviors (roles) expected of women and men (as well as girls and boys). For example, until recent decades, many occupations were not open to women in the United States and similar societies. Women were underrepresented in politics, business, science, technologically, and various other fields. In turn, girls were not expected to develop interests and skills that would lead toward professions in those fields. Thus, somewhat similar to the bioecological systems model, social role theory highlights ways that institutionalized roles impose both opportunities and constraints on people's behavior and beliefs in the home, schools, the labor force, and political institutions. Accordingly, social role theory is useful when interpreting variations across societies in women's and men's relative status and power (see Wood & Eagly, 2002).

review:

In trying to explain gender differences in behavior, some researchers emphasize the role of biological factors. Those who adopt an evolutionary perspective argue that differences in gender behavior emerged over the course of human evolution because they offered reproductive advantages to males and females. Other proponents of the biological view limit their focus to the possible influences of such factors as sex differences in brain structure and hormone effects. Researchers who focus on cognitive-motivational influences emphasize how children's gender-related beliefs, expectations, and preferences guide their behavior.

Children are intrinsically motivated to acquire interests, values, and behavior in accord with their social identity as girls or boys. Self-socialization plays a prominent role in cognitive theories because it is primarily children themselves who initiate and enforce many forms of gender-typed behavior. Finally, cross-cultural comparisons and historical change within the United States underscore ways that gender roles are tied to culture. Societal values and cultural practices can limit or enhance the role models and opportunities that girls and boys experience during development.

Milestones in Gender Development

Developmental psychologists have identified some general patterns that tend to occur over the course of children's gender development. During infancy and toddlerhood, these patterns are quite simple, involving, first, the ability to distinguish gender and, later, the tendency to associate particular actions and objects with one gender or the other. Thereafter, children's awareness of gender deepens greatly, and developmental trends in their understanding of gender and in their practice of gender-typed behaviors become apparent. In our discussion of gender development in the preschool years, middle childhood, and adolescence, we will begin each section by outlining children's typical gender knowledge and beliefs and then survey their typical gender-typed behavior.

Infancy and Toddlerhood

During the first year of life, infants' perceptual abilities allow them to figure out that there are two groups of people in the world: males and females. As we saw in Chapter 5, much research indicates that infants are able to detect complex regularities in perceptual information. Clothing, hairstyle, height, body shape, motion patterns, vocal pitch, and activities all tend to vary with gender, and these differences provide infants with gender cues. For example, habituation studies of infant perception and categorization indicate that by about 6 to 9 months of age, infants can distinguish males and females, usually on the basis of hairstyle (Intons-Peterson, 1988). Infants can also distinguish male and female voices and make intermodal matches on the basis of gender (Martin, Ruble, & Szkrybalo, 2002). For example, they expect a female voice to go with a female face rather than with a male face. Although we cannot conclude that infants understand anything about what it *means* to be male or female, it does appear that older infants can tell the physical difference between females and males using multiple perceptual cues.

Shortly after entering toddlerhood, children begin exhibiting distinct patterns of gender development. By the latter half of their second year, children have begun to form gender-related expectations about the kinds of objects and activities that are typically associated with males and females. For example, 18-month-olds looked longer at a doll than at a toy car after viewing a series of female faces, and looked longer at a toy car than at a doll after being habituated to male faces (Serbin, Poulin-Dubois, Colburne, Sen, & Eichstedt, 2001). Another study with 24-month-olds found that "mismatches" of gender and action (e.g., a man putting on lipstick) led to longer looking times, as if the children were surprised by the gender inconsistency of the action (Poulin-Dubois, Serbin, Eichstedt, Sen, & Beissel, 2002).

The clearest evidence that children have acquired a concept of gender occurs when they begin to label people's gender. Between 2 and 2½ years of age, about 25% of children can actively classify people by gender, for example, by putting photos of children into "boys" and "girls" piles. Toddlers can also make simple gender matches, such as choosing a toy train over a doll when asked to point to the "boy's toy" (Campbell, Shirley, & Caygill, 2002). Children typically begin to show understanding of their own gender within a few months after labeling other people's gender. This attainment of gender identity seems to emerge between the 2nd and 3rd birthday. By age 3, most children are using gender terms such as "boy" and "girl" in their speech (some do this even earlier) and correctly refer to themselves as a boy or girl (Fenson et al., 1994).

Preschool Years

During the preschool years, children quickly learn gender stereotypes regarding the activities, traits, and roles associated with each gender. By around 3 years of age, they begin to attribute certain toys and play activities to each gender. By around 5 years of age, they typically stereotype affiliative characteristics to females and assertive characteristics to males (Best & Thomas, 2004; Biernat, 1981; Liben & Bigler, 2002; Serbin, Powlishta, & Gulko, 1993). During this period, children usually lack gender constancy (page 590); that is, they do not understand that gender remains stable across time and is consistent across situations. For example, a preschooler might think that a girl becomes a boy if she cuts her hair, or that a boy becomes a girl if he wears a dress.

MICHELLE D. BRIDWELL / PHOTOEDIT

In the United States, children's play becomes differentiated by gender during the preschool period, with most girls preferring to play with soft toys and to spend time in the "housekeeping" area, and most boys preferring to play with blocks and transportation toys.

Gender-Typed Behavior

Many children begin to demonstrate preferences for gender-typed toys by around 2 years of age. These preferences become stronger for most children during the preschool years (Cherney & London, 2006; Pomerleau, Bolduc, Malcuit, & Cossette, 1990; Rheingold & Cook, 1975). As noted earlier, girls, on average, are more likely than boys to favor such toys as dolls, cooking sets, and dress-up materials. Girls are also more likely to invoke domestic themes, such as playing house, in their fantasy play. In contrast, boys are more likely not only to prefer such toys as cars, trucks, building toys, and sports equipment but also, along with rough-and-tumble play, to enact action-and-adventure plots, such as playing superheroes, in their fantasy play.

The preschool period is also when **gender segregation** emerges, as children start to prefer playing with same-gender peers (Leaper, 1994; Maccoby, 1998). Gender segregation increases steadily—including the active avoidance of other-gender peers—until around 6 years of age, and then remains stable throughout childhood (see Figure 15.2). Children's preference for same-gender peers is seen across cultures, although there are some cultural variations in the degree that children play exclusively with their own gender (Whiting & Edwards, 1988).

gender segregation children's tendency to associate with same-gender peers and avoid other-gender peers

Peers are both role models and reinforcers of gender-typed behavior, making gender-segregated peer groups a laboratory for children to learn what it means to be a girl or a boy. Carol Martin and Richard Fabes (2001) identified what they termed a "social dosage effect" of belonging to same-gender peer groups during early childhood. The amount of time that preschool or kindergarten children spent with same-gender peers predicted subsequent increases in gender-typed behavior over six months.

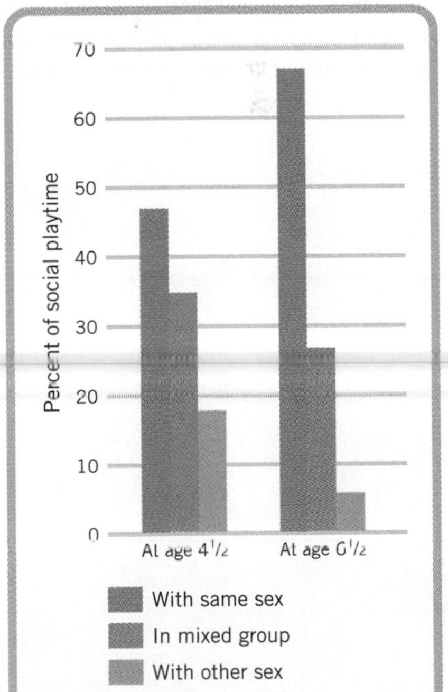

FIGURE 15.2 Gender segregation in play This graph shows the percent of social playtime that preschool and 1st-grade children spent with children of their own or the other gender. (Adapted from Maccoby, 1998)

The reasons for children's same-gender peer preferences seem to involve a combination of temperamental, cognitive, and social forces (Maccoby, 1998), with the relative influences of these forces often changing over time. At first, children appear to prefer same-gender peers because they have more compatible behavioral styles and interests. For example, girls may avoid boys because they tend to be rough and unresponsive, and boys may prefer the company of other boys because they share similar activity levels. Around the time that children begin to exhibit same-gender peer preference, they also are establishing a gender identity and therefore are further drawn to peers who belong to the same ingroup. As children get older, peer pressures may additionally motivate children to favor same-gender peers. Thus, behavioral compatibility may be a less important factor with age; for example, physically active girls may frequently play with boys during early childhood but shift their affiliations more toward girls as they get older.

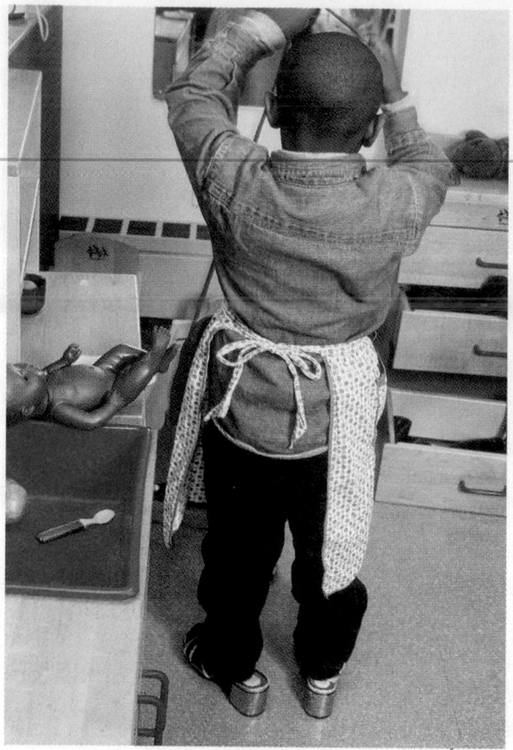

LAURA DWIGHT

During preschool, children begin to avoid peers who violate gender-role norms, and by age 5 to 7 years, they will actively tease peers who cross gender-role boundaries. This is especially true for boys: the one in this photo is likely to experience peer rejection if he continues to play with "girls' toys" and wear aprons and women's shoes.

Middle Childhood

By around 7 years of age, children have attained gender constancy, and their ideas about gender are more consolidated. At this point, children often show more flexibility in their gender stereotypes and attitudes (Katz & Ksansnak, 1994; Liben & Bigler, 2002; Serbin, Powlishta, & Gulko, 1993).

Around 9 or 10 years of age, children start to show a clear understanding that gender is a social category and that gender roles are social conventions as opposed to biological outcomes (Carter & Patterson, 1982; Stoddart & Turiel, 1985). As they come to appreciate the social basis of gender roles, they may recognize that some children may not want to do things that are typical for their gender: they will even argue that in such cases, children should be allowed to follow their personal preferences. For example, Damon (1977) found that children would say that a boy who liked to play with dolls should be allowed to do so. However, children also recognized that the boy would probably be teased and that they themselves would not want to play with him. That is, children understood the notion of individual variations in gender typing, but they were also aware that violating gender role norms would have social costs.

Another development in children's thinking is realizing that gender discrimination is unfair and noticing when it occurs (Brown & Bigler, 2005; Killen, 2007). This was demonstrated when Melanie Killen and Charles Stangor (2001) told children stories about a child who was excluded from a group because of the child's gender. Examples included a boy who was kept out of a ballet club and a girl who was kept out of a baseball-cards club. Eight- and ten-year-olds consistently judged it unfair for a child to be excluded from a group solely due to gender.

Christia Brown and Rebecca Bigler (2005) identified various factors that affect whether children recognize gender discrimination. First among them are cognitive prerequisites such as having an understanding of cultural stereotypes, being able to make social comparisons, and having a moral understanding of fairness and equity. These abilities are typically reached by middle childhood. People's awareness of sexism can also be influenced by individual factors such as their self-concepts or beliefs. For example, girls with gender-egalitarian beliefs were more likely to recognize sexism (Brown & Bigler, 2004; Leaper & Brown, 2008). Finally, the specific situation can affect children's likelihood of noticing discrimination. For example, children are more likely to notice discrimination directed toward someone else than toward themselves. Also, they are more apt to recognize gender discrimination when it is being committed by someone known to be prejudiced (Brown & Bigler, 2005).

Gender-Typed Behavior

In middle childhood, boys' and girls' peer groups tend to establish somewhat different gender-role norms for behavior (Rose & Rudolph, 2006). For this reason, some researchers have suggested that each gender constructs its own "culture" (Maccoby, 1998; Maltz & Borker, 1982; Thorne & Luria, 1986). In line with their tendency to value self-assertion over affiliation, boys' peer groups are more likely to reflect norms of dominance, self-reliance, and hiding vulnerability. In contrast, girls' peer groups, in line with their greater tendency to value affiliative goals (or a balance of affiliative and assertive goals), are more likely to reflect norms of intimacy, collaboration, and emotional sharing. As we have noted, when children violate gender-role norms, their peers often react negatively (Fagot, 1977), including mercilessly teasing someone who has crossed gender "borders." The degree to which children enforce gender segregation on their own is clearly illustrated in the following description of an event in an American elementary school:

> In the lunchroom, when the two second-grade tables were filling, a high-status boy walked by the inside table, which had a scattering of both boys and girls, and said loudly, "Oooo, too many girls," as he headed for a seat at the far table. The boys at the inside table picked up their trays and moved, and no other boys sat at the inside table, which the pronouncement had effectively made taboo.
>
> (Thorne, 1986, p. 171)

During the elementary school years, boys' and girls' groups rarely mix. Children themselves enforce gender segregation; this tendency does not seem to be due to adult influences.

© ELLEN SENISI / THE IMAGE WORKS

It should be noted that there are certain contexts in which friendly cross-gender contacts often occur (Sroufe, Bennett, Englund, Urban, & Shulman, 1993; Strough & Covatto, 2002; Thorne, 1993; Thorne & Luria, 1986). In the home and local neighborhood, the choice of play companions is frequently limited. As a result, girls and boys often play cooperatively with one another (until possibly more same-gender friends become available). In more public settings, the implicit convention is that girls and boys can be friendly if they can attribute the reason for their cross-gender contact to an external cause. For example, this might occur when a teacher assigns them to work together on a class project or when they are waiting in line together at the cafeteria. But, again, beyond such exceptions, the risk of peer rejection is high when children violate the convention to avoid cross-gender contact (Sroufe et al., 1993).

Overall, gender typing during childhood tends to be more rigid among boys than among girls (Leaper, 1994; Levant, 2005). Boys, for example, are more likely to endorse gender stereotypes than are girls, who tend to endorse gender-egalitarian attitudes (Brown & Bigler, 2004). In addition, girls are less gender-typed in their behavior. For example, girls commonly coordinate both affiliative and assertive goals in their actions (Leaper, 1991; Leaper & Smith, 2004). That is, girls are more likely than boys to use collaborative communication that affirms both the self and the other (e.g., proposals for joint activity), whereas boys are more likely than girls to use power-assertive communication that primarily affirms the self (e.g., giving commands). Girls also frequently pursue play activities traditionally associated with boys, as in sports such as soccer and basketball. In contrast, it is relatively rare to see boys to engage in activities traditionally associated with girls, such as playing house.

ANTON VENGO / SUPERSTOCK

Gender segregation persists through childhood. Cross-gender teasing is used to maintain gender boundaries.

Adolescence

For some girls and boys, adolescence can be a period of either increased *gender-role intensification* (Galambos, Almeida, & Petersen, 1990; Hill & Lynch, 1983) or

gender-role intensification refers to heightened concerns with adhering to traditional gender roles

gender-role flexibility refers to advances in cognitive development that can allow adolescents (more often girls than boys) to transcend traditional conventions and pursue a more flexible range of interests

increased *gender-role flexibility* (Carter & Patterson, 1982; Katz & Ksansnak, 1994). **Gender-role intensification** refers to heightened concerns with adhering to traditional gender roles. Factors associated with adolescence, such as concerns with romantic attractiveness or conventional beliefs regarding adult gender roles, may intensify some youths' adherence to traditional gender roles. Alternatively, advances in cognitive development can lead to greater **gender-role flexibility,** allowing adolescents to transcend traditional conventions and pursue a more flexible range of interests. As in childhood, greater gender-role flexibility during adolescence is more likely among girls than among boys. For example, in recent decades, girls' interest and achievement in formerly male-dominated domains such as athletics, mathematics, and science have dramatically increased. At the same time, there has been little change in boys' interest and achievement in traditionally female-dominated domains such as reading and writing (Leaper & Friedman, 2007).

During late childhood and adolescence, as children increasingly develop an understanding that norms about gender roles are social conventions, they may nevertheless endorse the conventions. Thus, adolescents may believe it is legitimate to exclude cross-gender peers from their peer group because they are perceived as violating the group's gender norms and social conventions (Killen, 2007). Researchers also find that girls tend to perceive more gender discrimination during the course of adolescence (Leaper & Brown, 2008). This trend is likely due to a combination of increased experiencing of sexist events (American Association of University Women, 2001; Goldstein, Malanchuk, Davis-Kean, & Eccles 2007; McMaster, Connolly, Pepler, & Craig, 2002) and an increased awareness of sexism (Brown & Bigler, 2005).

Gender-Typed Behavior

During early adolescence, peer contacts are primarily with members of the same gender. However, cross-gender interactions and friendships are usually more common than they are in childhood (Poulin & Pedersen, 2007). As described in Chapter 13, these interactions can open the way to romantic relationships. Adolescence is also a period of increased intimacy in same-gender friendships. For many girls and boys, increased emotional closeness is often attained through sharing personal feelings and thoughts, although there appears to be more variability among boys in the ways they experience and express closeness in friendships (Camarena, Sarigiani, & Petersen, 1990). While some boys attain intimacy through shared disclosures with same-gender friends, many others tend to avoid self-disclosure with same-gender friends due to the wish to appear strong. Instead, they usually attain a feeling of emotional closeness with friends through shared activities, such as playing sports together. At the same time, many boys who avoid expressing feelings with male friends will do so with their female friends or girlfriends (Leaper & Anderson, 1997).

Self-disclosure and supportive listening are generally associated with relationship satisfaction and emotional adjustment (Leaper & Anderson, 1997; Rubin, Bukowski, & Parker, 2006). However, it is possible to have too much of a good thing. This occurs when friends dwell too long on upsetting events, talking to each other about them over and over. Amanda Rose and her colleagues (Rose, Carlson, & Waller, 2007) referred to this process as *co-rumination* and found that it was more common among girls than among boys. Although it may foster feelings of closeness between friends, co-rumination appears to increase depression and anxiety in girls (but not in boys).

Gender Flexibility and Asymmetry

As suggested by our discussion so far, at all ages, boys are more rigidly gender-typed than girls are (Carter & McClosky, 1984), engaging almost exclusively in activities that are considered to be either masculine or gender-neutral, while girls fairly often engage in activities stereotyped for boys (Bussey & Bandura, 1992; Fagot & Leinbach, 1993). This difference in gender flexibility seems to stem in large part from males' *avoidance* of feminine-stereotyped activities, not just from their preference for masculine-stereotyped ones (Bussey & Bandura, 1992; Martin et al., 1995; Powlishta, Serbin, & Moller, 1993). By age 5, boys are more likely than girls to say that they *dislike* other-gender toys (Bussey & Bandura, 1992; Eisenberg, Murray, & Hite, 1982). The preference for objects and activities deemed appropriate for one's own gender, along with the bias against those deemed appropriate for the other gender, declines during the school years, although much more so for girls than for boys (Serbin et al., 1993).

JIM CUMMINS / CORBIS

Parents, peers, and teachers are much more tolerant of girls who engage in masculine-stereotyped activities than they are of boys who engage in feminine-stereotyped activities.

One reason for boys' greater avoidance of feminine-stereotyped activities is that there is an asymmetry in the extent to which most people find it acceptable for boys and girls to engage in activities deemed more appropriate for the other gender. Generally, parents, peers, and teachers respond more negatively to boys who do "girl things" than vice versa. One of the authors' children, for instance, attended preschool with a girl who spent most of her time in the block-building area and a boy who, almost every day, selected a pink tutu from the dress-up corner to wear over his clothes. The teachers, parents, and other adults who observed these two children were concerned about the boy's behavior but not the girl's.

Recall the children in the photos at the beginning of this chapter. If they were your children, which would you find less acceptable—for the girl to don the helmet and pick up the gun, or for the boy to strike the starlet pose? Would you be more upset to hear another child call your daughter a "tomboy" or to hear someone refer to your son as a "sissy"? In our experience, most people report that they find the image of a tomboy girl considerably more acceptable than that of the effeminate boy.

Fathers play a particularly active role in instilling male behaviors in their sons and in enforcing the avoidance of feminine behaviors (Jacklin, DiPietro, & Maccoby, 1984; Leve & Fagot, 1997; Turner & Gervai, 1995). They generally react negatively to their son for doing anything, such as crying, that they think of as "feminine." Consider the contrasting reactions of this mother and father to their toddler son's falling and hurting himself:

> *Mother:* "Come here, honey. I'll kiss it better."
> *Father:* "Oh toughen up. Quit your bellyaching."
>
> (Gable, Belsky, & Crnic, 1993, p. 32)

CORBIS IMAGES / PICTUREQUEST

Fathers play an important role in encouraging boys to learn masculine-stereotyped behaviors and to avoid feminine-stereotyped behaviors.

Why are parents and other adults more upset when boys engage in cross-gender-typed behaviors than they are when girls do? According to social identity theory (page 592), the asymmetry is tied to men's dominant status in society. Related to this difference is the notion that men need to be tough. As noted earlier, when boys show interest in feminine-stereotyped characteristics, people with traditional attitudes view the boys' behavior as a loss in status. Conversely, when girls exhibit certain masculine-stereotyped qualities, those qualities are more likely to be seen as conferring status. For example, a boy who wants to babysit may be ridiculed for being "soft," but a girl who wants to play ice hockey may be praised for being "strong." But can't caring for children also be viewed as a strength? In many cultures it is. As discussed in Chapter 12, for example, among the Aka in Africa, child care is not viewed as a solely feminine activity and is in fact shared by men and women (Hewlett, 1991).

review:

By about the age of 6 to 9 months, infants can distinguish between males and females on the basis of perceptual cues. Between the ages of 2 and 3 years, children identify their own gender and begin acquiring stereotypes regarding "gender-appropriate" behavior, characteristics, and activities. They also begin to demonstrate gender-stereotypical play preferences. During the preschool period, children begin a process of self-initiated gender segregation that lasts through childhood and is strongly enforced by peers. Around 7 years of age, children have acquired gender constancy, and their understanding of gender is consolidated. During middle childhood, children are capable of recognizing gender discrimination. Adolescence is a period that can involve increased gender-role rigidity or flexibility. It is also a time when girls are more likely to experience gender discrimination. Friendship intimacy also increases during adolescence, although intimacy is more common among girls than among boys. Throughout childhood and adolescence, gender-role flexibility also tends to be more common among girls.

Gender Comparisons

Given the gender stereotypes that exist, as well as children's early adoption of gender-typed behavior, one might assume that the actual differences between girls and boys are many and deep. However, as we will see in this section, there are actually only a few areas of cognitive and social behavior that show consistent gender differences, and these differences tend to be fairly small. Figure 15.3 depicts the

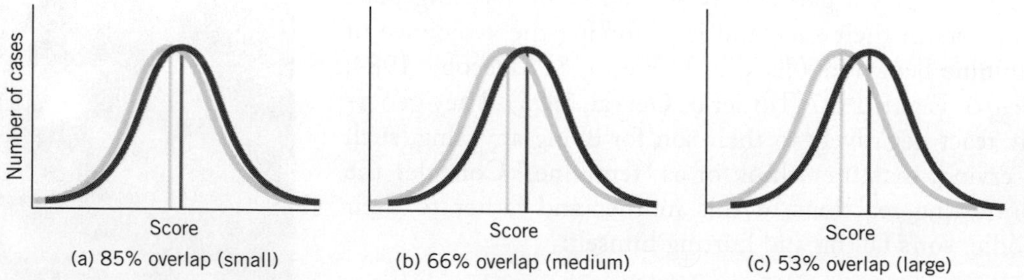

FIGURE 15.3 A typical distribution of scores This graph depicts a typical distribution of scores for males and females on a hypothetical dimension. On many attributes, there is a statistically significant difference in average performance, but the difference is very small and there is considerable overlap between the scores for girls and boys. Also, there is considerable variation within each gender. This pattern is typical for most psychological gender differences.

pattern that is usually observed, in which the average performance of one gender on a given psychological measure is *slightly* higher than that of the other gender. The most salient feature of the graph is the considerable overlap in the distribution of scores for females and males, indicating that, in most cases, girls and boys are much more similar psychologically than they are different. Therefore, besides knowing whether a group difference is statistically significant, it is important to consider the *magnitude* of similarity and difference. This is known as the **effect size.**

effect size the magnitude of similarity and difference between groups

meta-analysis a statistical technique used to summarize the average effect size across studies

Researchers generally categorize effect sizes in the following way: *trivial* if the two distributions overlap more than 85%; *small* but meaningful if the distributions overlap between 67 and 85%; *medium* if the distributions overlap between 53 and 66%; and *large* if the overlap is less than 53% (Cohen, 1988). In studies with large sample sizes, a very small group difference can be statistically significant (in other words, unlikely due to chance).

Across different research studies, there are often contradictory findings regarding gender differences or similarities in particular outcomes. This can occur because researchers use different samples and methods. To infer overall patterns, scientists use a statistical technique known as **meta-analysis** to summarize the average effect size across studies. When available, we have used meta-analyses to summarize the research on gender differences and similarities in this chapter.

Because most average gender differences in cognitive abilities and social behaviors are in the small range, Janet Hyde (2005) has advocated "the gender similarities hypothesis." She argued that when comparing girls and boys, it is important to appreciate that similarities far outweigh differences. When reviewing research findings, we will acknowledge this importance by noting whether the size of any average gender differences in behavior or cognition are trivial, small, medium, or large. Keep in mind, however, that even with large average differences in any particular domain, there are many females and males who are similar to one another in that domain; and there are also some members of the group with the lower average who exceed some members of the group with the higher average. For example, there is a large average gender difference in adult height, but many women and men are the same height, and some women are taller than the average man.

Physical Growth: Infancy through Adolescence

Early in life, males and females are quite similar in size, appearance, and abilities. At birth, males, on average, weigh only about half a pound more than females do; through infancy, male and female babies look so similar that, if they are dressed in gender-neutral clothing, people cannot guess their gender. Not surprisingly, it is quite easy to mislead people by dressing, say, an infant boy in a girl's outfit and calling him by a girl's name. In fact, this "Baby X" technique has frequently been used to demonstrate the power of gender stereotypes. Adults who believe that they are playing with a boy are likely to encourage the infant to play with blocks and to offer the infant a toy football, even though the infant is really a girl (Bell & Carver, 1980). The technique is successful at revealing the influence of stereotyped expectations because there are no consistent or obvious differences in how female and male infants actually look (when they are clothed in a neutral manner) or in how they behave.

As discussed in Chapter 3, during childhood, boys and girls grow at roughly the same rate and are essentially equal in height and weight, though boys are notably stronger. With the changes in body composition that occur in early adolescence, particularly in the substantial increase in muscle mass in boys, the gap that has

puberty the developmental period marked by the ability to reproduce and other dramatic bodily changes

menarche the onset of menstruation

spermarche the onset of males' capacity for ejaculation

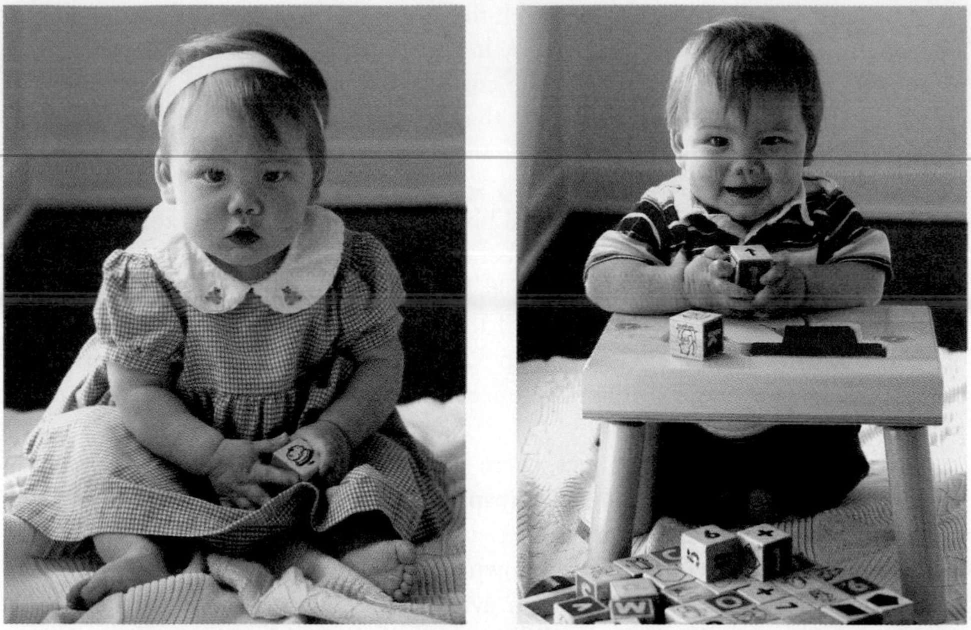

BOTH: DAVID YOUNG-WOLFF / PHOTOEDIT

The same baby is shown in these photographs. Most adults would offer a doll to the "girl" and a toy car or football to the "boy," revealing the influence of stereotyped expectations about the sexes.

existed for years in the sports-related skills of boys and girls greatly increases. After puberty, average gender differences in strength, speed, and size are very large: that is, few adolescent girls can run as fast or throw a ball as far as most boys can (Malina & Bouchard, 1991; Thomas & French, 1985).

Another average gender difference that increases in magnitude during childhood is activity level (Eaton & Enns, 1986). As described in Chapter 10, activity level is a temperamental quality that refers to how much children tend to move and expend energy. On average, boys' activity level tends to be higher than that of girls. In infancy, the difference is small, meaning that there is a lot of overlap between the distributions of the two genders (see Figure 15.3). During childhood, the average gender difference in activity level increases to medium. This increase may result from a combination of practice effects and the greater encouragement commonly given to boys to participate in sports and other physical activities (Leaper & Friedman, 2007). At the same time, average gender differences in activity level also may contribute to children's preferences for gender-typed play activities.

In early puberty, girls are typically taller than boys due to girls' earlier physical maturation. Boys catch up and surpass girls in average height and weight by the end of adolescence.

LAURA DWIGHT

In adolescence, a series of dramatic bodily transformations are associated with **puberty,** which is defined as the development of the ability to reproduce: for boys, to impregnate, and for girls, to menstruate, gestate, and lactate. In girls, puberty typically begins with enlargement of the breasts and the general growth spurt in height and weight, followed by the appearance of pubic hair and then the onset of menstruation, known as **menarche.** Menstruation is triggered in part by the increase in body fat that typically occurs in adolescence. In boys, puberty generally starts with the growth of the testes, followed by the appearance of pubic hair, the general growth spurt, growth of the penis, and the capacity for ejaculation, known as **spermarche** (Gaddis & Brooks-Gunn, 1985; Jorgensen & Keiding, 1991).

For both sexes, there is considerable variability in physical maturation. Compared with their Euro-American peers, for example, African-American children mature somewhat earlier, and the onset of puberty is slightly earlier for African-American girls. Girls with a very low proportion of body fat, such as long-distance runners, gymnasts, and dancers, often experience a delay in menarche (Brooks-Gunn, 1987). The variability in physical development is due to both genetic and environmental factors. Genes affect growth and sexual maturation in large part by influencing the production of hormones, especially growth hormone (secreted by the pituitary gland) and thyroxine (released by the thyroid gland). The influence of environmental factors is particularly evident in secular trends, or changes in physical development that have occurred over generations (see page 117). In the United States today, girls begin menstruating several years earlier than their ancestors did 200 years ago. This change is thought to reflect improvement in nutrition over the generations.

The physical changes that boys and girls experience as they go through puberty are accompanied by psychological and behavioral changes. For example, in some cultures, the increase in body fat that girls experience in adolescence may be related to gender differences in **body image,** that is, how an individual perceives and feels about his or her physical appearance. Currently, American girls tend to have more negative attitudes toward their bodies than boys do, and teenage girls typically want to lose several pounds regardless of how much they actually weigh (Tyrka, Graber, & Brooks-Gunn, 2000). A survey of over 10,000 U.S. adolescents found that roughly half of boys and two-thirds of girls were dissatisfied with their body. Girls were mostly concerned about losing weight; boys, with being more pumped up (Field et al., 2005). Dissatisfaction with body image has long been known to be associated with a host of difficulties, ranging from low self-esteem and depression to eating disorders. This survey added another to the list: the use of unproven and potentially harmful substances to control weight or build muscle—a practice acknowledged by 12% of the boys and 8% of the girls surveyed.

Another change that accompanies physical maturation is in how girls and boys feel about each other. Although boys and girls avoid each other for much of their childhood, sexual attraction begins well before the physical process of puberty is complete. According to the recollections of a sample of American adults, sexual attraction is first experienced at around 10 years of age, regardless of whether the attraction is for individuals of the other sex or the same sex (McClintock & Herdt, 1996). The onset of sexual attraction correlates with the maturation of the adrenal glands, the major source of sex steroids other than the testes and ovaries. This stage has been termed **adrenarche,** which some researchers consider to be an early stage of puberty, although the child's body does not yet show any outside signs of maturation.

body image an individual's perception of, and feelings about, his or her own body

adrenarche the period, prior to the emergence of visible signs of puberty, during which the adrenal glands mature, providing a major source of sex steroids. This period correlates with the onset of sexual attraction.

The onset of sexual interest has been linked to the maturation of the adrenal glands, a source of sex steroids in both males and females.

DAVID YOUNG-WOLFF / PHOTOEDIT

Cognitive Abilities and Academic Achievement

Although average gender differences have been reported for certain aspects of mental functioning, the amount of difference between girls' and boys' averages on these measures is usually small. Thus, there is a lot of overlap between the two distributions, with girls as well as boys scoring at the top and the bottom. In the following discussion, we will summarize the current evidence comparing boys' and girls' cognitive abilities and then examine biological, cognitive-motivational, and cultural influences that might account for these findings.

General Intelligence

Despite widespread belief to the contrary, boys and girls are equivalent in most aspects of intelligence and cognitive functioning. The average IQ scores of girls and boys are virtually identical (Halpern, 2004; Hyde & McKinley, 1997). Although girls and boys show the same average in IQ scores, there are proportionally more boys than girls at both the lower and the upper range of scores. That is, somewhat more boys than girls are diagnosed with intellectual disabilities or classified as intellectually gifted (Halpern, 2000).

Overall Academic Achievement

Although girls and boys are similar in general intelligence, they tend to differ in academic achievement from elementary school through college. Recent statistics in the United States indicate that girls tend to show higher levels of school adjustment and achievement than do boys (U.S. Department of Education and National Center for Education Statistics, 2007). For example, in 2001, the high school dropout rate was higher for boys (12%) than for girls (9%). In addition, in that same year, 57% of bachelor's degrees were awarded to women. In terms of ethnic groups, the magnitude of gender difference in academic achievement is higher among Latino-American or African-American youth than it is among Euro-American or Asian-American youth.

As you will now see, in addition to the overall differences in academic achievement, there are some specific cognitive abilities and academic subjects in which one gender tends to excel slightly more than the other.

Verbal Skills

On average, girls tend to be slightly advanced in early language development, including fluency and clarity of articulation and vocabulary development (Gleason & Ely, 2002). In reading and writing, girls tend to achieve higher performances from elementary school into high school, with the size of the average differences being small for reading and medium for writing (Hedges & Nowell, 1995; Nowell & Hedges, 1998). Boys are more likely to suffer speech-related problems, such as poor articulation and stuttering (Halpern, 2000), as well as more reading-related problems such as dyslexia (Halpern, 2000).

Spatial Skills

Boys, as a group, tend to perform better than girls do in some aspects of visual-spatial processing. This difference emerges between 3 and 4 years of age and becomes more substantial during adolescence (Halpern, 2004; Masters & Sanders, 1993). Gender differences are most pronounced on tasks that involve mental rotation of a complex geometric figure in order to decide if it matches another figure presented in a different orientation (see Figure 15.4a). However, other spatial tasks, such as finding a hidden figure embedded within a larger image, show much smaller gender differences (see Figure 15.4b). And on some spatial tasks, such as remembering the position of various objects that were arranged on a surface,

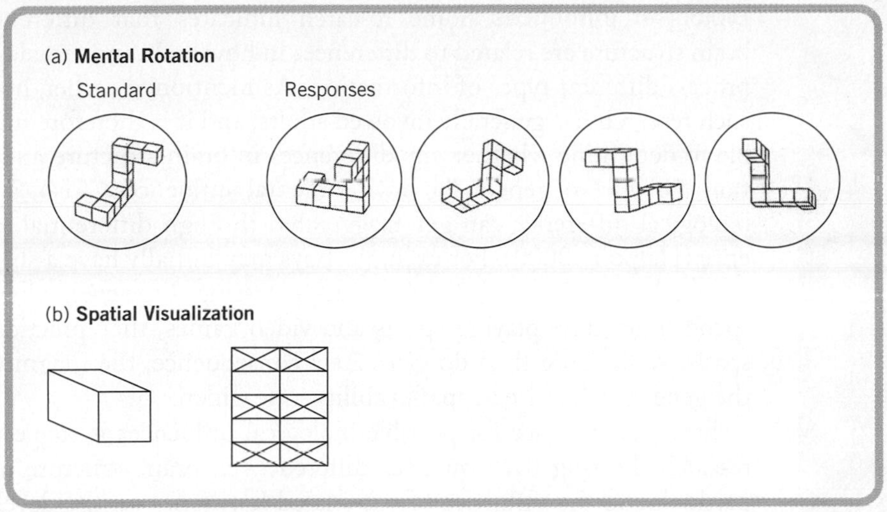

FIGURE 15.4 Gender differences in spatial abilities Tests of spatial skills show that gender differences vary according to the type of task in question. Boys tend to perform better than girls do on tasks that involve mental rotation, such as the one in (a), in which children have to determine which of the responses matches the standard. In contrast, gender differences are small or nonexistent on tasks like that in (b), which require children to find the simple geometric figure to the left embedded in the adjoining complex figure. (Adapted from Linn & Peterson, 1985)

females outperform males (Blakemore, Berenbaum, & Liben, 2009). Thus, the conclusion that males have superior spatial ability depends on the particular type of spatial ability that is being considered.

Mathematical and Related Skills

Until recent decades, boys tended to perform somewhat better on standardized tests of mathematical ability than did girls. However, as a result of efforts made by schools to improve girls' math achievement, the gender gap in mathematics achievement has closed dramatically, with boys and girls currently being near parity in performance on standardized tests at the high school level (Halpern et al., 2007; Nowell & Hedges, 1998). Furthermore, girls and women are maintaining their interest in math beyond high school at rates higher than seen in earlier decades. The percentage of bachelor's degrees in mathematics awarded to women increased from 37% in 1970 to 48% in 2001 (National Science Foundation, 2008; U.S. Department of Education and National Center for Education Statistics, 2007).

Mathematics is considered a pipeline for science, technology, and engineering (Halpern et al., 2007). Patterns of gender differences in these areas are mixed. At the high school level, there is a small average difference favoring boys in achievement in physical sciences (e.g., physics), while in the life sciences (e.g., biology), there is no average gender difference. At the college level, 62% of recent bachelor's degrees in life sciences were earned by women, but women's share of degrees in other scientific fields was much lower: 22% in physics, 22% in computer science, and 20% in engineering (National Science Foundation, 2008). Following the attention paid to the gender gap in math achievement a few decades ago, educators and researchers are now addressing the gender gap in these other disciplines.

Explanations for Gender Differences in Cognitive Abilities and Achievement

Depending on their perspective, researchers emphasize biological, cognitive-motivational, or cultural influences that may contribute to gender-related variations in cognitive abilities and achievement. We will examine each of these areas of influence in turn.

Attention problems in girls may often go unrecognized because girls' symptoms do not match the standard descriptions of attention problems that are based on male symptoms. A girl with attention difficulties may be overlooked or described as "just dreamy" by her teacher because her behavior is not disruptive to the class.

Biological influences Some research indicates that differences in brain structure are related to differences in how male and female brains process different types of information. As mentioned earlier, however, such research has generally involved adults, and it is therefore impossible to determine whether any differences in brain structure and function are due to genetic or environmental influences. Also, a slight biological difference can get exaggerated through differential experience (Halpern, 2000). For example, boys may initially have a slight average advantage over girls in spatial processing. However, when boys spend more time playing sports and video games, they practice their spatial skills more than do girls. As a consequence, the magnitude of the gender difference in spatial ability may widen.

Stronger evidence for possible biological influences is suggested by research showing that some sex differences in brain structure may be partly due to the influence of sex-related hormones on the developing fetal brain (Hines, 2004). Thus, one strategy for inferring sex-linked biological influences on brain functioning is to see if sex-related differences in prenatal hormone levels predict later cognitive abilities. For example, androgens may affect parts of the brain associated with spatial skills; indeed, the area of the brain associated with processing spatial information is rich with androgen receptors (Gron, Wunderlich, Spitzer, Tomczak, & Riepe, 2000). Since males are exposed to higher levels of androgens during normal prenatal development than are females, this difference may lead to greater hemispheric specialization in the male brain and more proficiency in spatial ability later in life.

Support for this hypothesis comes from studies that have linked very high levels of prenatal androgens in girls with above-average spatial ability (Grimshaw, Sitarenios, & Finegan, 1995; Hines et al., 2003; Mueller et al., 2008). Conversely, it has been found that males with androgen insensitivity (a disorder in which the body is unresponsive to androgens) tend to score lower-than-average in spatial ability (Imperato-McGinley, Pichardo, Gautier, Voyer, & Bryden, 2007).

As discussed in Chapters 2 and 8, males are more vulnerable than females to developmental problems, including disorders of mental functioning such as autism, attention-deficit hyperactivity disorder, language-related disabilities, and mental retardation (Thompson, Caruso, & Ellerbeck, 2003). Some researchers have argued that these differences may be linked to differences in brain organization and sex hormones. For example, higher rates of attention problems and language-related disorders in boys might be linked to unusually high levels of androgen exposure during prenatal development (Tallal & Fitch, 1993).

Cognitive and motivational influences The process of self-socialization that is emphasized in social cognitive theory and gender schema theory also plays a role in children's academic achievement. Many children, for example, internalize gender stereotypes pertaining to the idea that science, technology, and math are for boys and that reading, writing, and the arts are for girls (Archer & Macrae, 1991; Whitehead, 1996). Perhaps it is not surprising, then, that there are small average gender differences in interest and self-efficacy in these academic areas (Wigfield et al., 1997; Wilgenbusch & Merrell, 1999) or that these self-concepts predict academic achievement and occupational aspirations (Bussey & Bandura, 1999; Eccles & Wigfield, 2002; Halpern et al., 2007). As discussed below, parents, teachers, peers, and the surrounding culture can influence the development of girls' and boys' academic self-concepts and achievement through the role models, opportunities, and motivations that they provide for practicing, or not practicing, particular behaviors.

PARENTAL INFLUENCES As noted in Chapter 6, parents' talking to their children is a strong predictor of children's language learning. Researchers generally find that mothers tend to have higher rates of verbal interaction with daughters than with sons (Leaper, Anderson, & Sanders, 1998). (Most studies have been conducted with mothers, although similar patterns should occur with fathers.) Thus, young girls may learn language a bit faster than boys do simply because their parents spend more time talking with them. At the same time, it may be that girls' relative language proficiency encourages parents to talk more to them than to their sons (Leaper & Smith, 2004).

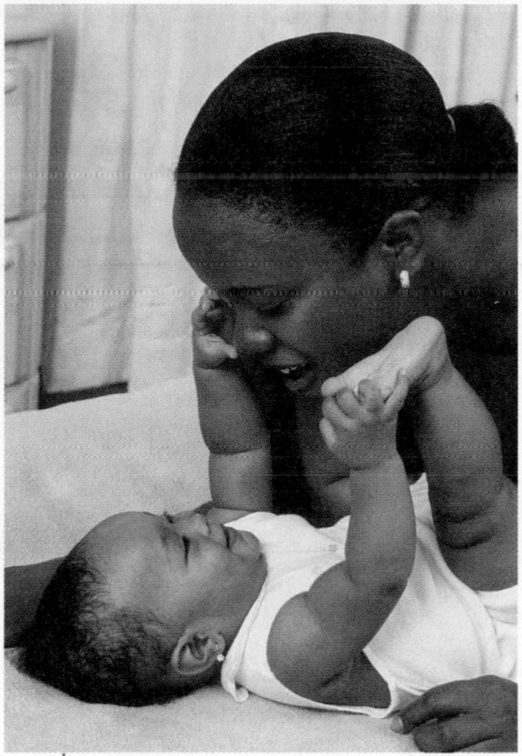

LAURA DWIGHT

Some studies find that mothers are more talkative with daughters than with sons. Studies also find that, on average, girls acquire language at a faster rate than do boys. Does mothers' greater talkativeness with girls contribute to girls' faster language acquisition? Or does girls' faster language acquisition influence mothers' talkativeness with them?

Parents' gender-stereotyped beliefs may also affect children's academic achievement. Many parents accept the prevailing stereotypes about boys' and girls' relative interest in and aptitude for various academic subjects (Eccles et al., 2000; Leaper & Friedman, 2007), and these gender-typed expectations can affect children's achievement motivation (Eccles et al., 2000). Observational research suggests that parents' gender-stereotyped expectations may be communicated to their children through differential encouragement (Bhanot & Jovanovic, 2005; Crowley, Callanan, Tenenbaum, & Allen, 2001; Tenenbaum & Leaper, 2003). One might think that parents' beliefs about their children's academic potential would be based primarily on their children's own self-concepts and achievement. However, researchers find that parents often hold these beliefs before any average gender differences in academic interest or performance occur. In fact, longitudinal research indicates that parents' expectations can be a stronger predictor of children's later achievement than the children's earlier performance in particular subject areas (Bleeker & Jacobs, 2004).

TEACHER INFLUENCES Teachers can influence gender differences in children's academic motivation and achievement in two important ways. First, they themselves are sometimes influential gender-role models. Having women as science teachers, for example, may increase girls' interest in science careers (Evans, Whigham, & Wang, 1995). Second, many teachers hold gender-stereotyped beliefs about girls' and boys' abilities. They may, for example, expect overall higher school achievement in girls than in boys (Jones & Myhill, 2004), or they may stereotype boys as being better at math and science (Shepardson & Pizzini, 1992; Tiedemann, 2000). Such expectations may lead teachers to unintentionally assess, encourage, and pay attention to students differentially according to their gender. In this manner, teachers can lay the groundwork for self-fulfilling prophecies that affect children's later academic achievement (see Halpern et al., 2007; Jussim, Eccles, & Madon, 1996).

Reviewing the research on teachers' differential treatment of girls and boys in elementary and high school classrooms, Jones and Dindia (2004) found that, across studies, there was a small average gender difference indicating that teachers initiated interactions with boys more often than they did with girls. Further analyses in terms of positive and negative interactions revealed that there was no significant average gender difference in praise and other positive interactions but that boys were significantly more likely than girls to be the focus of criticism and other negative interactions. Therefore, one reason that boys may tend to get more of the teacher's attention is because they are more disruptive. Moreover, this negative attention can become a habit for some teachers, who begin to focus more on boys even when they are not misbehaving (Sadker & Sadker, 1994).

Teachers are more likely to call on boys than on girls. One reason may be that, on average, girls earn higher grades than boys, and teachers tend to focus their attention on lower-achieving students. Another reason is that boys are more assertive in raising their hands and shouting out answers.

ELLEN SENISI / THE IMAGE WORKS

Teachers' paying greater attention to boys than to girls is also influenced by gender differences in the rates of student-initiated class participation. For example, in science classes, boys were observed to volunteer more often than girls did, and this led to higher rates of teacher responsivity to boys (Altermatt, Jovanovic, & Perry, 1998).

PEER INFLUENCES The types of play activities that children practice with their peers may contribute to the development of some gender differences in achievement. As we have noted, many activities favored by boys—including construction play, sports, and video games—provide them opportunities to develop their spatial abilities as well as math- and science-related skills (Serbin et al., 1990; Subrahmanyam, Kraut, Greenfield, & Gross, 2001). The types of play more common among girls—such as domestic role play—are talk-oriented and exercise the participants' verbal skills (Taharally, 1991).

Peer norms can have a strong impact on girls' and boys' achievement motivation. For example, research indicates that girls are more likely to maintain their interest in science and computers when their friends support achievement in these subjects.

ELLEN SENISI / THE IMAGE WORKS

Gender-typed social norms in peer groups may also affect how girls and boys approach school and achievement. For example, boys who apply themselves in school may experience pressure to excel in masculine-stereotyped domains such as science and to devalue feminine-stereotyped subjects such as reading (Andre, Whigham, Hendrickson, & Chambers, 1999; Whitehead, 1996). Many other boys may feel a different kind of pressure—the pressure to maintain an image of masculinity based on power and dominance. Adhering to this role may contribute to some boys' difficulties in school adjustment and academic achievement (Levant, 2005; Renold, 2001; Steinmayr & Spinath, 2008; Van Houtte, 2004). That is, some boys may view doing well at school generally or, in certain subjects, as not masculine. These attitudes may be related to lower average performances in reading and writing (Van de gaer, Pustjens, Van Damme, & De Munter, 2006). At the same time, there is research suggesting that gender-role flexibility in adolescent boys is related to holding more positive scholastic self-concepts (Rose & Montemayor, 1994), as well as to greater self-efficacy and interest in nontraditional college majors (Jome & Tokar, 1998; Leaper & Van, 2008).

In contrast, girls' traditional concerns with getting along with others may facilitate their greater likelihood of compliance and school adjustment (Serbin et al., 1990). Other gender-typed norms, however, may impede some girls' achievement. This possibility was revealed in a study of academically gifted girls in grades 3 through 6 who were asked if they experienced any obstacles to school achievement (Bell, 1989). Two major issues that many girls raised pertained to perceived gender-typing pressures: they wanted to be seen as physically attractive, and they did not want to be viewed as overly competitive. Thus, some girls' traditional concerns with looking pretty and acting nice may lead them to downplay their academic accomplishments. However, these concerns may be less likely when girls experience support from peers for academic achievement. For example, one study found that girls who felt peer support in science demonstrated positive expectations for their science achievement 6 months later (Stake & Nickens, 2005).

CULTURAL INFLUENCES As discussed earlier, social role theory maintains that socialization practices prepare children for their adult roles in society. If women and men tend to hold different occupations, then different abilities and preferences are apt to be encouraged in girls and boys. Therefore, where there are cultural variations in girls' and boys' academic achievement, there should be corresponding differences in socialization.

Baker and Jones (1993) support this interpretation in their review of studies of the math performance of 8th graders in different countries. Gender differences on standardized math tests varied quite a bit across nations: in some, boys scored higher; in others, girls scored higher; and in still others, there was no gender difference. To assess possible cultural influences, the researchers considered various measures of educational and occupational opportunities for females and males in each society. They found gender differences in math-test performance to be negatively related to the percentage of women in higher levels of education and the percentage of women in the labor force. Furthermore, gender differences in math had declined over time (1964 to 1982) in virtually every nation sampled. Typical of this pattern is the U.S. one we described earlier, in which a closing of the gender gap in math achievement over the past half century was accompanied by a steady increase in the proportion of women in science and engineering (National Science Foundation, 2008).

Other cultural factors have also been found to predict gender-related variations in academic achievement within American society. Average gender differences in overall academic success and verbal achievement tend to be less common among children from higher-income neighborhoods and among children of highly educated parents (Burkam, Lee, & Smerdon, 1997; DeBaryshe, Patterson, & Capaldi, 1993; Ferry, Fouad, & Smith, 2000). Gender differences in achievement may also be less common among children of gender-egalitarian parents. One study found that adolescent girls raised by egalitarian parents maintained higher levels of academic achievement in middle school—especially in math and science—compared with girls raised by traditional parents (Updegraff, McHale, & Crouter, 1996).

Personality and Social Behavior

Gender differences in personality and social development have attracted considerable research attention, including studies of emotional expressiveness,

DENNIS MACDONALD / PHOTOEDIT

Boys tend to be less compliant with adult instructions and expectations than girls are. Boys are also more likely than girls to engage in risky behaviors, leading to higher rates of injury and death for males.

self-regulation, risk taking, and aggression. In these areas, researchers often have observed differences between males and females, although the differences are not as great as popularly believed.

Self-Regulation and Risk Taking

As discussed in Chapter 10, an important part of development is self-regulation—that is, children's ability to comply with adult directions, to control their own behavior, and to make good decisions when adults are not around. Research indicates that girls tend to show higher levels of self-regulation than do boys of the same age, with the average gender difference being in the moderate-to-large range (Else-Quest, Hyde, Goldsmith, & Van Hulle, 2006).

On average, girls are more compliant with adult directives and expectations than boys are (Smith, Calkins, Keane, Anastopoulos, & Shelton, 2004). Beginning in the preschool years, girls are also more likely to resist the temptation to touch or play with an attractive toy that an experimenter has told them not to handle (although girls and boys who violate the prohibition are equally likely to lie about their transgression) (Silverman, 2003). Consistent with this pattern, there is a small average gender difference indicating that boys are more likely than girls to engage in certain risky behaviors (Byrnes, Miller, & Schafer, 1999). When boys and girls encounter the same hazardous situation, for example, girls are more cautious, on average, and often point out the hazard to a parent. In contrast, boys are more likely to approach and explore the hazard (Fabes, Martin, & Hanish, 2003).

Explanations for Gender Differences in Self-Regulation and Risk Taking

As with other aspects of gender development, there is evidence for both biological and cognitive-motivational influences on average gender differences in self-regulation and risk taking. The ability to control one's impulses is considered a temperamental quality that is partly based on genetic predispositions (see Chapter 10). As noted earlier, evolutionary psychologists argue that a tendency to respond impulsively might have offered certain advantages for males, whereas the ability to inhibit impulses might have been beneficial for females.

Environmental factors, such as parents' and peers' reactions, can exaggerate or attenuate temperamental dispositions (Goldsmith, Buss, & Lemery, 1997). As described in Chapter 12, parenting styles can foster or impede children's self-regulation development. One relevant pattern is that parents and other adults tend to monitor girls more closely than they do boys (Leaper, 2002). Consequently, girls have more opportunities to learn impulse control because they spend more time near adults. Another factor underlying these differences may be that many parents believe that boys must be independent and step up to challenges, and they socialize their sons accordingly.

Aggressive Behavior

A common belief is that boys are more aggressive than girls are. Is there any truth to this view? The answer is yes, although the actual gender difference is not as great as most people believe. As explained as follows, the answer depends partly on the type of aggression being considered.

In Chapter 13, we indicated that researchers distinguish between direct and indirect (relational) forms of aggression (Archer & Coyne, 2005; Bjorkqvist, Osterman, & Kaukiainen, 1992). *Direct aggression,* you will recall, refers to overt physical or verbal acts openly intended to cause harm. In contrast, *indirect aggression* refers to attempts to damage a person's social standing or group acceptance through covert means such as negative gossip and social exclusion.

SPENCER GRANT/ PHOTOEDIT

Rates of indirect aggression are higher for girls than for boys. Indirect aggression includes behaviors such as criticizing another girl, spreading rumors about her, and excluding her from the friendship group.

Average gender differences in the incidence of physical aggression emerge gradually during the preschool years (Hay, 2007). In a comprehensive review of studies comparing boys' and girls' aggressive behavior, John Archer (2004) found that both physical and verbal forms of direct aggression occurred more often among boys than among girls, with the difference being small during childhood and moderate-to-large during adolescence. This widening gap is due largely to the fact that although direct aggression generally declines for both boys and girls with age, the decline is more pronounced for girls than for boys. In terms of the use of indirect aggression, there appears to be no average gender difference during childhood; but there is a small average difference during adolescence, with girls resorting to indirect aggression more frequently. Being the target of indirect aggression appears to cause more problems for girls than it does for boys (Crick & Grotpeter, 1996), in part because girls' friendships tend to be exclusive and intimate, whereas boys' friendships tended to be embedded within a larger boys' group (Benenson et al., 2002; Rose & Rudolph, 2006).

Average gender differences in aggression have been found primarily in research on same-gender interactions. Different rules may apply when girls and boys have conflicts with one another. Beginning in early childhood, boys are more likely than girls to ignore the other gender's attempts to exert influence (Jacklin & Maccoby, 1978; Serbin, Sprafkin, Elman, & Doyle, 1982). As a consequence, boys, being more assertive and less affiliative, often get their way in unsupervised mixed-gender groups (Charlesworth & LaFreniere, 1983). Studies comparing children's behavior in same-gender versus cross-gender conflicts reveal an interesting pattern, however. Whereas in same-gender conflicts, boys are more likely to use power-assertive strategies (e.g., threats, demands) and girls are more likely to use conflict mitigation strategies (e.g., compromise, change topic), in cross-gender conflicts, girls' use of power-assertive strategies increases, but boys' use of conflict-mitigation strategies does not change (Miller et al., 1986; Sims, Hutchins, & Taylor, 1998). Thus, girls may find it necessary to play by the boys' rules to gain influence.

Sexual harassment Sexual harassment commonly affects both boys and girls. It can include direct physical or verbal aggression, as well as indirect aggression. Physical sexual harassment involves inappropriate touching or forced sexual activity. Verbal sexual harassment involves unwanted, demeaning, or homophobic sexual comments. Also, verbal harassment can be spoken directly to the target or behind her or his back; and now verbal harassment also occurs in Internet chat rooms and through text messaging (Ybarra & Mitchell, 2007).

Recent surveys in the United States and Canada indicate that the vast majority of both girls and boys have experienced sexual harassment during adolescence

(American Association of University Women, 2001; Leaper & Brown, 2008; McMaster, Connolly, Pepler, & Craig, 2002). In the American Association of University Women (AAUW) survey (2001), 83% of girls and 79% of boys reported having experienced sexual harassment. Also, 30% of girls and 24% of boys reported that these experiences occurred often (as opposed to occasionally, rarely, or not at all). Other surveys suggest that rates of sexual harassment may be higher for sexual-minority youth (Williams, Connolly, Pepler, & Craig, 2005).

Most sexual harassment occurs in school hallways and classrooms, with the perpetrators most likely being peers (versus teachers or other adults). In the AAUW report, both girls and boys indicated that sexual harassment was more apt to come from other-gender peers than from same-gender peers. However, rates of same-gender peer harassment were higher among boys than girls.

Although the rates for most forms of sexual harassment (e.g., sexual comments or gestures, being brushed against in a sexual manner, being the subject of sexual rumors) are similar for girls and boys, girls are more likely than boys to indicate that they are afraid of being harassed and are more likely to feel distressed following sexual harassment (American Association of University Women, 2001). Also, there are some average gender differences in rates for specific types of harassment. Most notably, girls are more likely than boys to be targets of inappropriate sexual touching, whereas boys are more apt to be targets of homophobic comments. In these ways, girls are treated as sexual objects, while boys are pressured to conform to traditional norms for masculinity (Murnen & Smolak, 2000).

Sexual harassment and violence also occur in dating relationships. It is estimated that physical aggression occurs in one-fourth of adolescent dating relationships (Hickman, Jaycox, & Aronoff, 2004; O'Leary, Slep, Avery-Leaf, & Cascardi, 2008), with boys, not surprisingly, being more likely to be the perpetrators in heterosexual dating relationships (Swahn, Simon, Arias, & Bossarte, 2008; Wolitzky-Taylor et al., 2008).

Repeated experiences with sexual harassment and dating violence can have negative consequences on self-esteem and adjustment (American Association of University Women, 2001; Goldstein et al., 2007; Gruber & Fineran, 2008; Holt & Espelage, 2003; Lindberg, Grabe, & Hyde, 2007). These negative effects may be stronger for girls and for sexual-minority youth (Gruber & Fineran, 2008; Timmerman, 2005). Also, many girls come to regard demeaning male behaviors as normal in heterosexual relationships (Witkowska & Gadin, 2005) and may be at risk for dysfunctional and abusive relationships in adulthood (Larkin & Popaleni, 1994; Leaper & Anderson, 1997).

Explanations for Gender Differences in Aggression

Possible explanations for gender differences in aggression range from the effects of biological factors to the socializing influences of family, peers, the media, and the culture at large. It seems likely that each has a contributing role.

Biological influences It is well known that, on average, males have higher baseline levels of testosterone than do females, and many people assume that this is what accounts for gender differences in aggression. Contrary to this popular belief, there is *not* a direct association between aggression and baseline testosterone levels (Archer, Graham-Kevan, & Davies, 2005). However, there is an indirect one: the body increases its production of testosterone in response to perceived threats and challenges, and this increase can lead to more aggressive behavior

(Archer, 2006). Furthermore, people who are impulsive and less inhibited are more likely to perceive the behavior of others as threatening. Thus, because boys, on average, have more difficulty regulating emotion (Else-Quest et al., 2006), they may be more prone to direct aggression (Hay, 2007). Conversely, greater emotion regulation among girls may contribute to higher rates of prosocial behavior.

Cognitive and motivational influences Average gender differences in aggression may be related to average differences in empathy and prosocial behavior (Knight, Fabes, & Higgins, 1996; Lemerise & Arsenio, 2000; Levant, 2005; Mayberry & Espelage, 2007). On average, girls are somewhat more likely than boys to report feelings of empathy and sympathy in response to people's distress (Eisenberg & Fabes, 1998), and they also tend to display more concern in their behavioral reactions (e.g., looks of concern and attempts to help). Direct aggression may be more likely among children who are less empathetic and have fewer prosocial skills. In support of this explanation, one study found average gender differences with boys scoring higher on direct aggression and lower on empathy compared with girls; but both aggressive girls and aggressive boys scored lower on empathy than did nonaggressive youth (Mayberry & Espelage, 2007).

The gender-typed social norms and goals that we discussed earlier regarding assertion and affiliation may also contribute to the average gender difference in direct and indirect aggression (Miller et al., 1986; Rose & Rudolph, 2006). As noted, boys, on average, are more likely to endorse assertive over affiliative goals (e.g., being dominant), and girls are more likely to endorse affiliative traits and goals or a combination of affiliative and assertive traits and goals (e.g., maintaining intimacy). By focusing on dominance goals, boys may be more likely than girls to appraise conflicts as competitions that require the use of direct aggression. In addition, some boys may initiate direct aggression as a way to enhance their status.

In contrast, by emphasizing intimacy and nurturance goals, girls may be more likely to view relationship conflicts as threats that need to be resolved through compromise that preserves harmony. The normative social pressures on girls to act "nice" may also lead them to avoid direct confrontation. Alternatively, when girls are unable to resolve a conflict, they may try to hurt one another through indirect strategies such as those mentioned earlier—criticizing or excluding the offender or sharing secret information about the offender with other girls (Crick, Bigbee, & Howes, 1996; Galen & Underwood, 1997). This may be why girls' same-gender friendships, although more intimate than those of boys, are less stable over time (Benenson & Christakos, 2003).

Parental and other adult influences Although U.S. parents and other adults generally disapprove of physical aggression in both boys and girls, they tend, after the preschool years, to be more tolerant of aggression in boys, adopting a "boys will be boys" view (Martin & Ross, 2005). In an experimental demonstration of this effect, researchers asked people to watch a short film of two children engaged in rough-and-tumble play in the snow and to rate the level of the play's aggressiveness (Condry & Ross, 1985). The children were dressed in gender-neutral snowsuits and filmed at a distance that made their gender undeterminable. Some viewers were told that both children were male; others, that they were both female; and still others, that they were a boy and girl. Viewers who thought that both children were boys rated their play as much less aggressive than did viewers who thought that both children were girls.

Children also appear aware of this "boys will be boys" bias and believe that physical aggression is more acceptable, and less likely to be punished, when enacted by boys than when enacted by girls (Giles & Heyman, 2005; Perry et al., 1989). Thus, girls' reliance on strategies of aggression that are covert, and easily denied if detected, may reflect their recognition that displays of physical aggression on their part will attract adult attention and punishment.

Parenting style may also be a factor in children's manifestations of aggression. Harsh, inconsistent parenting and poor monitoring increase the likelihood of physical aggression in childhood (Leve, Pears, & Fisher, 2002; Vitaro, Barker, Boivin, Brendgen, & Tremblay, 2006). Children who experience this kind of parenting may learn to mistrust others and make hostile attributions about other people's intentions (Crick & Dodge, 1996). The association between harsh parenting and later physical aggression is stronger for boys than for girls. Also, as noted in Chapter 14, poor parental monitoring increases children's susceptibility to negative peer influences and is correlated with higher rates of aggression and delinquency (Jacobson & Crockett, 2000). Thus, the fact that parents monitor daughters more closely than they do sons may contribute to gender differences in aggression.

Peer influences A number of the discussions in this chapter make it clear that gender differences in aggression are consistent with the gender-typed social norms of girls' and boys' same-gender peer groups. However, it is worth noting that children who are high in aggression *and* low in prosocial behavior are typically rejected in both male and female peer groups (Hawley, Little, & Card, 2008). These children tend to seek out marginal peer groups of other similarly rejected peers, and these contacts strengthen the likelihood of physical aggression over time (Werner & Crick, 2004).

Michael Messner (1998) has also highlighted how boys' regular participation in aggressive contact sports, such as football, sanctions the use of physical force and may contribute to higher rates of direct aggression among boys. Support for this proposal is the finding that participation in aggressive sports, such as football, in high school is correlated with a higher likelihood of sexual aggression in college (Forbes, Adams-Curtis, Pakala, & White, 2006).

Media influences In our discussion of media violence in Chapter 9, it was made clear that watching aggression in movies, TV programming, and video games is associated with levels of children's aggressive behavior and that this holds true for girls as well as boys. As might be expected, boys are more likely than girls to spend time watching violent TV programming and playing violent video games (Cherney & London, 2006). Recent research also confirmed what might be expected for girls: they are more likely than boys to prefer TV shows depicting indirect aggression (Coyne & Archer, 2005). Furthermore, an experimental study demonstrated that observing indirect aggression on TV increased the subsequent likelihood of indirect aggressive behavior (Coyne, Archer, & Eslea, 2004).

Other cultural influences Although gender differences in aggression are observed in all cultures, cultural norms also play an important role in determining the levels of aggression that are observed in boys and girls. Douglas Fry (1988) studied rural communities in the mountains of Mexico and found that the levels of childhood aggression that were considered normal varied widely from one area to another. Although boys in each community showed more aggression than girls did, girls in

SYRACUSE NEWSPAPERS / AL CAMPANIE / THE IMAGE WORKS

Rates of violence are high in many American communities, and boys are more likely to witness violent events. These experiences may contribute to higher rates of aggression for boys compared with girls.

the high-aggression communities were more aggressive than boys in the low-aggression communities.

The community context must also be considered in relation to the emergence of differential aggression in U.S. youth. Levels of violence are high in many American communities, particularly in inner-city areas where an estimated 40 to 60% of children have witnessed violent crimes within the previous year (Osofsky, 1995). When children are exposed to violence in their homes and communities, boys and girls both experience an increased risk of emotional and behavioral problems and show an increase in aggressive behaviors. However, boys are more likely than girls to be exposed to the highest levels of violence, and the impact of exposure is also greater for boys than for girls (Guerra, Huesmann, & Spindler, 2003).

review: Although the common impression is that girls and boys are inherently and deeply different, in most respects, the similarities between them outweigh the differences. Even when differences are consistently reported, they tend to be fairly small. Also, many of the average differences do not emerge until later in childhood or adolescence. The most substantial differences are found in physical strength and speed, certain specific cognitive abilities (e.g., mental rotation), academic achievement, self-control, and physical aggression. Small average gender differences are seen in verbal ability, math ability, risk taking, empathy, and indirect aggression. A combination of biological, cognitive-motivational, and cultural influences are implicated to differing degrees to explain most of these differences.

Chapter Summary

Theoretical Perspectives on Gender Development

- One major perspective on gender development is the biological perspective. According to evolutionary psychology theory, differences in male and female behavior served an adaptive function in our evolutionary past, and this led to the gender differences in behavioral dispositions. For example, direct aggression in males is interpreted as an advantage in mating competition, whereas nurturance in females is viewed as facilitating the survival of offspring. Biosocial theory focuses on the impact of evolved physical differences between females (childbearing and nursing capacities) and males (greater strength, speed, and size) in relation to the social ecology.

For example, men's strength and women's childbearing may have made certain roles more appropriate for women and men in hunter-gatherer societies, but these physical differences impose fewer constraints in today's modern society.

- Other researchers take a neuroscience approach to gender development, emphasizing sex differences in brain organization and the influence of sex hormones such as androgens, both before birth and after. Among the most striking examples of the role of hormones involves cases of girls with CAH, who tend to show a stronger inclination toward "male" activities than do girls without CAH, as well as somewhat better spatial abilities.
- A second set of theories address the cognitive and motivational influences on gender development. These theories emphasize children's active participation in learning gender roles and adopting the preferences and behaviors considered appropriate for their gender.
- According to cognitive developmental theory, once children realize that their gender is consistent across situations (gender constancy), they pay close attention to same-gender models to learn how to behave.
- Gender schema theory maintains that children construct gender schemas based on their own experience and the gender-related ideas they are exposed to. Unlike Kohlberg's cognitive theory, gender schema theory proposes that children begin to acquire same-gender interest and values as soon as they can identify their own gender. They subsequently pay greater attention to, and learn more about, those things that they regard as "for my gender."
- Social identity theory also stresses the importance of adopting a gender identity. Children tend to form an ingroup bias favoring attributes associated with their own gender and also enforce conformity to gender-role norms.
- Social cognitive theory addresses many of the processes involved in learning gender-typed values and behaviors, including the observation of others' behavior and of the kinds of responses that others' behavior (or their own) evokes. Children internalize standards (gender-typed norms) that they use to monitor their behavior. Social cognitive theory also stresses the importance of opportunities to practice behaviors and develop a sense of self-efficacy. All four cognitive theories are based on the premise that gender development is largely a process of self-socialization.
- The third set of theories focuses on cultural influences. The bioecological model characterizes children's development as embedded in nested systems ranging from the microsystem (immediate environment) to the macrosystem (society). A key feature of the macrosystem is its opportunity structure and the corresponding roles available for women and men; these opportunities shape the ways in which girls and boys are socialized. Social role theory similarly addresses the division of labor by gender in society and how it affects girls' and boys' development.

Milestones in Gender Development

- During their first year, infants learn to distinguish males and females through a variety of perceptual cues, such as hairstyle. Between ages 2 and 3, children learn to identify their own gender and start to acquire stereotypes about males and females. Around this age, children also begin to prefer gender-typed toys and play activities.
- During preschool, children begin to gravitate toward same-gender peers, and a strong tendency for children to self-segregate by gender persists until adolescence. Preschool children also stereotype certain traits and activities for each gender. Preferences for gender-typed play become stronger.
- Around 7 years of age, children understand that gender is a stable and consistent attribute (gender constancy). During middle childhood, children come to understand that gender roles are social conventions. They also may understand that gender discrimination is unfair and notice when it occurs. Average gender differences in social behavior begin to emerge, with boys more likely to stress assertion over affiliation, and girls more apt to emphasize affiliation (or a combination of affiliation and assertion).
- Adolescence is a period when gender roles sometimes become more flexible (due to increased cognitive flexibility) or more rigid (due to concerns with heterosexual roles and adoption of conventional gender attitudes). Intimacy in friendships and romantic relationships also increases during adolescence for both girls and boys, although friendship intimacy is more common among girls.
- Throughout childhood and adolescence, gender flexibility is more likely among girls than among boys. Peers and parents tend to react more negatively to cross-gender-typed behavior in boys than in girls. This asymmetry may be related to the higher status and power traditionally accorded males.

Gender Comparisons

- The actual differences in boys' and girls' psychological functioning are decidedly fewer and much less strong than commonly portrayed by gender stereotypes. Even on measures in which, on average, one gender scores higher than the other, the differences are slight, and there is considerable overlap in the distribution of scores for males and females.
- Boys and girls are quite similar in physical development until puberty, which begins earlier for girls than for boys. Some of the largest average gender differences are in physical strength, speed, and size after puberty. In addition, there is a moderate difference in physical activity level.
- Girls and boys are similar on general intelligence. Slight to small average gender differences have been reported in specific cognitive abilities, with boys showing higher proficiency with certain types of spatial reasoning and mathematic ability, and girls tending to show a small advantage in verbal ability. In academic achievement, girls have tended to do better than boys in reading and writing, whereas boys have tended to do better than girls in math and physical sciences. Also, girls tend to do better in overall school performance. There is some indication that biological influences, such as prenatal

hormones, may play a role in these differences, possibly affecting girls' and boys' brain development and cognitive functioning. However, the evidence for cognitive-motivational and cultural influences is very strong. Researchers find academic achievement in particular domains is related to the expectations of parents, peers, and teachers. Also, the gender gap in math achievement has dramatically closed in recent decades and is smaller in societies characterized by greater overall gender equality.

- Average gender differences in personality and social behavior vary in magnitude. The largest average differences are seen in self-regulation (girls higher) and direct aggression (boys higher). Small average differences are associated with risk taking (boys higher), empathy (girls higher), and indirect aggression (girls higher during adolescence). Average gender differences in self-regulation reflect corresponding differences in temperament. This factor may also be related to the higher incidence of direct aggression among boys. Cognitive and motivational factors are also important: children are usually motivated to conform to stereotyped views regarding the traits and social behaviors expected for each gender. Moreover, peers, parents, and the media reinforce these expectations. Some cultural variations are also indicated in the kinds of social behaviors that girls and boys tend to enact.

Critical Thinking Questions

1. Colin and Catherine, the two children pictured at the start of the chapter, have gender-typed differences in their behavior and interests. How would the different theories outlined in this chapter attempt to explain these differences and similarities? How would different theories account for other children who have more flexible gender-typed behaviors and interests?
2. Think about how males and females were portrayed in the television shows, movies, and computer games that you watched while growing up. How might these depictions have affected your gender development?
3. Imagine that you wanted to raise your own children to be as minimally gender-typed as possible. Which of the theoretical perspectives outlined in the chapter would you rely on most? Do you think you would be more likely to achieve your goal with a daughter or a son?
4. Suppose you are speaking with an evolutionary psychology theorist who tells you that biology makes males and females different and that gender differences in behavior are inevitable. What pieces of evidence could you use to challenge this view? What pieces of evidence could you use to support it?

Key Terms

assertion, p. 584
affiliation, p. 584
collaboration, p. 584
androgens, p. 588
congenital adrenal hyperplasia (CAH), p. 588
organizational hormonal influences, p. 588
activational hormonal influences, p. 588
gender self-socialization, p. 589
gender identity, p. 590
gender stability, p. 590
gender constancy, p. 590
gender schemas, p. 591
ingroup bias, p. 592
ingroup assimilation, p. 592
tuition, p. 593
enactive experience, p. 593
gender-essentialist statements, p. 594
opportunity structure, p. 596
gender segregation, p. 599
gender-role intensification, p. 602
gender-role flexibility, p. 602
effect size, p. 605
meta-analysis, p. 605
puberty, p. 606
menarche, p. 606
spermarche, p. 606
body image, p. 607
adrenarche, p. 607

PABLO PICASSO, *Paul Drawing Françoise and Paloma,* 1954

16

Conclusions

THEMES

Nature and Nurture

The Active Child

Continuity/Discontinuity

Mechanisms of Change

The Sociocultural Context

Individual Differences

Research and Children's Welfare

In the preceding 15 chapters, you have been presented with a great deal of information about how children develop. You have learned about the development of perception, attachment, conceptual understanding, language, intelligence, emotional regulation, peer relations, aggression, morality, gender, and a host of other vital human characteristics. Although these are all important parts of child development, the sheer amount of information may seem daunting: getting lost in the trees and losing a sense of the forest is a real danger. We therefore devote this final chapter to providing an overview of the forest by organizing the many specifics that you have learned into an integrative framework. A likely side benefit of reading this chapter is that you probably will discover that you understand much more about child development than you realized.

The integrative framework that organizes this chapter consists of the seven themes that were introduced in Chapter 1 and highlighted throughout the book. As we have noted, most child-development research is ultimately aimed at understanding fundamental issues related to these themes. This is true regardless of the type of development that the research addresses and regardless of whether the research focuses on fetuses, infants, toddlers, preschoolers, school-age children, or adolescents. Beneath the myriad details, the seven themes emerge again and again.

Theme 1: Nature and Nurture: All Interactions, All the Time

When people think of a child's nature, they typically focus on the biological characteristics with which the child enters the world. When they think of the child's nurture, they focus on the child-rearing experiences provided by parents, caregivers, and other adults. Within this view, nurture is like a sculptor, shaping the raw material provided by the child's nature into closer and closer approximations of its final form.

Although this metaphor is appealing, the reality is much more complex. Unlike the sculptor's passive media of marble and clay, children are active participants in their own development. They seek out their own experiences, based on their inclinations and interests. They also influence other people's behavior toward them: from birth onward, their nature influences the nurture they receive. In addition, rather than nature doing its work before birth and nurture doing its work after, nurture influences development even before birth, and nature is just as influential in adolescence and adulthood as earlier. In this section, we review how nature and nurture interact to produce development.

Nature and Nurture Begin Interacting Before Birth

When prenatal development proceeds normally, it is easy to think of it as a simple unfolding of innate potential, one in which the environment matters little. When things go wrong, however, the interaction of nature and nurture is all too evident. Consider the effects of teratogens. Prenatal exposure to these potentially harmful substances—which include toxins in the general environment, such as mercury, radiation, and air pollution, and also toxins that depend on parental behavior, such as cigarettes, alcohol, and illegal drugs—can cause a wide variety of physical and cognitive impairments. However, whether a given baby will actually be affected depends on innumerable interactions among the genetics of the mother, the genetics of the fetus, and a host of environmental factors such as the particular teratogen and the timing and amount of exposure.

The interaction of nature and nurture during the prenatal period is also evident in fetal learning. The experience of hearing their mother's voice while they are in the womb leads newborns to prefer her voice to that of other women once they enter the world. Fetuses can also learn taste preferences from their mother's diet during pregnancy. Thus, even qualities that are present at birth, which are often thought of as being determined purely by nature, reflect the fetus's experience as well.

LAURA DWIGHT

Rather than sitting back passively, waiting for parents and others to teach them, infants and toddlers actively explore their world. Even the most mundane explorations, such as pulling a shoelace, provide them not only with entertainment but also with information about the environment around them.

Infants' Nature Elicits Nurture

Nature equips babies with a host of qualities that elicit appropriate nurture from parents and other caregivers. One big factor in babies' favor is that they are cute; most people enjoy watching and interacting with them. Their looking and smiling at other people motivates others to feel warmly toward them and to care for them. Their emotional expressions—cries, coos, and smiles—guide caregivers' efforts to figure out what to do to make them happy and comfortable. In addition, their attentiveness to sights and sounds that they find interesting encourages others to talk to them and to provide the stimulation necessary for learning. One simple example of this interactive relationship is the fact that parents everywhere sing to their infants; infants throughout the world find singing to be soothing, bounce in response to rhythm, and respond positively to melodies.

Timing Matters

The effects of an experience on development depend on the state of the organism at the time of the experience. As already noted, timing of exposure to teratogens greatly influences their effects on prenatal development. For example, if a pregnant woman comes down with rubella early in pregnancy, when the developing visual and auditory systems are at a particularly sensitive point, her baby may be born deaf or blind; if she comes down with the same disease later in pregnancy, no damage will occur.

Timing also influences many aspects of development in the months and years following birth. The development of perceptual capabilities presents numerous illustrations of the importance of appropriate experience at the appropriate time. The general rule in such cases is "use it or lose it": for normal development to occur, children must encounter the relevant experiences during a certain window of time.

Binocular depth perception provides a good example. For normal depth perception, both eyes must focus on the same point. By age 4 months, most infants' eyes do this; however, some infants are born with strabismus (they are cross-eyed), and each of their eyes focuses on a different point, preventing them from obtaining binocular cues to depth. Cross-eyedness is correctable through surgery, but depth perception develops normally only if the surgery is done early. Performing the operation before age 4 months virtually guarantees development of normal depth perception, because it allows normal development of relevant neural pathways in the brain. In contrast, performing the surgery after age 3 years usually does no good.

Auditory development involves similar sensitive periods. Until 8 months of age, infants can discriminate between phonemes regardless of whether they appear in the language the infants hear daily. By age 12 months, however, infants lose the ability to hear the difference between similar sounds that they do not ordinarily encounter or that are not meaningfully different in their native language.

Similar sensitive periods occur in grammatical development. Children from East Asia who move to the United States and begin to learn English as a second language before age 7 acquire grammatical competence in English that eventually matches that of native-born American children. Those who arrive between ages 7 and 11 learn almost as well. However, individuals who emigrate at later ages to the United States rarely gain comparable mastery of English grammar, even after many years of hearing and speaking the language in their adopted land. Deaf children's learning of American Sign Language shows a similar pattern: early exposure results in more complete grammatical mastery.

The importance of normal early experience is also evident in social, emotional, and intellectual development. Infants and toddlers who do not have an emotional connection with any caregiver, such as those children who spent their first years in the infamous orphanages of Romania in the 1980s or in concentration camps during World War II, often continue to interact abnormally with other people, even after being placed in loving homes. Those who spent their first two years or more in the Romanian orphanages also had unusually high rates of intellectual retardation years after they were adopted into loving homes in Great Britain. Thus, in many aspects of the development of perception, language, intelligence, emotions, and social behavior, the timing of experience is crucial: normal early experience is vital for successful later development.

Nature Does Not Reveal Itself All at Once

Many genetically influenced properties do not become evident until middle childhood, adolescence, or adulthood. One obvious example is the physical changes that occur at puberty. A less obvious example involves nearsightedness. Many children are born with genes that predispose them to become nearsighted, but most do not become so until late childhood or early adolescence. The more close work, including reading, that they do during childhood, the more likely that the genetic predisposition will eventually be realized. A third example involves children who are born with certain types of brain damage. These children's performance on IQ tests is comparable to that of other children through age 6 years, but falls considerably behind thereafter.

The development of schizophrenia follows a similar path. Schizophrenia is highly influenced by genes inherited at conception, but most people who become schizophrenic do not do so until late adolescence or early adulthood. As with other aspects of development, the emergence of schizophrenia reflects a complex interplay between nature and nurture. Children with a schizophrenic biological parent who are raised by nonschizophrenic parents are more likely to become schizophrenic themselves than are the biological children of the nonschizophrenic parents. Children who are raised in troubled homes are also more likely than others to become schizophrenic. However, the only children with a substantial likelihood of becoming schizophrenic are those who have a biological parent who is schizophrenic and who also grow up in a troubled family. As in other contexts, the interaction between the children's nature and the nurture they receive is crucial.

Everything Influences Everything

One common reaction to learning about the complex interactions between nature and nurture is "It sounds like everything influences everything else." This reaction is basically accurate. Consider some of the factors that influence children's and adolescents' self-esteem. Genes matter; the closer the biological relation between two children or adolescents, the more similar their degree of self-esteem is likely to be. A large part of the reason for this genetic influence on self-esteem is that genes influence a wide range of other characteristics that themselves influence self-esteem. For example, genes strongly affect attractiveness, athletic talent, and academic success, all of which contribute to self-esteem.

Factors other than genes also play large roles in the development of self-esteem. Support from one's family and peers contribute in a positive way; poverty and unpopularity contribute in a negative way. Values of the broader society also are influential. East Asian societies tend to emphasize the importance of self-criticism, and children and adolescents in those societies express less self-esteem than do peers in Western societies. Institutional practices also interact with characteristics of the child. For example, in the United States, physically mature girls show increased resistance to authority during junior high school, apparently because they chafe under the tight discipline characteristic of junior high schools.

Complex interactions are not limited to the development of self-esteem or to social development; they are characteristic of development in all areas. For example, in the development of intelligence, the influence of genetics seems to be greater than that of shared environment for children from affluent backgrounds, but the relation is reversed for children from impoverished backgrounds. Similarly, parental involvement in school is more closely related to academic achievement in low-income and African-American families than in more affluent and Euro-American families. Thus, children's nature—their genes, personal characteristics,

DAVID YOUNG-WOLFF / PHOTOEDIT

Differences in running speeds are partially attributable to genetic differences that are present at birth, but nature takes time to reveal itself: Who could have looked at these children when they were newborns and predicted which would be the best runners?

and behavioral tendencies—interact with the nurture they receive from parents, teachers, peers, the broader society, and the physical environment in ways that shape their self-esteem, intellect, actions, and other qualities.

Theme 2: Children Play Active Roles in Their Own Development

Children are physically active even before they leave the womb; the kicking that thrills prospective parents is just the most obvious example. Less obvious is how early in life children become mentally active. While still in the womb, fetuses can learn enough about the sounds in a story their mother repeatedly reads aloud that, as newborns, they are able to discriminate that story from ones their mother did not read aloud. From their first minutes outside the womb, infants selectively focus on objects and events that interest them, rather than passively gazing at whatever appears before their eyes.

Infants' and older children's actions also produce reactions in other people, which further shape the children's development. In this section, we examine four ways in which children contribute to their own development—through physically interacting with the environment, interpreting their experience, regulating their behavior, and eliciting reactions from other people.

Self-Initiated Activity

Even in the womb, normal development depends on the fetus's being active. Fetuses make breathing movements that strengthen their lungs and swallow amniotic fluid, preparing their digestive system to function properly after birth. They also "work out" various muscles, tugging on their umbilical cord, sucking their thumb, kicking, and turning somersaults.

From the day they are born, infants display looking preferences that guide their attention to the most informative aspects of the environment and thus enhance their learning. They like looking at objects rather than at blank fields. They like looking at moving objects rather than at stationary ones and at the edges of objects rather than at their interiors. And they particularly like looking at faces, especially their mother's.

Infants' ability to interact with the environment expands greatly during the first year. At around 3 months, most infants become able to follow moving objects fairly smoothly with their eyes, which improves their ability to follow the actions occurring around them. At 6 or 7 months, most become able to crawl on their bellies and soon after, on their hands and knees; as a result, they no longer have to wait for the world to come to them. By 8 or 9 months, most can hold up their heads, which allows them to reach accurately for objects even when they are not being supported. And by 13 or 14 months, most begin to walk independently, opening a new era in their exploration of the world.

As this infant's eager gaze suggests, children's choices of where to look are among the ways in which they shape their own development.

COURTESY OF ALICE & ROBERT SIEGLER

COURTESY OF ALICE & ROBERT SIEGLER

Children's choices of activities shape their development. This child's interest in print led him to learn to read and write at age 3; the fact that he is one of the authors' children also probably had something to do with his early interest in these skills. (He also is now the father of the baby shown on the previous page.)

As development proceeds, children's self-initiated activity extends to new domains such as language. Toddlers delight in telling their parents the names of objects for no apparent reason beyond the joy of doing so. They also practice talking in their cribs, even when nobody else is present to hear them. They and older children, both deaf and hearing, invent gestures and words to represent objects and events. As their language proficiency develops, children become skilled at initiating conversations that bring them information, allow them to express their feelings and desires, and help them regulate their emotions.

The effects of self-initiated activities also are seen at older ages in other areas, such as self-socialization and antisocial behavior. Throughout the world, boys and girls choose to play predominantly with members of their own gender, especially between the ages of 6 and 10 years. The play patterns reflect the children's own choices: gender segregation is rarely imposed by adults but, rather, arises from differences in the kinds of play that boys and girls tend to prefer and is reinforced by criticism from peers when a child crosses the "gender border."

In later childhood and adolescence, children's choices of friends and peer groups become important influences on whether they engage in criminal activity, drinking, drug use, and so on. More generally, children who belong to cliques tend to increasingly act like other members of the clique in both positive and negaive ways. Thus, from the prenatal period through adolescence, children's self-initiated activities contribute to their development.

Active Interpretation of Experience

Children also contribute to their development by trying to understand the world around them. Even in the first year, infants develop a sense of what is possible in the physical world. Thus, they look longer at an "impossible" event—such as when one solid object appears to move through the space occupied by another object, or when an object seems to be suspended in midair without support—than they do at a physically possible event. Toddlers' and preschoolers' continuous "why" questions, and preschoolers' searching for the explanations of magic tricks, provide other compelling examples of children's eagerness to understand the world.

This desire to understand also motivates young children to construct informal theories concerning inanimate objects, living things, and people. These theories allow children to go beyond the data provided by their senses to infer underlying causes. For example, preschoolers reason that there must be something inside animals that causes them to grow, breathe, have babies, get sick, and so on, even though they do not know what that something is. They also reason that inanimate objects must have different material inside them than living things do.

Children's and adolescents' interpretation of their experience extends to inferences about themselves as well as about the external world. When some children fail on a task, for example, they feel sad and question their ability. Other children who fail on the same task take the failure as a challenge and an opportunity to learn. Similarly, in ambiguous situations, children who are aggressive tend to attribute hostile intentions to others even when the motives of others are unclear; this interpretation sometimes leads the aggressive children to lash out before the other person can hurt them. Thus, subjective interpretations of experiences, as well as objective reality, shape development.

Self-Regulation

Another way in which children contribute to their development is by regulating their behavior. Consider how they regulate their emotions. In the first months after they are born, infants rely almost totally on parents and other caregivers to help them cope with fright and frustration. By age 6 months, they learn to cope with some upsetting situations by turning away from them or by rubbing their bodies to soothe themselves. During the toddler and preschool periods, children become increasingly adept at using physical strategies, such as looking away, when faced with stressors or temptation. During elementary school, they increasingly use cognitive strategies, such as reminding themselves that an unpleasant experience will soon be over, to cope with negative situations. During adolescence, they become increasingly able to deal with emotional stress by discussing their problems with peers. Children who successfully regulate their emotions tend to be more popular and more socially competent than those who are less skilled at emotional regulation, regardless of the children's ages.

Over the course of childhood and adolescence, children increasingly regulate their development through their choice of activities. Whether young children go to sports events, for example, or to movies or the library or religious services, depends mainly on whether their parents take them there. Whether adolescents engage in the same activities depends mainly on whether they want to do so. Selecting moral values, choosing a romantic partner, pursuing an occupation, and deciding whether to have children are just a few of the major decisions that adolescents and young adults face. As noted in Sternberg's theory of intelligence, the wisdom with which people make these choices is an important determinant of their success in life.

Eliciting Reactions from Other People

From the first days of life, infants' behavior influences other people's behavior toward them, which in turn further influences the infants' behavior. For example, infants' smiling and cooing elicits smiling and talking from mothers; these maternal responses, in turn, elicit further smiling and cooing from infants. Because children differ individually in behavior and appearance, they evoke different reactions from other people. For example, babies with easy temperaments elicit more positive reactions from their parents than do cranky or fussy babies. Similarly, attractive babies elicit more affectionate and playful mothering than do less attractive ones. And in trying times, attractive children are less likely to suffer parental rejection and punishment than are less attractive ones. As children develop, their interests and abilities also begin to influence their interactions with their parents. For example, mothers are more likely to entrust children with helping to care for a younger sibling if they are responsible and sympathetic to the younger child.

The effects that children's initial inclinations have on their parents' behavior toward them tend to multiply over time. Most parents of children who are disobedient, angry, and challenging try to be supportive but firm with them. However, if the bad behavior and defiance continue, many parents give up and become hostile and

It is all too easy for relations between parents and children to spiral downward, with disobedience and anger from children eliciting anger and hostility from parents, which then elicits more disobedience and anger from children, and so on.

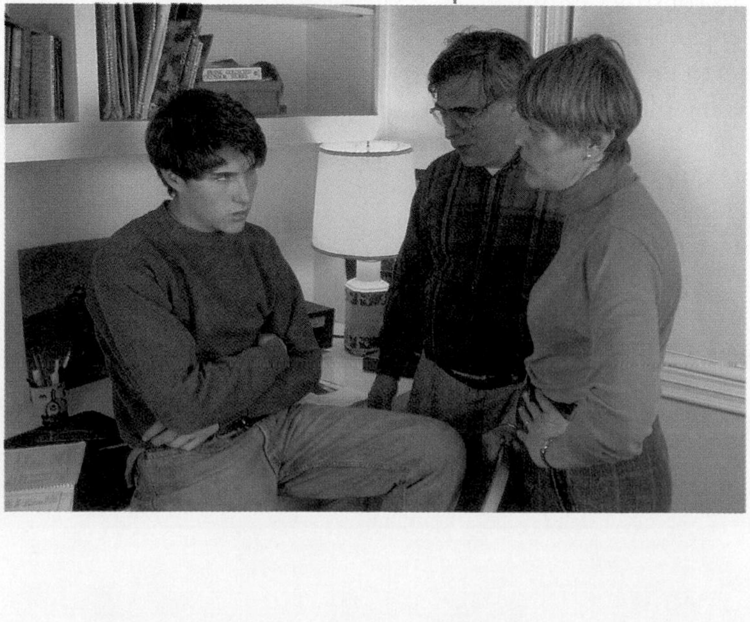

JOHNATHAN NOUROK / PHOTOEDIT / PICTUREQUEST

punitive. Other parents, faced with belligerence and aggression, back down from confrontations and increasingly give in to their children's demands. Once such negative cycles are established, they are difficult to stop. If teenagers act disruptively, and parents respond with hostility, problems generally worsen over the course of adolescence.

Children's characteristics and behavior influence not just their parents' reactions but also those of their peers. At all ages, children who are cooperative, friendly, sociable, and sensitive to others tend to be popular with their peers, whereas those who are aggressive or disruptive tend to be disliked and rejected. In some cases, peers' reactions to each other's behavior change with age; for example, kindergartners tend to neither like nor dislike unaggressive withdrawn peers, but older elementary and middle school students tend to dislike such children. Peer reactions to children's behavior often have long-term consequences; thus, rejected children are more likely than popular children to later have difficulty in school and to engage in criminal activity. In many ways, then, children influence their development, not only by initiating actions, interpreting their experiences, and regulating their emotions, but also by eliciting certain kinds of reactions from other people that then shape their own behavior.

Theme 3: Development Is Both Continuous and Discontinuous

Long before there was a scientific discipline of child development, philosophers and others interested in human nature argued about whether development is continuous or discontinuous. Current disputes between those who believe that development is continuous, such as social learning theorists, and those who believe it is discontinuous, such as stage theorists, are part of the same tradition. There is a good reason why both positions have endured so long: each captures important truths about development. Two particularly important issues in this longstanding debate involve continuity/discontinuity of individual differences and continuity/discontinuity of the standard course of development with age.

Continuity/Discontinuity of Individual Differences

One sense of continuity/discontinuity involves stability of individual differences over time. The basic question is whether children who initially are higher or lower than most peers in some quality continue to be higher or lower in that quality years later. It turns out that many individual differences in psychological properties are moderately stable over the course of development, but the stability is always far from 100%.

Consider the development of intelligence. Some stability is present from infancy onward. For example, the faster that infants habituate to repeated presentation of the same display, the higher their IQ scores tend to be 10 or more years later. Infants' patterns of electrical brain activity (EEGs) also are related to their speed of processing and attention regulation more than 10 years later. The amount of stability increases with age. IQ scores show some stability from age 3 to age 13, considerable stability from age 5 to age 15, and substantial stability from age 8 to age 18. However, even at older ages, IQ scores vary somewhat from occasion to occasion.

For example, when the same children take IQ tests at ages 8 and 17, the two scores differ on average by 9 points. Part of this variability reflects random fluctuations in how sharp the person is on the particular day of testing and in the person's knowledge of the particular questions on each test. Another part of the variability reflects the fact that even if two children start out with equal intelligence, one may show greater intellectual growth over time.

Individual differences in social and personality characteristics also show some continuity over time. Shy toddlers tend to grow into shy children, fearful toddlers into fearful children, aggressive children into aggressive adolescents, generous children into generous adults, and so on. The continuity also carries over into situations quite different from any that the children faced at the earlier time; for example, secure attachments in infancy predict positive romantic relationships in adolescence.

Although there is some continuity of individual differences in social, emotional, and personality development, the degree of continuity is generally lower than in intellectual development. For example, whereas children who are high in reading and math achievement in 5th grade generally remain so in 7th grade, children who are popular in 5th grade may or may not be popular in 7th grade. In addition, aspects of temperament such as fearfulness and shyness often change considerably over early and middle childhood.

Regardless of whether the focus is on intellectual, social, or emotional development, the stability of individual differences is influenced by the stability of the environment. For example, an infant's attachment to his or her mother correlates positively with the infant's long-term security, but the correlation is higher if the home environment stays consistent than if serious disruptions occur. Similarly, IQ scores are more stable if the home environment remains stable. Thus, continuities in individual differences reflect continuities in children's environments as well as in their genes.

Continuity/Discontinuity of Overall Development: The Question of Stages

Many of the most prominent theories of development divide childhood and adolescence into a small number of discrete stages. Piaget's theory of cognitive development, Freud's theory of psychosexual development, Erikson's theory of psychosocial development, and Kohlberg's theory of moral development all describe development in this way. The enduring popularity of these stage approaches is easy to understand: they simplify the enormously complicated process of development by dividing it into a few distinct periods; they point to important characteristics of behavior during each period; and they impart an overall sense of coherence to the developmental process.

Although stage theories differ in their particulars, they share four key assumptions: (1) development progresses through a series of qualitatively distinct stages; (2) when children are in a given stage, a fairly broad range of their thinking and behavior exhibits the features characteristic of that stage; (3) the stages occur in the same order for all children; and (4) transitions between stages occur quickly.

Development turns out to be considerably less tidy than stage approaches imply, however. Children who exhibit preoperational reasoning on some tasks often exhibit concrete operational reasoning on others; children who reason in a preconventional way about some moral dilemmas often reason in a conventional way about others; and so on. Rarely is a sudden change evident across a broad range of tasks.

In addition, developmental processes often show a great deal of continuity. Throughout childhood and adolescence, there are continuous increases in the ability to regulate emotions, make friends, take other people's perspectives, remember events, solve problems, and engage in many other activities.

This does not mean that there are no sudden jumps. When we consider specific tasks and processes, rather than broad domains, we see a number of discontinuities. Three-month-olds move from having almost no binocular depth perception to having adultlike levels within a week or two. Before age 7 months, infants rarely fear strangers; after this time, wariness develops quickly. Many toddlers move in a single day from being unable to walk without support to walking unsupported for a number of steps. After acquiring about one word per week between ages 12 and 18 months, toddlers undergo a vocabulary explosion in which they learn roughly 10 words per day for years thereafter. Thus, although broad domains, such as intelligence and personality, rarely show discontinuous changes, specific aspects of development fairly often do.

Whether development appears to be continuous or discontinuous often varies with whether the focus is on behavior or on underlying processes. Behaviors that emerge or disappear quite suddenly may reflect continuous underlying processes. Recall the case of infants' stepping reflex. For the first two months after birth, if infants are supported in an upright position with their feet touching the ground, they will first lift one leg and then the other in a pattern similar to walking. At around age 2 months, this reflex suddenly disappears. Underlying the abrupt change in behavior, however, are gradual changes in two dimensions that underlie the behavioral change—weight and leg strength. As babies grow, their gain in weight temporarily outstrips their gain in leg strength, and they become unable to lift their legs without help. Thus, when babies who have stopped exhibiting the stepping reflex are supported in a tank of water, making it easier for them to lift their legs, the stepping reflex reappears.

Whether development appears continuous or discontinuous also depends on the time scale being considered. Recall that when a child's height was measured every 6 months from birth to 18 years, the growth looked continuous (see Figure 1.2, page 17). When height was measured daily, however, development looked discontinuous, with occasional "growth days" sprinkled among numerous days without growth.

One useful framework for thinking about developmental continuities and discontinuities is to envision development as a road trip through the United States, from New York City to San Francisco. In one sense, the drive is a continuous progression westward along Interstate 80. In another sense, the drive starts in the East and then proceeds (in an invariant order, without the possibility of skipping a region) through the Midwest and the Rocky Mountains before reaching its end point in California. The East includes the Atlantic Coast and the Appalachians, and it tends to be hilly, cloudy, and green; the Midwest tends to be flatter, dryer, and sunnier; the Mountain States are dryer and sunnier still, with extensive mountainous areas; and most of California is dry and sunny, with both extensive flat and extensive mountainous areas. The differences between regions in climate, color, and topography are large and real, but the boundaries between them are arbitrary. Is Ohio the westernmost eastern state or the easternmost midwestern state? Is eastern Colorado part of the Midwest or part of the Rocky Mountain region?

The continuities and discontinuities in development are a lot like those on the road trip. Consider children's conceptions of the self. At one level of analysis, the development of the self is continuous. Over the course of development, children

A trip along I-80 from New York to San Francisco takes a driver through four time zones in which the main features of the land change dramatically. The changes in topography, like those in development, however, are not discontinuous. Adjacent areas tend to be highly similar, and classification of a border area as being in one zone or another are often quite arbitrary. In all of these ways, the journey resembles psychological development.

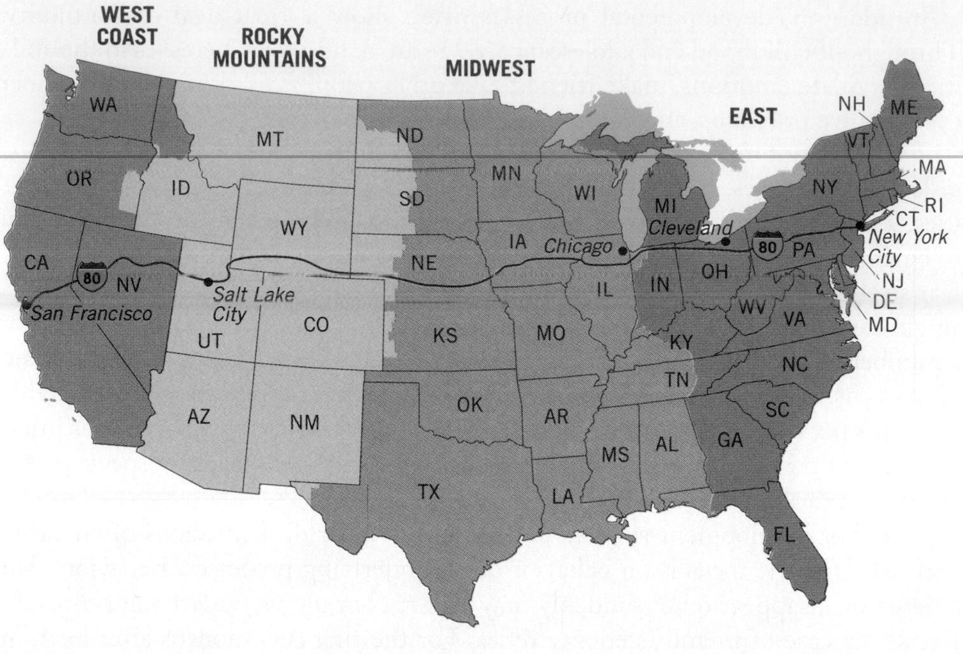

(and adults) understand more and more about themselves. At another level of analysis, milestones characterize each period of development. During infancy, children come to distinguish between themselves and other people, but they rarely if ever see themselves from another person's perspective. During the toddler period, children increasingly view themselves as others might, which allows them to feel such emotions as shame and embarrassment. During the preschool period, children realize that certain of their personal characteristics, such as their gender, are fundamental and permanent, and they use this knowledge to guide their behavior. During the elementary school years, children increasingly think of themselves in terms of their competencies relative to other children's (intelligence, athletic skill, popularity, etc.). During adolescence, children come to recognize that, to an extent, who we are as individuals reflects our own choices.

Thus, any statement about when a given competency emerges is somewhat arbitrary, much like a statement about where a geographic region begins. Nonetheless, identifying the milestones helps us understand where we are on the map.

Theme 4: Mechanisms of Developmental Change

As with so many issues, contemporary thinking about developmental change owes a large debt to the ideas of Jean Piaget. Within Piaget's theory, change occurs through the interaction of assimilation and accommodation. Through assimilation, children interpret new experiences in terms of their existing mental structures; through accommodation, they revise their existing mental structures in accord with the new experiences. Thus, when we hear a truly unfamiliar type of music (for most of us, Javanese twelve-tone music would fit this description), we assimilate the sounds to more familiar musical patterns, to the extent we can. At the same time, our understanding accommodates to the experience, so that when we next encounter the unfamiliar music, it will be a little easier to grasp and will feel a little less strange.

A great deal has been learned about developmental mechanisms since Piaget formulated his theory. Some of the advances have come in understanding change at the biological level, others in understanding it at the behavioral level, and still others in understanding it at the level of cognitive processes.

Biological Change Mechanisms

Biological change mechanisms come into play from the moment a sperm unites with an egg. Each of these cells contains half of the DNA that will constitute the child's genotype throughout life. The genotype contains instructions that specify the rough outline of development, but all particulars are filled in by subsequent interactions between the genotype and the environment.

The way in which the brain forms following conception illustrates the complexity of change at the biological level. The first key process in brain development is *neurogenesis,* which by the 3rd or 4th week after conception is producing roughly 10,000 brain cells *per minute.* About 100 days later, the brain contains just about all of the neurons it ever will have. As neurons form, a process of *cell migration* causes many of them to travel from where they were produced to their long-term location.

Once neurons reach their destination, they undergo a process of *differentiation,* in which dendrites and axons grow out from the original cell body. Later in the prenatal period, the process of *myelination* adds an insulating sheath over certain axons, which speeds up the rate of transmission of electrical signals along them. Myelination continues through childhood and into adolescence.

Yet another process, *synaptogenesis,* involves formation of synapses between the end of axons and the beginning of dendrites that allow neurotransmitters to transmit signals from neuron to neuron. From the prenatal period to early or middle childhood (depending on the particular area of the brain), the number of synapses increases rapidly. By the end of this period of explosive growth, the number of synapses in the area far exceeds the number in the brains of adults. A process of *pruning* then reduces the number of synapses in the area. The greatest pruning occurs at different times in different areas of the brain. Those synapses that are frequently used are maintained; those that are not are eliminated ("use it or lose it" at the biological level). The pruning of unused synapses makes information processing more efficient.

The brain includes a number of areas that are specialized for particular psychological functions. This specialization makes possible rapid and universal development of these functions and thus enhances learning of the relevant type of information. Some of the functions are closely linked to sensory and motor systems. The visual cortex and lateral geniculate are particularly active in processing sights, the auditory cortex is particularly active in processing sounds, the motor cortex is particularly active in making movements, and so on.

Other brain areas are specialized for functions that are not specific to any one sensory or motor system. The limbic system, located in the lower part of the brain, is particularly prominent in producing emotions. Certain areas of the occipital and temporal lobes of the cortex are especially crucial for recognizing faces, whether through vision or touch. Broca's and Wernicke's areas are especially active in processing spoken and written language. Some areas toward the back of the right hemisphere are especially active in processing spatial configurations. All of these areas are involved in numerous other types of processing, and all types of processing involve numerous brain areas, but each of the areas is especially active in processing the type of information associated with it. Thus, biological mechanisms underlie both very specific and very general changes.

This fMRI image, taken while a person in a scanner was reading a sentence projected on a screen, shows that diverse areas of the brain contribute to reading comprehension. The large cluster of red toward the front of the brain (the middle of the scan) includes Broca's area, which tends to be especially active in the processing of grammar and meaning. The smaller cluster of red at the back of the brain (the rightmost area of the scan) likely is involved in visual processing of the text. The red area located low and central in the scan corresponds to Wernicke's area, which is particularly involved in processing the meaning of words and sentences. The red area in the upper right part of the image probably reflects processing of the spatial location of the text on the screen.

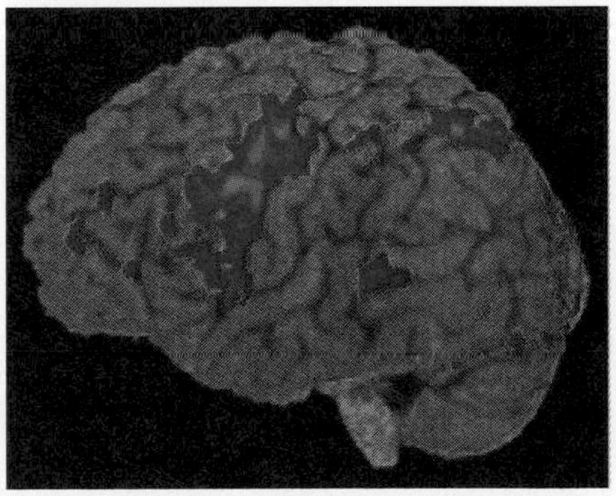

COURTESY OF DRS. SHARLENE NEWMAN AND MARCEL JUST

Behavioral Change Mechanisms

Behavioral change mechanisms describe responses to environmental contingencies that contribute to development. These mechanisms shape behavior from infants' first days onward.

Habituation, Conditioning, and Statistical Learning

The capacity to habituate to familiar stimuli begins before fetuses leave the womb. When simple syllables such as "ba-bi" are spoken into a microphone close to the belly of a woman in her 9th month of pregnancy, her fetus's heart rate decelerates. The fetus's heart rate returns to normal as the same pair of syllables is repeated in the same order several times. However, when the order of syllables is reversed, so that "bi-ba" is presented, the fetus's heart rate again decelerates, thus demonstrating that the fetus habituated to the original "word" and dishabituated to the novel one. Habituation continues after birth as well; for example, when a picture of a face is shown repeatedly, infants reduce their looking, but they show renewed interest when a different face appears. Habituation motivates babies to seek new stimulation and thus helps them learn.

From their first days in the outside world, infants also can learn through classical conditioning. If an initially neutral stimulus is repeatedly presented just before an unconditioned stimulus, it comes to elicit a similar response to that elicited by the unconditioned stimulus. Recall little Albert who, after repeatedly seeing a harmless white rat and then hearing a frightening loud noise immediately after, came to fear the white rat (as well as doctors and nurses wearing white lab coats).

The fact that an infant would become afraid not only of the white rat but also of the doctors and nurses illustrates the functioning of another key learning ability that is present from infancy: generalization. Although infants' learning tends to be less general than that of older children, it is never completely literal. Infants generalize the lessons of their past experience to new situations that differ at least in a few details from the original ones.

Like older children, infants also learn through instrumental conditioning; behaviors that are rewarded become more frequent, and behaviors that do not lead to rewards become less frequent. In the first few months after birth, infants learn from instrumental conditioning only when the reinforcement occurs immediately after the relevant behavior; over the next several months, infants become able to learn when reinforcement is delayed as well.

Yet another mechanism that allows infants to acquire information rapidly is statistical learning. From as early as 2 months of age, infants quickly learn the likelihood that one sight or sound will follow another. Because many events, including the sounds within words and certain daily activities, occur in predictable orders, statistical learning helps infants anticipate other people's actions and generate similar sequences of behavior themselves. Thus, basic behavioral learning mechanisms—habituation, generalization, classical conditioning, instrumental conditioning, and statistical learning—allow children to learn from their interactions with the environment from the first days onward.

Social Learning

Children (and adults) learn a great deal from observing and interacting with other people. This social learning pervades our life to such an extent that it is difficult to think of it as a specific learning capability. However, when we compare humans with other animals, even close relatives such as apes and chimpanzees, the omnipresence of social learning in people's lives becomes apparent. Humans are far more skillful than any other animal in learning what others are trying to teach them; they also are far more inclined to teach others what they know. Among the crucial contributors to this social learning are imitation, social referencing, language, and guided participation.

JUDITH KRAMER / THE IMAGE WORKS

Imitation starts in infancy.

The first discernible form of social learning is imitation. At first, the imitation seems limited to behaviors that infants sometimes produce on their own, such as sticking out their tongue. However, by age 6 months, infants begin to imitate novel behaviors that they never make spontaneously. By 15 months, toddlers not only learn novel behaviors but can remember them and continue to produce them for at least a week. This imitation is not just "monkey see, monkey do." When children of this age see a model try to do something but fail, they imitate what the model was trying to do rather than what the model actually did.

Social learning influences socioemotional development as well as acquisition of knowledge. When an unfamiliar person enters the room, 12-month-olds look to their mother for guidance. If the mother's face or voice shows fear, the baby tends to stay close to her; if the mother smiles, the baby is more likely to approach the stranger. Similarly, in the laboratory, a baby of this age will cross the visual cliff if the mother smiles but not if she looks apprehensive. Social learning also shapes children's standards and values. From the second year of life, toddlers internalize their parents' values and standards and use them to guide and evaluate their own conduct. Later in development, peers, teachers, and other adults also influence children's standards and values through the process of social learning. Peers, in particular, play a steadily increasing role over the course of childhood and adolescence.

The likelihood of children's imitating other people varies with the quality of their relationship with them. Children are more likely to imitate the behavior of adults with whom they have positive relationships than the behavior of other adults. They also are more likely to imitate friends' behaviors than those of other children that they see doing the same thing; even 1-year-olds prefer to imitate their friends.

Imitation is not the only mechanism of social learning, however. Another is social scaffolding. In this change mechanism, an older and more knowledgeable person provides a learner with an overview of a given task, demonstrates how to do the most difficult parts of it, and offers suggestions to the learner on how to proceed. Such scaffolding allows a beginner to do more than he or she could without help. Then, as the learner masters the basics of the task, the scaffolder transfers increasing responsibility to the learner until the learner is doing the entire task. Thus, adults and children work together to produce social learning.

Changing a doll's diaper while Mom changes that of the baby is a common activity among children in many homes. Such imitation of parents usually reflects a positive parent–child relationship.

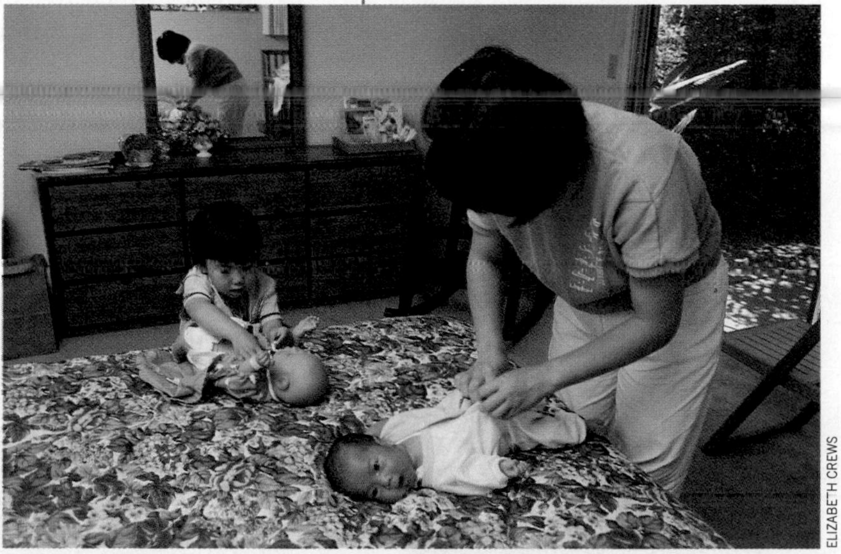

ELIZABETH CREWS

Cognitive Change Mechanisms

Many of the most compelling analyses of developmental change are at the level of cognitive processes. Both general and specific information-processing mechanisms play important roles.

General Information-Processing Mechanisms

Numerous cognitive mechanisms can be applied to all kinds of information. These general information-processing mechanisms fall into four main categories: basic processes, strategies, metacognition, and content knowledge.

Basic processes are the simplest, most broadly applicable, and earliest-developing general information-processing mechanisms. They include associating events with each other, recognizing objects as familiar, recalling facts and procedures, encoding key features of events, and generalizing from one instance to another. Changes with age occur in the speed and efficiency of these basic processes, but all of the basic processes are present from infancy onward. The fundamental organization of memory into sensory, working, and long-term components also is constant throughout life. These basic processes and structures provide a foundation that allows infants to learn about the world from their very first days.

Strategies also contribute to many types of development. Toddlers, for example, form strategies for achieving such goals as obtaining a toy that is out of reach or descending a steep surface; preschoolers form strategies for counting and solving arithmetic problems; school-age children form strategies for playing games and getting along with others; and so on. Often, children acquire multiple strategies for solving a single kind of problem—for example, strategies for approaching unfamiliar children on a playground or for solving arithmetic problems. Knowing multiple strategies allows children to adapt to the demands of different problems and situations.

Metacognition is a third general process that contributes to development in large ways. For example, increasing use of memory strategies stems in large part from children's increasing realization that they are unlikely to remember large amounts of material verbatim without using such strategies. Among the most important applications of metacognition is adaptive choice among alternative strategies. The memory strategy of rehearsal presents one clear example. Children often rehearse when they need to remember information verbatim, as with remembering a phone number or a locker combination. However, they almost never rehearse when the literal information does not matter, as with summarizing a story. Reflection is another metacognitive process that contributes to development; for example, asking students to reflect on the relative quality of essays written by other children, and to analyze why some essays are better than others, can improve the students' own writing.

Exceptional content knowledge can outweigh all of adults' usual intellectual advantages over children. On the day this photograph was taken, this 8-year-old boy became the youngest person ever to defeat a Chess Grand Master (the ranking awarded to the greatest chess players in the world).

TOPHAM / THE IMAGE WORKS

Content knowledge is a fourth pervasive contributor to cognitive change. The more children know about any topic—whether it be chess, soccer, dinosaurs, or language—the better able they are to learn and remember new information about it. Knowledge also facilitates learning of unfamiliar content by allowing children to draw analogies between the new content and content that is familiar to them.

Domain-Specific Learning Mechanisms

Infants acquire some complex competencies surprisingly rapidly, including basic perception and understanding of the physical world, language comprehension and production, interpretation of emotions, and attachment to caregivers. What seems to unite the varied capabilities that children acquire especially rapidly is their apparent evolutionary importance. Evolution seems to have provided us with specialized learning mechanisms that ensure that virtually everyone will quickly and easily acquire abilities that are important to survival.

One type of mechanism that enhances learning in these areas is accurate assumptions about the experiences that the world will provide. Even infants in their first year seem to assume that bigger moving objects will produce stronger effects than smaller moving objects. Similarly, toddlers' word learning is aided by the whole-object assumption (the idea that words used to label objects refer to the whole object rather than to a part of it) and the mutual exclusivity assumption (the idea that each object has a single name). These assumptions are usually correct for the words that young children hear, thus helping them learn what the words mean.

Children's informal theories about the main types of entities in the world—inanimate objects, people, and other living things—also facilitate their learning about them. The value of learning rapidly about the properties of people, other living things, and inanimate objects is clear; saying "More juice" to another person, for example, is considerably more likely to be successful than is saying the same words to the family dog. Crucial in children's informal theories, as in scientists' formal ones, are causal relations that explain a large number of observations in terms of a few basic concepts.

Possessing basic understanding of key concepts—such as inertia and solidity for inanimate objects; goal-directed movement and growth for living things; and intentions, beliefs, and desires for people—helps children act appropriately in new situations. For example, when preschoolers meet an unfamiliar child, they assume that the child will have intentions, beliefs, and desires—an assumption that helps them understand the other child's actions and react appropriately to them. These assumptions about other people's minds aid the social understanding of children in all societies. Thus, both general and domain-specific cognitive learning mechanisms help children understand the world around them.

Change Mechanisms Work Together

Although it is often easiest to discuss different change mechanisms separately, it is crucial to remember that biological, cognitive, and behavioral mechanisms all reflect interactions between the person and the environment and that all work together to produce change. For example, consider the development of effortful attention. Development of this capability reflects contributions of genes, neurotransmitters, interconnections among brain areas, and the external environment. Genes influence the production of neurotransmitters, which, in turn, affects children's ability to concentrate and ignore distractions. The development of connections between two parts of the brain—the anterior cingulate, which is active in attention to goals, and the limbic area, which is active in emotional reactions—also influences the development of effortful attention. Quality of parenting is another influence on development of this capability. However, the impact of parenting depends on the child's genes; quality of parenting influences development of effortful attention for children with one form of a relevant gene but has little if any effect on children with another form of the gene.

Conversely, experiences playing specially designed computer games increases the activity of the anterior cingulate and thus the ability to sustain attention on both experimental tasks and intelligence tasks. In short, varied types of mechanisms work together to produce development of even a single capability.

Theme 5: The Sociocultural Context Shapes Development

Children develop within a personal context of other people: families, friends, neighbors, teachers, and classmates. They also develop within an impersonal context of historical, economic, technological, and political forces, as well as societal beliefs, attitudes, and values. The impersonal context is as important as the personal one in shaping development. There is little reason to think that parents in developed societies in the twenty-first century care more about their children's development than parents of the past did. Yet their children die less often, get sick less often, eat a more varied and nutritious diet, receive more formal schooling, and see more of the world than did children from even the wealthiest families of 100 or 200 years ago. Thus, when and where children grow up profoundly influences their lives.

Growing Up in Societies with Different Values

The culture of Mexican villages successfully encourages cooperation and caring among children.

WESLEY BOCKE / PHOTO RESEARCHERS, INC

Values and practices that people within a society take for granted as "natural" often vary substantially among societies. These variations considerably influence the rate and form of development. Throughout the book, you encountered examples of this in every aspect of development, including in domains that are commonly thought of as governed by maturation. For example, people often assume that the timing of walking and other motor skills in infancy is determined solely by biology. However, babies who grow up in African tribes that strongly encourage infants' motor development tend to walk and reach other motor milestones earlier than do infants in the United States. Conversely, babies who grow up in South American tribes that discourage early motor activity reach the motor milestones later than do infants in the United States.

Emotional reactions provide another example of how cultural attitudes and values influence behavior even when we might not expect them to do so. Infants in all societies that have been studied show the same attachment patterns, but the frequency of occurrence of each pattern varies with the values of the society. Relative to babies in the United States, for instance, Japanese babies who are placed in the Strange Situation more often become very upset, showing the insecure-resistant attachment pattern. These differences in attachment patterns appear to be due to differing cultural values and practices. Japanese mothers encourage dependence in children and rarely leave their babies alone, which may lead to the babies' becoming especially upset when they are left alone in the Strange Situation. In contrast, U.S. parents emphasize independence to a greater degree and more often leave babies with other adults and children.

Cultural influences such as these continue well beyond infancy. Japanese culture, for example, places a higher value on hiding negative emotions than does American culture; correspondingly, Japanese preschoolers express negative emotions less often than do American preschoolers. Child rearing in rural Mexican villages emphasizes cooperation and caring about others; children raised in these areas are more likely to share their possessions than are children from Mexican cities or the United States, a pattern that continues among Mexican-American children whose parents moved from Mexican villages to the United States.

Although authoritarian parenting is generally associated with negative outcomes for adolescents in the United States, the negative outcomes do not generally hold for African-American adolescents.

Culture influences not only parents' actions but also children's interpretations of those actions. For example, Chinese-American mothers use a great deal of scolding and guilt to control their children. In the broader U.S. population, use of this disciplinary approach is associated with negative outcomes, but the association is not present among Chinese-American children. Similarly, authoritarian parenting is generally associated with negative outcomes for adolescents, but it does not seem to have this effect on African-American adolescents. In both cases, the differing effectiveness of the disciplinary approaches may reflect children's interpretations of the parents' behavior. If children believe that scolding or authoritarian parenting is in their best interest, the behaviors can be effective. However, if children see such disciplinary approaches as reflecting negative parental feelings toward them, the discipline tends to be ineffective or harmful.

Sociocultural differences exert a similar influence on cognitive development. They help determine which skills and knowledge children acquire—for example, whether children learn to operate abacuses or pocket calculators. They also influence how well children learn skills that everyone acquires to some degree; for example, Australian Aboriginal children, whose lives will eventually depend on their ability to trek through the desert to distant oases, develop spatial skills superior to those of urban Australian children. Finally, cultural values influence the educational system, which in turn influences what and how deeply children learn. For example, students in community-of-learners classrooms learn about fewer scientific topics than do children in traditional classrooms, but they learn about them in greater depth.

Growing Up in Different Times and Places

When and where children grow up profoundly influences their development. As noted earlier, in modern societies, children's lives are greatly improved over what they were in the past in terms of health, nutrition, shelter, and so on. Not all of the changes in these societies have promoted children's well-being, however. For example, in North America and Europe, far more children grow up with divorced parents than in the past, and these children are at risk for many problems. On average, they are more prone to sadness and depression, have lower self-esteem, and are less socially competent than peers who live in intact families. Although most children from divorced families do not have serious problems, about 20 to 25% do: engaging in delinquent activities, dropping out of school, and having children out of wedlock all are more common among children whose parents are divorced.

Other historical changes may result in children's lives being different, but neither better nor worse. The great expansion of child care outside the home represents one such case. In the United States, about half of infants and three-fourths of 4-year-olds currently receive child care outside their homes—5 times the rates in 1965. As this change was occurring, many people feared that such care would weaken attachment between babies and mothers. Others expressed hopes that such care would greatly stimulate cognitive development, especially of children from impoverished backgrounds, because of the greater opportunities for interaction with other children and adults. In fact, the data indicate that neither the fears nor the exaggerated hopes were justified. Overall, children who receive care outside the home tend to develop very similarly, both emotionally and cognitively, to those who do not. Thus, some of the effects of growing up now rather than in the past are positive, others are negative, and still others make life different but neither better nor worse.

Growing Up in Different Circumstances Within a Society

Even among children growing up at the same time in the same society, differences in economic circumstances, family relationships, and peer groups lead to large differences in children's lives.

Economic Influences

In every society, the economic circumstances of a child's family considerably influence the child's life. However, the degree of economic inequality within each society influences just how large a difference the economic circumstances make. In societies with large income inequalities, such as the United States, poor children's academic achievement is far lower than that of children from wealthier families. In societies with smaller inequalities, such as Japan and Sweden, children from affluent families also do better academically than children from poorer families, but the differences are smaller.

This evocative photograph makes us wonder how the severe poverty this Depression Era family faced affected the children's subsequent lives.

DOROTHEA LANGE / FSA / ARCHIVE PHOTOS

It is not just academic achievement that is influenced by economic circumstances; all aspects of development are. Infants from impoverished families more often are insecurely attached to their mothers. Children and adolescents from impoverished families more often are rejected as friends and more often say they are lonely. Illegal substance use, crime, and depression also are more common among poor adolescents than among peers from wealthier backgrounds.

These negative outcomes are unsurprising, given the many disadvantages that poor children face. Relative to children who grow up in more affluent environments, poor children more often live in dangerous neighborhoods; grow up in homes with one or no biological parents; attend inferior day-care centers and schools; and have few books, magazines, and other intellectually stimulating material in their homes. The cumulative effect of these disadvantages, rather than any one of them, poses the greatest obstacle to successful development.

Influences of Family and Peers

Families and peer groups vary considerably, and the differences among them have a substantial influence on development. In some families, regardless of income, parents are sensitive to babies' needs and form close attachments with them; in others, this does not occur. In some families, again regardless of income, parents read to their children each night, thus helping the children to learn to read; in others, this does not occur. The influence of friends, other peers, teachers, and other adults vary in as many ways as those of families. Friends, for example, can provide companionship and feedback, contribute to self-esteem, and serve as a buffer against stress; during adolescence, they can be particularly important sources of sympathy and support. On the other hand, friends can also have a negative influence, drawing children and adolescents into reckless and aggressive behavior, including crime, drinking, and drug use. Thus, personal relationships, like economic circumstances, history, and culture, vary in a multitude of ways that influence development.

Theme 6: Individual Differences

Children differ on an infinite number of dimensions—demographic characteristics (gender, race, ethnicity, SES), psychological characteristics (intellect, personality, artistic ability), experiences (where they grow up, whether their parents are divorced, whether they participate in organized sports), and so on. How can we tell which individual differences are the crucial ones for understanding children and predicting their futures?

As illustrated in Figure 16.1, three characteristics—breadth of related characteristics, stability over time, and predictive value—are crucial in determining the importance of a dimension of individual differences. First, as shown by the dotted vertical arrows, children's status on the most important dimensions is associated with their status at that time on other important dimensions. Thus, one reason why intelligence is considered a central individual difference is that the higher a child's IQ at a given age, the higher the child's grades, achievement test scores, and general knowledge tend to be at the same time. A second key characteristic is stability over time (the solid arrows). A dimension of individual differences is of greater interest if the higher or lower that children score on it early in development, the higher or lower they are likely to score on it later. Thus, another reason for interest in IQ is that children with high IQs usually grow into adults with high IQs, and vice versa. A third characteristic of major dimensions of individual differences is that a child's status on the dimension predicts outcomes on other important characteristics in the future (dashed arrows). Thus, a third reason for interest in IQ scores is that a person's IQ during middle childhood and adolescence predicts that person's later earnings, occupational status, and years of education.

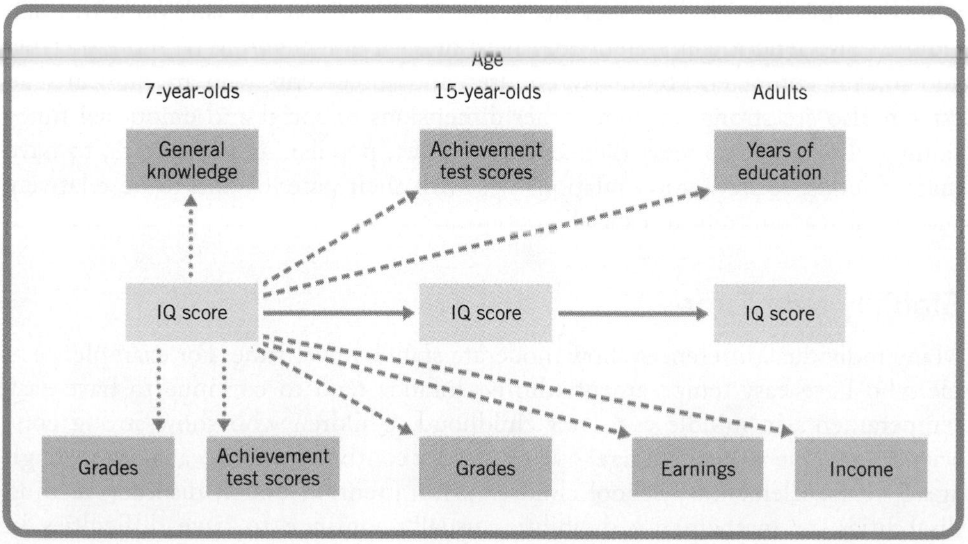

FIGURE 16.1 Intelligence and individual differences Intelligence is considered a crucial dimension of individual differences because IQ scores (1) correlate with other conceptually related dimensions such as general knowledge and grades at any one age (dotted arrows extending from IQ to other outcomes at age 7); (2) show considerable continuity over age (solid arrows); and (3) predict future outcomes, such as years of education and income in adulthood (dashed arrows connecting IQ score at age 7 to other later outcomes).

These three characteristics make clear why demographic variables such as gender, race, ethnicity, and SES are studied so often. Consider gender, for example. Gender differences are related to a wide variety of other differences. Boys tend to be larger, stronger, more physically active, and more aggressive; to play in larger groups; to be better at some forms of spatial thinking; and to more often have attention-deficit hyperactivity disorder (ADHD) and math or reading disabilities. Girls tend to be more verbal, quicker to perceive emotions, better at writing, and more likely to express sympathy and empathy for people in distress. Gender also is completely stable over time: our gender is part of who we are throughout life. Finally, gender predicts future individual differences. Knowing a baby's gender to be female, for example, allows us to predict that, compared with males, she will be more likely, among other things, to have an easy time learning to read, to be self-revealing with friends, to be vulnerable to depression, to be inclined to prosocial behavior, and to engage in relational rather than overt aggression.

We next consider the extent to which several other variables show these three key characteristics of major individual differences.

Breadth of Individual Differences at a Given Time

Individual differences are not randomly distributed. Children who are high on one dimension also tend to be high on other, conceptually related dimensions. Thus, children who do well on one measure of intellect—language, memory, conceptual understanding, problem solving, reading, or mathematics—tend to do well on others. Similarly, children who do well on one measure of social or emotional functioning—relations with parents, relations with peers, relations with teachers, self-esteem, prosocial behavior, and lack of aggression and lying—also tend to do well on others. Sometimes, as with the relation between intelligence and school achievement, the connections are very strong. More often, the relations are moderate. Thus, although children who get along well with their parents also tend to get along well with peers, there are many exceptions.

Certain dimensions of psychological functioning seem crucial for an especially broad range of other outcomes. Intelligence is one such dimension, as described above. Two other crucial dimensions of individual differences are attachment and self-esteem. Toddlers who are securely attached to their mother tend to be more enthusiastic and positive about solving problems with her, to comply more often with her directives, and to obey her requests even when she isn't present. Such children also tend to get along better with other toddlers and to be more sociable and socially competent. Similarly, children and adolescents who are high in self-esteem also are strong on many other dimensions of social and emotional functioning. They tend to view themselves as smart, popular, and attractive; to have many friends; to have good relationships with their parents; and to be relatively successful academically and socially.

Stability over Time

Many individual differences show moderate stability over time. For example, people who have easy temperaments during infancy tend to continue to have easy temperaments in middle and later childhood. Children who show strong consciences relative to peers at age 2 years usually continue to do so at least through age 5 years. Elementary school children with attention-deficit disorder, reading disabilities, or mathematics disabilities usually continue to have difficulties in those areas into adulthood.

The reasons for such stability of psychological characteristics are to be found in the stability of both genes and environment. A child's genotype remains identical over the course of development (though particular genes switch on and off at different times). Most children's environments remain fairly stable as well. Families that are middle-class when a child is born tend to remain middle-class; families that value education when the child is born usually continue to value education; families that are sensitive and supportive generally remain that way; and so on. Major changes, such as divorce and unemployment, do occur, and they affect children's happiness, self-esteem, and other variables. Nonetheless, the relative stability of children's environments, like the stability of their genes, contributes to the stability over time of their psychological functioning.

Predicting Future Individual Differences on Other Dimensions

Individual differences on some dimensions are related not only to future status on that dimension but also to future status on other dimensions. For example, children who are securely attached as infants tend as toddlers and preschoolers to have more social ties to their peers than do children who were insecurely attached as infants. When they reach school age, they tend to understand other children's emotions relatively well and to be relatively skilled in resolving conflicts. When they reach adolescence and adulthood, they tend to form close attachments with romantic partners. All of these outcomes are consistent with the view that secure early attachment provides a working model that influences subsequent relationships with other people.

As with stability over time of a single dimension, the relative stability of most children's environments contributes to these long-term continuities of psychological functioning. If children's environments change in important ways, the typical continuities may be disrupted accordingly. Thus, stressful events such as divorce reduce the likelihood that children who were securely attached during infancy will continue to show the positive relations with peers usually associated with secure attachment.

Determinants of Individual Differences

Individual differences, like all aspects of development, are ultimately attributable to the interaction of children's genes and the environments they encounter.

Genetics

For a number of important characteristics—including IQ, prosocial behavior, and empathy—about 50% of the differences among individuals in a given population are attributable to differences in genetic inheritance. The degree of genetic influence on individual differences tends to increase over the course of development. For example, correlations between the IQs of adopted children and their biological parents, whom the adopted children never see, steadily increase over the course of childhood and adolescence. One reason for this is that many genes related to intellectual functioning do not exercise their effects until late childhood or adolescence. Another reason is that over the course of development, children become increasingly free to choose environments that are in accord with their genetic predispositions.

Genetic similarities sometimes produce a striking physical resemblance between parent and child. We can only wonder whether this baby, as she develops, will come to resemble her father in other ways as well.

COURTESY OF BETHANY RITTLE-JOHNSON

Experience

Individual differences reflect children's experiences as well as their genes. Consider just one major environmental influence: one's parents. The more speech that parents address to their toddlers, the more rapidly the toddlers learn new words. The more that parents read to their toddlers, the better readers the children become. The more stimulating and responsive the home intellectual environment, the higher children's IQ and school achievement tend to be.

Parents exert at least as large an influence on their children's social and emotional development as on their intellectual development. For example, the likelihood that children will adopt their parents' standards and values appears to be influenced by the type of discipline their parents use with them. Similarly, parents influence their children's willingness to share, especially if they discuss the reasons for such prosocial activities with their children and have good relationships with them.

The effect of different types of parenting, like those of children's other experiences, depends on the nature of the child. One example of this involves the development of conscience. For fearful children, the key factor determining whether the child internalizes the parents' moral values is gentle discipline. Fearful children may become so anxious in the face of rigorous discipline that they cannot focus on the moral values that the parents are trying to instill. For fearless children, on the other hand, the key factor is a positive relationship with one's parents. Such fearless children often do not respond to gentle discipline; they tend to internalize the parents' values only if they feel positive toward them. As an old adage states, "It's a wise parent who knows his child."

Theme 7: Child-Development Research Can Improve Children's Lives

One of the few goals shared by virtually everyone is that children be as happy and healthy as possible. Understanding how children develop can lead to progress toward this goal. Theories of development provide general principles for interpreting children's behavior and for analyzing their problems. Empirical studies yield specific lessons regarding how to promote children's physical well-being, positive relationships with other people, and learning. In this section, we review practical implications of child-development research for raising and educating children and helping them overcome problems.

Implications for Parenting

Several principles of good parenting are so obvious it might seem as though they hardly need to be pointed out. Yet the number of children who experience difficulties related to poor parenting make it clear that these principles cannot be emphasized too often.

Pick a Good Partner

The practical lessons of child-development research for parents begin even before they become parents. Given the importance of genetics, pick a partner whose physical, intellectual, and emotional characteristics suggest that he or she will provide your child with good genes. Given the importance of the environment, pick a partner who will be a good mother or father. In terms of long-term impact on your child, this choice almost certainly will be the most important decision you ever make.

Ensure a Healthy Pregnancy

An expectant mother should maintain a healthy diet, have regular checkups, and keep stress levels low to increase the likelihood of a successful pregnancy. Equally important is avoiding teratogens such as tobacco, alcohol, and illegal drugs.

Know Which Decisions Are Likely to Have a Long-Term Impact

In addition to the joy they feel when their baby is born, new parents face a daunting number of decisions. Fortunately, babies are quite resilient. In the context of a loving and supportive home, a wide range of choices work out about equally well. Some decisions that seem minor, however, can have important effects. One such decision involves the baby's sleeping position: having a baby sleep on his or her back, rather than on his or her stomach, reduces the possibility of SIDS.

In other cases, the lesson of child-development research is that early problems are often transitory, so there is no reason to worry about them. Colic, which affects about 10% of babies, is one such problem. A colicky baby's frequent, high-pitched, grating, sick-sounding cries are difficult for parents to bear, but they have no long-term implications for the baby's development. In the short run, the best approach is to soothe the baby to the extent possible; the combination of holding, rocking, and talking or singing seems to be the most effective. In the longer run, the best path for parents is to relax, seek social support, and obtain babysitting help to allow some time off from caregiving—and to remember that colic usually ends by the time babies are 3 months old.

Form a Secure Attachment

Most parents have no difficulty forming a secure attachment with their baby. Some parents and babies, however, do not form such bonds. Parents can maximize the likelihood of their baby's becoming securely attached by maintaining a positive approach in their caregiving and by being responsive to the baby's needs. This is easier said than done, of course, and the baby's temperament, as well as the parents' attitude and responsiveness, influence the quality of attachment. However, even when babies are initially irritable and difficult, programs that teach parents how to be responsive and positive with them can lead to more secure attachments.

Provide a Stimulating Environment

The home environment has a great deal to do with children's learning, particularly in early childhood. One good example involves reading acquisition. Telling stories to toddlers and preschoolers, being responsive when they tell stories, and reading to them all are positively related to later reading achievement. One reason is that such activities promote phonological awareness (the ability to identify the component sounds within words). Nursery rhymes seem to be particularly effective in this regard; children who repeatedly hear *Green Eggs and Ham*, for example, generally learn to appreciate the similarities and differences in *Sam, ham, am,* and related words. Phonological awareness helps children learn to sound out words, which, in turn, helps them learn to retrieve the words' identities quickly and effortlessly. Successful early reading leads children to read more, which helps them improve

RICHARD HUTCHINGS / PHOTO RESEARCHERS, INC

Family activities, such as looking at photo albums and reminiscing about the people and settings they depict, provide both stimulation and warm, positive feelings for many children.

their reading further over the course of schooling. More generally, the more stimulating the environment, the more eager children will be to learn.

Implications for Education

Theories and research on child development hold a number of further lessons for how to educate children most effectively. Consider the instructional implications of several major theories of cognitive development.

Piaget's theory emphasizes the importance of the child's active involvement, both mental and physical, in the learning process. This active involvement is especially important in helping children master counterintuitive ideas. For example, the physical experience of walking around a pivot while holding a long metal rod at points close to and far from the pivot allowed children to overcome a widely held misconception that previous paper and pencil physics lessons had failed to correct—the misconception that all parts of an object must move at the same speed.

Information-processing theories suggest methods for identifying the sources of children's misunderstandings. The basic idea is to choose problems on which children with systematic misconceptions will generate distinctive patterns of errors. Then, if a child's responses to such problems reveal a particular misconception, instruction can be directed at the source of the difficulty. (Recall the example of children's thinking that 12 is the answer to 3 + 4 + 5 = ___ + 5.)

Core-knowledge approaches emphasize children's informal theories. Knowing about these theories can help teachers interpret children's comments and correct their confusions. For example, young children's relatively advanced knowledge of human beings plays a central role in their initial theories of biology and leads them to draw both correct and incorrect inferences about plants and animals. For instance, 1st and 2nd graders often believe that water provides nutrition for plants, just as food does for people. This view makes it difficult for the children to understand that plants actually create food through photosynthesis. When teachers understand the source of children's confusion, they can explain both the similarities and differences in the way that people and plants obtain nutrition.

Sociocultural theories emphasize the need to turn classrooms into communities of learners in which children cooperate with each other in their pursuit of knowledge. Rather than following the traditional model of instruction in which teachers lecture and children take notes, community-of-learners classrooms follow an approach in which teachers provide the minimum guidance needed for children to learn and gradually decrease their directive role as children's competence increases. Such programs also encourage children to make use of the resources of the broader community—children and teachers at other schools, outside experts, Web sites, reference books, and so on. The approach can be effective not only in building intellectual skills but also in promoting desirable values, such as personal responsibility and mutual respect.

Implications for Helping Children at Risk

Several principles that have emerged from empirical research offer valuable guidance for helping children at risk for serious developmental problems.

The Importance of Timing

As in the case of cross-eyedness noted earlier in this chapter, providing treatment at the optimal time is crucial in a variety of developmental contexts. Treatments for low-birth-weight babies are one important example. About 8% of babies in the United States, and as many as 50% of babies in poor countries such as Bangladesh, are born weighing 5½ pounds or less. Relative to babies of normal size, babies born this small have higher rates of many problems, including poor hearing, language impairments, hyperactivity, and learning disabilities. However, the number of low-birth-weight babies who develop such problems can be reduced through stimulation techniques, such as massaging and moving the babies' arms and legs. Starting such gentle stimulation soon after birth is crucial to the success of the approach.

Timing also is important in helping children at risk for learning difficulties. All theories of cognitive development indicate that such difficulties should be addressed early, before children lose confidence in their ability to learn or become resentful toward schools and teachers. This realization, together with research documenting the difficulty that many children from impoverished backgrounds have in school, laid the groundwork for Project Head Start and a variety of experimental preschool programs. Evaluations of the programs' effects indicate that both the small experimental programs and Head Start increase

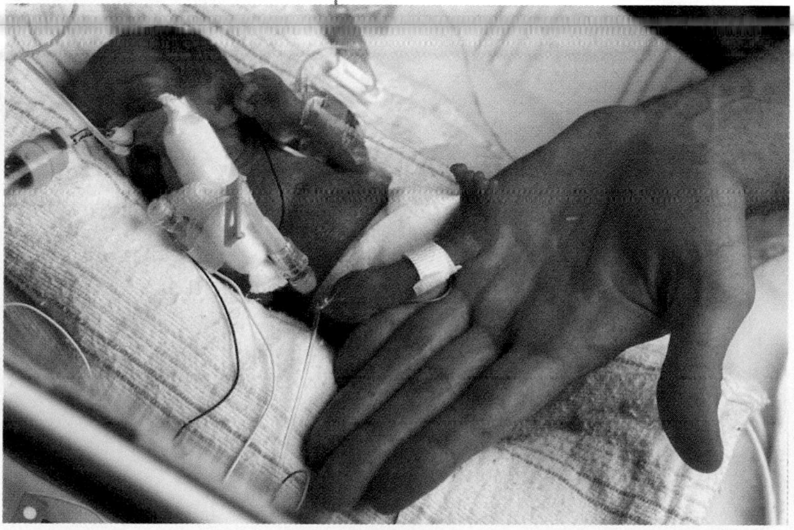

With the increased survival rate of extremely premature, low birth weight babies, research on how to help such babies has become increasingly important.

AP / WIDE WORLD PHOTOS

LAURA DWIGHT

The intellectual stimulation children receive and the academic skills they acquire in Head Start classrooms such as this one boost their IQ and achievement test scores not only at program completion but for several years thereafter.

children's IQs and achievement test scores by the end of the programs and for several years thereafter. Subsequently, the positive effects on IQ and academic achievement usually fade, but other positive effects continue. Fewer children who participate in such programs are ever held back in school or assigned to special-education classes, and more graduate from high school.

Even greater positive effects of early educational programs are possible, as illustrated by the Abecedarian Project. Designed to show what could be achieved through an optimally staffed, carefully designed program that started during infancy and lasted through age 5, the Abecedarian Project produced gains in both academic achievement and social skills that continued throughout childhood and adolescence. Its results demonstrate that it is possible for intensive programs that start early to have substantial, lasting benefits on poor children's academic achievement.

Early detection of child maltreatment, and rapid intervention to put an end to it, is also crucial. In the United States, roughly 4% of children age 17 and younger are abused or neglected in a given year. Inadequate care, physical abuse, and sexual abuse are the three most common problems. Parents who are stressed economically, have few friends, use alcohol and illegal drugs, and are being abused by their partner are the most likely to maltreat their children.

Knowing the characteristics of abused and neglected children can help teachers and others who come into contact with children recognize potential problems early and alert social service agencies so that they can investigate and remedy the problems. Children who are maltreated tend to have difficult temperaments, to have few friends, to be in poor physical or mental health, to do poorly in school, and to show abnormal aggressiveness or passivity. Adolescents who are maltreated may be depressed or hyperactive, use drugs or alcohol, and have sexual problems such as promiscuity or abnormal fearfulness. Early recognition of such signs of abuse can literally save a child's life.

ELIZABETH CREWS

In addition to their traditional mission of helping children learn, teachers in contemporary classrooms also need to be aware of signs of children being maltreated, so that they can alert the proper authorities to potential cases of abuse and neglect.

Biology and Environment Work Together

Another principle with important practical implications is that biology and environment work together to produce all behavior. This principle has proved important in designing treatments for ADHD. Although stimulant drugs such as Ritalin are the best-known treatment for this problem, research has shown that when medications are used alone, their benefits usually end as soon as children stop taking them. Longer-lasting benefits require behavioral therapy as well as medication. One effective behavioral treatment is to teach the children strategies for screening out distractions. The medications calm children with ADHD sufficiently that they can benefit from the therapy; the therapy helps them learn effective ways for dealing with their problems and for interacting with other people.

Every Problem Has Many Causes

An additional principle that has proved useful for helping children with developmental problems is that trying to identify *the* cause of any particular problem is futile; problems invariably have multiple causes. The greater the number of risks, the more likely children will have low IQs, poor socioemotional skills, and psychiatric disorders. Accordingly, providing effective treatment often requires addressing many particular difficulties. This principle has provided useful guidance for intervening with children who are rejected by other children. Helping these children gain better social skills requires increasing their understanding of other people. It also requires helping them learn new strategies, such as how to enter an ongoing group interaction unobtrusively and how to resolve conflicts without resorting to aggression. It also requires helping them learn from their own experience, for example, by monitoring the success of the different strategies they try. Together, these approaches can help rejected children make friends and become better accepted.

Improving Social Policy

Even if you do not have children of your own and rarely interact with them, your actions as a citizen can influence their lives. Votes in elections and referenda, opinions expressed in informal discussions, and participation in advocacy organizations all can make a difference. Knowledge of child-development research can inform your stances on many issues relevant to children. The conclusions that you reach will, and should, reflect your values as well as the evidence. For example, reductions in class size in kindergarten through 3rd grade classrooms have had variable effects on student achievement. A large-scale, well-implemented study in Tennessee, for example, indicated positive effects on student achievement (Krueger, 1999), whereas a large-scale, well-implemented study in California did not show any effect on achievement (Stecher, McCaffrey, & Bugliari, 2003). Teachers and parents appeared to be pleased with the class size reductions in both cases and believed that the smaller classes helped their children. Are these outcomes worth the substantial cost of hiring the number of teachers needed to implement such reform (roughly $1.7 billion per year in California)?

Research cannot answer this question, because the answer depends on values as well as data. Nonetheless, as the example illustrates, knowing the scientific evidence can help us, as citizens, make better-informed decisions.

Maternity Leave

Should society require employers to grant maternity leave in the months after a baby is born? Knowing that long hours of day care before an infant is 9 months old may have negative effects on early cognitive development argues in favor of society's making it easier for parents to take maternity leave. However, other considerations such as economic costs are also important; as noted above, the scientific evidence alone can never be decisive.

Day Care

Similar debates have arisen about whether the general society should subsidize day-care payments for parents of young children. One argument against such a policy has been the claim that children develop more successfully if they stay at home than if they attend day care. This argument has turned out to be false, however. Children who attend good-quality day care develop quite similarly to children who receive care at home from their parents.

Eyewitness Testimony

Understanding child development also is vital for deciding whether children should be allowed to testify in court cases and for obtaining the most accurate testimony possible from them. Each year, more than 100,000 children in the United States testify in court, many of them in trials involving allegations of abuse. Often, the child and the accused are the only ones who witnessed the events. Research indicates that, in general, the accuracy of testimony increases with age; 8-year-olds recall more than do 6-year-olds, and 6-year-olds recall more than do 4-year-olds. However, when children are shielded from misleading and repeated questioning, even 4- and 5-year-olds usually provide accurate testimony about the types of issues that are central in court cases. Given the high stakes in such cases, using the lessons of research to elicit the most accurate possible testimony from children is essential for justice to be done.

Child-development research holds lessons for numerous other social problems as well. Research on the causes of aggression has led to programs such as Fast Track, which are designed to teach aggressive children to manage their anger and

ELIZABETH CREWS

Children are naturally curious about the world; encouraging this curiosity, and channeling it in fruitful directions, is among the most vital goals facing parents and society alike.

avoid violence. Research on the roots of morality has led to programs such as the Child Development Project, designed to encourage students to help others who are in need. Research on the effects of poverty has provided the basis for the Abecedarian Project and other early education efforts. There is no end of social problems that need to be addressed. Understanding child development can help us address them more effectively.

Critical Thinking Questions

1. What qualities of children influence the way that other people act toward them, and how do these actions influence their development?
2. Individual differences show some stability over time. How do both genes and environment contribute to this stability?
3. How would growing up in one developed society rather than another, for example, the United States rather than Japan, be expected to influence a child's development?
4. How have the changes that have taken place in the United States over the past century influenced children's development? Has the overall effect of the changes been predominantly beneficial or predominantly harmful?
5. What practical lessons have you learned from this course that will influence the way that you raise your children if you have them?

Glossary

A-not-B error the tendency to reach for a hidden object where it was last found rather than in the new location where it was last hidden (p. 134)

accommodation the process by which people adapt current knowledge structures in response to new experiences (p. 131)

activational hormonal influences the potential result of certain fluctuations in sex-linked hormone levels affecting the contemporaneous activation of certain brain and behavioral responses (p. 588)

adaptation the tendency to respond to the demands of the environment in ways that meet one's goals (p. 131)

ADHD (attention-deficit hyperactivity disorder) a syndrome that involves difficulty in sustaining attention (p. 370)

adrenarche the period, prior to the emergence of visible signs of puberty, during which the adrenal glands mature, providing a major source of sex steroids. This period correlates with the onset of sexual attraction. (p. 607)

adult attachment models working models of attachment in adulthood that are believed to be based upon adults' perceptions of their own childhood experiences—especially their relationships with their parents—and of the influence of these experiences on them as adults (p. 430)

affiliation the tendency to affirm connection with others through being emotionally open, empathetic, or cooperative (p. 584)

affordances the possibilities for action offered by objects and situations (p. 201)

aggression behavior aimed at harming or injuring others (p. 567)

aggressive-rejected children a category of sociometric status that refers to children who are especially prone to physical aggression, disruptive behavior, delinquency, and negative behavior such as hostility and threatening others (p. 525)

alleles two or more different forms of a gene (p. 89)

altruistic motives helping others for reasons that initially include empathy or sympathy for others and, at later ages, the desire to act in ways consistent with one's own conscience and moral principles (p. 559)

amniotic sac a transparent, fluid-filled membrane that surrounds and protects the fetus (p. 49)

anal stage the second stage in Freud's theory, lasting roughly from 1 to 3 years of age, in which the primary source of pleasure comes from defecation (p. 346)

androgens a class of hormones that normally occur at higher levels in males than in females and that affect physical development and functioning from the prenatal period onward (p. 588)

apoptosis genetically programmed cell death (p. 48)

assertion the tendency to take action on behalf of the self through competitive, independent, or aggressive behaviors (p. 584)

assimilation the process by which people translate incoming information into a form that fits concepts they already understand (p. 131)

association areas parts of the brain that lie between the major sensory and motor areas and that process and integrate input from those areas (p. 104)

attachment an emotional bond with a specific person that is enduring across space and time. Usually, attachments are discussed in regard to the relation between infants and specific caregivers, although they can also occur in adulthood. (p. 425)

attachment theory theory based on John Bowlby's work that posits that children are biologically predisposed to develop attachments with caregivers as a means of increasing the chances of their own survival (p. 426)

auditory localization perception of the location in space of a sound source (p. 185)

authoritarian parenting a parenting style that is high in demandingness and low in responsiveness. Authoritarian parents are nonresponsive to their children's needs and tend to enforce their demands through the exercise of parental power and the use of threats and punishment. They are oriented toward obedience and authority and expect their children to comply with their demands without question or explanation. (p. 470)

authoritative parenting a parenting style that is high in demandingness and supportiveness. Authoritative parents set clear standards and limits for their children and are firm about enforcing them; at the same time, they allow their children considerable autonomy within those limits, are attentive and responsive to their children's concerns and needs, and respect and consider their children's perspective. (p. 470)

autostimulation theory the idea that brain activity during REM sleep in the fetus and newborn facilitates the early development of the visual system (p. 71)

axons neural fibers that conduct electrical signals away from the cell body to connections with other neurons (p. 102)

basic level the middle level, and often the first level learned, within a category hierarchy, such as "dog" in the animal/dog/poodle example (p. 264)

basic processes the simplest and most frequently used mental activities (p. 147)

behavior genetics the science concerned with how variation in behavior and development results from the combination of genetic and environmental factors (p. 95)

behavior modification a form of therapy based on principles of operant conditioning in which reinforcement contingencies are changed to encourage more adaptive behavior (p. 353)

behavioral inhibition a temperamentally based style of responding characterized by the tendency to be particularly fearful and restrained when dealing with novel or stressful situations (p. 406)

bidirectionality of parent–child interactions the idea that parents and their children are mutually affected by each other's characteristics and behaviors (p. 474)

bilingualism the ability to use two languages (p. 224)

binocular disparity the difference between the retinal image of an object in each eye that results in two slightly different signals being sent to the brain (p. 185)

body image an individual's perception of, and feelings about, his or her own body (p. 607)

Carolina Abecedarian Project a comprehensive and successful enrichment program for children from low-income families (p. 318)

categorical perception the perception of speech sounds as belonging to discrete categories (p. 226)

category hierarchy categories that are related by set–subset relations, such as animal/dog/poodle (p. 262)

cell body a component of the neuron that contains the basic biological material that keeps the neuron functioning (p. 102)

centration the tendency to focus on a single, perceptually striking feature of an object or event (p. 137)

cephalocaudal development the pattern of growth in which areas near the head develop earlier than areas farther from the head (p. 50)

cerebral cortex the "gray matter" of the brain that plays a primary role in what is thought to be particularly humanlike functioning, from seeing and hearing to writing to feeling emotion (p. 103)

cerebral hemispheres the two halves of the cortex; for the most part, sensory input from one side of the body goes to the opposite hemisphere of the brain (p. 104)

cerebral lateralization the specialization of the hemispheres of the brain for different modes of processing (p. 104)

child maltreatment intentional abuse or neglect that endangers the well-being of anyone under the age of 18 (p. 369)

chromosomes molecules of DNA that transmit genetic information; chromosomes are made up of DNA (p. 87)

chronosystem in the bioecological model, historical changes that influence the other systems (p. 368)

classical conditioning a form of learning that consists of associating an initially neutral stimulus with a stimulus that always evokes a particular reflexive response (p. 202)

clinical interview a procedure in which questions are adjusted in accord with the answers the interviewee provides (p. 27)

cliques friendship groups that children voluntarily form or join themselves (p. 519)

cognitive development the development of thinking and reasoning (p. 16)

colic excessive, inconsolable crying by a young infant for no apparent reason (p. 74)

collaboration a blending of the assertion and affiliation styles of behavior. Associated with gender-role flexibility, it is more common among girls than among boys. (p. 584)

collective monologue conversation beween children that involves a series of non sequiturs, the content of each child's turn having little or nothing to do with what the other child has just said (p. 244)

comprehension monitoring the process of keeping track of one's understanding of a verbal description or text (p. 328)

conception the union of an egg from the mother and a sperm from the father (p. 44)

concepts general ideas or understandings that can be used to group together objects, events, qualities, or abstractions that are similar in some way (p. 260)

concrete operational stage the period (7 to 12 years) within Piaget's theory in which children become able to reason logically about concrete objects and events (p. 133)

conditioned response (CR) in classical conditioning, the originally reflexive response that comes to be elicited by the conditioned stimulus (p. 202)

conditioned stimulus (CS) in classical conditioning, the neutral stimulus that is repeatedly paired with the unconditioned stimulus (p. 202)

conduct disorder (CD) a disorder that involves severe antisocial and aggression behaviors that inflict pain on others or involve destruction of property or denial of the rights of others (p. 570)

cones the light-sensitive neurons that are highly concentrated in the fovea (the central region of the retina) (p. 178)

congenital adrenal hyperplasia (CAH) a condition in which the adrenal glands produce high levels of hormones that have androgen-like effects (p. 588)

connectionism a type of information-processing approach that emphasizes the simultaneous activity of numerous interconnected processing units (p. 251)

conscience an internal regulatory mechanism that increases the individual's ability to conform to standards of conduct accepted in his or her culture (p. 556)

conservation concept the idea that merely changing the appearance of objects does not change their key properties (p. 137)

continuous development the idea that changes with age occur gradually, in small increments, like that of a pine tree growing taller and taller (p. 14)

contrast sensitivity the ability to detect differences in light and dark areas in a visual pattern (p. 178)

control group the group of children in an experimental design who are not presented the experience of interest but in other ways are treated similarly (p. 33)

controversial peer status a category of sociometric status that refers to children or adolescents who are liked by quite a few peers and are disliked by quite a few others (p. 529)

core-knowledge theories approaches that emphasize the sophistication of infants' and young children's thinking in areas that have been important throughout human evolutionary history (p. 154)

corpus callosum a dense tract of nerve fibers that enable the two hemispheres of the brain to communicate (p. 104)

correlation the association between two variables (p. 30)

correlation coefficient a statistic that indicates the direction and strength of a correlation (p. 31)

correlational designs studies intended to indicate how variables are related to each other (p. 30)

counting-on strategy counting up from the larger addend the number of times indicated by the smaller addend (p. 35)

critical period for language the time during which language develops readily and after which (sometime between age 5 and puberty) language acquisition is much more difficult and ultimately less successful (p. 221)

crossing over the process by which sections of DNA switch from one chromosome to the other; crossing over promotes variability among individuals (p. 88)

cross-sectional design a research method in which children of different ages are compared on a given behavior or characteristic over a short period of time (p. 34)

crowds groups of adolescents who have similar stereotyped reputations. Among American high school students, typical crowds may include the "brains," "jocks," "loners," "burnouts," "punks," "populars," "elites," "freaks," or "nonconformists." (p. 520)

crystallized intelligence factual knowledge about the world (p. 300)

cultural tools the innumerable products of human ingenuity that enhance thinking (p. 159)

cultural training a function of the family that pertains to teaching children the basic values in their culture (p. 466)

deferred imitation the repetition of other people's behavior a substantial time after it originally occurred (p. 135)

dendrites neural fibers that receive input from other cells and conduct it toward the cell body in the form of electrical impulses (p. 102)

dependent variable a behavior that is measured to determine whether it is affected by exposure to the independent variable (p. 33)

developmental resilience successful development in spite of multiple and seemingly overwhelming developmental hazards (p. 79)

differentiation the extraction from the constantly changing stimulation in the environment of those elements that are invariant, or stable (p. 200)

direction-of-causation problem the concept that a correlation between two variables does not indicate which, if either, variable is the cause of the other (p. 31)

discontinuous development the idea that changes with age include occasional large shifts, like the transition from caterpillar to cocoon to butterfly (p. 14)

discrete emotions theory a theory about emotions, held by Tomkins, Izard, and others, in which emotions are viewed as innate and discrete from one another from very early in life, and each emotion is believed to be packaged with a specific and distinctive set of bodily and facial reactions (p. 384)

disorganized/disoriented attachment a type of insecure attachment in which infants or young children have no consistent way of coping with the stress of the Strange Situation. Their behavior is often confused or even contradictory, and they often appear dazed or disoriented (p. 429)

display rules a social group's informal norms about when, where, and how much one should show emotions and when and where displays of emotion should be suppressed or masked by displays of other emotions (p. 417)

distributional properties the phenomenon that in any language, certain sounds are more likely to appear together than are others (p. 229)

DNA (deoxyribonucleic acid) molecules that carry all the biochemical instructions involved in the formation and functioning of an organism (p. 87)

domain specific limited to a particular area, such as living things or people (p. 156)

dominant allele the allele that, if present, gets expressed (p. 89)

dose-response relation a relation in which the effect of exposure to an element increases with the extent of exposure (prenatally, the more exposure a fetus has to a potential teratogen, the more severe its effect is likely to be) (p. 61)

dual representation the idea that a symbolic artifact must be represented mentally in two ways at the same time—both as a real object and as a symbol for something other than itself (p. 252)

dynamic-systems theories a class of theories that focus on how change occurs over time in complex systems (p. 165)

dyslexia inability to read well despite normal intelligence (p. 327)

economic function a function of the family that pertains to providing the means for children to acquire the skills and other resources they need to be economically productive as adults (p. 466)

effect size the magnitude of similarity and difference between groups (p. 605)

ego in psychoanalytic theory, the second personality structure to develop. It is the rational, logical, problem-solving component of personality. (p. 345)

egocentric representations coding of spatial locations relative to one's own body, without regard to the surroundings (p. 280)

egocentrism the tendency to perceive the world solely from one's own point of view (p. 136)

Electra complex Freud's term for the conflict experienced by girls in the phallic stage when they develop unacceptable romantic feelings for their father and see their mother as a rival. (The complex is named after a figure in Greek mythology who arranged for the murder of her mother.) (p. 347)

embryo the name given to the developing organism from the 3rd to 8th week of prenatal development (p. 47)

emotion emotion is characterized by physiological responses, subjective feelings, cognitions related to those feelings, and the desire to take action (p. 383)

emotional intelligence a set of abilities that contribute to competence in the social and emotional domains (p. 383)

emotional self-regulation the process of initiating, inhibiting, or modulating internal feeling states and related physiological processes, cognitions, and behaviors (p. 396)

enactive experience learning about gender through experiencing the reactions one's behavior evokes in others (p. 593)

encoding the process of representing in memory information that draws attention or is considered important (p. 147)

entity theory a theory that a person's level of intelligence is fixed and unchangeable (p. 360)

entity/helpless orientation a general tendency to attribute success and failure to enduring aspects of the self and to give up in the face of failure (p. 360)

environment every aspect of an individual and his or her surroundings other than genes (p. 86)

epigenesis the emergence of new structures and functions in the course of development (p. 44)

equilibration the process by which children (or other people) balance assimilation and accommodation to create stable understanding (p. 131)

erogenous zones in Freud's theory, areas of the body that become erotically sensitive in successive stages of development (p. 344)

ERPs (event-related potentials) changes in the brain's electrical activity that occur in response to the presentation of a particular stimulus (p. 106)

essentialism the view that living things have an essence inside them that makes them what they are (p. 276)

ethnic identity individuals' sense of belonging to an ethnic or racial group, including the degree to which they associate their thinking, perceptions, feelings, and behavior with membership in that group (p. 446)

ethology the study of the evolutionary bases of behavior (p. 363)

exosystem in the bioecological model, environmental settings that a person does not directly experience but that can affect the person indirectly (p. 368)

experience-dependent plasticity the process through which neural connections are created and reorganized throughout life as a function of an individual's experiences (p. 112)

experience-expectant plasticity the process through which the normal wiring of the brain occurs in part as a result of experiences that every human who inhabits any reasonably normal environment will have (p. 111)

experimental control the ability of researchers to determine the specific experiences that children have during the course of an experiment (p. 33)

experimental designs a group of approaches that allow inferences about causes and effects to be drawn (p. 32)

experimental group a group of children in an experimental design who are presented the experience of interest (p. 33)

expressive (holistic) style speech strategy that gives more attention to the overall sound of language—its rhythmic and intonational patterns—than to the phonetic elements of which it is composed (p. 234)

external validity the degree to which results can be generalized beyond the particulars of the research (p. 26)

failure-to-thrive (nonorganic) (FTT) a condition in which infants become malnourished and fail to grow or gain weight for no obvious medical reason (p. 117)

false-belief problems tasks that test a child's understanding that other people will act in accord with their own beliefs even when the child knows that those beliefs are incorrect (p. 268)

family dynamics the way in which the family operates as a whole (p. 466)

fast mapping the process of rapidly learning a new word simply from hearing the contrastive use of a familiar and unfamiliar word (p. 237)

fetal alcohol spectrum disorder (FASD) the harmful effects of maternal alcohol consumption on a developing fetus. Fetal alcohol syndrome (FAS) involves a range of effects, including facial deformities, mental retardation, attention problems, hyperactivity, and other defects. Fetal alcohol effects (FAE) is a term used for individuals who show some, but not all, of the standard effects of FAS. (p. 62)

fetus the name given to the developing organism from the 9th week to birth (p. 47)

fluid intelligence ability to think on the spot to solve novel problems (p. 299)

Flynn effect the rise in average IQ scores that has occurred over the past 75 years in many countries (p. 313)

foreclosure status a category of identity status in which the individual is not engaged in any identity experimentation and has established a vocational or ideological identity based on the choices or values of others (p. 444)

formal operational stage the period (12 years and beyond) within Piaget's theory in which people become able to think about abstractions and hypothetical situations (p. 133)

fraternal twins twins that result when two eggs happen to be released into the fallopian tube at the same time and are fertilized by two different sperm. Fraternal twins have only half their genes in common. (p. 49)

friendships intimate, reciprocated positive relationships between two people (p. 507)

frontal lobe associated with organizing behavior; the one that is thought responsible for the human ability to plan ahead (p. 104)

functionalist approach a theory of emotion, proposed by Campos and others, that argues that the basic function of emotions is to promote action toward achieving a goal. In this view, emotions are not discrete from one another and vary somewhat based on the social environment. (p. 384)

***g* (general intelligence)** the part of intelligence that is common to all intellectual tasks (p. 299)

gametes (germ cells) reproductive cells—egg and sperm—that contain only half the genetic material of all the other cells in the body (p. 44)

gang a loosely organized group of adolescents or young adults who identify as a group and often engage in illegal activities (p. 521)

gender constancy the realization that gender is invariant despite superficial changes in a person's appearance or behavior (p. 590)

gender identity awareness of one's own gender (p. 590)

gender schemas organized mental representations (concepts, beliefs, memories) about gender, including gender stereotypes (p. 591)

gender segregation children's tendency to associate with same-gender peers and avoid other-gender peers (p. 599)

gender self-socialization the process through which children's biases to behave in accord with their gender identity is strengthened by their greater attention to and involvement with entities and activities deemed appropriate to their gender (p. 589)

gender stability awareness that gender is stable over time (p. 590)

gender-essentialist statements statements about males and females that imply that the descriptions and characterizations contained therein generally apply to all members of the gender in question and always will (p. 594)

gender-role flexibility refers to advances in cognitive development that can allow adolescents (more often girls than boys) to transcend traditional conventions and pursue a more flexible range of interests (p. 602)

gender-role intensification refers to heightened concerns with adhering to traditional gender roles (p. 602)

generativity refers to the idea that through the use of the finite set of words in our vocabulary, we can put together an infinite number of sentences and express an infinite number of ideas (p. 217)

genes sections of chromosomes that are the basic unit of heredity in all living things (p. 87)

genital stage the fifth and final stage in Freud's theory, beginning in adolescence, in which sexual maturation is complete and sexual intercourse becomes a major goal (p. 347)

genome the complete set of genes of any organism (p. 85)

genotype the genetic material an individual inherits (p. 86)

gesture–speech mismatches a phenomenon in which hand movements and verbal statements convey different ideas (p. 335)

glial cells cells in the brain that provide a variety of critical supportive functions (p. 103)

goodness of fit the degree to which an individual's temperament is compatible with the demands and expectations of his or her social environment (p. 406)

guided participation a process in which more knowledgeable individuals organize activities in ways that allow less knowledgeable people to learn (p. 159)

habituation a simple form of learning that involves a decrease in response to repeated or continued stimulation (p. 56)

heritability a statistical estimate of the proportion of the measured variance on a trait among individuals in a given population that is attributable to genetic differences among those individuals (p. 98)

heritable refers to any characteristics or traits that are influenced by heredity (p. 96)

heterozygous having two different alleles for a trait (p. 89)

holophrastic period the period when children begin using the words in their small productive vocabulary one word at a time (p. 236)

homozygous having two of the same allele for a trait (p. 89)

hostile attributional bias in Dodge's theory, the tendency to assume that other people's ambiguous actions stem from a hostile intent (p. 359)

hypotheses educated guesses (p. 25)

id in psychoanalytic theory, the earliest and most primitive personality structure. It is unconscious and operates with the goal of seeking pleasure. (p. 345)

identical twins twins that result from the splitting in half of the zygote, resulting in each of the two resulting zygotes having exactly the same set of genes (p. 49)

identity achievement an integration of various aspects of the self into a coherent whole that is stable over time and across events (p. 443)

identity confusion an incomplete and sometimes incoherent sense of self that often occurs in Erikson's stage of identity versus identity confusion (p. 443)

identity foreclosure premature commitment to an identity without adequate consideration of other options (p. 444)

identity versus identity confusion Erikson's psychosocial stage of development that occurs during adolescence. During this stage, the adolescent or young adult either develops an identity or experiences an incomplete and sometimes incoherent sense of self. (p. 443)

identity-achievement status a category of identity status in which, after a period of exploration, the individual has achieved a coherent and consolidated identity based on personal decisions regarding occupation, ideology, and the like. The individual believes that these decisions were made autonomously and is committed to them. (p. 445)

identity-diffusion status a category of identity status in which the individual does not have firm commitments and is not making progress toward them (p. 444)

imaginary audience the belief, stemming from adolescent egocentrism, that everyone else is focused on the adolescent's appearance and behavior (p. 441)

imprinting a form of learning in which the young of some species of newborn birds and mammals become attached to and follow adult members of the species (usually their mother) (p. 363)

incremental theory a theory that a person's intelligence can grow as a function of experience (p. 361)

incremental/mastery orientation a general tendency to attribute success and failure to the amount of effort expended and to persist in the face of failure (p. 360)

independent variable the experience that children in the experimental group receive and that children in the control group do not receive (p. 33)

infant mortality death during the first year after birth (p. 74)

infant-directed talk (IDT) the distinctive mode of speech that adults adopt when talking to babies and very young children (p. 223)

ingroup assimilation process whereby individuals are socialized to conform to the group's norms, demonstrating the characteristics that define the ingroup (p. 592)

ingroup bias tendency to evaluate individuals and characteristics of the ingroup as superior to those of the outgroup (p. 592)

insecure attachment a pattern of attachment in which infants or young children have a less positive attachment to their caregiver than do securely attached children. Insecurely attached children can be classified as insecure/resistant (ambivalent), insecure/avoidant, or disorganized/disoriented. (p. 429)

insecure/avoidant attachment a type of insecure attachment in which infants or young children seem somewhat indifferent toward their caregiver and may even avoid the caregiver. In the Strange Situation, they seem indifferent toward their caregiver before the caregiver leaves the room and indifferent or avoidant when the caregiver returns. If they get upset when left alone, they are as easily comforted by a stranger as by a parent. (p. 429)

insecure/resistant (or ambivalent) attachment a type of insecure attachment in which infants or young children are clingy and stay close to their caregiver rather than exploring their environment. In the Strange Situation, insecure/resistant infants tend to get very upset when the caregiver leaves them alone in the room, and they are not readily comforted by strangers. When their caregiver returns, they are not easily comforted and both seek comfort and resist efforts by the caregiver to comfort them. (p. 429)

instrumental aggression aggression motivated by the desire to obtain a concrete goal (p. 568)

instrumental or operant conditioning learning the relation between one's own behavior and the consequences that result from it (p. 203)

intermittent reinforcement inconsistent response to the behavior of another person, for example, sometimes punishing an unacceptable behavior and sometimes ignoring it (p. 353)

intermodal perception the combining of information from two or more sensory systems (p. 188)

internal validity the degree to which effects observed within experiments can be attributed to the variables that the researcher intentionally manipulated (p. 26)

internal working model of attachment the child's mental representation of the self, of attachment figure(s), and of relationships in general that is constructed as a result of experiences with caregivers. The working model guides children's interactions with caregivers and other people in infancy and at older ages. (p. 427)

internalization the process of adopting as one's own the attributes, beliefs, and standards of another person (p. 346)

interrater reliability the amount of agreement in the observations of different raters who witness the same behavior (p. 26)

intersubjectivity the mutual understanding that people share during communication (p. 161)

IQ (intelligence quotient) a summary measure used to indicate a child's intelligence relative to that of other children of the same age (p. 304)

joint attention a process in which social partners intentionally focus on a common referent in the external environment (p. 162)

language comprehension understanding what others say (or sign or write) (p. 217)

language production speaking (or writing or signing) to others (p. 217)

latency period the fourth stage in Freud's theory, lasting from age 6 to age 12, in which sexual energy gets channeled into socially acceptable activities (p. 347)

lobes major areas of the cortex associated with general categories of behavior (p. 104)

longitudinal design a method of study in which the same children are studied twice or more over a substantial period of time (p. 34)

long-term memory information retained on an enduring basis (p. 146)

low birth weight (LBW) a birth weight of less than $5\frac{1}{2}$ pounds (2500 grams) (p. 75)

macrosystem in the bioecological model, the larger cultural and social context within which the other systems are embedded (p. 368)

mathematical equality the concept that the values on each side of the equal sign must be equivalent (p. 334)

menarche the onset of menstruation (p. 606)

mental model processes used to represent a situation or sequence of events (p. 328)

mesosystem in the bioecological model, the interconnections among immediate, or microsystem, settings (p. 368)

meta-analysis a statistical technique used to summarize the average effect size across studies (p. 605)

metalinguistic knowledge an understanding of the properties and function of language—that is, an understanding of language as language (p. 219)

microgenetic design a method of study in which the same children are studied repeatedly over a short period of time (p. 35)

microsystem in the bioecological model, the immediate environment that an individual personally experiences (p. 366)

modularity hypothesis the idea that the human brain contains an innate, self-contained language module that is separate from other aspects of cognitive functioning (p. 249)

monocular or pictorial cues the perceptual cues of depth (such as relative size and interposition) that can be perceived by one eye alone (p. 185)

moral judgments decisions that pertain to issues of right and wrong, fairness, and justice (p. 554)

moratorium status a category of identity status in which the individual is in the phase of experimentation with regard to occupational and ideological choices and has not yet made a clear commitment to them (p. 445)

morphemes the smallest units of meaning in a language, composed of one or more phonemes (p. 218)

multifactorial refers to traits that are affected by a host of environmental factors as well as genetic ones (p. 96)

multiple intelligence theory Gardner's theory of intellect, based on the view that people possess at least eight types of intelligence (p. 321)

mutation a change in a section of DNA (p. 88)

myelin sheath a fatty sheath that forms around certain axons in the body and increases the speed and efficiency of information transmission (p. 103)

myelination the formation of myelin (a fatty sheath) around the axons of neurons that speeds and increases information-processing abilities (p. 108)

naïve psychology a commonsense level of understanding of other people and oneself (p. 266)

narratives descriptions of past events that have the basic structure of a story (p. 245)

naturalistic observation examination of ongoing behavior in an environment not controlled by the researcher (p. 28)

nature our biological endowment; the genes we receive from our parents (p. 11)

negative identity identity that stands in opposition to what is valued by people around the adolescent (p. 444)

neglected peer status a category of sociometric status that refers to children or adolescents who are infrequently mentioned as liked or disliked; they simply are not noticed much by peers (p. 527)

neural tube a groove formed in the top layer of differentiated cells in the embryo that eventually becomes the brain and spinal cord (p. 49)

neurogenesis the proliferation of neurons through cell division (p. 104)

neurons cells that are specialized for sending and receiving messages between the brain and all parts of the body, as well as within the brain itself (p. 102)

neurotransmitters chemicals involved in communications among brain cells (p. 18)

non-REM sleep a quiet or deep sleep state characterized by the absence of motor activity or eye movements and regular, slow brain waves, breathing, and heart rate (p. 71)

norm of reaction all the phenotypes that can theoretically result from a given genotype in relation to all the environments in which it can survive and develop (p. 90)

normal distribution a pattern of data in which scores fall symmetrically around a mean value, with most scores falling close to the mean and fewer and fewer scores farther from it (p. 304)

numerical equality the realization that all sets of N objects have something in common (p. 289)

nurture the environments, both physical and social, that influence our development (p. 11)

object permanence the knowledge that objects continue to exist even when they are out of view (p. 134)

object segregation the identification of separate objects in a visual array (p. 182)

object substitution a form of pretense in which an object is used as something other than itself (p. 271)

occipital lobe the lobe of the cortex that is primarily involved in processing visual information (p. 104)

Oedipus complex Freud's term for the conflict experienced by boys in the phallic period because of their sexual desire for their mother and their fear of retaliation by their father. (The complex is named for the king in Greek mythology who unknowingly murdered his father and married his mother.) (p. 346)

opportunity structure the economic resources offered by the macrosystem in Bronfenbrenner's bioecological model, and people's understanding of those resources (p. 596)

oppositional defiant disorder (ODD) a disorder characterized by age-inappropriate and persistent displays of angry, defiant, and irritable behaviors (p. 570)

optical expansion a depth cue in which an object occludes increasingly more of the background, indicating that the object is approaching (p. 184)

oral stage the first stage in Freud's theory, occurring in the first year, in which the primary source of satisfaction and pleasure is oral activity (p. 345)

organization the tendency to integrate particular observations into coherent knowledge (p. 131)

organizational hormonal influences the potential result of certain sex-linked hormones affecting brain differentiation and organization during prenatal development or at puberty (p. 588)

overextension the use of a given word in a broader context than is appropriate (p. 236)

overlapping-waves theories an information-processing approach that emphasizes the variability of children's thinking (p. 150)

overregularization speech errors in which children treat irregular forms of words as if they were regular (p. 243)

parental sensitivity an important factor contributing to the security of an infant's attachment. Parental sensitivity can be exhibited in a variety of ways, including responsive caregiving when an infant is distressed or upset and engaging in coordinated play with the infant. (p. 433)

parental-investment theory a theory that stresses the evolutionary basis of many aspects of parental behavior, including the extensive investment parents make in their offspring (p. 365)

parenting styles parenting behaviors and attitudes that set the emotional climate in regard to parent–child interactions, such as parental responsiveness and demandingness (p. 469)

parietal lobe governs spatial processing as well as integrating sensory input with information stored in memory (p. 104)

peers people of approximately the same age and status (p. 506)

perceived self-efficacy an individual's beliefs about how effectively he or she can control his or her own behavior, thoughts, and emotions in order to achieve a desired goal (p. 356)

perception the process of organizing and interpreting sensory information (p. 177)

perceptual categorization the grouping together of objects with similar appearances (p. 263)

perceptual constancy the perception of objects as being of constant size, shape, color, etc., in spite of physical differences in the retinal image of the object (p. 182)

permissive parenting a parenting style that is high in responsiveness but low in demandingness. Permissive parents are responsive to their children's needs and do not require their children to regulate themselves or act in appropriate or mature ways. (p. 471)

personal fable a form of adolescent egocentrism that involves beliefs in the uniqueness of one's own feelings and thoughts (p. 441)

personal judgments decisions that refer to actions in which individual preferences are the main consideration (p. 554)

personality the pattern of behavioral and emotional propensities, beliefs and interests, and intellectual capacities that characterize an individual. Personality has its roots in temperament (and thus has a constitutional basis) but is shaped by interactions with the social and physical world. (p. 407)

personification generalizing knowledge about people to infer properties of other animals (p. 158)

phallic stage the third stage in Freud's theory, lasting from age 3 to age 6, in which sexual pleasure is focused on the genitalia (p. 346)

phenotype the observable expression of the genotype, including both body characteristics and behavior (p. 86)

phenylketonuria (PKU) a disorder related to a defective recessive gene on chromosome 12 that prevents metabolism of phenylalanine (p. 91)

phonemes the elementary units of meaningful sound used to produce languages (p. 218)

phonemic awareness ability to identify component sounds within words (p. 323)

phonological development the acquisition of knowledge about the sound system of a language (p. 218)

phonological processing ability to discriminate and remember sounds within words (p. 327)

phonological recoding skills ability to translate letters into sounds and to blend sounds into words (p. 323)

phylogenetic continuity the idea that because of our common evolutionary history, humans share many characteristics, behaviors, and developmental processes with other animals, especially mammals (p. 48)

placenta a support organ for the fetus; it keeps the circulatory systems of the fetus and mother separate, but as a semipermeable membrane permits the exchange of some materials between them (oxygen and nutrients from mother to fetus and carbon dioxide and waste products from fetus to mother) (p. 50)

plasticity the capacity of the brain to be affected by experience (p. 110)

polygenic inheritance inheritance in which traits are governed by more than one gene (p. 90)

popular peer status a category of sociometric status that refers to children or adolescents who are viewed positively (liked) by many peers and are viewed negatively (disliked) by few peers (p. 524)

positive reinforcement a reward that reliably follows a behavior and increases the likelihood that the behavior will be repeated (p. 203)

practical intelligence mental abilities not measured on IQ tests but important for success in many situations, such as accurately reading other people's emotions and intentions and motivating others to work effectively as a team (p. 307)

pragmatic cues aspects of the social context used for word learning (p. 239)

pragmatic development the acquisition of knowledge about how language is used (p. 218)

preferential-looking technique a method for studying visual attention in infants that involves showing infants two patterns or two objects at a time to see if the infants have a preference for one over the other (p. 178)

Pre-K mathematics a program designed for preschoolers, especially those from low-income families, to prevent mathematics disabilities through exposure to a variety of numerical activities (p. 334)

premature any child born at 35 weeks after conception or earlier (as opposed to the normal term of 38 weeks) (p. 75)

preoperational stage the period (2 to 7 years) within Piaget's theory in which children become able to represent their experiences in language, mental imagery, and symbolic thought (p. 133)

prereaching movements clumsy swiping movements by young infants toward the general vicinity of objects they see (p. 195)

pretend play make-believe activities in which children create new symbolic relations, for example, using a broom to represent a horse (p. 271)

primary mental abilities seven abilities said by Thurstone to be crucial to intelligence (p. 300)

private speech the second phase of Vygotsky's internalization-of-thought process, in which children develop their self-regulation and problem-solving abilities by telling themselves aloud what to do, much as their parents did in the first stage (p. 160)

proactive aggression unemotional aggression aimed at fulfilling a need or desire (p. 572)

problem solving the process of attaining a goal by using a strategy to overcome an obstacle (p. 145)

processes the specific mental activities, such as rules and strategies, that people use to remember and to solve problems (p. 144)

prosocial behavior voluntary behavior intended to benefit another, such as helping, sharing, and comforting of others (p. 552)

prosody the characteristic rhythm, tempo, cadence, melody, intonational patterns, and so forth with which a language is spoken (p. 226)

psychic energy Freud's term for the collection of biologically based instinctual drives that he believed fuel behavior, thoughts, and feelings (p. 344)

psychosocial moratorium a time-out during which the adolescent is not expected to take on adult roles and can pursue activities that lead to self-discovery (p. 444)

puberty the developmental period marked by the ability to reproduce and other dramatic bodily changes (p. 606)

random assignment a procedure in which each child has an equal chance of being assigned to each group within an experiment (p. 32)

reactive aggression emotionally driven, antagonistic aggression sparked by one's perception that other people's motives are hostile (p. 572)

recessive allele the allele that is not expressed if a dominant allele is present (p. 89)

reciprocal determinism Bandura's concept that child–environment influences operate in both directions; children are affected by aspects of their environment, but they also influence the environment (p. 355)

reciprocated best friendship a friendship in which two children view each other as best or close friends (p. 512)

reference in language and speech, the associating of words and meaning (p. 232)

referential (analytic) style speech strategy that analyzes the speech stream into individual phonetic elements and words; the first utterances of children who adopt this style tend to use isolated, often monosyllabic words (p. 234)

reflexes innate, fixed patterns of action that occur in response to particular stimulation (p. 190)

regulator genes genes that control the activity of other genes (p. 89)

rehearsal the process of repeating information over and over to aid memory of it (p. 148)

rejected peer status a category of sociometric status that refers to children or adolescents who are liked by few peers and disliked by many peers (p. 525)

rejecting-neglecting (disengaged) parenting a parenting style that is low in both responsiveness and demandingness. Rejecting-neglecting parents do not set limits for or monitor their children's behavior, are not supportive of them, and sometimes are rejecting or neglectful. They tend to be focused on their own needs rather than their children's. (p. 471)

relational aggression a kind of aggression that involves exclusion from the social group or attempting to do harm to another's relationships with others. It includes spreading rumors about peers, withholding friendship to inflict harm, and ignoring and excluding peers when a child is angry or wants his or her own way. (p. 525)

reliability the degree to which independent measurements of a given behavior are consistent (p. 26)

REM (rapid eye movement) sleep an active sleep state characterized by quick, jerky eye movements under closed lids and associated with dreaming in adults (p. 70)

role taking being aware of the perspective of another person, thereby better understanding that person's behavior, thoughts, and feelings (p. 358)

scale error the attempt by a young child to perform an action on a miniature object that is impossible due to the large discrepancy in the relative sizes of the child and the object (p. 199)

scientific method an approach to testing beliefs that involves choosing a question, formulating a hypothesis, testing the hypothesis, and drawing a conclusion (p. 25)

secular trends marked changes in physical development that have occurred over generations (p. 117)

secure attachment a pattern of attachment in which infants or young children have a high-quality, relatively unambivalent relationship with their attachment figure. In the Strange Situation, a securely attached infant, for example, may be upset when the caregiver leaves but may be happy to see the caregiver return, recovering quickly from any distress. When children are securely attached, they can use caregivers as a secure base for exploration. (p. 429)

secure base referes to the idea that the presence of a trusted caregiver provides an infant or toddler with a sense of security that makes it possible for the child to explore the environment (p. 426)

selective attention the process of intentionally focusing on the information that is most relevant to the current goal (p. 149)

self a conceptual system made up of one's thoughts and attitudes about oneself (p. 437)

self-conscious emotions emotions such as guilt, shame, embarrassment, and pride that relate to our sense of self and our consciousness of others' reactions to us (p. 390)

self-discipline the ability to inhibit actions, follow rules, and avoid impulsive reactions (p. 307)

self-esteem one's overall evaluation of the worth of the self and the feelings that this evaluation engenders (p. 454)

self-locomotion the ability to move oneself around in the environment (p. 196)

self-socialization the idea that children play a very active role in their own socialization through their activity preferences, friendship choices, and so on (p. 358)

semantic development the learning of the system for expressing meaning in a language, including word learning (p. 218)

sensation the processing of basic information from the external world by the sensory receptors in the sense organs (eyes, ears, skin, etc.) and brain (p. 177)

sensitive period the period of time during which a developing organism is most sensitive to the effects of external factors; prenatally, the sensitive period is when the fetus is maximally sensitive to the harmful effects of teratogens (p. 59)

sensorimotor stage the period (birth to 2 years) within Piaget's theory in which intelligence is expressed through sensory and motor abilities (p. 133)

sensory memory the fleeting retention of sights, sounds, and other sensations that have just been experienced (p. 146)

separation anxiety feelings of distress that children, especially infants and toddlers, experience when they are separated, or expect to be separated, from individuals to whom they are emotionally attached (p. 389)

sex chromosomes the chromosomes (X and Y) that determine an individual's gender (p. 87)

sexual orientation a person's preference in regard to males or females as objects of erotic feelings (p. 449)

sexual-minority youth young people who experience same-sex attractions and for whom the question of personal sexual identity is often confusing and painful (p. 450)

SIDS (sudden infant death syndrome) the sudden, unexpected death of an infant less than 1 year of age that has no identifiable cause (p. 63)

small for gestational age babies that weigh substantially less than is normal for whatever their gestational age (p. 75)

social comparison the process of comparing aspects of one's own psychological, behavioral, or physical functioning to that of others in order to evaluate oneself (p. 439)

social competence the ability to achieve personal goals in social interactions while simultaneously maintaining positive relationships with others (p. 398)

social conventional judgments decisions that pertain to customs or regulations intended to secure social coordination and social organization (p. 554)

social referencing the use of a parent's or other adult's facial expression or vocal cues to decide how to deal with novel, ambiguous, or possibly threatening situations (p. 414)

social scaffolding a process in which more competent people provide a temporary framework that supports children's thinking at a higher level than children could manage on their own (p. 162)

social skills training training programs designed to help rejected children gain peer acceptance; they are based on the assumption that rejected children lack important knowledge and skills that promote positive interaction with peers (p. 528)

social smiles smiles that are directed at people. They first emerge as early as 6 to 7 weeks of age. (p. 386)

socialization the process through which children acquire the values, standards, skills, knowledge, and behaviors that are regarded as appropriate for their present and future role in their particular culture (p. 408)

sociocultural context the physical, social, cultural, economic, and historical circumstances that make up any child's environment (p. 19)

sociocultural theories approaches that emphasize that other people and the surrounding culture contribute to children's development (p. 158)

sociodramatic play activities in which children enact minidramas with other children or adults, such as "mother comforting baby" (p. 272)

socioeconomic status (SES) a measure of social class based on income and education (p. 20)

sociometric status a measurement that reflects the degree to which children are liked or disliked by their peers as a group (p. 524)

spermarche the onset of males' capacity for ejaculation (p. 606)

spines formations on the dendrites of neurons that increase the dendrites' capacity to form connections with other neurons (p. 108)

stage theories approaches that propose that development involves a series of discontinuous, age-related phases (p. 16)

standard deviation a measure of the variability of scores in a distribution; in a normal distribution, 68% of scores fall within 1 standard deviation of the mean and 95% of scores fall within 2 standard deviations (p. 304)

state level of arousal and engagement in the environment, ranging from deep sleep to intense activity (p. 70)

stem cells embryonic cells, which can develop into any type of body cell (p. 47)

stepping reflex a neonatal reflex in which an infant lifts first one leg and then the other in a coordinated pattern like walking (p. 194)

stereopsis the process by which the visual cortex combines the differing neural signals caused by binocular disparity, resulting in the perception of depth (p. 185)

Strange Situation a procedure developed by Mary Ainsworth to assess infants' attachment to their primary caregiver (p. 427)

strategy-choice process procedure for selecting among alternative ways of solving problems (p. 325)

structure the basic organization of the cognitive system, including its main components and their characteristics (p. 144)

structured interview a research procedure in which all participants are asked to answer the same questions (p. 27)

structured observation a method that involves presenting an identical situation to each child and recording the child's behavior (p. 29)

style the strategies that young children enlist in beginning to speak (p. 234)

subitizing a process by which adults and children can look at a few objects and almost immediately know how many objects are present (p. 291)

subordinate level the most specific level within a category hierarchy, such as "poodle" in the animal/dog/poodle example (p. 264)

superego in psychoanalytic theory, the third personality structure, consisting of internalized moral standards (p. 346)

superordinate level the most general level within a category hierarchy, such as "animal" in the animal/dog/poodle example (p. 264)

survival of offspring a function of the family that pertains to ensuring the survival of offspring by providing for their needs (p. 466)

swaddling a soothing technique, used in many cultures, that involves wrapping a baby tightly in cloths or a blanket (p. 73)

symbolic representation the use of one object to stand for another (p. 136)

symbols systems for representing our thoughts, feelings, and knowledge and for communicating them to other people (p. 216)

synapses microscopic junctions between the axon terminal of one neuron and the dendritic branches or cell body of another (p. 103)

synaptic pruning the normal developmental process through which synapses that are rarely activated are eliminated (p. 109)

synaptogenesis the process by which neurons form synapses with other neurons, resulting in trillions of connections (p. 108)

syntactic bootstrapping the strategy of using the grammatical structure of whole sentences to figure out meaning (p. 240)

syntactic development the learning of the syntax of a language (p. 218)

syntax rules in a language that specify how words from different categories (nouns, verbs, adjectives, etc.) can be combined (p. 218)

systematic desensitization a form of therapy based on classical conditioning, in which positive responses are gradually conditioned to stimuli that initially elicit a highly negative response. This approach is especially useful in the treatment of fears and phobias. (p. 352)

task analysis the research technique of identifying goals, relevant information in the environment, and potential processing strategies for a problem (p. 144)

telegraphic speech the term describing children's first sentences that are generally two-word utterances (p. 241)

temperament constitutionally based individual differences in emotional, motor, and attentional reactivity and self-regulation that demonstrate consistency across situations, as well as relative stability over time (p. 400)

temporal lobe the lobe of the cortex that is associated with memory, visual recognition, and the processing of emotion and auditory information (p. 104)

teratogen an external agent that can cause damage or death during prenatal development (p. 59)

test–retest reliability the degree of similarity of a child's performance on two or more occasions (p. 26)

theory of mind a basic understanding of how the mind works and how it influences behavior (p. 267)

theory of mind module (TOMM) a hypothesized brain mechanism devoted to understanding other human beings (p. 269)

theory of successful intelligence Sternberg's theory of intellect, based on the view that intelligence is the ability to achieve success in life (p. 322)

third-variable problem the concept that a correlation between two variables may stem from both being influenced by some third variable (p. 31)

three-stratum theory of intelligence Carroll's model of intelligence, including *g* at the top of the hierarchy, eight moderately general abilities in the middle, and many specific processes at the bottom (p. 300)

tuition learning about gender through direct teaching (p. 593)

umbilical cord a tube containing the blood vessels connecting the fetus and placenta (p. 50)

unconditioned response (UCR) in classical conditioning, a reflexive response that is elicited by the unconditioned stimulus (p. 202)

unconditioned stimulus (UCS) in classical conditioning, a stimulus that evokes a reflexive response (p. 202)

universal grammar a set of highly abstract, unconscious rules that are common to all languages (p. 248)

validity the degree to which a test measures what it is intended to measure (p. 26)

variables attributes that vary across individuals and situations, such as age, gender, and expectations (p. 29)

vicarious reinforcement observing someone else receive a reward or punishment (p. 354)

victimized peer status with respect to peer relations, this term refers to children who are targets of their peers' aggression and demeaning behavior (p. 532)

violation-of-expectancy a procedure used to study infant cognition in which infants are shown an event that should evoke surprise or interest if it violates something the infant knows or assumes to be true (p. 207)

visual acuity the sharpness of visual discrimination (p. 178)

visually based retrieval proceeding directly from the visual form of a word to its meaning (p. 325)

voice onset time (VOT) the length of time between when air passes through the lips and when the vocal cords start vibrating (p. 226)

wait-and-see style speech strategy that typically involves a late start in speaking, but a large vocabulary once speaking begins (p. 234)

Wechsler Intelligence Scale for Children (WISC) a widely used test designed to measure the intelligence of children 6 years and older (p. 302)

withdrawn-rejected children a category of sociometric status that refers to rejected children who are socially withdrawn, wary, and often timid (p. 526)

working (short-term) memory a kind of workspace in which information from sensory memory and long-term memory is brought together, attended to, and processed (p. 146)

zygote a fertilized egg cell (p. 46)

References

AAUW (American Association of University Women). (2001). *Hostile hallways: Bullying, teasing, and sexual harassment in school.* Washington, DC: Author.

Abela, J. R. Z. (2001). The hopelessness theory of depression: A test of the diathesis-stress and causal mediation components in third and seventh grade children. *Journal of Abnormal Child Psychology, 29,* 241–254.

Abelson, P., & Kennedy, D. (2004). The obesity epidemic. *Science, 304,* 1413.

Aboud, F. E., & Mendelson, M. J. (1996). Determinants of friendship selection and quality: Developmental perspectives. In W. M. Bukowski, A. F. Newcomb, & W. W. Hartup (Eds.), *The company they keep: Friendship in childhood and adolescence* (pp. 87–112). Cambridge, UK: Cambridge University Press.

Abramovitch, R., Corter, C., & Lando, B. (1979). Sibling interaction in the home. *Child Development, 4,* 997–1003.

Achenbach, T. M., Phares, V., Howell, C. T., Rauh, V. A., & Nurcombe, B. (1990). Seven-year outcome of the Vermont intervention program for low-birthweight infants. *Child Development, 61,* 1672–1681.

Acredolo, C., & Schmidt, J. (1981). The understanding of relative speeds, distances, and durations of movement. *Developmental Psychology, 17,* 490–493.

Acredolo, L. P. (1978). The development of spatial orientation in infancy. *Developmental Psychology, 14,* 224–234.

Acredolo, L. P., & Goodwyn, S. W. (1990). Sign language in babies: The significance of symbolic gesturing for understanding language development. In R. Vasta (Ed.), *Annals of child development: A research annual* (Vol. 7, pp. 1–42). London: Jessica Kingsley.

Adam, E. K., Gunnar, M. R., & Tanaka, A. (2004). Adult attachment, parent emotion, and observed parenting behavior: Mediator and moderator models. *Child Development, 75,* 110–122.

Adams, M. J. (1990). *Beginning to read: Thinking and learning about print.* Cambridge, MA: The MIT Press.

Adams, M. J., Treiman, R., & Pressley, M. (1998), Reading, writing, and literacy. In W. Damon (Series Ed.) and I. E. Sigel & K. A. Renninger (Vol. Eds.), *Handbook of child psychology: Vol.4. Child psychology in practice.* (5th ed., pp. 275–355). New York: Wiley.

Adams, R. J. (1995). Further exploration of human neonatal chromatic-achromatic discrimination. *Journal of Experimental Child Psychology, 60,* 344–360.

Adamson, L. B., Bakeman, R., & Deckner, D. F. (2004). The development of symbol-infused joint engagement. *Child Development, 75,* 1171–1187

Adler, S. A., Haith, M. M., Arehart, D. M., & Lanthier, E. C. (2008). Infants' visual expectations and the processing of time. *Journal of Cognition and Development, 9,* 1–25.

Adolph, K. E. (1997). Learning in the development of infant locomotion. *Monographs of the Society for Research in Child Development, 62*(3, Serial No. 251).

Adolph, K. E. (2000). Specificity of learning: Why infants fall over a veritable cliff. *Psychological Science, 11,* 290–295.

Adolph, K. E., & Berger, S. E. (2006). Motor development. In W. Damon & R. M. Lerner (Series Eds.) & D. Kuhn & R. S. Siegler (Vol. Eds.), *Handbook of child psychology: Volume 2: Cognition, perception, and language* (6th ed., pp. 161–213). Hoboken, NJ: Wiley.

Adolph, K. E., Eppler, M., & Gibson, E. (1993). Crawling versus walking infants' perception of affordances for locomotion over sloping surfaces. *Child Development, 64,* 1158–1174.

Adolph, K. E., Vereijken, B., & Denny, M. A. (1998). Learning to crawl. *Child Development, 69,* 1299–1312.

Adolph, K. E., Vereikjen, B., & Shrout, P. E. (2003). What changes in infant walking and why? *Child Development, 74(2),* 475–497.

Aguilar, B., Sroufe, L. A., Egeland, B., & Carlson, E. (2000). Distinguishing the early-onset/persistent and adolescence-onset antisocial behavior types: From birth to 16 years. *Development and Psychopathology, 12,* 109–132.

Ainsworth, M. D. S. (1967). *Infancy in Uganda: Infant care and the growth of attachment.* Baltimore, MD: Johns Hopkins Press.

Ainsworth, M. D. S. (1973). The development of infant-mother attachment. In B. Caldwell & H. Ricciuti (Eds.), *Review of child development research* (Vol. 3, pp. 1–94). Chicago: University of Chicago Press.

Ainsworth, M. D. S., Blehar, M. C., Waters, E., & Wall, S. (1978). *Patterns of attachment: A psychological study of the strange situation.* Hillsdale, NJ: Erlbaum.

Akhtar, N. (2005). The robustness of learning through overhearing. *Developmental Science, 8,* 199–209.

Akhtar, N., & Gernsbacher, M. A. (2008). On privileging the role of gaze in infant social cognition. *Child Development Perspectives, 2,* 59–65.

Aksan, N., & Kochanska, G. (2005). Conscience in childhood: Old questions, new answers. *Developmental Psychology, 41,* 506–516.

Aksan, N., Kochanska, G., & Ortmann, M. R. (2006). Mutually responsive orientation between parents and their young children: Toward methodological advances in the science of relationships. *Developmental Psychology, 42,* 833–848.

Aldous, J., Mulligan, G. M., & Bjarnason, T. (1998). Fathering over time: What makes the difference? *Journal of Marriage and the Family, 60,* 809–820.

Alexander, G. M. (2003). An evolutionary perspective of sex-typed toy preferences: Pink, blue, and the brain. *Archives of Sexual Behavior, 32,* 7–14.

Alexander, K. L., & Entwistle, D. R. (1996). Schools and children at risk. In A. Booth & J. F. Dunn (Eds.), *Family-school links: How do they affect educational outcomes?* (pp. 67–88). Mahwah, NJ: Erlbaum.

Alibali, M. W., & Goldin-Meadow, S. (1993). Gesture-speech mismatch and mechanisms of learning: What the hands reveal about a child's state of mind. *Cognitive Psychology, 25*, 468–523.

Alink, L. R. A., Mesman, J., van Zeijl, J., Stolk, M. N., Juffer, F., Koot, H. M., et al. (2006). The early childhood aggression curve: Development of physical aggression in 10- to 50-month-old children. *Child Development, 77*, 954–966.

Allen, J. P., Marsh, P., McFarland, C., McElhaney, K. B., Land, D. J., Jodl, K. M., & Peck, S. (2002). Attachment and autonomy as predictors of the development of social skills and delinquency during midadolescence. *Journal of Consulting and Clinical Psychology, 70*, 56–66.

Allen, J. P., McElhaney, K. B., Kuperminc, G. P., & Jodl, K. M. (2004). Stability and change in attachment security across adolescence. *Child Development, 75*, 1792–1805.

Allen, J. P., Porter, M. R., McFarland, F. C., Marsh, P., & McElhaney, K. B. (2005). The two faces of adolescents' success with peers: Adolescent popularity, social adaptation, and deviant behavior. *Child Development, 76*, 747–760.

Allen, J. P., Porter, M. R., & McFarland, F. C. (2006). Leaders and followers in adolescent close friendships: Susceptibility to peer influence as a predictor of risky behavior, friendship instability, and depression. *Development and Psychopathology, 18*, 155–172.

Allen, J. P., Porter, M., MacFarland, C., & McElhaney, K. B. (2007). The relation of attachment security to adolescents' paternal and peer relationships, depression, and externalizing behavior. *Child Development, 78*, 1222–1239.

Allison, D. B., & Pi-Sunyer, F. X. (1994, May/June). Fleshing out obesity. *The Sciences*, 38–43.

Als, H. (1995). The preterm infant: A model for the study of fetal brain expectation. In J. Lecanuet & W. P. Fifer (Eds.), *Fetal development: A psychobiological perspective* (pp. 439–471). Hillsdale, NJ: Erlbaum.

Als, H., et al. (2003). A three-center randomized controlled trial of individualized developmental care for very low-birth-weight preterm infants: Medical, neurodevelopmental, parent and care giving effects. *Journal of Developmental Behavioral Pediatrics, 24*, 399–408.

Altermatt, E. R., Jovanovic, J., & Perry, M. (1998). Bias or responsivity? Sex and achievement-level effects on teachers' classroom questioning practices. *Journal of Educational Psychology, 90*, 516–527.

Altermatt, E. R., & Pomerantz, E. M. (2003). The development of competence-related and motivational beliefs: An investigation of similarity and influence among friends. *Journal of Educational Psychology, 95*, 111–123.

Altshuler, J. L., Genevro, J. L., Ruble, D. N., & Bornstein, M. H. (1995). Children's knowledge and use of coping strategies during hospitalization for elective surgery. *Journal of Applied Developmental Psychology, 16*, 53–76.

Alwin, D. F. (1984). Trends in parental socialization: Detroit, 1958–1983. *American Journal of Sociology, 90*, 359–381.

Amato, P. R. (2001). Children of divorce in the 1990s: An update of the Amato and Keith (1991) meta-analysis. *Journal of Family Psychology, 15*, 355–370.

Amato, P. R., & Gilbreth, J. G. (1999). Nonresident fathers and children's well being: A meta-analysis. *Journal of Marriage and Family, 61*, 557–573.

Amato, P. R., & Keith, B. (1991). Parental divorce and the well-being of children: A meta-analysis. *Psychological Bulletin, 110*, 26–46.

American Academy of Pediatrics. (2000). Clinical practice guideline: Diagnosis and evaluation of the child with attention-deficit/hyperactivity disorder. *Pediatrics, 105*, 1158–1170.

American Psychiatric Association. (1994). *Diagnostic and statistical manual of mental disorders* (4th ed.). Washington, DC: Author.

Amsterlaw, J., & Wellman, H. M. (2006). Theories of mind in transition: A microgenetic study of the development of false belief understanding. *Journal of Cognition and Development, 7*, 139–172.

Anderson, C. A., Berkowitz, L., Donnerstein, E., Huesmann, L. R., Johnson, J. D., Linz, D., Malamuth, N. M., & Wartella, E. (2003). The influence of media violence on youth. *Psychological Sciences in the Public Interest, 4*, 81–110.

Anderson, C. A., & Bushman, B. J. (2001). Effects of violent video games on aggressive behavior, aggressive cognition, aggressive affect, physiological arousal, and prosocial behavior: A meta-analytic review of the scientific literature. *Psychological Science, 12*, 353–359.

Anderson, D. R., Huston, A. C., Schmitt, K. L., Linebarger, D. L., & Wright, J. C. (2001). Early childhood television viewing and adolescent behavior. *Monographs of the Society for Research in Child Development, 68* (1, Serial No. 264).

Anderson, J. R. (2000). *Learning and memory: An integrated approach.* New York: Wiley.

Anderson, J. R. (2005). Human symbol manipulation within an integrated cognitive architecture. *Cognitive Science, 29*, 313–341.

Anderson, J. R., Albert, M. V., & Fincham, J. M. (2005). Tracing problem solving in real time: fMRI analysis of the subject-paced Tower of Hanoi. *Journal of Cognitive Neuroscience, 17*, 1261–1274.

Anderson, M. E., Johnson, D. C., & Batal, H. A. (2005). Sudden infant death syndrome and prenatal maternal smoking: Rising attributed risk in the Back to Sleep era. *BMC Medicine*, 3:4.

Anderson, R. C., Wilson, P. T., & Fielding, L. G. (1988). Growth in reading and how children spend their time outside school. *Reading Research Quarterly, 23*, 285–303.

Anderson, V., Jacobs, R., & Harvey, A. S. (2005). Prefrontal lesions and attentional skills in childhood. *Journal of the International Neuropsychological Society, 11*, 817–831.

Andre, T., Whigham, M., Hendrickson, A., & Chambers, S. (1999). Competency beliefs, positive affect, and gender stereotypes of elementary students and their parents about science versus other school subjects. *Journal of Research in Science Teaching, 36*, 719–747.

Angier, N. (1999). *Woman: An intimate geography.* Houghton Mifflin Company, New York.

Anglin, J. M. (1993). Vocabulary development: A morphological analysis. *Monographs of the Society for Research in Child Development, 58*(10, Serial No. 238).

Ansari, D. (2008). Effects of development and enculturation on number representation in the brain. *Nature Reviews, Neuroscience, 9*, 278–291.

Anthony, J. L., & Francis, D. J. (2005). Development of phonological awareness. *Current Directions in Psychological Science, 14*, 255–259.

Aptehar, L., & Ciano-Federoff, L. M. (1999). Street children in Nairobi: Gender differences in mental health. *New Directions in Child Development, 85*, 35–46.

Archer, J. (1991). The influence of testosterone on human aggression. *British Journal of Psychology, 81*, 1–28.

Archer, J. (2004). Sex differences in aggression in real-world settings: A meta-analytic review. *Review of General Psychology, 8*, 291–291.

Archer, J. (2006). Testosterone and human aggression: An evaluation of the challenge hypothesis. *Neuroscience & Biobehavioral Reviews, 30*, 319–345.

Archer, J., & Coyne, S. M. (2005). An integrated review of indirect, relational, and social aggression. *Personality and Social Psychology Review, 9*, 212–212.

Archer, J., Graham-Kevan, N., & Davies, M. (2005). Testosterone and aggression: A reanalysis of Book, Starzyk, and Quinsey's (2001) study. *Aggression and Violent Behavior, 10*, 241–241.

Archer, J., & Lloyd, B. (2002). *Sex and gender* (2nd ed.). New York, NY: Cambridge University Press.

Archer, J. & Macrae, M. (1991). Gender-perceptions of school subjects among 10–11 year olds. *British Journal of Educational Psychology, 61*, 99–103.

Arduini, D., Rizzo, G., & Romanini, C. (1995). Fetal behavioral states and behavioral transitions in normal and compromised fetuses. In J. Lecanuet, W. P. Fifer, N. A. Krasnegor, & W. P. Smotherman (Eds.), *Fetal development: A psychobiological perspective*. Hillsdale, NJ: Erlbaum.

Aristotle. (1954). *Nicomachean ethics* (D. Ross, Trans.). London: Oxford University Press.

Arndorfer, C. L., & Stormshak, E. A. (2008). Same-sex versus other-sex best friendship in early adolescence: Longitudinal predictors of antisocial behavior throughout adolescence. *Journal of Youth and Adolescence, 37*, 1059–1070.

Arnett, J. J. (1999). Adolescent storm and stress, a reconsideration. *American Psychologist, 54*, 317–328.

Aronson, E. (2000). *Nobody left to hate: Teaching compassion after Columbine*. New York: Worth.

Arsenault, L., Moffitt, T. E., Caspi, A., Taylor, A., Rijsdijk, F. V., Jaffee, S. R., Ablow, J. C., & Measelle, J. R. (2003). Strong genetic effects on cross-situational antisocial behaviour among 5-year-old children according to mothers, teachers, examiner-observers, and twins' self reports. *Journal of Child Psychology & Psychiatry, 44*, 832–848.

Asbury, K., Dunn, J. F., Pike, A., & Plomin, R. (2003). Nonshared environmental influences on individual differences in early behavioral development: A monozygotic twin differences study. *Child Development, 74*, 933–943.

Asendorpf, J. B. (1990). Development of inhibition during childhood: Evidence for situational specificity and a two-factor model. *Developmental Psychology, 26*, 721–730.

Asendorpf, J. B., Warkentin, V, & Baudonniere, P.-M. (1996). Self-awareness and other-awareness: II. Mirror self-recognition, social contingency awareness, and synchronic imitation. *Developmental Psychology, 32*, 313–321.

Ashcraft, M. H., Kirk, E. P., & Hopko, D. (1998). On the cognitive consequences of mathematics anxiety. In C. Donlan (Ed.), *The development of mathematical skills* (pp. 175–196). East Sussex: Psychology Press.

Ashcraft, M. H., Krause, J. A., & Hopko, D. R. (2007). Math anxiety as a mathematics learning disability. In D. B. Berch & M. M. M. Mazzocco (Eds.), *Why is math so hard for some children? The nature and origins of mathematical learning difficulties and disabilities* (pp. 329–348). New York: Plenum.

Asher, S. R., & Dodge, K. A. (1986). Identifying children who are rejected by their peers. *Developmental Psychology, 22*, 444–449.

Asher, S. R., & Paquette, J. A. (2003). Loneliness and peer relations in childhood. *Current Directions in Psychological Science, 12*, 75–78.

Ashman, S. B., Dawson, G., Panagiotides, H., Yamada, E., & Wilkinson, C. W. (2002). Stress hormone levels of children of depressed mothers. *Development and Psychopathology, 14*, 333–349.

Aslin, R. N. (1981). Development of smooth pursuit in human infants. In D. F. Fisher, R. A. Monty & J. W. Senders (Eds.), *Eye movements: Cognition and visual perception* (pp. 31–51). Hillsdale, NJ: Erlbaum.

Aslin, R. N., Jusczyk, P. W., & Pisoni, D. B. (1998). Speech and auditory processing during infancy: Constraints on and precursors to language. In W. Damon (Series Ed.), D. Kuhn, & R. S. Siegler (Vol. Eds.), *Handbook of child psychology: Vol. 2. Cognition, perception, and language* (5th ed., pp. 147–198). New York: Wiley.

Aslin, R. N., Saffran, J. R., & Newport, E. L. (1998). Computation of conditional probability statistics by 8-month-old infants. *Psychological Science, 9*(4), 321–324.

Atran, S. (1990). *Cognitive foundations of natural history*. Cambridge, UK: Cambridge University Press.

Atran, S. (2002). Modular and cultural factors in biological understanding: An experimental approach to the cognitive basis of science. In P. Carruthers, S. Stich, & M. Siegal, (Eds.), *The cognitive basis of science* (pp. 41–72). New York: Cambridge University Press.

Attili, G., Vermigli, P., & Schneider, B. H. (1997). Peer acceptance and friendship patterns among Italian schoolchildren within a cross-cultural perspective. *International Journal of Behavioral Development, 21*, 277–288.

Augusta, D., & Hakuta, K. (1998). *Educating language-minority children*. Washington, DC: National Academy Press.

Augustine, St. (398/1963). *The Confessions of St. Augustine*. New York: The Catholic Book Company.

Awong, T., Grusec, J. E., & Sorenson, A. (2008). Respect-based control and anger as determinants of children's socio-emotional development. *Social Development, 17*, 941–959.

Ayduk, O., Mendoza-Denton, R., Downey, G., Peake, P. K., & Rodriguez, M. (2000). Regulating the interpersonal self: Strategic self-regulation for coping with rejection sensitivity. *Journal of Personality and Social Psychology, 79*, 776–792.

Azmitia, M., & Montgomery, R. (1993). Friendship, transactive dialogues, and the development of scientific reasoning. *Social Development, 2*, 202–221.

Backscheider, A. G., Shatz, M., & Gelman, S. A. (1993). Preschoolers' ability to distinguish living kinds as a function of regrowth. *Child Development, 64*, 1242–1257.

Bagwell, C. L., Newcomb, A. F., & Bukowski, W. M. (1998). Preadolescent friendship and peer rejection as predictors of adult adjustment. *Child Development, 69*, 140–153.

Baham, M. E., Weimer, A. A., Braver, S. L., & Fabricius, W. V. (2008). Sibling relationships in blended families. In J. Pryor (Ed.), *The international handbook of stepfamilies: Policy and practice in legal, research, and clinical environments* (pp. 175–207). Hoboken, NJ: John Wiley & Sons, Inc.

Bahrick, H. P. (1987). Functional and cognitive memory theory: An overview of some key issues. *Memory and learning: The Ebbinghaus centennial conference.* Hillsdale, NJ: Erlbaum, pp. 387–395.

Bahrick, H. P., Hall, L. K., Goggin, J. P., Bahrick, L. E., & Berger, S. A. (1994). Fifty years of language maintenance and language dominance in bilingual Hispanic immigrants. *Journal of Experimental Psychology: General, 123,* 264–283.

Bahrick, L. E., Lickliter, R., & Flom, R. (2004). Intersensory redundancy guides the development of selective attention, perception, and cognition in infancy. *Current Directions in Psychological Science, 13*(3), 99–102.

Bailey, J. M., Bobrow, D., Wolfe, M., & Mikach, S. (1995). Sexual orientation of adult sons and gay fathers. *Developmental Psychology, 31,* 124–129.

Bailey, H. N., Moran, G., Pederson, D. R., & Bento, S. (2007). Understanding the transmission of attachment using variable- and relationship-centered approaches. *Development and Psychopathology, 19,* 313–343.

Bailey, J. M., & Pillard, R. C. (1991). A genetic study of male sexual orientation. *Archives of General Psychiatry, 43,* 808–812.

Bailey, J. M., Pillard, R. C., Neale, M. C., & Agyes, Y. (1993). Heritable factors influence sexual orientation in women. *Archives of General Psychiatry, 50,* 217–223.

Baillargeon, R. (1987a). Object permanence in 3.5- and 4.5-month-old infants. *Developmental Psychology, 23,* 655–664.

Baillargeon, R. (1987b). Representing the existence and the location of hidden objects: Object permanence in 6- and 8-month-old infants. *Cognition, 23,* 21–41.

Baillargeon, R. (1993). The object concept revisited: New directions in the investigation of infants' physical knowledge. In C. E. Granrud (Ed.), *Visual perception and cognition in infancy.* Hillsdale, NJ: Erlbaum.

Baillargeon, R. (1994). How do infants learn about the physical world? *Current Directions in Psychological Science, 3,* 133–140.

Baillargeon, R. (1998). Infants' understanding of the physical world. In M. Sabourin, F. Craik, & M. Robert (Eds.), *Advances in psychological science* (Vol. 2, pp. 503–529). London: Psychology Press.

Baillargeon, R. (2004). Infants' reasoning about hidden objects: Evidence for event-general and event-specific expectations. *Developmental Science, 7*(4), 391–424.

Baillargeon, R., DeVos, J., & Graber, M. (1989). Location memory in 8-month-old infants in a non-search AB task: Further evidence. *Cognitive Development, 4,* 345–367.

Baillargeon, R., Kotovsky, L., & Needham, A. (1995). The acquisition of physical knowledge in infancy. In G. Lewis, D. Premack, & D. Sperber (Eds.), *Causal understandings in cognition and culture.* Oxford, UK: Oxford University Press.

Baillargeon, R., Needham, A., & DeVos, J. (1992). The development of young infants' intuitions about support. *Early Development and Parenting, 1,* 69–78.

Baillargeon, R., Spelke, E. S., & Wasserman, S. (1985). Object permanence in 5-month-old infants. *Cognition, 20,* 191–208.

Baker, D. P. & Jones, D. P. (1993). Creating gender equality: Cross-national gender stratification and mathematical performance. *Sociology of Education, 66,* 91–103.

Baker, L. A., Raine, A., Liu, J., & Jacobson, K. C. (2008). Differential genetic and environmental influences on reactive and proactive aggression in children. *Journal of Abnormal Child Psychology, 36,* 1265–1278.

Bakermans-Kranenburg, M. J., van IJzendoorn, M. H., & Juffer, F. (2003). Less is more: Meta-analyses of sensitivity and attachment interventions in early childhood. *Psychological Bulletin, 129,* 195–215.

Bakermans-Kranenburg, M. J., & van IJzendoorn, M. H. (2006). Gene-environment interaction of the dopamine D4 receptor (DRD4) and observed maternal insensitivity predicting externalizing behavior in preschoolers. *Developmental Psychobiology, 48,* 406–409.

Balaban, M. T., Anderson, L. M., & Wisniewski, A. B. (1998). Lateral asymmetries in infant melody perception. *Developmental Psychology, 34,* 39–48.

Baldwin, D. A. (1991). Infants' contribution to the achievement of joint reference. *Child Development, 62,* 875–890.

Baldwin, D. A. (1993). Early referential understanding: Infants' ability to recognize referential acts for what they are. *Developmental Psychology, 29,* 832–843.

Baldwin, D. A., Markman, E. M., & Mellartin, R. L. (1993). Infants' ability to draw inferences about nonobvious object properties: Evidence from exploratory play. *Child Development, 64,* 711–728.

Ball, W., & Tronick, E. (1971). Infant responses to impending collision: Optical and real. *Science, 171,* 818–820.

Bámaca, M. Y., Umaña-Taylor, A. J., Shin, N., & Alfaro, E. C. (2005). Latino adolescents' perception of parenting behaviors and self-esteem: Examining the role of neighborhood risk. *Family Relations, 54,* 621–632.

Bandura, A. (1965). Influence of models: Reinforcement contingencies on the acquisition of imitative behaviors. *Journal of Personality and Social Psychology, 1,* 589–595.

Bandura, A. (1977). *Social learning theory.* Upper Saddle River, NJ: Prentice-Hall.

Bandura, A. (1986). *Social foundations of thought and action.* Upper Saddle River, NJ: Prentice-Hall.

Bandura, A. (1997). *Self-efficacy: The exercise of control.* New York: W. H. Freeman.

Bandura, A., Caprara, G. V., Barbaranelli, C., Gerbino, M., & Pastorelli, C. (2003). Role of affective self-regulatory efficacy in diverse spheres of psychosocial functioning. *Child Development, 74,* 769–782.

Bandura, A., Ross, D., & Ross, S. A. (1963). Imitation of film-mediated aggressive models. *Journal of Abnormal Social Psychology, 66,* 3–11.

Bandura, A., & Walters, R. H. (1963). *Social learning and personality development.* New York: Holt, Rinehart & Winston.

Banerjee, M. (1997). Hidden emotions: Preschoolers' knowledge of appearance-reality and emotion display rules. *Social Cognition, 15,* 107–132.

Banerjee, R. & Lintern, V. (2000). Boys will be boys: The effect of social evaluation concerns on gender-typing. *Social Development, 9,* 397-408.

Banich, M. T. (1997). *Neuropsychology: The neural bases of mental function.* New York: Houghton Mifflin.

Banich, M. T., Levine, S., Kim, H., & Huttenlocher, P. (1990). The effects of developmental factors on IQ in hemiplegic children. *Neuropsychologia, 28,* 35–47.

Bank, L., Patterson, G. R., & Reid, J. B. (1996). Negative sibling interaction patterns as predictors of later adjustment problems in adolescent and young adult males. In G. H. Brody (Ed.), *Sibling relationships: Their causes and consequences* (pp. 197–229). Norwood, NJ: Ablex Press.

Banks, M. S., & Dannemiller, J. L. (1987). Infant visual psychophysics. In P. Salapatek & L. Cohen (Eds.), *Handbook of infant perception. Vol. 1. From sensation to perception* (pp. 115–184). Orlando, FL: Academic Press.

Banks, M. S., & Shannon, E. S. (1993). Spatial and chromatic visual efficiency in human neonates. In C. Granrud (Ed.), *Visual perception and cognition in infancy.* Hillsdale, NJ: Erlbaum.

Barbaresi, W. J. (2007). Stimulant treatment of children with AD/HD was associated with improved reading achievement, decreased school absenteeism, and decreased grade retention. *Journal of Developmental and Behavioral Pediatrics, 28,* 265–287.

Barbaresi, W. J., Katusic, S. K., Colligan, R. C., Weaver, A.L., & Jacobsen, S. J. (2007). Modifiers of long-term school outcomes for children with attention-deficit/hyperactivity disorder: Does treatment with stimulant medication make a difference? Results from a population-based study. *Journal of Developmental and Behavioral Pediatrics, 4,* 274–287.

Barber, B. K. (1996). Parental psychological control: Revisiting a neglected construct. *Child Development, 67,* 3296–3319.

Barden, R. C., Zelko, F. A., Duncan, S. W., & Masters, J. C. (1980). Children's consensual knowledge about the experiential determinants of emotion. *Journal of Personality and Social Psychology, 39,* 968–976.

Barker, E. D., Boivin, M., Brendgen, M., Fontaine, N., Arseneault, L., Vitaro, F., et al. (2008). Predictive validity and early predictors of peer-victimization trajectories in preschool. *Archives of General Psychiatry, 65*(10), 1185–1192.

Barkley, R. A. (1994). Impaired delayed responding: A unified theory of attention-deficit hyperactivity disorder. In R. A. Barkley (Ed.), *Disruptive behavior disorders in childhood* (pp. 11–57). New York: Plenum Press.

Barkley, R. A. (1997). Behavioral inhibition, sustained attention, and executive functions. Constructing a unifying theory of ADHD. *Psychological Bulletin, 121,* 65–94.

Baron-Cohen, S. (1991). The development of a theory of mind in autism: Deviance and delay? *Psychiatric Clinics of North America, 14,* 33–51.

Baron-Cohen, S. (1993). From attention-goal psychology to belief-desire psychology: The development of a theory of mind, and its dysfunction. In S. Baron-Cohen, H. Tager-Flusberg, & D. J. Cohen (Eds.), *Understanding other minds: Perspectives from autism.* Oxford, UK: Oxford University Press.

Baron-Cohen, S. (1995). *Mindblindness: An essay on autism and theory of mind.* Cambridge, MA: The MIT Press.

Baron-Cohen, S. (2003). *The essential difference: The truth about the male and female brain.* New York: Basic Books.

Barr, R. G. (1998). Colic and crying syndromes in infants. In J. G. Warhol and S. P. Shelov (Eds.), *New Perspectives in Early Emotional Development* (pp. 147–157). Calverton, New York: Johnson & Johnson Pediatric Institute, LLC.

Barr, R., Dowden, A., & Hayne, H. (1996). Developmental changes in deferred imitation by 6- to 24-month-old infants. *Infant Behavior and Development, 19,* 159–170.

Barr, R., & Hayne, H. (1999). Developmental changes in imitation from television during infancy. *Child Development, 70,* 1067–1081.

Barr, R. G., Quek, V. S., Cousineau, D., Oberlander, T. F., Brian, J. A., & Young, S. N. (1994). Effects of intra-oral sucrose on crying, mouthing and hand-mouth contact in newborn and six-week-old infants. *Developmental Medicine & Child Neurology, 36,* 608–618.

Barrett, D. E., & Yarrow, M. R. (1977). Prosocial behavior, social inferential ability, and assertiveness in young children. *Child Development, 48,* 475–481.

Barrett, K. C., Zahn-Waxler, C., & Cole, P. M. (1993). Avoiders versus amenders: Implications for the investigation of guilt and shame during toddlerhood? *Cognition and Emotion, 7,* 481–505.

Barsalou, L. W. (2005). Abstraction as dynamic interpretation in perceptual symbol systems. In L. Gershkoff-Stowe & D. H. Rakison (Eds.), *Building object categories in developmental time* (pp. 389–431). Mahwah, NJ: Erlbaum.

Barsalou, L. W. (2005). Continuity of the conceptual system across species. *Trends in Cognitive Sciences, 9,* 309–311.

Bartlett, N. H., Vasey, P. L., & Bukowski, W. M. (2000). Is gender identity disorder in children a mental disorder? *Sex Roles, 43,* 753–758.

Bartrip, J., Morton, J., & de Schonen, S. (2001). Responses to mother's face in 3-week to 5-month-old infants. *British Journal of Developmental Psychology, 19,* 219–232.

Bartsch, K., & Wellman, H. M. (1995). *Children talk about the mind.* New York: Oxford University Press.

Bassen, C. R., & Lamb, M. E. (2006). Gender differences in adolescents' self-concepts of assertion and affiliation. *European Journal of Developmental Psychology, 3,* 71–94.

Bates, E. (1990). Language about me and you: Pronominal reference and the emerging concept of self. In D. Cicchetti & M. Beeghly (Eds.), *The self in transition: Infancy to childhood* (pp. 165–182). Chicago: University of Chicago Press.

Bates, E., Dale, P., & Thal, D. (1995). Individual differences and their implications for theories of language development. In P. Fletcher & B. MacWhinney (Eds.), *Handbook of child language* (pp. 96–151). Oxford: Basil Blackwell.

Bates, E., & Elman, J. L. (1993). Connectionism and the study of change. In M. H. Johnson (Ed.), *Brain development and cognition: A reader* (pp. 623–642). Cambridge, MA: Blackwell.

Bates, J. E., Bayles, K., Bennett, D. S., Ridge, B., & Brown, M. M. (1991). Origins of externalizing behavior problems at eight years of age. In D. Pepler & K. Rubin (Eds.), *Development and treatment of childhood aggression* (pp. 93–120). Hillsdale, NJ: Erlbaum.

Bates, J. E., Marvinney, D., Kelly, T., Dodge, K. A., Bennett, D. S., & Pettit, G. S. (1994). Child-care history and kindergarten adjustment. *Developmental Psychology, 30,* 690–700.

Bates, J. E., Pettit, G. S., Dodge, K. A., & Ridge, B. (1998). Interaction of temperamental resistance to control and restrictive parenting in the development of externalizing behavior. *Developmental Psychology, 34,* 982–995.

Bates, L., Luster, T., & Vandenbelt, M. (2003). Factors related to social competence in elementary school among children of adolescent mothers. *Social Development, 12,* 107–124.

Battin, S. R., Hill, K. G., Abbott, R. D., Catalano, R. F., & Hawkins, J. D. (1998). The contribution of gang membership to delinquency beyond delinquent friends. *Criminology, 36,* 93–115.

Battistich, V., Schaps, E., Watson, M., Solomon, D., & Lewis, C. (2000). Effects of the Child Development Project on students' drug use and other problem behaviors. *Journal of Primary Prevention, 21,* 75–99.

Battistich, V., Schaps, E., Wilson, N. (2004). Effects of an elementary school intervention on students' "connectedness" to school and social adjustment during middle school. *Journal of Primary Prevention, 24,* 243–262.

Battistich, V., Solomon, D., Watson, M., & Schaps, E. (1997). Caring school communities. *Educational Psychologist,* 32, 137–151.

Battistich, V., Watson, M., Solomon, D., Schaps, E., & Solomon, J. (1991). The Child Development Project: A comprehensive program for the development of prosocial character. In W. M. Kurtines & J. L. Gerwirtz (Eds.), *Handbook of moral behavior and development. Vol. 3. Application* (pp. 1–34). New York: Erlbaum.

Bauer, P. J. (1995). Recalling past events: From infancy to early childhood. *Annals of Child Development, 11,* 25–71.

Bauer, P. J. (2002). Long-term recall memory: Behavioral and neurodevelopmental changes in the first 2 years of life. *Current Directions in Psychological Science, 11*(4), 137–141.

Bauer, P. J. (2007). *Remembering the times of our lives: Memory in infancy and beyond.* Mahwah, NJ: Erlbaum.

Bauer, P. J., Wenner, J. A, & Kroupina, M. G. (2002). Making the past present: Later verbal accessibility of early memories. *Journal of Cognition & Development, 3,* 21–47.

Bauminger, N., Finzi-Dottan, R., Chason, S., & Har-Even, D. (2008). Intimacy in adolescent friendship: The roles of attachment, coherence, and self-disclosure. *Journal of Social and Personal Relationships, 25,* 409–428.

Baumrind, D. (1972). An exploratory study of socialization effects on black children: Some black-white comparisons. *Child Development, 43,* 261–267.

Baumrind, D. (1973). The development of instrument competence through socialization. In A. D. Pick (Ed.), *Minnesota symposia on child psychology* (Vol. 7, pp. 3–46). Minneapolis: University of Minnesota Press.

Baumrind, D. (1991a). The influence of parenting style on adolescent competence and substance use. *Journal of Early Adolescence, 11,* 56–95.

Baumrind, D. (1991b). Parenting styles and adolescent development. In R. M. Lerner, A. C. Petersen, & J. Brooks-Gunn (Eds.), *Encyclopedia of adolescence,* (Vol. 11, pp. 746–758). New York: Garland.

Bauserman, R. (2002). Child adjustment in joint-custody versus sole-custody arrangements: A meta-analytic review. *Journal of Family Psychology, 16,* 91–102.

Beardsall, L., & Dunn, J. (1989). *Life events in childhood: Shared and nonshared experiences of siblings.* Unpublished manuscript.

Beauchaine, T. (2001). Vagal tone, development, and Gray's motivational theory: Toward an integrated model of autonomic nervous system functioning in psychopathology. *Development and Psychopathology, 13,* 183–214.

Beck, A. T. (1983). Cognitive therapy of depression: New perspectives. In P. J. Clayton & J. E. Barrett (eds.), *Treatment of depression: Old controversies and new approaches* (pp. 265–290). New York: Raven Press.

Becker-Bryant, J., & Polkosky, M. D. (2001, April). *Parents' responses to preschoolers' lexical innovations.* Paper presented at the biennial meeting of the Society for Research in Child Development, Minneapolis, MN.

Becker-Stoll, F., Delius, A., & Scheitenberger, S. (2001). Adolescents' nonverbal emotional expressions during negotiation of a disagreement with their mothers: An attachment approach. *International Journal of Behavioral Development, 25,* 344–353.

Beckett, C., Maughan, B., Rutter, M., Castle, J., Colvert, E., Groothues, C., Kreppner, J., Stevens, S., O'Connor, T. G., & Sonuga-Barke, E. J. S. (2006). Do the effects of early severe deprivation on cognition persist into early adolescence? Findings from the English and Romanian adoptees study. *Child Development, 77,* 696–711.

Behl-Chadha, G. (1996). Basic-level and superordinate-like categorical representations in early infancy. *Cognition, 60,* 105–141.

Behrend, D. A., Rosengren, K. S., & Perlmutter, M. (1992). The relation between private speech and parental interactive style. In R. M. Diaz & L. E. Berk (Eds.), *Private speech: From social interaction to self-regulation* (pp. 85–100). Hillsdale, NJ: Erlbaum.

Behrens, K. Y., Hesse, E., & Main, M. (2007). Mothers' attachment status as determined by the adult attachment interview predicts their 6-year-olds' reunion responses: A study conducted in Japan. *Developmental Psychology, 43,* 1553–1567.

Bell, L. A. (1989). Something's wrong here and it's not me: Challenging the dilemmas that block girls' success. *Journal for the Education of the Gifted, 12,* 118–130.

Bell, N. J., & Carver, W. (1980). A reevaluation of gender label effects: Expectant mothers' responses to infants. *Child Development, 51,* 925–927.

Bellugi, U., Mills, D., Jernigan, T., Hickok, G., & Galaburda, A. (1999). Linking cognition, brain structure, and brain function in Williams syndrome. In H. Tager-Flusberg (Ed.), *Neurodevelopmental disorders: Developmental cognitive neuroscience* (pp. 111–136). Cambridge, MA: The MIT Press.

Bellugi, U., Poizner, H., & Klima, E. S. (1989). Language, modality and the brain. *Trends in Neurosciences, 12,* 380–388.

Belsky, J. (1986). Infant day care: A cause for concern? *Zero to Three, 6,* 1–9.

Belsky, J. (1993). Etiology of child maltreatment: A developmental-ecological analysis. *Psychological Bulletin, 114,* 413–433.

Belsky, J., Bakermans-Kranenburg, M., & van IJzendoorn, M. (2007). For better and for worse: Differential susceptibility to environmental influences. *Current Directions in Psychological Science, 16,* 305–309.

Belsky, J., Fearon, R. M. P., & Bell, B. (2007). Parenting, attention and externalizing problems: Testing mediation longitudinally, repeatedly and reciprocally. *Journal of Child Psychology and Psychiatry, 48,* 1233–1242.

Belsky, J., Rosenberger, K., & Crnic, K. (1995). Maternal personality, marital quality, social support and infant temperament: Their significance for infant-mother attachment in human families. In C. R. Pryce & R. D. Martin (Eds.), *Motherhood in human and nonhuman primates: Biosocial determinants* (pp. 115–124). Basel, Switzerland: Karger.

Belsky, J., Vandell, D. L., Burchinal, M., Clarke-Stewart, K. A., McCartney, K., & Owen, M. T. and the NICHD Early Child Care Research Network. (2007). Are there long-term effects of early child care? *Child Development, 78,* 681–701.

Bem, D. (1996). Exotic becomes erotic: A developmental theory of sexual orientation. *Psychological Review, 103,* 320–335.

Bem, S. L. (1981). Gender schema theory: A cognitive account of sex typing. *Psychological Review, 88,* 354–364.

Bem, S. L. (1989). Genital knowledge and gender constancy in preschool children. *Child Development, 60,* 649–662.

Bem, S. L. (1993). *The lenses of gender.* New Haven, CT: Yale University Press.

Benbow, C. P. (1988). Sex differences in mathematically talented preadolescents: Their nature, effects, and possible causes. *Behavioral and Brain Sciences, 11,* 169–183.

Bender, H. L., Allen, J. P., McElhaney, K. B., Antonishak, J., Moore, C. M., Kelly, H. O., et al. (2007). Use of harsh physical discipline and developmental outcomes in adolescence. *Development and Psychopathology, 19,* 227–242.

Benedict, H. (1979). Early lexical development: Comprehension and production. *Journal of Child Language, 6,* 183–200.

Benedict, R. (1934). *Patterns of culture.* Boston: Houghton Mifflin.

Benenson, J. F., & Christakos, A. (2003). The greater fragility of female's versus male's closest same-sex friendships. *Child Development, 74,* 1123–1129.

Benenson, J. F., Maiese, R., Dolenszky, E., Dolensky, N., Sinclair, N., & Simpson, A. (2002). Group size regulates self-assertive versus self-deprecating responses to interpersonal competition. *Child Development, 73,* 1818–1829.

Benenson, J. F., Markovits, H., Roy, R., & Denko, P. (2003). Behavioural rules underlying learning to share: Effects of development and context. *International Journal of Behavioral Development, 27,* 116–121.

Benenson, J. F., Morganstein, T., & Roy, R. (1998). Sex differences in children's investment in peers. *Human Nature, 9,* 369–390.

Benoit, D., & Parker, K. C. H. (1994). Stability and transmission of attachment across three generations. *Child Development, 65,* 1444–1456.

Bereiter, C., & Scardamalia, M. (1982). From conversation to composition: The role of instruction in a developmental process. In R. Glaser (Ed.), *Advances in instructional psychology* (Vol. 2, pp. 1–64). Mahwah, NJ: Erlbaum.

Berenbaum, S. A. (1998). How hormones affect behavioral and neural development: Introduction to the special issue on "Gonadal hormones and sex differences in behavior." *Developmental Neuropsychology, 14,* 175–196.

Berenbaum, S. A., & Hines, M. (1992). Early androgens are related to childhood sex-typed toy preferences. *Psychological Science, 3,* 203–206.

Berg, C. A. (1989). Knowledge of strategies for dealing with everyday problems from childhood through adolescence. *Developmental Psychology, 25,* 607–618.

Berg, C. A., Strough, J., Calderone, K., Meegan, S. P., & Sansone, C. (1997). Planning to prevent everyday problems from occurring. In S. L. Friedman & E. K. Scholnick (Eds.), *The developmental psychology of planning: Why, how and when do we plan?* (pp. 209–236). Mahwah, NJ: Erlbaum.

Berg, N. E., & Mussen, P. (1975). Origins and development of concepts of justice. *Journal of Social Issues, 31,* 183–201.

Berger, L., Brooks-Gunn, J., Paxson, C., & Waldfogel, J. (2008). First-year maternal employment and child outcomes: Differences across racial and ethnic groups. *Children and Youth Services Review, 30,* 365–387.

Berk, L. E. (1994). Why children talk to themselves. *Scientific American, 271,* 78–83.

Berkel, Cady, Murry, Velma McBride, Hurt, Tera R., Chen, Yi-fu, Brody, Gene H., Simons, Ronald L., Cutrona, Carolyn, Gibbons, Frederick X. (2009). It takes a village: Protecting African American youth in the context of racism. *Journal of Youth and Adolescence, 38*(2), 175–188.

Berko, J. (1958). The child's learning of English morphology. *Word, 14,* 150–177.

Bernal, M. E., Knight, G. P., Garza, C. A., Ocampo, K. A., & Cota, M. K. (1990). The development of ethnic identity in Mexican American children. *Hispanic Journal of Behavioral Sciences, 12,* 3–24.

Bernal, M. E., Knight, G. P., Ocampo, K. A., Garza, C. A., & Cota, M. K. (1993). Development of Mexican American identity. In M. E. Bernal & G. P. Knight (Eds.), *Ethnic identity: Formation and transmission among Hispanics and other minorities* (pp. 31–46). Albany: State University of New York Press.

Berndt, T. J. (1979). Developmental changes in conformity to peers and parents. *Developmental Psychology, 15,* 608–616.

Berndt, T. J., Hawkins, J. A., & Jiao, Z. (1999). Influences of friends and friendships on adjustment to junior high school. *Merrill-Palmer Quarterly, 45,* 13–41.

Berninger, V. W., & Richards, T. L. (2002). *Brain literacy for educators and psychologists.* San Diego, CA: Academic Press.

Berrill, K. T. (1990). Anti-gay violence and victimization in the United States: An overview. *Journal of Interpersonal Violence, 5,* 274–294.

Bertenthal, B. I. (1993). Infants' perception of biomechanical motions: Intrinsic image and knowledge-based constraints. In C. Granrud (Ed.), *Visual perception and cognition in infancy* (pp. 175–214). Hillsdale, NJ: Erlbaum.

Bertenthal, B. I., Campos, J. J., & Haith, M. M. (1980). Development of visual organization: The perception of subjective contours. *Child Development, 51,* 1077–1080.

Bertenthal, B. I., Campos, J. J., & Kermoian, R. (1994). An epigenetic perspective on the development of self-produced locomotion and its consequences. *Current Directions in Psychological Science, 5,* 140–145.

Bertenthal, B. I., & Clifton, R. K. (2006). Perception and action. In W. Damon (Series Ed.), D. Kuhn, & R. Siegler (Vol. Eds.), *Handbook of child psychology: Vol. 2. Cognition, perception and language* (6th ed., pp. 51–102). New York: Wiley.

Bertenthal, B. I., Proffitt, D. R., & Kramer, S. J. (1987). Perception of biomechanical motions by infants: Implementation of various processing constraints. *Journal of Experimental Psychology, 13,* 577–585.

Berzonsky, M. D., & Adams, G. R. (1999). Reevaluating the identity status paradigm: Still useful after 35 years. *Developmental Review, 19,* 557–590.

Best, D. L., & Thomas, J. J. (2004). Cultural diversity and cross-cultural perspectives. In A. H. Eagly, A. E. Beall, & R. J. Sternberg (Eds.), *The psychology of gender* (2nd ed., pp. 296–327). New York: Guilford.

Beyer, S. (1995). Maternal employment and children's academic achievement: Parenting styles as mediating variables. *Developmental Review, 15,* 212–253.

Bhanot, R., & Jovanovic, J. (2005). Do parents' academic gender stereotypes influence whether they intrude on their children's homework? *Sex Roles, 52,* 597–607.

Bialystok, E. (2000). Symbolic representation across domains in preschool children. *Journal of Experimental Child Psychology, 76,* 173–189.

Bialystok, E. (2009). Bilingualism: The good, the bad, and the indifferent. *Bilingualism: Language and Cognition, 12,* 3–11.

Bialystok, E., Shenfield, T., & Codd, J. (2000). Languages, scripts, and the environment: Factors in developing concepts of print. *Developmental Psychology, 36,* 66–76.

Biederman, J., Petty, C. R., Dolan, C., Hughes, S., Mick, E., Monuteaux, M. C. et al. (2008). The long-term longitudinal course of oppositional defiant disorder and conduct disorder in ADHD boys: Findings from a controlled 10-year prospective longitudinal follow-up study. *Psychological Medicine, 38,* 1027–1036.

Biederman, J., Rosenbaum, J. F., Hirshfeld, D. R., Faraone, S. V., Bolduc, E. A., Gersten, M., et al. (1990). Psychiatric correlates of behavioral inhibition in young children of parents with and without psychiatric disorders. *Archives of General Psychiatry, 47,* 21–26.

Bierman, K. L., Coie, J. D., Dodge, K. A., Foster, E. M., Greenberg, M. T., Lochman, J. E., et al. (2004). The effects of the Fast Track program on serious problem outcomes at the end of elementary school. *Journal of Clinical Child and Adolescent Psychology, 33,* 650–661.

Bierman, K. L., Coie, J. D., Dodge, K. A., Foster, E. M., Greenberg, M. T., Lochman, J. E. et al. (2007). Fast track randomized controlled trial to prevent externalizing sychiatric disorders: Findings from grades 3 to 9. *Journal of the American Academy of Child & Adolescent Psychiatry, 46,* 1250–1262.

Biernat, M. (1981). Gender stereotypes and the relationship between masculinity and femininity: A developmental analysis. *Journal of Personality & Social Psychology, 61,* 351–365.

Bigelow, B. J. (1977). Children's friendship expectations: A cognitive developmental study. *Child Development, 48,* 246–253.

Bigler, R., & Liben, L. S. (1987). Reformulating children's gender schemata. In L. S. Liben & M. L. Signorella (Eds.), *Children's gender schemata* (New directions in child development, No. 38, pp. 85–109). San Francisco CA: Jossey-Bass.

Bigler, R. S., & Liben, L. S. (1990). The role of attitudes and interventions in gender-schematic processing. *Child Development, 61,* 1440–1452.

Bigler, R. S., & Liben, L. S. (2007). Developmental intergroup theory: Explaining and reducing children's social stereotyping and prejudice. *Current Directions in Psychological Science, 16,* 162–166.

Birch, L. L., & Fisher, J. A. (1996). The role of experience in the development of children's eating behavior. In E. D. Capaldi (Ed.), *Why we eat what we eat: The psychology of eating* (pp. 113–141). Washington, DC: American Psychological Association.

Bird, A., Reese, E., & Tripp, G. (2006). Parent-child talk about past emotional events: Associations with child temperament and goodness-of-fit. *Journal of Cognition and Development, 7,* 189–210.

Bishop, J. B. (2000). An environmental approach to combat binge drinking on college campuses. *Journal of College Student Psychotherapy, 15,* 15–30.

Bithoney, W. G., & Newberger, E. H. (1987). Child and family attributes of failure-to-thrive. *Journal of Developmental and Behavioral Pediatrics, 8,* 32–36.

Bjerregaard, B., & Smith, C. (1993). Gender differences in gang participation, delinquency, and substance use. *Journal of Quantitative Criminology, 9,* 329–355.

Bjorklund, D. F. (1997). The role of immaturity in human development. *Psychological Bulletin, 122,* 153–169.

Bjorklund, D. F. (2007). *Why youth is* not *wasted on the young: Immaturity in human development.* Oxford: Blackwell

Bjorklund, D. F., Miller, P. H., Coyle, T. R., & Slawinsky, J. L. (1997). Instructing children to use memory strategies: Evidence of utilization deficiencies in memory training studies. *Developmental Review, 17,* 411–442.

Bjorklund, D. F., & Pellegrini, A. D. (2002). *The origins of human nature: Evolutionary developmental psychology.* Washington, DC: American Psychological Association.

Bjorkqvist, K., & Niemela, P. (Eds.) (1992). *Of mice and women: Aspects of female aggression.* San Diego, CA: Academic Press.

Bjorkqvist, K., Osterman, K., & Kaukiainen, A. (1992). The development of direct and indirect aggressive strategies in males and females. In K. Bjorkqvist & P. Niemela (Eds.), *Of mice and women: Aspects of female aggression* (pp. 51–64). San Diego, CA: Academic Press.

Blachman, B. A., Schatschneider, C., Fletcher, J. M., Francis, D. J., Clonan, S. M., Shaywitz, B. A., & Shaywitz, S. E. (2004). Effects of intensive reading remediation for second and third graders and a 1-year follow-up. *Journal of Educational Psychology, 96,* 444–461.

Black, B., & Logan, A. (1995). Links between communication patterns in mother-child, father-child, and child-peer interactions and children's social status. *Child Development, 66,* 255–271.

Blackwell, L. S., Trzesniewski, K. H., & Dweck, C. S. (2007). Implicit theories of intelligence predict achievement across an adolescent transition: A longitudinal study and an intervention. *Child Development, 78,* 246–263.

Blair, K. A., Denham, S. A., Kochanoff, A., & Whipple, B. (2004). Playing it cool: Temperament, emotion regulation, and social behavior in preschoolers. *Journal of School Psychology, 42,* 419–443.

Blair, C., Granger, D. A., Kivlighan, K. T., Mills-Koonce, R., Willoughby, M., Greenberg, M. T., Hibel, L. C., Fortunato, C. K., & Family Life Project Investigators. (2008). Maternal and child contributions to cortisol response to emotional arousal in young children from low-income, rural communities. *Developmental Psychology, 44,* 1095–1109.

Blair, C., & Razza, R. P. (2007). Relating effortful control, executive function, and false belief understanding to emerging math and literacy ability in kindergarten. *Child Development, 78,* 647–663.

Blakemore, J. E. O., Berenbaum, S. A., & Liben, L. S. (2009). *Gender development.* Mahwah, NJ: Erlbaum.

Blakemore, S.-J., & Choudhury, S. (2006). Development of the adolescent brain: Implications for executive function and social cognition. *Journal of Child Psychology and Psychiatry, 47,* 296–312.

Blandon, A. Y., Calkins, S. D., Keane, S. P., & O'Brien, M. (2008). Individual differences in trajectories of emotion regulation processes: The effects of maternal depressive symptomatology and children's physiological regulation. *Developmental Psychology, 44,* 1110–1123.

Blasi, A. (1980). Bridging moral cognition and moral action: A critical review of the literature. *Psychological Bulletin, 88,* 1–45.

Blass, E. M. (1990). Suckling: Determinants, changes, mechanisms, and lasting impressions. *Developmental Psychology, 26,* 520–533.

Blass, E. M., & Camp, C. A. (2003). Biological bases of face preference in 6-week-old infants. *Developmental Science, 6,* 524–536.

Blass, E. M., & Hoffmeyer, L. B. (1991). Sucrose as an analgesic in newborn humans. *Pediatrics, 87,* 215–218.

Blass, E. M., & Teicher, M. H. (1980). Suckling. *Science, 210,* 15–22.

Blauw-Hospers, C. H., & Hadders-Algra, M. A. (2005). A systematic review of the effects of early intervention on motor development. *Developmental Medicine & Child Neurology, 47,* 421–432.

Bleeker, M. M. & Jacobs, J. E. (2004). Achievement in math and science: Do mothers' beliefs matter 12 years later. *Journal of Educational Psychology, 96,* 97–109.

Block, J. H., Block, J., & Gjerde, P. F. (1986). The personality of children prior to divorce: A prospective study. *Child Development, 57,* 827–840.

Bloom, L. (1970). *Language development: Form and function in emerging grammars.* Cambridge, MA: The MIT Press.

Bloom, L. (1975). Language development. In F. Horowitz (Ed.), *Review of child development research* (Vol. 4, pp. 245–303). Chicago: University of Chicago Press.

Bloom, L. (1991). *Language development from two to three.* Cambridge, UK: Cambridge University Press.

Bloom, L. (1998). Language acquisition in its developmental context. In D. Kuhn & R. S. Siegler (Eds.), *Handbook of child psychology,. Vol. 2. Cognition, perception, and language.* (5th ed.) New York: Wiley.

Bloom, L., Rocissano, L., & Hood, L. (1976). Adult-child discourse: Developmental interaction between information processing and linguistic knowledge. *Cognitive Psychology, 8,* 521–552.

Bloom, L., & Tinker, E. (2001). The intentionality model and language acquisition: Engagement, effort, and the essential tension in development. *Monographs of the Society for Research in Child Development, 66*(4, Serial No. 267).

Bloom, P. (2004). *Descartes' baby: How the science of child development explains what makes us human.* New York: Basic Books.

Boden, J. M., Fergusson, D. M., & Horwood, L. J. (2008). Does adolescent self-esteem predict later life outcomes? A test of the causal role of self-esteem. *Development and Psychopathology, 20,* 319–339.

Bohlin, G., Hagekull, B., & Rydell, A-M. (2000). Attachment and social functioning: A longitudinal study from infancy to middle childhood. *Social Development, 9,* 24–39.

Bohon, C., Stice, E., Burton, E., Fudell, M., Nolen-Hoeksema, S. (2008). A prospective study of cognitive vulnerability models of depression with adolescent girls. *Behavior Therapy, 39,* 79–90.

Boismeyer, J. D. (1977). Visual stimulation and wake-sleep behavior in human neonates. *Developmental Psychobiology, 10,* 219–227.

Bokhorst, C. L., Bakermans-Kranenburg, M. J., Fearon, R. M., van IJzendoorn, M. H., Fonagy, P., & Schuengel, C. (2003). The importance of shared environment in mother-infant attachment security: A behavioral genetic study. *Child Development, 74,* 1769–1782.

Boland, A. M., Haden, C. A., & Ornstein, P. A. (2003). Boosting children's memory by training mothers in the use of an elaborative conversational style as events unfold. *Journal of Cognition and Development, 4,* 39–64.

Bolger, K. E., & Patterson, C. J. (2001). Developmental pathways from child maltreatment to peer rejection. *Child Developmental, 72,* 549–568.

Bolger, K. E., & Scarr, S. (1995). Not so far from home: How family characteristics predict child care quality. *Early Development and Parenting, 4,* 103–112.

Bonica, C., Arnold, D. H., Fisher, P. H., Zeljo, A., & Yershova, K. (2003). Relational aggression, relational victimization, and language development in preschoolers. *Social Development, 12,* 551–562.

Bonner, J. T. (1988). *The evolution of culture in animals.* Princeton, NJ: Princeton University Press.

Book, A. S., Starzyk, K. B., & Quinsey, V. L. (2001). The relationship between testosterone and aggression: A meta-analysis. *Aggression and Violent Behavior, 6,* 579–599.

Booth, J. L., & Siegler, R. S. (2006). Developmental and individual differences in pure numerical estimation. *Developmental Psychology, 41,* 189–201.

Booth, J. L., & Siegler, R. S. (2008). Numerical magnitude representations influence arithmetic learning. *Child Development, 79,* 1016–1031.

Booth-LaForce, C., & Oxford, M. (2008). Trajectories of social withdrawal from grades 1 to 6: Prediction from early parenting, attachment, and temperament. *Developmental Psychology, 144,* 1298–1313.

Borge, A. I. H., Rutter, M., Côté, S., & Tremblay, R. E. (2004). Early childcare and physical aggression: Differentiating social selection and social causation. Journal of Child Psychology and Psychiatry, 45, 367–376.

Borke, H. (1971). Interpersonal perception of young children: Egocentrism or empathy? *Developmental Psychology, 5,* 263–269.

Bornstein, M. H. (1975). Qualities of color vision in infancy. *Journal of Experimental Child Psychology, 19,* 401–419.

Bornstein, M. H. (2006). On the significance of social relationships in the development of children's earliest symbolic play: An ecological perspective. In A. Göncü & S. Gaskins (Eds.), *Play and development: Evolutionary, sociocultural, and functional perspectives* (pp. 101–130). Mahwah, NJ: Erlbaum.

Bornstein, M. H., & Bradley, R. H. (Eds.) (2003). *Socioeconomic status, parenting, and child development.* Mahwah, NJ: Erlbaum.

Bornstein, M. H., Kessen, W., & Weiskopf, S. (1976). Color vision and hue categorization in young human infants. *Journal of Experimental Psychology: Human Perceptions and Performance, 2,* 115–129.

Borstelmann, L. J. (1983). Children before psychology: Ideas about children from antiquity to the late 1800s. In P. H. Mussen (Series Ed.) & W. Kessen (Vol. Ed.), *Handbook of child psychology: Vol. 1. History, theory, and methods* (4th ed., pp. 1–40). New York: Wiley.

Bortfeld, H., Morgan, J., Golinkoff, R., & Rathbun, K. (2005). Mommy and me: Familiar names help launch babies into speech stream segmentation. *Psychological Science, 16,* 298–304.

Bos, H. M. W., Sandfort, T. G. M., de Bruyn, E. H., & Hakvoort, E. M. (2008). Same-sex attraction, social relationships, psychosocial functioning, and school performance in early adolescence. *Developmental Psychology, 44,* 59–68.

Bos, H. M. W., & van Balen, F. (2008). Children in planned lesbian families: Stigmatisation, psychological adjustment and protective factors. *Culture, Health & Sexuality, 10,* 221–236.

Bosma, H. A., & Kunnen, E. S. (2001). Determinants and mechanisms in ego identity development: A review and synthesis. *Developmental Review, 21,* 39–66.

Bouchard Jr., T. J. (2004). Genetic influence on human psychological traits: A survey. *Current Directions in Psychological Science, 13,* 148–151.

Bouchard, T. J., Jr., Lykken, D. T., McGue, M., Segal, N. L., & Tellegen, A. (1990). Sources of human psychological differences: The Minnesota Study of Twins Reared Apart. *Science, 250,* 223–228.

Bound, J., Duncan, G. J., Laren, D. S., & Oleinick, L. (1991). Poverty dynamics in widowhood. *Journals of Gerontology, 46,* S115–S124.

Bowerman, M. (1978). The acquisition of word meaning: An investigation into some current conflicts. In N. Waterson & C. Snow (Eds.), *The development of communication.* Chichester, England, Wiley.

Bowerman, M. (1979). The acquisition of complex sentences. In P. Fletcher & M. Garman (Eds.), *Language acquisition* (pp. 285–306). Cambridge, UK: Cambridge University Press.

Bowker, A., Bukowski, W. M., Zargarpour, S., & Hoza, B. (1998). A structural and functional analysis of a two-dimensional model of social isolation. *Merrill-Palmer Quarterly, 44*, 447–463.

Bowlby, J. (1953). *Child care and the growth of love*. London: Penguin Books.

Bowlby, J. (1969). *Attachment and loss: Vol. 1. Attachment*. New York: Basic Books.

Bowlby, J. (1973). *Attachment and loss: Vol. 2. Separation*. New York: Basic Books.

Bowlby, J. (1980). *Attachment and loss: Vol. 3. Loss: Sadness and depression*. New York: Basic Books.

Boysson-Bardies, B. de (1999). *How language comes to children: From birth to two years* (M. DeBevoise, Trans.). Cambridge, MA: The MIT Press. (Original work published 1996.)

Boysson-Bardies, B. de, Sagart, L., & Durant, C. (1984). Discernable differences in the babbling of infants according to target language. *Journal of Child Language, 11,* 1–15.

Bozett, F. W. (1980). *A secure base: Parent-child attachment and healthy human development*. New York: Basic Books.

Bozett, F. W. (1987). Children of gay fathers. In F. W. Bozett (Ed.), *Gay and lesbian parents* (pp. 39–57). New York: Praeger.

Braaksma, M. A. H., Rijlaarsdam, G., van den Bergh, H., van Hout-Wolters, B. H. A. M. (2004). Observational learning and its effects on the orchestration of writing process. *Cognition and Instruction, 22*, 1–36.

Brackbill, Y., McManus, K., & Woodward, L. (1985). *Medication in maternity: Infant exposure and maternal information*. Ann Arbor: University of Michigan Press.

Bradbard, M. R., Martin, C. L., Endsley, R. C., & Halverson, C. F. (1986). Influence of sex stereotypes on children's exploration and memory: A competence versus performance distinction. *Developmental Psychology, 22,* 481–486.

Bradley, R. H. (1989). The use of the HOME inventory in longitudinal studies of child development. In M. H. Bornstein & N. A. Krasnegor (Eds.), *Stability and continuity in mental development: Behavioral and biological perspectives* (pp. 191–215). Mahwah, NJ: Erlbaum.

Bradley, R. H. (1994). The HOME Inventory: Review and reflections. In H. W. Reese (Ed.), *Advances in child development and behavior* (Vol. 25, pp. 241–288). San Diego, CA: Academic Press.

Bradley, R. H., Corwyn, R. F., Burchinal, M., McAdoo, H. P., & Coll, C. G. (2001). The home environments of children in the United States: Part II: Relations with behavioral development through age thirteen. *Child Development, 72*, 1868–1886.

Bradley, R. H., Whiteside, L., Mundfrom, D. J., Casey, P. H., Kelleher, K. J., & Pope, S. K. (1994). Contribution of early intervention and early caregiving experiences to resilience in low-birthweight, premature children living in poverty. *Journal of Clinical Child Psychology, 23*, 425–434.

Braine, M. D. S. (1963). The ontogeny of English phrase structure. *Language, 39,* 1–13.

Braine, M. D. S. (1976). Review of *The acquisition of phonology* by N. V. Smith. *Language, 52,* 489–498.

Bramlett, M. D., & Mosher, W. D. (2002). Cohabition, marriage, divorce, and remarriage in the United States. National Center for Health Statistics. *Vital Health Statistics, 23* (22).

Brannon, E. M. (2002). The development of ordinal numerical knowledge in infancy. *Cognition, 83*, 223–240.

Brannon, E. M. (2006). The representation of numerical magnitude. *Current Opinion in Neurobiology, 16*, 222–229.

Brannon, E. M., Suanda, S., & Libertus, K. (2007). Temporal discrimination increases in precision over development and parallels the development of numerosity discrimination. *Developmental Science, 10*, 770–777.

Braver, S. L., Ellman, I. M., & Fabricius, W. V. (2003). Relocation of children after divorce and children's best interests: New evidence and legal considerations. *Journal of Family Psychology, 17*, 206–219.

Bray, J. H., Adams, G. J., Getz, J. G., & McQueen, A. (2003). Individuation, peers, and adolescent alcohol use: A latent growth analysis. *Journal of Consulting and Clinical Psychology, 71,* 553–564.

Bray, J. H., & Berger, S. H. (1993). Developmental issues in Stepfamilies Research Project: Family relationships and parent-child interactions. *Journal of Family Psychology, 7*, 76–90.

Brazelton, T. B., Nugent, J. K., & Lester, B. M. (1987). Neonatal Behavioral Assessment Scale. In J. D. Osofsky (Ed.), *Handbook of infant development* (2nd ed., pp. 780–817). New York: Wiley.

Breazeal, C. L. (2002). *Designing sociable robots*. Cambridge, MA: The MIT Press.

Bremner, J. G., Knowles, L., & Andreasen, G. (1994). Processes underlying young children's spatial orientation during movement. *Journal of Experimental Child Psychology, 57*, 355–376.

Brendgen, M., Boivin, M., Vitaro, F., Bukowski, W.M., Dionne, G., Tremnlay, R. E. et al. (2008). Linkages between children's and their friends' social and physical aggression: Evidence for a gene-environment interaction? *Child Development, 70*, 13–29.

Brendgen, M., Vitaro, F., & Bukowski, W. M. (2000). Deviant friends and early adolescents' emotional and behavioral adjustment. *Journal of Research on Adolescence, 10*, 173–189.

Brendgen, M., Vitaro, F., Bukowski, W. M., Boyle, A. B., & Markiewicz, C. (2001). Developmental profiles of peer social preference over the course of elementary school: Associations with trajectories of externalizing and internalizing behavior. *Developmental Psychology, 37,* 308–320.

Brennan, P. A., Hammen, C., Katz, A. R., & Le Brocque, R. M. (2002). Maternal depression, paternal psychopathology, and adolescent diagnostic outcomes. *Journal of Consulting and Clinical Psychology, 70*, 1075–1085.

Brenner, E. M., & Salovey, P. (1997). Emotion regulation during childhood: Developmental, interpersonal, and individual considerations. In P. Salovey & D. Sluyter (Eds.), *Teaching in the heart of the classroom: Emotional development, emotional literacy, and emotional intelligence* (pp. 168–192). New York: Basic Books.

Bretherton, I., & Beeghly, M. (1982). Talking about internal states: The acquisition of an explicit theory of mind. *Developmental Psychology, 18,* 906–921.

Bretherton, I., Golby, B., & Cho, E. Y. (1997). Attachment and the transmission of values. In J. E. Grusec & L. Kuczynski (Eds.), *Parenting and children's internalization of values* (pp. 103–134). New York: Wiley.

Bretherton, I., & Munholland, K. A. (1999). Internal working models in attachment relationships: A construct revisited. In J. Cassidy & P. R. Shaver (Eds.), *Handbook of attachment: Theory, research, and clinical implications* (pp. 89–111). New York: Guilford.

Bretherton, I., & Page, T. F. (2004). Shared or conflicting working models? Relationships in postdivorce families seen through the eyes of mothers and their preschool children. *Development and Psychopathology, 16,* 551–575.

Brewis, A., Schmidt, K. L. & Casas, C. A. S. (2003). Cross-cultural study of the childhood developmental trajectory of attention and impulse control. *International Journal of Behavioral Development,* 27, 2, 174–181.

Bridges, L. J., & Grolnick, W. S. (1995). The development of emotional self-regulation in infancy and early childhood. In N. Eisenberg (Ed.), *Review of personality and psychology: Vol. 15. Social development* (pp. 185–211). Thousand Oaks, CA: Sage.

Bril, B., & Sabatier, C. (1986). The cultural context of motor development: Postural manipulations in the daily life of Bambara babies (Mali). *International Journal of Behavioral Development, 9,* 439–453.

Broaders, S. C., Cook, S. W., Mitchell, Z., & Goldin-Meadow, S. (2007). Making children gesture brings out implicit knowledge and leads to learning. *Journal of Experimental Psychology: General, 136,* 539–550.

Brody, G. H., & Ge, X. (2001). Linking parenting processes and self-regulation to psychological functioning and alcohol use during early adolescence. *Journal of Family Psychology, 15,* 82–94.

Brody, G. H., Ge, X., Kim, S. Y., Murry, V. M., Simons, R. L., Gibbons, F. X., et al. (2003). Neighborhood disadvantage moderates associations of parenting and older sibling problem attitudes and behavior with conduct disorders in African American children. *Journal of Consulting and Clinical Psychology, 71,* 211–222.

Brody, G. H., Stoneman, Z., Flor, D., McCrary, C., Hastings, L., & Conyers, O. (1994). Financial resources, parent psychological functioning, parent co-caregiving, and early adolescent competence in rural two-parent African-American families. *Child Development, 65,* 590–605.

Brody, G. H., Stoneman, Z., MacKinnon, C. E., & MacKinnon, R. (1985). Role relationships and behavior between preschool-aged and school-aged sibling pairs. *Developmental Psychology, 21,* 124–129.

Brody, G. H., Stoneman, Z., & McCoy, J. K. (1994). Forecasting sibling relationships in early adolescence from child temperament and family processes in middle childhood. *Child Development, 65,* 771–784.

Brody, G. H., Stoneman, Z., McCoy, J. K., & Forehand, R. (1992). Contemporaneous and longitudinal associations of sibling conflict with family relationship assessments and family discussions about sibling problems. *Child Development, 63,* 391–400.

Brody, N. (1992). *Intelligence* (2nd ed.). San Diego, CA. Academic Press.

Broidy, L. M., Nagin, D. S., Tremblay, R. E., Bates, J. E., Brame, B., Dodge, K. A., Fergusson, D., Horwood, J. L., Loeber, R., Laird, R., Lynam, D. R., Moffitt, T., & Pettit, G. S., & Vitaro, F. (2003). Developmental trajectories of childhood disruptive behaviors and adolescent delinquency: A six-site, cross-national study. *Developmental Psychology, 39,* 222–245.

Bronfenbrenner, U. (1979). *The ecology of human development: Experiments by nature and design.* Cambridge, MA: Harvard University Press.

Bronfenbrenner, U. (1993). The ecology of cognitive development: Research models and fugitive findings. In R. H. Wozniak & K. W. Fisher (Eds.), *Development in context* (pp. 3–44). Hillsdale, NJ: Erlbaum.

Bronfenbrenner, U., & Morris, P. A. (1998). The ecology of developmental processes. In R. M. Lerner (Ed.), *Handbook of child psychology: vol. 1. Theoretical models of human development* (5th ed., pp. 535–584). New York: Wiley.

Bronfenbrenner, U. & Morris, P. A. (2006). The bioecological model of human development. In R. M. Lerner (Ed.), *Handbook of child psychology: Vol. 1: Theoretical models of human development* (6th edition, pp. 297–342). Hoboken, NJ: Wiley.

Bronson, G. W. (1972). Infants' reactions to unfamiliar persons and novel objects. *Monographs of the Society for Research in Child Development, 37*(3, Serial No. 148).

Brooks, R., & Meltzoff, A. N. (2008). Infant gaze following and pointing predict accelerated vocabulary growth through two years of age: A longitudinal, growth curve modeling study. *Journal of Child Language, 35,* 207–220.

Brooks-Gunn, J. (1987). Pubertal processes and girls' psychological adaptation. In R. M. Lerner & T. L. Foch (Eds.), *Biological psychosocial interactions in early adolescence.* Hillsdale NJ: Erlbaum.

Brooks-Gunn, J. (2003). Do you believe in Magic?: What we can expect from early childhood intervention programs. *Social Policy Report, 17,* 3–14.

Brooks-Gunn, J., Han, W. J., & Waldfogel, J. (2002). Maternal employment and child cognitive outcomes in the first three years of life: The NICHD study of early child care. *Child Development, 73,* 1052–1072.

Brophy-Herb, H. E., Lee, R. E., Nievar, M. A., & Stollak, G. (2007). Preschoolers' social competence: Relations to family characteristics, teacher behaviors and classroom climate. *Journal of Applied Developmental Psychology, 28,* 134–148.

Broughton, J. M. (1978). The development of the concepts of self, mind, reality, and knowledge. In W. Damon (Ed.), *New directions for child development: Social cognition* (pp. 75–100). San Francisco: Jossey-Bass.

Brown, A. L. (1997). Transforming schools into communities of thinking and learning about serious matters. *American Psychologist, 52,* 300–413.

Brown, A. S., Begg, M. D., Gravenstein, S., Schaefer, C. A., Wyatt, R. J., Bresnahan, M., Babulas, V. P., & Susser, E. S. (2004). Serologic evidence of prenatal influenza in the etiology of schizophrenia. *Archives of General Psychiatry, 61,* 774–780.

Brown, B. B. (1990). Peer groups and peer cultures. In S. S. Feldman & G. R. Elliott (Eds.), *At the threshold: The developing adolescent* (pp. 171–196). Cambridge, MA: Harvard University Press.

Brown, B. B. (2004). Adolescents' relationships with peers. In R. M. Lerner & L. Steinberg (Eds.), *Handbook of Adolescent Psychology* (2nd ed.; pp. 363–394). New York: Wiley.

Brown, B. B., Clasen, D. R., & Eicher, S. A. (1986). *Developmental Psychology, 22,* 521–530.

Brown, B. B. & Klute, C. (2003). Friends, cliques, and crowds. In G. R. Adams & M. D. Berzonsky (Eds.), *Blackwell Handbook of Adolescence* (pp. 330–348). Malden, MA: Blackwell.

Brown, B. B., von Bank, H., & Steinberg, L. (2008). Smoke in the looking glass: Effects of discordance between self- and peer rated crowd affiliation on adolescent anxiety, depression and self-feelings. *Journal of Youth and Adolescence, 37,* 1163–1177.

Brown, C. S., & Bigler, R. S. (2004). Children's perceptions of gender discrimination. *Developmental Psychology, 40,* 714–726.

Brown, C. S., & Bigler, R. S. (2005). Children's perceptions of discrimination: A developmental model. *Child Development, 76,* 533–553.

Brown, J. L., & Pollitt, E. (1996, February). Malnutrition, poverty, and intellectual development. *Scientific American,* 38–43.

Brown, J. R., & Dunn, J. (1996). Continuities in emotion understanding from three to six years. *Child Development, 67,* 789–802.

Brown, R. (1957). Linguistic determinism and the part of speech. *Journal of Abnormal and Social Psychology, 55,* 1–5.

Brown, R. (1973). *A first language: The early stages.* Cambridge, MA: Harvard University Press.

Brown, R., & Fraser, C. (1963). The acquisition of syntax. In C. N. Cofer & B. S. Musgrave (Eds.), *Verbal behavior and learning* (pp. 158–196). New York: McGraw-Hill.

Brown, R., & Hanlon, C. (1970). Derivational complexity and order of acquisition in child speech. In J. R. Hayes (Ed.), *Cognition and the development of language* (pp. 11–53). New York: Wiley.

Brownell, C. A., Ramani, G. B., & Zerwas, S. (2006). Becoming a social partner with peers: Cooperation and social understanding in one- and two-year-olds. *Child Development, 77,* 803–821.

Brownell, C. A., Zerwas, S., & Ramani, G. B. (2007). "So big": The development of body self-awareness in toddlers. *Child Development, 78,* 1426–1440.

Brownell, K. D. (2003). Diet, obesity, public policy, and defiance. In R. J. Sternberg (Ed.), *Psychologists defying the crowd: Stories of those who battled the establishment and won* (pp. 47–64). Washington, DC: American Psychological Association.

Brownell, K. D. (2004). Overfeeding the future. In A. Heintzman & E. Solomon (Eds.), *Feeding the future, from fat to famine: How to solve the world's food crises.* Toronto: Anansi.

Bruck, M., Ceci, S. J., Francoeur, E., & Renick, A. (1995). Anatomically detailed dolls do not facilitate preschoolers' reports of a pediatric examination involving genital touching. *Journal of Experimental Psychology, 1,* 95–109.

Bruck, M., Ceci, S. J., & Principe, G. F. (2006). The child and the law. In W. Damon & R. M. Lerner (Book Eds.) & K. A. Renninger & I. E. Sigel (Vol. Eds.), *Handbook of child psychology: Vol. 4. Child psychology in practice* (6th ed., pp. 776–816). New York: Wiley.

Bruner, J. S. (1973). *Beyond the information given: Studies in the psychology of knowing.* New York: Norton.

Bruner, J. S. (1975). The ontogenesis of speech acts. *Journal of Child Language, 2,* 1–19.

Bruner, J. S. (1977). Early social interaction and language acquisition. In H. R. Schaffer (Ed.), *Studies in mother-infant interaction* (pp. 271–289). London: Academic Press.

Bruner, J. S. (1996). *The culture of education.* Cambridge, MA: Harvard University Press.

Bryan, J. H., & Walbek, N. H. (1970). Preaching and practicing generosity: Children's actions and reactions. *Child Development, 41,* 329–353.

Buchanan, C. M., Eccles, J. S., & Becker, M. B. (1992). Are adolescents the victims of raging hormones: Evidence for activational effects of hormones on moods and behavior at adolescence. *Psychological Bulletin, 111,* 62–107.

Buchanan, C. M., Maccoby, E. E., & Dornbusch, S. M. (1991). Caught between parents: Adolescents' experience in divorced families. *Child Development, 62,* 1008–1029.

Buchanan, C. M., Maccoby, E. E., & Dornbusch, S. M. (1996). *Adolescents after divorce.* Cambridge, MA: Harvard University Press.

Buckner, J. C., Bassuk, E. L., Weinreb, L. F., & Brooks, M. G. (1999). Homelessness and its relation to the mental health and behavior of low-income school-age children. *Developmental Psychology, 35,* 246–257.

Buehler, C., Anthony, C., Krishnakumar, A., Stonge, G., Gerard, J., & Pemberton, S. (1997). Interparental conflict and youth problem behaviors: A meta-analysis. *Journal of Child and Family Studies, 6,* 233–247.

Buehler, C., Lange, G., & Franck, K. L. (2007). Adoelscents' cognitive and emotional responses to marital hostility. *Child Development, 78,* 775–789.

Bugental, D. B. (2003). *Thriving in the face of childhood adversity.* New York: Psychology Press.

Bugental, D. B., Blue, J. B., & Cruzcosa, M. (1989). Perceived control over caregiving outcomes: Implications for child abuse. *Developmental Psychology, 25,* 532–539.

Bugental, D. B., Ellerson, P. C., Lin, E. K., Rainey, B., Kokotovic, A., & O'Hara, N. O. (2002). A cognitive approach to child abuse prevention. *Journal of Family Psychology, 16,* 243–258.

Bugental, D. B., & Happaney, K. (2004). Predicting infant maltreatment in low-income families: The interactive effects of maternal attributions and child status at birth. *Developmental Psychology, 40,* 234–243.

Bugental, D. B., & Johnston, C. (2000). Parental and child cognitions in the context of the family. In S. T. Fiske, D. L. Schacter, & C. Zahn-Waxler (Eds.), *Annual Review of Psychology, 51,* 315–344.

Bugental, D. B., Martorell, G. A., & Barraza, V. (2003). The hormonal costs of subtle forms of infant maladjustment. *Hormones and Behavior, 43,* 237–244.

Bukowski, W. M., Gauze, C., Hoza, B., & Newcomb, A. F. (1993). Differences and consistency between same-sex and other-sex peer relationships during early adolescence. *Developmental Psychology, 29,* 255–263.

Bukowski, W. M., Newcomb, A. F., & Hartup, W. W. (1996). Friendship and its significance in childhood and adolescence: Introduction and comment. In W. M. Bukowski, A. F. Newcomb, & W. W. Hartup (Eds.), *The company they keep: Friendship in childhood and adolescence* (pp. 1–15). Cambridge, UK: Cambridge University Press.

Bullock, M., & Lutkenhaus, P. (1990). Who am I? Self-understanding in toddlers. *Merrill-Palmer Quarterly, 36,* 217–238.

Bullock, M., & Russell, J. A. (1985). Further evidence on preschoolers' interpretation of facial expressions. *International Journal of Behavioral Development, 8,* 15–38.

Bumpass, L. L., Martin, T. C., & Sweet, J. A. (1991). The impact of family background and early marital factors on marital disruption. *Journal of Family Issues, 12,* 22–42.

Burchinal, M. R., Campbell, F. A., Bryant, D. M., Wasik, B. H., & Ramey, C. T. (1997). Early intervention and mediating processes in cognitive performance of children of low-income African American families. *Child Development, 68,* 935–954.

Burchinal, M. R., & Clarke-Stewart, K. A. (2007). Maternal employment and child cognitive outcomes: The importance of analytic approach. *Developmental Psychology, 43,* 1140–1155.

Burgess, K. B., Marshall, P., Rubin, K. H., & Fox, N. A. (2003) Infant attachment and temperament as predictors of subsequent behavior problems and psychophysiological functioning. *Journal of Child Psychology and Psychiatry and Allied Disciplines, 44,* 1–13.

Burkam, D. T., Lee, V. T., & Smerdon, B. A. (1997). Gender and science learning early in high school: Subject matter and laboratory experiences. *American Educational Research Journal, 34,* 297–331.

Burleson, B. R. (1982). The development of comforting communication skills in childhood and adolescence. *Child Development, 53,* 1578–1588.

Burmeister, D. (1996). Need fulfillment, interpersonal competence, and the developmental contexts of early adolescent friendship. In W. M. Bukowski, A. F. Newcomb, & W. W. Hartup (Eds), *The company they keep. Friendship in childhood and adolescence* (pp. 66–86). Cambridge, UK: Cambridge University Press.

Burt, S. A., Barnes, A. R., McGue, M., & Iacono, W. G. (2008). Parental divorce and adolescent delinquency: Ruling out the impact of common genes. *Developmental Psychology, 44,* 1668–1677.

Burt, S. A., McGue, M., Krueger, R. F., & Iacono, W. G. (2005). How are parent-child conflict and childhood externalizing symptoms related over time? Results from a genetically informative cross-lagged study. *Development and Psychopathology, 17,* 145–165.

Busch, A. L., Cowan, P. A., & Cowan, C. P. (2008). Unresolved loss in the adult attachment interview: Implications for marital and parenting relationships. *Development and Psychopathology, 20,* 717–735.

Bushnell, E. W., & Boudreau, J. P. (1991). The development of haptic perception during infancy. In M. A. Heller & W. Schiff (Eds.), *The psychology of touch* (pp. 139–161). Hillsdale, NJ: Erlbaum.

Bushnell, E. W., McKenzie, B. E., Lawrence, D. A., & Connell, S. (1995). The spatial coding strategies of 1-year-old infants in a locomotor search task. *Child Development, 66,* 937–958.

Bushnell, I. W. R. (1998). The origins of face perception. In F. Simion & G. Butterworth (Eds.), *The development of sensory, motor, and cognitive capacities in early infancy: From perception to cognition* (pp. 69–86). Hove, UK: Psychology Press.

Bushnell, I. W. R., Sai, F., & Mullin, J. T. (1989). Neonatal recognition of the mother's face. *British Journal of Developmental Psychology, 7,* 3–15.

Buss, D. M. (1999). *Evolutionary Psychology: The New Science of the Mind.* Boston: Allyn & Bacon.

Buss, K. A., Davidson, R. J., Kalin, N. H., & Goldsmith, H. H. (2004). Context-specific freezing and associated physiological reactivity as a dysregulated fear response. *Developmental Psychology, 40,* 583–594.

Busseri, M. A., Willoughby, T., Chalmers, H., & Bogaert, A. F. (2008). On the association between sexual attraction and adolescent risk behavior involvement: Examining mediation and moderation. *Developmental Psychology, 44,* 69–80.

Bussey, K., & Bandura, A. (1992). Self-regulatory mechanisms governing gender development. *Child Development, 63,* 1236–1250.

Bussey, K., & Bandura, A. (1999). Social cognitive theory of gender development and differentiation. *Psychological Review, 106,* 676–713.

Buttelmann, D., Carpenter, M., Call, J., & Tomasello, M. (2008). Rational tool use and tool choice in human infants and great apes. *Child Development, 79,* 609–626.

Butterworth, G. E. (1998). What is special about pointing in babies? In F. Simion & G. Butterworth (Eds.), *The development of sensory, motor and cognitive capacities in early infancy: From perception to cognition* (pp. 171–190). Hove, UK: Psychology Press/Erlbaum.

Butterworth, G. E., & Grover, L. (1988). The origins of referential communication in human infancy. In L. Weiskrantz (Ed.), *Thought without language* (pp. 5–24). Oxford, UK: Clarendon Press.

Byrnes, J. P., Miller, D. C. & Schafer, W. D. (1999). Gender differences in risk taking: A meta-analysis. *Psychological Bulletin, 125,* 367–383.

Cahan, S., & Cahan, N. (1989). Age versus schooling effects on intelligence development. *Child Development, 60,* 1239–1249.

Cahill, L. (2005). His brain, her brain. *Scientific American, 292*(5), 41–47.

Cai, H., Brown, J. D., Deng, C., & Oakes, M. A. (2007). Self-esteem and culture; Differences in cognitive self-evaluations or affective self-regard? *Asian Journal of Social Psychology, 10,* 162–170.

Cain, K. M., & Dweck, C. S. (1995). The relation between motivational patterns and achievement cognitions through the elementary years. *Merrill-Palmer Quarterly, 41,* 25–52.

Cairns, R. B., Cairns, B. D., Neckerman, H. J., Ferguson, L. L., & Gariepy, J. L. (1989). Growth and aggression: 1. Childhood to early adolescence. *Developmental Psychology, 25,* 320–330.

Cairns, R. B., Leung, M-C., Buchanan, L., & Cairns, B. D. (1995). Friendships and social networks in childhood and adolescence: Fluidity, reliability, and interrelations. *Child Development, 66,* 1330–1345.

Caldwell, B. M., & Bradley, R. (1979). *Home observation for measurement of the environment.* Unpublished manuscript, University of Arkansas, Little Rock.

Caldwell, C. H., Zimmerman, M. A., Bernat, D. H., Sellers, R. M., & Notaro, P. C. (2002). Racial identity, maternal support, and psychological distress among African American adolescents. *Child Development, 73,* 1322–1336.

Caldwell, M. S., Rudolph, K. D., Troop-Gordon, W., & Kim, D-Y. (2004). Reciprocal influences among relational self-views, social disengagement, and peer stress during early adolescence. *Child Development, 75,* 1140–1154.

Calkins, S. D. (1997). Cardiac vagal tone indices of temperamental reactivity and behavioral regulation in young children. *Developmental Psychobiology, 31,* 125–135.

Calkins, S. D. (2002). Does aversive behavior during toddlerhood matter? The effects of difficult temperament on maternal perceptions and behavior. *Infant Mental Health Journal, 23,* 381–402.

Calkins, S. D., & Dedmon, S. E. (2000). Physiological and behavioral regulation in two-year-old children with aggressive/destructive behavior problems. *Journal of Abnormal Child Psychology, 28,* 103–118.

Calkins, S. D., Fox, N. A., & Marshall, T. R. (1996). Behavioral and physiological antecedents of inhibited and uninhibited behavior. *Child Development, 67,* 523–540.

Calkins, S. D. & Keane, S. P. (2004). Cardiac vagal regulation across the preschool period: Stability, continuity, and implications for childhood adjustment. *Developmental Psychobiology, 45,* 101–112.

Callaghan, T., Rochat, P., Lillard, A., Claux, M. L., Odden, H., Itakura, S., Tapanya, S., & Singh, S. (2005). Synchrony in the onset of mental-state reasoning: Evidence from five cultures. *Psychological Science, 16,* 378–384.

Callanan, M. A. (1990). Parents' descriptions of objects: Potential data for children's inferences about category principles. *Cognitive Development, 5,* 101–122.

Callanan, M. A., & Sabbagh, M. A. (2004). Multiple labels for objects in conversations with young children: Parents' language and children's developing expectations about word meanings. *Developmental Psychology, 40,* 746–763.

Calvert, S. L., & Huston, A. C. (1987). Television and children's gender schemata. In L. S. Liben & M. L. Signorella (Eds.), *Children's gender schemata* (pp. 75–88). San Francisco: Jossey-Bass.

Camarena, P. M., Sarigiani, P. A. & Petersen, A. C. (1990). Gender-specific pathways to intimacy in early adolescence. *Journal of Youth and Adolescence, 19,* 19–32.

Campbell, A., Shirley, L., & Caygill, L. (2002). Sex-typed preferences in three domains: Do two-year-olds need cognitive variables? *British Journal of Psychiatry, 93,* 203–217.

Campbell, F. A., Pungello, E. P., Miller-Johnson, S., Burchinal, M., & Ramey, C. T. (2001). The development of cognitive and academic abilities: Growth curves from an early childhood educational experiment. *Developmental Psychology, 37,* 231–242.

Campbell, F. A., & Ramey, C. T. (2007). *Carolina Abecedarian project.* Presentation at the National Invitation Conference of the Early Childhood Research Collaborative, University of Minnesota Center for Early Education and Development and the Federal Reserve Bank of Minneapolis; Human Capital Conference Series on Early Childhood Development: Critical Issues in cost effectiveness in children's first decade, Minneapolis, MN.

Campbell, S. B. (2000). Attention-deficit/hyperactivity disorder: A developmental view. In A. Sameroff, M. Lewis, & S. M. Miller (Eds.), *Handbook of developmental psychopathology* (2nd ed.). New York: Plenum.

Campbell, S. B., Cohn, J. F., & Meyers, T. (1995). Depression in first-time mothers: Mother-infant interaction and depression chronicity. *Developmental Psychology, 31,* 349–357.

Campbell, S. B., Matestic, P., von Stauffenberg, C., Mohan, R., & Kirchner, T. (2007). Trajectories of maternal depressive symptoms, maternal sensitivity, and children's functioning at school entry. *Developmental Psychology, 43,* 1202–1215.

Campos, J. J., Anderson, D. I., Barbu-Roth, M. A., Hubbard, E. M., Hertenstein, M. J., & Witherington, D. (2000). Travel broadens the mind. *Infancy, 1,* 149–220.

Campos, J. J., Bertenthal, B. I., & Kermoian, R. (1992). Early experience and emotional development: The emergence of wariness of heights. *Psychological Science, 3,* 61–64.

Campos, J. J., Frankel, C. B., & Camras, L. (2004). On the nature of emotion regulation. *Child Development,* 75, 377–394.

Campos, J. J., Kermoian, R., & Zumbahlen, M. R. (1992). Socioemotional transformations in the family system following infant crawling onset. In N. Eisenberg & R. A. Fabes (Eds.), *New directions for child development: No. 55. Emotion and its regulation in early development* (pp. 25–40). San Francisco: Jossey-Bass.

Campos, J. J., Mumme, D. L., Kermoian, R., & Campos, R. G. (1994). A functionalist perspective on the nature of emotion. *Monographs of the Society for Research in Child Development, 59*(2–3, Serial No. 240), 284–303.

Campos, J. J., Witherington, D., Anderson, D. I., Frankel, C. I., Uchiyama, I., & Barbu-Roth, M. (2008). Rediscovering development in infancy. *Child Development, 79,* 1625–1632.

Campos, R. G. (1989). Soothing pain-elicited distress in infants with swaddling and pacifiers. *Child Development, 60,* 781–792.

Camras, L. A. (1992). Expressive development and basic emotions. *Cognition and Emotion, 6,* 269–283.

Camras, L. A., Malatesta, C., & Izard, C. (1991). The development of facial expressions in infancy. In R. Feldman & B. Rime (Eds.), *Fundamentals of nonverbal behavior* (pp. 73–105). New York: Cambridge University Press.

Camras, L. A., Oster, H., Bakeman, R., Meng, Z., Ujiie, T., & Campos, J. J. (2007). Do infants show distinct negative facial expressions for fear and anger? Emotional expression in 11-month-old European American, Chinese, and Japanese infants. *Infancy, 11,* 131–155.

Camras, L. A., Oster, H., Campos, J., Campos, R. Ujiie, T., Miyake, K., Wang, L., & Meng, Z. (1998). Production of emotional facial expression in European American, Japanese, and Chinese infants. *Developmental Psychology, 34,* 616–628.

Camras, L. A., & Witherington, D. C. (2005). Dynamical systems approaches to emotional development. *Developmental Review, 25,* 328–350.

Canli, T. Omura, K., Haas, B. W., Fallgatter, A., Todd, R., Constable, R. T., et al. (2005). Beyond affect: A role for genetic variation of the serotonin transporter in neural activation during a cognitive attention task. *Proceedings of the National Academy of Science, 102,* 12224–12229.

Canobi, K. H., Reeve, R. A., & Pattison, P. E. (2002). Young children's understanding of addition. *Educational Psychology, 22,* 513–532.

Capaldi, D. M., & Patterson, G. R. (1991). Relation of parental transitions to boys' adjustment problems: I. A linear hypothesis. II. Mothers at risk for transitions and unskilled parenting. *Developmental Psychology, 27,* 489–504.

Capizzano, J., Tout, K., & Adams, G. (2002). Child care patterns of school-age children with employed mothers: A report from the Urban Institute. Retrieved December 20, 2002, from http://www.urban.org/template.cfm?Template=/TaggedContent/ViewPublication.cfm&PublicationID=7259&NavMenuID=95.

Card, N. A., Stucky, B. D., Sawalani, G.M., & Little, T. D. (2008). Direct and indirect aggression during childhood and adolescence: A meta-analytic review of gender differences, intercorrelations, and relations to maladjustment. *Child Development, 79,* 1185–1229.

Card, N. A., Stucky, B. D., Sawalani, G. M., & Little, T. D. (2008). Direct and indirect aggression during childhood and adolescence: A meta-analytic review of gender differences, intercorrelations, and relations to maladjustment. *Child Development, 79,* 1185–1229.

Carey, S. (1978). The child as a word learner. In M. Halle, J. Bresnan, & G. A. Miller (Eds.), *Linguistic theory and psychological reality* (pp. 264–293). Cambridge, MA: The MIT Press.

Carey, S. (1985). *Conceptual change in childhood.* Cambridge, MA: The MIT Press.

Carey, S. (1999). Sources of conceptual change. In In E. K. Scholnick, K. Nelson, S. A. Gelman, & P. H. Miller (Eds.), *Conceptual development: Piaget's legacy* (pp. 293–326). Mahwah, NJ: Erlbaum.

Carey, S., & Bartlett, E. (1978). Acquiring a single new word. *Papers and Reports on Child Language Development, 15,* 17–29.

Carey, S., & Spelke, E. S. (1994). Domain-specific knowledge and conceptual change. In L. S. Hirschfeld & S. A. Gelman (Eds.), *Mapping the mind: Domain specificity in cognition and culture* (pp. 169–220). Cambridge, UK: Cambridge University Press.

Carlo, G., Koller, S. H., Eisenberg, N., DaSilva, M. S., & Frohlich, C. B. (1996). A cross-national study on the relations among prosocial moral reasoning, gender role orientations, and prosocial behaviors. *Developmental Psychology, 32,* 231–240.

Carlson, E. A. (1998). A prospective longitudinal study of attachment disorganization/disorientation. *Child Development, 69,* 1107–1128.

Carlson, E. A., Sroufe, L. A., & Egeland, B. (2004). The construction of experience: A longitudinal study of representation and behavior. *Child Development, 75,* 66–83.

Carlson, S., Hyvarinen, L., & Raninen, A. (1986). Persistent behavioral blindness after early visual deprivation and active visual rehabilitation: A case report. *British Journal of Ophthalmology, 70,* 607–611.

Carlson, S. M., Gum, J., Davis, A., & Malloy, A. (2003). *Predictors of imaginary companion in early childhood.* Poster presented at the annual meeting of the Jean Piaget Society, Chicago, June.

Carlson, S. M., Mandell, D. J., & Williams, L. (2004). Executive function and theory of mind: Stability and prediction from ages 2 to 3. *Developmental Psychology, 40,* 1105–1122.

Carlson, S. M., Moses, L. J., & Nix, H. R. (1998). The role of inhibitory control in young children's difficulties with deception and false belief. *Child Development, 69,* 672–691.

Carlson, W., & Rose, A. J. (2007). The role of reciprocity in romantic relationships in middle childhood and early adolescence. *Merrill-Palmer Quarterly, 53,* 262–290.

Carpenter, M., Nagell, K., & Tomasello, M. (1998). Social cognition, joint attention, and communicative competence from 9 to 15 months of age. *Monographs of the Society for Research in Child Development, 63*(4, Serial No. 255).

Carpenter, P. A., Just, M. A., & Shell, P. (1990). What one intelligence test measures: A theoretical account of the processing in the Raven Progressive Matrices Test. *Psychological Review, 97,* 404–431.

Carroll, J. B. (1993). *Human cognitive abilities: A survey of factor-analytic studies.* New York: Cambridge University Press.

Carroll, J. B. (2005). The three-stratum theory of cognitive abilities. In D. P. Flanagan & P. L. Harrison (Eds.), *Contemporary intellectual assessment: Theories, tests, and issues* (2nd ed., pp. 69–76). New York: Guilford.

Carroll, J. J., & Steward, M. S. (1984). The role of cognitive development in children's understandings of their own feelings. *Child Development, 55,* 1486–1492.

Carter, C. A., & Kahnweiler, W. M. (2000). The efficacy of the social norms approach to substance abuse prevention applied to fraternity men. *Journal of American College Health, 49,* 66–71.

Carter, C. S. (1986). The reproductive and adrenal systems. In M. G. H. Coles, E. Donchin, & S. E. Porges (Eds.), *Psychophysiology: Systems, processes, and applications* (pp. 172–182). New York: Guilford.

Carter, D. B., & McClosky, L. A. (1984). Peers and maintenance of sex typed behavior: The development of children's conceptions of cross-gender behavior in their peers. *Social Cognition, 2,* 294–314.

Carter, D. B., & Patterson, C. J. (1982). Sex roles as social conventions: The development of children's conceptions of sex-role stereotypes. *Developmental Psychology, 18,* 812–824.

Carver, K., Joyner, K., & Udry, J. R. (2003). national estimates of adolescent romantic relationships. In P. Florsheim (Ed.), *Adolescent romantic relations and sexual behavior: Theory, research, and practical implications* (pp. 23–56) Mahwah, NJ: Erlbaum.

Carver, L. J., & Bauer, P. J. (1999). When the event is more than the sum of its parts: 9-month-olds' long-term ordered recall. *Memory, 7,* 147–174.

Carver, L. J., & Bauer, P. J. (2001). The dawning of a past: The emergence of long-term explicit memory in infancy. *Journal of Experimental Psychology: General, 130,* 726–745.

Carver, L. J., Bauer, P. J., & Nelson, C. A. (2000). Associations between infant brain activity and recall memory. *Developmental Science, 3,* 234–246.

Carver, L. J., & Vaccaro, B. G. (2007). 12-month-old infants allocate increased neural resources to stimuli associated with negative adult emotion. *Developmental Psychology, 43,* 54-69.

Carver, P. R., Egan, S., & Perry, D. G. (2004). Children who question their heterosexuality. *Developmental Psychology, 40,* 43–53.

Casasola, M. (2008). The development of infants' spatial categories. *Current Directions in Psychological Science, 17,* 21–25.

Case, R., Griffin, S., & Kelley, W. M. (1999). Socioeconomic gradients in mathematical ability and their responsiveness to intervention during early childhood. In D. P. Keating & C. Hertzman (Eds.), *Developmental health and the wealth of nations: Social, biological, and educational dynamics* (pp. 125–149). New York: Guilford.

Casey, B. J. (1999). Maturation in brain activation. *American Journal of Psychiatry, 156,* 504.

Casey, B. J., Cohen, J. D., Jezzard, P., Turner, R., Noll, D. C., Trainor, R. J., et al. (1995). Activation of prefrontal cortex in children during a non-spatial working memory task with functional MRI. *NeuroImage, 2,* 221–229.

Casey, B. J., Tottenham, N., Liston, C., & Durston, S. (2005). Imaging the developing brain: What have we learned about cognitive development? *Trends in Cognitive Sciences, 9,* 105–110.

Casiglia, A. C., Lo Coco, A., & Zappulla, C. (1998). Aspects of social reputation and peer relationships in Italian children: A cross-cultural perspective. *Developmental Psychology, 34,* 723–730.

Caspi, A. (1998). Personality development across the life course. In W. Damon (Series Ed.) & N. Eisenberg (Vol. Ed.), *Handbook of child psychology: Vol. 3. Social, emotional, and personality development* (5th ed., pp. 311–388). New York: Wiley.

Caspi, A. (2000). The child is father of the man: Personality continuities from childhood to adulthood. *Journal of Personality and Social Psychology, 78,* 158–172.

Caspi, A., Elder, G., Jr., & Bem, D. (1988). Moving away from the world: Lifecourse patterns of shy children. *Developmental Psychology, 24,* 824–831.

Caspi, A., Harrington, H., Milne, B., Amell, J. W., Theodore, R. F., & Moffitt, T. E. (2003). Children's behavioral styles at age 3 are linked to their adult personality traits at age 26. *Journal of Personality, 71,* 495–513.

Caspi, A., Henry, B., McGee, R. O., Moffitt, T. E., & Silva, P. A. (1995). Temperamental origins of child and adolescent behavior problems: From age three to age fifteen. *Child Development, 66,* 55–68.

Caspi, A., McClay, J., Moffitt, T., Mill, J., Martin, J., Craig, I. W., Taylor, A., & Poulton, R. (2002). Role of genotype in the cycle of violence in maltreated children. *Science, 297,* 851–854.

Caspi, A., Moffitt, T. E., Morgan, J., Rutter, M., Taylor, A., Arseneault, L., Tully, L., Jacobs, C., Kim-Cohen, J., & Polo-Tomas, M. (2004). Maternal expressed emotion predicts children's antisocial behavior: Using MZ-twin differences to identify environmental effects on behavioral development. *Developmental Psychology , 40,* 149–161.

Caspi, A., & Shiner, R. L. (2006). Personality development. In W. Damon & R. L. Lerner (Series Eds.) & N. Eisenberg (Vol. Ed.), *Handbook of child psychology, Vol. 3. Social, emotional, and personality development* (6th ed., pp. 300–365). Hoboken, NJ: Wiley.

Caspi, A., & Silva, P. A. (1995). Temperamental qualities at age 3 predict personality traits in adulthood: Longitudinal evidence from a birth cohort. *Child Development, 66,* 486–498.

Cassidy, J. (1994). Emotion regulation: Influences of attachment relationships. *Monographs of the Society for Research in Child Development, 59*(2–3, Serial No. 240), 228–249.

Cassidy, J., Ziv, Y., Mehta, T. G., & Feeney, B. C. (2003). Feedback seeking in children and adolescents: Associations with self-perceptions, attachment representations, and depression. *Child Development, 74,* 612–628.

Cassidy, K. W., Fineberg, D. S., Brown, K., & Perkins, A. (2005). Theory of mind may be contagious, but you don't catch it from your twin. *Child Development, 76,* 97–106.

Cattell, R. B. (1987). *Intelligence: Its structure, growth and action.* Amsterdam: North-Holland.

CDC. (2007). *Prevalence of autism spectrum disorders: Autism and developmental disabilities monitoring network, 14 sites, United States, 2002.* CDC online report, http://www.cdc.gov/MMWR/preview/mmwrhtml/ss5601a2.htm.

Ceballo, R., & McLoyd, V. C. (2002). Social support and parenting in poor, dangerous neighborhoods. *Child Development, 73,* 1310–1321.

Ceci, S. J. (1991). How much does schooling influence general intelligence and its cognitive components? A reassessment of the evidence. *Developmental Psychology, 27,* 703–722.

Ceci, S. J. (1993). Contextual trends in intellectual development. *Developmental Review, 13,* 403–435.

Ceci, S. J. (1996). *On intelligence: A biological treatise on intellectual development* (Expanded ed.). Cambridge, MA: Harvard University Press.

Ceci, S. J., & Bruck, M. (1998). Children's testimony: Applied and basic issues. In W. Damon (Series Ed.), I. Sigel & K. A. Renninger (Vol. Eds.), *Handbook of child psychology: Vol. 4. Child psychology in practice* (5th ed., pp. 713–774). New York: Wiley.

Ceci, S. J., Rosenblum, T. B., & Kumpf, M. (1998). The shrinking gap between high- and low-scoring groups: Current trends and possible causes. In U. Neisser (Ed.), *The rising curve* (pp. 287–302). Washington, DC: American Psychological Association.

Chabris, C. F., & Kosslyn, S. M. (1998). How do the cerebral hemispheres contribute to encoding spatial relations? *Current Directions in Psychological Science, 7,* 8–14.

Chall, J. S. (1979). The great debate: Ten years later, with a modest proposal for reading stages. In L. B. Resnick & P. A. Weaver (Eds.), *Theory and practice of early reading* (Vol. 1, pp. 29–55). Mahwah, NJ: Erlbaum.

Chalmers, D., & Lawrence, J. (1993). Investigating the effects of planning aids on adults' and adolescents' organization of a complex task. *International Journal of Behavioral Development, 16,* 191–214.

Chan, A., & Poulin, F. (2007). Monthly changes in the composition of friendship networks in early adolescence. *Merrill-Palmer Quarterly, 53,* 578–602.

Chan, R. W., Brooks, R. C., Raboy, B., & Patterson, C. J. (1998). Division of labor among lesbian and heterosexual parents: Associations with children's adjustment. *Journal of Family Psychology, 12,* 402–419.

Chan, R. W., Raboy, B., & Patterson, C. J. (1998). Psychosocial adjustment among children conceived via donor insemination by lesbian and heterosexual mothers. *Child Development, 69,* 443–457.

Chandler, M., Fritz, A. S., & Hala, S. (1989). Small-scale deceit: Deception as a marker of two-, three-, and four-year-olds' early theories of mind. *Child Development, 60,* 1263–1277.

Chandler, M. J., Greenspan, S., & Barenboim, C. (1973). Judgments of intentionality in response to videotaped and verbally presented moral dilemmas: The medium is the message. *Child Development, 44,* 315–320.

Chang, Lei, Lansford, Jennifer E., Schwartz, David, Farver, JoAnn M. (2004). Marital quality, maternal depressed affect, harsh parenting, and child externalising in Hong Kong Chinese families. *International Journal of Behavioral Development, 28*(4), 311–318.

Chang, H. W., & Trehub, S. E. (1977). Auditory processing of relational information by young infants. *Journal of Experimental Child Psychology, 24,* 324–331.

Changeux, J. P. (1985). *Neuronal man: The biology of mind.* Princeton, NJ: Princeton University Press.

Changeux, J. P., & Danchin, A. (1976). Selective stabilization of developing synapses as a mechanism for the specification of neuronal networks. *Nature, 264,* 705–712.

Chao, R. K. (1994). Beyond parental control and authoritarian parenting style: Understanding Chinese parenting through the cultural notion of training. *Child Development, 65,* 1111–1119.

Charlesworth, W. R., & La Freniere, P. (1983). Dominance, friendship, and resource utilization in preschool children's groups. *Ethology & Sociobiology, 4,* 175–186.

Chase-Lansdale, P. L., Cherlin, A. J., & Kiernan, K. E. (1995). The long-term effects of parental divorce on the mental health of young adults: A developmental perspective. *Child Development, 66,* 1614–1634.

Chassin, L., Pitts, S. C., & Prost, J. (2002). Binge drinking trajectories from adolescence to emerging adulthood in a high-risk sample: Predictors and substance abuse outcomes. *Journal of Consulting and Clinical Psychology, 70,* 67–78.

Chen, C., Greenberger, E., Lester, J., Dong, Q., & Guo, M-S. (1998). A cross-cultural study of family and peer correlates of adolescent misconduct. *Developmental Psychology, 34,* 770–781.

Chen, E., Matthews, K. A., & Boyce, T. (2002). Socioeconomic status differences in health: What are the implications for children? *Psychological Bulletin, 128,* 295–329.

Chen, X., Cen, G., Li, D., & He, Y. (2005). Social functioning and adjustment in Chinese children: The imprint of historical time. *Child Development, 76,* 182–195.

Chen, X., Chang, L., & He, Y. (2003). The peer group as a context: Mediating and moderating effects on the relations between academic achievement and social functioning in Chinese children. *Child Development, 74,* 710–727.

Chen, X., Chang, L., He, Y., & Liu, H. (2005). The peer group as a context: Moderating effects on relations between maternal parenting and social and school adjustment in Chinese children. *Child Development, 76,* 417–434.

Chen, X., He, Y., & Li, D. (2004). Self-perceptions of social competence and self-worth in Chinese children: Relations with social and school performance. *Social Development, 13,* 570–589.

Chen, X., Rubin, K. H., & Li, B. (1995a). Social functioning and adjustment in Chinese children: A longitudinal study. *Developmental Psychology, 31,* 531–539.

Chen, X., Rubin, K. H., & Li, B. (1995b). Social and school adjustment of shy and aggressive children in China. *Development and Psychopathology, 7,* 337–349.

Chen, X., Rubin, K. H., & Li, D. (1997). Relations between academic achievement and social adjustment: Evidence from Chinese children. *Developmental Psychology, 33*, 518–525.

Chen, X., Rubin, K. H., Li, B., & Li, D. (1999). Adolescent outcomes of social functioning in Chinese children. *International Journal of Behavioral Development, 23*, 199–223.

Chen, X., Rubin, K. H., & Sun, Y. (1992). Social reputation and peer relationships in Chinese and Canadian children: A cross-cultural study. *Child Development, 63*, 1336–1343.

Chen, Z., Dong, Q., & Zhou, H. (1997). Authoritative and authoritarian parenting practices and social and school performance in Chinese children. *International Journal of Behavioral Development, 21*, 855–873.

Chen, Z., Mo, L. & Honomichl, R. (2004). Having the memory of an elephant: Long-term retrieval and the use of analogues in problem solving. *Journal of Experimental Psychology, 133*, 415–433.

Chen, Z., Sanchez, R. P., & Campbell, T. (1997). From beyond to within their grasp: The rudiments of analogical problem solving in 10- and 13-month-olds. *Developmental Psychology, 33*, 790–801.

Chen, Z., & Siegler, R. S. (2000). Across the great divide: Bridging the gap between understanding of toddlers' and older children's thinking. *Monographs of the Society for Research in Child Development, 65*(2, Serial No. 261).

Cheour, M., Martynova, O., Naeaetaenen, R., Erkkola, R., Sillanpaeae, M., Kero, P., Raz, A., Kaipio, M.-L., Hiltunen, J., Aaltonen, O., Savela, J., & Haemaelaeinen, H. (2002). Speech sounds learned by sleeping newborns. *Nature, 415*, 599–600.

Cherney, I. D., & London, K. (2006). Gender-linked differences in the toys, television shows, computer games, and outdoor activities of 5- to 13-year-old children. *Sex Roles, 54*, 717–726.

Chess, S., & Thomas, A. (1990). Continuities and discontinuities in temperament. In L. Robins & M. Rutter (Eds.), *Straight and devious pathways from childhood to adulthood* (pp. 182–220). Cambridge, UK: Cambridge University Press.

Chi, M. T. H., & Ceci, S. J. (1987). Content knowledge: Its role, representation, and restructuring in memory development. In H. W. Reese (Ed.), *Advances in child development and behavior, 20*, 91–142. San Diego, CA: Academic Press.

Child Health. (2006). Maternal and Child Health Bureau. U.S. Department of Health and Human Services. http://www.mchb.hrsa.gov/chusa_06/popchar/0206wmcc.htm.

ChildStats. (2001). *America's children 2001*. Retrieved from http://www.ChildStats.gov.

ChildStats. (2005). *America's children: Key national indicators of well-being, 2005: Child poverty and family income.* Retrieved August 16, 2005, from http://www.childstats.gov/americaschildren/eco1.asp.

ChildStats. (2007). *America's children: Key national indicators of well-being, 2007.* www.childstats.gov.

Childstats.gov. (2008). *American's children in brief: Key national indicators of well-being, 2008.* www.childstats.gov/americaschldren.

Child Trends, 2007. http://www.childtrendsdatabank.

Chisolm, J. S. (1963). *Navajo infancy: An ethological study of child development.* New York: Aldine.

Chomsky, N. (1957). *Syntactic structures.* The Hague: Mouton.

Chomsky, N. (1988). *Language and problems of knowledge.* Cambridge, MA: The MIT Press.

Christian, R. E., Frick, P. J., Hill, N. L., Tyler, L., & Frazer, D. R. (1997). Psychopathy and conduct problems in children: II. Implications for subtyping children with conduct problems. *Journal of the American Academy of Child and Adolescent Psychiatry, 36*, 233–241.

Chugani, H. T., Phelps, M. E., & Mazziotta, J. C. (1987). Positron emission tomography study of human brain functional development. *Annals of Neurology, 22*, 487–497.

Church, R. B. (1999). Using gesture and speech to capture transitions in learning. *Cognitive Development, 14*, 313–342.

Church, R. B., & Goldin-Meadow, S. (1986). The mismatch between gesture and speech as an index of transitional knowledge. *Cognition, 23*, 43–71.

Cianciolo, A. T., Matthew, C., Sternberg, R. J., & Wagner, R. K. (2006). Tacit knowledge, practical intelligence, and expertise. In K. A. Cricsson, N. Charness, P. J. Feltovich, & R. R. Hoffman (Eds.), *The Cambridge handbook of expertise and expert performance* (pp. 613–632). New York: Cambridge University Press.

Cicchetti, D., & Toth, S. L. (1998). Perspectives on research and practice in developmental psychopathology. In W. Damon (Series Ed.) and I. E. Sigel & K. A. Renninger (Vol. Eds.), *Handbook of child psychology, Vol. 4: Child psychology in practice* (5th ed., pp. 479–583). New York: Wiley.

Cicchetti, D., & Toth, S. L. (2006). Developmental psychopathology and preventive intervention. In K. A. Renninger & I. E. Sigel (Vol. Eds) and W. Damon & R. M. Lerner (Eds.), *Handbook of child psychology* (6th ed., pp. 497–547). New York: Wiley.

Cillessen, A. H. N., & Mayeux, L. (2004). From censure to reinforcement: Developmental changes in the association between aggression and social status. *Child Development, 75*, 147–163.

Cillessen, A. H., van IJzendoorn, H. W., van Lieshout, C. F., & Hartup, W. W. (1992). Heterogeneity among peer-rejected boys: Subtypes and stabilities. *Child Development, 63*, 893–905.

Clark, C. A. C., Woodward, L. J., Horwood, L. J., & Moor, S. (2008). Development of emotional and behavior regulation in children born extremely preterm and very preterm: Biological and social influences. *Child Development, 79*, 1444–1462.

Clark, E. V. (1979). Building a vocabulary: Words for objects, actions, and relations. In P. Fletcher & M. Garman (Eds.), *Language acquisition* (pp. 149–160). Cambridge, UK: Cambridge University Press.

Clark, E. V. (1993). *The lexicon in acquisition.* Cambridge, UK: Cambridge University Press.

Clarke-McLean, J. (1996). Social networks among incarcerated juvenile offenders. *Social Development, 5*, 203–217.

Clarke-Stewart, K. A. (1981). Observation and experiment: Complementary strategies for studying day care and social development. In S. Kilmer (Ed.), *Advances in early education and day care* (Vol. 2, pp. 227–250). Greenwich, CT: JAI Press.

Clarke-Stewart, K. A., Vandell, D. L., McCartney, K., Owen, M. T., & Booth, C. (2000). Effects of parental separation and divorce on very young children. *Journal of Family Psychology, 14*, 304–326.

Clarkson, M. G., & Clifton, R. K. (1991). Acoustic determinants of newborn orienting. In M. J. S. Weiss & P. R. Zelazo (Eds.), *Newborn attention: Biological constraints and the influence of experience* (pp. 99–119). Stamford, CT: Ablex.

Clary, E. G., & Miller J. (1986). Socialization and situational influences on sustained altruism. *Child Development, 57*, 1358–1369.

Claxton, L. J., Keen, R., & McCarty, M. E. (2003). Evidence of motor planning in infant reaching behavior. *Psychological Science, 14(4)*, 354–356.

Clearfield, M. (2006). A dynamic account of infant looking behavior in small and large number tasks. In F. Columbus (Ed.), *Trends in cognitive psychology research*. Hauppague, NY: Nova Science Publishers.

Clearfield, M. W., Diedrich, F. J., Smith, L. B., & Thelen, E. (2006). Young infants reach correctly in A-not-B tasks: On the development of stability and perseveration. *Infant Behavior and Development, 29*, 435–444.

Clearfield, M. W., & Mix, K. S. (1999). Number versus contour length in infants' discrimination of small visual sets. *Psychological Science, 10*, 408–411.

Clearfield, M. W., Smith, L. B., Diedrich, F. J., & Thelen, E. (2006). Young infants reach correctly on the A-not-B task: On the development of stability and perseveration. *Infant Behavior and Development, 29*, 435–444.

Clifton, R. K., Rochat, P., Litovsky, R. Y., & Perris, E. E. (1991). Object representation guides infants' reaching in the dark. *Journal of Experimental Psychology: Human Perception and Performance, 17*, 323–329.

Clore, G. (1981). *The wit and wisdom of Benjamin Clore.* Unpublished manuscript.

Coe, C. L., & Lubach, G. R. (2008). Fetal programming: Prenatal origins of health and illness. *Current Directions in Psychological Science, 17*, 36–41.

Cohen, J. (1988). *Statistical power analysis for the behavioral sciences* (2nd ed.). Hillsdale, NJ: Lawrence Erlbaum.

Cohen, L. B., & Cashon, C. H. (2006). Infant cognition. In W. Damon & R. M. Lerner (Series Eds.) & D. Kuhn & R. S. Siegler (Vol. Eds.), *Handbook of child psychology: Volume 2: Cognition, perception, and language* (6th ed., pp. 214–251). Hoboken, NJ: Wiley.

Cohen, L. B., Chaput, H. H., & Cashon, C. H. (2002). A constructivist model of infant cognition. *Cognitive Development, Special Issue: Constructivism Today, 17*, 1323–1343.

Cohen, L. B., & Marks, K. S. (2002). How infants process addition and subtraction events. *Developmental Science, 5*, 186–201.

Cohen, P., & Brook, J. S. (1995). The reciprocal influence of punishment and child behavior disorder. In J. McCord (Ed.), *Coercion and punishment in long-term perspectives* (pp. 154–164). Cambridge, UK: Cambridge University Press.

Cohen, R. W., & Martinez, M. E. (2006). Health insurance coverage: Estimates from the National Health Interview Survey, January–September 2005. *Center for Disease Control and Prevention*, p. 76.

Coie, J. D., & Dodge, K. A. (1983). Continuities and changes in children's social status: A five-year longitudinal study. *Merrill-Palmer Quarter, 29*, 261–282.

Coie, J. D., & Dodge, K. A. (1988). Multiple sources of data on social behavior and social status in the school: A cross-age comparison. *Child Development, 59*, 815–829.

Coie, J. D., & Dodge, K. A. (1998). Aggression and antisocial behavior. In W. Damon (Series Ed.) and N. Eisenberg (Vol. Ed.), *Handbook of child psychology. Vol. 3. Social, emotional, and personality development* (pp. 779–862). New York: Wiley.

Coie, J. D., Dodge, K. A., & Kupersmidt, J. B. (1990). Peer group behavior and social status. In S. R. Asher & J. D. Coie (Eds.), *Peer rejection in childhood* (pp. 17–59). Cambridge, UK: Cambridge University Press.

Coie, J. D., & Kupersmidt, J. (1983). A behavioral analysis of emerging social status in boys' groups. *Child Development, 54*, 1400–1416.

Coie, J. D., Lochman, J. E., Terry, R., & Hyman, C. (1992). Predicting early adolescent disorder from childhood aggression and peer rejection. *Journal of Consulting and Clinical Psychology, 60*, 783–792.

Coie, J. D., Terry, R., Lenox, K., Lochman, J., & Hyman, C. (1995). Childhood peer rejection and aggression as predictors of stable patterns of adolescent disorder. *Development and Psychopathology, 7*, 697–713.

Colby, A., & Kohlberg, L. (1987a). *The measurement of moral judgment. Vol. 1.* Cambridge, UK: Cambridge University Press.

Colby, A., & Kohlberg, L. (1987b). *The measurement of moral judgment. Vol. 2.* Cambridge, UK: Cambridge University Press.

Colby, A., Kohlberg, L., Gibbs, J., & Lieberman, M. (1983). A longitudinal study of moral judgment. *Monographs of the Society for Research in Child Development, 48* (Serial No. 200), 1–124.

Colder, C. R., Lochman, J. E., & Wells, K. C. (1997). The moderating effects of children's fear and activity level of relations between parenting practices and childhood symptomatology. *Journal of Abnormal Child Psychology, 25*, 251–263.

Coldwell, J., Pike, A., & Dunn, J. (2008). Maternal differential treatment and child adjustment: A multi-informant approach. *Social Development, 17*, 596–612.

Cole, D. A., Martin, J. M., & Powers, B. (1997). A competency-based model of child depression: A longitudinal study of peer, parent, teacher, and self-evaluations. *Journal of Child Psychology and Psychiatry, 38*, 505–514.

Cole, P. M. (1986). Children's spontaneous control of facial expression. *Child Development, 57*, 1309–1321.

Cole, P. M., Bruschi, C. J., & Tamang, B. L. (2002). Cultural differences in children's emotional reactions to difficult situations. *Child Development, 73*, 983–996.

Cole, P. M., & Dennis, T. A. (1998). Variations on a theme: Culture and the meaning of socialization practices and child competence. *Psychological Inquiry, 9*, 276–278.

Cole, P. M., Luby, J., & Sullivan, M. W. (2008). Emotions and the development of childhood depression: Bridging the gap. *Child Development Perspectives.*

Cole, P. M., & Tamang, B. L. (1998). Nepali children's ideas about emotional displays in hypothetical challenges. *Developmental Psychology, 34*, 640–646.

Cole, P. M., Tamang, B. L., & Shrestha, S. (2006). Cultural variations in the socialization of young children's anger and shame. *Child Development, 77*, 1237–1251.

Cole, P. M., & Tan, P. Z. (2007). Emotion socialization from a cultural perspective. In J. E. Grusec & P. D. Hastings (Eds.), *Handbook of socialization: Theory and research* (pp. 516–542). New York: Guilford.

Coleman, M., Wheeler, L., & Webber, J. (1993). Research on interpersonal problem-solving training: A review. *Remedial and Special Education, 14*, 25–37.

Coley, J. D. (2000). On the importance of comparative research: The case of folkbiology. *Child Development, 71*, 82–90.

Coley, R. L., & Chase-Lansdale, P. L. (1998). Adolescent pregnancy and parenthood: Recent evidence and future directions. *American Psychologist, 53*, 152–166.

Collaer, M. L., & Hines, M. (1995). Human behavioral sex differences: A role for gonadal hormones in early development? *Psychological Bulletin, 118,* 55–107.

Colley, A., & Comber, C. (2003). School subject preferences: Age and gender differences revisited. *Educational Studies, 29,* 59–67.

Collie, R., & Hayne, H. (1999). Deferred imitation by 6- and 9-month-old infants: More evidence for declarative memory. *Developmental Psychobiology, 35,* 83–90.

Collins, W. A. (1990). Parent-child relationships in the transition to adolescence: Continuity and change in interaction, affect, and cognition. In R. Montemayor, G. R. Adams, & T. P. Gullotta (Eds.), *From childhood to adolescence: A transitional period?* (pp. 85–106). Newbury Park, CA: Sage.

Collins, W. A. (2003). More than a myth: The developmental significance of romantic relationships during adolescence. *Journal of Research on Adolescence, 13,* 1–24.

Collins, W. A., Hennighausen, K. H., Schmit, D. T., & Sroufe, L. A. (1997). Developmental precursors of romantic relationships: A longitudinal analysis. In S. Shulman & W. A. Collins (Eds.), *Romantic relationships in adolescence: Developmental perspectives* (pp. 69–84). San Francisco: Jossey-Bass.

Collins, W. A., Maccoby, E. E., Steinberg, L., Hetherington, E. M., & Bornstein, M. H. (2000). Contemporary research on parenting: The case for nature and nurture. *American Psychologist, 55,* 218–232.

Collins, W. A., & Steinberg, L. (2006). Adolescent development in interpersonal context. In W. Damon & R. M. Lerner (Series Eds.) & N. Eisenberg (Vol. Ed.), *Handbook of child psychology: Vol. 3. Social, emotional, and personality development.* (6th ed., pp. 1003–1068). Hoboken, NJ: Wiley.

Collins, W. A., Welsh, D. P., & Furman, W. (2009). Adolescent romantic relationships. *Annual Review of Psychology, 60,* 631–652.

Colombo, J. (2001). Infant's detection of contingency: A cognitive-neuroscience perspective. *Bulletin of the Menninger Clinic* Special Issue: Cognitive and Interactional Foundations of Attachment, *65,* 321–334.

Colombo, J. (2001). The development of visual attention in infancy. *Annual Review of Psychology, 52,* 337–367.

Colombo, J., & Frick, J. (1999). Recent advances and issues in the study of preverbal intelligence. In M. Anderson (Ed.), *The development of intelligence* (pp. 43–71). Hove, East Sussex: Psychology Press.

Colombo, J., & Richman, W. A. (2002). Infant timekeeping: Attention and temporal estimation in 4-month-olds. *Psychological Science, 13,* 475–479.

Colombo, J., Shaddy, D. J., Richman, W. A., Maikranz, J. M., & Blaga, O. (2004). Developmental course of visual habituation and preschool cognitive and language outcome. *Infancy, 5,* 1–38.

Coltrane, S. (1996.) *Family man.* New York: Oxford University Press.

Colwell, J., Grady, C., & Rhiati, S. (1995). Computer games, self-esteem, and gratification of needs in adolescents. *Journal of Community and Applied Social Psychology, 5,* 195–206.

Compas, B. E., Connor-Smith, J. K., Saltzman, H., Thomsen, A. H., & Wadsworth, M. E. (2001). Coping with stress during childhood and adolescence: Problems, progress, and potential in theory and research. *Psychological Bulletin, 127,* 87–127.

Compian, L., Gowen, L. K., & Hayward, C. (2004). Peripubertal girls' romantic and platonic involvement with boys: Associations with body image and depression symptoms. *Journal of Research on Adolescence, 141,* 23–47.

Compton, K., Snyder, J., Schrepferman, L., Bank, L. & Shortt, J. W. (2003). The contribution of parents and siblings to antisocial and depressive behavior in adolescents: A double jeopardy coercion model. *Development and Psychopathology, 15,* 163–182.

Condry, J., & Ross, D. F. (1985). Sex and aggression: The influence of gender label on the perception of aggression in children. *Child Development, 56,* 225–233.

Conduct Problems Prevention Research Group. (1999a). Initial impact of the Fast Track Prevention Trial for conduct problems: I. The high-risk sample. *Journal of Consulting and Clinical Psychology, 67,* 619–647.

Conduct Problems Prevention Research Group. (1999b). Initial impact of the Fast Track Prevention Trial for conduct problems: II. Classroom effects. *Journal of Consulting and Clinical Psychology, 67,* 648–657.

Conduct Problems Prevention Research Group. (2002a). Evaluation of the first 3 years of the Fast Track Prevention trial with children at high risk for adolescent conduct problems. *Journal of Abnormal Child Psychology, 30,* 19–35.

Conduct Problems Prevention Research Group. (2002b). Using the Fast Track randomized prevention trial to test the early-starter model of the development of serious conduct problems. *Development and Psychopathology, 14,* 925–943.

Conduct Problems Prevention Research Group (2004). The effects of the Fast Track program on serious problem outcomes at the end of elementary school. *Journal of Clinical Child and Adolescent Psychology, 33,* 650–661.

Conduct Problems Prevention Research Group. (in press). The effects of the Fast Track Program on serious problem outcomes at the end of elementary school. *Journal of Clinical Child and Adolescent Psychology.*

Conger, R. D., Conger, K. J., Elder, G. H., Jr., Lorenz, F. O., Simons, R. L., & Whitbeck, L. B. (1993). Family economic stress and adjustment of early adolescent girls. *Developmental Psychology, 29,* 206–219.

Conger, R. D., & Ge, X. (1999). Conflict and cohesion in parent-adolescent relations: Changes in emotional expression from early to midadolescence. In M. J. Cox & J. Brooks-Gunn (Eds.), *Conflict and cohesion in families: Courses and consequences* (pp. 183–206). Mahwah, NJ: Erlbaum.

Conger, R. D., Ge, X., Elder, G. H. Jr., Lorenz, F. O., & Simons, R. L. (1994). Economic stress, coercive family process, and developmental problems of adolescents. *Child Development, 65,* 541–561.

Conger, R. D., Wallace, L. E., Sun, Y., Simmons, R. L., McLoyd, V. C., & Brody, G. H. (2002). Economic pressure in African American families: A replication and extension of the family stress model. *Developmental Psychology, 38,* 179–193.

Conley, D., & Bennett, N. (2002). Comment: Outcomes in young adulthood for very-low-birth weight infants. *New England Journal of Medicine, 347,* 141–143.

Connell, A., Bullock, B. M., Dishion, T. J., Shaw, D., Wilson, M., & Gardner, F. (2008). Family intervention effects on co-occurring early childhood behavioral and emotional problems: A latent transition analysis approach. *Journal of Abnormal Child Psychology, 36,* 1211–1225.

Connell, J. P., & Wellborn, J. G. (1991). Competence, autonomy, and relatedness: A motivational analysis of self-system processes. In M. R. Gunnar & L. A. Sroufe (Eds.), *The Minnesota Symposium on Child Development: Vol. 23. Self processes and development* (pp. 43–78). Hillsdale, NJ: Erlbaum.

Connellan, J., Baron-Cohen, S., Wheelwright, S., Ba'tki, A., & Ahluwalia, J. (2001). Sex differences in human neonatal social perception. *Infant Behavior and Development, 23,* 113–118.

Conner, D. B., Knight, D. K., & Cross, D. R. (1997). Mothers' and fathers' scaffolding of their 2-year-olds during problem solving and literacy interactions. *British Journal of Developmental Psychology, 15,* 323–338.

Connolly, J. A., Craig, W., Goldberg, A., & Pepler, D. (1999). Conceptions of cross-sex friendships and romantic relationships in early adolescence. *Journal of Youth and Adolescence, 28,* 481–494.

Connolly, J. A., Craig, W., Goldberg, A., & Pepler, D. (2004). Mixed-gender groups, dating, and romantic relationships in early adolescence. *Journal of Research on Adolescence, 14,* 185–207.

Connolly, J. A., & Konarski, R. (1994). Peer self-concept in adolescence: Analysis of factor structure and of associations with peer experience. *Journal of Research on Adolescence, 4,* 385–403.

Consortium for Longitudinal Studies (1983). *As the twig is bent: Lasting effects of preschool programs.* Hillsdale, NJ: Erlbaum.

Conway, M. A., & Holmes, A. (2004). Psychosocial stages and the accessibility of autobiographical memories across the life cycle. *Journal of Personality, 72,* 461–480.

Cook, W. L., Kenny, D. A., & Goldstein, M. J. (1991). Parental affective style risk and the family system: A social relations model analysis. *Journal of Abnormal Psychology, 100,* 492–501.

Cooley, C. H. (1902). *Human nature and the social order.* New York: Charles Schribner & Sons.

Cooney, T. M., Pedersen, F. A., Indelicato, S., & Palkovitz, R. (1993). Timing of fatherhood: Is "on-time" optimal? *Journal of Marriage and the Family, 55,* 205–215.

Cooper, P. J., & Goodyer, I. (1993). A community study of depression in adolescent girls: I. Estimates of symptom and syndrome prevalence. *British Journal of Psychiatry, 163,* 369–374.

Cooper, R. P., & Aslin, R. N. (1994). Developmental differences in infant attention to the spectral properties of infant-directed speech. *Child Development, 65,* 1663–1677.

Corballis, M. C. (1999). The gestural origins of language. *American Scientist, 87,* 138–145.

Corbetta, D., & Thelen, E. (1999). Lateral biases and fluctuations in infants' spontaneous arm movements and reaching. *Developmental Psychobiology, 34,* 237–255.

Cornell, E. H., Heth, C. D., Kneubuhler, Y., & Sehgal, S. (1996). Serial position effects in children's route reversal errors: Implications for police search operations. *Applied Cognitive Psychology, 10,* 301–326.

Costello, D. M., Swendsen, J., Rose, J. S., & Dierker, L. C. (2008). Risk and protective factors associated with trajectories of depressed mood from adolescence to early adulthood. *Journal of Consulting and Clinical Psychology, 76,* 173–183.

Côté, S. M., Borge, A. I., Georffroy, M-C., Rutter, M., & Tremblay, R. E. (2008). Nonmaternal care in infancy and emotional/behavioral difficulties at 4 years old: Moderation by family risk characteristics. *Developmental Psychology, 44,* 155–168.

Côté, S., Zoccolillo, M., Tremblay, R. E., Nagin, D., & Vitaro, F. (2001). Predicting girls' conduct disorder in adolescence from childhood trajectories of disruptive behaviors. *Journal of the American Academy of Child and Adolescent Psychiatry, 40,* 678–684.

Coulton, C. J., Korbin, J. E., Su, M., & Chow, J. (1995). Community level factors and child maltreatment rates. *Child Development, 66,* 1262–1276.

Courage, M. L., & Howe, M. L. (2002). From infant to child: The dynamics of cognitive change in the second year of life. *Psychological Bulletin, 128,* 250–277.

Cowan, N., Nugent, L. S., Elliott, E. M., Ponomarev, I., & Sautls, J. S. (1999). The role of attention in the development of short-term memory: Age differences in the verbal span of apprehension. *Child Development, 70,* 1082–1097.

Cowan, P. A., Powell, D., & Cowan, C. P. (1998). Parenting interventions: A family systems perspective. In I. E. Sigel & K. A. Renninger (Eds.), *Handbook of child psychology: Vol. 4. Child psychology in practice* (5th ed., pp. 3–72). New York: Wiley.

Cox, M. J., Owen, M. T., Lewis, J. M., & Henderson, V. K. (1989). Marriage, adult adjustment, and early parenting. *Child Development, 60,* 1015–1024.

Coyne, S. M., & Archer, J. (2005). The relationship between indirect and physical aggression on television and in real life. *Social Development, 14,* 324–324.

Coyne, S. M., Archer, J., & Eslea, M. (2004). Cruel intentions on television and in real life: Can viewing indirect aggression increase viewers' subsequent indirect aggression? *Journal of Experimental Child Psychology, 88,* 234–234.

Craig, W. M., Vitaro, F., Gagnon, G., & Tremblay, R. E. (2002). The road to gang membership: Characteristics of stable and unstable male gang members from ages 10 to 14. *Social Development, 11,* 53–68.

Crain, W. C. (1985). *Theories of development: Concepts and applications* (2nd ed.). Upper Saddle River, NJ: Prentice-Hall.

Crawford, J. (1997). *Best evidence: Research foundations of the Bilingual Education Act.* Washington, DC: National Clearinghouse for Bilingual Education.

Crick, N. R., Bigbee, M. H., & Howes, C. (1996). Gender differences in children's normative beliefs about aggression: How do I hurt thee? Let me count the ways. *Child Development, 67,* 1003–1014.

Crick, N. R., Casas, J. F., & Mosher, M. (1997). Relational and overt aggression in preschool. *Developmental Psychology, 33,* 579–588.

Crick, N. R., & Dodge, K. A. (1994). A review and reformulation of social information-processing mechanisms in children's social adjustment. *Psychological Bulletin, 115,* 74–101.

Crick, N. R., & Dodge, K. A. (1996). Social information-processing mechanisms in reactive and proactive aggression. *Child Development, 67,* 993–1002.

Crick, N. R., & Grotpeter, J. K. (1995). Relational aggression, gender, and social psychological adjustment. *Child Development, 66,* 710–722.

Crick, N. R., & Grotpeter, J. K. (1996). Children's treatment by peers: Victims of relational and overt aggression. *Development and Psychopathology, 8,* 367–380.

Crick, N. R., Werner, N. E., Casas, J. F., O'Brien, K. M., Nelson, D. A., Grotpeter, J. K., & Markon, K. (1999). Childhood aggression and gender: A new look at an old problem. In D. Bernstein (Ed.), *Gender and motivation: Nebraska Symposium on Motivation* (pp. 75–141). Lincoln: University of Nebraska Press.

Criss, M. M., Pettit, G. S., Bates, J. E., Dodge, K. A., & Lapp, A. L. (2002). Family adversity, positive peer relationships, and children's externalizing behavior: A longitudinal perspective on risk and resilience. *Child Development, 73,* 1220–1237.

Crockenberg, S., & Langrock, A. (2001). The role of specific emotions in children's responses to interparental conflict: A test of the model. *Journal of Family Psychology, 15,* 163–182.

Crocker, J. (2001). Self-esteem in adulthood. In N. Smelser & P. Baltes (Eds.), *International Encyclopedia of the Social and Behavioral Sciences.* Oxford, UK: Elsevier.

Crockett, L., Losoff, M., & Peterson, A. C. (1984). Perceptions of the peer group and friendship in early adolescence. *Journal of Early Adolescence, 4,* 155–181.

Crosbie-Burnett, M., & Helmbrecht, L. (1993). A descriptive empirical study of gay male stepfamilies. *Family Relations,* 42, 256–262.

Crosnoe, R., & Needham, B. (2004). Holism, contextual variability, and the study of friendships in adolescent development. *Child Development, 75,* 264–279.

Crosnoe, R., Riegle-Crumb, C., Field, S., Frank, K., & Muller, C. (2008). Peer group contexts of girls' and boys' academic experiences. *Child Development, 79,* 139–155.

Crouter, A. C., & Booth, A. (Eds.) (2003). *Children's influence on family dynamics: The neglected side of family relationships.* Mahwah, NJ: Erlbaum.

Crowley, K., Callanan, M. A., Tenenbaum, H. R., & Allen, E. (2001). Parents explain more often to boys than to girls during shared scientific thinking. *Psychological Science, 12*(3), 258–261.

Csibra, G., Bíró, S., Koós, O., & Gergely, G. (2003). One-year-old infants use teleological representations of actions productively. *Cognitive Science, 27,* 111–133.

Csibra, G., Gergely, G., Bíró, S., Koós, O., & Brockbank, M. (1999). Goal attribution without agency cues: The perception of "pure reason" in infancy. *Cognition, 72,* 237–267.

Csikszentmihalyi, M., & Schneider, B. (2000). *Becoming adult: How teenagers prepare for the world of work.* New York: Basic Books.

Cui, M., Donnellan, M. B., & Conger, R. D. (2007). Reciprocal influences between parents' marital problems and adolescent internalizing and externalizing behavior. *Developmental Psychology,* 43, 1544–1552.

Culp, R. E., Appelbaum, M. I., Osofsky, J. D., & Levy, J. A. (1988). Adolescent and older mothers: Comparison between prenatal maternal variables and newborn interaction measures. *Infant Behavior and Development, 11,* 353–362.

Cummings, E. M., & Davies, P. T. (2002). Effects of marital conflict on children: Recent advances and emerging themes in process-oriented research. *Journal of Child Psychology and Psychiatry and Allied Disciplines, 43,* 31–63.

Cunningham, A. E., & Stanovich, K. E. (1997). Early reading acquisition and its relation to reading experience and ability 10 years later. *Developmental Psychology, 33,* 934–945.

Curry, D., Schmitt, M.J., & Waldron, S. (1996). *A framework for adult numeracy standards: The mathematical skills and abilities adults need to be equipped for the future.* Retrieved April 15, 2009, from Adult Numeracy Network Web site: http://shell04.TheWorld.com/std/anpn//framewk. html.

Curtiss, S. (1977). *Genie: A psycholinguistic study of a modern-day "wild child."* London: Academic Press.

Curtiss, S. (1989). The independence and task-specificity of language. In M. H. Bornstein & J. S. Bruner (Eds.), *Interaction in human development* (pp. 105–138). Hillsdale, NJ: Erlbaum.

Custodero, L. A., Britto, P. R., & Brooks-Gunn, J. (2003). Musical lives: A collective portrait of American parents and their young children. *Applied Developmental Psychology, 24,* 553–572.

Cutrona, C. E., Hessling, R. M., Bacon, P. L., & Russell, D. W. (1998). Predictors and correlates of continuing involvement with the baby's father among adolescent mothers. *Family Psychology, 12,* 369–387.

Dallaire, D. H., & Weinraub, M. (2007). Infant-mother attachment and children's anxiety and aggression at first grade. *Journal of Applied Developmental Psychology, 28,* 477–492.

Daly, M., & Wilson, M. I. (1996). Violence against stepchildren. *Current Directions in Psychological Science, 5,* 77–81.

Damasio, A. (1999). *The feeling of what happens: Body and emotion in the making of consciousness.* New York: Harcourt Brace & Company.

Damon, W. (1977). *The social world of the child.* San Francisco: Jossey-Bass.

Damon, W. (1983). *Social and personality development: Infancy through adolescence.* New York: Norton.

Damon, W., & Hart, D. (1988). *Self-understanding in childhood and adolescence.* Cambridge, UK: Cambridge University Press.

Darling, N., & Steinberg, L. (1993). Parenting style as context: An integrative model. *Psychological Bulletin, 113,* 487–496.

Darwin, C. (1877). A biographical sketch of an infant. *Mind, 2,* 285–294.

D'Augelli, A. R. (1998). Developmental implications of victimization of lesbian, gay, and bisexual youth. In G. M. Herek (Ed.), *Stigma and sexual orientation: Understanding prejudice against lesbians, gay men, and bisexuals* (pp. 187–210). Thousand Oaks, CA: Sage.

D'Augelli, A. R., & Hershberger, S. L. (1993). Lesbian, gay, and bisexual youth in community settings: Personal challenges and mental health problems. *American Journal of Community Psychology, 21,* 421–448.

D'Augelli, A. R., Hershberger, S. L., & Pilkington, N. W. (1998). Lesbian, gay, and bisexual youth and their families: Disclosure of sexual orientation and its consequences. *American Journal of Orthopsychiatry, 68,* 361–371.

Davidson, R. J. (1994). Asymmetric brain function, affective style, and psychopathology. *Development and Psychopathology, 6,* 741–758.

Davidson, R. J., Scherer, K. R., Goldsmith, H. H., Pizzagalli, D., Nitschke, J. B., Kalin, N. H., Berridge, K. C., LaBar, K. S., LeDoux, J. E., Damasio, A. R., Adolphs, R., Damasio, H., McGaugh, J. L., Cahill, L., Elliot, R., & Dolan, R. J. (2003). Part I. Neuroscience. In R. J. Davidson, K. R. Scherer, et al. (Eds.), *Handbook of affective sciences. Series in affective science* (pp. 3–128). London: Oxford University Press.

Davies, P. T., & Cummings, E. M. (1994). Marital conflict and child adjustment: An emotional security hypothesis. *Psychological Bulletin, 116,* 387–411.

Davies, P. T., Cummings, E. M., & Winter, M. A. (2004). Pathways between profiles of family functioning, child security in the interparental subsystem, and child psychological problems. *Development and Psychopathology, 16,* 525–550.

Davies, P. T., Sturge-Apple, M. L., Cicchetti, D., & Cummings, E. M. (2007). The role of child andrenocortical functioning in pathways between interparental conflict and child maladjustment. *Developmental Psychology, 43*, 918–930.

Davies, P. T., & Windle, M. (2000). Middle adolescents' dating pathways and psychosocial adjustment. *Merrill-Palmer Quarterly, 46(1),* 90–118.

Davis, B. E., Moon, R. Y., Sachs, H. C., & Ottolini, M. C. (1998). Effects of sleep position on infant motor development. *Pediatrics, 102,* 1135–1140.

Dawson, G., Klinger, L. G., Panagiotides, H., Spieker, S., & Frey, K. (1992). Infants of mothers with depressive symptoms: Electrophysiological and behavioral findings related to attachment status. *Development and Psychopathology, 4,* 67–80.

Dearing, E. (2004). The developmental implications of restrictive and supportive parenting across neighborhoods and ethnicities: Exceptions are the rule. *Journal of Applied Developmental Psychology, 25,* 555–575.

Deák, G. O., Flom, R. A., & Pick, A. D. (2000). Effects of gesture and target on 12- and 18-month-olds' joint visual attention to objects in front or behind them. *Developmental Psychology, 36*, 511–523.

Deary, I. J. (2000). *Looking down on human intelligence: From psychometrics to the brain.* (Oxford Psychology Series No. 34.) Oxford, UK: Oxford University Press.

Deary, I. J., Strand, S., Smith, P., & Fernandes, C. (2007). Intelligence and educational achievement. *Intelligence, 35*, 13–21.

Deater-Deckard, K. (2000). Parenting and child behavioral adjustment in early childhood: A quantitative genetic approach to studying family processes. *Child Development, 71*, 468–484.

Deater-Deckard, K., & Dodge, K. A. (1997). Externalizing behavior problems and discipline revisited: Nonlinear effects and variation by culture, context, and gender. *Psychological Inquiry, 8*, 161–175.

Deater-Deckard, K., Dodge, K. A., Bates, J. E., & Pettit, G. S. (1995, March–April). *Risk factors for the development of externalizing behavior problems: Are there ethnic group differences in process?* Paper presented at the biennial meeting of the Society for Research in Child Development, Indianapolis, IN.

Deater-Deckard, K., Dodge, K. A., Bates, J. E., & Pettit, G. S. (1996). Physical discipline among African American and European American mothers: Links to children's externalizing behaviors. *Developmental Psychology, 32*, 1065–1072.

Deater-Deckard, K., Dodge, K. A., Bates, J. E., & Pettit, G. S. (1998). Multiple risk factors in the development of externalizing behavior problems: Group and individual differences. *Development and Psychopathology, 10*, 469–493.

Deater-Deckard, K., & O'Connor, T. G. (2000). Parent-child mutuality in early childhood: Two behavioral genetic studies. *Developmental Psychology, 36,* 1–10.

Deater-Deckard, K., Petrill, S. A., & Thompson, L. A. (2007). Anger/frustration, task persistence, and conduct problems in childhood: a behavioral genetic analysis. *Journal of Child Psychology and Psychiatry, 48,* 80–87.

DeBaryshe, B. D., Patterson, G. R., & Capaldi, D. M. (1993). A performance model for academic achievement in early adolescent boys. *Developmental Psychology, 29*(5), 795–804.

DeCasper, A. J., & Fifer, W. P. (1980). Of human bonding: Newborns prefer their mothers' voices. *Science, 208*, 1174–1176.

DeCasper, A. J., & Spence, M. J. (1986). Prenatal maternal speech influences newborns' perception of speech sounds. *Infant Behavior and Development, 9*, 133–150.

Decker, S. H. (1996). Collective and normative features of gang violence. *Justice Quarterly, 13*, 243–264.

Decker, S. H., & van Winkle, B. (1996). *Life in the gang: Family, friends, and violence.* Cambridge, UK: Cambridge University Press.

DeFries, J. C., & Gillis, J. J. (1993). Genetics of reading disability. In R. Plomin & G. E. McClearn (Eds.), *Nature, nurture, and psychology* (pp. 121–145). Washington, DC: American Psychological Association.

de Guzman, M. R. T., Carlo, G., & Edwards, C. P. (2008). Prosocial behaviors in context: Examining the role of children's social companions. *International Journal of Behavioral Development, 32*, 522–530.

de Haan, M., Johnson, M. H., & Halit, H. (2003). Development of face-sensitive event-related potential during infancy: A review. *International Journal of Psychophysiology, 51,* 45–58.

deHouwer, A. (1995). Bilingual language acquisition. In P. Fletcher & B. MacWhinney (Eds.), *The handbook of child language* (pp. 219–250). Oxford, UK: Basil Blackwell.

Delaney, C. (2000). Making babies in a Turkish village. In J. S. DeLoache & A. Gottlieb (Eds.), *A world of babies: Imagined childcare guides for seven societies.* New York: Cambridge University Press.

DeLoache, J. S. (1987). Rapid change in the symbolic functioning of very young children. *Science, 238,* 1556–1557.

DeLoache, J. S. (2000). Dual representation and young children's use of scale models. *Child Development, 71,* 329–338.

DeLoache, J. S. (2002). The symbol-mindedness of young children. In W. Hartup & R. Weinberg (Eds.), *The Minnesota Symposium on Child Psychology* (Vol. 32). Mahwah, NJ: Erlbaum.

DeLoache, J. S. (2004). Becoming symbol-minded. *Trends in Cognitive Sciences, 8*, 66–70.

DeLoache, J. S. (2005). Mindful of symbols. *Scientific American,* 72–77.

DeLoache, J. S., Cassidy, D. J., & Carpenter, C. J. (1987). The three bears are all boys: Mothers' labeling of gender-neutral picture book characters. *Sex roles, 17*, 163–178.

DeLoache, J. S., & Ganea, P. A. (2009). Symbol-based learning in infancy. In A. Woodward & A. Needham (Eds.), *Learning and the Infant Mind.* New York: Oxford University Press.

DeLoache, J. S., & Gottlieb, A. (Eds.). (2000). *A world of babies: Imagined childcare guides for seven societies*. Cambridge, UK: Cambridge University Press.

DeLoache, J. S., & Marzolf, D. P. (1995). The use of dolls to interview young children. *Journal of Experimental Child Psychology, 60,* 155–173.

DeLoache, J. S., Miller, K. F., & Rosengren, K. S. (1997). The credible shrinking room: Very young children's performance with symbolic and non-symbolic relations. *Psychological Science, 8,* 308–313.

DeLoache, J. S., Pierroutsakos, S. L., Uttal, D. H., Rosengren, K. S., & Gottlieb, A. (1998). Grasping the nature of pictures. *Psychological Science, 9,* 205–210.

DeLoache, J. S., Simcock, G., & Macari, S. (2005). Planes, trains, automobiles—and tea sets: Extremely intense interests in very young children. Unpublished manuscript.

DeLoache, J. S., Strauss, M. S., & Maynard, J. (1979). Picture perception in infancy. *Infant Behavior and Development, 2,* 77–89.

DeLoache, J. S., Uttal, D. H., & Rosengren, K. S. (2004). Scale errors offer evidence for a perception-action dissociation early in life. *Science, 304*, 1027–1029.

DeLoache, J. S., Uttal, D. H., & Pierroutsakos, S. L. (2000). What's up? The emergence of an orientation preference for picture books. *Journal of Cognition and Development, 1,* 81–95.

Delsing, M. J. M. H., ter Bogt, T. F. M., Engels, R. C. M. E., & Meeus, W. H. J. (2007). Adolescents' peer crowd identification in the Netherlands: Structure and associations with problem behaviors. *Journal of Research on Adolescence, 17,* 467–480.

Deluty, R. H. (1985). Cognitive mediation of aggressive, assertive, and submissive behavior in children. *International Journal of Behavioral Development, 8,* 355–369.

DeMarie-Dreblow, D., & Miller, P. H. (1988). The development of children's strategies for selective attention: Evidence for a transitional period. *Child Development, 59,* 1504–1513.

Dempster, F. N. (1995). Interference and inhibition in cognition: An historical perspective. In F. N. Dempster & C. J. Brainerd (Eds.), *Interference and inhibition in cognition* (pp. 3–26). San Diego, CA: Academic Press.

Dempster, F. N., & Corkill, A. J. (1999). Interference and inhibition in cognition and behavior: Unifying themes for educational psychology. *Educational Psychology Review, 11,* 1–88.

DeMulder, E. K., Denham, S., Schmidt, M., & Mitchell, J. (2000). Q-sort assessment of attachment security during the preschool years: Links from home to school. *Developmental Psychology, 36,* 274–282.

Denham, S. A. (1986). Social cognition, prosocial behavior, and emotion in preschoolers: Contextual validation. *Child Development, 57,* 194–201.

Denham, S. A. (1998). *Emotional development in young children.* New York: Guilford.

Denham, S. A. (2006). The emotional basis of learning and development in early childhood education. In B. Spodek & O. N. Saracho (Eds.), *Handbook of research on the education of young children,* (2nd ed., pp. 85–103). Mahwah, NJ: Erlbaum.

Denham, S. A., Blair, K. A., DeMulder, E., Levitas, J., Sawyer, K., Auerbach-Major, S., & Queenan, P. (2003). Preschool emotional competence: Pathway to social competence. *Child Development, 74,* 238–256.

Denham, S. A., Blair, K., Schmidt, M., & DeMulder, E. (2002). Compromised emotional competence: Seeds of violence sown early? *American Journal of Orthopsychiatry, 72,* 70–82.

Denham, S. A., & Burton, R. (1996). A social-emotional intervention program for at-risk four-year-olds. *Journal of School Psychology, 34,* 225–245.

Denham, S. A., Caverly, S., Schmidt, M., Blair, K., DeMulder, E., Caal, S., Hamada, H., & Mason, T. (2002). Preschool understanding of emotions: Contributions to classroom anger and aggression. *Journal of Child Psychology and Psychiatry, 43,* 901–916.

Denham, S. A., & Couchoud, E. A. (1990). Young preschoolers' understanding of emotions. *Child Study Journal, 20,* 171–192.

Denham, S. A., & Couchoud, E. A. (1991). Social-emotional predictors of preschoolers' responses to adult negative emotion. *Journal of Child Psychology and Psychiatry, 32,* 595–608.

Denham, S. A., Zoller, D., & Couchoud, E. A. (1994). Socialization of preschoolers' emotion understanding. *Developmental Psychology, 30,* 928–936.

Dennis, S. (1992). Stage and structure in the development of children's spatial representations. In R. Case (Ed.), *The mind's staircase: Exploring the conceptual underpinnings of children's thought and knowledge.* Hillsdale, NJ: Erlbaum.

Dennis, T., Bendersky, M., Ramsay, D., & Lewis, M. (2006). Reactivity and regulation in children prenatally exposed to cocaine. *Developmental Psychology, 42,* 688–697.

Dennis, W., & Najarian, P. (1957). Infant development under environmental handicap. *Psychological Monographs, 71*(7, Whole No. 436).

DeRosier, M. E., Kupersmidt, J. B., & Patterson, C. J. (1994). Children's academic and behavioral adjustment as a function of the chronicity and proximity of peer rejection. *Child Development, 65,* 1799–1813.

Dettling, A. C., Parker, S. W., Lane, S., Sebanc, A., & Gunnar, M. R. (2000). Quality of care and temperament determine changes in cortisol concentrations over the day for young children in childcare. *Psychoneuroendocrinology, 25,* 819–836.

Deutsch, F. M. (2005). Filial piety, patrilineality, and China's one-child policy. *Journal of Family Issues, 27,* 366–389.

deVilliers, J. G., & deVilliers, P. A. (1973). A cross-sectional study of the acquisition of grammatical morphemes in child speech. *Journal of Psycholinguistic Research, 2,* 267–278.

De Vries, J. I. P., Visser, G. H. A., & Prechtl, H. F. R. (1982). The emergence of fetal behavior: I. Qualitative aspects. *Early Human Development, 7,* 301–322.

DeVries, M. W. (1984). Temperament and infant mortality among the Masai of East Africa. *American Journal of Psychiatry, 141,* 1189–1194.

De Wolff, M. S., & van IJzendoorn, M. H. (1997). Sensitivity and attachment: A meta-analysis on parental antecedents of infant attachment. *Child Development, 68,* 571–591.

Diamond, A. (1985). Development of the ability to use recall to guide action as indicated by infants' performance on AB. *Child Development, 56,* 868–883.

Diamond, A. (1991). Neuropsychological insights into the meaning of object concept development. In S. Carey & R. Gelman (Eds.), *The epigenesis of mind: Essays on biology and cognition* (pp. 67–110). Hillsdale, NJ: Erlbaum.

Diamond, A., Briand, L., Fossella, J., & Gehlbach, L. (2004). Genetic and neurochemical modulation of prefrontal cognitive functions in children. *American Journal of Psychiatry, 161,* 125–132.

Diamond, A., & Goldman-Rakic, P. (1989). Comparison of human infants and rhesus monkeys on Piaget's A-not-B task: Evidence for dependence on dorsolateral prefrontal cortex. *Experimental Brain Research, 74,* 24–40.

Diamond, A., & Amso, D. (2008). Contributions of neuroscience to our understanding of cognitive development. *Current Directions in Psychological Science,* 136–141.

Diamond, A., Kirkham, N., & Amso, D. (2002). Condition under which young children can hold two rules in mind and inhibit a prepotent response. *Developmental Psychology, 38,* 352–362.

Diamond, L. M. (1998). Development of sexual orientation among adolescent and young adult women. *Developmental Psychology, 34,* 1085–1095.

Diamond, L. M. (2008). Female bisexuality from adolescence to adulthood: Results from a 10-year longitudinal study. *Developmental Psychology, 44,* 5–14.

Diamond, L. M., & Lucas, S. (2004). Sexual-minority and heterosexual youths' peer relationships: Experiences, expectations, and implications for well-being. *Journal of Research on Adolescence, 14,* 313–340.

Diamond, L. M., Savin-Williams, R. C., & Dube, E. M. (1999). Sex, dating, passionate friendships and romance: Intimate peer relations among lesbian, gay, and bisexual adolescents. In W. Furman, B. B. Brown, & C. Feiring (Eds.), *The development of romantic relationships in adolescence* (pp. 175–210). Cambridge, UK: Cambridge University Press.

Diamond, M., & Sigmundson, H. K. (1997). Sex reassignment at birth: Long term review and clinical implications. *Archives of Pediatric and Adolescent Medicine, 151,* 298–304.

DiBiase, R., & Waddell, S. (1995). Some effects of homelessness on the psychological functioning of preschoolers. *Journal of Abnormal Child Psychology, 23*, 783–792.

Dichtelmiller, M., Meisels, S. J., Plunkett, J. W., Bozynski, M. E., & Mangelsdorf, S. (1992). The relationship of parental knowledge to the development of extremely low birth weight infants. *Journal of Early Intervention, 16*, 210–220.

Dick, D. M., Pagan, J. L., Holliday, C., Viken, R., Pulkkinen, L., Kaprio, J., & Rose, R. J. (2007). Gender differences in friends' influences on adolescent drinking: A genetic epidemiological study. *Alcoholism: Clinical and Experimental Research, 31*, 2012–2019.

Dickens, W. T., & Flynn, J. R. (2001). Heritability estimates versus large environmental effects: The IQ paradox resolved. *Psychological Review, 108*, 346–369.

Dickens, W. T., & Flynn, J. R. (2006). Black Americans reduce the racial IQ gap: Evidence from standardization samples. *Psychological Science, 17*, 913–920.

Diedrich, F. J., Thelen, E., Smith, L. B., & Corbetta, D. (2000). Motor memory is a factor in infant perseverative errors. *Developmental Science, 3*, 479–494.

Diener, M. (2000). Gift from the Gods: A Balinese guide to early child rearing. In J. DeLoache & A. Gotlieb (Eds.), *A world of babies: Imagined childcare guides for seven societies.* Cambridge, UK: Cambridge University Press.

Diener, M., & Kim, D-Y. (2004). Maternal and child predictors of preschool children's social competence. *Applied Developmental Psychology, 25*, 3–24.

Dijkstra, J. K., Lindenberg, S., Veenstra, R. A. (2008). Beyond the class norm: Bullying behavior of popular adolescents and its relation to peer acceptance and rejection. *Journal of Abnormal Child Psychology, 36*, 1289–1299.

Dilworth-Bart, J. E., & Moore, C. F. (2006). Mercy mercy me: Social injustice and the prevention of environmental pollutant exposures among ethnic minority and poor children. *Child Development, 77*, 247–265.

Dionne, G., Tremblay, R., Boivin, M., Laplante, D., & Pérusse, D. (2003). Physical aggression and expressive vocabulary in 19-month-old twins. *Developmental Psychology*, 39, 261–273.

DiPietro, J. A. (1981). Rough and tumble play: A function of gender. *Developmental Psychology*, *17*, 50–58.

DiPietro, J. A. (2004). The role of prenatal maternal stress in child development. *Current Directions in Psychological Science, 13,* 71–74.

DiPietro, J. A., Bornstein, M. H., Costigan, K. A., Pressman, E. K., Hahn, C-S., Painter, K., Smith, B. A., & Yi, L. J. (2002). What does fetal movement predict about behavior during the first two years of life? *Developmental Psychobiology, 40,* 358–371.

DiPietro, J. A., Costigan, K. A., Shupe, A. K., Pressman, E. K., & Johnson, T. R. B. (1998). Fetal neurobehavioral development: Associations with socioeconomic class and fetal sex. *Developmental Psychobiology, 33*, 79–91.

DiPietro, J. A., Hilton, S. C., Hawkins, M., Costigan, K. A., & Pressman, E. K. (2002). Maternal stress and affect influence fetal neurobehavioral development. *Developmental Psychology, 38,* 659–668.

DiPietro, J. A., Suess, P. A., Wheeler, J. S., Smouse, P. H., & Newlin, D. B. (1995). Reactivity and regulation in cocaine-exposed infants. *Infant Behavior and Development, 18*, 407–414.

Dirks, J., & Gibson, E. (1977). Infants' perception of similarity between live people and their photographs. *Child Development, 48,* 124–130.

Dishion, T. J. (1990). The family ecology of boys' peer relations in middle childhood. *Child Development, 61,* 874–892.

Dishion, T. J., Andrews, D. W., & Crosby, L. (1995). Antisocial boys and their friends in early adolescence: Relationship characteristics, quality, and interactional process. *Child Development, 66*, 139–151.

Dishion, T. J., Eddy, J. M., Haas, E., Li, F., & Spracklen, K. (1997). Friendships and violent behavior during adolescence. *Social Development, 6*, 207–223.

Dishion, T. J., Shaw, D., Connell, A., Gardner, F., Weaver, C., & Melvin, W. (2008). The family check-up with high-risk indigent families: Preventing problem behavior by increasing parents' positive behavior support in early childhood. *Child Development, 79*, 1395–1414.

Diversi, M., Filho, N. M., & Morelli, M. (1999). Daily reality on the streets of Campinas, Brazil. *New Directions in Child Development, 85*, 19–34.

DiVitto, B., & Goldberg, S. (1979). The effects of newborn medical status on early parent-infant interaction. In T. M. Field, A. M. Sostch, S. Goldberg, & H. H. Shuman (Eds.), *Infants born at risk: Behavior and development* (pp. 311–332). New York: Spectrum.

Dix, T., & Grusec, J. E. (1983). Parental influence techniques: An attributional analysis. *Child Development, 54*, 645–652.

Dobzhansky, T. (1955). *Evolution, genetics, and man.* New York: Wiley.

Dodge, K. A. (1980). Social cognition and children's aggressive behavior. *Child Development, 51*, 162–170.

Dodge, K. A. (1986). A social information processing model of social competence in children. In M. Perlmutter (Ed.), *Minnesota Symposium on Child Psychology: Vol. 18. Cognitive perspectives on children's social and behavioral development* (pp. 77–125). Mahwah, NJ: Erlbaum.

Dodge, K. A., Coie, J. D., & Lynam, D. (2006). Aggression and antisocial behavior in youth. In W. Damon & R. L. Lerner (Senior Eds.) and N. Eisenberg (Vol. Ed.), *Handbook of child psychology. Vol. 3. Social, emotional, and personality development* (6th ed.). Hoboken, NJ.: Wiley.

Dodge, K. A., Coie, J. D., Pettit, G. S., & Price, J. M. (1990). Peer status and aggression in boys' groups: Developmental and contextual analyses. *Child Development, 61*, 1289–1309.

Dodge, K. A., Greenberg, M. T., & Malone, P. S. (2008). Testing an idealized dynamic cascade model of the development of serious violence in adolescence. *Child Development, 79*, 1907–1927.

Dodge, K. A., Lansford, J. E., Burks, V. S., Bates, J. E., Pettit, G. S., Fontaine, R., & Price, J. M. (2003). Peer rejection and social information-processing factors in the development of aggressive behavior problems in children. *Child Development, 74 (2)*, 374–393.

Dodge, K. A., Lansford, J. E., & Dishion, T. J. (2006). The problem of deviant peer influences in intervention programs. In K. A. Dodge, T. J. Dishion, & J. E. Lansford (Eds.), *Deviant Peer Influences in Programs for Youth: Problems and Solutions*. New York: Guilford.

Dodge, K. A., Lochman, J. E., Harnish, J. D., Bates, J. E, & Pettit, G. S. (1997). Reactive and proactive aggression in school children and psychiatrically impaired chronically assaultive youth. *Journal of Abnormal Psychology, 106*, 37–51.

Dodge, K. A., Murphy, R. R., & Buchsbaum, K. (1984). The assessment of intention-cue detection skills in children: Implications for developmental psychopathology. *Child Development, 55*, 163–173.

Dodge, K. A., & Pettit, G. S. (2003). A biophychosocial model of the development of chronic conduct problems in adolescence. *Developmental Psychology*, 39(2), 349–371.

Dodge, K. A., Pettit, G. S., & Bates, J. E. (1994). Socialization mediators of the relation between socioeconomic status and child conduct problems. *Child Development, 65*, 649–665.

Dodge, K. A., Pettit, G. S., Bates, J. E., & Valente, E. (1995). Social information processing patterns partially mediate the effect of early physical abuse on later conduct problems. *Journal of Abnormal Psychology, 104*, 632–643.

Dodge, K. A., Pettit, G. S., McClaskey, C. L., & Brown, M. M. (1986). Social competence in children. *Monographs of the Society for Research in Child Development, 51*(2, Serial No. 213), 1–85.

Dodge, K. A., Schlundt, D. G., Schocken, I., & Delugach, J. D. (1983). Social competence and children's social status: The role of peer group entry strategies. *Merrill-Palmer Quarterly, 29*, 309–336.

Dogan, S. J., Conger, R. D., Kim, K. J., & Masyn, K. E. (2007). Cognitive and parenting pathways in the transmission of antisocial behavior from parents to adolescents. *Child Development, 78*, 335–349.

Dohnt, H. & Tiggemann, M. (2006). The contribution of peer and media influences to the development of body satisfaction and self-esteem in young girls: A prospective study. *Developmental Psychology, 42*(5), 929–936.

Domitrovich, C. E., Cortes, R. C., & Greenberg, M. T. (2007). Improving young children's social and emotional competence: A randomized trial of the preschool "PATHS" curriculum. *Journal of Primary Prevention, 28*, 67–91.

Donaldson, S. K., & Westerman, M. A. (1986). Development of children's understanding of ambivalence and causal theories of emotions. *Developmental Psychology, 22*, 655–662.

Dong, M., Giles, W. H., Felitti, V. J., Dube, S. R., Williams, J. E., Chapman, D. P., & Anda, R. F. (2004). Insights into causal pathways for ischemic heart disease: Adverse childhood experiences study. *Circulation, 110*, 1761–1766.

Donnellan, M. B., Trzesniewski, K. H., Robins, R. W., Moffitt, T. E., & Caspi, A. (2005). Low self-esteem is related to aggression, antisocial behavior, and delinquency. *Psychological Science, 16*, 328–335.

Dorval, B., & Eckerman, C. O. (1984). Developmental trends in the quality of conversation achieved by small groups of acquainted peers. *Monographs of the Society for Research in Child Development, 49* (Serial No. 206).

Douglas, E. (2001). The ABCs of early child care research: Keeping Congress accurately informed. *Psychological Science Agenda, 14*, 10–11.

Downey, G., & Coyne, J. C. (1990). Children of depressed parents: An integrative review. *Psychological Bulletin, 108*, 50–76.

Dreves, C. & Jovanovic, J. (1998). Male dominance in the classroom: Does it explain the gender difference in young adolescents' science ability perceptions? *Applied Developmental Science, 2*, 90–98.

Driesen, N. R., & Raz, N. (1995). The influence of sex, age, and handedness on corpus callosum morphology: A meta analysis. *Psychobiology, 23*, 240 247.

Drillien, C. M. (1964). *The growth and development of the prematurely born infant*. Edinburgh & London: Livingstone.

Driscoll, A. K., Russell, S. T., Crockett, L. J. (2008). Parenting styles and youth well-being across immigrant generations. *Journal of Family Issues, 29*, 185–209.

Drotar, D. (1992). Personality development, problem solving, and behavior problems among preschool children with early histories of nonorganic failure-to-thrive: A controlled study. *Developmental and Behavioral Pediatrics, 13*, 266–273.

Drummond, K. D., Bradley, S. J., Peterson-Badali, M., & Zucker, K. J. (2008). A follow-up study of girls with gender identity disorder. *Developmental Psychology, 44*, 34–45.

Dubas, J. S., & Gerris, J. R. M. (2002). Longitudinal changes in the time parents spend in activities with their adolescent children as a function of child age, pubertal status, and gender. *Journal of Family Psychology, 16*, 415–427.

Duckett, E., & Richards, M. H. (1995). Maternal employment and the quality of daily experience for young adolescents of single mothers. *Journal of Family Psychology, 9*, 418–432.

Duckworth, A. L., & Seligman, M. E. P. (2005). Self-discipline outdoes IQ in predicting academic performance of adolescents. *Psychological Science, 16*, 939–944.

Dumka, L. E., Roosa, M. W., & Jackson, K. M. (1997). Risk, conflict, mothers' parenting, and children's adjustment in low-income, Mexican immigrant and Mexican American families. *Journal of Marriage and the Family, 59*, 309–323.

Duncan, G. J., Brooks-Gunn, J., & Klebanov, P. K. (1994). Economic deprivation and early childhood development. *Child Development, 65*, 296–318.

Duncan, G. J., Dowsett, C. J., Claessens, A., Magnuson, K., Huston, A. C., Klebanov, P., Pagani, L., Feinstein, L., Engel, M., Brooks-Gunn, J., Sexton, H., Duckworth, K., & Japel, C. (2007). School readiness and later achievement. *Developmental Psychology, 43*, 1428–1446.

Duncan, G. J., Yeung, W., Brooks-Gunn, J., & Smith, J. (1998). How much does poverty affect the life chances of children? *American Sociological Review, 63*, 406–423.

Dunn, J. (1988). *The beginnings of social understanding*. Cambridge, MA: Harvard University Press.

Dunn, J. (1992). Siblings and their development. *Current Directions in Psychological Science, 1*, 6–9.

Dunn, J. (1999). Personal communication.

Dunn, J. (2004). *Children's friendships: The beginning of intimacy*. Oxford: Blackwell Publishing.

Dunn, J., & Brown, J. (1994). Affect expression in the family, children's understanding of emotions, and their interactions with others. *Merrill-Palmer Quarterly, 40*, 120–137.

Dunn, J., Brown, J., & Beardsall, L. (1991). Family talk about feeling states and children's later understanding of others' emotions. *Developmental Psychology, 27*, 448–455.

Dunn, J., Brown, J., Slomkowski, C., Tesla, C., & Youngblade, L. (1991). Young children's understanding of other people's feelings and beliefs: Individual differences and their antecedents. *Child Development, 62,* 1352–1366.

Dunphy, D. C. (1963). The social structure of urban adolescent peer groups. *Sociometry, 26,* 230–246.

Dunsmore, J. C., & Halberstadt, A. G. (1997). How does family emotional expressiveness affect children's schemas? *New Directions for Child Development, 77,* 45–68.

Dupéré, F., Lacourse, E., Willms, J. D., Vitaro, F., & Tremblay, R. E. (2007). Affiliation to youth gangs during adolescence: The interaction between childhood psychopathic tendencies and neighborhood disadvantage. *Journal of Abnormal Child Psychology, 35,* 1035–1045.

Durbin, C. E., Hayden, E. P., Klein, D., & Olino, T. M. (2007). Stability of laboratory-assessed temperamental emotionality traits from ages 3 to 7. *Emotion, 7,* 388–399.

Durrett, M. E., Otaki, M., & Richards, P. (1984). Attachment and the mother's perception of support from the father. *International Journal of Behavioral Development, 72,* 167–176.

Durston, S., Hulshoff Pol, H. E., Casey, B. J., Giedd, J. N., Buitelaar, J. K., & van Engeland, H. (2001). Anatomical MRI of the developing human brain: What have we learned? *Journal of the American Academy of Child and Adolescent Psychiatry, 40,* 1012–1020.

Dweck, C. S. (1999). *Self-theories: Their role in motivation, personality, and development.* Philadelphia: Psychology Press.

Dweck, C.S. (2006). *Mindset.* New York: Random House.

Dweck, C. S., & Leggett, E. L. (1988). A social-cognitive approach to motivation and personality. *Psychological Review, 95,* 256–273.

Eagly, A. H. (1987). *Sex differences in social behavior: A social-role interpretation.* Hillsdale, NJ: Lawrence Erlbaum Associates.

Eagly, A. H., Wood, W., & Diekman, A. B. (2000). Social role theory of sex differences and similarities: A current appraisal. In T. Eckes & H. M. Trautner (eds.), *The developmental social psychology of gender* (pp. 123–174). Mahwah, NJ: Erlbaum.

East, P. L., Felice, M. E., & Morgan, M. C. (1993). Sisters' and girlfriends' sexual and childbearing behavior: Effects on early girls' sexual outcomes. *Journal of Marriage and the Family, 55,* 953–963.

East, P. L., & Jacobson, L. J. (2001). The younger siblings of teenage mothers: A follow-up of their pregnancy risk. *Developmental Psychology, 37,* 254–264.

Eaton, W. O. & Enns, L. R. (1986). Sex differences in motor activity level. *Psychological Bulletin, 100,* 19–28.

Eaton, W. O., & Saudino, K. J. (1992). Prenatal activity level as a temperament dimension? Individual differences and developmental functions in fetal movement. *Infant Behavior and Development, 15,* 57–70.

Eccles, J., Barber, B., Jozefowicz, D., Malenchuk, O., & Vida, M. (1999). Self-evaluations of competence, task values, and self-esteem. In N. G. Johnson, & M. C. Roberts (Eds.), *Beyond appearance: A new look at adolescent girls* (pp. 53–83). Washington, DC: American Psychological Association.

Eccles, J. S., Freedman-Doan, C., Frome, P., Jacobs, J., & Yoon, K. S. (2000). Gender-role socialization in the family: A longitudinal approach. In T. Eckes and H. M. Trautner (Eds.), *The developmental social psychology of gender* (pp. 333–360). Mahwah, NJ: Lawrence Erlbaum Associates, Inc.

Eccles, J. S., & Midgley, C. (1989). Stage/environment fit: Developmentally appropriate classrooms for early adolescents. In R. Ames & C. Ames (Eds.), *Research on motivation in education* (Vol. 3, pp. 139–181). Orlando, FL: Academic Press.

Eccles, J. S., & Wigfield, A. (2002). Motivational beliefs, values, and goals. *Annual Review of Psychology, 53,* 109–132.

Eccles, J. S., Wigfield, A., Flanagan, C., Miller, C., Reuman, D., & Yee, D. (1989). Self-concepts, domain values, and self-esteem: Relations and changes at early adolescence. *Journal of Personality, 57,* 283–310.

Eckenrode, J., Laird, M., & Doris, J. (1993). School performance and disciplinary problems among abused and neglected children. *Developmental Psychology, 29,* 53–62.

Eckert, P. (1989). *Jocks and burnouts: Social categories and identity in the high school.* New York: Teachers' College Press.

Edelman, G. M. (1987). *Neural Darwinism: The theory of neuronal group selection.* New York: Basic Books.

Eder, D. (1985). The cycle of popularity: Interpersonal relations among female adolescents. *Sociology of Education, 58,* 154–165.

Edwards, C. P. (1992). Cross-cultural perspective on family-peer relations. In R. D. Parke & G. W. Ladd (Eds.), *Family-peer relationships: Modes of linkage* (pp. 285–316). Hillsdale, NJ: Erlbaum.

Edwards, G. D., Bangert, A. W., Cooch, G., Shinfuku, N., Chen, T., Bi, Y., & Rappe, P. (2005). The impact of sibling status on Chinese college students' quality of life. *Social Behavior and Personality, 33,* 227–242.

Egan, S. K. & Perry, D. G. (2001). Gender identity: A multidimensional analysis with implications for psychosocial adjustment. *Developmental Psychology, 37,* 451–463.

Egley, A. (2002, February). National Youth Gangs Survey trends from 1996 to 2000. OJJDP Fact Sheet. U.S. Department of Justice, Office of Juvenile Justice and Delinquency Prevention.

Egley, A., Jr., & O'Donnell, C. E. (2009, April). Highlights of the 2007 National Youth Gang Survey. OJJDP Fact Sheet. U.S. Department of Justice, Office of Juvenile Justice and Delinquency Prevention.

Ehri, L. C., Nunes, S. R., Willows, D. M., Schuster, B. V., Yaghoub Zadeh, Z., & Shanahan, T. (2001). Phonemic awareness instruction helps children learn to read: Evidence from the National Reading Panel's meta-analysis. *Reading Research Quarterly, 36,* 250–287.

Eichenbaum, H. (2003). Learning and memory: Brain systems. In L. R. Squire, F. E. Bloom, S. K. McConnell, J. L. Roberts, N. C. Spitzer, & M. J. Zigmond (Eds.), *Fundamental neuroscience* (2nd ed., pp. 1299–1327). New York: Academic Press.

Eiden, R. D., Colder, C., Edwards, E. P., & Leonard, K. E. (2009). A longitudinal study of social competence among children of alcoholic and nonalcoholic parents: Role of parental psychopathology, parental warmth, and self-regulation. *Psychology of Addictive Behaviors, 23,* 36–46.

Eigsti, I-M., Zayas, V., Mischel, W., Shoda, Y., Ayduk, O., Dadlani, M. B., Davidson, M. C., Aber, J. L., & Casey, B. J. (2006). Predicting cognitive control from preschool to late adolescecence and young adulthood. *Psychological Science, 17,* 478–484.

Eimas, P. D., Siqueland, E. R., Jusczyk, P., & Vigorito, J. (1971). Speech perception in infants. *Science, 171,* 303–306.

Eisenberg, A. R. (1999). Emotion talk among Mexican American and Anglo American mothers and children from two social classes. *Merrill-Palmer Quarterly, 45,* 267–284.

Eisenberg, M. E., Neumark-Sztainer, D., & Story, M. (2003). Associations of weight-based teasing and emotional well-being among adolescents. *Archives of Pediatrics & Adolescent Medicine, 157,* 733–738.

Eisenberg, N. (1986). *Altruistic emotion, cognition, and behavior.* Hillsdale, NJ: Erlbaum.

Eisenberg, N. (2000). Emotion, regulation, and moral development. In S. T. Fiske, D. L. Schacter, & C. Zahn-Waxler (Eds.), *Annual review of psychology* (Vol. 51; pp. 665–697). Palo Alto, CA: Annual Reviews.

Eisenberg, N., Boehnke, K., Schuhler, P., & Silbereisen, R. K. (1985). The development of prosocial behavior and cognitions in German children. *Journal of Cross-Cultural Psychology, 16,* 69–82.

Eisenberg, N., Carlo, G., Murphy, B., & Van Court, P. (1995). Prosocial development in late adolescence: A longitudinal study. *Child Development, 66,* 911–936.

Eisenberg, N., Chang, L., Ma, Y., & Huang, X. (2009). Relations of parenting style to Chinese children's effortful control, ego resilience, and maladjustment. *Development and Psychopathology, 21,* 455–477.

Eisenberg, N., Cialdini, R., McCreath, H., & Shell, R. (1987). Consistency-based compliance: When and why do children become vulnerable? *Journal of Personality and Social Psychology, 52,* 1174–1181.

Eisenberg, N., Cumberland, A., & Spinrad, T. L. (1998). Parental socialization of emotion. *Psychological Inquiry, 9,* 241–273.

Eisenberg, N., & Fabes, R. A. (1998). Prosocial development. In W. Damon (Series Ed.) & N. Eisenberg (Vol. Ed), *Handbook of child psychology: Vol. 3. Social, emotional, and personality development* (5th ed., pp. 701–778). New York: Wiley.

Eisenberg, N., Fabes, R. A., Bernzweig, J., Karbon, M., Poulin, R., & Hanish, L. (1993). The relations of emotionality and regulation to preschoolers' social skills and sociometric status. *Child Development, 64,* 1418–1438.

Eisenberg, N., Fabes, R. A., Guthrie, I. K., & Reiser, M. (2000). Dispositional emotionality and regulation: Their role in predicting quality of social functioning. *Journal of Personality and Social Psychology, 78,* 136–157.

Eisenberg, N., Fabes, R. A., & Murphy, B. C. (1996). Parents' reactions to children's negative emotions: Relations to children's social competence and comforting behavior. *Child Development, 67,* 2227–2247.

Eisenberg, N., Fabes, R. A., Murphy, B., Karbon, M., Smith, M., & Maszk, P. (1996). The relations of children's dispositional empathy-related responding to their emotionality, regulation, and social functioning. *Developmental Psychology, 32,* 195–209.

Eisenberg, N., Fabes, R. A., Schaller, M., Carlo, G., & Miller, P. A. (1991). The relations of parental characteristics and practices to children's vicarious emotional responding. *Child Development, 62,* 1393–1408.

Eisenberg, N., Fabes, R. A., Schaller, M., & Miller, P. A. (1989). Sympathy and personal distress: Development, gender differences, and interrelations of indexes. *New Directions in Child Development, 44,* 107–126.

Eisenberg, N., Fabes, R. A., Shepard, S. A., Guthrie, I. K., Murphy, B. C., & Reiser, M. (1999). Parental reactions to children's negative emotions: Longitudinal relations to quality of children's social functioning. *Child Development 70,* 513–534.

Eisenberg, N., Fabes, R. A., Shepard, S. A., Murphy, B. C., Jones, J., & Guthrie, I. K. (1998). Contemporaneous and longitudinal prediction of children's sympathy from dispositional regulation and emotionality. *Developmental Psychology, 34,* 910–924.

Eisenberg, N., Fabes, R. A., & Spinrad, T. L. (2006). Prosocial behavior. In W. Damon & R. L. Lerner (Series Eds.) & N. Eisenberg (Vol. Ed.), *Handbook of child psychology, Vol. 3. Social, emotional, and personality development* (6th ed., pp. 646–718). Hoboken, NJ: Wiley.

Eisenberg, N., Gershoff, E. T., Fabes, R. A., Shepard, S. A., Cumberland, A. J., Lososya, et al. (2001). Mothers' emotional expressivity and children's behavior problems and social competence: Mediation through children's regulation. *Developmental Psychology, 37,* 475–490.

Eisenberg, N., Guthrie, I., Cumberland, A., Murphy, B. C., Shepard, S. A., Zhou, Q., & Carlo, G. (2002). Prosocial development in early adulthood: A longitudinal study. *Journal of Personality and Social Psychology, 82,* 993–1006.

Eisenberg, N., Guthrie, I. K., Murphy, B. C., Shepard, S. A., Cumberland, A., & Carlo, G. (1999). Consistency and development of prosocial dispositions: A longitudinal study. *Child Development, 70,* 1360–1372.

Eisenberg, N., Hofer, C., Spinrad, T., Gershoff, E., Valiente, C., Losoya, S. L., Zhou, Q., Cumberland, A., Liew, J., Reiser, M., & Maxon, E. (2008). Understanding parent-adolescent conflict discussions: Concurrent and across-time prediction from youths' dispositions and parenting. *Monographs of the Society for Research in Child Development, 73* (Serial No. 290, No. 2), 1–160.

Eisenberg, N., Michalik, N., Spinrad, T. L., Hofer, C., Kupfer, A., Valiente, C., et al. (2007). The relations of effortful control and impulsivity to children's symptoms: A longitudinal study. *Cognitive Development, 22,* 544–567.

Eisenberg, N., Miller, P. A., Shell, R., McNalley, S., & Shea, C. (1991). Prosocial development in adolescence: A longitudinal study. *Developmental Psychology, 27,* 849–857.

Eisenberg, N., Murphy, B., & Shepard, S. (1997). The development of empathic accuracy. In W. Ickes (Eds.), *Empathic accuracy* (pp. 73–116). New York: Guilford.

Eisenberg, N., Murray, E., & Hite, T. (1982). Children's reasoning regarding sex typed toy choices. *Child Development, 53,* 81–86.

Eisenberg, N., & Mussen, P. (1989). *The roots of prosocial behavior in children.* Cambridge, UK: Cambridge University Press.

Eisenberg, N., Sadovsky, A., & Spinrad, T. L. (2005). Associations among emotion-related regulation, language skills, emotion knowledge, and academic outcomes. *New Directions in Child and Adolescent Development, 109,* 109–118.

Eisenberg, N., Spinrad, T. L., & Eggum, N. D. (in press). Emotion-related self-regulation and its relation to children's maladjustment. *Annual Review of Clinical Psychology.*

Eisenberg, N., Spinrad, T. L., Fabes, R. A., Reiser, M., Cumberland, A., Shepard, S. A., Valiente, C., Losoya, S. H., Guthrie, I. K., & Thompson, M. (2004). The relations of effortful control and impulsivity to children's resiliency and adjustment. *Child Development, 75,* 25–46.

Eisenberg, N., Valiente, C., Spinrad, T. L., Cumberland, A., Liew, J., Reiser, M., Zhou, Q., & Losoya, S. H. (2009). Longitudinal relations of children's effortful control, impulsivity, and negative emotionality to their externalizing, internalizing, and co-occurring behavior problems. *Developmental Psychology, 45,* 988–1008.

Eisenberg-Berg, N., & Geisheker, E. (1979). Content of preachings and power of the model/preacher: The effects on children's generosity. *Developmental Psychology, 15,* 168–175.

Eisenberg-Berg, N., & Hand, M. (1979). The relationship of preschooler's reasoning about prosocial moral conflicts to prosocial behavior. *Child Development, 50,* 356–363.

Ekeus, C., Christensson, K., & Hjern, A. (2004). Unintentional and violent injuries among pre-school children of teenage mothers in Sweden: A national cohort study. *Journal of Epidemiology & Community Health, 58,* 680–685.

Elder, G. H., Jr., Van Nguyen, T., & Caspi, A. (1985). Linking family hardship to children's lives. *Child Development, 56,* 361–375.

Elicker, J., Englund, M., & Sroufe, L. A. (1992). Predicting peer competence and peer relationships in childhood from early parent-child relationships. In R. D. Parke & G. W. Ladd (Eds.), *Family-peer relationships: Modes of linkage* (pp. 77–106). Hillsdale, NJ: Erlbaum.

Elkind, D. (1967). Egocentrism in adolescence. *Child Development, 38,* 1025–1034.

Elliott, D. S. (1994). Serious violent offenders: Onset, developmental course, and termination: The American Society of Criminology 1993 Presidential Address. *Criminology, 32,* 1–21.

Ellis, B. J., Bates, J. E., Dodge, K. A., Fergusson, D. M., Horwood, L. J., Pettit, G. S., & Woodward, L. (2003). Does father absence place daughters at special risk for early sexual activity and teenage pregnancy? *Child Development, 74,* 801–821.

Ellis, W. E., Crooks, C. V., & Wolfe, D. A. (2009). Relational aggression in peer and dating relationships: Links to psychological and behavioral adjustment. *Social Development, 18,* 253–269.

Ellsworth, C., Muir, D., & Hains, S. (1993). Social competence and person-object differentiation: An analysis of the still-face effect. *Developmental Psychology, 29,* 63–73.

Elman, J. L., Bates, E. A., Johnson, M. H., Karmiloff-Smith, A., Parisi, D., & Plunkett, K. (1996). *Rethinking innateness: A connectionist perspective on development.* Cambridge, MA: The MIT Press.

Else-Quest, N., Hyde, J., Goldsmith, H. & Van Hulle, C. (2006). Gender differences in temperament: A meta-analysis. *Psychological Bulletin, 132,* 33–72.

El-Sheikh, M., & Elmore-Staton, L. (2004). The link between marital conflict and child adjustment: Parent-child conflict and perceived attachments as mediators, potentiators, and mitigators of risk. *Development and Psychopathology, 16,* 631–648.

El-Sheikh, M., Harger, J., & Whitson, S. M. (2001). Exposure to interparental conflict and children's adjustment and physical health: The moderating role of vagal tone. *Child Development, 72,* 1617–1636.

El-Sheikh, M., & Whitson, S. A. (2006). Longitudinal relations between marital conflict and child adjustment: Vagal regulation as a protective factor. *Journal of Family Psychology, 20,* 30–39.

Ely, R., & McCabe, A. (1994). The language play of kindergarten children. *First Language, 14,* 19–35.

Emde, R. N. (1994). Individual meaning and increasing complexity: Contributions of Sigmund Freud and René Spitz to developmental psychology. In R. D. Parke, P. A. Ornstein, J. J. Rieser, & C. Zahn-Waxler (Eds.), *A century of developmental psychology* (pp. 203–231). Washington, DC: American Psychological Association.

Emde, R. N., Plomin, R., Robinson, J., Corley, R., DeFries, J., Fulker, D. W., et al. (1992). Temperament, emotion, and cognition at fourteen months: The MacArthur Longitudinal Twin Study. *Child Development, 63,* 1437–1455.

Eme, R. F. (2007). Sex differences in child-onset, life-course persistent conduct disorder. A review of biological influences. *Clinical Psychology Review, 27,* 607–627.

Emery, R. E. (1989). Family violence. *American Psychologist, 44,* 321–328.

Emery, R. E., & Forehand, R. (1994). Parental divorce and children's well-being: A focus on resilience. In R. J. Haggerty, L. R. Sherrod, N. Garmezy, & M. Rutter (Eds.), *Stress, risk, and resilience in children and adolescents: Processes, mechanisms, and interventions* (pp. 64–99). Cambridge, UK: Cambridge University Press.

Emery, R. E., & Laumann-Billings, L. (1998). An overview of the nature, causes, and consequences of abusive family relationships. *American Psychologist, 53,* 121–135.

Emery, R. E., Waldron, M., Kitzmann, K. M., & Aaron, J. (1999). Delinquent behavior, future divorce or nonmarital childrearing, and externalizing behavior among offspring: A 14-year prospective study. *Journal of Family Psychology, 13,* 568–579.

Engle, R. W. (2002). Working memory capacity as executive attention. *Current Directions in Psychological Science, 11,* 19–23.

Ensor, R., & Hughes, C. (2998). Content or connectedness? Mother-child talk and early social understanding. *Child Development, 79,* 201–216.

Entwistle, D., & Alexander, K. (1992). Summer setback: Pace, poverty, school composition, and mathematics achievement in the first two years of school. *American Sociological Review, 57,* 72–84.

Eppler, M. A., Adolph, K. E., & Weiner, T. (1996). The developmental relationship between infants' exploration and action on sloping surfaces. *Infant Behavior and Development, 19,* 259–264.

Epstein, L. H., Valoski, A., Wing, R. R., & McCurley, J. (1994). Ten-year outcomes of behavioral family-based treatment for childhood obesity. *Health Psychology, 13,* 373–383.

Erdley, C. A., Nangle, D. W., Newman, J. E., & Carpenter, E. M. (2001). Children's friendship experiences and psychological adjustment: Theory and research. *New Directions for Child and Adolescent Development, 91,* 5–24.

Erel, O., Margolin, G., & John, R. S. (1998). Observed sibling interaction: Links with the marital and the mother-child relationship. *Developmental Psychology, 34,* 288–298.

Erel, O., Oberman, Y., & Yirmiya, N. (2000). Maternal versus nonmaternal care and seven domains of children's development. *Psychological Bulletin, 126,* 727–747.

Erickson, M., Egeland, B., & Pianta, R. (1989). The effects of maltreatment on the development of young children. In D. Cicchetti & V. Carlson (Eds.), *Child maltreatment: Theory and research on the causes and consequences of child abuse and neglect* (pp. 647–684). New York: Cambridge University Press.

Erickson, M. F., Sroufe, L. A., & Egeland, B. (1985). The relationship between quality of attachment and behaviour problems in preschool in a high-risk sample. In I. Bretherton & E. Waters (Eds.), *Growing points of attachment theory and research. Monographs of the Society of Research in Child Development, 50* (1–2, Serial No. 209), 147–166.

Ericsson, K. A., & Ward, P. (2007). Capturing the naturally occurring superior performance of experts in the laboratory: Toward a science of expert and exceptional performance. *Current Directions in Psychological Science, 16,* 346–350.

Erikson, E. H. (1950). *Childhood and society.* New York: Norton.

Erikson, E. H. (1968). *Identity: Youth and crisis.* New York: Norton.

Erikson, E. H. (1969). *Gandhi's truth.* New York: Norton.

Erikson, E. H. (1994). *Identity and the life cycle.* New York: Norton.

Erkut, S., Marx, F., Fields, J. P., & Sing, R. (1998). Raising confident and competent girls: One size does not fit all. In L. A. Peplau, S. C. DeBro, R. Veniegas, & P. L. Taylor (Eds.), *Gender, culture, and ethnicity: Current research about women and men.* Mountain View, CA: Mayfield.

Eron, L. D., Huesmann, L. R., Dubow, E., Romanoff, R., & Yarmel, P. W. (1987). Aggression and its correlates over 22 years. In D. H. Crowell, I. M., Evans, & C. R. O'Donnell (Eds.), *Childhood aggression and violence: Sources of influence, prevention, and control* (pp. 249–262). New York: Plenum Press.

Esbensen, F.-A., & Huizinga, D. (1993). Gangs, drugs, and delinquency in a survey of urban youth. *Criminology, 31*, 565–589.

Espelage, D. L., Aragon, S. R., Birkett, M. & Koenig, B. W. (2008). Homophobic teasing, psychological outcomes, and sexual orientation among high school students: What influence do parents and schools have? *School Psychology Review, 37*, 202–216.

Espelage, D., Holt, M., & Henkel, R. (2003). Examination of peer-group contextual effects on aggression during early adolescence. *Child Development, 74*, 205–220.

Estell, D. B., Cairns, R. B., Farmer, T. W., & Cairns, B. D. (2002). Aggression in inner-city early elementary classrooms: Individual and peer group configurations. *Merrill-Palmer Quarterly, 48*, 52–76.

Estes, K. G., Evans, J. L., Alibali, M. W., & Saffran, J. R. (2007). Can infants map meaning to newly segmented words? *Psychological Science, 18*, 254–260.

Etkin, A., Egner, T., Peraza, D. M., Kandel, E. R., & Hirsch, J. (2006). Resolving emotional conflict: A role for the rostral anterior cingulate cortex in modulating activity in the amygdala. *Neuron, 51, 871–882.*

Evans, E. M. (2008). In S. Vosniadou (Ed.), *International Handbook of Research on Conceptual Change.* New York: Routledge/Taylor & Francis Group, pp. 263–294.

Evans, E. M. (2008). Conceptual change and evolutionary biology: A developmental analysis. In S. Vosniadou (Ed.), *International Handbook of Research on Conceptual Change* (pp. 263–294). New York: Routledge/Taylor & Francis.

Evans, G. W. (2004). The environment of childhood poverty. *American Psychologist, 59*, 77–92.

Evans, G. W., Gonnella, C., Marcynyszyn, L. A., Gentile, L., & Salpekar, N. (2005). The role of chaos in poverty and children's socio-emotional adjustment. *Psychological Science, 16*, 560–565.

Evans, M. A., Whigham, M. & Wang, M. C. (1995). The effect of a role model project upon the attitudes of ninth-grade science students. *Journal of Research in Science Teaching, 32*, 195–204.

Evans, S. W., Pelham, W. E., Smith, B. H., Bukstein, O., Gnagy, E. M., Greiner, A. R., Altenderfer, L., & Baron-Myak, C. (2001). Dose-response effects of methylphenidate of ecologically valid measures of academic performance and classroom behavior in adolescents with ADHD. *Experimental & Clinical Psychopharmacology, 9*, 163–175.

Eveleth, P. B., & Tanner, J. M. (1990). *Worldwide variation in human growth* (2nd ed.). Cambridge, UK: Cambridge University Press.

Ewart, C. K., & Suchday, S. (2002). Discovering how urban poverty and violence affect health: Development and validation of a neighborhood stress index. *Health Psychology, 21*, 254–262.

Eyberg, S. M., Nelson, M. M., & Boggs, S. R. (2008). Evidence-based psychosocial treatments for children and adolescents with disruptive behavior. *Journal of Clinical Child and Adolescent Psychology. Special Issue: Evidence-based psychosocial treatments for children and adolescents: A ten year update, 37*, 215–237.

Fabes, R. A., & Eisenberg, N. (1992). Young children's coping with interpersonal anger. *Child Development, 63*, 116–128.

Fabes, R. A., Eisenberg, N., McCormick, S. E., & Wilson, M. S. (1988). Preschoolers' attributions of the situational determinants of others' naturally occurring emotions. *Developmental Psychology, 24*, 376–385.

Fabes, R. A., Eisenberg, N., Nyman, M., & Michealieu, Q. (1991). Young children's appraisals of others' spontaneous emotional reactions. *Developmental Psychology, 27*, 858–866.

Fabes, R. A., Eisenberg, N., Smith, M. C., & Murphy, B. (1996). Getting angry at peers: Associations with liking of the provocateur. *Child Development, 67*, 942–956.

Fabes, R. A., Fultz, J., Eisenberg, N., May-Plumlee, T., & Christopher, F. S. (1989). The effects of reward on children's prosocial motivation: A socialization study. *Developmental Psychology, 25*, 509–515.

Fabes, R. A., Leonard, S. A., Kupanoff, K., & Martin, C. L. (2001). Parental coping with children's negative emotions: Relations with children's emotional and social responding. *Child Development, 72*, 907–920.

Fabes, R. A., Martin, C. L., & Hanish, L. D. (2003). Young children's play quality in same-, other- and mixed-sex play. *Child Development, 74*, 921–932.

Fagan, J., Bernd, E., & Whiteman, V. (2007). Adolescent fathers' parenting stress, social support, and involvement with infants. *Journal of Research on Adolescence, 17*, 1–22.

Fagot, B. I. (1977). Consequences of moderate cross-gender behavior in preschool children. *Child Development, 48*, 902–907.

Fagot, B. I. (1985). Stages in thinking about early sex role development. *Developmental Review, 5*, 83–98.

Fagot, B. I. (1997). Attachment, parenting, and peer interactions of toddler children. *Developmental Psychology, 33*, 489–499.

Fagot, B. I., & Leinbach, M. D. (1989). The young child's gender schema: Environmental input, internal organization. *Child Development, 60*, 663–672.

Fagot, B. I., & Leinbach, M. D. (1993). Gender role developments in young children: From discrimination to labeling. *Developmental Review, 13*, 205–224.

Fagot, B. I., Pears, K. C., Capaldi, D. M., Crosby, L., & Leve, C. S. (1998). Becoming an adolescent father: Precursors and parenting. *Developmental Psychology, 34*, 1209–1219.

Falbo, T., & Polit, D. F. (1986). A quantitative review of the only-child literature: Research evidence and theory development. *Psychological Bulletin, 100*, 176–189.

Falbo, T., & Poston, D. L. (1993). The academic, personality, and physical outcomes of only children in China. *Child Development, 64*, 18–35.

Falbo, T., Poston, D. L., & Jiao, S. (1989). Physical achievement and personality characteristics of Chinese children. *Journal of Biosocial Science, 21*, 483–495.

Falci, C. (2006). Family structuve, closeness to residential and nonresidential parents, and psychological distress in early and middle adolescence. *The Sociological Quarterly, 47*, 123–146.

Fallang, B., Saugstad, O. D., Grøgaard, J., & Hadders-Algra, M. (2003). Kinematic quality of reaching movements in preterm infants. *Pediatric Research, 53,* 836–842.

Family Safe Media. (2009). Pornography Statistics. http://familysafe media.com/pornography_statistics.

Fantz, R. L. (1961). The origin of form perception. *Scientific American, 204,* 66–72.

Farmer, T. W., & Rodkin, P. C. (1996). Antisocial and prosocial correlates of classroom social positions: The social network centrality perspective. *Social Development, 5,* 174–188.

Farrant, K., & Reese, E. (2002). *Attachment security and mother-child reminiscing: Reflections on a shared past.* Unpublished manuscript.

Farrell, A. D., & White, K. S. (1998). Peer influences and drug use among urban adolescents: Family structure and parent-adolescent relationship as protective factors. *Journal of Consulting and Clinical Psychology, 66,* 248–258.

Farrell, J. N., & McDaniel, M. A. (2001). The stability of validity coefficients over time: Ackerman's (1988) model and the General Aptitude Test Battery. *Journal of Applied Psychology, 86,* 60–79.

Fass, S., & Cauthen, N. K. (November, 2007). Who are America's Poor Children? The Official Story. National Center for Children in Poverty. http://www.nccp.org/publications/pub_787.html

Fausto-Sterling, A. (1992). *Myths of gender: Biological theories about women and men* (2nd ed.). New York: Basic Books.

Fearon, R. M. P., van IJzendoorn, M. H., Fonagy, P., Bakermans-Kranenburg, M. J. Schuengel, C., & Bokhorst, C. L. (2006). In search of shared and nonshared environmental factors in security of attachment: A behavior-genetic study of the association between sensitivity and attachment security. *Developmental Psychology, 2006,* 1026–1040.

Federal Bureau of Investigation. (2009a). Crimes against children. http://www.fbi.gov/hq/cid/cac/crimesmain.htm.

Federal Bureau of Investigation. (2009b). Innocent images national initiative. http://www.fbi.gov/publications/innocent.htm.

Fehr, E., Bernhard, H., & Rockenbach, B. (2008). Egalitarianism in young children. *Nature, 454* (7208), 1079–1083.

Feigenson, L., Carey, S., & Hauser, M. (2002). The representations underlying infants' choice of more: Object files versus analog magnitudes. *Psychological Science, 13,* 150–156.

Feigenson, L., Carey, S., & Spelke, E. (2002). Infants' discrimination of number vs. continuous extent. *Cognitive Psychology, 44,* 33–66.

Feinberg, M., & Hetherington, E. M. (2001). Differential parenting as a within-family variable. *Journal of Family Psychology, 15,* 22–37.

Feitelson, D., & Goldstein, Z. (1986). Patterns of book ownership and reading to young children in Israeli school-oriented and nonschool-oriented families. *The Reading Teacher, 39,* 924–930.

Feldman, H., Goldin-Meadow, S., & Gleitman, L. R. (1978). Beyond Herodotus: The creation of language by linguistically deprived deaf children. In A. Locke (Ed.), *Action, gesture, and symbol: The emergence of language* (pp. 351–414). London: Academic Press.

Feldman, R. & Masalha, S. (2007). The role of culture in moderating the links between early ecological risk and young children's adaptation. *Development and Psychopathology, 19,* 1–21.

Feldman, R. S., Philippot, P., & Custrini, R. J. (1991). Social competence and nonverbal behavior. In R. S. Feldman & B. Rime (Eds.), *Fundamentals of nonverbal behavior* (pp. 329–350). Cambridge, UK: Cambridge University Press.

Feldman, S. S., & Weinberger, D. A. (1994). Self-restraint as a mediator of family influences on boys' delinquent behavior. *Child Development, 65,* 195–211.

Felsman, J. K., & Vaillant, G. E. (1987). Resilient children as adults: a 40-year study. In E. J. Anderson & B. J. Cohler (Eds.), *The invulnerable child* (pp. 211–228). New York: Guilford.

Fenson, L., Dale, P. S., Resnick, J. S., Bates, E., Thale, D. J., & Pethick, S. J. (1994). Variability in early communicative development. *Monographs of the Society for Research in Child Development, 59*(5).

Ferguson, C. J. (2007). Evidence for publication bias in video game violence effects literature: A meta-analytic review. *Aggression & Violent Behavior, 12,* 470–482.

Fergusson, D. M., Woodward, L. J., & Horwood, L. J. (1999). Childhood peer relationship problems and young people's involvement with deviant peers in adolescence. *Journal of Abnormal Child Psychology, 27,* 357–370.

Fernald, A. (1989). Intonation and communicative intent in mothers' speech to infants: Is the melody the message? *Child Development, 60,* 1497–1510.

Fernald, A., & McRoberts, G. (1995). *Infants' developing sensitivity to language-typical word order patterns.* Paper presented at the 20th annual Boston University Conference on Child Language Development, Boston.

Fernald, A., & Morikawa, H. (1993). Common themes and cultural variations in Japanese and American mothers' speech to infants. *Child Development, 64,* 637–656.

Ferrier, L. J. (1978). Some observations of error in context. In N. Waterson & C. Snow (Eds.), *The development of communication* (pp. 301–309). Chichester: Wiley.

Ferry, T., Fouad, N. A., & Smith, P. L. (2000). The role of family context in social cognitive model for math and science. *Journal of Vocational Behavior, 57,* 348–364.

Feshbach, N. D. (1978). Studies of empathic behavior in children. In B. A. Maher (Ed.), *Progress in experimental personality research* (Vol. 8, pp. 1–47). New York: Academic Press.

Feshbach, S., & Tangney, J. (2008). Television viewing and aggression: Some alternative perspectives. *Psychological Science, 3,* 387–389.

Field, A. E., Austin, S. B., Camargo, C. A. Jr., Taylor, C. B., Striegel-Moore, R. H., Loud, K. J., & Colditz, G. A. (2005). Exposure to the mass media, body shape concerns, and use of supplements to improve weight and shape among male and female adolescents. *Pediatrics, 116,* e214–e220.

Field, D. (1987). A review of preschool conservation training: An analysis of analyses. *Developmental Review, 7,* 210–251.

Field, T. (2001). Massage therapy facilitates weight gain in preterm infants. *Current Directions in Psychological Science, 10,* 51–54.

Field, T. (1995). Infants of depressed mothers. *Infant Behavior and Development, 18,* 1–13.

Field, T., Hernandez-Reif, M., & Freedman, J. (2004). Stimulation program for preterm infants. *Social Policy Report, 18,* 3–19.

Field, T. M., Grizzle, N., Scafidi, F., Abrams, S., Richardson, S., Kuhn, C., & Schanberg, S. (1996). Massage therapy for infants of depressed mothers. *Infant Behavior and Development, 19,* 107–112.

Fifer, W. P., & Moon, C. M. (1995). The effects of fetal experience with sound. In J. P. Lecanuet, W. P. Fifer, N. A. Krasnegor, & W. P. Smotherman (Eds.), *Fetal development: A psychobiological perspective.* Hillsdale, NJ: Erlbaum.

Filardo, E. M. (1996). Gender patterns in African American and white adolescents' social interactions in same-race, mixed-gender groups. *Journal of Personality & Social Psychology, 71*, 71–82.

Fine, S. E., Izard, C., Mostow, A., Trentacosta, C. J., & Ackerman, B. P. (2003). First grade emotion knowledge as a predictor of fifth grade self-reported internalizing behaviors in children from economically disadvantaged families. *Development and Psychopathology, 15*, 331–342.

Finnie, V., & Russell, A. (1988). Preschool children's social status and their mothers' behavior and knowledge in the supervisory role. *Developmental Psychology, 24,* 789–801.

Fischer, A. H., Rodriguez Mosquera, P. M., van Vianen, A. E., & Manstead, A. S. (2004). Gender and culture differences in emotion. *Emotion, 4,* 87–94.

Fischer, A. R., & Shaw, C. M. (1999). African Americans' mental health and perceptions of racist discrimination: The moderating effects of racial socialization experiences and self-esteem. *Journal of Counseling Psychology, 46*, 395–407.

Fischer, J. L., Sollie, D. L., & Morrow, K. B. (1986). Social networks in male and female adolescents. *Journal of Adolescent Research, 1,* 1–14.

Fischer, K. W., & Bidell, T. R. (2006). Dynamic development of action and thought. In W. Damon & R. M. Lerner (Series Eds.) & R. M. Lerner (Vol. Ed.), *Handbook of child psychology: Volume 1: Theoretical models of human development* (6th ed., pp. 313–399). Hoboken, NJ: Wiley.

Fisher, C. (2000). From form to meaning: A role for structural alignment in the acquisition of language. *Advances in Child Development and Behavior, 27,* 1–53.

Fisher, C., Gleitman, H., & Gleitman, L. R. (1991). On the semantic content of subcategorization frames. *Cognitive Psychology, 23,* 331–392.

Fisher, E. P. (1992). The impact of play on development: A meta-analysis. *Play and Culture, 5*, 159–181.

Fisher-Thompson, D. (1993). Adult toy purchase for children: Factors affecting sex-typed toy selection. *Journal of Applied Developmental Psychology, 14,* 385–406.

Fitzgerald, J. (1992). Variant views about good thinking during composing: Focus on revision. In M. Pressley, K. R. Harris, & J. T. Guthrie (Eds.), *Promoting academic competence and literacy in school* (pp. 337–358). San Diego, CA: Academic Press.

Fivush, R. (1989). Exploring sex differences in the emotional content of mother-child conversations about the past. *Sex Roles, 20*, 675–691.

Fivush, R. (1991). The social construction of personal narratives. *Merrill-Palmer Quarterly, 37*, 59–81.

Fivush, R., Brotman, M. A., Buckner, J. P., & Goodman, S. H. (2000). Gender differences in parent-child emotion narratives. *Sex Roles, 42,* 233–253.

Flanagan, D. P., & Kaufman, A. S. (Eds.) (2004). *Essentials of WISC-IV Assessment* (2nd ed.), *Essentials of Psychological Assessment*, A. S. Kaufman & N. L. Kaufman (Series Eds). Hoboken, NJ: Wiley & Sons.

Flavell, J. H. (1971). Stage-related properties of cognitive development. *Cognitive Psychology, 2,* 421–453.

Flavell, J. H. (1982). On cognitive development. *Child Development, 53,* 1–10.

Flavell, J. H. (1986). The development of children's knowledge about the appearance-reality distinction. *American Psychologist, 41,* 418–425.

Flavell, J. H., Flavell, E. R., Green, F. L., & Korfmacher, J. E. (1990). Do young children think of television images as picture or real objects? *Journal of Broadcasting & Electronic Media, 34*, 399–419.

Floyd, F. J., Stein, T. S., Harter, K. S. M., Allison, A., & Ney, C. L. (1999). Gay, lesbian, and bisexual youths: Separation, individuation, parental attitudes, identity consolidation, and well-being. *Journal of Youth and Adolescence, 28,* 719–739.

Flynn, J. R. (1987). Massive IQ gains in 14 nations: What IQ tests really measure. *Psychological Bulletin, 101*, 171–191.

Flynn, J. R. (2007). *What is intelligence? Beyond the Flynn effect.* New York: Cambridge University Press.

Flynn, J. R., & Weiss, L. G. (2007). American IQ gains from 1931 to 2002: The WISC subtests and educational progress. *International Journal of Testing, 7*, 209–224.

Fodor, J. A. (1983). *The modularity of mind.* Cambridge, MA: The MIT Press.

Fodor, J. A. (1992). A theory of the child's theory of mind. *Cognition, 44*, 283–296.

Foehr, U. G. (December, 2006). *Media Multitasking Among American Youth: Prevalence, Predictors and Pairings.* Kaiser Family Foundation.

Fogel, A., Nwokah, E., Dedo, J. Y., Messinger, D., Dickson, K. L., Matusov, E., & Holt, S. A. (1992). Social process theory of emotion: A dynamic systems approach. *Social Development, 1,* 122–142.

Fontaine, N., Carbonneau, R., Vitaro, F., Barker, E. D., & Tremblay, R. E. (2009). Research review: A critical review of studies on the developmental trajectories of antisocial behavior in females. *Journal of Child Psychology and Psychiatry, 50*, 363–385.

Fontaine, R. G., Yang, C., Dodge, K. A., Bates, J. E., & Pettit, G. S. (2008). Testing an individual systems model of response evaluation and decision (RED) and antisocial behavior across adolescence. *Child Development, 79*, 462–475.

Fonzi, A., Schneider, B. H., Tani, F., & Tomada, G. (1997). Predicting children's friendship status from their dyadic interaction in structured situations of potential conflict. *Child Development, 68*, 496–506.

Forbes, G. B., Adams-Curtis, L. E., Pakala, H. A. & White, K. B. (2006). Dating aggression, sexual coercion, and aggression supporting attitudes among college men as a function of participating in aggressive high school sports. *Violence Against Women, 12*, 441–455.

Forbes, L. M., Evans, G., Moran, G., & Pederson, D. R. (2007). Change in atypical maternal behavior predicts change in attachment disorganization from 12 to 24 months in a high-risk sample. *Child Development, 78*, 955–971.

Foster, E. M., & Jones, D. E. (2007). The economic analysis of prevention: An illustration involving children's behavior problems. *Journal of Mental Health Policy and Economics, 10*, 165–175.

Fox, N. A. (1995). Of the way we were: Adult memories about attachment experiences and their role in determining infant-parent relationships: A commentary on van IJzendoorn (1995). *Psychological Bulletin, 117*, 404–410.

Fox, N. A., & Calkins, S. D. (1993). Pathways to aggression and social withdrawal: Interactions among temperament, attachment, and regulation. In K. H. Rubin & J. Asendorpf (Eds.), *Social withdrawal, inhibition, and shyness in childhood* (pp. 81–100). Hillsdale, NJ: Erlbaum.

Fraisse, P. (1982). The adaptation of the child to time. In W. J. Friedman (Ed.), *The developmental psychology of time*. New York: Academic Press.

Fraley, R. C. (2002). Attachment stability from infancy to adulthood: Meta-analysis and dynamic modeling of developmental mechanisms. *Personality and Social Psychology Review, 6*, 123–151.

Frank, D. A., Augustyn, M., Knight, W. G., Pell, T., & Zuckerman, B. (2001). Growth, development and behavior in early childhood following prenatal cocaine exposure. *Journal of the American Medical Association, 285*, 1613–1625.

Frankenburg, W. K., Fandal, A. W., Sciarillo, W., & Burgess, D. (1981). The newly abbreviated and revised Denver Developmental Screening Test. *Journal of Pediatrics, 99*, 995–999.

Franz, M., Lensche, H., & Schmitz, N. (2003). Psychological distress and socioeconomic status in single mothers and their children in a German city. *Social Psychiatry and Psychiatric Epidemiology, 38*, 59–68.

Freedman, D. G., & Freedman, N. C. (1969). Behavioral differences between Chinese-American and European-American newborns. *Nature, 224*, 1227.

Freitag, M. K., Belsky, J., Grossmann, K., Grossmann, K. E., & Scheuerer-Englisch, H. (1996). Continuity in parent-child relationships from infancy to middle childhood and relations with friendship competence. *Child Development, 67*, 1437–1454.

Freitas, G. V. S., Cais, C. F. S., Stefanello, S., & Botega, N. J. (2008). Psychosocial conditions and suicidal behavior in pregnant teenagers. *European Child and Adoelscent Psychiatry, 17*, 336–342.

French, Doran C., Pidada, Sri, Denoma, Jill, McDonald, Kristina, Lawton, Allison. (2005). Reported peer conflicts of children in the United States and Indonesia. *Social Development, 14*(3), 458–472.

French, D. C., Setiono, K., & Eddy, J. M. (1999). Bootstrapping through the cultural comparison minefield: Childhood social status and friendship in the United States and Indonesia. In W. A. Collins & B. Laursen (Eds.), *Relationships as developmental contexts: The Minnesota Symposia on Child Psychology. Vol. 30* (pp. 109–131). Mahwah, NJ: Erlbaum.

French, L. A., Lucariello, J., Seidman, S., & Nelson, K. (1985). The influence of discourse content and context on preschoolers' use of language. In L. Galda & A. Pellegrini (Eds.), *Play, language and stories.* Norwood, NJ: Albex.

French, S. E., Seidman, E., Allen, L. & Aber, J. L. (2006). The development of ethnic identity during adolescence. *Developmental Psychology, 42*, 1–10.

Freud, A., & Dann, S. (1951/1972). An experiment in group upbringing. In U. Bronfenbrenner (Ed.), *Influences on human development* (pp. 449–473). Hinsdale, IL: Dryden Press. (Original work published 1951 in *The Psychoanalytic Study of the Child*, Vol. 6, pp. 127–168).

Freud, S. (1920/1965). *A general introduction to psychoanalysis* (J. Riviere, trans.). New York: Washington Square Press. (Original work published 1920.)

Freud, S. (1923/1960). *The ego and the id* (J. Riviere, trans.). New York: W. W. Norton & Co. (Original work published 1923.)

Freud, S. (1926/1959). Inhibitions, symptoms and anxiety. In J. Strachey (Ed. & Trans.), *The standard edition of the complete works of Sigmund Freud* (Vol. 12, pp. 145–156). London: Hogarth Press. (Original work published 1926.)

Freud, S. (1933/1964). *New introductory lectures on psychoanalysis* (J. Strachey, trans.). New York: W. W. Norton & Co. (Original work published 1933.)

Freud, S. (1940/1964). An outline of psychoanalysis. In J. Strachey (Ed. & Trans.), *The standard edition of the complete psychological works of Sigmund Freud* (Vol. 23). London: Hogarth Press. (Original work published 1940.)

Freund, L. S. (1990). Maternal regulation of children's problem-solving behavior and its impact on children's performance. *Child Development, 61*, 113–126.

Frey, K. S., & Ruble, D. N. (1985). What children say when the teacher is not around: Conflicting goals in social comparison and performance assessment in the classroom. *Journal of Personality and Social Psychology, 48*, 550–562.

Frick, P. J. (1998). Callous-unemotional traits and conduct problems: Applying the two-factor model of psychopathy to children. In D. J. Cooke et al. (Eds.), *Psychopathy: Theory, research and implications for society* (pp. 161–187). Amsterdam: Kluwer Academic Publishers.

Frick, P. J., Christian, R. E., & Wooten, J. M. (1999). Age trends in the association between parenting practices and conduct problems. *Behavior Modification, 23*, 106–128.

Frick, P. J, & Morris, A. S. (2004). Temperament and developmental pathways to conduct problems. *Journal of Clinical and Adolescent Psychology, 33*, 54–68.

Fried, P. A., & Smith, A. M. (2001). A literature review of the consequences of prenatal marijuana exposure: An emerging theme of a deficiency in aspects of executive function. *Neurotoxicology and Teratology, 23*, 1–11.

Friedman, C. K., Leaper, C., & Bigler, R. S. (2007). Do mothers' gender-related attitudes or comments predict young children's gender beliefs? *Parenting: Science and Practice, 7*, 357–366.

Friedman, M. A., & Brownell, K. D. (1995). Psychological correlates of obesity: Moving to the next research generation. *Psychological Bulletin, 117*, 3–20.

Friedman, W. J. (1991). The development of children's memory for the time of past events. *Child Development, 62*, 139–155.

Friedman, W. J. (2000). The development of children's knowledge of the times of future events. *Child Development, 71*, 913–932.

Friedman, W. J. (2003). The development of a differentiated sense of the past and the future. *Advances in Child Development and Behavior, 31*, 229–269.

Friedman, W. J. (2008). Developmental perspectives on the psychology of time. In S. Grondin (Ed.), *The psychology of time* (pp. 246–366), Amsterdam: Elsevier.

Friedman, W. J., & Lyon, T. D. (2005). Development of temporal-reconstructive abilities. *Child Development, 76*, 1202–1216.

Friend, A., DeFries, J. C., & Olson, R. K. (2008). Parental education moderates genetic influences on reading disability. *Psychological Science, 19*, 1124–1130.

Frodi, A. M., & Lamb, M. E. (1980). Child abusers' responses to infant smiles and cries. *Child Development, 51*, 238–241.

Frosch, C. A., Mangelsdorf, S. C., & McHale, J. L. (2000). Marital behavior and the security of preschooler-parent attachment relationships. *Journal of Family Psychology, 14*, 144–161.

Fry, A. F., & Hale, S. (2000). Relationships among processing speed, working memory, and fluid intelligence in children. *Biological Psychology, 54*, 1–34.

Fry, D. (1988). Intercommunity differences in aggression among Zapotec children. *Child Development, 59,* 1008–1019.

Fry, D. P. (1998). Anthropological perspectives on aggression: Sex differences and cultural variation. Aggressive Behavior, 24, 81–95.

Frye, D., Braisby, N., Lowe, J., Maroudas, C., & Nicholls, J. (1989). Young children's understanding of counting and cardinality. *Child Development, 60*, 1158–1171.

Frye, D., Zelazo, P. D., Brooks, P. J., & Samuels, M. C. (1996). Inference and action in early causal reasoning. *Developmental Psychology, 32*, 120–131.

Fuchs, D., & Thelen, M. H. (1988). Children's expected interpersonal consequences of communicating their affective state and reported likelihood of expression. *Child Development, 58,* 1314–1322.

Fuchs, I., Eisenberg, N., Hertz-Lazarowitz, R., & Sharabany, R. (1986). Israeli city and American children's moral reasoning about prosocial moral conflicts. *Merrill-Palmer Quarterly, 32*, 37–50.

Fujisawa, K. K., Kutsukake, N., & Hasegawa, T. (2008a). Reciprocity of prosocial behavior in Japanese preschool children. *International Journal of Behavioral Development, 32*, 89–97.

Fujisawa, K. K., Kutsukake, N., & Hasegawa, T. (2008b). Individual differences in gender development: Associations with parental sexual orientation, attitudes, and division of labor. *Sex Roles, 58*, 330–341.

Fuligni, A. (2007). Family obligation, college enrollment, and emerging adulthood in Asian and Latin American families. *Child Development Perspectives, 1*, 96–100.

Fuligni, A. J. (1998). Authority, autonomy, and parent-adolescent conflict and cohesion: A study of adolescents from Mexican, Chinese, Filipino, and European backgrounds. *Developmental Psychology, 34*, 782–792.

Fuligni, A. J., Eccles, J. S., Barber, B. L., & Clements, P. (2001). Early adolescent peer orientation and adjustment during high school. *Developmental Psychology, 37*, 28–36.

Fuligni, A., & Stevenson, H. (1995). Time use and mathematics achievement among American, Chinese, and Japanese high school students. *Child Development, 66*, 830–842.

Fuligni, A. J., Yip, T., & Tseng, V. (2002). The impact of family obligation on the daily activities and psychological well-being of Chinese American adolescents. *Child Development, 73*, 302–314.

Fuligni, A. J., & Zhang, W. (2004). Attitudes toward family obligation among adolescents in contemporary urban and rural China. *Child Development, 74,* 180–192.

Fung, H., & Chen, E. Ch-H. (2001). Across time and beyond skin: Self and transgression in the everyday socialization of shame among Taiwanese preschool children. *Social Development, 10*, 420–437.

Furman, W., & Bierman, K. L. (1984). Children's conceptions of friendship: A multimethod study of developmental changes. *Developmental Psychology, 20*, 925–931.

Furman, W., & Buhrmester, D. (1985). Children's perceptions of the personal relationships in their social networks. *Developmental Psychology, 21*, 1016–1024.

Furman, W., & Buhrmester, D. (1992). Age and sex differences in perceptions of networks of personal relationships. *Child Development, 63*, 103–115.

Furman, W., Simon, V. A., Shaffer, L., & Bouchey, H. A. (2002). Adolescents' working models and styles for relationships with parents, friends, and romantic partners. *Child Development, 73*, 241–255.

Furstenberg, F. F., Jr. (1988). Child care after divorce and remarriage. In E. M. Hetherington & J. D. Arasteh (Eds.), *Impact of divorce, single parenting, and stepparenting on children* (pp. 245–261). Hillsdale, NJ: Erlbaum.

Furstenberg, F. F., Jr., & Harris, K. M. (1993). When and why fathers matter: Impacts of father involvement on children of adolescent mothers. In R. I. Lerman & T. J. Ooms (Eds.), *Young unwed mothers* (pp. 117–138). Philadelphia: Temple University Press.

Gable, S., Belsky, J. & Crnic, K. (1993, March). *Coparenting in the child's second year: Stability and change from 15 to 21 months.* Paper presented at the biennial meeting of the Society for Research in Child Development, New Orleans, LA.

Gaddis, A., & Brooks-Gunn, J. (1985). The male experience of pubertal change. *Journal of Youth and Adolescence, 14*, 61–69.

Gaertner, B. M., Spinrad, T. L., Eisenberg, N. & Greving, A. K. (2007). Parental childrearing attitudes as correlates of father involvement during infancy. *Journal of Marriage and Family, 69*, 962–976.

Galambos, N. L., Almeida, D. M. & Petersen, A. C. (1990). Masculinity, femininity, and sex role attitudes in early adolescence: Exploring gender intensification. *Child Development, 61*, 1905–1914.

Galambos, N. L, Leadbeater, B. J., & Barker, E. T. (2004). Gender differences in and risk factors for depression in adolescence: A 4-year longitudinal study. *International Journal of Behavioral Development, 28*, 16–25.

Galen, B. R., & Underwood, M. K. (1997). A developmental investigation of social aggression among children. *Developmental Psychology, 33*, 589–600.

Gallup, G. H., & Newport, F. (1991). Belief in paranormal phenomena among adult Americans. *Skeptical Inquirer, 15*, 137–146.

Galton, F. (1869/1962). *Hereditary genius: An inquiry into its laws and consequences.* London: Macmillan. Cleveland, OH: World. (Original work published 1869.)

Gandelman, R. (1992). *The psychobiology of behavioral development.* Oxford, UK: Oxford University Press.

Ganiban, J. M., Saudino, K. J., Ulbricht, J., Neiderhiser, J. M., & Reiss, D. (2008). Stability and change in temperament during adolescence. *Journal of Personality and Social Psychology, 95*, 222–236.

Garbarino, J., & Kostelny, K. (1992). Child maltreatment as a community problem. *Child Abuse and Neglect, 16*, 455–467.

Garber, J., Keiley, M. K., & Martin, N. C. (2002). Developmental trajectories of adolescents' depressive symptoms: Predictors of change. *Journal of Consulting and Clinical Psychology, 70*, 79–95.

Gardner, D., Harris, P. L., Ohmoto, M., & Hamazaki, T. (1988). Japanese children's understanding of the distinction between real and apparent emotion. *International Journal of Behavioral Development, 11*, 203–218.

Gardner, H. (1993). *Multiple intelligences: The theory in practice.* New York: Basic Books.

Gardner, R. A., & Gardner, B. T. (1969). Teaching sign language to a chimpanzee. *Science, 165*, 664–672.

Garmezy, N. (1983). Stressors of childhood. In N. Garmezy & M. Rutter (Eds.), *Stress, coping, and development in children* (pp. 43–84). New York: McGraw-Hill.

Garmon, L. C., Basinger, K. S., Gress, V. R., & Gibbs, J. C. (1996). Gender differences in stage and expression of moral judgment. *Merrill-Palmer Quarterly, 42*, 418–437.

Gassman-Pines, A., & Yoshikawa, H. (2006). The effects of antipoverty programs on children's cumulative level of poverty-related risk. *Developmental Psychology, 42*, 981–999.

Gass, K., Jenkins, J., & Dunn D. (2007). Are sibling relationships protective? A longitudinal study. *Journal of Child Psychology and Psychiatry, 48*, 167–175.

Gathercole, S. E., Pickering, S. J., Ambridge, B., & Wearing, H. (2004). The structure of working memory from 4 to 15 years of age. *Developmental Psychology, 40*, 177–190.

Gatzke-Kopp, L. M., Beauchaine, T. P., Shannon, K. E., Chipman, J., Fleming, A. P., Crowell, S. E., et al. (2009). Neurological correlates of reward responding in adolescents with and without externalizing behavior disorders. *Journal of Abnormal Psychology, 118*, 203–213.

Gaub, M., & Carlson, C. L. (1997). Gender differences in ADHD: A meta-analysis and critical review. *Journal of the American Academy of Child and Adolescent Psychiatry, 36*, 1036–1045.

Gauvain, M. (2001). *The social context of cognitive development*. New York: Guilford.

Gavin, L. A., & Furman, W. (1989). Age differences in adolescents' perceptions of their peer groups. *Developmental Psychology, 25*, 827–834.

Gavin, L. A., & Furman, W. (1996). Adolescent girls' relationships with mothers and best friends. *Child Development, 67*, 375–386.

Gazelle, H. (2008). Behavioral profiles of anxious solitary children and heterogeneity in peer relations. *Developmental Psychology, 144*(6), 1604–1624.

Gazelle, H. & Ladd, G. W. (2003). Anxious solitude and peer exclusion: A diathesis-stress model of internalizing trajectories in childhood. *Child Development*, 74, 257–278.

Ge, X., Conger, R. D., & Elder, G. H., Jr. (1996). Coming of age too early: Pubertal influences on girls' vulnerability to psychological distress. *Child Development, 67*, 3386–3400.

Ge, X., Kim, I. J., Brody, G. H., Conger, R. D., Simons, R. L., Gibbons, F. X., & Cutrona, C. E. (2003). It's about timing and change: Pubertal transition effects on symptoms of major depression among African American youths. *Developmental Psychology, 39*, 430–439.

Ge, X., Natsuaki, M. N., & Conger, R. D. (2006). Trajectories of depressive symptoms and stressful life events among male and female adolescents in divorced and nondivorced families. *Development and Psychopathology, 18*, 253–273.

Geary, D. C. (1998). *Male, female: The evolution of human sex differences.* Washington, DC: American Psychological Association.

Geary, D. C. (1999). Evolution and developmental sex differences. *Current Directions in Psychological Science, 8*, 115–120.

Geary, D. C. (2004). Mathematics and learning disabilities. *Journal of Learning Disabilities, 37*, 4–15.

Geary, D. C. (2005). *The origin of mind: Evolution of brain, cognition, and general intelligence.* Washington, DC: American Psychological Association.

Geary, D. C. (2006). Development of mathematical understanding. In W. Damon & R. M. Lerner (Series Eds.) & D. Kuhn & R. S. Siegler (Vol. Eds.), *Handbook of child psychology: Volume 2: Cognition, perception, and language* (6th ed., pp. 777–810). Hoboken, NJ: Wiley.

Geary, D. C. (2009). *Male, female: The evolution of human sex differences* (2nd ed.). Washington, DC: American Psychological Association.

Geary, D. C., Hoard, M. K., Byrd-Craven, J., Nugent, L., & Numtee, C. (2007). Cognitive mechanisms underlying achievement deficits in children with mathematical learning disability. *Child Development, 78*, 1343–1359.

Gelman, R. (2002). Animates and other worldly things. In N. Stein, P. Bauer, & M. Rabinowitz (Eds). *Representation, Memory, and Development: Essays in Honor of Jean Mandler*. Mahwah, NJ: Lawrence Erlbaum Associates. (pp. 75–87).

Gelman, R., & Gallistel, C. R. (1978). *The child's understanding of number*. Cambridge, MA: Harvard University Press.

Gelman, R., Meck, E., & Merkin, S. (1986). Young children's numerical competence. *Cognitive Development, 1*, 1–29.

Gelman, R., & Williams, E. (1998). Enabling constraints for cognitive development and learning: Domain specificity and epigenesis. In W. Damon (Series Ed.), D. Kuhn, & R. Siegler (Vol. Eds.), *Handbook of child psychology: Vol. 2. Cognition, perception, and language* (5th ed., pp. 575–630). New York: Wiley.

Gelman, S. (2003). *The essential child*. New York: Oxford University Press.

Gelman, S. A., Coley, J. D., Rosengren, K. S., Hartman, E., & Pappas, A. (1998). Beyond labeling: The role of maternal input in the acquisition of richly structured categories. *Monographs of the Society for Research in Child Development, 63*(1, Serial No. 253).

Gelman, S. A., Taylor, M. G., & Nguyen, S. P. (2004). Mother-child conversations about gender. *Monographs of the Society for Research in Child Development, 69*(1, Serial No. 275). Boston, MA: Blackwell Publishing.

Gentner, D. (1982). Why nouns are learned before verbs: Linguistic relativity versus natural partitioning. In S. A. Kuczaj (Ed.), *Language development: Syntax and semantics*. Hillsdale, NJ: Erlbaum.

Gentner, D., & Boroditsky, L. (2001). Individuation, relativity and early word learning. In M. Bowerman & S. Levinson (Eds.), *Language acquisition and conceptual development* (pp. 215–256). Cambridge, UK: Cambridge University Press.

Gentner, D., & Markman, A. B. (1997). Structure mapping in analogy and similarity. *American Psychologist, 52*, 45–56.

Gentner, D., Ratterman, M. J., Markman, A., & Kotovsky, L. (1995). Two forces in the development of relational similarity. In T. J. Simon & G. S. Halford (Eds.), *Developing cognitive competence: New approaches to process modeling* (pp. 263–313). Hillsdale, NJ: Erlbaum.

Gergely, G., Bekkering, H., & Kiraly, I. (2002). Rational imitation in preverbal infants. *Nature, 415*, 755.

Gerken, L. A. (1994). Child phonology: Past research, present questions, future directions. In M. A. Gernsbacher (Ed.), *Handbook of psycholinguistics* (pp. 781–820). New York: Academic Press.

German, T. P., & Nichols, S. (2003). Children's counterfactual inferences about long and short causal chains. *Developmental Science, 6*, 514–523.

Gershkoff-Stowe, L., Connell, B., & Smith, L. (2006). Priming overgeneralizations in two- and four-year-old children. *Journal of Child Language, 33*, 461–486.

Gershoff, E. T. (2002). Parental corporal punishment and associated child behaviors and experiences: A meta-analytic and theoretical review. *Psychological Bulletin, 128,* 539–579.

Gesell, A., & Thompson, H. (1938). *The psychology of early growth including norms of infant behavior and a method of genetic analysis.* New York: Macmillan.

Gest, S. D., Graham-Bermann, S. A., & Hartup, W. W. (2001). Peer experience: Common and unique features of number of friendships, social network centrality, and sociometric status. *Social Development, 10,* 23–40.

Gianino, A., & Tronick, E. Z. (1988). The mutual regulation model: The infant's self and interactive regulation, coping, and defense. In T. Field, P. McCabe, & N. Schneiderman (Eds.), *Stress and coping* (pp. 47–68). Hillsdale, NJ: Erlbaum.

Gibbs, N. (1999, May 3). In sorrow and disbelief. *Time.*

Gibson, E. J. (1988). Exploratory behavior in the development of perceiving, acting, and the acquiring of knowledge, *Annual Review of Psychology, 39,* 1–41.

Gibson, E. J. (1994). Has psychology a future? *Psychological Science, 5,* 69–76.

Gibson, E. J., & Pick, A. D. (2000). *An ecological approach to perceptual learning and development.* New York: Oxford University Press.

Gibson, E. J., Riccio, G., Schmuckler, M. A., Stoffgren, T. A., Rosenberg, D., & Taormina, J. (1987). Detection of the traversability of surfaces by crawling and walking infants. *Journal of Experimental Psychology: Human Perception and Performance, 13,* 533–544.

Gibson, E. J., & Schmuckler, M. A. (1989). Going somewhere: An ecological and experimental approach to the development of mobility. *Ecological Psychology, 1,* 3–25.

Gibson, E. J., & Walk, R. D. (1960). The "visual cliff." *Scientific American, 202,* 64–71.

Giedd, J. N., Blumenthal, J., Jeffries, N. O., Castellanos, F. X., Liu H., Zijdenbos, A., et al. (1999). Brain development during childhood and adolescence: A longitudinal MRI study. *Nature Neuroscience, 2,* 861–863.

Giedd, J. N., Blumenthal, J., Molloy, E., & Castellanos, F. X. (2001). Brain imaging of attention deficit/hyperactivity disorder. *Annals of the New York Academy of Sciences, 931,* 33–49.

Giles, J. W., & Heyman, G. D. (2005). Young children's beliefs about the relationship between gender and aggressive behavior. *Child Development, 76,* 107–121.

Gillham, J. E., Reivich, K. J., Jaycox, L. H., & Seligman, M. E. P. (1995). Prevention of depressive symptoms in schoolchildren: Two-year follow up. *Psychological Science, 6,* 343–350.

Gilligan, C. (1982). *In a different voice: Psychological theory and women's development.* Cambridge, MA: Harvard University Press.

Gilligan, C., & Attanucci, J. (1988). Two moral orientations: Gender differences and similarities. *Merrill-Palmer Quarterly, 34,* 223–238.

Ginsburg, H. P., & Opper, S. (1988). *Piaget's theory of intellectual development* (3rd ed.). Englewood Cliffs, NJ: Prentice Hall.

Gleason, J. B., & Ely, R. (2002). Gender differences in language development. In A. M. De Lisi & R. De Lisi (Eds.), *Biology, society, and behavior: The development of sex differences in cognition* (pp. 127–154). Westport, CT: Ablex.

Gleitman, L., Gleitman, H., Landau, B., & Wanner, E. (1988). Where the learning begins: Initial representations for language learning. In F. Newmeyer (Ed.), *The Cambridge Linguistic Survey* (Vol. 3, pp. 150–193). Cambridge, MA: Harvard University Press.

Gnepp, J., & Hess, D. L. R. (1986). Children's understanding of verbal and facial display rules. *Developmental Psychology, 22,* 103–108.

Gogtay, N., Sporn, A., Clasen, L. S., Nugent, T. F. III, Greenstein, D., Nicolson, R., Giedd, J. N., Lenane, M., Gochman, P., Evans, A., & Rapoport, J. L. (2004). Comparison of progressive cortical gray matter loss in childhood-onset schizophrenia with that in childhood-onset atypical psychoses. *Archives of General Psychiatry, 61,* 17–22.

Goldberg, Carey. (July 5, 2007). With rise in autism, programs strained. *The Boston Globe.*

Goldfield, B. A., & Reznick, J. S. (1990). Early lexical acquisition: Rate, content, and the vocabulary spurt. *Journal of Child Language, 17,* 171–184.

Goldin-Meadow, S. (1999). The role of gesture in communication and thinking. *Trends in Cognitive Sciences, 3,* 419–429.

Goldin-Meadow, S. (2001). Giving the mind a hand: The role of gesture in cognitive change. In J. L McClelland, & R. S. Siegler, (Eds.), *Mechanisms of cognitive development: Behavioral and neural perspectives* (pp. 5–31). Mahwah, NJ: Erlbaum.

Goldin-Meadow, S. (2003). *The resilience of language: What gesture creation in deaf children can tell us about how all children learn language.* New York: Psychology Press.

Goldin-Meadow, S., & Alibali, M. W. (2002). Looking at the hands through time: A microgenetic perspective on learning and instruction. In N. Grannott & J. Parziale (Eds.), Microdevelopment: Transition processes in development and learning (pp. 80–105). Cambridge, UK: Cambridge University Press.

Goldin-Meadow, S., Cook, S. W., & Mitchell, Z. A. (2009). Gesturing gives children new ideas about math. *Psychological Science, 20,* 267–272.

Goldin-Meadow, S., & Mylander, C. (1998). Spontaneous sign systems created by deaf children in two cultures. *Nature, 391,* 279–281.

Goldin-Meadow, S., Seligman, M. E. P., & Gelman, R. (1976). Language in the two-year-old. *Cognition, 4,* 189–202.

Goldsmith, H. H., Buss, K. A., & Lemery, K. S. (1997). Toddler and childhood temperament: Expanded content, stronger genetic evidence, new evidence for the importance of environment. *Developmental Psychology, 33,* 891–905.

Goldsmith, H. H., Lemery, K. S., Buss, K. A., & Campos, J. J. (1999). Genetic analyses of focal aspects of infant temperament. *Developmental Psychology, 35,* 972–985.

Goldsmith, H. H., Pollak, S. D., & Davidson, R. J. (in press). Developmental neuroscience perspectives on emotion regulation. *Child Development Perspectives.*

Goldstein, S. E., Malanchuk, O., Davis-Kean, P. E., & Eccles, J. S. (2007). Risk factors of sexual harassment by peers: A longitudinal investigation of African American and European American adolescents. *Journal of Research on Adolescence, 17,* 285–300.

Goleman, D. (1995). *Emotional intelligence.* New York: Bantam Books.

Golinkoff, R. M., & Alioto, A. (1995). Infant-directed speech facilitates lexical learning in adults hearing Chinese: Implications for language acquisition. *Journal of Child Language, 22,* 703–726.

Golinkoff, R. M., Alioto, A., & Hirsh-Pasek, K. (1996). Infants' word learning is facilitated when novel words are presented in infant-direct speech and in either sentence-medial or sentence-final position. In D. Cahana-Arnitay, L. Hughes, A. Stringfellow, & A. Zukowske (Eds.),

Proceedings of the 20th Boston University Conference on Language Development. Somerville, MA: Cascadilla Press.

Golish, T. D. (2003). Stepfamily communication strengths: Understanding the ties that bind. *Human Communication Research, 29,* 41–80.

Golombok, S., Perry, B., Burston, A., Golding, J., Murray, C., Mooney-Somers, J., & Stevens, M. (2003). Children with lesbian parents: A community study. (2003). *Developmental Psychology, 19,* 20–33.

Golombok, S., Spencer, A., & Rutter, M. (1983). Children in lesbian and single-parent households: Psychosexual and psychiatric appraisal. *Journal of Child Psychology and Psychiatry, 24,* 551–572.

Goncu, A. (1993). Development of intersubjectivity in the dyadic play of preschoolers. *Early Childhood Research Quarterly, 8,* 99–116.

Goncu, A., Mistry, J., & Mosier, C. (2000). Cultural variations in the play of toddlers. *International Journal of Behavioral Development, 24,* 321–329.

Gonzales, N. A., Pitts, S. C., Hill, N. E., & Roosa, M. W. (2000). A mediational model of the impact of interparental conflict on child adjustment in a multiethnic, low-income sample. *Journal of Family Psychology, 14,* 365–379.

Gonzales, P., Guzmán, J. C., Partelow, L., Pahlke, E., Jocelyn, L., Kastberg, D., & Williams, T. (2004, December). *Highlights from the trends in international mathematics and science study (TIMSS) 2003.* National Center for Education Statistics, U. S. Department of Education, Institute of Education Sciences.

Good, T. L., & Brophy, J. E. (1996). *Looking in classrooms* (7th ed.). New York: Addison-Wesley.

Goodenough, F. C. (1931). *Anger in young children.* Minneapolis: University of Minnesota Press.

Goodglass, H. (1979). Effect of aphasia on the retrieval of lexicon and syntax. In. C. J. Fillmore, D. Kempler, & W. S.-Y. Wang (Eds.), *Individual differences in language ability and language behavior* (pp. 253–260). New York: Academic Press.

Goodglass, H. (1993). *Understanding aphasia.* San Diego, CA: Academic Press.

Goodman, G. S., & Aman, C. (1990). Children's use of anatomically detailed dolls to recount an event. *Child Development, 61,* 1859–1871.

Goodnow, J. J. (1977). *Children drawing.* Cambridge, MA: Harvard University Press.

Goodnow, J. J., Cashmore, J., Cotton, S., & Knight, R. (1984). Mothers' developmental timetables in two cultural groups. *International Journal of Psychology, 19,* 193–205.

Goodwin, M. H. (1990). *He-Said-She-Said: Talk as social organization among black children.* Bloomington, IN: Indiana University Press.

Goodwin, M. H. (2001). Organizing participation in cross-sex jump rope: Situating gender differences within longitudinal studies of activities. *Research on Language and Social Interaction, 34,* 1, 75–106.

Goodwin, P., McGill, B., & Chandra, A. (2009). Who marries and when? Age at first marriage in the United States: 2002. NCHS Data Brief, no. 19. National Center for Health Statistics. http://www.cdc.gov/nchs/data/databriefs/db19.htm.

Gopnik, A., & Astington, J. W. (1988). Children's understanding of representational change and its relation to the understanding of false belief and the appearance-reality distinction. *Child Development, 59,* 26–37.

Gopnik, A., & Slaughter, V. (1991). Young children's understanding of changes in their mental states. *Child Development, 62,* 98–110.

Gordon, R. A., Lahey, B. B., Kawai, E., Loeber, R., Stouthamer-Loeber M., & Farrington, D. P. (2004). Antisocial behavior and youth gang membership: Selection and socialization. *Criminology, 42,* 55–87.

Gosselin, J., & David, H. (2007). Risk and resilience factors linked with the psycosocial adjustment of adolescents, stepparents and biological parents. *Journal of Divorce and Remarriage, 48,* 29–53.

Goswami, U. (2001). Analogical reasoning in children. In D. Gentner, K. J. Holyoak, & B. N. Kokinov, (Eds.), *The analogical mind: Perspectives from cognitive science* (pp. 437–470). Cambridge, MA: The MIT Press.

Gottesman, I. I. (1991). *Schizophrenia genesis: The origins of madness.* New York: Freeman.

Gottesman, I. I., & Goldsmith, H. H. (1994). Developmental psychopathology of antisocial behavior: Inserting genes into its ontogenesis and epigenesis. In C. Nelson (Ed.), *Minnesota Symposium on Child Psychology: Vol. 27. Threats to optimal development: Integrating biological, psychological, and social risk factors* (pp. 69–104). Hillsdale, NJ: Erlbaum.

Gottfried, A. E., Gottfried, A. W., & Bathurst, K. (2002). Maternal and dual-earner employment status and parenting. In M. H. Bornstein (Ed.), Handbook of parenting (2nd ed.; Vol. 2): *Biology and ecology of parenting* (pp. 207–229). Mahwah, NJ: Erlbaum.

Gottlieb, A. (2004). *The afterlife is where we come from: The culture of infancy in West Africa.* Chicago: University of Chicago Press.

Gottlieb, G. (1992). *Individual development and evolution.* New York: Oxford University Press.

Gottlieb, G., Wahlsten, D., & Lickliter, R. (1997). The significance of biology for human development: A developmental psychobiological systems view. In W. Damon (Series Ed.) & R. M. Lerner (Vol. Ed.), *Handbook of child psychology: Vol. 1. Theoretical models of human development* (5th ed., pp. 233–273). New York: Wiley.

Gottman, J. M. (1986). The world of coordinated play: same- and cross-sex friendship in young children. In J. M. Gottman & J. G. Parker (Eds.), *Conversations of friends: Speculations on affective development* (pp. 139–191). Cambridge, UK: Cambridge University Press.

Gottman, J. M., Katz, L. F., & Hooven, C. (1997). *Meta-emotion: How families communicate emotionally.* Mahwah, NJ: Erlbaum.

Gottman, J. M., & Mettetal, G. (1986). Speculations about social and affective development: friendship and acquaintanceship through adolescence. In J. M. Gottman & J. G. Parker (Eds.), *Conversations of friends: Speculations on affective development* (pp. 192–237). Cambridge, UK: Cambridge University Press.

Gougoux, F., Lepore, F., Lassonde, M., Voss, P., Zatorre, R. J., & Belin, P. (2004). Pitch discrimination in the early blind: People blinded in infancy have sharper listening skills than those who lost their sight later. *Nature, 430,* 309.

Gould, S. J. (1981). *The mismeasure of man.* New York: W. W. Norton & Co.

Gould, S. J. (1997, June 12). Darwinian fundamentalism. *The New York Review of Books, 44,* No. 10.

Gove, W. R., & Zeiss, C. (1987). Multiple roles and happiness. In F. Crosby (Ed.), *Spouse, parent, worker* (pp. 125–137). New Haven, CT: Yale University Press.

Graham, J. A., & Cohen, R. (1997). Race and sex as factors in children's sociometric ratings and friendship choices. *Social Development, 6,* 355–372.

Graham. S., & Harris, K. R. (1996). Self-regulation and strategy instruction for students who find writing and learning challenging. In C. M. Levy & S. Ransdell (Eds.), *The science of writing: Theories, methods, individual differences, and applications* (pp. 347–360). Mahwah, NJ: Erlbaum.

Graham, S., & Hudley, C. (1994). Attributions of aggressive and nonaggressive African-American male early adolescents: A study of construct accessibility. *Developmental Psychology, 28*, 731–740.

Graham-Bermann, S. A., & Brescoll, V. (2000). Gender, power, and violence: Assessing the family stereotypes of the children of batterers. *Journal of Family Psychology, 14*, 600–612.

Granger, D. A., Serbin, L. A., Schwartzman, A., Lehoux, P., Cooperman, J., & Ikeda, S. (1998). Children's salivary cortisol, internalising behaviour problems, and family environment: Results from the Concordia longitudinal risk project. *International Journal of Behavioral Development, 22*, 707–728.

Granger, Douglas A., Stansbury, Kathy, Henker, Barbara. (1994). Preschoolers' behavioral and neuroendocrine responses to social challenge. *Merrill-Palmer Quarterly: Journal of Developmental Psychology, 40*(2), 190–211.

Granot, D., & Mayseless, O. (2001). Attachment security and adjustment to school in middle childhood. *International Journal of Behavioral Development, 25*, 530–541.

Granrud, C. E. (1987). Size constancy in newborn human infants. *Investigative Ophthalmology and Visual Science, 28*(Suppl.), 5.

Graves, N. B., & Graves, T. D. (1983). The cultural context of prosocial development: An ecological model. In D. L. Bridgeman (Ed.), *The nature of prosocial development* (pp. 243–264). New York: Academic Press.

Gray, E. (1993). *Unequal justice: The prosecution of child sexual abuse.* New York: Macmillan.

Gray, J. R., Chabris, C. F., & Braver, T. S. (2003). Neural mechanisms of general fluid intelligence. *Nature Neuroscience, 6*, 316–322.

Gray-Little, B., & Hafdahl, A. R. (2000). Factors influencing racial comparisons of self-esteem: A quantitative review. *Psychological Bulletin, 126*, 26–54.

Green, C. S., & Bavelier, D. (2003). Action video game modifies visual attention. *Nature, 423*, 534–537.

Green, J. A., Jones, L. E., & Gustafson, G. E. (1987). Perception of cries by parents and nonparents: Relation to cry acoustics. *Developmental Psychology, 23*, 370–382.

Green, R. W., Biederman, J., Faraone, S. V., Sienna, M., & Garcia-Jetton, J. (1997). Adolescent outcome of boys with attention-deficit/hyperactivity disorder and social disability: Results from a 4-year longitudinal follow-up study. *Journal of Consulting and Clinical Psychology, 65*, 758–767.

Greenberg, M. T., Domitrovich, C., & Bumbarger, B. (2001). The prevention of mental disorders in school-age children: Current state of the field. *Prevention and Treatment, 4*, Article 001a. Online article available at http://journals.apa.org/prevention/volume4/pre004001a.html.

Greenberg, M. T., Kusche, C. A., Cook, E. T., & Quamma, J. P. (1995). Promoting emotional competence in school-aged children: The effects of the PATHS curriculum. *Development and Psychopathology, 7*, 117–136.

Greenberg, M. T., & Kusche, C. A. (2006). Building social and emotional competence: The PATHS curriculum. In S. R. Jimerson & M. Furlong (Eds.), *Handbook of school violence and school safety: From research to practice* (pp. 395–412). Mahwah, NJ: Erlbaum.

Greenberger, E., Chen, C., Tally, S. R., & Dong, Q. (2000). Family, peer, and individual correlates of depressive symptomatology among U.S. and Chinese adolescents. *Journal of Consulting and Clinical Psychology, 68*, 209–219.

Greenberger, E., O'Neil, R., & Nagel, S. K. (1994). Linking workplace and homeplace: Relations between the nature of adults' work and their parenting behaviors. *Developmental Psychology, 30*, 990–1002.

Greene, J. G., Fox, N. A., & Lewis, M. (1983). The relationship between neonatal characteristics and three-month mother-infant interaction in high risk infants. *Child Development, 54*, 1286–1296.

Greene, M., Way, N., & Pahl, K. (2006). Trajectories of perceived adult and peer discrimination among Black, Latino, and Asian American adolescents: Patterns and psychological correlates. *Developmental Psychology, 42*, 218–238.

Greenfield, P. M. (2004). Inadvertent exposure to pornography on the Internet: Implications of peer-to-peer file-sharing networks for child development and families. *Applied Developmental Psychology, 25*, 741–750.

Greenfield, P. M., deWinstanley, P., Kilpatrick, H., & Kaye, D. (1994). Action video games and informal education: Effects on strategies for dividing visual attention. *Journal of Applied Developmental Psychology, 15*, 105–123.

Greenfield, P. M., Suzuki, L. K., & Rothstein-Fisch, C. (2006). Cultural pathways through human development. In W. Damon & R. M. Lerner (Book Eds.) & K. A. Renninger & I. E. Sigel (Vol. Eds.), *Handbook of child psychology: Vol. 4. Child psychology in practice* (6th ed., pp. 655–699). Hoboken, NJ: Wiley.

Greenwald, A. G., & Banaji, M. R. (1995). Implicit social cognition: Attitudes, self-esteem, and stereotypes. *Psychological Review, 102*, 4–27.

Greif, M. L., Kemler-Nelson, D. G., Keil, F. C., & Guitierrez, F. (2006). What do children want to know about animals and artifacts? *Psychological Science, 17*, 455–459.

Gregory, A. M., Light-Häusermann, J. H., Rijsdijk, F., & Eley, T. C. (2009). Behavioral genetic analyses of prosocial behavior in adolescents. *Developmental Science, 12*, 165–174.

Gregory, A. M., Rijsdijk, F., Lau, J. Y. F., Napolitano, M., McGuffin, P., & Eley, T. C. (2007). Genetic and environmental influences on interpersonal cognitions and associations with depressive symptoms in 8-year-old twins. *Journal of Abnormal Psychology, 116*, 762–775.

Griffin, S. (2004). Number worlds: A research-based mathematics program for young children. In. D. H. Clements & J. Sarama (Eds.), *Engaging young children in mathematics: Standards for early mathematics education* (pp. 325–342). Mahwah, NJ: Erlbaum.

Grimshaw, G. M., Sitarenios, G., & Finegan, J. K. (1995). Mental rotation at 7 years: Relations with prenatal testosterone levels and spatial play experience. *Brain and Cognition, 29*, 85–100.

Grolnick, W. S., Bridges, L. J., & Connell, J. P. (1996). Emotion regulation in two-year-olds: Strategies and emotional expression in four contexts. *Child Development, 67*, 928–941.

Gron, G., Wunderlich, A. P., Spitzer, M., Tomczak, R., & Riepe, M. W. (2000). Brain activation during human navigation: Gender different neural networks as substrate of performance. *Nature Neuroscience, 3*, 404–408.

Gross, D., & Harris, P. L. (1988). False beliefs about emotion: Children's understanding of misleading emotional displays. *International Journal of Behavioral Development, 11*, 475–488.

Gross, R. T., Spiker, D., & Haynes, C. W. (1997). *Helping low birth weight, premature babies: The infant health and development program.* Palo Alto: Stanford University Press.

Grotevant, H. D. (1998). Adolescent development in family contexts. In W. Damon (Series Ed.) & N. Eisenberg (Vol. Ed.), *Handbook of child psychology: Vol. 3. Social, emotional, and personality development* (5th ed., pp. 1097–1149). New York: Wiley.

Gruber, J. E., & Fineran, S. (2008). Comparing the impact of bullying and sexual harassment victimization on the mental and physical health of adolescents. *Sex Roles, 59,* 1–13.

Grueneich, R. (1982). Issues in the developmental study of how children use intention and consequence information to make moral evaluations. *Child Development, 53,* 29–43.

Grusec, J. E., Goodnow, J. J., & Cohen, L. (1996). Household work and the development of concern for others. *Developmental Psychology, 32,* 999–1007.

Grusec, J. E., Goodnow, J. J., & Kuczynski, L. (2000). New directions in analyses of parenting contributions to children's acquisition of values. *Child Development, 81,* 205–211.

Grych, J. H., & Fincham, F. D. (1997). Children's adaptation to divorce: From description to explanation. In S. A. Wolchik & I. N. Sandler (Eds.), *Handbook of children's coping: Linking theory and intervention* (pp. 159–193). New York: Plenum Press.

Grych, J. H., Harold, G. T., & Miles, C. J. (2003). A prospective investigation of appraisals as mediators of the link between interparental conflict and child adjustment. *Child Development, 74,* 1176–1193.

Grych, J. H., Raynor, S. R., & Fosco, G. M. (2004). Family processes that shape the impact of interparental conflict on adolescents. *Development and Psychopathology, 16,* 649–665.

Guerin, D. W., & Gottfried, A. W. (1994). Developmental stability and change in parent reports of temperament: A ten-year longitudinal investigation from infancy through preadolescence. *Merrill-Palmer Quarterly, 40,* 334–355.

Guerin, D. W., Gottfried, A. W., & Thomas, C. W. (1997). Difficult temperament and behaviour problems: A longitudinal study from 1.5 to 12 years of age. *International Journal of Behavioral Development, 21,* 71–90.

Guerra, N. G., Huesmann, L. R., & Spindler, A. (2003). Community violence exposure, social cognition, and aggression among urban elementary school children. *Child Development, 74,* 1561–1576.

Gummerum, M., & Keller, M. (2008). Affection, virtue, pleasure, and profit: Developing an understanding of friendship closeness and intimacy in western and Asian societies. *International Journal of Behavioral Development, 32,* 218–231.

Gunnar, M. R. (1994). Psychoendocrine studies of temperament and stress in early childhood: Expanding current models. In J. E. Bates & T. D. Wachs (Eds.), *Temperament: Individual differences at the interface of biology and behavior* (pp. 175–198). Washington, DC: American Psychological Association.

Gunnar, M. R., & Cheatham, C. L. (2003). Brain and behavior interface: Stress and the developing brain. *Infant Mental Health Journal, 24,* 195–211.

Gunnar, M. R., Sebanc, A. M., Tout, K., Donzella, B., & van Dulmen, M. M. H. (2003). Peer rejection, temperament, and cortisol activity in preschoolers. *Developmental Psychobiology, 43,* 346–358.

Gunnar, M. R., & Vazquez, D. (2006). Stress neurobiology and developmental psychopathology. In D. Cicchetti & D. J. Cohen (Eds.), *Developmental psychopathology* (Vol. 2) *Developmental neuroscience* (2nd ed., pp. 533–577). Hoboken, NJ: John Wiley & Sons.

Gunnoe, M. L., & Hetherington, E. M. (2004). Stepchildren's perceptions of noncustodial mothers and noncustodial fathers: Differences in socioemotional involvement and associations with adolescent adjustment problems. *Journal of Family Psychology, 18,* 555–563.

Gustafson, G. E., & Green, J. A. (1988, April). *A role of crying in the development of prelinguistic communicative competence.* Paper presented at the International Conference on Infant Studies, Washington, DC.

Guthrie, J. T., Wigfield, A., Metsala, J. L., & Cox, K. E. (1999). Motivational and cognitive predictors of text comprehension and reading amount. *Scientific Studies of Reading, 3,* 231–256.

Gutman, L. M., Sameroff, A. J., & Cole, R. (2003). Academic growth curve trajectories from 1st grade to 12th grade: Effects of multiple social risk factors and preschool child factors. *Developmental Psychology, 39,* 777–790.

Haden, C. A., Hayne, R. A., & Fivush, R. (1997). Developing narrative structure in parent–child reminiscing across the preschool years. *Developmental Psychology, 33,* 295–307.

Haith, M. M. (1980). *Rules that babies look by: The organization of newborn visual activity.* Hillsdale, NJ: Erlbaum.

Haith, M. M., & Benson, J. B. (1998). Infant cognition. In W. Damon (Series Ed.), D. Kuhn, & R. S. Siegler (Vol. Eds.), *Handbook of child psychology: Vol. 2. Cognition, perception, and language* (5th ed., pp. 199–254). New York: Wiley.

Haith, M. M., Bergman, T., & Moore, M. J. (1977). Eye contact and face scanning in early infancy. *Science, 198,* 853–855.

Haith, M. M., Wentworth, N., & Canfield, R. L., (1993). The formation of expectations in early infancy. In C. Rovee-Collier & L. P. Lipsitt (Eds.), *Advances in infancy research.* Norwood, NJ: Ablex.

Hakuta, K. (1999). The debate on bilingual education. *Journal of Developmental & Behavioral Pediatrics, 20,* 36–37.

Halberstadt, A. G., Cassidy, J., Stifter, C. A., Parke, R. D., & Fox, N. A. (1995). Self-expressiveness within the family context: Psychometric support for a new measure. *Psychological Assessment, 7,* 93–103.

Halberstadt, A. G., Crisp, V. W., & Eaton, K. L. (1999). Family expressiveness: A retrospective and new directions for research. In P. Philippot, R. S. Feldman, & E. Coats (Eds.), *The social context of nonverbal behavior.* New York: Cambridge University Press.

Halberstadt, A. G., Denham, S. A., & Dunsmore, J. C. (2001). Affective social competence. *Social Development, 10,* 79–119.

Hall, D. G., Waxman, S. R., & Hurwitz, W. M. (1993). How 2- and 4-year-old children interpret adjectives and count nouns. *Child Development, 64,* 1661–1664.

Hall, J. A. & Halberstadt, A. G. (1980). Masculinity and femininity in children: Development of the Children's Personal Attributes Questionnaire. *Developmental Psychology, 16,* 270–280.

Halpern, C. T., Udry, J. R., & Suchindran, C. M. (1997), Testosterone predicts initiation of coitus in adolescent females, *Psycohosomatic Medicine, 50,* 161–171.

Halpern, D. F. (2000). *Sex differences in cognitive abilities* (3rd ed.). Mahwah, NJ: Erlbaum.

Halpern, D. F. (2004). A cognitive-process taxonomy for sex differences in cognitive abilities. *Current Directions in Psychological Science, 13,* 135–139.

Halpern, D. F., Benbow, C. P., Geary, D. C., Gur, R. C., Hyde, J. S. & Gernbacher, M. A. (2007). The science of sex differences in science and mathematics. *Psychological Science in the Public Interest, 8,* 1–51.

Halpern-Meekin, S., & Tach, L. (2008). Heterogeneity in two-parent families and adolescent well-being. *Journal of Marriage and Family, 70,* 435–451.

Hamalainen, M., & Pulkkinen, L. (1996). Problem behavior as a precursor of male criminality. *Development and Psychopathology, 8,* 443–455.

Hamamura, T., Heine, S. J., & Paulhus, D. L. (2008). Cultural differences in response styles: The role of dialectical thinking. *Personality and Individual Differences, 44,* 932–942.

Hamer, D. H., Hu, S., Magnuson, V. L., Hu, N., & Pattatucci, A. M. L. (1993). A linkage between DNA markers on the X chromosome and male sexual orientation. *Science, 261,* 311–327.

Hamilton, B. E., Martin, J. A., & Ventura, S. J. (2007, December 5). Births: Preliminary data for 2006. *National Vital Statistics Reports, 56,* 7, 1–18.

Hamilton, C. E. (2000). Continuity and discontinuity of attachment from infancy through adolescence. *Child Development, 71,* 690–694.

Hamlin, J. K., Wynn, K., & Bloom, P. (2007). Social evaluation by preverbal infants. *Nature, 450,* 557–559.

Hammen, C., & Rudolph, K. D. (2003). Childhood mood disorders. In E. J. Mash & R. A. Barkley (Eds.), *Child psychopathology* (2nd ed., pp. 233–278). New York: Guilford.

Han, W. J. (2005). Maternal nonstandard work schedules and child cognitive outcomes. *Child Development, 76,* 137–154.

Hanish, L. D., & Guerra, N. G. (2000a). Predictors of peer victimization among urban youth. *Social Development, 9,* 521–543.

Hanish, L. D., & Guerra, N. G. (2000b). The roles of ethnicity and school context in predicting children's victimization by peers. *American Journal of Community Psychology, 28,* 201–223.

Hanish, L. D., & Guerra, N. G. (2002). A longitudinal analysis of patterns of adjustment following peer victimization. *Development and Psychopathology, 14,* 69–89.

Hanish, L. D., & Guerra, N. G. (2004). Aggressive victims, passive victims, and bullies: Developmental continuity or developmental change? *Merrill-Palmer Quarterly, 50*(1), 17–38.

Hanish, L. D., & Tolan, P. H. (2001). Patterns of change in family-based aggression prevention. *Journal of Marital and Family Therapy, 27,* 213–226.

Hankin, B. L., & Abramson, L. Y. (1999). Development of gender differences in depression: description and possible explanations. *Annals of Medicine, 31,* 372–379.

Hankin, B. L., Abramson, L. Y., Moffitt, T. E., Silva, P. A., McGree, R., & Angell, K. E. (1998). Development of depression from preadolescence to young adulthood: Emerging gender differences in a 10-year-longitudinal study. *Journal of Abnormal Psychology, 107,* 128–140.

Hankin, B. L., Meremelstin, R., & Roesch, L. (2007). Sex differences in adolescent depression: Stress exposure and reactivity models. *Child Development, 78,* 279–295.

Hanna, N. A. (1998). Predictors of friendship quality and peer group acceptance at summer camp. *Journal of Early Adolescence, 18,* 291–318.

Hanna, E., & Meltzoff, A. N. (1993). Peer imitation by toddlers in laboratory, home, and day-care contexts: Implications for social learning and memory. *Developmental Psychology, 29,* 701–710.

Happé, F. G. E. (1995). The role of age and verbal ability in the theory-of-mind task performance of subjects with autism. *Child Development, 66,* 843–855.

Harada, M. (1995). Minamata disease: Methylmercury poisoning in Japan caused by environmental pollution. *Critical Reviews in Toxicology, 25,* 1–24.

Harden, K. P., Turkheimer, E., Emery, R. E., D'Onofrio, B. M., Slutske, W. S., Heath, A. C., & Martin, N. G. (2007). Marital conflict and conduct problems in children of twins. *Child Development, 78,* 1–18.

Hardy, C. L., Bukowski, W. M., & Sippola, L. K. (2002). Stability and change in peer relationships during the transition to middle-level school. *Journal of Early Adolescence, 22,* 117–142.

Hardy, J. B., Astone, N. M., Brooks-Gunn, J., Shapiro, S., & Miller, T. L. (1998). Like mother, like child: Intergenerational patterns of age at first birth and association with childhood and adolescent characteristics and adult outcomes in the second generation. *Developmental Psychology, 34,* 1220–1232.

Harkness, S. & Super, C. M. (1985). The cultural context of gender segregation in children's peer groups. *Child Development, 56,* 219–224.

Harkness, S., & Super, C. (1995). Culture and parenting. In M. Bornstein (Ed.), *Handbook of parenting* (Vol. 2, pp. 211–234). Hillsdale, NJ: Erlbaum.

Harkness, S., Super, C., Keefer, C. H., Raghavan, C. S., & Campbell, E. K. (1996). Ask the doctor: The negotiation of cultural models in American parent-pediatrician discourse. In S. Harkness & C. M. Super (Eds.), *Parents' cultural belief systems: Their origins, expressions, and consequences.* New York: Guilford.

Harlaar, N., Dale, P. S., & Plomin, R. (2007). From learning to read to reading to learn: Substantial and stable genetic influence. *Child Development, 78,* 116–131.

Harley, K., & Reese, E. (1999). Origins of autobiographical memory. *Developmental Psychology, 35,* 1338–1348.

Harlow, H. F., & Harlow, M. K. (1965). The affectional systems. In A. M. Schrier, H. F. Harlow, & F. Stollnitz (Eds.), *Behavior of nonhuman primates: Vol. 2.* New York: Academic Press.

Harlow, H. F., & Zimmerman, R. (1959). Affectional responses in the infant monkey. *Science, 130,* 421–432.

Harman, C., Rothbart, M. K., & Posner, M. I. (1997). Distress and attention interactions in early infancy. *Motivation & Emotion, 21,* 27–43.

Harold, G. T., & Conger, R. D. (1997). Marital conflict and adolescent distress: The role of adolescent awareness. *Child Development, 68,* 333–350.

Harris, F. R., Wolf, M. M., & Baer, D. M. (1967). Effects of adult social reinforcement on child behavior. In W. W. Hartup and N. L. Smothergill (Eds.), *The young child: Reviews of research.* Washington, DC: National Association for the Education of Young Children.

Harris, J. F. (1995). Where is the child's environment? A group socialization theory of development. *Psychological Review, 102,* 458–489.

Harris, P. L. (2000). *The work of the imagination.* Oxford: Blackwell.

Harris, P. L. (2002). What do children learn from testimony? In P. Carruther, S. Stitch, & M. Siegal (Eds.), *The cognitive basis of science* (pp. 316–334). Cambridge, UK: Cambridge University Press.

Harris, P. L. (2006). Social cognition. In W. Damon & R. M. Lerner (Series Eds.) & D. Kuhn & R. S. Siegler (Vol. Eds.), *Handbook of child* *psychology: Volume 2: Cognition, perception, and language* (6th ed., pp. 811–858). Hoboken, NJ: Wiley.

Harris, P. L., Olthof, T., Terwogt, M. M., & Hardman, C. E. (1987). Children's knowledge of the situations that provoke emotion. *International Journal of Behavioral Development, 10,* 319–343.

Harris-Britt, A., Valrie, C. R., Kurtz-Costes, B., & Rowley, S. J. (2007). Perceived racial discrimination and self-esteem in African American youth: Racial socialization as a protective factor. *Journal of Research on Adolescence, 17,* 669–682.

Harrison, Y. (2004). The relationship between daytime exposure to light and night-time sleep in 6–12-week-old infants. *Journal of Sleep Research, 13,* 345–352.

Harrist, A. W., Zaia, A. F., Bates, J. E., Dodge, K. A., & Pettit, G. S. (1997). Subtypes of social withdrawal in early childhood: Sociometric status and social-cognitive differences across four years. *Child Development, 68,* 278–294.

Hart, B., & Risley, T. R. (1995). *Meaningful differences in the everyday experience of young American children.* Baltimore: Brookes.

Hart, C. H., DeWolf, D. M., Wozniak, P., & Burts, D. C. (1992). Maternal and paternal disciplinary styles: Relations with preschoolers' playgroup behavioral orientations and peer status. *Child Development, 63,* 879–892.

Hart, C. H., Ladd, G. W., & Burleson, B. R. (1990). Children's expectations of the outcomes of social strategies: Relations with sociometric status and maternal disciplinary styles. *Child Development, 61,* 127–137.

Hart, D., Donnelly, T. M., Youniss, J., & Atkins, R. (2007). High school predictors of adult civic engagement: The roles of volunteering, civic knowledge, extracurricular activities, and attitudes. *American Educational Research Journal, 44,* 197–219.

Hart, D., & Fegley, S. (1995). Altruism and caring in adolescence: Relations to self-understanding and social judgment. *Child Development, 66,* 1346–1359.

Harter, S. (1983). Developmental perspectives on the self-system. In P. H. Mussen (Series Ed.) & E. M. Hetherington (Vol. Ed.), *Handbook of child psychology: Vol. 4. Socialization, personality, and social development* (pp. 275–385). New York: Wiley.

Harter, S. (1985). *Manual for the self-perception profile for children.* Unpublished manuscript, University of Denver, Denver, CO.

Harter, S. (1993). Causes and consequences of low self-esteem in children and adolescents. In R. F. Baumeister (Ed.), *Self-esteem: The puzzle of low self-regard* (pp. 87–116). New York: Plenum Press.

Harter, S. (1998). The development of self-representations. In W. Damon (Series Ed.) & N. Eisenberg (Vol. Ed.), *Handbook of child psychology: Vol. 3. Social, emotional, and personality development* (5th ed., pp. 553–617). New York: Wiley.

Harter, S. (1999). *The cognitive and social construction of the developing self.* New York: Guilford.

Harter, S. (2006). The self. In N. Eisenberg (Vol. Ed.) and W. Damon & R. M. Lerner (Series Eds.), *Handbook of child psychology. Vol. 3. Social, emotional, and personality development* (6th ed., pp. 505–570). Hoboken, NJ: Wiley.

Harter, S., Bresnick, S., Bouchey, H. A., & Whitsell, N. R. (1998). The development of multiple role-related selves during adolescence. *Development and Psychopathology, 9,* 835–854.

Harter, S., & Buddin, B. J. (1987). Children's understanding of the simultaneity of two emotions: A five-stage developmental acquisition sequence. *Developmental Psychology, 23,* 388–399.

Harter, S., & Monsour, A. (1992). Developmental analysis of conflict caused by opposing attributes in the adolescent self-portrait. *Developmental Psychology, 28,* 251–260.

Harter, S., & Pike, R. (1984). The Pictorial Scale of Perceived Competence and Social Acceptance for young children. *Child Development, 55,* 1969–1982.

Hartshorn, K., & Rovee-Collier, C. (1997). Infant learning and long-term memory at 6 months: A confirming analysis. *Developmental Psychology, 30,* 71–85.

Hartup, W. W. (1974). Aggression in childhood: Developmental perspectives. *American Psychologist, 27,* 336–341.

Hartup, W. W. (1983). Peer relations. In P. H. Mussen (Ed.), *Handbook of child development: Vol. 4. Socialization personality and social development* (4th ed., pp. 103–196). New York: Wiley.

Hartup, W. W. (1996). The company they keep: Friendships and their developmental significance. *Child Development, 67,* 1–13.

Hartup, W. W., French, D. C., Laursen, B., Johnston, M. K., & Ogawa, J. R. (1993). Conflict and friendship relations in middle childhood: Behavior in a closed-field situation. *Child Development, 64,* 445–454.

Hartup, W. W., Laursen, B., Stewart, M. A., & Eastenson, A. (1988). Conflicts and the friendship relations of young children. *Child Development, 59,* 1590–1600.

Hartup, W. W., & Stevens, N. (1997). Friendships and adaptation in the life course. *Psychological Bulletin, 121,* 355–370.

Harvey, E. (1999). Short-term and long-term effects of early parental employment on children of the National Longitudinal Survey of youth. *Developmental Psychology, 35,* 445–459.

Haselager, G. J. T., Hartup, W. W., van Lieshout, C. F. M., & Riksen-Walraven, J. M. A. (1998). Similarities between friends and nonfriends in middle childhood. *Child Development, 69,* 1198–1208.

Haskins, R. (1985). Public school aggression among children with varying day care experience. *Child Development, 56,* 689–703.

Haskins, R. (1989). Beyond metaphor: The efficacy of early childhood education. *American Psychologist, 44,* 274–282.

Hastings, P. D., & De, I. (2008). Parasympathetic regulation and parental socialization of emotion: Biopsychosocial processes of adjustment in preschoolers. *Social Development, 17,* 211–238.

Hastings, P. D., McShane, K. E., Parker, R., & Ladha, F. (2007). Ready to make nice: Parental socialization of young sons' and daughters' prosocial behaviors with peers. *Journal of Genetic Psychology, 168,* 177–200.

Hastings, P. D., Zahn-Waxler, C., & McShane, K. (2005). We are, by nature, moral creatures: Biological bases of concern for others. In M. Killen & J. Smetana (Eds.), *Handbook of moral development* (pp. 483–516). Hillsdale, NJ: Erlbaum.

Hastings, P. D., Zahn-Waxler, C., Robinson, J., Usher, B., & Bridges, D. (2000). The development of concern for others in children with behavior problems. *Developmental Psychology, 35,* 531–546.

Hatano, G., & Inagaki, K. (1996). Cognitive and cultural factors in the acquisition of intuitive biology. In D. R. Olson & N. Torrance (Eds.), *Handbook of education and human development: New models of learning, teaching and schooling.* Cambridge, UK: Blackwell.

Hatano, G., Siegler, R. S., Richards, D. D., Inagaki, K., Stavy, R., & Wax, N. (1993). The development of biological knowledge: A multinational study. *Cognitive Development, 8*, 47–62.

Hatzichristou, C., & Hopf, D. (1996). A multiperspective comparison of peer sociometric status groups in childhood and adolescence. *Child Development, 67*, 1085–1102.

Hawker, D. S. J., & Boulton, M. J. (2000). Twenty years' research on peer victimization and psychosocial maladjustment: A meta-analytic review of cross-sectional studies. *Journal of Child Psychology and Psychiatry, 41*, 441–455.

Hawley, P. H., Little, T. D., & Card, N. A. (2008). The myth of the alpha male: A new look at dominance-related beliefs and behaviors among adolescent males and females. *International Journal of Behavioral Development, 32*, 76–88.

Hawley, T. L., & Disney, E. R. (1992, Winter). Crack's children: The consequences of maternal cocaine abuse. *Social Policy Report: Society for Research in Child Development, 6*.

Hay, D. F. (2007). The gradual emergence of sex differences in aggression: Alternative hypotheses. *Psychological Medicine, 37*, 1527–1537.

Hay, D. F., Caplan, M., & Nash, A. (2009). The beginnings of peer relations. In K. H. Rubin, W. M. Bukowski, & B. Laursen (Eds.), *Handbook of peer interactions, relationships, and groups* (pp. 121–142). New York: Guilford Press.

Hay, D. F., Castle, J., Stimson, C. A., & Davies, L. (1995). The social construction of character in toddlerhood. In M. Killen & D. Hart (eds.), *Moral in everyday life* (pp. 23–51). Cambridge, UK: Cambridge University Press.

Hay, D. F., Nash, A., & Pedersen, J. (1981). Responses of six-month-olds to the distress of their peers. *Child Development, 52*, 1071–1075.

Hay, D. F., & Ross, H. S. (1982). The social nature of early conflict. *Child Development, 53*, 105–113.

Hayes, K. J., & Hayes, C. (1951). The intellectual development of a home-raised chimpanzee. *Proceedings of the American Philosophical Society, 95*, 105–109.

Hayne, H. (2004). Infant memory development: Implications for childhood amnesia. *Developmental Review, 24*, 33–73.

Hayne, H., Barr, R., & Herbert, J. (2003). The effect of prior practice on memory reactivation and generalization. *Child Development, 74(6)*, 1615–1627.

Head Start Bureau. (2007). *Head Start Program Performance Standards and Other Regulations*. Washington, DC.

Heathcock, J. C., Lobo, M., & Galloway, J. C. (2008). Movement training advances the emergence of reaching in infants born at less than 33 weeks of gestational age: A randomized clinical trial. *Physical Therapy, 88*, 1–13.

Heaven, P., & Ciarrochi, J. (2008). Parental styles, gender and the development of hope and self-esteem. *European Journal of Personality, 22*, 707–724.

Hedges, L. V., & Nowell, A. (1995). Sex differences in mental test scores, variability, and numbers of high-scoring individuals. *Science, 269*, 41–45.

Heine, S. J., Lehman, D. R., Markus, H. R., & Kitayama, S. (1999). Is there a universal need for positive self-regard? *Psychological Review, 106*, 766–794.

Held, R., Birch, E. E., & Gwiazda, J. (1980). Stereoacuity of human infants. *Proceedings of the National Academy of Sciences of the USA, 77*, 5572–5574.

Helsen, M., Vollebergh, W., & Meeus, W. (2000). Social support from parents and friends and emotional problems in adolescence. *Journal of Youth and Adolescence, 29*, 319–335.

Henry, B., Caspi, A., Moffitt, T. E., & Silva, P. A. (1994). Temperamental and familial predictors of violent and non-violent criminal convictions: From age 3 to age 18. *Developmental Psychology, 32*, 614–623.

Hepper, P. (1988). Adaptive fetal learning: Prenatal exposure to garlic affects postnatal preferences. *Animal Behaviour, 36*, 935–936.

Herdt, G., & Boxer, A. M. (1993). *Child of horizons: How gay and lesbian teens are leading a new way out of the closet.* Boston: Beacon Press.

Herman, M. (2004). Forced to choose: Some determinants of racial identification in multiracial adolescents. *Child Development, 75*, 730–748.

Hermans, E. J., Ramsey, N. F., & van Honk, J. (2008). Exogenous testosterone enhances responsiveness to social threat in the neural circuitry of social aggression in humans. *Biological Psychiatry, 63*, 263–270.

Hermer, L., & Spelke, E. (1996). Modularity and development: The case of spatial reorientation. *Cognition, 61*, 195–232.

Hernandez, D. J. (1993). America's children: Resources for family, government and the economy. New York: Russell Sage Foundation.

Hernandez, D. J., Denton, N. A., & Macartney, S. E. (2008). Children in immigrant families: Looking to America's future. *Social Policy Report of the Society for Research in Child Development, 22*, 3–22.

Hernandez, J. T., & DiClemente, R. J. (1992). Self control and ego identity development as predictors of unprotected sex in late adolescent males. *Journal of Adolescence, 15*, 437–447.

Herrera, C., & Dunn, J. (1997). Early experiences with family conflict: Implications for arguments with a close friend. *Developmental Psychology, 33*, 869–881.

Hertenstein, M. J., & Campos, J. J. (2004). The retention effects of an adult's emotional displays on infant behavior. *Child Development, 75*, 595–613.

Hesketh, T., Ding, Q. J. (2005). Anxiety and depression in adolescents in urban and rural China. *Psychological Reports, 96*, 435–444.

Hespos, S. J., & Spelke, E. S. (2004). Conceptual precursors to language. *Nature, 430*, 453–456.

Hess, R. D., Kashiwagi, K., Azuma, H., Price, G. G., & Dickson, W. P. (1980). Maternal expectations for mastery of developmental tasks in Japan and the United States. *International Journal of Psychology, 15*, 259–271.

Hesse, E. (1999). The adult attachment interview: Historical and current perspectives. In J. Cassidy & P. R. Shaver (Eds.), *Handbook of attachment: Theory, research, and clinical applications* (pp. 395–433). New York: Guilford.

Hesse, E., Main, M. (2006). Frightened, threatening, and dissociative parental behavior in low-risk samples: Description, discussion, and interpretations. *Development and Psychopathology, 18*, 309–343.

Hetherington, E. M. (1989). Coping with family transitions: Winners, losers, and survivors. *Child Development, 60*, 1–14.

Hetherington, E. M. (1993). An overview of the Virginia Longitudinal Study of Divorce and Remarriage with a focus on early adolescent. *Journal of Family Psychology, 7*, 39–56.

Hetherington, E. M. (1999). Social capital and the development of youth from nondivorced, divorced, and remarried families. In W. A. Collins & B. Laursen (Eds.), *Relationships as developmental contexts. The Minnesota Symposia on Child Psychology* (Vol. 30, pp. 177–209). Mahwah, NJ: Erlbaum.

Hetherington, E. M., Bridges, M., & Insabella, G. M. (1998). What matters? What does not? Five perspectives on the association between marital transitions and children's adjustment. *American Psychologist, 53*, 167–184.

Hetherington, E. M., & Clingempeel, W. G. (1992). Coping with marital transitions: A family systems perspective. *Monographs of the Society for Research in Child Development, 57* (Serial No. 227), 1–242.

Hetherington, E. M., Clingempeel, W. G., Anderson, E. R., Deal, J. E., Stanley-Hagen, M., Hollier, E. A., & Lindner, M. S. (1992). Coping with marital transitions: A family systems perspective. *Monographs of the Society for Research in Child Development, 57*(2–3, Serial No. 227).

Hetherington, E. M., Hagan, M. S., & Anderson, E. R. (1989). Marital transitions: A child's perspective. *American Psychologist, 44*, 303–312.

Hetherington, E. M., Henderson, S. H., & Reiss, D. (1999). Adolescent siblings in stepfamilies: Family functioning and adolescent adjustment. *Monographs of the Society for Research in Child Development, 64* (4, Serial No. 259), iv–209.

Hetherington, L., & Lavner, J. A. (2008). Coming to terms with coming out: Review and recommendations for family systems-focused research. *Journal of Family Psychology, 22*, 329–343.

Hetherington, E. M., & Stanley-Hagan, M. S. (1995). Parenting in divorced and remarried families. In M. Bornstein (Ed.), *Handbook of parenting* (Vol. 3, pp. 233–255). Hillsdale, NJ: Erlbaum.

Hetherington, E. M., & Stanley-Hagan, M. S. (2002). Parenting in divorced and remarried families. In M. Bornstein (Ed.), *Handbook of parenting*, Vol. 3 (2nd ed., pp. 287–315). Mahwah, NJ: Erlbaum.

Hetherington, E. M., Stanley-Hagan, M. S., & Anderson, E. R. (1989). Marital transitions: A child's perspective. *American Psychologist, 44*, 303–312.

Hewlett, B. S. (1991). Intimate fathers: The nature and context of Aka Pygmy paternal infant care. Ann Arbor, MI: University of Michigan Press.

Hewlett, B. S., Lamb, M. E., Shannon, D., Leyendecker, B., & Scholmerich, A. (1998). Culture and early infancy among central African foragers and farmers. *Developmental Psychology, 34*, 651–661.

Hiatt, S. W., Campos, J. J., & Emde, R. N. (1979). Facial patterning and infant emotional expression: Happiness, surprise, and fear. *Child Development, 50*, 1020–1035.

Hickling, A. K., & Gelman, S. A. (1995). How does your garden grow? Early conceptualization of seeds and their place in the plant growth cycle. *Child Development, 66*, 856–876.

Hickman, L. J., Jaycox, L. H., & Aronoff, J. (2004). Dating violence among adolescents: Prevalence, gender distribution, and prevention program effectiveness. *Trauma, Violence, & Abuse, 5*, 123–142.

Hiebert, J., Stigler, J. W., Jacobs, J. K., Givvin, K. B., Garnier, H., Smith, M., Hollingsworth, H., Manaster, A., Wearne, D., & Gallimore, R. (2005). Mathematics teaching in the United States today (and tomorrow): Results from the TIMMS 1999 video study. *Educational Evaluation and Policy Analysis, 27*, 111–132.

Higgins, E. T. (1991). Development of self-regulatory and self-evaluative processes: Costs, benefits, and tradeoffs. In M. R. Gunnar & L. A. Sroufe (Eds.), *The Minnesota Symposia on Child Development: Vol. 23. Self processes and development* (pp. 125–166). Hillsdale, NJ: Erlbaum.

Hill, J., Emery, R. E., Harden, K. P., Mendle, J., & Turkheimer, E. (2008). Alcohol use in adolescent twins and affiliation with substance using peers. *Journal of Abnormal Child Psychology, 36*, 81–94.

Hill, J. P., & Lynch, M. E. (1983). The intensification of gender-related role expectations during early adolescence. In J. Brooks-Gunn & A. C. Petersen (Eds.), *Girls at puberty: Biological and psychosocial perspectives* (pp. 201–228). New York: Plenum.

Hill, J. P. (1988). Adapting to menarche: Familial control and conflict. In M. R. Gunnar & W. A. Collins (Eds.), *Minnesota symposia on child psychology* (Vol. 21, pp. 43–77). Hillsdale, NJ: Erlbaum.

Hill, N. E., Bush, K. R., & Roosa, M. W. (2003). Parenting and family socialization strategies and children's mental health: Low-income Mexican-American and Euro-American mothers and children. *Child Development, 74*, 189–204.

Hill, N. E., Castellino, D. R., Lansford, J. E., Nowlin, P., Dodge, K. A., Bates, J. E., & Pettit, G. S. (2004). Parent academic involvement as related to school behavior, achievement, and aspirations: Demographic variations across adolescence. *Child Development, 75*, 1491–1509.

Hill, N. E., & Taylor, L. C. (2004). Parental school involvement and children's academic achievement. *Current Directions in Psychological Science, 13*, 161–164.

Hill, S. A., & Sprague, J. (1999). Parenting in black and white families: The interaction of gender with race and class. *Gender and Society, 13*, 480–502.

Hines, M. (2004). *Brain gender.* Oxford, UK: Oxford University Press.

Hines, M., Fane, B. A., Pasterski, V. L., Mathews, G. A., Conway, G. S., & Brook, C. (2003). Spatial abilities following prenatal androgen abnormality: targeting and mental rotations performance in individuals with congenital adrenal hyperplasia. *Psychoneuroendocrinology, 28*, 1010–1026.

Hinshaw, S. P., & Lee, S. S. (2003). In E. J. Mash & R. A Berkley (Eds.), *Child psychopathology* (2nd ed., pp. 144–198). New York: Guilford.

Hinshaw, S. P., Zupan, B. A., Simmel, C., Nigg, J. T., & Melnick, S. (1997). Peer status in boys with and without attention-deficit hyperactivity disorder: Predictions from overt and covert antisocial behavior, social isolation, and authoritative parenting beliefs. *Child Development, 68*, 880–896.

Hirsh-Pasek, K., & Golinkoff, R. M. (1991). Language comprehension: A new look at some old themes. In N. A. Krasnegor, D. M. Rumbaugh, R. I. Schiefelbusch, & M. Studdert-Kennedy (Eds.), *Biological and behavioral determinants of language development* (pp. 301–320). Hillsdale, NJ: Erlbaum.

Hirshfeld-Becker, D. R., Biederman, J., Henin, A., Faraone, S. V., Davis, S., Harrington, K., & Rosenbaum, J. F. (2007). Behavioral inhibition in preschool children at risk is a specific predictor of middle childhood social anxiety: A five-year follow-up. *Journal of Developmental & Behavioral Pediatrics, 28*, 225–233.

Ho, D. Y. F. (1986). Chinese patterns of socialization: A critical review. In M. H. Bond (Ed.), *The psychology of Chinese people* (pp. 1–37). New York: Oxford University Press.

Hoard, M. K., Geary, D. C., & Hamson, C. O. (1999). Numerical and arithmetical cognition: Performance of low- and average-IQ children. *Mathematical Cognition, 5*, 65–91.

Hobson, J. A., Harris, R., García-Peréz, R., & Hobson, R. P. (2009). Anticipatory concern: A study in autism. *Developmental Science, 12*, 249–263.

Hochberg, J., & Brooks, V. (1962). Pictorial recognition as an unlearned ability: A study of one child's performance. *American Journal of Psychology, 75,* 624–628.

Hodges, E. V. E., Boivin, M., Vitaro, F., & Bukowski, W. M. (1999). The power of friendship: Protection against an escalating cycle of peer victimization. *Developmental Psychology, 35,* 94–101.

Hodges, E. V. E., Malone, M. J., & Perry, D. G. (1997). Individual risk and social risk as interacting determinants of victimization in the peer group. *Developmental Psychology, 33,* 1032–1039.

Hofer, C., & Eisenberg, N. (in press). The role of socialization, effortful control, and resiliency in French adolescents' social functioning. *Journal of Research on Adolescence.*

Hoff, E. (2001). *Language development* (2nd ed.). Belmont, CA: Wadsworth.

Hoff, E., Laursen, B., & Tardif, T. (2002). Socioeconomic status and parenting. In M. H. Bornstein (Ed.), *Handbook of parenting. Vol. 3. Biology and ecology of parenting* (2nd ed., pp. 231–252). Mahwah, NJ: Erlbaum.

Hoff-Ginsberg, E., & Tardif, T. (1995). Socioeconomic status and parenting. In M. H. Bornstein (Ed.), *Handbook of parenting. Vol. 2. Biology and ecology of parenting* (pp. 161–188). Mahwah, NJ: Erlbaum.

Hoffman, K. B., Cole, D. A., Martin, J. M., Tram, J., & Seroczynski, A. D. (2000). Are discrepancies between self- and others' appraisals of competence predictive or reflective of depressive symptoms in children and adolescents: A longitudinal study, Part II. *Journal of Abnormal Psychology, 2000,* 109, 651–662.

Hoffman, L. W. (1984). Work, family, and the socialization of the child. In R. D. Parke (Ed.), *The family: Review of child development research* (Vol. 7, pp. 223–282). Chicago: University of Chicago Press.

Hoffman, L. W. (1989). Effects of maternal employment in the two-parent family. *American Psychologist, 44,* 283–292.

Hoffman, L. W., & Youngblade, L. (1999). *Mothers at work: Effects on children's well-being.* Cambridge, UK: Cambridge University Press.

Hoffman, M. L. (1963). Parent discipline and the child's consideration for others. *Child Development, 34,* 573–588.

Hoffman, M. L. (1976). Empathy, role-taking, guilt and development of altruistic motives. In T. Lickona (Ed.), *Moral development and behavior: Theory, research, and social issues.* New York: Holt, Rinehart, & Winston.

Hoffman, M. L. (1981). Is altruism part of human nature? *Journal of Personality and Social Psychology, 40,* 121–137.

Hoffman, M. L. (1982). Development of prosocial motivation: Empathy and guilt. In N. Eisenberg (Ed.), *The development of prosocial behavior* (pp. 281–313). New York: Academic Press.

Hoffman, M. L. (1983). Affective and cognitive processes in moral internalization. In E. T. Higgins, D. N. Ruble, & W. W. Hartup (Eds.), *Social cognition and social development: A sociocultural perspective* (pp. 236–274). Cambridge, MA: Cambridge University Press.

Hoffman, M. L. (2000). *Empathy and moral development: Implications for caring and justice.* Cambridge, UK: Cambridge University Press.

Hoffner, C. (1993). Children's strategies for coping with stress: Blunting and monitoring. *Motivation and Emotion, 17,* 91–106.

Hofstadter, M., & Reznick, J. S. (1996). Response modality affects human infant delayed-response performance. *Child Development, 67,* 646–658.

Hofstede, G. (2000). Masculine and feminine cultures. *Encyclopedia of Psychology, 5,* 115–118.

Hogue, A., & Steinberg, L. (1995). Homophily of internalized distress in adolescent peer groups. *Developmental Psychology, 31,* 897–906.

Holden, C. (1980). Identical twins reared apart. *Science, 207,* 1323–1325.

Holden, C. (2005). Sex and the suffering brain. *Science, 308,* 1574–1577.

Holt, M. K., & Espelage, D. L. (2003). A cluster analytic investigation of victimization among high school students: Are profiles differentially associated with psychological symptoms and school belonging? *Journal of Applied School Psychology, 19,* 81–98.

Hopkins, B., & Westra, T. (1988). Maternal handling and motor development: An intracultural study. *Genetic, Social, and General Psychology Monographs, 14,* 377–420.

Horn, S. (2003). Adolescents' reasoning about exclusion from social groups. *Developmental Psychology, 39,* 71–84.

Hosenfeld, B., van der Maas, H. L. J., & van den Boom, D. C. (1997). Indicators of discontinuous change in the development of analogical reasoning. *Journal of Experimental Child Psychology, 64,* 367–395.

Howe, M. L., & Courage, M. L. (1997). The emergence and early development of autobiographical memory. *Psychological Review, 104,* 499–523.

Howe, N., Aquan-Assee, J., & Bukowski, W. M. (2001). Predicting sibling relations over time: Synchrony between maternal management styles and sibling relationship quality. *Merrill-Palmer Quarterly, 47,* 121–141.

Howell, J. C. (1998). *Youth gangs: An overview.* Washington, DC: U.S. Department of Justice, Office of Justice Programs, Office of Juvenile Justice and Delinquency Prevention.

Howes, C. (1983). Patterns of friendship. *Child Development, 54,* 1041–1053.

Howes, C. (1996). The earliest friendships. In W. M. Bukowski, A. F. Newcomb, & W. W. Hartup (Eds.), *The company they keep. Friendship in childhood and adolescence* (pp. 66–86). Cambridge, UK: Cambridge University Press.

Howes, C., & Farver, J. (1987). Toddlers' responses to the distress of their peers. *Journal of Applied Developmental Psychology, 8,* 441–452.

Howes, C., & Matheson, C. C. (1992). Sequences in the development of competent play with peers: Social and social pretend play. *Developmental Psychology, 28,* 961–974.

Howes, C., & Phillipsen, L. (1998). Continuity in children's relations with peers. *Social Development, 7,* 340–349.

Howes, C., & Unger, O. A. (1989). Play with peers in child care settings. In M. Bloch & A. Pelligrini (Eds.), *The ecological contexts of children's play* (pp. 104–119). Norwood, NJ: Ablex.

Hoza, B., Molina, B. S. G., Bukowski, W. M., & Sippola, L. K. (1995). Peer variables as predictors of later childhood adjustment. *Development and Psychopathology, 7,* 787–802.

Hubbard, F. O. A., & van IJzendoorn, M. H. (1991). Maternal unresponsiveness and infant crying across the first 9 months: A naturalistic longitudinal study. *Infant Behavior and Development, 14,* 299–312.

Hudson, J. A., Sosa, B. B., & Shapiro, L. R. (1997). Scripts and plans: The development of preschool children's event knowledge and event planning. In S. L. Friedman & E. K. Scholnick (Eds.), *The developmental psychology of planning: Why, how, and when do we plan?* (pp. 77–102). Mahwah, NJ: Erlbaum.

Huebner, R. R., & Izard, C. E. (1988). Mothers' responses to infants' facial expressions of sadness, anger, and physical distress. *Motivation and Emotion, 12,* 185–196.

Huesmann, L. R., Guerra, N. G., Zelli, A., & Miller, L. (1992). Differing normative beliefs about aggression for boys and girls. In K. Bjoerkqvist & P. Niemelae (Eds.), *Of mice and women: Aspects of female aggression* (pp. 77–87). San Diego, CA: Academic Press.

Huffman, L.C., Bryan, Y., del Carmen, R., Pederson, F., Doussard-Roosevelt, J., & Porges, S. (1998). Infant temperament and cardiac vagal tone: Assessments at twelve weeks of age. *Child Development, 69*, 624–635.

Hughes, C., & Dunn, J. (1998). Understanding mind and emotion: Longitudinal associations with mental-state talk between young friends. *Developmental Psychology, 34*, 1026–1037.

Hughes, D., Rodriguez, J., Smith, E. P., Johnson, D. J., Stevenson, H. C., & Spicer, P. (2006). Parents' ethnic-racial socialization practices: A review of research and directions for future study. *Developmental Psychology, 42*, 747–770.

Huizinga, D. (1997). The volume of crime by gang and nongang members. Paper presented at the annual meeting of the American Society of Criminology, San Diego, DA. Cited in Howell, J.C. (1998). Youth Gangs: An Overview. Washington, D.C.: U.S. Department of Justice, Office of Justice Programs, Office of Juvenile Justice and Delinquency Prevention.

Huizink, A. C., Mulder, E. J. H., & Buitelaar, J. K. (2004). Prenatal stress and risk for psychopathology: Specific effects or induction of general susceptibility. *Psychological Bulletin, 130*, 115–142.

Humphreys, L. G. (1989) Intelligence: Three kinds of instability and their consequences for policy. In R. L. Linn (Ed.), *Intelligence* (pp. 193–216). Urbana: University of Illinois Press.

Hunt, E., Streissguth, A. P., Kerr, B., & Olson, H. C. (1995). Mothers' alcohol consumption during pregnancy: Effects on spatial-visual reasoning in 14-year-old children. *Psychological Science, 6*, 339–342.

Hunt, J. (1961). *Intelligence and experience.* New York: Ronald Press.

Hunter, F. T., & Youniss, J. (1982). Changes in functions of three relationships during adolescence. *Developmental Psychology, 18*, 806–811.

Hunziker, U. A., & Barr, R. G. (1986). Increased carrying reduces infant crying: A randomized control trial. *Pediatrics, 77*, 641–648.

Huston, A. C. (1983). Sex-typing. In E. M. Hetherington (Ed.), *Handbook of child psychology: Socialization, personality, and social development, Vol. 4* (pp. 387–467). New York: Wiley.

Huston, A. C. (1985). The development of sex typing: Themes from recent research. *Developmental Review, 5*, 1–17.

Huston, A. C., & Aronson, S. R. (2005). Mothers' time with infant and time in employment as predictors of mother-child relationships and children's early development. *Child Development, 76*, 467–482.

Huston, A. C., & Wright, J. C. (1998). Mass media and children's development. In W. Damon (Series Ed.) and I. E. Sigel & K. A. Renninger (Vol. Eds), *Handbook of child psychology. Vol. 4. Child psychology in practice* (5th ed., pp. 999–1058). New York: Wiley.

Huttenlocher, J., Haight, W., Bryk, A., Seltzer, M., & Lyons, T. (1991). Early vocabulary growth: Relation to language input and gender. *Developmental Psychology, 27*, 236–248.

Huttenlocher, J., Jordan, N. C., & Levine, S. C. (1994). A mental model for early arithmetic. *Journal of Experimental Psychology: General, 123*, 284–296.

Huttenlocher, J., Levine, S., & Vevea, J. (1998). Environmental input and cognitive growth: A study using time-period comparisons. *Child Development, 69*, 1012–1029.

Huttenlocher, P. R. (1994). Synaptogenesis in human cerebral cortex. In G. Dawson & K. W. Fischer (Eds.), *Human behavior and the developing brain* (pp. 137–152). New York: Guilford.

Huttenlocher, P. R., & Dabholkar, A. S. (1997). Regional differences in synaptogenesis in human cerebral cortex. *Journal of Comparative Neurology, 387*, 167–178.

Hwang, P. (1987). The change role of Swedish fathers. In M. E. Lamb (Ed.), *The father's role: Cross-cultural perspectives* (pp. 197–226). Hillsdale, NJ: Erlbaum.

Hyde, J. S. (1984). How large are gender differences in aggression? A developmental meta-analysis. *Developmental Psychology, 20*, 722–736.

Hyde, J. S. (2005). The gender similarities hypothesis. *American Psychologist, 60*, 581–592.

Hyde, J. S., & McKinley, N. M. (1997). Gender differences in cognition: results from meta-analyses. In P. J. Caplan, M. Crawford, J. S. Hyde, & J. T. E. Richardson (Eds.), *Gender differences in human cognition* (pp. 30–51). New York: Oxford University Press.

Hymel, S., Bowker, A., & Woody, E. (1993). Aggressive versus withdrawn unpopular children: Variations in peer and self-perceptions in multiple domains. *Child Development, 64*, 879–896.

Hymel, S., Comfort, C., Schonert-Reichl, K. & McDougall, P. (1996). Academic failure and school dropout: The influence of peers. In J. Juvonen & K. R. Wentzel (Eds.), *Social motivation: Understanding children's social adjustment* (pp. 313–345). New York: Cambridge University Press.

Hynd, G. W., Horn, K. L., Voeller, K. K., & Marshall, R. M. (1991). Neurobiological basis of attention-deficit hyperactivity disorder (ADHD). *School Psychology Review, 20*, 174–186.

Imperato-McGinley, J., Pichardo, M., Gautier, T., Voyer, D., & Bryden, M. P. (2007). Cognitive abilities in androgen-insensitive subjects: Comparison with control males and females from the same kindred. Cambridge, MA: The MIT Press.

Impett, E. A., Sorsoli, L., Schooler, D., Henson, J. M., & Tolman, D. L. (2008). Girls' relationship authenticity and self-esteem across adolescence. *Developmental Psychology, 44*, 722–733.

Inagaki, K., & Hatano, G. (1991). Constrained person analogy in young children's biological inference. *Cognitive Development, 6*, 219–231.

Inagaki, K., & Hatano, G. (1993). Young children's understanding of the mind-body distinction. *Child Development, 64*, 1534–1549.

Inagaki, K., & Hatano, G. (1996). Young children's recognition of commonalities between animals and plants. *Child Development, 67*, 2823–2840.

Inagaki, K., & Hatano, G. (2008). Conceptual change in naïve biology. In S. Vosniadou (Ed.), *International Handbook of Research on Conceptual Change* (pp. 240–262). New York: Routledge/Taylor & Francis.

Ingoldsby, E. M., Shaw, D. S., & Garcia, M. M. (2001). Intrafamily conflict in relation to boys' adjustment at school. *Development and Psychopathology, 13*, 35–52.

Ingoldsby, E. M., Shaw, D. S., Owens, E. B., & Winslow, E. B. (1999). A longitudinal study of interparental conflict, emotional and beahvioral reactivity, and preschoolers' adjustment problems among low-income families. *Journal of Abnormal Child Psychology, 27*, 343–356.

Inhelder, B., & Piaget, J. (1958). *The growth of logical thinking from childhood to adolescence.* New York: Basic Books.

Institute of Medicine (2004). *Preventing childhood obesity: Health in the balance.* Retrieved April 2005 from www.iom.edu.

Interagency Council on the Homeless (Department of Housing and Urban Development). (1999). *Homelessness: Programs and the people they serve.* The Urban Institute. Retrieved from http://www/huduser.org/publications/homeless/homelessness.

Intons-Peterson, M. J. (1988). *Children's concepts of gender.* Norwood, NJ: Ablex.

Isabella, R. A. (1993). Origins of attachment: Maternal interactive behavior across the first year. *Child Development, 64,* 605–621.

Ispa, J. M., Fine, M. A., Halgunseth, L. C. Harper, S., Robinson, J., Boyce, L., Brooks-Gunn, J., & Bradley-Smith, C. (2004). Maternal intrusiveness, maternal warmth, and mother-toddler relationship outcomes: Variations across low-income ethnic and acculturation groups. *Child Development, 75,* 1613–1631.

Iverson, J. M., & Goldin-Meadow, S. (1998). Why people gesture when they speak. *Nature, 396,* 228.

Izard, C. E. (1991). *The psychology of emotions.* New York: Plenum Press.

Izard, C. E., & Ackerman, B. P. (2000). Motivational, organizational, and regulatory functions of discrete emotions. In M. Lewis & J. M. Haviland-Jones (Eds.), *Handbook of emotions* (2nd ed.). New York: Guilford.

Izard, C. E., Fantauzzo, C. A., Castle, J. M., Haynes, O. M., Rayias, M. F., & Putnam, P. H. (1995). The ontogeny and significance of infants' facial expressions in the first 9 months of life. *Developmental Psychology, 31,* 997–1013.

Izard, C. E. (2007). Basic emotions, natural kinds, emotion schemas, and a new paradigm. *Perspectives on Psychological Science, 2,* 260–280.

Izard, C. E., Ackerman, B. P., Schoff, K. M., & Fine, S. E. (2000). Self-organization of discrete emotions, emotion patterns, and emotion-cognition relations. In M. D. Lewis & I. Granic (Eds.), *Emotion, development, and self-organization: Dynamic systems approaches to emotional development* (pp. 15–36). New York: Cambridge University Press.

Izard, C. E., Hembree, E. A., & Huebner, R. R. (1987). Infants' emotional expressions to acute pain: Developmental change and stability of individual differences. *Developmental Psychology, 23,* 105–113.

Izard, C. E., King, K. A., Trentacosta, C. J., Morgan, J. K., Laurenceau, J.-P., Krauthamer-Ewing, E. et al. (2008). Accelerating the development of emotion competence in Head Start children: Effects on adaptive and maladaptive behavior. *Development and Psychopathology, 20,* 369–397.

Jaccard, J., Blanton, H., & Dodge, T. (2005). Peer influences on risk behavior: An analysis of the effects of a close friend. *Child Development, 41,* 135–147.

Jacklin, C. N., DiPietro, J. A., & Maccoby, E. E. (1984). Sex typing behavior and sex typing pressure in parent-child interactions. *Archives of Sexual Behavior, 13,* 413–425.

Jacklin, C. N., & Maccoby, E. E. (1978). Social behavior at thirty-three months in same-sex and mixed-sex dyads. *Child Development, 49,* 557–569.

Jacobsen, T., & Hofmann, V. (1997). Children's attachment representations: Longitudinal relations to school behavior and academic competency in middle childhood and adolescence. *Developmental Psychology, 33,* 703–710.

Jacobson, J. L., & Jacobson, S. W. (1996). Intellectual impairment in children exposed to polychlorinated biphenyls in utero. *New England Journal of Medicine, 335,* 783–789.

Jacobson, J. L., & Jacobson, S. W. (2002). Effects of prenatal alcohol exposure on child development. *Alcohol Research & Health, 26,* 282–286.

Jacobson, J. L., Jacobson, S. W., Padgett, R. J., Brumitt, G. A., & Billings, R. L. (1992). Effects of prenatal PCB exposure on cognitive processing efficiency and sustained attention. *Developmental Psychology, 28,* 297–306.

Jacobson, K. C. & Crockett, L. J. (2000). Parental monitoring and adolescent adjustment: An ecological perspective. *Journal of Research on Adolescence, 10,* 65–97.

Jacquez, F., Cole, D. A., & Searle, B. (2004). Self-perceived competence as a mediator between maternal feedback and depressive symptoms in adolescents. *Journal of Abnormal Child Psychology, 32,* 355–367.

Jaffee, S. R. (2002). Pathways to adversity in young adulthood among early childbearers. *Journal of Family Psychology, 16,* 38–49.

Jaffee, S. R., Caspi, A., Moffitt, T. E., Belsky, J., & Silva, P. (2001). Why are children born to teen mothers at risk for adverse outcomes in young adulthood? Results from a 20-year longitudinal study. *Development and Psychopathology, 13,* 377–397.

Jaffee, S. R., Caspi, A., Moffitt, T. E., Polo-Tomas, M., Price, T. S., & Taylor, A. (2004a). The limits of child effects: Evidence for genetically mediated child effects on corporal punishment, but not on physical maltreatment. *Developmental Psychology, 40,* 1047–1058.

Jaffee, S. R., Caspi, A., Moffitt, T. E., & Taylor, A. (2004b). Physical maltreatment victim to antisocial child: Evidence of an environmentally mediated process. *Journal of Abnormal Psychology, 113.*

Jaffee, S., & Hyde, J. S. (2000). Gender differences in moral orientation: A meta-analysis. *Psychological Bulletin, 126,* 703–726.

Jaffee, S. R., Moffitt, T. E., Caspi, A., Taylor, A., & Arseneault, L. (2002). Influence of adult domestic violence on children's internalizing and externalizing problems: An environmentally informative twin study. *Journal of the American Academy of Child and Adolescent Psychiatry, 41,* 1095–1103.

Jahromi, L. B., Putnam, S. P., & Stifter, C. A. (2004). Maternal regulation of infant reactivity from 2 to 6 months. *Developmental Psychology, 40,* 477–487.

Jakobson, R. (1941). *Child language, aphasia and phonological universals.* The Hague: Mouton. (English translation 1968.)

James, D., Pillai, M., & Smoleniec, J. (1995). Neurobehavioral development in the human fetus. In J. Lecanuet, W. P. Fifer, N. A. Krasnegor, & W. P. Smotherman (Eds.), *Fetal development: A psychobiological perspective.* Hillsdale, NJ: Erlbaum.

Jamison, J., & Meyers, L. B. (2008). Peer-group and price influence student drinking along with planned behavior. *Alcohol and Alcoholism, 43,* 492–497.

Janssens, J. M. A. M., & Dekovic, M. (1997). Child rearing, prosocial moral reasoning, and prosocial behaviour. *International Journal of Behavioral Development, 20,* 509–527.

Jaser, S. S., Champion, J. E., Reeslund, K. L., Keller, G., Merchant, M. J., Benson, M., & Compas, B. E. (2007). Cross-situational coping with peer and family stressors in adolescent offspring of depressed parents. *Journal of Adolescence, 30,* 917–932.

Jaswal, V. K. (2004). Don't believe everything you hear: Preschoolers' sensitivity to speaker intent in category induction. *Child Development, 75,* 1871–1885.

Jaswal, V. K., & Fernald, A. (2002). Learning to communicate. In A. Slater & M. Lewis (Eds.), *Introduction to infant development* (pp. 244–265). Oxford, UK: Oxford University Press.

Jaycox, L. H., Reivich, K. J., Gillham, J., & Seligman, M. E. (1994). Prevention of depressive symptoms in school children. *Behavior Research and Therapy, 32,* 801–816.

Jegalian, K., & Lahn, B. T. (2001, February). Why the Y is so weird. *Scientific American, 284*(2), 56–61.

Jencks, C. (1979). *Who gets ahead? The determinants of economic success in America.* New York: Basic Books.

Jenkins, J. (1992). Sibling relationships in disharmonious homes: Potential difficulties and protective effects. In F. Boer & J. Dunn (Eds.), *Children's sibling relationships: Developmental and clinical issues* (pp. 125–138). Hillsdale, NJ: Erlbaum.

Jenkins, J. M., & Astington, J. W. (1996). Cognitive factors and family structure associated with theory of mind development in young children. *Developmental Psychology, 32,* 70–78.

Jensen, A. R. (1973). *Educability and group differences.* New York: Harper & Row.

Jensen, A. R. (1998). *The g factor: The science of mental ability.* New York: Praeger.

Jiao, S., Ji, G., & Jing, Q. (1986). Comparative study of behavioral qualities of only children and sibling children. *Child Development, 57,* 367–361.

Jiao, S., Ji, G., & Jing, Q. (1996). Cognitive development of Chinese urban only children and children with siblings. *Child Development, 67,* 387–395.

Jochlin, V., McGue, M., & Lykken, D. T. (1996). Personality and divorce: A genetic analysis. *Journal of Personality and Social Psychology, 71,* 288–299.

Joh, A. S., Adolph, K. E., Campbell, M. R., & Eppler, M. A. (2006). Why walkers slip: Shine is not a reliable cue for slippery ground. *Perception & Psychophysics, 68,* 339–352.

Joh, A. S., Adolph. K. E., Narayanan, P., & Dietz, V. (2007). Gauging possibilities for action based on friction underfoot. *Journal of Experimental Psychology: Human Perception & Performance, 33,* 1145–1157.

Johnson, D. J., Jaeger, E., Randolph, S. M., Cauce, A. M., & Ward, J. (2003). Studying the effects of early child care experiences on the development of children of color in the United States: Toward a more inclusive research agenda. *Child Development, 74,* 1227–1244.

Johnson, F. A. (1993). *Dependence and Japanese socialization: Psychoanalytic and anthropological investigation into amae.* New York: New York University Press.

Johnson, J., & Newport, E. L. (1989). Critical period effects in second language learning: The influence of maturational state on the acquisition of English as a second language. *Cognitive Psychology, 21,* 60–99.

Johnson, J. E., & Martin, C. (1985). Parents' beliefs and home learning environments: Effects on cognitive development. In I. E. Sigel (Ed.), *Parental belief systems: The psychological consequences for children* (pp. 25–50). Hillsdale, NJ: Erlbaum.

Johnson, K. E., & Mervis, C. B. (1994). Microgenetic analysis of first steps in children's acquisition of expertise on shorebirds. *Developmental Psychology, 30,* 418–435.

Johnson, M., Beebe, T., Mortimer, J., & Snyder, M. (1998). Volunteerism in adolescence: A process perspective. *Journal of Research on Adolescence, 8,* 309–330.

Johnson, M. H. (1992). Imprinting and the development of face recognition: From chick to man. *Current Directions in Psychological Science, 1,* 52–55.

Johnson, M. H. (1998). The neural basis of cognitive development. In W. Damon (Series Ed.), D. Kuhn, & R. S. Siegler (Vol. Eds.), *Handbook of child psychology: Vol. 2. Cognition, perception, and language* (5th ed., pp. 1–49). New York: Wiley.

Johnson, M. H., & Morton, J. (1991). *Biology and cognitive development: The case of face recognition.* Oxford, U.K.: Blackwell.

Johnson, S. C. (2003). Detecting agents. *Philosophical Transactions of the Royal Society B, 358,* 549–559.

Johnson, S. C., Dweck, C. S., & Chen, F. S. (2007). Evidence for infants' internal working models of attachment. *Psychological Science, 18,* 501–502.

Johnson, S. C., Slaughter, V., & Carey, S. (1998). Whose gaze will infants follow? Features that elicit gaze-following in 12-month-olds. *Developmental Science, 1(2),* 233–238.

Johnson, S. C., & Solomon, G. E. A. (1996). Why dogs have puppies and cats have kittens: The role of birth in young children's understanding of biological origins. *Child Development, 68,* 404–419.

Johnson, S. L., & Birch, L. L. (1994). Parents' and children's adiposity and eating style. *Pediatrics, 94,* 653–661.

Johnson, S. P. (2010). (Ed.), *Neoconstructivism: The new science of cognitive development.* New York: Oxford University Press.

Johnson, S. P., Amso, D., & Slemmer, J. A. (2003). Development of object concepts in infancy: Evidence for early learning in an eye-tracking paradigm. *PNAS, 100(18),* 10568–10573.

Johnson, S. P., & Aslin, R. N. (1995). Perception of object unity in 2-month-old infants. *Developmental Psychology, 31,* 739–745.

Johnson, W., McGue, M., & Iacono, W. G. (2006). Genetic and environmental influences on academic achievement trajectories during adolescence. *Developmental Psychology, 42,* 514–532.

Jome, L. M., & Tokar, D. M. (1998). Dimensions of masculinity and major choice traditionality. *Journal of Vocational Behavior, 52,* 120–134.

Jones, D. C., Abbey, B. B., & Cumberland, A. (1998). The development of display rule knowledge: Linkages with family expressiveness and social competence. *Child Development, 69,* 1209–1222.

Jones, K. L., & Smith, D. W. (1973). Recognition of the fetal alcohol syndrome in early infancy. *Lancet, 2,* 99–100.

Jones, M. (1990). Children's writing. In R. Grieve and M. Hughes (Eds.), *Understanding children: Essays in honor of Margaret Donaldson* (pp. 94–120). Oxford, UK: Blackwell.

Jones, M. C. (1924). A laboratory study of fear: The case of Peter. *Pedagogical Seminary, 31,* 308–315.

Jones, M. D., & Galliher, R. V. (2007). Ethnic identity and psychosocial functioning in Navajo adolescents. *Journal of Research on Adolescence, 17,* 683–696.

Jones, R. M. (1992). Ego identity and adolescent problem behavior. In G. R. Adams, T. P. Gulotta, & R. Montemayor (Eds.), *Advances in adolescent development: Vol. 4. Adolescent identity formation* (pp. 216–233). Newbury Park, CA: Sage.

Jones, S. M. & Dindia, K. (2004). A meta-analytic perspective on sex equity in the classroom. *Review of Educational Research, 74,* 443–471.

Jones, S. M., & Myhill, D. (2004). "Troublesome boys" and "compliant girls": Gender identity and perceptions of achievement and underachievement. *British Journal of Sociology of Education, 25,* pp. 547–561.

Jordan, N. C. (2007). Do words count? Connections between mathematics and reading difficulties. In D. B. Berch, & M. M. M. Mazzocco (Eds.), *Why is math so hard for some children? The nature and origins of mathematical learning difficulties and disabilities* (pp. 107–120). New York: Plenum.

Jorgensen, M., & Keiding, N. (1991). Estimation of spermarche from longitudinal spermaturia data. *Biometrics, 47,* 177–193.

Joshi, M. S., & MacLean, M. (1994). Indian and English children's understanding of the distinction between real and apparent emotion. *Child Development, 65,* 1372–1384.

Joshi, P. T., & O'Donnell, D. A. (2003). Consequences of child exposure to war and terrorism. *Clinical Child and Family Psychology Review 6,* 275–291.

Joussemet, M., Vitaro, F., Barker, E. D., Cotes, S., Nagin, D. S., Zoccolillo, M., et al. (2008). Controlling parenting and physical aggression during elementary school. *Child Development, 79,* 411–425.

Juel, C. (1988). Learning to read and write: A longitudinal study of 54 children from first through fourth grades. *Journal of Educational Psychology, 80,* 417–447.

Juel, C. (1994). *Learning to read and write in one elementary school.* New York: Springer-Verlag.

Julian, T. W., McKenry, P. C., & McKelvey, M. W. (1994). Cultural variations in parenting: Perceptions of Caucasian, African-American, Hispanic, and Asian-American parents, *Family Relations, 43,* 30–37.

Juraska, J. M., Henderson, C., & Muller, J. (1984). Differential rearing experience, gender and radial maze performance. *Developmental Psychobiology, 17,* 209–215.

Jusczyk, P. W. (1997). *The discovery of spoken language.* Cambridge, MA: The MIT Press.

Jusczyk, P. W., & Aslin, R. N. (1995). Infants' detection of sound patterns of words in fluent speech. *Cognitive Psychology, 29,* 1–23.

Jusczyk, P. W., Cutler, A., & Redanz, N. (1993). Preference for the predominant stress patterns of English words. *Child Development, 64,* 675–687.

Jusczyk, P. W., & Hohne, E. A. (1997). Infants' memory for spoken words. *Science, 277,* 1984–1986.

Jussim, L., Eccles, J. & Madon, S. (1996). Social perception, social stereotypes, and teacher expectations: Accuracy and the quest for the powerful self-fulfilling prophecy. In M. Zanna (Ed.), *Advances in Experimental Social Psychology* (Vol. 28, pp. 281–388). San Diego, CA: Academic.

Juvonen, J., Nishina, A., & Graham, S. (2000). Peer harassment, psychological adjustment, and school functioning in early adolescence. *Journal of Educational Psychology, 92,* 349–359.

Kagan, J. (1972). Do infants think? *Scientific American, 226,* 74–82.

Kagan, J. (1976). Emergent themes in human development. *American Scientist, 64,* 186–196.

Kagan, J. (1997). Temperament and the reactions to unfamiliarity. *Child Development, 68,* 139–143.

Kagan, J. (1998). Biology and the child. In W. Damon (Series Ed.) & N. Eisenberg (Vol. Ed.), *Handbook of child psychology: Vol. 3. Social, emotional, and personality development* (5th ed., pp. 177–235). New York: Wiley.

Kagan, J. (2008). In defense of qualitative changes in development. *Child Development, 79,* 1606–1624.

Kagan, J., & Fox, N. (2006). Biology, culture, and temperamental biases. In W. Damon & R. M. Lerner (Series Eds.) & N. Eisenberg (Vol. Ed.), *Handbook of child psychology: Vol. 3. Social, emotional, and personality development* (6th ed., pp. 167–225). Hoboken, NJ: Wiley.

Kagan, J., Kearsley, R. B., & Zelazo, P. (1978). *Infancy: Its place in human development.* Cambridge, MA: Harvard University Press.

Kagan, J., Snidman, N., & Arcus, D. (1998). Childhood derivatives of high and low reactivity in infancy. *Child Development, 69,* 1483–1493.

Kahen, V., Katz, L. F., & Gottman, G. M. (1994). Linkages between parent-child interaction and conversations of friends. *Social Development, 3,* 238–254.

Kail, R. (1984). *The development of memory in children* (2nd ed.). New York: Freeman.

Kail, R. (1991). Developmental changes in speed of processing during childhood and adolescence. *Psychological Bulletin, 109,* 490–501.

Kail, R. (1997). Processing time, imagery, and spatial memory. *Journal of Experimental Child Psychology, 64,* 67–78.

Kaiser Family Foundation (2009). New study finds children age zero to six spend as much time with TV, computers and video games as playing outside. http://www.kff.org/entmedia/upload/7593.pdf.

Kalil, A., Levine, J. A., Ziol-Guest, K. M. (2005). Following in their parents' footsteps: How characteristics of parental work predict adolescents' interest in parents' jobs. In B. Schneider & L. J. Waite (Eds.), *Being together, working apart: Dual-career families and the work-life balance* (pp. 422–442). New York: Cambridge University Press.

Kalil, A., & Ziol-Guest, K. M. (2005). Single mothers' employment dynamics and adolescent well-being. *Child Development, 76,* 196–211.

Kalish, C. W. (1996). Preschoolers' understanding of germs as invisible mechanism. *Cognitive Development, 11,* 83–106.

Kalish, C. W. (1997). Preschoolers' understanding of mental and bodily reactions to contamination: What you don't know can hurt you, but cannot sadden you. *Developmental Psychology, 33,* 79–91.

Kalmar, M. (1996). The course of intellectual development in preterm and fullterm children: An 8-year longitudinal study. *International Journal of Behavioral Development, 19,* 491–516.

Kamin, L. J. (1974). *The science and politics of I.Q.* Oxford, UK: Erlbaum.

Kanner, A. D., Feldman, S. S., Weinberger, D. A., & Ford, M. E. (1987). Uplifts, hassles, and adaptational outcomes in early adolescents. *Journal of Early Adolescence, 7,* 371–394.

Kaplan, H., & Dove, H. (1987). Infant development among the Ache of Eastern Paraguay. *Developmental Psychology, 23,* 190–198.

Karriker-Jaffe, K. J., Foshee, V. A., Ennett, S. T., & Suchindran, C. (2008). The development of aggression during adolescence: Sex differences in trajectories of physical and social aggression among youth in rural areas. *Journal of Abnormal Child Psychology, 36,* 1227–1236.

Katz, L. F., & Low, S. M. (2004). Marital violence, co-parenting, and family-level processes in relation to children's adjustment. *Journal of Family Psychology, 18,* 372–382.

Katz, L. F., & Windecker-Nelson, B. (2004). Parental meta-emotion philosophy in families with conduct disordered children: Links with peer relations. *Journal of Abnormal Child Psychology, 32,* 385–398.

Katz, P. A., & Ksansnak, K. R. (1994). Developmental aspects of gender role flexibility and traditionality in middle childhood and adolescence. *Developmental Psychology, 30,* 272–282.

Kavanaugh, R. D., & Engel, S. (1998). The development of pretense and narrative in early childhood. In O. N. Saracho & B. Spodek (Eds.), *Multiple perspectives on play in early childhood education* (pp. 80–99). Albany: State University of New York Press.

Kavsêk, M. (2004). Predicting later IQ from infant visual habituation and dishabituation: A meta-analysis. *Journal of Applied Developmental Psychology, 25,* 369–393.

Kawabata, Y., & Crick, N. R. (2008). The role of cross-racial/ethnic friendships in social adjustment. *Developmental Psychology, 44,* 1177–1183.

Kaye, K. L., & Bower, T. G. R. (1994). Learning and intermodal transfer of information in newborns. *Psychological Science, 5,* 286–288.

Kearins, J. M. (1981). Visual spatial memory in Australian aboriginal children of desert regions. *Cognitive Psychology, 13,* 434–460.

Keating, D., & Clark, L. V. (1980). Development of physical and social reasoning in adolescence. *Developmental Psychology, 16,* 23–30.

Keating, D. P., & Hertzman, C. (Eds.) (1999). *Developmental health and the wealth of the nations: Social, biological, and educational dynamics.* New York: Guilford.

Keen, R. (2003). Representation of objects and events: Why do infants look so smart and toddlers look so dumb? *Current Directions in Psychological Science, 12,* 79–83.

Keen, R. E., & Berthier, N. E. (2004). Continuities and discontinuities in infants' representation of objects and events. In R. V. Kail (Ed.), *Advances in child development and behavior, 32* (pp. 243–379). San Diego, CA: Elsevier.

Keenan, K., Loeber, R., Zhang, Q., Stouthamer-Loeber, M., & Van Kammen, W. B. (1995). The influence of deviant peers on the development of boys' disruptive and delinquent behavior: A temporal analysis. *Development and Psychopathology, 7,* 715–726.

Keil, F. C. (1979). *Semantic and conceptual development: An ontological perspective.* Cambridge, MA: Harvard University Press.

Keil, F. C. (1992). The origins of an autonomous biology. *Minnesota Symposium on Child Psychology, 25,* 103–138.

Keil, F. C. (2005). Foreword: Categories, cognitive development, and cognitive science. In D. H. Rakison & L. M. Oakes (Eds.), *Early category and concept development: Making sense of blooming, buzzing confusion.* New York: Oxford University Press.

Keiley, M., Bates, J. E., Dodge, K. A., & Pettit, G. (2000). A cross-domain growth analysis: Externalizing and internalizing behaviors during 8 years of childhood. *Journal of Abnormal Child Psychology, 28,* 161–179.

Keiley, M., Howe, T. R., Dodge, K. A., Bates, J. E., & Pettit, G. S. (2001). The timing of child physical maltreatment: A cross-domain growth analysis of impact on adolescent externalizing and internalizing problems. *Development and Psychopathology, 13,* 891–912.

Kelemen, D. (1999). Why are rocks pointy? Children's preference for teleological explanations of the natural world. *Developmental Psychology, 35,* 1440–453.

Kelemen, D., & DiYanni, C. (2005). Intuitions about origins: Purpose and intelligent design in children's reasoning about nature. *Journal of Cognition and Development, 6,* 3–31.

Keller, P. S., Cummings, E. M., Davies, P. T., & Mitchell, P. M. (2008). Longitudinal relations between parental drinking problems, family functioning, and child adjustment. *Development and Psychopathology, 20,* 195–212.

Kelley, M. L., Sanchez-Hucles, J., & Walker, R. (1993). Correlates of disciplinary practices in working- to middle-class African-American mothers. *Merrill-Palmer Quarterly, 39,* 252–264.

Kellman, P., & Arterberry, M. (2006). Infant visual perception. To appear in W. Damon and R. Lerner (Series Eds.), & D. Kuhn & R. S. Siegler (Vol. Eds.), *Handbook of child psychology: Vol. 2. Cognition, perception, and language* (6th ed.). Hoboken, NJ: Wiley.

Kellman, P. J., & Spelke, E. S. (1983). Perception of partly occluded objects in infancy. *Cognitive Psychology, 15,* 483–524.

Kellman, P. J., Spelke, E. S., & Short, K. (1986). Infant perception of object unitary from translatory motion in depth and vertical translation. *Child Development, 57,* 72–86.

Kellogg, R. T. (1994). *The psychology of writing.* New York: Oxford University Press.

Kemler-Nelson, D. G., Egan, L. C., & Holt, M. B. (2004). When children ask, "What is it?" what do they want to know about artifacts? *Psychological Science, 15,* 384–389.

Kemler-Nelson, D. G., Greif, M. L., Keil, F. C., & Gutierrez, F. (2006). What do children want to know about animals and artifacts? Domain-specific requests for information. *Psychological Science, 17,* 455–459.

Kendler, K. S., Jacobson, K., Myer, J. M., & Eaves, L. J. (2008). A genetically informative developmental study of the relationship between conduct disorder and peer deviance in males. *Psychological Medicine, 38,* 1001–1011.

Kenny, P., & Turkewitz, G. (1986). Effects of unusually early visual stimulation on the development of homing behavior in the rat pup. *Developmental Psychobiology, 19,* 57–66.

Kenrick, Douglas T., Trost, Melanie R., & Sundie, Jill M. (2004). Sex-roles as adaptations: An evolutionary perspective on gender differences and similarities. In Alice R. Eagly, Anne E. Beall, and Robert J. Sternberg (Eds.), *The Psychology of Gender.* New York: Guilford.

Kerkman, D. D., & Siegler, R. S. (1993). Individual differences and adaptive flexibility in lower-income children's strategy choices. *Learning and Individual Differences, 5,* 113–136.

Kerns, K. A., Abraham, M. M., Schlegelmilch, A., & Morgan, T. A. (2007). Mother-child attachment in later middle childhood: Assessment approaches and associations with mood and emotion regulation. *Attachment & human Development, 9,* 33–53.

Kerns, K. A., Klepac, L., & Cole, A. (1996). Peer relationships and preadolescents' perceptions of security in the child-mother relationship. *Developmental Psychology 32,* 457–466.

Kessen, W. (1965). *The child.* New York: Wiley.

Kessler, R. C. (2002). Epidemiology of depression. In J. H. Gotlib & C. L. Hammen (Eds.), *Handbook of depression* (pp. 23–42). New York: Guilford.

Kestenbaum, R., Farber, E. A., & Sroufe, L. A. (1989). Individual differences in empathy among preschoolers: Relation to attachment history. In N. Eisenberg (Ed.), *Empathy and related emotional responses. New directions for child development: Vol. 44* (pp. 51–64). San Francisco: Jossey-Bass.

Kety, S. S., Wender, P. H., Jacobsen, B., Ingraham, L. J., Jansson, L., Faber, B., & Kinney, D. K. (1994). Mental illness in the biological and adoptive relatives of schizophrenic adoptees: Replication of the Copenhagen study in the rest of Denmark. *Archives of General Psychiatry, 51,* 442–455.

Kiang, L., Yip, T., & Fuligni, A. J. (2008). Multiple social identities and adjustment in young adults from ethnically diverse backgrounds. *Journal of Research on Adolescence, 18*, 643–670.

Kiang, L., Yip, T., Gonzales-Backen, M., Witkow, M., & Fuligni, A. J. (2006). Ethnic identity and the daily psychological well-being of adolescents from Mexican and Chinese backgrounds. *Child Development, 77*, 1338–1350.

Kiesner, J., Poulin, F., & Nicotra, E. (2003). Peer relations across contexts: Individual network homophily and network inclusion in and after school. *Child Development, 74*, 1328–1343.

Killen, M. (2007). Children's social and moral reasoning about exclusion. *Current Directions in Psychological Science, 16*, 32–36.

Killen, M., & Stangor, C. (2001). Children's social reasoning about inclusion and exclusion in gender and race peer group contexts. *Child Development, 72*, 174–186.

Killen, M., & Turiel, E. (1998). Adolescents' and young adults' evaluations of helping and sacrificing for others. *Journal of Research on Adolescence, 8*, 355–375.

Kilpatrick, D. G., Acierno, R., Saunders, B., Resnick, H. S., Best, C. L., & Schnurr, P. P. (2000). Risk factors for adolescent substance abuse and dependence: Data from a national sample. *Journal of Consulting and Clinical Psychology, 68*, 19–30.

Kim, H. K., Capaldi, D. M., & Stoolmiller, M. (2003). Depressive symptoms across adolescence and young adulthood in men: Predictions from parental and contextual risk factors. *Development and Psychopathology, 15*, 469–495.

Kim, I. J., Ge, X., Brody, G. H., Conger, R. D., Gibbons, F. X., & Simons, R. L. (2003). Parenting behaviors and the occurrence and co-occurrence of depressive symptoms and conduct problems among African American Children. *Journal of Family Psychology, 17*, 571–583.

Kim, J. K., Conger, R. D., Lorenz, F. O., & Elder, G., Jr. (2001). Parent-adolescent reciprocity in negative affect and its relation to early adult social development. *Developmental Psychology, 37*, 775–790.

Kim, J-Y., McHale, S. M., Osgood, D. W., & Crouter, A. C. (2006). Longitudinal course and family correlates of sibling relationships from childhood through adolescence. *Child Development, 77*, 1746–1761.

Kim, K., & Spelke, E. S. (1992). Infants' sensitivity to effects of gravity on visible object motion. *Journal of Experimental Psychology: Human Perception and Performance, 18*, 385–393.

Kindermann, T. A. (1993). Natural peer groups as contexts for individual development: The case of children's motivation in school. *Developmental Psychology, 29*, 970–977.

Kindermann, T. A. (2007). Effects of naturally existing peer groups on changes in academic engagement in a cohort of sixth graders. *Child Development, 78*, 1186–1203.

Kirkham, N. Z., Slemmer, J. A., & Johnson, S. P. (2002). Visual statistical learning in infancy: Evidence for a domain general learning mechanism. *Cognition, 83*, B35–B42.

Kisilevsky, B. S., Fearon, I., & Muir, D. W. (1998). Fetuses differentiate vibroacoustic stimuli. *Infant Behavior and Development, 21*, 25–46.

Kisilevsky, B. S., Hains, S. M. J., Leen, K., Muir, D. W., Xu, F., Fu, G., et al. (1998). The still-face effect in Chinese and Canadian 3- and 6-month-old infants. *Developmental Psychology, 34*, 629–639.

Kisilevsky, B. S., & Muir, D. W. (1991). Human fetal and subsequent newborn responses to sound and vibration. *Infant Behavior and Development, 14*, 1–26.

Kiuru, N., Nurmi, J-E., Aunola, K., & Salmela-Aro, K. (2009). Peer group homogeneity in adolescents' school adjustment varies according to peer group type and gender. *International Journal of Behavioral Development, 33*, 65–76.

Klahr, D. (1978). Goal formation, planning, and learning by preschool problem solvers or: "My socks are in the dryer." In R. S. Siegler (Ed.), *Children's thinking: What develops?* Hillsdale, NJ: Erlbaum.

Klahr, D., & Wallace, J. G. (1976). *Cognitive development: An information processing view.* Hillsdale, NJ: Erlbaum.

Klima, E. S., & Bellugi, U. (1967). Syntactic regularities in the speech of children. In J. Lyons & R. Wales (Eds.), *Psycholinguistic papers. Proceedings of the Edinburgh Conference* (pp. 183–208). Edinburgh: Edinburgh University Press.

Klima, T., & Repetti, R. L. (2008). Children's peer relations and their psychological adjustment: Differences between close friendships and the larger peer group. Merrill-Palmer Quarterly, 54, 151–178.

Klimes-Dougan, B., Brand, A. E., Zahn-Waxler, C., Usher, B., Hastings, Pl D., Kendziora, K., & Garside, R. B. (2007). Parental emotion socialization in adolescence: Differences in sex, age and problem status. *Social Development, 16*, 326–342.

Klimes-Dougan, B., & Kopp, C. B. (1999). Children's conflict tactics with others: A longitudinal investigation of the toddler and preschool years. *Merrill-Palmer Quarterly, 45*, 226–241.

Klin, A., Jones, W., Schultz, R., & Volkmar, F. (2004). The enactive mind, or from actions to cognition: Lessons from autism. In U. Frith & E. Hill (Eds.), *Autism: Mind and brain* (pp. 127–160). Oxford, UK: Oxford University Press.

Kling, K. C., Hyde, J. S., Showers, C. J., & Buswell, B. N. (1999). Gender differences in self-esteem: A meta-analysis. *Psychological Bulletin, 125* 470–500.

Kloos, H., & Keen, R. (2005). An exploration of toddlers' problems in a search task. *Infancy, 7(1)*, 7–34.

Knafo, A., & Plomin, R. (2006a). Parental discipline and affection and children's prosocial behavior: Genetic and environmental links. *Journal of Personality and Social Psychology, 90*, 147–164.

Knafo, A., & Plomin, R. (2006b). Prosocial behavior from early to middle childhood: Genetic environmental influences on stability and change. *Developmental Psychology, 42*, 771–786.

Knafo, A., Zahn-Waxler, C., Van Hulle, C., Robinson, J. L., & Rhee, S. H. (2008). The developmental origins of a disposition toward empathy: Genetic and environmental contributions. *Emotion, 8*, 737–752.

Knight, G. P., Cota, M. K., & Bernal, M. E. (1993). The socialization of cooperative, competitive, and individualistic preferences among Mexican American children: The mediating role of ethnic identity. *Hispanic Journal of Behavioral Sciences, 15*, 291–309.

Knight, G. P., Fabes, R. A., & Higgins, D. A. (1996). Concerns about drawing causal inferences from meta-analyses: An example in the study of gender differences in aggression. *Psychological Bulletin, 119*, 410–421.

Kobak, R., Cassidy, J., & Ziv, Y. (2004). Attachment-related trauma and posttraumatic stress disorder: Implications for adult adaptation. In W. S. Rholes & J. A. Simpson *(Eds.), Adult attachment: Theory, research, and clinical implications* (pp. 388–407). New York: Guilford.

Kobasigawa, A., Ransom, C. C., & Holland, C. J. (1980). Children's knowledge about skimming. *Alberta Journal of Educational Research, 26*, 169–182.

Kobiella, A., Grossmann, T., Reid, V., & Striano, T. (2008). The discrimination of angry and fearful facial expressions in 7-month-old infants: An event-related potential study. *Cognition and Emotion, 22*, 134–146.

Kochanska, G. (1993). Toward a synthesis of parental socialization and child temperament in early development of conscience. *Child Development, 64*, 325–347.

Kochanska, G. (1995). Children's temperament, mothers' discipline, and security of attachment: Multiple pathways to emerging internalization. *Child Development, 66*, 597–615.

Kochanska, G. (1997a). Multiple pathways to conscience for children with different temperaments: From toddlerhood to age 5. *Developmental Psychology, 33*, 228–240.

Kochanska, G. (1997b). Mutually responsive orientation between mothers and their young children: Implications for early socialization. *Child Development, 68*, 94–112.

Kochanska, G. (2001). Emotional development in children with different attachment histories: The first three years. *Child Development, 72*, 474–490.

Kochanska, G. (2002). Committed compliance, moral self, and internalization: A mediational model. *Developmental Psychology, 38*, 339–351.

Kochanska, G., & Aksan, N. (2006). Children's conscience and self-regulation. *Journal of Personality, 74*, 1587–1617.

Kochanska, G., Aksan, N., Knaack, A., & Rhines, H. (2004). Maternal parenting and children's conscience: Early security as a moderator. *Child Development, 75*, 1229–1242.

Kochanska, G., Aksan, N., & Nichols, K. (2003). Maternal power assertion in discipline and moral discourse contexts: Commonalities, differences, and implications for children's moral conduct and cognition. *Developmental Psychology, 39*, 949–963.

Kochanska, G., Barry, R. A., Aksan, N., & Boldt, L. J. (2008). A developmental model of maternal and child contributions to disruptive conduct: The first six years. *Journal of Child Psychology and Psychiatry, 49*, 1220–1227.

Kochanska, G., & Coy, K. C. (2002). Child emotionality and maternal responsiveness as predictors of reunion behaviors in the Strange Situation: Links mediated and unmediated by separation distress. *Child Development, 73*, 228–240.

Kochanska, G., Coy, K. C., & Murray, K. T. (2001). The development of self-regulation in the first four years of life. *Child Development, 72*, 1091–1111.

Kochanska, G., Forman, D. R., Aksan, N., & Dunbar, S. B. (2005). Pathways to conscience: Early mother-child mutually responsive orientation and children's emotion, conduct, and cognition. *Journal of Child Psychology and Psychiatry, 46*, 19–34.

Kochanska, G., Forman, D. R., & Coy, K. C. (1999). Implications of the mother-child relationship in infancy for socialization in the second year of life. *Infant Behavior & Development, 22*, 249–265.

Kochanska, G., Gross, J., Lin, M.-H., & Nichols, K. (2002). Guilt in young children: Development, determinants, and relations with a broader system of standards. *Child Development, 73*, 461–482.

Kochanska, G., & Murray, K. T. (2000). Mother-child mutually responsive orientation and conscience development: From toddler to early school age. *Child Development, 71*, 417–431.

Kochanska, G., Murray, K. T., & Harlan, E. T. (2000). Effortful control in early childhood: Continuity and change, antecedents, and implications for social development. *Developmental Psychology, 36*, 220–232.

Kochanska, G., Philibert, R. A., & Barry, R. A. (in press). Interplay of genes and early mother-child relationship in the development of self-regulation from toddler to preschool age. *Journal of Child Psychology and Psychiatry.*

Kochenderfer, B. J., & Ladd, G. W. (1996). Peer victimization: Cause or consequence of school maladjustment? *Child Development, 67*, 1305–1317.

Kodama, H., Shinagawa, F., & Motegi, M. (1978). *WISC-R manual: Standardized in Japan*. New York: Psychological Corporation.

Kohen, D. E., Leventhal, T., Dahinten, V. S., & McIntosh, C. N. (2008). Neighborhood disadvantage: Pathways of effects for young children. *Child Development, 79*, 156–169.

Kohlberg, L. A. (1966). A cognitive-developmental analysis of children's sex role concepts and attitudes. In E. E. Maccoby (Ed.), *The development of sex differences* (pp. 82–173). Palo Alto: Stanford University Press.

Kohlberg, L. (1969). Stage and sequence: The cognitive-developmental approach to socialization. In D. A. Goslin (Ed.), *Handbook of socialization theory and research* (pp. 325–480). New York: Rand McNally.

Kohlberg, L. (1976). Moral stage and moralization: The cognitive-developmental approach. In T. Lickona (Ed.), *Moral development and behavior: Theory, research, and social issues* (pp. 84–107). New York: Holt, Rinehart, & Winston.

Kohlberg, L. (1978). Revisions in the theory and practice of moral development. *New Directions for Child Development, 2*, 83–88.

Kohlberg, L., & Candee, D. (1984). The relationship of moral judgment to moral action. In W. M. Kurtines & J. L. Gewirtz (Eds.), *Morality, moral behavior, and moral development* (pp. 52–73). New York: Wiley.

Kopp, C. B. (1990). Risks in infancy: Appraising the research. *Merrill-Palmer Quarterly, 36*, 117–139.

Kopp, C. B. (1992). Emotional distress and control in young children. In N. Eisenberg & R. A. Fabes (Eds.), *Emotion and its regulation in early development (New Directions in Child Development)* (pp. 41–56). San Francisco: Jossey-Bass.

Kopp, C. B. (2001). Self regulation in childhood. *International Encyclopedia of the Social and Behavioral Sciences*. London: Elsevier.

Kopp, C. B., & Kaler, S. R. (1989). Risk in infancy: Origins and implications. *American Psychologist, 44*, 224–230.

Koren, G., Nulman, I., Rovet, J., Greenbaum, R., Loebstein, M., & Einarson, T. (1998). Long-term neurodevelopmental risks in children exposed in utero to cocaine. The Toronto Adoption Study. *Annals of the New York Academy of Sciences, 846*, 306–313.

Korner, A. F., & Thoman, E. (1970). Visual alertness in neonates as evoked by maternal care. *Journal of Experimental Child Psychology, 10*, 67–78.

Kortenhaus, C. M., & Demorest, J. (1993). Gender role stereotyping in children's literature: An update. *Sex Roles, 28*, 219–232.

Kovas, Y., & Plomin, R. (2007). Learning abilities and disabilities: Generalist genes, specialist environments. *Current Directions in Psychological Science, 16*, 284–288.

Kovacs, M., Joormann, J., Gotlib, & I. H. (in press). Emotion (dys) regulation and links to depressive disorders. *Child Development Perspectives.*

Kowal, A., & Kramer, L. (1997). Children's understanding of parental differential treatment. *Child Development, 68*, 113–126.

Kowal, A. K., Krull, J. L., & Kramer, L. (2004). How the differential treatment of siblings is linked with parent-child relationship quality. *Journal of Family Psychology, 18*, 658–665.

Krascum, R. M., & Andrews, S. (1998). The effects of theories on children's acquisition of family resemblance categories. *Child Development, 69*, 333–346.

Kreager, D. A. (2007). When it's good to be "bad": Violence and adolescent peer acceptance. *Criminology, 45*, 893–923.

Krebs, D. L. (2003). Fictions and facts about evolutionary approaches to human behavior. Comment on Lickliter and Honeycutt (2003). *Psychological Bulletin, 129*, 842–847.

Kreider, R. M., & Fields, J. M. (2002). Number, timing, and duration of marriages and divorces: 1996. *U.S. Census Bureau Current Population Reports*. Retrieved from: http://www.census.gov/prod/2002pubs/p70-80.pdf.

Kreppner, J. M., Rutter, M., Beckett, C., Castle, J., Colvert, E., Groothues, C., Hawkins, A., O'Connor, T. G., Stevens, S., & Sonuga-Barke, E. J. S. (2007). Normality and impairment following profound early institutional deprivation: A longitudinal follow-up into early adolescence. *Developmental Psychology, 43*, 931–946.

Krevans, J., & Gibbs, J. C. (1996). Parents' use of inductive discipline: Relations to children's empathy and prosocial behavior. *Child Development, 67*, 3263–3277.

Krishnamoorthy, J. S., Hart, C., & Jelalian, E. (2006). The epidemic of childhood obesity: Review of research and implications for public policy. *Social Policy Report, 19*(2), 1–17.

Krueger, A. B. (1999). Experimental estimates of educational production functions. *Quarterly Journal of Economics, 114*, 497–532.

Kruger, A. C., & Tomasello, M. (1986). Transactive discussions with peers and adults. *Developmental Psychology, 22*, 681–685.

Krumhansl, C. L., & Jusczyk, P. W. (1990). Infants' perception of phrase structure in music. *Psychological Science, 1*, 70–73.

Kuczaj, S. A., II (1977). The acquisition of regular and irregular past tense forms. *Journal of Verbal Learning and Verbal Behavior, 16*, 589–600.

Kuhl, P. K. (1991). Human adults and human infants show a "perceptual magnet effect" for the prototypes of speech categories, monkeys do not. *Perception and Psychophysics, 50*, 93–107.

Kuhl, P. K., & Meltzoff, A. N. (1982). The bimodal perception of speech in infancy. *Science, 218*, 1138–1141.

Kuhl, P. K., & Meltzoff, A. N. (1984). The intermodal representation of speech in infants. *Infant Behavior and Development, 7*, 361–381.

Kuhl, P. K., Williams, K. A., Lacerda, F., Stevens, K. N., & Lindbloom, B. (1992). Linguistic experiences alter phonetic perception in infants by 6 months of age. *Science, 255*, 606–608.

Kuhlmeier, V., Wynn, K., & Bloom, P. (2003). Attribution of dispositional states by 12-month-olds. *Psychological Science, 14(5)*, 402–408.

Kuhn, D., & Franklin, S. (2006). The second decade: What develops (and how). In W. Damon & R. M. Lerner (Series Eds.) & D. Kuhn & R. S. Siegler (Vol. Eds.), *Handbook of child psychology: Volume 2: Cognition, perception, and language* (6th ed., pp. 953–993). Hoboken, NJ: Wiley.

Kupersmidt, J. B., & Coie, J. D. (1990). Preadolescent peer status, aggression, and school adjustment as predictors of externalizing problems in adolescence. *Child Development, 61*, 1350–1362.

Kurdek, L. A. (1993). Predicting marital dissolution: A 5-year prospective longitudinal study of newlywed couples. *Journal of Personality and Social Psychology, 64*, 221–242.

Kurdek, L. A., & Fine, M. A. (1993). Parent and nonparent residential family members as providers of warmth, support, and supervision to young adolescents. *Journal of Family Psychology, 7*, 245–249.

Kuschel, C. (2007). Managing drug withdrawal in the newborn infant. *Seminar in Fetal Neonatal Medicine, 12*, 127–133.

Kutnick, P. (1985). The relationship of moral judgment and moral action: Kohlberg's theory, criticism and revision. In S. Modgil & C. Modgil (Eds.), *Lawrence Kohlberg: Consensus and controversy* (pp. 125–148). Philadelphia: Falmer Press.

Kwon, K., & Lease, A. M. (2007). Clique membership and social adjustment in children's same-gender cliques: The contribution of the type of clique to children's self-reported adjustment. *Merrill-Palmer Quarterly, 53*, 216–242.

Kwong, T., & Varnhagen, C. (2005). Strategy development and learning to spell new words: Generalization of a process. *Developmental Psychology, 41*, 148–159.

Kyratzis, A. & Guo, J. (2001). Preschool girls' and boys' verbal conflict strategies in the U.S. and China: Cross-cultural and contextual considerations. *Research on Language & Social Interaction, 34*, 45–74.

LaBounty, J., Wellman, H. M., Olson, S., Lagattuta, K., & Liu, D. (2008). Mothers' and fathers' use of internal state talk with their young children. *Social Development, 17*, 757–775.

Lacourse, E., Nagin, D., Tremblay, R. E., Vitaro, F., & Claes, M. (2003). Developmental trajectories of boys' delinquent group membership and facilitation of violent behaviors during adolescence. *Development and Psychopathology, 15*, 183–197.

Ladd, G. W., & Coleman, C. C. (1997). Children's classroom peer relationships and early school attitudes: Concurrent and longitudinal associations. *Early Education and Development, 8*, 51–66.

Ladd, G. W., & Golter, B. S. (1988). Parents' management of preschooler's peer relations: Is it related to children's social competence? *Developmental Psychology, 24*, 109–117.

Ladd, G. W., Herald-Brown, S. L., & Reiser, M. (2008). Does chronic classroom peer rejection predict the development of children's classroom participation during the grade school years? *Child Development, 79*, 1001–1015.

Ladd, G. W., & Hart, C. H. (1992). Creating informal play opportunities: Are parents' and preschoolers' initiations related to children's competence with peers? *Developmental Psychology, 28*, 1179–1187.

Ladd, G. W., & Kochenderfer, B. J. (1996). Linkages between friendship and adjustment during early school transition. In W. M. Bukowski, A. F. Newcomb, & W. W. Hartup (Eds.), *The company they keep. Friendship in childhood and adolescence* (pp. 322–345). Cambridge, UK: Cambridge University Press.

Ladd, G. W., Kochenderfer, B. J., & Coleman, C. C. (1996). Friendship quality as a predictor of young children's early school adjustment. *Child Development, 67*, 1103–1118.

Ladd, G. W., & Troop-Gordon, W. (2003). The role of chronic peer difficulties in the development of children's psychological adjustment problems. *Child Development, 74*, 5, 1344–1367.

LaFreniere, P. J., & Sroufe, L. A. (1985). Profiles of peer competence in the preschool: Interrelations between measures, influence of social ecology, and relations to attachment history. *Developmental Psychology, 21*, 56–69.

LaFreniere, P. J., Strayer, F. F., & Gauthier, R. (1984). The emergence of same-sex affiliative preferences among preschool peers: A developmental ethological perspective. *Child Development, 55,* 1958–1965.

LaFromboise, T., Coleman, H. L., & Gerton, J. (1993). Psychological impact of biculturalism: Evidence and theory. *Psychological Bulletin, 114,* 395–412.

Lagattuta, K. H. (2007). Thinking about the future because of the past: Young children's knowledge about the causes of worry and preventative decisions. *Child Development, 78,* 1492–1509.

Lagattuta, K. H., Wellman, H. M., & Flavell, J. H. (1997). Preschoolers' understanding of the link between thinking and feeling: Cognitive cuing and emotional change. *Child Development, 68,* 1081–1104.

Lagercrantz, H., & Slotkin, T. A. (1986). The "stress" of being born. *Scientific American, 254,* 100–107.

La Greca, A. M., & Lopez, N. (1998). Social anxiety among adolescents: Linkages with peer relations and friendships. *Journal of Abnormal Child Psychology, 26,* 83–94.

La Greca, A. M., Prinstein, M. J., & Fetter, M. D. (2001) Adolescent peer crowd affiliation: Linkages with health risk behaviors and close friendships. *Journal of Pediatric Psychology, 26,* 131–143.

Lahey, B. B., Goodman, S. H., Waldman, I. D., Bird, H., Canino, G., Jensen, P., et al. (1999). Relation of age of onset to the type and severity of child and adolescent conduct problems. *Journal of Abnormal Child Psychology, 27,* 247–260.

Lahey, B. B., Gordon, R. A., Loeber, R., Stouthamer-Loeber, M., & Farrington, D. P. (1999). Boys who join gangs: A prospective study of predictors of first gang entry. *Journal of Abnormal Child Psychology, 27,* 261–276.

Lahey, B. B., Schwab-Stone, M., Goodman, S. H., Waldman, I. D., Canino, G., Rathouz, P. J., Miller, T. L., Dennis, K. D., Bird, H., & Jensen, P. S. (2000). Age and gender differences in oppositional behavior and conduct problems: A cross-sectional household study of middle childhood and adolescence. *Journal of Abnormal Psychology, 109,* 488–503.

Lahey, B. B., Van Hulle, C. A., Rathouz, P. J., Rodgers, J. L., D'Onofrio, B. M., & Waldman, I. D. (2009). Are oppositional-defiant and hyperactive-inattentive symptoms developmental precursors to conduct problems in late childhood? Genetic and environmental links. *Journal of Abnormal Psychology, 37,* 45–58.

Laible, D. J. (2004). Mother-child discourse surrounding a child's past behavior at 30 months: Links to emotional understanding and early conscience development at 36 months. *Merrill-Palmer Quarterly, 50,* 159–180.

Laible, D. J., & Carlo, G. (2004). The differential relations of maternal and paternal support and control to adolescent social competence, self-worth, and sympathy. *Journal of Adolescent Research, 19,* 759–782.

Laible, D., Eye, J., & Carlo, G. (2005). Dimensions of conscience in mid-adolescence: Links with social behavior, parenting, and temperament. *Journal of Youth and Adolescence, 37,* 875–887.

Laible, D. J., & Thompson, R. A. (1998). Attachment and emotional understanding in preschool children. *Developmental Psychology, 24,* 1038–1045.

Laird, R. D., Pettit, G. S., Bates, J. E., & Dodge, K. A. (2003). Parents' monitoring-relevant knowledge and adolescents' delinquent behavior: Evidence of correlated developmental changes and reciprocal influences. *Child Development, 74,* 752–768.

Lamb, B., & Lang, R. (1992). Aetiology of cerebral palsy. *British Journal of Obstetrics and Gynecology, 99,* 176–178.

Lamb, M. E. (1998). Nonparental child care: Context, quality, correlates, and consequences. In W. Damon (Series Ed.) and I. E. Sigel & K. A. Renninger (Vol. Eds.), *Handbook of child psychology: Vol. 4. Child psychology in practice* (5th ed., pp. 73–133). New York: Wiley.

Lamb, M. E., & Ketterlinus, R. D. (1991). Parental behavior, adolescent. In R. M. Lerner, A. C. Petersen, & J. Brooks-Gunn (Eds.), *Encyclopedia of adolescence* (pp. 735–738). New York: Garland.

Lamb, M. E., & Teti, D. M. (1991). Parenthood and marriage in adolescence: Associations with educational and occupational attainment. In R. M. Lerner, A. C. Petersen, & J. Brooks-Gunn (Eds.), *Encyclopedia of adolescence* (pp. 742–745). New York: Garland.

Lamb, M. E., Thompson, R. A., Gardner, W., & Charnov, E. L. (1985). *Infant-mother attachment: The origins and developmental significance of individual differences in Strange Situation behavior*. Hillsdale, NJ: Erlbaum.

Lamb, S., & Zakhireh, B. (1997). Toddlers' attention to the distress of peers in a daycare setting. *Early Education and Development, 8,* 105–118.

Lamborn, S. D., Dornbusch, S. M., & Steinberg, L. (1996). Ethnicity and community context as moderators of the relations between family decision making and adolescent adjustment. *Child Development, 67,* 283–301.

Lamborn, S. D., Mounts, N. S., Steinberg, L., & Dornbusch, S. M. (1991). Patterns of competence and adjustment among adolescents from authoritative, authoritarian, indulgent, and neglectful families. *Child Development, 62,* 1049–1065.

Landau, B., Smith, L. B., & Jones, S. S. (1988). The importance of shape in early lexical learning. *Cognitive Development, 3,* 299–321.

Landau, B., Smith, L., & Jones, S. (1998) Object perception and object naming in early development. *Trends in Cognitive Sciences, 2,* 19–24.

Landau, S., Lorch, E. P., & Milich, R. (1992). Visual attention to and comprehension of television in attention-deficit hyperactivity disordered and normal boys. *Child Development, 63,* 928–937.

Landerl, K., Bevan, A., & Butterworth, B. (2004). Developmental dyscalculia and basic numerical capacities: A study of 8–9-year-old students. *Cognition, 93,* 99–125.

Landry, S. H., Chapieski, M. L., Richardson, M. A., Palmer, J., & Hall, S. (1990). The social competence of children born prematurely: Effects of medical complications. *Child Development, 61,* 1605–1616.

Lane, H. (1976). *The wild boy of Aveyron*. Cambridge, MA: Harvard University Press.

Langlois, J. H., Kalakanis, L., Rubenstein, A. J., Larson, A., Hallam, M., & Smoot, M. (2000). Maxims or myths of beauty? A meta-analytic and theoretical review. *Psychological Bulletin, 126,* 390–423.

Langlois, J. H., Ritter, J. M., Casey, R. J., & Sawin, D. B. (1995). Infant attractiveness predicts maternal behaviors and attitudes. *Developmental Psychology, 31,* 464–472.

Langlois, J. H., Ritter, J. M., Roggman, L. A., & Vaughn, L. S. (1991). Facial diversity and infant preferences for attractive faces. *Developmental Psychology, 27,* 79–84.

Langlois, J. H., Roggman, L. A., Casey, R. J., Ritter, J. M., Rieser-Danner, L. A., & Jenkins, V. Y. (1987). Infant preferences for attractive faces: Rudiments of a stereotype? *Developmental Psychology, 23,* 363–369.

Langlois, J. H., Roggman, L. A., & Rieser-Danner, L. A. (1990). Infants' differential social responses to attractive and unattractive faces. *Developmental Psychology, 26,* 153–159.

Lansford, J. E., Chang, L., Dodge, K. A., Malone, P. S., Oburu, P., Palmérus, K., et al. (2005). Physical discipline and children's adjustment: Cultural normativeness as a moderator. *Child Development, 76,* 1234–1246.

Lansford, J. E., Deater-Deckard, K., Dodge, K. A., Bates, J. E., & Petit, G. S. (2004). Ethic differences in the link between physical discipline and later adolescent externalizing behaviors. *Journal of Child Psychology and Psychiatry, 45,* 801–812.

Lansford, J. E., Putallaz, M., Grimes, C. L., Schiro-Osman, K. A., Kupersmidt, J. B., & Coie, J. D. (2006). Perceptions of friendship quality and observed behaviors with friends: How do sociometrically rejected, average, and popular girls differ? *Merrill-Palmer Quarterly, 52,* 694–720.

LAPD (Los Angeles Police Department). (2004). http://www.lapdonline.org/general_information/crime_statistics/gang_stats/2004_gang_stats/04_03_sum.htm.

Lapsley, D. K. (2006). Moral stage theory. In M. Killen & J. G. Smetana (Eds.), *Handbook of moral development* (pp. 37–66). Mahwah, NJ: Erlbaum.

Largo, R. H., Pfister, D., Molinari, L., Kundu, S., Lipp, A., & Duc, G. (1989). Significance of prenatal, perinatal and postnatal factors in the development of AGA preterm infants at five to seven years. *Developmental Medicine and Child Neurology, 31,* 440–456.

Larkin, June, & Popaleni, Katherine. (1994). Heterosexual courtship violence and sexual harassment: The private and public control of young women. *Feminism and Psychology, 4*(2), 213–227.

Larson, R., & Lampman-Petraitis, C. (1989). Daily emotional states as reported by children and adolescents. *Child Development, 60,* 1250–1260.

Larson, R. W., Moneta, G., Richards, M. H., & Wilson, S. (2002). Continuity, stability, and a change in daily emotional experience across adolescence. *Child Development, 73,* 1151–1165.

Larson, R. W., & Richards, M. H. (1991). Daily companionship in late childhood and early adolescence: Changing developmental contexts. *Child Development, 62,* 284–300.

Larson, R. W., & Verma, S. (1999). How children and adolescents spend time across the world: Work, play, and developmental opportunities. *Psychological Bulletin, 125,* 701–736.

Lau, J. Y., Rijsdijk, F., Gregory, A. M., McGuffin, P., Eley, T. C. (2007). Pathways to childhood depressive symptoms: the role of social, cognitive, and genetic risk factors. *Developmental Psychology, 43*(6), 1402–1414.

Laub, J. H., & Sampson, R. J. (1988). Unraveling families and delinquency: A reanalysis of the Glueck's data. *Criminology, 26,* 355–379.

Laursen, B., Bukowski, W. M., Aaunola, K., & Nurmi, J.-E. (2007). Friendship moderates prospective associations between social isolation and adjustment problems in young children. *Child Development, 78,* 1395–1404.

Laursen, B., & Collins, W. A. (1994). Interpersonal conflict during adolescence. *Psychological Bulletin, 115,* 197–209.

Laursen, B., Coy, K. C., & Collins, W. A. (1998). Reconsidering changes in parent-child conflict across adolescence: A meta-analysis. *Child Development, 69,* 817–832.

Laursen, B., Finkelstein, B. D., & Betts, N. T. (2001). A developmental meta-analysis of peer conflict resolution. *Developmental Review, 21,* 423–449.

Lavelli, M., & Fogel, A. (2005). Developmental changes in the relationship between infant's attention and emotion during early face-to-face communication: The 2-month transition. *Developmental Psychology, 41,* 265–280.

Lawford, H., Pratt, M. W., Hunsberger, B., Pancer, S. M. (2005). Adolescent generativity: A longitudinal study of two possible contexts for learning concern for future generations. *Journal of Research on Adolescence, 15,* 261–273.

Lazar, I., Darlington, R., Murray, H., Royce, J., & Snipper, A. (1982). Lasting effects of early education: A report from the Consortium for Longitudinal Studies. *Monographs of the Society for Research in Child Development, 47*(Serial No. 195).

Le, H. N. (2000). Never leave your little one alone: Raising an Ifaluk child. In J. S. DeLoache & A. Gottlieb (Eds.), *A world of babies: Imagined childcare guides for seven societies.* Cambridge, UK: Cambridge University Press.

Leaper, C. (1991). Influence and involvement in children's discourse: Age, gender, and partner effects. *Child Development,* 62, 797–811.

Leaper, C. (1994). Exploring the correlates and consequences of gender segregation: Social relationships in childhood, adolescence, and adulthood. In W. Damon (Series Ed.) & C. Leaper (Vol. Ed.), *New directions for child development. The development of gender relationships.* San Francisco: Jossey-Bass.

Leaper, C. (2000a). Gender, affiliation, assertion, and the interactive context of parent-child play. *Developmental Psychology, 36,* 381–393.

Leaper, C. (2000b). The social construction and socialization of gender. In P. H. Miller & E. K. Scholnick (Eds.), *Towards a feminist developmental psychology* (pp. 127–152). New York: Routledge Press.

Leaper, C. (2002). Parenting girls and boys. In M. H. Bornstein (Ed.), *Handbook of parenting: Vol. 1: Children and parenting* (2nd ed., pp. 189–225). Mahwah NJ: Erlbaum.

Leaper, C., & Anderson, K. J. (1997). Gender development and heterosexual romantic relationships during adolescence. In W. Damon (Series Ed.) & S. Shulman & W. A. Collins (Issue Eds.), *Romantic relationships in adolescence: Developmental perspectives* (*New Directions for Child Development*, No. 78, pp. 85–103). San Francisco: Jossey-Bass.

Leaper, C., Anderson, K. J. & Sanders, P. (1998). Moderators of gender effects on parents' talk to their children: A meta-analysis. *Developmental Psychology, 34,* 3–27.

Leaper, C. & Ayres, M. M. (2007). A meta-analytic review of gender variation in adults' language use: Talkativeness, affiliative speech, and assertive speech. *Personality & Social Psychology Review, 11,* 328–363.

Leaper, C. & Bigler, R. S. (2004). Gendered language and sexist thought. *Monographs of the Society for Research in Child Development, 69,* 1, 128–142.

Leaper, C., Breed, L., Hoffman, L., & Perlman, C. A. (2002). Variations in the gender-stereotyped content of children's television cartoons across genres. *Journal of Applied Social Psychology, 32,* 1653–1662.

Leaper, C., & Brown, C. S. (2008). Perceived experiences with sexism among adolescent girls. *Child Development, 79,* 685–704.

Leaper, C., Carson, M., Baker, C., Holliday, H. & Myers, S. B. (1995). Self-disclosure and listener verbal support in same-gender and cross-gender friends' conversations. *Sex Roles, 33,* 387–404.

Leaper, C., & Friedman, C.K. (2007). The socialization of gender. In J. Grusec & P. Hastings (Eds.), *Handbook of socialization: Theory and research* (pp. 561–587). New York: Guilford.

Leaper, C. & Holliday, H. (1995). Gossip in same-gender and cross-gender friends' conversations. *Personal Relationships, 2,* 237–246.

Leaper, C. & Smith, T. E. (2004). A meta-analytic review of gender variations in children's language use: Talkativeness, affiliative speech, and assertive speech. *Developmental Psychology, 40,* 993–1027.

Leaper, C., Tenenbaum, H. R. & Shaffer, T. G. (1999). Communication patterns of African American girls and boys from low-income, urban backgrounds. *Child Development, 70,* 1489–1503.

Leaper, C., & Van, S. R. (2008). Masculinity ideology, covert sexism, and perceived gender typicality in relation to young men's academic motivation and choices in college. *Psychology of Men & Masculinity, 9,* 139–153.

Lecanuet, J. P., Granier-Deferre, C., & Busnel, M. C. (1995). Human fetal auditory perception. In J. P. Lecanuet, W. P. Fifer, N. A. Krasnegor, & W. P. Smotherman (Eds.), *Fetal development: A psychobiological perspective.* Hillsdale, NJ: Erlbaum.

Lee, H., & Barratt, M. (1993). Cognitive development of preterm low birth weight children at 5 to 8 years old. *Journal of Developmental and Behavioral Pediatrics, 14,* 242–249.

Lee, K., & Karmiloff-Smith, A. (2002). Macro- and microdevelopmental research: Assumptions, research strategies, constraints, and utilities. In N. Granott & J. Parziale (Eds.), *Microdevelopment: Transition processes in development and learning* (pp 243–265). Cambridge, UK: Cambridge University Press.

Lee, L., Howes, C., & Chamberlain, B. (2007). Ethnic heterogeneity of social networks and cross-ethnic friendships of elementary school boys and girls. *Merrill-Palmer Quarterly, 53,* 325–346.

Lee, L. C., & Zhan, G. Q. (1991). Political socialization and parental values in the People's Republic of China. *International Journal of Behavioral Development, 14,* 337–373.

Leerkes, E., & Crockenberg, S. C. (2003). The impact of maternal characteristics and sensitivity on the concordance between maternal reports and laboratory observations of infant negative emotionality. *Infancy, 4,* 517–539.

LeFevre, J. A., Sadesky, G. S., & Bisanz, J. (1996a). Selection of procedures in mental addition: Reassessing the problem-size effect in adults. *Journal of Experimental Psychology: Learning, Memory, and Cognition, 22,* 216–230.

LeFevre, J. A., Bisanz, J., Daley, K. E., Buffone, L., Greenham, S. L., & Sadesky, G. S. (1996b). Multiple routes to solution of single-digit multiplication problems. *Journal of Experimental Psychology: General, 125,* 284–306.

Le Grand, R., Mondloch, C. J., Maurer, D., & Brent, H. P. (2001). Early visual experience and face processing. *Nature, 410,* 890.

Le Grand, R., Mondloch, C. J., Maurer, D., & Brent, H. P. (2003). Expert face processing requires input to the right hemisphere during infancy. *Nature Neuroscience, 6,* 1108–1112.

Leichtman, M. D., Pillemer, D. B., Wang, Q., Koreishi, A., & Han, J. J. (2000). When Baby Maisy came to school: Mothers' interview styles and preschoolers' event memories. *Cognitive Development, 15,* 99–114.

Lemerise, E. A., & Arsenio, W. F. (2000). An integrated model of emotion processes and cognition in social information processing. *Child Development, 71,* 107–118.

Lemery, K. S., Essex, M. J., & Smider, N. A. (2002). Revealing the relationship between temperament and behavior problem symptoms by eliminating measurement confounding: Expert ratings and factor analyses. *Child Development, 73,* 867–882.

Lemery, K. S., Goldsmith, H. H., Klinnert, M. D., & Mrazek, D. A. (1999). Developmental models of infant and childhood temperament. *Developmental Psychology, 35,* 189–204.

Lengua, L. J., Bush, N., Long, A. C., Kovacs, E. A., & Trancik, A. M. (2008). Effortful control as a moderator of the relation between contextual risk factors and growth in adjustment problems. *Development and Psychopathology, 20,* 509–528.

Lengua, L. J., Honorado, E., Bush, N. (2007). Contextual risk and parenting as predictors of effortful control and social competence in preschool children. *Journal of Applied Developmental Psychology, 28,* 40–55.

Lengua, L. J., Wolchik, S. A., Sandler, I. N., & West, S. G. (2000). The additive and interactive effects of parenting and temperament in predicting adjustment problems of children of divorce. *Journal of Clinical Child Psychology, 29,* 232–244.

Lenneberg, E. H. (1967). *Biological foundations of language.* New York: Wiley.

Lerner, I. M., & Libby, W. J. (1976). *Heredity, evolution, and society.* (2nd ed.). San Francisco: Freeman.

Lerner, R. (1995). The limits of biological influence: Behavioral genetics as the Emperor's New Clothes. *Psychological Inquiry, 6,* 145–156.

Leslie, A. M. (1986). Getting development off the ground. Modularity and the infant's perception of causality. In P. v. Geert (Ed.), *Theory building in developmental psychology* (pp. 406–437). Amsterdam: North Holland.

Leslie, A. M. (1991). The theory of mind impairment in autism: Evidence for a modular mechanism of development? In A. Whiten (Ed.), *Natural theories of mind: Evolution, development and simulation of everyday mindreading.* Oxford, UK: Basil Blackwell.

Leslie, A. M. (2000). How to acquire a "representational theory of mind." In D. Sperber (Ed.), *Metarepresentations: A multidisciplinary perspective* (pp. 197–223). Oxford, UK: Oxford University Press.

Lester, B. M. (1998). The maternal lifestyles study. *Annals of the New York Academy of Sciences, 846,* 296–305.

Lester, B. M., Anderson, L. T., Boukydis, C. F. Z., Garcia-Coll, C. T., Vohr, B., & Peucker, M. (1989). Early detection of infants at risk for later handicap through acoustic cry analysis. *Birth Defects: Original Article Series, 26,* 99–118.

Lester, B. M., & Tronick, E. Z. (1994). The effect of prenatal cocaine exposure and child outcome. *Infant Mental Health Journal, 15,* 107–120.

Leung, M.-C. (1996). Social networks and self enhancement in Chinese children: A comparison of self reports and peer reports of group membership. *Social Development, 5,* 146–157.

Levant, R. F. (2005). The crises of boyhood. In G. E. Good & G. R. Brooks (Eds.), The new handbook of psychotherapy and counseling with men: A comprehensive guide to settings, problems, and treatment approaches (2nd ed., pp. 161–171). San Francisco, CA: Jossey-Bass.

Leve, L. D., & Fagot, B. I. (1997). Prediction of positive peer relations from observed parent-child interactions. *Social Development, 6,* 254–269.

Leve, D. L., Pears, K. C., & Fisher, P. A. (2002). Competence in early development. In J. B. Reid, G. R. Patterson, & J. Snyder (Eds.), *Antisocial behavior in children and adolescents* (pp. 45–64). Washington, DC: American Psychological Association.

Levin, I. (1982). The nature and development of time concepts in children: The effects of interfering cues. In W. J. Friedman (Ed.), *The developmental psychology of time.* New York: Academic Press.

Levin, I. (1989). Principles underlying time measurement: The development of children's constraints on counting time. In I. Levin & D. Zakay (Eds.), *Time and human cognition: A life-span perspective*. Amsterdam: Elsevier.

Levin, I., & Korat, O. (1993). Sensitivity to phonological, morphological, and semantic cues in early reading and writing in Hebrew. *Merrill-Palmer Quarterly, 39*, 213–232.

Levin, I., Siegler, R. S., & Druyan, S. (1990). Misconception about motion: Development and training effects. *Child Development, 61*, 1544–1557.

Levine, J., & Suzuki, D. (1993). *The secret of life*. Boston: WGBH Educational Foundation.

LeVine, R. A. (1988). Human parental care: Universal goals, cultural strategies, individual behavior. In R. A. Le Vine, P. M. Miller, & M. M. West (Eds.). *Parental behavior in diverse societies: New directions for child development, Vol. 40* (pp. 3–12). San Francisco: Jossey-Bass.

LeVine, R. A., Dixon, S., LeVine, S., Richman, A., Leiderman, P. H., Keefer, C. H., & Brazelton, T. B. (1996). *Childcare and culture: Lessons from Africa*. Cambridge, UK: Cambridge University Press.

Levitt, M. J., Weber, R. A., Clark, M. C., & McDonnell, P. (1985). Reciprocity of exchange in toddler sharing behavior. *Developmental Psychology, 21*, 122–123.

Lew, A. R., Foster, K. A., Crowther, H. L., & Green, M. (2004). Indirect landmark use at 6 months of age in a spatial orientation task. *Infant Behavior and Development, 27*, 81–90.

Lewinsohn, P. M. (1974). A behavioral approach to depression. In R. Friedman & M. Katz (Eds.), *The psychology of depression: Contemporary theory and research* (pp. 157–185). Washington, DC: Winston-Wiley.

Lewinsohn, P. M., Joiner, T. E., & Rohde, P. (2001). Evaluation of cognitive diathesis-stress models in predicting major depressive disorder in adolescents. *Journal of Abnormal Psychology, 110*, 203–215.

Lewis, E E., Dozier, M., Ackerman, J., & Sepulveda-Kozakowski, S. (2007). The effect of placement instability on adopted children's inhibitory control abilities and oppositional behavior. *Developmental Psychology, 43*, 1415–1427.

Lewis, M. (1995). Embarrassment: The emotion of self-exposure and evaluation. In J. P. Tangney & K. W. Fischer (Eds.), *Self-conscious emotions* (pp. 198–218). New York: Guilford.

Lewis, M. (1998). Emotional competence and development. In D. Pushkar, W. M. Bukowski, A. E. Schwartzman, D. M. Stack, & D. R. White (Eds.), *Improving competence across the lifespan* (pp. 27–36). New York: Plenum Press.

Lewis, M. (2007). Self-conscious emotional development. In J. L. Tracy, R. W. Robins, J. P., Tangney (Eds.), *The self-conscious emotions: Theory and research* (pp. 134–1490). New York: Guilford Press.

Lewis, M., Alessandri, S. M., & Sullivan, M. W. (1990). Violation of expectancy, loss of control, and anger expressions in young infants. *Developmental Psychology, 26*, 745–751.

Lewis, M., Alessandri, S. M., & Sullivan, M. W. (1992). Differences in shame and pride as a function of children's gender and task difficulty. *Child Development, 63*, 630–638.

Lewis, M., & Brooks-Gunn, J. (1979). *Social cognition and the acquisition of self*. New York: Plenum Press.

Lewis, M., Feiring, C., & Rosenthal, S. (2000). Attachment over time. *Child Development, 71*, 707–720.

Lewis, M., Sullivan, M. W., Stanger, C. & Weiss, M. (1989). Self-development and self-conscious emotions. *Child Development, 60*, 146–156.

Lewis, M. D. (2005). Bridging emotion theory and neurobiology through dynamic systems modeling (target article). *Behavioral and Brain Sciences, 28*, 169–194.

Lewis, T. L., & Maurer, D. (2005). Multiple sensitive periods in human visual development: Evidence from visually deprived children. *Developmental Psychobiology* Special Issue: Critical Periods Re-examined: Evidence from Human Sensory Development, *46*, 163–183.

Lewkowicz, D. J. (2004). Perception of serial order in infants. *Developmental Science, 7*, 175–184.

Lewkowicz, D. J., Karmel, B. Z., & Gardner, J. M. (1998). Effects of prenatal cocaine exposure on responsiveness to multimodal information in infants between 4 and 10 months of age. *Annals of the New York Academy of Sciences, 846*, 408–411.

Lewontin, R. (1982). *Human diversity*. New York: Scientific American Books.

Li-Grining, C. P. (2007). Effortful control among low-income preschoolers in three cites: Stability, change, and individual differences. *Developmental Psychology, 43*, 208–221.

Liaw, F. R., & Brooks-Gunn, J. (1993). Patterns of low birth weight on children's cognitive development. *Developmental Psychology, 29*, 1024–1035.

Liben, L. S. (1999). Developing an understanding of external spatial representations. In I. E. Sigel (Ed.), *Development of mental representation: Theories and applications* (pp. 297–321). Mahwah, NJ: Erlbaum.

Liben, L. S., & Bigler, R. S. (2002). The developmental course of gender differentiation: Conceptualizing, measuring, and evaluating constructs and pathways. *Monographs of the Society for Research in Child Development, 67*(2), vii–147.

Liben, L. S. & Myers, L. J. (2007). Children's understanding of maps: What develops? In J. Plumert & J. Spencer (Eds.), *The emerging spatial mind* (pp. 193–218). Oxford, UK: Oxford University Press.

Liben, L. S., & Signorella, M. L. (1993). Gender-schematic processing in children: The role of initial interpretations of stimuli. *Developmental Psychology, 29*, 141–149.

Lichter, D. T., & Lansdale, N. S. (1995). Parental work, family structure, and poverty among Latino children. *Journal of Marriage and the Family, 57*, 346–354.

Lickliter, R. (1995). Embryonic sensory experience and intersensory development in precocial birds. In J. Lecanuet & W. P. Fifer (Eds.), *Fetal development: A psychobiological perspective* (pp. 281–294). Hillsdale, NJ: Erlbaum.

Lickliter, R., & Honeycutt, H. (2003). Developmental dynamics: Toward a biologically plausible evolutionary psychology. *Psychological Bulletin, 129*, 819–835.

Lickona, T. (1976). Research on Piaget's theory on moral development. In T. Lickona (Ed.), *Moral development and behavior: Theory, research, and social issues* (pp. 219–240). New York: Holt, Rinehart, and Winston.

Lieven, E. V. M. (1994). Crosslinguistic and crosscultural aspects of language addressed to children. In C. Gallaway & B. J. Richards (Eds.), *Input and interaction in language acquisition* (pp. 56–73). Cambridge, UK: Cambridge University Press.

Lillard, A. (2006). Children's play as cultural interpretation. In A. Göncü & S. Gaskins (Eds.), *Play and development: Evolutionary, sociocultural, and functional perspectives* (pp. 131–154). Mahwah, NJ: Erlbaum.

Lillard, A. S., & Flavell, J. H. (1992). Young children's understanding of different mental states. *Developmental Psychology, 28*, 626–634.

Limber, J. (1973). The genesis of complex sentences. In T. Moore (Ed.), *Cognitive development and the acquisition of language* (pp. 169–186). New York: Academic Press.

Linares, L. O., Heeren, T., Bronfman, E., Zuckerman, B., Augustyn, M., & Tronick, E. (2001). A mediational model for the impact of exposure to community violence on early child behavior problems. *Child Development, 72*, 639–652.

Lindahl, K. M., Malik, N. M., Kaczynski, K., & Simons, J. S. (2004). Couple power dynamics, systemic family functioning, and child adjustment: A test of a mediational model in a multiethnic sample. *Development and Psychopathology, 16*, 609–630.

Lindberg, M. A. (1980). Is knowledge base development a necessary and sufficient condition for memory development? *Journal of Experimental Child Psychology, 30,* 401–410.

Lindberg, M. A. (1991). A taxonomy of suggestibility and eyewitness memory: Age, memory process, and focus of analysis. In J. L. Doris (Ed.), *The suggestibility of children's recollections.* Washington, DC: American Psychological Association.

Lindell, S. G. (1988). Education for childbirth: A time for change. *Journal of Obstetrics, Gynecology, and Neonatal Nursing, 17*, 108–112.

Lindberg, S. M., Grabe, S., & Hyde, J. S. (2007). Gender, pubertal development, and peer sexual harassment predict objectified body consciousness in early adolescence. *Journal of Research on Adolescence, 17*, 723–742.

Lindsey, E. W., Caldera, Y. M., & Tankersley, L. (2009). Marital conflict and the quality of young children's peer play behavior: The mediating and moderating role of parent-child emotional reciprocity and attachment security. *Journal of Family Psychology, 23*, 130–145.

Lindsey, E. W., & Mize, J. (2001). Interparental agreement, parent-child responsiveness and children's peer competence. *Family Relations: Interdisciplinary Journal of Applied Family Studies, 50*, 348–354.

Linkletter, A. (1957). *Kids say the darnedest things*. Englewood Cliffs, NJ: Prentice-Hall.

Linn, M., & Petersen, A. (1985). Emergence and characterization of sex differences in spatial ability: A meta-analysis. *Child Development, 56*, 1479–1498.

Lins-Dyer, M. T., & Nucci, L. (2007). The impact of social class and social cognitive domain on northeastern Brazilian mothers' and daughters' conceptions of parental control. *International Journal of Behavioral Development, 31*, 105–114.

Lipsitt, L. P. (1977). Taste in human neonates: Its effect on sucking and heart rate. In J. M. Weiffenbach (Ed.), *Taste and development: The genesis of sweet preference* (DHEW Publication No. NIH 77-1068, pp. 125–141). Washington, DC: U. S. Government Printing Office.

Lipsitt, L. P. (2003). Crib death: A biobehavioral phenomenon? *Current Directions in Psychological Science, 12,* 164–170.

Lipton, J. S., & Spelke, E. S. (2003). Origins of number sense: Large number discrimination in human infants. *Psychological Science, 14*, 396–401.

Little, J. F., Hepper, P. G., & Dornan, J. C. (2002). Maternal alcohol consumption during pregnancy and fetal startle behaviour. *Physiology & Behavior, 76*, 691–694.

Little, S. A., & Garber, J. (1995). Aggression, depression, and stressful life events predicting peer rejection in children. *Development and Psychopathology, 7*, 845–856.

Llewellyn, C. H., van Jaarsveld, Cornelia H. M., Boniface, David, Carnell, Susan, & Wardle, Jane. (2008). Eating rate is a heritable phenotype related to weight in children. *American Journal of Clinical Nutrition, 88*(6), 1560–1566.

Lobo, M. A., Galloway, J. C., & Savelsbergh, G. J. (2004). General and task-related experiences affect early object interaction. *Child Development, 75*, 1268–1281.

Lochman, J. E., Coie, J. D., Underwood, M. K., & Terry, R. (1993). Effectiveness of a social relations intervention program for aggressive and nonaggressive, rejected children. *Journal of Consulting and Clinical Psychology, 61*, 1053–1058.

Lockman, J. J., Ashmead, D., & Bushnell, E. (1984). The development of anticipatory hand orientation during infancy. *Journal of Experimental Child Psychology, 37,* 176–186.

Lockman, J. J., & McHale, J. P. (1989). Object manipulation in infancy: Developmental and contextual determinants. In J. J. Lockman & N. L. Hazen (Eds.), *Action in social context: Perspectives on early development* (pp. 129–167). New York: Plenum Press.

Lockman, J. J., & Thelen, E. (1993). Developmental biodynamics: Brain, body, behavior connections. *Child Development, 64,* 953–959.

Loeber, R. (1982). The stability of antisocial and delinquent child behavior: A review. *Child Development, 53*, 1431–1446.

Loeber, R., & Hay, D. F. (1993). Developmental approaches to aggression and conduct problems. In M. Rutter & D. F. Hay (Eds.), *Development through life: A handbook for clinicians* (pp. 488–516). Oxford, UK: Blackwell.

Loeber, R., & Schmaling, K. B. (1985). Empirical evidence for overt and covert patterns of antisocial conduct problems: A meta-analysis. *Journal of Abnormal Child Psychology, 13*, 315–336.

Loeber, R., & Stouthamer-Loeber, M. (1986). Family factors as correlates and predictors of juvenile conduct problems and delinquency. In M. Tonry & N. Morris (Eds.), *Crime and justice* (Vol. 17, pp. 29–149). Chicago: University of Chicago Press.

Loeber, R., Wung, P., Keenan, K., Giroux, B., Stouthamer-Loeber, M., Van Kammen, W. B., & Maughan, B. (1993). Developmental pathways in disruptive child behavior. *Development and Psychopathology, 5*, 103–133.

Lonardo, R., Giordano, P. C., Longmore, M. A., & Manning, W. D. (2009). Parents, friends, and romantic partners: Enmeshment in deviant networks and adolescent delinquency involvement. *Journal of Youth and Adolescence, 38*, 367–383.

Loomis, J. M, Klatzky, R. L., Golledge, R. G., Cicinelli, J. G., Pellegrino, J. W., & Fry, P. A. (1993). Nonvisual navigation by blind and sighted: Assessment of path integration ability. *Journal of Experimental Psychology: General, 122*, 73–91.

Lorenz, K. Z. (1935). Der Kumpan in der Umwelt das Vogels. *Journal of Ornithology, 83*, 137–213.

Lorenz, K. Z. (1952). *King Solomon's ring*. New York: Crowell.

Loukas, A., Prelow, H., Suizzo, M.-A., & Allua, S. (2008). Mothering and peer associations mediate cumulative risk effects for Latino youth. *Journal of Marriage and Family, 70*, 76–85.

Love, J. M., Chazan-Cohen, R., & Raikes, H. (2007). Forty years of research knowledge and use: From Head Start to early Head Start and beyond. In J. L. Aber, S. J. Bishop-Josef, S. M. Jones, K. T. McLearn, & D. A. Phillips (Eds.). *Child development and social policy: Knowledge for action* (pp. 79–95). Washington, DC: American Psychological Association.

Love, J. M., Harrison, L., Sagi-Schwartz, A., van IJzendoorn, M. H., Ross, C., Ungerer, J. A., Raikes, H., Brady-Smith, C., Boller, K., Brooks-Gunn, J., Constantine, J., Kisker, E. E., Paulsell, D., & Chazan-Cohen, R. (2003). Child care quality matters: How conclusions may vary with context. *Child Development, 74,* 1021–1033.

Lovejoy, C. M., Graczyk, P. A., O'Hare, E., & Neuman, G. (2000). Maternal depression and parenting behavior: A meta-analytic review. *Clinical Psychology Review, 20,* 561–592.

Lovett, M. W., Borden, S. L., DeLuca, T., Lacerenza, L., Benson, N. J., & Blackstone, D. (1994). Treating the core deficits of developmental dyslexia: Evidence of transfer of learning after phonologically- and strategy-based reading training programs. *Developmental Psychology, 30,* 805–822.

Lozoff, B. (1989). Nutrition and behavior. *American Psychologist, 44,* 231–236.

Lubinski, D., Benbow, C. P., Webb, R. M., & Bleske-Rechek, A. (2006). Tracking exceptional human capital over two decades. *Psychological Science, 17,* 194–199.

Lubinski, D., & Humphreys, L. G. (1997). Incorporating general intelligence into epidemiology and the social sciences. *Intelligence, 24,* 159–202.

Lubinski, D., Webb, R. M., Morelock, M. J., & Benbow, C. P. (2001). Top 1 in 10,000: A 10-year follow-up of the profoundly gifted. *Journal of Applied Psychology, 86,* 718–729.

Lucas-Thompson, R., & Clarke-Stewart, K. A. (2007). Forecasting friendship: How martial quality, maternal mood, and attachment security are linked to children's peer relationships. *Journal of Applied Developmental Psychology, 28,* 499–514.

Luna, B., Garver, K. E., Urban, T. A., Lazar N. A., & Sweeney, J. A. (2004). Maturation of cognitive processes from late childhood to adulthood. *Child Development, 75,* 1357–1372.

Lunkenheimer, E. S., Shields, A. M., & Cortina, K. S. (2007). Parental emotion coaching and dismissing in family interaction. *Social Development*, 16, 232–248.

Luntz, B. K., & Widom, C. S. (1994). Antisocial personality disorders in abused and neglected children grown up. *American Journal of Psychiatry, 151,* 670 674.

Luster, T., & McAdoo, H. (1996). Family and child influences on educational attainment: A secondary analysis of the High/Scope Perry Pre-school data. *Developmental Psychology, 32,* 26–39.

Luster, T., Rhoades, K., & Haas, B. (1989). The relation between parental values and parenting behavior: A test of the Kohn hypothesis. *Journal of Marriage and the Family, 51,* 139–147.

Lutchmaya, S., & Baron-Cohen, S. (2002). Human sex differences in social and non-social looking preferences, at 12 months of age. *Infant Behavior and Development, 25,* 319–325.

Lutchmaya, S., Baron-Cohen, S., & Raggatt, P. (2002). Foetal testosterone and eye contact in 12 month old human infants. *Infant Behavior and Development, 24,* 418–424.

Luthar, S. S. (1999). *Poverty and children's adjustment.* Thousand Oaks, CA: Sage Publications.

Luthar, S. S. (2003). The culture of affluence: Psychological costs of material wealth. *Child Development, 74,* 1581–1593.

Luthar, S. S., & Becker, B. E. (2002). Privileged but pressured: A study of affluent youth. *Child Development, 73,* 1593–1610.

Luthar, S. S., & D'Avanzo, K. (1999). Contextual factors in substance use: A study of suburban and inner-city adolescents. *Development and Psychopathology, 11,* 845–867.

Luthar, S. S., & Latendresse, S. J. (2005). Children of the affluent: Challenges to well-being. *Current Directions in Psychological Science, 14,* 49–53.

Luxen, M. F. (2007). Sex differences, evolutionary psychology and biosocial theory: Biosocial theory is no alternative. *Theory & Psychology, 17,* 383–394.

Lynam, D. R. (1996). Early identification of chronic offenders: Who is the fledgling psychopath? *Psychological Bulletin, 120,* 209–234.

Lynam, D. R. (1997). Pursuing the psychopathy: Capturing the fledgling psychopath in a nomological net. *Journal of Abnormal Psychology, 106,* 425–438.

Lynch, M., & Cicchetti, D. (1998). An ecological-transactional analysis of children and contents: The longitudinal interplay among child maltreatment, community violence, and children's symptomatology. *Development and Psychopathology, 10,* 235–257.

Lynn, R., and Hampson, S. L. (1986). The rise of national intelligence: Evidence from Britain, Japan and the USA. *Personality and Individual Differences, 7,* 323–332.

Lyon, G. R. (1995). Toward a definition of dyslexia. *Annals of Dyslexia, 45,* 20–45.

Lyons-Ruth, K., Easterbrooks, M. A., & Cibelli, C. D. (1997). Infant attachment strategies, infant mental lag, and maternal depressive symptoms: Predictors of internalizing and externalizing problems at age 7. *Developmental Psychology, 33,* 681–692.

Mabbott, D. J., & Bisanz, J. (2003). Developmental change and individual differences in children's multiplication. *Child Development, 74,* 1091–1107.

MacBrayer, E. K., Milich, R., & Hundley, M. (2003). Attributional biases in aggressive children and their mothers. *Journal of Abnormal Psychology, 112,* 698–708.

Macchi Cassia, V., Turati, C., & Simion, F. (2004). Can a nonspecific bias toward top-heavy patterns explain newborns' face preference? *Psychological Science, 15*(6), 379–383.

Maccoby, E. E. (1998). *The two sexes: Growing up apart, coming together.* Cambridge, MA: Harvard University Press.

Maccoby, E. E. (2000). Perspectives on gender development. *International Journal of Behavioral Development, 24,* 398–496.

Maccoby, E. E. (2002). Gender and group process: A developmental perspective. *Current Directions, 11,* 54–58.

Maccoby, E. E., Buchanan, C. M., Mnookin, R. H., & Dornbusch, S. M. (1993). Postdivorce roles of mothers and fathers in the lives of their children. *Journal of Family Psychology, 7,* 24–38.

Maccoby, E. E., & Jacklin, C. N. (1987). Gender segregation in childhood. In W. R. Hayne (Ed.), *Advances in child development and behavior* (Vol. 20, pp. 239–287). Orlando FL: Academic Press.

Maccoby, E. E., & Martin, J. A. (1983). Socialization in the context of the family: Parent-child interaction. In P. H. Mussen (Ed.) & E. M. Hetherington (Vol. Ed.), *Handbook of child psychology. Vol 4. Socialization, personality, and social development* (pp. 1–101). New York: Wiley.

MacDonald, W. G., & Cornwall, A. (1995). The relationship between phonological awareness and reading and spelling achievement eleven years later. *Journal of Learning Disabilities, 28,* 523–527.

MacDonald, K., & Parke, R. D. (1984). Bridging the gap: Parent-child play interaction and peer interactive competence. *Child Development, 55,* 1265–1277.

MacFarlane, A. (1975). Olfaction in the development of social preferences in the human neonate. *Parent–infant interaction* (CIBA Foundation Symposium, No. 33, pp. 103–117). Amsterdam: Elsevier.

MacKinnon-Lewis, C., Starnes, R., Volling, B., & Johnson, S. (1997). Perceptions of parenting as predictors of boys' sibling and peer relations. *Developmental Psychology, 33,* 1024–1031.

Maclean, M., Bryant, P., & Bradley, L. (1987). Rhymes, nursery rhymes and reading in early childhood. *Merrill-Palmer Quarterly, 33,* 255–281.

Macmillan, R., McMorris, B. J., & Kruttschnitt, C. (2004). Linked lives: Stability and change in maternal circumstances and trajectories of antisocial behavior in children. *Child Development, 75,* 205–220.

McMurray, B. (2007). Defusing the childhood vocabulary explosion. *Science, 317,* 5838.

MacPhee, D., Fritz, J., & Miller-Heyl, J. (1996). Ethnic variations in personal social networks and parenting. *Child Development, 67,* 3278–3295.

Madigan, S., Moran, G., & Pederson, D. R. (2006). Unresolved states of mind, disorganized attachment relationships, and disrupted interactions of adolescent mothers and their infants. *Developmental Psychology, 42,* 293–304.

Madigan, S., Moran, G., Schuengel, C., Pederson, D. R., & Otten, R. (2007). Unresolved maternal attachment representations, disrupted maternal behavior and disorganized attachment in infancy: Links to toddler behavior problems. *Journal of Child Psychology and Psychiatry, 48,* 1042–1050.

Madole, K. L., & Oakes, L. M. (1999). Making sense of infant categorization: Stable processes and changing representations. *Developmental Review, 19,* 263–296.

Maes, H. H., Silberg, J. L., Neale, M. C., & Eaves, L. J. (2007). Genetic and cultural transmission of antisocial behavior: An extended twin parent model. *Twin Research and Human Genetics, 10,* 136–150.

Magai, C., Hunziker, J., Mesias, W., & Culver, L. C. (2000). Adult attachment styles and emotional biases. *International Journal of Behavioral Development, 24,* 301–309.

Maguire, M. C., & Dunn, J. (1997). Friendships in early childhood and social understanding. *International Journal of Behavioral Development, 21,* 669–686.

Mahler, M. S., Pine, F., & Bergman, A. (1975). *The psychological birth of the human infant: Symbiosis and individuation.* New York: Basic Books.

Mahoney, J. L. (2000). School extracurricular activity participation as a moderator in the development of antisocial patterns. *Child Development, 71,* 502–516.

Main, M. (2000). The organized categories of infant, child, and adult attachment: Flexible vs. inflexible attention under attachment-related stress. *Journal of the American Psychoanalytic Association, 4,* 1055–1096.

Main, M., & George, C. (1985). Responses of abused and disadvantaged toddlers to distress in agemates: A study in the day care setting. *Developmental Psychology, 21,* 407–412.

Main, M., Kaplan, N., & Cassidy, J. (1985). Security infancy, childhood and adulthood: A move to the level of representation. *Monographs of the Society for Research in Child Development, 50*(1–2, Serial No. 209).

Main, M., & Solomon, J. (1990). Procedures for identifying infants as disorganized/disoriented during the Ainsworth Strange Situation. In M. T. Greenberg, D. Cicchetti, & E. M. Cummings (Eds.), *Attachment in the preschool years* (pp. 121–160). Chicago: University of Chicago Press.

Maldonado-Duran, J. M. (2000). A new perspective on failure to thrive. *Bulletin of Zero to Three, 21,* 14.

Malina, R. M. (1975). *Growth and development: The first twenty years in man.* Minneapolis: Burgess Publishing.

Malina, R. M., & Bouchard, C. (1991). *Growth, maturation and physical activity.* Champaign, IL: Human Kinetics Academic.

Malone, P. S., Lansford, J. E., Castellino, D. R., Berlin, L. J., Dodge, K. A., Bates, J. E., & Pettit, G. S. (2004). Divorce and child behavior problems: Applying latent change score models to life event data. *Structural Equation Modeling, 11*(3), 401–423.

Maltz, D. N., & Borker, R. (1982). A cultural approach to male-female miscommunication. In J. J. Gumperz (Ed.), *Language and social identity* (pp. 195–216). Cambridge, UK: Cambridge University Press.

Mandel, D. R., Jusczyk, P. W., & Pisoni, D. B. (1995). Infants' recognition of the sound patterns of their own names. *Psychological Science, 6,* 315–318.

Mandler, J. M., & McDonough, L. (1998). Studies in inductive inference in infancy. *Cognitive Psychology, 37,* 60–96.

Mangelsdorf, S. C., Shapiro, J. R., & Marzolf, D. (1995). Developmental and temperamental differences in emotion regulation in infancy. *Child Development, 66,* 1817–1828.

Manis, F. R., Seidenberg, M. S., Doi, L. M., McBride-Chang, C., & Peterson, A. (1996). On the bases of two subtypes of developmental dyslexia. *Cognition, 58,* 157–195.

Maratsos, M. (1998). The acquisition of grammar. In D. Kuhn & R. S. Siegler (Eds.), *Handbook of child psychology: Vol. 2. Cognition, perception, and language* (5th ed., pp. 421–466). New York: Wiley.

Marcia, J. E. (1980). Identity in adolescence. In J. Adelson (Ed.), *Handbook of adolescent psychology* (pp. 159–187). New York: Wiley.

Marcia, J. E., & Friedman, M. L. (1970). Ego identity status in college women. *Journal of Personality, 38,* 249–263.

Marcus, D. E., & Overton, W. F. (1978). The development of cognitive gender constancy and sex role preferences. *Child Development, 49,* 434–444.

Marcus, G. F. (1996). Why do children say "breaked"? *Current Directions in Psychological Science, 5,* 81–85.

Marcus. G. F. (2004). *The birth of the mind.* New York: Basic Books.

Marcus, G. F., & Fisher, S. E. (2003). FOXP2 in focus: What can genes tell us about speech and language? *Trends in Cognitive Sciences, 7,* 257–262.

Marcus, G. F., Pinker, S., Ullman, M., Hollander, M., Rosen, T. J., & Zu, F. (1992). Overregularization in language acquisition. *Monographs of the Society for Research in Child Development, 57*(4, Serial No. 228).

Margolin, G., Gordis, E. B., & John, R. S. (2001). Coparenting: A link between marital conflict and parenting in two-parent families. *Journal of Family Psychology, 15,* 3–21.

Mark, M. A., & Greer, J. E. (1995). The VCR tutor: Effective instruction for device operation. *Journal of the Learning Sciences, 4,* 209–246.

Markman, E. M. (1989). *Categorization and naming in children.* Cambridge, MA: The MIT Press.

Markman, E. M., & Hutchinson, J. E. (1984). Children's sensitivity to constraints on word meaning: Taxonomic vs. thematic relations. *Cognitive Psychology, 16,* 1–27.

Markman, E. M., & Wachtel, G. A. (1988). Children's use of mutual exclusivity to constrain the meanings of words. *Cognitive Psychology, 20,* 121–157.

Markus, H. R., & Kitayama, S. (1991). Culture and the self: Implications for cognition, emotion, and motivation. *Psychological Review, 98,* 224–253.

Marler, P. (1970). Birdsong and speech development: Could there be parallels? *American Scientist, 58,* 669–673.

Marlier, L., & Schaal, B. (2005). Human newborns prefer human milk: Conspecific milk odor is attractive without postnatal exposure. *Child Development, 76(1),* 155–168.

Marlier, L., Schaal, B., & Soussignon, R. (1998). Neonatal responsiveness to the odor of amniotic and lacteal fluids: A test of perinatal chemosensory continuity. *Child Development, 69,* 611–623.

Marsh, H. W., Craven, R., & Debus, R. (1998). Structure, stability, and development of young children's self-concepts: A multicohort-multioccasion study. *Child Development, 69,* 1030–1053.

Marsiglio, W., Amato, P., Day, R. D., & Lamb, M. (2000). Scholarship on fatherhood in the 1990s and beyond. *Journal of Marriage and the Family, 62,* 1173–1191.

Martin, C. L. (1993). New directions of investigating children's gender knowledge. *Developmental Review, 13,* 184–204.

Martin, C. L., Eisenbud, L., & Rose, H. (1995). Children's gender-based reasoning about toys. *Child Development, 66,* 1453–1471.

Martin, C. L., & Fabes, R. A. (2001). The stability and consequences of young children's same-sex peer interactions. *Developmental Psychology, 37,* 431–446.

Martin, C. L., Fabes, R. A., Evans, S. M., & Wyman, H. (1999). Social cognition on the playground: Children's beliefs about playing with girls versus boys and their relation to sex segregated play. *Journal of Social & Personal Relationships, 16,* 751–771.

Martin, C. L., & Halverson, C. (1981). A schematic processing model of sex typing and stereotyping in children. *Child Development, 52,* 1119–1134.

Martin, C. L., & Halverson, C. (1983). The effects of sex typing schemas on young children's memory. *Child Development, 54,* 563–574.

Martin, C. L., Ruble, D. N., & Szkrybalo, J. (2002). Cognitive theories of early gender development. *Psychological Bulletin, 128,* 903–933.

Martin, J. L., & Ross, H. S. (2005). Sibling aggression: Sex differences and parents' reactions. *International Journal of Behavioral Development, 29,* 129–138.

Martin, J. H., Choy, M., Pullman, S., & Meng, Z. (2004). Corticospinal system development depends on motor experience. *Journal of Neuroscience, 24,* 2122–2132.

Masataka, N. (1992). Motherese in a signed language. *Infant Behavior and Development, 15,* 453–460.

Mascolo, M. F., Fischer, K. W., & Li, J. (2003). Dynamic development of component systems of emotions: Pride, shame, and guilt in China and the United States. In R. J. Davidson, K. R. Scherer, & H. H. Goldsmith (Eds.), *Handbook of affective sciences* (pp. 375–408). Oxford, UK: Oxford University Press.

Mason, M. G., & Gibbs, J. C. (1993). Social perspective taking and moral judgment among college students. *Journal of Adolescent Research, 8,* 109–123.

Masten, A. S. (2007). Resilience in developing systems: Progress and promise as the fourth wave rises. *Development and Psychopathology, 19,* 921–930.

Masten, A., Best, K., & Garmezy, N. (1990). Resilience and development: Contributions from the study of children who overcame adversity. *Development and Psychopathology, 2,* 425–444.

Masten, A. S., Sesma, A., Si-Asar, R., Lawrence, C., Miliotis, D., & Dionne, J. A. (1997). Educational risks for children experiencing homelessness. *Journal of School Psychology, 35,* 27–46.

Masters, M. S., & Sanders, B. (1993). Is the gender difference in mental rotation disappearing? *Behavior Genetics, 23,* 337–341.

Masur, E. (1982). Mothers' responses to infants' object-related gestures: Influences on lexical development. *Journal of Child Language, 9,* 23–30.

Maszk, P., Eisenberg, N., & Guthrie, I. K. (1999). Relations of children's social status to their emotionality and regulation: A short-term longitudinal study. *Merrill-Palmer Quarterly, 45,* 468–492.

Maternal and Child Health Bureau (2002). *Child Health USA 2002.* www.mchb.hrsa.gov.

Matheny, A. P., Jr. (1990). Developmental behavior genetics: Contributions from the Louisville Twin Study. In M. E. Hahn, J. K. Hewitt, N. D. Henderson, & R. H. Benno (Eds.), *Developmental behavior genetics: Neural, biometrical, and evolutionary approaches* (pp. 25–39). New York: Oxford University Press.

Matsumoto, D. (1996). *Unmasking Japan.* Stanford, CA: Stanford University Press.

Matthews, G., Zeidner, M., & Roberts, R. D. (2002). *Emotional intelligence: Science & myth.* Cambridge, MA: The MIT Press.

Mattson, S. N., Riley, E. P., Delis, D. C., & Jones, K. L. (1998). Neuropsychological comparison of alcohol-exposed children with or without physical features of fetal alcohol syndrome. *Neuropsychology, 12,* 146–153.

Maurer, D. (1985). Infant's perception of facedness. In T. M. Field & N. A. Fox (Eds.), *Social perception in infants.* Norwood, NJ: Ablex.

Maurer, D., & Lewis, T. L. (2001). Visual acuity: the role of visual input in inducing postnatal change. *Clinical Neuroscience Research, 1,* 239–247.

Maurer, D., Lewis, T. L., Brent, H. P., & Levin, A. V. (1999). Rapid improvement in the acuity of infants after visual input. *Science, 286,* 108–110.

Maurer, D., & Maurer, C. (1988). *The world of the newborn.* New York: Basic Books.

Maurer, D., & Mondloch, C. (2004). Neonatal synesthesia: A re-evaluation. In L. Robertson & N. Sagiv (Eds.), *Attention on synesthesia: Cognition, development and neuroscience* (pp. 193–213). New York: Oxford University Press.

Maurer, D., & Salapatek, P. (1976). Developmental changes in the scanning of faces by young infants. *Child Development, 47,* 523–527.

Mayberry, M. L., & Espelage, D. L. (2007). Associations among empathy, social competence, and reactive/proactive aggression subtypes. *Journal of Youth & Adolescence, 36*, 787–798.

Mayer-Smith, J., Pedretti, E., & Woodrow, J. (2000). Closing of the gender gap in technology-enriched science education: A case study. *Computers and Education, 35*, 51–63.

Mayeux, L., & Cillessen, A. H. N. (2008). It's not just being popular, it's knowing it too: The role of status in associations between peer status and aggression. *Social Development, 17*, 879–888.

McBride-Chang, C. (2004). *Children's literacy development. Texts in Developmental Psychology*. P. Smith, (Series Ed.). New York: Oxford University Press.

McCabe, A., & Peterson, C. (1991). Getting the story: A longitudinal study of parental styles in eliciting narratives and developing narrative skill. In A. McCabe & C. Peterson (Eds.), *Developing narrative structure* (pp. 217–253). Hillsdale, NJ: Erlbaum.

McCabe, K. M., Hough, R., Wood, P. A., & Yeh, M. (2001). Childhood and adolescent onset conduct disorder: A test of the developmental taxonomy. *Journal of Abnormal Child Psychology, 29*, 305–316.

McCabe, K. M., Rodgers, C., Yeh, M., Hough, R. (2004). Gender differences in childhood onset conduct disorder. *Development and Psychopathology, 16*, 179–192.

McCall, R. B., & Carriger, M. S. (1993). A meta-analysis of infant habituation and recognition memory performance as predictors of later IQ. *Child Development, 64*, 57–79.

McCarton, C. M., Brooks-Gunn, J., Wallace, I. F., & Bauer, C. R. (1997). Results at age 8 years of intervention for low-birth-weight premature infants: The infant health and development program. *Journal of the American Medical Association, 277*, 126–132.

McCarty, C. A., & McMahon, R. J. (2003). Mediators of the relation between maternal depressive symptoms and child internalizing and disruptive behavior disorders. *Journal of Family Psychology, 17*, 545–556.

McClelland, M. M., Cameron, C. E., Connor, C. M., Farris, C. L., Jewkes, A. M., Morrison, F. J. (2007). Links between behavioral regulation and preschoolers' literacy, vocabulary, and math skills. *Developmental Psychology, 43*, 947–959.

McClintock, M. K., & Herdt, G. (1996). Rethinking puberty: The development of sexual attraction. *Current Directions, 5*, 178–183.

McCloskey, M. (2007). Quantitative literacy and developmental dyscalculias. In D. B. Berch & M. M. M. Mazzocco (Eds.), *Why is math so hard for some children? The nature and origins of mathematical learning difficulties and disabilities* (pp. 415–429). New York: Plenum.

McCloskey, L. A., & Stuewig, J. (2001). The quality of peer relationships among children exposed to family violence. *Development and Psychopathology, 13*, 83–96.

McClure, E. B. (2000). A meta-analytic review of sex differences in facial expression processing and their development in infants, children, and adolescents. *Psychological Bulletin, 126*, 424–453.

McCormick, M. C., Brooks-Gunn, J., et al. (2006). Early intervention in low-birth-weight premature infants: Results at 18 years of age for the Infant Health and Development Program. *Pediatrics, 117*, 771–780.

McCrae, R. R., Costa, P. T., Jr., Ostendorf, F., Angleitner, A., Hrebickova, M., Avia, M. D., et al. (2000). Nature over nurture: Temperament, personality, and life-span development. *Journal of Personality and Social Psychology, 78*, 173–186.

McDonald, K. L., Putallaz, M., Grimes, C., Kupersmidt, J. B., & Coie, J D. (2007). Girl talk: Gossip, friendship, and sociometric status. *Merrill-Palmer Quarterly. Special Issue: Gender and Friendships, 53*, 381–411.

McDougall, P., & Hymel, S. (2007). Same-gender versus cross-gender friendship conceptions. *Merrill-Palmer Quarterly, 53*, 347–380.

McDowell, D. J., & Parke, R. D. (2000). Differential knowledge of display rules for positive and negative emotions: Influences from parents, influences on peers. *Social Development, 9*, 415–432.

McDowell, D. J., & Parke, R. D. (2009). Parental correlates of children's peer relations: An empirical test of the tripartite model. *Developmental Psychology, 45*(1), 224–235.

McEwen, B. S., & Schmeck, H. M. (1994). *The hostage brain*. New York: Rockefeller University Press.

McFadyen-Ketchum, S. A., Bates, J. E., Dodge, K. A., & Pettit, G. S. (1996). Patterns of change in early childhood aggressive-disruptive behavior: Gender differences in predictions from early coercive and affectionate mother-child interactions. *Child Development, 67*, 2417–2433.

McGhee, P. E., & Frueh, T. (1980). Television viewing and the learning of sex-role stereotypes. *Sex Roles, 6*, 179–188.

McGrath, E. P., & Repetti, R. L. (2002). A longitudinal study of children's depressive symptoms, self-perceptions, and cognitive distortions about the self. *Journal of Abnormal Psychology, 111*, 77–87.

McGraw, M. B. (1943). *Neuromuscular maturation of the human infant*. New York: Hafner.

McGue, M., Bouchard, T. J., Jr., Iacono, W. G., & Lykken, D. T. (1993). Behavioral genetics of cognitive ability: A life-span perspective. In R. Plomin & G. E. McClearn (Eds.), *Nature, nurture, and psychology* (pp. 59–76). Washington, DC: American Psychological Association.

McGue, M., & Lykken, D. T. (1992). Genetic influence on risk of divorce. *Psychological Science, 3*, 368–373.

McGue, M., Sharma, A., & Benson, P. (1996). Parent and sibling influences on adolescent alcohol use and misuse: Evidence in a U.S. adoption cohort. *Journal of Studies on Alcohol, 57*, 8–18.

McGuigan, F., & Salmon, K. (2004). The time to talk: The influence of the timing of adult-child talk on children's event memory. *Child Development, 75*, 669–686.

McGuire, S. (2003). The heritability of parenting. *Parenting: Science and Practice, 3*, 73–94.

McGuire, S., McHale, S. M., & Updegraff, K. (1996). Children's perceptions of the sibling relationship in middle childhood: Connections within and between family relationships. *Personal Relationships, 3*, 229–239.

McGuire, S., Neiderhiser, J. M., Reiss, D., Hetherington, E. M., & Plomin, R. (1994). Genetic and environmental influences on perceptions of self-worth and competence in adolescence: A study of twins, full siblings, and step-siblings. *Child Development, 65*, 785–799.

McHale, J. P., Kazali, C., Rotman, T., Talbot, J., Carleton, M., & Lieberson, R. (2004). The transition to coparenthood: Parents' prebirth expectations and early coparental adjustment at 3 months postpartum. *Development and Psychopathology, 16*, 711–733.

McHale, S., Crouter, A. C., Kim, J-Y., Burton, L. M., Davis, K. D., Dotterer, A. M., & Swanson, D. P. (2006). Mothers' and fathers' racial socialization in African American families: Implications for youth. *Child Development, 77,* 1387–1402.

McHale, S. M., Crouter, A. C., McGuire, S. A., & Updegraff, K. A. (1995). Congruence between mothers' and fathers' differential treatment of siblings: Links with family relations and children's well being. *Child Development, 66,* 116–128.

McHale, S. M., Updegraff, K. A., Jackson-Newsom, J., Tucker, C. E., & Crouter, A. C. (2000). When does parents' differential treatment have negative implications for siblings? *Social Development, 9,* 149–172.

McHale, S. M., Updegraff, K. A., Shanahan, L., Crouter, A. C., & Killoren, S. E. (2005). Gender, culture, and family dynamics: Differential treatment of siblings in Mexican American families. *Journal of Marriage and the Family, 67,* 1259–1274.

McHale, S. M., Whiteman, S. D., Kim, J-Y., & Crouter, A. C. (2007). Characteristics and correlates of sibling relationships in two-parent African American families. *Journal of Family Psychology, 21,* 227–235.

McKey, R. H., Condelli, L., Ganson, H., Barrett, B. J., McConkey, C., & Plantz, M. C. (1985). *The impact of Head Start on children, families, and communities.* Washington, DC: U.S. Government Printing Office.

McLean, J. F., & Hitch, G. J. (1999). Working memory impairments in children with specific arithmetic learning disabilities. *Journal of Experimental Child Psychology, 74,* 240–260.

McLean, K. C., & Pratt, M. W. (2006). Life's little (and big) lesions: Identity statuses and meaning-making in the turning point narratives of emerging adults. *Developmental Psychology, 42,* 714–722.

McLoughlin, C. S. (2005). The coming-of-age of China's single-child policy. *Psychology in the Schools, 42,* 305–313.

McLoyd, V. C. (1998). Children in poverty: Development, public policy, and practice. In W. Damon (Series Ed.) & I. E. Sigel & K. A. Renninger (Vol. Eds.), *Handbook of child psychology: Vol. 4. Child psychology in practice* (5th ed., pp. 135–208), New York: Wiley.

McLoyd, V. C., Jayaratne, T. E., Ceballo, R., & Borquez, J. (1994). Unemployment and work interruption among African American single mothers: Effects on parenting and adolescent socioemotional functioning. *Child Development, 65,* 562–589.

McLoyd, V. C., Kaplan, R., Hardaway, C. R., & Wood, D. A. (2007). Does endorsement of physical discipline matter? Assessing moderating influences on the maternal and child psychological correlates of physical discipline in African American families. *Journal of Family Psychology, 21(2),* 165–175.

McMahon, A. W., Iskander, J. K., Haber, P., Braun, M. M., & Ball, R. (2008). Inactivated influenza vaccine (IIV) in children less than 2 years of age: Examination of selected adverse events reported to the Vaccine Adverse Event Reporting System (VAERS) after thimerosal-free or thimerosal-containing vaccine. *Vaccine, 26,* 427–429.

McMaster, L. E., Connolly, J., Pepler, D., & Craig, W. M. (2002). Peer to peer sexual harassment in early adolescence: A developmental perspective. *Development and Psychopathology, 14,* 91–105.

McNeil, N. M. (2008). Limitations to teaching children 2 + 2 = 4: Typical arithmetic problems can hinder learning of mathematical equivalence. *Child Development, 79,* 1524–1537.

McNeil, N. M., & Alibali, M. W. (2005). Knowledge change as a function of mathematics experience: All contexts are not created equal. *Journal of Cognition and Development, 6,* 285–306.

Mcquaid, N., Bigelow, A. E., Mclaughlin, J., & MacLean, K. (2007). Maternal mental state language and preschool children's attachment security: Relation to children's mental state language and expessions of emotional understanding. *Social Development, 17,* 61–83.

Meeus, W., Iedema, J., Helsen, M., & Vollebergh, W. (1999). Patterns of adolescent identity development: Review of literature and longitudinal analyses. *Developmental Review, 19,* 419–461.

Mehler, J., Jusczyk, P., Lambertz, G., Halsted, N., Bertoncini, J., & Amiel-Tison, C. (1988). A precursor of language acquisition in young infants. *Cognition, 29,* 143–178.

Meilman, P., Leichliter, J. S., & Presley, C. A. (1999). Greeks and athletes: Who drinks more? *Journal of American College Health, 47,* 187–190.

Meisels, S. J., & Plunkett, J. W. (1988). Developmental consequences of preterm birth: Are there long-term effects? In P. B. Baltes, D. L. Featherman, & R. M. Lerner (Eds.), *Life-span development and behavior* (Vol. 9). Hillsdale, NJ: Erlbaum.

Meltzoff, A. N. (1988a). Imitation of televised models by infants. *Child Development, 59,* 1221–1229.

Meltzoff, A. N. (1988b). Infant imitation and memory: Nine-month-olds in immediate and deferred tests. *Child Development, 59,* 217–225.

Meltzoff, A. N. (1995a). Apprehending the intentions of others: Re-enactment of intended acts by 10-month-old children. *Developmental Psychology, 31,* 838–850.

Meltzoff, A. N. (1995b). What infant memory tells us about infantile amnesia: Long-term recall and deferred imitation. *Journal of Experimental Child Psychology, 59,* 497–515.

Meltzoff, A. N., & Borton, R. W. (1979). Intermodal matching by human neonates. *Nature, 282,* 403–404.

Meltzoff, A. N., & Moore, M. K. (1977). Imitation of facial and manual gestures by human neonates. *Science, 198,* 75–78.

Meltzoff, A. N., & Moore, M. K. (1983). Newborn infants imitate adult facial gestures. *Child Development, 54,* 702–709.

Meltzoff, A. N., & Moore, M. K. (1994). Imitation, memory, and the representation of persons. *Infant Behavior and Development, 17,* 83–99.

Meltzoff, A. N., & Moore, M. K. (2000). Resolving the debate about early imitation. In D. Muir & A. Slater (Eds.), *Infant development: The essential readings* (pp. 176-181). Boston, MA: Blackwell Science.

Menaghan, E. G., & Parcel, T. L. (1995). Social sources of change in children's home environments: The effects of parental occupational experiences and family conditions. *Journal of Marriage and the Family, 57,* 69–84.

Menella, J. A., & Beauchamp, G. K. (1993a). Beer, breast feeding, and folklore. *Developmental Psychobiology, 26,* 459–466.

Menella, J. A., & Beauchamp, G. K. (1993b). The effects of repeated exposure to garlic-flavored milk on the nursling's behavior. *Pediatric Research, 34,* 805–808.

Menella, J. A., & Beauchamp, G. K. (1996). The human infant's response to vanilla flavor in mother's milk and formula. *Infant Behavior and Development, 19,* 13–19.

Mennella, J. A., Jagnow, C. P., & Beauchamp, G. K. (2001). Prenatal and postnatal flavor learning by human infants. *Pediatrics, 107,* e88.

Mennella, J. A., Johnson, A., & Beauchamp, G. K. (1995). Garlic ingestion by pregnant women alters the odor of amniotic fluid. *Chemical Senses, 20,* 207–209.

Mereu, G., Fà, M., Ferraro, L., Cagiano, R., Antonelli, T., Tattoli, M., Ghiglieri, V., Tanganelli, S., Gessa, G. L., & Cuomo, V. (2003). Prenatal exposure to a cannabinoid agonist produces memory deficits linked to dysfunction in hippocampal long-term potentiation and glutamate release. *Proceedings of the National Academy of Sciences, 100,* 4915–4920.

Merton, D. E. (1997). The meaning of meanness: Popularity, competition, and conflict among junior high school girls. *Sociology of Education, 70,* 175–191.

Mervis, C. B. (1987). Child-basic object categories and early lexical development. In U. Neisser (Ed.), *Concepts and conceptual development: Ecological and intellectual factors in categorization.* Cambridge, UK: Cambridge University Press.

Mervis, C. B., Robinson, B. F., Bertrand, J., Morris, C. A., Klein-Tasman, B. P., & Armstrong, S. C. (2000). The Williams Syndrome cognitive profile. *Brain & Cognition, 44,* 604–628.

Messner, M. A. (1998). Boyhood, organized sports, and the construction of masculinities. In M.A. Messner (Ed.), *Men's lives* (pp. 109–121). Boston, MA: Allyn & Bacon.

Mesquita, B., & Frijda, N. H. (1992). Cultural variations in emotions: A review. *Psychological Bulletin, 112,* 179–204.

Metz, E., & Youniss, J. (2003). A demonstration that school-based required service does not deter, but heightens, volunteerism. *Political Science and Politics, 36,* 281–286.

Michalik, N. M., Eisenberg, N., Spinrad, T. L., Ladd, B., Thompson, M., & Valiente, C. (2007). Longitudinal relations among parental emotional expressivity and sympathy and prosocial behavior in adolescence. *Social Development, 16,* 286–309.

Michalson, L., & Lewis, M. (1985). What do children know about emotions and when do they know it. In M. Lewis & C. Saarni (Eds.), *The socialization of emotions* (pp. 117–139). New York: Plenum.

Miell, D. (2000). Children's creative collaborations: The importance of friendship when working together on a musical composition. *Social Development, 9,* 348–369.

Milberger, S., Biederman, J., Faraone, S. V., Guite, J., & Tsuang, M. T. (1997). Pregnancy, delivery, and infancy complications and attention deficit hyperactivity disorder: Issues of gene-environment interaction. *Biological Psychiatry, 41,* 65–75.

Miles, D. R., & Carey, G. (1997). Genetic and environmental architecture of human aggression. *Journal of Personality and Social Psychology, 72,* 207–217.

Milewski, A. E. (1976). Infants' discrimination of internal and external pattern elements. *Journal of Experimental Child Psychology, 22,* 229–246.

Millar, W. S. (1990). Span of integration for delayed-reward contingency learning in 6- to 8-month-old infants. In A. Diamond (Ed.), *The development and neural bases of higher cognitive functions* (pp. 239–259). New York: New York Academy of Sciences.

Miller, B. C., Benson, B., & Galbraith, K. A. (2001). Family relationships and adolescent pregnancy risk: A research synthesis. *Developmental Review, 21,* 1–38.

Miller, C. L., Miceli, P. J., Whitman, T. L., & Borkowski, J. G. (1996). Cognitive readiness to parent and intellectual-emotional development in children of adolescent mothers. *Developmental Psychology, 32,* 533–541.

Miller, G. A., & Gildea, P. M. (1987). *How* children learn words. *Scientific American, 257*(3).

Miller, J. G., & Bersoff, D. M. (1992). Culture and moral judgment: How are conflicts between justice and interpersonal responsibilities resolved? *Journal of Personality and Social Psychology, 62,* 541–554.

Miller, J. G., & Bersoff, D. M. (1995). Development in the context of everyday family relationships: Culture, interpersonal morality, and adaptation. In M. Killen & D. Hart (Eds.), *Morality in everyday life: Developmental perspectives* (pp. 259–282). Cambridge, UK: Cambridge University Press.

Miller, J. G., Bersoff, D. M., & Harwood, R. L. (1990). Perceptions of social responsibilities in India and in the United States: Moral imperatives or personal decisions? *Journal of Personality and Social Psychology, 58,* 33–47.

Miller, K. (1984). Child as the measurer of all things: Measurement of procedures and the development of quantitative concepts. In C. Sophian (Ed.), *Origins of cognitive skills: The eighteenth annual Carnegie symposium on cognition* (pp. 193–228). Hillsdale, NJ: Erlbaum.

Miller, K. (1989). Measurement as a tool for thought: The role of measuring procedures in children's understanding of quantitative invariance. *Developmental Psychology, 25,* 589–600.

Miller, K. F., Smith, C. M., Zhu, J., & Zhang, H. (1995). Preschool origins of cross-national differences in mathematical competence: The role of number-naming systems. *Psychological Science, 6,* 56–60.

Miller, L. C., Putcha-Bhagavatula, A., & Pedersen, W. C. (2002). Men's and women's mating preferences: Distinct evolutionary mechanisms? *Psychological Science, 11,* 88–93.

Miller, P. A., Eisenberg, N., Fabes, R. A., & Shell, R. (1989). Socialization of empathic and sympathetic responding. In N. Eisenberg (Ed.), *The development of empathy and related vicarious responses. New Directions in Child Development* (pp. 65–83). San Francisco: Jossey-Bass.

Miller, P. H. (2000). How best to utilize a deficiency. *Child Development, 71,* 1013–1017.

Miller, P. H. (2002). *Theories of developmental psychology* (4th ed.). New York: Worth.

Miller, P. H., & Coyle, T. R. (1999). Developmental change: Lessons from microgenesis. In E. K. Scholnick, K. Nelson, S. A. Gelman, & P. H. Miller (Eds.), *Conceptual development: Piaget's legacy* (pp. 209–239). Mahwah, NJ: Erlbaum.

Miller, P. H., & Seier, W. L. (1994). Strategy utilization deficiencies in children: When, where, and why. In H. W. Reese (Ed.), *Advances in child development and behavior* (*Vol. 25,* pp. 108–156). New York: Academic Press.

Miller, P. J., & Sperry, L. L. (1987). The socialization of anger and aggression. *Merrill-Palmer Quarterly, 33,* 1–31.

Miller, P. J., & Sperry, L. L. (1988). Early talk about the past: The origins of conversational stories of personal experience. *Journal of Child Language, 15,* 293–315.

Miller, P. M., Danaher, D. L. & Forbes, D. (1986). Sex-related strategies for coping with interpersonal conflict in children aged five and seven. *Developmental Psychology, 22,* 543–548.

Miller-Johnson, S., Winn, D-M. C., Coie, J. D., & Lochman, J. (2004). Risk factors for adolescent pregnancy reports among African American males. *Journal of Research on Adolescence, 14,* 471–495.

Mills, C. M., & Keil, F. C. (2004). Knowing the limits of one's understanding: The development of an awareness of an illusion of explanatory depth. *Journal of Experimental Child Psychology, 87,* 1–32.

Mills, D. L., Coffey-Corina, S., & Neville, H. J. (1997). Language comprehension and cerebral specialization from 13 to 20 months. *Developmental Neuropsychology, 13,* 397–445.

Mills, R. S. L., & Rubin, K. H. (1993). Socialization factors in the development of social withdrawal. In K. H. Rubin & J. Asendorpf (Eds.), *Social withdrawal, inhibition and shyness in childhood* (pp. 117–150). Hillsdale, NJ: Erlbaum.

Minde, K. (1993). Prematurity and illness in infancy: Implications for development and intervention. In C. H. Zeanah Jr. (Ed.), *Handbook of infant development.* New York: Guilford.

Miner, J. L., & Clarke-Stewart, K. A. (2008). Trajectories of externalizing behavior from age 2 to age 9: Relations with gender, temperament, ethnicity, parenting, and rater. *Developmental Psychology, 44,* 771–786.

Mischel, W. (1970). Sex typing and socialization. In P. H. Mussen (Ed.), *Carmichael's handbook of child psychology* (Vol. 2, pp. 3–72). New York: Wiley.

Mischel, W. (1981). Metacognition and the rules of delay. In J. H. Flavell & L. Ross (Eds.), *Social cognitive development* (pp. 240–271). Cambridge, UK: Cambridge University Press.

Mischel, W. (2000, June). *Attention control in the service of the self: Harnessing willpower in goal pursuit.* Paper presented at the Self Workshop, National Institutes of Mental Health, Bethesda, MD.

Mischel, W. & Ayduk, O. (2004). Willpower in a cognitive-affective processing system: The dynamics of delay of gratification. In R. F. Baumeister & K. D. Vohs (Eds.), *Handbook of self-regulation: Research, theory, and applications.* New York: Guilford.

Mischel, W., Shoda, Y., & Peake, P. K. (1988). The nature of adolescent competencies predicted by preschool delay of gratification. *Journal of Personality and Social Psychology, 54,* 687–696.

Mitchell, E. (1985). The dynamics of family interaction around home video games. *Marriage and Family Review, 8,* 121–135.

Mix, K. S., Huttenlocher, J., & Levine, S. C. (2002). *Quantitative development in infancy and early childhood.* Oxford, UK: Oxford University Press.

Mize, J., & Ladd, G. W. (1990). Toward the development of successful skills training for preschool children. In S. R. Asher & J. D. Coie (Eds.), *Peer rejection in childhood* (pp. 338–361). Cambridge, UK: Cambridge University Press.

Mizuta, I., Zahn-Waxler, C., Cole, P. M., & Hiruma, N. (1996). A cross-cultural study of preschoolers' attachment: Security and sensitivity in Japanese and US Dyads. *International Journal of Behavioral Development, 19,* 141–159.

Moffitt, T. E. (1990). Juvenile delinquency and attention deficit disorder: Boys' developmental trajectories from age 3 to age 15. *Child Development, 61,* 893–910.

Moffitt, T. E. (1993a). Adolescence-limited and life-course-persistent antisocial behavior: A developmental taxonomy. *Psychological Review, 100,* 674–701.

Moffitt, T. E. (1993b). The neuropsychology of conduct disorder. *Development and Psychopathology, 5,* 135–151.

Moffitt, T. E., & Caspi, A. (2001). Childhood predictors differentiate life-course persistent and adolescence-limited antisocial pathways among males and females. *Development and Psychopathology, 13,* 135–151.

Moffitt, T. E., Caspi, A., Harrington, H., & Milne, B. J. (2002). Males on the life-course-persistent and adolescence-limited antisocial pathways: Follow-up at age 26 years. *Development and Psychopathology, 14,* 179–207.

Moffitt, T. E., Caspi, A., Harrington, H., Milne, B. J., Melchior, M., Goldberg, D., & Poulton, R. (2007). Generalized anxiety disorder and depression: Childhood risk factors in a birth cohort followed to age 32. *Psychological Medicine, 37,* 441–452.

Molfese, D. L., & Betz, J. (1988). Electrophysiological indices of the early development of lateralization for language and cognition, and their implications for predicting later development. In D. L. Molfese & S. J. Segalowitz (Eds.), *Brain lateralization in children: Developmental implications* (pp. 171–190). New York: Guilford.

Molfese, D. L., & Molfese, V. J. (1994). Short-term and long-term developmental outcomes: The use of behavioral and electrophysiological measures in early infancy as predictors. In G. Dawson & K. W. Fischer (Eds.), *Human behavior and the developing brain* (pp. 493–517). New York: Guilford.

Moncur, L. (2008). Motivational Quotations. Available at http://www.quotationspage.com/collections.html.

Money, J., & Ehrhardt, A. A. (1972). Rearing of a sex-reassigned normal male infant after traumatic loss of the penis. In J. Money & A. A Ehrhardt, *Man and woman/boy and girl: The differentiation and dimorphism of gender identity from conception to maturity* (pp. 46–51). Baltimore, MD: Johns Hopkins University Press.

Moon, C., Cooper, R. P., & Fifer, W. P. (1993). Two-day-olds prefer their native language. *Infant Behavior and Development, 16*(4), 495–500.

Moon, C., & Fifer, W. (1990, April). *Newborns prefer a prenatal version of mother's voice.* Presented at the biannual meeting of the International Society of Infant Studies, Montreal, Canada.

Moon, M., & Hoffman, C. D. (2008). Mothers' and fathers' differential expectancies and behaviors: Parent X child gender effects. *Journal of Genetic Psychology, 164,* 261–279.

Moore, C. (2008). The development of gaze following. *Child Development Perspectives, 2,* 66–70.

Moore, C., & D'Entremont, B. (2001). Developmental changes in pointing as a function of attentional focus. *Journal of Cognition and Development, 2,* 109–129.

Moore, C. F. (2003). *Silent scourge: Children, pollution, and why scientists disagree.* New York: Oxford University Press.

Moore, D. R., & Florsheim, P. (2001). Interpersonal processes and psychopathology among expectant and nonexpectant adolescent couples. *Journal of Consulting and Clinical Psychology, 69,* 101–111.

Moore, K. A., Manlove, J., Glei, D., & Morrison, D. R. (1998). Nonmarital school-age motherhood: Family, individual, and school characteristic. *Journal of Adolescent Research, 13,* 433–457.

Moore, K. L., & Persaud, T. V. N. (1993). *Before we are born* (4th ed.). Philadelphia: Saunders.

Moore, M. R., & Brooks-Gunn, J. (2002). Adolescent parenthood. In M. H. Bornstein (Ed.), Handbook of parenting. *Vol. 3. Biology and ecology of parenting* (2nd ed., pp. 173–214). Mahwah, NJ: Erlbaum.

Morales, J. R., & Guerra, N. G. (2006). Effects of multiple context and cumulative stress on urban children's adjustment in elementary school. *Child Development, 77,* 907–923.

Morelli, G. A., Rogoff, B., Oppenheim, D., & Goldsmith, D. (1992). Cultural variation in infants' sleeping arrangements: Questions of independence. *Developmental Psychology, 28,* 604–613.

Moreno, A. J., Klute, M. M., & Robinson, J. L. (2008). Relational and individual resources as predictors of empathy in early childhood. *Social Development, 17,* 613–637.

Morris, A. S., Silk, J. S., Steinberg, L., Myers, S. S., & Robinson, L. R. (2007). The role of the family context in the development of emotion regulation. *Social Development, 16,* 361–388.

Morris, A. S., Silk, J. S., Steinberg, L., Sessa, F. M., Avenevoli, S., & Essex, M. J. (2002). Temperamental vulnerability and negative parenting as interacting predictors of child adjustment. *Journal of Marriage and Family, 64,* 461–471.

Morrongiello, B. A., Fenwick, K. D., Hillier, L., & Chance, G. (1994). Sound localization in newborn human infants. *Developmental Psychobiology, 27,* 519–538.

Morrow, M. T., Hubbard, J. A., Rubin, R. M., & McAuliffe, M. D. (2008). The relation between childhood aggression and depressive symptoms. *Merrill-Palmer Quarterly, 54,* 316–340.

Moses, L. J., Baldwin, D. A., Rosicky, J. G., & Tidball, G. (2001). Evidence for referential understanding in the emotions domain at twelve and eighteen months. *Child Development, 72,* 655–948.

Moss, E., Cyr, C., & Dubois-Comtois, K. (2004). Attachment at early school age and developmental risk: Examining family contexts and behavior problems of controlling-caregiving, controlling-punitive, and behaviorally disorganized children. *Developmental Psychology, 40,* 519–532.

Mounts, N. S. (2002). Parental management of adolescent peer relationships in context: The role of parenting style. *Journal of Family Psychology, 16,* 58–69.

Mounts, N. S., & Steinberg, L. (1995). An ecological analysis of peer influence on adolescent grade point average and drug use. *Developmental Psychology, 31,* 915–922.

Mrug, S., Hoza, B., & Bukowski, W. M. (2004). Choosing or being chosen by aggressive-disruptive peers: Do they contribute to children's externalizing and internalizing problems? *Journal of Abnormal Child Psychology, 32,* 53–65.

Mueller, S. C., Temple, V., Oh, E., Vanryzin, C., Williams, A., & Cornwell, B. (2008). Early androgen exposure modulates spatial cognition in congenital adrenal hyperplasia (CAH). *Psychoneuroendocrinology, 33,* 973–980.

Muller, C. (1995). Maternal employment, parent involvement, and mathematics achievement among adolescents. *Journal of Marriage and the Family, 57,* 85–100.

Mulvaney, M. K., & Mebert, C. J. (2007). Parental corporal punishment predicts behavior problems in early childhood. *Journal of Family Psychology, 21,* 389–397.

Mumme, D. L., Fernald, A., & Herrera, C. (1996). Infants' responses to facial and vocal emotional signals in a social referencing paradigm. *Child Development, 67,* 3219–3237.

Munakata, Y., McClelland, J. L., Johnson, M. H., & Siegler, R. S. (1997). Rethinking infant knowledge: Toward an adaptive process account of successes and failures in object permanence tasks. *Psychological Review, 104,* 686–713.

Munekata, H., & Ninomiya, K. (1985). Development of prosocial moral judgments. *Japanese Journal of Educational Psychology, 33,* 157–164.

Munn, D., & Dunn, J. (1989). Temperament and the developing relationship between siblings. *International Journal of Behavioral Development, 12,* 433–451.

Munroe, R. H., Shimmin, H. S., & Munroe, R. L. (1984). Gender understanding and sex role preference in four cultures. *Developmental Psychology, 20,* 673–682.

Munson, J. A., McMahon, R. J., & Spieker, S. J. (2001). Structure and variability in the developmental trajectory of children's externalizing problems: Impact of infant attachment, maternal depressive symptomatology, and child sex. *Development and Psychopathology, 13,* 277–296.

Muraskas, J., Hasson, A., & Besinger, R. E. (2004). Girl with a birth weight of 280 g, now 14 years old. *New England Journal of Medicine, 351,* 836–837.

Murnen, S. K., & Smolak, L. (2000). The experience of sexual harassment among grade-school students: Early socialization of female subordination? *Sex Roles, 43,* 1–17.

Murphy, B. C., Eisenberg, N., Fabes, R. A., Shepard, S., & Guthrie, I. K. (1999). Consistency and change in children's emotionality and regulation: A longitudinal study. *Merrill-Palmer Quarterly, 45,* 413–444.

Murphy, S. M., & Faulkner, D. (2006). Gender differences in verbal communication between popular and unpopular children during an interactive task. *Social Development, 15,* 82–108.

Murray, L., & Trevarthen, C. (1985). Emotional regulation of interactions between two-month-olds and their mothers. In T. M. Field & N. A. Fox (Eds.), *Social perception in infants* (pp. 177–197). Norwood, NJ: Ablex.

Myowa-Yamakoshi, M., & Takeghita, H. (2006). Do human fetuses anticipate self-oriented actions? A study by four-dimensional (4D) ultrasonography. *Infancy, 10,* 289–301.

Naigles, L. (1990). Children use syntax to learn verb meanings. *Journal of Child Language, 17,* 357–374.

Naigles, L., & Gelman, S. A. (1995). Overextensions in comprehension and production revisited: Preferential looking in a study of dog, cat, and cow. *Journal of Child Language, 22,* 19–46.

Namy, L. L. (2001). What's in a name when it isn't a word? 17-month-olds' mapping of nonverbal symbols to object categories. *Infancy, 2,* 73–86.

Namy, L. L., & Waxman, S. R. (1998). Words and gestures: Infants' interpretations of different forms of symbolic reference. *Child Development, 69,* 295–308.

Nanez, J., Sr., & Yonas, A. (1994). Effects of luminance and texture motion on infant defensive reactions to optical collision. *Infant Behavior and Development, 17,* 165–174.

Nangle, D. W., Erdley, C. A., Zeff, K. R., Stanchfield, L. L., & Gold, J. A. (2004). Opposites do not attract: Social status and behavioral-style concordances and discordances among children and the peers who like or dislike them. *Journal of Abnormal Child Psychology, 32,* 425–434.

Narusyte, J., Neiderhiser, J. M., D'Onofrio, B. M., Reiss, D., Spotts, E. L., & Ganiban, J. (2008). Testing different types of genotype-environment correlaton: An extended children-of-twins model. *Developmental Psychology, 44,* 1591–1603.

Nathanielsz, P. W. (1994). *A time to be born.* Oxford, UK: Oxford University Press.

Nation, K. (2008). Learning to read words. *The Quarterly Journal of Experimental Psychology, 61,* 1121–1133.

National Association for the Education of Young Children. (1986). Washington, DC: Author.

National Center for Children in Poverty. (May, 2004). Low-income children in the United States. www.nccp.org.

National Center for Health Statistics. (1998). *Health, United States, 1998: With socioeconomic status and health chartbook.* Retrieved from http://www.cdc.gov/nchs/data/hus/hus98.pdf.

National Center for Health Statistics. (1999). *America's children 1999. Part 1. Population and family characteristics.* Retrieved from http://www/childstats.gov/ac1999/poptxt.asp.

National Center for Health Statistics. (2003). Births: Final data for 2002. *National Vital Statistics Reports, 52,* No. 10.

National Center for Health Statistics. (2004). *Prevalence of overweight among children and adolescents: United States, 1999–2002.* Washington, DC: U.S. Department of Health and Human Services.

National Law Center on Homelessness and Poverty (2009). http://www.nlchp.org/hapia.cfm.

National Reading Advisory Panel (2000). *Teaching children to read: An evidence-based assessment of the scientific research literature on reading and its implications for reading instruction.* Washington, DC: National Institute of Child Health and Human Development.

National Research Council. (2001). *Knowing what student know: The science and design of education assessment.* Washington, DC: National Academy Press.

National Science Foundation (2008). *Women, minorities, and persons with disabilities in science and engineering.* Washington, DC: National Science Foundation. Document available online http://www.nsf.gov/statistics/wmpd/start.htm.

Neblett, E. W. Jr., Smalls, C. P., Ford, K. R., Nguyen, H. X., & Sellers, R. M. (2009). Racial socialization and racial identity: African American parents' messages about race as precursors to identity. *Journal of Youth and Adolescence, 38,* 189–203.

Neblett, E. W., Jr., White, R. L., Ford, K. R., Philip, C. L., Nguyen, H. X., & Sellers, R. M. (2008). Patterns of racial socialization and psychological adjustment: Can parental communications about race reduce the impact of racial discrimination? *Journal of Research on Adolescence, 18*(3), 477–515.

Neckerman, H. J. (1996). The stability of social groups in childhood and adolescence: The role of the classroom social environment. *Social Development, 5,* 131–145.

Needham, A. (1997). Factors affecting infants' use of featural information in object segregation. *Current Directions in Psychological Science, 6*(2), 26–33.

Needham, A., & Baillargeon, R. (1993). Intuitions about support in 4.5-month-old infants. *Cognition, 47,* 121–148.

Needham, A., & Baillargeon, R. (1997). Object segregation in 8-month-old infants. *Cognition, 62,* 121–149.

Needham, A., Baillargeon, R., & Kaufman, L. (1997). Object segregation in infancy. In C. Rovee-Collier & L. Lipsitt (Eds.), *Advances in infancy research* (Vol. 11, pp. 1–44). Norwood, NJ: Ablex.

Needham, A., Barrett, T., & Peterman, K. (2002). A pick me up for infants' exploratory skills: Early simulated experiences reaching for objects using "sticky" mittens enhances young infants' object exploration skills. *Infant Behavior and Development, 25,* 279–295.

Neiderhiser, J. M., Pike, A., Hetherington, E. M., & Reiss, D. (1998). Adolescent perceptions as mediators of parenting: Genetic and environmental contributions. *Developmental Psychology, 34,* 1459–1469.

Neiderhiser, J. M., Reiss, D., Pedersen, N. L., Lichtenstein, P., Spotts, E. L., Hansson, K., Cederblad, M., & Elthammer, O. (2004). Genetic and environmental influences on mothering of adolescents: A comparison of two samples. *Developmental Psychology, 40,* 335–351.

Neisser, U. (2004). Memory development: New questions and old. *Developmental Review, 24,* 154–158.

Nelson, A. (2000). The pink dragon is female: Halloween costumes and gender markers. *Psychology of Women Quarterly, 24,* 137–144.

Nelson, C. A. (1987). The recognition of facial expressions in the first two years of life: Mechanisms of development. *Child Development, 58,* 889–909.

Nelson, C.A., de Haan, M., & Thomas, K. M. (2006). *Neuroscience of cognitive development: The role of experience and the developing brain.* Hoboken, NJ: Wiley.

Nelson, C. A., III, Thomas, K. M., & de Haan, M. (2006). Neural bases of cognitive development. In W. Damon & R. M. Lerner (Series Eds.) & D. Kuhn & R. S. Siegler (Vol. Eds.), *Handbook of child psychology: Volume 2: Cognition, perception, and language* (6th ed., pp. 3–57). Hoboken, NJ: Wiley.

Nelson, C. A., III, Zeanah, C. H., Fox, N. A., Marshall, P. J., Smyke, A. T., & Guthrie, D. (2007). Cognitive recovery in socially deprived young children: The Bucharest early intervention project. *Science, 318,* 1937–1940.

Nelson, David A., Hart, Craig H., Yang, Chongming, Olsen, Joseph A., Jin, Shenghua. (2006). Aversive parenting in China: Associations with child physical and relational aggression. *Child Development, 77*(3), 554–572.

Nelson, D. A., Mitchell, C., & Yang, C. (2008). Intent attributions and aggression: A study of children and their parents. *Journal of Abnormal Child Psychology, 36,* 793–806.

Nelson, E. A. S., Schiefenhoevel, W. & Haimerl, F. (2000). Child care practices in nonindustrialized societies. *Pediatrics, 105,* e75.

Nelson, J., & Aboud, F. E. (1985). The resolution of social conflict between friends. *Child Development, 56,* 1009–1017.

Nelson, J. K. (2006). Interference resolution in the left nferior frontal gyrus. *Dissertation Abstracts International: Section B: The Sciences and Engineering, 66,* 5703.

Nelson, J. R., Smith, D. J., & Dodd, J. (1990). The moral reasoning of juvenile delinquents: A meta-analysis. *Journal of Abnormal Child Psychology, 18,* 231–239.

Nelson, K. E. (1973). Structure and strategy in learning to talk. *Monographs of the Society for Research in Child Development, 38*(1–2, Serial No. 149).

Nelson, K. E. (1993). The psychological and social origins of autobiographical memory. *Psychological Science, 4,* 7–14.

Nelson, K. E., Denninger, M. M., Bonvillian, J. D., Kaplan, B. J., & Baker, N. D. (1984). Maternal input adjustments and nonadjustments as related to children's linguistic advances and to language acquisition theories. In A. D. Pellegrini & T. D. Yawkey (Eds.), *The development of oral and written languages: Readings in developmental and applied linguistics* (pp. 31–56). New York: Ablex.

Nelson, K., & Fivush, R. (2000). Socialization of memory. In E. Tulving, & F. I. M. Craik, (Eds.), *The Oxford handbook of memory.* New York: Oxford University Press.

Nelson, K., & Fivush, R. (2004). The emergence of autobiographical memory: A social cultural developmental theory. *Psychological Review, 111,* 486–511.

Nelson, K. E., & Gruendel, J. M. (1979). At morning it's lunchtime: A scriptal view of children's dialogues. *Discourse Processes, 2,* 73–94.

Nelson, T. F., & Wechsler, N. (2001). Alcohol and college athletes. *Medicine and Science in Sports and Exercise, 33,* 43–47.

Neville, B., & Parke, R. D. (1997). Waiting for paternity: Interpersonal and contextual implications of the timing of fatherhood. *Sex Roles, 37,* 45–89.

Neville, H. J. (1990). Intermodal competition and compensation in development: Evidence from studies of the visual system in congenitally deaf adults. *Annals of the New York Academy of Sciences, 608,* 71–91.

Neville, H. J., & Bavelier, D. (1999). Specificity and plasticity in neurocognitive development in humans. In M. S. Gazzaniga (Ed.), *The cognitive neurosciences* (2nd ed., pp. 83–98). Cambridge, MA: The MIT Press.

Newcomb, A. F., & Bagwell, C. L. (1995). Children's friendship relations: A meta-analytic review. *Psychological Bulletin, 117,* 306–347.

Newcomb, A. F., & Bukowski, W. M. (1984). A longitudinal study of the utility of social preference and social impact sociometric classification schemes. *Child Development, 55,* 1434–1447.

Newcomb, A. F., Bukowski, W. M., & Pattee, L. (1993). Children's peer relations: A meta-analytic review of popular, rejected, neglected, controversial, and average sociometric status. *Psychological Bulletin, 113,* 99–128.

Newcombe, N. S., & Huttenlocher, J. (2000). *Making space: The development of spatial representation and reasoning.* Cambridge, MA: The MIT Press.

Newcombe, N., & Huttenlocher, J. (2006). Development of mathematical understanding. In W. Damon & R. M. Lerner (Series Eds.) & D. Kuhn & R. S. Siegler (Vol. Eds.), *Handbook of child psychology: Volume 2: Cognition, perception, and language* (6th ed., pp. 734–776). Hoboken, NJ: Wiley.

Newcombe, N., Huttenlocher, J., Drummey, A. B., & Wiley, J. G. (1998). The development of spatial location coding: Place learning and dead reckoning in the second and third years. *Cognitive Development, 13,* 185–200.

Newell, K. M., Scully, D. M., McDonald, P. V., & Baillargeon, R. (1989). Task constraints and infant grip configurations. *Developmental Psychobiology, 22,* 817–832.

Newland, M. C., & Rasmussen, E. B. (2003). Behavior in adulthood and during aging is affected by contaminant exposure in utero. *Current Directions in Psychological Science, 12,* 212–217.

Newman, J. (1995, December). How breast milk protects newborns. *Scientific American, 273*(6), 76–79.

Newman, R. S. (2005). The cocktail party effect in infants revisited: Listening to one's name in noise. *Developmental Psychology, 41,* 352–362.

Newport, E. L. (1990). Maturational constraints on language learning. *Cognitive Science, 14,* 11–28.

Newport, E. L. (1991). Contrasting concepts of the critical period for language. In S. Carey & R. Gelman (Eds.), *The epigenesis of mind: Essays on biology and cognition. The Jean Piaget Symposium series* (pp. 111–130). Hillsdale, NJ: Erlbaum.

Newport, E. L., Gleitman, H., & Gleitman, L. (1977). Mother, I'd rather do it myself: Some effects and noneffects of maternal speech style. In C. E. Snow & C. A. Ferguson (Eds.), *Talking to children: Language input and acquisition* (pp. 109–150). Cambridge, UK: Cambridge University Press.

Nguyen, S. P., & Gelman, S. A. (2002). Four- and 6-year-olds' biological concept of death: The case of plants. *British Journal of Developmental Psychology, 20,* 495–513.

NICHD Early Child Care Research Network. (1997a). The effects of infant child care on infant-mother attachment security: Results of the NICHD study of early child care. *Child Development, 68,* 860–879.

NICHD Early Child Care Research Network. (1997b). Familial factors associated with the characteristic of nonmaternal care for infants. *Journal of Marriage and the Family, 59,* 389–408.

NICHD Early Child Care Research Network. (1998a). Early child care and self-control, compliance, and problem behavior at 24 and 36 months. *Child Development, 69,* 1145–1170.

NICHD Early Child Care Research Network. (1998b). *When child-care classrooms meet recommended guidelines for quality.* Paper submitted for publication.

NICHD Early Child Care Research Network. (1999). Child care and mother-child interaction in the first three years of life. *Developmental Psychology, 35,* 1399–1413.

NICHD Early Child Care Research Network. (2000a). Factors associated with fathers' caregiving activities and sensitivity with young children. *Journal of Family Psychology, 14,* 200–219.

NICHD Early Child Care Research Network. (2000b). The relation of child care to cognitive and language development. *Child Development, 71,* 960–980.

NICHD Early Child Care Research Network. (2002). Early child care and children's development prior to school entry: Results from the NICHD study of early child care. *American Education Research Journal,* 39, 133–164.

NICHD Early Child Care Research Network. (2003a). Does amount of time spend in child care predict socioemotional adjustment during the transition to kindergarten? *Child Development, 74,* 976–1005.

NICHD Early Child Care Research Network, & Duncan, G. J. (2003b). Modeling the impacts of child care quality on children's preschool cognitive development. *Child Development, 74,* 1454–1475.

NICHD Early Child Care Research Network. (2003c). Social functioning in first grade: Associations with earlier home and child care predictors and with current classroom experiences. *Child Development, 74,* 1639–1662.

NICHD Early Child Care Research Network. (2004). Trajectories of physical aggression from toddlerhood to middle childhood: Predictors, correlates, and outcomes. *Monographs of the Society for Research in Child Development, 69* (Serial No. 278; No. 4), 1–144.

NICHD Early Childhood Research Network. (2006). Infant-mother attachment classification: Risk and protection in relation to changing maternal caregiving quality. *Developmental Psychology, 42,* 38–58.

NICHD Early Child Care Research Network. (2006). Child-care effect sizes for the NICHD Study of Early Child Care and Youth Development. *American Psychologist, 61,* 99–116.

Nicholson, T. (1999). Reading comprehension processes. In G. B. Thompson & T. Nicholson (Eds.), *Learning to read: Beyond phonics and whole language* (pp. 127–149). New York: Teachers College Press.

Nicolopoulou, A. (2006). The interplay of play and narrative in children's development: Theoretical reflections and concrete examples. In A.

Göncü & S. Gaskins (Eds.), *Play and development: Evolutionary, sociocultural, and functional perspectives* (pp. 247–274). Mahwah, NJ: Erlbaum.

Nieder, A. (2005). Counting on neurons: The neurobiology of numerical competence. *Nature Reviews Neuroscience, 6*, 177–190.

Nielsen, M., Suddendorf, T., & Slaughter, V. (2006). Mirror self-recognition beyond the face. *Child Development, 77*, 175–185.

Nievar, M. A., & Becker, B. J. (2007). Sensitivity as a privileged predictor of attachment: A second perspective on de Wolff and van IJzendoorn's meta-analysis. *Social Development, 17*, 102–114.

Nisan, M., & Kohlberg, L. (1982). Universality and variation in moral judgment: A longitudinal and cross-sectional study in Turkey. *Child Development, 53*, 865–876.

Nolen-Hoeksema, S. (1991). Sex differences in control of depression. In J. W. Pennebaker & D. M. Wegner (Eds.), *Handbook of mental control* (pp. 306–324). Saddle River, NJ: Prentice-Hall.

Nolen-Hoeksema, S. (2001). Gender differences in depression. *Current Directions in Psychological Science, 10*, 173-176.

Nolen-Hoeksema, S., Larson, J., & Grayson, C. (1999). Explaining the gender differences in depressive symptoms. *Journal of Personality and Social Psychology, 77*, 1061–1072.

Nolen-Hoeksema, S., Stice, E., Wade, E., & Bohon, C. (2007). Reciprocal relations between rumination and bulic, substance abuse, and depressive symptoms in female adolescents. *Journal of Abnormal Psychology, 116*, 198–207.

Nordenstrom, A., Servin, A., Bohlin, G., Larsson, A., & Wedell, A. (2002). Sex-typed toy play behavior correlates with the degree of prenatal androgen exposure assessed by CYP21 genotype in girls with congenital adrenal hyperplasia. *Journal of Clinical Endocrinology and Metabolism, 87*, 5119–5124.

Nosek, B. A., & Banaji, M. R. (2009). Implicit attitude. In P. Wilken, T. Bayne, & A. Cleeremans (Eds.), *Oxford Companion to Consciousness* (pp. 84–85). Oxford, UK: Oxford University Press.

Nosek, B. A., Greenwald, A. G., & Banaji, M. R. (in press). The Implicit Association Test at age 7: A methodological and conceptual review. In J. A. Bargh (Ed.), *Automatic processes in social thinking and behavior*. Psychology Press.

Nowell, A., & Hedges, L.V. (1998). Trends in gender differences in academic achievement from 1960 to 1994: An analysis of differences in mean, variance and extreme scores. *Sex Roles, 39*, 21–43.

Nucci, L. P. (1981). Conceptions of personal issues: A domain distinct from moral or societal concepts. *Child Development, 52*, 114–121.

Nucci, L. P. (1997). Culture, universals, and the personal. *New Directions in Child Development, 76*, 5–22.

Nucci, L. P., Camino, C., & Sapiro, C. M. (1996). Social class effects on northeastern Brazilian children's conceptions of areas of personal choice and social regulation. *Child Development, 67*, 1223–1242.

Nucci, L. P., & Weber, E. K. (1995). Social interactions in the home and the development of young children's conceptions of the personal. *Child Development, 66*, 1438–1452.

Nunes, T., & Bryant, P. (1996). *Children doing mathematics*. Cambridge, MA: Blackwell.

Nunes, T., Schliemann, A.-L., and Carraher, D. (1993). *Street mathematics and school mathematics*. New York: Cambridge University Press.

Nurmi, J. E. (2004). Socialization and self-development. Channeling, selection, adjustment, and reflection. In R. Lerner & L. Steinberg (Eds.), *Handbook of adolescent psychology* (2nd ed., pp. 85–124). New York: Wiley.

Nylund, K., Bellmore, A., Nishina, A., & Graham, S. (2007). Subtypes, severity, and structural stability of peer victimization: What does latent analysis say? *Child Development, 78*(6), 1706–1722.

Oakes, L. M., & Cohen, L. B. (1995). Infant causal perception. In C. Rovee-Collier & L. P. Lipsitt (Eds.), *Advances in infancy research* (Vol. 9). Norwood, NJ: Ablex.

Oakhill, J. V., & Cain, K. E. (2000). Children's difficulties in text comprehension: Assessing causal issues. *Journal of Deaf Studies & Deaf Education, 5*, 51–59.

Ocampo, K. A., Bernal, M. E., & Knight, G. P. (1993). Gender, race, and ethnicity: The sequencing of social constancies. In M. E. Bernal & G. P. Knight (Eds.), *Ethnic identity: Formation and transmission among Hispanics and other minorities* (pp. 11–30). Albany: State University of New York Press.

Ocampo, K. A., Knight, G. P., & Bernal, M. E. (1997). The development of cognitive abilities and social identities in children: The case of ethnic identity. *International Journal of Behavioral Development, 21*, 479–500.

O'Connor, T. G., Caspi, A., DeFries, J. C., & Plomin, R. (2000). Are associations between parental divorce and children's adjustment genetically mediated? An adoption study. *Developmental Psychology, 36*, 429–437.

O'Connor, T. G., Heron, J., Golding, J., Beveridge, M., & Glover, V. (2002). Maternal antenatal anxiety and children's behavioural/emotional problems at 4 years: Report from the Avon Longitudinal Study of Parents and Children. *British Journal of Psychiatry, 180*, 502–508.

O'Connor, T. G., Hetherington, E. M., & Reiss, D. (1998). Family systems and adolescent development: Shared and nonshared risk and protective factors in nondivorced and remarried families. *Development and Psychopathology, 10*, 353–375.

O'Connor, T. G., & Rutter, M. (2000). Attachment disorder behavior following early severe deprivation: Extension and longitudinal follow-up. *Journal of the American Academy of Child and Adolescent Psychiatry, 39*, 703–712.

O'Connor, T. G., Rutter, M., Beckett, C., Keaveney, L., Kreppner, J. M., & The English and Romanian Adoptees Study Team. (2000). The effects of global severe privation on cognitive competence: Extension and longitudinal follow-up. *Child Development, 71*, 376–390.

Oden, S., & Asher, S. R. (1977). Coaching children in social skills for friendship making. *Child Development, 48*, 498–506.

Offord, D. R., Alder, R. J., & Boyle, M. H. (1986). Prevalence and sociodemographic correlates of conduct disorders. *American Journal of Social Psychiatry, 4*, 272–278.

Ogbu, J. U. (1981). Origins of human competence: A cultural-ecological perspective. *Child Development, 52*, 413–429.

Oh, W., Rubin, K. H., Bowker, J. C., Booth-LaForce, C., Rose-Krasno, L., & Laursen, B. (2008). Trajectories of social withdrawal from middle childhood to early adolescence. *Journal of Abnormal Child Psychology, 36*, 553–566.

Ohman, A., & Mineka, S. (2001). Fears, phobias, and preparedness: Toward an evolved module of fear and fear learning. *Psychological Review, 108*, 483–522.

Okagaki, L., & Frensch, P. A. (1996). Effects of video game playing on measures of spatial performance: Gender effects in late adolescence. In P. M. Greenfield & R. R. Cocking (Eds.), *Interacting with video* (pp. 115–140). Norwood, NJ: Ablex.

O'Leary, K. D., Slep, A. M. S., Avery-Leaf, S., & Cascardi, M. (2008). Gender differences in dating aggression among multiethnic high school students. *Journal of Adolescent Health, 42*, 473–479.

Oliner, S. P., & Oliner, P. M. (1988). *The altruistic personality: Rescuers of Jews in Nazi Europe*. New York: Free Press.

Oliver, B., Dale, P. S., & Plomin, R. (2004). Verbal and nonverbal predictors of early language problems: An analysis of twins in early childhood back to infancy. *Journal of Child Language, 31*, 609–631.

Ollendick, T. H., Weist, M. D., Borden, M. C., & Greene, R. W. (1992). Sociometric status and academic, behavioral, and psychological adjustment: A five-year longitudinal study. *Journal of Consulting and Clinical Psychology, 60*, 80–87.

Oller, D. K., & Eilers, R. E. (1988). The role of audition in infant babbling. *Child Development, 59*, 441–449.

Oller, D. K., & Pearson, B. Z. (2002). Assessing the effects of bilingualism. In D. K. Oller (Ed.), *Language and literacy in bilingual children*. Clevedon, UK: Multilingual Matters.

Olson, R. K., Wise, B., Ring, J., & Johnson, M. (1997). Computer-based remedial training in phoneme awareness and phonological decoding: Effects on the post-training development of work recognition. *Scientific Studies of Reading, 1*, 235–253.

Olson, S. (2004). Making sense of Tourette's. *Science, 305*, 1390–1392.

Olson, S. L., Bates, J. E., & Kaskie, B. (1992). Caregiver-infant interaction antecedents of children's schoolage cognitive ability. *Merrill-Palmer Quarterly, 38*, 309–330.

Olson, S. L., Bates, J. E., Sandy, J. M., & Lanthier, R. (2000). Early developmental precursors of externalizing behavior in middle childhood and adolescence. *Journal of Abnormal Child Psychology, 28*, 119–133.

Olweus, D. (1979). Stability and aggressive reaction patterns in males: A review. *Psychological Bulletin, 86*, 852–875.

Olweus, D. (1994). Annotation: Bullying at school: Basic facts and effects of a school based intervention program. *Journal of Child Psychology and Psychiatry, 35*, 1171–1190.

O'Neil, D. K. (1996). Two-year-old children's sensitivity to a parent's knowledge state when making requests. *Child Development, 67*, 659–677.

Onishi, K. H., & Baillargeon, R. (2005). Do 15-month-old infants understand false beliefs? *Science, 308*, 255–258.

Ontai, L. & Thompson, R. A. (2002). Patterns of attachment and maternal discourse effects on children's emotion understanding from 3 to 5 years of age. *Social Development, 11*, 433–450.

Opfer, J. E., & Gelman, S. A. (2001). Children's and adults' models of teleological action: The development of biology-based models. *Child Development, 72*, 1367–1381.

Opfer, J. E., & Siegler, R. S. (2004). Revisiting preschoolers' *living things* concept: A microgenetic analysis of conceptual change in basic biology. *Cognitive Psychology, 49*, 301–332.

Oppliger, P. A. (2007). Effects of gender stereotyping on socialization. In Preiss, Raymond W.; Gayle, Barbara Mae; Burrell, Nancy; Allen, Mike; Bryant, Jennings (2007). *Mass media effects research: Advances through meta-analysis* (pp. 199–214). Mahwah, NJ: Lawrence Erlbaum Associates.

O'Reilly, A. W., & Bornstein, M. H. (1993). Caregiver-child interaction in play. In M. H. Bornstein & A. W. O'Reilly (Eds.), *The role of play in the development of thought* (New Directions for Child Development, No. 59). San Francisco: Jossey–Bass.

Organization for Economic Co-operation and Development. (2004). *OECD Health Data 2004: A comparative analysis of 30 countries*. Paris, France: Organization for Economic Co-operation and Development. Available at: www.oecd.org/health.

Orlofsky, J. L. (1978). Identity formation: Achievements and fear of success in college men and women. *Journal of Youth and Adolescence, 7*, 49–62.

Ormerod, A. J., Collinsworth, L. L., & Perry, L. A. (2008). Critical climate: Relations among sexual harassment, climate, and outcomes for high school girls and boys. *Psychology of Women Quarterly, 32*, 113–125.

Orth, U., Robins, R. W., & Roberts, B. W. (2008). Low self-esteem prospectively predicts depression in adolescence and young adulthood. *Journal of Personality and Social Psychology, 95*, 695–708.

Osborne, L. (1999, October 24). A linguistic big bang. *The New York Times Magazine*, pp. 84–89.

Osofsky, J. D. (1995). The effects of exposure to violence on young children. *American Psychologist, 50*, 782–788.

Oster, H., Hegley, D., & Nagel, L. (1992). Adult judgments and fine-grained analysis of infant facial expressions: Testing the validity of a priori coding formulas. *Developmental Psychology, 28*, 1115–1131.

Ostrov, J. M. (2008). Forms of aggression and peer victimization during early childhood: A short-term longitudinal study. *Journal of Abnormal Child Psychology, 36*, 311–322.

Ostrov, J. M., Ries, E. E., Stauffacher, K., Godleski, S. A., & Mullins, A. D. (2008). Relational aggression, physical aggression and deception during early childhood: A multimethod, multi-informant short-term longitudinal study. *Journal of Clinical Child and Adolescent Psychology, 37*, 664–675.

Otake, M., & Schull, W. J. (1984). In utero exposure to A-bomb radiation and mental retardation: A reassessment. *British Journal of Radiology, 57*, 409–414.

Overman, W. H., Pate, B. J., Moore, K., & Peleuster, A. (1996). Ontogeny of place learning in children as measured in the radial arm maze, Morris search task, and open field task. *Behavioral Neuroscience, 110*, 1205–1228.

Ozonoff, S., Cook, I., Coon, H., Dawson, G., Joseph, R. M., Klin, A., et al. (2004). Performance on CANTAB subtests sensitive to frontal lobe function in people with autistic disorder: Evidence from the CPEA Network. *Journal of Autism and Developmental Disorders, 34*, 139–150.

Pacifici, C., & Bearison, D. J. (1991). Development of children's self-regulations in idealized and mother-child interactions. *Cognitive Development, 6*, 261–277.

Pagani, L., Tremblay, R. E., Vitaro, F., Kerr, M., & McDuff, P. (1998). The impact of family transition on the development of delinquency in adolescent boys: A 9-year longitudinal study. *Journal of Child Psychology and Psychiatry, 39*, 489–499.

Paik, H. & Comstock, G. (1994). The effects of television violence on antisocial behavior: A meta-analysis. *Communication Research, 21*, 516–546.

Paley, V. G. (1981). *Wally's stories.* Cambridge, MA: Harvard University Press.

Palincsar, A. S., & Magnusson, S. J. (2001). The interplay of first-hand and text-based investigations to model and support the development of scientific knowledge and reasoning. In D. Klahr & S. Carver (Eds.), *Cognition and instruction: 25 years of progress.* Mahwah, NJ: Erlbaum.

Palmer, C. F. (1989). The discriminating nature of infants' exploratory actions. *Developmental Psychology, 25,* 885–893.

Palmer, E. J., & Hollin, C. R. (1998). A comparison of patterns of moral development in young offenders and non-offenders. *Legal and Criminological Psychology, 3,* 225–235.

Papini, D. R., & Sebby, R. A. (1988). Variations in conflictual family issues by adolescent pubertal status, gender, and family member. *Journal of Early Adolescence, 8,* 1–15.

Park, G., Lubinski, D., & Benbow, C. P. (2008). Ability differences among people who have commensurate degrees matter for scientific creativity. *Psychological Science, 19,* 957–961.

Parke, R. D. (1996). *Fatherhood.* Cambridge, MA: Harvard University Press.

Parke, R. D., & Buriel, R. (1998). Socialization in the family: Ethnic and ecological perspectives. In W. Damon (Series Ed.) and N. Eisenberg (Vol. Ed.), *Social, emotional and personality development. Vol. 3. Handbook of child psychology* (pp. 463–552). New York: Wiley.

Parke, R. D., & Buriel, R. (2006). Socialization in the family: Ethnic and ecological perspectives. In W. Damon & R. M. Lerner (Series Ed.) & N. Eisenberg (Vol. Ed.), *Handbook of child psychology: Vol. 3. Social, emotional, and personality development* (6th ed. 429–504). Hoboken, NJ: Wiley.

Parke, R. D., & Collmer, C. (1975). Child abuse: An interdisciplinary review. In E. M. Hetherington (Ed.), *Review of child development research* (Vol. 5). Chicago: University of Chicago Press.

Parke, R. D., Coltrane, S., Duffy, S. Buriel, R., Dennis, J., Powers, J., French, S., & Widaman, K. F. (2004). Economic stress, parenting, and child adjustment in Mexican American and European American families. *Child Development, 75,* 1632–1656.

Parke, R. D., & Kellam, S. (Ed.). (1994). *Advances in family research. Vol. 4. Family relationships with other social systems.* Hillsdale, NJ: Erlbaum.

Parke, R. D., O'Neil, R., Spitzer, S., Isley, S., Welsh, M., Wang, S., et al. (1997). A longitudinal assessment of sociometric stability and the behavioral correlates of children's social status. *Merrill-Palmer Quarterly, 43,* 635–662.

Parke, R. D., & Slaby, R. G. (1983). The development of aggression. In P. H. Mussen (Series Ed.) and E. M. Hetherington (Vol. Ed.), *Handbook of child psychology, Vol. 4. Socialization, personality, and social development* (pp. 547–641). New York: Wiley.

Parker, J. G., & Asher, S. R. (1987). Peer relations and later personal adjustment: Are low-accepted children at risk. *Psychological Bulletin, 102,* 357–389.

Parker, J. G., & Asher, S. R. (1993). Friendship and friendship quality in middle childhood: Links with peer group acceptance and feelings of loneliness and social dissatisfaction. *Developmental Psychology, 29,* 611–621.

Parker, J. G., & Gottman, J. M. (1989). Social and emotional development in a relational context. In T. J. Berndt & G. W. Ladd (Eds.), *Peer relationships in child development* (pp. 95–131). New York: Wiley.

Parker, J. G., & Herrera, C. (1996). Interpersonal processes in friendship: A comparison of maltreated and nonmaltreated children's experience. *Developmental Psychology, 32,* 1025–1038.

Parker, J. G., Rubin, K. H., Price, J. M., & DeRosier, M. E. (1995). In D. Cicchetti & D. Cohen (Eds.), *Developmental psychopathology. Vol. 2: risk, disorder, and adaptation* (pp. 96–161). New York: Wiley.

Parritz, R. H. (1996). A descriptive analysis of toddler coping in challenging circumstances. *Infant Behavior and Development, 19,* 171–180.

Pascalis, O., de Haan, M., Nelson, C. A. (2002). Is face processing species-specific during the first year of life? *Science, 296,* 1321–1323.

Pascalis, O., de Schonen, S., Morton, J., Deruelle, C., & Fabre-Grenet, H. (1995). Mother's face recognition by neonates: A replication and an extension. *Infant Behavior and Development, 18,* 79–85.

Pascalis, O., Scott, L. S., Kelly, D. J., Shannon, R. W., Nicholson, E., Coleman, M., & Nelson, C. A. (2005). Plasticity of face processing in infancy. *PNAS, 102(14),* 5297–5300.

Paschall, M. J., & Hubbard, M. L. (1998). Effects of neighborhood and family stressors on African American male adolescents' self-worth and propensity for violent behavior. *Journal of Consulting and Clinical Psychology, 66,* 825–831.

Pascual-Leone, A., Cammarota, A., Wasserman, E. M., Brasil-Neto, J. P., Cohen, L. G., & Hallett, M. (1993). Modulation of motor cortical outputs to the reading hand of braille readers. *Annals of Neurology, 34,* 33–37.

Patterson, C. J. (1995). Families of the lesbian baby boom: Parents' division of labor and children's adjustment. *Developmental Psychology, 31,* 115–123.

Patterson, C. J. (1997). Children of lesbian and gay parents. In T. H. Ollendick & R. J. Prinz (Eds.), *Advances in clinical child psychology* (Vol. 19, pp. 235–282). New York: Plenum Press.

Patterson, C. J. (2002). Lesbian and gay parenthood. In M. H. Bornstein (Ed.), *Handbook of parenting. Vol. 3. Biology and ecology of parenting* (2nd ed., pp. 317–338). Mahwah, NJ: Erlbaum.

Patterson, C. J., & Chan, R. W. (1997). Gay fathers. In M. Lamb (Ed.), *The role of the father in child development* (3rd ed., pp. 245–260). New York: Wiley.

Patterson, C. J., Griesler, P. C., Vaden, N. A. & Kupersmidt, J. B. (1992). Family economic circumstances, life transitions, and children's peer relations. In R. D. Parke & G. W. Ladd (Eds.), *Family-peer relationships: Modes of linkage.* Hillsdale, NJ: Erlbaum.

Patterson, C. J., Kupersmidt, J. B., & Griesler, P. C. (1990). Children's perceptions of self and of relationships with others as a function of sociometric status. *Child Development, 61,* 1335–1349.

Patterson, F., & Linden, E. (1981). *The education of Koko.* New York: Holt, Rinehart, & Winston.

Patterson, G. R. (1982). *Coercive family processes.* Eugene, OR: Castilla Press.

Patterson, G. R. (1995). Coercion—A basis for early age of onset for arrest. In J. McCord (Ed.), *Coercion and punishment in long-term perspective* (pp. 81–105). New York: Cambridge University Press.

Patterson, G. R., Capaldi, D., & Bank, L. (1991). An early starter model for predicting delinquency. In D. J. Pepler & K. H. Rubin (Eds.), *The development and treatment of childhood aggression* (pp. 139–168). Hillsdale, NJ: Erlbaum.

Patterson, G. R., Reid, J. B., & Dishion, T. J. (1992). *A social learning approach: Vol. 4. Antisocial boys.* Eugene, OR: Castalia Press.

Patteson, D. M., & Barnard, K. E. (1990). Parenting of low birth weight infants: A review of issues and interventions. *Infant Mental Health Journal, 11*, 37–56.

Paulson, S. E. (1996). Maternal employment and adolescent achievement revisited: An ecological perspective. *Family Relations, 45*, 201–208.

Pazzanchera, C. (2009, April). Juvenile arrests: 2007. *Juvenile Justice Bulletin.* www.ojp.usdoj.gov.

Peake, P. K., Hebl, M., & Mischel, W. (2002). Strategic attention deployment for delay of gratification in working and waiting situations. *Developmental Psychology, 38*, 313–326.

Peake, P. K., & Mischel, W. (2000). *Adult correlates of preschool delay of gratification.* Unpublished data. Smith College, Northampton, MA.

Pearson, B. Z., & Fernández, S. C. (1994). Patterns of interaction in the lexical growth in two languages of bilingual infants and toddlers. *Language Learning, 44*, 617–653.

Pederson, D. R., Gleason, K. E., Moran, G., & Bento, S. (1998). Maternal attachment representations, maternal sensitivity, and the infant-mother attachment relationship. *Developmental Psychology, 34*, 925–933.

Pederson, D. R., & Moran, G. (1996). Expressions of attachment relationship outside of the Strange Situation. *Child Development, 67*, 915–927.

Pedersen, N. L., Plomin, R., Nesselroade, J. R., & McClearn, G. E. (1992). A quantitative genetic analysis of cognitive abilities during the second half of the life span. *Psychological Science, 3*, 346–353.

Pedersen, P. A., & Blass, E. M. (1982). Prenatal and postnatal determinants of the 1st suckling episode in albino rats. *Developmental Psychobiology, 15*, 349–355.

Pedersen, S., Vitaro, F., Barker, E. D., & Borge, A .I. H. (2007). The timing of middle-childhood peer rejection and friendship: Linking early behavior to early-adolescent adjustment. *Child Development, 78*, 1037–1051.

Pegg, J. E., Werker, J. F., & McLeod, P. J. (1992). Preference for infant-directed over adult-directed speech: Evidence from 7-week-old infants. *Infant Behavior and Development, 15*, 325–345.

Peisner-Feinberg, E. S., Burchinal, M. R., Clifford, R. M., Culkin, M. L., Howes, C., Kagan, S. L., & Yazejian, N. (2001). The relation of preschool child-care quality to children's cognitive and social developmental trajectories through second grade. *Child Development, 72*, 1534–1553.

Peláez-Nogueras, M., Field, T. M., Hossain, Z., & Pickens, J. (1996). Depressed mothers' touching increases infants' positive affect and attention in still-face interactions. *Child Development, 67*, 1780–1792.

Pelham, W. E., & Hoza, B. (1996). Intensive treatment: A summer treatment program for children with ADHD. In E. D. Hibbs & P. S. Jensen (Eds.), *Psychosocial treatments for child and adolescent disorders: Empirically based strategies for clinical practice* (pp. 311–340). Washington, DC: American Psychological Association.

Pellegrini, A. D., & Long, J. D. (2003). A sexual selection theory analysis of sexual segregation and integration in early adolescence. *Journal of Experimental Child Psychology, 85*, 257–278.

Pellegrini, A. D., & Long, J. D. (2007). An observational study of early heterosexual interaction at middle school dances. *Journal of Research on Adolescence, 17*, 613–638.

Pellegrini, A. D. (2004). Sexual segregation in childhood: A review of evidence for two hypotheses. *Animal Behaviour, 68*, 435–443.

Pellizzoni, S., Siegal, M., & Surian, L. (2009). Foreknowledge, caring, and the side-effect effect in young children. *Developmental Psychology, 45*, 289–295.

Pelphrey, K. A., Reznick, J. S., Goldman, B. D., Sasson, N., Morrow, J., Donahoe, A., & Hodgson, K. (2004). Development of visuospatial short-term memory in the second half of the first year. *Developmental Psychology, 40*, 836–851.

Pennisi, E. (2003). A low number wins the gene sweep pool. *Science,* 300, 1484.

Perkins, S. A., & Turiel, E. (2007). To lie or not to lie: To whom and under what circumstances. *Child Development, 78*, 609–621.

Perris, E. E., & Clifton, R. K. (1988). Reaching in the dark toward sound as a measure of auditory localization in infants. *Infant Behavior and Development, 11*, 473–492.

Perry, D. G., & Bussey, K. (1979). The social learning theory of sex differences: Imitation is alive and well. *Journal of Personality and Social Psychology, 37*, 1699–1712.

Perry, D. G., & Bussey, K. (1984). *Social development.* Upper Saddle River, NJ: Prentice Hall.

Perry, D. G., Perry, L. C., & Weiss, R. (1989). Sex differences in the consequences that children anticipate for aggression. *Developmental Psychology, 25*, 312–319.

Perry, D. G., Bussey, K., & Freiberg, K. (1981). Impact of adults' appeals for sharing on the development of altruistic dispositions in children. *Journal of Experimental Child Psychology, 32*, 127–138.

Perry, D. G., Perry, L. C., & Rasmussen, P. (1986). Cognitive social learning mediators of aggression. *Child Development, 57*, 700–711.

Perry, M., & Lewis, J. L. (1999). Verbal imprecision as an index of knowledge in transition. *Developmental Psychology, 35*, 749–759.

Petersen, A. C., Sarigiani, P. A., & Kennedy, R. E. (1991). Adolescent depression: Why more girls? *Journal of Youth and Adolescence, 20*, 247–271.

Peterson, C. C., Wellman, H. M., & Liu, D. (2005). Steps in theory-of-mind development for children with deafness or autism. *Child Development, 76*, 502–517.

Peterson, C. L., & McCabe, A. (1988). The connective "and" as discourse glue. *First Language, 8*, 19–28.

Petitto, L. A., Holowka, S., Sergio, L. E., & Ostry, D. (2001). Language rhythms in baby hand movements. *Nature, 413*, 35–36.

Petitto, L. A., & Marentette, P. F. (1991). Babbling in the manual mode: Evidence for the ontogeny of language. *Science, 251*, 1493–1496.

Petrill, S. A., Lipton, P. A., Hewitt, J. K., Plomin, R., Cherny, S. S., Corley, R., & DeFries, J. C. (2004). Genetic and environmental contributions to general cognitive ability through the first 16 years of life. *Developmental Psychology, 40*, 805–812.

Petrill, S. A., Deater-Deckard, K., Schatschneider, C., & Davis, C. (2005). Measured environmental influences on early reading: Evidence from an adoption study. *Scientific Studies of Reading, 9*, 237–259.

Petrill, S. A., Deater-Deckard, K., Thompson, L. A., Schatschneider, C., & DeThorne, L. S. (2006). Longitudinal genetic analysis of early reading: The Western Reserve Reading Project. *Reading & Writing,* May 25.

Pettit, G. S., Brown, E. G., Mize, J., & Lindsey, E. (1998). Mothers' and fathers' socializing behavior in three contexts: Links with children's peer competence. *Merrill-Palmer Quarterly, 44,* 173–193.

Pettit, G. S., Laird, R. D., Dodge, K. A., Bates, J. E., & Criss, M. M. (2001). Antecedents and behavior-problem outcomes of parental monitoring and psychological control in early adolescence. *Child Development, 72,* 583–598.

Pew Internet (2008). http://www.pewinternet.org/Reports/2008/Teens-Video-Games-and-Civics.aspx.

Pfeifer, M., Goldsmith, H. H., Davidson, R. J., & Rickman, M. (2002). Continuity and change in inhibited and uninhibited children. *Child Development, 73,* 1474–1485.

Phillips, A., Wellman, H. M., & Spelke, E. (2002). Infants' ability to connect gaze and emotional expression to intentional action. *Cognition, 85,* 53–78.

Phillips, S., King, S., & DuBois, L. (1978). Spontaneous activities of female versus male newborns. *Child Development, 49,* 590–597.

Phinney, J. S. (1993). Multiple group identities: differentiation, conflict, and integration. In J. Kroger (Ed.), *Discussions on ego identity* (pp. 47–73). Hillsdale, NJ: Erlbaum.

Phinney, J. S., Cantu, C. L., & Kurtz, D. A. (1997). Ethnic and American identity as predictors of self-esteem among African American, Latino, and White adolescents. *Journal of Youth and Adolescence, 26,* 165–185.

Phinney, J. S., & Kohatsu, E. L. (1997). Ethnic and racial identity development and mental health. In J. Schulenberg, J. L. Maggs, & K. Hurrelmann (Eds.), *Health risks and developmental transitions during adolescence* (pp. 420–443). Cambridge, UK: Cambridge University Press.

Phipps, M. G., Blume, J. D., & DeMonner, S. M. (2002). Young maternal age associated with increased risk of postneonatal death. *Obstetrics and Gynecology, 100,* 481–486.

Piaget, J. (1926). *The language and thought of the child.* New York: Harcourt, Brace & World. (Original work published 1923.)

Piaget, J. (1928/1959). *Judgment and reasoning in the child.* Patterson, NJ: Littlefield, Adams. (Original work published in 1928 by Routledge & Kegan Paul, London.)

Piaget, J. (1932/1965). *The moral judgment of the child.* New York: Free Press.

Piaget, J. (1951). *Play, dreams, and imitation in childhood.* New York: Norton.

Piaget, J. (1952a). *The child's concept of number.* New York: Norton.

Piaget, J. (1952b). *The origins of intelligence in children.* New York: Int. University Press.

Piaget, J. (1954). *The construction of reality in the child.* New York: Basic Books.

Piaget, J. (1964). Development and learning. In R. E. Ripple & V. N. Rockcastle (Eds.), *Piaget rediscovered.* Ithaca, NY: Cornell University Press.

Piaget, J. (1969). *The child's conception of time.* New York: Ballantine.

Piaget, J. (1970). *Psychology and epistemology.* New York: W. W. Norton.

Piaget, J. (1971). *The construction of reality in the child.* New York: Ballantine.

Piaget, J., & Inhelder, B. (1956). *The child's conception of space* (F. J. Langdon & J. L. Lunzer, Trans.). Atlantic Highlands, NJ: Humanities Press. (Reprinted in *The essential Piaget: An interpretive reference and guide,* pp. 576–642, by H. E. Gruber & J. J. Voneche, Eds., 1977, New York: Basic Books.)

Piehler, T. F., & Dishion, T. J. (2007). Interpersonal dynamics within adolescent friendships: Dyadic mutuality, deviant talk, and patterns of antisocial behavior. *Child Development, 78,* 1611–1624.

Pierroutsakos, S. L., & DeLoache, J. S. (2003). Infants' manual exploration of pictorial objects varying in realism. *Infancy, 4,* 141–156.

Pilgrim, C., Luo, Q., Urberg, K. A. & Fang, X. (1999). Influence of peers, parents, and individual characteristics on adolescent drug use in two cultures. *Merrill-Palmer Quarterly, 45,* 85–107.

Pilkington, N. W., & D'Augelli, A. R. (1995). Victimization of lesbian, gay, and bisexual youth in community settings. *Journal of Community Psychology, 23,* 33–56.

Pillow, B. H. (1988). The development of children's beliefs about the mental world. *Merrill-Palmer Quarterly, 34,* 1–32.

Pinderhughes, E. E., Dodge, K. A., Bates, J. E., Pettit, G. S., & Zelli, A. (2000). Discipline responses: Influences of parents' socioeconomic status, ethnicity, beliefs about parenting, stress, and cognitive-emotional processes. *Journal of Family Psychology, 14,* 380–400.

Pine, J. M. (1994). Environmental correlates of variation in lexical style: Interactional style and the structure of the input. *Applied Psycholinguistics, 15,* 355–370.

Pinker, S. (1994). *The language instinct: The new science of language and mind.* Harmondsworth, Middlesex: Alan Lane, Penguin.

Pinker, S. (1997, October 9). Evolutionary psychology: An exchange. *The New York Review of Books, 44,* No. 15.

Pipe, M.-E., Gee, S., Wilson, J. C., Egerton, J. M. (1999). Children's recall 1 or 2 years after an event. *Developmental Psychology, 35,* 781–789.

Plato. (1980). *The laws of Plato* (T. L. Pangle, Trans.). New York: Basic Books.

Plomin, R. (1990). *Nature and nurture.* Belmont, CA: Brooks/Cole.

Plomin, R. (2004). Genetics and developmental psychology. *Merrill-Palmer Quarterly,* 50, 341–352.

Plomin, R., & Bergeman, C. S. (1991). The nature of nurture: Genetic influence on "environmental" measures. *Behavioral and Brain Sciences, 14,* 373–427.

Plomin, R., Corley, R., DeFries, J. C., & Fulker, D. W. (1990). Individual differences in television viewing in early childhood: Nature as well as nurture. *Psychological Science, 6,* 371–377.

Plomin, R., & Daniels, D. (1987). Why are children in the same family so different from each other? *Behavioral and Brain Sciences, 10,* 1–16.

Plomin, R., DeFries, J. C., McClearn, G. E., & McGuffin, P. (2001). *Behavioral genetics* (4th ed.). New York: Worth.

Plomin, R., DeFries, J. C., McClearn, G. E., & Rutter, M. (1997). *Behavioral genetics* (3rd ed.). New York: Freeman.

Plomin, R., Fulker, D. W., Corley, R., & DeFries, J. C. (1997). Nature, nurture, and cognitive development from 1 to 16 years: A parent-offspring adoption study. *Psychological Science, 8,* 442–447.

Plumert, J. M. (1995). Relation between children's overestimation of their physical abilities and accident proneness. *Developmental Psychology, 31,* 866–876.

Plumert, J. M., Kearney, J. K., & Cremer, J. F. (2004). Children's perception of gap affordances: Bicycling across traffic-filled intersections in an immersive virtual environment. *Child Development, 75,* 1243–1253.

Podd, M. H., Marcia, J. E., & Rubin, B. M. (1970). The effects of ego identity and partner perception on a prisoner's dilemma game. *Journal of Social Psychology, 82,* 117–126.

Polka, L., & Werker, J. F. (1994). Developmental changes in perception of non-native vowel contrasts. *Journal of Experimental Psychology: Human Perception and Performance, 20,* 421–435.

Pollitt, E., Golub, M., Grantham-McGregor, S., Levitsky, D., Schurch, B., Strupp, B., & Wachs, T. (1996). A reconceptualization of the effects of undernutrition on children's biological, psychosocial, and behavioral development. *SRCD Social Policy Report, 10*(5), 1–21.

Pollitt, E., Gorman, K. S., Engle, P., Martorell, R., & Rivera, J. (1993). Early supplementary feeding and cognition: Effects over two decades. *Monographs of the Society for Research in Child Development, 58*(7, Serial No. 238), 1–99.

Pomerleau, A., Bolduc, D., Malcuit, G., & Cossette, L. (1990). Pink or blue: Environmental gender stereotypes in the first two years of life. *Sex Roles, 22,* 359–367.

Pons, F., & Harris, P. L. (2005). Longitudinal change and longitudinal stability of individual differences in children's emotion understanding. *Cognition & Emotion, 19,* 1158–1174.

Poole, D. A., & Lindsay, D. S. (1995). Interviewing preschoolers: Effects of nonsuggestive techniques, parental coaching, and leading questions on reports of nonexperienced events. *Journal of Experimental Child Psychology, 60,* 129–154.

Popkin, B. M., & Doan, R. M. (1990). Women's roles, time allocation and health. In J. Caldwell, S. Findley, P. Caldwell, G. Santow, W. Cosford, J. Braid, & D. Broers-Freeman (Eds.), *What we know about health transition: The cultural, social, and behavioral determinants of health transition* (Vol. 2, No. 2, pp. 683–706). Canberra: Australian National University Press.

Popp, D., Laursen, B., Kerr, M., Stattin, H., & Burk, W. J. (2008). Modeling homophily over time with actor-partner interdependence model. *Developmental Psychology, 44,* 1028–1039.

Poremba, A., Malloy, M., Saunders, R. C., Carson, R. E., Herscovitch, P., & Mishkin, M. (2004). Species-specific calls evoke asymmetric activity in the monkey's temporal poles. *Nature, 427,* 448–451.

Porges, S. W. (1991). Vagal tone: An autonomic mediator of affect. In J. Garber & K. A. Dodge (Eds.), *The development of emotion regulation and dysregulation* (pp. 111–128). Cambridge, UK: University of Cambridge Press.

Porges, S.W. (2007). The polyvagal perspective. *Biological Psychology, 74,* 116–143.

Porges, S. W., Doussard-Roosevelt, J. A., & Maiti, A. K. (1994). Vagal tone and the physiological regulation of emotion. *Monographs of the Society for Research in Child Development, 59*(2–3, Serial No. 240), 167–186.

Porter, R. H., Makin, J. W., Davis, L. B., & Christensen, K. M. (1992). Breast-fed infants respond to olfactory cues from their own mother and unfamiliar lactating females. *Infant Behavior & Development, 15,* 85–93.

Posada, G., Carbonell, O. A., Alzate, G. & Plata, S. J. (2004). Through Colombian lenses: Ethnographic and conventional analyses of maternal care and their associations with secure base behavior. *Developmental Psychology, 40,* 508–518.

Posada, G., Jacobs, A., Carbonell, O., Alzate, G., Bustemante, M., & Arenas, A. (1999). Maternal care and attachment security in ordinary and emergency contexts. *Developmental Psychology, 35,* 1379–1388.

Posada, R., & Wainryb, C. (2008). Moral development in a violent society: Columbian children's judgments in the context of survival and revenge. *Child Development, 79,* 882–898.

Posner, M. I., Rothbart, M. K., Farah, M., & Bruer, J. (Eds.). (2001). The developing human brain [Special issue]. *Developmental Science, 4*(3).

Posner, M. I., Rothbart, M. K., & Sheese, B. E. (2007). Attention genes. *Developmental Science, 10,* 24–29.

Poston, D. L., Jr., & Falbo, T. (1990). Academic performance and personality traits of Chinese children: "Onlies" versus others. *American Journal of Sociology, 96,* 433–451.

Poulin, F., Cillessen, A. H. N., Hubbard, J. A., Coie, J. D., Dodge, K. A., & Schwartz, D. (1997). Children's friends and behavioral similarity in two social contexts. *Social Development, 6,* 224–236.

Poulin, F., & Pedersen, S. (2007). Developmental changes in gender composition of friendship networks in adolescent girls and boys. *Developmental Psychology, 43,* 1484–1498.

Poulin-Dubois, D. (1999). Infants' distinction between animate and inanimate objects: The origins of naive psychology. P. Rochat (Ed.), *Early social cognition: Understanding others in the first months of life* (pp. 257–280). Mahwah, NJ: Erlbaum.

Poulin-DuBois, D., Serbin, L. A., Eichstedt, J. A., Sen, M. G., & Beissel, C. F. (2002). Men don't put on make-up: Toddlers' knowledge of the gender stereotyping of household activities. *Social Development, 11,* 166–181.

Powell, G. F., Brasel, J. A., & Blizzard, R. M. (1967). Emotional deprivation and growth retardation simulating idiopathic hypopituitarism: I. Clinical evaluation of the syndrome. *New England Journal of Medicine, 276,* 1272–1278.

Power, Thomas G. (2004). Stress and coping in childhood: The parents' role. *Parenting: Science and Practice, 4*(4), 271–317.

Power, N., & Valiente, C. (2004). Stress and coping in childhood: The parents' role. *Parenting: Science and Practice, 4,* 271–317.

Powlishta, K. K. (1995). Intergroup processes in childhood: Social categorization and sex role development. *Developmental Psychology, 31,* 5, 781–788.

Powlishta, K. K., Serbin, L. A., & Moller, L. C. (1993). The stability of individual differences in gender typing: Implications for understanding gender segregation. *Sex Roles, 29,* 723–737.

Pratt, M. W., Kerig, P., Cowan, P. A., & Cowan, C. P. (1988). Mothers and fathers teaching 3-year-olds: Authoritative parenting and adult scaffolding of young children's learning. *Developmental Psychology, 24,* 832–839.

Preissler, M. A., & Carey, S. (2004). Do both pictures and words function as symbols for 18- and 24-month-old children? *Journal of Cognition and Development, 5*(2), 185–212.

Pressley, M., & Hilden, D. (2006). Cognitive strategies. In W. Damon & R. M. Lerner (Series Eds.) & D. Kuhn & R. S. Siegler (Vol. Eds.), *Handbook of child psychology: Volume 2: Cognition, perception, and language* (6th ed., pp. 511–556). Hoboken, NJ: Wiley.

Pressley, M., Levin, J. R., & McDaniel, M. A. (1987). Remembering versus inferring what a word means: Mnemonic and contextual approaches. In M. G. McKeown & M. E. Curtis (Eds.), *The nature of vocabulary aquisition.* Mahwah, NJ: Erlbaum.

Prinstein, M. J., & Cillessen, A. H. (2003). Forms and functions of adolescent peer aggression associated with high levels of peer status. *Merrill-Palmer Quarterly, 49,* 310–342.

Prinstein, M. J., Rancourt, D., Guerry, J. D., & Browne, C. B. (2009). Peer reputations and psychological adjustment. In K. H. Rubin, W. M. Bukowski, & B. Laursen (Eds.), *Handbook of peer interactions, relationships, and groups* (pp. 548–567). New York: Guilford Press.

Pruett, M. K., Williams, T., Insabella, G., & Little, T. D. (2003). Family and legal indicators of child adjustment of divorce among families with young children. *Journal of Family Psychology, 17,* 169–180.

Public Health Policy Advisory Board. (2001). *Health and the American child: A focus on mortality among children.* Washington, DC.

Puffenberger, E. G., Hu-Lince, D., Parod, J. M., Craig, D. W., Dobrin, S. E., Conway, A. R., Donarum, E. A., Strauss, K. A., Dunckley, T., Cardenas, J. F., Melmed, K. R., Wright, C. A., Liang, W., Stafford, P., Flynn, C. R., Morton, D. H., & Stephan, D. A. (2004). Mapping of sudden infant death with dysgenesis of the testes syndrome (SIDDT) by a SNP genome scan and identification of TSPYL loss of function. *Proceedings of the National Academy of Sciences of the United States of America,* 101, 11689–11694.

Puhl, R. M., & Schwartz, M. B. (2003). If you are good you can have a cookie: How memories of childhood food rules link to adult eating behaviors. *Eating Behaviors, 4,* 283–293.

Putallaz, M. (1983). Predicting children's sociometric status from their behavior. *Child Development, 54,* 1417–1426.

Putnam, S. P., Gartstein, M. A., & Rothbart, M. K. (2006). Measurement of fine-grained aspects of toddler temperament: The Early Childhood Behavior Questionnaire. *Infant Behavior & Development, 29,* 386–401.

Qin, D. B. (2009). Being "good" or being "popular." *Journal of Adolescent Research, 24,* 37–66.

Quiggle, N. L., Garber, J., Panak, W. F., & Dodge, K. A. (1992). Social information processing in aggressive and depressed children. *Child Development, 63,* 1305–1320.

Quine, W. V. O. (1960). *Word and object.* Cambridge, UK: Cambridge University Press.

Quinn, P. C. (2005). Developmental constraints on the representation of spatial relation information: Evidence from preverbal infants. In L. A. Carlson & E. van der Zee (Eds.), *Functional features in language and space: Insights from perception, categorization, and development.* New York: Oxford University Press.

Quinn, P. C., & Eimas, P. D. (1996). Peceptual organization and categorization. In C. Rovee-Collier & L. P. Lipsitt (Eds.), *Advances in infancy research:* Vol. 10, pp. 1–36. Norwood, NJ: Ablex.

Quinn, P. C., Westerlund, A., & Nelson, C. A. (2006). Neural markers of categorization in 6-month-old infants. *Psychological Science, 17,* 59–66.

Quinn, P. C., Yahr, J., Kuhn, A., Slater, A. M., & Pascalis, O. (2003) Representation of the gender of human faces by infants: A preference for female. *Perception, 31(9),* 1109–1121.

Radke-Yarrow, M., & Kochanska, G. (1990). Anger in young children. In N. L. Stein, B. Leventhal, & T. Trabasso (Eds.), *Psychological and biological approaches to emotion* (pp. 297–310). Hillsdale, NJ: Erlbaum.

Radke-Yarrow, M., & Zahn-Waxler, C. (1984). Roots, motives, and patterns in children's prosocial behavior. In E. Staub, D. Bar Tal, J. Karylowski, & J. Reykowski (Eds.), *Development and maintenance of prosocial behavior: International perspectives on positive behavior* (pp. 81–99). New York: Plenum Press.

Radziszewska, B., & Rogoff, B. (1988). Influence of adult and peer collaborators on the development of children's planning skills. *Developmental Psychology, 24,* 840–848.

Raevuori, A., Dick, D. M., Keski-Rahkonen, A., Pulkkinen, L., Rose, R. J., Rissanen, A., Kaprio, J., Viken, R. J., Silventoinen, K. (2007). Genetic and environmental factors affecting self-esteem from age 14 to 17: A longitudinal study of Finnish twins. *Psychological Medicine, 37,* 1625–1633.

Rafferty, Y., & Shinn, M. (1991). The impact of homelessness on children. *American Psychologist, 46,* 1170–1179.

Ragozin, A. S., Basham, R. B., Crnic, K. A., Greenberg, M. T., & Robinson, N. M. (1982). Effects of maternal age on parenting roles. *Developmental Psychology, 18,* 627–634.

Raikes, H., Pan, B. A., Luze, G., Tamis-LeMonda, C. S., Brooks-Gunn, J., Constantine, J., Tarullo, L. B., Raikes, H. A., & Rodriguez, E. T. (2006). Mother-child bookreading in low-income families: Correlates and outcomes during the first three years of life. *Child Development, 77,* 924–953.

Raikes, H. A., & Thompson, R. A. (2006). Family emotional climate, attachment security and young children's emotion knowledge in a high risk sample. *British Journal of Developmental Psychology, 24,* 89–104.

Raikes, H. A., & Thompson, R.A. (2008). Attachment security and parenting quality predict children's problem-solving, attributions, and loneliness with peers. *Attachment & Human Development, 10,* 319–344.

Rakic, P. (1995). Corticogenesis in human and nonhuman primates. In M. S. Gazzaniga (Ed.), *The cognitive neurosciences* (pp. 127–145). Cambridge, MA: The MIT Press.

Rakison, D. H. (2005). The perceptual to conceptual shift in infancy and early childhood: A surface or deep distinction? In L. Gershkoff-Stowe & D. H. Rakison (Eds.), *Building object categories in developmental time* (pp. 131–158). Mahwah, NJ: Erlbaum.

Rakison, D. H., & Derringer, J. (2008). Do infants possess an evolved spider-detection mechanism? *Cognition, 107,* 381–393.

Rakison, D. H., & Lupyan, G. (2008). Developing object concepts in infancy: An associative learning perspective. Monographs of SRCD.

Rakison, D. H., & Poulin-Dubois, D. (2001). The developmental origin of the animate inanimate distinction. *Psychological Bulletin, 2,* 209–238.

Ramados, J., et al. (2008). Acid-sensitive channel inhibition prevents fetal alcohol spectrum disorders cerebellar Purkinje cell loss. *AJP Regulatory Integrative and Comparative Physiology, 295,* R597–R603.

Ramani, G. B., & Siegler, R. S. (2008). Promoting broad and stable improvements in low-income children's numerical knowledge through playing number board games. *Child Development, 79,* 375–394.

Ramey, C. T., & Campbell, F. A. (1992). Poverty, early childhood education, and academic competence: The Abecedarian experiment. In A. C. Huston (Ed.), *Children in poverty: Child development and public policy.* Cambridge, UK: Cambridge University Press.

Ramey, C. T., Campbell, F. A., Burchinal, M., Skinner, M. L., Gardner, D. M., & Ramey, S. L. (2000). Persistent effects of early childhood education on high-risk children and their mothers. *Applied Developmental Science, 4,* 2–14.

Ramey, C. T., & Ramey, S. L. (2004). Early learning and school readiness: Can early intervention make a difference? *Merrill-Palmer Quarterly, 50,* 471–491.

Ramey, C. T., Yates, K. O., & Short, E. J. (1984). The plasticity of cognitive performance: Insights from preventive intervention. *Child Development, 55,* 1913–1925.

Rao, N., & Stewart, S. M. (1999). Cultural influences on sharer and recipient behavior: Sharing in Chinese and Indian preschool children. *Journal of Cross-Cultural Psychology, 30,* 219–241.

Ratner, N., & Bruner, J. (1978). Games, social exchange and the acquisition of language. *Journal of Child Language, 5,* 391–401.

Raver, C. C., Gershoff, E. T., & Aber, J. (2007). Lawrence testing equivalence of mediating models of income, parenting, and school readiness for white, black, and Hispanic children in a national sample. *Child Development, 78,* 96–115.

Rayner, K., Foorman, B. R., Perfetti, C. A., Pesetsky, D., & Seidenberg, M. S. (2001). How psychological science informs the teaching of reading. *Psychological Science in the Public Interest, 2*(2), 31–74.

Rayner, K., & Pollatsek, A. (1989). *The psychology of reading.* Englewood Cliffs, NJ: Prentice Hall.

Reardon, P., Bushnell, E. W. (1988). Infants' sensitivity to arbitrary pairings of color and taste. *Infant Behavior and Development, 11,* 245–250.

Reed, M. A., Pien, D. P., & Rothbart, M. K. (1984). Inhibitory self-control in preschool children. *Merrill-Palmer Quarterly, 30,* 131–147.

Reese, E., & Fivush, R. (1993). Parental styles of talking about the past. *Developmental Psychology, 29,* 596–606.

Reid, M. J., Webster-Stratton, C., Hammond, M. (2007). Enhancing a classroom social competence and problem-solving curriculum by offering parent training to families of moderate- to high-risk elementary school children. *Journal of Clinical Child and Adolescent Psychology, 36,* 605–620.

Reinisch, J. M., & Sanders, S. A. (1992). Prenatal hormonal contributions to sex differences in human cognitive and personality development. In A. A. Gerall, M. Moltz, & I. I. Ward (Eds.), *Sexual differentiation: Vol. 11. Handbook of behavioral neurobiology* (pp. 221–243). New York: Plenum Press.

Reis, H. T., Lin, Y., Bennett, M. E., & Nezlek, J. B. (1993). Change and consistency in social participation during early adulthood. *Developmental Psychology, 29,* 633–645.

Reissland, N. (1985). The development of concepts of simultaneity in children's understanding of emotions. *Journal of Child Psychology and Psychiatry, 26,* 811–824.

Rende, R., & Plomin, R. (1995). Nature, nurture, and the development of psychopathology. In D. Ciccetti & D. J. Cohen (Eds.), *Developmental psychopathology. Vol. 1. Theory and methods* (pp. 291–314). New York: Wiley.

Renken, B., Egeland, B., Marvinney, D., Sroufe, L. A., & Mangelsdorf, S. (1989). Early childhood antecedents of aggression and passive-withdrawal in early elementary school. *Journal of Personality, 57,* 257–281.

Renold, E. (2001). "Square-girls," femininity and the negotiation of academic success in the primary school. *British Educational Research Journal, 27,* 577–588.

Rescorla, L. A. (1980). Overextension in early language. *Journal of Child Language, 7,* 321–335.

Rest, J. R. (1979). *Development in judging moral issues.* Minneapolis: University of Minnesota Press.

Rest, J. R. (1983). Morality. In P. Mussen (Ed.), *Handbook of child psychology. Vol. 3. Cognitive development* (pp. 556–629). New York: Wiley.

Reynolds, A. J., Mavrogenes, N. A., Bezruczko, N., & Hagemann, M. (1996). Cognitive and family-support mediators of preschool effectiveness: A confirmatory analysis. *Child Development, 67,* 1119–1140.

Reynolds, A. J., Temple, J. A., Robertson, D. L., & Mann, E. A. (2001). Long-term effects of an early childhood intervention on educational achievement and juvenile arrest: A 15-year follow-up of low-income children in public schools. *The Journal of the American Medical Association, 285,* 2339–2346.

Rhee, S. H., & Waldman, I. D. (2002). Genetic and environmental influences on antisocial behavior: A meta-analysis of twin and adoption studies. *Psychological Bulletin, 128,* 490–529.

Rhee, S. H., Waldman, I. D., Hay, D. A., & Levy, F. (1999). Sex differences in genetic and environmental influences on DSM-III-R attention deficit/hyperactivity disorder. *Journal of Abnormal Psychology, 108,* 24–41.

Rheingold, H. L. (1982). Little children's participation in the work of adults, a nascent prosocial behavior. *Child Development, 53,* 114–125.

Rheingold, H. L., & Cook, K. V. (1975). The contents of boys' and girls' rooms as an index of parents' behavior. *Child Development, 46,* 445–463.

Rheingold, H. R., & Eckerman, C. O. (1970). The infant separates himself from his mother. *Science, 168,* 78–90.

Rhoades, K. A. (2008). Children's responses to interparental conflict: A meta-analysis of their associations with child adjustment. *Child Development, 79,* 1942–1956.

Ricard, M., & Allard, L. (1993). The reaction of 9- to 10-month-old infants to an unfamiliar animal. *Journal of Genetic Psychology, 154,* 5–16.

Rice, M. L., Huston, A. C., Truglio, R., & Wright, J. C. (1990). Words from Sesame Street: Learning vocabulary while viewing. *Developmental Psychology, 26,* 421–428.

Richards, D. D., & Siegler, R. S. (1984). The effects of task requirements on children's life judgments. *Child Development, 55,* 1687–1696.

Richards, M. H., Crowe, P. A., Larson, R., & Swarr, A. (1998). Developmental patterns and gender differences in the experience of peer companionship during adolescence. *Child Development, 69,* 154–163.

Richman, C. L., Berry, C., Bittle, M., & Himan, M. (1988). Factors related to helping behavior in preschool-age children. *Journal of Applied Developmental Psychology, 9,* 151–165.

Ridderinkhof, K., van der Molen, M., Band, G., & Bashore, T. (1997). Sources of interference from irrelevant information: A developmental study. *Journal of Experimental Child Psychology, 65,* 315–341.

Rideout, V. J., Vandewater, E. A., & Wartella, E. A. (2003). *Zero to six: Electronic media in the lives of infants, toddlers and preschoolers.* Menlo Park, CA: The Kaiser Family Foundation.

Ridley, M. (2003). *Nature via nurture.* New York: Harper-Collins.

Rieser, J. J., Garing, A. E., & Young, M. F. (1994). Imagery, action, and young children's spatial orientation: it's not being there that counts, it's what one has in mind. *Child Development, 65*, 1262–1278.

Riggs, N. R., Greenberg, M. T., Kusché, C. A., & Pentz, M. A. (2006). The meditational role of neurocognition in the behavioral outcomes of a social-emotional prevention program in elementary school students: Effects of the PATHS curriculum. Prevention Scinece, 7, 91–202.

Rittle Johnson, B. R., & Siegler, R. S. (1999). Learning to spell: Variability, choice, and change in children's strategy use. *Child Development, 70*, 332–349.

Rivera-Gaxiola, M., Silva-Pereyra, J., & Kuhl, P. K. (2005). Brain potentials to native and non-native speech contrasts in 7- and 11-month-old American infants. *Developmental Science, 8*, 162–172.

Roberts, B. W., Kuncel, N. R., Shiner, R., Caspi, A., & Goldberg, L. R. (2007). The power of personality: The comparative validity of personality traits, socio-economic status, and cognitive ability for predicting important life outcomes. *Perspectives of Psychological Science, 2*, 313–345.

Roberts, D. F. & Foehr, U. G. (2008). Trends in media use. In Brooks-Gunn, J. & Donahue, E. (Eds), *The future of children: Children and Electronic Media, 18*(1), 11–38.

Roberts, R. E., Phinney, J. S., Masse, L. C., Chen, Y. R., Roberts, C. R., & Romero, A. (1999). The structure of ethnic identity of young adolescents from diverse ethnocultural groups. *Journal of Early Adolescence, 19*, 301–322.

Robertson, J., & Robertson, J. (1971). *Young children in brief separation: Thomas, 2 years 4 months, in fostercare for 10 days* [Film]. London: Tavistock Institute of Human Relations.

Robertson, S. S. (1990). Temporal organization in fetal and newborn movement. In H. Bloch & B. I. Bertenthal (Eds.), *Sensory-motor organizations and development in infancy and early childhood* (pp. 105–122). Dordrecht, The Netherlands: Kluwer Academic.

Robin, D. J., Berthier, N. E., & Clifton, R. K. (1996). Infants' predictive reaching for moving objects in the dark. *Developmental Psychology, 32*, 824–835.

Robinson, J. L., Kagan, J., Reznick, J. S., & Corley, R. (1992). The heritability of inhibited and uninhibited behavior: A twin study. *Developmental Psychology, 28*, 1030–1037.

Robinson, K. M., Ninowski, J. E., & Gray, M. L. (2006). Children's understanding of the arithmetic concepts of inversion and associativity. *Journal of Experimental Child Psychology, 94*, 349–362.

Robinson, N. M., & Robinson, H. B. (1992). The use of standardized tests with young gifted children. In P. S. Klein & A. Tannenbaum (Eds.), *To be young and gifted* (pp. 141–170). Norwood, NJ: Ablex.

Robinson, T. N. (2001). Television viewing and childhood obesity. *Pediatric Clinic of North America, 48*(4), 1017–1025.

Rochat, P. (1989). Object manipulation and exploration in 2- to 5-month-old infants. *Developmental Psychology, 25*, 871–884.

Rochat, P. (1992). Self-sitting and reaching in 5- to 8-month-old infants: The impact of posture and its development on early eye-hand coordination. *Journal of Motor Behavior, 24*, 210–220.

Rochat, P., & Goubet, N. (1995). Development of sitting and reaching in 5- to 6-month-old infants. *Infant Behavior and Development, 18*, 53–68.

Rochat, P., & Morgan, R. (1995). Spatial determinants in the perception of self-produced leg movements by 3- to 5-month-old infants. *Developmental Psychology, 31*, 626–636.

Rochat, P., & Striano, T. (2002). Who's in the mirror? Self-other discrimination in specular images by four- and nine-month-old infants. *Child Development, 73*, 35–46.

Rodgers, B., Power, C., & Hope, S. (1997). Parental divorce and adult psychological distress: Evidence from a national birth cohort: A research note. *Journal of Child Psychology and Psychiatry, 38*, 867–872.

Rodier, P. M. (2000, Feb.). The early origins of autism. *Scientific American, 56–63.*

Rodkin, P. C., Farmer, T. W., Pearl, R., & Van Acker, R. (2000). Heterogeneity of popular boys: Antisocial and prosocial configurations. *Developmental Psychology, 36*, 14–24.

Rodkin, P. C., Farmer, T. W., Pearl, R., & Van Acker, R. (2006). They're cool: Social status and peer group supports for aggressive boys and girls. *Social Development, 15*, 175–204.

Rodriguez, M. L., Mischel, W., & Shoda, Y. (1989). Cognitive person variables in the delay of gratification of older children at risk. *Journal of Personality and Social Psychology, 57*, 358–367.

Roffwarg, H. P., Muzio, J. N., & Dement, W. C. (1966). Ontogenetic development of the human sleep-dream cycle. *Science, 152*, 604–619.

Rogers, F. (1996). *Dear Mr. Rogers, does it ever rain in your neighborhood? Letters to Mister Rogers*. New York: Penguin Books.

Rogers, T. T. & McClelland, J. L. (2004). *Semantic cognition: A parallel distributed processing approach*. Cambridge, MA: The MIT Press.

Rogoff, B. (2003). *The cultural nature of human development*. Oxford, UK: Oxford University Press.

Rogosch, F., Cicchetti, D., & Aber, J. L. (1995). The role of child maltreatment in early deviations in cognitive and affective processing abilities and later relationship problems. *Development and Psychopathology, 7*, 591–609.

Rohner, R. P. (1975). *They love me, they love me not*. HRAF Press.

Roisman, G. I., & Fraley, R. C. (2006). The limits of genetic influence: A behavior-genetic analysis of infant-caregiver relationship quality and temperament. *Child Development, 77*, 1656–1667.

Roisman, G. I., & Fraley, R. C. (2008). A behavior-genetic study of parenting quality, infant attachment security, and their covariation in a nationally representative sample. *Developmental Psychology, 44*, 831–839.

Rolls, B. J., Morris, E. L., & Roe, L. S. (2002). Portion size of food affects energy intake in normal-weight and overweight men and women. *American Journal of Clinical Nutrition, 76*, 1207–1213.

Rommetveit, R. (1985). Language acquisition as increasing linguistic structuring of experience and symbolic behavior control. In J. V. Wertsch (Ed.), *Culture, communication, and cognition: Vygotskian perspectives* (pp. 183–204). Cambridge, UK: Cambridge University Press.

Roopnarine, J. L., & Hossain, Z. (1992). Parent-child interaction patterns in urban Indian families in New Delhi: Are they changing? In J. L. Roopnarine & D. B. Carter (Eds.), *Parent-child socialization in diverse cultures. Annual advances in applied developmental psychology.* (Vol. 5, pp. 1–16). Norwood, NJ: Ablex Publishing.

Roopnarine, J. L., Lu, M., & Ahmeduzzaman, M. (1989). Parental reports of early patterns of caregiving play and discipline in India and Malaysia. *Early Child Development and Care, 50*, 109–120.

Ropelato, J. (2009). Internet Pornography Statistics - 2009. *Top Ten Reviews.com.*

Rosch, E., Mervis, C. B., Gray, W. D., Johnson, D. M. & Boyes-Braem, P. (1976). Basic objects in natural categories. *Cognitive Psychology, 8*, 382–439.

Rose, A. (2002). Co-rumination in the friendships of girls and boys. *Child Development, 73*, 1830–1843.

Rose, A. J., Carlson, W., & Waller, E. M. (2007). Prospective associations of co-rumination with friendship and emotional adjustment: Considering the socioemotional trade-offs of co-rumination. *Developmental Psychology, 43*, 1019–1031.

Rose, A. J., & Montemayor, R. (1994). The relationship between gender role orientation and perceived self-competency in male and female adolescents. *Sex Roles, 31*, 579–595.

Rose, A. J. & Rudolph, K. D. (2006). A review of sex differences in peer relationship processes: Potential tradeoffs for the emotional and behavioral development of girls and boys. *Psychological Bulletin, 132*, 98–131.

Rose, A. J., Swenson, L. P., & Carlson, W. (2003). Friendships of aggressive youth: Considering the influences of being disliked and of being perceived as popular. *Journal of Experimental Child Psychology, 88*, 25–45.

Rose, A. J., Swenson, L. P., & Waller, E. M. (2004). Overt and relational aggression and perceived popularity: Developmental differences in concurrent and prospective relations. *Developmental Psychology, 40*, 378–387.

Rose, J. S., Chassin, L., Presson, C. C., & Sherman, S. J. (1999). Peer influences on adolescent cigarette smoking: A prospective sibling analysis. *Merrill-Palmer Quarterly, 45*, 62–84.

Rose, S. A., & Feldman, J. F. (1995). Prediction of IQ and specific cognitive abilities at 11 years from infancy measures. *Developmental Psychology, 31*, 531–539.

Rose, S. A., & Feldman, J. F. (1997). Memory and speed: Their role in the relation of infant information processing to later IQ. *Child Development, 68*, 630–641.

Rosen, W. D., Adamson, L. B., & Bakeman, R. (1992). An experimental investigation of infant social referencing: Mothers' messages and gender differences. *Developmental Psychology, 28*, 1172–1178.

Rosenberg, M. (1979). *Conceiving the self.* New York: Basic Books.

Rosenfeld, A., & Wise, N. (2000). *The overscheduled child: Avoiding the hyper-parenting trap.* New York: St. Martin's Griffin.

Rosengren, K. S., Gelman, S. A., Kalish, C. W., & McCormick, M. (1991). As time goes by: Children's early understanding of growth in animals. *Child Development, 62*, 1302–1320.

Rosengren, K. S., & Hickling, A. K. (2000). Metamorphosis and magic: The development of children's thinking about possible events and plausible mechanisms. In K. S. Rosengren, C. N. Johnson, & P L. Harris (Eds.), *Imagining the impossible: Magical, scientific, and religious thinking in children* (pp. 75–98). Cambridge, UK: Cambridge University Press.

Rosenshine, B., & Meister, C. (1994). Reciprocal teaching: A review of nineteen experimental studies. *Review of Educational Research, 64*, 479–530.

Rosenstein, D., & Oster, H. (1988). Differential facial responses to four basic tastes in newborns. *Child Development, 59*, 1555–1568.

Ross, H. S., & Lollis, S. (1989). A social relations analysis of toddler peer relations. *Child Development, 60*, 1082–1091.

Ross, N., Medin, D., Coley, J. D., & Atran, S. (2003). Cultural and experiential differences in the development of folkbiological induction. *Cognitive Development, 18*, 25–47.

Rossi, A. S. (1977). A biosocial perspective on parenting. *Daedalus, 106*, 1–31.

Rotenberg, K., & Eisenberg, N. (1997). Developmental differences in the understanding of and reaction to others' inhibition of emotional expression. *Developmental Psychology, 33*, 526–537.

Rothbart, M. K., Ahadi, S. A., & Evans, D. E. (2000). Temperament and personality: Origins and outcomes. *Journal of Personality and Social Psychology, 78*, 122–135.

Rothbart, M. K., & Bates, J. E. (1998). Temperament. In W. Damon (Series Ed.) & N. Eisenberg (Vol. Ed.), *Handbook of child psychology: Vol. 3. Social, emotional, and personality development* (5th ed., pp. 105–176). New York: Wiley.

Rothbart, M. K., & Bates, J. E. (2006). Temperament. In W. Damon & R. M. Lerner (Series Eds.) & N. Eisenberg (Vol. Ed.), *Handbook of child psychology: Vol. 3. Social, emotional, and personality development.* (6th ed., pp. 99–166). Hoboken, NJ: Wiley.

Rothbart, M. K., Derryberry, D., & Hershey, K. (2000). Stability of temperament in childhood: Laboratory infant assessment to parent report at seven years. In V. J. Molfese & D. L. Molfese (Eds.), *Temperament and personality development across the life span* (pp. 85–119). Hillsdale, NJ: Erlbaum.

Rothbart, M. K., & Gartstein, M. A. (2000). Infant Behavior Questionnaire—Revised. Retrieved January 27, 2002, from http://www.uoregon.edu/~maryroth.

Rothbart, M. K., & Rueda, M. R. (2005). The development of effortful control. In U. Mayr, E. Awh, & S. Keele (Eds.), *Developing individuality in the human brain: A festschrift honoring Michael I Poser—May, 2003* (pp. 167–188). Washington, DC: American Psychological Assocation.

Rothbart, M. K., Sheese, B. E., & Posner, M. I. (2007). Executive attention and effortful control: Linking temperament, brain networks, and genes. *Child Development Perspectives, 1*, 2–7.

Rothbaum, F., Pott, M., Azuma, H., Miyake, K., & Weisz, J. (2000). The development of close relationships in Japan and the United States: Paths of symbiotic harmony and generative tension. *Child Development, 71*, 1121–1142.

Rothbaum, F., & Weisz, J. R. (1994). Parental caregiving and child externalizing behavior in nonclinical samples: A meta-analysis. *Psychological Bulletin, 116*, 55–74.

Rotheram, M. J., & Phinney, J. S. (1987). Introduction: Definitions and perspectives in the study of children's ethnic socialization. In J. S. Phinney & M. J. Rotheram (Eds.), *Children's ethnic socialization* (pp. 10–28). Newbury Park, CA: Sage.

Rotheram-Borus, M. J., & Langabeer, K. A. (2001). Developmental trajectories of gay, lesbian, and bisexual youths. In A. R. D'Augelli, & Patterson, C. (Eds.), *Lesbian, gay and bisexual identities among youth: Psychological perspectives* (pp. 97–128). New York: Oxford University Press.

Rovee-Collier, C. (1997). Dissociations in infant memory: Rethinking the development of implicit and explicit memory. *Psychological Review, 104*, 467–498.

Rowe, D. C. (1994). *The limits of family influence: Genes, experience, and behavior.* New York: Guilford.

Rowe, M., & Goldin-Meadow, S. (2009) Early gesture selectively predicts later language learning. *Developmental Science, 12*, 182–187.

Rowe, M. L., Ozcaliskan, S., & Goldin-Meadow, S. (2008). Learning words by hand: Gesture's role in predicting vocabulary development. *First Language, 28*, 182–199.

Rowley, S. J., Kurtz-Costes, B., Mistry, R., & Feagans, L. (2007). Social status and a predictor of race and gender stereotypes in late childhood and early adolescence. *Social Development, 16*, 150–168.

Rubenstein, A. J., Kalakanis, L., & Langlois, J. H. (1999). Infant preferences for attractive faces: A cognitive explanation. *Developmental Psychology, 35,* 848–855.

Rubin, K. H., Bukowski, W., & Parker, J. G. (1998). Peer interactions, relationships, and groups. In W. Damon (Series Ed.) & N. Eisenberg (Vol. Ed.), *Handbook of child psychology. Vol. 3. Social, emotional, and personality development* (5th ed.). New York: Wiley.

Rubin, K. H., Bukowski, W., & Parker, J. (2006). Peer interactions, relationships, and groups. In N. Eisenberg (Vol. Ed.) and W. Damon & R. M. Lerner (Series Eds.), *Handbook of child psychology. Vol.3. Social, emotional, and personality development.* (6th ed., pp. 571-645). Hoboken, NJ: Wiley.

Rubin, K. H., Chen, X., McDougall, P., Bowker, A.,& McKinnon, J. (1995). The Waterloo Longitudinal Project: Predicting internalizing and externalizing problems in adolescence. *Development and Psychopathology, 7,* 751–764.

Rubin, K. H., Coplan, R. J., & Bowker, J. C. (2009). Social withdrawal in childhood. *Annual Review of Psychology, 60,* 141–171.

Rubin, K. H., Dwyer, K. M., Booth, C. L., Kim, A. H., Burgess, K. B., & Rose-Krasnor, L. (2004). Attachment, friendship, and psychosocial functioning in early adolescence. *Journal of Early Adolescence, 24,* 326–356.

Rubin, K. H., Fein, G. G., & Vandenberg, B. (1983). Play. In E. M. Hetherington (Ed.), *Handbook of child psychology: Vol. 4. Socialization, personality, and social development* (4th ed., pp. 693–744). New York: Wiley.

Rubin, K. H., Hastings, P., Chen, X., Stewart, S., & McNichol, K. (1998). Intrapersonal and maternal correlates of aggression, conflict, and externalizing problems in toddlers. *Child Development, 69*, 1614–1629.

Rubin, K. H., Lynch, D., Coplan, R., Rose-Krasnor, L., & Booth, C. L. (1994). "Birds of a feather . . .": Behavioral concordances and preferential personal attraction in children. *Child Development, 65*, 1778–1785.

Rubin, K. H., Nelson, L. J., Hastings, P., & Asendorpf, J. (1999). The transaction between parents' perceptions of their children's shyness and their parenting styles. *International Journal of Behavioral Development, 23,* 937–957.

Ruble, D. (2004, March). *Gender development.* Paper presented at the Gender Development conference, San Francisco, CA.

Ruble, D. N., Grosovsky, E. H., Frey, K. S., & Cohen, R. (1992). Developmental changes in competence assessment. In A. K. Boggiano & T. S. Pittman (Eds.), *Achievement and motivation: A social developmental perspective.* New York: Cambridge University Press.

Ruble, D., & Martin, C. L. (1998). Gender development. In N. Eisenberg (Ed.), *Handbook of child psychology: Vol. 3, Social, emotional and personality development* (5th ed., pp. 933–1016). New York: Wiley.

Ruble, D. N., Martin, C. L., & Berenbaum, S. (2006). Gender development. In W. Damon & R. L. Lerner (Series Eds.) & N. Eisenberg (Vol. Ed.), *Handbook of child psychology, Vol. 3. Social, emotional, and personality development* (6th ed., pp. 858–932). Hoboken, NJ: Wiley.

Rudolph, K. D., & Clark, A. G. (2001). Conceptions of relationships in children with depressive and aggressive symptoms: Social-cognitive distortion or reality? *Journal of Abnormal Child Psychology, 29*, 41–56.

Rudolph, K. D., Dennig, M. D., & Weisz, J. R. (1995). Determinants and consequences of children's coping in the medical setting: Conceptualization, review, and critique. *Psychological Bulletin, 118,* 328–357.

Rudolph, K. D., & Flynn, M. (2007). Childhood adversity and youth depression: Influence of gender and subertal status. *Development and Psychopathology, 19*, 497–521.

Rudolph, K. D., Ladd, G., & Dinella, L. (2007). Gender differences in the interpersonal consequences of early-onset depressive symptoms. *Merrill-Palmer Quarterly, 53*, 461–488.

Rudolph, K. D., Lambert, S. M., Clark, A. G., & Kurlakowsky, K. D. (2001). Negotiating the transition to middle school: The role of self-regulatory processes. *Child Development, 72,* 929–946.

Rudy, D., & Grusec, J. E. (2006). Authoritarian parenting in individualist and collectivist groups: Associatons with maternal emotion and cognition and children's self-esteem. *Journal of Family Psychology, 20,* 68–78.

Rueda, M. R., Posner, M. I., & Rothbart, M. K. (2004). Attentional control and self-regulation. In R. F. Baumeister & K. D. Vohs (Eds.), *Handbook of self-regulation: Research, theory, and applications* (pp. 283–300). New York: Guilford.

Rueda, M. R., Rothbart, M. K., McCandliss, B. D., Saccamanno, L., & Posner, M. I. (2005). Training, maturation and genetic influences on the development of executive attention. *Proceedings of the National Academy of Sciences of the USA, 102,* 14931–14936.

Rueter, M. A., & Conger, R. D. (1998). Reciprocal influences between parenting and adolescent problem-solving behavior. *Developmental Psychology, 34,* 1470–1482.

Ruff, H. A. (1986). Components of attention during infants' manipulative exploration. *Child Development, 57,* 105–114.

Ruff, H. A., & Capozzoli, M. C. (2003). Development of attention and distractibility in the first 4 years of life. *Developmental Psychology, 39,* 877–890.

Ruffman, T., Slade, L., & Crowe, E. (2002). The relation between children's and mothers' mental state language and theory-of-mind. *Child Development, 73,* 734–751.

Rumelhart, D. E., & McClelland, J. L. (1986). On learning the past tense of English verbs. In J. L. McClelland, D. E. Rumelhart, & the PDP Research Group (Eds.), *Parallel distributed processing: Explorations in the microstructure of cognition: Vol. 2. Psychological and biological models.* Cambridge, MA: Bradford Books/The MIT Press.

Rushton, J. P. (1975). Generosity in children: Immediate and long term effects of modeling, preaching, and moral judgment. *Journal of Personality and Social Psychology, 31,* 459–466.

Rushton, J. P., Fulker, D. W., Neale, M. C., Nias, D. K. B., & Eysenck, H. J. (1986). Altruism and aggression: The heritability of individual differences. *Journal of Personality and Social Psychology, 50,* 1192–1198.

Russell, A., & Finnie, V. (1990). Preschool children's social status and maternal instructions to assist group entry. *Developmental Psychology, 26,* 603–611.

Russell, A., Pettit, G. S., & Mize, J. (1998). Horizontal qualities in parent-child relationships: Parallels with and possible consequences for children's peer relationships. *Developmental Review, 18,* 313–352.

Russell, G., & Russell, A. (1987). Mother-child and father-child relationships in middle childhood. *Child Development, 58,* 1573–1585.

Russell, J. A., & Bullock, M. (1986). On dimensions preschoolers use to interpret facial expressions of emotion. *Developmental Psychology, 22,* 97–102.

Russell, J. A., & Widen, S. C. (2002). A label superiority effect in children's categorization of facial expressions. *Social Development, 11,* 30–52.

Russell, S. T., Crockett, L. J., Shen, Y-L., & Lee, S-A. (2008). Cross-ethnic invariance of self-esteem and depression measures for Chinese, Filipino, and European American adolescents. *Journal of Youth and Adolescence, 37,* 50–61.

Rutter, M. (1979). Protective factors in children's responses to stress and disadvantage. In M. W. Kent & J. E. Rolf (Eds.), *Primary prevention of psychopathology: Social competence in children* (Vol. 3). Hanover, Austrailia: University of New England.

Rutter, M., O'Connor, T. G., & the English and Romanian Adoptees (ERA) Study Team (2004). Are there biological programming effects for psychological development? Findings from a study of Romanian adoptees. *Developmental Psychology, 40,* 81–94.

Rymer, R. (1993). *Genie: An abused child's flight from silence.* New York: HarperCollins.

Saarni, C. (1979). Children's understanding of display rules for expressive behavior. *Developmental Psychology, 15,* 424–429.

Saarni, C. (1984). An observational study of children's attempts to monitor their expressive behavior. *Child Development, 55,* 1504–1513.

Saarni, C., Campos, J. J., Camras, L. A., & Witherington, D. W. (2006). Emotional development: Action, communication, and understanding. In W. Damon & R. L. Lerner (Series Eds.) & N. Eisenberg (Vol. Ed.), *Handbook of child psychology, Vol. 3. Social, emotional, and personality development* (6th ed., pp. 226–299). Hoboken, NJ: Wiley.

Saarni, C., Mumme, D. L., & Campos, J. J. (1998). Emotional development: Action, communication, and understanding. In W. Damon (Series Ed.) & N. Eisenberg (Vol. Ed.), *Handbook of child psychology: Vol. 3. Social, emotional, and personality development* (5th ed., pp. 237–309). New York: Wiley.

Sabongui, A. G., & Bukowski, W. M., & Newcomb, A. F. (1998). The peer ecology of popularity: The network embeddedness of a child's friend predicts the child's subsequent popularity. In W. Bukowski & T. Cillessen (Eds.) *Sociometry then and now: Six decades of the sociometric study of children in peer groups.* (Volume in the New Directions for Child Development Series) (pp. 83–92). San Francisco: Jossey Bass.

Sackett, P. R., Borneman, M. J., & Connelly, B. S. (2008). High-stakes testing in higher education and employment: Appraising the evidence for validity and fairness. *American Psychologist, 63,* 215–227.

Sadato, N., Pascual-Leone, A., Grafman, J., & Deiber, M. P. (1998). Neural networks for Braille reading by the blind. *Brain, 121,* 1213–1229.

Sadker, M., & Sadker, D. (1994). *Failing at fairness: How America's schools cheat girls.* New York: Scribner.

Saffran, J. R. (2003). Statistical language learning; Mechanisms and constraints. *Current Directions in Psychological Science, 12,* 110–114.

Saffran, J. R., Aslin, R. N., & Newport, E. L. (1996). Statistical learning by 8-month-old infants. *Science, 274,* 1926–1928.

Saffran, J. R., & Thiessen, E. D. (2007). Domain-general learning capacities. In E. Hoff & M. Shatz (Eds.). *Blackwell handbook of language development* (pp. 68–86). Malden, MA: Blackwell.

Safren, S. A., & Heimberg, R. G. (1999). Depression, hopelessness, suicidality, and related factors in sexual minority and heterosexual adolescents. *Journal of Consulting and Clinical Psychology, 67,* 859–866.

Sagi, A., Koren-Karie, N., Gini, M., Ziv, Y., & Joels, T. (2002). Shedding further light on the effects of various types and quality of early child care on infant-mother attachment relationship: The Haifa study of early child care. *Child Development, 73,* 1166–1186.

Salapatek, P., & Kessen, W. (1966). Visual scanning of triangles by the human newborn. *Journal of Experimental Child Psychology, 3,* 155–167.

Sallquist, J., Eisenberg, N., Spinrad, T. L., Gaertner, B. M., Eggum, N., D., & Zhou, N. (in press). Mothers' and children's positive emotion: Relations and trajectories across four years. *Social Development.*

Sallquist, J. V., Eisenberg, N., Spinrad, T. L., Reiser, M., Hofer, C, Zhou, Q., Liew, J., & Eggum, N. (2009). Positive and negative emotionality: Trajectories across six years and relations with social competence. *Emotion, 9,* 15–28.

Salmivalli, C., & Voeten, M. (2004). Connections between attitudes, group norms, and behaviour in bullying situations. *International Journal of Behavioral Development, 28,* 246–258.

Salmon, K. (2001). Remembering and reporting by children: The influence of cues and props. *Clinical Psychology Review, 21,* 267–300.

Salthouse, T. A. (2009). Decomposing age correlations on neuropsychological and cognitive variables. *Journal of the International Neuropsychological Society, 15,* 650–661.

Salthouse, T. A. (2009). When does age-related cognitive decline begin? *Neurobiology of Aging, 30,* 507-514.

Salzinger, S., Feldman, R. S., Ng-Mak, D. S., Mojica, E., & Stockhammer, T. F. (2001). The effect of physical abuse on children's social and affective status: A model of cognitive and behavioral processes explaining the association. *Developmental and Psychopathology, 13,* 805–825.

Sameroff, A. J. (1986). Environmental context of child development. *Journal of Pediatrics, 109,* 102–200.

Sameroff, A. J. (1998). Environmental risk factors in infancy. In J. G. Warhol (Ed.), *New Perspectives in Early Emotional Development.* Skillman, NJ: Johnson & Johnson. pp. 159–171.

Sameroff, A. J., Seifer, R., Baldwin, A., & Baldwin, C. (1993). Stability of intelligence from preschool to adolescence: The influence of social and family risk factors. *Child Development, 64,* 80–97.

Sameroff, A. J., Seifer, R., Zax, M., & Barocas, R. (1987). Early indicators of developmental risk: The Rochester Longitudinal Study. *Schizophrenia Bulletin, 13,* 383–394.

Sampa, A. (1997). Street children of Lusaka: "A case of the Zambia Red Cross drop-in centre." *Journal of Psychology in Africa; South of the Sahara, the Caribbean and Afro-Latin-America, 2,* 1–23.

Sampson, R. J., & Laub, J. H. (1994). Urban poverty and the family context of delinquency: A new look at structure and process in a classic study. *Child Development, 65,* 523–540.

Samuelson, L. K., & Horst, J. S. (2008). Confronting complexity: Insights from the details of behavior over multiple timescales. *Developmental Science, 11,* 209–215.

Samuelson, L. K., & Smith, L. B. (2005). They call it like they see it: Spontaneous naming and attention to shape. *Developmental Science, 8,* 182–198.

Samuolis, J., Layburn, K., & Schiaffino, K. (2001). Identity development and attachment to parents in college students. *Journal of Youth and Adolescence, 30,* 373–384.

Sandman, C. A., Wadhwa, P., Hetrick, W., Porto, M., & Peeke, H. V. S. (1997). Human fetal heart rate dishabituation between thirty and thirty-two weeks gestation. *Child Development, 68,* 1031–1040.

Santangelo, S. L., & Folstein, S. E. (1999). Autism: A genetic perspective. In H. Tager-Flusberg (Ed.), *Neurodevelopmental disorders: Developmental cognitive neuroscience* (pp. 431–447). Cambridge, MA: The MIT Press.

Saraswathi, T. S., & Dutta, R. (1988). *Invisible boundaries: Grooming for adult roles.* New Delhi, India: Northern Book Centre.

Sarigiani, P. A., Heath, P. A., & Camarena, P. M. (2003). The significance of parental depressed mood for young adolescents' emotional and family experiences. *Journal of Early Adolescence, 23,* 241–267.

Saudino, K. J. (2005). Behavioral genetics and child temperament. *Developmental and Behavioral Pediatrics, 26,* 214–223.

Saudino, K. J., & Eaton, W. O. (1991). Infant temperament and genetics: An objective twin study of motor activity level. *Child Development, 62,* 1167–1174.

Saudino, K., McGuire, S., Reiss, D., Hetherington, E. M., & Plomin, R. (1995). Parent ratings of EAS temperaments in twins, full siblings, half siblings, and step siblings. *Journal of Personality and Social Psychology, 68,* 723–733.

Savage-Rumbaugh, E. S., Murphy, J., Sevcik, R. A., Brakke, K. E., Williams, S. L., & Rumbaugh, D. M. (1993). Language comprehension in ape and child. *Monographs of the Society for Research in Child Development, 58*(3–4, Serial No. 233).

Savin-Williams, R. C. (1989a). Coming out to parents and self-esteem among gay and lesbian youths. *Journal of Homosexuality, 18,* 1–35.

Savin-Williams, R. C. (1989b). Parental influences on the self-esteem of gay and lesbian youths: A reflected appraisals model. *Journal of Homosexuality, 17,* 93–109.

Savin-Williams, R. C. (1994). Verbal and physical abuse as stressors in the lives of lesbian, gay male, and bisexual youths: Associations with school problems, running away, substance abuse, prostitution, and suicide. *Journal of Consulting and Clinical Psychology, 62,* 261–269.

Savin-Williams, R. C. (1996) Self-labeling and disclosure among gay, lesbian, and bisexual youths. In J. Laird & R-J. Green (Eds)., *Lesbians and gays in couples and families* (pp. 153–182). San Francisco: Jossey-Bass.

Savin-Williams, R. C. (1998a). *". . . And then I became gay": Young men's stories.* New York: Routledge.

Savin-Williams, R. C. (1998b). The disclosure to families of same-sex attractions by lesbian, gay, and bisexual youths. *Journal of Research on Adolescence, 8,* 49–68.

Savin-Williams, R. C. (2001a). A critique of research on sexual minority youths. *Journal of Adolescence, 24,* 5–13.

Savin Williams, R. C. (2001b). *Mom, Dad, I'm gay: How families negotiate coming out.* Washington, DC: American Psychological Association Press.

Savin-Williams, R. C. (2006). Who's gay? Does it matter? *Current Directions in Psychological Science, 15,* 40–44.

Savin-Williams, R. C., & Cohen, K. M. (2004). Homoerotic development during childhood and adolescence. *Child and Adolescent Psychiatric Clinics, 13,* 529–549.

Savin-Williams, R. C. & Cohen, K. M. (2007). Development of same-sex attracted youth. In I. H. Meyers & M. E. Northridge (Eds.), *The health of sexual minorities: Public health perspectives on lesbian, gay, bisexual, and transgender populations* (pp. 27–47). New York: Springer.

Savin-Williams, R. C., & Diamond, L. M. (2000). Sexual identity trajectories among sexual-minority youths: Gender comparisons. *Archives of Sexual Behavior, 29,* 419–440.

Savin-Williams, R. C., & Ream, G. (2003a). Sex variations in the disclosure to parents of same-sex attractions. *Journal of Family Psychology, 17,* 429–438.

Savin-Williams, R. C., & Ream, G. (2003b). Suicide attempts among sexual-minority male youth. *Journal of Clinical Child and Adolescent Psychology, 32,* 509–522.

Savin-Williams, R. C., & Ream, G. L. (2007). Prevalence and stability of sexual orientation components during adolescence and young adulthood. *Archives of Sexual Behavior, 36,* 385–394.

Saxe, G. B., Guberman, S. R., & Gearhart, M. (1987). Social processes in early number development. *Monographs of the Society for Research in Child Development, 52*(2, Serial No. 216).

Saxe, R., Carey, S., & Kanwisher, N. (2004). Understanding other minds: Linking developmental psychology and functional neuroimaging. *Annual Review of Psychology, 55,* 87–124.

Saxe, R., & Powell, L. J. (2006). It's the thought that counts: Specific brain regions for one component of theory of mind. *Psychological Science, 17,* 692–699.

Scaramella, L. V., Conger, R. D., Simons, R. L., & Whitbeck, L. B. (1998). Predicting risk for pregnancy by late adolescence: A social contextual perspective. *Developmental Psychology, 34,* 1233–1245.

Scaramella, L. V., Conger, R. D., Spoth, R. & Simmons R. L. (2002). Evaluation of a social contextual model of delinquency: A cross-study replication. *Child Development, 73,* 175–195.

Scaramella, L. V., Neppl, T. K., Ontai, L. L., & Conger, R. D. (2008). Consequences of socioeconomic disadvantage across three generations: Parenting behavior and child externalizing problems. *Journal of Family Psychology, 22,* 725–733.

Scarr, S. (1992). Developmental theories for the 1990s: Development and individual differences. *Child Development, 63,* 1–19.

Scarr, S. (1998). American child care today. *American Psychologist, 53,* 95–108.

Scarr, S., & McCartney, K. (1983). How people make their own environments: A theory of genotype-environment effects. *Child Development, 54,* 424–435.

Scarr, S., & Salapatek, P. (1970). Patterns of fear development during infancy. *Merrill-Palmer Quarterly, 16,* 53–90.

Scarr, S., & Weinberg, R. A. (1976). I. Q. test performance of black children adopted by white families. *American Psychologist, 31,* 726–739.

Scarr, S., & Weinberg, R. A. (1983). The Minnesota Adoption Studies: Genetic differences and malleability. *Child Development, 54,* 260–267.

Schaal, B., Orgeur, P., & Rognon, C. (1995). Odor sensing in the human fetus: Anatomical, functional, and chemoecological bases. In J. P. Lecanuet, W. P. Fifer, N. A. Krasnegor, & W. P. Smotherman (Eds.), *Fetal development: A psychobiological perspective.* Hillsdale, NJ: Erlbaum.

Schaeffer, C. M., Petras, H., Ialongo, N., Poduska, J., & Kellam, S. (2003). Modeling growth in boys' aggressive behavior across elementary school: Links to later criminal involvement, conduct disorder, and antisocial personality disorder. *Developmental Psychology, 39,* 1020–1035.

Schauble, L. (1996). The development of scientific reasoning in knowledge-rich contexts. *Developmental Psychology, 32,* 102–119.

Schellenberg, E. G., & Trehub, S. E. (1996). Natural musical intervals: Evidence from infant listeners. *Psychological Science, 7,* 272–277.

Scheper-Hughes, N. (1992). *Death without weeping: The violence of everyday life in Brazil.* Los Angeles: University of California Press.

Schieffelin, B. B., & Ochs, E. (1987). *Language socialization across cultures.* New York: Cambridge University Press.

Schlaggar, B. L., & Church, J. A. (2009). Functional neuroimaging insights into the development of skilled reading. *Current Directions in Psychological Science, 18,* 21–26.

Schmidt, F. L., & Hunter, J. (2004). General mental ability in the world of work: Occupational attainment and job performance. *Journal of Personality & Social Psychology, 86,* 162–173.

Schmidt, F. L., & Hunter, J. E. (1998). The validity and utility of selection methods in personnel psychology: Practical and theoretical implications of 85 years of research findings. *Psychological Bulletin, 124,* 262–274.

Schmidt, M. E., & Bagwell, C. L. (2007). The protective role of friendships in overtly and relationally victimized boys and girls. *Merrill-Palmer Quarterly, 53,* 439–460.

Schmidt, M. E., Pempek, T. A., Kirkorian, H. L., Frankenfield, A. E., & Anderson, D. R. (2008). The effects of background television on the toy play behavior of very young children. *Child Development, 79,* 1137–1151.

Schmuckler, M. A. (1996). Visual-proprioceptive intermodal perception in infancy. *Infant Behavior and Development, 19,* 221–232.

Schneider, B. H., Atkinson, L., & Tardif, C. (2001). Child-parent attachment and children's peer relations: A quantitative review. *Developmental Psychology, 37,* 86–100.

Schneider, M. S. (2001). Toward a reconceptualization of the coming-out process for adolescent females. In A. R. D'Augelli & C. Patterson (Eds.), *Lesbian, gay and bisexual identities among youth: Psychological perspectives* (pp. 71–96). New York: Oxford University Press.

Schneider, W. (1998). Performance prediction in young children: Effects of skill, metacognition and wishful thinking. *Developmental Science, 1,* 291–297.

Schneider, W., & Bjorklund, D. F. (1998). Memory. In D. Kuhn & R. S. Siegler (Vol. Eds.) *Volume 2: Cognition, perception, and language.* In W. Damon (Series Ed.), *Handbook of child psychology* (5th ed., pp. 467–521). New York: Wiley.

Schneider, W., Korkel, J., & Weinert, F. E. (1989). Domain-specific knowledge and memory performance: A comparison of high- and low-aptitude children. *Journal of Educational Psychology, 81,* 306–312.

Schneider, W., & Pressley, M. (1997). *Memory development between 2 and 20* (2nd ed). New York: Springer-Verlag.

Schniering, C. A., & Rapee, R. M. (2004). The relationship between automatic thoughts and negative emotions in children and adolescents: A test of the cognitive content-specificity hypothesis. *Journal of Abnormal Psychology, 113,* 464–470.

Schoeber-Peterson, D., & Johnson, C. J. (1991). Non-dialogue speech during preschool interactions. *Journal of Child Language, 18,* 153–170.

Scholl, B. J., & Leslie, A. M. (1999). Modularity, development and "theory of mind." *Mind & Language, 14,* 131–153.

Scholl, B. J., & Leslie, A. M. (2002). Minds, modules, and meta-analysis. Commentary on "Meta-analysis of theory-of-mind development: The truth about false belief." *Child Development, 72,* 696–701.

Scholnick, E. K., Friedman, S. L., & Wallner-Allen, K. E. (1997). What do they really mean? A comparative analysis of planning tasks. In S. L. Friedman & E. K. Scholnick (Eds.), *The developmental psychology of planning: Why, how, and when do we plan?* (pp. 127–156). Mahwah, NJ: Erlbaum.

Scholte, R. H. J., Poelen, E. A. P., Willemsin, G., Boomsma, D., & Engels, R. C. M. E. (2008). Relative risks of adolescent and young adult alcohol use: The role of drinking fathers, mothers, siblings, and friends. *Addictive Behaviors, 33,* 1–14.

Schoppe-Sullivan, S. J., Brown, G. L., Cannon, E. A., Mangelsdorf, S. C., & Sokolowski, M. S. (2008). Maternal gatekeeping, coparenting quality, and fathering behavior in families with infants. *Journal of Family Psychology, 22,* 389–398.

Schuetze, P., Eiden, R. D., & Dombkowski, L. (2006). The association between cigarette smoking during pregnancy and maternal behavior during the neonatal period. *Infancy, 10,* 267–288.

Schulenberg J., Maggs, J. L., Dielman, T. E., Leech, S. L., Kloska, D. D., Shope, J. T., & Laetz, V. B. (1999). On peer influences to get drunk: A panel study of young adolescents. *Merrill-Palmer Quarterly, 45,* 108–142.

Schult, C. A., & Wellman, H. M. (1997). Explaining human movements and actions. *Cognition, 62,* 291–324.

Schultz, D., Izard, C. E., Ackerman, B. P., & Yungstrom, E. A. (2001). Emotion knowledge in economically disadvantaged children: Self-regulatory antecedents and relations to social difficulties and withdrawal. *Development and Psychopathology, 13,* 53–67.

Schulz, L. E., & Sommerville, J. (2006). God does not play dice: Causal determinism and preschoolers' causal inferences. *Child Development, 77,* 427–442.

Schutte, A. R., Spencer, J. P., & Schöner, G. (2003). Testing the dynamic field theory: Working memory for locations becomes more spatially precise over development. *Child Development, 74,* 1393–1417.

Schwarz, S. J., Mason, C. A., Pantin, H., & Szapocznik, J. (2009). Longitudinal relationships between family functioning and identity development in Hispanic adolescents: Continuity and change. *Journal of Early Adolescence, 29,* 177–211.

Schwartz, D., McFadyen-Ketchum, S. A., Dodge, K. A., Pettit, G. S., & Bates, J. E. (1998). Peer group victimization as a predictor of children's behavior problems at home and in school. *Development and Psychopathology, 10,* 87–99.

Schwartz, D., McFadyen-Ketchum, S., Dodge, K. A., Pettit, G. S., & Bates, J. E. (1999). Early behavior problems as a predictor of later peer group victimization: Moderators and mediators in the pathways of social risk. *Journal of Abnormal Child Psychology, 27,*191–201.

Schwartz, S., & Johnson, J. J. (1985). *Psychopathology of childhood.* New York: Pergamon.

Seaton, E. K., Caldwell, C. H., Sellers, R. M., & Jackson, J. S. (2008). The prevalence of perceived discrimination among African American and Caribbean black youth. *Developmental Psychology, 44,* 1288–1297.

Seaton, E. K., & Yip, T. (2009). School and neighborhood contexts, perceptions of racial discrimination, and psychological well-being among African American adolescents. *Journal of Youth and Adolescence, 38,* 153–163.

Sebanc, A. M., Kearns, K.T., Hernandez, M. D., & Galvin, K. B. (2007). Predicting having a best friend in young children: Individual characteristics and friendship features. *Journal of Genetic Psychology, 168,* 81–95.

Segal, N. L., McGuire, S. A., Havlena, J., Gill, P., & Hershberger, S. L. (2007). Intellectual similarity of virtual twin pairs: Developmental trends. *Personality and Individual Differences, 42,* 1209–1219.

Seidman, E., Allen, L., Aber, J. L., Mitchell, C., & Feinman, J. (1994). The impact of school transitions in early adolescence on the self-system and perceived social context of poor urban youth. *Child Development 65,* 507–522.

Seifer, R., Sameroff, A. J., Barrett, L. C., & Krafchuk, E. (1994). Infant temperament measured by multiple observations and mother report. *Child Development, 65,* 1478–1490.

Seifer, R., Schiller, M., Sameroff, A. J., Resnick, S., & Riordan, K. (1996). Attachment, maternal sensitivity, and infant temperament during the first year of life. *Developmental Psychology, 32,* 12–25.

Selfe, L. (1995). Nadia reconsidered. In C. Golomb (Ed.), *The development of artistically gifted children: Selected case studies* (pp. 197–236). Hillsdale, NJ: Erlbaum.

Selfhout, M. H.W., Branje, S. J. T., Meeus, W. H. J. (2008). The development of delinquency and perceived friendship quality in adolescent best friendship dyads. *Journal of Abnormal Child Psychology*, 36, 471–485.

Seligman, M. E. P. (1975). *Helplessness: On depression, development, and death.* San Francisco: Freeman.

Selman, R. L. (1980). *The growth of interpersonal understanding: Developmental and clinical analysis.* New York: Academic Press.

Senghas, A., & Coppola, M. (2001). Children creating language: How Nicaraguan sign language acquired a spatial grammar. *Psychological Science, 12,* 323–328.

Serbin, L. A., Moller, L. C., Gulko, J., Powlishta, K. K., & Colburne, K. A. (1994). The emergence of gender segregation in toddler playgroups. In C. Leaper (Ed.), *Childhood gender segregation: Causes and consequences. New directions for child development* (Vol. 65, pp. 7–17). San Francisco: Jossey-Bass.

Serbin, L. A., Poulin-Dubois, D., Colburne, K. A., Sen, M. G., & Eichstedt, J. A. (2001). Gender stereotyping in infancy: Visual preferences for and knowledge of gender stereotyped toys in the second year. *International Journal of Behavioral Development, 25,* 7–15.

Serbin, L. A., Powlishta, K. K., & Gulko, J. (1993). The development of sex typing in middle childhood. *Monographs of the Society for Research in Child Development, 58*(2, Serial No. 232).

Serbin, L. A., Sprafkin, C., Elman, M. & Doyle, A. B. (1982). The early development of sex-differentiated patterns of social influence. *Canadian Journal of Behavioural Sciences, 14,* 350–363.

Serbin, L. A., Zelkowitz, P., Doyle, A., Gold, D., & Wheaton, B. (1990). The socialization of sex-differentiated skills and academic performance: A mediational model. *Sex Roles, 23,* 613–628.

Serrano, J. M., Iglesias, J., & Loeches, A. (1993). Visual discrimination and recognition of facial expressions of anger, fear and surprise in four- to six-month-old infants. *Developmental Psychobiology, 25,* 411–425.

Seyfarth, R. M., & Cheney, D. L. (1993). Meaning, reference, and intentionality in the natural vocalizations of monkeys. In H. L. Roitblat, L. M. Herman, & P. E. Nachtigall (Eds.), *Language and communication: Comparative perspectives* (pp. 195–220). Hillsdale, NJ: Erlbaum.

Shahinfar, A., Kupersmidt, J. B., & Matza, L. S. (2001). The relation between exposure to violence and social information processing among incarcerated adolescents. *Journal of Abnormal Psychology, 110,* 136–141.

Shalev, R. S. (2007). Prevalence of developmental dyscalculia. In D. B. Berch, & M. M. M. Mazzocco (Eds.), *Why is math so hard for some children? The nature and origins of mathematical learning difficulties and disabilities* (pp. 49–60). New York: Plenum.

Shanahan, L., McHale, S. M., Crouter, A. C., & Osgood, D. W. (2007). Warmth with mothers and fathers from middle childhood to late adolescence: Within- and between-families comparisons. *Developmental Psychology, 43,* 551–563.

Shanahan, L., McHale, S. M., Crouter, A. C., & Osgood, D. W. (2008). Parents' differential treatment and youth depressive symptoms and sibling relationships: Longitudinal linkages. *Journal of Marriage and the Family, 70,* 480–495.

Shantz, C. U. (1987). Conflicts between children. *Child Development, 58,* 283–305.

Shapiro, L. R., & Hudson, J. A. (1991). Tell me a make-believe story: Coherence and cohesion in young children's picture-elicited narratives. *Developmental Psychology, 27,* 960–974.

Share, D. L. (2004). Knowing letter names and learning letter sounds: A causal connection. *Journal of Experimental Child Psychology, 88,* 213–233.

Share, D. L., & Gur, T. (1999). How reading begins: A study of preschoolers' print identification strategies. *Cognition and Instruction, 17,* 177–313.

Share, D. L., & Silva, P. A. (2003). Gender bias in IQ-discrepancy and post-discrepancy definitions of reading disability. *Journal of Learning Disabilities, 36,* 4–15.

Shatz, M., & Gelman, R. (1973). The development of communication skills: Modifications in the speech of young children as a function of listener. *Monographs of the Society for Research in Child Development, 38,* 1–37.

Shaw, D. S., Criss, M. M., Schonberg, M. A., & Beck, J. E. (2004). The development of family hierarchies and their relation to children's conduct problems. *Development and Psychopathology, 16,* 483–500.

Shaw, D. S., Gilliom, M., Ingoldsby, E. M., & Nagin, D. S. (2003). Trajectories leading to school-age conduct problems. *Developmental Psychology, 39,* 189–200.

Shaw, J. A. (2003). Children exposed to war/terrorism. *Clinical Child and Family Psychology Review, 6,* 237–246.

Shaywitz, S. E., Mody, M., & Shaywitz, B. A. (2006). Neural mechanisms in dyslexia. *Current Directions in Psychological Science, 15,* 278–281.

Shaywitz, S. E., Shaywitz, B. A., Fletcher, J. M., & Escobar, M. D. (1990). Prevalence of reading disability in boys and girls. *Journal of the American Medical Association, 264,* 998–1002.

Shaywitz, B. A., Shaywitz, S. E., Pugh, K. R., Constable, R. T., Skudlarski, P., Fulbright, R. K., et al. (1995). Sex differences in the functional organization of the brain for language. *Nature, 373,* 607–609.

Shaywitz, S. E., Shaywitz, B. A., Pugh, K. R., Fulbright, R. K., Constable, R. T., Mencl, W. E., Shankweiler, D. P., Liberman, A. M., Skudlarski, P., Fletcher, J. M., Katz, L., Marchione, K. E., Lacadie, C., Gatenby, C., & Gore, J. C. (1998). Functional disruption in the organization of the brain for reading in dyslexia. *Proceedings of the National Academy of Science USA, 95,* 2636–2641.

Sheehan, M. J., & Watson, M. W. (2008). Reciprocal influences between maternal discipline techniques and aggression in children and adolescents. *Aggressive Behavior, 34,* 245–255.

Sheese, B. W., Voelker, P. M., Rothbart, M. K., & Posner, M. I. (2007). Parenting quality interacts with genetic variation in dopamine receptor D4 to influence temperament in early childhood. *Development and Psychopathology*: Special Issue: Gene–Environment Interaction, *19*, 1039–1046.

Shell, R., & Eisenberg, N. (1990). The role of peers' gender in children's naturally occurring interest in toys. *International Journal of Behavioral Development, 13,* 373–388.

Shepardson, D. P. & Pizzini, E. L. (1992). Gender bias in female elementary teachers' perceptions of the scientific ability of students. *Science Education, 76,* 147–153.

Shields, A., & Cicchetti, D. (1998). Reactive aggression among maltreated children: The contributions of attention and emotion dysregulation. *Journal of Clinical Child Psychology, 27,* 381–395.

Shiller, V. M., Izard, C. E., & Hembree, E. A. (1986). Patterns of emotion expression during separation in the strange-situation procedure. *Developmental Psychology, 22*(3), 378–382.

Shinn, M., Knickman, J. R., & Weitzman, B. C. (1991). Social relationships and vulnerability to becoming homeless among poor families. *American Psychologist, 46,* 1180–1187.

Shirtcliff, E. A., Granger, D. A., Booth, A., & Johnson, D. (2005). Low salivary cortisol levels and externalizing behavior problems in youth. *Development and Psychopathology, 17,* 167–184.

Shoal, G. D., Giancola, P. R., & Kirillova, G. P. (2003). Salivary cortisol, personality, and aggressive behavior in adolescent boys: A 5-year longitudinal study. *Journal of the American Academy of Child & Adolescent Psychiatry, 42,* 1101–1107.

Shoda, Y., Mischel, W., & Peake, P. K. (1990). Predicting adolescent cognitive and self-regulatory competencies from preschool delay of gratification: Identifying diagnostic conditions. *Journal of Personality and Social Psychology, 26,* 978–986.

Short, J. F., Jr. (1996). Personal, gang, and community careers. In C. R. Huff (Ed.), *Gangs in America* (2nd ed, pp. 221–240). Thousand Oaks, CA: Sage.

Shrum, W., & Cheek, N. H. (1987). Social structure during the school years: Onset of the degrouping process. *American Sociological Review, 52,* 218–223.

Shweder, R. A., Balle-Jensen, L., & Goldstein, W. (1995). Who sleeps by whom revisited: A method for extracting the moral goods implicit in praxis. In J. J. Goodnow, P. J. Miller, & F. Kessell (Eds.), *Cultural practices as contexts for development: New directions for child development.* San Francisco: Jossey-Bass.

Shweder, R. A., Mahapatra, M., & Miller, J. G. (1987). Culture and moral development. In J. Kagan & S. Lamb (Eds.), *The emergence of morality in young children* (pp. 1–83). Chicago: University of Chicago Press.

Siegal, M. (2004). Signposts to the essence of language. *Science, 305,* 1720–1721.

Siegel, L. S. (1993). The cognitive basis of dyslexia. In R. Pasnak & M. L. Howe (Eds.), *Emerging themes in cognitive development: Vol. 2. Competencies.* New York: Springer-Verlag.

Siegler, R. S. (1976). The effects of simple necessity and sufficiency relationships on children's causal inferences. *Child Development, 47,* 1058–1063.

Siegler, R. S. (1981). Developmental sequences within and between concepts. *Society for Research in Child Development Monographs, 46,* (Whole No. 189).

Siegler, R. S. (1986). Unities in strategy choices across domains. In M. Perlmutter (Ed.), *Minnesota symposium on child psychology,* (Vol. 19). Mahwah, NJ: Erlbaum, 1–48.

Siegler, R. S. (1988). Strategy choice procedures and the development of multiplication skill. *Journal of Experimental Psychology: General, 117,* 258–275.

Siegler, R. S. (1988). Individual differences in strategy choices: Good students, not-so-good students, and perfectionists. *Child Development, 59,* 833–851.

Siegler, R. S. (1995). How does change occur: A microgenetic study of number conservation. *Cognitive Psychology, 28,* 225–273.

Siegler, R. S. (1996). *Emerging minds: The process of change in children's thinking.* New York: Oxford University Press.

Siegler, R. S. (2006). Microgenetic analyses of learning. In W. Damon & R. M. Lerner (Series Eds.) & D. Kuhn & R. S. Siegler (Vol. Eds.), *Handbook of child psychology: Volume 2: Cognition, perception, and language* (6th ed., pp. 464–510). Hoboken, NJ: Wiley.

Siegler, R. S., & Chen, Z. (1998). Developmental differences in rule learning: A microgenetic analysis. *Cognitive Psychology, 36,* 273–310.

Siegler, R. S., & Jenkins, E. A. (1989). *How children discover new strategies.* Hillsdale, NJ: Erlbaum.

Siegler, R. S., & McGilly, K. (1989). Strategy choices in children's time-telling. In I. Levin and D. Zakay (Eds.) *Time and human cognition: A life span perspective*, (pp. 185–218). The Netherlands: Elsevier Science Publishers.

Siegler, R. S., & Mu, Y. (2008). Chinese children excel on novel mathematics problems even before elementary school. *Psychological Science, 19,* 759–763.

Siegler, R. S., & Ramani, G. B. (2009). Playing linear number board games – but not circular ones – improves low-income preschoolers' numerical understanding. *Journal of Educational Psychology, 101,* 545–560.

Siegler, R. S., & Shrager, J. (1984). Strategy choices in addition and subtraction: How do children know what to do? In C. Sophian (Ed.), *The origins of cognitive skills* (pp. 229–293). Mahwah, NJ: Erlbaum.

Siegler, R. S., & Svetina, M. (2006). What leads children to adopt new strategies? A microgenetic/cross sectional study of class inclusion. *Child Development, 77,* 996–1015.

Sigman, M. (1995). Nutrition and child development: More food for thought. *Current Directions in Psychological Science, 4,* 52–55.

Sigman, M., Cohen, S. E., & Beckwith, L. (1997). Why does infant attention predict adolescent intelligence? *Infant Behavior and Development, 20,* 133–140.

Sigman, M., & Ruskin, E. (1999). Continuity and change in the social competence of children with autism, Down syndrome, and developmental delays. *Monographs of the Society for Research in Child Development, 64* (1, Serial No. 256).

Signorella, M. L., Bigler, R. S., & Liben, L. S. (1997). A meta-analysis of children's memories for own-sex and other-sex information. *Journal of Applied Developmental Psychology, 18,* 429–445.

Signorielli, N. (1993). Television, the portrayal of women, and children's attitudes. In G. Berry & J. K. Asmen (Eds.), *Children and television: Images in a changing sociocultural world.* Newbury Park, CA: Sage.

Signorielli, N. (2001). Televisions's gender role images and contribution to stereotyping: Past present, future. In D. G. Singer & J. L. Singer (Eds.). *Handbook of children and the media* (pp. 341–358). Thousand Oaks, CA: Sage.

Signorielli, N. & Lears, M. (1992). Children, television, and conceptions about chores: Attitudes and behaviors. *Sex Roles, 27*, 157–170.

Signorielli, N., McLeod, D., & Healy, E. (1994, winter). Gender stereotypes in MTV commercials: The beat goes on. *Journal of Broadcasting & Electronic Media, 38*, 91–101.

Sijtsema, J. J., Veenstra, R., Lindenberg, S., & Salmivalli, C. (2009). Empirical test of bullies' status goals: Assessing direct goals, aggression, and prestige. *Aggressive Behavior, 35*, 57–67.

Silk, J. S., Steinberg, L., & Morris, A. S. (2003). Adolescents' emotion regulation in daily life: Links to depressive symptoms and problem behavior. *Child Development, 74*, 186–1880.

Silver, L. B. (1999). *Attention-deficit hyperactivity disorder* (2nd ed.). Washington, DC: American Psychiatric Press.

Silverman, I. W. (2003). Gender differences in resistance to temptation: Theories and evidence. *Developmental Review, 23*, 219–259.

Silverman, W. K., La Greca, A. M., & Wasserstein, S. (1995). What do children worry about? Worries and their relation to anxiety. *Child Development, 66*, 671–686.

Simcock, G. & DeLoache, J. (2006). Get the Picture? The effects of iconicity on toddlers' re-enactment from picture books. *Developmental Psychology, 42*, 1352–1357.

Simcock, G., & Hayne, H. (2002). Breaking the barrier? Children fail to translate their preverbal memories into language. Psychological Science, 13, 225–231.

Simion, F., Valenza, E., Macchi Cassia, V., Turati, C., & Umilta, C. (2002). Newborns' preference for up-down asymmetrical configurations. *Developmental Science, 5*, 427–434.

Simon, T. J. (1997). Reconceptualizing the origins of number knowledge: A "non-numerical" account. *Cognitive Development, 12*, 349–372.

Simon, T. J., Hespos, S. J., & Rochat, P. (1995). Do infants understand simple arithmetic: A replication of Wynn (1992). *Cognitive Development, 10*, 253–269.

Simon, T. J., & Rivera, S. M. (2007). Neuroanatomical approaches to the study of mathematical ability and disability. In D. B. Berch & M. M. M. Mazzocco (Eds.), *Why is math so hard for some children? The nature and origins of mathematical learning difficulties and disabilities* (pp. 283–305). New York: Plenum.

Simon, V. A., Aikins, J. W., & Prinstein, M. J. (2008). Romantic partner selection and socialization during early adolescence. *Child Development, 79*, 1676–1692.

Simons, L. G., & Conger, R. D. (2007). Linking mother-father differences in parenting to a typology of family parenting styles and adolescent outcomes. *Journal of Family Issues, 28*, 212–241.

Simons, R. L., & Associates (Eds.). (1996). *Understanding differences between divorced and intact families: Stress, interaction, and child outcome* (pp. 81–93). Thousand Oaks, CA: Sage.

Simons, R. L., & Johnson, C. (1996). Mother's parenting. In R. L. Simons & Associates (Eds.), *Understanding differences between divorced and intact families: Stress, interaction, and child outcome* (pp. 81–93). Thousand Oaks, CA: Sage.

Simpkins, S. D., Eccles, J. S., & Becnel, J. N. (2008). The meditational role of adolescents' friends in relations between activity breadth and adjustment. *Developmental Psychology, 44*, 1081–1094.

Simpkins, S. D., & Parke, R. D. (2001). The relations of parental friendships and children's friendships: Self-report and observational analysis. *Child Development, 72*, 569–582.

Simpson, E. L. (1974). Moral development research: A case study of scientific cultural bias. *Human Development, 17*, 81–106.

Simpson, J. S., Collins, W. A., Tran, S. S., & Haydon, K. C. (2007). Attachment and the experience and expression of emotions in romantic relationships: A developmental perspective. *Journal of Personality and Social Psychology, 92*, 355–367.

Sims, M., Hutchins, T. & Taylor, M. (1998). Gender segregation in young children's conflict behavior in child care settings. *Child Study Journal*, 28, 1, 1–16.

Singer, L. T., Arendt, R., Minnes, S., Farkas, K., Salvator, A., Kirchner, H. L., & Kliegman, R. (2002). Cognitive and motor outcomes of cocaine-exposed infants. *Journal of the American Medical Association, 287*, 1952–1960.

Singleton, J. L., & Newport, E. L. (2004). When learners surpass their models: The acquisition of American Sign Language from inconsistent input. *Cognitive Psychology.*

Siok, W. T., Perfetti, C. A., Jin, Z., & Tan, L. H. (2004). Biological abnormality of impaired reading is constrained by culture. *Nature, 431*, 71–76.

Sippola, L. K., Bukowski, W. M., & Noll, R. B. (1997). Dimensions of liking and disliking underlying the same-sex preference in childhood and early adolescence. *Merrill-Palmer Quarterly, 43*, 591–609.

Siqueland, E. R., & DeLucia, C. A. (1969). Visual reinforcement of non-nutritive sucking in human infants. *Science, 165*, 1144–1146.

Siqueland, E. R., & Lipsitt, L. P. (1966). Conditioned head-turning in the human newborn. *Journal of Experimental Child Psychology, 3*, 356–376.

Skinner, B. F. (1953). *Science and human behavior.* New York: Macmillan.

Skinner, B. F. (1971). *Beyond freedom and dignity.* New York: Bantam.

Skinner, E. A. (1985). Determinants of mother-sensitive and contingent-responsive behavior: The role of childbearing beliefs and socioeconomic status. In I. E. Sigel (Ed.), *Parental belief systems: The psychological consequences for children* (pp. 51–82). Hillsdale, NJ: Erlbaum.

Skinner, E. A., & Zimmer-Gembeck, M. J. (2007). The development of coping. *Annual Review of Psychology, 58*, 119–144.

Skinner, E. A., Zimmer-Gembeck, M. J., & Connell, J. P. (1998). Individual differences and the development of perceived control. *Monographs of the Society for Research in Child Development, 63*(2-3, Serial No. 254).

Skoe, E. E. A. (1998). The ethic of care: Issues in moral development. In E. E. A. Skoe, & A. L. von der Lippe (Eds.), *Personality development in adolescence: A cross national and life span perspective* (pp. 143–171). London: Routledge.

Slaby, R. G., & Frey, K. S. (1975). Development of gender constancy and selective attention to same-sex models. *Child Development, 52*, 849–856.

Slaby, R. G., & Guerra, N. G. (1988). Cognitive mediators of aggression in adolescent offenders: Assessment. *Developmental Psychology, 24*, 580–588.

Slater, A. M., Bremner, G., Johnson, S. P., Sherwood, P., Hayes, R., & Brown, E. (2000). Newborn infants' preference for attractive faces: The role of internal and external facial features. *Infancy, 1*, 265–274.

Slater, A. M., Johnson, S. P., Brown, E., & Badenoch, M. (1996). Newborn infants' perception of partly occluded objects. *Infant Behavior and Development, 19*, 145–148.

Slater, A. M., Mattock, A., & Brown, E. (1990). Size constancy at birth: Newborn infants' responses to retinal and real size. *Journal of Experimental Child Psychology, 49,* 314–322.

Slater, A. M., & Morison, V. (1985). Shape constancy and slant perception at birth. *Perception, 14,* 337–344.

Slater, A. M., Rose, D., & Morison, V. (1984). New-born infants' perception of similarities and differences between two- and three-dimensional stimuli. *British Journal of Developmental Psychology, 2,* 287–294.

Slater, A. M., Von der Schulenburg, C., Brown, E., Badenoch, M., Butterworth, G., Parsons, S., & Samuels, C. (1998). Newborn infants prefer attractive faces. *Infant Behavior and Development, 21,* 345–354.

Slaughter, V., Jaakkola, R., & Carey, S. (1999). Constructing a coherent theory: Children's biological understanding of life and death. In M. Siegal & C. C. Peterson (Eds.), *Children's understanding of biology and health* (pp. 71–96). Cambridge, UK: Cambridge University Press.

Slobin, D. I. (Ed.). (1985). *The crosslinguistic study of language acquisition* (Vols. 1–2). Hillsdale, NJ: Erlbaum.

Slomkowski, C., Rende, R., Conger, K. J., Simons, R. L., & Conger, R. D. (2001). Sisters, brothers, and delinquency: Evaluating social influence during early and middle adolescence. *Child Development, 72,* 271–283.

Slough, N. M., McMahon, R. J., & the Conduct Problems Prevention Research Group. (2008). Preventing serious conduct problems in school-age youth: The Fast Track Program. *Cognitive and Behavioral Practice, 15,* 3–17.

Smeeding, T. M. (2008). Access to the Income Safety Net for Children of Immigrants, *Social Policy Report, Society for Research on Child Development* 23(3): 13–15.

Smetana, J. G. (1988). Adolescents' and parents' conceptions of parental authority. *Child Development, 59,* 321–335.

Smetana, J. G. (1995). Context, conflict, and constraint in adolescent-parent authority relationships. In M. Killen & D. Hart (Eds.), *Morality in everyday life: Developmental perspectives* (pp. 225–255). Cambridge, UK: Cambridge University Press.

Smetana, J. G., & Asquith, P. (1994). Adolescents' and parents' conceptions of parental authority and personal autonomy. *Child Development, 65,* 1147–1162.

Smetana, J. G., & Braeges, J. L. (1990). The development of toddlers' moral and conventional judgments. *Merrill-Palmer Quarterly, 36,* 329–346.

Smider, N. A., Essex, M. J., Kalin, N. H., Buss, K. A., Klein, M. H., Davidson, R. J., et al. (2002). Salivary cortisol as a predictor of socio-emotional adjustment during kindergarten: A prospective study. *Child Development, 73,* 75–92.

Smiley, P. A., & Dweck, C. S. (1994). Individual differences in achievement goals among young children. *Child Development, 65,* 1723–1743.

Smith, B. A., & Blass, E. M. (1996). Taste-mediated calming in premature, preterm, and full-term human infants. *Developmental Psychology, 32,* 1084–1089.

Smith, C. L., Calkins, S. D., Keane, S. P., Anastopoulous, A. D., & Shelton, T. L. (2004). Predicting stability and change in toddler behavior problems: Contributions of maternal behavior and child gender. *Developmental Psychology, 40,* 29–42.

Smith, E. E., & Jonides, J. (1998). Neuroimaging analyses of human working memory. *Proceedings of the National Academy of Sciences*, U.S.A., *95*, 12061–12068.

Smith, L. B. (1999). Do infants possess innate knowledge structures? The con side. *Developmental Science, 2,* 133–144.

Smith, L. B. (2003). Learning to Recognize Objects. *Psychological Science, 14,* 244–251.

Smith, L. B. (2005). Action alters shape categories. *Cognitive Science, 29,* 665–679.

Smith, L. B., & Breazeal, C. (2007). The dynamic lift of developmental process. *Developmental Science, 10,* 61–68.

Smith, L. B., Jones, S., & Landau, B. (1992). Count nouns, adjectives and perceptual properties in novel word interpretations. *Developmental Psychology, 28,* 273–288.

Smith, L. B., & Thelen, E. (2003). Development as a dynamic system. *Trends in Cognitive Sciences, 7*, 343–348.

Smith, L. B., Thelen, E., Titzer, R., & McLin, D. (1999). Knowing in the context of acting: The task dynamics of the A-not-B error. *Psychological Review, 106,* 235–260.

Smith, L. M., LaGasse, L. L., Derauf, C., Grant, P., Shah, R., Arria, A., Huestis, M., Haning, W., Strauss, A., Della Grotta, S., Liu, J., & Lester, B. M. (2006). The infant development, environment, and lifestyle study: Effects of prenatal methamphetamine exposure, polydrug exposure, and poverty on intrauterine growth. *Pediatrics, 118,* 1149–1156.

Smith, M., & Walden, T. (1998). Developmental trends in emotion understanding among a diverse sample of African-American preschool children. *Journal of Applied Developmental Psychology, 19,* 177–197.

Smith, M., & Walden, T. (1999). Understanding feelings and coping with emotional situations: A comparison of maltreated and nonmaltreated preschoolers. *Social Development, 8,* 93–116.

Smith, P. K. (2003). Play and peer relations. In A. Slater & G. Bremner (Eds.), *An introduction to developmental psychology* (pp. 311–333). Malden, MA: Blackwell.

Smith, T. E. & Leaper, C. (2006). Self-perceived gender typicality and the peer context during adolescence. *Journal of Research on Adolescence, 16*, 91–104.

Smith, W. E., & Smith, A. M. (1975). *Minamata.* New York: Holt, Rinehart, and Winston.

Smotherman, W. P., & Robinson, S. R. (1987). Psychobiology of fetal experience in the rat. In N. A. Krasnegor, E. M. Blass, M. A. Hofer, & W. P. Smotherman (Eds.), *Perinatal development: A psychobiological perspective* (pp. 39–60). Orlando, FL: Academic Press.

Snarey, J. R. (1985). Cross-cultural universality of socio moral development: A critical review of Kohlbergian review. *Psychological Bulletin, 97*, 202–232.

Snow, C. (1999). Social perspectives on the emergence of language. In B. MacWhinney (Ed.), *The emergence of language* (pp. 257–276). Mahwah, NJ: Erlbaum.

Snow, C. E. (1990). Building memories: The ontogeny of autobiography. In D. Cicchetti & M. Beeghly (Eds.), *The self in transition: Infancy to childhood* (pp. 213–242). Chicago: University of Chicago Press.

Snyder, D. K., Simpson, J., Hughes, J. N. (2006). *Emotion regulation in couples and families: Pathways to dysfunction and health.* (pp. 163–182). Washington, DC: American Psychological Association. xiv, 332 pp.

Snyder, H. N. (2003). *Juvenile arrests 2001.* Washington, DC: U.S. Department of Justice, Office of Justice Programs, Office of Juvenile Justice and Delinquency Prevention.

Snyder, H. N., & Sickmund, M. (1999). *Juvenile offenders and victims.* 1999 National Report. National Center for Juvenile Justice.

Snyder, J., Brooker, M., Renee, P. M., Snyder, A., Schrepferman, L., & Stoolmiller, M. (2003). Observed peer victimization during early elementary school: Continuity, growth, and relation to risk for child antisocial and depressive behavior. *Child Development, 74*, 1881–1898.

Snyder, J., Cramer, A., Afrank, J., & Patterson, G. R. (2005). The contributions of ineffective discipline and parental hostile attributions of child misbehavior to the development of conduct problems at home and school. *Developmental Psychology, 41,* 30–41.

Snyder, J., Reid, J., & Patterson, G. (2003). A social learning model of child and adolescent antisocial behavior. In B. B. Lahey, T. E., Moffitt, & A. Caspi (Eds.), *Causes of conduct disorder and juvenile delinquency* (pp. 27–48). New York: Guilford.

Snyder, J., Schrepferman, L., McEachern, A., Barner, S., Johnson, K., & Provines, J. (2008). Peer deviancy training and peer coercion: Dual processes associated with early-onset conduct problems. *Child Development, 79,* 252–268.

Snyder, J., Stoolmiller, M., Wilson, M., & Yamamoto, M. (2003). Child anger regulation, parental responses to children's anger displays, and early child antisocial behavior. *Social Development, 12,* 335–360.

Sobel, D. M., & Kirkham, N. Z. (2006). Blickets and babies: The development of causal reasoning in toddlers and infants. *Developmental Psychology, 42,* 1103–1115.

Society for Research in Child Development. (1999). *Directory of members, 1999–2000.* Ann Arbor, MI: Author.

Soenens, B., Luyckx, K., Vansteenkiste, M., Luyten, P., Duriez, B., & Goossens, L. (2008). Maladaptive perfectionism as an intervening variable between psychological control and adolescent depressive symptoms: A three-wave longitudinal study. *Journal of Family Psychology, 22,* 465–474.

Soken, N. H., & Pick, A. D. (1992). Intermodal perception of happy and angry expressive behaviors by seven-month-old infants. *Child Development, 63,* 787–795.

Sokol, R. J., Delaney-Black, V., & Nordstrom, B. (2003). Fetal alcohol spectrum disorder. *Journal of the American Medical Association, 290,* 2996–2999.

Solomon, D., Battistich, V., & Watson, M. (1993, March). *A longitudinal investigation of the effects of a school intervention program on children's social development.* Paper presented at the biennial meeting of the Society for Research in Child Development. New Orleans, LA.

Solomon, D., Battistich, V., Watson, M., Schaps, E., & Lewis, C. (2000). A six-district study of educational change: Direct and mediated effects of the child development project. *Social Psychology of Education, 4,* 3–51.

Solomon, D., Watson, M. S., Delucchi, K. L., Schaps, E., & Battistich, V. (1988). Enhancing children's prosocial behavior in the classroom. *American Educational Research Journal, 25,* 527–554.

Solomon, G. E. A., Johnson, S. C., Zaitchik, D., & Carey, S. (1996). Like father, like son: Young children's understanding of how and why offspring resemble their parents. *Child Development, 67,* 151–171.

Solomon, J., & George, C. (1999). The measurement of attachment security in infancy and childhood. In J. Cassidy & P. R. Shaver (Eds.), *Handbook of attachment: Theory, research, and clinical applications* (pp. 287–316). New York: Guilford.

Solomon, J., George, C., De Jong, A. (1995). Children classified as controlling at age six: Evidence of disorganized representational strategies and aggression at home and at school. *Development and Psychopathology,* 7(3), 447–463.

Sommerville, J. A., & Crane, C. C. (2009). Ten-month-old infants use prior information to identify an actor's goal. *Developmental Science, 12,* 314–325.

Sommerville, J. A., Woodward, A. L., & Needham, A. (2005). Action experience alters 3-month-old infants' perception of others' actions. *Cognition, 96,* B1-B11.

Sophian, C., & Yengo, L. (1985). Infants' search for visible objects: Implications for the interpretation of early search errors. *Journal of Experimental Child Psychology, 40,* 260–278.

Sophie, J. (1985/1986). A critical examination of stage theories of lesbian identity development. *Journal of Homosexuality, 12,* 39–51.

Sorce, J. F., Emde, R. N., Campos, J. J., & Klinnert, M. D. (1985). Maternal emotional signaling: Its effect on the visual cliff behavior of 1-year-olds. *Developmental Psychology, 21,* 195–200.

Sosinsky, L. S., Lord, H., & Zigler, E. (2007). For-profit/nonprofit differences in center-based child care quality: Results from the National Institute of Child Health and Human Development Study of Early Child Care and Youth Development. *Journal of Applied Developmental Psychology, 28,* 390–410.

Spearman, C. (1927). *The abilities of man: Their nature and measurement.* New York: Macmillan.

Spelke, E. S. (1976). Infants' intermodal perception of events. *Cognitive Psychology, 8,* 553–560.

Spelke, E. S. (1979). Perceiving bimodally specified events in infancy. *Developmental Psychology, 15,* 626–636.

Spelke, E. S. (2000). Core knowledge. *American Psychologist, 55,* 1233–1243.

Spelke, E. S. (2003). What makes us smart? Core knowledge and natural language. In D. Gentner & S. Goldin-Meadow (Eds.), *Language in mind: Advances in the study of language and thought* (pp. 277–311). Cambridge, MA: The MIT Press.

Spelke, E. S., Breinlinger, K., Macomber, J., & Jacobson, K. (1992). Origins of knowledge. *Psychological Review, 99,* 605–632.

Spelke, E. S., & Cortelyou, A. (1980). Perceptual aspects of social knowing: Looking and listening in infancy. In M. E. Lamb & L. R. Sherrod (Eds.), *Infant social cognition* (pp. 61–84). Hillsdale, NJ: Erlbaum.

Spelke, E. S., & Kinzler, K. (2007). Core Knowledge. *Developmental Science, 10,* 89–96.

Spelke, E. S. & Kinzler, K. D. (2009). Innateness, learning and rationality. *Child Development Perspectives.*, *3,* 96–98.

Spelke, E. S., & Newport, E. L. (1998). Nativism, empiricism, and the development of knowledge. In W. Damon (Series Ed.) & R. M. Lerner (Vol. Ed.), *Handbook of child psychology: Vol. 1. Theoretical models of human development* (5th ed., pp. 275–340). New York: Wiley.

Spelke, E. S., & Owsley, C. (1979). Intermodal exploration and knowledge in infancy. *Infant Behavior and Development, 2,* 13–17.

Speltz, M. L., DeKlyen, M., Calderon, R., Greenberg, M. T., & Fisher, P. A. (1999). Neuropsychological characteristics and test behaviors of boys with early onset conduct problems. *Journal of Abnormal Psychology, 108,* 315–325.

Spence, J. T., & Helmreich, R. (1978). *Masculinity and femininity: Their psychological dimensions, correlates, and antecedents.* Austin, TX: University of Texas Press.

Spence, M. J., & Freeman, M. S. (1996). Newborn infants prefer the maternal low-pass filtered voice, but not the maternal whispered voice. *Infant Behavior and Development, 19,* 199–212.

Spence, S. H., Sheffield, J. K., & Donovan, C. L. (2003). Preventing adolescent depression: An evaluation of the Problem Solving for Life Program. *Journal of Consulting and Clinical Psychology, 71,* 3–13.

Spencer, J. P., Clearfield, M., Corbetta, D., Ulrich, B., Buchanan, P., & Schöner, G. (2006). Moving toward a grand theory of development: In memory of Esther Thelen, *Child Development, 77,* 1521–1538.

Spencer, J. P., & Schutte, A. R. (2004). Unifying representations and responses: Perseverative biases arise from a single behavioral system. *Psychological Science, 15,* 187–193.

Spencer, J. P., Smith, L. B., & Thelen, E. (2001). Tests of a dynamic systems account of the A-not-B error: The influence of prior experience on the spatial memory abilities of two-year-olds. *Child Development, 72,* 1327–1346.

Spencer, J. P., & Thelen, E. (2000). Spatially specific changes in infants' muscle coactivity as they learn to reach. *Infancy, 1,* 275–302.

Spencer, J. P., & Thelen, E. (2003). Introduction to the special issue: Why this question and why now? *Developmental Science, 6,* 375–377.

Spencer, J. P., Vereijken, B., Diedrich, F. J., & Thelen, E. (2000). Posture and the emergence of manual skills. *Developmental Science, 3,* 216–233.

Spencer, M. B., & Markstrom-Adams, C. (1990). Identity processes among racial and ethnic minority children in America. *Child Development, 61,* 290–310.

Spencer-Rodgers, J., Peng, K., Wang, L., & Hou, Y. (2004). Dialectical self-esteem and East-West differences in psychological well-being. *Personality and Social Psychology Bulletin, 30,* 1416–1432.

Spilich, G. J., Vesonder, G. T., Chiesi, H. L., & Voss, J. F. (1979). Text processing of domain-related information for individuals with high and low domain knowledge. *Journal of Verbal Learning & Verbal Behavior, 18,* 275–290.

Spinrad, T. L., Eisenberg, N., Gaertner, B., Popp, T., Smith, C. L., Kupfer, A., Greving, K., Liew, J. & Hofer, C. (2007). Relations of maternal socialization and toddlers' effortful control to children's adjustment and social competence. *Developmental Psychology, 43,* 1170–1186.

Spitz, R. A. (1945). Hospitalism: An inquiry into the genesis of psychiatric conditions in early childhood. *The Psychoanalytic Study of the Child, 1,* 53–74.

Spitz, R. A. (1946). Hospitalism, a follow-up report. *The Psychoanalytic Study of the Child, 2,* 113–117.

Spitz, R. A. (1949). Motherless infants. *Child Development, 20,* 145–155.

Sprenger-Charolles, L. (2003). Linguistic processes in reading and spelling: The case of alphabetic writing systems: English, French, German and Spanish: In T. Nunes & P. Bryant (Eds.), *Handbook of children's literacy* (pp. 43–65). Dordrecht: Kluwer Academic Publishers.

Springer, K. (1996). Young children's understanding of a biological basis for parent-offspring relations. *Child Development, 67,* 2841–2856.

Springer, K., & Keil, F. C. (1991). Early differentiation of causal mechanisms appropriate to biological and nonbiological kinds. *Child Development, 62,* 767–781.

Springer, K., Nguyen, T., & Samaniego, R. (1996). Early understanding of age- and environment-related noxiousness in biological kinds: Evidence for a naive theory. *Cognitive Development, 11,* 65–82.

Sroufe, L. A. (1979). Socioemotional development. In J. Osofsky (Ed.), *The handbook of infant development* (pp. 462–516). New York: Wiley.

Sroufe, L. A. (1995). *Emotional development: The organization of emotional life in the early years.* Cambridge, UK: Cambridge University Press.

Sroufe, L. A., Bennett, C., Englund, M., Urban, J. & Shulman, S. (1993). The significance of gender boundaries in preadolescence: Contemporary correlates and antecedents of boundary violation and maintenance. *Child Development, 64,* 455–466.

Sroufe, L. A., Egeland, B., & Kreutzer, T. (1990). The fate of early experience following developmental change: Longitudinal approaches to individual adaptation in childhood. *Child Development, 61,* 1363–1373.

Sroufe, L. A., & Waters, E. (1976). The ontogenesis of smiling and laughter: A perspective on the organization of development in infancy. *Psychological Review, 83,* 173–189.

St. James-Roberts, I., Conroy, S., & Wilsher, C. (1998). Stability and outcome of persistent infant crying. *Infant Behavior and Development, 21,* 411–435.

St. James-Roberts, I., & Halil, T. (1991). Infant crying patterns in the first year: Normal community and clinical findings. *Journal of Child Psychology and Psychiatry, 32,* 951–968.

Stack, D. M., & Arnold, S. L. (1998). Changes in mothers' touch and hand gestures influence infant behavior during face-to-face interchanges. *Infant Behavior and Development, 21,* 451–468.

Stack, D. M., & Muir, D. W. (1990). Tactile stimulation as a component of social interchange: New interpretations for the still-face effect. *British Journal of Developmental Psychology, 8,* 131–145.

Stack, D. M., & Muir, D. W. (1992). Adult tactile stimulation during face-to-face interactions modulates five-month-olds' affect and attention. *Child Development, 63,* 1509–1525.

Stack, D., Muir, D., Sherriff, F., & Roman, J. (1989). Development of infant reaching in the dark to luminous objects and "invisible sounds." *Perception, 18,* 69–82.

Stake, J. E. & Nickens, S. D. (2005). Adolescent girls' and boys' science peer relationships and perceptions of the possible self as a scientist. *Sex Roles, 52,* 1–11.

Stams, G. J., Brugman, D., Dekovic, M., van Rosmalen, L., van der Laan, P., & Gibbs, J. C. (2006). The moral judgment of juvenile delinquents: A meta-analysis. *Journal of Abnormal Child Psychology, 34,* 697–713.

Stanger, J. D., & Gridina, N. (1999). *Media in the home 1999: The fourth annual survey of parents and children.* Philadelphia: Annenberg Public Policy Center, University of Pennsylvania.

Stangor, C., & McMillan, D. (1992). Memory for expectancy-congruent and expectancy-incongruent information: A review of the social and social developmental literatures. *Psychological Bulletin, 111,* 42–61.

Stangor, C., & Ruble, D. N. (1989). Differential influences of gender schemata and gender constancy on children's information processing and behavior. *Social Cognition, 7,* 353–372.

Stanovich, K. E. (2000). *Progress in understanding reading.* London: Guilford.

Stark, R. I., & Myers, M. M. (1995). Breathing and hiccups in the fetal baboon. In J. P. Lecanuet, W. P. Fifer, N. A. Krasnegor, & W. P. Smotherman (Eds.), *Fetal development: A psychobiological perspective.* Hillsdale, NJ: Erlbaum.

Starkey, P. (1992). The early development of numerical reasoning. *Cognition, 43*, 93–126.

Starkey, P., Klein, A., & Wakeley, A. (2004). Enhancing young children's mathematical knowledge through a pre-kindergarten mathematics intervention. *Early Childhood Research Quarterly, 19*, 99–120.

Starkey, P., Spelke, E. S., & Gelman, R. (1990). Numerical abstraction by human infants. *Cognition, 36*, 97–128.

Staub, E. (1979). *Positive social behavior and morality: Vol 2: Socialization and development.* New York: Academic Press.

Stecher, B. M., McCaffrey, D. F., & Bugliari, D. (2003, November 10). The relationship between exposure to class size reduction and student achievement in California. *Education Policy Analysis Archives, 11*(40). Retrieved June 2, 2005 from http://epaa.asu.edu/epaa/v11n40/.

Steele, H., Steele, M., Croft, C., & Fonagy, P. (1999). Infant-mother attachment at one year predicts children's understanding of mixed emotions at six years. *Social Development, 8,* 161–178.

Steele, H., Steele, M., & Fonagy, P. (1996). Associations among attachment classifications of mothers, fathers, and their infants. *Child Development, 67,* 541–555.

Steenbeek, H. & van Geert, P. (2008). An empirical validation of a dynamic systems model of interaction: Do children of different sociometric statuses differ in their dyadic play? *Developmental Science, 11*, 253–281.

Stein, N. L. (1988). The development of children's storytelling skill. In M. B. Franklin & S. Barten (Eds.), *Child language: A book of readings* (pp. 282–297). New York: Oxford University Press.

Stein, Z., Susser, M., Saenger, G., & Marolla, F. (1975). *Famine and human development: The Dutch hunger winter of 1944–1945.* New York: Oxford University Press.

Steinberg, L. (1987). Impact of puberty on family relations: Effects of pubertal status and pubertal timing. *Developmental Psychology, 23*, 451–460.

Steinberg, L. (1988). Reciprocal relation between parent-child distance and pubertal maturation. *Developmental Psychology, 24,* 122–128.

Steinberg, L. (1990). Autonomy, harmony, and conflict in the family relationship. In S. S. Feldman & G. R. Elliott (Eds.), *At the threshold: The developing adolescent* (pp. 54–89). Cambridge, MA: Harvard University Press.

Steinberg, L., Darling, N. E., & Fletcher, A. C. (1995). Authoritative parenting and adolescent development: An ecological journey. In P. Moen, G. H. Elder, & K. Luscher (Eds.), *Examining lives in context* (pp. 423–466). Washington, DC: American Psychological Association.

Steinberg, L., Lamborn, S. D., Darling, N., Mounts, N. S., & Dornbusch, S. M. (1994). Over-time changes in adjustment and competence among adolescents from authoritative, authoritarian, indulgent, and neglectful families. *Child Development, 65*, 754–770.

Steinberg, L., & Morris, A. S. (2001). Adolescent development. *Annual Review of Psychology, 52,* 83–110.

Steinberg, L., Mounts, N. S., Lamborn, S. D., & Dornbush, S. M. (1991). Authoritative parenting and adolescent adjustment across varied ecological niches. *Journal of Research on Adolescence, 1*, 19–36.

Steinberg, L., & Silverberg, S. B. (1986). The vicissitudes of autonomy in early adolescence. *Child Development, 57*, 841–851.

Steiner, J. E. (1979). Human facial expressions in response to taste and smell stimulation. In H. Reese & L. Lipsitt (Eds.), *Advances in child development and behavior* (Vol. 13, pp. 257–295). New York: Academic Press.

Steinmayr, Ricarda, & Spinath, Birgit. (2008). What explains boys' stronger confidence in their intelligence? *Sex Roles, 61*(9–10), 736–749.

Stemmler, M., & Petersen, A. C. (1999). Reciprocity and change within the affective family environment in early adolescence. *International Journal of Behavioral Development, 23*, 185–198.

Stenberg, C., Campos, J., & Emde, R. (1983). The facial expression of anger in seven-month-old infants. *Child Development, 54*, 178–184.

Stennes, L. M., Burch, M. M., Sen, M. G., & Bauer, P. J. (2005). A longitudinal study of gendered vocabulary and communicative action in young children. *Developmental Psychology, 41*, 75–88.

Stern, D. (1985). *The interpersonal world of the infant.* New York: Basic Books.

Sternberg, R. J. (2000). The theory of successful intelligence. *Review of General Psychology, 3*, 292–316.

Sternberg, R. J. (2003). A broad view of intelligence: The theory of successful intelligence. *Consulting Psychology Journal: Practice and Research, 55*, 139–154.

Sternberg, R. J. (2004). Culture and intelligence. *American Psychologist, 59*, 325–338.

Sternberg, R. J. (2007). *g*, g's, or Jeez: Which is the best model for developing abilities, competencies, and expertise? In P. C. Kyllonen, R. D. Roberts, & L. Stankov (Eds.), *Extending intelligence: Enhancement and new constructs* (pp. 250–265). Mahwah, NJ: Erlbaum.

Steuer, F. B., Applefield, J. M., & Smith, R. (1971). Televised aggression and the interpersonal aggression of preschool children. *Journal of Experimental Child Psychology, 11,* 442–447.

Stevens, T., Wang, K., Olivarez, A., Jr., & Hamman, D. (2007). Use of self-perspectives and their sources to predict the mathematics enrollment intentions of girls and boys. *Sex Roles, 56*, 351–363.

Stevenson, H. W. (1991). The development of prosocial behavior in large-scale collective societies: China & Japan. In R. A. Hinde & J. Groebel (Eds.), *Cooperation and prosocial behaviour* (pp. 89–105). Cambridge: Cambridge University Press.

Stevenson, H. W., Chen, C., & Lee, S-Y. (1993). Mathematics achievement of Chinese, Japanese, and American children: Ten years later. *Science, 259*, 53–58.

Stevenson, H. W., & Newman, R. S. (1986). Long-term prediction of achievement and attitudes in mathematics and reading. *Child Development, 57,* 646–659.

Stewart, S. M., Kennard, B. D., Lee, P. W. H., Hughes, C. W., Mayes, T. L., Emslie, G. J., & Lewinsohn, P. M. (2004). A cross-cultural investigation of cognitions and depression in adolescents. *Journal of Abnormal Psychology, 113,* 548–557.

Stewart, S. M., & McBride-Chang, C. (2000). Influences on children's sharing in a multicultural setting. *Journal of Cross-Cultural Psychology, 31*, 333–348.

Stice, E., & Barrera, M. (1995). A longitudinal examination of the reciprocal relations between perceived parenting and adolescents' substance use and externalizing behavior. *Developmental Psychology, 31*, 322–334.

Stifter, C. A., Bono, M., & Spinrad, T. (2003). Parent characteristics and conceptualizations associated with the emergence of infant colic. *Journal of Reproductive and Infant Psychology, 21,* 309–322.

Stifter, C. A., & Braungart, J. (1992). Infant colic: A transient condition with no apparent effects. *Journal of Applied Developmental Psychology, 13,* 447–462.

Stigler, J. W., & Hiebert, J. (1999). *The teaching gap.* New York: Free Press.

Stiles, J. (2008). *The Fundamentals of Brain Development: Integrating Nature and Nurture.* Cambridge, MA: Harvard University Press.

Stipek, D., Gralinski, H., & Kopp, C. (1990). Self-concept development in the toddler years. *Developmental Psychology, 26,* 972–977.

Stipek, D. J., Roberts, T. A., & Sanborn, M. E. (1984). Preschool-age children's performance expectations for themselves and another child as function of the incentive value of success and the salience of past performance. *Child Development, 55,* 1982–1989.

Stocker, C. M., Burwell, R. A., & Briggs, M. L. (2002). Sibling conflict in middle childhood predicts children's adjustment in early adolescence. *Journal of Family Psychology, 16,* 50–57.

Stocker, C. M., & Richmond, M. K. (2007). Longitudinal associations between hostility in adolescents' family relationships and friendships and hostility in their romantic relationships. *Journal of Family Psychology, 21,* 490–497.

Stocker, C. M., Richmond, M. K., & Rhoades, G. K. (2007). Family emotional processes and adolescents' adjustment. *Social Development, 16,* 310–325.

Stoddart, T., & Turiel, E. (1985). Children's concepts of cross-gender activities. *Child Development, 56,* 1241–1252.

Stone, J. L., & Church, J. (1957). *Childhood and adolescence: A psychology of the growing person.* New York: Random House.

Stoneman, Z., & Brody, G. H. (1993). Sibling temperaments, conflict, warmth, and role asymmetry. *Child Development, 64,* 1786–1800.

Stouthamer-Loeber, Loeber, R., Wei, E., Farrington, D. P., & Wikstrom, P-O. H. (2002). Risk and promotive effects in the explanation of persistent serious delinquency in boys. *Journal of Consulting and Clinical Psychology, 70,* 111–123.

Strauch, B. (2003). *The primal teen: What the new discoveries about the teenage brain tell us about our kids.* New York: Doubleday.

Strauss, M. S., & Curtis, L. E. (1984). Development of numerical concepts in infancy. In C. Sophian (Ed.), *Origins of cognitive skills* (pp. 131–155). Mahwah, NJ: Erlbaum.

Strauss, R. S., & Pollack, H. A. (2003). Social marginalization of overweight children. *The Archives of Pediatric & Adolescent Medicine, 157,* 746–752.

Strayer, F. F., & Strayer, J. (1976). An ethological analysis of social agonism and dominance relations among preschool children. *Child Development, 47,* 980–989.

Strayer, J. (1986). Children's attributions regarding the situational determinants of emotion in self and others. *Developmental Psychology, 22,* 649–654.

Strayer, J., & Roberts, W. (2004). Children's anger, emotional expressiveness, and empathy: Relations with parents' empathy, emotional expressiveness, and parenting practices. *Social Development, 13,* 229–254.

Streeter, L. A. (1976). Language perception of 2-month-old infants shows effects of both innate mechanisms and experience. *Nature, 259,* 39–41.

Streissguth, A. P. (2001). Recent advances in fetal alcohol syndrome and alcohol use in pregnancy. In D. P. Agarwal & H. K. Seitz (Eds), *Alcohol in health and disease* (pp. 303–324*)*. New York: Marcel Dekker, Inc.

Streissguth, A. P., Aase, J. M., Clarren, S. K., Randles, S. P., Ladue, R. A., & Smith, D. F. (1991). Fetal alcohol syndrome in adolescents and adults. *Journal of American Medical Association, 265,* 1961–1967.

Streissguth, A. P., Barr, H. M., & Martin, D. C. (1983). Maternal alcohol use and neonatal habituation assessed with the Brazelton scale. *Child Development, 54,* 1109–1118.

Streissguth, A. P., Bookstein, F. L., Sampson, P. D., & Barr, H. M. (1993). *The enduring effects of prenatal alcohol exposure on child development: Birth through seven years, a partial least squares solution.* Ann Arbor: University of Michigan Press.

Streitmatter, J. L. (1988). Ethnicity as a mediating variable of early adolescent identity development. *Journal of Adolescence, 11,* 335–346.

Streri, A., & Spelke, E. S. (1988). Haptic perception of objects in infancy. *Cognitive Psychology, 20,* 1–23.

Strough, J. & Berg, C. A. (2000). Goals as a mediator of gender differences in high-affiliation dyadic conversations. *Developmental Psychology, 36,* 117–125.

Strough, J. & Covatto, A. M. (2002). Context and age differences in same- and other-gender peer preferences. *Social Development, 11,* 346–361.

Stukas, A. A., Snyder, M., & Clary, E. G. (1999). The effects of "mandatory volunteerism" on intentions to volunteer. *Psychological Science, 10,* 59–64.

Stukas, A. A., Jr., Switzer, G. E., Dew, M. A., Goycoolea, J. M., & Simmons, R. G. (1999). Parental helping models, gender, and service-learning. *Journal of Prevention & Intervention in the Community, 18,* 5–18.

Stunkard, A. J., Foch, T. T., & Hrubeck, Z. (1986). A twin study of human obesity. *Journal of the American Medical Association, 256,* 51–54.

Stunkard, A. J., Sorenson, T. I. A., Hanis, C., Teasdale, T. W., Chakraborty, R., Schull, W. J., & Schulsinger, F. (1986). An adoption study of human obesity. *New England Journal of Medicine, 314,* 193–198.

Sturge-Apple, Davies, P. T., & Cummings, E. M. (2006). Hostility and withdrawal in marital conflict: Effects on parental emotional unavailability and inconsistent discipline. *Journal of Family Psychology, 20,* 227–238.

Subbotsky, E. B. (1993). *Foundations of the mind: Children's understanding of reality.* Cambridge, MA: Harvard University Press.

Subbotsky, E. B. (1994). Early rationality and magical thinking in preschoolers: Space and time. *British Journal of Developmental Psychology, 12,* 97–108.

Subbotsky, E. (2005). The permanence of mental objects: Testing magical thinking on perceived and imaginary realities. *Developmental Psychology, 41,* 301–318.

Subrahmanyam, K., & Greenfield, P. M. (1994). Effect of video game practice on spatial skills in girls and boys. *Journal of Applied Developmental Psychology, 15,* 13–32.

Subrahmanyam, K., & Greenfield, P. M. (1996). Effect of video game practice on spatial skills in girls and boys. In P. M. Greenfield & R. R. Cocking (Eds.), *Interacting with video* (pp. 95–114). Norwood, NJ: Ablex.

Subrahmanyam, K., Kraut, R. E., Greenfield, P. M., & Gross, E. F. (2000). The impact of home computer use on children's activities and development. *The Future of Children, 10,* 123–144.

Subrahmanyam, K., Kraut, R., Greenfield, P. M., & Gross, E. F. (2001). New forms of electronic media: The impact of interactive games and the Internet on cognition, socialization, and behavior. In D. L. Singer, & J. L. Singer (Eds.), *Handbook of children and the media* (pp. 73–99). Thousand Oaks, CA: Sage Publications.

Substance Abuse and Mental Health Services Administration. (2004). *Results of the 2003 national survey on drug use and health.* Washington, DC: Department of Health and Human Services.

Sue, S., & Okazaki, S. (1990). Asian-American educational achievements: A phenomenon in search of an explanation. *American Psychologist, 45*, 913–920.

Suess, P. E., Porges, S. W., & Plude, D. J. (1994). Cardiac vagal tone and sustained attention in school-age children. *Psychophysiology, 31*, 17–22.

Sullivan, H. S. (1953). *The interpersonal theory of psychiatry.* New York: Norton.

Sullivan, K., & Winner, E. (1993). Three-year-olds' understanding of mental states: The influence of trickery. *Journal of Experimental Child Psychology, 56*, 135–148.

Sullivan, M. W., & Lewis, M. (2003). Contextual determinants of anger and other negative expressions in young infants. *Developmental Psychology, 39*, 693–705.

Sullivan, M. W., Lewis, M., & Alessandri, S. M. (1992). Cross-age stability in infant emotional expressions during learning and extinction. *Developmental Psychology, 28*, 58–63.

Sulloway, F. J. (1996). *Born to rebel: Birth order, family dynamics, and creative lives.* New York: Pantheon Books.

Sundet, J. M., Barlaug, D. G., Torjussen, T. M. (2004). The end of the Flynn effect?: A study of secular trends in mean intelligence test scores of Norwegian conscripts during half a century. *Intelligence, 32*, 349–362.

Suomi, S., & Harlow, H. F. (1972). Social rehabilitation of isolate-reared monkeys. *Developmental Psychology, 6*, 487–496.

Super, C. (1976). Environmental effects on motor development: The case of "African infant precocity." *Developmental Medicine and Child Neurology, 18*, 561–567.

Super, C. M., & Harkness, S. (1986). The developmental niche: A conceptualization at the interface of child and culture. *International Journal of Behavioral Development, 9*, 545–569.

Sutton, P. D., & Mathews, T. J. (2004, May 10). Trends in characteristics of births by state: United States, 1990, 1995, and 2000–2002. *National Vital Statistics Reports, 52*, No. 19, 1–152. www.cdc.gov/nchs/births.htm.

Sutton, S. K., & Davidson, R. J. (1997). Prefrontal brain asymmetry: A biological substrate of the behavioral approach and inhibition systems. *Psychological Science, 8*, 204–210.

Suzuki, L. A., & Valencia, R. R. (1997). Race ethnicity and measured intelligence: Educational implications. *American Psychologist, 52*, 1103–1114.

Suzuki, L. K., & Calzo, J. P. (2004). The search for peer advice in cyberspace: An examination of online teen bulletin boards about health and sexuality. *Applied Developmental Psychology, 25*, 685–698.

Swahn, M. H., Simon, T. R., Arias, I., & Bossarte, R. M. (2008). Measuring sex differences in violence victimization and perpetration within date and same-sex peer relationships. *Journal of Interpersonal Violence, 23*, 1120–1138.

Swain, R. C., Oetting, E. R., Thurman, P. J., Beauvais, F., & Edwards, R. (1993). American Indian adolescent drug use and socialization characteristics. *Journal of Cross-Cultural Psychology, 24*, 53–70.

Szalacha, L. A., Erkut, S., Coll, C. G., Alarcón, O., Fields, J. P., & Ceder, I. (2003). Discrimination and Puerto Rican children's and adolescents' mental health. *Cultural Diversity and Ethnic Minority Psychology, 9*, 141–155.

Szynal-Brown, C., & Morgan, R. R. (1983). The effects of reward on tutor's behaviors in a cross-age tutoring context. *Journal of Experimental Child Psychology, 36*, 196–208.

Tager-Flusberg, H. (2003). Developmental disorders of genetic origin. In M. de Haan and M. H. Johnson (Eds.), *The cognitive neuroscience of development* (pp. 237–261). New York: Psychology Press.

Tager-Flusberg, H. (2007). Evaluating the theory-of-mind hypothesis of autism. *Current Directions in Psychological Science, 16*, 311–315.

Taharally, L. C. (1991). Fantasy play, language and cognitive ability of four-year-old children in Guyana, South America. *Child Study Journal, 21*, 37–56.

Tajfel, H., & Turner, J. (1979). An integrative theory of intergroup conflict. In W. G. Austin, & S. Worchel (Eds.), *The social psychology of intergroup relations* (pp. 94–109). Monterey, CA: Brooks-Cole.

Takahashi, K. (1986). Examining the Strange-Situation procedure with Japanese mothers and 12-month-old infants. *Developmental Psychology, 22*, 265–270.

Talbot, M. (1998, May 24). Attachment theory: The ultimate experiment. *New York Times Magazine,* 24–30, 38, 46, 50, 54.

Tallal, P., & Fitch, R. H. (1993). Hormones and cerebral organization: Implications for the development and transmission of language and learning disabilities. In A. M. Galaburda (Ed.), *Dyslexia and development: Neurobiological aspects of extra-ordinary brains* (pp. 168–186). Cambridge, MA: Harvard University Press.

Tallal, P., Miller, S. L., Bedi, G., Byma, G., Wang, X., Nagarajan, S. S., et al. (1996). Language comprehension in language-learning impaired children improved with acoustically modified speech. *Science, 271*, 81–84.

Tamis-LeMonda, C. S., Adolph, K. E., Lobo, S. A., Karasik, L. B., Ishak, S., & Dimitropoulou, K. A. (2008). When infants take mothers' advice: 18-month-olds integrate perceptual and social information to guide motor action. *Developmental Psychology, 44*, 734–746.

Tamis-LeMonda, C. S., & Bornstein, M. H. (1994). Specificity in mother-toddler language-play relations across the second year. *Developmental Psychology, 30*, 283–292.

Tamis-LeMonda, C. S., Briggs, R. D., McClowry, S. G., & Snow, D. L. (2008). Challenges to the study of African American parenting: Conceptualization, sampling, research approaches, measurement, and design. *Parenting: Science and Practice, 8*, 319–358.

Tangney, J., & Dearing, R. (2002). *Shame and guilt.* New York: Guilford.

Tangney, J. P. (1998). How does guilt differ from shame? In J. Bybee (Ed.), *Guilt and children* (pp. 1–17). San Diego, CA: Academic Press.

Tangney, J. P., Stuewig, J., & Mashek, D. J. (2007). Moral emotions and moral behavior. *Annual Review of Psychology, 58*, 345-372.

Tanner, J. M. (1961). *Education and physical growth: Implications of the study of children's growth for educational theory and practice.* New York: International Universities Press.

Tardif, T., et al. (2008). Baby's first 10 words. *Developmental Psychology, 44*, 929–938.

Task Force on Sleep Position and Sudden Infant Death. (2000). Report at year 2000. *Pediatrics: American Academy of Pediatrics, 105,* 650–656.

Tasker, F., & Golombok, S. (1995). Adults raised as children in lesbian families. *American Journal of Orthopsychiatry, 65,* 203–215.

Taumoepeau, M., & Huffman, T. (2006). Mother and infant talk about mental states relates to desire language and emotion understanding. *Child Development, 77,* 465–481.

Taumoepeau, M., & Ruffman, T. (2008). Stepping stones to others' minds: Maternal talk relates to child mental state language and emotion understanding at 15, 24, and 33 months of age. *Child Development, 79,* 284–302.

Taylor, J., Iacono, W. G., & McGue, M. (2001). Evidence for a genetic etiology of early-onset delinquency. *Journal of Abnormal Behavior, 109,* 634–643.

Taylor, M. (1999). *Imaginary companions and the children who create them.* New York: Oxford University Press.

Taylor, M. G. (1993). *Children's beliefs about the biological and social origins of gender differences.* Unpublished doctoral dissertation, University of Michigan, Ann Arbor.

Taylor, M. G. (1996). The development of children's beliefs about social and biological aspects of gender differences. *Child Development, 67,* 1555–1557.

Taylor, M., & Carlson, S. M. (1997). The relation between individual differences in fantasy and theory of mind. *Child Development, 68,* 436–455.

Taylor, M., Carlson, S. M., Maring, B. L., Gerow, L., & Charley, C. M. (2004). The characteristics and correlates of fantasy in school-age children: Imaginary companions, impersonation, and social understanding. *Developmental Psychology, 40,* 1173–1187.

Taylor, M., & Gelman, S. A. (1989). Incorporating new words into the lexicon: Preliminary evidence for language hierarchies in two-year-old children. *Cognitive Development, 60,* 625–636.

Taylor, M., & Mannering, A. M. (2007). Of Hobbes and Harvey: The imaginary companions created by children and adults. In A. Göncü & S. Gaskins (Eds.), *Play and development: Evolutionary, sociocultural, and functional perspectives* (pp. 227–246). Mahwah, NJ: Erlbaum.

Taylor, T. J., Freng, A., Esbensen, F., & Peterson, D. (2008). Youth gang membership and serious violent victimization: The importance of lifestyles and routine activities. *Journal of Interpersonal Violence, 23,* 1441–1464.

Taylor, R. D., & Roberts, D. (1995). Kinship support and maternal and adolescent well-being in economically disadvantaged African-American families. *Child Development, 66,* 1585–1597.

Taylor, R. D., Seaton, E., & Dominguez, A. (2008). Kinship support, family relations, and psychological adjustment among low-income African American mothers and adolescents. *Journal of Research on Adolescence, 18,* 1–22.

Taylor, R. L., & Richards, S. B. (1991). Patterns of intellectual differences of Black, Hispanic, and White children. *Psychology in the Schools, 28,* 5–8.

Taylor, T. J., Peterson, D., Esbensen, F., & Freng, A. (2007). Gang membership as a risk factor for adolescent violent victimization. *Journal of Research in Crime and Delinquency, 44,* 351–380.

Teasdale, T. W., & Owen, D. R. (2005). A long-term rise and recent decline in intelligence test performance: The Flynn Effect in reverse. *Personality and Individual Differences, 39,* 837–843.

Teig, S., & Susskind, J. E. (2008). Truck driver or nurse? The impact of gender roles and occupational status on children's occupational preferences. *Sex Roles, 58,* 848–863.

Tenenbaum, H. R., & Leaper, C. (2002). Are parents' gender schemas related to their children's gender-related cognitions? A meta-analysis. *Developmental Psychology, 38,* 615–630.

Tenenbaum, H. R., & Leaper, C. (2003). Parent-child conversations about science: The socialization of gender inequities? *Journal of Applied Developmental Psychology, 26,* 1–19.

Terrace, H. S., Petitto, L. A., Sanders, R. J., & Bever, T. G. (1979). Can an ape create a sentence? *Science, 206,* 891–902.

Thatcher, R. W. (1992) Cyclic cortical reorganization during childhood. *Brain & Cognition, 20,* 24–50.

Thiessen, E. D., Hill, E., & Saffran, J. R. (2005). Infant-directed speech facilitates word segmentation. *Infancy, 7,* 53–71.

Thelen, E. (1986). Treadmill-elicited stepping in seven-month-old infants. *Child Development, 57,* 1498–1506.

Thelen, E. (1995). Motor development: A new synthesis. *American Psychologist, 50,* 79–95.

Thelen, E. (2001). Dynamic mechanisms of change in early perceptual-motor development. In McClelland, J. L., & Siegler, R. S. (Eds.), *Mechanisms of cognitive development: Behavioral and neural perspectives* (pp. 161–184). Mahwah, NJ: Erlbaum.

Thelen, E., & Corbetta, D. (1994). Exploration and selection in the early acquisition of skills. *International Review of Neurobiology, 37,* 75–102.

Thelen, E., & Corbetta, D. (2002). Microdevelopment and dynamic systems: Applications to infant motor development. In N. Granott & J. Parziale (Eds.), *Microdevelopment: Transition processes in development and learning* (pp 59–79). Cambridge, UK: Cambridge University Press.

Thelen, E., Corbetta, D., Kamm, K., Spencer, J. P., Schneider, K., & Zernicke, R. F. (1993). The transition to reaching: Mapping intention and intrinsic dynamics. *Child Development, 64,* 1058–1098.

Thelen, E., & Fisher, D. M. (1982). Newborn stepping: An explanation for the "disappearing reflex." *Developmental Psychology, 18,* 760–775.

Thelen, E., Fisher, D. M., & Ridley-Johnson, R. (1984). The relationship between physical growth and a newborn reflex. *Infant Behavior and Development, 7,* 479–493.

Thelen, E., & Smith, L. B. (1994). *A dynamic systems approach to the development of cognition and action.* Cambridge, MA: The MIT Press/Bradford Books.

Thelen, E. & Smith, L. B. (1998). Dynamic systems theory. In W. Damon (Series Ed.) & R. M. Lerner (Vol. Ed.), *Handbook of child psychology: Vol. 1. Theoretical models of human development* (5th ed., pp. 563–634). New York: Wiley.

Thelen, E., & Smith, L. B. (2006). Dynamic systems theories. In W. Damon & R. M. Lerner (Series Eds.) & R. M. Lerner (Vol. Ed.), *Handbook of child psychology: Volume 1: Theoretical models of human development* (6th ed., pp. 258–312). Hoboken, NJ: Wiley.

Thiessen, E. D., Hill, E. A., & Saffran, J. R. (2005). Infant-directed speech facilitates word segmentation. *Infancy, 7,* 53–71.

Thinus-Blanc, C., & Gaunet, F. (1997). Representation of space in blind persons: Vision as a spatial sense? *Psychological Bulletin, 121,* 20–42.

Thomas, A., & Chess, S. (1977). *Temperament and development.* New York: Brunner/Mazel.

Thomas, A., Chess, S., & Birch, H. G. (1963). *Temperament and behavior disorders in children.* New York: New York University Press.

Thomas, J. R., & French, K. E. (1985). Gender differences across age in motor performance: A meta-analysis. *Psychological Bulletin, 98,* 260–282.

Thompson, E. M., & Morgan, E. M. (2008). "Mostly straight" young women: Variations in sexual behavior and identity development. *Developmental Psychology, 44,* 15–21.

Thompson, J. R., & Chapman, R. S. (1977). Who is "Daddy" revisited: The status of two-year-olds' over-extended words in use and comprehension. *Journal of Child Language, 4,* 359–375.

Thompson, R. A. (1987). Development of children's inferences of the emotions of others. *Developmental Psychology, 23,* 124–131.

Thompson, R. A. (1998). Early sociopersonality development. In W. Damon (Series Ed.) & N. Eisenberg (Vol. Ed), *Handbook of child psychology: Vol. 3. Social, emotional, and personality development* (5th ed., pp. 23–104). New York: Wiley.

Thompson, R. A. (2000). The legacy of early attachments. *Child Development, 71,* 145–152.

Thompson, R. A. (2006). The development of the person: Social understanding, relationships, conscience, self. In W. Damon & R. M. Lerner (Series Eds.) & N. Eisenberg (Vol. Ed.), *Handbook of child psychology: Vol. 3. Social, emotional, and personality development.* (6th ed., pp. 24–98). Hoboken, NJ: Wiley.

Thompson, R. A., Laible, D. J., & Ontai, L. L. (2003). Early understanding of emotion, morality, and the self: Developing a working model. In R. V. Kail (Ed.), *Advances in child development and behavior,* (vol. 31, pp. 137–171). San Diego: Academic.

Thompson, R. A., Lewis, M. D., & Calkins, S. D. (2008). Reassessing emotion regulation. *Child Development Perspectives, 2,* 121–208.

Thompson, R. F. (2000). *The brain: A neuroscience primer* (3rd ed.). New York: Worth.

Thompson, R. F., & Spencer, W. A. (1966). Habituation: A model for the study of neuronal substrates of behavior. *Psychological Review, 73,* 16–43.

Thompson, T., Caruso, M., & Ellerbeck, K. (2003). Sex matters in autism and other developmental disabilities. *Journal of Learning Disabilities, 7,* 345–362.

Thompson, T. L., & Zerbinos, E. (1995). Gender roles in animated cartoons: Has the picture changed in 20 years? *Sex Roles, 32,* 651–673.

Thornberry, T. P., Freeman-Gallant, A., Lizotte, A. J., Krohn, M. D., & Smith, C. A. (2003). Linked lives: The intergenerational transmission of antisocial behavior. *Journal of Abnormal Child Psychology, 31,* 171–184.

Thornberry, T. P., Lizotte, A. J., Krohn, M. D., Farnworth, M., & Jang, S. J. (1994). Delinquent peers' beliefs and delinquent behavior: A longitudinal test of interactional theory. *Criminology, 32,* 47–83.

Thornburgh, D., Lin, H. S., et al. (2002). Youth, pornography, and the Internet. Washington, DC: National Academy Press.

Thorne, B. (1986). Girls and boys together . . . but mostly apart: Gender arrangements in elementary schools. In W. W. Hartup & Z. Rubin (Eds.), *Relationships and development.* Mahwah, NJ: Erlbaum.

Thorne, B., & Luria, Z. (1986). Sexuality and gender in children's daily worlds. *Social Problems, 33,* 176–190.

Thurstone, L. L. (1938). *Primary mental abilities.* Chicago: University of Chicago Press.

Tiedemann, J. (2000). Parents' gender stereotypes and teachers' beliefs as predictors of children's concept of their mathematical ability in elementary school. *Journal of Educational Psychology, 92,* 144–151.

Tienari, P. L., Lahti, I., Sorri, A., Naarala, M., Moring, J., Kaleva, M., et al. (1990). Adopted away offspring of schizophrenics and controls. In L. Robins & M. Rutter (Eds.), *Straight and devious pathways from childhood to adulthood.* Cambridge, UK: Cambridge University Press.

Tietjen, A. (1986). Prosocial reasoning among children and adults in a Papua New Guinea society. *Developmental Psychology, 22,* 861–868.

Tietjen, A. M. (2006). Cultural influences on peer relations: An ecological perspective. In X. Chen, D. C. French, & B. H. Schneider (Eds.), *Peer relationships in cultural context* (pp. 52–74). Cambridge, UK: Cambridge University Press.

Timmerman, G. (2005). A comparison between girls' and boys' experiences of unwanted sexual behaviour in secondary schools. *Educational Research, 47,* 291–306.

Tincoff, R., & Jusczyk, P. W. (1999). Some beginnings of word comprehension in 6-month-olds. *Psychological Science, 10,* 172–175.

Tisak, M. S. (1995). Domains of social reasoning and beyond. In R. Vista (Ed.), *Annals of child development* (Vol. 11, pp. 95–130). London: Jessica Kingsley.

Tognoli, J., Pullen, J., & Lieber, J. (1994). The privilege of place: Domestic and work locations of characters in children's books. *Children's Environments Quarterly, 11,* 272–280.

Tolan, P. H., Gorman-Smith, D., & Henry, D. B. (2003). The developmental ecology of urban males' youth violence. *Developmental Psychology, 39,* 274–291.

Tolchnisky, L. (2003). *The cradle of culture and what children know about writing and numbers before being taught.* Mahwah, NJ: Erlbaum.

Tomada, G., & Schneider, B. H. (1997). Relational aggression, gender, and peer acceptance: Invariance across culture, stability over time, and concordance among informants. *Developmental Psychology, 33,* 601–609.

Tomasello, M. (1988). Learning to use prepositions: A case study. *Journal of Child Language, 14,* 79–98.

Tomasello, M. (1992). The social bases of language acquisition. *Social Development, 1,* 68–87.

Tomasello, M. (1994). Can an ape understand a sentence? A review of *Language comprehension in ape and child* by E. S. Savage-Rumbaugh et al. *Language & Communication, 14,* 377–390.

Tomasello, M. (1995). Language is not an instinct. *Cognitive Development, 10,* 131–156.

Tomasello, M. (2001). Perceiving intentions and learning words in the second year of life. In M. Bowerman & S. C. Levinson (Eds.), Language acquisition and conceptual development. New York: Cambridge University Press.

Tomasello, M. (2007). *Constructing a Language: A Usage-Based Theory of Language Acquisition.* Harvard University Press.

Tomasello, M. (2008). *Origins of Human Communication.* Cambridge, MA: The MIT Press.

Tomasello, M., & Barton, M. (1994). Learning words in non-ostensive context. *Developmental Psychology, 30,* 639–650.

Tomasello, M., & Farrar, M. J. (1986). Joint attention and early language. *Child Development, 57,* 1454–1463.

Tomasello, M., Strosberg, R., & Akhtar, N. (1996). Eighteen-month-old children learn words in non-ostensive contexts. *Journal of Child Language, 23,* 157–176.

Tomkins, S. S. (1962). *Affect, imagery, consciousness: Vol. 1. The positive emotions.* New York: Springer.

Tooby, J., & Cosmides, L. (2005). Evolutionary psychology: Conceptual foundations. In D. M. Buss (Ed.), *Handbook of Evolutionary Psychology.* New York: Wiley.

Toth, S. L., Rogosch, F. A., Manly, J. T., & Cicchetti, D. (2006). The efficacy of toddler-parent psychotherapy to reorganize attachment in the young offspring of mothers with major depressive disorder: A randomized prevention trial. *Journal of Consulting and Clinical Psychology, 74,* 1006–1016.

Trainor, L. J., & Heinmiller, B. M. (1998). The development of evaluative responses to music: Infants prefer to listen to consonance over dissonance. *Infant Behavior and Development, 21,* 77–88.

Travis, J. (2003). Mining the mouse: A rodent's DNA sheds light on the human genome. *Science News, 163,* 122.

Trehub, S. E. (1993). Temporal auditory processing in infancy. *Annals of the New York Academy of Sciences, 682,* 137–149.

Trehub, S. E., & Schellenberg, E. G. (1995). Music: Its relevance to infants. *Annals of Child Development, 11,* 1–24.

Tremblay, R. E., Pihl, R., Vitaro, F., & Dobkin, P. L. (1994). Predicting early onset of male antisocial behavior from preschool behavior. *Archives of General Psychiatry, 51,* 732–739.

Trentacosta, C. J., Hyde, L. W., Shaw, D. S., Dishion, T. J., Gardner, F., & Wilson, M. (2008). The relations among cumulative risk, parenting, and behavior problems during early childhood. *Journal of Child Psychology and Psychiatry, 49,* 1211–1219.

Trentacosta, C. J., & Izard, C. E. (2007). Kindergarten children's emotion competence as a predictor of their academic competence in first grade. *Emotion, 7,* 77–88.

Trinder, L., Kellet, J., & Swift, L. (2008). The relationship between contact and child adjustment in high conflict cases after divorce or separation. *Child and Adolescent Mental Health, 13,* 181–187.

Trivers, R. (1972). Parental investment and sexual selection. In B. Campbell (Ed.), *Sexual selection and the descent of man 1871–1971* (pp. 136–179). New York: Aldine de Gruyter.

Trivers, R. L. (1983). The evolution of cooperation. In D. L. Bridgeman (Ed.), *The nature of prosocial development* (pp. 95–112). NY: Academic Press.

Trommsdorff, G., Friedlmeier, W., & Mayer, B. (2007). Sympathy, distress, and prosocial behavior of preschool children in four cultures. *International Journal of Behavioral Development, 31,* 284–293.

Tronick, E. Z., Thomas, R. B., & Daltabuit, M. (1994). The Quechua manta pouch: A caretaking practice for buffering the Peruvian infant against the multiple stressors of high altitude. *Child Development, 65,* 1005–1013.

Troy, M., & Sroufe, L. A. (1987). Victimization among preschoolers: Role of attachment relationship history. *Journal of the American Academy of Child and Adolescent Psychiatry, 26,* 166–172.

Trzesniewski, K. H., Donnellan, M. B., Moffitt, T., Robins, R. W., Poulton, R., & Caspi, A. (2006). Low self-esteem during adolescence predicts poor health, criminal behavior, and limited economic prospects during adulthood. *Developmental Psychology, 42,* 381–390.

Tsao, F.-M., Liu, H.-M., & Kuhl, P. K. (2004). Speech perception in infancy predicts language development in the second year of life: A longitudinal study. *Child Development, 75,* 987–1297.

Tully, L. A., Arseneault, L., Caspi, A., Moffitt, T. E., & Morgan, J. (2004). Does maternal warmth moderate the effects of birth weight on twins' attention-deficit/hyperactivity disorder (ADHD) symptoms and wow IQ? *Journal of Consulting & Clinical Psychology, 72,* 218–226.

Tunteler, E., & Resing, W. C. M. (2002). Spontaneous analogical transfer in 4-year-olds: A microgenetic study. *Journal of Experimental Child Psychology, 83,* 149–166.

Turiel, E. (1987). Potential relations between the development of social reasoning and childhood aggression. In D. H. Crowell, I. M., Evans, & C. R. O'Donnell (Eds.), *Childhood aggression and violence: Sources of influence, prevention, and control* (pp. 95–114). New York: Plenum Press.

Turiel, E. (1998). The development of morality. In W. Damon (Series Ed.) and N. Eisenberg (Vol. Ed.), *Handbook of child psychology. Vol. 3. Social, emotional, and personality development* (pp. 863–932). New York: Wiley.

Turiel, E. (2006). The development of morality. In N. Eisenberg (Vol. Ed.) and W. Damon and R. M. Lerner (Series Eds.), *Handbook of child psychology* (6th ed.): *Social, emotionality, and personality development* (pp. 789–857). Hoboken, NJ: Wiley.

Turiel, E. (2008). Thought about actions in social domains: Morality, social conventions, and social interactions. *Cognitive Development, 23,* 136–154.

Turiel, E. (in press). The development of morality. In W. Damon & R. L. Lerner (Senior Eds.) and N. Eisenberg (Vol. Ed.), *Handbook of child psychology.* (Vol. 3; 6th ed.). *Social, emotional, and personality development.* Hoboken, NJ: Wiley.

Turkheimer, E. (2000). Three laws of behavior genetics and what they mean. *Current Directions in Psychological Science, 9,* 160–164.

Turkheimer, E., Haley, A., Waldron, M., D'Onofrio, B., & Gottesman, I. I. (2003). Socioeconomic status modifies heritability of IQ in young children. *Psychological Science, 14,* 623–628.

Turley, R. N. (2003a). Are children of young mothers disadvantaged because of their mother's age or family background? *Child Development, 74,* 465–474.

Turley, R. N. (2003b). When do neighborhoods matter? The role of race and neighborhood peers. *Social Science Research, 32,* 61–79.

Turnbull, C. M. (1972). *The mountain people.* New York: Simon & Schuster.

Turner-Bowker, D. M. (1996). Gender stereotyped descriptions in children's picture books: Does "curious Jane" exist in the literature? *Sex Roles, 35,* 461–488.

Turner, C. M., & Barrett, P. M. (2003). Does age play a role in the structure of anxiety and depression in children and youths? An investigation of the tripartite model in three age cohorts. *Journal of Consulting and Clinical Psychology, 71,* 826–833.

Turner, P. J., & Gervai, J. (1995). A multidimensional study of gender typing in preschool children and their parents. *Developmental Psychology, 31,* 759–772.

Tversky, B., & Hemenway, D. (1984). Objects, parts, and categories. *Journal of Experimental Psychology: General, 113,* 169–193.

Twenge, J. M., & Crocker, J. (2002). Race and self-esteem: Meta-analyses comparing Whites, Blacks, Hispanics, Asians, and American Indians and comment on Gray-Little and Hafdahl (2000). *Psychological Bulletin, 128*(3), 371–408.

Twenge, J. M., & Nolen-Hoeksema, S. (2002). Age, gender, race, socioeconomic status, and birth cohort differences on the Children's Depression Inventory: A meta-analysis. *Journal of Abnormal Psychology, 111,* 578–588.

Tyler, K. A., & Bersani, B. E. (2008). A longitudinal study of early adolescent precursors to running away. *Journal of Early Adolescence, 28,* 230–251.

Tyler, K. A., Whitbeck, L. B., Hoyt, D. R., & Johnson, K. D. (2003). Self-mutilation and homeless youth: The role of family abuse, street experiences, and mental disorders. *Journal of Research on Adolescence, 13,* 457–474.

Tyrka, A. R., Graber, J. A., & Brooks-Gunn, J. (2000). The development of disordered eating: Correlates and predictors of eating problems in the context of adolescence. In A. J. Sameroff, M. Lewis, et al. (Eds.), *Handbook of developmental psychopathology* (2nd ed., pp. 607–624). New York: Kluwer Academic/Plenum Press.

Uller, C., Carey, S., Huntley-Fenner, G., & Klatt, L. (1999). What representations might underlie infant numerical knowledge? *Cognitive Development, 14,* 1–36.

Umaña-Taylor, A., Diversi, M., & Fine, M. (2002). Ethnic identity and self-esteem among Latino adolescents: Distinctions among Latino populations. *Journal of Adolescent Research, 17,* 303–327.

Umaña-Taylor, A. J., Bhanot, R., & Shin, N. (2006). Ethnic identity formation during adolescence: The critical role of families. *Journal of Family Issues, 27,* 390–414.

Umaña-Taylor, A. J., & Updegraff, K. A. (2007). Latino adolescents' mental health: Exploring the interrelations among discrimination, ethnic identity, cultural orientation, self-esteem, and depressive symptoms. *Journal of Adolescence, 30,* 549–567.

Umaña-Taylor, A. J., Vargas-Chanes, D., Garcia, C. D., & Gonzales-Backen, M. (2008). A longitudinal examination of Latino adolescents' ethnic identity, coping with discrimination, and self-esteem. *Journal of Early Adolescence, 28,* 16–50.

Umiltà, M. A., Kohler, E., Gallese, V., Fogassi, L., Fadigo, L., Keysers, C., & Rizzolatti, G. (2001). I know what you are doing: A neurophysiological study. *Neuron, 31,* 155–165.

Underwood, B., & Moore, B. (1982). Perspective-taking and altruism. *Psychological Bulletin, 91,* 143–173.

Underwood, M. K. (2003). *Social aggression among girls.* New York: Guilford.

Underwood, M. K. (2004). Gender and peer relations: Are the two gender cultures really all that different? In J. B. Kupersmidt, & K. A. Dodge (Eds.), *Children's peer relations: From development to intervention* (pp. 21–36). Washington, DC: American Psychological Association.

Unger, J. B., Simon, T. R., Newman, T. L., Montgomery, S. B., Kipke, M. D., & Albornoz, M. (1998). Early adolescent street youth: An overlooked population with unique problems and service needs. *Journal of Early Adolescence, 18,* 325–348.

UNICEF Statistics. (2001). Low birthweight. Retrieved July 12, 2002, from http://www.childinfo.org/eddb/lbw/index.htm.

Updegraff, K. A., McHale, S. M., & Crouter, A. C. (1996). Egalitarian and traditional families: What do they mean for girls' and boys' achievement in math and science? *Journal of Youth and Adolescence, 25,* 73–88.

Urberg, K. A., Degirmencioglu, S. M., & Pilgrim, C. (1997). Close friend and group influence on adolescent cigarette smoking and alcohol use. *Developmental Psychology, 33,* 834–844.

Urberg, K. A., Degirmencioglu, S. M., Tolson, J. M., & Halliday-Scher, K. (1995). The structure of adolescent peer networks. *Developmental Psychology, 31,* 540–547.

Urbina, I. (2009). Running in the shadows: Recession drives surge in youth runaways. *New York Times,* October 26.

U.S. Bureau of the Census. (1992). *Marital status and living arrangements: March, 1992: Current population reports,* Series P-20, No. 468, Tables G. & 5. Washington, DC: U.S. Government Printing Office.

U.S. Bureau of the Census. (2003a). Current Population Reports, P60-222. *Poverty in the United States: 2002.* Washington, DC: U.S. Government Printing Office.

U.S. Bureau of the Census. (2003b). *Custodial mothers and fathers and their child support: 2001.* Current Population Reports, October.

U.S. Bureau of the Census. (2003c). *Families and Living Arrangements.* www.census.gov/population/socdemo/hh-fam-cps2003/tabc3-all.csv.

U.S. Bureau of the Census. (2004). POV07: Families with related children under 18 by member of working family members and family structure—all races. Online report available at http://ferret.bls.census.gov/macro/032004/pov/toc.htm. Last revised: July 14, 2004.

U.S. Bureau of the Census, Facts for Features, May 2, 2005. http://www.census.gov/Press-Release/www/releases/archives/cb05-ff.05-2.pdf.

U.S. Bureau of the Census (2007). Families by age of householder, number of children, and family structure (Table Number POV04). Available: http://pubdb3.census.gov/macro/032007/pov/new04_100.htm.

U.S. Department of Education and National Center for Education Statistics (2007). *Digest of Education Statistics.* Retrieved from http://nces.Ed.gov/index/asp.

U.S. Department of Health and Human Services. (1999). *America's children.* Retrieved November 12, 2002, from http:// www.childstats.gov/ac1999asp.

U.S. Department of Health and Human Services. (2005). Head Start family and child experiences survey (FACES), 1997 cohort. ICPSR version Rockville, MD: Westat, Inc. Retrieved from http://www.child carere search.org/location/ccrca5552.

U.S. Department of Health and Human Services, Administration on Children, Youth and Families. (2009). *Child Maltreatment 2007.* Washington, DC: U.S. Government Printing Office.

U.S. Department of Transportation. (2002). *Traffic safety facts 2002: Children.*

Usher, J. A., & Neisser, U. (1993). Childhood amnesia and the beginning of memory for four early life events. *Journal of Experimental Psychology: General, 122,* 155–165.

Uttal, D. H., Liu, L. L., & DeLoache, J. S. (1999). Taking a hard look at concreteness: Do real objects help children learn? In C. Tamis-LeMonda & L. Balter (Eds.), *Child psychology: A handbook of contemporary issues* (pp. 177–192). Hamden, CT: Garland.

Uttal, D. H., Liu, L. L., & DeLoache, J. S. (2006). Concreteness and symbolic development. In L. Balter and C. S. Tamis-LeMonda (Eds.), *Child psychology: A handbook of contemporary issues* (2nd Ed.) (pp. 167–184). Philadelphia, PA: Psychology Press.

Vaillancourt, T., Brendgen, M., Boivin, M., & Tremblay, R. E. (2003). A longitudinal confirmatory factor analysis of indirect and physical aggression: Evidence of two factors over time? *Child Development, 74,* 1628–1638.

Vaish, A., Carpenter, M., & Tomasello, M. (2009). Sympathy through affective perspective taking and its relation to prosocial behavior in toddlers. *Developmental Psychology, 45*, 534–543.

Valenzuela, M. (1997). Maternal sensitivity in a developing society: The context of urban poverty and infant chronic undernutrition. *Developmental Psychology, 33*, 845–855.

Valeski, T. N., & Stipek, D. J. (2001). Young children's feelings about school. *Child Development, 72*, 1198–1213.

Valiente, C., Eisenberg, N., Fabes, R. A., Shepard, S. A., Cumberland, A., & Losoya, S. H. (2004). Prediction of children's empathy-related responding from their effortful control and parents' expressivity. *Developmental Psychology, 40*, 911–926.

Valiente, C., Fabes, R. A., Eisenberg, N., & Spinrad, T. L. (2004). The relations of parental expressivity and support to children's coping with daily stress. *Journal of Family Psychology, 18*, 97–106.

Valiente, C., Lemery-Chalfant, K., & Castro, K. S. (2007). Children's effortful control and academic competence. *Merrill-Palmer Quarterly, 53*, 1–25.

Van Beek, Y., van Dolderen, M. S. M., Dubas, J. J. S. D. (2006). Gender-specific development of nonverbal behaviors and mild depression in adolescence. *Journal of Child Psychology and Psychiatry*, 47, 1272–1283.

Van de gaer, E., Pustjens, H., Van Damme, J., & De Munter, A. (2006). Tracking the effects of school-related attitudes on the language achievement of boys and girls. *British Journal of Sociology of Education, 27*, 293–309.

van den Boom, D. C. (1994). The influence of temperament and mothering on attachment and exploration: An experimental manipulation of sensitive responsiveness among lower-class mothers with irritable infants. *Child Development, 65*(5), 1457–1477.

van den Boom, D. C. (1995). Do first-year intervention effects endure? Follow-up during toddlerhood of a sample of Dutch irritable infants. *Child Development, 66*, 1798–1816.

van den Boom, D. C., & Hoeksma, J. B. (1994). The effect of infant irritability on mother-infant interaction: A growth curve analysis. *Developmental Psychology, 30*, 581–590.

Van den Oord, E. J. C. G., Boomsma, D. I., & Verhulst, F. C. (2000). A study of genetic and environmental effects on the co-occurrence of problem behaviors in three-year-old twins. *Journal of Abnormal Psychology, 109*, 360–372.

van der Maas, H. L. J., & Molenaar, P. C. M. (1992). Stagewise cognitive development: An application of catastrophe theory. *Psychological Review, 99*, 395–417.

Van Doesum, K. T. M., Riksen-Walraven, J. M., Hosman, C. M. H., & Hoefnagels, C. (2008). A randomized controlled trial of a home-visiting intervention aimed at preventing relationship problems in depressed mothers and their infants. *Child Development, 79*, 547–561.

Van Doorn, M. D., Branje, S. J. T., & Meeus, W. H. J. (2008). Conflict resolution in parent-adolescent relationships and adolescent delinquency. *Journal of Early Adolescence, 28*, 503–527.

van Houtte, M. (2004). Why boys achieve less at school than girls: The difference between boys' and girls' academic culture. *Educational Studies, 30*(2), 159–173.

van IJzendoorn, M. H. (1995). Adult attachment representations, parental responsiveness, and infant attachment: A meta-analysis on the predictive validity of the adult attachment interview. *Psychological Bulletin, 117*, 387–403.

van IJzendoorn, M. H. (1997). Attachment, emergent morality, and aggression: Toward a developmental socioemotional model of antisocial behaviour. *International Journal of Behavioral Development, 21*, 703–727.

van IJzendoorn, M. H., & De Wolff, M. S. (1997). In search of the absent father—Meta-analyses of infant-father attachment: A rejoinder to our discussants. *Child Development, 68*, 604–609.

van IJzendoorn, M. H., Juffer, F., & Duyvesteyn, M. G. C. (1995). Breaking the intergenerational cycle of insecure attachment: A review of the effects of the effects of attachment-based interventions on maternal sensitivity and infant security. *Journal of Child Psychology and Psychiatry, 36*, 225–248.

van IJzendoorn, M. H., & Kroonenberg, P. M. (1988). Cross-cultural patterns of attachment: A meta-analysis of the strange situation. *Child Development, 59*, 147–156.

van IJzendoorn, M. H., & Sagi, A. (1999). Cross-cultural patterns of attachment: Universal and contextual dimensions. In J. Cassidy & P. R. Shaver (Eds.), *Handbook of attachment: Theory, research, and clinical applications* (pp. 713–734). New York: Guilford.

van IJzendoorn, M. H., Schuengel, C., & Bakermans-Kranenburg, M. J. (1999). Disorganized attachment in early childhood: Meta-analysis of precursors, concomitants, and sequelae. *Development and Psychopathology, 11*, 225–249.

van IJzendoorn, M. H., Vereijken, C. M. J. L., Bakermans-Kranenburg, M. J., & Riksen-Walraven, J. M. (2004). Assessing attachment security with the attachment Q sort: Meta-analytic evidence for the validity of the observer AQS. *Child Development, 75*, 1188–1213.

van Loosbroek, E., & Smitsman, A. W. (1990). Visual perception of numerosity in infancy. *Developmental Psychology, 26*, 916–922.

Vance, H. B., Hankins, N., & McGee, H. (1979). A preliminary study of Black and White differences on the revised Wechsler Intelligence Scale for Children. *Journal of Clinical Psychology, 35*, 815–819.

Vandell, D. L. (1987). Baby sister/baby brother: Reactions to the birth of a sibling and patterns of early sibling relations. *Journal of Children in Contemporary Society, 19*, 13–37.

Vaquera, E., & Kao, G. (2008). Do you like me as much as I like you? Friendship reciprocity and its effects on school outcomes among adolescents. *Social Science Research, 37*, 55–72.

Varendi, H., Porter, R. H., & Winberg, J. (2002). The effect of labor on olfactory exposure learning within the first postnatal hour. *Behavioral Neuroscience, 116*, 206–211.

Vasek, M. E. (1986). Lying as a skill: The development of deception in children. In R. W. Mitchell & N. S. Thompson (Eds.), *Deception: Perspectives on human and non-human deceit.* (pp. 271–292). New York: SUNY Press.

Vaughn, B. E., Goldberg, S., Atkinson, L., Marcovith, S., MacGregor, D., & Seifer, R. (1994). Quality of toddler-mother attachment in children with Down syndrome: Limits to interpretation of Strange Room behavior. *Child Development, 65*, 95–108.

Vaughn, B. E., Vollenweider, M., Bost, K. K., Azria-Evans, M. R., & Snider, J. B. (2003). Negative interactions and social competence for preschool children in two samples: Reconsidering the interpretation of aggressive behavior for young children. *Merrill-Palmer Quarterly, 49*, 245–278.

Vaughn, C. (1996). *How life begins.* New York: Times Books.

Vellutino, F. R., & Scanlon, D. M. (1987). Phonological coding, phonological awareness, and reading ability: Evidence from a longitudinal and experimental study. *Merrill-Palmer Quarterly, 33*, 321–363.

Vellutino, F. R., Scanlon, D. M., & Spearing, D. (1995). Semantic and phonological coding in poor and normal readers. *Journal of Experimental Child Psychology, 59,* 76–123.

Ventura, S. J., Martin, J. A., Curtin, S. C., & Mathews, T. J. (1997). Report of final natality statistics, 1995. *Monthly Vital Statistics Report, 45* (11, Suppl. 2). Hyattsville, MD: National Center for Health Statistics.

Vera, E. M., & Quintana, S. M. (2004). Ethnic identity development in Chicana/o youth. In R. J. Valasquez, L. M. Arellano, & B. W. McNeill (Eds.), *The handbook of Chicana/o psychology and mental health.* Mahwah, NJ: Erlbaum.

Verkuyten, M. (1990). Self-esteem and the evaluation of ethnic identity among Turkish and Dutch adolescents in the Netherlands. *Journal of Social Psychology, 130,* 285–297.

Verma, S. (1999). Socialization for survival: Developmental issues among working street children in India. *New Directions in Child Development, 85,* 5–18.

Vernon, P. A., Wickett, J. C., Bazana, P. G., & Stelmack, R. M. (2000). The neuropsychology and psychophysiology of human intelligence. In R. J. Sternberg (Ed.), *Handbook of intelligence* (pp. 245–264). Cambridge, UK: Cambridge University Press.

Verschueren, K., Marcoen, A., & Schoefs, V. (1996). The internal working model of the self, attachment, and competence in five-year-olds. *Child Development, 67,* 2493–2511.

Vikan, A., & Clausen, S. E. (1993). Freud, Piaget, or neither? Beliefs in controlling other by wishful thinking and magical behavior in young children. *Journal of Genetic Psychology, 154,* 297–314.

Vitaro, F., Barker, E. D., Boivin, M., Brendgen, M., & Tremblay, R. E. (2006). Do early difficult temperament and harsh parenting differentially predict reactive and proactive aggression. *Journal of Abnormal Child Psychology, 34,* 685–695.

Vitaro, F., Brendgen, M., Pagani, L., Tremblay, R. E., & McDuff, P. (1999). Disruptive behavior, peer association, and conduct disorder: Testing the developmental links through early intervention. *Development and Psychopathology, 11,* 287–304.

Vitaro, F., Pedersen, S., & Brendgen, M. (2007). Children's disruptiveness, peer rejection, friends' deviancy, and delinquent behaviors: A process-oriented model. *Development and Psychopathology, 19,* 433–453.

Vitaro, F., Tremblay, R. E., Kerr, M., Pagani, L., & Bukowski, W. M. (1997). Disruptiveness, friends' characteristics, and delinquency in early adolescence: A test of two competing models of development. *Child Development, 68,* 676–689.

Vittori, J. (2007). The gang's all here: The globalization of gang activity. *Journal of Gang Research, 14,* 6–39.

Vohr, B. R., & Garcia-Coll, C. T. (1988). Follow-up studies of high risk low-birthweight infants: Changing trends. In H. E. Fitzgerald, B. M. Lester, & M. W. Yogman (Eds.), *Theory and research in behavioral pediatrics* (Vol. 4). New York: Plenum Press.

Volbrecht, M. M., Lemery-Chalfant, K., Aksan, N., Zahn-Waxler, C., & Goldsmith, H. H. (2007). Examining the familial link between positive affect and empathy development in the second year. *Journal of Genetic Psychology, 168,* 105–130.

Volling, B. L., & Belsky, J. (1991). Multiple determinants of father involvement during infancy in dual-earner and single-earner families. *Journal of Marriage and the Family, 53,* 461–474.

Volling, B. L., & Feagans, L. V. (1995). Infant day care and children's social competence. *Infant Behavior and Development, 18,* 177–188.

Volling, B. L., Mahoney, A., & Rauer, A. J. (2009). Sanctification of parenting, moral socializations, and young children's conscience development. *Psychology of Religion and Spirituality, 1,* 53–68.

von der Lippe, A. L. (1999). The impact of maternal schooling and occupation on child-rearing attitudes and behaviours in low income neighbourhoods in Cairo, Egypt. *International Journal of Behavioural Development, 23,* 703–729.

von Hofsten, C. (1979). Development of visually guided reaching: The approach phase. *Journal of Human Movement Studies, 5,* 160–178.

von Hofsten, C. (1980). Predictive reaching for moving objects by human infants. *Journal of Experimental Child Psychology, 30,* 369–382.

von Hofsten, C. (1982). Eye-hand coordination in the newborn. *Developmental Psychology, 18,* 450–461.

von Hofsten, C. (1991). Structuring of early reaching movements: A longitudinal study. *Journal of Motor Behavior, 23,* 280–292.

von Hofsten, C. (2004). An action perspective on motor development. *Trends in Cognitive Sciences, 8*(6), 266–272.

von Hofsten, C. (2007). Action in development. *Developmental Science, 10,* 54–60.

von Hofsten, C., Dahlström, E., & Fredricksson, Y. (2005). 12-month-old infants' perception of attention direction in static video images. *Infancy, 8,* 217–231.

von Hofsten, C., & Spelke, E. S. (1985). Object perception and object-directed reaching in infancy. *Journal of Experimental Psychology: General, 114,* 198–212.

von Hofsten, C., Vishton, P., Spelke, E. S., Feng, Q., & Rosander, K. (1998). Predictive action in infancy: Tracking and reaching for moving objects. *Cognition, 67,* 255–285.

Vondra, J. I., Shaw, D. S., Swearingen, L., Cohen, M., & Owens, E. B. (2001). Attachment stability and emotional and behavioral regulation from infancy to preschool age. *Development and Psychopathology, 13*(1), 13–33.

Votruba-Drzal, E., Coley, R. L., & Chase-Lansdale, P. L. (2004). Child care and low-income children's development: Direct and moderated effects. *Child Development, 75,* 296–312.

Vouloumanos, A., & Werker, J. F. (2004). Tuned to the signal: The privileged status of speech for young infants. *Developmentl Science, 7,* 270–276.

Vouloumanos, A., & Werker, J. F. (2007). Why voice melody alone cannot explain neonates' preference for speech. *Developmental Science, 10,* 170–172.

Voyer, D., Postma, A., Brake, B., & Imperato-McGinley, J. (2007). Gender differences in object location memory: A meta-analysis. *Psychonomic Bulletin & Review, 14,* 23–38.

Voyer, D., Voyer, S., & Bryden, M. P. (1995). Magnitude of sex differences in spatial abilities: A meta-analysis and consideration of critical variables. *Psychological Bulletin, 117,* 250–270.

Vraniak, D. (1994). Native Americans. In R. J. Sternberg (Ed.) *Encyclopedia of human intelligence* (pp. 747–754). New York: Macmillan.

Vygotsky, L. S. (1934/1962). *Thought and language.* Cambridge, MA: The MIT Press.

Vygotsky, L. S. (1978). *Mind in society: The development of higher mental processes.* Cambridge, MA: Harvard University Press. (Original works published 1930, 1933, 1935.)

Wadsworth, S. J., Corley, R. P., Plomin, R., Hewitt, J. K., & DeFries, J. C. (2006). Genetic and environmental influences on continuity and change in reading achievement in the Colorado Adoption Project. In A. Huston & M. Ripke (Eds.), *Developmental contexts in middle childhood: Bridges to adolescence and adulthood* (pp. 87–106). Cambridge, UK: Cambridge University Press.

Wagner, R. K., Torgesen, J. K., Rashotte, C. A., Hecht, S. A., Barker, T. A., Burgess, S. R., et al. (1997). Changing relations between phonological processing abilities and word-level reading as children develop from beginning to skilled readers: A 5-year longitudinal study. *Developmental Psychology, 33,* 468–479.

Wainright, J. L., & Patterson, C. J. (2006). Delinquency, victimization, and substance use among adolescents with female same-sex parents. *Journal of Family Psychology, 20,* 526–530.

Wainright, J. L., & Patterson, C. J. (2008). Peer relations among adolescents with female same-sex parents. *Developmental Psychology, 44,* 117–126.

Wainright, J. L., Russell, S. T., & Patterson, C. J. (2004). Psychological adjustment, school outcomes, and romantic relationships of adolescents with same-sex parents. *Child Development, 75,* 1886–1898.

Wainryb, C., & Turiel, E. (1995). Diversity of social development: Between and within cultures? In M. Killen & D. Hart (Eds.), *Morality in everyday life: Developmental perspectives* (pp. 283–313). Cambridge, UK: Cambridge University Press.

Waizenhofer, R. N., Buchanan, C. M., & Jackson-Newsom, J. (2004). Mothers' and fathers' knowledge of adolescents' daily activities: Its sources and its links with adolescent adjustment. *Journal of Family Psychology, 18,* 348–360.

Wakeley, A., Rivera, S., & Langer, J. (2000). Can young infants add and subtract? *Child Development, 71,* 1525–1534.

Wakschlag, L. S., Gordon, R. A., Lahey, B. B., Loeber, R., Green, S. M., & Leventhal, B. L. (2001). Maternal age at first birth and boys' risk for conduct disorder. *Journal of Research on Adolescence, 10,* 417–441.

Walden, T. A., & Baxter, A. (1989). The effect of context and age on social referencing. *Child Development, 60,* 1511–1518.

Waldman, I. D. (1996). Aggressive boys' hostile perceptual and response biases: The role of attention and impulsivity. *Child Development, 67,* 1015–1033.

Waldrip, A. M., Malcolm, K. T., & Jensen-Campbell, L. A. (2008). With a little help from your friends: The importance of high-quality friendships on early adolescent adjustment. *Social Development, 17,* 832–852.

Walker, B. E., & Quarles, J. (1962). Palate development in mouse fetuses after tongue removal. *Archives of Oral Biology, 21,* 405–412.

Walker, K., Taylor, E., McElroy, A., Phillip, D.-A., & Wilson, M. N. (1995). Familial and ecological correlates of self-esteem in African American children. *New Directions in Child Development, 68,* 23–34.

Walker, L. J. (1980). Cognitive and perspective taking prerequisites for moral development. *Child Development, 51,* 131–139.

Walker, L. J. (1984). Sex differences in the development of moral reasoning: A critical review. *Child Development, 55,* 677–691.

Walker, L. J. (1991). Sex differences in moral reasoning. In W. M. Kurtines & J. L. Gewirtz (Eds.), *Handbook of moral behavior and development: Vol. 2. Research* (pp. 333–364). Hillsdale, NJ: Erlbaum.

Walker-Andrews, A. S. (1997). Infants' perception of expressive behaviors: Differentiation of multimodal information. *Psychological Bulletin, 121,* 437–456.

Walker-Andrews, A. S., & Dickson, L. R. (1997). Infants' understanding of affect. In S. Hala (Ed.), *The development of social cognition* (pp. 161–186). West Sussex, UK: Psychology Press.

Wall, J. A., Power, T. G., & Arbona, C. (1993). Susceptibility to antisocial peer pressure and its relation to acculturation in Mexican-American adolescents. *Journal of Adolescent Research, 8,* 403–418.

Wallace, I., & McCarton, C. (1997). Neurodevelopmental outcomes of the premature, small-for-gestational infant through age 6. *Clinical Obstetrics and Gynecology, 40,* 843–852.

Wallerstein, J. S., & Blakeslee, S. (1989). *Second changes: Men, women and children a decade after divorce.* New York: Ticknor & Fields.

Wallerstein, J., & Lewis, J. M. (2007). Sibling outcomes and disparate parenting and stepparenting after divorce: Report from a 10-year longitudinal study. *Psychoanalytic Psychology, 24,* 445–458.

Wallman, J. (1992). *Aping language.* Cambridge, UK: Cambridge University Press.

Wang, D., Kato, N., Inaba, Y., Tango, T., Yoshida, Y., Kusaka, Y., et al. (2000). Physical and personality traits of preschool children in Fuzhou, China: Only child vs sibling. *Child: Care, Health and Development, 26,* 49–60.

Wang, Q. (2004). The emergence of cultural self-constructs: Autobiographical memory and self-description in European American and Chinese children. *Developmental Psychology, 40,* 3–15.

Wang, Q. (2006). Earliest recollections of self and others in European American and Taiwanese young adults. *Psychological Science, 17,* 708–714.

Wang, Q. (2007). "Remember when you got the big, big bulldozer?" Mother-child reminiscing over time and across cultures. *Social Cognition, 25,* 455–471.

Ware, E., Uttal, D. H., Wetter, E. K., & DeLoache, J. S. (2006). Young children make scale errors when playing with dolls. *Developmental Science, 9,* 40–45.

Wark, G. R., & Krebs, D. L. (1996). Gender and dilemma differences in real-life moral judgment. *Developmental Psychology, 32,* 220–230.

Warneken, F., Chen, F., & Tomasello, M. (2006). Cooperative activities in young children and chimpanzees. *Child Development, 77,* 640–663.

Warneken, F., & Tomasello, M. (2006). Altruistic helping in human infants and young chimpanzees. *Science, 311,* 1301–1303.

Warneken, F., & Tomasello, M. (2007). Helping and cooperation at 14 months of age. *Infancy, 11,* 271–294.

Warneken, F., & Tomasello, M. (2008). Extrinsic rewards undermine altruistic tendencies in 20-month-olds. *Developmental Psychology, 44,* 1785–1788.

Waterman, A. S. (1999). Issues of identity formation revisited: United States and the Netherlands. *Developmental Review, 19,* 462–497.

Waterman, A. S., & Waterman, C. K. (1971). A longitudinal study of changes in ego identity status during the freshman year at college. *Developmental Psychology, 5,* 167–173.

Waters, E., & Cummings, E. M. (2000). A secure base from which to explore close relationships. *Child Development, 71,* 164–173.

Waters, E., Merrick, S., Treboux, D., Crowell, J., & Albersheim, L. (2000). Attachment security in infancy and early adulthood: A twenty-year longitudinal study. *Child Development, 71,* 684–689.

Waters, H. S. (1980). Class news: A single subject longitudinal study of prose production and schema formation during childhood. *Journal of Verbal Learning and Verbal Behavior, 19,* 152–167.

Waters, H. S. (1989, April). *Problem-solving at two: A year-long naturalistic study of two children.* Paper presented at the Society for Research in Child Development Conference, Kansas City, MO.

Watson, J. B. (1924). *Behaviorism.* New York: Norton.

Watson, J. B. (1928). *Psychological care of infant and child.* New York: Norton.

Watson, J. B., & Rayner, R. (1920). Conditioned emotional reactions. *Journal of Experimental Psychology, 3,* 1–14.

Watson-Gegeo, K. A., & Gegeo, D. W. (1986). Calling-out and repeating routines in Kwara'ae children's language socialization. In B. B. Schieffelin & E. Ochs (Eds.), *Language socialization across cultures* (pp. 17–50). *Studies in the social and cultural foundations of language, No. 3.* New York: Cambridge University Press.

Watt, H. M. G. (2008). What motivates females and males to pursue sex-stereotyped careers? In H. M. G. Watt & J. S. Eccles (Eds.), *Gender and occupational outcomes: Longitudinal assessments of individual, social, and cultural influences* (pp. 87–113). Washington, DC: APA books.

Waxman, S. R. (1990). Linguistic biases and the establishment of conceptual hierarchies: Evidence from preschool children. *Cognitive Development, 5,* 123–150.

Waxman, S. R., & Hall, D. G. (1993). The development of a linkage between count nouns and object categories: Evidence from 15- to 21-month-old infants. *Child Development, 64,* 1224–1241.

Waxman, S. R., & Markow, D. B. (1995). Words as invitations to form categories: Evidence from 12- to 13-month-old infants. *Cognitive Psychology, 29,* 257–302.

Waxman, S. R., & Markow, D. B. (1998). Object properties and object kind: Twenty-one-month-old infants' extension of novel adjectives. *Child Development, 69,* 1313–1329.

Waxman, S. R., & Senghas, A. (1992). Relations among word meanings in early lexical development. *Developmental Psychology, 28,* 862–873.

Way, N., & Greene, M. L. (2006). Trajectories of perceived friendship quality during adolescence: The patterns and contextual predictors. *Journal of Research on Adolescence, 16,* 293–320.

Webb, R. M., Lubinski, D., & Benbow, C. P. (2002). Mathematically facile adolescents with math/science aspirations: New perspectives on their educational and vocational development. *Journal of Educational Psychology, 94,* 785–794.

Weber-Fox, C., & Neville, H. J. (1996). Maturational constraints on functional specializations for language processing: ERP and behavioral evidence in bilingual speakers. *Journal of Cognitive Neuroscience, 8,* 231–256.

Webster-Stratton, C. (1998). Preventing conduct problems in Head Start children: Strengthening parenting competencies. *Journal of Consulting and Clinical Psychology, 66,* 715–730.

Webster-Stratton, C., Reid, M. J., & Stoolmiller, M. (2008). Preventing conduct problems and improving school readiness: Evaluation of the Incredible Years teacher and child training programs in high-risk schools. *Journal of Child Psychology and Psychiatry, 49,* 471–488.

Wegner, D. M. (2002). *The illusion of conscious will.* Cambridge, MA: The MIT Press.

Weinberg, M. K., & Tronick, E. Z. (1994). Beyond the face: An empirical study of infant affective configurations of facial, vocal, gestural, and regulatory behaviors. *Child Development, 65,* 1503–1515.

Weinburgh, M. (1995). Gender differences in student attitudes toward science: A meta-analysis of the literature from 1970 to 1991. *Journal of Research in Science Teaching, 32,* 387–398.

Weinstein, S. M., Mermelstein, R. J., Hankin, B. L., Hedeker, D., & Flay, B. R. (2007). Longitudinal patterns of daily affect and global mood during adolescence. *Journal of Research on Adolescence, 17,* 587–600.

Weir, R. H. (1962). *Language in the crib.* The Hague: Mouton.

Weisgram, E. S., & Bigler, R. S. (2007). Effects of learning about gender discrimination on adolescent girls' attitudes towards and interest in science. *Psychology of Women Quarterly, 31,* 262–269.

Whitaker, D. J., Morrison, S., Lindquist, C., Hawkins, S. R., O'Neil, J. A., Nesius, A. M., Mathew, A. & Reese, L. (2006). A critical review of interventions for the primary prevention of perpetration of partner violence. *Aggression and Violence Behavior, 11,* 151–166.

Whitehead, J. M. (1996). Sex stereotypes, gender identity and subject choice at A-level. *Educational Research,* 38, 147–160.

Whiting, B. B., & Edwards, C. P. (1988). *Children of different worlds: The formation of social behavior.* Cambridge, MA: Harvard University Press.

Wiesner, M., & Kim, H. K. (2006). Co-occurring delinquency and depressive symptoms of adolescent boys and girls: A dual trajectory modeling approach. *Developmental Psychology, 42,* 1220–1235.

Wigfield, A., Eccles, J. S., Yoon, K. S., Harold, R. D., Arbreton, A. J. A., Freedman-Doam, C. & Blumenfeld, P. C. (1997). Change in children's competence beliefs and subjective task values across the elementary school years: A 3-year study. *Journal of Educational Psychology, 89,* 451–469.

Wilgenbusch, T. & Merrell, K. W. (1999). Gender differences in self-concept among children and adolescents: A meta-analysis of multidimensional studies. *School Psychology Quarterly, 14,* 101–120.

Williams, T., Connolly, J., Pepler, D., & Craig, W. (2005). Peer victimization, social support, and psychosocial adjustment of sexual minority adolescents. *Journal of Youth & Adolescence, 34,* 471–482.

Wilson, S. P., & Kipp, K. (1998). The development of efficient inhibition: Evidence from directed-forgetting tasks. *Developmental Review, 18,* 86–123.

Witkowska, E., & Gådin, K. G. (2005). Have you been sexually harassed in school? What female high school students regard as harassment. *International Journal of Adolescent Medicine and Health, 17,* 391–406.

Weiss, B., Dodge, K. A., Bates, J. E., & Pettit, G. S. (1992). Some consequences of early harsh discipline: Child aggression and a maladaptive social information processing style. *Child Development, 63,* 1321–1335.

Weissman, M. D., & Kalish, C. W. (1999). The inheritance of desired characteristics: Children's view of the role of intention in parent-offspring resemblance. *Journal of Experimental Child Psychology, 73,* 245–265.

Wellman, H. M. (1990). *Children's theories of mind.* Cambridge, MA: The MIT Press.

Wellman, H. M., Cross, D., & Bartsch, K. (1987). Infant search and object permanence: A meta-analysis of the A-not-B error. *Monographs of the Society for Research in Child Development, 51*(3, Serial No. 214).

Wellman, H. M., Cross, D., & Watson, J. (2001). Meta-analysis of theory-of-mind development: The truth about false belief. *Child Development, 72*, 655–684.

Wellman, H. M., & Gelman, S. (1998). Knowledge acquisition in foundational domains. In W. Damon (Series Ed.) & D. Kuhn & R. S. Siegler (Vol. Eds.), *Handbook of child psychology: Vol. 2: Cognition, Perception & Language.* (5th ed.). New York: Wiley.

Wellman, H. M., & Inagaki, K. (Eds.) (1997). The emergence of core domains of thought: Children's reasoning about physical, psychological, and biological phenomena. *New Directions for Child Development, No. 75.* San Francisco: Jossey-Bass.

Wellman, H. M., & Wooley, J. D. (1990). From simple desires to ordinary beliefs: The early development of everyday psychology. *Cognition, 35*, 245–275.

Wentzel, K. R. (2003). Sociometric status and adjustment in middle school: A longitudinal study. *Journal of Early Adolescence, 23*, 5–28.

Wentzel, K. R. (2009). Peers and academic functioning at school. In K. H. Rubin, W. M. Bukowski, & B. Laursen (Eds.), *Handbook of peer interactions, relationships, and groups* (pp. 531–547). New York: Guilford Press.

Wentzel, K. R., & Asher, S. R. (1995). The academic lives of neglected, rejected, popular, and controversial children. *Child Development, 66*, 754–773.

Wentzel, K. R., & Caldwell, K. (1997). Friendships, peer acceptance, and group membership: Relations to academic achievement in middle school. *Child Development, 68*, 1198–1209.

Werebe, M. J., & Baudonniere, P. (1991). Social pretend play among friends and familiar peers. *International Journal of Behavioral Development, 14*, 411–428.

Werker, J. F. (1989). Becoming a native listener. *American Scientist, 77*, 54–69.

Werker, J. F., & Lalonde, C. E. (1988). Cross-language speech perception: Initial capabilities and developmental change. *Developmental Psychology, 24*, 672–683.

Werker, J. F., Pegg, J. E., & McLeod, P. J. (1994). A cross-language investigation of infant preference for infant-directed communication. *Infant Behavior and Development, 17*, 323–333.

Werker, J. F., & Tees, R. C. (1984). Cross-language speech perception: Evidence for perceptual reorganization during the first year of life. *Infant Behavior and Development, 7*, 49–63.

Werner, E. E. (1989). Children of the Garden Island. *Scientific American, 260*(4), 106–111.

Werner, E. E. (1993). Risk, resilience, and recovery: Perspectives from the Kauai Longitudinal Study. *Development and Psychopathology, 5*, 503–515.

Werner, N. E., & Crick, N. R. (2004). Maladaptive peer relationships and the development of relational and physical aggression during middle childhood. *Social Development, 13*(4), 495–514.

Wertheimer, M. (1961). Psychomotor coordination of auditory and visual space at birth. *Science, 134,* 1692.

Wessel, M. A., Cobb, J. C., Jackson, E. B., Harris, G. S., & Detwiler, A. C. (1954). Paroxysmal fussing in infancy, sometimes called "colic." *Pediatrics, 14*, 421–433.

West, J., Denton, K., & Germino-Hausken, E. (2000). *America's kindergarteners.* National Center for Education Statistics Statistical Analysis Report, U. S. Department of Education, Office of Educational Research and Improvement (NCES 2000-0070, can be downloaded at http://nces.ed.gov/pubsearch/pubsinfo.asp?pubid+2000070)

West, M. J., & Rheingold, H. L. (1978). Infant stimulation of maternal instruction. *Infant Behavior and Development, 1,* 205–215.

Westat, Inc. (producer) (2005). *Head Start Family and Child Experiences (FACES) Survey, 2003 Cohort.* U. S. Department of Health and Human Service, Administration for Children and Families, Rockville, MD.

Westinghouse Learning Center (1969). *The impact of Head Start: An evaluation of the effects of Head Start on children's cognitive and affective development.* Washington, DC: Clearinghouse for Federal Scientific and Technical Information.

Weston, D. R., Ivins, B., Zuckerman, B., Jones, C., & Lopez, R. (1989). Drug exposed babies: Research and clinical issues. *Zero-to-Three, 9*, 1–7.

Weyandt, L. L., Iwaszuk, W., Fulton, K., Ollerton, M., Beatty, N., Fouts, H., Schepman, S., & Greenlaw, C. (2003). The Internal Restlessness Scale: Performance of college students with and without ADHD. *Journal of Learning Disabilities, 36*, 382–340.

White, B. L. (1985). *The first three years of life.* New York: Prentice-Hall.

White, J. L., Moffit, T. E., Earls, F., Robins, L., & Silva, P. (1990). How early can we tell? Predictors of childhood conduct disorder and adolescent delinquency. *Criminology, 28*, 507–533.

White, M. I., & LeVine, R. A. (1986). What is an ii do (good child)? In H. Stevenson, H. Azuma, & K. Hakuta (Eds.), *Child development and education in Japan* (pp. 55–62). New York: W. H. Freeman.

Whitehead, K. A., Ainsworth, A. T., Wittig, M. A., & Gadino, B. (2009). Implications of ethnic identity exploration and ethnic identity affirmation and belonging for intergroup attitudes among adolescents. *Journal of Adolescent Research, 19*, 123–135.

Whitehurst, G. J., & Lonigan, C. J. (1998). Child development and emergent literacy. *Child Development, 69*, 848–872.

Whitehurst, G. J., Zevenbergen, A. A., Crone, D. A., Schultz, M. S., Velting, O. N., & Fischel, J. E. (1999). Outcomes of an emergent literacy intervention from Head Start through second grade. *Journal of Educational Psychology, 91*, 261–272.

Whitesell, N. R., & Harter, S. (1996). The interpersonal context of emotion: Anger with close friends and classmates. *Child Development, 67*, 1345–1359.

Whiteside, M. F., & Becker, B. J. (2000). Parental factors and the young child's postdivorce adjustment: A meta-analysis with implications for parenting arrangements. *Journal of Family Psychology, 14*, 5–26.

Whiteside-Mansell, L., Bradley, R. H., Owen, M. T., Randolph, S. M., & Cauce, A. M. (2003). Parenting and children's behavior at 36 months: Equivalence between African American and European American mother-child dyads. *Parenting: Science and Practices, 3*, 197–234.

Whiting, B. B., & Edwards, C. (1988). *Children of different worlds: The formation of social behavior.* Cambridge, MA: Harvard University Press.

Whiting, B. B., & Whiting, J. W. M. (1975). *Children of six cultures: A psychocultural analysis.* Cambridge, MA: Harvard University Press.

Whitney, M. P., & Thoman, E. B. (1994). Sleep in premature and full-term infants from 24-hour home recordings. *Infant Behavior and Development, 17,* 223–234.

Whorf, B. L. (1956). *Language, Thought, and reality: Selected Writings of Benjamin Lee Whorf.* Cambridge: The MIT Press.

Wichmann, C., Coplan, R. J., & Daniels, T. (2004). The social cognitions of socially withdrawn children. *Social Development, 13,* 377–392.

Wichstrom, L. (1999). The emergence of gender difference in depressed mood during adolescence: The role of intensified gender socialization. *Developmental Psychology, 35,* 232–245.

Wickrama, K. A. S., Lorenz, F. O., Conger, R. D., Elder, G. H., Jr., Abraham, W. T., & Fang, S-A. (2006). Changes in family financial circumstances and the physical health of married and recently divorced mothers. *Social Science & Medicine, 63,* 123–136.

Wickett, J. C., Vernon, P. A., & Lee, D. H. (2000). Relationships between factors of intelligence and brain volume. *Personality and Individual Differences, 29,* 1095–1122.

Widen, S. C., & Russell, J. A. (2003). A closer look at preschoolers' feely produced labels for facial expressions. *Developmental Psychology, 39,* 114–128.

Wigfield, A., Eccles, J. S., Schiefele, U., Roeser, R. W., & Davis-Kean, P. (2006). In N. Eisenberg (Vol. Ed.) and W. Damon & R. M. Lerner (Series Eds.), *Handbook of child psychology. Vol. 3. Social, emotional, and personality development* (6th ed., pp. 933–1002). New York: Wiley.

Wigfield, A., Eccles, J. S., Schiefele, U., Roeser, R., & Davis-Kean, P. (in press). Development of achievement motivation. In W. Damon & R. M. Lerner (Series Eds.), and N. Eisenberg (Vol. Ed.), *The handbook of child psychology. Vol. 3. Social, personality, and emotional development.* (6th ed.) Hoboken, NJ: Wiley.

Wiggers, M., & van Lieshout, C. F. M. (1985). Development of recognition of emotions: Children's reliance on situational and facial expressive cues. *Developmental Psychology, 21,* 338–349.

Wilk, S. L., Desmarais, L. B., & Sackett, P. R. (1995). Gravitation to jobs commensurate with ability: Longitudinal and cross-sectional tests. *Journal of Applied Psychology, 80,* 79–85.

Willatts, P. (1990). Development of problem solving strategies in infancy. In D. Bjorklund (Ed.), *Children's strategies: Contemporary views of cognitive development* (pp. 23–66). Hillsdale, NJ: Erlbaum.

Williams, B. R., Ponesse, J. S., Schachar, R. J., Logan, G. D., & Tannock, R. (1999). Development of inhibitory control across the life span. *Developmental Psychology, 35,* 205–213.

Williams, S. T., Conger, K. J., & Blozis, S. A. (2007). The development of interpersonal aggression during adolescence: The importance of parents, siblings, and family economics. *Child Development, 78,* 1526–1542.

Williams, T. (Ed.). (1986). *The impact of television: A natural experiment in three communities.* Orlando, FL: Academic Press.

Willinger, M. (1995). SIDS prevention. *Pediatric Annals, 24,* 358–364.

Willingham, W. W., & Cole, L. S. (1997). *Gender and fair assessment.* Mahwah, NJ: Erlbaum.

Wilson, B. J. (2003). The role of attentional processes in children's prosocial behavior with peers: Attention shifting and emotion. *Development and Psychopathology, 15,* 313–329.

Wilson, B. J., Kunkel, D., Linz, D., Potter, J., Donnerstein, E., Smith, E. L., Blumenthal, E., & Gray, T. (1997). Violence in television programming overall: University of California, Santa Barbara study. In M. Seawall (Ed.), *National Television Violence Study* (Vol. 1, pp. 3–184). Thousand Oaks, CA: Sage Publications.

Wilson, E. O. (1975). *Sociobiology: The new synthesis.* Cambridge, MA: Harvard University Press.

Wilson, E. O. (2002) *The Future of Life.* New York: Knopf.

Wilson, J. B., & Brooks-Gunn, J. (2001). Health status and behaviors of unwed fathers. *Children and Youth Services Review, 23,* 377–401.

Wilson, T. D. (2002). *Strangers to ourselves: Discovering the adaptive unconscious.* Cambridge, MA: Harvard University Press.

Wilson, T. D., & Dunn, E. (2004). Self-knowledge: Its limits, value and potential for improvement. *Annual Review of Psychology, 55,* 493–518.

Wimmer, H., Mayringer, H., & Raberger, T. (1999). Reading and dual-task balancing: Evidence against the automatization deficit explanation of developmental dyslexia. *Journal of Learning Disabilities, 32,* 473–478.

Windle, M. (1992). A longitudinal study of stress buffering for adolescent problem behaviors. *Developmental Psychology, 28,* 522–530.

Windle, M. (1994). A study of friendship characteristics and problem behaviors among middle adolescents. *Child Development, 65,* 1764–1777.

Winner, E. (1996). *Gifted children: Myths and realities.* New York: Basic Books.

Winsler, A., De León, J. R., Wallace, B. A., Carlton, M. P., & Willson-Quayle, A. (2003). Private speech in preschool children: Developmental stability and change, across-task consistency, and relations with classroom behavior. *Journal of Child Language, 30,* 583–608.

Winsler, A., Dias, R. M., McCarthy, E. M., Atencio, D. J., & Chabay, L. (1999). Mother-child interactions, private speech, and task performance in preschool children with behavior problems. *Journal of Child Psychology and Psychiatry, 40,* 891–904.

Wintre, M. G., & Vallance, D. D. (1994). A developmental sequence in the comprehension of emotions: Intensity, multiple emotions, and valence. *Developmental Psychology, 30,* 509–514.

Witelson, S. F. (1987). Neurobiological aspects of language in children. *Child Development, 58,* 653–688.

Witelson, S. F., Glezer, I. I., & Kigar, D. L. (1995). Women have greater density of neurons in posterior temporal cortex. *Journal of Neuroscience, 15,* 3418–3428.

Witherington, D. C., Campos, J. J., & Hertenstein, M. J. (2001). Principles of emotion and its development in infancy. In G. Bremner & A. Fogel (Eds), *Blackwell handbook of infant development: Handbooks of developmental psychology* (pp. 427–464). Malden, MA: Blackwell Publishers.

Wittelson, S. F., & Swallow, J. A. (1988). Neuropsychological study of the development of spatial cognition. In J. Stiles-Davis, M. Kritchevsky, & U. Bellugi (Eds.), *Spatial cognition: Brain bases and development.* Mahwah, NJ: Erlbaum.

Wittmann, B., Daw, N., Seymour, B., & Dolan, R. (2008). Striatal activity underlies novelty-based choice in humans. *Neuron, 58,* 967–973.

Wolchik, S. A., Ruehlman, L. S., Braver, S., & Sandler, I. N. (1989). Social support of children of divorce: Direct and stress buffering effects. *American Journal of Community Psychology, 17,* 485–501.

Wolfe, S. M., Toro, P. A., & McCaskill, P. A. (1999). A comparison of homeless and matched housed adolescents on family environment variables. *Journal of Research on Adolescence, 9,* 53–66.

Wolfer, L. T., & Moen, P. (1996). Staying in school: Maternal employment and the timing of black and white daughters' school exit. *Journal of Family Issues, 17,* 540–560.

Wolff, P. (1987). *The development of behavioral states and expression of emotions in early infancy.* Chicago: University of Chicago Press.

Wolpert, L. (1991). *The triumph of the embryo.* Oxford, UK: Oxford University Press.

Wood, C. C. (1976). Discriminability, response bias, and phoneme categories in discrimination of voice onset time. *Journal of the Acoustical Society of America*, 1381–1389.

Wood, D. (1986). Aspects of teaching and learning. In M. Richards & P. Light (Eds.), *Children of social worlds.* Cambridge, UK: Polity Press.

Wood, D. J., Bruner, J. S., & Ross, G. (1976). The role of tutoring in problem-solving. *Journal of Child Psychology and Psychiatry, 17,* 89–100.

Wood, J. N., & Spelke, E. S. (2005). Infants' enumeration of actions: Numerical discrimination and its signature limits. *Developmental Science, 8*, 173–181.

Wood, W., & Eagly, A. H. (2002). A cross-cultural analysis of the behavior of women and men: Implications for the origins of sex differences. *Psychological Bulletin, 128*, 699–727.

Woodard, E. H., & Gridina, N. (2000). *Media in the home 2000: The fifth annual survey of parents and children.* Philadelphia: University of Pennsylvania, The Annenberg Public Policy Center. Retrieved January 19, 2002, from http://www.appcpenn.org/mediainhome/survey/survey.pdf.

Woodward, A. L. (1998). Infants selectively encode the goal object of an actor's reach. *Cognition, 69(1),* 1–34.

Woodward, A. L., & Hoyne, K. L. (1999). Infants' learning about words and sounds in relation to objects. *Child Development 70,* 65–77.

Woodward, A. L., & Markman, E. M. (1998). Early word learning. In D. Kuhn & R. S. Siegler (Eds.), *Handbook of child psychology: Vol. 2. Cognition, perception, and language* (5th ed., pp. 371–420). New York: Wiley.

Woodward, A. L., Markman, E. M., & Fitzsimmons, C. M. (1994). Rapid word learning in 13- and 18-month-olds. *Developmental Psychology, 30,* 553–566.

Woodward, L. J., & Fergusson, D. M. (1999). Childhood peer relationship problems and psychosocial adjustment in late adolescence. *Journal of Abnormal Child Psychology, 27*, 87–104.

Woolley, J. D. (1997). Thinking about fantasy: Are children fundamentally different thinkers and believers from adults? *Child Development, 68*, 991–1011.

Woolley, J. D., & Phelps, K. E. (1994). Young children's practical reasoning about imagination. *British Journal of Developmental Psychology, 12*, 53–67.

Wu, P., Robinson, C. C., Yang, C., Hart, C. H., Olsen, S. F., Porter, C. L., Jin, S., Wo, J., & Wu, X. (2002). Similarities and differences in mothers' parenting of preschoolers in China and the United States. *International Journal of Behavioral Development, 26*, 481–491.

Wynn, K. (1992). Addition and subtraction by human infants. *Nature, 358*, 749–750.

Wynn, K. (1995). Infants possess a system of numerical knowledge. *Current Directions in Psychological Science, 4*, 172–177.

Wynn, K. (2000). Findings of addition and subtraction in infants are robust and consistent: Reply to Wakeley, Rivera, and Langer. *Child Development, 71*, 1535–1536.

Wynn, K. (2008). Some innate foundations of social and moral cognition. In P. Carruthers, S. Laurence & S. Stich (Eds.), *The innate mind: Foundations and the future.* Oxford, UK: Oxford University Press.

Xu, F. (1999). Object individuation and object identity in infancy: The role of spatio-temporal information, object property information, and language. *Acta Psychologica, 102,* 113–136.

Xu, F., & Carey, S. (1996). Infants' metaphysics: The case of numerical identity. *Cognitive Psychology, 30,* 111–153.

Xu, F., & Pinker, S. (1995). Weird past tense forms. *Journal of Child Language, 22,* 531–556.

Xu, F., & Spelke, E. S. (2000). Large number discrimination in 6-month-old infants. *Cognition, 74*, B1–B11.

Xu, Y., Farver, J. A. M., Schwartz, D., & Chang, L. (2004). Social networks and aggressive behaviour in Chinese children. *International Journal of Behavioral Development, 28*, 401–410.

Xu, Y., Farver, J. A. M., & Zhang, Z. (2009). Temperament, harsh and indulgent parenting, and Chinese children's proactive and reactive aggression. *Child Development, 90*, 244–258.

Xue, Y., & Meisels, S. J. (2004). Early literacy instruction and learning in kindergarten: Evidence from the Early Childhood Longitudinal Study—Kindergarten Class of 1998–1999. *American Educational Research Journal, 41,* 191–229.

Yamagata, K. (1997). Representational activity during mother-child interaction: The scribbling stage of drawing. *British Journal of Developmental Psychology, 15,* 355–366.

Yap, M. B. H., Allen, N. B., & Ladouceur, C. D. (2008). Maternal socialization of positive affect: The impact of invalidation on adolescent emotion regulation and depressive symptomatology. *Child Development, 79*, 1415–1431.

Yarrow, M. R., Scott, P. M., & Zahn-Waxler, C. (1973). Learning concern for others. *Developmental Psychology, 8*, 240–260.

Yates, M. & Youniss, J. (1996). A developmental perspective on community service in adolescence. *Social Development, 5*, 85–111.

Yau, J., & Smetana, J. G. (1996). Adolescent-parent conflict among Chinese adolescents in Hong Kong. *Child Development, 67*, 1262–1275.

Yau, J., Smetana, J. G., & Metzger, A. (2009). Young Chinese children's authority concepts. *Social Development, 18*, 210–229.

Ybarra, M. L., & Mitchell, K. J. (2007). Prevalence and frequency of Internet harassment instigation: Implications for adolescent health. *Journal of Adolescent Health, 41*, 189–195.

Yeates, K. O., & Selman, R. L. (1989). Social competence in the schools: Toward an integrative developmental model for intervention. *Developmental Review, 9*, 64–100.

Yip, T., & Fuligni, A. J. (2002). Daily variation in ethnic identity, ethnic behaviors, and psychological well-being among American adolescents of Chinese descent. *Child Development, 73*, 1557–1572.

Yip, T., Seaton, E. K., & Sellers, R. M. (2006). African American racial identity across the lifespan: Identity status, identity content, and depressive symptoms. *Child Development, 77*, 1504–1517.

Yonas, A. (1981). Infants' responses to optical information for collision. In R. N. Aslin, J. Alberts, & M. Petersen (Eds.), *Development of perception: Psychobiological perspectives: The visual system.* New York: Academic Press.

Yonas, A., Cleaves, W. T., & Pettersen, L. (1978). Development of sensitivity to pictorial depth. *Science, 200,* 77–79.

Yonas, A., Elieff, C. A., & Arterberry, M. E. (2002). Emergence of sensitivity to pictorial depth cues: Charting development in individual infants. *Infant Behavior and Development, 25,* 495–514.

Young, L. D., Suomi, S. J., Harlow, H. F., & McKinney, W. T. (1973). Early stress and later response to separation in rhesus monkeys. *American Journal of Psychiatry, 130*(4), 400–405.

Youngblade, L. M., & Belsky, J. (1992). Parent-child antecedents of 5-year-olds' close friendships: A longitudinal analysis. *Developmental Psychology, 28,* 700–713.

Youngblade, L. M., & Dunn, J. (1995). Individual differences in young children's pretend play with mother and siblings: Links to relationships and understanding of other people's feelings and beliefs. *Child Development, 66,* 1472–1492.

Youniss, J. (1980). *Parents and peers in social development: A Sullivan-Piaget perspective.* Chicago: University of Chicago Press.

Youniss, J. & Smollar, J. (1985). *Adolescents' relations with mothers, fathers, and friends.* Chicago: University of Chicago Press.

Yuan, S. & Fisher, C. (2009). "Really? She blicked the baby?": Two-year-olds learn combinatorial facts about verbs by listening. *Psychological Science, 20,* 619–626.

Yuill, N., & Perner, J. (1988). Intentionality and knowledge in children's judgments of actor's responsibility and recipient's emotional reaction. *Developmental Psychology, 24,* 358–365.

Zacks, J. M., Rypma, B., Gabrielli, J. Tversky, B., & Glover, G. (1999). Imagined transformation of bodies: An fMRI study. *Neuropsychologia, 37*(9), 1029–1040.

Zahn-Waxler, C., Friedman, R. J., Cole, P. M., Mizuta, I., & Hiruma, N. (1996). Japanese and United States preschool children's responses to conflict and distress. *Child Development, 67,* 2462–2477.

Zahn-Waxler, C., Radke-Yarrow, M., & King, R. A. (1979). Child rearing and children's prosocial initiations toward victims of distress. *Child Development, 50,* 319–330.

Zahn-Waxler, C., Radke-Yarrow, M., Wagner, E., & Chapman, M. (1992). Development of concern for others. *Developmental Psychology, 28,* 126–136.

Zahn-Waxler, C., & Robinson, J. (1995). Empathy and guilt: Early origins of feelings of responsibility. In J. P. Tangney & K. W. Fischer (Eds.), *Self conscious emotions. The psychology of shame, guilt, embarrassment, and pride* (pp. 143–174). New York: Guilford.

Zahn-Waxler, C., Robinson, J., & Emde, R. N. (1992). The development of empathy in twins. *Developmental Psychology, 28,* 1038–1047.

Zahn-Waxler, C., Schiro, K., Robinson, J. L., Emde, R. N., & Schmitz, S. (2001). Empathy and prosocial patterns in young MZ and DZ Twins: Development and genetic and environmental influences. In R. N. Emde & J. K. Hewitt (Eds.), *Infancy to early childhood* (pp. 141–162). New York: Oxford University Press.

Zakay, D. (1992). The role of attention in children's time perception. *Journal of Experimental Child Psychology, 54,* 355–371.

Zakay, D. (1993). The roles of non-temporal information processing load and temporal expectations in children's prospective time estimation. *Acta Psychologica, 84,* 271–280.

Zani, B. (1991). Male and female patterns in the discovery of sexuality during adolescence. *Journal of Adolescence, 14,* 163–178.

Zarbatany, L., McDougall, P., & Hymel, S. (2000). Gender-differentiated experience in the peer culture: Links to intimacy in preadolescence. *Social Development, 9,* 62–79.

Zawaiza, T. R., & Gerber, M. (1993). Effects of explicit instruction on math word-problem solving by community college students with learning disabilities. *Learning Disability Quarterly, 16,* 64–79.

Zelazo, P. D., Reznick, J. S., & Spinazzola, J. (1998). Representational flexibility and response control in a multistep multilocation search task. *Developmental Psychology, 34,* 203–214.

Zelazo, P. R., Zelazo, N. A., & Kolb, S. (1972). "Walking" in the newborn. *Science, 117,* 1058–1059.

Zeman, J., & Garber, J. (1996). Display rules for anger, sadness, and pain: It depends on who is watching. *Child Development, 67,* 957–973.

Zeman, J., & Shipman, K. (1996). Expression of negative affect: Reasons and methods. *Developmental Psychology, 32,* 842–849.

Zentall, S. S., & Ferkis, M. A. (1993). Mathematical problem solving for youth with ADHD, with and without learning disabilities. *Learning Disability Quarterly, 16,* 6–18.

Zentner, M. R., & Kagan, J. (1996). Perception of music by infants. *Nature, 383,* 29.

Zentner, M. R., & Kagan, J. (1998). Infants' perception of consonance and dissonance in music. *Infant Behavior and Development, 21,* 483–492.

Zevalkink, J., Riksen-Walraven, J. M., & Van Lieshout, C. F. M. (1999). Attachment in the Indonesian caregiving context. *Social Development, 8*(1), 21–40.

Zevenburgen, A. A., & Whitehurst, G. J. (2003). Dialogic reading: A shared picture book reading intervention for preschoolers. In A. van Kleeck, S. A. Stahl, & E. B. Bauer (Eds.), *On reading books to children: Parents and teachers* (pp. 177–200). Mahwah, NJ: Erlbaum.

Zhang, S. (1997). Investigation of behaviour problem of only child in kindergarten children in a Beijing urban area. *International Medical Journal, 4,* 117–118.

Zhou, Q., Eisenberg, N., Wang, Y., & Reiser, M. (2004). Chinese children's effortful control and dispositional anger/frustration: Relations to parenting styles and children's social functioning. *Developmental Psychology, 40,* 352–366.

Zhou, Q., Wang, Y., Eisenberg, N., Wolchik, S., Tein, J W., & Deng, X. (2008). Relations of parenting and temperament to Chinese children's experience of negative life events, coping efficacy, and externalizing problems. *Child Development, 79,* 493–513.

Zigler, E. F., & Finn-Stevenson, M. (1999). Applied developmental psychology. In M. H. Bornstein, & M. E. Lamb (Eds.), *Developmental psychology: An advanced textbook* (4th ed.). Mahwah, NJ: Erlbaum.

Zigler, E., & Styfco, S. J. (2004). The wisdom of a federal effort on behalf of impoverished children and their families. In E. Zigler, & S. J. Styfco (Eds.), *The Head Start debates.* Baltimore: Brookes Publishing Co.

Zill, N., Davies, E., & Daly, M. (1994). *Viewing Sesame Street by preschool children in the United States and its relation to school readiness.* Rockville, MD: Westat.

Zimmer, E. Z., Chao, C. R., Guy, G. P., Marks, F., & Fifer, W. P. (1993). Vibroacoustic stimulation evokes human fetal micturition. *Obstetrics and Gynecology, 81*(2), 178–180.

Zimmer-Gembeck, M. J., Siebenbruner, J., & Collins, W. A. (2001). Diverse aspects of dating: Associations with psychosocial functioning from early to middle adolescence. *Journal of Adolescence, 24,* 313–336.

Zimmer-Gembeck, M. J., Siebenbruner, J., & Collins, W. A. (2004). A prospective study of intraindividual and peer influences on adolescents' heterosexual romantic and sexual behavior. *Archives of Sexual Behavior*, 33, 381–394.

Zimmermann, P., Maier, M. A., Winter, M., & Grossmann, K. E. (2001). Attachment and adolescents' emotion regulation during a joint problem-solving task with a friend. *International Journal of Behavioral Development, 25*, 321–343.

Zlotnick, C., Kronstadt, D., & Klee, L. (1998). Foster care children and family homelessness. *American Journal of Public Health, 88*, 1368–1370.

Zucker, K. J. (2006). Commentary on Langer and Martin's (2004) "How dresses can make you mentally ill: Examining gender identity disorder in children." *Child & Adolescent Social Work Journal, 23*, 533–555.

Zucker, K. J., & Bradley, S. (1995). *Gender identity disorder and psychosexual problems in children and adolescents.* New York: Guilford.

Name Index

A

Aaltonen, O., 72
Aaron, J., 488
Aaunola, K., 512
Abbey, B. B., 417, 419
Abbott, R. D., 577
Abela, J. R. Z., 395
Abelson, P., 119
Aber, J., 535
Aber, J. L., 370, 448, 457
Ablow, J. C., 572
Aboud, F. E., 513, 516
Abraham, M. M., 435
Abraham, W. T., 486
Abramovitch, R., 568
Abrams, S., 73
Abramson, L. Y., 393
Achenbach, T. M., 76
Acierno, R., 371
Ackerman, B. P., 385, 415
Ackerman, J., 400
Acredolo, C., 285
Acredolo, L. P., 248, 280
Adam, E. K., 431
Adams, G., 376
Adams, G. J., 516
Adams, G. R., 445
Adams, M. J., 324–325, 326
Adams, R. J., 179
Adams-Curtis, L. E., 618
Adamson, L. B., 162
Adler, S. A., 283
Adolph, K. E., 151, 170, 196, 197, 201, 281, 471, 472, 475, 476
Adolphs, R., 405
Afrank, J., 574
Aguilar, B., 570
Ahadi, S. A., 403, 404
Ahluwalia, J., 364
Ahmeduzzaman, M., 479
Aikins, J. W., 522
Ainsworth, A. T., 449
Ainsworth, M. D. S., 427, 429, 433
Akhtar, N., 162, 239, 241
Aksan, N., 390–391, 403, 474, 557, 558
Alarcón, O., 448
Albersheim, L., 431
Alder, R. J., 570
Aldous, J., 477
Alessandri, S. M., 73, 204, 386, 388, 390, 391
Alexander, G. M., 588
Alexander, K. L., 312
Alfaro, E. C., 458
Alibali, M., 228
Alibali, M. W., 151, 169, 334, 335
Alink, L. R. A., 567
Alioto, A., 225
Allard, L., 275
Allen, E., 594, 611
Allen, J. P., 349, 435, 516, 573, 576
Allen, L., 448, 457
Allen, N. B., 394
Allison, A., 453
Allison, D. B., 121
Allua, S., 521
Almeida, D. M., 601
Als, H., 366
Altenderfer, L., 371
Altermatt, E. R., 518, 612
Altshuler, J. L., 398
Alwin, D. F., 475
Alzate, G., 433
Aman, C., 253
Amato, P. R., 483, 485, 487, 488, 490
Ambridge, B., 147
Amell, J. W., 406
Amiel-Tison, C., 58
Amso, D., 153, 280
Amsterlaw, J., 151
Anastopoulous, A. D., 614
Anda, R. F., 371
Anderson, C. A., 356, 373
Anderson, D. I., 191, 261, 280
Anderson, D. R., 372
Anderson, D. R., 33
Anderson, E. R., 490, 575
Anderson, J. R., 147
Anderson, K. J., 602, 611, 616
Anderson, L. M., 187
Anderson, L. T., 76
Anderson, M. E., 64
Anderson, R. C., 328
Andre, T., 612
Andreasen, G., 282
Andrews, D. W., 516
Andrews, S., 265
Angell, K. E., 393
Angier, N., 587
Anglin, J. M., 237, 246
Ansari, D., 289
Anthony, C., 489, 575
Anthony, J. L., 325, 327
Antonelli, T., 64
Antonishak, J., 573
Appelbaum, M. I., 483
Aptehar, L., 477
Aquan-Assee, J., 480
Arbona, C., 577
Archer, J., 573, 587, 610, 615, 616, 617, 618
Arcus, D., 403, 404, 406
Arduini, D., 55
Arehart, D. M., 283
Arendt, R., 64
Arias, I., 616
Aristotle, 8–9, 43–44
Armstrong, S. C., 93
Arndorfer, C. L., 516
Arnett, J. J., 468
Arnold, D. H., 567
Arnold, S. L., 73
Aronoff, J., 616
Aronson, E., 544
Aronson, S. R., 493
Arria, A., 64
Arseneault, L., 370, 532, 572
Arsenio, W. F., 617
Arterberry, M., 178, 179, 185
Asbury, K., 565
Asendorpf, J. B., 438, 529, 536
Ashcraft, M. H., 334
Asher, S. R., 512, 514, 528, 529, 530
Ashman, S. B., 405
Ashmead, D., 195
Aslin, R. N., 179, 202, 225, 227, 229, 232
Asquith, P., 555
Astington, J. W., 268, 271
Astone, N. M., 482
Atencio, D. J., 153
Atkins, R., 565
Atkinson, L., 435, 535
Atran, S., 275, 277
Attanucci, J., 552
Attili, G., 529
Auerbach-Major, S., 415
Augusta, D., 224
Augustyn, M., 64, 576
Aunola, K., 519
Austin, S. B., 607
Avenevoli, S., 406
Avery-Leaf, S., 616
Awong, T., 456
Ayduk, O., 382
Azmitia, M., 513
Azria-Evans, M. R., 525
Azuma, H., 432, 517

B

Babulas, V. P., 66
Backscheider, A. G., 275, 277
Bacon, P. L., 483
Badenoch, M., 181
Baer, D. M., 353
Bagwell, C. L., 512, 514
Baham, M. E., 480
Bahrick, H. P., 147
Bahrick, L. E., 188
Bailey, H. N., 431
Bailey, J. M., 450, 491
Baillargeon, R., 128, 142, 157, 183, 195, 206, 207, 208, 210
Baily, H. N., 430
Bakeman, R., 162, 388
Baker, D. P., 613
Baker, L. A., 572
Baker, N. D., 244
Bakermans-Kranenburg, M. J., 375, 407, 429, 431, 433, 434
Balaban, M. T., 187
Baldwin, A., 21, 79, 305, 316, 317
Baldwin, C., 21, 79, 305, 316, 317
Baldwin, D. A., 162, 239, 264, 414
Ball, R., 93
Ball, W., 184
Bámaca, M. Y., 458
Banaji, M. R., 350
Bandura, A., 354, 356, 357, 585, 593, 603, 610
Banerjee, M., 417, 418
Banerjee, R., 592
Bangert, A. W., 464
Banich, M. T., 102, 114
Bank, L., 479, 574
Banks, M. S., 178

C

D

E

I

J

Klute, M. M., 565
Knafo, A., 558, 560, 561, 562, 563, 565
Kneubuhler, Y., 282
Knickman, J. R., 477
Knight, D. K., 163
Knight, G. P., 447, 564, 617
Knight, R., 517
Knight, W. G., 64
Knowles, L., 282
Kobak, R., 349
Kobasigawa, A., 328
Kobiella, A., 414, 558
Kochanoff, A., 399
Kochanska, G., 12, 29, 390–391, 397, 403, 407, 408, 474, 557, 558
Kochenderfer, B. J., 512, 532, 533
Kodama, H., 315
Kohatsu, E. L., 448
Kohen, D. E., 476
Kohlberg, L., 16, 548, 549, 550, 551, 590
Kohler, E., 167
Kokotovic, A., 372
Kolb, B., 102, 109, 114
Kolb, S., 194
Koller, S. H., 553
Konarski, R., 522
Koós, O., 210
Koot, H. M., 567
Kopp, C. B., 77, 79, 390, 397, 557
Korat, O., 330
Korbin, J. E., 369
Koreishi, A., 163
Koren, G., 65
Koren-Karie, N., 496
Korkel, J., 150
Korner, A. F., 73
Kortenhaus, C. M., 595
Kosslyn, S. M., 279
Kostelny, K., 369
Kotovsky, L., 153, 206
Kovacs, E. A., 399
Kovacs, M., 395
Kovas, Y., 327
Kowal, A. K., 480
Krafchuk, E., 405
Kramer, S. J., 179
Krascum, R. M., 265
Krause, J. A., 334
Kraut, R., 374, 612
Krauthamer-Ewing, E., 415, 528
Kreager, D. A., 525
Kreider, R. M., 481
Kreppner, J. M., 6, 7
Kreutzer, T., 435, 436
Krevans, J., 565
Krishnakumar, A., 489, 575
Krishnamoorthy, J. S., 121
Krohn, M. D., 576, 579
Kronstadt, D., 477
Kroonenberg, P. M., 432
Kroupina, M. G., 349
Krueger, A. B., 651
Krueger, R. F., 409
Kruger, A. C., 506
Krull, J. L., 480
Krumhansl, C. L., 187
Kruttschnitt, C., 575
Ksansnak, K. R., 599, 602
Kuczaj, S. A., II, 243
Kuczynski, L., 471
Kuhl, P. K., 189, 228
Kuhn, A., 180
Kuhn, C., 73
Kuhn, D., 35, 36, 151
Kumpf, M., 315
Kuncel, N. R., 307
Kundu, S., 79
Kunkel, D., 373
Kunnen, E. S., 445
Kupanoff, K., 410
Kuperminc, G. P., 349
Kupersmidt, J. B., 513, 524, 527, 529, 530, 531, 538, 573
Kupfer, A., 563
Kurdek, L. A., 488, 490
Kurlakowsky, K. D., 395
Kurtz, D. A., 449
Kurtz-Costes, B., 449, 592
Kusaka, Y., 464
Kusche, C. A., 4, 528, 578
Kuschel, C., 64
Kutnick, P., 551
Kutsukake, N., 562
Kwon, K., 519

L

LaBar, K. S., 405
LaBounty, J., 410
Lacerda, F., 228
Lacerenza, L., 327
Lacourse, E., 521, 576, 577
Ladd, B., 565
Ladd, G., 394
Ladd, G. W., 512, 526, 530, 532, 533, 535, 537
Ladha, F., 566
Ladouceur, C. D., 394
Laetz, V. B., 515
LaFreniere, P. J., 535, 615
LaFromboise, T., 449
LaGasse, L. L., 64
Lagattuta, K., 410
Lagattuta, K. H., 416
Lagercrantz, H., 68
La Greca, A. M., 392, 520, 521, 532
Lahey, B. B., 483, 568, 569, 570, 577
Lahn, B. T., 88
Lahti, I., 12
Laible, D. J., 408, 435, 456, 557
Laird, M., 371
Laird, R. D., 471, 569, 574
Lalonde, C. E., 228
Lamb, M. E., 76, 412, 435, 483, 496, 497, 498, 584
Lamb, S., 561
Lambert, S. M., 395
Lambertz, G., 58
Lamborn, S. D., 456, 470, 471, 486
Lampman-Petraitis, C., 392
Land, D. J., 435
Landau, B., 240, 242, 264
Landerl, K., 334
Lando, B., 568
Landry, S. H., 77
Lane, H., 222
Lane, S., 405
Langabeer, K. A., 450, 452, 453
Langer, J., 290
Langer, S. J., 589
Langlois, J. H., 181, 455, 473, 474, 524
Langrock, A., 409
Lansdale, N. S., 493
Lansford, J. E., 312, 359, 360, 472, 485, 524, 527, 531, 573, 575
Lanthier, E. C., 283
Lanthier, R., 571
Laplante, D., 567
Lapp, A. L., 538
Lapsley, D. K., 549
Laren, D. S., 314
Largo, R. H., 79
Larkin, J., 616
Larson, A., 455, 473, 474, 524
Larson, J., 393
Larson, J. R., 112
Larson, R., 392, 521, 522
Larson, R. W., 392, 468, 517
Larsson, A., 588
Lassonde, M., 112
Latendresse, S. J., 376
Lau, J. Y. F., 394
Laub, J. H., 574
Laumann-Billings, L., 368, 369
Laurenceau, J.-P., 415, 528
Laursen, B., 392, 467, 468, 475, 509, 512, 516, 526, 574
Lavelli, M., 13
Lavner, J. A., 452
Lawford, H., 565
Lawrence, C., 477
Lawrence, D. A., 282
Lawrence, J., 153
Lawton, A., 509
Layburn, K., 445
Lazar, I., 317
Lazar, N. A., 148
Leadbeater, B. J., 393
Leaper, C., 584, 585, 592, 594, 595, 597, 599, 600, 601, 602, 606, 611, 613, 614, 616
Lears, M., 595
Lease, A. M., 519
Le Brocque, R. M., 394
Lecanuet, J. P., 56, 57
LeDoux, J. E., 405
Lee, D. H., 299
Lee, H., 79
Lee, K., 151
Lee, L., 516
Lee, L. C., 564
Lee, P. W. H., 395
Lee, R. E., 538
Lee, S. S., 570
Lee, S-A., 460
Lee, S-Y., 368
Leech, S. L., 515
Leerkes, E., 467
LeFevre, J. A., 333
Leggett, E. L., 23, 360
Le Grand, R., 111, 181, 281
Lehman, D. R., 459
Lehoux, P., 405
Leichliter, J. S., 522
Leichtman, M. D., 163
Leiderman, P. H., 479
Leinbach, M. D., 590, 603
Lemerise, E. A., 617
Lemery, K. S., 99, 100, 403, 407, 474, 614
Lemery-Chalfant, K., 399
Lenane, M., 109, 110
Lengua, L. J., 399, 406, 538
Lenox, K., 531, 532
Lensche, H., 476
Leonard, K. E., 403, 535
Leonard, S. A., 410
Lepore, F., 112
Lerner, R., 99
Leslie, A. M., 206, 260, 266, 269, 285, 286
Lester, B. M., 64, 65, 67, 76
Lester, J., 523
Leung, M-C., 519, 521
Levant, R. F., 601, 612, 617
Leve, C. S., 483
Leve, D. L., 618
Leve, L. D., 603
Leventhal, B. L., 483

M

Marsh, H. W., 440
Marsh, P., 435, 576
Marshall, P., 535
Marshall, P. J., 6
Marshall, R. M., 370
Marshall, T. R., 405
Marsiglio, W., 483
Martin, C. L., 410, 418, 475, 585, 590, 591, 592, 598, 599, 603, 614
Martin, J., 94
Martin, J. A., 69, 465, 469, 481, 482
Martin, J. H., 170
Martin, J. I., 589
Martin, J. L., 617
Martin, J. M., 390, 391, 394, 559
Martin, N. C., 393, 394
Martin, N. G., 489
Martin, T. C., 485
Martinez, M. E., 75
Martorell, R., 123
Martynova, O., 72
Marvinney, D., 234, 495, 534
Marx, F., 455
Marzolf, D. P., 253, 397
Masalha, S., 476
Masataka, N., 225
Mascolo, M. F., 390, 391
Mashek, D. J., 391
Mason, M. G., 549
Mason, T., 415
Masten, A. S., 21, 79, 477
Masters, J. C., 416
Masters, M. S., 608
Masur, E., 237
Masyn, K. E., 573–574, 579
Maszk, P., 526
Matestic, P., 394
Matheson, C. C., 13, 272, 508
Mathews, G. A., 610
Mathews, T. J., 465, 481
Matsumoto, D., 412
Matthew, C., 307
Matthews, G., 383
Mattock, A., 181, 182
Mattson, S. N., 63
Matusov, E., 385
Maughan, B., 7
Maurer, C., 55, 68, 185
Maurer, D., 23, 55, 68, 108, 111, 181, 185, 281
Mavrogenes, N. A., 497
Maxon, E., 403, 468
Mayberry, M. L., 617
Mayer, B., 563
Mayes, T. L., 395
Mayeux, L., 525, 526
Maynard, J., 186
May-Plumlee, T., 565
Mayringer, H., 327
Mayseless, O., 535
Mazziotta, J. C., 106
McAdoo, H. P., 311, 368
McAuliffe, M. D., 395
McBride-Chang, C., 325, 327, 564
McCabe, A., 245, 246
McCabe, K. M., 570, 571
McCaffrey, D. F., 651
McCandliss, B. D., 18
McCarthy, E. M., 153
McCartney, K., 13, 22, 95, 97, 485
McCarton, C. M., 79
McCarty, C. A., 394
McCarty, M. E., 195
McCaskill, P. A., 477
McClaskey, C. L., 572
McClay, J., 94
McClearn, G. E., 97, 100, 309, 311
McClelland, J. L., 128, 206, 251, 285
McClelland, M. M., 18
McClintock, M. K., 607
McCloskey, L. A., 370
McCloskey, M., 334
McClosky, L. A., 603
McConkey, C., 317, 320
McCormick, M., 276
McCormick, M. C., 78
McCormick, S. E., 416
McCoy, J. K., 479
McCrary, C., 476, 479
McCreath, H., 565
McCurley, J., 121
McDaniel, M. A., 246
McDonald, K., 509
McDonald, K. L., 513
McDonald, P. V., 195
McDonough, L., 264
McDougall, P., 510, 513, 530
McDowell, D. J., 535
McDuff, P., 575
McEachern, A., 515
McElhaney, K. B., 349, 435, 573, 576
McElroy, A., 457, 458
McEwen, B. S., 103
McFadyen-Ketchum, S. A., 512, 532, 574
McFarland, C., 435
McFarland, F. C., 516, 576
McGaugh, J. L., 405
McGee, H., 315
McGee, R. O., 403, 571
McGhee, P. E., 595
McGill, B., 481
McGrath, E. P., 395
McGraw, M. B., 193
McGree, R., 393
McGue, M., 22, 97, 98, 99, 309, 409, 479, 485, 488, 490, 572
McGuffin, P., 309, 394
McGuigan, F., 163
McGuire, S., 456, 467, 480
McGuire, S. A., 312, 479
McHale, J. L., 436, 489
McHale, J. P., 188, 476
McHale, S. M., 449, 468, 479, 480, 613
McIntosh, C. N., 476
McKelvey, M. W., 473
McKenry, P. C., 473
McKenzie, B. E., 282
McKey, R. H., 317, 320
McKinley, N. M., 608
McKinney, W. T., 425–426
McLaughlin, J., 408
McLean, J. F., 334
McLean, K. C., 445
McLeod, D., 595
McLeod, P. J., 225
McLin, D., 168
McLoughlin, C. S., 464
McLoyd, V. C., 21, 318, 320, 472, 476, 538
McMahon, A. W., 93
McMahon, R. J., 394, 578
McManus, K., 67
McMaster, L. E., 602, 616
McMillan, D., 591
McMorris, B. J., 575
McMurray, B., 237
McNalley, S., 554
McNeil, N. M., 335
McNichol, K., 530
McQuaid, N., 408
McQueen, A., 516
McRoberts, G., 241
McShane, K. E., 562, 566
Measelle, J. R., 572
Mebert, C. J., 573
Meck, E., 292
Medin, D., 275
Meegan, S. P., 152
Meeus, W., 445, 513
Meeus, W. H. J., 468, 516, 520
Mehler, J., 58
Mehta, T. G., 456
Meilman, P., 522
Meisels, S. J., 76, 77, 79, 326
Meister, C., 328
Melchior, M., 406
Mellartin, R. L., 264
Melnick, S., 370, 525
Meltzoff, A. N., 163, 188, 189, 204, 205, 209
Melvin, W., 579
Menaghan, E. G., 494
Mendel, G., 85
Mendelson, M. J., 516
Mendle, J., 516
Mendoza-Denton, R., 382
Menella, J. A., 118
Meng, Z., 170, 388, 411
Mennella, J. A., 54, 55
Merchant, M. J., 399
Meremelstin, R., 393
Mereu, G., 64
Merkin, S., 292
Mermelstein, R. J., 392
Merrell, K. W., 610
Merrick, S., 431
Merton, D. E., 525
Mervis, C. B., 93, 150, 264
Mesias, W., 430
Mesman, J., 567
Mesquita, B., 412
Messinger, D., 385
Messner, M. A., 618
Metsala, J. L., 30, 328
Mettetal, G., 510
Metz, E., 565
Metzger, A., 556
Meyers, L. B., 523
Meyers, T., 204
Miceli, P. J., 483
Michalik, N. M., 563, 565
Michalson, L., 415
Michealieu, Q., 416
Mick, E., 570
Midgley, C., 54, 457
Miell, D., 513
Mikach, S., 491
Milberger, S., 370
Miles, C. J., 489
Milewski, A. E., 179
Milich, R., 571
Miliotis, D., 477
Mill, J. S., 85, 94
Millar, W. S., 203
Miller, B. C., 482
Miller, C. L., 483
Miller, D. C., 614
Miller, J., 563
Miller, J. G., 554, 555
Miller, K., 138, 246
Miller, K. F., 253, 289, 292, 293
Miller, L. C., 587
Miller, P. A., 554, 563
Miller, P. H., 35, 140, 149, 151, 170
Miller, P. J., 413
Miller, P. M., 615, 617
Miller, T. L., 482, 568
Miller-Heyl, J., 476
Miller-Johnson, S., 319, 483

Q

R

S

T

U

V

Verhulst, F. C., 579
Verkuyten, M., 455
Verma, S., 477, 517
Vermigli, P., 529
Vernon, P. A., 299
Verschueren, K., 456
Vevea, J., 312
Vigorito, J., 227
Vikan, A., 288
Viken, R., 516
Viken, R. J., 456
Vishton, P., 195
Visser, G. H. A., 53, 54
Vitaro, F., 35, 512, 515, 521, 522, 525, 531, 532, 568, 569, 570, 571, 575, 576, 577, 618
Vittori, J., 577
Voelker, P. M., 18, 407
Voeller, K. K., 370
Voeten, M., 519
Vohr, B., 76
Vohr, B. R., 77
Volkmar, F., 270
Vollebergh, W., 445, 513
Vollenweider, M., 525
Volling, B. L., 484, 494, 557
von Bank, H., 521
von der Lippe, A. L., 475
Von der Schulenburg, C., 181
Vondra, J. I., 435
von Hofsten, C., 167, 190, 193, 195, 280
von Stauffenberg, C., 394
Voss, P., 112
Votruba-Drzal, E., 497, 498
Vouloumanos, A., 223
Voyer, D., 610
Vygotsky, L. S., 159, 160, 161, 244, 506

W

Wachs, T., 65
Waddell, S., 477
Wade, E., 393
Wadhwa, P., 57
Wadsworth, M. E., 399
Wadsworth, S. J., 329
Wagner, E., 561
Wagner, R. K., 307, 327
Wahlsten, D., 99
Wainright, J. L., 491
Wainryb, C., 555
Wakeley, A., 290, 334
Wakschlag, L. S., 483
Walbek, N. H., 565
Walden, T., 370, 415
Waldfogel, J., 493
Waldman, I. D., 370, 568, 569, 570, 572
Waldrip, A. M., 512
Waldron, M., 12, 99, 312, 488
Waldron, S., 334
Walk, R. D., 197
Walker, B. E., 54
Walker, K., 457, 458
Walker, L. J., 552
Walker, R., 472
Walker-Andrews, A. S., 180, 189, 414
Wall, J. A., 577
Wall, S., 433
Wallace, B. A., 160
Wallace, I. F., 79
Wallace, J. G., 144
Wallace, L. E., 476
Waller, E. M., 514, 525, 602
Wallerstein, J. S., 487, 489, 491
Wallman, J., 220
Wang, D., 464
Wang, K., 593
Wang, L., 411, 459
Wang, M. C., 611
Wang, Q., 161, 163, 368, 459
Wang, Y., 399, 470, 472
Wanner, E., 242
Ware, E., 199
Warkentin, V., 438
Warneken, F., 561, 565
Wartella, E. A., 373
Wasik, B. H., 319
Wasserman, E. M., 113
Wasserman, S., 207
Wasserstein, S., 392
Waterman, A. S., 444, 445
Waterman, C. K., 445
Waters, E., 386, 426, 431, 433
Waters, H. S., 145
Watson, J., 11, 85, 269
Watson, J. B., 351–352
Watson, M. S., 566
Watson, M. W., 574
Watson-Gegeo, K. A., 225
Wax, N., 274, 275, 278
Waxman, S. R., 240, 241, 265
Way, N., 448, 458, 511
Wearing, H., 147
Wearne, D., 336
Weaver, C., 579
Webb, R. M., 306
Webber, J., 528
Weber, E. K., 554
Weber-Fox, C., 222
Webster-Stratton, C., 497, 528
Wechsler, N., 523
Wedell, A., 588
Wegner, D. M., 350
Wei, E., 475, 575
Weimer, A. A., 480
Weinberg, M. K., 387
Weinberg, R. A., 315
Weinberger, D. A., 520, 574
Weiner, T., 197
Weinert, F. E., 150
Weinraub, M., 435
Weinreb, L. F., 477
Weinstein, S. M., 392
Weir, R. H., 242
Weiskopf, S., 179
Weiss, B., 573
Weiss, L. G., 313
Weiss, R., 618
Weissman, M. D., 276
Weist, M. D., 530, 531
Weisz, J. R., 398, 432
Weitzman, B. C., 477
Wellborn, J. G., 457
Wellman, H. M., 151, 157, 262, 267, 268, 269, 270, 275, 410, 416
Wells, K. C., 579
Welsh, D. P., 522
Wender, P. H., 12, 101
Wenner, J. A., 349
Wentworth, N., 283
Wentzel, K. R., 527, 530
Werebe, M. J., 508
Werker, J. F., 223, 225, 228
Werner, E. E., 2, 3, 314
Werner, N. E., 618
Wertheimer, M., 185
West, J., 324
West, M. J., 437
West, S. G., 406
Westat, Inc., 320
Westerlund, A., 263
Westerman, M. A., 416
Weston, D. R., 78
Westra, T., 192
Wetter, E. K., 199
Wheaton, B., 612, 613
Wheeler, J. S., 64
Wheeler, L., 528
Wheelwright, S., 364
Whigham, M., 611, 612
Whipple, B., 399
Whishaw, I. Q., 102
Whitbeck, L. B., 477, 482
White, B. L., 386
White, K. B., 618
White, K. S., 523
White, M. I., 517
White, R. L., 449
Whitehead, J. M., 610, 612
Whitehead, K. A., 449
Whitehurst, G. J., 329
Whiteman, S. D., 479
Whiteman, V., 483
Whitesell, N. R., 509
Whiteside, L., 314
Whiteside, M. F., 488
Whiteside-Mansell, L., 473
Whiting, B. B., 19, 517, 564, 565, 597, 599
Whiting, J. W. M., 564, 565
Whitman, T. L., 483
Whitney, M. P., 72
Whitsell, N. R., 442
Whitson, S. A., 405
Whitson, S. M., 405
Wichmann, C., 527
Wichstrom, L., 393
Wickett, J. C., 299
Wickrama, K. A. S., 486
Widaman, K. F., 476
Widen, S. C., 414
Widom, C. S., 573
Wienbruch, C., 113
Wiesner, M., 394
Wigfield, A., 30, 328, 457, 610
Wiggers, M., 415
Wikstrom, P-O. H., 475, 575
Wiley, J. G., 282
Wilgenbusch, T., 610
Wilk, S. L., 307
Wilkinson, C. W., 405
Willatts, P., 151
Willemsin, G., 515
Williams, A., 610
Williams, B. R., 397
Williams, E., 155, 206, 290
Williams, J. E., 371
Williams, K. A., 228
Williams, L., 271
Williams, S. T., 576
Williams, T., 336, 485, 595, 616
Willinger, M., 63
Willms, J. D., 577
Willoughby, M., 405
Willoughby, T., 453
Willows, D. M., 25
Willson-Quayle, A., 160
Wilsher, C., 74
Wilson, B. J., 373, 399
Wilson, E. O., 562
Wilson, J. B., 483
Wilson, J. C., 5
Wilson, M., 410, 576, 579
Wilson, M. I., 365
Wilson, M. N., 457, 458
Wilson, M. S., 416
Wilson, N., 566
Wilson, P. T., 328
Wilson, S., 392
Wilson, S. P., 148
Wilson, T. D., 27, 350
Wimmer, H., 327
Winberg, J., 54
Windecker-Nelson, B., 411
Windle, M., 522
Wing, R. R., 121

Subject Index

Bold page numbers indicate material in tables and figures.

A

AAUW (American Association of University Women), 616
Abecedarian Project, 318–319, 650
Aborigines, Australian, spatial representation development, 283, 641
Abortion, spontaneous, 58, 80
Abstract thinking, 133, 136, 141
  counting principles, 292–293
  language development in connection with, 250
  in mathematics, 332–336
Abuse. *See* Child maltreatment
Abusive punishment and socialization of aggression, 573–574
  See also Child maltreatment
Academic achievement
  ADHD and, 370–371
  conflict in ethnic identity and, 448
  cultural influences, 613
  Dweck's theory of self-attributions and achievement motivation, 360–361
  gender difference in, 608
  IQ score and value of, 305
  in mathematics, 332–336, 609
  only children in China, 464–465
  peer status, 530–531, **531**, 612–613
  poverty and, 21, 313–314
  in reading, 323–329
  self-esteem, 457
  in writing, 329–332
  See also Education
Accommodation, in Piaget's theory of cognitive development, 131
Achievement. *See* Academic achievement
Achievement motivation
  current perspectives, 361–362
  Dweck's theory of, 360–361
Actions, learning from, 167–168
Activational influences, 588
Active child, as development theme
  active interpretation of experience, 629
  attachment, 425
  basic questions about child development, **11**
  biology and behavior, 84, 95
  caregiving
    behavior and temperament, 474, 630–631
    infant social smiling, 386–387
  child's contribution to development, 12–13, 22, 585
  cognitive development, 128–129, 133–136
  conceptual development, 260
  core-knowledge theories, 154
  divorce, 488
  eliciting reactions from others, 630–631
  emotional development, 383
  families, 465
  gender difference, 585
  infant exploration of environment, 176–177
  instrumental (operant) conditioning, 202, 203–204
  integrated review of, 628–631
  intelligence, 298–299, 310
  language development, 217
  moral development, 545
  parenting styles, 474
  peer relationships, 506
  physical appeal, 474
  Piaget's cognitive development theory, 128–129
  prenatal development and, 42
  research and children's welfare, 648–649
  self-initiated activity, 628–629
  self-regulation, 630
  sensorimotor stage of cognitive development, 133–136
  social cognitive theories, 358
  social development, 343
Active effects of genotype, 310
Activity level
  as a dimension of temperament, 401
  gender difference in, 611–612
  as heritable, 99
  See also Motor development
Adaption, in Piaget's theory of cognitive development, 131
ADD. *See* Attention-deficit disorder (ADD) and attention-deficit hyperactivity disorder (ADHD)
Addend, counting from, 332
Addition
  counting-on strategy, 35–36
  infant understanding of, 290–291
  memory in, **149**
ADHD. *See* Attention-deficit disorder (ADD) and attention-deficit hyperactivity disorder (ADHD)
Adolescence and adolescents
  active-child theme in, 13
  adjustment to middle school, 457
  aggression and antisocial behavior, 571–572
    aggressive-rejected, **531**
    characteristics of, 571–572
    frequency of, 568
    gangs, 521, 577–579
    origins of, 572–579
    peer status, 525, 527, 529
  brain development in, 109–110
  cliques, 520–521
  cognitive development, formal operations stage of, 133, 139–140, **141**
  dating behavior, 522, 616
  delinquency and criminal behavior, 570, 571, 576
  depression, 393, 607
  egocentrism, 441
  emotional development, 391–392
  ethnic identity, 448–449
  family dynamics, 468
  friendships, 510–511, 515–516, 518
  gender development, 601–602
  gender-typed behavior in, 602
  growth during adolescence
    continuity/discontinuity theme, 16–17, **17**
    maturity and, 16–17, **17**, 115–116, 606–607
  homelessness, 477
  identity formation in, 443–446
  intelligence, genetic contributions to, 309
  interests during, 518
  moral development
    Kohlberg's view, **550**
    prosocial reasoning, 553–554
  multiple selves and, 440–442, **442**
  obesity, 119, 121, 374
  parent–adolescent relationships, 468
  parenting style, 445
  as parents, 65, 319, 482–483
  parents' divorce or remarriage, 482, 487
  peer groups, 520–521
  poverty and, 21, 477
  pregnancy, 2–3, 65, 319, 482–483
  prosocial activities, opportunities for, 565

Adolescence *(cont.)*
puberty
defined, 606
physical growth, 116, 606–607
race and ethnicity, 448–449
remarriage, effects of, 487
self, conception of, 440–443
self-esteem, **455**
sexual-minority youth, 450–454
sibling relationships, 479–480
social judgment, 555
social networks, 520–521
Adoption studies
family environmental conditions, 309
IQ, heritability of, 97, 309
personality as heritable, 98
as research design, 97–98
Romanian orphans, 6–8, **107**, 112, 626
schizophrenia, 12, 100–101, 626–627
Adrenarche, 607
Adult attachment models, 430–431
Adults. *See* Parents and caregiving
Affiliation, defined, 584
Affordances in perceptual learning, 201
Africa
!Kung San, separation anxiety, 389
Aka, emotional development in, 411–412
Beng people, life beginnings and, 43
Ngandu, emotional development, 411–412
African-Americans
aggression and antisocial behavior, 571
authoritarian parenting styles, 471–472
Carolina Abecedarian Project, 318–319, 650
community-of-learners program, 164
early-intervention program, effects of, 164, 317–318
emotional development, 413
employment, maternal, effects of, 493–494
fear recognition, in children, 414–415
friendship, ethnic preferences in, 517
infant mortality, 74–75
IQ
group differences, 315
heritability of, 100
intelligence and, 315–316
race as risk, **316**
low birth weight (LBW), 75
maternal employment, effects of, 493–494
obesity, 119
parental interactions with children, 478
parenting styles, 471–472
physical growth, 119
physical maturation rate, 116, 607
poverty and children, **21**, 79, 314, 317–320
programs for poor children, 317–320
Project Head Start, 318–320, 497, 649
self-esteem, 458
sickle-cell anemia, 92
socioeconomic status of, **21**, 79, 314
Age
analogical reasoning, 153
body composition, 116, 606–607
brain damage and recovery, 114–115
of childbearing, 65, 319, 481–484
conversation skills, **246**
friends, number of, 34
gender segregation, 599–601, **599**
impact of divorce on children, 487
information-processing theories and speed of processing, **149**
intimate disclosure and, 512–513, **513**
IQ score continuity, 305, **309**, 311–312
Kohlberg's moral development summary, 549–552, **549**
of marriage, 481
milestones in gender development, **569**, 597–604
motor milestones, 191–192, **192**
physical growth, continuity, and discontinuity in development, 16–17, **17**
Piaget's theory of cognitive development, **137**
popularity, developmental trends, 35, 526–527
at pregnancy, 2–3, 65, 319, 481–484
prosocial behavior development, 560–562, **561**
REM (rapid eye movement) sleep, 52, 55, 70–72, **71**
Romanian orphan adoption outcomes, 6–8
social scaffolding quality, 163
speed of processing and information-processing theories, **149**
temperament and, 404
withdrawn behavior and peer rejection, 526–527
Age factors, prenatal development and, 65
Aggression
biology and socialization, 579
child care and, 497
consistency of, 568–571
cultural differences in, 410, 411, 564, 618–619
defined, 567
development of, 567–568
direct aggression, 615
Dodge's information-processing theory of social problem solving, 359–360
employment, maternal, effects of, 493
friend and peer influence on, 515, 518, 520, 576–579
gender difference in, 568–569, 614–619
genotype–environment interaction and, 94, **94**
hostile attributional bias, 359, 571
indirect aggression, 615, 618
instrumental, 568
media influences on, 618
observational learning of, 373–374, 573–574, 576
oppositional defiant disorder (ODD), 570
origins of, 572–579
parental influences on, 617–618
in popular children, 525
preschooler expression of, 568
proactive, 572
reactive, 572
relational, 525, 615
sexual harassment, 616
television violence and, 373–374, 618
Aggressive-rejected children, 525–526, 528, **531–532**
AIDS, as a prenatal hazard, 66
Ainsworth's Strange Situation, 427–431, **428**, 640
Aka (Africa), emotional development in, 411–412
Alaska (Inuit), sex selection of children, 46
Alcohol abuse
binge drinking, 522–523
child maltreatment and, 369, 650
fetal alcohol syndrome (FAS), 48, 62–64, **64**
friend and peer influence on, 515–516, 522–523
as prenatal hazard, 62–64
Alleles, 89–90
Altruistic motives, 559
Ambivalent (insecure/restraint) attachment, 429
America. *See* United States
American Academy of Pediatrics, 498
American Association of University Women (AAUW), 616
American Indians. *See* Native Americans
American Public Health Association, 498
American Sign Language (ASL), 111, 219, 222, 230, 626
Amnesia, infantile, 346, 349
Amniotic fluid, 48, 50–53, 55–56, 57
Amniotic sac, 49
Analogical reasoning, 150, 153, 161
Anal stage, Freud's psychosexual theory, 346
Analytical abilities, in successful intelligence theory, 322
Analytic style, in language development, 234
Androgens and gender differences, 588, 610
Anemia, sickle-cell, 92
Anencephalic, 54
Anger
early affect system and, **385**
as early negative emotion, 384, 387–388, 390
gender difference in toddlers, **390**
parental assistance in management of, 3–4
parents' expression of emotion and children's socialization, 408–411
parents' reaction to children's, 409–410, 413

B

Bangladesh, low birth weight (LBW), 649
Basic level, category hierarchies, 264–265
Basic processes, mental, information-processing theories, 147–148
Basic trust, in Erikson's psychosocial theory, 347–348
Battered children. *See* Child maltreatment
Behavioral cycles, in prenatal development, 54–55
Behavioral inhibition and temperament, 406
Behavior genetics, 95–101
 defined, 95
 environmental effects, 100–101
 heritability, 98–101
 research design, 96–98
Behaviorism
 classical conditioning, 202–203, 351–352, 636
 generalization, 636
 instrumental (operant) conditioning, 202, 203–204, 352–353, 636
 Watson's, 10, 351–352
Behavior modification, 352, 353
Beliefs and theory of mind, 267–269
Beng (Ivory Coast, Africa), prenatal development, 43
Between-group heritability measures, 100
Bias
 attractiveness bias, 180–181, 455–456, 473–474, 524
 gender schemas, 591, 596
 gender self-socialization, 358, 589, 593–596
 hostile attributional bias, 359, 571
 ingroup bias, 592
 in interviews, 27–28
 shape bias, **240**
 in valuing of male and female offspring, 46, 464–465, 611
Bicultural identity, 449
Bidirectionality of parent–child interactions, 474, **475**
Bilingualism, 222–223, 224
Binet-Simon Intelligence Test, 298
Binge drinking, peer influence in college, 522–523
Binocular disparity, depth perception, 185, 625–626
Bioecological model of social development (Bronfenbrenner), 366–377, **367**, 596–597
A Biographical Sketch of an Infant (Darwin), 9
Biology, primitive theory of
 core-knowledge theories, 156–157
 preschooler knowledge of living things, 273–278
Biosocial theory of gender development, 587
Birth. *See* Childbirth
Birth rates
 among adolescents, 482–483
 gender difference, 46, 464–465
 outside marriage, 481, **481**
Bisexual identity, 450–454
Bitter taste, food preferences and eating regulation, 118
Blacks. *See* African-Americans
Blindness
 gesturing with speech, 248
 spatial coding and, 281–282
Bodily-kinesthetic intelligence (Gardner), 321
Body composition and age, 116, 606–607
Body development. *See* Physical growth
Body image, gender differences, 393, 456, 607
Bonding. *See* Attachment
Bowlby's attachment research, 424, 426–427
Boys. *See* Gender differences
Brain, 102–115
 anencephalic, 54
 cerebral cortex
  language development, 220–221
  spatial reasoning and, 279
  structure and function, 103–104
  visual processing, 178
 cerebral lateralization, 104
 cortex, 103–104
 damage and recovery, 114–115
 developmental processes, 104–110
 development in adolescence, 109–110
 dysfunction, and antisocial and aggressive behavior, 573
 dyslexia studies, 327
 evolutionary psychology and, 364–365, **365**
 experience and, 110–113
  experience-dependent processes, 112–113
  experience-expectant processes, 111–112
 fetal, 49, **50**, 52–53
  auditory development and preferences, 56, 57
  fetal alcohol syndrome (FAS), 48, 62–64, **64**
  gender difference, 588–589
 formation of, 102–115
 glial cells, 103
 language development, 219–225
 lateralization, 104, 220–221
 mapping, 105–107
 memory and, 147, **147**
 music, as infant auditory experience, 187
 neural tube development, 49, **50**, 104
 neurogenesis, 104–108, 635
 neuroimaging, 105–107
 neuron development, 104–108
 neurons, 102–103
 plasticity, 110–113
 sensitive periods, 112
 structures of, 102–104
 synapse elimination, 108–110
 synaptic pruning, 109–110, 635
 synaptogenesis, 108, 635
Brazil, research in
 childbirth experience in, 69
 child street vendors and mathematics, 335–336
 infant mortality rate, 75
 moral vs. social conventions, 553
 obligation to parents and friends, 555–556
Breast milk, 117
Breathing, development of, 54, 56
Breathing, fetal, 54
Broca's aphasia, 220–221
Broca's area, 105, 220–221, **221**, 635
Bronfenbrenner's ecological systems approach, 366–377
Bullying
 in active isolates, 526
 proactive aggression, 571

C

Canada, research in
 child care, impact of, 497
 math achievement and fathers' occupation, **314**
 ODD and CD, rates of, 570
 poverty and children, 314
 self-esteem, 459
 sexual harassment, 615–616
Cancer, as prenatal teratogen impact, 61, 62
Cardinality, counting principles, 292
Career. *See* Employment
Caregivers. *See* Child care and child-care programs; Parents and caregiving
Carolina Abecedarian Project, 318–319, 650
Categorical perception, 226–228, **226**, **227**
Category hierarchies, 262–266, **262**
The Cat in the Hat (Seuss), 57
Causality
 causal understanding and categorization, 265–266
 conceptual development, 285–288
 correlation in research, 31–32
 domain-specific learning mechanisms, 156, 638–639
 multicausality of developmental problems, 651
Cell body, of neuron, 102, **102**
Cell differentiation, 47, 635
Cell division, 47
Cell migration, 47
Center-based programs for poor children, 317–320

Distributional properties of speech, 229
Diversity
birth experience and, 68–70
genetic perspective on, 88
Division, cellular, 47
Divorce, 484–489
changes in families and, 482
child custody arrangements, 486, 487–489
children's contribution to problem behavior, 488
factors affecting impact of, 485–488
as heritable, 99, 101
marital conflict vs., 489
potential impact of, 484–485
of reserved adults, 532
self-regulation and social behavior, 488
sibling relationships, 480
socialization of aggression and antisocial behavior, 575
stepparenting, 489–491
Dizygotic (fraternal) twins, 49, 96–97, 327
DNA (deoxyribonucleic acid), 87
Dodge's information-processing theory of social problem solving, 359–360
Domains of social judgment, 554–556
Domain-specific learning mechanisms, 156, 638–639
Dominance patterns in genetic expression, 89–90
Dominant allele, 89, 92
Dominant gene, 89, 92
Dominant-recessive patterns, 92
Dose–response relations, teratogen, 61
Doubt, in Erikson's psychosocial theory, 348
Doulas, in birth experience, 69
Down syndrome, 92–93
Drawing, language development and, 253–254, **253**, **254**, **255**
Drives (Freud), 11
Drugs, fertility drugs, 75
Drug use/abuse
antidepressant, 395
childbirth and, 67
cocaine, 64–65
cost of friendship and, 515–516
gang membership and, 577, 579
identity formation and, 445
marijuana, 64
nicotine, 62, 63
as prenatal hazard, 59–60, 61, 64–65
Ritalin, 370–371, 651
thalidomide, 59–60, 61, 89
See also Alcohol abuse
Dual representation and symbols, 252–253
Duchenne's muscular dystrophy, 92
Dweck's theory of self-attributions and achievement motivation, 360–361
Dynamics, family, 466–467
Dynamic-systems theories, 164–171
central developmental issues, 168–170
defined, 165
education application, 170
motor development and, 194
self-organization, 168–169
view of children's nature, 166–168
Dyslexia, 93, 113, 327

E

Easy temperament, 401
Eating
food preferences and eating regulation, 118
healthy habits, encouraging, 119
obesity, 118–121, 374
See also Nutrition
Ecological theories
gender development, 586–587
biosocial theory, 587
evolutionary theories, 363, 586–587
social development, 362–378
bioecological model, 366–377, 596–597
central developmental issues, 362
ethological theories, 363–366
evolutionary psychology, 364–366
evolutionary theories, 363–366
view of children's nature, 362
systems approach (Bronfenbrenner), 366–367
Economic function of family, 466
Economic influences on development
changes in families, 481
growing up in different economic influences, 642
remarriage, 490
stress and parenting, 476
See also Poverty; Socioeconomic status (SES)
Edges, infant visual preference for, 179
Education
African-American maternal employment, 494
bilingualism, 222–223, 224
Carolina Abecedarian Project, 318–319, 650
child-development research applied to, 23
classroom as community of learners, 164, 564
continuity of IQ scores, 305
core-knowledge theories, application to, 158, 648–649
cultural influences, 613
divorce or remarriage, effects on, 482–483
dynamic-systems theories, application to, 170
early-intervention program, 164, 317–320
family value placed on, 311–312
Fast Track intervention program, 578, 652
individual differences and student treatment, 22
information-processing theories, application to, 152, 648
IQ as predictor of outcomes, 307, **308**
jigsaw approach, 164
low-birth-weight (LBW) infant outcomes, 78, 649–650
maternal, vocabulary development of child and, 236
mathematics. *See* Mathematics
middle school transition, difficulty of, 457, 512
philosophical history of, 8–9
Piaget's theory, application to, 648–649
Project Head Start, 318–320, 497, 649
prosocial behavior and, 566
reading. *See* Reading
school as caring community, 566
SES and parenting styles, 475
sociocultural theories, application to, 164, 649
special curriculum, "turtle technique," 4
teachers, children as, 160–161
teacher valuing of gender-stereotyped behavior, 611–612
See also Academic achievement; School and school-age children
EEG. *See* Electroencephalogram (EEG)
Effect size, statistical analysis, 605
Effortful attention, 18
Egg, female human, 44–46, **45**, 88
Ego, 345
Egocentrism
adolescent, 441
egocentric representation, 280–281
preconventional morality (Kohlberg), 549, **550**
preoperational stage of cognitive development, 136–137, **137**
Electra complex (Freud), 347
Electroencephalogram (EEG)
brain imaging technique, 105, **105**
left-hemisphere specialization for language, 220
temperament and, 405
Embarrassment, development of, 390–391
Embryo
defined, 47
development
early development, 49–50
hand plate, **49**
illustrated summary of, 50–53
Emotional development, 382–421
adolescent, 391–392, 393
attachment. *See* Attachment
childhood, 383–395
emotional knowledge, 413–419
identifying emotions of others, 414–415
negative emotions, 3–4, 387–390, 398
normal emotional development, 391–392
positive emotions, 386–387
self-conscious emotions, 390–391
theories on nature and emergence of emotion, 384–385

H

J

K

L

N

O

Q

R

Raising children, 3–4
Random assignment in experimental design, 32, **34**
Random assortment, of chromosomes, 88
Rapid eye movement (REM) sleep, 52, 55, 70–72, **71**
Reaching, 195, **195**, 209, **209**
Reactive aggression, 572
Reading
 acquisition of skills, 323–329
  attention-deficit hyperactivity disorder (ADHD), 370
  comprehension, 328–329
  dyslexia, 93, 113, 327
  prereading skills, 324–325
  word identification, 325–326
 disabilities
  dyslexia, 93, 113, 327
  as heritable, 99
  individual differences as stable, 644–645
 hours spent, correlated with reading-test scores, 30
 preschooler knowledge of sounds, 25
 reading aloud to children, 329, 647
Reality principle (Freud), 345
Recessive allele, 89, 92
Recessive gene, 89, 92
Recessive patterns in genetic expression, 92–93
Reciprocal causation, triadic model of, 593
Reciprocal determinism, 354, 355, **356**
Reciprocal relationship
 attachment development, 427
 defined, 512
 in friendship, 507–508, 510–511, 515–516
Reciprocated best friendship, 512
Red-green color blindness, 92
Reference, first words and, 232
Referential style, in language development, 234
Reflexes
 defined, 190
 in infants, 190, **191**, 194
 motor development, 190
 sensorimotor stage of cognitive development and, 134
Regulation
 and active-child theme, 630
 divorce and, 488
 emotional, 398–399
 food preferences and eating regulation, 118
 gender difference, 614
 preschooler emotional development, 398
Regulator genes
 defects in, 93
 defined, 89
Rehearsal, memory and, 148–149
Reinforcement
 Bobo doll and learning theory, 354–355
 instrumental (operant) conditioning, 203–204, 636
 intermittent, 352, 353
 learning theories, 354–357
 vicarious, 354–355
Rejected peer status, 525–527
Rejecting-neglecting parenting style, 470, 471
Relational aggression, 525, 526, 615
Relative size, pictorial cues, **184**, 185
Relativism, moral, in Piaget's stages of moral development, 547
Reliability, defined, 26
Religion, social judgments, 555
REM (rapid eye movement) sleep, 52, 55, 70–72, **71**
Remarried families
 effects on adolescents, 487
 prevalence, 482
 sibling relationships in, 479
Reproduction, sexual, and conception, 44–46
Reputations, and peer crowd, 521
Research and children's welfare, as developmental theme, **11**, 23–24, 567
Research and research methods, 24–38
 adoption. *See* Adoption studies
 antisocial behavior, 567
 attachment, 425
 benefits of study of child development, 23–24
 causation, 31–32
 central developmental issues, 351
 data gathering, 27–29
  interviews, 27–28
  naturalistic observation, 28–29, **30**
  structured observation, 29, **30**
 design, 30–31
  behavior genetics, 96–97
  correlational, 30–31, **34**
  cross-sectional, 34, **37**
  experimental, 32–34, **34**
  longitudinal, 34–35, **37**
  microgenetic, 35–36, **37**
 developmental theories as framework and motivation for, 128–129
 effect size, statistical analysis, 605
 ethical issues in, 36–37
 families, 466
 friendships, 506
 historical foundations for, 8–11
 integrated review of, 646–653
 intelligence, 299
 meta-analysis, 605
 moral judgment and reasoning, 545
 nonhuman animals and, 48
 orphan studies. *See* Orphan studies
 peer relationships, 506
 prenatal development and birth, 43
 scientific method, 25–26
 twin studies. *See* Twin studies
Reserved children, long-term outlook, 532
Resilience
 at-risk children and, 2–3, 21, 79
 developmental, 2–3, 21, 79, 314
 poverty and, 21, 79, 314
Respiratory system, development of, 54, 56
Response to distress, newborns', 74
Rest–activity cycles, fetal, 55
Retina, 182
Rhythm
 musical, as infant auditory preference for, 187
 rhythmicity, as temperamental dimension, 401
Right-brain, spatial location, 279
Risks, newborns and, 78–79
Risk-taking, gender differences in, 614
Ritalin, 370–371, 651
Role confusion, in Erikson's psychosocial theory, 349
Role taking, Selman's stage theory of, 358–359
Romanian orphan adoption studies, 6–8, **107**, 112, 626
Rooting reflex, 190, **191**
Rubella (German measles), 66
Rules. *See* Moral development

S

Sadness
 infant, as early negative emotion, **385**, 390
 parents' reaction to children's, 410
Same-sex friendships, 516
Same-sex play patterns, 594–595
Scaffolding
 narratives, 245–246
 social, 163
Scale errors, 199, **199**
Scanning, infant visual, 179–181, **179**
Schizophrenia
 heritability, 12, 100–101, 626–627
 nature and nurture in, 12, 626–627
 polygenic inheritance of, 92
School and school-age children
 academic achievement. *See* Academic achievement
 aggression, frequency in, 568
 attachment, effects of, 434–436
 classroom as community of learners, 164, 564
 employment, maternal, effects of, 493–494
 environmental contributions to intelligence, 312–313
 extracurricular participation, 376
 Fast Track intervention for preventing antisocial behavior, 578, 652
 friend selection, 516–518
 friendship interactions, 509–511
 gender difference, 594–595, 611–612
 and IQ as predictor of outcomes, 305–306

U

V